TEACHING STANDARDS ALIGNMENT

D0085748

InTASC Standards | InTASC

The Interstate Teacher Assessment and Support Consortium (InTASC) is part of the Council of Chief State School Officers (CCSSO). In April 2011, the CCSSO published the InTASC Model Core Teaching Standards, which define effective teaching. They cut across age levels (K–12) and content areas. They were developed in collaboration with most major teaching-related national organizations. They are aligned with other national standards such as the Common Core State Standards, the National Board for Professional Teaching Standards (NBPTS) and the National Council for Accreditation of Teacher Education (NCATE). They are the most widely used national standards of teaching, and many state teaching standards are based on these national standards. There are 10 standards, with several aspects of essential knowledge (EK) within each standard. The following table shows the alignment between content in this text and InTASC standards.

InTASC Standard InTASC		Chapter in Text
Standard 1: Learner Development The teacher understands how learners grow and develop, recognizing that patterns of learning and development vary individually within and across the cognitive, linguistic, social, emotional, and physical areas, and designs and implements developmentally appropriate and challenging learning experiences.		
EK 1(d)	The teacher understands how learning occurs—how learners construct knowledge, acquire skills, and develop disciplined thinking processes—and knows how to use instructional strategies that promote student learning.	2, 3, 4, 5, 7, 12, 13
EK 1(e)	The teacher understands that each learner's cognitive, linguistic, social, emotional, and physical development influences learning and knows how to make instructional decisions that build on learners' strengths and needs.	All chapters
EK 1(f)	The teacher identifies readiness for learning, and understands how development in any one area may affect performance in others.	All chapters
EK 1(g)	The teacher understands the role of language and culture in learning and knows how to modify instruction to make language comprehensible and instruction relevant, accessible, and challenging.	1, 3, 4, 5, 6, 7, 12, 13
Standard 2: Learning Differences The teacher uses understanding of individual differences and diverse cultures and communities to ensure inclusive learning environments that enable each learner to meet high standards.		
EK 2(g)	The teacher understands and identifies differences in approaches to learning and performance and knows how to design instruction that uses each learner's strengths to promote growth.	3, 4, 5, 7, 12, 13
EK 2(h)	The teacher understands students with exceptional needs, including those associated with disabilities and giftedness, and knows how to use strategies and resources to address these needs.	4, 5, 7, 8, 9, 12
EK 2(i)	The teacher knows about second language acquisition processes and knows how to incorporate instructional strategies and resources to support language acquisition.	12
EK 2(j)	The teacher understands that learners bring assets for learning based on their individual experiences, abilities, talents, prior learning, and peer and social group interactions, as well as language, culture, family, and community values.	1, 3, 4, 5, 6, 7, 9, 10, 11, 12, 13
EK 2(k)	The teacher knows how to access information about the values of diverse cultures and communities and how to incorporate learners' experiences, cultures, and community resources into instruction.	1, 5, 6, 7, 12, 13
Standard 3: Learning Environments The teacher works with others to create environments that support individual and collaborative learning, and that encourage positive social interaction, active engagement in learning, and self motivation.		
EK 3(i)	The teacher understands the relationship between motivation and engagement and knows how to design learning experiences using strategies that build learner self-direction and ownership of learning.	7, 12, 13
EK 3(j)	The teacher knows how to help learners work productively and cooperatively with each other to achieve learning goals.	3, 7, 8, 9, 10, 11, 13
EK 3(k)	The teacher knows how to collaborate with learners to establish and monitor elements of a safe and productive learning environment including norms, expectations, routines, and organizational structures.	7, 8, 10, 11
EK 3(l)	The teacher understands how learner diversity can affect communication and knows how to communicate effectively in differing environments.	1, 7, 9, 12, 13
EK 3(m)	The teacher knows how to use technologies and how to guide learners to apply them in appropriate, safe, and effective ways.	14

InTASC Standard **InTASC**	Chapter in Text

Standard 5: Application of Content
The teacher understands how to connect concepts and use differing perspectives to engage learners in critical thinking, creativity, and collaborative problem solving related to authentic local and global issues.

EK 5(m)	The teacher understands critical thinking processes and knows how to help learners develop high level questioning skills to promote their independent learning.	3, 4, 5

Standard 6: Assessment
The teacher understands and uses multiple methods of assessment to engage learners in their own growth, to monitor learner progress, and to guide the teacher's and learner's decision making.

EK 6(p)	The teacher understands how to prepare learners for assessments and how to make accommodations in assessments and testing conditions, especially for learners with disabilities and language learning needs.	5, 8

Standard 7: Planning for Instruction
The teacher plans instruction that supports every student in meeting rigorous learning goals by drawing upon knowledge of content areas, curriculum, cross-disciplinary skills, and pedagogy, as well as knowledge of learners and the community context.

EK 7(i)	The teacher understands learning theory, human development, cultural diversity, and individual differences and how these impact ongoing planning.	All chapters
EK 7(j)	The teacher understands the strengths and needs of individual learners and how to plan instruction that is responsive to these strengths and needs.	1, 3, 4, 5, 6, 7, 8, 9, 10, 11, 12, 13, 14
EK 7(m)	The teacher knows when and how to access resources and collaborate with others to support student learning (e.g., special educators, related service providers, language learner specialists, librarians, media specialists, community organizations).	5, 6, 7, 8, 9, 10, 11

Standard 8: Instructional Strategies
The teacher understands and uses a variety of instructional strategies to encourage learners to develop deep understanding of content areas and their connections, and to build skills to apply knowledge in meaningful ways.

EK 8(j)	The teacher understands the cognitive processes associated with various kinds of learning (e.g., critical and creative thinking, problem framing and problem solving, invention, memorization and recall) and how these processes can be stimulated.	3, 4, 5, 13
EK 8(m)	The teacher understands how multiple forms of communication (oral, written, nonverbal, digital, visual) convey ideas, foster self-expression, and build relationships.	12

Standard 9: Professional Learning and Ethical Practice
The teacher engages in ongoing professional learning and uses evidence to continually evaluate his/her practice, particularly the effects of his/her choices and actions on others (learners, families, other professionals, and the community), and adapts practice to meet the needs of each learner.

EK 9(g)	The teacher understands and knows how to use a variety of self-assessment and problem-solving strategies to analyze and reflect on his/her practice and to plan for adaptations/adjustments.	All chapters (self-reflection checklists)
EK 9(i)	The teacher understands how personal identity, worldview, and prior experience affect perceptions and expectations, and recognizes how they may bias behaviors and interactions with others.	1, 5, 6, 7, 8, 9, 10, 12, 13
EK 9(j)	The teacher understands laws related to learners' rights and teacher responsibilities (e.g., for educational equity, appropriate education for learners with disabilities, confidentiality, privacy, appropriate treatment of learners, reporting in situations related to possible child abuse).	5, 7, 13

Standard 10: Leadership and Collaboration
The teacher seeks appropriate leadership roles and opportunities to take responsibility for student learning, to collaborate with learners, families, colleagues, other school professionals, and community members to ensure learner growth, and to advance the profession.

EK 10(m)	The teacher understands that alignment of family, school, and community spheres of influence enhances student learning and that discontinuity in these spheres of influence interferes with learning.	1, 6, 7, 12, 13, 14

continued in the back

Child and Adolescent Development in Your Classroom

TOPICAL APPROACH

Third Edition

Christi Crosby Bergin
University of Missouri

David Allen Bergin
University of Missouri

CENGAGE
Learning·

Australia • Brazil • Mexico • Singapore • United Kingdom • United States

Child and Adolescent Development in Your Classroom, **Third Edition,**
Christi Crosby Bergin, David Allen Bergin

Product Director: Marta Lee-Perriard

Senior Product Manager: Cheri-Ann Nakamaru

Content Developer: Julia White

Product Assistant: Kimiya Hojjat

Marketing Manager: Andrew Miller

Content Project Manager: Samen Iqbal

Art Director: Helen Bruno

Manufacturing Planner: Doug Bertke

Production Service and Composition:
  MPS Limited, Lynn Lustberg

Intellectual Property Project Manager:
  Nick Barrows

Photo Researcher: Lumina Datamatics,
  Veerabaghu Nagarajan

Text Researcher: Lumina Datamatics,
  Aruna Sekar

Text and Cover Designer: Lisa Buckley

Cover Images: Rubberball/Mark Andersen/
Getty Images; ImagesBazaar/Brand X Pictures/
Getty Images; Luca Cappelli/E+/Getty Images;
Gilbert Laurie/Getty Images; Blend Images/
Alamy Stock Photo.

© 2018, 2015 Cengage Learning

ALL RIGHTS RESERVED. No part of this work covered by the copyright herein may be reproduced or distributed in any form or by any means, except as permitted by U.S. copyright law, without the prior written permission of the copyright owner.

For product information and technology assistance, contact us at
Cengage Learning Customer & Sales Support, 1-800-354-9706.
For permission to use material from this text or product,
submit all requests online at **www.cengage.com/permissions**
Further permissions questions can be e-mailed to
permissionrequest@cengage.com

Library of Congress Control Number: 2016938743

Student Edition:

ISBN: 978-1-305-96424-2

Loose-leaf Edition:

ISBN: 978-1-305-96426-6

Cengage Learning
20 Channel Center Street
Boston, MA 02210
USA

Cengage Learning is a leading provider of customized learning solutions with employees residing in nearly 40 different countries and sales in more than 125 countries around the world. Find your local representative at **www.cengage.com**

Cengage Learning products are represented in Canada by Nelson Education, Ltd.

To learn more about Cengage Learning Solutions, visit **www.cengage.com**

Purchase any of our products at your local college store or at our preferred online store **www.cengagebrain.com**

Printed in the United States of America
Print Number: 01   Print Year: 2016

Dedication

This book is dedicated to our grandchildren, Ian, Anna, Bridget, William, and Nathan, who bring sparkle to this work.

Contents

4 Information Processing, Memory, and Problem Solving   131

5 Cognitive Ability: Intelligence, Talent, and Achievement 179

SECTION 4 THE SOCIAL CHILD 351

9 Social Cognition 351

9-1 Theory of Mind 352

9-2 Humor 362

14 The Child in Context: Family Structure, Child Care, and Media   573

Preface

Understanding child development is important to becoming an effective teacher. In Chapter 10 you will be introduced to Josh, who was one of the most difficult children in Mrs. Wentz's 25-year career as a teacher. He was involved in fighting, lying, skipping school, defying authority, and failing to complete work. After altercations involving the juvenile court officer, Josh was suspended—sent home where his mother used drugs and his father was angry and punitive. Other students were afraid of Josh. Mrs. Wentz was in Christi's child development class when we were test-driving the first edition manuscript for this textbook, and she began putting the concepts to use in her classroom with Josh. Mrs. Wentz began to feel more confident about how to help Josh, and subsequently, Josh began to complete his schoolwork and became helpful in the class. Mrs. Wentz said that learning about child development caused her to look at each student with more insight and that she had become a better teacher—and human being—as a result.

This textbook is designed for prospective teachers of infants through adolescents. Teachers of different age groups need to collaborate in order to provide seamless education as children transition from preschool through high school. When teachers of all age groups study child development together, they create a shared understanding of children that will promote children's success.

This textbook is about child development. However, it has some content that is traditionally found in "educational psychology" texts. Thus, teacher education programs that combine child development and educational psychology into a single course may find this text appropriate.

Our Goal: Promote Outstanding Teaching

If there is a silver bullet in education, it is teaching quality. Effective teachers raise the achievement of all children and narrow the achievement gap. Even one outstanding teacher can influence the course of a child's life. Children who are lucky enough to have many outstanding teachers across the years receive a substantially better education than children who are less lucky.

How does a teacher learn to be outstanding? One key pathway is to learn the science of child development and know how to apply it in the classroom. This provides teachers with the information they need to problem solve how to best educate each child. To be successful, teachers must understand each child as a learning, feeling, relating human being. The goal of this text is to help teachers create classrooms that optimize children's development.

A Distinctive Text

This text is "research-based," incorporating the latest science. Several thousand articles in peer-reviewed journals are summarized in the text. We have worked to make this research accessible to prospective teachers with everyday language and authentic vignettes of children of all ages, from infants to adolescents. Previous courses in psychology are not required to understand the text. Still, many research-based child development textbooks are available. What makes this one unique? The answer: the strong bridge between research and classroom application.

Classroom Application

In 2007 the National Institute of Child Health and Human Development and the National Council for the Accreditation of Teacher Education jointly reported that child development courses do not consistently offer realistic illustrations of developmental concepts or adequately tie concepts to classroom settings (NICHD & NCATE, 2007). This textbook is designed to overcome this problem through the following features:

- Research-based strategies that teachers can use in their classrooms are provided for each major topic.
- Authentic classroom vignettes are used to illustrate concepts.
- Topics are covered that are of keen interest to teachers, but that are not included in traditional child development texts (e.g., discipline, teacher–student relationships, how emotions affect learning).
- Explicit connections are made between theories and the teaching of mathematics and literacy in Chapters 4 and Chapters 12.
- Each chapter ends with a *Reflections on Practice* page that asks teachers to reflect on their behavior in the classroom and how it influences children.

This text is child-centered, putting the development of the child at the forefront of the content, providing readers with research- and theory-based knowledge of developmental psychology, while also providing strong practical skills for applying that knowledge in their classrooms.

Diversity

This text emphasizes diversity. Each major topic discusses both individual diversity and group diversity. Understanding diversity helps teachers differentiate pedagogy for students who come to class with widely different experiences and cultural backgrounds. Culture is introduced at the beginning of the text, and then discussed in subsequent chapters when relevant, rather than presented as a stand-alone topic in an isolated chapter.

Text Organization

Child development textbooks take either a chronological or a topical approach. We have combined the approaches—the text is organized topically across chapters, but age trends are highlighted within chapters. We took this approach because, while it is important for teachers to have a snapshot of children at a particular age, it is critically important for teachers to understand where their students have been and where they are going developmentally if they are to promote optimal development in children. In addition, children of the same age in the same classroom can be at remarkably different points in their development.

This textbook is organized into five sections.

1. The first section, "Foundations of Child Development," deals with foundational issues in child development. It introduces key themes in the study of child development and scientific foundations of the field. It discusses key biological topics relevant to teachers.

2. The second section, "The Cognitive Child," deals with major theories and research related to learning and cognition, including memory and problem solving. It models theory application by applying those theories to mathematics education. It also discusses intelligence, academic achievement, and the development of expertise.

3. The third section, "The Emotional Child," deals with attachment, self-control, and emotion regulation in the classroom.

4. The fourth section, "The Social Child," deals with social cognition (e.g., theory of mind, moral judgment, and humor), prosocial and antisocial behavior, conflict resolution, peer interaction, and play.

5. The fifth section, "The Whole Child," highlights the interrelatedness of each of the other domains of the child. Language, literacy, the self-system, and motivation are the result of interactions of biology, cognition, emotions, and social behavior. This section also deals with contexts of child development.

The Content Balance

No textbook can cover all the important topics in child development with adequate thoroughness to please all readers. Trying too hard to please everyone's priorities can result in "inch deep, mile wide" coverage. Weighing what to include and what to leave out is a dilemma for any textbook author. It was particularly challenging for this book. We wanted the length of this textbook to be manageable while offering classroom applications in enough depth to be useful to teachers. We also included teacher-relevant topics that are not in traditional textbooks. Something had to go in order to make room for an emphasis on classroom application.

We opted to forgo discussion of prenatal development and some other topics in order to make room for a chapter on self-control and discipline and more exten-sive coverage of social–emotional development. Why? Teachers' promotion of social and emotional well-being in students may have a larger effect than the quality of their instruction (Reyes, Brackett, Rivers, White, & Salovey, 2012). Furthermore, on September 8, 2014, a memorandum was released by the U.S. Administration for Children and Families stating that only 20% of early childhood teachers reported having received training focusing on children's social and emotional development in the past year, although this was a high priority for teachers. Teachers need more information on how to help students behave well and become emotionally and socially well adjusted in the classroom. Thus, while we cannot claim to have covered all the content that every instructor may deem important, this text provides a solid foundation in child development to which you may add your own emphases.

Prospective teachers sometimes see no point in learning theories of development. There are at least two reasons for this. One is that few texts make the connection between theory and practice explicit. The other is that theories are discussed in an opening chapter, divorced from the research that they spawned or the practice that they suggest. To remedy this, we have embedded theories throughout the text. Chapters 3 and 4 provide extensive discussion of learning and cognitive theories that are directly applied to classroom practice. Chapter 12 revisits each of these theories and directly applies them to literacy education. In each of the other chapters, embedded boxes describe theories or theorists that pertain to the topic at hand.

Learning Features of the Text

This textbook has features designed to facilitate learning. The features are based on principles derived from the field of educational psychology.

Consistent Chapter Structure

Chapters have a consistent structure to aid comprehension. Chapters 2 through 14 have the following general structure:

> Age Trends in [topic]
>
> Individual Diversity in [topic]
>> Stability of individual differences
>>
>> What do individual differences predict?
>>
>> What predicts individual differences?
>
> Group Diversity in [topic]
>
> Classroom Implications of [topic]

Special Features

In addition, pedagogical features that promote deep processing are included. Features have been kept to a minimum because too many features disrupt readers. The pedagogical features include the following:

- **Think About This** questions are dispersed throughout each chapter in the margins. These ask readers to process and apply content to current issues or personal experience. These questions can be used in small-group discussion, as assignments for short papers, or as Think-Pair-Share class activities.

MindTap easily integrates into your existing Learning Management System. MindTap is designed to save you time while allowing you to improve your course through fully customizing any aspect of the Learning Path. You can change the order of the student learning activities, hide activities you don't want to use in your course, and—most importantly—create custom assessments and add any standards, outcomes, or content to your course (e.g., YouTube videos, Google docs). Learn more at **www.cengage.com/mindtap**.

Instructor's Manual

The instructor's manual provides **Authentic Case Studies** that address topics across multiple chapters. They allow you to ask your students to interpret the situation and apply content. They can be used for extended discussions or papers. The instructor's manual also provides multiple **Field Observation** activities for each chapter. These ask students to actively connect content to real-world experiences. These activities can be used in field observations, lab sessions, journaling, or small-group discussions. They can be readily adapted to observing family and friends if there is no field component attached to your class. The instructor's manual has additional **"Think About This"** items to facilitate class discussions or assignments. It also lists additional resources with weblinks.

Test Bank

The Test Bank is available electronically or through a computerized testing program called Cognero. Instructors can use the Test Bank to create exams in just minutes by selecting from the existing database of questions, editing questions, or writing original questions.

PowerPoint Lecture Slides

These vibrant, Microsoft PowerPoint lecture slides for each chapter assist you with your lecture, by providing concept coverage using images, figures, and tables directly from the textbook.

Cengage Learning Testing Powered by Cognero

Cognero is a flexible, online system that allows you to do the following: author, edit, and manage test bank content from multiple Cengage Learning solutions; create multiple test versions in an instant; and deliver tests from your LMS, your classroom or wherever you want.

New to This Edition

This 3rd edition has retained the same key strengths of the previous editions—a strong research base with clear guidance on how to apply the research to practice in real classrooms, presented in a well-organized, highly readable style. However, there are some new features and enhancements in this edition.

Thoroughly Updated Research

Over 800 new citations have been incorporated across all chapters. Topics that have been revised and updated incorporating the latest research include the following:

- Chapter 1: Heritability estimates; cultural influences; ethnic group population census data; avoidance of deficit thinking; common risk and protective factors; achievement of poor versus wealthy students; strengths of low-income individuals.

- Chapter 2: Effects of adverse childhood experiences on brain development; music training as a stimulating environment for brain development; motor development in early childhood and markers of motor delays; exercise guidelines and rates of inactivity; rates of obesity among children; effects of obesity on academic achievement; sleep needs by age and rise in sleep deprivation; body dissatisfaction among boys; substance use rates and patterns, including ethnic group differences; low birth weight causes and interventions.

- Chapter 3: Use of applied behavior analysis; outcomes of constructivist instruction; smartphones as cultural tools; teaching in the zone of proximal development.

- Chapter 4: Updated views of the components of executive functions; cognitive flexibility; attention control and classroom implications for teachers on focusing learners' attention; relationship between executive functions and poverty, and their link to the achievement gap; childhood amnesia; scientific thinking in elementary school; computational thinking in secondary school; restructured section on antecedents of reasoning, with more content on classroom implications; updated content on reasoning, particularly the rapidly expanding research on infant reasoning that demonstrates they are better at reasoning than previously thought.

- Chapter 5: Fluid and crystallized intelligence; heritability of intelligence; music and intelligence; boys and spatial ability; biased test items; relationship between assignment of Black students to gifted services who have Black versus non-Black teachers; expert teachers, with new research and examples; high correlation between teacher judgment and performance on standardized achievement tests; gender and achievement; testing effect and how to use it; effects of homework; retention; learning disabilities.

- Chapter 6: Antecedents of attachment reflect new emphasis on autonomy support; interventions for attachment; father–child attachment; mechanisms for the far-reaching effects of attachment; achievement effects of teacher–student relationships; lifespan change in personality; the issue of missing heritability.

- Chapter 7: Use of social media while studying; self-control predicting well-being; strategies for improving self-control; corporal punishment; the Collaborative and Proactive Solutions approach to misbehavior ; ethnic differences in punishment at school; discipline gap; ethnic differences in parenting; collectivist and individualist cultures; child abuse.

- Chapter 8: Streamlined coverage of the functions of emotions; streamlined coverage of depression and anxiety, which strongly co-occur; math anxiety; embarrassment in adolescence; the challenges of military-connected children.

- Chapter 9: Infant and toddler theory of mind (ToM); adolescent ToM; moral identity; infants' sense of fairness; age trends in lying; the moral judgement-behavior gap.

- Chapter 10: Creating prosocial identity in children; infant precursors of aggression; cyberbullying; methods schools can use to reduce bullying.

- Chapter 11: Perceived popularity and why some aggressive children have peer status; aggression as functional; classroom seating arrangements' effect on peer status; social skills training for cooperative learning; support for LGBTQ youth in school.

- Chapter 12: Language development of deaf and hard of hearing children; code switching; academic language; learning from speech alone compared with speech plus gestures; teacher expectation effect; print exposure; handwriting; Twitter as an example of literacy; dyslexia.

- Chapter 13: High quality goals and goal setting; methods of triggering situational interest; the importance of relevance for motivating students; gender differences in self-concept; sex-typed play; goal setting and achievement in elementary and secondary students; autonomy support in the classroom.

- Chapter 14: Geography affects probability of marriage; effects of grandparent divorce on children *and* grandchildren; children of adolescent mothers; children of lesbian mothers; effects of marital conflict; effects of parent involvement; academic socialization; discussion of childcare; educational and non-educational screen media use; video game use and outcomes of use of various media; influence of media use on relational aggression; compulsive use of media; problems with multi-tasking; how to choose educational apps.

Visual Learning Aids

Thirty new figures and tables have been created to convey important concepts visually to readers. Figure captions provide questions to foster reflection and discussion among readers. New figures and tables include:

1. Correlations between Identical (MZ) and Fraternal (DZ) Twins (Chapter 1)
2. Kindergarten Readiness by SES (Chapter 1)
3. Black–White and Rich–Poor Achievement Gap by Year (Chapter 1)
4. Long-Term Outcomes from the Abecedarian Project (Chapter 1)
5. Views of Risky Activities by Age (Chapter 2)
6. Brain Plasticity (Chapter 2)
7. Dietary Guidelines (Chapter 2)
8. Adolescent Sleep Deprivation over Time (Chapter 2)
9. Exercise Promotes Brain Functioning (Chapter 2)
10. Applied Behavior Analysis during Recess (Chapter 3)
11. Teaching in the Zone of Proximal Development (Chapter 3)
12. Cognitive Flexibility by Age (Chapter 4)
13. Individual Differences in Executive Functions (Chapter 4)
14. Memory Improves with Age (Chapter 4)

Alignment with National Standards and Licensure Exam

Alignments of topics with InTASC and NAEYC standards are provided in a Standards Correlation Grid on the inside front and back covers. This allows you to quickly locate coverage of standards and licensure exam guidelines throughout the text.

Acknowledgments

All the vignettes describing children's behavior in this text are real classroom experiences. They are based on our own observations and on narratives written by students and colleagues. It is customary to acknowledge the author of any narrative, including informal portrayals such as the vignettes used in this text, immediately adjacent to the narrative. However, in the interest of a higher ethical purpose—that of protecting the privacy of children, teachers, and schools—we have chosen instead to list our sources here (in alphabetical order):

Alison Ausmus, Kevin Bishop, Carolyn Boswell, Russ Crane, Jerry Crosby, Brittany Dickman, Amy DeBacker, Nora Duffy, Katie Hams, Jennifer Greenway, Todd Gutschow, Stan Hernacki, Bethany Hintz, J.D. Hunter, Jennifer Kurt, Michelle Long, Clarissa Montz, Leah Morgan, Michael Norman, Kathleen O'Toole, Vashanti Rahaman, Dorothy Rohde-Collins, Gwen Roush, Emily Simon, Barbara Zimmerman

We have used false names in all the vignettes. We have also taken the liberty to adapt the narratives to fit the purpose of the chapter, or to shorten them because of space limitations. We express our gratitude for the narratives that each of these keen child-observers has contributed in order to help the next generation of teachers understand their students.

A number of reviewers offered excellent guidance and made key contributions to the organization and content of this text along the way. Special thanks to Nelson Cowan for advice on Chapter 4 and to the following reviewers:

Billi Bromer, Brenau University–Augusta

April Grace, Madisonville Community College

Marilyn Grave, University of Minnesota Crookston

Caryn Huss, Manhattanville College

Matthew Irvin, University of South Carolina

James Jurica, Texas A&M University–San Antonio

Kurt Kreassig, Regent University

Tina Kruse, Macalester College

Laura Lamper, Central Texas College

Elizabeth McCarroll, Texas Woman's University

Beth Moore, Franklin College

Michelle Morris, Wor–Wic Community College

Dawn Munson, Elgin Community College

Lisa Newland, The University of South Dakota

Grace Paradis, California State University, Stanislaus

Rachelle Powell, North Lake College

Jana Sanders, Texas A&M University–Corpus Christi

Lydia Smith, University of North Carolina at Charlotte

Dawn Tafari, Winston–Salem State University

Michelle Tichy, University of Northern Iowa

Merideth Van Namen, Delta State University

Stephen Whitney, University of Missouri

Victoria Zascavage, Xavier University

At Cengage Learning, we thank Cheri-Ann Nakamaru, Brady Golden, Drew Kennerley, and Julia White for their excellent editorial insight; Helen Bruno and Samen Iqbal for design and production; Joshua Taylor for supplement production; and Andrew Miller for marketing.

chapter **1**

© Cengage Learning

Ways of Thinking about Children

What factors have made you who you are today? Does your answer emphasize genes or experiences in your family, school, or culture? Did these factors make you similar or different from others your age? In this chapter, we will discuss how research helps answer questions like these. **After you read this chapter, you will be able to:**

1-1   Describe methods of scientific research in child development.

1-2   Recognize how genes and the environment interact to influence development.

1-3   Recognize risk factors and foster protective factors that influence development.

1-4   Use risk and protective factors to analyze the effects of preschool.

1-1 The Science of Child Development

An 18-month-old boy is left at preschool. When his mother returns, he runs to her and wants to be picked up. She picks him up briefly and puts him down. He cries and clamors to be picked up. She turns from him. He cries strongly. She intentionally refuses to pick him up because she says she doesn't want him to be too dependent on her, "Him being a boy and all." She doesn't want him to get "funny" by having to feel secure. She says she thinks he might "go gay" if she spoils him. (Adapted from Smyke, 1997)

toddler
a child between 1 and 3 years of age; so-called because of recent mastery of walking, often with a wobbly gait.

You may be amused or outraged by this mother's view of what causes overdependency and homosexuality. Do you believe that feeling secure is bad for **toddlers**? Can you "spoil" a child by picking him up when he cries? Your belief about how a crying toddler should be handled is your personal theory. Throughout this text you will learn about formal, research-based theories of child development that will help make your personal theories clearer to you and challenge the accuracy of some, so that you can provide the best possible classroom for your students.

Theories are developed from careful, systematic study as scientists seek to discover basic principles of child development. You might ask, "Are there general principles? Isn't each child unique?" While each child is unique, there are still principles of development that apply across children. What might these be? The answer depends on your theory of child development.

1-1a Child Development Theories: A Brief Overview

theory
an organized group of concepts or principles used to explain a particular aspect of human development.

A **theory** of development is simply an organized group of principles used to explain some aspect of children's development. Theories help you interpret what you observe in children, and suggest the best way to promote their development. In later chapters, you will be introduced to major theories of child development and some of their most influential proponents. To get started, we present here a brief overview of these theories.

Views of child development have changed over time. In the early 1900s, for example, many psychologists believed that children are genetically endowed with abilities that just need to unfold as children mature (Collins, 2002). Believers in this maturation perspective thought that how children change across time is genetically determined for all children, regardless of their different experiences.

Other psychologists are environmentalists who emphasize the role of the environment and claim that children's development is driven by experience within the family and culture. Early environmentalists tended to see children as relatively *passive* as they received influence from their environment, like clay being molded in the hands of an artist. A new view arose that recognized that children *actively* contribute to their own development by the way they think about their experiences. Jean Piaget, a key figure we will discuss in Chapter 3, was a primary proponent of this view.

Table 1.1 gives a simplified overview of contemporary theories. These theories differ in their view of what drives children's development. Some theories give greater emphasis to maturation (i.e., nature) as a cause of behavior and others to the environment (i.e., nurture). These theories also differ in what aspect of child development they

TABLE 1.1 Overview of major theories of child development

Theory and major theorist	Basic aim	Emphasis: general age trends for all children versus how individuals are different	Forces that drive development	Emphasis: nature or nurture?	Domains of development the theory explains well
Bioecological Model Urie Bronfenbrenner (Chapters 1 & 14)	To highlight the multiple layers of influence on the child	Both	Heredity and environment act together to influence development. Does not specify particular processes.	Both	Any
Ethology Konrad Lorenz and Nikolaas Tinbergen (Chapter 6)	To understand the functions of behavior in different species	Focuses on species-wide age trends, but not individual differences.	Genetically based processes shaped by evolution drive development. Behavior becomes incorporated into the biology of a species because it promotes breeding success. Compares human and animal behavior. Emphasis is on innate behaviors.	Nature	Attachment Emotions Aggression Language
Behaviorism B. F. Skinner (Chapters 3 & 7)	To explain learned behavior	Focuses on individual differences, which are the result of different histories of reinforcement.	The child is passive; reinforcement and punishment drive development. Behaviors that are reinforced are more likely to reoccur. Emphasis is on observable behavior. Concepts of mind, cognition, and inner experiences are ignored. Useful for managing children's behavior problems.	Nurture	Any learned behavior. Does not explain innate behaviors, like smiling, or why some things are reinforcing.
Social Cognitive (or Social Learning) Theory Albert Bandura (Chapters 3 & 13)	To explain acquisition of behavior and cognitions such as attitudes	Greater emphasis on individual differences, especially on behavior and attitude change, not age trends.	An expansion of behaviorism/learning theory. Children learn from models or others who are reinforced. This requires children to remember and interpret things they have observed—which means cognition is involved. The child actively interprets reinforcement.	Nurture	Any learned behavior

(continued)

TABLE 1.1 Overview of major theories of child development (continued)

Theory and major theorist	Basic aim	Emphasis: general age trends for all children versus how individuals are different	Forces that drive development	Emphasis: nature or nurture?	Domains of development the theory explains well
Cognitive Developmental Theory Jean Piaget (Chapter 3)	To explain the development of logical thought and moral judgment	Age trends are strongly emphasized and age-based "stages" of cognitive development are outlined.	Innate cognitive maturation (with some social interaction) drives development. Children actively "construct" their own knowledge through exploration. Abilities are similar, even with different cultural experience. Maturation limits logical reasoning ability, so children's cognitive development is stage-like.	Nature Maturation (with some environmental influences)	Knowledge Logical reasoning
Sociocultural Theory Lev Vygotsky (Chapter 3)	To explain acquisition of knowledge and language ability	Age trends are not emphasized. Individual differences are a result of unique social experiences.	Development occurs through interaction with others. Cognitive growth is collaborative (not within the child). The child's thought is the result of internalizing dialogue with others. Development cannot be separated from social and cultural interaction.	Nurture	Knowledge Culturally valued skills Language
Information Processing Various theorists (Chapter 4) **Social Information Processing** Kenneth Dodge (Chapter 11)	The step-by-step processing of information	Age trends are the result of faster and more efficient processing. Individual differences are the result of innate capacity and experience (i.e., prior knowledge).	Like a computer, the child receives sensory input, manipulates information, and then responds with output. This view focuses predominantly on what is happening inside the child's mind, but includes input from the environment. What is studied is narrow (i.e., logical flow of information). Useful for targeting interventions for specific processing problems.	Both	Problem solving Memory Decision making Attention Aggression
Psychodynamic Sigmund Freud (Chapter 9)	To explain personality and neurosis	Age trends are emphasized with age-based "stages" of psychosexual development. Individual differences in personality are the result of early parent–child interaction.	How parents gratify (vs. frustrate) biologically based drives influences personality. Children can become fixated at a particular stage. A newer version, the neo-psychoanalytic view, asserts that the goal of behavior is to regulate and maintain internal and interactional harmony with others. Early parent–child interaction is internalized and influences later experience. Emphasizes the unseen workings of the mind.	Both	Personality Attachment Emotions Morality Humor The unconscious

seek to explain and whether they see children as active or passive contributors to their own development. Spend a few minutes examining this table to compare the theories, but do not try to memorize them. We will discuss each theory in greater detail in later chapters. Revisit the table for a review when you finish the text.

Theories are important to teachers because they guide decisions about classroom practices and because they guide research. Indeed, all of your behavior as a teacher is based upon your own theory of instruction. If you believe children learn best by imitating an expert, your theory is different from someone who believes children learn best by trying things out on their own. In developmental science, research results are used to test and improve theories. In the next section, we explain the research methods on which formal child development theories are based.

1-1b Research Methods

Why does a teacher need to know research methods? Federal mandates require educators to use "scientifically based research" to guide decisions about how to teach. To help, the federal Department of Education maintains a *What Works Clearinghouse* website. Imagine that you are a preschool teacher and want to try a new reading program to help a bilingual student learn to read, or you might be a high school teacher looking for a curriculum to help struggling teen readers. Imagine you are on a committee looking for a bullying prevention program for your school. In any of these roles, you could search the clearinghouse for a program. It would tell you if there was research on the program, the caliber of the research, and the effectiveness of the program. In this section, we will introduce you to basics of research methods so that you can learn to assess the quality of research, a professional skill that is now important for teachers. To begin, let's look at the three basic research designs— experimental, nonexperimental, and qualitative designs.

Experimental Designs

While people commonly use the term *experiment* to refer to any kind of research, for psychologists the term has a very specific meaning. In a simple experiment, you change something in the learner's environment and measure the results. For example, a teacher could try a different phonics approach to see if students learn to read more easily. Such informal experiments can be useful, but cannot pinpoint the cause of an outcome like improved reading skills. To determine the *cause* of outcomes, scientists use controlled **experiments**.

In a controlled experiment, learners are placed in at least two groups: an intervention group or a **control group**. The intervention group gets a special treatment, but the control group does not. Outcomes for the two groups are compared. For example, to determine whether a phonics program results in better reading skills, you could place half of your 1st-graders in a phonics program and the other half in a different program. If learners in the phonics program develop better reading skills compared to the control group, you have evidence (not proof) that the phonics program might work.

However, what if the learners in the phonics program were "smarter" or already had better skills than the control group? For an experiment to demonstrate cause-and-effect—that the intervention and not something else *caused* an outcome like improved reading skills—the control group should be similar to the intervention

experiment
a controlled study comparing outcomes between people randomly assigned to a treatment group and to a control group.

control group
in an experiment, the group that does not receive the special treatment in order to provide a comparison group.

random assignment
each research participant has an equal chance of being assigned to the treatment or control group.

group in all attributes. To increase the probability that groups are similar, researchers use **random assignment**. This means each learner has an equal chance of being put in the intervention group or the control group. Even with random assignment, you might conclude that a phonics program is *more likely* to produce literate children, but not that the phonics program makes *all* children literate. Thus, research is about probability, not certainty.

Nonexperimental Correlational Designs

Experiments cannot always be used because they may be unethical or impractical. For example, if you want to understand the effect of prenatal alcohol exposure on children, it would not be ethical to randomly assign some pregnant mothers to drink five beers a day and other mothers to drink none. In a case like this, nonexperimental correlational research designs are used in which researchers measure variables as they naturally occur, without intervention. (A *variable* is an attribute of the child or environment that can be measured, like number of ounces of alcohol per day.) Researchers might, for example, measure how much mothers drank during their pregnancies and compare that to their children's reading ability to determine whether the two variables are related.

A correlation is a measure of the relationship between two variables. The **correlation coefficient**, or *r*, indicates the statistical strength of the relationship. A perfect positive correlation, or *r* = +1.00, means that a plot of the variables follows a straight line (see Figure 1.1). That is, if you know a value for one variable, you

correlation coefficient
a statistic that measures the relationship between two variables.

FIGURE 1.1 Correlation Coefficients.

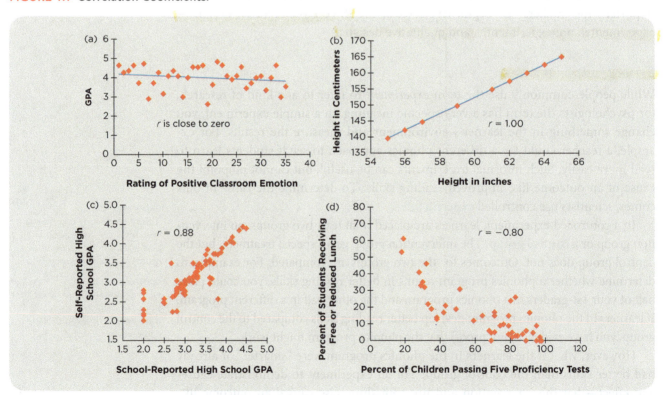

If you covered up the "r" statistic, could you guess it approximately? Explain correlation to a friend, and then test him or her.

can predict with perfect accuracy the corresponding value for the other variable. A *positive* correlation means that higher values on one variable go with higher values on the other. For example, *higher* levels of fathers' education predict *higher* levels of children's reading ability. If there is a perfect negative correlation, then $r = -1.00$. A *negative* correlation means that higher values on one variable go with lower values on the other. For example, *higher* levels of prenatal alcohol exposure predict *lower* levels of children's reading ability. Strong correlations can be either positive (e.g., $+0.60$) or negative (e.g., -0.60). If there is no association between the variables, then $r = 0$. Correlation coefficients *are not percentages*; a correlation of 0.40 does *not* mean 40% of anything.

Correlations between any two variables in child development research are rarely close to 1.00. In fact, very few are even as large as 0.50, and a correlation of 0.35 is considered large enough to draw attention. This is because important child outcomes are influenced by many variables—not just the one being measured in a study. For example, good reading ability is not the result of a single variable, like intelligence, involved parents, or effective schools. Rather, each of these variables (and many others) combines to influence reading ability.

Qualitative Designs

In experiments and correlational studies, scientists apply *numbers* to variables, such as fathers' education and children's reading ability, and then use statistics to analyze their relationship. This is a quantitative approach. In contrast, qualitative research involves interviews, observations of natural behavior, and other forms of data that are usually reported in words rather than numbers. The researcher may spend anywhere from hours to years observing and interacting with youth in order to accurately tell their story. For example, in one study researchers investigated the emotions that students felt—especially pride—as they developed understanding of science concepts (Bellocchi & Ritchie, 2015). Another study investigated how kindergarten students thought that being "smart" meant obeying teachers (Hatt, 2012). Qualitative studies like these can provide rich insight into learners' thoughts and behavior not captured in quantitative designs.

Studies of Change over Time

Imagine you want to know how children's aggression changes with age. You could follow one group of children for 12 years, assessing the *same* children at ages 4, 10, and 16. This is a **longitudinal research design**. What if you can't wait for 12 years? You could assess groups of 4-, 10-, and 16-year-olds at one time, which would not really study change over time, but would suggest whether children of different ages differ in their aggression. This is a **cross-sectional research design**. A cross-sectional design gathers data from different age groups at one point in time, and a longitudinal design gathers data from one group over multiple points in time.

Each research design has strengths and limitations. For example, longitudinal studies allow you to identify factors that might improve children's lives over time. However, they take a long time before results are available, and it is difficult to keep children involved over multiple years. Experiments can establish what causes a particular outcome; however, sometimes they are not ethical or practical, so

think about this

In a study of children adopted from Romanian orphanages, the longer the time spent in the orphanage before being adopted, the lower the cognitive ability (O'Connor et al., 2000). Would this be a positive or negative r? How would you graph this?

qualitative research
nonquantitative research characterized by the researcher being the instrument of data collection (rather than a test or questionnaire). May involve observations and interviews as data.

longitudinal research design
data are collected from the same individuals two or more times, separated by some period of time (e.g., months or years).

cross-sectional research design
data are collected at one point in time from two or more age groups to investigate age trends.

correlational designs are used instead. Qualitative studies provide rich descriptions and deep insight into a small group of young people's lives, but may not generalize to most other youth. Because each design has limitations, a mature field of science uses multiple designs.

In addition to the design of research, there are four other key issues to understand when you read research findings: (1) causality, (2) measurement, (3) generalizability, and (4) effect size. We'll discuss these next.

Causality

Most studies of child development are correlational. Therefore, it is important to understand their critical weakness: they cannot demonstrate that one variable causes another variable. If variables A and B are correlated, A could cause B, or B could cause A, or both could cause each other, or C could cause both A and B. For example: (1) hostile mothers could cause hostile children; (2) hostile children could cause hostile mothers; (3) the variables could be **bidirectional,** meaning that hostile children and hostile mothers influence each other; or (4) a third variable, like hostile fathers or a genetic predisposition to be hostile, could cause both children's and mothers' hostility.

bidirectional
variable A influences variable B, while B also influences A.

It is common for people to mistakenly assume causality from correlational studies. For example, years ago, research found that as they read, poor readers make more erratic eye movements than good readers. Interventions using special equipment and specially trained teachers attempted to teach poor readers improved eye movements (Stanovich, 1992). Later it was found that erratic eye movements do not cause poor reading, but rather poor reading causes erratic eye movements because poor readers have trouble recognizing words and understanding their meaning. Millions of dollars were wasted on special interventions. The critical lesson is that you cannot assume causation from correlational studies, although such studies can tell you the size of the relationship between two variables. As a teacher, you will probably be asked to help choose a curriculum or program for your school, so be prepared to think about what kind of evidence you would need to justify your selection. The What Works Clearinghouse gives precedence to controlled experiments over correlational studies because policy makers are usually interested in whether programs *cause* specific outcomes. When scientists use terms such as *predict*, *linked*, *correlated*, and *associated*, they are usually referring to correlational studies. Watch for these terms throughout this text.

Measurement

Researchers measure development in many ways: observations of behavior, ratings by a teacher or parent, self-report, and physiological markers such as level of hormones or brain images. Each form of measurement has weaknesses and strengths. For example, self-report (when respondents tell you what they think or fill out a survey) allows you to get inside the minds of those who respond, but children and youth can be biased, have trouble communicating, or misunderstand questions. Direct observations by researchers may be more objective, but they are costly, may not capture rare but important behaviors such as fights in school, and can change behavior because of the observer's presence. If learners are observed in an artificial, controlled setting, results may not apply to real-world settings. Parent or teacher questionnaires are inexpensive and easy to administer, but they can be biased and may be different from youths' self-reports. Again, a mature field of science uses multiple methods to compensate for the weaknesses of any single method.

Reliability and validity are two ways of describing how "good" a measure is. Validity refers to the accuracy of a test or measurement: does it really measure what it claims to measure? The validity of a measure depends on the purpose for which it is used. For example, a proficiency test might be valid for deciding whether students are mastering grade-level content, but not for deciding which students would benefit from special education.

Reliability refers to the consistency of a test or measurement. A reliable measure yields nearly the same results across time, so that you get about the same results today as next week. A reliable measure also yields the same results if administered by two different teachers under the same conditions. Short tests tend to be less reliable, so when you design a test, it is better to use 20 items than 10 items. A test cannot be valid if it is not reliable.

Validity and reliability are important because many decisions are made on the basis of measures. Such decisions include who receives special education services, who gets into which colleges, and what instructional strategy you use with a particular child. You should always ask whether a test is valid and reliable. For example, are IQ tests valid for selecting gifted students? Are readiness tests valid for deciding who is ready for kindergarten? Are your classroom tests valid and reliable enough to use for assigning grades?

Generalizability

It is not possible to include all learners in a study. Instead, a sample or subgroup is studied with the intent of generalizing the results to a larger group. When samples of learners are carefully selected to represent larger groups, research results should apply to other learners in the larger group. In the past, most research focused on White, middle-class learners. It was not clear if these results could be generalized to other learners. In recent decades, researchers have been careful to sample low-income learners, learners of color, and learners outside North America so that results are more generalizable (Hagen, 2007).

One factor that limits generalizability is the cohort effect. A cohort is a group of children born about the same time who experience unique political, economic, and social trends. You are a member of a cohort. A cohort effect, also called a *generation effect*, is an outcome caused by the particular era in which the cohort grows up. Some cohorts are labeled, like Baby Boomers and Millennials. There are cohort effects for intelligence (Chapter 5), personality (Chapter 6), and aggression (Chapter 10). That is, today's children on the average have higher intelligence, but they are more anxious, neurotic, and aggressive than past generations. Research conducted on one cohort might not generalize to a different cohort.

Effect Size

The concept of effect size has become increasingly important for teachers because of recent emphasis on raising test scores and using evidence-based curricula. Effect size is a measure of the strength of the relationship between two variables, or how much more effective one intervention is than another. The What Works Clearinghouse website reports the effect size of interventions to help you make decisions about your

validity
the extent to which a measurement assesses what it is supposed to measure for a specific purpose.

reliability
consistency of a test or measurement.

cohort effect
an effect upon development whose cause is specific to the particular time period in which the cohort grew up.

Effect size
a measure of the strength of the relationship between two variables, or the size of the difference between the treatment and control group.

TABLE 1.2 Effect sizes of interventions in different fields

Intervention	Effect size
Medical treatments (life-threatening illness)	0.08–0.47
Medical treatments (non-life-threatening illness)	0.24–0.80
Counseling interventions (social skills training, drug use prevention, career education, in-school prevention programs)	0.27–1.20
Parent involvement in education	0.14–0.30
Active learning (compared to passive lecture)	0.47
Study skills and strategies	0.59–0.69
Spaced practice rather than massed practice (cramming)	0.71
Direct instruction	0.59
Inquiry-based teaching	0.31
Cooperative learning	0.41
Retention (holding students back a grade)	−0.16 (outcomes are worse)

Adapted from Freeman et al. (2014), Hattie (2009), Jeynes (2012), Kim and Hill (2015), and Lipsey and Wilson (1993).

classroom practices. For example, you could compare the effect size of different curricula designed to help bilingual students, or struggling teens, learn to read.

Effect size is reported in decimal numbers. Effect sizes of 0.10 to 0.20 are commonly considered as small, 0.25 to 0.40 as medium, 0.50 to 0.80 or greater as large, and anything over 1.0 as quite large, but this is only a fuzzy standard. An effect size of 0.30 means that the 50th-ranked student in a group of 100 would move to 39th place if only he or she experienced the intervention (Cooper, 2008). Table 1.2 shows effect sizes of interventions in different fields.

Whether an effect size is meaningful depends on the situation. Even a small effect can be important if the stakes are high. For example, the effect size of taking aspirin to prevent heart attacks is only 0.07, or a 3 to 4% difference between those who get heart attacks after using aspirin compared to those that do not (Lipsey & Wilson, 1993), yet many physicians recommend aspirin therapy to save lives. Similarly, although maternal sensitivity has a modest effect on attachment, you might consider it important if *your* child's emotional well-being is at stake. As a teacher, you may want to change classroom practices that have a small effect if the outcomes are important, the changes are cheap or easy to make, and you do not have more effective alternatives. Thus, interpreting the importance of effect sizes requires judgment.

One major topic of research is the relative contribution of, or effect size for, genes and the environment. This is the nature-versus-nurture question. *Nature* refers to the influence of a child's genes on development. *Nurture* refers to the influence of a child's physical and social environment on development. It is important that you understand the influences of nature and nurture on development, because this understanding will help you create an optimal environment for your learners. In the next section, we take an in-depth look at the nature-and-nurture balance.

1-2 Nature and Nurture

Crystal and Garth are twins in the same kindergarten class. Garth likes to point out his superiority in sports and school. He says, "I scored two goals in our last game, and Crystal didn't score any." He says, "My teacher always tells me I am a good reader, but she has to help Crystal all the time." Garth does not get praised for doing well in school, but his sister does; in fact, she got a bracelet for improving her reading. When their mother picks them up from school, she always asks to see Garth's schoolwork, but just tells Crystal that she looks cute. Garth does better in all academic subjects. He can read and write his name. Crystal does not read, and writes her name poorly. Their puzzled teacher asks about these differences. Mother explains that Crystal has always liked to dress up and was never interested in books. She says that Crystal was "just born that way," implying the twins' differences are genetic. She does not seem to notice that she treats her children differently.

Could Crystal and Garth's differences be due to genetics (nature) or to the way their mother treats them (nurture), or both? The bioecological model (see Box 1.1) helps frame an answer to this question. In this model, *nature* refers to the innermost biological circle of influence, which includes genes. *Nurture* refers to all circles beyond the learner, which can include parent–child relationships, peer interaction, school experiences, and culture. In this section we will discuss how both genes and culture—the two extremes in the bioecological model—influence development.

1-2a Nature: The Role of Genes in Individual Diversity

Behavioral genetics is the study of how genes and the environment contribute to differences among people. According to behavioral genetics, differences in any trait are due to three sources (Pike, 2002): (1) genes, (2) shared environment, and (3) nonshared environment.

Genes and Heritability

Heritability is a statistical estimate of the amount of *variation* of a trait in a population that is due to genes. Heritability is commonly misunderstood, so remember that it is *not* an estimate of the percent of genetic influence on the trait. Instead, it is about amount of variation that is due to genes. Thus, if intelligence has a heritability of 0.50 among White, middle-class adolescents, then 50% of the *variation* in intelligence within that population is due to genes and the remaining variation is due to shared or nonshared environment.

behavioral genetics
the study of how genes and the environment contribute to individual differences in behavior.

BOX 1.1   theories & theorists

The Bioecological Model

The bioecological model presented a change in thinking from a "nature vs. nurture" tug-of-war to a view that they interact over time to influence children's development. It was developed by Urie Bronfenbrenner (1917–2005), a Russian-born psychologist who pointed out that children are influenced by social, economic, and political forces as well as their family. The model is portrayed with concentric circles (see Figure 1.2) that represent nested systems. Each system is an ecological level, with the biological child at the core, hence the name *bioecological*. The child is at the core because the effects of any other factor in the model are modified by the child's traits (Bronfenbrenner & Morris, 2006). The child's traits can be biological (e.g., low birth weight) or psychological (e.g., temperament or intelligence).

The next level is the *microsystem*. This includes the interactions, activities, and relationships of the child in settings that physically contain the child, such as the family, school, neighborhood, and peer group. The *mesosystem* is a system of two or more microsystems, such as home

and school. The *exosystem* refers to the linkages between two settings, one of which does not physically contain the child but influences the child indirectly, such as the parent's workplace.

The *macrosystem* refers to culture, which contains specific patterns of micro-, meso-, and exosystems. Culture determines what is acceptable and possible in the other levels. Public policy may be thought of as macrosystem. For example, welfare policy may not affect children directly, but affects them by changing the childcare environment (Yoshikawa & Hsueh, 2001). The *chronosystem* adds the dimension of time. It refers to change and consistency across the life course of a particular child, as well as cohort effects over historical time.

These ecological levels form a hierarchy of influence on children's development from proximal (near) to distal (far) factors. Proximal processes exist in the immediate environment, such as parent–child interaction; *they are the most powerful processes* (Bronfenbrenner & Morris, 1998; Rosa & Tudge, 2013). A key proposition of the model is that both the child and the environment influence these proximal processes.

In later chapters you will see how each of these levels influences child outcomes. For the time being, consider the case of drug use. *The child:* Children's traits like decision-making skills and attitude toward drug use are associated with drug use, as are children's genetic factors. *The microsystem:* Children's drug use is higher in families where parents use and the family environment is dysfunctional. Children's drug use is lower in schools that are caring and where children feel bonded. *The mesosystem:* Children are more vulnerable to attending an uncaring school if they also come from a dysfunctional family (Ennett et al., 2008). *The exosystem:* Children's drug use is higher in communities that approve of use among adults (Coate & Grossman, 1985). One implication of this model is that interventions will be most effective if they target multiple levels of the child's environment. Thus, an effective intervention for drug use would alter children's attitudes about drugs, change parents' drug use, create more caring schools, and change community acceptance of use.

FIGURE 1.2   Bioecological Model.

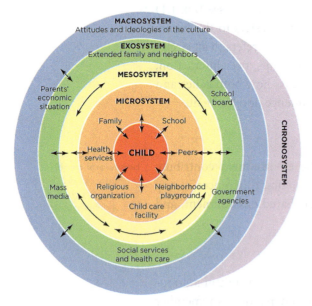

According to the bioecological model, the child is embedded within a series of increasingly distal sets of influences. *Based on Bronfenbrenner and Morris (2006).*

How do scientists make such estimates? They compare children with different genetic relatedness, such as twin, adopted, and half siblings. A common approach is to compare identical twins with fraternal twins. Identical twins share 100% of their genes, and fraternal twins share about 50% of their genes, as do non-twin full siblings (see Photo 1.1). Half siblings share about 25% of their genes. Adopted and stepsiblings are genetically unrelated.

If genes affect variation in a trait, then siblings who share more genes should be more similar in that trait. This means that identical (monozygotic) twins should be more similar than fraternal (dizygotic) twins, and biological siblings should be more similar than adopted siblings. This is the pattern that research consistently finds (see Figure 1.3). A recent study of thousands of traits found that the average heritability was 49% (Polderman et al., 2015). Studies of specific traits have found that shyness is about 40 to 50% heritable, cognitive abilities are about 47% heritable, psychiatric conditions are about 46% heritable, and antisocial behavior is about 40% heritable (Bouchard, 2004; Polderman et al., 2015). Thus, estimates of heritability can vary depending on the trait and the group being studied.

PHOTO 1.1 Heritable traits should be more similar for identical twins than for non-twin siblings.

Shared (SE) and Nonshared Environment (NSE)

Environmental influences can be shared or nonshared among family members. **Shared environment (SE)** refers to any factors that make siblings residing in the same family similar. SE effects are moderate for mental illness (10–30%) and personality traits. However, SE effects are large for delinquency, alcohol use, and college attendance (Burt, 2009; Pike, 2002).

shared environment (SE) factors that make individuals residing in the same family similar to each other.

nonshared environment (NSE) factors that make individuals in the same family different from each other.

Nonshared environment (NSE) refers to factors that make siblings living in the same family different from each other. A learner's peers are a powerful part of NSE. Imagine that Garth, as he enters high school, has friends who enjoy music and coax him to join a jazz band. Crystal may have friends who coax her to join the school soccer team. These peer influences will lead them to develop different talents and social networks, making them even more different. NSE effects are often larger than SE effects (Burt, 2009; Pike, 2002). Does this seem counterintuitive to you? It should if you assume that siblings share the same family environment. But do they?

FIGURE 1.3 Correlations between Identical (MZ) and Fraternal (DZ) Twins.

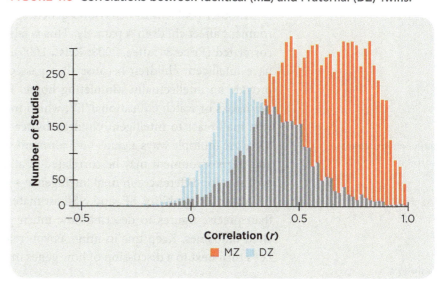

This graph depicts data from 2,748 studies that investigated correlations between twins for many different traits. Identical twins have more correlations close to 1.0 than do fraternal twins. On average, are identical or fraternal twins more similar across various traits? *Source: Adapted from Polderman et al. (2015).*

think
about this

Who are more accurate observers, researchers or parents? Keep in mind that observers typically watch children for a limited time in a specific environment. Parents watch children for years across many environments. Does this make them better observers? How might they compare to teachers?

Is the Family a Shared or Nonshared Environment?

Family is mostly a nonshared environment. There are at least two reasons for this. First, families do not influence all children in the same way. For example, in a family with an alcoholic mother, children could react differently—one could become the family caretaker and another could become a drug user. This would be a *nonshared* environment factor, because the outcome is sibling differences. Notice that NSE is *defined by outcome*, not by whether or not you think the environments are the same.

Second, families change. The firstborn may live in poverty and go to low-cost childcare as her parents struggle to get a family business going, and she may experience her mother's postpartum depression when a second child is born. The third child may be born 10 years later, after the family business is thriving, the father has completed a college degree, the mother has become much warmer in her parenting style, and the family has moved to a high-income neighborhood with good schools. If there is a divorce, one child may spend 14 years in a two-parent household, whereas another may spend only 4 years. These children are *not* growing up in identical families, even though they are siblings.

Problems with Estimating Heritability

There are several problems with estimating heritability, SE, and NSE effects. One problem is that they depend on variation of a trait in a population. If there is no variation in a trait—like having two eyes—then the **heritability estimate** would be zero because identical twins are no more similar than strangers. Yet, this trait is under strong genetic control (Sternberg, Grigorenko, & Kidd, 2005). Heritability can only tell you how much *variation of an attribute within a population* is linked to genes—not how much that trait is actually under genetic control: "heritability does not imply genetic determinism" (Plomin, 2013, p. 110).

Another problem in behavioral genetics is the assumption that genes and environment affect children separately. This is false, because genes and environment are correlated (Price & Jaffee, 2008; Reiss, 2005). For example, intelligent parents may have intelligent children because they pass on intelligent genes *and* because they provide an intellectually stimulating home. Further, intelligent children may seek out books or watch educational TV, which increases their intelligence. Finally, parents may react to intelligent children by teaching them advanced concepts. Thus, there are multiple ways a **gene–environment correlation** may evolve. Because genes and the environment may be correlated in all these ways, it is difficult to tell which accounts for differences in final intelligence—genes or the environment.

At best, heritability, SE, and NSE estimates should be considered ballpark rather than precise figures to describe how much genes and environment contribute to child outcomes. Keep this in mind as you read about heritability in later chapters. Let's turn next to a discussion of how genes might influence behavior.

How Can Genes Influence Behavior?

Your **genotype** is the set of genes in every cell that is directly inherited by you and transmitted to your descendants. Your **phenotype** is your observable characteristics. Is everything in your genes expressed in who you have become? Whether

heritability estimate
the amount of variation in a trait in a population (not individuals) that is attributable to genetic influences. Notated as h^2.

gene–environment correlation
genes influence the aspects of the environment that children experience which then further activates the genes.

genotype
the set of genes that is directly inherited and transmitted to descendants.

phenotype
observable characteristics of a person.

a genotype becomes a phenotype depends on the environment. For example, individuals who have genes for depression may only become depressed if they also have rejecting mothers or major life stress (Haeffel et al., 2008; Monroe & Reid, 2008). Both genotype and environment set limits on phenotype. The limits set by genes are probably very broad. You'll learn more about gene–environment interaction in Chapter 6.

Genes do not determine or cause behavior (except in the case of rare diseases), but they do influence probability. For example, genes do not dictate reading ability in Crystal or Garth. Instead, genes dictate things like the building of proteins. A gene is a region of DNA on a chromosome. The gene is activated when the environment (at the cellular level) asks for information. This is typically done by chemicals (e.g., hormones). Chemical levels, in turn, are affected by your biological and psychological environment. No *behavior* is directly inherited; what is inherited is the potential structure of specific proteins that can regulate the nervous system, hormones, and other body processes. For example, the *DRD4* gene that is linked to behavior problems might dampen the effect of chemicals in the brain, which might make children less responsive to the threat of discipline, but it does not directly cause misbehavior (Bakermans-Kranenburg, Van IJzendoorn, Pijlman, Mesman, & Juffer, 2008). A behavioral tendency may be associated with many different genes, and individual genes account for only a small percentage of how people vary in their behavior (Chabris, Lee, Cesarini, Benjamin, & Laibson, 2015).

The human genome contains about 20,000 protein-coding genes (Plomin, 2013). You share all but about 2% of your DNA material with apes (Johnson, Smith, Pobiner, & Schrein, 2012). The vast majority of human DNA is shared by everyone; you share about 99.9% of your genes with every other human on the planet. That leaves only 0.1% of genes to create human diversity (Quartz & Sejnowski, 2002). The genes that are free to vary are called **segregating genes**. When we said full siblings share an average 50% of their genes, we meant 50% of their segregating genes; full siblings actually differ only 0.05% genetically.

What does this mean? There is little room for genetically based individual differences (Bjorklund & Pellegrini, 2000). Natural selection preserves any successful phenotypes that result from these genetic differences. Any attribute that contributes to survival would quickly spread through the species. Thus, attributes important for survival will have less genetic variation than attributes that are not important for survival.

With so small a genome, how is it possible that humans are radically more adaptable and intelligent than apes and so different from one another? Part of the answer is that your DNA dictates the construction of a brain that is *designed to adapt to your environment*. Natural selection favors organisms that can adapt. If personality, behavior, and language were minutely prescribed by DNA, you would be less adaptable and would need substantially more DNA. Instead, your nervous system adapts and *changes biologically* as a result of experience (see Chapter 2). Gross brain structure is genetically programmed, but experience can change the fine structure and chemistry of your brain permanently. Because humans are designed for adaptability, you should expect differences between siblings like Crystal and Garth to result from NSE or unique environmental experiences (e.g., illness, quality of parenting, schooling). This is what behavioral geneticists generally find.

segregating genes
genes that are free to vary and that dictate individual differences.

What cultures and subcultures have influenced your own experiences, beliefs, and values? Do your classmates share your culture? Can you identify ways your subcultures are different and the same?

1-2b Nurture: The Role of Culture in Group Diversity

You are a product not only of your genes, but also of the culture in which you live. According to the bioecological model, both genes and culture work together to create variation among people. Genes operate at the level of the cell, at the innermost circle of the model. Culture, on the other hand, operates at the level of large groups, at the outermost circle of the model.

What Is Culture?

Culture is the pattern of values, beliefs, institutions, and behaviors shared by a group of people, a pattern that is different from that of other groups and is communicated from one generation to the next (Cohen, 2009). Culture dictates physical contexts (e.g., types of school buildings), social contexts (e.g., mixed-gender classrooms), customs for childrearing (e.g., spanking), and beliefs about the nature of children (e.g., they are inherently naughty or nice). Culture influences how much time children spend with their mothers versus fathers versus peers. You may be surprised to know that whether you believe that small or large classes are better for children is largely a matter of your culture. Small classes are valued in cultures where children are expected to develop independence, such as the United States, but large classes are valued in cultures where children are expected to develop interdependence and learn to function as part of a large group, such as Japan.

Culture can refer to large groups such as whole countries or to smaller subgroups within a country; within each country there are varied subcultures based on ethnicity, class, region, and religion. Each of us participates in multiple cultures, and we adopt aspects of new cultures. For example, Mexican immigrants to the United States may prefer their heritage language, food, and music, but they also adopt local language, food, and music. White European Americans may participate in multiple cultures such as Black hip-hop music and Latino foods.

Ethnicity

Ethnic group refers to a group that shares a cultural heritage and/or a common ancestry. The United States is comprised of many different ethnic groups. Collectively, non-White groups are sometimes referred to as **ALANA** (African, Latino, Asian, and Native American). The 2010 U.S. Census estimated ethnic group populations as follows: 64% White, non-Hispanic; 13% African American; 16% Latino; 5% Asian; 1% American Indian, Alaska Native, Native Hawaiian, and other Pacific Islander; and 3% two or more races. The population of the United States is expected to go from about 319 million in 2014 to 417 million in 2060. The Census Bureau projects that by 2060 the nation's children will be 56% ALANA and 29% Latino (up from 38% and 17% in 2014). Each major ethnic group has distinct subgroups. For example, among Latinos, there is cultural variation among Puerto Rican, Salvadoran, and Mexican Americans. Among Asian Americans there is variation among Chinese, Indian, and Filipino. Among African Americans, there is variation among those who have been in the United States for centuries and those who have recently emigrated from Africa.

Ethnicity is linked to success in school (see Chapter 5). For example, Figure 1.4 displays group differences in scores on the National Assessment of Educational Progress (NAEP), which is often called the Nation's Report Card. Hispanic and African American students have lower average achievement than White and Asian American

ALANA
an acronym that stands for the most populous non-White ethnic groups in the United States: African, Latino, Asian, and Native American.

FIGURE 1.4 Average Mathematics Scores by Ethnic Group for 4th and 8th Grades on the National Assessment of Educational Progress.

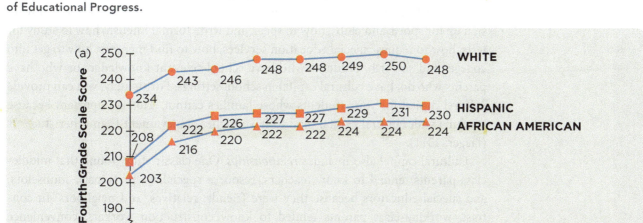

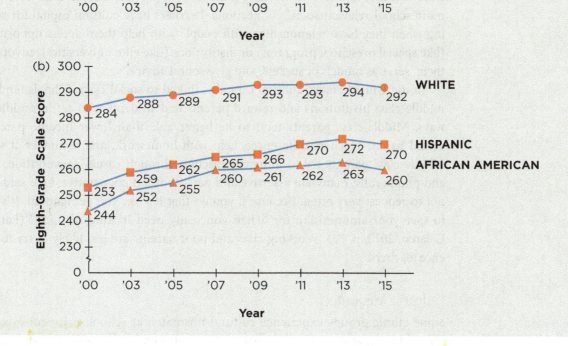

Graphs depict the achievement gap between White students and African American and Hispanic students. *Source: 2015 mathematics assessment national score gaps, www.nationsreportcard.gov.*

students throughout K–12 schooling (García & Jensen, 2009; Planty et al., 2009). The difference between White and minority students' achievement is often referred to as an *achievement gap*, which emerges as early as 3 years of age (Burchinal et al., 2011).

Why do learners from some ethnic groups have lower achievement? We will discuss two explanations next: cultural capital and cultural mismatch. In Chapter 5, we will discuss other explanations.

Cultural Capital

Financial capital refers to possessions like money and property that can be invested to gain wealth. Cultural capital refers to knowledge and relationships[1] that can

cultural capital
knowledge and social relationships that allow people to reap benefits within their culture.

---

[1] Some researchers use the term *social* capital to refer to relationships that foster benefits (Horvat, Weininger, & Lareau, 2003; Ream & Palardy, 2008), but for simplicity we will use the term *cultural* capital to include relationships.

be "invested" and passed on to the next generation to gain benefits (Lareau & Calarco, 2012). In school settings, cultural capital includes *knowledge* about how to sign up for sports and clubs, how to speak and write formal English, how to study for tests, how to request special education services, how to find mentors, how to get into college, and so forth. Students who have school-relevant knowledge, or who have parents who do, have cultural capital in school settings. Fortunately, you can provide cultural capital for your students whose families cannot. This is important because students with cultural capital tend to have higher achievement than other students (Jaeger, 2011).

Cultural capital also includes *relationships*. One classic study found that middle-class parents tended to know teachers, resource specialists, principals, counselors, and special educators because they were friends, relatives, and neighbors. In contrast, working-class parents tended to know construction workers, convenience store cashiers, and factory workers (Lareau, 1989). Thus, middle-class families had more school-relevant social connections. Learners have cultural capital for schooling when they have relationships with people who help them access opportunities (like special preschool programs) or institutions (like elite universities), advocate for them, serve as models of success, and give sound advice.

In the United States, cultural capital is linked to social class. Schools tend to be middle-class institutions and reward parents and students who act in middle-class ways. Middle-class parents tend to be better able than lower income parents to attend parent–teacher conferences, help with homework, and volunteer at school. Middle-class parents try to influence teachers through casual conversation, notes, and phone calls; many are assertive and persistent but cooperative. One said, "I try not to request very often. Because if you do that it's like you get ignored. It's better to save your ammunition for 'when you really need it' kind of thing" (Lareau & Calarco, 2012, p. 73). Working class and poor parents are less likely to try to influence teachers.

Cultural Mismatch

Some ethnic groups experience cultural mismatch at school. Cultural mismatch refers to a pattern of incompatibilities between home and school. Cultural mismatch can be subtle, like how close you stand when talking with other people, or more obvious, like attention to punctuality. It also includes language and narrative style.

Language

A learner may speak a different language than the one used in school. A learner may also use language in a different way from teachers, textbooks, or tests. An example is African American Vernacular English, which involves different pronunciation and syntax from the school's language. We will discuss this vernacular in Chapter 12.

Narrative structure

Within U.S. school culture, stories follow a traditional format of telling who was involved, what happened, and when. Typical stories build a series of events, in chronological order, up to a climax and problem solution. Think of fairy tales like

cultural mismatch
a pattern of incompatibilities between home and school.

Cinderella. However, not all cultures share this conception of story. For example, Japanese children's stories may resemble Haiku—a succinct, short, and restrained form of poetry. They may combine two or three similar events into one story, and are taught to value brevity. African American children's stories may weave multiple events into a long, out-of-order account in a way that has been compared to jazz (Bliss & McCabe, 2008; Gardner-Neblett, Pungello, & Iruka, 2012). The alternative story formats are not wrong within their cultures, but may be unexpected and considered wrong by some teachers.

Classroom Implications of Culture

Sonia is Mexican American. Her mother wants her to do well in school but does not know how to help. Sonia's friends reject academic achievement; they skip classes and get in trouble together. At school no one ever talks with her about her future or speaks positively about Mexican culture. In fact, teachers and non-Mexican peers are negative about her ethnicity. Not surprisingly, although she had good grades until 8th grade, her grades in high school are terrible. (Adapted from Phelan, Davidson, & Cao, 1991)

Sonia is experiencing cultural mismatch; she sees school as having no connection to her home world. Cultural mismatch is stressful. It can lead to poor adjustment to school and placement in special education. This is partly because teachers and students from different cultures may misunderstand each other. As a teacher, you will need to be careful not to hold your own culture as the "standard" and judge students who diverge as substandard. When persons assume that their own group is the best, and that groups that are different are inferior or deficient, this is called *deficit thinking*. Learners who lack cultural capital, who experience cultural mismatch at school, and who are the targets of deficit thinking may need support. There are several things you can do to help:

- Become aware of your students' cultural capital and how it affects their achievement. For example, when given an assignment to develop a travel brochure for France in a social studies class, some students have home access to computers, high-speed Internet, color printers, and relatives who traveled to France and speak French. Their brochures make them look "smarter" than other students who may be equally adept at writing, using the library, and asking questions, but have fewer resources. A study in Chicago found that when academic coaches provided cultural capital by guiding high school students through the college application process and reminding them of the tasks they needed to complete, students were more likely to actually enroll in college, particularly disadvantaged students (Stephan & Rosenbaum, 2013). You will need to provide ways for students with little cultural capital or material resources to be successful in your classroom.

- Be careful as you think about cultural capital, because it can lead to a deficit view that highlights what children lack. Think about the strengths of your students and their cultural backgrounds. For example, Latino children may develop a particularly strong sense of family connection and be more likely

Tony Freeman/PhotoEdit

Tony Freeman/PhotoEdit

PHOTO 1.2 Learn about your students' home cultures in order to build bridges between school and home.

than European American children to help around the house by cooking, cleaning, and babysitting (Telzer & Fuligni, 2009).

- Become knowledgeable about and accept the language and dialect of your students, but at the same time teach standard English so they will experience success in school and careers. This is discussed in Chapter 12. When directly asked, "Do you understand?" students with limited English want to appear competent, so they may say yes even when they do not understand. Some students report that they guess because they don't want to ask for help (Monzó & Rueda, 2009). Thus, you will need to be perceptive.

- Become aware of your students' narrative style. Do not assume that different styles do not "make sense," but also teach school narrative style so that your students will be successful in school.

- Build bridges between home and school. For example, in the play section of a preschool, the kitchen area should include items familiar in your students' home cultures, like tortillas or pita, not just hamburgers and pancakes. Be able to talk about current events in immigrants' home countries because their relatives will likely be experiencing the events (elections, natural disasters, armed conflicts, etc.). See Photo 1.2.

- Do not try to be colorblind. One principal told us he will not hire a teacher who claims to be colorblind. Why? Such a perspective leaves in place racial structures that have created inequity without challenging them, and does not acknowledge the unique experiences of children of color (Morris et al., 2015).

You may not know the different cultural values and practices of all your students, but genuinely trying to understand and value different perspectives will help you overcome mismatches in your classroom. While addressing cultural and ethnic differences is important, you should be careful not to stereotype your students or lower your expectations based on the fact that certain groups have lower average test scores than others. Learn about your students through your experiences with each of them, not based on generalizations about their ethnic group.

1-2c Reconciling the Role of Genes and Culture

Recall from the bioecological model that multiple levels of influence, such as genes and culture, act together to predict child outcomes. "Underlying the bioecological model is a cardinal theoretical principle…that genetic material does not produce finished traits but rather interacts with environmental experience in determining developmental outcomes" (Bronfenbrenner & Ceci, 1994, p. 571). Culture (the macrosystem or outer circle) determines what genes will be manifest by the opportunities that are available in the culture. For example, heavy alcohol use is partially heritable, but heritability is lower in religious households and in communities that spend less money on alcohol (Dick & Rose, 2002). Heritability of a trait may depend on culture-based opportunities for the trait to be manifest.

Some environments place children at risk for poor outcomes regardless of their genotype, whereas others are protective of children, fostering optimal outcomes. We will turn to a discussion of risk and protective factors next. Two risk factors will be used as examples: *socioeconomic status* is a part of culture (in the macrosystem) that affects large groups of children, whereas *maternal depression* affects proximal processes (in the microsystem) and fosters differences among individual children. Other risk and protective factors will be discussed in later chapters.

1-3 Risk and Resilience

Kathleen is a lively, smiling toddler with five older siblings who dote on her. Suddenly, her father leaves the family for a teenage girlfriend. Her mother begins drinking heavily, but denies that she is an alcoholic. Kathleen's siblings take care of her, until one by one they graduate from high school and leave home. As a teenager, Kathleen becomes her mother's caretaker when her mom is "sick." One of her brothers returns to live at home when he is not in jail. Kathleen manages to be tidy, but not stylish, in appearance. She attends a low-achieving inner-city high school. She pays attention during class, turns in homework on time, and earns good grades. Teachers like her. She is a member of the school choir and her church's youth group. Kathleen feels depressed and anxious about her mother and her own future, but she keeps these feelings to herself. Through hard work, she later receives a scholarship to nursing school. By her late twenties Kathleen is married, has two children, and is a practicing nurse.

Why do some children, like Kathleen, seem to fare well even when they have adverse lives? This is the question of risk and resilience. A risk factor is an aspect of the child or environment that increases the probability of poor outcomes (see Photo 1.3). Risk factors can be *biological*, such as low birth weight; *cognitive*, such as low intelligence; *social* or *emotional*, such as aggression or depression; *part of the family*, such as an alcoholic parent; or *part of the community*, such as neighborhood violence. In the bioecological model, risk factors in the microsystem (e.g., parenting quality) have a stronger impact than risk factors in the macrosystem (e.g., neighborhood violence), but risk factors at any level can undermine children's development. Common risk factors for children include the following:[2]

risk factor
a variable associated with negative child outcomes.

Little positive mother–child interaction	*Negative parental attitude toward child*
Low maternal affection	*Physical or hostile discipline*

---

[2] This list is derived from many studies, a few of which are listed here: Brennan, Hall, Bor, Najman, and Williams (2003); Cooper, Osborne, Beck, and McLanahan (2011); Crosnoe et al. (2010); Evans, Li, and Whipple (2013); Heberle, Thomas, Wagmiller, Briggs-Gowan, and Carter (2014); Kujawa, Proudfit, Laptook, and Klein (2015); Lucio, Hunt, and Bornovalova (2012); Miller and Chen, (2010); Miller et al. (2011); Scher and Mayseless (2000); Ziol-Guest and McKenna (2014).

Abuse

Low parental education

Unstimulating home environment

Low family income—receive welfare

Unskilled head of household

Parental anxiety or depression

Antisocial parent

Low birth weight

Low intelligence

Parental drug use

Single parent

Change in parent's marital status

Mother works long hours

Low parental monitoring

Conflict or separation between parents

Parent has multiple sexual partners

Long hours in childcare

Overcrowding or large family

Frequent moves

Foster care or living with another family

Negative, stressful life events

Changing schools

Poor relationships with teachers

Exposure to violence or conflict

resilience
positive development despite adversity or risk.

protective factor
a factor that decreases the likelihood of poor outcomes in children at risk.

Rob Crandall/SCPhotos/Alamy Stock photo

PHOTO 1.3 Poverty is a powerful risk factor.

You probably know resilient children like Kathleen, who succeeded in school in spite of risk factors. **Resilience** refers to the ability to adapt and flourish in the face of adversity and includes the ability to recover from trauma.

1-3a Protective Factors

Resilient children usually have one or more protective factors in their lives. **Protective factors** decrease the likelihood of poor outcomes in children at risk and include the following:[3]

- High-quality parenting—especially a warm, nurturing mother.

- High intelligence, reading ability, and achievement.

- Special talents and participation in extracurricular activities.

- A strong relationship with a father figure or surrogate parent like a favorite teacher or relative.

- Social competence, outgoing personality, and peer acceptance.

- Religious involvement.

Can educators be protective factors for children? Listen to the story of Olly Neal, who grew up African American in Arkansas during the segregated 1950s.

---

[3] There are many studies that describe protective factors, just a few of which are listed here: Bernat, Oakes, Pettingell, and Resnick, (2012); Burchinal, Roberts, Zeisel, and Rowley (2008); Criss, Pettit, Bates, Dodge, and Lapp (2002); Grant et al. (2000); Hardy, Steelman, Coyne, and Ridge (2013); Kim-Cohen, Moffitt, Caspi, and Taylor (2004); Luthar (2006); Pearce, Jones, Schwab-Stone, and Ruchkin (2003).

During his senior year in high school, Olly cut class one day and was hanging around in the library when he noticed a book with a provocative woman on the cover. He wanted to read the book, but was afraid to check it out because his friends might find out that he was reading. He said he wanted to be known for fighting and cussing, not reading, so he stole the book. Weeks later when he returned the book to its place on the shelf, he noticed another book by the same author. He stole that one too, and ended up reading four books by Frank Yerby, an African American author. Olly Neal became a reader, went to law school, and became an appellate judge in the Arkansas Court of Appeals. He learned a hidden part of his own story for the first time at his thirteenth high school reunion. The librarian had noticed him stealing the first book, realized why he was stealing, drove to Memphis to buy another Yerby book, and placed the new book on the shelf where he would find it. She made three trips to Memphis. Her self-less legacy extended to Judge Neal's daughter, who earned a PhD in genetics. (Adapted from Kristof, 2012; Taing, 2009)

This school librarian served as a protective factor for Judge Neal. Many teachers serve as similar protective factors when they promote their students' success at school.

Even resilient children may experience depression and anxiety or stress-related health problems. That is, something that protects children from one negative outcome does not necessarily protect them from all problems. High-risk children are more likely to be resilient in academic achievement than in social or emotional well-being. For example, Kathleen did well in school, but still struggled with depression through adolescence and into adulthood.

Throughout this text you will learn how specific risk and protective factors influence children. You may personally know exceptions to the research. This is because research tells us what *probably* happens for most children, not what definitely happens for each child. For example, children's risk status when they enter school predicts school problems with about 75% accuracy (Pianta, Nimetz, & Bennett, 1997). While this accuracy is substantial, there is clearly room for exceptions.

Typically, a single risk factor has only a small effect size because a particular child's development is a complex array of risk and protective factors. The more risk factors a child experiences, the greater the likelihood that one or more problems will emerge. The *combined number of risk factors* better predicts child outcomes than a single risk factor.

1-3b Accumulation of Risk

Risk factors tend to go together—they are correlated. For example, in a study of African American 4th-, 5th-, and 6th-graders, several risk factors—unmarried mother, low maternal education, poverty, many siblings, maternal depression, many poor classmates—were highly correlated in the 0.79–0.97 range (Burchinal et al., 2008). This means that a child who had one of these risk factors was likely to have some of the other risk factors as well.

When risk factors accumulate, they have a stronger effect. For example, one study found that each additional risk factor in kindergarten predicted higher odds

FIGURE 1.5 Relationship Between Number of Risk Factors and School Outcomes.

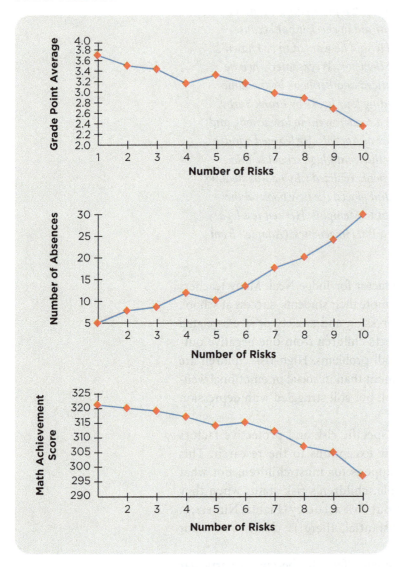

Risk factors included low maternal education (high school diploma or less), maternal depression, unmarried mother, three or more children in the household, unskilled work, living in high-poverty neighborhoods, and stressful events like victim of a crime or lost a job. *Source: Gutman, Sameroff, and Eccles (2002).*

in 5th grade of misbehavior, failing grades, and low academic achievement (Lanza, Rhoades, Nix, & Greenberg, 2010). Among older youth (ages 11–17) a study found that the more risk factors, the greater the likelihood of anxiety, depression, ADHD, and substance use (Roberts, Roberts, & Chan, 2009). Similarly, a study of 95,000 youth found that about 48% had experienced at least one major trauma (e.g., parental divorce, abuse, neglect, witness of violence, parent served time in jail), and 22% had experienced two or more. Youth with two or more traumas were more than twice as likely as youth with zero traumas to have chronic health problems and to have repeated a grade (Bethell, Newacheck, Hawes, & Halfon, 2014). Having only one trauma did not portend these problems. Other studies have found that numbers of risk factors predict students' aggression, school absence, misbehavior, GPA, and math, reading, and social studies test scores.[4] See Figure 1.5.

Risk factors can reside within a child biologically or within the social environment. Biological risks include low birth weight, neurological problems, prenatal drug exposure, and not being breastfed. Social risks include poor-quality parenting, mother's depression, and parental divorce. Some risk factors are more potent than others. Among typical children, *social risk factors are generally more powerful in predicting outcomes than biological risk factors* (Rouse & Fantuzzo, 2009), though an exception is severe biological problems that delay development. Children with *both* social and biological risk are most likely to develop problem behavior, like serious aggression (Belsky, Bakermans-Kranenburg, & Van IJzendoorn, 2007; Brennan et al., 2003). While you might think that it would be ideal to have zero risk factors, there is evidence that children are less likely to develop resilience if they don't have anything to overcome; some adversity, but not too much, may predict greater well-being in adulthood (Seery, 2011).

---

[4] Burchinal et al. (2008); Dearing, McCartney, and Taylor (2009); Fantuzzo, LeBoeuf, and Rouse (2014); Gutman, Sameroff, and Eccles (2002); Lengua, Bush, Long, Kovacs, and Trancik (2008); Yumoto, Jacobson, and Jacobson (2008).

There are three key points for teachers: (1) when risk accumulates, there is a steep increase in the odds of poor outcome; (2) learners may fare well if only one or two risk factors operate in their lives; and (3) a high quality social environment can foster protective factors. Keep these key points in mind as you read about risk and protective factors throughout this text.

1-3c Stability in Development

Does risk or resilience in early childhood have effects into adulthood? Overall there is stability in development because there tends to be stability in risk and protective factors in the environment.

Stability of Risk across Childhood

Children's risk status is quite stable. However, despite this general stability of risk factors, some children's life circumstances do change. Major family turning points such as marriage, a new job, a move to a different community, and religious conversion change a child's life course. A child may be developing poorly but make a dramatic recovery when circumstances improve dramatically. Another child may be doing fine, but experience major life traumas, such as the death of a parent, from which the child may not recover. More mundane changes can also alter a child's risk, such as moving, entry and exit of parents' partners, parents' drug use, and decrease in income (Ackerman, Brown, & Izard, 2004a). Intermittent risk, such as moving in and out of poverty, can be as toxic as stable, persistent risk (Ackerman, Brown, & Izard, 2004b).

Canalization protects children from early risk factors for a short time. Canalization refers to the tendency of genes to restrict development to a limited range of outcomes, despite quite different environments. For example, children learn to walk at about 13 months whether parents help their infants practice walking or not. Canalization often leads children to "self-right" in spite of early deprivation. We experienced an example when one of our sons developed a medical problem at 2 weeks old. His stomach was not functioning properly, so he began to starve. After the condition was corrected surgically, he quickly "self-righted" to a normal weight.

Canalization is stronger for physical development than for social, emotional, or cognitive development. For example after adoption, severely deprived Romanian orphans were more likely to catch up in physical growth than in social behavior, language, or cognitive ability (see Chapter 14).

canalization
genetically based restriction or channeling of development to a limited range of outcomes despite differences in environment.

The Importance of Early Experience

Early experiences are important because they influence later opportunities and color interpretation of later experiences. For example, imagine that Ahmad bumps 15-year-old Duane in the hallway. If Duane experienced hostile, angry parenting as a toddler, he is likely to assume that Ahmad bumped him on purpose. He will slug Ahmad. His aggression will make other youth avoid him, which will prevent him from developing better social skills. In contrast, if Duane experienced soothing, compassionate parenting as a toddler, he is likely to assume Ahmad's bump was an accident, behave kindly toward Ahmad, and be sought out by other youth, which will provide him with the opportunity to develop even better social skills.

Duane could take widely different developmental paths depending on his early experiences.

In spite of the power of early experience to influence later experience, children are flexible and adjust to the quality of their environment at any age. In some instances, children can remain scarred from severe early deprivation, but improvement is always possible, although it may be small. Thus, at any age both the child's historical and current profile of risk and protective factors are important. We next turn to a discussion of the effects of two of the most powerful risk factors—maternal depression and poverty.

1-3d Maternal Depression as a Risk Factor

When a mother is clinically depressed, she may experience sadness, loss of interest in daily activities, fatigue, and inability to think clearly. This may affect her children. Research shows that maternal depression is associated with children's *biological* and *cognitive* problems, such as failure to thrive, behavior problems, poor sleep, limited play, poor language ability, high heart rate, and abnormal brain functioning. Maternal depression is also associated with children's *social* and *emotional* problems, such as irritability, depression, wariness, unresponsiveness to others, slow response to psychological interventions, ADHD (attention-deficit/hyperactivity disorder), suicidal thoughts, aggression, and social withdrawal.[5]

Some negative social and emotional effects appear as early as 2 months of age. They have been found in diverse families, from children of low-income teenage mothers to middle-class adult mothers (Dawson et al., 1999). Children's behavior problems tend to wax and wane as the mother's depression waxes and wanes (Nicholson, Deboeck, Farris, Boker, & Borkowski, 2011). Effects depend on the severity and longevity of the mother's depression (see Photo 1.4). However, early effects can be long-lasting. Effects of maternal depression in the first few years of life are still evident in adolescence, even if the mother has recovered by then (Karevold, Rxysamb, Ystrom, & Mathiesen, 2009). Interestingly, some children with depressed mothers take on the caretaking of their depressed mothers—as Kathleen did (Champion et al., 2009).

How does maternal depression influence such a wide array of outcomes? Perhaps through other risk factors such as divorce, marital conflict, and low education that are linked to maternal depression. Perhaps children "catch" emotional negativity by imitating their depressed mothers. Depressed parents model and reinforce depressed behavior in their children (Webster-Stratton & Herman, 2008). Perhaps depression

PHOTO 1.4 Maternal depression can interfere with quality of parenting.

Denise Hager/Catchlight Visual Services/Alamy stock photo

[5] There are many studies that support these conclusions, just a few of which are listed here: Claessens, Engel, and Chris Curran (2015); Dawson et al. (2003); Kersten-Alvarez et al. (2012); Lesesne, Visser, and White (2003); Mennen et al. (2015); Shaw, Gilliom, Ingoldsby, and Nagin (2003); Wachs, Black, and Engle (2009); Weinberg and Tronick (1998).

compromises the mother–child relationship. Depressed mothers tend to be more intrusive, more critical, and less responsive to their children (Dix & Meunier, 2009; Milan, Snow, & Belay, 2009). These parent–child interactions are among the most powerful processes discussed in the bioecological model.

Are there protective factors? Children are less likely to develop problems despite a depressed mother if they have:

- A positive mother–child relationship where the mother is warm and sensitive despite her depression (Pargas, Brennan, Hammen, & Le Brocque, 2010).

- Affluence. Depressed but high-income mothers are more likely to be sensitive to their children (NICHD ECCRN, 1999; Petterson & Albers, 2001).

- A mentally healthy, nondepressed father in the home (Field, Hossain, & Malphurs, 1999; Radke-Yarrow, Cummings, Kuczynski, & Chapman, 1985).

- High IQ (Pargas et al., 2010).

- A warm and positive classroom emotional environment (Yan, Zhou, & Ansari, 2015), which you can help create.

Most research on maternal depression is nonexperimental, making it hard to determine what causes what. Does maternal depression cause problems in children, or do problems in children cause their mothers to be depressed? Experimental studies can help answer this question. It turns out that interventions that help depressed mothers improve their parenting skills result in better outcomes in their children. This suggests that maternal depression causes child problems (Baydar, Reid, & Webster-Stratton, 2003; Field, 1998).

1-3e Poverty as a Risk Factor

Poverty is another powerful and all-too-common risk factor for children. Almost one in five children live in poverty, which is twice the rate of elderly people (Hernandez, Denton, & Macartney, 2008). About 37% of children will experience poverty at some time during their childhood or adolescence (Ratcliffe & McKernan, 2010). In 2015, the federal government defined *poverty* as an annual income below $24,250 for a family of two parents and two related children.

The term *poverty* is often used broadly to refer to very low socioeconomic status, rather than strictly adhering to the federal definition. Socioeconomic status (SES) refers to a combination of parental education, occupation, and income. Families are designated as low, middle, or high in SES. You may think income is the key component of SES, but as you will learn in later chapters, parent education more strongly predicts child outcomes. SES influences many things that you think and do. When did you start to think about attending college (and what type of college)? What sports have you participated in? What kinds of food do you eat? What jobs have you considered? Low- and high-SES persons may answer each of those questions differently.

Low SES is a risk factor for many problems. For example, low SES is linked to *health* problems like drug exposure, rlespiratory illness, cavities, obesity, and complications following injuries or infections. These health problems continue into adulthood (John-Henderson, Stellar, Mendoza-Denton, & Francis, 2015). Low SES is also

socioeconomic status (SES) categorization based on parental education, income, and occupational status; often simplified as low, middle, and upper class.

FIGURE 1.6 **Kindergarten Readiness by SES.**

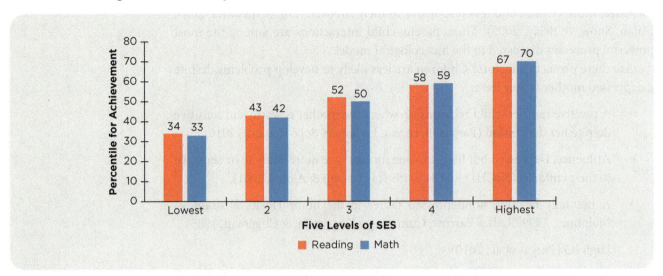

This graph depicts reading and math scores for 6600 children at entry to kindergarten for five levels of SES. *Source: Larson, Russ, Nelson, Olson, and Halfon (2015).*

linked to *socioemotional* problems like depression, delinquency, psychiatric problems, low self-control, and especially aggression. Lower income individuals are more likely to express anger, especially if frustrated (Park et al., 2013). Low SES is also linked to *cognitive* problems like low verbal ability, low intelligence, poor memory, and low achievement (see Figure 1.6). Even families who are working class but not in poverty tend to have children with lower achievement than middle-class families (Roksa & Potter, 2011). Poverty undermines self-regulation, which undermines children's achievement (Blair & Raver, 2015). We will return to this topic in later chapters.

The Black–White achievement gap you learned about earlier, while large, has declined somewhat. In contrast, the rich–poor achievement gap has increased (see Figure 1.7). Why might this be? One possibility is that income inequality has risen dramatically, creating a greater divide between families who have money to spend on school-relevant activities and those who do not (Reardon, 2013). The rich–poor gap is not only for test scores, but also for college attendance and extracurricular activities.

FIGURE 1.7 **Black–White and Rich–Poor Achievement Gap by Year.**

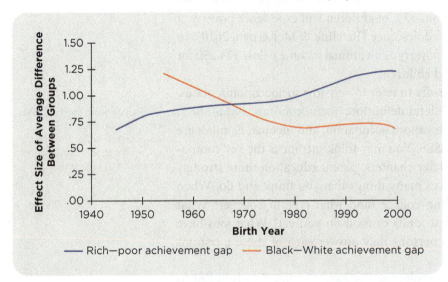

This graph depicts the size of the achievement gap between Black and White students and the achievement gap between low-income and high-income students, for different cohorts. For which cohort were there steeper changes? How might you explain this? *Source: Reardon (May 2013).*

There is evidence that increasing family income, even if the money is not earned and comes from tribal casino payments or poverty assistance programs, improves child outcomes such as higher academic achievement, fewer behavioral disorders, greater conscientiousness, and more enjoyable relationships with parents, as well as reductions in parental drug and alcohol use (Akee, Simeonova, Costello, & Copeland, 2015; Duncan, Morris, & Rodrigues, 2011).

If you teach in an elite private school, you will see that the top rungs of the income ladder are not ideal; wealth poses risk for children. High-SES youth have higher levels of stress, pressure to achieve, anxiety, depression, and drug use than inner-city youth (Luthar & Latendresse, 2008). Furthermore, high-SES individuals tend to be less compassionate, generous, trusting, and helpful—and even donate a lower proportion of their income to charity—compared to low-SES (Kraus, Piff, Mendoza-Denton, Rheinschmidt, & Keltner, 2012). As one researcher argued, "To be compassionate, you have to carefully attend to other people—to what they're thinking, feeling and saying. The wealthy don't do that as well as poorer people" (De Angelis, 2015, p. 65). Children may fare best in middle-income, *but not wealthy*, neighborhoods (Caspi, Taylor, Moffitt, & Plomin, 2000). This is right where you are likely to be with a teacher's salary!

How Does Poverty Have These Effects?

Two major models have been proposed to explain the many effects of poverty on children.

Family investment model

According to the family investment model, poverty is associated with less access to cultural or financial capital that the family can "invest" in children, which leads to poorer health and a low-quality learning environment in the home (Duncan & Brooks-Gunn, 2000). Home-learning environment refers to time spent reading, preschool experience, language stimulation, number of puzzles and books, outings to museums or theaters, and family meal routines. The quality of the home-learning environment, in turn, predicts achievement and behavior problems among Latino, African American, and White children (Bradley, Corwyn, Burchinal, McAdoo, & Garcia Coll, 2001; Linver, Brooks-Gunn, & Kohen, 2002).

Family stress model

According to the family stress model, poverty is associated with conditions that stress parents, such as lack of food, single parenthood, divorce, frequent moves, and job loss. This leads to depression, marital conflict, and other problems. These, in turn, lead to *diminished quality of parenting* (Bradley & Corwyn, 2002). Home or job stress tends to result in parents' emotional and physical withdrawal from children (Repetti, Wang, & Saxbe, 2009). The family stress model has been supported for Latino, African American, and White families (Lugo-Gil & Tamis-LeMonda, 2008; Raver, Gershoff, & Aber, 2007; White, Liu, Nair, & Tein, 2015). Both of these models may be true—the family stress model may explain behavior problems better, while

think
about this
Stanford University has a "housing project" for graduate students with children. Many children live there for years, with stressed parents and incomes well below the poverty level. How do you predict the children fare? Weigh risk and protective factors.

the family investment model may explain academic problems better (Gershoff, Aber, Raver, & Lennon, 2007).

In addition to the family investment and stress models, the effects of poverty could result from a simple accumulation of risk factors. Poor children are exposed to more risk factors—such as family violence and instability, low-quality parenting, heavy TV watching, pollution, lead, parental smoking, and a variety of other risk factors (Dilworth-Bart & Moore, 2006; Evans, 2004). Major risk factors for impoverished children include having a single parent, frequent moving, and stress (Adam, 2004; Blair et al., 2011). Another is household chaos—noise, crowding, and few household routines. In fact, when chaos levels are statistically accounted for, the effect of poverty on children almost disappears, suggesting that chaos may be a key path through which poverty affects children (Evans, Gonnella, Marcynyszyn, Gentile, & Salpekar, 2005).

Ethnicity and Poverty

In most countries, poverty and ethnicity go hand in hand. In the United States, children of color are more likely to be poor than White children, though the majority of poor children are White. For example, about 77% of African American children compared to 30% of White children will experience poverty (Ratcliffe & McKernan, 2010). Families that are persistently poor are more likely to be headed by an African American than are families that are able to increase their income (Wagmiller, 2015).

Classroom Implications of Poverty

Poor children are more likely than wealthier children to develop problems that undermine their achievement in school. However, keep in mind that this is only a probability, not destiny. Many poor children will do well in school. Let's listen to an adult who grew up poor.

> *Poverty is like a gravity that pulls you down to earth. There's no way to jump high enough to overcome gravity by "hard work." Effort alone won't make you fly. I was aware that people judged my mother negatively because she did not have a job. I was torn between wanting to side with those who judged my mother as lazy and irresponsible—and wanting to protect her from those judgments because I loved her and saw all the good things she did do and the intelligence inside her, the beautiful bright interesting person she is. (Adapted from Summer, 2003, pp. 3, 33–34)*

This was written by a girl who was so poor she was homeless in childhood but later attended Harvard. How did she come to be successful in school (and write so well)? She may have had protective factors that offset her poverty.

Family protective factors include a married mother, a mother with high intelligence, stimulating care at home, income adequate to meet basic needs, a family that provides structure, and social support. Personal protective factors include optimism, sense of humor, emotional competence, and intelligence (Bradley & Corwyn, 2002;

Dearing, McCartney, & Taylor, 2001). How can you be a protective factor to your students?

1. Amplify their protective factors and highlight their strengths. Children like Kathleen have remarkable skills. Recognize them. Recognize that many low-SES children are taking care of parents or raising younger siblings.

2. Teach an engaging curriculum. Low-SES children tend to get less exposure to academic content. This may be partly due to low-SES students being pulled out of class for special services.

3. Don't wait to be asked for help. Low SES students are less likely to request or demand teacher help, so you may need to be observant and offer help instead of waiting for requests (Calarco, 2011).

Each chapter throughout this text will provide you with additional tools to help you be a protective factor for your students. High-quality school experiences can compensate for lower school readiness among poor children. Indeed, this is the aim of some preschools.

1-4 Classroom Implications: The Case of School Readiness and Preschool

Some preschool programs, like Head Start, are designed to promote better-than-expected school readiness for children at risk for low achievement, or in other words, to be a *protective factor*. Because risks accumulate, interventions targeting a single factor are not very successful (Masten & Reed, 2002). Thus, preschools for children at risk often include services that go beyond traditional preschools, like parent education and job training. Such preschools typically target children based on either low income or low birth weight (see Chapter 2).

It is important to place children on a positive developmental path as early as possible. It was a common, but mistaken, belief during the years when Head Start was begun that much of a child's crucial brain development was over by age 6, or even age 3. In fact, intervention can help children throughout the lifespan. However, change is more rapid in younger children. The use of preschool to foster school readiness in poor children touches upon each of the major topics of this chapter—the science of child development, the nature–nurture balance, and risk and resilience—so we will use it as a case to illustrate how ways of thinking about children influence your teaching experience.

1-4a School Readiness

School readiness refers to skills that prepare children for formal instruction, such as being able to follow directions; having self-control; and knowing the alphabet, basic numbers, and colors. While only 10% of teachers say that children should know their alphabet and be able to count to 20 to be ready for kindergarten, 60% say they need to have self-control, that is, be able to follow directions and not be disruptive

(Blair, 2002). Interestingly, several large studies across several countries show that math skills, like knowing numbers, predict later academic success with an effect size of 0.34 (Duncan et al., 2007). Early math scores predicted later pre-reading *and* math scores with about the same accuracy, and early math scores predicted later pre-reading *better* than early reading scores, which is surprising. This does not mean that social and emotional skills are not important to how children get along later in school—indeed, you will learn in subsequent chapters that these are important skills—but rather that preschool math knowledge is a particularly important predictor of later achievement.

Young children vary in school readiness. Some enter kindergarten reading at a 5th-grade level or counting to 100, but others have no reading skills and can't count to 10. Some enter kindergarten with good self-regulation—the ability to focus and maintain attention, control their emotions, and maintain positive social interactions with teachers and peers—but others have poor self-regulation (Blair & Raver, 2015). Self-regulation is considered a key aspect of school readiness. It partially explains why some enter kindergarten with school-appropriate behavior, but others have social and behavior problems that are linked to low achievement several years later (Sabol & Pianta, 2012). About 16% have serious problems adjusting to kindergarten, another 32% have some problems, and the rest do fine according to kindergarten teachers (Rimm-Kaufman, Pianta, & Cox, 2000). Low SES is a risk factor for entering school unprepared, but low SES children fare well if they have effective teachers and parents who support their learning (Crosnoe & Cooper, 2010; Crosnoe et al., 2010).

Measuring School Readiness

Some states require tests of kindergarten readiness. Some readiness tests measure beginning academic skills, like knowledge of letters, numbers, or shapes. Many readiness tests do not meet standards for validity or reliability, yet are still used by schools (La Paro & Pianta, 2000). Some experts object to their use as gatekeepers to school because children with low scores have the greatest need to be in school and because they encourage advantaged parents to hold back their children so they will be at the top of their class. This inflates teachers' concepts of what a typical kindergartener is capable of, which pushes excessively academic curricula onto younger children (Shepard, 1997).

Many districts use age as a gatekeeper to school. Should parents place their September-birthday son in kindergarten where he will be the youngest, or wait until next year when he will be the oldest? Research shows that "underage" kindergarteners perform well in high school (Vecchiotti, 2003). The youngest 1st-graders may be a little behind the oldest 1st-graders in reading and math, but this effect washes out by the middle of elementary school (Morrison, Griffith, & Alberts, 1997). Furthermore, when children who are placed in school young are later tested in first grade, they are more advanced than their same-age peers who are in kindergarten. School makes kids smarter. Some parents have their children start kindergarten a year late, assuming that this will give them an academic advantage; evidence suggests it does not, and it may even create disadvantage (Martin, 2009). Thus, entrance age is not a good predictor of academic success.

What Should Be Done for Children Who Are Not Ready for School?

The answer to this question depends on your theory of children's development. A *maturationist* assumes that school readiness depends on abilities driven by a genetic timetable. Thus, waiting for the child to mature biologically is the logical answer. The practice of holding back children in kindergarten is evidence that this view is common in schools. In contrast, an *environmentalist* would assume that school readiness is driven by having the right experiences. Thus, providing preschool experiences would be the logical answer. The difference in these views is the nature–nurture contrast.

What does the research say about this contrast? The maturationist view is undermined by two lines of research. First, kindergarten retention does not have an academic payoff; children learn more if they are promoted (Hong & Yu, 2008b). Second, quality of the home environment affects school readiness. A major twin study shows that shared environment makes a substantial contribution to school readiness—even bigger than genes or nonshared environment (Forget-Dubois et al., 2009; Lemelin et al., 2007). Aspects of the environment that affect school readiness include mothers' education, preschool experience, and books at home. School readiness can be promoted for children at risk by providing enriched preschool experiences (Huang & Invernizzi, 2013).

think about this

If the quality of the environment affects children's school readiness, should children who perform poorly on readiness tests be kept out of school? Describe how another year in their home environment might affect the school readiness of children from different backgrounds.

1-4b What Does the Research on Preschools for Children at Risk Say?

One approach to helping poor children become ready for formal schooling is to provide publicly funded preschool, like Head Start and prekindergarten.

Head Start

The most famous preschool program is Head Start. Eligibility for Head Start is based on family income. The largest single federal program exclusively for poor children, Head Start provides health, education, and social services. Most programs are half day and operate on a school-year calendar. Most children enrolled in Head Start are 3 or 4 years old. Roughly one-third of Head Start children are African American, another one-third are Latino, another one-third are White, and a small number are other ethnicities (Administration for Children & Families, 2007).

How effective is Head Start? Evidence from the 1990s and before suggests Head Start was associated with short-term cognitive gains that diminished over time (Lamb, 1998). Head Start children also behaved worse in school than children in no preschool or other preschools, but the effect was small (Lee, Brooks-Gunn, Schnur, & Liaw, 1990). Because these effects of Head Start were modest at best, some programs were extended up to 3rd grade and down to toddlers, like Early Head Start, in order to increase impact.

Did these innovations help? Scientists have used randomized experiments to answer this question. In a national experiment mandated by Congress, the researchers concluded:

Head Start has benefits for both 3-year-olds and 4-year-olds in the cognitive, health, and parenting domains, and for 3-year-olds in the social–emotional

> *domain. However, the benefits of access to Head Start at age four are largely absent by 1st grade . . . . For 3-year-olds, there are few sustained benefits, although access to the program may lead to improved parent–child relationships through first grade, a potentially important finding for children's longer term development. (Puma et al., 2010, p. xxxviii)*

This conclusion that Head Start has neutral to positive effects that improve school readiness and last for a few years but generally not more has been found repeatedly in previous studies (e.g., Goodson, Layzer, St. Pierre, Bernstein, & Lopez, 2000; Love et al., 2005; Puma, Bell, Cook, Heid, & Lopez, 2005).

Prekindergarten

Elementary schools serving large numbers of poor children often have compensatory prekindergarten programs at the school site. Some are funded by Title I (also called Chapter 1), a federal program for schools with high rates of poverty. They tend to have more highly educated teachers than other preschools, including Head Start (Lee, Loeb, & Lubeck, 1998). Some pre-K programs result in better readiness skills at school entry, but few results last beyond 1st grade (e.g., Gormley, Gayer, Phillips, & Dawson, 2005; Weiland & Yoshikawa, 2013). A review of pre-K programs found that of 11 outcomes, the only robust long-term effect was less grade retention (Gilliam & Zigler, 2000). For example, in Maryland, 44% of pre-K attenders, but 64% of nonattenders, had been retained at some point by tenth grade. Yet, some studies find positive long-term effects on delinquent behavior and educational achievement. For example, in Chicago, children in pre-K were more likely to finish high school (56% versus 47%) and not be arrested for crimes (13% versus 22%) by age 20 than nonattendees (Reynolds, Ou, & Topitzes, 2004). Some programs also find an effect on math and reading achievement beyond third grade, but the effect is very small (Gilliam & Zigler, 2000). There is little effect on behavior problems, parent involvement, self-esteem, or health. Effects may depend on the instructional quality of the preschool. A study of over 2700 preschoolers found that children who mainly engaged in free play had smaller learning gains than children who had more instructional time with teachers (Chien et al., 2010). Play is important, but so is effective instruction.

To summarize, the research suggests that Head Start and pre-K programs have small, short-term benefits. Once intervention children enter school, their test scores drop and often the control group children's rise (Barnett, 1995; Magnuson et al., 2004). Similar effects are found for full- versus half-day kindergarten; small gains in achievement for full-day kindergarten wash out by third grade (Cooper, Allen, Patall, & Dent, 2010).

Intensive, model programs generally have stronger effects, with effect sizes of 0.15 to 0.43 (Magnuson, Meyers, Ruhm, & Waldfogel, 2004; Reynolds et al., 2004). Model programs also tend to have more extensive components, such as beginning earlier in infancy instead of at age 3 and using highly trained staff at a university childcare facility. Positive effects of intensive, model programs have been documented into the middle school and high school years (Dearing, McCartney,

FIGURE 1.8 Long-Term Outcomes from the Abecedarian Project.

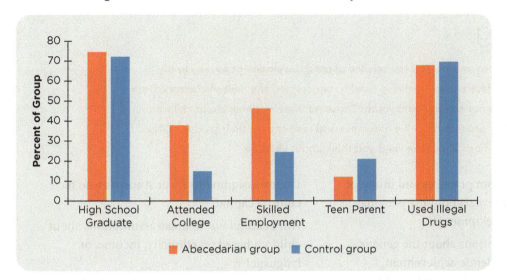

Children were randomly assigned to the Abecedarian Project or to a control group as infants. Both groups were followed longitudinally. Results suggest that the project had a long-term impact on some outcomes. Which outcomes differed for the two groups and which did not? Which outcomes were high or low for both groups? *Source: Data are from Pungello et al. (2010).*

& Taylor, 2009; Vandell et al., 2010). One of the most successful is the *Abecedarian Project*, which provided educational child care of exceptional quality 8 hours daily for 5 years and home visits from a resource teacher for the first 3 years of school. Researchers have followed children in this project, and a control group, into adulthood. The project resulted in better cognitive and academic ability, less depression, increased college attendance and graduation, more highly skilled employment, and higher income, but no difference in illegal drug use (Campbell et al., 2012; McLaughlin, Campbell, Pungello, & Skinner, 2007; Pungello et al., 2010). (See Figure 1.8.) Similar effects were found for a model program in Chicago (Reynolds, Temple, Ou, Arteaga, & White, 2011). Children who fare best over the long run are those who continue to have enrichment into the elementary years—either by continuing in an intervention program or by entering high-quality elementary schools (Reynolds et al., 2004, 2011).

In conclusion, preschool can enhance the development of high-risk children if it is of high quality and extensive. Effects may be strongest for African American and Hispanic children compared to White children (Bassok, 2010; Tucker-Drob, 2012). Some programs are more effective than others, but even among successful programs, effects on achievement diminish over time and cannot fully compensate for disparities between poor and advantaged children. Although the effects are small, they have important benefits for individuals and society and, over the long run, may outweigh costs if they result in less special education placement, lower crime rates, and better adult employment. The fact that children's outcomes can be modestly improved by preschool suggests a role for nurture beyond the family (Rutter, 2000). You can enhance the development of your high-risk students by providing optimal education environments.

reflections on practice

My Teaching

It is important for teachers to understand the science of child development as they apply research findings to their classrooms. They also need to understand the multiple factors, from genes to culture, that influence children and youth. The ways teachers think about children will influence whether they promote positive outcomes and resilience in their students. Ask yourself the following questions about the ways you think about children:

1. What do my classroom practices and image of an ideal classroom reveal about my personal theories of child development?

2. What are my assumptions about the genetic basis of a child's academic achievement, athletic prowess, or social competence? What is my role as teacher in fostering ability in these domains?

3. Am I a careful consumer of information about supposedly effective interventions? Do I check to see if the information is research based and whether the research was carefully conducted? Do I consider whether causal factors can be determined, if results should generalize to my students, and whether effect size is adequate?

4. When I use information from tests, am I careful to consider reliability and the validity for their use?

5. What factors are operating on my students in each ring of the bioecological model? What personal and cultural strengths does each child bring to the classroom?

6. What is the cultural capital of my students? What can I do to provide cultural capital?

Do my assignments favor students who have cultural capital?

7. Am I careful not to make assumptions about children based on ethnicity, income, or language?

8. Are my students comfortable at school? Is there a cultural mismatch between my students and my classroom? Do I genuinely celebrate the strengths of different cultures?

9. What is the profile of risk and protective factors for each of my students? Do I facilitate resilience by enhancing their protective factors?

10. Do the at-risk, low-income children in my classroom spend as much academic time-on-task as their more affluent peers? Do I have appropriately high expectations for them?

11. What is my school's vision of school readiness (maturationist or environmentalist)? Do we use age or readiness tests to keep children out even though they need school experience? What are my district and school doing to improve readiness in preschoolers?

Professional Resource Download

Chapter Summary

1-1 The Science of Child Development

- There are many different theories of child development. Theories vary in the emphasis given to biological processes (i.e., maturationist) or the environment (i.e., environmentalist).

- Research designs include experiments, correlational studies, and qualitative studies. Experiments use random assignment and control groups to make strong claims about causality that correlational studies cannot. Longitudinal designs document change across time, and cross-sectional studies simulate change across time.

- Use of reliable and valid measures is fundamental to research and education.

- Research should be crafted to generalize to a variety of children. Research in recent decades has included more diverse populations than in the past.

- Effect size refers to the size of difference between groups, or correlation between variables, and helps you judge how important a research finding may be.

1-2 Nature and Nurture

- The bioecological model suggests that nested systems influence the child, with proximal processes like the family being the most powerful.

- Behavioral geneticists attribute variation in any trait to heritability, shared environment, or nonshared environment. Estimates of their relative contribution are based on indirect methods, such as comparing twins or adopted siblings.

- Genes make a contribution to many aspects of development, but environment typically makes a greater contribution.

- Families can be a nonshared environment, because children react differently to the family environment and because families change over time.

- Whether a genotype becomes a phenotype depends on the environment. Genes do not minutely program behavior or the brain, which makes adaptation possible.

- Genes and environment interact. Gene–environment correlation means that children may select environments that match their genetic dispositions. Culture can influence whether a genotype is manifest.

- Within the United States, Asian children tend to have the highest achievement, followed by White, African American, and then Latino children. However, within ethnic groups there are large differences in achievement. Plausible explanations include cultural capital and cultural mismatch (e.g., language and narrative style).

1-3 Risk and Resilience

- Risk factors predict poor outcomes for children. Social risk factors are usually more powerful than biological risk factors. A single risk factor is not likely to strongly predict poor outcomes. Risk factors tend to accumulate, greatly increasing the likelihood of a poor outcome. Protective factors reduce the likelihood of poor outcomes among children at risk, leading to resilience.

- Development is generally stable because early development influences later development and because risk factors tend to be stable across childhood. In spite of early risk, canalization leads children to "self-right" to a species-typical trajectory. Canalization is strongest in the first 2 years, and for physical development.

- Maternal depression and poverty are major risk factors that have pervasive effects on child outcomes. Both may affect children by compromising the quality of parent–child interaction. Poverty may also affect children through parents' limited ability to invest in the children, and through chaos and stress.

1-4 Classroom Implications: The Case of School Readiness and Preschool

- School readiness refers to social and emotional skills as well as basic knowledge that help children experience success in school. Many children are not ready for school, but keeping children out of school based upon readiness tests or age does not promote their development.

- Large-scale, community-based preschools for low-SES children (e.g., Head Start and pre-K programs) generally have positive short-term cognitive effects, but slight or no long-term effects, although participants are less likely to be retained in grade. In contrast, intensive, high-quality programs can produce long-term benefits, but participants do not continue to make academic gains after they enter school, and they still perform below grade level. Long-term benefits include more education, better employment, and higher income.

chapter

2

Rob Mattingley/iStock/Getty Images Plus/Getty Images

Physical Development and Health

Should you be concerned about your students' physical well-being, such as nutrition, physical activity, drug use, and sleep? We think you will answer with a resounding yes at the end of this chapter. **After you read this chapter, you will be able to:**

2-1 Describe how the brain develops from infancy through adolescence and analyze how experiences in your classroom may influence brain architecture in learners.

2-2 Identify how individual and group differences in motor skills contribute to learners' success in your classroom, and create an environment that fosters optimal physical well-being in your students.

2-3 Describe three health challenges today's children face—sleep, obesity and other eating disorders, and substance use and exposure—and what you can do to address these challenges.

2-1 The Brain

> *All of Mrs. Z's kindergarten students receive a free breakfast, which they eat at 8:45 in the morning. Their assigned lunchtime is 12:40. Even if you assume they actually ate their breakfast, 4 hours is a long time without food or drink. Mrs. Z decided to provide a 10:30 snack. She reports, "I have seen a big difference in the children's ability to stay on task, greater desire to complete their work to the best of their abilities, and there seems to be less conflict in the centers or during free time just before lunch. I cannot believe the difference it has made."*

Your students are biological beings. This may seem obvious, but it is easy for teachers to overlook physical needs, as Mrs. Z initially did. Abraham Maslow, a psychologist, argued that children cannot attend to classroom tasks unless their basic physical needs are met first (see Box 2.1). Meeting the needs of one part of the body—the brain—is especially important because the brain regulates learning, behavior, and other physical functions.

Interest in the brain has surged thanks to technology that allows neuroscientists to view the brain in action. Neuroscience is the study of how the brain is involved in perception, memory, and emotions. Among the most important discoveries of neuroscience is that *the brain is constructed by experience.* This means that as a teacher, the way that you interact with your students will contribute to their brain development. Before we discuss how this happens, let's begin with a quick lesson on how the brain works.

2-1a Structure and Function of the Brain

The basic unit of the brain is the nerve cell, or neuron. There are about 100 billion neurons in the brain (Beatty, 2001). A neuron has three parts: the cell body (with a nucleus much like other cells in the body), the dendrites (receiving units that bring information from other cells), and the axons (sending units that carry information away to other neurons or to muscle cells). See Figure 2.2.

Neurons communicate with each other through electrical signals. These signals are affected by **myelin**, a fatty substance that forms an insulating sheath around axons. This myelin sheath makes the electrical signals more efficient, increasing their speed. Some diseases, such as multiple sclerosis (known as MS), damage the myelin sheath; this may result in muscle weakness or thinking problems.

Neurons also communicate with each other chemically at synapses. A **synapse** has three parts: the sending end of one neuron, the receiving end of another, and the space between them. When prompted by an electrical signal, neurons release a chemical, called a **neurotransmitter**, which is then received by another neuron. This occurs at the synapse. Some neurotransmitters you will commonly hear of are dopamine, serotonin, noradrenaline, and norepinephrine. A single neuron may receive input from tens of thousands of synapses. There are more than 100 trillion synapses in the brain (Beatty, 2001). The synapse is where many drugs operate, including drugs that are abused (such as heroin), as well as psychiatric drugs. For example, Ritalin, used to treat ADHD, inhibits the activity of dopamine and norepinephrine.

myelin
a fatty substance that forms an insulating coating, called a myelin sheath, around axons that allows them to function efficiently.

synapse
a junction where neurons communicate with each other, or with other kinds of cells.

neurotransmitter
a chemical that allows neurons to communicate across synapses.

self-actualization
the process of fulfilling one's potential in a way that shows concern for society.

BOX 2.1 theories & theorists

Maslow's Hierarchy of Needs

Abraham Maslow (1908–1970) was the oldest of seven children of uneducated Russian Jews who immigrated to the United States. He was encouraged by his parents to excel in school. He did not; his grades were mediocre. Yet he read voraciously, which may explain why he got into the University of Wisconsin to study psychology. He became a professor at Brooklyn College in his home state of New York in 1937.

Maslow was a leader of humanistic psychology, which was quite different from two prevailing theories of his time: Freudian psychology and behaviorism. Humanistic psychology emphasizes growth and fulfillment. Maslow wanted to know what makes people mentally healthy, rather than mentally ill. He studied exceptional people, such as Abraham Lincoln, Jane Addams, and Albert Einstein. His studies led him to develop the concept of a hierarchy of needs.

Maslow's hierarchy of needs is usually portrayed like a pyramid (see Figure 2.1). The most basic human needs are at the bottom of the pyramid. These are physical needs like air, water, food, and sleep. At the next level are safety needs. These include psychological safety (e.g., stability, security, and order) as well as physical safety. Then come social needs, such as love and acceptance. At the next level are esteem needs, such as admiration from others and self-respect. The highest level is self-actualization.

FIGURE 2.1 **Maslow's Hierarchy of Needs.**

Can you identify where you currently are in this pyramid? Which of your needs are mostly met, and which are pressing issues for you now? Do the same for a child in your class. *Based on Maslow (1970).*

Self-actualization is the process of fulfilling one's potential. This is not a self-centered state. Rather, self-actualizing people are concerned with issues that affect humanity. Self-actualizing people are unpretentious, ethical, compassionate, and creative. However, they are not perfect, nor do they display these attributes at all times. Most people do not become self-actualized; perhaps less than 5% of people truly achieve it. Self-actualization is a very long process. Maslow believed college students are too young to reach this level (Maslow, 1970, p. 150).

According to Maslow, your students' first concern is to fulfill the lowest level of unsatisfied need. When a need is met, it becomes unimportant, and the next level of need becomes pressing. After physiological needs are met, safety needs become pressing. When these needs are met, belonging becomes pressing, and so on. In contrast, when basic needs are not met, children will not go on to higher steps. Needs are not "all or nothing," but rather they emerge gradually. That is, a child does not have to have 100% of each lower need met before the next level of need becomes relevant. Motivation to satisfy needs produces growth as the child comes to pursue higher needs.

According to Maslow, unmet needs are the root of misbehavior and most mental illnesses. For example, hungry learners may become distractible, selfish, and aggressive, as Mrs. Z's students did. Older youth with unmet belongingness needs may join violent gangs.

There are many criticisms of Maslow's work. It was not scientific, because he decided who were self-actualizers and studied their life stories in retrospect. In addition, people can behave as self-actualizers even when lower needs are not met. For example, there were individuals in World War II concentration camps who were deprived of food but were still creative, compassionate, and ethical.

Despite these criticisms, Maslow's hierarchy of needs is useful for teachers. In Maslow's view children are inherently good. If a student misbehaves in your classroom, it may mean that the student's needs are not being met. In Maslow's view, you do not need to control negative impulses as much as to help satisfy basic needs so that your students are free to become all that they can be. Children must be well fed, rested, and feel cared for if they are to achieve in school. This is why understanding children's physical and socioemotional needs will help you become a more effective teacher.

FIGURE 2.2 Anatomy of a Neuron.

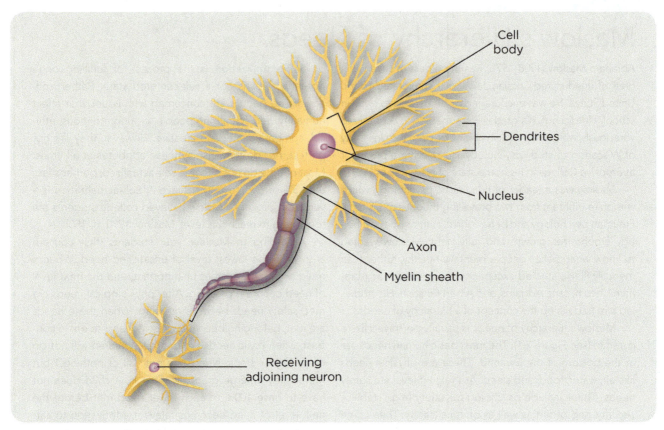

Notice the myelin sheath; this is an important component of the neuron. The neuron is floating in a chemical soup that includes transmitters.

You can think of the brain as a mass of these neurons. This mass has two sides, or hemispheres. The left hemisphere is biased toward language, analytical, and sequential processing. The right hemisphere is biased toward spatial, holistic, and integrative processing (Hopkins & Cantalupo, 2008). Within each hemisphere there are specialized regions. However, there is no such thing as a single place where complex functions, like memory or language, occur. Instead, they use both hemispheres and draw on a network of interconnected systems (Blumstein & Amso, 2013; Cabeza & Moscovitch, 2013). The particular function of a region in the brain depends on which systems it belongs to and where it is in the system. We will briefly describe some key regions next:

- The *brainstem* (midbrain and hindbrain) is part of the lower brain, which is believed to be an evolutionarily old region that regulates body functions like the sleep–wake cycle (Joseph, 2000). It develops around 6 weeks after conception. The *hypothalamus* is located in the midbrain. It regulates internal organs, hormones, body temperature, hunger, emotion, and many other activities. See Figure 2.3.

- The *limbic system* is a collection of structures that sit like a donut on the brainstem; it is considered the reward center of the brain because it is involved in attention, motivation, and emotion. Important structures include the *hippocampus,* the *cingulate gyrus,* and the *amygdala.* The hippocampus is essential to memory. The cingulate gyrus is involved in problem solving. The amygdala is involved in emotions.

- The *cerebellum* is a latticework of neurons at the back of the brain. It is involved in movement, muscle tone, concentration, and learning from errors. It works with the cortex in producing finely coordinated movements, like speech.

FIGURE 2.3 **The Brain.**

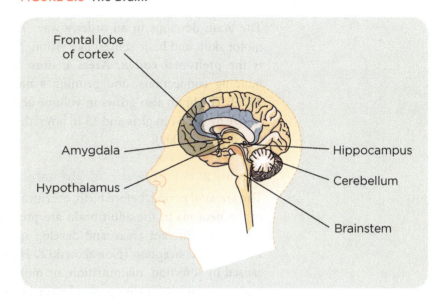

Notice that the prefrontal cortex sits just behind your forehead. This is the last area of your brain to reach maturity.

- The *cerebral cortex* is like a cap covering the other regions of the brain. It takes many years to develop fully. Complex functions like language and abstract thinking are coordinated in the cortex. The cerebral cortex has four lobes, or areas: frontal, parietal, temporal, and occipital. The frontal lobe is especially important for teachers to know about.

- The *frontal lobe* is the largest part of the cortex and is disproportionately large in humans as compared with other species (Rubenstein, 2011). It is involved in organizing information in your mind as you read this text, resisting distraction, and inhibiting impulses. A portion of the frontal lobe, the *prefrontal cortex,* is particularly important in working memory and emotions, which you will read about in later chapters. The prefrontal cortex comprises about one-third of the entire cortex. It directs activity in other parts of the brain, like the conductor of a symphony (Huey, Krueger, & Grafman, 2006).

When a task activates the prefrontal cortex, it also activates the cerebellum. This is why cognitive and motor problems often go together. For example, poor balance or poor handwriting (i.e., motor problems) are found in more than half of learners with ADHD. Motor problems are also found in learners with dyslexia and autism. Thus, many, but not all, children in your classroom who have cognitive problems may also have motor problems (e.g., Roebers & Kauer, 2009).

Age does not bring changes in the overall structure of the brain, but it does bring changes in the brain's fine architecture and functioning. Let's look at age trends next.

2-1b Age Trends in Brain Development

The brain develops in an orderly way. The first areas to mature are involved in motor skills and basic senses, like vision. Next come language areas. Last to mature is the prefrontal cortex. Areas mature by increasing myelination, specializing, building connections, and pruning synapses (Johnson, Grossmann, & Kadosh, 2009). The brain also grows in volume across childhood; the cerebral cortex peaks in size by age 11 in girls and 15 in boys; the cerebellum peaks a couple of years later (Giedd et al., 2009).

Infancy and Toddlerhood (Prenatal to 2 Years)

The *prenatal* period, before birth, is critically important in brain development. Most of the neurons in the adult brain are produced before birth. Neurons proliferate, migrate to different areas, and develop specialized functions beginning just a few weeks after conception (Nowakowski & Hayes, 2002). Errors in this process can be caused by infection, malnutrition, or mother's alcohol use during pregnancy. The brain is capable of learning even before birth, such as an infant's learning to recognize the mother's voice (Joseph, 2000).

A dramatic change during this period is the explosive growth of synapses. **Synaptogenesis** is an extreme overproduction of synapses that occurs from about 3 months before birth until about age 2 (see Figure 2.4). The number of brain cells does not increase substantially after birth, but there are many more neuron branches and synaptic connections between cells. **Myelination** also begins during the last 3 months of pregnancy and is completed in the sensory and motor areas in the first few years after birth (Blakemore & Choudhury, 2006). Myelination increases the connections between key areas of the brain.

Glucose fuels the brain. At birth, the glucose consumption rate is about two-thirds that of adults, but it increases steadily. The consumption of glucose indicates energy use in the brain.

synaptogenesis
a spurt in synaptic connections of the brain that occurs from the third trimester of gestation until about 2 years of age.

myelination
the development of myelin.

glucose rate
the rate of consumption of glucose, an indicator of energy use in the brain.

FIGURE 2.4 **Synaptogenesis.**

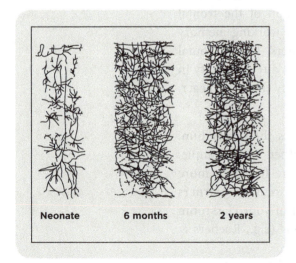

Neonate   **6 months**   **2 years**

The remarkable increase in neuron connections across the synapses in the first 2 years allows the brain to be shaped by experience.

Early Childhood (3 to 5 Years)

The brain's consumption of glucose continues to increase so that by 4 years of age, both **glucose rate** and blood flow to the cortex are *twice that of adults* (Chugani, 1998). This is a dramatic increase in energy demand in the cortex. In contrast, the brainstem remains fairly stable in glucose use throughout childhood.

Some areas of the prefrontal cortex become more interconnected, which is linked to young children's increasing ability to follow rules, sit still, and raise their hands during group time (Bunge & Zelazo, 2006). When children enter kindergarten, they have more synapses than when they were born, and more than you have now, thanks to synaptogenesis. Why would young children have more synapses than you do? Your neurons have been "pruned" of their branches. Pruning is not random. It is based on experience. When enough electrical signals are sent to a synapse, and the chemical environment of the synapse is favorable, the synapse gets stronger. If neurons are repeatedly activated together, they form stable circuits; *those that are not used are pruned.* A saying you may hear is, "Neurons that fire together wire together." When you interact with your students in ways that cause specific neurons to fire together often, you influence which brain cells remain connected; you contribute to the final architecture of your students' brains.

Middle Childhood (6 to 12 Years)

The glucose rate in the brain tends to plateau at twice the rate of adults until 9 to 10 years of age. After this, it gradually *declines.* There is a second wave of synaptogenesis in the prefrontal cortex at the start of puberty, and then it plateaus until after puberty (Blakemore & Choudhury, 2006). Some neuroscientists believe that the first 10 years may be a **sensitive period** in brain development (see Chapter 6) because of this intense activity. While it is true that early experience shapes the architecture of the brain, it is important to remember that critical brain development continues beyond middle childhood (Fox, Levitt, & Nelson, 2010).

sensitive period
a biologically determined time period, typically early in life, in which a child readily develops specific abilities. Change is less likely before or after the sensitive period.

Adolescence (13 to 19 Years)

The brain becomes more efficient in adolescence. The glucose rate slows to adult levels at 16 to 18 years, indicating less energy use. There are three key changes that make the brain more efficient: (1) Different areas of the brain become more interconnected. (2) Pruning continues—synapses in the frontal cortex diminish to adult levels. (3) Myelination of the prefrontal cortex increases. Axons gradually get thicker from ages 4 to 17, particularly in speech and motor-skill areas. Both myelination and thick axons make information flow more quickly and precisely (Giedd et al., 2009; Paus, 2005). By midadolescence, your students have adultlike memory and information-processing ability.

There is also a chemical shift in the adolescent brain. Some neurotransmitters are reduced, but dopamine increases (Bjork, Lynne-Landsman, Sirocco, & Boyce, 2012). Dopamine affects motivation by changing how rewarding something feels, like driving fast or listening to loud music. Adolescents in many species, including humans, increase their social interactions, sensation seeking, and risk taking, perhaps because of this chemical shift. Figure 2.5 shows how positive views of risk

FIGURE 2.5 Views of Risky Activities by Age.

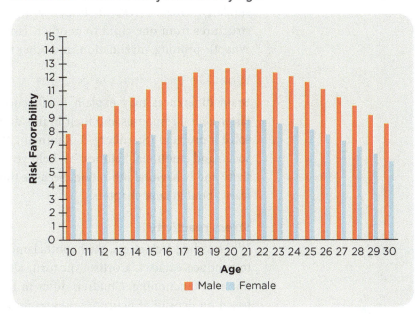

This graph shows average ratings by age of whether respondents said an activity (e.g., riding a bike down stairs, surfing on very high waves, getting drunk) is a "good idea" or a "bad idea." Higher scores indicate a more positive view of risky behaviors. What is the peak age for viewing risky behavior in a positive light? How do males and females differ? *Source: Shulman and Cauffman (2014).*

think
about this

The tendency for teens to view risky behavior as overly rewarding before they have fully developed self-control has implications for many social policies. Discuss how this might affect age-based policies like when youth can get a driver's license, buy alcohol, vote, enter the military, or be tried as an adult for crimes.

taking increase through adolescence, peaking at age 20 (Shulman & Cauffman, 2014). This increase may help with leaving the home nest, but in excess can be a problem. Dopamine is also linked to psychopathology, such as depression (see Chapter 8), and many mental illnesses emerge in adolescence. The combination of risk taking and mental illness has led some people to perpetuate negative stereotypes of teens by blaming the adolescent brain. Some psychologists counterargue that teens who use drugs, are promiscuous, or commit crimes are just imitating adults in their lives (Males, 2009).

Nevertheless, adolescent brain development does present a challenge. Dopamine increases in *early* adolescence (before about age 16), but the prefrontal cortex does not fully mature until the mid-20s. The prefrontal cortex manages thinking processes such as reasoning, impulse control, motor coordination, controlling emotions, weighing risks with rewards, and long-term planning. Can you see the potential problem? Teens may see risky behaviors as overly rewarding before they have adult-like self-control (Bjork et al., 2012). For example, when some boys are discussing racing their bikes down the stadium bleachers, their teenage brains are more likely to register "Great FUN! Let's do it!" whereas adult brains are likely to register "Maybe a little bit fun, but not enough to risk breaking my neck."

Are adult brains, like yours, done developing? Animal research shows that adult brains continue to develop; as a result of learning, they can grow synapses, dendrites, and supportive tissue like blood vessels (Kolb & Whishaw, 1998). However, early life experience may have disproportionate influence on brain architecture because it literally dictates the basic framework.

2-1c Individual Diversity in Brain Development

We have discussed brain structure and age trends as though all brains develop similarly. There is *general* similarity in size, shape, and location of specific brain structures from one child to another. However, there are individual differences in synaptic pruning, myelination, and other factors.

What Do Individual Differences in the Brain Predict?

Brain differences may explain intelligence. That is, more intelligent people have faster neural responses and their brains do not have to consume as much glucose to solve a problem (Sternberg & Kaufman, 1998). Brain differences may also explain social and emotional abilities. To help you understand this, let's look at stress reactivity and behavioral inhibition, because they are the basis of characteristics you will learn about in later chapters.

Stress reactivity

When a child feels stress, the hypothalamus secretes a hormone that causes the body to produce cortisol. Cortisol, in turn, alters energy level, emotions, learning, and immune functioning. Children differ in how easily this stress response is activated based on density of neurons and amount of chemicals in their brains. These brain differences may be caused by adverse childhood experiences (ACE). ACE include the cumulative risk factors you learned about in Chapter 1, such as poverty, discrimination, child abuse, parental drug use, exposure to violence, or negative family environments (Shonkoff et al., 2012).

cortisol
a hormone that the body generates as a response to stress.

adverse childhood experience (ACE)
early toxic experience resulting in prolonged and intense stress, which leaves a mark on long-term brain architecture and well-being.

Children who have an *underreactive* stress response tend to be aggressive, impulsive, delinquent, and have ADHD (Blair, Granger, & Razza, 2005; van Goozen, Fairchild, & Harold, 2008). They do not feel stress as readily as other children and so are not as deterred by the negative consequences of their misbehavior. Children who have an *overreactive* stress response tend to have depression, anxiety, or anorexia. They have higher levels of cortisol after mildly stressful events, such as a 6-minute discussion with their parents about getting homework done (Granger, Weisz, McCracken, & Ikeda, 1996). Balance is ideal; the right amount of cortisol helps you focus attention and control thought and emotion.

Behavioral inhibition

Children with an overreactive stress response may have behavioral inhibition, or a tendency to avoid new people, events, or objects. In social situations, behavioral inhibition is commonly called shyness. During mild stress, inhibited children's hearts speed up, pupils dilate, muscles tense, and cortisol flows more than other children's do (Schmidt & Fox, 2002). When you see shy learners hang back in your classroom, it is likely that their hearts are racing.

Behavioral inhibition is linked to brain differences. Inhibited children have more electrical activity in the right hemisphere and less in the left as early as 4 months of age (Hane, Fox, Henderson, & Marshall, 2008). Children with more *right* hemisphere activity tend to become inhibited toddlers who cry at separation from their mother, or shy older learners whose hearts pound when they have to make a class presentation (Davidson, 2000). On the other hand, children with more *left* activity tend to be outgoing. The left frontal lobe is involved in positive emotions and approaching novel things.

In summary, individual differences in brain function are linked to intelligence, coping with stress, and greeting strangers, as well as many other outcomes. Let's discuss next where these brain differences may come from.

What Predicts Individual Differences in Brain Development?

Brain differences occur in infancy and have a biological base, so you might assume they are caused by genes. This is not necessarily true. They may be caused by differences in experience. The brain adapts to experience, so that experience becomes biology. Both nature and nurture shape the brain.

Genetics

In coming chapters you will learn that most traits have some heritability. Heritability presumably works through genetically caused brain differences. The size of some areas of the brain may be 60 to 80% heritable (Giedd et al., 2009). However, as you learned in Chapter 1, there are not enough genes to specify the precise architecture of the trillions of synapses in the brain. Instead, genes tell the brain to overproduce synapses and then prune them. *The purpose of synaptogenesis is to capture experience and incorporate it into brain architecture.* This is genetically efficient—it requires fewer genes than if all important connections had to be precisely coded in the genes.

Experience

brain plasticity
the brain's ability to change structure and function as a result of experience.

The brain's ability to change as a result of experience is known as **brain plasticity**. Brain plasticity has been studied more in animals than in humans. For example, in monkeys each finger is served by a different area in the cortex. If a monkey loses a finger, the cortex reorganizes itself so the neurons in the area that once served the missing finger now respond to the adjacent fingers instead (Beatty, 2001). Also, when monkeys are trained to pick up a small object from a cup, the cortex area for that finger increases. Human brains also respond to experience—jugglers and musicians develop greater density in areas of the brain related to those skills (Paus, 2005). Similarly, in blind people, the area of the brain that processes vision adapts to process other things instead (Amedi, Merabet, Bermpohl, & Pascual-Leone, 2005). Much of the cortex is *not* dedicated to a specific function and can adapt to other functions.

Is there an age at which the brain no longer responds to experience? There is a subtle, gradual diminishment in the brain's plasticity. Some neuroscientists speculate that the pruning that makes brains more efficient occurs at the cost of plasticity. Learning is not equally easy over time (Thomas & Johnson, 2008). This is why early deprivation can have long-lasting effects in spite of later intervention. Plasticity begins to be lost at about 10 years of age. For example, if there is damage to the language areas of the brain before age 10, there is better recovery of language skills than if damage occurs after age 10. The ability to acquire language is not completely lost after age 10, but the potential is diminished. The plasticity of children's brains may help them learn subjects like algebra or second languages more efficiently than adults (Luna, 2004). However, keep in mind that the brain remains plastic across the life span to some extent, or you could not be learning about child development right now.

Experiences that shape the brain can include *biological* factors. We will discuss the role of exercise, nutrition, sleep, and drug exposure later in this chapter. Experiences can also include *social* factors (Fox et al., 2010). In other chapters you will learn how experiences like attachment and stress affect the brain. Another social factor that is relevant to you as a teacher is whether the environment is stimulating.

Stimulating environments promote brain development. In a classic experiment, Hebb and his students showed that when baby rats were raised in laboratory cages, they could not solve problems as adults as well as rats raised in more stimulating environments. The "more stimulating environment" was free range of his house with the enthusiastic help of his 7- and 5-year-old daughters (Forgays & Forgays, 1952; Hebb, 1949). Other researchers later found similar results in monkeys, chicks, mice, squirrels, and cats, although they used elaborate cages with toys rather than letting animals roam their houses. The brains of animals in stimulating cages have more chemical activity, a thicker cortex, larger synapses, more cells, more blood vessels, and more dendrites as compared with the brains of isolated animals in barren cages (Kolb & Whishaw, 1998).

Stimulating environments also promote human brain development. (See Figure 2.6.) For example, people with a college education have more dendrites in the language area of the cortex than other people (Kolb & Whishaw, 1998). Such effects been studied most with music. Children with music training have more connections between sensory and motor areas of their brain, have more efficient

FIGURE 2.6 Brain Plasticity.

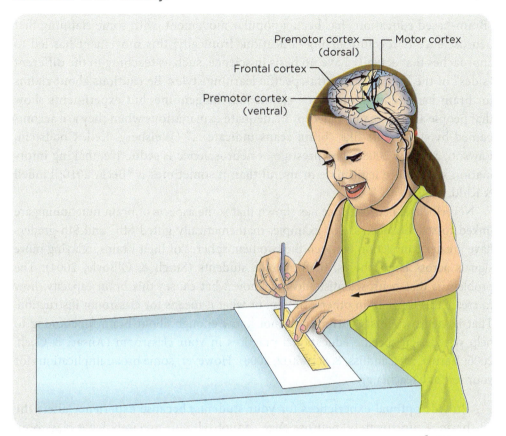

Premotor cortex (dorsal)
Motor cortex
Frontal cortex
Premotor cortex (ventral)

One of the most important lessons for teachers about the brain is that it is changed through use. Good instruction builds better brains.

brain systems for hearing, and tend to be better at reading, language, memory, and paying attention (White, Hutka, Williams, & Moreno, 2013). In one experiment, 4- to 6-year-olds were given music training for just 4 weeks. Changes in brain functioning were detected at the end of the brief training, and *again a year later* (Moreno, Lee, Janus, & Bialystok, 2015). Timing matters. Musicians who begin learning an instrument before age 7 have different brain architecture from those who learn at a later age. The effect of childhood music training on brain architecture can be lifelong, even when adults have not played the instrument for many years (White et al., 2013).

Unfortunately adverse childhood experience can also have a lifelong effect on brain architecture. Chronic stress can result in a brain that is anxious, fearful, impulsive, and less able to cope with future stress. It can result in poor memory, as well as behavior or learning problems at school (Shonkoff et al., 2012). In Chapter 14 you will learn that children in unstimulating orphanages have less brain activity than other children. This might be due to overpruning of the synapses (Nelson, 2007).

The key lesson is that brains are built over time by both genes and experience. Genes determine the basic architecture of the brain, but experience fine-tunes how circuits are formed.

2-1d Classroom Implications of Brain Development

"Brain-based education" has been a popular movement, with some claiming that neuroscience is revolutionizing education. Ironically, this movement has led to approaches that actually have no basis in science, such as teaching to the different "sides" of the brain or to brain-specific learning styles. Be cautious about claims for brain-based education. Some claims may be genuine, but experiments show that people are too ready to accept inadequate explanations when they are accompanied by statements like "brain scans indicate ..." (Weisberg, Keil, Goodstein, Rawson, & Gray, 2008). The prestige of neuroscience is seductive, making information seem more legitimate or useful than it sometimes is (Beck, 2010; Lindell & Kidd, 2013).

Nevertheless, neuroscience has shown that some aspects of brain functioning are linked to school success. For example, mathematically gifted 8th- and 9th-graders have greater connection between the two hemispheres of their brains, relaying more signals across hemispheres, than average students (Singh & O'Boyle, 2004). The problem is that neuroscientists do not know what causes this brain capacity, how to create this capacity in other children, or what it means for classroom instruction. That is, neuroscientists currently do not know enough about brain functioning to help you design specific educational practices in your classroom (Ansari & Coch, 2006; Varma, McCandliss, & Schwartz, 2008). However, some broad implications for your role as a teacher are:

1. Provide optimal experiences for your students, because experience alters the brain. Unfortunately, neuroscience cannot tell you precisely what classroom experiences are optimal. The "stimulating" environment of rats with well-developed brains simply mimicked their natural environment. This could mean that a merely "adequate" environment is ideal for children. In fact, children may be over stimulated by a "too-rich" environment filled with many distractions.

2. Keep the brain well nourished. Throughout the day your students need plenty of oxygen (stretching, movement) and glucose to fuel the brain. In the opening vignette, Mrs. Z found that providing a snack improved her students' ability to stay on task. Teachers at the secondary level may need to give special emphasis to keeping their students nourished because teens often skip lunch.

3. Reduce stress at school by creating nurturing and predictable environments. Toxic levels of stress interfere with learning and may lead to aggression and negative emotions. Children with chronically high levels of cortisol have more cognitive, motor, and social delays than other children (American Academy of Pediatrics, 1999).

4. Give children repetitive practice of important skills in order to strengthen synaptic connections.

5. Capitalize on teens' hyperresponse to rewards by emphasizing the rewards of learning and appropriate behavior. Capitalize on older teens' reasoning and planning abilities by emphasizing the implications of learning and appropriate behavior for their futures.

6. Advocate for high-quality early childhood education. The first 10 years of life are a sensitive period in brain development. By the time children enter elementary schools, half of that period is over. This period when children are avid learners could be more fully exploited for many children whose first 5 years are spent in unstimulating environments. Preschoolers are capable of learning skills in language, mathematics, music, and art when taught in developmentally appropriate ways.

The importance of early childhood for brain development is not a myth, but it is sometimes exaggerated. Early childhood education has rightfully benefited from media attention on early brain development and the push to provide quality programs for young children. However, remediation is possible, and quality programs are needed for struggling students at older ages as well.

In summary, the view from neuroscience is that actions, thoughts, and experiences alter the brain, rather than genes strictly dictating brain development. In Chapter 1 you learned that genes and environment interact to affect development. In Chapter 6 you will learn the latest remarkable research showing that experience can change genes, so stay tuned. The key message is that what happens in your classroom can alter your students' brain development. Let's turn now to other aspects of physical development that also have implications for your classroom.

2-2 Growth and Motor Development

At age 4 Ben said to his mother: "I'm all growed up now." A little surprised, his mother asked how he knew this. He replied, "Cuz I can cross the street all by myself; I can turn on the light all by myself; and I have hair on my arm just like Daddy—so I'm growed up."

Ben is now 16. He is 100 pounds heavier and 4 feet taller. Not only can he reach the light switch, he now has the coordination to wire an electric circuit. Not only can he cross the street, he now drives a car on it. Yet, he is still not quite "growed up" because he has not reached the final stage of puberty. The next 2 years will bring a few more inches of height and more muscle mass. In this section, we discuss normal growth and motor development.

Growth refers to changes in height, weight, and body composition. *Motor development* refers to changes in control and proficiency in movement. At first, infants have very little motor control, but will develop *fine* motor skills. These involve small muscle movements, like picking up a bean. They will also develop *gross* motor skills. These involve large muscle movements, like walking or throwing.

2-2a Age Trends in Growth and Motor Development

The rate of growth changes with age. The U.S. Centers for Disease Control and Prevention (CDC) publishes growth charts indicating average height and weight at each age. Figure 2.7 illustrates this growth. Coordination of movement also increases with age.

FIGURE 2.7 **Growth in Boys and Girls.**

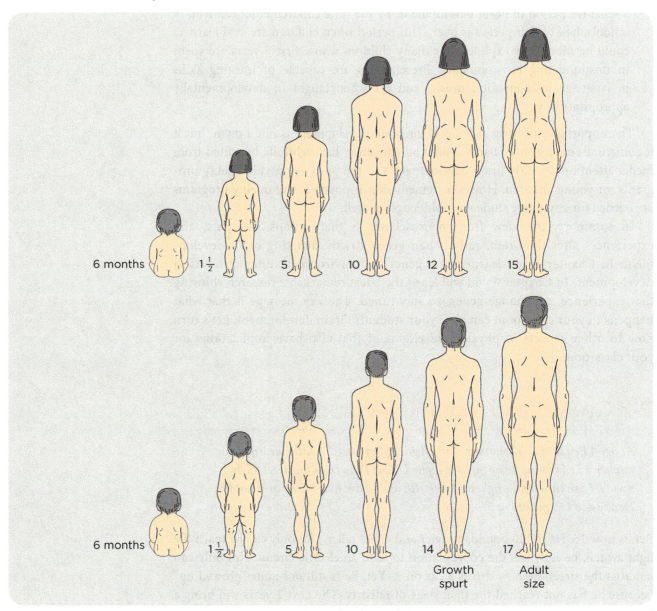

What do you notice about change in proportion and shape, as well as size? *Adapted from Tanner (1973).*

Infancy and Toddlerhood (Prenatal to 2 Years)

The last 3 months of pregnancy are primarily a period of rapid fetal growth, because most major body structures already function. Normal birth size can range from 5.5 to 10 pounds, but birth size does not predict adult size. For example, one of our sons was born very large, weighing 9.3 pounds, but he grew to be about average in height.

Growth is dramatic in infancy. After birth, infants gain more than a pound a month, so that birth weight is doubled by 5 months of age. Infants grow about 10 inches in the first year and 5 inches in the second year (Rogol, Roemmich, & Clark, 2002).

Motor development is also dramatic. Newborns cannot grasp a toy you hold in front of them or sit up by themselves, yet by age 2 they are walking and stooping over to pick up a bean off the floor. This remarkable motor development is portrayed in Table 2.1.

TABLE 2.1	Motor milestones from infancy to 10 years	
Age	**Fine motor skill**	**Gross motor skill**
2–3 months	• Sweeping or batting motions with the arm • Try to grasp, but poorly coordinated	• Hold head up when on stomach* • Roll from stomach to side
4–6 months	• Hands become unclenched* • Reach and grasp for objects* • Hold objects in the palms with all fingers (ulnar–palmar grasp) • Play with fingers in the center of torso*	• Hold entire upper torso up when on stomach* • Begin to sit without help • Reach for feet to play with • Roll from stomach to back*
6–10 months	• Coordinate both hands, transfer objects between hands* • Bang objects together across chest* • Poke with index finger • Rake small objects with 4 fingers*	• Crawl or creep* • Sit without help, then come to sit from lying* • Roll from back to stomach* • Stand while holding onto objects, then pull to standing*
10–14 months	• Use thumb and index finger to pick up small objects (pincer grasp)* • Drink from cup • Turn pages of book • Stack two cubes • Put one block in cup*	• Climb up stairs • Stand* • Walk with support, then walk independently*
15–24 months	• Use spoon or fork • Scribble in imitation, then spontaneously* • Stack two cubes, then three or more* • Put 10 blocks in a cup* • Hold pencil with all four fingers, forming a fist around it. Movement of the pencil comes from the shoulder.	• Squat to pick up objects • Walk up stairs with hand held* • Walk backward* • Run, but stiff-legged* • Climb up on furniture • Kick ball • Throw ball with overhead motion
2–3 years	• Build tower of 3, then 4 blocks* • Eat with spoon • Put puzzle pieces together • Roll clay into shapes • Imitate horizontal and vertical lines, then a circle* • Draw people with a head, and one other body part*	• Squat in play • Walk up steps alternating feet* • Walk down stairs • Run forward • Jump with both feet • Begin to stand on one foot • Ride toys without pedals*
3–4 years	• Unscrew lids • Grasp toward the tip of the pencil • Print recognizable letters. Letters are large, uppercase, uneven, and get larger toward the end of a word. • Draw "tadpole" people with 6 parts or a simple cross* • Paint • Cut with scissors • Button medium-sized buttons*	• Walk down stairs • Hop on one foot* • Ride toys with pedals* • Climb on and off furniture* • Begin to catch a bouncing ball • Walk up stairs without support*

(continued)

TABLE 2.1	Motor milestones from infancy to 10 years (continued)	
Age	**Fine motor skill**	**Gross motor skill**
5–7 years	• Zip zippers and lace shoes • Able to learn to play piano or violin • Control pencil with the finger and thumb. Movement comes from the elbow. • Write and draw with more control, but writing looks choppy and uneven. Letters are getting smaller. Uppercase letters are somewhat mastered, but lowercase letters continue to be challenging through 3rd grade, especially letters with slants or curves.	• Hop • Skip on alternating feet • Jump rope • Walk on a balance beam • Throwing, catching, and kicking become smoother • Begin to participate in organized games (e.g., hopscotch) and sports (e.g., soccer or baseball) • Skate, ski, bike, and other specialized skills with training
10 years	• Pencils are controlled by rotating the forearm and bending the index finger less when writing. Properly spacing letters is mastered around 4th grade.	• Fully participates in sports; can do same activities as adults but has less strength and somewhat less coordination

* These are approximate age trends. Do not use this table for diagnosis of delays. The online Additional Resources lists websites that give more information about motor delays if there is a child you are concerned about. Adapted from Payne and Issacs (1994) and Johnson and Blasco (1997). Skills with an asterisk are used by pediatricians to document motor milestones (Noritz et al., 2013).

Early Childhood (3 to 5 Years)

Compared to infants, preschoolers grow more slowly. Their rate of growth slows to about 2 to 3 inches in height and 5 pounds per year. (See Figure 2.8.) Most children double their birth height by age 3 to 4 (Rogol et al., 2002). Unlike birth size, children's size at age 4 strongly correlates ($r = 0.80$) with adult size (Tanner, 1985); that is, tall 4-year-olds will likely become tall adults.

Gross and fine motor skills continue to be refined; by age 5, children can throw a ball and stack cubes. However, the most dramatic motor development may be in the quality of walking. The toddler's teetering walk becomes a stable, smooth movement by 4 years of age, similar to the quality of adults' walk.

Middle Childhood (6 to 12 Years)

Growth in middle childhood is less dramatic than in infancy, but keeps to an average of 2 to 3 inches and 5 to 6 pounds per year for both boys and girls until puberty (Rogol et al., 2002). In addition, the rate of growth slows just before puberty.

Quality of fine motor skills increases dramatically in middle childhood. This is why the writing of a 1st-grader is clearly distinguishable from that of older children (see Figure 2.9). There is also improvement, although less dramatic, in speed, agility, and control of gross motor skills like jumping, throwing, balancing, and hanging (Malina, Bouchard, & Bar-Or, 2004). One of the amusing and endearing aspects of teaching 1st-graders is how often

FIGURE 2.8 Rate of Growth for Boys and Girls by Age.

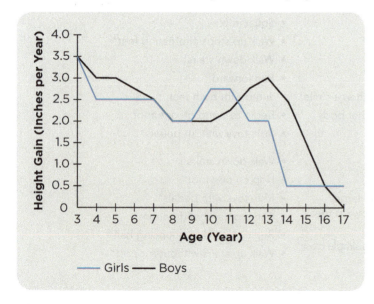

What conclusions would you draw about how the rate of growth changes across childhood? At what age do girls and boys diverge in growth patterns? At what age do girls and boys have their adolescent growth spurts? *Source: Retrieved from www.cdc.gov/growthcharts.*

FIGURE 2.9 Writing Samples.

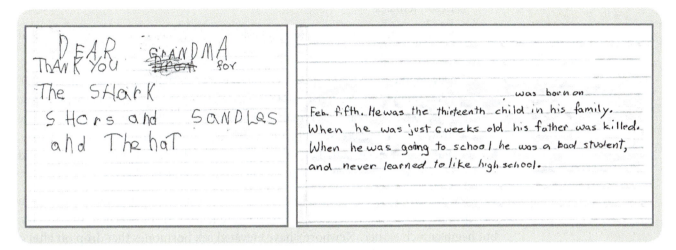

These writing samples are from the same boy, at ages 6 and 10. The first note says, "Dear Grandma thank you for the shark shorts and sandals and the hat." What attributes in his writing have changed over the 4 years?

they fall out of their seats. They have trouble raising their hand while maintaining balance in their seat. During middle childhood they will become better at coordinating movement with perception so they can maintain balance, catch a ball, or write their name (Thelen, 1995). They will also become coordinated enough to play sports like baseball and games with rules, like hopscotch and tag.

Many people believe preschoolers are the most active of any age. Actually, physical activity peaks in middle childhood. Motion recorders (actometers) strapped to arms and legs have been used to record round-the-clock movement in people from toddler age to young adults. Results indicate that movement increases from infancy, peaks at ages 7 to 9 years, and then decreases (see Figure 2.10).

puberty
physical changes that occur as children move into adulthood, including development of primary and secondary sex characteristics and capacity for reproduction.

Adolescence (13 to 19 Years)

Adolescents experience a dramatic spurt or acceleration in growth (refer back to Figure 2.8). The timing and speed of the adolescent growth spurt varies. Variation in this spurt does not correlate with final adult height. That is, teens who spurt early do not necessarily become taller adults.

Puberty

The adolescent growth spurt is part of **puberty**, which refers to physical changes that occur as children move into adulthood. The changes include:

- The growth spurt.

- Changes in proportion of muscle and fat. Boys gain more muscle than fat and girls gain more fat (Ogden, Yi, Freedman, Borrud, & Flegal, 2011).

FIGURE 2.10 Activity Level by Age.

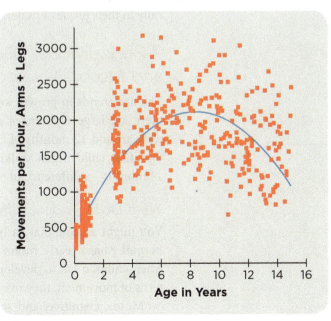

Dots represent children, showing wide individual differences. The line represents the average for each age. What age is the most active on average? *Source: Eaton, McKeen, and Campbell (2001).*

think about this

Children's movement peaks at the same age when there is a peak in diagnosis of ADHD—around 7 to 9 years. What might this mean for whether you view hyperactivity as normal or pathological? What might this imply for the structure of school at this age?

- Development of primary sex characteristics, such as testes in males and ovaries in females.

- Sexual maturation, such as menarche, or first menstruation, for girls and spermarche, or first ejaculation, for boys.

- Development of secondary sex characteristics (Shirtcliff, Dahl, & Pollak, 2009). Girls follow this sequence: acne, breast development, height increase, pubic hair, weight increase, and finally menarche. Boys follow this sequence: testicle growth, height increase, pubic hair, strength spurt, spermarche, voice change, and finally facial hair. For boys, puberty also brings hormone changes and increased cardiovascular capacity that enhance athletic skills.

Puberty is a *gradual process* over several years. Puberty is not sudden, as though a switch were turned on. It is also not just menarche for girls or spermarche for boys, but begins much earlier. Newborns have elevated sex hormones that drop off after a few months and stay low for several years. Then at 6 to 11 years of age—or around 4th grade—*adrenarche* begins, which is the maturation of the adrenal glands. These glands secrete androgens. During adrenarche children develop body odor, oily skin, and pubic hair; have mini–growth spurts; and have some external genitalia changes. The hormones then plateau until *gonadarche* triggers another rise in hormones to the adult level. Gonadarche brings the final maturation of the testes or ovaries, which secrete the hormones estrogen (girls) or androgen (boys).

Height spurts can occur rapidly, and menarche or spermarche can occur suddenly. Other developments, such as breast or testicle growth, tend to take 3 to 5 years, with differences in tempo or speed among individual children (Marceau, Ram, Houts, Grimm, & Susman, 2011). On average, menarche occurs for girls at ages 12 to 13 and spermarche for boys at ages 14 to 15 (Chumlea et al., 2003; Rogol et al., 2002). Thus, you can think of puberty as hormonally starting about 6 to 8 years of age and finishing about 15 to 22 years of age. Youth of the same age can vary radically in their phase of puberty.

2-2b Individual Diversity in Growth and Motor Development

The age trends in growth and motor development just described are averages, but there are large differences among children. For example, most children learn to walk around 12 months of age, but anywhere between 9 and 17 months is normal. Our first child began walking at 8 months. Our second child began walking at 14 months—a difference of 6 months!

What Do Individual Differences in Growth and Motor Skills Predict?

You might assume that early walkers are more intelligent. This is not true. *Within normal ranges,* early motor development does not reflect intelligence. However, when children fail to develop within the normal age range, or develop unusual patterns of movement, they may have cognitive problems as well.

Motor, cognitive, and social problems may occur together because they share an underlying neurological cause, such as the link between ADHD and motor skills you learned about earlier. In addition, serious motor delays can cause other delays because children learn about the world through movement. For example, infants who are walking retrieve an object from further away—touching, banging, and exploring it—and then share it with their caretakers more than same-age infants who are still crawling (Karasik, Tamis-LeMonda, & Adolph, 2011). Motor skills make it possible for children to connect with other people. Motor skills also make possible other abilities—like talking, reading, and writing—that are critical for school success. That is why pediatricians routinely note motor milestones at checkups.

Pediatricians also routinely measure children. This is because when children fail to grow within normal ranges, there may be problems. One type of growth problem is being born very small, which is linked to later school problems. This is discussed in Box 2.2. Another type of problem is going through puberty unusually early or late.

BOX 2.2 challenges in development

Low Birth Weight

Low birth weight (LBW) is defined as less than 5.5 pounds (2,500 grams). About 8% of infants are LBW—14% of African American infants, but 6 to 8% of other ethnic groups.[1] The most common cause of LBW is being born before 37 weeks of gestation, or preterm. However, infants can also be small for their gestational age (SGA), regardless of whether they are preterm or not. Infants who are *both* preterm and SGA are at greater risk than infants who are preterm but of normal size. LBW, SGA, and prematurity are each risk factors, and they often occur together.

Other common causes of LBW are drug use by the mother during pregnancy, having a teenaged mother, and being a twin (FIFCFS, 2009). However, the cause is unknown for about 40% of infants who are born preterm and/or SGA. Some scientists believe that stress during pregnancy may account for many of these preterm infants (Coussons-Read, 2012). Stress could be caused by experiencing discrimination, domestic violence, worry over taking care of the baby, and so on.

Why Does It Matter if Infants Are Born Small? LBW, SGA, and prematurity are associated with many developmental problems, including:[2]

- Somewhat smaller size, including head size, into adolescence.
- Delayed motor development. There may be catch-up for some children, but motor delays are often evident at school age.

- Socioemotional problems such as difficulty controlling emotions and behavior, low self-esteem, and peer rejection, particularly for boys.
- Cognitive problems such as low IQ, poor memory, slow processing speed, and attention deficits.
- School problems such as low math and reading test scores, learning disabilities (particularly math), grade retention, and special education placement.

These problems are detectable in infancy through adolescence, although some problems may become more pronounced in early adolescence (Rose & Feldman, 2000; Taylor, Klein, & Hack, 2000).

The lower the birth weight, the greater the likelihood of these problems (Aarnoudse-Moens, Weisglas-Kuperus, van Goudoever, & Oosterlaan, 2009). That is, infants weighing 1.5 pounds tend to achieve less later in their school years than infants weighing 3.5 pounds. They are also more likely to have serious medical problems such as bleeding in the head or lung disease, and immature myelination and brain development (see, for example, Clark, Woodward, Horwood, & Moor, 2008).

Not all LBW, SGA, or preterm infants will develop problems. Thanks to improvement in neonatal medicine, even very LBW children may now fare well (Rickards, Kelly, Doyle, & Callanan, 2001). In one study, 32% of infants weighing 1.5 pounds or less did not develop obvious problems (Taylor, Klein, Minich, & Hack, 2000). LBW children fare worse if they have both medical problems and insensitive parents (Landry, Smith, Miller-Loncar, & Swank, 1997).

---

[1] For updated statistics see www.childstats.gov.
[2] There are many studies that support these conclusions, just a few of which are listed here: Aarnoudse-Moens, Weisglas-Kuperus, van Goudoever, and Oosterlaan (2009); Basten, Jaekel, Johnson, Gilmore, and Wolke (2015); Clark, Woodward, Horwood, and Moor (2008); Goosby and Cheadle (2009); Li-Grining (2007).

Low Birth Weight (continued)

What Can Be Done to Help LBW Children? A good home environment can do much to compensate for LBW (Goosby & Cheadle, 2009). LBW children may develop well if they have responsive, sensitive caregivers and a stimulating home. Thus, one way to help LBW children is to improve quality of parenting. This needs to occur early, because the gap in academic achievement is already in place at school entry.

Improving quality of parenting is difficult. Even well-funded, intensive programs may result in only very small effects over the long run (see, for example, McCormick et al., 2006). However, in an experiment in Norway, parents were taught to "read" their preterm infants' cues and to interact sensitively (Landsem et al., 2015). At 7 and 9 years of age, the children were better able to pay attention, had fewer difficulties at school, and were less likely to be referred for special services, compared to other preterm children.

A few simpler programs have also shown promise for helping LBW or preterm infants thrive. One of these is called "Kangaroo Care." Tiny infants are positioned on the mother's chest with direct skin-to-skin contact, like a kangaroo, rather than in incubators (Baley et al., 2015). Another approach is to massage infants (Field, Hernandez-Reif, & Freedman, 2004). Breastfeeding is another simple yet particularly important intervention for preterm infants.

Implications for Teachers Some learners who were born LBW may have difficulties in understanding arithmetic, grasping new concepts, and thinking flexibly. These difficulties occur as early as kindergarten and continue or grow worse as schoolwork gets more abstract in high school (Aarnoudse-Moens et al., 2009; Goosby & Cheadle, 2009). The learners may need more time processing classroom tasks and need help with organizing work. However, not all LBW learners will have these difficulties. Other risk factors, such as a single mother with a low education level, have a stronger effect than birth weight (Breslau, Johnson, & Lucia, 2001; Goosby & Cheadle, 2009). Many more students are in special education because of a negative environment than because of LBW.

think about this

Across countries, the effect size for very LBW infants doing more poorly than other children in math, reading, spelling, and controlling attention was 0.43 to 0.76 (Aarnoudse-Moens et al., 2009). What does this mean? Should you assume that your students who were born very small will have problems in your classroom? Defend your answer using what you learned about research and effect sizes in Chapter 1.

Girls who mature earlier than their peers are more likely to have behavior problems, feel depressed and socially anxious, use drugs, and view themselves as less attractive than later-maturing girls (Blumenthal et al., 2011; Ge & Natsuaki, 2009). Early maturing may lead to associating with older boys, dating, and promiscuous sexual activity. However, girls who mature early are not any different in academic achievement than on-time peers. To be late in puberty is not ideal either. Late-maturing girls experience more depression than on-time peers.

Early and late maturing can also be a challenge for boys, but effects are inconsistent and short-lived. For example, body image is poor for late-maturing boys, but it improves by late adolescence. Still, early- and late-maturing boys are more likely to be depressed and delinquent than on-time peers (Negriff & Susman, 2011).

Early maturing has negative outcomes primarily for children who already have other problems. That is, early maturing alone may not cause negative outcomes, but it can magnify difficulties for children who have risk factors like harsh parents, a poor neighborhood, or deviant friends (Negriff & Susman, 2011).

As a teacher you can help children avoid the pitfalls of early puberty by conveying that being "different" is only temporary—their peers will catch up to them. You may also need to respond to sexual harassment that may be directed at your students.

Most importantly, you can treat them as the children that they are; do not expect adult abilities even if they look like adults. An 11-year-old who is "fully developed" is still only an 11-year-old.

What Predicts Individual Differences in Growth and Motor Skills?

There are many factors that influence growth and motor development. We will discuss four here—genes, exercise, nutrition, and quality of parent–child relationships.

Genes

Beginning in 1925, Arnold Gesell identified an orderly sequence of normal growth and motor development in young children (e.g., Gesell, 1933). This is the foundation for "motor milestones" still used by pediatricians today. Gesell was a *maturationist,* meaning that he believed motor development was so strongly genetically programmed that the environment was not able to speed it up or slow it down.

There is some support for this maturationist view. For example, restricting infant's movements by strapping them to a cradle board, as Hopis once did, does not delay normal motor skills (Thelen, 1995). In addition, you learned in Chapter 1 that growth is strongly canalized. When a child is ill or undernourished to a degree that slows growth, growth may accelerate to catch up once the problem is resolved. Yet an extreme maturationist view is not entirely correct. While genes may dictate the basic sequence of physical development, children are susceptible to their environment. For example, a poor diet over several years will permanently retard growth. Thus, the environment contributes to physical development, as you will see next.

Exercise

Ardent maturationists, like Gesell, believe that there is no point in training children until they are developmentally ready to learn a skill. In 1935, Myrtle McGraw tested this belief in a famous study of twins named Johnny and Jimmy (Photo 2.1). The twins were children 6 and 7 and from an American Irish-Catholic family that lived in five "dark, poorly ventilated rooms" heated by a single coal stove in the kitchen, as was typical of middle-class urban tenements then (McGraw, 1935, p. 35). The children played in the street, and the family was described as happy and intelligent. McGraw took the twins to her lab 5 days a week, from 1 to 26 months of age. At the lab, Jimmy was kept in a crib, but Johnny was given special training in motor skills. Johnny learned these skills—reaching, swimming, climbing up a slide, and roller skating—at a younger age than Jimmy. However, Jimmy learned some skills at roughly the same age—walking, sitting up, and riding a tricycle. In addition, Jimmy learned some skills (e.g., roller skating) *more quickly* than Johnny when given a chance at an older age than Johnny.

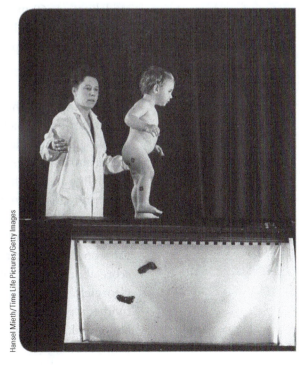

Hansel Mieth/Time Life Pictures/Getty Images

PHOTO 2.1 Myrtle McGraw observing one of the twins exercising.

The conclusion of this experiment was that you can speed children's motor development with exercise, but only to a limited extent. Older children will acquire motor skills at a faster rate, and some skills will not be mastered until there is biologically based maturation regardless of training. Ben, from our opening story, could not do a single pull-up when he was 14, although he tried hard. A year later, after puberty improved muscle mass, he could do seven pull-ups. Thus, there is a role for both exercise and maturation.

Exercise does more than promote motor skills. It also improves strength and endurance, builds healthy bones and muscles, increases positive emotions, and reduces anxiety and stress. It can promote socializing with other children, as well as self-esteem and attractiveness. However, it is possible to overdo exercise. The intense training of elite, national-caliber child athletes can be stressful and disrupt peer relationships. It can also delay growth and delay puberty in girls (Georgopoulos et al., 2010) and lead to overuse injuries (DiFiori et al., 2014).

Unfortunately, many children do not exercise enough. Almost two decades ago, the U.S. Surgeon General called physical inactivity a major epidemic, and the situation is growing worse (Morrow, Jackson, & Payne, 1999). A new term has even been coined: exercise deficit disorder (Faigenbaum, Best, MacDonald, Myer, & Stracciolini, 2014). Many babies are deprived of exercise because they are increasingly "packaged," meaning that they spend much of their time in baby seats, strollers, and other equipment that keep them from moving. Many preschoolers are remarkably sedentary at school (W. H. Brown et al., 2009). Sedentary behavior of more than 2 hours per day in school-age children predicts overweight, poor fitness, low self-esteem, and low academic achievement (Tremblay et al., 2011). More than 70% of 6-to-17-year-olds do not meet national guidelines for physical activity. The guidelines are 60 minutes of aerobic activity intense enough to make you sweat or breathe hard every day (DHHS, 2008). On the other hand, some youth do get plenty of exercise through play and team sports.

Nutrition

Undernutrition is the single most common cause of stunted growth in the world. Undernutrition delays puberty, while obesity accelerates it. This means that overweight youth develop secondary sex characteristics earlier than other youth. Undernutrition is also associated with low intelligence, poor academic achievement, irritability, and apathy (Wachs, 2000). Undernutrition affects brain cell growth, neurotransmitters, and myelination.

Two common nutritional deficiencies affecting the brain are iron and protein deficiencies. In the United States, toddlers and teenage girls are most at risk for iron deficiency; about 9% of them are iron-deficient. Iron-deficient infants score about 10 to 12 points lower on intelligence tests than other infants (Rao & Georgieff, 2000). Effects can be permanent if the deficiency occurs during the mother's pregnancy or during early infancy, but if the deficiency occurs in later childhood, iron supplements can help. This is one of many reasons breastfeeding is important.

Breast milk has a unique profile of nutrients that meet an infant's needs. Substitutes, like formula, are adequate for growth, and babies do not need to be breastfed

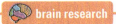 **brain research**

Exercise Builds Better Brains

Exercise promotes brain functioning and growth (Figure 2.11). Studies find that active, physically fit children control their attention better, have better memory, and have higher test scores than nonfit children, beyond the effects of IQ and SES (Castelli et al., 2014; Hillman & Drobes, 2012). Most of these studies are correlational, but randomized experiments (see Chapter 1) with adults and children show that exercise causes better brain functioning. For example,

in one study sedentary, overweight 7- to 11-year-olds exercised in an after-school program for 40 minutes per day for 12 weeks. After 3 months, they had better cognitive functioning, higher math test scores, and more activity in the prefrontal cortex than a comparison group (Davis et al., 2011). How might this happen? One possibility found in animal studies is that brains form more new neurons after exercise (Bryck & Fisher, 2012).

FIGURE 2.11 **Exercise Promotes Brain Functioning.**

BRAIN AFTER SITTING
QUIETLY

BRAIN AFTER 20 MINUTE
WALK

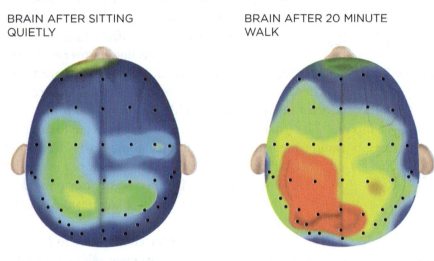

This figure depicts typical differences in electric activity in the brain of 9- to 10-year-olds after sitting quietly (such as in a classroom) compared with walking for 20 minutes. They had better attention control and test scores after walking. How does this fit with research on the relationship between learning and exercise? What does it suggest for learners in your classroom? *Source: Hillman, Ponitfex, Raine, Castelli, Hall, and Kramer (2009).*

to develop a strong mother–child bond, but infants who are breastfed have some advantages,[3] such as:

- Fewer illnesses in infancy (e.g., diarrhea, earaches, asthma) as well as later in life (e.g., allergies, digestive problems).

- Lower rates of obesity later in childhood.

- Better problem-solving skills in infancy, and slightly higher intelligence test scores through young adulthood (regardless of parental IQ).

- Lower rates of depression in adolescence.

---

[3] There are many studies that support these conclusions, just a few of which are listed here: Drover, Hoffman, Castañeda, Morale, and Birch (2009); Jansen, de Weerth, and Riksen-Walraven (2008); Kanazawa (2015); Kramer and Kakuma (2004); Soliday (2007). See also the American Academy of Pediatrics (AAP), official policy statement of 2012.

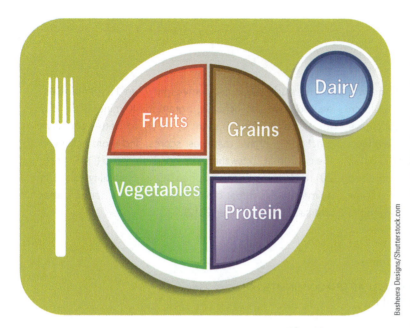

Basheera Designs/Shutterstock.com

PHOTO 2.2 The U.S. Department of Agriculture's "MyPlate," showing a healthy, balanced meal.

FIGURE 2.12 Dietary Guidelines for Vegetables.

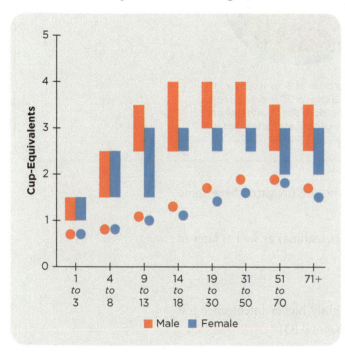

Bars indicate recommended ranges for eating; circles indicate average consumption. On average children do not consume as many healthy foods, such as vegetables, as federal dietary guidelines suggest they should. Which age group has the largest gap? Is it the same for boys and girls? Why are recommendations different for boys and girls at some ages? *Source: DDHS (2015).*

Health benefits to mother from breastfeeding include delayed menstruation, faster shedding of pregnancy pounds, lower risk of cancer, and healthier bones, as well as financial savings.

Scientists have tried to imitate breast milk, but these efforts have not been entirely successful. Specific fatty acids needed for brain growth are present in breast milk (Soliday, 2007). Formula-fed infants have less of these fatty acids in their brain. Experiments in which these fatty acids are added to formula have found that infants may develop better memory, attention, and problem–solving skills, but these effects have not always been found, and there may be negative side effects such as increased incidence of infection (Drover et al., 2009).

Both the World Health Organization and the U.S. government are trying to increase breastfeeding. The U.S. goal is for infants to get exclusively breast milk the first 6 months and then breast milk plus additional foods with iron supplements until 12 months. This goal is not yet being met. There are many reasons mothers or infants cannot breastfeed. In addition, mothers who have specific illnesses like AIDS or who are drug users should not breastfeed, because toxins can pass through the milk to the infant (American Academy of Pediatrics, 2001).

What should older children eat to be healthy? In 2015, the U.S. government released new dietary guidelines to support their *MyPlate* campaign (DHHS, 2015). See Photo 2.2. The basic message is that children should eat more fruits, vegetables, and whole grains, augmented with low-fat meats and dairy products, and drink water rather than sugary drinks. (Sorry, but French fries, ketchup, and chips do not count as vegetables.) Ideally, less than 30% of calories would come from fat.

Based on these guidelines, most U.S. children eat too much fat and sugar and not enough fruits and vegetables (DHHS, 2015). See Figure 2.12. As children get older, their diet quality gets worse. About 27% of 2- to 5-year-olds, and less than 10% of 6- to 9-year-olds, have a good diet (FIFCFS, 2009). Adolescent girls are less likely than boys to get sufficient milk, fruits, and vegetables, which can cause them to have inadequate calcium for their developing bones (Grunbaum et al., 2002). Carbonated soft drinks make matters worse. Teenage girls who drink such beverages have a higher risk of bone fracture than other girls and a greater risk for adult osteoporosis (Wyshak, 2000).

It is a common myth that sugar makes children "hyper." Research shows that sugary treats do not affect the behavior of typical children (Sciutto, Terjesen, & Frank, 2000). This is an opportunity for a lesson on research. Early *correlational* studies found a link between sugar and overly active behavior. However, later research using well-controlled *experiments,* in which the control group received a placebo instead of sugar, found no connection. The simplest explanation is that when children act wild during a class party, it is more likely due to having a party than to sugar. However, some children may react to other chemicals in a sugary treat, such as caffeine or dyes.

Parent–child relationship

The effects of genes, exercise, and nutrition on physical development should not surprise you. However, you may be surprised to learn that parent–child relationships also affect physical development. A few decades ago, physicians at Johns Hopkins Medical School had 13 children between 3 and 11 years referred for growth failure. Their height was 30 to 66% of normal, which is a huge deficit. They had delayed speech and delayed walking. They had protruding stomachs. Yet, they were not malnourished. The children almost all stole food, gorged themselves (like eating a whole loaf of bread), and ate from garbage cans. The physicians suspected pituitary problems at first, but later realized the problem was the parents (Powell, Brasel, & Blizzard, 1967). Most of the children's parents abused alcohol, were promiscuous, and quarreled.

When the children were placed in a convalescent hospital, they grew rapidly. Their average growth in the hospital was 0.65 inches per month; the typical rate is 0.20 (see Figure 2.13). They also quit stealing food, their speech developed, and they appeared happier and less withdrawn. When the children were returned to their homes, growth slowed again. Similar growth failure occurs for children in bleak orphanages. Many children surge in growth when caregivers develop warmer relationships with children or when the children are adopted out of the orphanage (St. Petersburg–USA Orphanage Research Team, 2008).

Growth failure can also occur in less-extreme environments, such as those of children who are raised by their mother but have an insecure attachment to her (Valenzuela, 1990). Low-quality parenting is a key cause of **nonorganic failure to thrive**. This is a medical label for children who fail to grow adequately without any apparent medical reason. Children who have this

nonorganic failure to thrive failure to grow adequately without any apparent medical reason.

FIGURE 2.13 Growth of a Boy from a Negative Home.

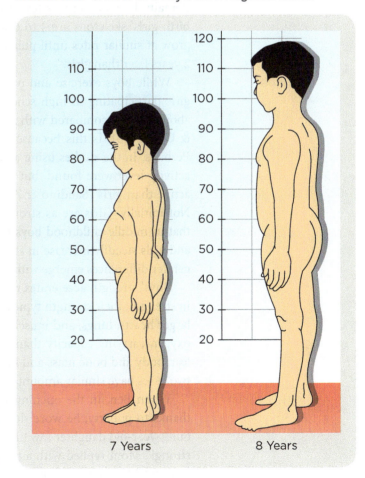

This boy was delayed in growth when brought to a medical center. At age 7 he looked like a substantially younger child. He grew dramatically after he was removed from his negative home.

condition may catch up to peers mentally once they begin school, but usually remain physically small (Boddy, Skuse, & Andrews, 2000).

Although poor parent–child relationships are linked to *delayed* growth, they are also linked to *accelerated* puberty. Girls experience puberty earlier in cold, harsh families, and in father-absent families in which the mother is single, depressed, has conflict with her romantic partner, or exposes her daughter to a boyfriend (Archibald, Graber, & Brooks-Gunn, 2003; Belsky, Steinberg, Houts, & Halpern-Felsher, 2010). In contrast, when fathers and mothers are affectionate and supportive, their daughters are likely to experience later puberty (Ellis & Essex, 2007).

2-2c Group Diversity in Growth and Motor Development

There are strong gender differences in growth and motor development, particularly after puberty. There are fewer, but some, socioeconomic status (SES) and ethnic differences in physical development. Let's look at these next.

Gender

There are greater gender differences in physical development than in any other domain discussed in this text. Gender differences in growth begin before birth. At birth girls' skeletons are 4 to 6 weeks more mature than boys'. Boys and girls then grow at similar rates until puberty. Boys experience some aspects of puberty about 2 years later than girls.

While boys exercise and participate in team sports more than girls, the rate of girls participating in high school sports has increased since the 1970s and is now about 35%, as compared with about 50% for boys (Bassett, John, Conger, Fitzhugh, & Coe, 2015). Is this because boys need an outlet for their higher activity level? Perhaps. In the studies using actometers discussed earlier, no gender differences in activity level were found, but some studies do find that boys are somewhat more active than girls (Saudino & Zapfe, 2008). Is this because boys are better athletes? Not initially. Girls are as strong as boys of similar body size until puberty, except that in middle childhood boys throw farther and girls are more flexible. Both boys and girls steadily increase in strength and athletic skill from ages 4 to 14. However, gender differences emerge with puberty.

Boys' strength accelerates rapidly with puberty. Girls have no comparable spurt in strength; their strength typically plateaus around age 14. After puberty, boys have larger hearts, lungs, and muscles (particularly in the upper body), as well as greater oxygen-carrying capacity than girls (Malina et al., 2004). They have 1.5 times the lean body and bone mass and half the body fat of girls, whereas prior to puberty the two sexes have similar amounts (Archibald et al., 2003).

When Ben, in the opening vignette, was suddenly able to do several pull-ups, thanks to puberty, he wore sleeveless T-shirts to show off his new muscles. When our 9-year-old daughter saw his bulging biceps, she said, "Mommy, that boy is really strong!" Mom replied with a twinkle in her eye, "That's exactly what he wants you to think." Not surprisingly, studies find that boys feel positive about their gains in strength and growth. In contrast, girls tend to dislike their normal puberty-caused weight gain (Archibald et al., 2003).

Socioeconomic Status

There is no relationship between motor development and SES in school-aged children in the United States (Malina et al., 2004). However, there is a relationship between nutrition and SES. Low-SES children eat more high-fat, high-sugar foods. This may be because they live in neighborhoods with convenience carryout stores instead of supermarkets, making healthy food less accessible (Morland, Wing, Diez Roux, & Poole, 2002).

As many as one-third of children in developing countries are undernourished, making it one of the most common risks of childhood worldwide. However, in the United States, children go hungry in less than 1% of households. What is more common is food insecurity, or periodic lack of adequate-quality food; this occurs for 21% of children (FIFCFS, 2015).

What happens when children lack food security? They are more likely to be anxious, aggressive, friendless, suspended from school, and quarrelsome than well-fed, low-income children. They are also more likely to be in special education, have low math scores, and be retained a grade. They have more colds, stomachaches, and headaches, but are not absent from school more often (Alaimo, Olson, Frongillo, & Briefel, 2001; Council on Community Pediatrics, 2015). Hunger may cause these problems, or both the problems and the food insecurity may be the result of some other underlying problem, such as a mentally ill parent.

Ethnicity

Within the United States there are some ethnic differences in growth. African American infants are smaller at birth and are less likely to be breastfed than White or Latino infants (Ruowei, Zhao, Mikdad, Barker, & Grummer-Strawn, 2003). However, African American infants grow more quickly during the first few years of life and tend to be more advanced in skeletal development (Rogol et al., 2002). They are slightly larger in childhood, but not in adulthood.

There are also ethnic differences in puberty. African American children have their adolescent growth spurt and puberty earlier than other children (Archibald et al., 2003; Malina et al., 2004). At age 8, a total of 48% of African American and 15% of White girls have begun pubertal development. Smaller differences occur for menarche. The average age of menarche is 12.1, 12.3, and 12.7 for African American, Latina, and White girls, respectively (Chumlea et al., 2003).

There are also some ethnic differences in motor development. For example, African American children have more advanced motor development up to 2 years of age than White children; thus, African American children walk earlier. African American school-age children, especially boys, tend to run faster and jump farther than White children, but there are no differences in other motor skills like throwing, balance, or sit-ups. There are not much data comparing motor development of other ethnic groups within the United States (Malina et al., 2004).

African American and Latino children, particularly girls, get less exercise than White and Asian children and participate less in school sports (Grunbaum et al., 2002). However, one of our Latina neighbors was the junior high soccer star. There are many such exceptions to these group trends. In fact, ethnic differences are small compared to SES differences (Malina et al., 2004). Some ethnic differences may be the result of SES. Children in high-crime neighborhoods are less likely to exercise vigorously (Gordon-Larsen, McMurray, & Popkin, 2000). In contrast, children with highly educated mothers are more likely to get vigorous exercise, regardless of ethnicity.

2-2d Classroom Implications of Growth and Motor Development

There are several ways you can help your students be physically healthy. One is to *prevent the school climate from becoming stressful to children.* A famous experiment occurred after World War II in Germany when food was rationed. British researchers gave children in orphanage A additional bread and juice for 6 months. Children in orphanage B were not given supplements, yet the children in orphanage B grew larger (Widdowson, 1951). Why these surprising results? At the time of the experiment, orphanage A just happened to get a new headmistress, Frauline Schwarz, who was mean and used mealtime to berate children. The children's growth slowed. Yet, she had eight favorite children in the orphanage who escaped her wrath and grew robustly. The moral of the story is to maintain low stress by keeping Frauline Schwarz out of your school. We will discuss school climate in more depth in Chapter 6.

Two other ways to help your students be physically healthy are to promote: (1) good nutrition and (2) physical activity. You should also become aware of the role of motor development in your classroom. Let's discuss these next.

In-School Nutrition

Since 1946, the U.S. Department of Agriculture (USDA) has provided cash subsidies to schools and child care centers to feed low-income children. In 2012, the National School Lunch program provided free or low-cost breakfast to 12 million and low-cost lunch to 31 million children. This is because research suggests that school nutrition affects learning for low-income children, such as increasing their test scores (Weaver-Hightower, 2011). You may help your students by following these guidelines:

1. Encourage your students to eat breakfast on all days, not just the week of standardized testing. This is especially important for low-SES learners; only half of learners who qualify for free breakfast at school actually participate in the program. In a national study, three-fourths of White and one-half of African American 9-year-olds ate breakfast regularly; these fractions dropped to a dismal one-third and one-fifth among 19-year-olds (Basch, 2011a). Eating a high-protein breakfast keeps glucose available to the brain and reduces unhealthy snacking later.

2. Advocate for better nutrition in the breakfasts and lunches served to your students. Support your school's compliance with the Healthy Hunger-Free Kids Act of 2010 that calls for healthier school meals, access to drinking water (rather than sugary drinks), farm-to-school food sources, and increased breastfeeding. School programs alone are not likely to overcome home influences on diet and weight gain, but they can help (Van Hook & Altman, 2012). In a clever, but simple, experiment, scientists simply renamed food in the lunchroom to "X-ray Vision Carrots" and "Power Punch Broccoli." Learners bought and ate dramatically more of these well-named vegetables (Wansink, Just, Payne, & Klinger, 2012).

3. In secondary schools where snack foods and beverages are sold, advocate for healthier options than candy, sport drinks, or soda pop. Students will choose healthier products from vending machines if they are accessible (Kocken et al., 2012). Schools are getting better about providing healthy snacks, but more improvement is needed (AAP Committee on Nutrition, 2015).

4. If needed, allow children to bring a healthy snack, as Mrs. Z did in the opening vignette. At class parties, have healthy treats like apple slices instead of cupcakes.

5. Be a good nutrition role model yourself and directly teach principles of good nutrition in class.

Physical Activity at School

In a Head Start classroom, 3-year-old Markeet is fidgety, boisterous, and agitating other children during group time. As punishment, his teacher says, "It's time to go outside and play, but Markeet you'll have to stay inside with Ms. Jenny until you are ready to join us." Once they are alone in the room, Ms. Jenny (the aide) tells Markeet, "You need to sit still, criss-cross legs, and be quiet for 2 minutes. If you talk, I'll have to start your timer all over." Markeet is successfully mute and still for 30 seconds, but then asks "Can I have a book?" Ms. Jenny says, "No. You know the rules. Now I have to start the timer again." Again he is quiet, but 10 seconds later asks, "Can I go now?" Again Ms. Jenny starts the timer over. This pattern is repeated until Markeet misses 12 minutes of the 30-minute outside play period.

Is this an appropriate discipline approach? It is in conflict with a U.S. national goal of *Healthy People 2020* that children have daily physical education (PE) at school, in which at least 50% of the time is spent in vigorous exercise. This goal will be challenging to meet. In preschools, children tend to be sedentary (sitting, lying down, or standing); even outdoors they may be vigorously active only a small percentage of the time (Brown et al., 2009). Older children don't fare much better. A study of hundreds of 3rd-graders across the country found that they averaged only two PE classes per week; in those classes they spent only 5 minutes in vigorous exercise and 12 minutes in moderate exercise. Most of the time, they did things like wait for a turn or listen to instructions (NICHD Early Child Care Research Network [NICHD ECCRN], 2003b).

PE and recess have been reduced in many schools for at least two reasons:

1. Need for more time on academics. This is misguided. In Chapter 11 you will learn that physical play and recess *enhance* learning from preschool through high school. When schools double or triple PE time, test scores do not go down, and they often rise (Basch, 2011b; CDC, 2010). Physically active children have higher test scores, better attendance, and fewer discipline problems.

2. Budget crunches reduce money for PE teachers, facilities, and playground supervisors. In our local high school of 1,700 students, there is one gym and one weight room that was converted from a storage closet. Students can only take one semester of PE in their high school career because there simply is not enough room for more PE classes.

What can you do to help children get active? Try the following:

1. In preschools, give children balls and plenty of space for vigorous physical activity. Children tend to be more active in games they have initiated, but if they are not active, you may need to initiate games that involve running, jumping, or climbing (W. H. Brown et al., 2009).

2. In elementary and secondary schools, advocate for *daily* physical education, even for high school students. The percentage of high school students in daily PE dropped from 42% in 1991 to 29% in 2013.[4] Students who are involved in extracurricular sports could be exempted. For younger students, provide school time for unstructured physical activity such as jumping rope or running around the play yard.

   • Offer PE classes that emphasize enjoyable activities that are done throughout life, not just competitive sports. Some high schools offer "Fitness for Life" classes that include jogging, bicycling, and other activities that students can do after they leave school.

   • Make sure that during PE classes each child is active for most of the class period. For example, in dodge ball most participants do not participate most of the time because they are "out."

3. Discourage withholding of physical activity as a punishment. Withholding vigorous physical play from an overactive child is not only unkind, it is counterproductive, as it was for Markeet.

4. Provide diverse extracurricular activities appropriate for different abilities that involve physical activity. For example, a junior high Earth Club could take hikes to study nature, or a preschool class could walk to a nearby park to play.

5. Build physical activity into classroom lessons when appropriate. Short 5- to 20-minute breaks for physical activity improve mood, concentration, time-on-task, and test scores (CDC, 2010). For example, one teacher had her 2nd-graders gather at a start line. She would call out a vocabulary word. The children had to briskly walk to their seat to spell the word, then return to the start line for the next word.

Your school may be interested in model programs to improve the health of learners that can be found on the Centers for Disease Control and Prevention (CDC) website. Effective programs combine improved in-school nutrition with increased physical activity, as well as classroom lessons on healthy lifestyles. Parents are often involved through homework and family fun nights. The CDC publishes a "School Health Index" to help your school assess current practices and implement better practices.

Motor Skills in the Classroom

Movement can support learning. For example, preschoolers learn their letters better when they physically write them, as compared with when they type them on a keyboard (James & Engelhardt, 2012). (The same may be true for you when learning a new alphabet, such as Armenian.) In addition, good motor skills help learners be more

---

[4] You can see updated state data for different grades at http://www.cdc.gov/healthyyouth/data/yrbs. Data come from the Centers for Disease Control and Prevention, "Youth Risk Behavior Surveillance System."

successful in school. For example, children who enter kindergarten with better fine motor skills—like stacking blocks and imitating line drawings—have higher achievement in elementary school (Gissmer, Grimm, Aiyer, Murrah, & Steele, 2010). About 30 to 60% of classroom activities require motor skills. These are mostly fine motor skills using paper and pencil, but also some less obvious skills like posture control. Furthermore, most classroom learning is measured with motor output, such as writing, playing an instrument, making an art project, or using a keyboard (Pape & Ryba, 2004). Imagine how difficult school would be if you struggled with these skills.

Young children do struggle with these skills. Before age 6, they have difficulty moving their eyes deliberately across lines of small print and controlling hand movements, which makes reading and writing challenging. Even some older children have motor problems. They may have difficulty writing letters, fastening clothing, using scissors, folding papers, opening containers at lunch, or finding a folder in a messy desk. They may appear clumsy and disorganized and may be the last ones chosen for a team. When writing, they cannot stay on a line and may mush words together. Tasks that require them to listen and write at the same time (such as taking notes) are especially difficult. Motor problems can lead to further language and social problems.

You are likely to have children with motor problems in your classroom. Under the Individuals with Disabilities Education Act (or PL 101-476), children with physical difficulties are to be educated in the *least restrictive environment*. This is often interpreted to mean a regular classroom. Your school may have access to an occupational or physical therapist whose job is to help children who have motor problems adapt to your classroom. The occupational therapist will help you make classroom accommodations, as well as provide exercises to help increase motor skills in targeted children.

2-3 Contemporary Health Challenges

Several common children's health issues that affect classroom performance will be discussed in other chapters: child abuse (Chapter 7), ADHD (Chapter 4), depression (Chapter 8), and sexually transmitted diseases (Chapter 11). In this chapter, we focus on sleep deprivation, obesity, and drug use. These threats to children's health are preventable, and teachers can help.

2-3a Sleep Deprivation

During the summer, 10th-grader Jay routinely stayed up until 3 a.m. and woke up at noon. In the fall, when school began, he tried to go to bed at 10 p.m., but couldn't fall asleep until 3 a.m. He was anxious about school beginning, which made it harder to sleep. He got up at 6 a.m. for school the first week, but was exhausted. When the weekend came, he stayed up late and slept until 3 p.m. on Saturday to "catch up." He continued this pattern for several weeks. Sometimes he would oversleep and miss class or fall asleep during class. This made his teachers and parents angry. He became irritable, had difficulty paying attention, and began failing his classes. This increased his anxiety, which made it harder to sleep, creating a vicious cycle. Eventually he was diagnosed with ADHD and depression; sleep deprivation symptoms mirror these psychiatric disorders. (Adapted from Dahl & Lewin, 2002)

In addition to masquerading as depression and ADHD, sleep deprivation can trigger mental illness. Sleep deprivation and emotional disorders, like depression or anxiety, are bidirectional, meaning each can cause the other (El-Sheikh, Bub, Kelly, & Buckhalt, 2013). Children with unhealthy sleep habits, like sleeping less than 7 hours a night or having more than a 2-hour difference between school-night and weekend bedtimes, tend to be more depressed than other children (Short, Gradisar, Lack, & Wright, 2013).

Sleep deprivation decreases motivation, ability to concentrate or reason, speed and accuracy of information processing, memory, motor control, and emotion regulation (which makes children sillier, angrier, or sadder). It increases restlessness, irritability, illness, injuries, impulsivity, mistakes, drug use to stay awake (such as caffeine or nicotine), daytime sleepiness (such as dozing off during class), and tardiness for morning classes. Some of these effects occur even if people are not aware of feeling sleepy, because they have adapted to sleep deprivation (Horowitz, Cade, Wolfe, & Czeisler, 2003).

Age Trends in Sleep Patterns

Newborns sleep more than they are awake. Overall, children sleep more than half of their first 2 years of life, including daytime naps. By school age, children no longer need naps; sleepy children may need to go to bed earlier rather than nap. As they grow older, youth gradually need less sleep until they reach adult levels. One way to remember children's sleep needs is "10 for 10," or 10 hours for 10-year-olds—younger learners need more, older learners need less (Table 2.2). An important exception is that adolescents need more sleep during growth spurts; if they do not increase their amount of sleep, they feel more tired (Photo 2.3).

Many U.S. children do not get enough sleep, particularly adolescents like Jay, and the situation is getting worse (see Figure 2.14). From ages 3 to 17, children

TABLE 2.2 Sleep needs by age

Age	Average number of hours of sleep needed daily	
	Nighttime	Daytime
0–3 months (full term)	8–12	4–9 (14–17 total per day)
6 months	8–10	4–6 (about two naps per day)
1–2 years	10–12	1–2 (one midday nap)
3–5 years	9–11	1–2 (one midday nap)
6 years	11–12	None
10 years	9–11	None
Adolescence	8–10	None
Adults	7–9	None

Adapted from Iglowstein, Jenni, Molinari, and Largo (2003); Mindell and Owens (2010); and Ollendick and Schroeder (2003).

tend to get up at the same time. However, as they enter adolescence, they stay up 2.5 hours later, on average (Snell, Adam, & Duncan, 2007). They work more—in sports, homework, and employment—which keeps them up too late. They also wake more easily during the night than younger children (Owens et al., 2014). As a result about 85% of adolescents are mildly sleep-deprived, with 10 to 40% significantly so. Adolescents often go to bed later on weekends than school nights, creating a jet-lag effect each week. Keeping consistent bed and wake times eliminates this effect. To make up for sleep loss, adolescents may sleep excessively on weekends so that their total sleep time is similar to that of younger children (Owens et al., 2014). Still, many high school students function at a level of sleep deprivation characteristic of people with sleep disorders.

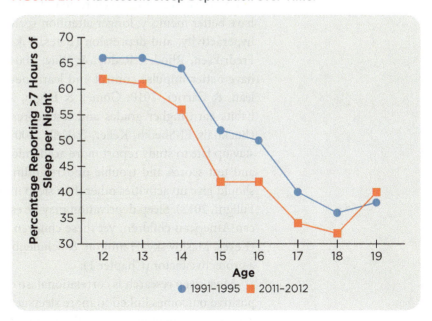

PHOTO 2.3 Adolescents may need more sleep than adults.

apnea
a sleep disturbance that consists of repeated periods without breathing, and snoring or gasping for breath.

sudden infant death syndrome (SIDS)
the sudden death of an infant for whom a cause of death cannot be determined.

Sleep Disorders

Children with sleep disorders can go to bed at a reasonable hour and still not be refreshed because their sleep is of poor quality or they wake frequently. Occasional nighttime waking is normal, but excessive waking is not. Nightmares are the most common sleep disturbance in preschoolers. Sleep talking (22 to 60% of children) and sleepwalking (15 to 75%) are common in middle childhood. A delayed sleep–wake cycle (i.e., the night owl) is the most common (7%) sleep disorder in adolescence. Overall, studies have found that about 20 to 40% of children have some sleep problem (Mindell & Owens, 2010).

Sleep **apneas**, or repeated periods without breathing during sleep, are another common sleep disturbance. Apnea is characterized by snoring, restlessness or gasping for breath during sleep, sleeping with the mouth open, morning headaches, crankiness, and daytime sleepiness. Brief apneas are common in healthy people, but not periods long enough to disturb sleep. In children, apneas are typically caused by enlarged tonsils or adenoids or obesity.

Sleep apnea may be linked to **sudden infant death syndrome (SIDS)**, or crib death. SIDS refers to the sudden death of an infant for whom a cause of death cannot be determined. SIDS typically occurs at night, but 20% of cases may occur in childcare settings

FIGURE 2.14 **Adolescent Sleep Deprivation over Time.**

This graph depicts the percentage of adolescents who report regularly getting 7 hours or more of sleep per night in two cohorts. What does this graph tell you about how sleep patterns have changed over 20 years (blue to orange lines)? What does it tell you about how sleep changes from age 12 to age 19? What do you think happens at age 14 that might be linked to a steep decrease in sleep? *Source: Data from Keyes, Maslowsky, Hamilton, and Schulenberg (2015).*

(Moon, Patel, & McDermott Shaefer, 2000). It is a leading cause of infant death. It is most common for boys; preterm, low-SES, and African American and Latino infants; and infants with young mothers who smoke or have little prenatal care. However, the cause of SIDS is still unknown. The probability of SIDS can be reduced if infants sleep on firm surfaces without pillows, on their backs, and in the same room (but not the same bed) as their parents (American Academy of Pediatrics, 2011).

Improving Sleep

Sleep *needs* may not be under voluntary control, but sleep *amount* and *schedule* are. If a child, like Jay, has an unhealthy sleep cycle, it can be gradually changed by changing bedtime in increments of 15 to 30 minutes over several weeks (Ollendick & Schroeder, 2003). If parents seek your advice about how to help their child sleep better, suggest that the child: (1) have the same bedtime and wake time 7 days a week; (2) have a bedtime routine that is calming, with dimmed lights; (3) wake up without the use of an alarm; and (4) if school-age, keep daytime naps to a maximum of 30 minutes. They will also need to eliminate conditions that disturb sleep, including noise, light, stress, anxiety, overtiredness, lack of exposure to daylight, and some medicines. They also include eating a large meal, exercising, and consuming caffeine or alcohol within an hour of bedtime. Caffeine disrupts sleep even in the small amounts found in soft drinks, chocolate, and over-the-counter drugs (Roehrs & Roth, 2008). The more children use electronics (text messaging, watching TV, playing computer games) just before bedtime, the more trouble they have sleeping (Owens et al., 2014).

Classroom Implications of Sleep Deprivation

Sleep affects learning. Well-rested children do better mentally and socially—they have better memory; longer attention spans; higher self-esteem; and less aggression, hyperactivity, and depression (Bates, Viken, Alexander, Beyers, & Stockton, 2002; Fredriksen, Rhodes, Reddy, & Way, 2004). Toddlers with more night-time sleep have better impulse control and learn new words better (Bernier, Carlson, Bordeleau, & Carrier, 2010; Gomez & Edgin, 2015). Older students with healthy sleep habits earn higher grades and test scores, beyond the effect of earlier test scores (Buckhalt, El-Sheikh, Keller, & Kelly, 2009). In contrast, high school students who stay up late to study report more academic problems the next day, such as poor quiz and test scores and trouble understanding course content; this suggests that they should give up activities other than sleep in order to study (Gillen-O'Neel, Huynh, & Fuligni, 2013). Sleep deprivation may be especially detrimental to low-SES and African American children, yet these children are also more likely to be sleep-deprived (Keyes, Maslowsky, Hamilton, & Schulenberg, 2015). Adequate high-quality sleep is a protective factor (Chapter 1).

Most sleep research is correlational, so direction of causation is not clear. Perhaps positive outcomes linked to more sleep actually result from healthy family routines. To test this possibility, researchers randomly assigned toddlers to miss a nap and then tested them with a puzzle-solving task. On nap-deprived days, compared to napping days, toddlers were more anxious, less happy and proud when they solved a puzzle, and less likely to realize when a puzzle was unsolvable (Berger, Miller, Seifer, Cares, & LeBourgeois, 2011). In another experiment, researchers asked parents to put their 4th-, 5th-, and 6th-graders to bed thirty to forty minutes earlier, or later, than usual for three nights in a row (Sadeh, Gruber, & Raviv, 2003). The children who slept more improved in memory, motor speed, and attention. The size of effect was equivalent to 2 years' development. These studies suggest that ample sleep *causes* improved academic achievement and classroom behavior.

Sleep is not idle time. Learning depends on sleep; you remember information and solve problems better when you have had a chance to "sleep on it" (Strickgold & Walker, 2004). Sleep helps you remember information because memories are consolidated during sleep (Rasch & Born, 2008). What can you do about your student's sleep deprivation? The following tips may help:

1. Watch for signs of sleepiness so that you know which learners might be sleep-deprived. In one 8th-grade science class, five students were sleeping at 10:15 in the morning! They were not high achievers.

2. Teach parents about age-specific sleep needs from Table 2.1. Watch for learners who have been diagnosed with ADHD, learning disability, or depression who may actually suffer from sleep deprivation. If a student is having trouble in class, inform parents and ask about sleep patterns.

3. Avoid contributing to sleep deprivation. End school-sponsored activities, like open houses or play practices, early enough that children can be in bed on time. Give homework assignments that do not require staying up late.

4. Avoid early start times for secondary schools. Typically, when adolescents transition from middle schools to high schools that have an earlier start time, they do not go to bed earlier. Thus, after starting high school they may sleep an hour less each night, becoming significantly sleep-deprived. In high schools that change their start time, say from 7:30 to 8:30 a.m., teens get substantially more sleep each week because they continue to go to bed at the same time as before (AAP Policy Statement, 2014).

2-3b Obesity and Other Eating Disorders

The Donovan family has four children. Both parents are obese. Their refrigerator is stocked with soda pop and hot dogs. The oldest child, Jacob, is tall and fit. He is on the football and basketball teams in high school. His dream is a Division 1 college athletic scholarship, which he attains. His 8th- and 5th-grade siblings are both obese and not involved in sports. His 1st-grade brother is very thin—nicknamed "skinny boy." If the children are good all week, they are rewarded on Friday night with a trip to a fast-food restaurant and a double-feature video at home. The real motive for the reward is that the parents are too tired to cook after they get home from work.

Families with weight problems, like the Donovans, are becoming common. The World Health Organization has declared obesity one of the top health problems in developed nations. In the United States, the number of overweight children has quadrupled since 1970 (see Figure 2.15). Roughly 8% of infants and toddlers are obese. Among 2- to 19-year-olds 20% are obese and 33% are overweight (Ogden, Carroll, Kit, & Flegal, 2014).

FIGURE 2.15 **Sharp Rise in U.S. Childhood Obesity.**

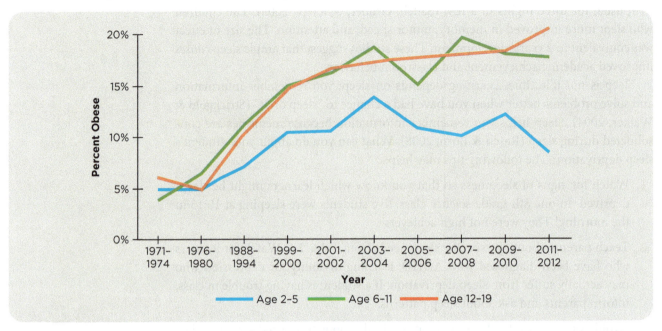

How would you describe the change in obesity across these four decades? Obesity is defined as BMI ≥95th percentile on age-specific CDC growth charts from 2000. *Source: Centers for Disease Control and Prevention.*

Obesity or *overweight* is defined by body-mass index (BMI). *BMI* is calculated as the weight in kilograms divided by the square of height in meters (kg/m²). For adults, overweight is a BMI ≥25, and obesity is a BMI ≥30. For an adult, this means being at least 30 pounds over ideal weight (Grunbaum et al., 2002). In children, the BMI indicators of obesity are similar, but vary by gender and age. (They can be found on the CDC's growth charts.)

Age Trends in Obesity

Fat level, or adiposity, naturally changes across the lifespan. There is an increase in adiposity from birth to about 1 year of age, then a decrease. A rebound in adiposity sets in between 4 and 8 years of age, then decreases again. The body peaks in leanness around age 25; after that age, adiposity increases again. While obesity can develop at any age, the primary grades are a risk period because of the adiposity rebound. The Donovans are typical. "Skinny boy" is not likely to deserve his nickname once the adipose rebound sets in, just as it did for his older, inactive siblings.

What Does Obesity Predict?

Obesity can cause serious health problems in both children and adults. In children, being overweight may cause type 2 (non–insulin-dependent) diabetes. There has been a dramatic increase in diabetes, which puts children at risk for hardening of the arteries, kidney problems, eye disease, and death. Obesity is also linked to early onset of puberty in girls, sleep apnea, asthma, and problems with joints and bones (Davison, Susman, & Birch, 2003; Krishnamoorthy, Hart, & Jelalian, 2006).

Obesity is linked to achievement problems in school. It is linked to poor working memory and lower reading, math, and intelligence scores. Obese learners may score a full grade lower on achievement tests than fit children. Does this mean that obesity causes impaired mental abilities, or vice versa? There is evidence for both directions of effect (Khan, Raine, Donovan, & Hillman, 2014; Pontifex et al., 2014).

Obesity can also cause social and emotional problems. Obese children are more lonely, depressed, and anxious and have less self-control in the classroom (Gable, Krull, & Chang, 2009). They are seen as less likable by their peers, even as young as age 3 (Bell & Morgan, 2000). Perhaps because of this, obesity is linked to lower self-esteem in school-age children (but not in preschoolers), particularly if peers tease and parents criticize the child's weight (BeLue, Francis, & Colaco, 2009). By early adolescence, not all obese teens have low self-esteem, but those who do are at risk for other problems, such as smoking and drinking (Strauss, 2000). The link between obesity and these problems is stronger for girls than for boys, and stronger for Latino and White children than for African American children (Khan et al., 2014; Pontifex et al., 2014).

What Predicts Obesity?

There are many factors linked to obesity. A few that help explain the rapid rise of the epidemic over the past few decades include:

- *Exercise.* BMI is a direct function of calorie intake (diet) relative to calorie output (exercise)—known as the *energy equation.* It only takes a small imbalance in the equation to become overweight. You learned earlier that many children today do not get enough exercise.

- *Diet.* More families, like the Donovans, often eat out and eat too much. In the United States, portion sizes have increased, particularly for soft drinks and salty snacks like crackers and chips (Nielsen & Popkin, 2003). Portion sizes are especially large at fast-food restaurants. Coke was originally served in 6-ounce glasses in the early 1900s; now it is served in 48-ounce cups. One additional serving of sugary drinks per day can increase obesity by 60% in 6th- and 7th-graders (Ludwig, Peterson, & Gortmaker, 2001).

- *Sleep deprivation.* Children who sleep fewer hours and go to bed later tend to have higher BMI than other children (Snell et al., 2007). Less than 10 hours of sleep per night is linked to obesity in children in countries around the world, such as the United States, China, Tunisia, and Brazil (Cappuccio et al., 2008). Sleep deprivation begins early and can have lasting effects. Toddlers who do not get enough sleep tend to become young adults who are overweight (Al Mamun et al., 2007).

- *Television viewing.* Television viewing reduces activity level and promotes calorie intake. Many children watch TV during meals; this habit is linked to eating fewer fruits and vegetables and eating more pizza, salty snacks, and soda pop (Coon, Goldberg, Rogers, & Tucker, 2001). Children who watch more than 2 hours daily tend to be more obese than their peers (Tremblay et al., 2011).

- *Parent behavior.* Parents influence their children's obesity in many ways, such as being obese themselves, skipping family mealtime, being negative during mealtime, or being highly controlling about eating (e.g., "No soda at any time") so that their children overeat the wrong foods when the controls are lifted (Harrison et al., 2011). See Photo 2.4. Parents who do not cook meals at home tend to purchase less-nutritious, higher-calorie food for their children (Krishnamoorthy et al., 2006).

Tim Boyle/Getty Images News/Getty Images

Group Diversity in Obesity

Obesity rates vary by ethnicity and SES in the United States. Ethnic differences in excessive BMI are small, with Asian children having the lowest rate and Latino and African American children having the highest rates (Ogden et al., 2014). In most countries, higher-SES children are taller and heavier than low-SES children. However, in developed countries, low-SES children with single parents, or a mother who did not finish high school, are more likely to be obese (Strauss & Knight, 1999). Mrs. Donovan did not finish high school.

It may seem ironic that low-SES children who are more likely to have food insecurity would be obese, but in the United States, high-calorie food is plentiful and cheap. For example, a box of cookies provides more calories per dollar than fresh fruit. Children living in poverty are more likely than high-SES children to eat cookies rather than fruit, although most nonpoor children do not have stellar diets either (DHHS, 2015).

PHOTO 2.4 Can you think of more than one reason why mothers' obesity is a powerful predictor of children's obesity?

Classroom Implications of Obesity

Children consume about 40% of their daily calories at school (AAP Committee on Nutrition, 2015). Doing the following may help your learners if they are overweight:

1. Help them reduce calorie intake and get more exercise, as discussed earlier. For example, where appropriate, suggest walking and biking instead of busing students to school.

2. Teach them about appropriate quantities and types of food. Emphasize nutrient-rich foods. Unfortunately, schools may offer unhealthy foods through vending machines, snacks, and fund-raising sales.

3. Advocate for longer lunch periods in a socially pleasant environment where learners are presented with choices among healthy foods. Nutritional foods take longer to eat.

4. Focus attention on becoming healthy, not on dieting or losing weight. Communicate to overweight learners that they are valued regardless of their weight.

Three federal agencies (USDA, CDC, and Department of Health and Human Services [DHHS]) have combined to identify success stories from schools that have become healthier.[5] These schools make healthy foods more accessible. Some offer healthy rewards such as a walk with the principal instead of a pizza party. Some adopt a "fruits and veggies only" policy for snacks. Some have removed all soda and candy from vending machines, replacing them with yogurt, string cheese, fruit, or beef jerky. Contrary to many people's beliefs, schools can make money selling healthy options.

---

[5] At cdc.gov, visit the "Making It Happen! School Nutrition Success Stories" page.

Should you encourage overweight students to diet? Generally, no. Food restriction can negatively affect later eating habits. If too stringent, diets can create a failure experience that further diminishes self-esteem. Diets can create nutritional deficiencies in growing bodies (Rogol et al., 2002). Instead, interventions should focus on teaching parents to use rewards other than food, developing healthy eating behavior, and reducing TV viewing. Some learners may need behavior therapy with a psychologist, especially family-based therapy, rather than dieting (Altman & Wilfley, 2015).

Although youth should not diet, many do. In a national study, a whopping 62% of high school girls and 28% of boys reported trying to lose weight in the past month. Generally they do this by exercising more or by eating fewer calories, but 14% went without food for more than 24 hours, 9% tried diet pills, and 5% used vomiting or laxatives (Grunbaum et al., 2002). Sometimes this attempt to lose weight can develop into an eating disorder (Rome et al., 2003).

Other Eating Disorders

Obesity is the most prevalent eating disorder. Less common eating disorders involve the extreme pursuit of thinness. Two of the most well-known disorders are *anorexia nervosa* and *bulimia nervosa,* which affect 1 to 4% of the U.S. population. Anorexia is self-starvation; it can be fatal. Youth with anorexia refuse to maintain minimal body weight, have a distorted perception of their size (think that they are fat when they are not), and base their value on their weight. Bulimia has similar psychological factors, but the person is *not underweight.* Bulimia is binge eating, followed by vomiting, use of laxatives, fasting, or excessive exercise. It is diagnosed when binge–purge episodes occur at least twice a week for 3 months (Smolak & Thompson, 2009). Bulimia is less apparent than anorexia because there is no emaciation, so it may go undiagnosed.

These eating disorders are more prevalent in girls than boys and emerge with puberty as girls' dissatisfaction with their increased fat level grows. Dissatisfaction with body weight is so common that it has become normal among American girls. However, not all girls who are dissatisfied with their bodies develop eating disorders. Boys' body dissatisfaction tends to focus on wanting bigger muscles, rather than on thinness (Field et al., 2014).

Besides body dissatisfaction, other risk factors for eating disorders include pressure to be thin, fat phobia, dieting, depression, low self-esteem, feelings of inadequacy, impulsiveness, drug use, and lack of social support. Families of youth with anorexia and bulimia may go to excessive lengths to avoid conflicts; they may be excessively enmeshed and overprotective; or they may be detached, hostile, disorganized, and conflict-ridden. The eating disorder may arise from adolescents' attempts to have some control over their own lives or from perfectionist strivings to please critical parents (Polivy, Herman, Mills, & Wheller, 2003). Daughters may learn distorted body perceptions from their mothers. In addition, there may be a genetic susceptibility to eating disorders (Striegel-Moore & Bulik, 2007). No single risk factor produces eating disorders, but an unfortunate combination of multiple risk factors may.

Eating disorders respond to some of the same treatments that are used for depression, anxiety, and panic disorders, such as medication and psychotherapy, because the conditions may share the same underlying causes (Rome et al., 2003; Stice & Shaw, 2004). Treatment may also involve hospitalization to foster weight gain.

2-3c Drug Use

Elaine's mother frequently got into physical fights with her boyfriend. Whenever he stormed from the house, Elaine's mother would smoke a blunt (cigar-sized marijuana) to help her calm down. One day she generously (in her view) invited 13-year-old Elaine to join her. That was Elaine's first drug use. When we met her, Elaine was a 35-year-old cocaine addict. Five of her seven children were exposed to cocaine while in the womb.

Drug use is one of society's most challenging problems. The term *drug use* refers to the use of alcohol and tobacco (which are legal), the use of illegal drugs, and the misuse of prescription medicine. Collectively they are known by the acronym ATOD (alcohol, tobacco, and other drugs).

The U.S. government sponsors national surveys of high school students[6] to monitor ATOD use (Johnson, O'Malley, Miech, Bachman, & Schulenberg, 2014). Among youth who use drugs, *alcohol is the most common drug*. Roughly 66% of 12th-graders report having tried alcohol at some time and 37% report drinking in the previous month. This means that *most youth are not consistent users and most abstain* in any given month, but some adolescents are heavy drinkers.

Tobacco and marijuana are the next most commonly used drugs. Roughly 34% of 12th-graders report having tried cigarettes at some time and 23% report having used some form of tobacco (including e-cigarettes and hookahs) in the past month. Roughly 44% report having tried marijuana and 21% report having used it in the past month. Additionally, 10% of 8th-graders and 23% of 12th-graders report having tried illegal drugs other than marijuana, including ecstasy, steroids, heroin, or cocaine, and 8% report having used them in the past month (Johnson et al., 2014). Youth who use these illegal drugs are likely to use more than one drug. That is, most youth who use marijuana or cocaine also smoke or drink alcohol. However, *most youth are not regular users of any drug*.

Age Trends in Drug Use

You might think drug use is a teen problem. This is both true and false. *Moderate* users typically begin drug use in late adolescence. However, *heavy* users typically begin drug use in elementary school (Grunbaum et al., 2002). This is why many school-based drug prevention programs begin in 3rd to 6th grade. In addition, the factors that lead to heavy use begin in early childhood (Dodge et al., 2009). We will discuss these factors later in this section.

You might also think that adolescents use drugs—and engage in other risky behavior (such as driving fast)—because they are irrational and do not understand the risk involved. Actually, their logical reasoning may be as good as that of adults. Instead, they engage in risky behavior because it feels more rewarding, especially in the presence of peers, and because they are imitating adults. Thus, merely "educating" teens about the risks is not likely to deter drug use.

---

[6] The numbers are updated annually. For the latest statistics and to find out about your state specifically, go to samhsa.gov and search for the "National Survey on Drug Use."

What Does Drug Use Predict?

Drug use is common in most countries, yet it is condemned by most. This is because drug use has negative outcomes that range from mild to severe, depending on whether it is short-lived experimentation or chronic, heavy use. At the severe end, drugs can cause death. Smoking is the leading preventable cause of death in the United States, including deaths attributable to secondhand smoke and infant death due to mothers' smoking. Moderate drug use can also cause physical illness and injury (Mokdad, Marks, Stroup, & Gerberding, 2004; Windle & Windle, 2003). Drug use leads to motor vehicle accidents, a leading cause of death among adolescents. More than 30% of high school students, particularly boys, report having ridden in a car with a driver who had been drinking (Grunbaum et al., 2002).

Alcohol and tobacco use are linked to poor grades (Busch et al., 2014). Drug use is also linked to social problems. Youth who use drugs are more likely to have risky sex and commit crimes than other youth (Fisher et al., 2000). Early involvement, before age 15, with *any* drug is a risk factor for later adult problems like crime, sexually transmitted diseases, dropping out of school, marital fights, and poor job performance (Odgers et al., 2008; Windle & Windle, 2003). The heavier the early drug use, the greater the risk of these problems.

What Predicts Drug Use?

One of the most powerful risk factors for drug use is parents' drug use (Ennett et al., 2008; Windle & Windle, 2003). Some children, like Elaine, use drugs with their parents as a time to bond (Lopez, Katsulis, & Robillard, 2009). Other children merely observe their parents' use and get their drugs from parents' stash. Cigarettes and alcohol are readily available in about 30% of homes. Some parents who want to be "cool" provide alcohol for their children's parties, even though it is a crime. Most teens who drink do so in their own or a friend's home (SAMHSA, 2008a). *Thus, many drug users are introduced to drug use by their parents.*

Another strong risk factor is whether the child's friends use drugs. This does not necessarily mean the child was introduced to drugs by the friends. Youth who use ATOD *select* friends who also use ATOD. Schools with large numbers of drug-using students make this selection easy. This is not to say that peers never cause drug use. If a child has a close friend who uses drugs, there is a small chance that the child will come to use drugs also, beyond the selection effect (e.g., Allen, Chango, Szwedo, Schad, & Martson, 2012; Cruz, Emery, & Turkheimer, 2012). Once drug-using cliques are formed, youth influence one another to continue use.

Another strong risk factor is mental health problems. Many youth who abuse ATOD also suffer from depression, ADHD, and conduct disorder (see Chapters 7, 8, and 10), particularly those who start using early. Perhaps this is because drug use is linked to family risk factors like domestic violence, harsh discipline, marital conflict, single parents, and mentally ill parents (Dodge et al., 2009). Additional risk factors include life stress, low school grades, early puberty, appearing older than peers, working at least 20 hours per week, low religiosity, and low self-esteem. Children with multiple risk factors are more likely to become drug users.

think about this

Children with a specific gene (called *5-HTTLPR*) are more likely to use drugs. However, even if they have this gene, they usually do not use drugs if they have a happy home. Children with *both* the gene and family problems are twice as likely to use drugs as children without the gene or without family problems (Brody, Beach, Philibert, Chen, & Murry, 2009). Which concepts from the "Nature and Nurture" and "Risk and Resiliency" sections of Chapter 1 does this support or refute? (You can fast-forward to Box 6.3 in Chapter 6 for more insights.)

On the other hand, parents really can be the "anti-drug" (Lac & Crano, 2009). Parents protect their children from drug use by monitoring them, being home, sharing activities with them, and being authoritative (see Chapter 7), disapproving of drug use, setting rules against drug use, and having a secure attachment with their children (see Chapter 6). These parenting factors may be especially powerful in protecting African American youth in high-risk neighborhoods (Cleveland, Gibbons, Gerrard, Pomery, & Brody, 2005). Several personal characteristics also protect children from drug use. These include having a valued skill, high IQ, high self-control, and strong school bonds (Windle & Windle, 2003; Zucker, Heitzeg, & Nigg, 2011). These personal protective factors—which you can influence as a teacher—are about as powerful as parenting factors.

Many people believe school sports protect children from drug use. This is not necessarily true. Sports participation is associated with an *increase* in the use of smokeless tobacco, alcohol, and performance-enhancing drugs; a *decrease* in cigarette use; and *no difference* in marijuana or barbiturate use (Lisha & Sussman, 2010; Naylor, Gardner, & Zaichkowsky, 2001). In one study, 38% of high school students reported violating the athletic association's rules against drug use (Naylor et al., 2001). Most were not caught, but among those that were, many were not sanctioned. Drug use is part of the culture of some sports. Youth are more likely to use ATOD if their teammates use ATOD (Fujimoto, Unger, & Valente, 2012). Professional athletes model ATOD use to youth. When we discussed avoiding drug use with a high school cross-country team, they responded with "look at Prefontaine!" Steve Prefontaine was an Olympic runner known to use alcohol.

Group Diversity in Drug Use

There are *gender differences* in drug use. While similar numbers of boys and girls report drinking and smoking, boys are more likely to binge drink and use illicit drugs than girls (Johnson et al., 2014). There are also *ethnic differences* in drug use. Until recently White youth used the most legal and illicit drugs, African American and Asian American youth the least. Latino youth were in between. However, there has been an increase in marijuana use among Latino and African American youth, such that the gap with White youth has decreased, and Latino 12th-graders now use more illicit drugs than other groups (Johnson et al., 2014). There are also small

brain research

Drug Use Harms Young Brains

Students' drug use is linked to lower grades and test scores, absences and dropping out, and misbehavior that interferes with learning (Jeynes, 2002). This may be due to compromised brain functioning. ATOD use affects the frontal cortex and the limbic system. For example, marijuana use diminishes motivation, short-term memory, judgment, and motor coordination (NIDA, 2010). Alcohol use hampers memory, attention, and information processing (S. Brown, Tapert, Granholm, & Delis, 2000). In fact, youth may be more susceptible to brain damage from drug use than are adults (Lubman, Yucei, & Hall, 2007). Remember that myelination and synapses continue to develop through adolescence.

socioeconomic differences in drug use. High-SES youth are less likely to use tobacco than low-SES youth, but not less likely to binge drink. These ethnic, SES, and gender differences have a small effect on drug use; personal and parenting factors are more powerful.

Classroom Implications of Drug Use

Most schools have policies that include notifying parents and police, and suspending or expelling students for using, possessing, or selling drugs (IES, 2012). Yet, nationally, 29% of youth report having been sold, offered, or given illegal drugs at school sometime during the year (Grunbaum et al., 2002). As many as 13% report coming to school under the influence (Jeynes, 2002). However, there is huge variation in this rate across schools (R. Rose et al., 2003). Some schools have greater need for ATOD interventions than others do. What can you do about ATOD use at your school? The following are some tips:

1. Avoid modeling acceptance of drug use by joking about it or using drugs yourself. Students know which teachers smoke, drink alcohol, or are addicted to caffeine, even when teachers try to hide it.

2. Convey that abstaining from drugs, including alcohol, is *normal.* Research shows *most youth do not use drugs.* Youth who believe that everyone else is doing it are more likely to use drugs.

3. Promote school bonding. In Chapter 6 you will learn how to do this. Children who feel cared for at school are less likely to abuse alcohol (Ennett et al., 2008).

4. Advocate for effective drug-use prevention programs. We will discuss these next.

Since enactment of the Drug-Free Schools and Communities Act in 1989, almost all schools have some type of ATOD prevention program. Most are aimed at resisting "peer pressure" to use drugs, even though peer pressure may be less powerful than family influences. The most common program was Drug Abuse Resistance Education (DARE), which was used in almost 75% of elementary schools. Dozens of studies indicated that DARE did not curb ATOD use and might even be counterproductive (Lilienfeld, 2007), so the program has been revised and debate continues about its effectiveness. Even the best peer pressure resistance programs have modest effects for only some children (Windle & Windle, 2003).

Does random drug testing work? Perhaps a little. An experiment in 36 high schools found that when schools test students who are involved in sports and extracurricular activities, 16% of students self-report drug use, as compared with 22% in schools that do not test. The good news is that drug testing does not deter youth from joining extracurricular activities. The bad news is that it does not reduce their intent to use drugs, nor does it reduce use in other students in the school (James-Burdumy, Goesling, Deke, & Einspruch, 2010).

Fortunately, there are school-based programs that are effective in reducing drug use. The most effective interventions address multiple levels of the bioecological model: individual, family, peers, school, and community (see Chapter 1). They teach the children social skills and coping strategies (see Chapter 8). They

Two sisters, ages 8 and 10, helped their mother carry several packs of beer from the grocery store to their car. The oldest girl asked, "Mommy, are these for the party or just for you?" What are the girls learning from their mother? As a teacher, what is your role in ATOD prevention with these girls? What type of school-based program is likely to prevent their ATOD use?

teratogen

an agent that harms the developing fetus.

encourage parents to set antidrug policies at home and strengthen families. They emphasize school bonding. They also change community norms for ATOD use. The U.S. government maintains websites that list research-based programs to help you select a program for your school.

Prenatal Drug Exposure—Behavioral Teratogens

One of the most serious consequences of children's drug use is that some continue drug use into their 20s, which are the prime childbearing years. Drugs are teratogens. A **teratogen** is an agent that harms the developing fetus. Teratogens include many things besides drugs, such as stress, pollutants, and illnesses (Hubbs-Tait, Nation, Krebs, & Bellinger, 2006).

Some teratogens have effects that are obvious at birth because they cause physical abnormalities, such as deformed limbs. However, other teratogens have effects that are not obvious at birth. For example, alcohol severely disrupts synaptogenesis (Ikonomidou et al., 2000). You cannot see this, but it will affect thought and behavior later in childhood. Such teratogens are called *behavioral teratogens.* They may affect infants by depriving them of oxygen, constricting blood flow, or altering neurotransmitters in their brain in the womb (Behnke et al., 2013).

Alcohol is one of the most powerful and common behavioral teratogens. Prenatal exposure to alcohol is the *leading preventable cause of intellectual disability.* It can result in fetal alcohol syndrome (FAS). Symptoms of FAS are small head size, facial abnormalities such as a thin upper lip and wide eyes, attention and behavior problems, and low intelligence (Williams et al., 2015). Children with less severe symptoms may have fetal alcohol spectrum disorders (FASDs). FASD symptoms are low birth weight (see Box 2.2), slow thinking, poor memory, difficulty focusing attention, and impulsive behavior, such as talking constantly in class. Alcohol-exposed children may also have poor motor development, particularly poor fine motor skills, making handwriting difficult.

Alcohol is linked to these problems even at common social levels of drinking and when the child is *not* diagnosed with FASDs (Behnke et al., 2013; Williams et al., 2015). For example, in one classic study, 14-year-olds' scores on a reasoning test were correlated with the number of drinks their mothers had at the beginning of pregnancy—before the mothers knew they were pregnant (Hunt, Streissguth, Kerr, & Olson, 1995). The more alcohol exposure, the faster, more impulsive, but inaccurate the child's responses 14 years later.

Tobacco is another common teratogen. Like alcohol, prenatal tobacco exposure is associated with low birth weight and with slightly smaller stature beyond birth as well. Tobacco exposure is robustly linked to low self-control, ADHD, aggression, and the child's own drug use in adolescence. It has also been linked to SIDS, poor language development, poor memory, slower learning, and lower IQ (e.g., Behnke et al., 2013; Farber et al., 2015).

These effects of prenatal ATOD exposure last beyond infancy into adolescence and adulthood. Generally, the effects are subtle. That is, *most exposed children tend to function within "normal" ranges, but at the low end of the range.* The degree of problems depends on the amount of exposure and whether exposure occurred early in pregnancy, when the brain is developing rapidly. There are no known safe periods of the pregnancy or safe quantities.

We have focused on how mothers' *prenatal* use of drugs affects children. However, *postnatal* (after birth) drug use can also affect children. For example, when parents smoke, their children are more likely to have ear infections, colds, and asthma and to miss school and have learning problems (Farber et al., 2015). Furthermore, ATOD use can diminish the quality of care parents give their children. For example, cocaine can cause parents to "crash" or be unwakable for several hours at a time, during which time no one is talking to, feeding, or supervising the children. Let's look at the classroom behavior of 4-year-old Jenny, whose mother uses alcohol daily:

> *Jenny chases imaginary children. She talks to objects. One day she sees a pumpkin in the room, stops to pat it, and asks how it is doing. She says, "You are a beautiful pumpkin—so big and fat!" One child says, "Nobody likes her; she's weird." Jenny plays alone unless someone feels bad for her and lets her into their group, usually at the teacher's urging. The other children say they don't play with her because they are afraid of hurting her. She looks fragile; she is very small for her age, awkward, and has a surgically corrected cleft palate. Unlike other children, she is not excited to go home after school and see her mother.*

Are Jenny's challenges due to prenatal drug exposure or the ongoing drug use of her mother? Probably both (Bergin & McCullough, 2009; Yumoto, Jacobson, & Jacobson, 2008). Parents who use drugs—even if they are *former* users who quit before having children—tend to be emotionally negative and have poor parenting skills, which leads to behavior problems in their children (Bailey et al., 2013).

The implications for you as a teachers are: (1) a key reason for preventing or reducing drug use in your students is to deflect them from becoming drug-using parents; (2) prenatal drug exposure can have long-term repercussions for some learners in your classroom; and (3) parents' current and past drug use can interfere with your students' success at school. If your school offers drug-prevention programs, try to get parents included in the programs.

At the conclusion of this chapter, it should be clear that physical well-being affects children's behavior and achievement at school. As a teacher, you have a vested interest in promoting the health of children. Many schools acknowledge this by having a nurse on staff. There is a movement in the United States to go a step further and create school-based health centers. (Other countries already have such centers.) The idea is to bring medical care to children where they are usually found—at school. This reduces costs and promotes better outcomes for ill children (Lear, 2003). For example, children with asthma had fewer costly hospitalizations and missed school less if their school had a health center (Webber et al., 2003). Asthma is the leading medical cause of school absence. Even in schools without health centers, you can promote the physical development of your students through the suggestions discussed in this chapter.

My Teaching

Brain architecture is influenced by the environment, including quality of your classroom. In addition, other aspects of children's physical development both influence and are influenced by experiences at school. To ensure you are promoting your students' physical well-being, periodically ask yourself:

1. Do I understand that brains change as a result of experience—such as the way I instruct or interact with each learner? Do I provide a stimulating environment that will foster brain development and learning, without being overstimulating?

2. Do I provide a relatively low-stress environment by being accepting and predictable? (See Chapter 8.) For example, do I provide a list of assignments and due dates well in advance? Do I avoid criticizing and punishing publicly?

3. Do I observe my students closely to verify that they are reaching appropriate physical milestones? Is my school screening the health, vision, and hearing of children?

4. Do I provide emotional support to children who are overweight or are unusually early or late to achieve puberty?

5. Are my students getting enough exercise? Do I encourage exercise, perhaps by providing physical activity in the classroom or by taking my class out to play? Does my school offer a safe approach for students who are walking or biking?

6. Do I model eating healthy food and encourage learners to do so also? Does my school offer healthy food? Do learners have adequate time for lunch in a pleasant space? Do I encourage learners, especially toddlers and teen girls, to get adequate iron and avoid soda? Should I allow healthy snacks in class?

7. Are my low-income students receiving free or reduced-price breakfast and lunch? If not, what can I do to help?

8. Are my students sleepy? Do I encourage them to get enough sleep? Does my school schedule events to end early enough?

9. Do I avoid inappropriately modeling or discussing smoking, drinking, or drug use with students? Do I convey the message that abstaining from drug use is normal (instead of talking as though all youth drink and will be doing so on the coming weekend)?

⌄⌄ Professional Resource Download

Chapter Summary

2-1 The Brain

- The brain has billions of nerve cells. Neurons communicate with each other through electrical impulses and neurotransmitters at synapses. Nerve cells have axons with a coating called a myelin sheath, which increases the speed of impulses.

- During infancy, synaptogenesis results in overproduction of synapses. During childhood, some connections are strengthened and others are pruned. Neurons that are repeatedly activated form stable circuits and brain structures.

- The brain has two sides, or hemispheres, and several major structures such as the brainstem, the limbic system, the cerebellum, and four lobes of the cortex. The prefrontal cortex carries on functions that make us uniquely human, like problem solving.

Summary of Age Trends in Physical Development

	Brain Development	Growth and Motor Development	Health Challenges
Infancy & Toddlerhood (Prenatal–2 Years)	• Brain development begins early in gestation. Myelination begins the last trimester. • Dramatic synaptogenesis occurs from before birth to age 2. • At birth, glucose rates are about two-thirds of adult rates. • Metabolic activity in the cortex is low, but in sensory, motor, and emotions areas it is high. These areas are fully myelinated around age 2 or 3.	• Normal birth size can range from 5.5 to 10 pounds. After birth, infants gain more than a pound a month. Birth weight doubles by 5 months and height doubles by 3 or 4 years. • The development of fine and gross motor skills follows a predictable sequence.	• Newborns sleep more than they are awake. Their sleep need gradually diminishes, until toddlers typically need just two naps a day. • SIDS is most likely to occur in infants under 1 year old. • Fat levels increase in infants until about 1 year and then decreases. • Prenatal drug exposure, including alcohol and nicotine, is linked to low birth weight.
Early Childhood (3–5 Years)	• The brain is almost adult-sized by age 5 to 7, but refinements continue. • At 4 years, glucose rates and blood flow are twice those of adults. Increased activity begins in the cerebral cortex. As it becomes interconnected, children gain self-control. • Kindergarteners have more synapses than adults.	• By preschool age, rate of growth is about 3 inches in height and 4 pounds per year. • The development of fine and gross motor skills follows a predictable sequence.	• Preschoolers need about 11 hours of sleep, and need one day-time nap until age 3 to 5. • Nightmares are common among preschoolers. • Roughly 8% of preschoolers are obese. The adiposity rebound may begin in preschool. Obesity is not yet linked to low self-esteem.
Middle Childhood (6–12 Years)	• Glucose rate plateaus until age 9 or 10, then gradually declines. • After a second wave of synaptogenesis, synaptic proliferation also plateaus. • Brain plasticity declines after age 10.	• Children grow about 2.5 inches and gain 5 to 6 pounds per year until puberty. • Coordination of movement with perception allows children to maintain balance, catch a ball, or write their name. • Amount of physical movement peaks around 7 to 9 years. • Hormones that trigger puberty begin about 6 to 8 years.	• At age 6, children need about 11 to 12 hours of sleep. • Fat increases at 4 to 8 years. Girls who are overweight at 5 to 7 tend to enter puberty early. • Roughly 18% of elementary students are obese. • Heavy drug users usually begin use in elementary school.
Adolescence (13–19 Years)	• Glucose rate declines to adult levels at about 16 to 18 years—less energy is required. • Synaptic pruning continues well into adolescence. Synaptic densities in the frontal cortex stabilize at adult levels in mid- to late adolescence. • Myelination of the prefrontal cortex becomes adultlike. • The cerebellum reaches full maturity. • A chemical shift in some neurotransmitters alters motivation and psychopathology. • Adult brains continue to grow synapses, dendrites, and supportive tissue because of learning.	• Puberty culminates during adolescence. This includes a growth spurt, changes in ratio of muscle and fat, and a spurt in strength for boys. It includes development of primary sex characteristics such as testes in males and ovaries in females and secondary sex characteristics such as pubic, facial, and body hair and breasts in women. On average, menarche occurs for girls at age 12 or 13 and spermarche for boys at age 14 or 15.	• Adolescents need about 8 to 10 hours of sleep, with the higher amount applying to rapidly growing or physically active teens. About 85% of teens get inadequate sleep. • About 7% of teens have delayed sleep, which is a sleep disorder. • Roughly 21% of teens are obese. • Girls become more dissatisfied with their body fat; this dissatisfaction is linked to anorexia nervosa and bulimia. • Most adolescents try ATOD, but are not consistent users. • The effects of behavioral teratogens may still be apparent.

✔ Professional Resource Download

- Genes do not specify the precise architecture of the brain. Instead, synaptogenesis allows the brain to capture experience, which shapes brain architecture. An enriched environment promotes brain development.
- There is a gradual loss of brain plasticity for some functions, but remediation is usually possible when early disadvantage occurs.

2-2 Growth and Motor Development

- Children develop gross and fine motor skills in a predictable sequence.
- Puberty is a long, gradual process that includes development of primary and secondary sex characteristics, as well as growth spurts and changes in body composition.
- Youth who mature early, especially girls, are at risk for behavior problems, substance use, and sexual activity.
- Genes and the environment combine to drive physical development. You can speed motor development, but only to a limited extent.
- Undernutrition causes stunted growth, delays puberty, and undermines brain development. Breast milk is the best nutrition for infants and is related to improved health and higher intelligence.
- Harsh or unresponsive caregiving can undermine physical growth and well-being.
- Most U.S. children consume too much fat and sugar and not enough fruits and vegetables. Nor do they get adequate exercise. Good nutrition and exercise are linked to success in school. Teachers can influence nutrition, exercise, and motor skills.

2-3 Contemporary Health Challenges

- Well-rested children behave better at school and have higher academic achievement. Unfortunately, many children, particularly adolescents, are sleep-deprived.
- Many American children are overweight, particularly low-SES children. Childhood obesity predicts type 2 diabetes, early onset of female puberty, and adult obesity, as well as learning, social, and emotional problems.
- Obesity is linked to low activity level, excessive television viewing, poor diet, and parent behaviors such as negativity during mealtime.
- Anorexia nervosa and bulimia are severe eating disorders that afflict girls more commonly than boys.
- Use of ATOD is predicted by parents' and friends' use. A sizable minority of adolescents are users, but at any given time most adolescents are abstainers. Among drug-using students, alcohol is the most common drug, followed by tobacco and then marijuana. Heavy drug users typically begin use in elementary school.
- White youth smoke and drink the most and African American youth the least, but Latino and African American youth have increased in marijuana use. Boys use illegal drugs more than girls and binge on alcohol more.
- Prenatal drug exposure undermines infant development and predicts negative outcomes through adolescence.

chapter **3**

Cengage Learning

Classic Theories of Learning and Cognition

How have the consequences of your behavior shaped the kind of student you are? Do you learn best by figuring out answers, or by being told the answers? In this chapter, we will discuss theories about how students learn. **After you read this chapter, you will be able to:**

3-1 Describe major concepts of behaviorism and apply them in the classroom.

3-2 Describe major concepts of Piaget's theory of cognitive development, describe how they are foundational to constructivism, and apply them in the classroom.

3-3 Describe major concepts of Vygotsky's sociocultural theory and apply them in the classroom.

3-4 Explain similarities and differences among the theories discussed in this chapter.

3-1 Behaviorism

In a 2nd-grade classroom, Naomi finishes her assignment and begins reading a book about Sacajawea. The class is supposed to be reading biographies in their free time, so the teacher announces to the whole class how happy she is to see that Naomi is reading. Her teacher then rewards Naomi with a ticket that she can use at the end of the week to buy candy, stickers, and small stuffed animals at the school store. Tickets are given out each time a child does something positive in class. The next day Naomi reads her biography during free time again—and so do several other children.

Naomi's teacher is using a behaviorist approach when she rewards Naomi for reading. When she gives Naomi a ticket, she influences Naomi to repeat the behavior and other students to follow Naomi's example. We will discuss behaviorism next. Two other influential theories that we will discuss in this chapter are cognitive developmental theory and sociocultural theory. The primary difference among these three classic theories is their perspective on what causes children to learn and reason better with age.

behaviorism
the scientific study of overt, observable behavior.

Behaviorism is the scientific study of observable behavior. According to behaviorists, control of behavior is located outside the child in the environment. John Watson (1878–1958), a leader of behaviorism, made the following assertion:

Give me a dozen healthy infants, well-formed, and my own specified world to bring them up in and I'll guarantee to take any one at random and train him to become any type of specialist I might select—doctor, lawyer, artist, merchant-chief and yes, even beggar-man and thief, regardless of his talents, penchants, tendencies, abilities, vocations, and race of his ancestors. (Watson, 1924, p. 82)

Do you agree with this statement? Watson is exaggerating the point that both the credit and the blame for what children become rest squarely on their environment. Behaviorists believe that children come to behave in their own unique ways because each has a unique learning history.

learning
according to behaviorists, a relatively permanent change in observable behavior that is the result of experience, not maturation or some other cause.

According to behaviorists, behavior is learned. In fact, **learning** is defined by behaviorists as a relatively permanent change in *behavior* that occurs as a result of experience. In a math class, you would know that student Monica has learned to solve math problems if she is able to *do* three-digit addition days or months after the lesson. You would know she had not learned if she were not able to add three-digit numbers. According to behaviorists, the same principles of learning apply to a 9-month-old as to a 19-year-old. Thus, whether you teach preschool or high school, the following discussion applies.

conditioning
learning, or creating conditions conducive to learning.

Behaviorists use the term **conditioning** to refer to creating situations that result in learning. Conditioned behavior is the same as learned behavior. In the vignette, Naomi and her classmates learned to read biographies as a result of their teacher's conditioning. We will discuss two forms of conditioning that are relevant to classrooms—classical conditioning and operant conditioning.

3-1a Classical Conditioning

classical conditioning
a form of conditioning in which a neutral stimulus is paired with a stimulus that causes an involuntary response until the neutral stimulus becomes a conditioned stimulus and also causes the response.

Classical conditioning is often called Pavlovian conditioning after Ivan Pavlov, a Russian physiologist who won the Nobel Prize in 1904. Classical conditioning starts

FIGURE 3.1 Pavlov's Cat.

Pavlov's research on salivating dogs is so well known that it even permeates cartoon culture. It appears that cats are not as predictable as dogs. *Mother Gooose & Grimm (new)* © 2002 Grimmy, *Inc. King Features Syndicate.*

with a stimulus that causes an *involuntary* response, without learning. In his most famous study, Pavlov placed meat powder in dogs' mouths, which caused them to salivate. The meat powder was an *unconditioned stimulus* (*UCS*). The salivation was an *unconditioned response*, meaning it was involuntary, not learned, and not under the dogs' control. At the same time, he presented a sound—for example, a bell. This was a *neutral stimulus* because it did not have anything to do with salivation. After repeatedly pairing the food and the sound, the dogs began salivating at the sound alone, so the sound changed from neutral stimulus to *conditioned stimulus* (*CS*). Salivation at the sound of the bell, without the food, became the *conditioned response.* The dogs had learned (changed their behavior) to salivate at the sound. Pavlov's studies are so famous that they even appear in cartoons (see Figure 3.1). Current research using classical conditioning focuses on anticipation. That is, the learner observes relations among events, *learns* to associate events with outcomes, and then anticipates those outcomes (Nilsson et al., 2012; Rescorla, 1988). Thus, a cognitive element has been added to some current theorizing.

Learned behavior can be unlearned. **Extinction** within the realm of classical conditioning refers to repeatedly providing the conditioned stimulus (bell) *without* the unconditioned stimulus (food) until the conditioned stimulus (bell) no longer elicits the conditioned response (salivation); that is, if conditioned dogs hear the bell repeatedly but do not receive food, after a while salivation will stop.

Classical conditioning occurs in humans as well as dogs. It explains some emotional responses, particularly fear and anxiety, such as math anxiety. If you are repeatedly humiliated (UCS) for doing poorly on math problems, you might be conditioned to associate math with humiliation and learn to feel anxious at the sight of math problems (CS). If you feel humiliated (UCS) for dropping fly balls, you may avoid baseball because you associate it with embarrassment (CS).

Classical conditioning can explain why some children dislike school. Children who have had negative experiences at school, like shame and embarrassment, have an unconditioned negative emotional response, which becomes paired with school. If this happens often, the mere sight, smell, and sounds of the school come

extinction (classical conditioning) the conditioned stimulus and unconditioned stimulus are repeatedly not paired until the conditioned stimulus no longer elicits the conditioned response.

to elicit sweaty palms, anxiety, shame, or anger. After conditioning, the negative emotional response to the school is automatic, not under the child's control. These feelings can apply to new situations, like other schools. Such children may grow up to become parents who will not attend back-to-school night because of the negative emotions school evokes. In contrast, learners who experience academic success and close friendships at school may be conditioned to feel happiness in school buildings. After reading this text, you will have the tools to condition your learners to enjoy school.

Conditioning applies to all ages. For example, if you play a musical tone (CS) every time infants reach for a colorful stick (UCS), they will reach out when they hear the tone, even in the dark where there is no stick (Keen, 2011). However, classical conditioning tends to be less effective with younger children than with adolescents and adults, perhaps because children don't always recognize the if-this-happens-then-that-will-happen contingency between the conditioned stimulus and the unconditioned stimulus (Hofmann, De Houwer, Perugini, Baeyens, & Crombez, 2010).

3-1b Operant Conditioning

While classical conditioning focuses on automatic or involuntary behavior, operant conditioning focuses on *voluntary* behavior like doing homework or getting in fights. **Operant conditioning** refers to learning voluntary behavior through consequences, which are either reinforcing or punishing.

Reinforcement and Punishment

A **reinforcer** is a consequence that increases the probability of a behavior. There are two types of reinforcers: positive and negative. Positive refers to *presenting something* and negative refers to *removing something*. Thus, **positive reinforcement** increases the probability that a behavior will occur again by *presenting* a consequence. A teacher may present learners with praise, treats, increased recess time, and good grades as positive reinforcers (Kodak, Northrup, & Kelley, 2007; Penrod, Wallace, & Dyer, 2008). If teens work hard on a class project, receive good grades, and then work hard on another project, they have been positively reinforced for hard work. If children on the playground push other children in order to get a ball, find that it works, and use pushing in the future to get what they want, they have been positively reinforced for pushing.

Positive reinforcement works on teachers also. Anthony Yom said he initially did not like teaching at his primarily Latino school in Los Angeles because so many student were unprepared and some tried to intimidate him (Lopez, 2016). Then, in 2016, one of his students earned a perfect score on the AP calculus AB exam. The student, from an immigrant family, credited Yom. Several other students told Yom that they appreciated his efforts and thought he was a good teacher. Thanks to these positive reinforcers, Yom continued to teach at the school. When was the last time you reinforced your instructors?

Negative reinforcement also *increases* the probability that a behavior will occur again by *removing* a negative or aversive stimulus. Seat-belt buzzers are an example of negative reinforcement. Drivers are reinforced to fasten their seat belt because

think about **this**

When people train dogs to roll over by giving them dog biscuits, or when they train dolphins to jump through hoops by giving them fish, are they using classical conditioning or operant conditioning? Explain.

operant conditioning
voluntary behavior is conditioned through its consequences.

reinforcer
a consequence that increases the probability of a response.

positive reinforcement
presentation of a consequence that increases the probability of a response.

negative reinforcement
removal of an aversive stimulus that increases the probability of a response. This is *not* punishment.

something negative (the buzzer) is removed when they fasten their seat belt, which increases the probability of the target behavior (fastening the seat belt). When people learn to escape aversive environments, they are being negatively reinforced (e.g., Gardner, Wacker, & Boelter, 2009). For example, when teens harass a teacher about too much homework, the teacher might reduce the homework in order to stop the harassment. When toddlers cry to get a cracker, the teacher may give it to them to stop the crying. In both cases, the teachers are negatively reinforced because they escape from a situation that is aversive for them. This is why negative reinforcement is sometimes referred to as *escape conditioning.*

You may confuse *negative reinforcement* with *punishment,* but they are not the same. **Punishment** refers to consequences that *reduce* the probability of a behavior. It does not necessarily refer to physical punishment, but can include scolding or having to sit in a less preferred seat. Punishment functions through *presenting* something or *removing* something. For example, presenting a student with an office referral could function as punishment. Removing outdoor playtime from a preschooler could function as punishment. These consequences would only qualify as punishment if they actually change the learner's behavior, regardless of the teacher's intention.

punishment
consequences that reduce the probability of a response.

Is it wise to punish learners? B. F. Skinner (1972), one of the most famous proponents of operant conditioning, was staunchly opposed to punishment (see Box 3.1). Skinner argued that behavior resulting from punishment was not as predictable as behavior resulting from reinforcement. It is better to reinforce appropriate behavior than to punish misbehavior. Nevertheless, punishment can be effective in stopping misbehavior. We will discuss the role of operant conditioning as a form of discipline in Chapter 7.

It is easy to misapply reinforcement and punishment in the classroom. Two common mistakes are ignoring behavior that deserves reinforcement and confusing punishment and reinforcement. For example, praise, intended as reinforcement, can actually be punishment for children who do not want praise. A teacher may intend reinforcement when she says, "Wallace, I am so glad to see that you did your homework today! And your score on the quiz was very good!" However, Wallace may be embarrassed and choose to do less homework. On the other hand, scolding, intended as punishment, can actually be reinforcement for children who seek attention. For some children even negative attention can reinforce.

How do you know whether you are correctly applying reinforcement and punishment in your classroom? If the consequence reduces the probability of a behavior, it is functioning as punishment. If the consequence increases the behavior, it is functioning as reinforcement. Let's see how this works in a 3rd-grade classroom:

Othman dislikes math work. Anytime Mr. Samms, his teacher, passes out difficult math work, Othman makes inappropriate noises and comments, flicks materials across the room, throws books, and instigates a commotion. Mr. Samms puts Othman in time-out for his misbehavior. Othman begins to act out every day in math, so that he will get sent to time-out.

Although Mr. Samms intends to punish Othman (decrease his misbehavior), the misbehavior continues or even increases, which means that *the intended punishment*

BOX 3.1 **theories & theorists**

B. F. Skinner

B. F. Skinner (1904–1990) was one of the most influential psychologists in history. Skinner studied rats in specially designed cages, which became known as *Skinner boxes*. A rat was put in a cage with a lever. If the rat pressed the lever, a pellet of food was released into the cage. No one told this to the rat beforehand, so it often made many movements before randomly pressing the lever. After being reinforced, the rat would press the lever again and again, until it was no longer hungry. If the lever only operated when a light was on, then the rat quickly learned to press the lever as soon as the light came on, and not at any other time. (Skinner also invented a teaching machine that reinforced human learners, but it did not involve rat-food pellets!) From these kinds of experiments, Skinner demonstrated the effects of reinforcement.

Skinner believed that the purpose of science is to predict and control behavior. Behavior is lawful. If you understand all the contingencies operating on a learner, you will understand the learner's behavior. The environment, not internal events like thoughts or feelings, is the primary cause of behavior. Skinner argued that internal events in the mind are not a complete cause of behavior, because you still have to understand where internal events come from, and ultimately the answer would be the environment. So why invoke the concept of internal events at all? In his last talk at the American Psychological Association, 8 days before he died, he ardently exclaimed that there was no need to invoke the concept of mind to explain behavior.

Skinner applied behaviorism in schools and any other situation where reinforcement was possible. He even began training pigeons to guide missiles. This led to animals being used in early space flight to determine whether being in space would alter behavior. He believed that

B. F. Skinner

Cengage Learning

advances in physical and medical science would never solve the world's problems. Only behavior change would. To convey this view, he wrote a utopian novel called *Walden Two* (1948). The book evoked many strong, and often angry, responses. People compared it with Orwell's totalitarians in *Nineteen Eighty-Four*, Hitler's Nazism, and Stalin's Communist regime because Skinner advocated controlling behavior. It was threatening to people who want to view themselves as masters of their own destiny rather than as robots controlled by their environments.

Skinner addressed his critics in another book, *Beyond Freedom and Dignity* (1971), in which he argued that lack of awareness of the forces controlling your behavior could make you feel free, but the feeling is illusory. It is dangerous to be controlled by forces you are not aware of. Skinner believed it was better to make control systematic rather than haphazard. To his credit, his methods have been applied to produce freedom for drug addicts, delinquents, and others, who, without behavior therapy, relinquish their freedom to prisons or mental hospitals. His books advocate that society eliminate punitive forms of control and use only positive reinforcement to change behavior.

is functioning as reinforcement. Othman was allowed to leave the aversive math lesson, so Mr. Samms is negatively reinforcing Othman, thus increasing misbehavior.

Shaping

As a teacher, one of your responsibilities is to get learners to enact specific behaviors. Yet, if a learner never displays a target behavior, like fully joining class activities, you cannot reinforce it. What can you do? Behaviorists use a technique called **shaping**, which means that you reinforce behaviors that are in the *direction* of the target behavior. Behaviorists call this *reinforcing successive approximations* to the target

shaping
reinforcement of successive approximations to a target behavior.

behavior. For example, 10-year-old Doug has illegible handwriting. He does not close the letters *d* or *a*, so they look like *cl* and *u*. His teacher describes how she uses shaping to help him:

> *Whenever I saw an "a" or a "d" on Doug's papers that was closer to the standard, I circled it and wrote "better" beside it. One time I asked Doug to look over one of his own papers and tell me which "a" he thought was best and which "d" best. I did not comment on the poorly written letters.... After 3 weeks his handwriting had improved markedly. I retrieved one of the papers he had written a month earlier, and we compared it with his current handwriting. He was impressed ... and could see how much he had improved. (Krumboltz & Krumboltz, 1972, p. 42)*

Be aware that you can inadvertently shape learner behavior in undesirable ways. If you ignore learners' requests for attention until they shout loudly, you are training them to shout; you will have extinguished quiet hand-raising, by ignoring it, and shaped a new behavior.

Stability and Extinction

Behavior tends to be stable as long as the system of reinforcement remains stable. If what is reinforced changes, new behaviors will appear. Thus, if Naomi in the opening vignette is reinforced for writing in her journal during free time, rather than silently reading, then she is likely to begin writing more and reading less in class.

Sometimes you will be interested in stopping a behavior. **Extinction** (in relation to operant conditioning) refers to eliminating or reducing a behavior by stopping reinforcement. In order to extinguish a behavior, you need to figure out what is reinforcing the behavior and then eliminate the reinforcer. For example, if Mr. Samms had ignored Othman's misbehavior, the misbehavior might have extinguished. However, when you attempt extinction, the misbehavior may *increase initially,* as the learner seeks the attention that he or she has come to expect. Thus, Othman probably would have intensified his misbehavior temporarily, when Mr. Samms first started to ignore it, but over time might have quit misbehaving during math.

If you want to teach a new behavior, it is best to use **continuous reinforcement**— that is, reinforce every correct response, and reinforce it immediately. However, if you want to maintain an existing behavior and make it less susceptible to extinction, it is best to use **intermittent reinforcement**—that is, reinforce some but not all appropriate responses. For example, gambling is reinforced on an intermittent schedule, and is highly resistant to extinction. Gamblers go for long periods without winning but continue to gamble. Thus, if you want your learners to maintain a behavior over the long term, like sitting on their assigned carpet square or bringing their books to class daily, reinforce them occasionally but not every time, after the behavior is reasonably stable.

3-1c Classroom Implications of Behaviorism

When applied well, behaviorism is a powerful tool for promoting learning and positive behavior. We will discuss general guidelines for applying operant conditioning in your classroom and then discuss a specific approach to instruction that evolved from behaviorism, called direct instruction.

extinction (operant conditioning) the elimination or decline in response caused by stopping reinforcement.

continuous reinforcement reinforcement occurs after every correct response.

intermittent reinforcement reinforcement occurs after some, but not all, responses.

think
about this

Teachers sometimes place misbehaving learners in time-out, like sitting on a solitary chair. Is extinction the goal of time-out? What other principles of conditioning might be at work in time-out? Is the intent to increase or decrease the target behavior? What do you think learners of different ages are thinking about during time-out? Use a concrete example to make your case.

Operant Conditioning in Classrooms

Operant conditioning has been effectively used to improve paying attention in class, completing assignments, and studying (Greenwood et al., 1992). To apply behaviorism successfully in your classroom, follow these guidelines:

1. Figure out what your learners find reinforcing. Your attention may be reinforcing for many, though not all, learners (Austin & Soeda, 2008). One teacher discovered that eating lunch with her was a reinforcer for her students. Another teacher found that helping a student compose an email to send to his jailed father was a strong reinforcer. Pride in new knowledge and problem solving may be reinforcing. Different learners may find different things reinforcing. One study found that when 17 items such as stickers, toy dinosaurs, and candy bars were ranked by teachers and elementary students, the items ranked highest by the teachers were not ranked highly by the students (Resetar & Noell, 2008). This suggests that you may have to problem solve about what is truly reinforcing to your students.

2. Grades are one of the key consequences that teachers control in classrooms, usually from 3rd through 12th grade. Grades can serve as reinforcement, punishment, or neither. One student may be thrilled to get a C, another student may be disappointed, and still another may not care. If good grades result in students studying and trying hard, they function as reinforcement.

3. Intentionally condition positive behavior in learners. Be careful not to mistakenly reinforce misbehavior, as Mr. Samms did with Othman, or extinguish good behavior by ignoring it.

4. Focus on reinforcement, not punishment. Be clear about what you want to reinforce, such as solving problems or continuing to try after failure.

5. Shape learners' behavior when teaching complex skills; that is, reinforce successive approximations to the target behavior. Earlier, we showed how this was done with handwriting. Shaping can also be applied to teaching toddlers to count and to coaching teens in sports (Photo 3.1). For example, novices were taught to golf by first hitting short putts. Then they progressed to longer putts, then to chip shots with irons, then to long drives with drivers. Compared with students who started with long drives, students whose skills were carefully shaped were more likely to win a playoff (Martin & Pear, 2003).

6. Use material rewards with care. While material rewards, like the tickets Naomi's teacher used, can be quite effective in classrooms, there are several drawbacks to their use. One is that managing them can become a burden for the teacher. Another is that learners come to expect them: "If I do my work, can I get a prize from the treasure box?" Teachers who used mechanical pencils as rewards said that they came to regret it because their learners soon expected rewards for good behavior and good grades. Another especially important drawback is that *material rewards do little to foster intrinsic motivation for the task.* This will be discussed more in Chapter 7.

If you follow these general guidelines from behaviorism in your classroom, learning should improve. However, you may not be able to apply operant conditioning in all situations, because you cannot always control the consequences of behavior.

You are likely to have more control of consequences in preschool, elementary school, or special education self-contained classrooms than in typical secondary classrooms, because adolescents can acquire their own reinforcers like food and money. Schools try to control teens' behavior using demerits, grades, exclusion from sports, or special honors, but many teens are not reinforced or punished by these consequences. Nevertheless, one powerful reinforcer that you control, and that most learners respond to, is caring from you. We will discuss this more in Chapter 6.

When teachers deliberately apply operant conditioning to children, it is called **behavior modification** or **applied behavior analysis**. One of us (CB) taught reading in

PHOTO 3.1 Shaping can improve golf and many other skills.

behavior modification
operant conditioning used to change human behavior, frequently applied in special education classrooms. Token economies may be used for reinforcement.

applied behavior analysis
controlled application of behaviorist principles to experimentally alter behavior. Overlaps with behavior modification.

a program that used behavior modification with high-risk 5-to-12-year-olds who had failed to learn to read in their regular classroom. Teachers sat at a table with six children. When a child correctly paired a sound with a letter, the teacher would place a chip in front of the child. After children mastered this basic skill, they were given a chip for a slightly more advanced skill, like blending sounds. When this was mastered, they were given a chip for sounding out simple words, and so on. Thus, their behavior was gradually *shaped* toward reading. Twice a day children turned in their chips for a prize. Because some of these children had experienced serious failure in school, they came to the program angry and frequently kicked the teachers under the table. The teachers wore shin guards so that they could ignore *all* disruptive behavior (*extinction*) and respond only to positive behavior (*reinforcement*). The approach was highly successful in that most students were soon reading at grade level. When behavior modification uses tokens like chips that children earn and use to pay for objects or privileges, it is called a *token economy*. In the opening vignette, Naomi's teacher was using a token economy.

Applied behavior analysis is especially common in the treatment of learners with autism, ADHD, and intellectual disabilities (e.g., Eikeseth, 2009). It has also been used to change a variety of behaviors in typically developing children, such as to be physically active during recess (Hayes & Van Camp, 2015), to move more quickly during classroom transitions (Hine, Ardoin, & Foster, 2015), to tackle properly in football (Stokes, Luiselli, & Reed, 2010), and to stay on-task in the classroom (Austin & Soeda, 2008). Figure 3.2 shows how 3rd-graders' physical activity increased when they were rewarded with small toys for increasing the number of steps they took during recess.

Direct Instruction

In addition to these general guidelines for applying behaviorism in your classroom, there is a particular approach to instruction, known as **direct instruction**, that has

direct instruction
a didactic form of instruction largely based on operant conditioning.

FIGURE 3.2 Applied Behavior Analysis during Recess.

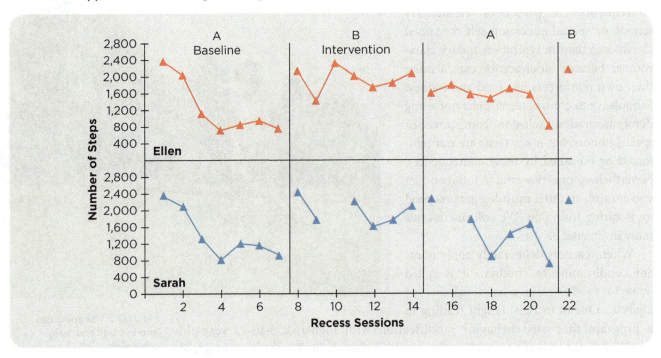

The authors of this study wanted to increase vigorous activity of 3rd-graders during 20-minute recesses. These data are from two girls, Ellen and Summer. During time A, the investigators just observed the two girls until their activity stabilized. During time B, the intervention, they gave the girls a Fitbit to count steps and set goals for the number of steps. They also reinforced the girls with small toys. Activity increased. During the second time A, the investigators stopped giving reinforcers or goals. Activity decreased. When reinforcers and goals were given again, activity increased again. *Data from Hayes and Van Camp (2015).*

its origin in behaviorism. There are two types of direct instruction. In the first type, a teacher follows this general format (Rosenshine, 1987):

1. Begin a lesson with a short statement of goals.

2. Begin with a short review of previous, prerequisite learning.

3. Present new material in small steps, with practice after each step.

4. Give clear and detailed instructions and explanations.

5. Ask a large number of questions to check for understanding.

6. Provide systematic feedback and corrections.

7. Obtain a success rate of 80% or higher during initial practice.

This is the approach commonly used in educational settings. When people refer to traditional instruction, they usually mean this sort of direct instruction.

The second type of direct instruction uses commercially prepared scripts. Some well-known direct instruction curricula include DISTAR, *Connecting Mathematics Concepts,* and *Reading Mastery*. In scripted direct instruction, teachers are provided with the *exact wording* to use when teaching. Both forms of direct instruction provide frequent and immediate feedback to every learner. Reinforcement should occur immediately after correct responses.

Direct instruction does not rely on discovery; everything that learners are expected to know is explicitly taught. No assumptions based on home life are made about what learners already know. The creed is: *if the learner has not learned, the teacher has not taught* (Adams & Engelmann, 1996). Thus, low income, poor motivation, or lack of family support cannot be used to explain low achievement; the teacher keeps instructing until the learner has learned.

There is clear evidence that direct instruction is effective, particularly for teaching *skills* like decoding words, reading comprehension, arithmetic, and basic science or social studies *facts*, although not all researchers agree (Borman, Hewes, Overman, & Brown, 2003; Dean & Kuhn, 2006; Rittle-Johnson, 2007). Direct instruction is also effective for teaching *concepts*. For example, in one study researchers taught 3rd- and 4th-graders how to use a controlled experiment, where they altered just one variable at a time, to determine which variable (e.g., smooth vs. rough surface, or steep vs. shallow incline) caused balls to roll the farthest (Klahr & Nigam, 2004). More students (77%) in the direct instruction group learned the concept of controlled experimentation than in the discovery group (23%). Direct instruction is sometimes mistakenly described as passive learning; in fact, good direct instruction requires learners to be cognitively active, thinking about what they are learning. Direct instruction is particularly effective when combined with hands-on activity (Lorch et al., 2010).

Some educators argue that direct instruction is effective for disadvantaged children who are unfairly burdened when left to discover academic knowledge on their own, in contrast to middle class children who are more likely to be taught academic knowledge at home. For example, Delpit (1988), an African American educator with extensive experience in inner city schools, pointed out that students of color and poor students who lack background knowledge about the sounds that go with specific letters or about how to speak and write Standard English should not have to discover the rules of literacy; they need to be *taught* the rules so that they too can experience the power that goes with knowledge. Yet, direct instruction, especially the scripted form, has critics. Some feel it is too heavy-handed, unresponsive to student differences, and developmentally inappropriate. Some research suggests that it results in learning that is less complex and less creative (Bonawitz et al., 2011; Dean & Kuhn, 2006). One study found that 5th-grade students wrote better essays about making a decision (considering both sides of a dilemma, describing varied reasons, and weighting some reasons as more important than others) if they participated in collaborative interaction groups than if they experienced direct instruction (Zhang et al., 2016). Let's turn to Piaget's theory next, which presents a different concept of how children learn and grow cognitively that leads to quite different approaches to instruction.

3-2 Piaget's Theory of Cognitive Development

We asked him why a boat floats on the water whilst a little stone, which is lighter, sinks immediately. Vern reflected and then said: "The boat is more intelligent than the stone.—What does 'to be intelligent' mean?—It doesn't do things it ought not to do." (Piaget, 1929/1963, p. 223)

This is an interview between Swiss researcher Jean Piaget (1896–1980) and a 6-year-old boy. Piaget used hundreds of interviews such as this one to develop a very

cognition
mental processes like thinking, planning, reasoning, and remembering.

complex theory of cognitive development that scientists are still debating (Müller, Berman, & Hutchinson, 2013). We'll discuss just a few concepts. The term **cognition** refers to mental processes like thinking, problem solving, categorizing, and remembering. *Cognitive development* means the orderly change across age in these mental processes. Piaget believed that to understand children's cognitive development, you must not only observe their behavior (as behaviorists do), but also consider *why* the child behaved that way. In particular, Piaget focused on why children give incorrect answers to questions, like why stones sink but boats do not. Because of children's consistent errors in reasoning, Piaget concluded that the logical structures of children's thought are different from those of adults.

Before Piaget developed his theory of cognitive development, a prominent view was that knowledge is simply a recording of something perceived in the environment; that is, the mind makes a copy of the perception and stores it. Piaget rejected this view. He said that knowledge is not just a copy of the world, but that it is an invention or construction in the mind of each person. He wrote, "In order to know objects, the [child] must act upon them, and therefore transform them: he must displace, connect, combine, take apart, and reassemble them" (Piaget, 1970, p. 704). This emphasis on each child constructing his or her own knowledge makes Piaget a **constructivist**, that is, someone who believes that each individual constructs his or her own understanding rather than merely making a mental copy of what was observed. Piaget also believed that learning involves assimilation. **Assimilation** refers to a learner incorporating a new perception into existing schemes. A **scheme** is a cognitive structure, such as an image, perception, or thought. For example, in a 4th-grade class the teacher was reading aloud from a book about pioneers in early Ohio. She read about a peddler coming to an isolated farm in the wilderness. She stopped to clarify her students' understanding:

constructivist
one who believes that knowledge acquisition is a process of construction rather than duplication (creating a mental copy of what is observed).

assimilation
the process by which children incorporate experience into existing mental structures or schemes, according to Piaget.

scheme
a cognitive structure or piece of understanding constructed through experience.

Teacher:	Who knows what "isolated" means? (Several hands wave.) Jorge?
Jorge:	There's a lot of ice there?
Teacher:	No. Lacey?
Lacey:	It is really, really, really cold there.

Through making the students' thinking public, the teacher has discovered that the children had constructed their own understanding of the word *isolated* based on their previous knowledge of the word *ice*. The children were mistakenly assimilating a new word, *isolated*, into their preexisting scheme of *ice*.

The counterpart to assimilation is accommodation. **Accommodation** refers to a child revising a scheme so that a new experience makes sense. In the 4th-grade class, the teacher helped the children accommodate their scheme of *isolated*:

accommodation
the process by which children modify existing mental structures or schemes in order to adapt to new experience, according to Piaget.

Teacher:	Scott, will you go stand in the corner by the sink for a minute? OK. Now Scott is isolated from the rest of us. What does "isolated" mean? (All hands go up.) Trevor?
Trevor:	Away from others?
Teacher:	Right. The author means they don't have any neighbors. No one lives within miles of them.

According to Piaget, every act of learning includes both assimilation and accommodation, though the amount of each may vary. Some experiences may involve more assimilation, and some more accommodation. For example,

> *Manny, a toddler who has a pet cat, sees a new cat. He assimilates the new experience into his existing scheme for* kitty. *At the same time, the new cat is not identical with his own, so his scheme of* kitty *expands to other small, four-legged furry animals. One day Manny cries, "Kitty, kitty!" as he runs toward a skunk. His mother cries, "No. It's a skunk!" and whisks Manny away.*

His mother's reaction then causes Manny to accommodate and modify the existing kitty scheme into separate *skunk* and *kitty* schemes. Two children with the same experience may construct different knowledge because they had different preexisting schemes.

The tug-of-war between assimilation and accommodation is the result of the need for **equilibrium**, a state of cognitive balance and comfort. Piaget suggested that as you experience the world, you become perplexed and wish to resolve your cognitive disequilibrium. You assimilate and accommodate as you seek a state of equilibrium, which results in cognitive development.

equilibrium
a state of cognitive balance or cognitive comfort.

3-2a Age Trends in Piaget's Cognitive Developmental Theory

According to Piaget, cognitive development happens in stages. He described four major stages: sensorimotor, preoperations, concrete operations, and formal operations. While Piaget gave approximate ages for each stage, he did not claim that specific ages go with each stage. Piaget believed that some children may reach a stage at a slightly younger or older age than average. The only way to infer a child's stage is by observing the child, not by merely knowing his or her age.

The four stages are linked with *qualitative,* as opposed to *quantitative,* differences in children's logic; that is, older children reason and solve problems in a different way than younger children. For example, a toddler who thinks that when her mother breaks a cookie in two she has more cookie, could be said to be reasoning in a different way than a teenager would. Piaget believed that a key difference between teens' and toddlers' cognitive ability is that teens can think accurately about abstract concepts, but younger children cannot. As children's experience with concrete objects accumulates, abstract concepts and higher-level knowledge develop. Let's examine each stage.

The Sensorimotor Stage (Birth to 2 Years)

When infants are born, they immediately begin to observe the world and attempt to make sense of it. Through rooting, sucking, grasping, and looking, they lay a foundation for cognitive growth. At this stage, thought and action are indistinguishable. The infant's first cognitions are sensory and motor oriented. A child learns about a new toy by grasping and chewing on it.

Later in this stage, children become capable of **symbolic thought**—that is, the ability to have one thing stand for another. Language is a key marker for symbolic thought because to use language, children must understand that words like *mama*

symbolic thought
the cognitive ability to have one thing stand for, or represent, another.

sensorimotor stage
children rely on senses and
behavioral schemes to acquire
knowledge. Roughly birth to
2 years.

deferred imitation
ability to mentally represent and
then imitate an action that was
observed in the past.

object permanence
the knowledge that objects that
are out of view continue to exist.

A-not-B error
children observe an object
being moved from hiding place
A to hiding place B, but they
search in hiding place A. Typical
of the sensorimotor stage.

and *juice* stand for objects. As they grow older, children engage in symbolic thought as they use rocks as dishes or colored blocks as cars. This makes symbolic, make-believe play possible. During the **sensorimotor stage**, children become capable of **deferred imitation**; that is, they can mentally represent, remember, and then imitate an action they observed in the past. This ability is also related to make-believe play, which requires that children remember and reproduce what they have observed, such as putting the baby doll to sleep, or leaping like Superman into the air.

Sensorimotor infants develop **object permanence**, or the knowledge that objects that are out of view continue to exist. Infants who lack object permanence behave as though an object that has gone out of view has ceased to exist. Object permanence follows a predictable sequence. Newborns may show interest in an object, say, an attractive toy, but do not visually search for the toy if it is removed from view, suggesting no mental representation of the toy. At 4 to 8 months, infants will visually track the toy and reach for it if it is partially hidden beneath a blanket, but not if it is fully hidden. At 8 to 12 months, infants will search for the toy if it is hidden before their eyes. But they make an interesting mistake consistently: They search for the object at point A even if the object is moved to point B in full view (Photo 3.2). For example, Piaget twice hid his 10-month-old daughter's toy parrot under her mattress at point A while she watched. Both times Jacqueline retrieved the parrot. Then, Piaget hid the toy parrot under the mattress in a different place, at point B, while she watched. Jacqueline searched for the parrot at point A instead of point B (Piaget, 1954). This is called the **A-not-B error**. Piaget believed this occurred

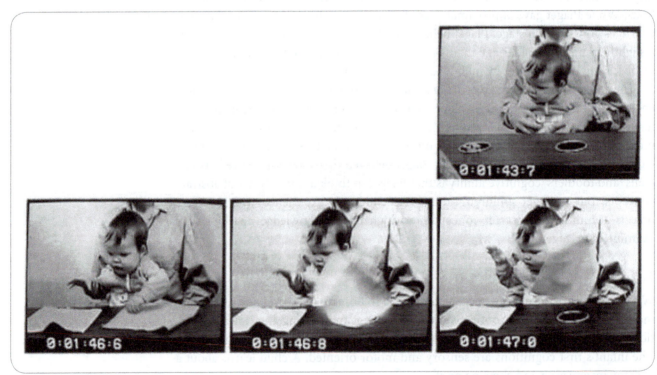

Adele Diamond

PHOTO 3.2 While the child was watching, a toy was placed in the opening to your right (location A, see top photo); then the toy was placed in the opening to your left (location B in top photo). In the next three photos, you can see the child reach for location A while looking intently at location B. The looking behavior suggests object permanence, but the reaching behavior suggests an inability to inhibit behavior.

because older infants still have an incomplete understanding of object permanence. Currently, there are alternative explanations, such as infants' difficulty inhibiting an impulse to reach where they found the object previously (Watanabe, Forssman, Green, Bohlin, & Hofsten, 2012).

The Preoperational Stage (About Ages 2 through 7)

Operations are mental actions that follow rules. You could think of an operation as an act of logic. The term *preoperational* refers to Piaget's view that children in this stage are not yet capable of thinking logically. He believed they have other limitations as well, like inability to think about how an object might look from different points of view, which requires mental manipulation. He believed they do not fully understand cause-and-effect sequences (Desrochers, 2008). According to Piaget, other cognitive deficits include those discussed below.

operation
according to Piaget, mental actions or manipulations that follow rules.

Animism

Animism is the belief that nonliving, inanimate objects have lifelike qualities. For example, children may think that boats are intelligent, that the sun is following them, that a single flower might get lonely, and that things that move, such as a flickering flame, are alive. They believe that objects or natural phenomena (rain, wind, snow) have intention, including intent to harm. For example, they might cry because they think that a leaf blowing toward them is chasing them.

animism
attribution of lifelike qualities, like intention, to nonliving, inanimate objects.

Lack of hierarchical classification

Hierarchical classification means that things can be members of multiple levels of categories at the same time. For example, a collie is a dog and a mammal at the same time. Preoperational children have trouble classifying objects in a hierarchy. They have trouble understanding that all collies are dogs, but not all dogs are collies. We heard a young child correct someone by saying, "That's no woman—that's my mommy!" indicating trouble with hierarchical classification.

hierarchical classification
the ability to classify or place objects into superordinate and subordinate categories.

How did Piaget study children's trouble with hierarchical classification? He used *class inclusion* tests (Piaget & Inhelder, 1964). For example, he presented children with two colors of beads—10 red and 5 blue. He asked, "Are there more red beads or more beads?" Preoperational children tend to answer more red beads even though there are clearly more beads. Piaget argued that this is because the child cannot at the same time think of the whole class of beads and the parts (red and blue) that compose it, which is part of a general deficiency in mental flexibility.

Egocentrism

Young children are **egocentric**, which is the tendency to see the world from their own point of view and to assume that other people do too (Piaget, 1926/1959, p. 9). Have you seen young children on the phone silently nod their head to say yes, when the person on the other end of the line cannot see the nod? Have you seen them close their eyes in order to hide from you? Preschoolers also show their egocentrism when they hold **collective monologues** in which they speak with another child and even take turns talking so they appear to be conversing, but neither is listening to the other.

egocentric
the tendency to see the world from your own point of view while failing to see other people's points of view.

collective monologues
children appear to be conversing with each other, but are really not addressing thoughts or adapting speech to their conversation partners.

One way that Piaget demonstrated children's egocentrism was with the "three-mountain task" (see Figure 3.3). A child is presented with a three-dimensional model

FIGURE 3.3 Piaget's Three-Mountain Task.

When preoperational children are asked to choose photos depicting the doll's view, they tend to choose photos of their own view.

of three mountains that are distinctive because they have different objects at each peak: snow, a cross, or a house. The child is given 10 pictures of different views of the three mountains. A doll is placed at various points around the model, and the child is asked to pick the picture that shows what the *doll* sees. Children in the **preoperational stage** tend to choose the picture that depicts *what the child sees,* not what the doll sees.

Lack of conservation

Conservation refers to the fact that the properties of objects such as mass, volume, and number do not change just because the objects' appearance changes. For example, if you have a ball of clay, the amount of clay in the ball does not change if you smash it down it into a pancake shape, though the appearance changes (see Figure 3.4). Preoperational children might say that the smashed lump of clay has more mass than the ball. This is because they **center** on the superficial attributes of objects. They are unable to **decenter** and simultaneously consider that the smashed clay covers more surface area but is thinner than it was. You can see this when you cut an apple in half for one child, but not the other. Listen to this conversation between two brothers:

preoperational stage
children are able to use symbolic thought, but unable to think logically, particularly to conserve or decenter. Roughly ages 2 to 7.

conservation
understanding that the properties of objects like mass, volume, and number do not change just because the objects' appearance changes.

center (or centration)
the child focuses on one aspect of a task to the exclusion of other aspects.

decenter (or decentration)
ability to think about multiple aspects of a task simultaneously.

5-year-old:	*Ha, ha, I got more than you!*
11-year-old:	*You did not. They are the same.*
5-year-old:	*Nut-uh. I got two and you only got one.*
11-year-old:	*It doesn't matter. They are still the same size.*
5-year-old:	*They are not! I have two, so that is bigger!*
11-year-old:	*Look, if you put your two pieces together, they are the same size as mine.*
5-year-old:	*Oh, I see. But I still have more!*

Piaget is probably most famous for his conservation tasks, even though they constituted a small part of his work. They are popular because they illustrate the apparent illogic of young children and are fun to replicate. The best-known task involves two identical glasses and a third taller, skinnier glass. You pour liquid carefully into the identical glasses until the child agrees that they have the same amount. You then pour the liquid from one glass into the glass that is taller and ask, "Do they still contain the same amount?" Preoperational children will say that there is more liquid in the tall skinny glass, even though no liquid has been added or subtracted. The child centers on the height of the liquid in the glass and cannot consider the height and width of the container at the same time. In addition, the child cannot **reverse operations**— that is, mentally consider that if the liquid were poured back into the glass from whence it came, the height would be the same as before. Figure 3.4 provides examples of conservation tasks and the ages at which they are typically mastered.

reverse operations
ability to mentally reverse or negate an operation.

FIGURE 3.4 **Piagetian Conservation Tasks.**

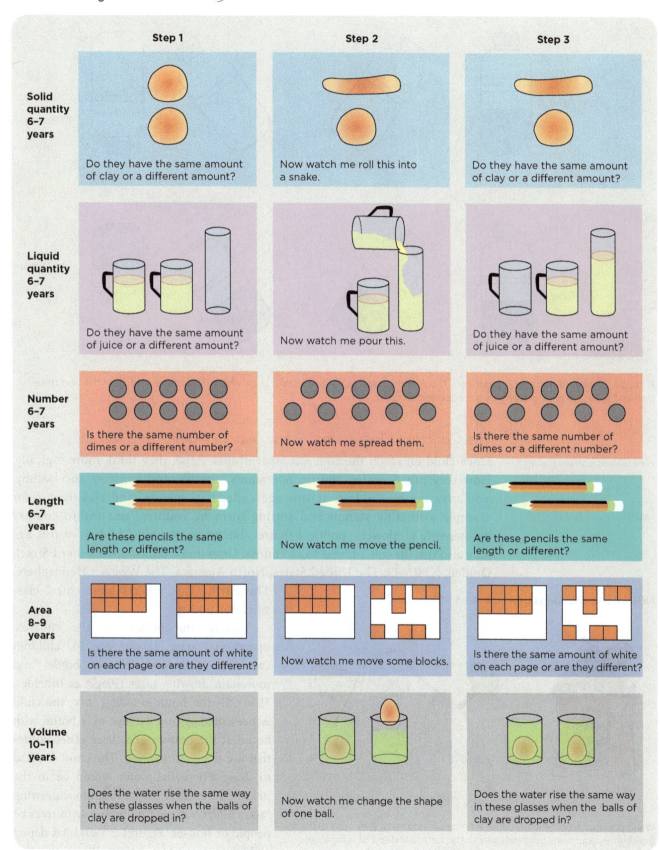

Examples of different types of conservation tasks. Notice that children master different types at different ages.

FIGURE 3.5 **Bottle Drawing Task.**

A child is presented with row A and asked, "Look at the water in the first bottle. Draw where the water would go in the next three bottles." Row B depicts drawing by a preoperational child.

The Concrete Operational Stage (About Ages 7 through 11)

concrete operational stage
children are able to decenter and think logically about concrete objects and experience. Roughly ages 7 to 11.

Once children reach the **concrete operational stage**, they think more logically. Now they can decenter, reverse operations, classify, and conserve successfully. You may notice children at this age collecting, sorting, and classifying—for example, collecting stamps and sorting them by country, and within country by theme (e.g., flowers, political figures, historical events). Children at this age may also use the full address to Grandma: Grandma Collins, 400 Orchard Street, Oradell, NJ 07649, The United States, North America, The Western Hemisphere, The Earth. This reflects hierarchical classification ability.

Toward the middle of the concrete operational stage (about age 9), children can successfully complete the bottle- and mountain-drawing tasks (Piaget & Inhelder, 1956). In the bottle-drawing task, the child is presented with a picture of a bottle with liquid at the bottom and three other bottles that are tilted or inverted. The child is asked to draw where the water would be in the next three bottles. In the mountain-drawing task, children draw a mountain with trees or people or houses. Figures 3.5 and 3.6 depict children's responses before they have this

FIGURE 3.6 **Drawings of a House and Mountain.**

When preoperational children draw a house or mountain, they tend to place the chimney and trees perpendicular to the surface instead of vertical. You may notice this in their art.

ability. Although children at this stage are now better at logical reasoning, they still are not skilled at abstract thinking, which comes with the next stage.

The Formal Operational Stage (About Age 12 and Older)

In the **formal operational stage**, youth can think in the abstract; that is, they can think about possibilities that may not physically exist. They can think about, manage, and monitor their own thinking, which we will discuss more in Chapter 4 (Kuhn, 2008). They can follow clear logic and reason in a hypothetical-deductive manner, even if the premises are not true. For example, if all New Yorks are Chicagos, and all Chicagos are Seattles, is it true that all New Yorks are Seattles? Young, concrete thinkers cannot see this as a pure logic problem: If all As are Bs, and all Bs are Cs, is it true that all As are Cs? In contrast, formal thinkers can reason that As must be Cs, and all New Yorks are Seattles.

> **formal operational stage** children are able to think abstractly about hypothetical events and systematically test hypotheses; roughly age 12 to adulthood.

Youth at the formal operational stage can systematically test possible solutions to problems. They can isolate variables, form multiple hypotheses about which variable is relevant, vary one factor at a time to test each one, and assess each in light of evidence. In one task, Piaget asked children to test what factor causes the rate of oscillation, or swinging, of a pendulum (see Figure 3.7). Possible variables are the length of string, the weight of the object at the end of the string, the height from which the weight is dropped, and the force of the push used to begin swinging. If you are a formal operational thinker, you might try different lengths of string while keeping all the other variables the same. Then, you would hold length of string and the other variables constant while varying only one other variable, such as weight. After such systematic testing, you would discover that only length of string affects oscillation rate. This sort of controlled experimentation is important in everyday life. For example, if a car won't start and the mechanic replaces both the starter motor and the battery at the same time, the car may start, but the owner may have paid for an unneeded repair.

The following two tasks measure formal operations (Gray, 1976). See if you can do them.

Task 1.

All of the following sentences are true. What determines whether or not the mice will fight with each other?

1. *The mice are not brown; the mice are not old; the mice have food; the mice do not fight.*

2. *The mice fight; the mice do not have food; the mice are old; the mice are brown.*

3. *The mice are not old; the mice do not fight; the mice are brown; the mice do not have food.*

4. *The mice have food; the mice are not brown; the mice fight; the mice are old.*

Task 2.

Teresa (T), Carol (C), Peggy (P), and Sharon (S) are going to form teams for a contest. Teams can have one, two, three, or four members. Write all of the possible teams that can be formed. Use the first letter of each girl's name in the answer.

FIGURE 3.7 **Piaget's Pendulum Problem.**

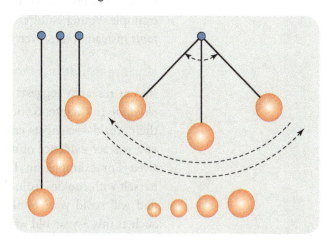

What determines how fast the pendulum swings? Length of the string? Weight of the object? Height from which the weight is dropped? Force of the push? Formal operational learners are able to vary one variable at a time, systematically, to determine what causes the rate of oscillation. *Adapted from Inhelder and Piaget (1958).*

To successfully solve the mice problem, you have to suppress knowledge of how mice really act, and you must reason only from the facts given in the task. Children who are not yet formal thinkers use personal experience rather than abstract logic to solve the problem. They tend to say that mice who do not have food will fight, which is wrong given the third proposition. The correct answer is that old mice fight. To be scored in the formal operational stage on the second task, the response must provide 14 or 15 teams (the correct answer is 15 teams) and the response must be *systematic*. One example of a systematic response is

T	TC	TCP	TCPS
C	TP	TCS	
P	TS	TPS	
S	CP	CPS	
	CS		
	PS		

Formal operational thought is important for understanding science, mathematics, history, literary analysis, and other school subjects. To understand the scientific process, students must be able to see the logic of controlled experimentation. To successfully solve mathematical problems, students must be able to think in the abstract. For example, in algebra the variable *x* is used to represent many different numbers, which is an abstract notion.

3-2b Advances in Knowledge since Piaget

Piaget's research was brilliant and groundbreaking. However, researchers have continued to move forward. Today, Piaget's stages are not widely accepted among researchers. Some researchers also challenge his notion that knowledge begins with experience through the five senses, which is then stored as concrete knowledge and later becomes the basis for abstract concepts (Uttal, Liu, & DeLoache, 2006). Children often acquire abstract concepts before the concrete examples of them. For example, young children apply abstract grammar rules to language when they say *foots* instead of feet, even though they have never heard adults say *foots*.

Underestimation and Overestimation of Abilities

Recent research suggests that Piaget *underestimated the cognitive abilities of young children.* In Chapter 5 you will learn that infants know many surprising things about their world—scientists call this *core knowledge.* In your interactions with toddlers, you will see evidence of nonegocentrism, or an ability to anticipate others' perspectives. For example, an 18-month-old hid under the kitchen table while stuffing herself with cookies from the cookie jar. Why hide if you cannot anticipate that your dad will scold you? Similarly, young children often show good reasoning ability, such as this 3-year-old who wants crackers:

Mother:	*They're all gone.*
Boy:	*No they aren't. I want some!*
Mother:	*Yes they are. What makes you think they aren't?*
Boy:	*'Cause if they was all gone, I seed them [the empty package] in the garbage. Look, nothing in the garbage!*

Or this conversation between two 7-year-old boys eating lunch in the school cafeteria, after one had been pondering an abstract concept:

> Boy 1:   *Everyone is related to each other.*
> Boy 2:   *Huh? Show me your logic.*
> Boy 1:   *Well, I have cousins. And they have cousins, who have cousins, who have cousins, who have cousins, who have cousins …*
> Boy 2:   *Stop! I get it.*

Piaget also *overestimated the ability of adolescents.* Adolescents can be remarkably egocentric, as in this conversation between two 14-year-olds after swim team practice at the high school:

> Boy: *What a bear of a practice. I'm wiped out.*
> Girl: *My hair smells good. I got this new shampoo. It smells like coconuts.*
> Boy: *If we keep working out like that, we ought to all be able to improve our times. If we're not wasted!*
> Girl: *Kendra's got this cool shampoo too. I like hers better.*
> Boy: *I could qualify for state if I could take two more seconds off my freestyle.*
> Girl: *Kendra's dad sells it. They won a trip to Hawaii for selling the most, or something like that. Her mom and dad, I mean.*

This example has the turn-taking quality of a dialogue, but it is really a collective monologue with neither youth attending to the other, which Piaget said was characteristic of preoperational children.

In the 1970s researchers began to demonstrate that with modest changes in the tasks used by Piaget, young children could reverse, decenter, use logic, and classify hierarchically (Donaldson, 1978; Gelman & Baillargeon, 1983). For example, the "Sleeping Cows Task" is a modified test of class inclusion. In this task, some black and white toy cows are placed on their sides as though they are sleeping. The standard Piagetian approach would be to ask the child, "Are there more black cows or more cows?" When asked in this way, only 25% of 6-year-olds respond correctly. If one word is added—"Are there more black cows or more *sleeping* cows?"—then 48% of 6-year-olds respond correctly. Only one word is changed, but responses are substantially different. Another example is the "Police Task," which tests egocentrism. A child is asked to hide a child doll from police dolls. Partitions are set up so that the child must consider two different points of view simultaneously (see Figure 3.8). Most (90%) 3-year-olds can do this task correctly, whereas few can do the three-mountain task, even though both tasks require the child to consider what another person would see.

FIGURE 3.8 **Hide-from-Police-Officer Task.**

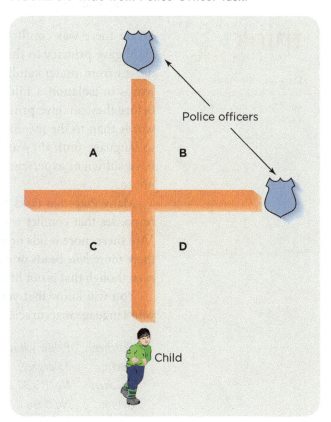

A child is given a doll and asked to hide it so that neither police officer can see it. About 90% of 3- to 5-year-olds get the task correct, even though results of the three-mountain task would predict a much lower proportion. *Source: Donaldson (1978).*

Thus, current evidence suggests that there is less difference between the logic of children and adults and that young children are not as egocentric or illogical as Piaget believed, though there continues to be some controversy (Kagan, 2008). However, it is also true that if you carry out Piagetian tasks in the same way that Piaget did, you will tend to get the same responses. This suggests that young children do have cognitive limitations. Their abilities are fragile. Their knowledge is often implicit, meaning the child cannot reflect on and discuss the knowledge. In addition, young children do not give primacy to language, which may cause them to fail at Piagetian tasks.

Primacy of Language

When children begin to learn language, they pay more attention to context than to words. In fact, they often learn words through clues from the context. The child first makes sense of the context and then uses that to make sense of what is said. For example, a 2-year-old is taking a bath "by herself" with instruction from her mother:

> Mom: *Take the wash cloth and wash your mouth.*
> *(Child does.)*
> Mom: *Good! Now wash your eyes.*
> *(Child does.)*
> Mom: *Good! Now wash your ears (while unconsciously scratching her nose).*
> *(The child washes her nose.)*

think about **this**

Do any of the Piagetian tasks seem like trick questions to you? Might they to a child? Explain.

When there was conflict between what her mother *said* and what she *did*, the child gave primacy to the mother's action. The language-learning child gradually moves from understanding words in conjunction with action to understanding words in isolation. Children must have a great deal of experience with language before they can give primacy to language—that is, more weight to the meaning of words than to the meaning of the context. Children are not able to give primacy to language until they are confident about their understanding of language and have sufficient experience to know when to give primacy to language and when not to.

Many Piagetian tasks require children to give primacy to language and require responses that conflict with contextual clues. For example, the class inclusion task "Are there more beads or more red beads?" is likely interpreted by the child as "Are there more *blue* beads or more red beads?" because that is what the context suggests, even though that is not literally what is asked.

You will know that your learners have primacy of language when they correct *your* language inaccuracies, as was the case in this 8th-grade classroom:

> Teacher: *Below what temperature does water freeze?*
> Devin: *33 degrees.*
> Teacher: *No. It's 32 degrees.*
> Devin: *No it isn't! You asked **below** what temperature does water freeze.*
> *It freezes **at** 32 degrees. So it freezes **below** 33 degrees.*

Imagine what Devin's answer will be after he takes physics!

3-2c Diversity in Cognitive Developmental Theory

Piaget believed that stages of cognitive development occur in a predictable sequence from child to child because each stage is necessary for the formation of the next stage. He was interested in universal patterns in how children think, so he paid little attention to individual differences. He did not investigate whether some children achieved a stage earlier than other children. Yet, listen as Lisa reacts to the conservation-of-liquid task in her 2nd-grade class:

Lisa:	*The tall glass has more water. It is bigger. The other one is short.*
Teacher:	*Does everyone agree with Lisa? (Some students nod yes, but others shake their heads no.) Aaron, you do not agree?*
Aaron:	*The glasses are not the same shape. The tall one is really skinny and the short one is really fat. I think they might be the same, or the short one might hold more.*
Teacher:	*How many of you thought about how big around the glasses are, and not just how tall they are? (Some hands shoot up, but it is clear that many 2nd-graders were just beginning to think about the possibility.)*

think
about **this**
Discuss parallels between the poor performance on concrete operations tasks for adults who are not familiar with the researcher's language or materials and a young child's poor performance.

Piaget's theory does not explain the differences in performance between Lisa and Aaron, or other children in your classroom.

Piaget also believed that the stages of cognitive development are the same across cultures. Members of some cultures may be faster or slower in their rate of development, but he believed that the sequence would be the same. He believed that nearly all people in all cultures would achieve concrete operations; that is, their thinking would become logical. However, early research *using Piaget's interview method* found that in some cultures many adults do *not* achieve concrete operations. This finding was met with skepticism. For example, Cole (1975) asked how people who experience water shortages could function if they thought water in tall thin cans was more than the same amount in short wide cans. Later research indicated that when people are interviewed in their native language, with familiar materials, they do achieve concrete operations across cultures and ethnic groups (Laboratory of Comparative Human Cognition, 1998). Thus, supposed cultural differences in logic may be a result of the research methods used, but not of real differences in cognitive ability.

The formal operations stage is a different story. In most cultures, many people never attain this stage when tested with standard Piagetian tasks. For example, even Americans who are in their teens or 20s have trouble with formal operational tasks (like the mice-fighting task), with only 30% to 40% being successful (Dimant & Bearison, 1991; Moshman, 1998). This raises the possibility that formal operations is not a stage, but rather a type of cognitive specialization linked to formal schooling. Some scientists dismiss Piaget's notion of formal operations altogether because evidence suggests that there are different types of reasoning—analogical, legal, logical, and scientific—that develop during adolescence and adulthood depending on one's area of specialized education (Moshman, 1998). Advanced schooling may be necessary, but not sufficient, to develop formal operations.

If Piaget is wrong about some things, why study him? For two reasons:

1. His theory is a good starting point because it caused scientists to try to understand why children respond so oddly to Piaget's tasks. Science evolves through our quest for understanding. As a result of newer research that tests Piaget's theory, we now understand more about children's cognitive development, which you will learn about in the next two chapters.

2. Piaget's theory continues to be widely applied in education. Let's look at these applications next.

3-2d Classroom Implications of Cognitive Developmental Theory

There are several school-based legacies from Piaget's theory. One legacy is the notion of school readiness (see Chapter 1). Piaget believed little can be done to accelerate development because each child has a biologically based rate of transition from one stage to the next. In fact, Piaget was annoyed with teachers who wanted to speed up cognitive development. In contrast to Piaget's view, current research does not support stage-based readiness for school, nor does it support the notion that some concepts should not be taught to young children because they are not yet at the appropriate stage (APA, 2015). Some researchers believe that a strong readiness stance can deprive children of valuable experiences. Unfortunately, Piaget's theory is sometimes mistakenly used as a rationale for not teaching children valued content, like history, because the children are supposedly not ready to learn it (Hinde & Perry, 2007).

Developmentally Appropriate Practice

Another concept that was influenced by Piaget's theory is *developmentally appropriate practice* (DAP), which is an approach to educating children from birth to age 8 that emphasizes the child as an active participant in learning, not just a passive receiver of knowledge. The teacher's role is to create an environment in which the child can construct meaning from interactions with people and objects. Young children learn through active exploration and play. A DAP position statement published by the National Association for the Education of Young Children (NAEYC, 2009) makes the following points:

1. Know children well, including their significant adults, so that you can scaffold their learning. Help them attain goals that are challenging but achievable.

2. Make instruction appropriate to children's age and developmental level, individualized to them, and fitting their social and cultural background.

3. Base practices on research about how children learn and develop, not on unfounded assumptions.

4. Use practices that are likely to reduce the achievement gap.

Is DAP actually beneficial to children? Little research has directly addressed this question. One study of more than 3,000 1st-, 2nd-, and 3rd-graders found that classrooms that were more developmentally appropriate did not foster greater academic achievement in diverse, low-income students than traditional classrooms (Van Horn & Ramey, 2003). Although children may not do better academically in

DAP classrooms, children may feel less stress and anxiety, be more physically active, and be more likely to be on-task, which are important (Alford, Rollins, Padrón, & Waxman, 2015; Van Horn, Karlin, Ramey, Aldridge, & Snyder, 2005).

Constructivist Teaching

A third legacy from Piaget's theory is constructivist teaching. While constructivism is a theory of learning, not of instruction or of curriculum design, it has been used to guide the development of instruction. Piaget asserted that learners construct their own knowledge and should be encouraged to do so. He stated that "each time one prematurely teaches a child something he could have discovered for himself, that child is kept from inventing it and consequently from understanding it completely" (Piaget, 1970, p. 715). Piaget was attacking the notion that learning is the transfer of knowledge from one person to another, where the teacher pours knowledge into children's minds. Instead, Piaget asserted that when children act on their own, they create their own understanding; when they are told the facts, they may just memorize them in a superficial way. Learning is a constructive process that depends on the prior experience and knowledge of the learner.

In **constructivist instruction** teachers minimize (but do not eliminate) adult authority. Instead of simply lecturing on facts, constructivist teachers provide experiences, ask questions, provoke discourse, and encourage experimentation and deep thought. This facilitates learners' personal construction of understanding. As constructivist math educators put it, "Piaget showed that children acquire logico-mathematical knowledge not by *internalizing* rules from the outside but by *constructing* (making or creating) relationships from within, in interaction with the environment. We, therefore, give problems to children and ask them to do their own thinking to solve them in their own ways" (Kamii, Pritchett, & Nelson, 1997, p. 5, emphasis in original).

constructivist instruction an approach to instruction in which teachers provide learners with experiences that facilitate their personal construction of knowledge.

Math instruction commonly involves learning algorithms. An algorithm is a procedure that, if followed, guarantees a correct answer. For example, in three-digit addition you add the ones column first, then carry over to the tens, then carry over to the hundreds. Some constructivists oppose teaching students algorithms because students can just memorize the procedure, without really understanding the underlying concept. If they follow an algorithm for three-digit addition with carrying, they do not have to keep an understanding of place value foremost in their minds.

There are many variations on constructivist instruction that you may hear about, such as project-based instruction, apprenticeship, whole language, discovery learning, inquiry approach, transformational approach, teaching for understanding, 5E learning cycle, and minds-on instruction. Common attributes of various versions of constructivism include the following:

1. Activating prior knowledge (helping learners realize what they already know about a topic).

2. Using hands-on materials when appropriate, particularly for novices (Kontra, Lyons, Fischer, & Beilock, 2015; Zacharia, Loizou, & Papaevripidou, 2012).

3. Encouraging learners to connect new material to familiar objects and events.

4. Following the learners' lead. Following up on their questions. Talking less and listening more.

5. Asking more questions than giving answers. Asking open-ended questions that foster deep thinking rather than questions that ask for a single-word answer.

6. Presenting learners with puzzling or unexpected information that causes them to question their existing schemas, such as asking, "What causes the seasons? It is *not* the distance from the sun."

7. Allowing a long wait time (at least 5 seconds) after asking questions.

8. Requiring learners to justify their answers regardless of whether their answers are correct or not. Ask "What is your evidence?" or "Why do you think that?"

9. Not stating that answers or reasons are correct or incorrect. Instead, ask more questions, or provide experiences that allow learners to correct their own errors.

10. Making thinking public. Encourage learners to explain their thinking process and how they came up with particular answers.

11. Conduct error analysis—that is, when children respond incorrectly, ask why they responded the way they did. This will give insight into what they do and do not know. For example, a 4-year-old was being tested for school readiness. The examiner asked her which shape among a triangle, square, circle, and rectangle was different from the others. The correct answer was the circle, because it does not have any straight lines or angles. The child responded, "the triangle." Fortunately, the examiner did not simply mark her answer wrong, but asked her why. The child said, "The others would be easier to divide into fourths." That ended the test. The examiner stated the child was ready for kindergarten (if not junior high).

12. Keep learning embedded in a context that makes sense and supports the child's use of language. This is especially important for children who are young, immigrant, or have poor verbal ability, and for children from subcultures that rarely use abstract language. Schools use a lot of abstract language that does not fit these children's experience. Learning may need to be grounded in a supportive context for an extended period of time for children who do not yet give primacy to language. This is why beginning reader books have pictures (context) to support the written word.

Making thinking public is important because your learners' misconceptions will remain hidden unless you attempt to understand their thinking process. In traditional instruction, teachers ask students questions in a recitation format or in tests, which makes students' *answers* public, but not their *thinking*. For example, Ms. Wilson was teaching 3rd-graders about state government. As she questioned them, she found that some students thought that being governor bestowed ownership of the whole state. She tried to use an analogy to correct them:

> *"Who is the leader of this school?" I asked, hopefully.*
> *"Dr. Tough," they replied in unison.*
> *"And what does that mean?" I probed.*
> *"That she owns the school. That's why she gets to tell everyone what to do. . . . "*
> *I felt like I was being sucked into a . . . veritable whirlpool of misconceptions.*
> *(Ball & Wilson, 1996, pp. 160–161)*

If Ms. Wilson had not asked for student thinking, she would not have discovered their misconceptions.

It is not always easy to get learners to reveal their misconceptions. Think about a time when you have been unwilling to answer a question in class. Were you trying to avoid showing your ignorance? If you give learners responsibility for their learning, as constructivists would recommend, but ask them to demonstrate their understanding before they actually understand, you may end up with learners who avoid making their thinking public and avoid seeking help.

Outcomes of effective constructivist instruction can include the following (adapted from Boaler & Staples, 2008; Boekaerts & Minnaert, 2006):

1. Deeper conceptual understanding.

2. Greater interest and positive attitude toward the topic.

3. Reduced labeling by students that other students are smart or dumb.

4. Increased perceptions that learners are responsible for their own learning and have some control over their own learning.

Piaget's theory was too lean in three ways. (1) He was vague about how children transition from one stage to another. In Chapter 4 you will learn what current research tells us about how children come to reason better with age. (2) He was silent on the issue of individual differences in cognitive abilities. You'll learn about individual differences in Chapter 5. (3) He commented on the importance of sociocultural influences on learning, but this was not his focus. Sociocultural influences are the focus of Vygotsky, who was also a constructivist.

3-3 Vygotsky's Sociocultural Theory

One morning, a 5th-grade class is working on long division. Most of the students grasp the concept, but not all. A new worksheet is passed out. Darius begins the first problem, but quickly becomes frustrated and gives up, saying, "I just don't know how to do these!" His teacher works through the first problem with him and realizes that Darius has all the component skills—how to multiply, divide, and subtract. But he cannot remember the complex steps in sequence. His teacher prompts him about when to apply each component (e.g., subtract or carry down) but lets Darius do the calculations himself. Darius can complete problems as long as the teacher guides him in this way. After a few problems, his teacher provides guidance only when Darius clearly needs it. By the time they reach the 20th problem, Darius remembers the steps himself.

Darius began the class without the cognitive ability to do long division, but he developed the ability, although still fragile, by the end of the class period. This newfound ability was a result of interaction with his teacher. Vygotsky believed that social interaction with others is the primary force driving cognitive development.

Lev Semenovich Vygotsky (1896–1934) was born in Belorussia in eastern Europe, lived through the Bolshevik revolution of 1917, and later became a major intellectual in Russia. He died of tuberculosis at age 37. For political reasons, his works were largely banned after his death, but in the 1960s and 1970s, some of his works began to appear in English. Since that time, his views on children's cognitive development have had a substantial impact on education.

Vygotsky's theory of cognitive development has been labeled sociocultural or *cultural-historical* because of his focus on how social relationships, social interaction, historical context, and culture interact to promote cognitive development. Like Piaget, he believed that knowledge cannot be directly communicated from the teacher's head to the learner's head; such attempts result in "meaningless acquisition of words," not understanding (Gredler, 2012). While Vygotsky emphasized interaction with *adults* to foster cognitive growth, most current sociocultural approaches also emphasize interaction with peers.

sociocultural theory
a theory of how children learn, largely based on Vygotsky's writings, that emphasizes social interaction, historical context, and culture.

3-3a The Role of Social Interaction

According to Vygotsky, children grow into the intellectual life of those around them. Vygotsky wrote, "Every function in the child's cultural development appears twice: first, on the social level, and later, on the individual level; first between people (interpsychological), and then inside the child (intrapsychological)" (Vygotsky, 1978, p. 57). That is, social interaction with a more competent person in a shared activity drives cognitive growth. The more competent person and the child first *co-construct* skills and understanding out of their interaction, which then is internalized by the child.

Whether a toddler is learning to count or an adolescent is learning to solve liquid dynamics problems, the learner may initially merely observe the expert. Next, the expert does most of the work, both cognitive and physical, while guiding the learner through the task. The learner may have the appearance of doing the task, but could make no progress without the expert's aid. As the learner gains increased competence, the expert gives more and more of the responsibility to the learner, who grows in expertise. The expert's support is reduced. The expert may still need to give hints and reminders for a time, until at last the learner can perform the task independently.

Darius's teacher was gradually placing more of the responsibility for solving the long division problems on him, as he was increasingly able to work independently. This is a one-lesson example. Some skills take substantially longer to develop. Learning to read, or to solve calculus problems, requires several months or years of working with more-competent others before developing proficiency. Whether you are teaching a skill within a single class period or across several years, the same mechanism is at work; a more competent individual scaffolds learners' performance within their zone of proximal development.

3-3b Zone of Proximal Development

zone of proximal development (ZPD)
the distance between what learners can do independently and what they can do with the assistance of a competent other.

The zone of proximal development (ZPD) is the level of competence between what a learner can do alone and what he or she can do with assistance. Darius's learning of long division occurred in his zone of proximal development. Without his teacher's assistance, he experienced failure. Yet, with a little help, he was successful. You can probably think of many activities in which novices struggle alone but vastly improve their performance with a little assistance or scaffolding, such as learning to walk or to drive. With assistance, the learner's performance reveals a level of development to come. In these day-to-day interactions are the roots of higher mental functions.

FIGURE 3.9 Teaching in the Zone of Proximal Development.

Knowledge Level at Kindergarten Entry (% of Students)	Content Level Taught			
	1 Basic Counting & Shapes	2 Patterns & Measurement	3 Place Value & Currency	4 Adding & Subtracting
<1 (5%)	+	−	∅	∅
1 (28%)	−	+	∅	∅
2 (42%)	−	−	+	+
3 (18%)	−	−	+	+
4 (7%)	∅	∅	∅	∅

In a study of kindergarteners, children scored higher (+) on mathematical knowledge at the end of kindergarten if the content level on which their teachers spent the most time was just above the level they already knew when they entered kindergarten. If their teacher focused on content that was at their existing (or a lower) level, they regressed (−) during the year, unless they had unusually strong math ability to begin with. If their teacher focused on content much above their current level, it didn't seem to have an effect (ϕ). Unfortunately, the majority of teachers focused on level 1 in kindergarten, which 95% of kindergarteners already knew. *Source: Data from Engel, Claessens, and Finch (2013).*

Teaching children in their zone of proximal development, which challenges them, promotes growth; teaching them skills they already know, or skills that are easy, does little to promote growth (see Figure 3.9).

3-3c Scaffolding

Scaffolding is support for learning and problem solving that comes from outside the learner (Wood, Bruner, & Ross, 1976); it usually includes social interaction with a more competent other, but could also include textbooks or prompting from a computer. Scaffolding occurs when an expert helps a novice master new skills by breaking the skill into small units and guiding performance to a higher level. Scaffolding can occur in the emotional, physical, social, or cognitive realm. Darius's teacher is providing scaffolding when she prompts him about when to apply basic skills he already has. So is the parent who holds the back of the bicycle while a child learns to ride. So is the coach who reminds the angry athlete to count to 10 before talking to the referee. An analysis of 37 studies found that students learning science benefited from an inquiry approach that included teacher scaffolding (Furtak, Seidel, Iverson, & Briggs, 2012). An inquiry approach asks students to ask questions, collect and analyze data, and develop explanations for patterns in the data. Just turning students loose to discover for themselves does not work well. They need guidance (Fisher, Hirsh-Pasek, Newcombe, & Golinkoff, 2013; Shneidman & Woodward, 2016). From the sociocultural perspective, a teacher's primary role is to scaffold children in their zone of proximal development. You will do this largely through language.

3-3d Language and Private Speech

Language is one of the most important tools of any culture because it provides an extremely efficient means of learning. For example, in Chapter 8 you will learn that when adults talk about emotions with children, the children become better

think about **this**

If a child is easily attaining straight A's in class, is he or she operating in the zone of proximal development? Explain your answer.

scaffolding
a more competent person helps a child master new skills by breaking the tasks or subskills into small units and guiding performance to a higher level.

at perceiving others' emotions. In Chapter 4, you will also learn that when adults talk about an event, the children remember the event better. That is, perceptions, memory, and reasoning are enhanced by talk.

According to Vygotsky, language first arises as a social/cultural tool a child uses to communicate with others. Subsequently, as language is converted to private speech, it becomes a tool for controlling one's own thoughts, emotions, and behavior (Day & Smith, 2013; Vygotsky, 1978). **Private speech** refers to talking to oneself out loud, partially out loud like mouthing words or whispering, or silently in one's mind. Private speech can be relevant to a task at hand (such as a teen mouthing instructions to herself about the steps in a science class experiment) or irrelevant (such as a boy yawning and saying, "I'm tired" to himself).

While all children use private speech, research shows they are more likely to use it when: (1) engaged in goal-directed activities, like academic work rather than play; (2) their task is challenging as opposed to easy; (3) an adult is aiding, as opposed to controlling, their problem solving; and (4) they are alone rather than with someone (Winsler, Carlton, & Barry, 2000). Let's see how private speech develops.

3-3e Age Trends in Sociocultural Theory

Vygotsky's sociocultural theory is not stage oriented. One aspect of Vygotsky's theory that does show age trends is private speech. Children progress from task-irrelevant out-loud talk, to relevant and self-regulatory out-loud talk, and then to partially silent inner speech, such as whispers and quiet muttering (Winsler, Diaz, Atencio, McCarthy, & Chabay, 2000). The out-loud talk increases during the preschool period, peaks around 4 to 6 years of age, and then becomes replaced by increasingly silent self-talk. Thus, private speech becomes more internal as children progress from preschool through the school years (Patrick & Abravanel, 2000).

However, adolescents, and even adults, revert to out-loud private speech as they attempt to solve problems or do difficult tasks. For example, let's peek at 12th-grader Zaheen in biology class:

> The task is complicated, and the room is overcrowded and noisy. Zaheen is working alone, but talking out loud. He reads the directions aloud to himself: "Obtain nine test tubes and place them in the rack. Fill each tube with five milliliters of the substance indicated on the label." He then mouths the directions to himself again as he touches each object referred to. Finally, he actually enacts the instructions.

Zaheen was clearly using private speech to regulate his own thought and behavior. Similarly, you probably mouth some phrases in this text as you try to master details (and you may learn more if you do), particularly if you are studying in a noisy place. In addition to using private speech to aid their thinking, learners use private speech to regulate their emotions, such as distracting themselves in order to avoid becoming angry (Day & Smith, 2013).

3-3f Diversity in Sociocultural Theory

According to Vygotsky, *what* a child learns is determined by the culture in which the child lives. That is, children learn what is valued in their culture, such as how

---

private speech
talking to oneself out loud, partially out loud, or silently in one's mind to help regulate one's own behavior or solve problems.

Private Speech Builds Brains

In Chapter 2 you learned about brain plasticity; brains can reorganize to compensate for deficiencies in some areas. Scientists help children with cognitive problems, such as ADHD, compensate for brain deficiencies by coaching them to talk to themselves (Bryck & Fisher, 2012). Private speech helps children regulate their thoughts and attention (Fuhs & Day, 2011). In a preschool curriculum, called *Tools of the Mind*, designed to improve cognitive functioning, children are taught to control themselves by talking out loud using private speech, among other things (Diamond, Barnett, Thomas, & Munro, 2007). Some studies indicate that the approach is effective, but others do not (e.g., Blair & Raver, 2014; Jacob & Parkinson, 2015). This approach is based on Vygotsky's view that language guides behavior.

to grow crops, compute algebra, or recite poems. In addition, *how* a child learns and the scaffolding the child receives is also influenced by culture. For example in one culture children may be directly instructed or formally trained, whereas in another they may be simply woven into activities with no direct instruction (Chavajay & Rogoff, 2002). This is relevant to teachers who work with immigrant children whose parents may have had very little formal schooling. Such children may be used to a collaborative, whole-group approach to work more than children of formally schooled parents.

The tools children have available for thinking are determined by the culture. **Cultural tools** can be concrete objects such as rulers, books, or computers (Photo 3.3). They can also be tools of the mind that are symbolic, such as written language or counting systems. Children's competence depends on the cultural tools available to them. For example, multiply 578 times 264. Is it difficult? If the equation were written in a vertical format with 578 below 264, you would probably have an easier time as you first multiply 8 times 4, then 8 times 6, and so forth. You would be benefiting from a cultural tool, an algorithm for multiplication, that was developed by others and made available to you through the culture of schooling.

Writing is a key cultural tool. It allows individuals to record and remember with more accuracy and less effort than was possible before its invention. Genres or types of writing are also cultural tools. For example, a story is a narrative that usually follows chronological order and often uses suspense, while a science report focuses

Richard Hutchings/PhotoEdit

PHOTO 3.3 How many cultural tools can you spot in this photo? Support your label of *cultural tool* for each.

cultural tools
concrete objects and symbolic tools that allow members of a culture to think, build, record, problem solve, and communicate.

on analysis of processes and seldom has elements of suspense. Young children lack these cultural tools of genre writing and often produce a story when asked to write a science report (Kamberelis & Bovino, 1999). They must be taught how to write a story versus a science report.

Written language is a school-learned cultural tool that transfers widely across many different contexts because it is seen in many contexts, not just school. Writing is used in stores, restaurants, street signs, and magazines. However, learners tend to see most cultural tools embedded in a single place and tend not to transfer those tools elsewhere. For example, our young daughter was baking cookies and asked, "Do two quarters make a half? I know they do in math class, but do they in cooking?" In another example, a high school chemistry teacher found that her students only used the study strategies that she taught when she was present; they would not even use them with the student teacher in the same classroom (Moje, 1996). If you want your learners to transfer the use of a cultural tool from one context to another, you will need to help them see how the tool is used in other settings.

A newer cultural tool is the smartphone, which has many uses. For example, GPS functions can improve your ability to find places, but also undermine your spatial skills if you just follow the instructions without orienting in space. There are apps for photography, audio and video production, finding information, creating concept maps, and many more functions. They change the ways in which we interact with each other and the world, and the sorts of problems that we can solve on the run.

In summary, culture influences what children learn, how they are taught, what tools they acquire, and where those tools are applied. One lesson for you is to be careful not to jump to conclusions about a learner's capability based on a single cultural context. Learners may appear unskilled in some contexts, but be quite skilled in others.

3-3g Classroom Implications of Sociocultural Theory

There are at least four general implications of Vygotsky's perspective on cognitive development for your role as a teacher:

1. Use language as a tool to help learners organize their thoughts and to consolidate memories. Private speech should be tolerated and encouraged, particularly for young children or during difficult problem solving in older students.

2. Teach learners in their zone of proximal development, using appropriate scaffolding. It is not easy to determine each learner's ZPD, and it is a moving target, always changing. It takes attention and insight on the part of the teacher to continually adjust to each learner's abilities.

3. Help learners actively observe and participate in activities with adults and peers through **apprenticeship** and **guided participation**. In an apprenticeship, a novice develops competence through interaction with a more expert person who guides or scaffolds participation in the developing activity. Children are apprentices in your classroom. The apprenticeship is directed by you, the teacher, as you plan specific learning experiences and help the learners understand the experiences.

4. Work together as a *community of learners* in which everyone contributes to the learning process. The teacher is not the only person who has knowledge, but

apprenticeship
a learner actively observes and participates with an expert in order to improve competence.

guided participation
a novice learns through an expert's scaffolding.

rather expertise is distributed among the members of the group. A community of learners experiences *distributed cognition* in which thinking and knowledge exist not only in the minds of individuals, but also in their social interaction and the artifacts that they use and create, like books and computers (Salomon, 1993). Learners can become experts in certain areas and know more than even the teacher in those areas; other learners and the teacher may look to them for help.

How might attachment to teachers and bonding to school affect cognitive development from a sociocultural perspective?

These broad implications for classrooms stem from sociocultural theory. In addition, you may want to apply a specific style of teaching that stems from this theory—social constructivism.

Social Constructivism

Social constructivism shares with Piagetian constructivism the assertion that knowledge is not poured into children's brains, but rather knowledge must be constructed. It uses the term *social* because it emphasizes social interaction as the source of knowledge construction. Social constructivist instruction includes scaffolding, classroom discussion, and reciprocal teaching.

social constructivism
the view that knowledge is not poured into learners' brains, but that knowledge is constructed through social interaction.

Scaffolding in the classroom

Recall that scaffolding involves a more competent individual (like a teacher) helping novices master new skills. You've already seen how Darius's teachers scaffolded his math skills. Scaffolding is important at other ages as well. Imagine that you want to teach preschoolers how to play number-oriented board games, like *Chutes and Ladders*™. (In Chapter 4, you will learn that this fosters children's understanding of numbers.) Initially you might model how to count and move the pieces, pointing to each square in turn. After several episodes of scaffolded play, children may be able to play with each other with no support from you.

Imagine you want to teach high school students how to write a research paper. You could tell the students what to do, and then turn them loose to apply what they've learned. Such a technique tends to lead to poor writing and weak papers from novice writers. A better technique is to use scaffolding to help the students construct, through interaction with others, a shared understanding of high-quality writing. One scaffolding technique is to break the tasks into small units. Thus, you might require students to choose a topic, then to read and write notes about references, then to write a research question or thesis statement for the paper, then to outline the major sections of the paper, and so forth. At each stage of the paper, you review the students' work and provide feedback. Social constructivism also involves interaction among peers, so you would have students provide feedback on each others' draft manuscripts. Students at all ages, from preschool to graduate school, can benefit from scaffolding.

Scaffolding can be indirect or direct. One study found that when learners revealed their lack of understanding and asked for help, successful teachers carefully scaffolded them through a solution process, sometimes by having peer learners help with the instruction (Turner et al., 2002). Teachers did not tell learners how to do the problem, but asked questions and gave hints until the learners understood what was being taught. However, the following is an example of a music teacher taking a more directive style while scaffolding 10-year-old Lauren in piano lessons:

> *Lauren is learning a complicated piano sonata that has a difficult rhythm and many chords, including some that require her to stretch her small hand across six keys. Looking at the piece, Lauren felt overwhelmed, and she quickly became frustrated trying to read the notes. She pounded the piano and her posture collapsed, communicating "I give up!" The teacher pointed her to a single measure with four chords in the left hand. The teacher modeled the first chord and had Lauren play just that chord. The teacher repeated this with each chord. Then she had Lauren play the four chords in succession, modeling when necessary. After Lauren mastered these four chords, the teacher asked Lauren to play them with her eyes closed several times. When Lauren was finished, the teacher enthusiastically congratulated Lauren and explained to her that anything is easy if you break it down into little steps. Lauren grinned with pride.*

In this example, the teacher had Lauren focus on only one hand, and one measure of music, at a time. The scaffolding took less than five minutes, yet it changed Lauren's whole perspective of her ability to master the sonata.

Classroom discussion

Through classroom discussion, learners can co-construct understanding in their zones of proximal development and achieve greater skill. When learners explain their thinking aloud, they may notice their errors and correct them. Deep discussion requires that learners agree, disagree, and critique each other's reasoning—hence, the social dimension of social constructivism. In constructivist classrooms, there should be a great deal of learner-to-learner commentary, rather than just teacher-to-learner commentary. Students report that they are more interested during such discussions and put out more effort (Wu, Anderson, Nguyen-Jahiel, & Miller, 2013).

In a constructivist 2nd-grade classroom, the teacher poses an arithmetic question: 19 + 13. One child gives her answer—26—and the classroom erupts into a loud cacophony of *"Agree!"* and *"Disagree!"* This sort of discussion is usually extolled as a virtue of social constructivist instruction. But how do students feel about it? Some like it, but some do not. According to a 5th-grader: "[I]t can get sort of embarrassing at times, because like … you say something and everybody will raise their hand and want to say something different or they all disagree with you. And it makes you sort of feel like you want to crawl into a hole and die" (Lampert, Rittenhouse, & Crumbaugh, 1996, p. 742).

Learners will not engage in the kind of classroom discussion that makes social constructivist instruction work if they feel vulnerable to ridicule, teasing, or appearing stupid. Teachers must work hard to provide a supportive environment and keep the discourse civil without squelching it. This means maintaining a neutral stance, using a warm tone, and providing supportive comments. It also means training the learners to be able to discuss respectfully.

In constructivist settings, children are given the opportunity to work together so that they will be confronted with different views. Learners of differing levels of ability are placed together so the more advanced students will clarify their knowledge by having to explain to others, and the less advanced will be challenged to understand thinking a bit above their own. However, you cannot assume that just because learners are discussing subject matter that they are learning; even if they are on-task, their conversations may not lead to understanding. In Chapter 11, you will learn how to implement group work in an effective way.

Reciprocal teaching

One of the best-known applications of the principles of Vygotsky's social constructivism is **reciprocal teaching**, which research suggests is effective (Palincsar & Brown, 1984; Spörer, Brunstein, & Kieschke, 2009). Reciprocal teaching puts the student in the teacher role (Photo 3.4). It is applied most often to reading comprehension. Students read a text in a group of two to six students with the teacher's expert scaffolding. The teacher introduces the reading by asking students to state what they already know about the topic and to predict what the passage is about based on the title. Then a student is assigned to be the student-teacher for a passage. After the group reads the passage, the student-teacher asks a *question* about the main point, *summarizes* the passage, seeks to *clarify* anything unclear, and then makes a *prediction* about what might come next. The teacher scaffolds the student-teacher's responses and provides feedback. Eventually the teacher can leave the reading groups alone to scaffold each other.

Michael Newman/PhotoEdit

PHOTO 3.4 Students engaged in reciprocal teaching.

reciprocal teaching
students take turns in the teacher role. A student-teacher summarizes, asks questions, clarifies, and predicts the content of a passage of text in a small group of other students.

The following is an example of reciprocal teaching by a 7th-grade student, Charles (from Palincsar & Brown, 1984, pp. 138–139).

Day 1.

TEXT: *The water moccasin, somewhat longer than the copperhead, is found in the southeastern states. It lives in swampy regions. It belongs, as do also the copperhead and the rattlesnakes, to a group of poisonous snakes called pit vipers. They have pits between their eyes and their nostrils which, because they are sensitive to heat, help the snakes tell when they are near a warm-blooded animal…*

Charles: *What is found in the southeastern snakes—also the copperhead, rattlesnakes, vipers—they have … I'm not doing this right.*

Teacher: *All right. Do you want to know about the pit vipers? What would be a good question about the pit vipers that starts with the word "why"?*

Charles: *(No response)*

Teacher: *How about, "Why are the snakes called pit vipers?"*

Charles: *Why do they want to know that they are called pit vipers?*

Teacher: *Try it again.*

Charles: *Why do they, pit vipers in a pit?*

Teacher: *How about, "Why do they call the snakes pit vipers?"*

Charles: *Why do they call the snakes pit vipers?*

Teacher: *There you go! Good for you.*

Reciprocal teaching is beneficial to reading comprehension because students, like Charles, are often unaware that they do not comprehend a reading passage. Even among our hundreds of university students, only a few have ever come to class asking for clarification of an obscure passage, although all textbooks (except this one) contain obscure passages.

You can apply reciprocal teaching to content areas besides reading. For example, students studying history can take on the student–teacher role to *summarize*, *question*, *clarify*, and *predict* as they read historical texts.

A Note of Caution about Constructivist Instruction

Both Piaget and Vygotsky present a theory of constructivist *learning*. This does not necessarily translate to a case for constructivist *instruction* as it is typically construed. Many teachers assume constructivist instruction must involve hands-on activities, group discussion, interactive games, and other behaviorally active forms of instruction. They view lectures, books, worksheets, and online presentations as too passive. They also assume constructivist instruction must be based on discovery learning, in which students are left to figure out (discover) things on their own. Neither is necessarily true. A constructivist teacher helps learners make sense of incoming information, organize it coherently, and integrate it with previous knowledge. Passive methods (such as lecture) can foster these processes, and active methods (such as hands-on experiments) can fail to foster these processes. It is *cognitive* activity rather than *behavioral* activity that matters. Children learn by thinking.

Some teachers are concerned about implementing a constructivist curriculum because they view it as incompatible with the proficiency exams and college entrance exams for which they need to prepare students. However, research shows that curricula that are based on constructivist methods do provide students with the skills to do well on standardized tests (McCaffrey et al., 2001; National Mathematics Advisory Panel, 2008). Any sort of activity that makes learning more cognitively active for the student, from group discussions to personal response systems (clickers, for example), tends to raise achievement (Freeman et al., 2014).

3-4 Comparing Theories of Learning and Cognition

Although John Watson (a behaviorist), Jean Piaget, and Lev Vygotsky were contemporaries, each advocated a different theory of how children learn and develop cognitively. Some aspects of their theories are simply unrelated because they address different issues. For example, both behaviorism and sociocultural theory say little about age trends in cognitive development. Instead, these theories focus on processes of learning such as reinforcement and scaffolding. In sharp contrast, Piaget had little to say about processes of learning—or *how* children move from stage to stage—yet he focused extensively on age trends in cognitive development.

Some aspects of the three theories are similar, and others directly contradict one another. One example of similarity is that both Piaget's and Vygotsky's theories are considered constructivist because they view children as active participants in constructing or co-constructing their own knowledge. Behaviorists have a more passive view of the child's mental role. Piaget's constructivism is sometimes called *cognitive constructivism* or *individual constructivism* to distinguish it from Vygotsky's *social constructivism*. However, many educators meld Piaget's cognitive constructivism with Vygotsky's social constructivism, so while researchers make distinctions among the various brands of constructivism, many educators do not.

Piaget's cognitive-developmental theory differs from the other two theories in two ways. First, both behaviorists and socioculturalists stress direct teaching by adults, but Piagetians stress self-directed learning through exploration. Second, Piagetians give greater emphasis to maturation (i.e., nature). In other words, Piaget believed mental maturation is a *prerequisite* for learning, not a result of learning. By contrast, Vygotsky believed learning and education *cause* mental maturation. Vygotsky believed that instruction that is oriented toward a level of cognitive development (or stage) that has already been reached is ineffective. *Good instruction pushes development* (Vygotsky, 1978). As you read in Chapter 1 regarding school readiness, research supports Vygotsky's view on this issue.

Behaviorism is one of the most commonly applied theories in classrooms. All classrooms use reinforcement and punishment, whether intentional or not. Behaviorism is powerful in promoting learning and altering behavior. However, children can learn without being directly reinforced. They can learn from watching other children being reinforced, as in the opening vignette when Naomi was rewarded for getting out a book to read during free time and several other children imitated her. Children learn rapidly from observing others, even as young as 6 months of age. Recognition of this has led to a revision of behaviorism, now called social cognitive theory. This theory is discussed in Box 3.2 and will be further discussed in Chapter 13.

Social cognitive theory moves behaviorism closer toward Piaget in that children are now viewed as actively influencing their own development through mental processes—they attend to, interpret, and select which behaviors to imitate depending on attributes of the models and their own feelings of confidence. The revised theory is also more similar to Vygotsky in that the social nature of learning is emphasized. Although all three theories may have moved closer toward one another as new research provides insight into how children develop, there currently is no single grand theory that adequately unifies them.

Although major theories differ in their view of what drives development, each is "true" in some ways and incomplete by itself. Reinforcement does lead to learning, as behaviorists claim. Children are innately motivated to explore the world and they do construct their own knowledge, as Piaget claimed. Children do learn through social interaction and dialogue with others, as socioculturalists claim.

Nevertheless, constructivism and behaviorism can lead to two very different approaches to instruction—direct instruction and discovery learning. Which is

BOX 3.2 **theories & theorists**

Social Cognitive Theory

In the opening vignette, Naomi's teacher wanted the children to read biographies in their free time, so she announced to the whole class how happy she was to see Naomi reading and gave Naomi a reward. The next day several other children read biographies during free time. This event highlights two key points: (1) Children can learn from watching others be reinforced without being directly reinforced themselves. (2) Children can learn without immediate behavior change; the learning might not be apparent until a day later, or years later. For example, when Elena's mother was 6, she watched her grandmother make tamales in Mexico, but was not allowed to help. At age 15 she made tamales herself. She had learned through observation despite nine years of no behavior change. These points may seem obvious to you, but they present a challenge for behaviorism.

Recall that behaviorists define learning as a change in behavior. Along with others, Albert Bandura questioned this.

Albert Bandura was born in 1925 in tiny Mundare, Alberta, Canada. He became a psychologist when behaviorism was dominant. Bandura began to study how children learn through observation. Perhaps his most famous studies were the Bobo-doll experiments. Bobo was an inflatable 4.5 foot high clown that was weighted in the bottom and bounced back up if you punched it down. See Figure 3.10. Children watched an adult act aggressively toward the Bobo doll (Bandura, 1965). The adult yelled, punched, kicked, and hit it with a mallet. The children were then invited to play alone with the Bobo doll. Children who had observed the aggressive adult were more aggressive toward the Bobo doll than children in a control

FIGURE 3.10 **Bandura's Bobo-Doll Experiments.**

Albert Bandura/Dept. of Psychology, Stanford University

Children watched a film of an adult being aggressive. They later imitated the same aggressive behaviors during free-play.

Social Cognitive Theory (continued)

group. In fact, they were aggressive in the very same ways as the adult. The children had clearly learned to be aggressive from a model.

Bandura's Bobo-doll experiments made him famous. In fact, he told of checking into a hotel where the desk clerk asked: "Aren't you the psychologist who did the Bobo-doll experiment?" Bandura replied, "I'm afraid that's going to be my legacy." The clerk replied, "That deserves an upgrade!" (Bandura, 2007). So there are some perks to being a psychologist.

Bandura developed a theory about how people learn from observation. He initially called it *social learning theory* because it added a social dimension to Skinner-style learning theory. Social learning theory claimed that in addition to direct reinforcement, behavior can also be changed when the child observes someone else being reinforced, termed *vicarious reinforcement*. In Chapter 8 you will learn that neuroscience shows that from birth, children's brains are designed for imitating others.

As Bandura's research developed, his theory became more *cognitive* as well as more *social*. His research showed that children's beliefs and expectations strongly influence their behavior. Thus, Bandura, like Piaget, came to view children as actively influencing their own development through mental processes—they attend to, interpret, and select which behaviors to imitate. Today Bandura's theory is called social cognitive theory.

A key mental process in social cognitive theory is self-efficacy. **Self-efficacy** refers to your belief that you can accomplish some behavior. It is a judgment about your competence. Self-efficacy powerfully influences behavior in both the social and academic domains. A boy who believes aggression works, and who has high self-efficacy for aggression (i.e., believes he is good at it), will tend to behave more aggressively. A boy who has self-efficacy for mathematics (i.e., believes he is good at it) will tend to work harder at difficult math problems, and earn higher grades.

Self-efficacy and vicarious reinforcement are linked. Learners come to feel greater self-efficacy if they watch a model they feel is *similar to themselves* being reinforced for success. For example, high school students learn physics from watching a peer successfully complete a problem better than if they just watch an expert work an example during a tutoring session (Craig, Chi, & VanLehn, 2009). This means that self-efficacy is not just a reflection of one's previous success and failure. Thus, one way that you can improve learners' self-efficacy in your classroom is to provide a successful model who is similar to themselves. High self-efficacy is linked with higher goals, preference for challenge, and improved performance (Bandura, 2012). In Chapter 13 we will discuss how you can enhance learners' self-efficacy in order to improve their motivation in your classroom.

most effective according to research? If only one approach is used and test scores are the outcome measure, there is some evidence that direct instruction tends to be more effective, particularly for weak learners and for basic skills (Kirschner, Sweller, & Clark, 2006), but the topic is controversial. A combined approach that draws on powerful elements of constructivism, such as cooperative learning and having learners explain their thinking out loud, may be ideal. We will compare these approaches in more detail for math instruction in Chapter 4 and literacy instruction in Chapter 12, so that you can judge how to apply each in your classroom in appropriate situations.

self-efficacy
belief that you have the capability to perform a specific task.

My Teaching

Behaviorism, cognitive developmental theory, and sociocultural theory each include important implications for the classroom. To determine if you are promoting learning according to these three theories, periodically ask yourself:

1. Am I aware of the full array of reinforcers operating on my learners? Are the reinforcers facilitating learning? Do I mistakenly reinforce inappropriate behaviors?

2. Do I avoid using punishment? If I do use punishment, does it actually stop the misbehavior? (If it does not, it may actually be reinforcing.)

3. Do I use direct instruction? Would my learners benefit?

4. Do I model how to think about problems? Am I aware of which models my learners imitate?

5. Do I help learners construct their own understanding by guiding experiences, encouraging experiments, asking questions, and provoking discourse? Do I wait at least five seconds after asking a question in order to promote thinking? Do I ask open-ended questions? Could I talk less and listen more?

6. Do I conduct error analysis? When learners make mistakes, do I try to understand why rather than just correcting them?

7. Do I keep learning embedded in a context that makes sense? Do I use context to support learning so that learners do not have to rely on language alone? (This is particularly important for young children, for English language learners, and for older youth with poor language skills.)

8. Do I connect new material to familiar objects and events? Do I use hands-on materials when appropriate, particularly for novices?

9. Do I make thinking (not just answers) public? Do I encourage learners to justify their answers regardless of whether they are correct?

10. Do I allow learners to choose some of their learning activities when possible? Do I follow the learners' lead? Do I follow up on their questions?

11. Do I know what each learner's zone of proximal development is for a particular task? Am I helping each operate in his or her zone of proximal development?

12. Do I encourage private speech when learners are solving difficult problems?

13. Do I scaffold classroom tasks by helping learners master subskills so that each learner can achieve success?

14. Am I taking advantage of opportunities to use reciprocal teaching in my classroom?

Professional Resource Download

Summary of Age Trends in Learning and Cognition

	Behaviorism	**Piaget's View**	**Vygotsky's View of Private Speech**
Infancy & Toddlerhood (Birth–2 Years)	• Newborn infants can be conditioned. Behaviorists have little to say about age trends in cognitive development. • Both classical and operant conditioning principles apply to this age, as well as other ages.	• The sensorimotor stage is roughly birth–24 months. In this stage thoughts and actions are not distinguishable. Mental schemes are based on sensory or motor input. • At 4–8 months children develop object permanence. • Between 8–12 months they make the A-not-B error in searching, but may have success by 12 months. • Children develop symbolic thought. They begin pretend play using symbols. • At the end of this stage, they are capable of deferred imitation.	• The principles of Vygotsky's theory, such as scaffolding in the ZPD, apply to all age groups. However, private speech changes with age. • During infancy, adult speech supports regulation of children's behavior. • Toddlers begin to use private speech to regulate their own behavior.
Early Childhood (3–5 Years)	• Language acquisition provides additional avenues for conditioning.	• The preoperational stage corresponds to roughly 2–7 years of age. In this stage children are capable of symbolic thought, but not of logic or mental manipulations. • They do not understand cause-and-effect or hierarchical classification. • They engage in animism, egocentrism, and centration. • They cannot reverse operations.	• Out-loud private speech peaks at about 4–6 years.
Middle Childhood (6–12 Years)	• Increases in self-control allow reinforcement to be more effective even after delay in older children.	• The concrete operational stage corresponds to roughly 7–11 years of age. Children are able to conserve and have mastered some of the limitations of preoperational thought. • They reason about objects in everyday life, but are still not skilled at abstract thinking.	• Private speech continues to become more internal and silent, and more task-relevant.
Adolescence (13–19 Years)	• Adolescents have access to their own sources of reinforcement (e.g., food and money), which limits adults' control over their behavior.	• The formal operational stage corresponds to roughly 12 years of age through adulthood. Some adolescents, but not all, are now capable of formal abstract logic. They can follow clear logic, and they reason in a hypothetical-deductive manner even if the premises are not true. • They can systematically generate possible solutions to problems. • They can isolate variables to test hypotheses.	• Private speech is typically "underground" or silent. However, adolescents and adults will talk out loud to themselves if the task is very difficult.

⌄⌄ Professional Resource Download

Chapter Summary

3-1 Behaviorism

- Behaviorism is the science of observable behavior. Control of behavior is located in the environment. For behaviorists, learning (also called conditioning) is synonymous with behavior change.

- Classical conditioning involves involuntary behavior. An unconditioned stimulus that evokes an unconditioned (involuntary) response is paired with a neutral stimulus until the neutral stimulus evokes the same response. This conditioning can be extinguished by ceasing to pair the unconditioned and conditioned stimuli.

- Operant conditioning involves voluntary behavior. Reinforcement increases the probability of a behavior occurring, and punishment decreases its probability. Negative reinforcement refers to increasing the probability of a behavior by removing an aversive stimulus.

- Shaping is used to train behavior that does not spontaneously occur, by reinforcing behaviors that come closer and closer to the target behavior.

- Continuous reinforcement is best for training new behavior. Intermittent reinforcement is best for maintaining existing behavior. Extinction results when reinforcement ceases.

- Teaching is viewed as the arrangement of reinforcers. One application of operant conditioning is direct instruction. It is effective for teaching basic skills and concepts, particularly with high-risk students.

- B. F. Skinner is one of the most famous behaviorists. He wanted to use science to make society better by carefully controlling behavior.

3-2 Piaget's Theory of Cognitive Development

- A key point in Piaget's theory is that children actively construct knowledge rather than passively copying what they perceive. Children construct knowledge as they assimilate new information into existing mental structures or accommodate those mental structures to fit new information. These processes result in cognitive balance or equilibrium.

- Piaget believed children progress in logical reasoning ability through qualitatively distinct, universal stages that follow an invariant sequence. Piaget believed that maturation combined with experience drives cognitive development.

- Research suggests Piaget underestimated the cognitive abilities of young children and overestimated those of adolescents and adults. Young children may fail to conserve on standard Piagetian tasks for reasons other than inability to think logically, such as inability to give primacy to language.

- Formal schooling, which varies by culture, is associated with differences in formal operational thinking.
- Constructivist instruction is an outgrowth of Piaget's theory. Constructivist instruction can include hands-on experiences, provoking discourse, asking questions, following learners' lead, guiding discovery learning, and making thinking public.

3-3 Vygotsky's Sociocultural Theory

- Vygotsky emphasized social and cultural influences on cognitive development. Cognitive growth is a function of social interaction with others. The learner's abilities are first *inter*personal and then become *intra*personal. Culture determines what learners learn, how it is taught, and what tools are available for learning.
- Private speech is typically out loud in younger children and then becomes internal and silent, but even teens will use audible self-talk to solve difficult problems.
- A more competent person scaffolds the learners' performance by guiding performance to a higher level. The more competent person provides less and less support as the learner becomes more expert.
- The zone of proximal development (ZPD) is the difference between what a learner can achieve alone and what the learner can achieve with the help of a more competent person. Vygotsky believed that instruction in the ZPD drives cognitive development.
- Instruction may emphasize reciprocal teaching and scaffolding in the zone of proximal development. Implementation of Vygotsky's views in the classroom are referred to as social constructivism, and Piaget's are referred to as cognitive constructivism. There is overlap between these two approaches.

3-4 Comparing Theories of Learning and Cognition

- Social cognitive theory includes elements of behaviorism. It also emphasizes the roles of vicarious reinforcement (or learning through observation) and self-efficacy beliefs in learning.
- Piaget's and Vygotsky's theories are considered constructivist, while direct instruction is not.
- Both behaviorists and socioculturalists stress direct teaching by adults; Piagetians stress children's self-directed learning through exploration.

chapter 4

Cengage Learning

Information Processing, Memory, and Problem Solving

Have you met people who seem exceptionally good at remembering information or solving problems? You may have wondered whether you can help your students develop these abilities to their fullest potential. **After you read this chapter, you will be able to:**

4-1 Discuss how information processing develops with age and varies across individuals, and apply these concepts to strengthen the information-processing abilities of your students, including learners with ADHD.

4-2 Identify age trends in memory, and teach your students effective memory strategies.

4-3 Analyze whether your students have age-appropriate reasoning abilities, and formulate a plan to promote reasoning abilities among your students, using evidence to support your plan.

4-4 Apply the major theories of learning and cognition to teaching, using the example of mathematics.

131

4-1 Information Processing

In a high school class, students are told they will silently read a passage from
The Crucible, after which they will write answers to five questions about themes,
symbols, and the moral behavior of each character. Their teacher briefly quizzes
them to make sure they understand the instructions; then they begin reading. Nick
is a struggling reader. The teacher gives him occasional help on difficult words.
After he finishes laboring through the passage, he asks, "What were we supposed
to write again?"

Why did Nick forget the instructions? One possibility is limited working memory. Nick had to remember what he was supposed to write about while also doing a difficult task—decoding words and comprehending text—which overloaded Nick's working memory. Working memory is a key component of the **information-processing model**.

This model describes how learners receive, reason with, and remember information. It clarifies the process by which children grow cognitively, which is not clear in the three classic theories—behaviorism, cognitive development, and sociocultural theory—you read about in Chapter 3. For example, behaviorism ignores thinking. Piaget is vague about how a child moves from one cognitive stage to the next. Vygotsky's sociocultural theory does not specify how growth occurs in the zone of proximal development. In contrast, the information-processing model outlines how learners become better at processing information.

information-processing model
a model of cognition that focuses on how children acquire, store, and use knowledge.

4-1a Components of the Information-Processing Model

There are different versions of the information-processing model. We will discuss the common three-layer model (Öztekin, Davachi, & McElree, 2010). Its key components are illustrated in Figure 4.1 and described next.[1]

Sensory Register

sensory register
the component of the information-processing model where initial stimuli from the environment are briefly held.

When you see, hear, feel, taste, and smell, information enters your **sensory register**. The sensory register takes in a great deal of information, but stores it for a very short period of time (perhaps a few seconds). As you are reading this text, your sensory register is taking in patterns of colors on the page, the feel of your clothes, food you may be chewing, your thoughts, noises in the room, and so forth. The fact that you cannot remember much of this information shows how briefly it is stored.

Long-Term Memory

long-term memory
the relatively permanent storage of information. Duration is long and capacity is very large, perhaps unlimited.

Long-term memory refers to the relatively permanent storage of information, also known as knowledge. Information might become stored in long-term memory—but much is lost. Later we will discuss strategies for increasing the odds that you will remember information over the long term. Scientists do not know whether long-term memory has limits. It may not be possible to have too much knowledge, although you may have felt cognitive overload in some classes.

---

[1] There is not yet consensus among scientists about the one best model, so we provide a common, simplified version that will help you understand classroom learning.

FIGURE 4.1 Three-Layer Model of Information Processing.

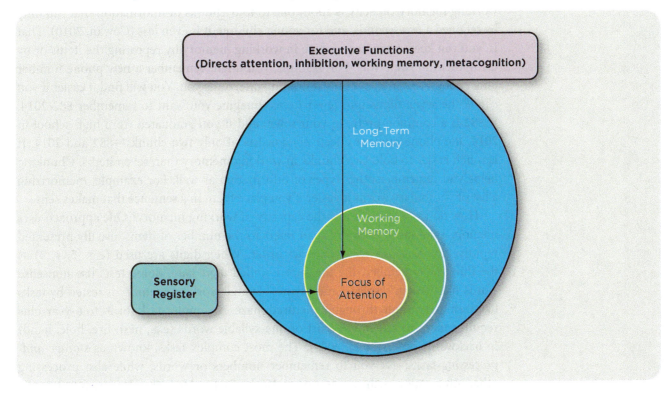

Your working memory (short-term storage and on-line processing) is active right now as you process this figure. Your executive functions are controlling your attention, inhibition of irrelevant information, and metacognition.

Executive Functions

The term **executive functions** refers to the brain's control of its own information processing. The brain must control attention and focus on a task, hold information during reasoning, retrieve information from long-term storage, monitor sequences of behavior, detect errors and make corrections, and shift ongoing functions to more urgent functions. Executive functions are essential for self-control and for high-level cognition, that is, any activity that requires effortful, complex thought. Let's take a look at a few important executive functions.

executive functions
the brain's control of its own information processing.

Working memory

Information in the sensory register that is given attention may enter **working memory**. Working memory contains small amounts of information that you are processing at a given moment. This information comes through your senses from what you are experiencing at that moment (e.g., watching a video about the Battle of the Bulge) or can be retrieved from your long-term memory (e.g., remembering what you know about the Battle of the Bulge), or information could come from both. Working memory allows you to maintain some information during the processing of other information. For example, you might compare what you are watching with what you know about the Battle of the Bulge. Thus, *working memory is where thinking occurs.*

working memory
the component of the information processing model where items of information are temporarily held for encoding or processing.

The capacity of working memory is relatively small and of short duration. Adult working memory capacity is about one to four chunks of information that can only be retained a few seconds, and for young children it is even less (Cowan, 2010). That is, you can keep a few items active in working memory by repeating the items or by using them in some way. For example, you might remember a new phone number long enough to dial it, but only if nothing interrupts you. You will find it easier if you *chunk* the seven digits into fewer items. Imagine you want to remember 882-2014. If 882 is a common prefix in your town, and if you graduated from high school in 2014, the phone number effectively consists of only two chunks—882 and 2014. It is much easier to hold two chunks in working memory than seven items. Chunking helps you remember other types of information as well. For example, memorizing a list of vocabulary words is easier if you place them in a sentence that makes sense.

How do researchers know the capacity of working memory? One approach uses memory-span tasks. Memory span refers to the number of items, usually presented rapidly, that you can recall in exact order. When digits are used (e.g., 5, 1, 3) as the thing to remember, the measure is called *digit span*. Some tests use nonsense words like "woog," "spleg," and "symo." Spatial working memory is tested by tasks like recalling a route through a pictured maze. A complex task for 3- to 6-year-olds requires them to remember a list of one-syllable words (e.g., nest, fire, hole, hand) in backwards order (Noël, 2009). The most complex tasks, known as *storage-and-processing* tasks, ask you to remember numbers or words, while also processing other information such as counting to 100 by 5s. For Nick, the classroom task in the opening vignette is equivalent to a storage-and-processing task.

Cognitive flexibility

cognitive flexibility
the ability to switch from one cognitive activity or perspective to another (also called attention shifting)

Cognitive flexibility (also called attention shifting) is the ability to change how you think about something, switch perspectives, and adjust to changing demands. One way scientists measure this is the Dimensional Change Card Sorting task. Children are given cards that can be sorted by either color, object, or number (e.g., 3 red trucks on one card, 2 blue trucks on another). They are asked to sort by one dimension, and then to switch and sort by another dimension. They are scored on accuracy and speed. That task can be made more difficult by increasing the frequency of switching. Cognitive flexibility supports creativity and problem solving.

Inhibitory control

inhibitory control
the ability to inhibit processing irrelevant information or to suppress a response.

selective attention
attending to task-relevant input while suppressing irrelevant input.

Inhibitory control is the ability to keep from processing irrelevant information, or to suppress a response. One way scientists measure this ability is by showing children cards that are either black with a moon and stars, or white with a yellow sun. Children must say *night* when shown a sun card and *day* when shown a moon card.

Inhibitory control includes **selective attention**, which helps you resist distractions that grab your attention. You attend to information for at least three reasons (Downing, 2000; Raymond, Fenskey, & Tavassoli, 2003): (1) it is new, (2) it is relevant to something you are actively processing, and (3) it has emotional importance. For example, if you gasp, you will immediately grab the attention of the class.

Most of the information you take in through your sensory register is forgotten because you do not pay attention to it. Attention acts as a gatekeeper of memory. Only information that receives some attention is remembered (Barrouillet & Camos, 2012).

Your executive functions control the shifting of attention from one task to another. In the opening vignette, Nick could not remember the worksheet instructions because he did not occasionally shift from the reading task to reactivate his fading memory of the instructions.

Metacognition

Sometimes you *think about your thinking*, which is called metacognition. Metacognition refers to your knowledge of your own learning processes and how to regulate them. It takes metacognition to choose a strategy to apply to a problem. It takes metacognition to answer the question, "What do you know and how do you know it?" When you finish reading a page of this textbook and suddenly realize that you have not processed a single word, that is metacognition at work. Planning and using effective learning strategies is part of metacognition.

Two types of metacognition are important for learning. *Metacomprehension* refers to judging when you have understood something. Even college students have difficulty with this. You can improve metacomprehension by practicing summarizing what you have read (Dunlosky & Lipko, 2007). *Metamemory* refers to what you know about your own memory and how to store or retrieve information from it. Children have metamemory when they know that learning precise historical facts takes more effort than learning the gist of history or that stories are easier to remember than lists. Children with better metamemory are better at recall and use better memory strategies (Pierce & Lange, 2000).

You may have noticed overlap between these executive functions. Scientists currently disagree about how distinct these different executive functions are, but agree that they are strongly intertwined (Diamond, 2013; Jacob & Parkinson, 2015). For example, working memory capacity is linked to attention control. Preschoolers who can hold more in working memory are particularly good at controlling their attention and are likely to become teenagers who are fast and accurate at inhibitory control tests (Eigsti et al., 2006). As you read this text, if you have larger working memory, you will more quickly disengage from distractions and get your attention back on task (Fukuda & Vogel, 2011).

4-1b Age Trends in Information Processing

Infants are born with rudimentary information-processing abilities that grow over time. Some of these abilities reach adult levels by 6th grade, others in adolescence, and still others continue to improve in adulthood.

Infancy and Toddlerhood (Birth to 2 Years)

Processing speed is relatively slow in young children because myelination, knowledge, and language are limited. Have you noticed that there is a brief delay between a painful event (e.g., pinching a finger) and infants' crying? Infants process such information more slowly than you because of incomplete myelination. Language affects processing speed because it organizes the storage and retrieval of information. Processing speed, in turn, limits working memory. As each of these factors improves, *working memory* capacity increases.

metacognition
cognition that reflects on, monitors, or regulates other cognition.

retrieval
finding items in long-term memory and placing them into working memory.

Infants have selective attention. How do we know? Imagine an infant is sitting on your lap in front of a monitor with an attractive animation in the center. Occasionally a white square appears at the side of the screen. Infants' ability to resist the distraction and focus attention on the animation assesses their selective attention and inhibitory control, and so does the A-not-B task described in Chapter 3 (Diamond, 2013; Holmboe et al., 2010). Voluntary control over attention is in place by infancy for everyday things that matter, such as an angry face, but it will increase substantially with age for abstract symbols, such as reading (Ristic & Enns, 2015). When infants pay attention to something, their posture stiffens, their heart slows down, and their brain's electrical signals change (Richards, Reynolds, & Courage, 2010). Over the first 2 years of life, infants look longer and prefer increasingly complex things to look at.

Early Childhood (3 to 5 Years)

Processing speed continues to improve in the preschool years. *Executive functions* improve dramatically. In fact, you can measure improvement within a year's time (Clark et al., 2013). This is apparent in the Dimensional Change Card Sort that was described earlier in this chapter. Recall that children are asked to first sort by one dimension (e.g., color). After sorting several cards, they are asked to switch and sort by a different dimension (e.g., shapes). You will find that 3-year-olds across the world will usually continue sorting by the old rule (color), even though they can tell you they should be sorting by the new rule (shape). Why is this task so difficult? They must pay attention to instruction, keep the new rule in working memory, and inhibit their original response. Most children become successful at this task and the day/night task described earlier by age 4 to 5 (Best & Miller, 2010). See Figure 4.2. However, inhibitory control continues to be challenging for young children (Diamond, 2013).

FIGURE 4.2 Cognitive Flexibility by Age.

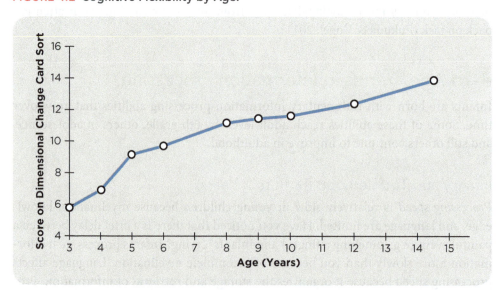

Children perform better on the Dimensional Change Card Sort test with age. At what age is there more rapid growth (i.e., where is the line steepest)? *Source: Zelazo et al. (2013).*

Middle Childhood (6 to 12 Years)

In middle childhood, *processing speed* continues to improve, although the rate of change eventually slows down. Figure 4.3 shows how processing speed increases from 5 to 18 years of age. (If you immediately thought, "Ah! That is a quadratic function," you were right. Negotiate for extra credit.)

Working memory improves substantially (Cowan et al., 2010). On simple memory span tests, children improve in roughly 2-year steps such that an average 3-year-old can remember one number or word, a 5-year-old two numbers or words, a 7-year-old three, a 9-year-old four, an 11-year-old five, a 13-year-old six, and a 15-year-old seven (Kemps, De Rammelaere, & Desmet, 2000). On more complex tasks, the number of "chunks" of information that can be processed increases steadily until adult capacity of about four chunks is reached.

Inhibition continues to improve, although at a slower rate than in early childhood. One way this is measured is with go/no-go tasks (Best & Miller, 2010) in which children are asked to push a button for every "go" indicator on a computer screen (e.g., all letters but X), but not for every "no-go" indicator (e.g., the letter X). *Cognitive flexibility* also improves steadily from ages 4 to 14 and then levels off. The improvement in working memory is partly due to better control of attention. Figure 4.4

FIGURE 4.3 Processing Speed by Age.

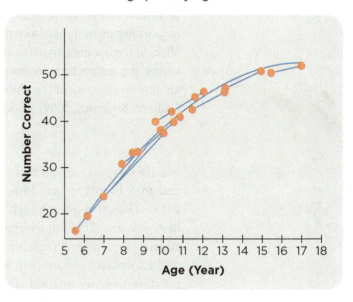

Children were given rows of six numbers, like 8, 9, 5, 3, 9, 7, and asked to circle the identical numbers. The number of rows they can do in a 3-minute period is a measure of processing speed. Can you describe how processing speed develops with age in this graph? Graphs of working memory tend to have the same shape (e.g., Dempster, 1981). Try this with children of different ages to see if you get a similar age trend. Be prepared with about 60 rows if you are testing intelligent adolescents! *Source: Kail and Ferrer (2007).*

FIGURE 4.4 Working Memory Capacity.

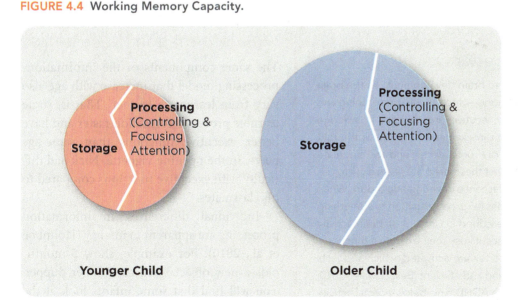

Working memory capacity increases with age, as indicated by a larger circle. At the same time, the proportion of that capacity that is needed for processing diminishes.

shows that children's working memory capacity gets larger, and control of attention becomes more efficient, freeing memory capacity as they get older. The improvement in working memory is also partly due to faster processing speed. The difficulty that Nick, in the opening vignette, had with shifting between the reading task and remembering the instructions is more typical of primary-grade children. Second-graders are just on the cusp of the ability to update memory (Barrouillet, Gavens, Vergauwe, Gaillard, & Camos, 2009). Older children should have less difficulty with it.

Adolescence (13 to 19 Years)

We are sorry to tell you that *processing speed* increases into adolescence, levels off, and then begins to get slower after age 18 (Coyle, Pillow, Snyder, & Kochunov, 2011). Thus, if you teach high school, you are likely to have students who are faster than you are. This improvement supports formal operational thinking and better athletic performance, reasoning, and impulse control compared to younger children.

Performance on complex *working memory* tasks that require strategy use, incorporating new information, and monitoring progress increases across adolescence, and peaks at about age 30 (Hartshorne & Germine, 2015). However, on simple working memory tasks, like recognizing a face you've seen before, adult levels of performance are reached as early as ages 9 to 10.

Other executive functions improve in adolescence. Adolescents are better at controlling their thinking. They are faster and more accurate on tests of inhibitory control, which peaks in the late teens (Sinopoli, Schachar, & Dennis, 2011). Task switching, like sorting cards by a new rule, is easy for typical adolescents. However, they will sort cards at a slower rate using the new rule compared to the old rule. A harder test of executive functions used with adolescents is the Stroop test (see Figure 4.5). Don't worry that it is all downhill for you; the amount of knowledge peaks in late middle age (Hartshorne & Germine, 2015).

 **brain research**

Mature Brains Have Better Executives

Information processing is linked to brain development. As the brain continues to mature across childhood—through synaptic pruning and myelination—processing speed, executive functions, and knowledge all steadily improve. Improvement in executive functions is thought to result from maturation of the prefrontal cortex and the cingulate gyrus. In Chapter 2 you learned that these brain areas are slow to develop, coming to maturity in adolescence or young adulthood. When infants use their executive functions (e.g., pay attention to something or engage in the A-not-B task described in Chapter 3), brain activity tends to be global. When adolescents use their executive functions, specific areas of the prefrontal cortex are activated, which suggests that their brains are more organized and efficient (Best & Miller, 2010; Richards et al., 2010). Children with ADHD have below-normal activity for their age in the prefrontal cortex.

4-1c Individual Diversity in Information Processing

The same components of the information-processing model that increase with age also vary from learner to learner. That is, some learners process information faster and have better executive functions than same-age peers. In the opening vignette, Nick had difficulty with executive functions compared to his classmates.

Individual differences in information processing are apparent in infancy (Holmboe et al., 2010). For example, show 5-month-olds a new object, such as a finger puppet. You will find that some infants look at the new object very briefly before shifting their attention to something else, whereas others

FIGURE 4.5 **The Stroop Test.**

In set 1 read the words out loud and time yourself. In set 2 time yourself saying the *color* the word is printed in. (You must inhibit the automatic tendency of skilled readers to *read* the word.) The difference in time between the sets is your "inhibitory control" score. Get friends and children of different ages to try it. Try it online. There are various Stroop test websites that will time you automatically. You can also try an online "Tower of Hanoi" test that assesses working memory.

will look for longer. The "short-lookers" may have faster processing speed and memory. Later in childhood they have better executive functions, language, memory, and intelligence (Cuevas & Bell, 2014; Rose, Feldman, & Jankowski, 2015). These individual differences tend to be stable from early childhood to late adolescence (Miyake & Friedman, 2012). However, individual differences are larger in adolescence than in early childhood. By adolescence, two students the same age can be quite dissimilar in their information processing skills (Kuhn, 2006).

Although the laboratory tasks used to measure information processing, like the Stroop test, seem trivial, performance on the tasks predicts a remarkable range of real-world outcomes over the long-term. Faster processing speed and better executive functions have been linked to academic success. For example, learners who have better information-processing abilities are better at solving math problems and comprehending what they read and get higher standardized test scores. This pattern has been found for multiple ages and in multiple countries.[2] Indeed, executive functions form the core of "school readiness" skills such as the ability to concentrate, pay attention, and follow instructions. They may be more important to school success than IQ or prereading skills (Diamond, 2013). Children who start kindergarten with these skills will make greater gains over the years (Li-Grinning, Votruba-Drzal, Maldonado-Carreño, & Haas, 2010). Learners with poor information-processing ability, like Nick, may struggle more as they progress through school because school tasks will increasingly demand these abilities.

Information-processing abilities are also linked to emotional and social skills at school. Students with poor attention control and other executive functions tend to have more problems like anxiety, depression, impulsiveness, aggression, and acting without thinking (e.g., Khurana et al., 2015).

---

[2] This has been found in many studies, including large national studies, just a few of which are listed here: Brock, Rimm-Kaufman, Nathanson, and Grimm (2009); Grimm, Steele, Mashburn, Burchinal, and Pianta (2010); Swanson (2008); Wanless et al. (2011); Welsh, Nix, Blair, Bierman, and Nelson (2010).

BOX 4.1   challenges in development

ADHD

In an 8th-grade history class, Clayton is supposed to be completing a worksheet. While looking at the paper, he constantly taps his pencil and drums the desk with his thumb. He gets out of his seat to throw away a piece of paper. He wanders the room and taps another student on the shoulder. He sits down, but in a few minutes gets up to read the classroom rules posted by the door. He sits down again, but soon walks over to talk to his friend. His teacher tells him to return to his seat. Clayton works on the worksheet for 2 minutes without interruption only when his teacher stands next to him.

Clayton has attention-deficit/hyperactivity disorder (ADHD), which is the most common neurobehavioral disorder in childhood. About 9% of school-age children have ADHD, and the rate of occurrence in boys is three times the rate in girls (Akinbami, Liu, Pastor, & Reuben, 2011; Getahun et al., 2013). Everyone varies in how easily distractible they are, but learners diagnosed with ADHD are at the extreme end of the continuum (Forster & Lavie, 2015).

The primary symptoms of ADHD are hyperactivity, impulsivity, and inattention. ADHD can be reliably diagnosed as young as 3, although children on average are diagnosed between 8 and 10 years of age (Getahun et al., 2013). For most children (70%) symptoms last into adulthood, but hyperactivity diminishes across childhood.

What Might Lead to ADHD? Both genes and environment contribute to ADHD. This means ADHD runs in families. Heritability estimates of 70% have been found; yet only small effects (1% to 3%) are linked with genome patterns (Nikolas, Klump, & Burt, 2015). This puzzling mismatch suggests a gene–environment interaction (see Chapter 1). That is, ADHD is substantially more likely in children who have *both* a genetic predisposition and environmental risk factors, rather than genetics alone (Pennington et al., 2009). For example, children whose mother smoked during pregnancy and who have genetic propensity are particularly likely to be distractible (Wiebe et al., 2009).

Prenatal experiences linked to ADHD include the mother feeling stress or using tobacco or alcohol during pregnancy and low birth weight (Schneider & Moore, 2000). ADHD is also linked to quality of parenting. Children with a mother who has chronic depression, anxiety, or other emotional disturbance are four times more likely to have ADHD. There is also higher prevalence among children in step, adoptive, foster, or single-parent households; households that move frequently; and negative, conflict-ridden households (Lesesne, Visser, & White, 2003). Children with insecure attachment to their parents are more likely to have ADHD symptoms (see Chapter 6).

In classrooms, students must ignore distractions when given a task that requires concentration, and they must suppress irrelevant information. Two-year-old Akiva is skilled at such selective attention:

In the toddler class, the teacher is presenting a brief lesson on fall leaves, with pictures and sample leaves. Two children are pushing chairs around the room, taking off their shoes, and jumping about. These two children capture the attention of other toddlers, but not Akiva. She listens to the teacher with unwavering attention, softly imitating occasional words like pretty, golden, fall down, *as though nothing else were happening in the room.*

In contrast to Akiva, some classmates are described by their teachers as "inattentive, easily distracted, can't concentrate, daydreams." Inability to control attention is a defining feature of **attention-deficit/hyperactivity disorder (ADHD)** (see Box 4.1). Scientists believe that poor executive functions are the core problem underlying some forms of ADHD (Nigg, 2010). However, mind wandering is common, and the larger your working memory capacity, the *more* your mind may

attention-deficit/hyperactivity disorder (ADHD)
a neurobehavioral disorder characterized by hyperactivity, low impulse control, and inattention.

Why Does it Matter if Children Have ADHD? Children with ADHD may have cognitive and behavior problems as early as age 3 (Loe et al., 2008). They are more likely to use drugs, be injured, and as teenagers to be involved in theft, assault, and use of a weapon. In school they are likely to underachieve, as they struggle to comply with classroom demands (Harstad et al., 2014). They are more likely to be retained a grade or drop out of school. Although symptoms of ADHD diminish with age, academic problems tend to persist and may increase (Barkley, 2006).

Practicing Inclusion—How Can You Help Learners with ADHD? Inclusion refers to creating a learning environment that is fully welcoming and accommodates diverse learners with special needs. Because ADHD is so prevalent, you will likely practice inclusion with learners like Clayton in your classroom. First, confirm that the learner does not have sleep deprivation, which mimics ADHD (Bonuck, Freeman, Chervin, & Zu, 2012). If sleep deprivation is ruled out, you may be called upon to provide evidence as part of a diagnosis. Teachers' assessments of ADHD may be more valid than parents' assessments (Mannuzza, Klein, & Moulton, 2002).

If the learner has ADHD, research suggests that the following may help: (1) give the learner a choice between two acceptable tasks, (2) incorporate the learner's interest into the task, (3) seat the learner away from objects or classmates that are distracting, (4) give instructions in short bouts rather than lengthy lists, (5) praise good behavior and success, and (6) make sure the learner gets periodic exercise, which helps the brain focus (Harrison, Bunford, Evans, & Owens, 2013). Don't try to over-control movement, if it is not distracting others. Learners with ADHD tend to perform better on tasks if they fidget a little, like tapping their foot or rocking their chair (Sarver, Rapport, Kofler, Rasiker, & Friedman, 2015).

Follow the guidelines on classroom implications for information processing in this chapter. Chapter 7 provides other suggestions to help learners control their impulses. In addition, you may be involved in a treatment plan that includes parents and a counselor. Treatment usually includes behavior therapy and/or medication. Behavior therapy typically involves applied behavior analysis (see Chapter 3), as well as therapy aimed at altering thoughts (e.g., "I need to pause before acting"). Medication reduces fidgety and impulsive behavior, but a large randomized experiment showed it does not reduce academic or behavior problems over the long run (Molina et al., 2009). Medication is controversial because all drugs have side effects. These may include growth deficits, muscle tics, sleep problems, lack of emotion, and possibly an increase in suicide (National Institute of Mental Health, 2008). The U.S. Food and Drug Administration requires that warnings be placed on ADHD drugs. In spite of these concerns, drug treatment is common and increasing, even among preschoolers. The American Academy of Pediatrics recommends combined medication and behavioral treatment for parent and child (American Academy of Pediatrics, 2011b).

wander during undemanding tasks—so don't assume daydreaming is always a problem (Levinson, Smallwood, & Davidson, 2012).

What might predict differences in information processing? One factor is genes. Executive functions have a very high heritability index in childhood (Engelhardt, Briley, Mann, Harden, & Tucker-Drob, 2015). However, this does not mean executive functions are not influenced by experience. Heritability is an estimate of how much variation among the children tested at a particular point in time might be attributed to genes, but says nothing about whether it can be changed. As you learned in Chapter 2, the brain is shaped by experience.

An important experience is the quality of a child's home (see Figure 4.6). Mothers and fathers who are sensitive, supportive, and provide activities that stimulate their children's cognitive and language development tend to have children who have better information-processing abilities (Fay-Stammbach, Hawes, & Meredith, 2014; Meuwissen & Carlson, 2015). For example, a national study found that quality of parenting when children were 4 years old predicted their executive functions and memory at that time and reading and mathematics test scores when they were in 3rd grade (Friedman et al., 2014). Akiva's mother is a former teacher who creates a

inclusion
creating learning environments that enable learners with special education needs to fully participate in the school community. Some groups (e.g., UNESCO) expand the term beyond students with disabilities to inclusion of marginalized groups, such as religious minorities or impoverished children.

FIGURE 4.6 Individual Differences in Executive Functions.

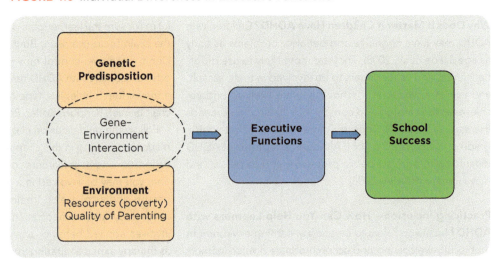

A child's executive functions are influenced by an interaction of genes and environment, which in turn influence school success. In other chapters, you will learn about several aspects of parenting quality that have been linked to executive functions. These include sensitivity (vs. hostility) and security of attachment (see Chapter 6), reading and talking to children (see Chapter 12), scaffolding children in challenging tasks (see Chapter 3), providing a stimulating home, and authoritative parenting (see Chapter 7). (See Deater-Deckard, 2014). Can you explain how genes and environment might interact to influence children's executive functions?

stable and stimulating home. In Box 4.1 you learned that ADHD is associated with several aspects of the home environment. There is likely a gene–environment interaction at work (see Chapter 1). That is, children with a genetic predisposition tend to develop low executive functions primarily when there is also insensitive parenting, household chaos, or more hours in child care (Deater-Deckard, 2014).

In addition to the home environment, your classroom environment influences development of the brain, where information processing takes place. Let's discuss this next.

4-1d Classroom Implications of Information Processing

Information-processing ability affects learners' academic and social success in your classroom. Academic tasks—such as correctly spelling words while keeping in mind the point of the essay you are writing—require strong information processing. So does computing math in your head, translating to another language, or coming to a conclusion (Fenesi, Sana, Kim, & Shore, 2015).

One hypothesis used to explain the income–achievement gap is outlined in Figure 4.6. That is, poverty may reduce quality of parenting due to stress and limited resources (see Chapter 1), which may compromise executive functions in children, which interferes with academic achievement. For example, in one study, poverty at 1 and 24 months predicted executive function problems in 3rd grade, which predicted low math and reading test scores in 5th grade, after controlling for IQ (Crook & Evans, 2014). Have you noticed that you have trouble thinking clearly or remembering things when your life is not going well? Executive functions are compromised when you are stressed, sad, sleep-deprived, or physically unfit, just as it is for your learners (Diamond, 2013).

If you have learners like Nick who have difficulty shifting between tasks, forget lengthy instructions, forget letters in words or words in sentences, are easily distracted or poorly organized, cannot complete a multistep task, or raise their hand but forget the response when called upon, they may have limited information-processing ability. There are a few things you can do as a teacher to help such learners be successful.

Reduce Working Memory and Executive Load

Your learners cannot process new information when their working memory capacity is overloaded. To reduce the load on working memory:

1. Limit your talking. If you keep talking after presenting important information, it will be forgotten. Present information at a speed that allows learners to fully process it.

2. Reduce distractions in your classroom. Distractions can be comings and goings, announcements, and even decorations that visually bombard learners. For example, in an experiment, kindergarteners were off-task and learned less in a highly decorated, versus spartan, room (Fisher, Godwin, & Seltman, 2014).

3. Increase your learners' expertise. The more automatic their processing, the less space is consumed by executive functions. If reading is automatic for you, you would not have been overwhelmed by the task in the opening vignette, but it would be overwhelming to young beginning readers and to struggling older readers, like Nick.

4. Provide external storage. A preschool teacher might post informational pictures on the wall. An elementary teacher might write on the board: "Read for 20 minutes. Write a summary of what you read. Look at the sample on the wall, if you need to." A secondary teacher might provide partial notes (i.e., a rough outline of the lesson, but not details), which frees students' working memory to attend to the information.

5. Carve problems into smaller subtasks that can be performed sequentially. In math and science this includes providing formulas or algorithms.

Imagine that you teach physics to 11th-graders, who have adultlike working memory capacity and speed. You ask your students, "What would be the acceleration of an object if the object travels the same distance again in half the time?" Solving complex problems that require processing three or four variables at once taxes their working memory. However, if your students know that velocity equals distance divided by time ($V = d/t$), they can determine what the new velocity is. They can then apply velocity as a single variable to compute acceleration, which is the difference between velocity at time 1 and time 2 ($A = V_1 - V_2$). These formulas take care of whole chunks of the problem. *Part of educating children toward expertise is to give them the tools to chunk problems into a manageable size that fits their processing capacity.*

Focus Attention

Selective attention is considered a gateway to learning (Bahrick & Lickliter, 2014). The better learners can control their attention, the higher their academic achievement (e.g., Claessens & Dowsett, 2014). You want your learners to concentrate, resist distractions, and not let their minds wander during instruction. This simple skill exists in infants but is strengthened through exercise. Over time, this simple skill develops into complex skills, such as computer programming or reading Dickens (Sörqvist & Marsh, 2015).

To be an effective teacher, you need to attract learners' attention and maintain it on important information, particularly if you teach students who have difficulty controlling their attention. It helps to make learning goals explicit and remind learners of the goal. Children often do not know the goal of a learning task, which is crucial to monitoring what to pay attention to and whether they are reaching the goal (Barker & Munakata, 2015; Chevalier, 2015). It also helps to give learners a break for physical activity. After 20 minutes of exercise, learners behave more attentively (Pontifex et al., 2014).

Strengthen Executive Functions

Using executive functions makes them stronger, just like muscles. You can strengthen your students' executive functions by following these guidelines:

think about **this**

A study of Swedish children with ADHD found that after playing a specially designed computer game for forty minutes per day for five weeks, executive functions increased (Klingberg et al., 2005). The effect size was 0.93. The effect size for ADHD medication is 0.4 to 1.2. What does this mean? Which intervention would you use and why?

1. Promote healthy habits—especially adequate sleep, good nutrition, and physical fitness (see Chapter 2). Executive functions require a large amount of glucose (the brain's fuel, as you undoubtedly remember from Chapter 2). Part of why you don't think clearly when you are tired or hungry is because your brain is depleted of fuel. The brain's store of glucose is replenished during sleep and after eating (Gailliot, 2008). Physical fitness is also linked to better brain functioning. More fit children have faster processing speed, better memory, and better executive functions, including attention control (Chaddock-Heyman, Hillman, Cohen, & Kramer, 2014). Aerobic and mindful exercise, like martial arts and yoga, may improve information processing in children (Diamond & Lee, 2011).

2. Help learners practice using their executive functions through mundane, daily activities like requiring them to sit up straight or persist in activities even when they want to stop. However, be aware that you can overtax executive functions. Learners may occasionally need a restorative break (Kaplan & Berman, 2010).

brain research

Brains Can Be Trained

Can you improve your students' brains by training their executive functions? Scientists are trying to through two approaches, both of which have been used with typical children and children with ADHD, language delays, or low socioeconomic status (SES). One approach is to intensively drill children in a narrow skill using a computer program. For example, programs may ask children to remember where an object is on a 4 × 4 grid, or find matching figures among many figures. This approach has been used with 4-year-olds to adults. Does it work? It improves performance on laboratory tests of executive functions, with impressive effect sizes ranging from 0.40 to 1.80. However, there is no robust evidence that it improves classroom performance, or that it lasts over the long run, but scientists are working on it. (Bryck & Fisher, 2012; Jacob & Parkinson, 2015; Shipstead, Hicks, & Engle, 2012).

The second approach is to improve the structure, discipline, and emotional supportiveness of the classroom. Does it work? It has only been tested in early childhood (3- to 7-year-olds), but it has been linked to better executive functions and academic skills (Bryck & Fisher, 2012; Jacob & Parkinson, 2015). How to do this is the focus of the next sections of the text, so stay tuned!

3. Help young children improve their verbal abilities, which are linked to executive functions. In Chapter 3 you learned that self-talk helps children regulate their thoughts and attention. Music training has also been shown to improve both verbal ability and executive functions, presumably because they share the same brain resources (Moreno et al., 2011).

4. Ask learners to think about their thinking, or practice metacognition, with questions such as: "How did you know … ? How have you improved your thinking about math (or history, or science)? How would you do it differently? What did you learn from doing this work? I noticed you erased a lot—how did you know it needed fixing?"

From an information-processing point of view, cognitive growth is the result of greater *knowledge* as well as greater processing speed and executive functions. Greater knowledge enhances these other components of information processing because knowledge that is overlearned and automatic frees resources and is processed more quickly. Greater knowledge is the focus of the next section.

4-2 Memory

Mr. Glazer helps his 6th-grade students learn new vocabulary words by reciting the definitions out loud several times throughout the week. They also do a worksheet matching definitions and words. At the end of the week, Mr. Glazer has the children write their own sentences using the vocabulary words.

Mr. Glazer is helping his students store vocabulary words in their long-term memory. Information in long-term memory can be stored unintentionally, like a conversation with a friend, or intentionally, like studying for a test. Deliberately attempting to remember is called *memorizing*. Schooling often requires memorizing, like these 6th-graders are doing. While education is not only about memorization, memorization is necessary for many types of problem solving and conceptual understanding.

4-2a Remember? Maybe, Maybe Not

In this section we will discuss limits in remembering and then strategies learners can use to overcome those limits and memorize important information.

Memory Errors

Memory is not an exact replica of an object, event, or experience. There are two types of memories: verbatim traces, which are detailed accurate memories, and **fuzzy traces**, which are general, vague memories, or the gist of an experience. Can you remember a lecture word-for-word from last week? Probably not, but you might remember the gist of it. Most of your remembering involves fuzzy, not verbatim, traces. This may not seem ideal, but in fact fuzzy traces are adequate for most endeavors.

> **fuzzy traces**
> a distilled gist of an experience rather than an exact memory.

You may have worked hard to teach students something—a piece of music, the names of colors, anatomy terms—which they appear to learn at one time, but later forget. Verbatim memories are forgotten more readily than gist memories. For example, if you have a verbatim trace of the algebra test scores for two students in your class (e.g., 97% and 84%), this would soon deteriorate such that you could not remember the exact scores but you could remember which student did better. Like you, children remember details only if they use them frequently.

There are at least three reasons learners forget things:

1. *Decay.* The memory decays over time and loses strength if it is not used.

2. *Retrieval failure.* Learners may know something but then go blank during a test. They cannot retrieve the information when they need it.

3. **Interference.** New knowledge can make retrieval of old knowledge difficult and vice versa. For example, Kevin is an English speaker who knows the word *embarrassed* (old knowledge). In Spanish class, he learns that *embarazada* means *pregnant* (new knowledge) but has trouble remembering the new definition because of interference from the word *embarrassed.* When he does something embarrassing, he says, "*Estoy embarazado,*" which unfortunately means "I am a pregnant boy" (adding to his embarrassment).

interference
existing information in long-term memory prevents accurate retrieval of new information, or information learned recently prevents accurate retrieval of older information.

While forgetting information you want to remember is frustrating, scientists argue that forgetting is good for you, to some extent. Forgetting painful experiences or failures helps you feel happier, and forgetting irrelevant, incorrect, or out-of-date information unclutters your mind for more efficient thinking (Nørby, 2015). It can help you see the forest, rather than the trees.

Another type of memory error, besides forgetting things that you once knew, is remembering things that never happened, or *false memories.* Our youngest daughter remembered family vacations that occurred before she was born. Apparently, she was a precocious child. (Actually, she saw photos and then created a "memory" of the vacation.) Other children do this, too. A sneaky researcher intentionally told another adult at a preschool—in front of some of the children—that an escaped rabbit was eating carrots in another classroom. Later 55% of the *classmates* of those children, not the children who overheard the story, reported having actually seen the rabbit, which did not exist (Principe, Kanaya, Ceci, & Singh, 2006)—that is, rumor-mongering caused false memories.

False memories occur in adolescents and adults as well. In fact, you may be more prone to false memories now compared to when you were a child (Brainerd, 2013). For example, researchers doctored family photographs into a picture of a hot air balloon ride, and family members remembered taking the ride, which never occurred (Garry & Gerrie, 2005). Just imagining doing something, or watching someone else do it, can create false memories that you actually did it (Lindner, Echterhoff, Davidson, & Brand, 2010).

Why do we have false memories? Memory contains pieces of reality mixed with creation. False memories are intelligent errors—that is, your mind makes sense of a situation and recalls details that were not there but logically fit your expectations. The memory learners construct is influenced by their previous experience, so different learners construct different memories of the same event. Just because learners express a memory with confidence, detail, and emotion does not necessarily mean it is factual.

source monitoring
memory of the source or origin of information.

One type of false memory you'll need to help learners with is the **source monitoring** error, or a false memory of the source of their information. For example, children may think they learned history facts from their teacher when they actually learned them from not-quite-accurate cartoons (Riggins, 2014). Source monitoring is crucial for critical thinking about the meaning and accuracy of information. A supposed "fact" is evaluated differently based on whether it came from a supermarket tabloid, a research journal, or an Internet advertisement.

Memory Strategies

Although memory has plenty of errors, it works reasonably well if you are not too concerned about precision. However, in some situations precise, accurate details must be consciously memorized. The process of putting information into long-term memory is called **encoding**. There are three types of effective strategies for encoding.

> **encoding**
> the process of forming mental representations of information for storage.

1. *Rehearsal.* **Rehearsal** refers to repeating items over and over again, which keeps them active in working memory. It is more effective than a one-shot exposure to material such as reading through a chapter once, but encoding can be transitory (Camos, 2015). The next two strategies are more effective.

> **rehearsal**
> mentally repeating information over and over in working memory.

2. *Organization.* Organizing or clustering related items into groups facilitates memory. For example, a student who is trying to remember the attributes of two civilizations in social studies class might create a Venn diagram that includes two overlapping circles to organize attributes that the civilizations share and attributes that are different.

3. *Elaboration.* **Elaboration** involves creating associations between what you are learning and things you already know, so it requires recognizing how the new information fits with information in your long-term memory. You can help learners elaborate by asking *why* questions and asking learners to put things into their own words, create verbal or visual links between items, generate examples, or apply information. Mr. Glazer, in the vignette, did this when he had his 6th-graders use new vocabulary words in sentences. Help learners see meaningful relations among the items, or make up relations solely for the purpose of remembering. For example, to remember that latitude lines are horizontal on a globe, learners might think LATitude sounds like LADder, and visualize ladder-like lines. Learners who use elaboration strategies tend to remember more.

> **elaboration**
> a method of enhancing memory that involves creating visual or verbal links or representations to associate two or more items.

How do you know if a strategy has been successful? An important next step in remembering is self-testing. Have you ever been sure you were ready for a test because you had the content down cold, yet when you actually took the test, you didn't do so well? Such misjudgments of memory are common. Self-testing helps students more accurately judge what they know—if they diligently check their answers without cheating (Dunlosky & Lipko, 2007). Self-testing, which is described again later in this chapter, improves both memory and metamemory. Thus, after reading this chapter, come back later and test yourself without the answers in front of you.

4-2b Age Trends in Memory

Children know more and become better at remembering and memorizing with age. They come to use memory strategies more effectively. Let's look at these age trends in greater detail.

Infancy and Toddlerhood (Prenatal to 2 Years)

Infants have some long-term memory. How do we know this? A graduate student, Carolyn Rovee-Collier, was trying to keep her infant son happy so she could study. She tied a ribbon from his foot to a mobile over his crib, so that when he kicked, the mobile moved. Soon he began kicking in anticipation, before the ribbon was tied to his foot, indicating that he remembered (Vigorito & Fagen, 2015). His mother went on to join the ranks of scientists who study infant memory. Through their work, we know that even during the last month of pregnancy, fetuses remember specific sounds or vibrations (Dirix, Nijhuis, Jongsma, & Hornstra, 2009). After birth they prefer to smell foods their mothers ate during pregnancy, which suggests prenatal memory (Mannella, Jagnow, & Beauchamp, 2001). When shown a familiar and a novel picture, infants will look more at the novel picture (Richards et al., 2010).

Deferred imitation studies show that older infants also remember complex information. In deferred imitation studies, the experimenter demonstrates actions that are unfamiliar to the infant—such as placing a toy car into a tunnel and then pushing it with a rod so it rolls to the end and turns on a light. The infant is given the opportunity to reproduce the same actions weeks later. Older infants learn faster, retain memories longer, and need less training than younger infants. By 9 to 12 months of age, infants may remember complex sequences for 4 to 6 weeks. Thus, long-term memory increases steadily through infancy (Schneider & Ornstein, 2015).

Despite this evidence that infants have memory, you probably can't remember anything from when you were a toddler. The average age of the first memory that adults can recall is around 3 or 4 years (Jack, Simcock, & Hayne, 2012). Early memories are likely to be sparse—like a snapshot without context. Most people have only a few memories before 6 to 8 years of age.

childhood amnesia
the inability to recall things that occurred during infancy, typically from birth to about 3.5 years of age.

The inability to remember things that occurred to you from infancy to your first memories is called **childhood amnesia**. There is currently no single explanation for childhood amnesia. One possibility is forgetting. At age 5, you could probably remember events from toddlerhood that you could no longer remember at age 7, *even if you were reminded of them* (Peterson, Warren, & Short, 2011). As you got older, the age of your earliest memory got older, until about age 8 to 10 when it stabilized. This suggests that earlier memories are fragile and fade. Another possibility is the absence of language. Language helps children encode memories so that they can tell you about events later. Yet another possibility is an immature brain, although key brain structures that support long-term memory are in place by age two (Jack et al., 2012).

Early Childhood (3 to 5 Years)

Preschoolers often display good long-term memory, but they may need adult support. For example, in a classic study scientists asked children who were 3 and 4 years old when they visited Disneyworld to recount their trips several months later (Hamond & Fivush, 1991). The children remembered a great deal of accurate information about their trip. However, the 3-year-olds needed cues to help them remember, such as "What rides did you go on?" and "What did you eat?" The 4-year-olds recalled more spontaneously, without cues, and they provided more details. In reminiscing, adults provide more scaffolding (see Chapter 3) with younger children, but need to provide less with older children (Schneider & Ornstein, 2015).

Young children's memories are fragile and susceptible to interference. That is, learning something new may override existing memories (Darby & Sloutsky, 2015). Young children often fail to use memory strategies. They may use rehearsal, but are not likely to use organizational strategies before age 5 or 6. You can teach kindergarteners memory strategies, but they are unlikely to apply them to situations outside the training context, may not see the value of using the strategies, and will need more time to learn the strategies than older children (Kuhn, 2000; Schneider, 2000).

Middle Childhood (6 to 12 Years)

Elementary-age children's memory improves in at least five ways. First, they know more; they have more items in long-term memory. Second, they get dramatically better at remembering the source of their information (Riggins, 2014). See Figure 4.7. Third, they get better at metamemory. That is, they understand that they are more likely to forget details than gist and that they can remember details better if they are linked to easy-to-remember events (Friedman, 2007; Jaswal & Dodson, 2009). For example, they can remember when they went to the zoo if that detail is linked to their summer visit to Grandma's house. Fourth, they get better at remembering to do something in the future, like return a permission slip or library book (Smith, Bayen, & Martin, 2010).

Fifth, they get better at using effective memory strategies. When presented with a task like remembering vocabulary words, younger children will use no strategy or they will use simple rehearsal. By age 7, but not younger, children will periodically shift their attention to reactivate their decaying memory in order to prevent forgetting (Camos & Barrouillet, 2011). This attention shifting is an executive function. Younger children have less capacity to actively use their executive functions to strategize about remembering. By about 3rd grade, children will use organization (Lehmann & Hasselhorn, 2007). They are not likely to generate elaboration spontaneously, but it becomes easier to get them to use it (Waters, 2000).

FIGURE 4.7 Memory Improves with Age.

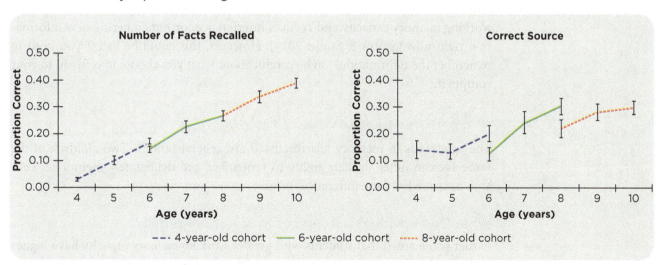

Children were taught several new facts (e.g., a group of goats is called a tribe) by an adult or a puppet. A week later children were tested on recall of the new facts, as well as facts they already knew (e.g., what color is grass). They were asked "From who did you learn that?" There was a steady increase in memory for facts and for monitoring the source of their information. Children with better processing speed and language skills learned more. *Adapted from Riggins (2014).*

One of the most effective memory strategies is to write something down. This is why you take notes during class. Do children use written notes, and do they actually help? Researchers asked 1st- through 7th-graders to play the game *Concentration*, in which they memorize the location of overturned cards with identical pictures (Eskritt & Lee, 2002). They were given paper and told they could write anything that would help them remember where each card was. Only 50% of the children, regardless of age, chose to use notes. Of the children who did use notes, many used notes that were not helpful. Those whose notes were helpful were mostly 5th-, 6th-, and 7th-graders. Thus, older children were not more likely to use notes, but if they did use notes they used them more effectively.

Children do not gradually transition from nonuse of memory strategies to full use, as you might expect. Instead, they inconsistently use strategies. Some children discover a strategy at one age, lose it at a later age, and then rediscover it still later. A child may use old and new strategies at the same period in time.

Adolescence (13 to 19 Years)

Two aspects of memory increase through adolescence. First, quality improves. Adolescents are better at remembering both verbatim traces and fuzzy traces (Reyna, Wilhelms, McCormick, & Weldon, 2015). As children move into adolescence they shift from vague to vivid recall. That is, 9th-graders are better able to recall specific, vivid details than 2nd-graders. This occurs for word lists, narratives, pictures, and numbers (Brainerd, Holliday, & Reyna, 2004).

Second, memory strategies improve. With age, children are more likely to use elaboration. Elaboration strategies develop later than rehearsal and organizational strategies, and seldom before adolescence. However, many adolescents, and even college students, may not use elaboration spontaneously or effectively.

One form of memory strategy, akin to taking notes as discussed above, is to "off-load" your memory to your computer. You may not be aware of this, but when you save information in a file on your computer, you are *more* likely to forget the information than if you did not save it in a file. This could be good; it frees up your working memory capacity and reduces interference for remembering new information right now (Storm & Stone, 2014). However, this could be bad if you need to remember the information—so be careful about what you choose to off-load to your computer.

4-2c Individual Diversity in Memory

The age trends in memory just discussed are generalizations. Two children of the same age can differ in their ability to remember and deliberately memorize. Let's look next at what these differences mean.

What Do Individual Differences in Memory Predict?

Earlier you learned that students with greater *working memory* capacity have higher achievement. Students who have greater *long-term memory*—or know more—also have higher achievement. This is obvious because achievement tests measure how much children know. Less obvious is that knowing more also makes children better problem solvers because memorized knowledge can be applied to the problem at hand, like solving math problems or writing a persuasive essay. Students with better *metamemory* also have higher achievement. That is, they know how and when to apply memory strategies to their advantage.

What Predicts Individual Differences in Memory?

Individual differences in long-term memory are the result of differences in exposure to information, resistance to memory error, and effective use of memory strategies. Some of these factors are linked to information-processing ability. For example, learners with better working memory use memory strategies more effectively, which helps them come to know more (Lehmann & Hasselhorn, 2007). Two additional factors that predict remembering, that teachers can influence, are prior knowledge and conversation.

Prior knowledge

Children who have prior knowledge about a topic learn new material about that same topic more easily—whether the topic is ant behavior, lowest common denominators, or *The Crucible*. This effect is so powerful that *low-ability students with prior knowledge about a topic may learn more effectively than high-ability students without prior knowledge.* In Chapter 5 you will learn that expertise in an area can compensate for low intelligence. Because of this, some scientists argue that increasing your learners' knowledge base is the most powerful source of cognitive growth (Schneider & Hardy, 2013).

Prior knowledge has a powerful influence on memory because knowledge is organized in long-term memory as webs or networks of related information. The more connections between individual items of knowledge, the better. When items of knowledge are encoded with many connections, they are easier to retrieve because more things can activate them. For example, if you learn that the Mexican author Mariano Azuela wrote *The Underdogs,* you are not likely to remember it if you have no other connections to it. Someone with a richer network might trigger *The Underdogs* from related pieces of information like the Mexican Revolution, Francisco Madero, Pancho Villa, and the novel *Maria Luisa.* Similarly, if you were raised in the United States, you might be able to trigger information about George Washington with cues such as first president, cherry tree, Mount Vernon, Valley Forge, and many others.

These networks of knowledge are called **schemas**. (They are sometimes called *schemata* and are similar to Piaget's schemes.) Much of education is an attempt to build accurate schemas for specific topics like British Romantic poets in high school or animal camouflage in preschool. One type of schema is a **script**. Scripts focus on *how to do something.* Much of education involves attempts to develop automatic scripts for behavior like counting, reading books, or solving algebra problems.

Conversation

Language is a powerful tool in helping learners store information and create schemas. If you talk about novel objects with learners as they are handling them, learners are more likely to remember the objects (Haden, Ornstein, Eckerman, & Didow, 2001). If you talk about an event, like a visit to a museum, as it is happening or shortly afterward, learners recall the event better.

schema
an organized network of information.

script
a schema for how to do something or for an event.

The fact that talking aids memory suggests that memory is a social event. How does this fit with Vygotsky's sociocultural theory?

How you converse matters. When adults elaborate as learners recall events, they develop better memories (Schneider & Ornstein, 2015). Ideally you should ask open-ended questions (e.g., "tell me about …") and follow the learner's lead by talking about things the learner brings up. For example, in one study, toddlers whose mothers elaborated, not merely repeated, what they talked about could remember things from early childhood at ages 12 to 13 better than could other teens (Jack, MacDonald, Reese, & Hayne, 2009).

Talking about things helps your students retain a memory longer. Talking about things also helps them understand the information better or focus their attention on important features. Thus, to help your students remember, talk with them about what you want them to remember.

4-2d Classroom Implications of Memory

Many college students *and teachers* have false conceptions about how best to remember important information (Bjork, Dunlosky, & Kornell, 2013). Most report never having been taught how to study and learn; they were just left to figure it out. Those with little cultural capital may not figure it out. You can change this situation by deliberately teaching memory skills, so that your students will learn more. How can you do this? Earlier you learned that conversation enhances memory. In addition, combining verbal and visual information enhances memory (Roediger, 2008). A picture may not actually be worth a 1,000 words (perhaps only 789 words?), but it helps. There are at least five more ways you may help your students remember: (1) help them connect knowledge, (2) teach memory strategies, (3) increase exposure to content, (4) provide spaced practice, and (5) test them. Let's discuss each next.

Connect Knowledge

Earlier you learned that prior knowledge promotes remembering new information. This is because rich networks of connections between new and old knowledge help learners store and retrieve information (Bjork et al., 2013). To help learners connect knowledge, use these guidelines:

1. *Help learners develop a broad knowledge base.*

2. *Help learners activate relevant prior knowledge* to show them what they already know about a new topic. One approach is known as KWL, which stands for what do you *know*, what do you *want* to know, and what have you *learned* (Photo 4.1). The *know* and *want* questions are asked before instruction, and the *learned* question comes after instruction. For example, if you are teaching about animal camouflage, ask children what they already know about it. They might talk about owls the color of snow or camouflage clothing for hunting. Then ask them what they want to know about animal camouflage, such as why zebras have stripes. This helps them connect prior and new knowledge.

3. *Refer to content from other classes or from different units within your own class.* For example, in history class, students may learn about World War II in the context of Pearl Harbor and connect the war with the end of the Depression. They could also connect World War II with literature published during the war, like Steinbeck's *The Moon Is Down* and Hemingway's *For Whom the Bell Tolls*, or with sports like Ted Williams batting .406, or with products like nylon.

In the past, secondary schools tended to compartmentalize content rather than build connections. For example, students might never discuss literature or popular culture in connection with World War II. Today, some schools actively try to connect content, such as combining social studies and English classes.

Facilitate Memory Strategies

Learners must sometimes memorize details like vocabulary, dates in history, or multiplication tables. Many learners do not know how to memorize, particularly young children. Research shows that effective teachers deliberately teach memorization strategies (Coffman, Ornstein, McCall, & Curran, 2008). To do this, use these guidelines:

PHOTO 4.1 An example of the KWL approach.

1. Let your students know which details must be memorized and why. Use phrases like "remember" and "don't forget."

2. Frequently demand remembering. For example, "Yesterday we talked about states of matter. What are the three forms that water can take?" In many cultures educators require young children to memorize poems, religious texts, or music. In an experiment, 1st- and 2nd-grade teachers were trained to regularly request that their learners remember facts, procedures, and events during science lessons. In addition to learning the science, the children randomly assigned to these memory-rich classes increased their memory skills in general (Grammer, Coffman, & Ornstein, 2013).

3. Ask your students to think about their memory strategies. For example, "How did you remember . . . ?" This exercises their metamemory skills.

4. Directly teach memory strategies. Unfortunately, observations of classrooms show that teachers seldom do this (Coffman et al., 2008).

There are a variety of ways to teach memory strategies. Teach your students to use flashcards, a type of *rehearsal,* to memorize things like multiplication facts. Teach them to *organize* items to be remembered. For example, memorizing anatomy terms is easier if they are organized by body regions. Teach them to use *elaboration.* For example, remembering when the California gold rush occurred is easier if it is paired with the San Francisco Forty-Niners football team, which is named after the 1849 gold-rush miners.

You can also teach your students to use **mnemonics** to memorize information such as the state capitals, vocabulary words, and ordered lists like the presidents of the United States or artists and their major works. Two types of mnemonics are acronyms and the keyword method.

An **acronym** takes the first letters of words to be remembered and combines them into a word or phrase. For example, *HOMES* is used to remember the Great

mnemonics
techniques for improving memory.

acronym
a mnemonic technique that takes the first letters of words to be remembered and combines them into a word or phrase.

Lakes, which are <u>H</u>uron, <u>O</u>ntario, <u>M</u>ichigan, <u>E</u>rie, and <u>S</u>uperior. Similarly, *sentence mnemonics* (sometimes called *acrostics*) use the first letter of each item to create a sentence that is more easily remembered. For example, <u>*P*</u>*lease* <u>*e*</u>*xcuse* <u>*my*</u> <u>*d*</u>*ear* <u>*A*</u>*unt* <u>*S*</u>*ally* is used to remember the order of operations in algebra (parentheses, exponents, multiplication, division, addition, and subtraction).

The **keyword method** is a two-stage mnemonic. First, the learner chooses a keyword that has a *sound* similar to the target word. Second, the learner creates an *image* that links the keyword with the target word. For example, Mrs. Patel used a keyword to help sophomores in her chemistry class remember whether cations or anions are positive.

> *Mrs. Patel draws a picture of a cat with a bib on the whiteboard. Then she draws a large plus sign on the bib. A student looked at the picture with a puzzled expression, then suddenly smiled, saying "Oh! I thought it was kay-shun, not cat-ion. And I guess it is an-ion, not an-yun—well, duh—they're ions! Well, that makes more sense!"*

Not only did this picture help the student remember cations are positive, it also resolved her confusion over reading about "kayshuns" in a chapter that was supposed to be about ions.

Mnemonic strategies can be complex. Young children, and low-ability older students, may need your scaffolding to use them, and you may need to convince them that the effort is worth the payoff. Over time they will be able to apply these strategies without support. Once learners become expert in a domain, they no longer need mnemonics because the information is encoded in so many ways and so deeply.

Increase Exposure to Material to Be Learned

Learners need multiple high-quality exposures to material in order to remember it effectively. For example, Mr. Glazer exposed his 6th-graders in the vignette to vocabulary words in three different ways. A study of middle school students learning about Antarctica found that in order to remember material over an 8-month period, students had to have at least three activities in which they had full exposure to the material (Nuthall, 2000). (Do not assume that three is a magical number or that learners will remember everything they come across three times.) If the exposure was partial, indirect, or not explicit, more exposure was necessary. A caution is that you should monitor understanding so that *misconceptions* do not have multiple exposures and become entrenched.

Spaced Practice

Exposure to material and practice with it needs to be spaced out over time. For example, Mr. Glazer had his students practice vocabulary words over a week's time, but he could have done all the learning activities back-to-back. Which is best? **Spaced practice** (also called *distributed practice*) is more effective than massed practice (all at one time). Whether you spaced or massed practice can influence how well you remember information several years later. Massed practice creates an illusion of learning, but the material is quickly forgotten; it creates false confidence rather than true competence (Bjork et al., 2013). The *spacing effect* applies to memorizing facts and to learning concepts (Kornell & Bjork, 2008).

keyword method
a mnemonic in which a keyword that *sounds* like the target word is chosen and then an *image* is linked with it.

spaced practice
multiple periods of practicing, or studying, over a period of time rather than in a single massed episode. Also referred to as distributed practice.

Spacing information over time helps reduce the effect of interference, to which young children are more prone. That is, when children have time to consolidate a memory before learning overlapping information, they remember better. In one study, 5-year-olds were given two sets of information, either one right after the other, or with a 48-hour delay between. The group with the delay remembered better when tested later (Darby & Sloutsky, 2015). The delay included a period of sleep. Recall from Chapter 2 that memory is consolidated during sleep.

The longer you want to remember something, the longer the spacing needs to be. Table 4.1 gives approximate lengths of spaced practice for optimal remembering based on research; these are suggestions, not surefire recipes. If Mr. Glazer wants his students to remember their vocabulary words permanently, he will need to do some of the same activities months later. In addition, he could test them—our next suggestion.

TABLE 4.1 Approximate interval of practice needed to remember for long periods	
Length of time to remember	Interval to space practice or review content
1 week	1 day apart
1 month	1 week apart
1 year	3–4 weeks apart
Several years	Several months apart

Adapted from Cepeda, Vul, Rohrer, Wixted, and Pashler (2008); and Rohrer and Pashler (2007).

Test Students

Finally, a fifth way to help your students remember is to test them. This may surprise you, but *testing can be more effective for learning than reviewing the content* or other study strategies (Bjork et al., 2013). Learners better remember content that they have been tested on. Working to recall information for a test boosts learning. It also exercises retrieval skills. Caregivers often test toddlers informally with questions such as "What sound does a cow make?" With older learners, follow these guidelines:

1. Teach your students about the benefits of testing. Learners' most common approach to studying is re-reading, which is not as effective as self-testing.

2. Test frequently. This tends to discourage cramming, to foster spaced practice, and to lower test anxiety because each test counts less. Cramming can result in good short-term, but not long-term, test scores.

3. Use recall rather than recognition tests, such as short-answer rather than multiple-choice. However, multiple-choice tests are better than no tests for enhancing memory.

4. Use cumulative tests. Learners are more likely to integrate new material with old if they know that tests will cover material that goes beyond the time period since the last test.

5. Provide feedback soon after the test. Do not allow learners to solidify the wrong information. For essays and other constructed responses, provide models of an ideal response, or ask learners to share their responses with each other so that they learn from other models.

In this section, you have learned several ways to improve the memory of your students. Helping learners remember important information is a key goal of education. Let's turn now to another key goal of education: helping them learn to reason and problem solve.

4-3 Reasoning and Problem Solving

A 3rd-grade teacher, committed to helping her students connect their mathematics problem-solving skills to the real-world, brings in grocery ads from the newspaper. Today the ads are for brownie mixes from two companies: Martha White's 10-oz for $0.99 and Pillsbury's 15-oz for 2/$3. She asks the students: "Which is a better deal?" An 8-year-old boy responds with great certainty—as though this were an easy task— "Martha White. Because it's 2 for 2 dollars. This other one is 2 for 3 dollars."

A 5th-grade teacher in the same school borrowed the ads. She also asks her students: "Which is a better deal?" An 11-year-old boy responds with less confidence, "They're the same. Thirty ounces would be 3 dollars for the Martha White, and 30 ounces would be 3 dollars for the Pillsbury. Am I right?"

The older boy is right; the younger boy does not take into account that the cheaper package is also smaller. Why do these boys use different problem-solving strategies to arrive at their answers? How can you help learners reason accurately? Before we delve into these questions, let's discuss what reasoning is and how it develops.

Reasoning includes important skills such as critical thinking and problem solving. Reasoning is goal-directed. The goal might be to simply understand something, like why wood floats, or be highly specific, like how to answer question 17 on the quiz. Reasoning often involves inference. You make an inference any time you go beyond the information you have to reach a new conclusion, generalize to a new situation, or find a solution to a problem. Thus, inference is one way to generate new knowledge; it is a source of learning. Inference is a key part of many classroom activities. For example, while you read a book to children, you may periodically ask "what is going to happen next?" Children who cannot make an inference will struggle with reading comprehension.

Problem solving is a type of reasoning. Problem solving in school is often artificial because the teacher or textbook sets up a series of problems in a constrained way that helps learners arrive at correct answers but does little to train them to solve real problems. For example, textbooks introduce a strategy for approaching one type of problem, such as three-digit addition or physics velocity problems. Students are then given practice problems that require the same strategy for solution. They do not have to figure out which strategies are relevant. These *well-structured* problems might be useful during early phases of learning, but *ill-structured* real-world problems that require students to draw upon all their knowledge, not only the strategy they just learned, should also be used. One teacher said of her lesson:

> It was set up too much for success . . . I made the lesson safe for the kids—no fail—which was my goal at the time. I now think I need to let them go through the frustration that goes with problem solving. The lesson probably wouldn't have looked as smooth, but I think it would have stretched the kids more.
> (M. S. Smith, 2000, p. 362)

Children have a repertoire of strategies that can be used to solve a problem. Development occurs when children gradually give up less-effective strategies and increase their use of more-effective, advanced strategies. For example, in one study children learning to multiply used two strategies: (1) retrieval from memory ($2 \times 5 = 10$; more advanced) and (2) adding one digit the number of times dictated by the other digit ($2 \times 5 = 2 + 2 + 2 + 2 + 2 = 10$; less advanced). Most children used both strategies across the school year, but the more-advanced strategy was used more frequently as the children grew older (Siegler, 2000). The advanced strategy was also used more for easier problems and the less advanced for more difficult problems. This is typical. Children select faster, less effortful strategies on easier tasks and slower, more effortful ones on difficult tasks.

Your students' development of problem-solving strategies may resemble overlapping waves. That is, some strategies are used initially and then used less frequently, others become more frequent, others rise from infrequent to frequent and back to infrequent, and still others are seldom ever used. The overlapping wave model is depicted in Figure 4.8. The essence of the model is that children know and use multiple strategies. Earlier, you learned that the same is true for the use of memory strategies. This model contrasts with a Piagetian view of problem-solving development, that children have stage-like improvements in strategy use with age.

4-3a Age Trends in Reasoning and Problem Solving

Reasoning improves with age. This is the result of improved strategies, knowledge, working memory capacity, and ability to manage the process using executive functions and metacognition.

Infancy and Toddlerhood (Birth to 2 Years)

Infants use simple forms of problem solving such as trial-and-error, where they try all possible strategies until one works. Give a 9-month-old a spoon with food, oriented in a way that the infant grasps it as in Figure 4.9. What will happen? The wrong end of the spoon will go in the mouth! Through trial-and-error infants will eventually get the food in their mouth. Around 14 months, they will come up with multiple strategies before it gets to the mouth, such as set the spoon down and rotate it (Keen, 2011).

FIGURE 4.8 Models of Problem-Solving Strategies.

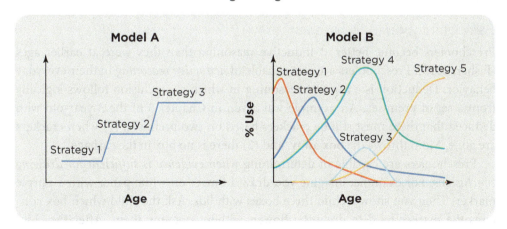

Model A is a stage-based model. According to this model, as children acquire a new, better strategy, they no longer use old, less-adequate strategies. Model B is an overlapping wave model. According to this model, children may use multiple strategies at any given time, but over time increasingly use more-adequate strategies. Research indicates model B more accurately describes children's strategy use. *Source: Siegler (1995).*

FIGURE 4.9 **Problem Solving in Infancy.**

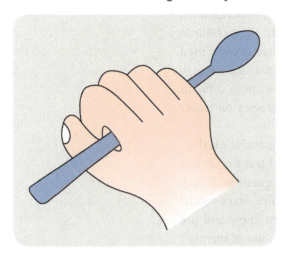

When handed a spoon with the wrong orientation, 9-month-olds put the wrong end in their mouths before realizing they need a different strategy, 14-month-olds realize this halfway to the mouth, and 19-month-olds realize it before picking up the spoon. Strategies include turning the spoon around before picking it up, or grabbing it with the nondominant hand. (It takes inhibitory control to resist using the dominant hand.) Try this out with infants you know. *Source: McCarty, Clifton, and Collard (2001).*

induction
a form of reasoning in which a child detects generalizations, rules, or regularities, often, but not always, through comparison and contrast.

Infants may be born with the ability to use **induction**, or a form of reasoning in which they generalize information from their experience to new situations. For example, when 7-month-olds are shown pictures of two things that are the same (e.g., two fish, two pigs) several times, but then are shown two things that are different (e.g., a pig and a fish), they will show interest in the "differentness." This indicates that they have generalized the concepts long before they know the words, "same" and "different" (Ferry, Hespos, & Gentner, 2015). For another example, when 14-month-olds are shown a toy that rattles, which they are told is a *flum,* they will try to rattle a different-looking toy that is also called a flum (Graham, Kilbreath, & Welder, 2004).

At 30 months (but not 24 months) toddlers use subtle language differences to make inferences. If you say "Bants have stripes," they will infer that another striped animal is a "bant," but they will not do this if you say "*This* bant has stripes" (Graham, Nayer, & Gelman, 2011). They infer stable, inherent attributes about "bants" (Cimpian & Markman, 2011). This means toddlers can take information about an object and use it to make inferences about a new object and they can use induction to generate a simple abstract rule.

Toddlers are notorious for asking "why?" over and over. You might think this is just a bid for conversation. However, if they ask you for an explanation (e.g., "Why are there only red crayons?") and you respond with a nonexplanation (e.g., "There are only red crayons."), they will frown and ask "Why?" again, suggesting they want more than mere conversation. Children seek logical, causal explanations about their world as early as 2 years, and spontaneously give explanations by 3 years (Wellman, 2011). In fact, you may think of young children as "natural scientists." While this is generally delightful, sometimes these little scientists develop misconceptions, which you will have to help them overcome.

Early Childhood (3 to 5 Years)

Preschoolers become better at inductive reasoning than they were at earlier ages (Fisher, 2015). Preschoolers are also capable of *deductive reasoning* in their everyday behavior. Deduction is a form of reasoning in which a conclusion follows logically from a set of premises. An example was given in Chapter 3 of the 3-year-old who deduced that there must still be crackers based on two premises: (1) when crackers are gone, Mom throws the box away, and (2) there is no box in the garbage.

Preschoolers are capable of determining *when evidence is sufficient for drawing conclusions.* For example, imagine you draw a flower on white paper with a purple marker. Then you show a child three boxes with lids. Ask the child which box contains the marker used to draw the flower, without opening them. After the child guesses, ask: "Do you know for sure, or do you have to guess?" Then open the boxes, one at a time, revealing a green, then purple, then red marker, repeating the question. Only when all three boxes are open can the child "know for sure" which box contains the marker used to draw the flower. A more complex version uses four boxes. The fourth box will contain another purple marker. Even when all four boxes are open, the child cannot determine which box contains the marker used to draw the flower. Most preschoolers can do the three-box task, and about 70% can do the four-box task (Klahr & Chen, 2003).

Preschoolers' logic is not flawless, however. When two boxes are open, and one reveals the purple marker, preschoolers often say that purple marker must be the one—even though the third, still-closed box may also contain a purple marker. The single positive instance captures the children's attention and blinds them to the fact that the third box might render the problem unsolvable. Even adults have this bias to some extent, which is why advanced scientific reasoning requires extensive education.

Reasoning can be improved through direct instruction. When children are told *why* their response is correct or incorrect, they improve in reasoning on the purple-marker task (Klahr & Chen, 2003). Five-year-olds, but not 4-year-olds, will improve with simple experience, even without feedback. They also learn faster from feedback, improve more dramatically, and transfer their improved ability to other similar tasks more than 4-year-olds. This is probably the result of better working memory and executive functions.

In summary, while preschoolers have trouble talking about it, their behavior shows that they reason and problem solve (Lucas, Bridgers, Griffiths, & Gopnik, 2014). They gradually become more reliable, systematic, and efficient in their reasoning with age, but there is not a stage-like shift. They are substantially more logical than Piaget believed them to be (Wellman, 2011).

Middle Childhood (6 to 12 Years)

In middle childhood, children become better at distinguishing reasoning from guessing or acting on a hunch (Amsterlaw, 2006). Their private speech becomes more internal (see Chapter 3), although children may still talk out loud to themselves when they try to solve difficult problems. Six to 7-year-olds become capable of "if-then" inference with concrete objects. For example, when told, "If something is a car, then it has a motor," they can answer questions like:

Suppose that something does not have a motor. Is it a car?

Suppose that something has a motor. Is it a car?

Suppose that something is not a car. Does it have a motor?

Such reasoning requires the child to retrieve relevant counterexamples from memory. For example, given the statement, "If something is a car, then it has a motor," children in middle childhood can recognize that something that has a motor does not have to be a car, because they know that boats have motors. They also recognize that the statement *if car then motor* is not the same as *if motor then car* or *only cars have motors*. Children's increased knowledge, speed in retrieving counterexamples, and increased size of working memory help them reason in tasks like these (Markovits & Lortie-Forgues, 2011).

By 2nd grade, learners are capable of limited *scientific thinking*—the ability to generate, test, and evaluate hypotheses against data. However, the ability will grow substantially over the next few years, and they will still struggle with systematically controlling variables (Koerber, Mayer, Oserhaus, Schwippert, & Sodian, 2015). Across middle childhood, learners will also get better at *counter-factual reasoning*. This involves imagining what the world be like now if things had been different in the past (e.g., if you hadn't surfed Facebook last night, would you have done better on today's test?). This type of reasoning is important for life success (to do better on tests and avoid future regrets). For example, imagine Carol walks around in dirty shoes, leaving footprints behind. Ask children, "If Carol had taken her dirty shoes off, would the floor be clean or dirty?" Most 3-year-olds correctly answer "clean." However, if both Carol and Max dirty the floor, and you ask the same question, 18% of 5-year-olds, 50% of 7- to 10-year-olds, and most adolescents correctly answer "dirty" rather than "clean," thanks to naughty Max (Rafetseder & Perner, 2014).

Adolescence (13 to 19 Years)

Younger learners can reason from what they know and experience, but adolescents can suspend what they know and reason from data (Legare, 2014). This helps adolescents become better at scientific thinking. Initially, most adolescents struggle to design a study, collect and analyze data, and draw conclusions. For example, in one study, 6th-, 7th-, and 8th-graders were asked to determine what factors affected flooding in a simulation—water pollution, temperature, soil, or elevation. A computer simulation program allowed them to alter each variable and see what happened to flooding. If they changed only one variable at a time, holding all others constant, they could figure out that temperature and soil affected flooding. Even after experience, not all the students could use logical strategies to find the solution (Kuhn, Black, Keselman, & Kaplan, 2000). However, some students did come to use effective strategies more frequently, suggesting that practice can cause strategy change. Older adolescents, and even adults, will continue to have trouble systematically controlling variables in experiments and anticipating what kind of evidence they will need to support a hypothesis. This is another reason that becoming a scientist takes many years of formal training.

computational thinking
a particular type of large-scale problem-solving using computers

Computational thinking is a problem-solving approach that is increasingly emphasized in secondary schools for career readiness (Grover & Pea, 2013). It involves applying reasoning skills to real-world, technology-oriented problems. You take a large problem and break it down into smaller problems, which you solve using a computer to systematically run repetitive algorithms on quantitative data over and over, and then put the big picture back together to draw conclusions. For example, in a biology class, learners investigate how an epidemic might spread through the school. Students decide what data to put in the model (e.g., how many students in the school, how many classrooms they visit in a day, etc.). They run the model many, many times to try it out, then evaluate and refine the model. This kind of problem solving is used for tasks like mapping the human genome, analyzing voting trends, and building "Google Earth."

Adolescents continue to struggle with two other types of reasoning: (1) Argumentation, or presenting evidence to support your position and counter opposing positions. (2) Reasoning with abstract premises, such as proving a mathematical theorem. The ability to reason with abstract premises emerges in late adolescence—if at all (Markovits & Lortie-Forgues, 2011). For example, consider the premises

"If P is true, then Q must be true. Q is true." Must P be true? Some people think so, but in fact one cannot tell. A nonabstract version of the same statement would be "If something is a car, then it has a motor. The thing has a motor." Does that mean it is a car? No, it might be a plane or boat. Piaget considers abstract reasoning part of formal operations. Later we'll discuss how you can promote these skills in your students.

4-3b Individual Diversity in Reasoning and Problem Solving

Learners of the same age can vary substantially in their reasoning ability. For example, in one study, 23% of 3rd- and 4th-graders discovered how to reason scientifically during a science experiment, but most needed direct instruction, and still others never got it. A precocious 7% were able to do it before the study began (Klahr & Nigam, 2004).

What Do Individual Differences in Reasoning Predict?

Reasoning ability influences academic achievement and is a key part of intelligence. It also influences antisocial behavior. For example, Steven may be frustrated on the school bus by Allen's loud talking. If he is poor at problem solving, he might slug Allen. Antisocial children tend to come from families with meager problem-solving abilities (Spotts, Neiderhiser, Hetherington, & Reiss, 2001). You will learn more about this in Chapter 10. Indeed, differences in reasoning ability influence all aspects of behavior. For example, reasoning ability influences how successful you are at parenting, as a citizen in a democracy, and in your career as a teacher—teachers must reason about how to teach, test, and discipline learners.

What Predicts Individual Differences in Reasoning?

Learners with faster processing speed and better executive functions have advanced reasoning ability. Thus, the home environment, which predicts these basic, underlying information processing skills, also affects reasoning ability. Children with college-educated parents score higher on reasoning tests than children with less-educated parents (Koerber et al., 2015). In addition, children with parents who talk with them about judging evidence have better reasoning ability. They may use statements such as "Some people have a different opinion because...." or "You could find out if you..." (Luce, Callanan, & Smilovic, 2013). As a teacher, you can use this same conversational style with students (Photo 4.2). Let's look at other classroom implications next.

Fuse/Jupiter Images

PHOTO 4.2 Teachers promote learning when they model or provide feedback to students.

4-3c Classroom Implications of Reasoning and Problem Solving

Reasoning ability promotes achievement because many school activities (e.g., solving an algebra equation or writing a persuasive essay) require reasoning. One of the K–12 Common Core Standards is that students become proficient in *logical arguments based on substantive claims, sound reasoning, and relevant evidence*. Great teachers do not just teach *what* to think, but also *how* to think. Figure 4.10 shows that learners' reasoning skills increase with schooling. You can promote reasoning ability in your learners in six ways: (1) increase knowledge, (2) require explanations, (3) teach more-effective strategies, (4) foster argument, (5) use inquiry-based lessons, and (6) directly train reasoning. Let's look at how to do this in more detail.

Increase Knowledge

Can you solve the following analogy? Beat is to 45 degrees as Reach is to _____.

The answer is "90 degrees." *Beat* and *reach* are sailing terms. If you are not familiar with sailing, you could not logically derive an answer. Analogy-based reasoning is heavily dependent on your prior knowledge. Indeed reasoning in any area is dependent on your knowledge in that area. This is one reason members of groups with less school-relevant knowledge have difficulty with problem solving on school tasks. (Do you recognize this as part of cultural capital from Chapter 1?) Some educators argue that education should focus more on reasoning abilities rather than on "rote" knowledge. Effective educators do both. While it is possible to increase knowledge without improving reasoning (Finn et al., 2014), it is very difficult to improve reasoning without increasing knowledge. Can you imagine a physician improving disease diagnosis without increased knowledge of diseases?

FIGURE 4.10 Schooling Improves Children's Thinking.

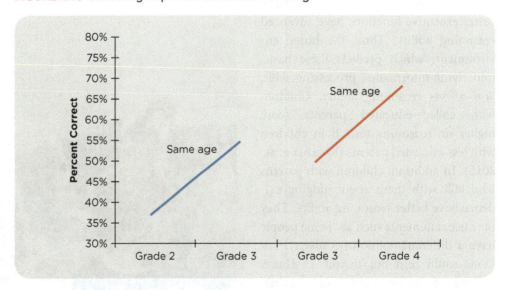

Two groups of children who were the same age, but in different grades, were compared. (They were either young for their grade, or old for their grade.) Children who had been in school a year longer performed higher on a test of scientific thinking than their same-age peers in the lower grade. *Source: Koerber, Mayer, Osterhaus, Schwippert, and Sodian (2015), p. 332.*

Require Explanations

When you ask learners to explain their own reasoning, or to explain another's reasoning, you promote cognitive development. This seemingly simple request forces learners to focus on what caused what and to make generalizations. It also guides further exploration with the content (Legare, 2014). Frequently ask, "How?" or "Why?" Preschoolers can answer questions like "Why did they do that?" and older students can answer the more difficult "Why did they think that?" (Wellman, 2011). *Asking for explanations may be the most important way to improve your students' reasoning ability.* It applies to the next point as well, because when learners must explain strategy use, their understanding of strategies grows (Rittle-Johnson, 2007).

Teach Effective Strategies

You will help your students learn more-effective strategies if you follow these guidelines:

1. Use feedback and modeling. Providing explicit feedback about whether the strategy was successful and allowing learners to observe models are both effective (Hattie & Timperley, 2007). For example, in a *Tic-Tac-Toe* game children watched a model use a more sophisticated strategy than the children themselves used. The strategy was to find two separate winning paths, or a fork, so that even if your opponent blocks one, you can win with the other path. Second-graders and some kindergarteners were able to learn the strategy whether the model directly explained the strategy or they inferred the explanation themselves (Rittle-Johnson, 2007). In another example, when a 10th-grader was struggling with literary analysis of *To Kill a Mockingbird*, her teacher modeled how he would extract themes and symbols and think about characterization. In Chapter 3 you learned that students learned by observing another student successfully solve physics problems, and that this was more effective than watching an expert work an example (Craig, Chi, & VanLehn, 2009).

2. Ask students to reflect on the problem and ask themselves "What strategy could be used to solve this problem?" or "How is this problem similar to the previous problem?" Students given this metacognitive-strategy training develop better reasoning ability (Kramarski & Mevarech, 2003).

3. Ask students to share and compare strategies. For example, 7th- and 8th-graders might be asked to compare two different strategies to solve algebra problems like $5(y + 1) = 3(y + 1) + 8$. Expert math teachers ask students: (1) "Describe how your strategies are different" and (2) "Which is the most efficient strategy?" This helps students learn procedures as well as abstract concepts. However, there are two important caveats. First, this approach is most effective when followed by direct instruction (Rittle-Johnson & Star, 2009). Second, for students who have no prior knowledge, it may be ideal to practice just one strategy for a while so their working memory is not overloaded (Rittle-Johnson, Star, & Durkin, 2009).

Don't expect that students will use a new strategy effectively right away. Sometimes when they try a new, better strategy they don't have better performance. However, if they keep using the strategy, it eventually leads to better performance (Schwenck, Bjorklund, & Schneider, 2007).

Knowing how to use a strategy to solve a problem does not guarantee that a student will choose to use it. For example, a strategy for ensuring you get the right answer in a physics problem is to write out the units as well as the numbers (e.g., 10 m/s $\times$ 15 s = 150 m), and make sure the units on both sides of the equal sign cancel out. Students resist using this strategy because it takes effort. As a teacher, you can convince them of the effectiveness of this strategy by providing examples from their own work showing incorrect responses because they did not use the strategy.

Foster Argument

Research supports both Piaget's and Vygotsky's views that argument promotes reasoning ability. Argument also promotes metacognition. Argumentation skills do not necessarily develop naturally by adolescence, but they can be trained by skilled teachers (Kuhn & Crowell, 2011). To foster rational argument in your class:

1. Require learners to respectfully defend their claims. Ask learners to elaborate on their reasons, support them with evidence, and evaluate them. This is effective in an approach known as "collaborative reasoning," where students engage in small group, student-led discussions to construct arguments within a rich web of evidence and logic (Wu, Anderson, Nguyen-Jahiel, & Miller, 2013).

2. Require students to respectfully identify and address weaknesses in the opponent's argument. This may be even more effective than having them explain their own position (Kuhn & Udell, 2003).

In one study teachers guided 6th-graders through a process of taking a stance on an issue, working with a partner to collect evidence to support their stance, blogging with same-stance and opposite-stance classmates, having a whole-class debate, and writing a final essay (Kuhn & Crowell, 2011). The students developed better reasoning skills compared to students who merely wrote an essay on the topic but did not have this rich argumentative experience. Similar effects have been found for 2nd- and 4th-graders (Lin et al., 2012; Walker, Wartenberg, & Winner, 2013).

Use Inquiry-Based Lessons

You promote reasoning skills when you involve learners in inquiry experiences. With young children this may take the form of informal exploration and play, or directed activities. For example, you might encourage learners to put objects with different weights in a toy truck on a ramp. You can guide experimentation with questions such as "how can you make it go further or faster?" You might ask preschoolers to predict whether small or large objects are more likely to float. They will often choose the larger one, because it is "stronger." Let them try it out. When they experience that they are wrong, 4-year-olds (but not 3-year-olds) will revise their hypotheses (Gropen, Clark-Chiarelli, Hoisington, & Ehrlich, 2011).

With older students, inquiry may take the form of science experiments that emphasize controlling variables, with multiple replications, peer review, and using data rather than preexisting beliefs to guide conclusions. *However, explicit guidance can be critically important.* For example, teachers in an urban 5th grade in New York had their students plant seeds in multiple cups that contained three different types of soil (Hogan & Corey, 2001). They wanted their students to investigate which soil was best for growth by applying the scientific method, such as treating all the plants identically so the only thing that varies is the soil, or replicating because if one plant died in soil A, it could have been a bad seed, but if many died, it might be poor soil. Many of the students never did understand these concepts. Some thought that the purpose of replication was to give everyone a turn, some focused only on the data from their own plants rather than from the whole class, some said that they already knew which soil was best and did not need an experiment, and some saw the experiment as a sort of race to see who would "win." This study, along with the experiment on flooding discussed earlier, and many other studies, suggest that direct instruction may be more effective than unguided inquiry for immediate learning and for applying the learning to new kinds of problems (Klahr, Zimmerman, & Jirout, 2011).

Directly Train Reasoning

When you foster argument in your classroom, ask challenging questions, and use inquiry-based lessons, you are giving students practice reasoning. For example, when you read a book about animals to toddlers, you might point to one animal and say, "This one has a wing. Does one of these other animals have a wing?" Children have to use reasoning through induction to figure out what a wing is (Gentner, Loewenstein, & Hung, 2007). Some media, like *Sesame Street* and *Highlights* magazine, have tasks designed to train reasoning in preschoolers, like those shown in Figure 4.11. Practice with such tasks improves reasoning if children are taught to ask questions like, "What do I have to look at? What should I do to find the solution? How should I check my solution?" After just ten 45-minute practice sessions, children score better on intelligence tests compared to control groups. (Induction tasks are part of many intelligence tests because induction is a critical component of intelligence.) After such training, children learn more during later academic lessons across subjects like biology, geography, grammar, and foreign languages. The effect size is impressive (0.50 to 0.70) and long lasting (Klauer & Phye, 2008).

With older children you can train one of the most challenging skills—reasoning from abstract premises—by asking them to reason from false premises. For example,

FIGURE 4.11 Tasks for Training Problem-Solving Ability.

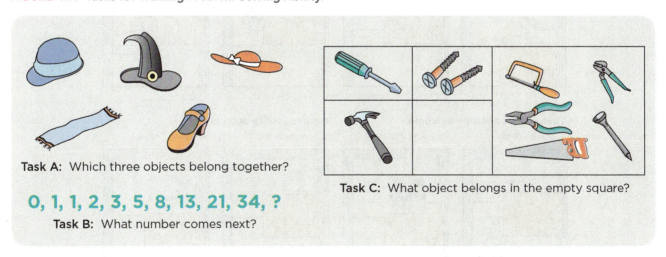

Task A: Which three objects belong together?

0, 1, 1, 2, 3, 5, 8, 13, 21, 34, ?

Task B: What number comes next?

Task C: What object belongs in the empty square?

Inductive reasoning involves comparison. Children make sense of the world by searching for similarities and differences in objects or the relationships between them. Tasks like these help children practice reasoning. Task A requires children to generalize attributes and classify. Tasks B and C require children to recognize relationships.

tell them "On another planet ketchup makes things clean. If ketchup touches your shirt, what will happen to it?" It will become clean, of course! This kind of mind-play promotes abstract reasoning because it forces reasoning based on pure logic rather than on personal experience. Reasoning from false premises is an intermediary step between reasoning with concrete and abstract premises. This approach works with students as young as 9 to 11, but generally not younger (Markovits & Lortie-Forgues, 2011). We'll talk more about mind play in Chapter 11.

In Chapter 3 and this chapter you have learned about four theories of learning and cognitive development that can be applied to your classroom. Let's finish our discussion of these theories by comparing how they might apply to learning mathematics, since increasing math achievement is currently a national priority. In Chapter 12 we will focus on how they might apply to learning reading and writing. If you do not teach math or literacy, you can use your reasoning ability to extrapolate to other content areas.

4-4 Putting the Theories to Work: The Case of Mathematics

A 5-month-old sits before a large box (see Figure 4.12). He sees a hand holding one mouse doll enter the box from a hole in the side and place the doll in the box. The hand retreats empty. A screen rotates up to hide the doll. The infant sees the hand enter from the side with a doll again. It presumably adds another doll behind the screen because it also retreats empty. The screen then rotates down to reveal only one doll. (A doll was removed through a trap door.) The infant looks longer at this impossible event than he did in preceding trials when two dolls were revealed.

FIGURE 4.12 Infant Number Sense.

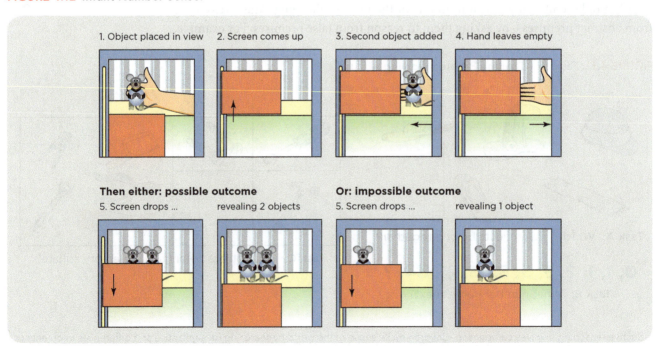

Infants look longer at the impossible event, suggesting rudimentary number sense. *Source: Wynn (1992).*

We suspect the infant looks longer at the impossible event because he is surprised that there are not two dolls in the box. Chimpanzees have similar reactions (Beran & Beran, 2004). Does this mean that infants and chimpanzees can count? Can they add? At age 3, our daughter enthusiastically announced a revelation: "6! There are 6 people in our family: 3 girls and 3 boys!" If infants, 3-year-olds, and chimpanzees can do basic math, why do children have so much difficulty learning math in school? In the following section, we briefly apply what you have learned in this and the previous chapter to the domain of mathematics. You will also be introduced to some concepts from Chapter 5. Key concepts are italicized. First, we will begin with an overview of math development.

4-4a Age Trends in Mathematics

Infants have an intuitive, imprecise sense of number (called the *approximate number system*) that stays with them across their lifetime. For example, some 6-month-olds will gaze longer at a screen that shows dots that change in number, than a screen that shows the same number of dots that change color (Starr, Libertus, & Brannon, 2013). This suggests they are able to detect changes in quantity. Because number sense is present as soon as infants are old enough to be testable, it may be a biologically determined, innate ability that does not depend on learning—or a *core domain* (Feigenson, Libertus, & Halberda, 2013). However, infants can succeed in these types of tasks only with small quantities (Desrochers, 2008). Furthermore, infants' innate number sense stands in stark contrast to other math concepts like propositions, percentages, and algebra that are acquired later with considerable effort and varied success.

Informal Math

Preschoolers' understanding of basic math concepts is referred to as "informal math" because it is acquired without formal schooling. What kinds of math abilities do preschoolers have? They understand that adding to a set produces more and taking away produces less. They can tell which quantities are larger. For example, they know a row of 12 has more than a row of 8 objects, even before they can count. Typical children begin counting around 2 years. For example, 22-month-old Connor counted his blocks by pointing to each one in turn and saying, "nine, nine, nine, nine." He had the concept of assigning a number to each object, but he did not yet know the number names except nine. Learning number names begins at 2 to 3 years. At 4 to 5 years, most children can count up to 20 or even 100, and may use a combination of finger and verbal counting. They can evenly divide treats. They can also solve simple arithmetic problems: "If you had 4 candies and someone gave you 3 more, how many candies would you have?" (Engel, Claessens, & Finch, 2013; Huntley-Fenner & Cannon, 2000).

Although most children will acquire these informal math skills before entering school, low-SES preschoolers may not (Jordan, Kaplan, Olah, & Locuniak, 2006). This is a concern because, as you learned in Chapter 1, a strong predictor of academic achievement—even stronger than reading ability—is math skills at entry into kindergarten (Duncan et al., 2007; Romano, Babchishin, Pagani, & Kohen, 2010). Given that other preschoolers are developmentally ready to reason about math, low-SES preschoolers' meager math skills may be due to less opportunity to learn these concepts.

Denise Hager/Catchlight Visual Services/Alamy Stock Photo

What can you do to help? First, use math talk with young children, such as "You can have three crackers" or "Count how many cups we need for snack" (Photo 4.3). Use math-related vocabulary often (e.g., minus, bigger, altogether, edge, short, middle). This helps children develop better number sense (e.g., Jordan et al., 2012). Second, play number-oriented board games. Playing games that involve counting pieces along a number line, like *Chutes and Ladders™*, or simple homemade games, helps preschoolers develop better math skills, particularly if you ask them to say the number they spun and count the spaces as they move along (Ramani, Siegler, & Hitti, 2012). Finally, directly teach math. There are several play-like math curricula such as *Big Math for Little Kids*, *Building Blocks*, *Number Worlds*, and *Rightstart* that are designed for 3- to 5-year-olds based on developmental science (Clements & Sarama, 2008; Ginsburg, Lee, & Boyd, 2008). The *Building Blocks* curriculum involves *asking children to explain their strategies* (e.g., "How did you know?"), and *spacing practice* over time. Some preschool teachers resist using math curricula, preferring that children learn through teachable moments in naturally emerging play. Unfortunately, many such moments are overlooked and those that are noticed may not provide enough opportunity to learn for low-SES children (Ginsburg et al., 2008).

PHOTO 4.3 Use math talk with toddlers and preschoolers, like "How many candies do you have?"

School-Age Math

As children enter kindergarten, most are skilled at counting, and understand numbers up to 10 (Engle et al., 2013). They commonly progress through the following strategies when solving a simple problem like 2 + 7: counting-all (1, 2, 3, 4, 5, 6, 7, 8, 9), to counting-on-from-the-first-number (2, 3, 4, 5, 6, 7, 8, 9), to counting-on-from-the-largest-number (7, 8, 9). Thus, children are *using more sophisticated strategies* and becoming faster and more accurate at addition. They are beginning to understand place value, and most master it by 2nd grade (Mix, Prather, Smith, & Stockton, 2014). If they do not, they are likely to have long-term math difficulties because this is foundational to higher-level mathematics (Byrge, Smith, & Mix, 2014).

To master fractions and other mathematical concepts, children must transition from additive to multiplicative reasoning. Children can be taught multiplication/division as young as age 4, like: "If 4 dogs want 3 treats each, how many treats do you need?" Typical children develop these concepts without instruction by age 6 for small numbers, perhaps because they have experience with division each time they share with peers. However, understanding the concept does not mean they will do computations correctly or use efficient strategies. This takes instruction and practice. In U.S. schools, relevant instruction usually begins in 2nd grade. Children who are going to have serious difficulties with math are usually identified by about 3rd grade.

Children's counting strategies are eventually replaced by *memorizing* facts like 2 + 3 = 5 and 3 × 4 = 12. Doubles (5 + 5 and 6 × 6) are memorized especially rapidly. These facts are stored in long-term memory as the result of frequent *spaced practice*. *Retrieval* is an efficient *problem-solving strategy*, as it becomes more rapid

think
about **this**

Compared to low-SES pre-schoolers, middle-SES pre-schoolers are twice as likely to play board games like *Chutes and Ladders* and card games like *Uno*, whereas low-SES preschoolers are twice as likely to play video games (Ramani & Siegler, 2008). How might this partially explain lower academic achievement of low-SES children? Most cultures have children's games that promote such basic skills. Why might low-SES children not engage in them? Defend your argument using the Family Investment and Family Stress models and cultural capital from Chapter 1.

children as thinking differently than adults, as Piaget does, they portray children as knowing less and having slower processing and more-limited working memory.

All aspects of information processing are involved in math. To solve the problem $2 + 3 = 4 + ?$ a child must access *long-term memory* to get $2 + 3 = 5$, then maintain this in *working memory* while again accessing long-term memory to get $5 - 4 = ?$. *Long-term memory* of addition facts helps them *reason* about the problem. *Working memory* allows children to compare previously solved problems with the current problem. *Executive functions* keep them moving through the steps of problem solving and flexibly selecting the most appropriate strategy. For example, mathematically skilled students use a mental approach on easy items and an algorithm on more difficult problems. Instead of using an algorithm for the problem $(736 \div 32)$, they might *chunk* the problem like this: $20 \times 32 = 640$, $3 \times 32 = 96$, therefore, $23 \times 32 = 736$ (Hickendorff et al., 2010). *Metacognition* acts on feedback about whether the strategy was useful or not.

Research shows that both age-related growth in math ability and individual differences in math ability are linked to each component of the information-processing model. For example, learners of all ages who have better *working memory* and *executive functions* are faster and more accurate at addition, multiplication, algebra, and solving word problems. In contrast, children with slow processing speed and limited working memory are likely to have math disability. *Knowledge* also makes a contribution. Learners who know their numbers and youth who can readily retrieve math facts or theorems from long-term memory have higher math achievement.[3]

This suggests that your role as a teacher is to help learners acquire better information-processing skills and more knowledge. You can help learners *memorize* math facts and procedures through *spaced practice* and *frequent tests.* Instead of practicing one type of problem in a massed block and then moving on to the next type, space practice of each type across time. Having more knowledge will help your students with problem solving, because one of the most efficient problem-solving strategies is simple retrieval of the answer from memory. You can help learners chunk problems to *reduce memory load.* You can teach other strategies through *direct instruction* and *modeling,* although you have to be careful not to overwhelm their working memory capacity with complex strategies (Swanson, 2014). The *overlapping wave model* suggests that children will gradually shift toward more efficient strategies. You can facilitate this shift by providing *feedback* to students. You can also make children aware of their strategies by having them *explain the strategy*, which facilitates metacognition.

In summary, some number sense is innate. However, children still have much to learn about math. While Piaget underestimated young children's mathematical reasoning ability, he was correct that children construct their own understandings (and misconceptions) of math. Contrary to Piaget's theory, children do not follow an orderly progression in moving from less-advanced to more-advanced strategies for solving problems, but rather follow an overlapping wave model. They also do not reinvent the numerical notation system; rather, as Vygotsky pointed out, they learn this cultural tool in informal interactions as well as in formal school settings. Behaviorists tend to focus on very specific behavioral objectives in math learning, with emphasis on skill and drill. Behaviorists and constructivists are often at odds with one another—educators

---

[3] Many studies have found this, some of which are listed here: Bull and Lee (2014); Clark, Pritchard, and Woodward (2010); Fenesi, Sana, Kim, and Shore (2015); Geary (2011); Viterbori, Usai, Traverso, and de Franchis (2015); Welsh et al. (2010).

tend to avoid one and support the other. The information-processing model, on the other hand, fits either perspective. Information-processing researchers have demonstrated that children learn by direct instruction, skill-and-drill practice, modeling from more-skilled others, and constructing their own knowledge through reasoning and metacognition as they receive feedback about the success of their strategies.

How to teach math has been a polarizing issue, particularly when traditional methods (often based on behaviorism) are compared with reform methods (often based on constructivism). Yet, when implemented well, both methods may be effective. Different math curricula are based on different theories, yet there are only small effect sizes on student achievement when researchers compare one curriculum with another (0.10 at elementary, 0.03 at secondary school), probably because most curricula are well designed (e.g., IES, 2011). The What Works Clearinghouse (see Chapter 1) has reviews of many curricula to help your school make good decisions. They also have practice guides for early childhood, elementary, and secondary school math instruction (see resource list). Other aspects of teaching, such as using cooperative learning, promoting time-on-task, and motivating students, have larger effect sizes than curricula (Harwell et al., 2009; Slavin, Cheung, Groff, & Lake, 2008; Slavin & Lake, 2008). You'll learn about these topics in later chapters, so stay tuned.

reflections on practice

My Teaching

Efficient information processing forms the basis of good memory and problem solving, which are important for success at school. You can influence each of these abilities in your students. Ask yourself the following questions as you think about your classroom practices:

1. Do I help learners focus attention on critical information?

2. Do I keep working memory load to a level that is appropriate for my students (e.g., by reducing distractions, repeating key points, speaking slowly when covering new ideas, providing partial notes)? Am I helping them develop a strong knowledge base so that some processing is "automatic"?

3. Do I exercise learners' executive functions through the kinds of activities I plan for them? Do I make sure children have food, sleep, and exercise so that their executive functioning is optimal?

4. Do I recognize that most memory exists as fuzzy traces and plan instruction accordingly? When learners need verbatim traces, do I help them memorize? Do I teach and use memory strategies like organization, elaboration, and mnemonics?

5. Do I teach in a way that shows connections between different topics and helps learners construct a rich mental web of information? Do I give learners multiple exposures to key concepts over time (i.e., spaced practice)?

6. Do I teach reasoning and problem solving in my classroom, in addition to content? Do I provide learners with both well-structured and ill-structured problems? Do I provide opportunities to practice problem solving?

7. Do I require learners to explain or justify their (or others') thinking? Do I provide feedback that will improve problem-solving ability rather than just indicate if learners are correct? Do I foster informed debate in the classroom when appropriate?

Summary of Age Trends in Information Processing

	Information Processing	Memory	Reasoning and Problem Solving
Infancy & Toddlerhood (Prenatal–2 Years)	• Processing speed is slow due to limited myelination, knowledge, and language. • Infants are capable of paying attention and resisting distractions. • The A-not-B task shows that infants have some inhibitory control. • Individual differences appear in infancy.	• Fetuses can remember simple things for a few weeks. • Deferred imitation studies suggest that infants can remember action sequences for several weeks and that their memory increases steadily. • Yet, early events are seldom verbally recalled due to childhood amnesia.	• Infants can do rudimentary problem solving, like trial and error. • Toddlers can induce a simple abstract rule or infer attributes of a thing based on subtle language distinctions. • They seek to explain and make sense of their world.
Early Childhood (3–5 Years)	• Speed of processing increases. • Executive functions improve dramatically from 3–5 years. Children become able to do the card rule-switching task.	• Long-term memory improves from 3 to 5 years, but may need to be supported by cues. • Children are particularly susceptible to interference. • Children make source monitoring errors. • Children are poor at using memory strategies.	• Between 3 and 5 years, children learn more effective problem-solving strategies through experience or instruction. • They understand that inference is a source of knowledge. • They can reason by analogy, and, in simple tasks, deduce when evidence is sufficient to draw conclusions. That is, preschoolers are logical.
Middle Childhood (6–12 Years)	• Speed of processing continues to increase, but the rate of increase slows. • Working memory improves substantially and reaches adult levels for simple tasks. • Metamemory becomes apparent. • Cognitive flexibility and inhibitory control steadily increases.	• Children have greater long-term memory than do preschoolers. They have larger webs of knowledge. • Metamemory, remembering to do something in the future, and source monitoring all improve. • Deliberate use of memory strategies improves. Rehearsal is most common, but children can use organization strategies effectively. They can use elaboration, but need scaffolding. They learn to take useful notes.	• Children become better at distinguishing guessing from inferences. • Private speech becomes more covert during problem solving. • Children develop formal "if-then" reasoning. Greater prior knowledge helps them generate counterexamples. • They are capable of simple scientific reasoning. • Children become more likely to try new strategies if old ones don't work.
Adolescence (13–19 Years)	• Processing speed peaks. • Working memory capacity (for complex tasks) and other executive functions increase dramatically (peaking in early adulthood). • Knowledge increases and peaks in late adulthood.	• Fuzzy and verbatim memory increase. • Adolescents continue to use rehearsal and organization strategies, but also become effective at using elaboration on their own. • Particularly susceptible to false memories.	• Some adolescents develop complex scientific reasoning—systematically varying only one factor at a time in order to draw conclusions. • Some can reason about abstract hypothetical propositions that may be counter to the real world. • They can distinguish logical from nonlogical statements given a set of premises.

⌄ **Professional Resource Download**

Chapter Summary

4-1 Information Processing

- The information-processing framework explains how learners acquire, store, and use information. The three-layer model includes the sensory register (large capacity, brief duration), long-term memory (unlimited capacity, long duration), and working memory (limited capacity, brief duration). Attention is usually required for information to be encoded (stored) into memory. Executive functions (working memory, cognitive flexibility, and inhibition) control flow of information, attention shifting, and metacognition.

- There are individual differences in each component of the model. These differences appear in infancy and are stable. They are linked to interactions of genes and environment (e.g., quality of parenting and poverty). These differences predict academic and social skills.

- Teachers should avoid overloading working memory and help learners focus their attention on important details. Teachers can also help learners exercise executive functions.

- Attention-deficit/hyperactivity disorder, the most common neurobehavioral disorder among children, is believed to result from poor executive functions. ADHD is linked to poorer academic achievement and to behavior problems.

4-2 Memory

- There are two common errors in memory: (1) Forgetting, which is due to decay, retrieval problems, and interference, and (2) False memories, which are intelligent constructions of things that did not happen. Source monitoring error refers to forgetting the source of information.

- Most memory is a fuzzy trace rather than a verbatim trace. To remember details, learners must use memory strategies.

- Memory strategies include rehearsal, organization, elaboration, and mnemonics. Mnemonics are particularly appropriate for material that is not yet meaningful to the student. Teachers should teach memory strategies.

- Prior knowledge facilitates remembering new knowledge and can compensate for low intelligence. Dense networks of related knowledge facilitate retrieval. Schemas and scripts, which are interconnected networks of information, facilitate learning.

- Teachers should help learners connect pieces of knowledge, provide multiple exposures to the material, space practice, and test frequently. Teachers should converse with learners about things to be remembered.

4-3 Reasoning and Problem Solving

- *Reasoning* usually involves some kind of inference. *Problem solving* is a type of reasoning. School-based problems tend to be artificial and well-structured, while real-world problems are ill-structured.

- The overlapping wave model represents the way that learners improve in the strategies that they use to solve problems and to memorize.

- Antecedents of individual differences in reasoning include information processing ability, prior knowledge, and quality of parenting. Poor reasoning ability can affect functioning in all domains of life, including academic and social domains.

- Teachers can promote reasoning skills by increasing knowledge, requiring explanations, teaching effective strategies (through modeling, feedback, and metacognition), fostering classroom argument, giving direct training, and guiding inquiry-based lessons.

4-4 Putting the Theories to Work: The Case of Mathematics

- Number sense may be a core domain; it is present in infants. Rudimentary concepts are acquired informally by preschoolers. However, schooling is necessary for more advanced math.

- The behaviorist view is that math learning is hierarchical, with basic skills learned first through drill-and-practice and direct instruction. The Piagetian constructivist view is that learners construct their own arithmetic. The sociocultural view is that mathematics is a cultural tool acquired in interaction with others. The information-processing view is that age trends and individual differences in math ability are due to prior knowledge, processing speed, and executive functions.

Steve Debenport/E+/Getty Images

Cognitive Ability: Intelligence, Talent, and Achievement

Are some children academically talented because they are intelligent, because they practice more, or for some other reason? In this chapter, we will discuss what intelligence and talent are and how they relate to achievement. **After you read this chapter, you will be able to:**

5-1   Define intelligence and describe what it predicts.

5-2   Discuss how talent and expertise develop.

5-3   Analyze how you can improve your students' achievement.

5-1 Intelligence

Alex and Chuck are two 12-year-old boys in the same suburban school, but in different 6th-grade classes. Alex's teacher presents a 20-minute group lesson on homonyms. He then passes out two worksheets to give students practice with homonyms. The homonym worksheets include items like: "I took (there, their, they're) book." and "He began to play the (bass, base)." Alex takes 25 minutes to complete the first worksheet. Then he notices that the rest of the class has already finished and has started other tasks. He quickly completes the second worksheet in 5 minutes. The first worksheet has three errors and the second has six errors.

Chuck is given the same two worksheets to complete during lunch in the cafeteria. Chuck completes both worksheets in 4 minutes while also joking and talking with friends. He completes the items he is sure about first, and then goes back to those he is less sure about. Chuck says the worksheets are "too easy" for 6th grade. He cannot remember having had a lesson on homonyms.

intelligence
a general mental capability including the ability to reason, plan, solve problems, think abstractly, comprehend complex ideas, adapt, and learn quickly.

What might account for the difference between how Alex and Chuck perform on this task? Neither seems to have a problem focusing attention on the task. Is it because Chuck reads more fluently, which results in greater prior knowledge of words, better memory for homonyms, and faster information processing? Why might Chuck have greater reading expertise? Perhaps these boys have different levels of **intelligence**.

None of the three classic theories that you read about in Chapter 3—behaviorism, cognitive developmental theory, or sociocultural theory—emphasizes individual differences in cognitive ability. Jean Piaget, founder of cognitive developmental theory, was not very interested in individual differences but focused on age trends instead. While he noticed individual differences in the rate at which children move from stage to stage, he described patterns of how *most* children develop rather than how they *differ*. Therefore, it is difficult to explain the difference in Alex's and Chuck's performances from a Piagetian perspective. Teachers, however, are keenly interested in such differences because it is a significant challenge to teach children with quite different levels of intelligence in the same classroom.

5-1a What Is Intelligence?

The following widely used definition appeared in a statement that was signed by 52 experts in intelligence:

Intelligence is a very general mental capability that, among other things, involves the ability to reason, plan, solve problems, think abstractly, comprehend complex ideas, learn quickly and learn from experience. It is not merely book learning, a narrow academic skill, or test-taking smarts. Rather, it reflects a broader and deeper capability for comprehending our surroundings—"catching on," "making sense" of things, or "figuring out" what to do (Gottfredson, 1997, p. 13).

These attributes of intelligence should feel familiar to you from Chapter 4. The basis of intelligence is fast, accurate information processing. In particular, working memory and executive functions may be the core of intelligence because they form the capacity to control attention and the capacity to zoom in and zoom out from the big picture to the small pieces of a task without losing track of the goal (Swanson, 2008). For example, 1st- through 5th-graders who were in a gifted program because they had high IQ scores had faster processing speed, larger working-memory capacity, and better executive functions, including attention control, than their peers in regular classrooms (Johnson, Im-Bolter, & Pascual-Leone, 2003). They tended to perform information-processing tasks comparable to average children who were 1 to 2 years older.

Two components of intelligence are fluid and crystallized intelligence. *Fluid intelligence* is the application of reasoning skills to novel situations and includes reasoning and problem solving; fluid intelligence is linked with working memory. The ability to use existing knowledge is sometimes referred to as *crystallized intelligence* and is linked with long-term memory.

Intelligence as *g*

Children who score highly on one cognitive test tend to score highly on other tests as well. This means that test scores correlate with each other across a wide range of cognitive abilities, such as intelligence tests, college entrance tests (e.g., the SAT and ACT), vocabulary tests, analogy tests, proficiency tests, and so forth. For example, the SAT correlates a whopping 0.82 with the military's IQ test (Frey & Detterman, 2004). You may know individuals who seem to be exceptions, such as someone who received a high score on the SAT math section but a low score on the SAT verbal section. However, individual exceptions do not invalidate the general finding that high scores tend to go with high scores.

Some researchers interpret the correlation among different tests as evidence that there is a *general cognitive ability* that underlies specific cognitive abilities. This general cognitive ability is called *g*, or general intelligence. General intelligence can be thought of as a cognitive capability that cannot be directly observed, but that accounts for all sorts of intelligent behavior and learning.

g
general intelligence.

Most experts would agree that intelligence can be domain-specific. For example, mathematics, literacy, and social competence are domains. Through experience and practice, learners can have high levels of expertise in some domains without having high *g*. They have high crystallized intelligence for that domain. Also, *expertise in a domain can compensate for low* g *in that domain.* Through effort, one can develop expertise in a domain without high *g*. Thus, when you have students who are particularly intelligent in a subject area, it may be the result of either high *g* or domain-specific crystallized ability that developed through experience and practice.

Two theories involving different components of intelligence that apply to your classroom are discussed next.

Theory of Successful Intelligence

Noted psychologist Robert Sternberg expands the common notion of intelligence. He points out that intelligence tests predict academic achievement because that is what they were designed to do, but it would be more useful to predict successful adaptation to life. He defines *successful intelligence* as "the use of an integrated set of abilities needed to attain success in life, however an individual defines it, within

Have you heard parents refer to a child with learning difficulties as smart? Is it possible for a child to have trouble with school learning yet be "bright" in other ways? If intelligence means to learn complex material quickly and easily, how is this possible?

his or her sociocultural context" (Sternberg, Grigorenko, & Zhang, 2008, p. 487). Success may be different if you are a Yup'ik Eskimo child in Alaska concerned with fishing, a Brazilian street child concerned with selling goods on the street, or a middle-class suburban American concerned with admission to an elite university. Success depends on taking advantage of one's strengths and compensating for one's weaknesses, and possibly changing weaknesses to strengths.

According to Sternberg there are three components to successful intelligence: (1) analytic, (2) practical, and (3) creative. The *analytic* component includes the ability to recognize and define a problem, generate a solution, and evaluate progress toward a solution. It is measured on typical intelligence tests. The *practical* component of intelligence includes putting ideas into practice in the real world, being street smart, selecting activities and settings that match one's abilities, and changing settings as much as possible to match one's abilities. For example, the following 6th-grade girl shows practical intelligence:

> *Just before band practice, students hurriedly take their instruments out of their cases and leave the cases in the hallway just outside class, which not only creates a safety hazard but also a cluttered mess. However, if students put their cases in their lockers, it takes so long to unlock their lockers that they are late to their next class. As a solution to this problem, a 6th-grade girl suggests that students put their cases in the lockers, but not lock them. The band teachers are so pleased with this suggestion that they make the girl "queen for the day" for solving a problem that had eluded them (even though in hindsight the solution seemed obvious).*

The *creative* component of intelligence involves generating new or different ideas—creating, inventing, discovering, or hypothesizing. Sternberg tells the true story of an executive in the automobile industry who was fed up with his boss. The executive hired a headhunting firm to find him a new job. His wife helped him redefine the problem; he asked the headhunter to find a job for the *boss,* which he did. The executive ended up much happier, and with the boss's job (Sternberg, 1996, pp. 208–209). All three components can operate simultaneously; thus, the executive who finds a job for his boss is showing analytic skills and practical street smarts while thinking creatively.

Sternberg believes that understanding the three components of intelligence can help teachers identify learners' strengths and weaknesses and potentially improve intelligence. When intelligence is considered a single factor that cannot be broken into component parts, like a *g* factor, there is little that you can do to improve intelligence. Another view that seeks to expand notions of intelligence beyond *g* is the multiple intelligences model.

Multiple Intelligences

multiple intelligences
Gardner's theory of intelligence that proposes that there are various independent intelligences rather than just a dominant *g* factor.

Howard Gardner asserts that there are **multiple intelligences** that explain human abilities (Gardner, 2006). According to Gardner there are eight intelligences, as depicted in Table 5.1. These multiple intelligences are fairly independent, meaning that a child could be strong in some intelligences and weak in others. Gardner's model arose partly from his dissatisfaction with the notion that the highest type of intelligence is the ability to reason like a scientist—logically, precisely, mathematically. That is the sort of reasoning that is assessed in most intelligence tests.

TABLE 5.1 Description of multiple intelligences

Intelligence	Attributes	Types of people who tend to manifest the intelligence
Linguistic	Capacity to use language to express oneself and to understand others	Poet, writer, speaker, lawyer, journalist
Logical/mathematical	Capacity to understand underlying principles of cause-and-effect, logic, number manipulation	Scientist, mathematician, engineer, computer scientist
Spatial	Capacity to represent the spatial world in one's mind, to mentally transform spatial relationships, to recreate visual images	Sailor, pilot, sculptor, architect, physician, navigator, painter, chess players
Musical	Capacity to think in music, hear, recognize, and perhaps manipulate aural patterns	Musician
Bodily/kinesthetic	Capacity to use whole body or parts of body to solve a problem, make something, or portray something	Athlete, actor, dancer, rock climber, surgeon, mechanic
Naturalist	Capacity to discriminate among living things like plants and animals, to notice natural features like geological features, to recognize patterns	Botanist, chef, farmer, biologist, naturalist
Interpersonal	Capacity to understand other people	Teacher, therapist, salesperson, politician
Intrapersonal	Capacity to understand oneself: knowing what you can do, what you desire, what you should avoid, what you should engage	Relevant to many careers or activities

Source: Adapted from Checkley and Gardner (1997), Gardner (1999), and Torff and Gardner (1999).

Gardner's theory has influenced educators at all levels to expand their curriculum focus from reading, writing, and arithmetic to emphasize art, music, athletics, and social skills as well (Photo 5.1). Reaction to Gardner's theory of multiple intelligences is mixed, with many intelligence experts finding his list of intelligences arbitrary and claiming that the types of intelligence are not separate and independent (Brody, 1992; Sternberg, 1988).

These two theories of intelligence are helpful because they emphasize that there are many kinds of abilities, not just general intelligence. However, *g* remains important because it is associated with academic success, which is valued by society and linked to socioeconomic advancement. Later we will discuss how these different views of intelligence might apply to your classroom.

While Sternberg's theory of successful intelligence and Gardner's theory of multiple intelligences have both been influential in thinking about intelligence and classroom curriculum, neither plays a part in how intelligence is typically measured.

PHOTO 5.1 Students may have different types of intelligence.

Measurement of Intelligence

Individual intelligence tests are administered by a trained psychologist to one child at a time. They are expensive to administer because they require several hours of a trained professional's time. *Group intelligence tests* are paper-and-pencil tests that can be administered to large groups. They are also referred to as *school ability tests* or as *academic aptitude tests*. They are cheap to administer and are objectively scored. That is, each item has a single correct answer. Group tests can be used with children as young as kindergarteners, but only if you make sure each child understands the directions. As a teacher, you should be more cautious about accepting low scores on a group test than on an individual test, because in group-test settings, children may know the answer but write it down incorrectly, get discouraged, or not care about the test.

The most commonly used intelligence tests are the *Wechsler scales* (Kaufman, 2000), which include the Wechsler Preschool and Primary Scale of Intelligence (WPPSI, used with children as young as 2.5 years), the Wechsler Intelligence Scale for Children (WISC), and the Wechsler Adult Intelligence Scale (WAIS). Additional commonly used individual intelligence tests are the Stanford–Binet, Woodcock–Johnson, Kaufman, and Das–Naglieri. Common group tests of intelligence include the Lorge–Thorndike, Otis–Lennon, and Cognitive Abilities Tests (CogAT).

While these tests are widely used to measure children's intelligence, some experts argue that they do not actually measure some of the key components of intelligence, such as ability to learn quickly or adapt, but rather measure *past learning* (Sternberg, Grigorenko, & Kidd, 2005). This is an important distinction because it implies that intelligence as measured by tests is the result of past opportunity to learn, not just innate processing capacity.

Intelligence, or IQ, is reported using scores that have a specific mean and standard deviation. Most intelligence tests are created so that the mean score is 100 and the standard deviation is 15. *Standard deviation* is a number that describes the spread in scores and is used to compute effect sizes that were discussed in Chapter 1. Most children's intelligence scores (about 68%) are between plus or minus one standard deviation from the mean, or between 85 and 115, so a student who scores 145 is three standard deviations above the mean and has very high intelligence. Learners vary in their measured intelligence, which brings up the next topic: individual differences.

5-1b Individual Diversity in Intelligence

Children vary in their ability to solve problems, think abstractly, comprehend complex ideas, and learn quickly. Are these differences stable? **Stability** refers to whether a child's rank on a trait remains the same over time. In the case of intelligence, do young children who score higher on intelligence tests than their peers remain more intelligent at a later age?

stability
a term psychologists use to refer to whether rank-ordering on a trait remains the same across time.

Stability of Intelligence

Generally, intelligence scores are among the most stable psychological attributes across the lifespan. One classic study of stability of intelligence took advantage of the fact that all 11-year-old Scottish children attending school on June 1, 1932, were given intelligence tests. When individuals were found and retested 69 years later with the same test, scores from age 11 to age 80 were correlated at 0.66, which indicates substantial stability from middle childhood to late adulthood. They were followed up again at age 90 and the correlation was 0.54 (with fewer people, obviously) (Deary, Pattie, & Starr, 2013).

Traditional intelligence tests do not attempt to measure intelligence before about age 2.5 years because young children may not understand questions or be able to respond. However, infant habituation tasks do predict later intelligence (see Box 5.1). Some infants may only need about ten seconds and others may need forty seconds to explore a novel picture thoroughly before they turn away, or some infants may remember a picture better than others do. Infants who habituate faster or have better recognition memory have higher intelligence scores up to twenty years later, suggesting a high level of stability (Fagan, Holland, & Wheeler, 2007; Kavšek, 2004). Habituation probably predicts later intelligence because it reflects stability in general information processing abilities like memory and executive functioning.

Can intelligence be changed? Yes and no. Removing children from seriously deprived environments, such as bleak orphanages, and placing them into enriched environments results in increased intelligence (O'Connor et al., 2000). On the other hand, programs aimed at trying to enhance cognitive ability, such as preschool programs (see Chapter 1) or programs aimed at older children, generally have little long-term effect on measured intelligence (Sternberg, Grigorenko, and Bundy, 2001). If preschool programs are intensive, high quality, and focus on language development, there is some evidence that they can raise intelligence 4 to 7 points, but only for low-income, disadvantaged children (Protzko, Aronson, & Blair, 2013); long-term gains have not been demonstrated. Thus, intelligence can be increased to some degree with intensive intervention, but improvements tend to decay over time if the environment does not improve. However, expertise and achievement can be substantially increased. We will discuss these topics later.

What Do Individual Differences in Intelligence Predict?

A comedian once bragged about how intelligent she was. Although she was only 42 years old, she could read at a 45-year-old level! Her joke underscores the emphasis people give to intelligence. Parents want to believe their children have a high IQ. Why this obsession with intelligence? Does intelligence really influence how well a child's life is lived? Somewhat. Intelligence does affect academic achievement, as well as other life outcomes. However, as you read this section, keep in mind that social and emotional well-being, and motivation (discussed in later chapters), may have an even greater effect on life outcomes.

Academic achievement

Academic achievement is measured by achievement tests and classroom grades. Achievement tests are standardized tests that measure what children have learned in school. They include tests such as the Iowa Test of Basic Skills (ITBS), Comprehensive Test of Basic Skills (CTBS), Metropolitan Achievement Test (MAT), Stanford Achievement Test (SAT10, not to be confused with the SAT college entrance exam), and state proficiency tests.

think
about this

In Chapter 1 you learned that correlation does not prove causation. Thus, it is not clear whether: (1) high intelligence causes achievement, (2) achievement causes high intelligence, or (3) something else causes both. Drawing on this chapter and Chapter 4, make a case for options 1, 2, and 3.

BOX 5.1 theories & theorists

Habituation and Core Knowledge

Have you ever wondered what babies know? Infants only a few months old cannot be tested through interviews or questionnaires, so scientists use habituation to test their knowledge. Infants look longer at new things than at familiar things. Habituation is a reduction in attention to a repeatedly presented or continuously available stimulus (the familiar stimulus), which could be a picture of a face or a checkerboard pattern. When infants' attention declines to 50% of the amount of time they first looked at the stimulus, we say they have habituated to the familiar stimulus. Then a new stimulus is presented, like a different face or a checkerboard with a slightly different pattern. Usually infants increase their looking time when the stimulus is changed. This is known as dishabituation. We know several things about infants' cognitive abilities from habituation and other memory studies:

- Infants have a sense of number, size, and amount. Infants habituate to repeated displays of the same number of objects, then dishabituate when a different number of objects is shown (Gelman & Williams, 1998).
- Infants form categories to organize objects and events. For example, 3-month-olds will look longer at pictures of furniture after habituating to pictures of animals (Haith & Benson, 1998).
- Infants perceive causal sequences (Mascalzoni, Regolin, Vallortigara, & Simion, 2013). For example, infants habituate to seeing a toy car bump another toy car into moving. Then, when they see the first toy car bump into the second, but the second car does not move for a few seconds (a delayed launch), the infant

dishabituates to this novel event and pays increased attention (Cohen, Rundell, Spellman, & Cashon, 1999).

- Infants know physical objects are continuous and solid. That is, they understand that objects cannot spontaneously appear or disappear and that they cannot occupy the same space as other objects (Baillargeon, 2008). Infants respond with interest to "impossible events" such as balls that fall through solid objects or a ball on a table that does not fall when the table is removed. Infants understand object permanence much earlier than Piaget believed, perhaps as early as 3 months. (See Figure 5.1.)
- Five-month-olds can distinguish liquids from solids (Hespos, Ferry, & Rips, 2009).

Infants do not reason correctly about everything. For example, under some conditions they are not surprised by objects suspended in midair (Baillargeon, Kotovsky, & Needham, 1995). Nevertheless, it is clear that infants know a surprising amount about the world, and *they know it without handling physical objects*, within the first months of life, suggesting the presence of core knowledge.

What is Core Knowledge? Core knowledge refers to innate ideas, or concepts and principles that are genetically preprogrammed in the human brain. Core knowledge is present early, is universal in normal children, and is triggered by a normal environment. It does not appear to depend on feedback or imitation. Core knowledge seems to be acquired effortlessly, presumably because the conceptual structures are already in the mind, which helps children

habituation
a reduction in attention to a continuously available or repeated stimulus.

dishabituation
attention that has become habituated is renewed after a change in the stimulus.

core knowledge
innate, skeletal conceptual structures that develop early and easily, without instruction, and are universal, but may require experience to fine-tune.

Intelligence tests generally predict achievement test scores with high correlations of about 0.70 to 0.90, and they predict grades with moderate correlations of about 0.50 to 0.60, but different studies range widely (Kaufman, Reynolds, Liu, Kaufman, & McGrew, 2012; Kubiszyn & Borich, 2003). Still, on average, children who score higher on intelligence tests learn more in school and tend to attain more years of schooling.

Life outcomes

Think about your relatives and friends. Are the intelligent ones more successful in life? That may depend on how you define success. Children with high intelligence are more likely to become adults with higher income and better job success (Spengler et al., 2015). A review of more than 50 longitudinal studies (Strenze, 2007) found that intelligence predicted three measures of success: amount of education

learn new content in that domain. Innate ideas are not easily explained by behaviorist or Piagetian views of cognitive development (Baillargeon, 2008; Gelman, 2006).

Nativists believe that the only role environment plays in core knowledge is to provide some minimal experience to trigger innate ideas (Newcombe, 2002). However, most psychologists adhere to an *interactionist* view that there is a role for both nature and nurture. Core knowledge may be like a muscle that has a genetic basis, but is modified by experience (Bremner, Slater, & Johnson, 2015; Gelman & Williams, 1998).

There are few core domains. They appear to include *number sense*, like understanding quantity, or what is more and what is less, and basic arithmetic as you learned in Chapter 4. They also include understanding the *physical movement of solid objects* (e.g., unsupported objects fall in space, objects cannot pass through other objects), *physical movement of nonsolid substances* like sand and water (Hespos, Ferry, Anderson, Hollenbeck, & Rips, 2016), *physical movement of hands* (e.g., looking longer if hands are bent backwards; Longhi et al., 2015), understanding *other people's thoughts* (see Chapter 9), and *language* (see Chapter 12). Noncore domains, which are most domains, do not have innate structures and are acquired through experience. These include the ability to read, use computer software, or play chess. All normal children should acquire knowledge in the core domains, but there is great variation in noncore domains.

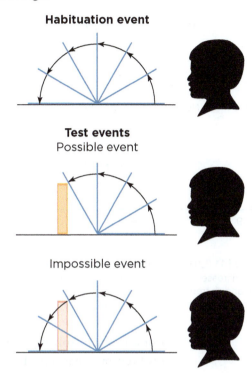

FIGURE 5.1 **Object Permanence May Exist before 4 Months of Age.**

Habituation event

Test events
Possible event

Impossible event

In a classic experiment, Renée Baillargeon (1987) used this technique to test whether infants 3.5 to 4.5 months of age understood object permanence. First the infant observed a screen flip back and forth like a book cover as in the first drawing. This process demonstrated that nothing was behind the screen and was continued until the infant showed habituation. Then a box was placed behind the screen, which stopped when it reached the box, as in the middle drawing. Then the researcher secretly removed the box, and the screen was moved all the way down, which would be impossible from the infant's perspective. The infants looked longer at the impossible event depicted in the last drawing.
Source: Baillargeon (1987).

(correlation = 0.56), job status (0.45), and income (0.23). Grades and parents' socioeconomic status (SES) also predicted these measures of success, but no better than intelligence. Low intelligence is linked to lower resiliency, poorer physical health, increased probability of injury and death, and increased risk of mental illness (Deary, Weiss, & Batty, 2010; Der, Batty, & Deary, 2009; Wraw, Deary, Gale, & Der, 2015).

What Predicts Individual Differences in Intelligence?

Higher *g* could be due to differences in information processing, such as working memory and processing speed, which could be due to brain differences, such as dendrite branching and myelination. These brain differences, in turn, may be caused by genes. A preponderance of evidence suggests that general intelligence, or *g*, is substantially heritable. Heritability estimates range from about 0.20 to 0.80, and they vary depending on age and environment of the group being studied (Deary, 2012).

nativists
those who believe that competence in core domains is largely innate and little influenced by the environment.

FIGURE 5.2 Variation in Intelligence Explained by Genes and Environment.

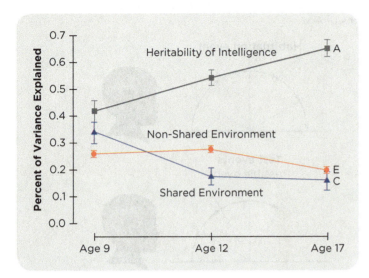

This meta-analysis of 11,000 pairs of twins showed that heritability of intelligence (A) increases over 8 years. Nonshared environment (E) is fairly stable, and shared environment (C) decreases. *Source: Adapted from Plomin, DeFries, Knopik, and Neiderhiser (2016).*

Figure 5.2 shows the surprising but well-established pattern of increasing heritability of intelligence from childhood to young adulthood (Briley & Tucker-Drob, 2013; Plomin, DeFries, Knopik, & Neiderhiser, 2016; Tucker-Drob & Bates, 2015). It is the only known trait for which heritability increases with age. This effect is probably due to gene–environment correlations (Chapter 1); that is, the effect of genes is amplified as children select environments that match their genetic propensities (Plomin et al., 2016).

While genes influence intelligence, so does the environment. You learned in Chapter 1 that children with multiple risk factors have lower intelligence than those with few risk factors. You learned in Chapter 2 that children exposed to prenatal teratogens have lower intelligence. Malnourished children have lower intelligence (Venables & Raine, 2015). You also learned that brains are built through experience. Rats in standard cages had less-developed brains and worse problem-solving ability than rats in elaborate cages. In fact, in 1958 researchers bred rats that were bright and dull at finding their way through mazes. They assumed that the differences were genetic, due to breeding. However, when they placed juvenile dull rats in enriched environments, and bright rats in impoverished environments, the differences disappeared (Champagne, 2009). This suggests that genetic effects depend on the environment—which you'll learn more about in Chapter 6. In addition, some researchers believe the effect of genes is overestimated, while the effect of shared environment is underestimated. Evidence to support this view is that brothers who are close in age, so that they probably had greater shared environment in the family, are more similar in intelligence than brothers who are far apart in age (Sundet, Eriksen, & Tambs, 2008). This suggests the importance of the home environment.

Home environment

The quality of a child's home environment predicts later intelligence (Nisbett et al., 2012). Home attributes linked to intelligence include learning materials in the home (e.g., books, magazines, computers), parent–child conversations, and trips, such as to museums (Photo 5.2). For example, a classic study of infants found that the amount that mothers talked to their babies predicted intelligence at 18 years (Sigman, Cohen, & Beckwith, 1997). Parental sensitivity and affection also predict children's later cognitive ability (Stams, Juffer, & van IJzendoorn, 2002). Such nurturance promotes feelings of security and self-regulation in children, which affects ability to cope with novelty and learn. Note that these findings are *correlational,* so it is possible that these home and parent attributes cause intelligence, or that intelligent children cause their parents to buy learning materials and provide nurturance.

Schooling

School attendance also affects intelligence. Students who drop out of school early, are chronically absent, and delay starting kindergarten have lower intelligence than comparable peers (Ceci, 2003; Nisbett et al., 2012). Some studies show that children who start out with an average IQ but miss a lot of school, due to illness or frequent moves, decline in intelligence as they miss more school. The effect of schooling on cognitive ability is one reason many experts object to readiness tests being used to exclude children from starting school. Children who are judged as not ready to begin school most need to be in school (see Chapter 1).

PHOTO 5.2 Children with access to books at home tend to have higher intelligence.

5-1c Group Diversity in Intelligence

Are there differences in intelligence based on gender, SES, or culture? The following sections deal with group differences in intelligence and also test bias and the rising trend in IQ scores.

Gender

Gender differences are seldom observed in *general* intelligence scores (Nisbett et al., 2012). However, boys score nearly a full standard deviation higher than girls on tests of *spatial* ability, particularly mental rotation (Halpern et al., 2007). Mental rotation is measured by tasks like the one depicted in Figure 5.3. In fact, there is evidence that as early as 3 months of age, infant boys are better than infant girls at mental rotation (Quinn & Liben, 2008). This superior spatial ability may explain their higher performance in some science domains, where boys tend to have higher test scores than girls, with effect sizes from 0.10 to 0.35 (Ganley, Vasilyeva, & Dulaney, 2014).

Why might boys have superior spatial ability? One probable reason is that they tend to play more with spatial toys such as puzzles and blocks (Jirout & Newcombe, 2015). The power of such playful practice is demonstrated by the fact that training can improve spatial ability with an average effect size of 0.47. This improvement is known to last at least several months and to transfer from the training situation to other situations (Uttal, Meadow, et al., 2013; Uttal, Miller, & Newcombe, 2013). Training has included shoot-'em-up action video games, computer-based training, and origami (Feng, Spence, & Pratt, 2007; Jaušovec & Jaušovec, 2012). Spatial ability is important because it can influence career choice. Adolescents who have high spatial ability are more likely than other students to go on to pursue science, technology, engineering, and mathematical (STEM) domains (Wai, Lubinski, & Benbow, 2009).

Children who take music lessons tend to have higher intelligence than other children. Given what you have learned about intelligence, is higher intelligence likely to be the cause of taking music lessons, or the result? What other factors might be involved? Can you explain the correlation between music lessons and IQ from a gene–environment correlation perspective?

FIGURE 5.3 **Example of Mental Rotation.**

Children are asked if the figure on the left and the one on the right are the same. This requires them to rotate the figures in their minds. Can you do it? *Source: Adapted from Halpern (1992).*

Boy vs. Girl Brains

Do boys outperform girls in high-level math and visual rotation because of brain differences? One theory in neuroscience is that the same hormones that cause fetuses to differentiate into baby boys and girls also cause their brains to develop differently (Valla & Ceci, 2011). This seems plausible. However, currently there is no sound evidence that structural differences in male and female brains are clearly linked to specific gender differences in abilities (Fine, 2010). This reality has not deterred many creative, but false, claims that perpetuate stereotypes, such as how men's "left" brains make them better at scientific precision than women.

Keep in mind that these differences are averages of many males and females and do not say anything about individuals. In addition, it is important to understand that aside from spatial ability, gender differences are small; there is much more variation in ability among boys and among girls than between boys and girls.

Socioeconomic Status

Middle- and high-SES children tend to score significantly higher on intelligence tests than low-SES children (Englund, Luckner, Whaley, & Egeland, 2004; Nisbett et al., 2012). In fact, a study of over 14,000 twins found that at age 2, children from low-SES families scored about 6 points lower than children from high-SES families, and by age 16 the difference was about 16 points (von Stumm & Plomin, 2015). How might SES influence intelligence? In Chapter 1 you learned about the family investment and family stress models. The family investment model suggests that a child's lack of access to material or social resources can lead to a low-quality learning environment in the home (e.g., fewer books, less conversation, less stimulation, more punishment), which in turn predicts lower intelligence. The family stress model suggests that low SES can result in diminished quality of parenting, which also predicts lower intelligence. In addition, low-SES children tend to experience high numbers of risk factors that can affect intelligence.

Risk factors linked to poverty can be so powerful that they overwhelm genetic predisposition for high intelligence. For example, one study found that among impoverished 7-year-olds, genes accounted for almost no variance in IQ, but shared environment accounted for 60% of variance (Turkheimer, Haley, Waldron, D'Onofrio, & Gottesman, 2003). The opposite pattern was found for advantaged children. That is, intelligence was less heritable for low-SES children and more heritable for higher-SES children. In a different study, the same pattern was found for infants (Tucker-Drob, Rhemtulla, Harden, Turkheimer, & Fask, 2011). This pattern suggests that when the environment is rich, genetic predispositions show through, but when the environment is very impoverished, nearly everyone experiences lower intelligence; genetic predispositions for high ability tend not to show through.

think about this

Think of the most intelligent person you know. Describe that person's attributes or behavior that led you to believe he or she is intelligent. What does this say about your personal view of what constitutes intelligence?

Ethnicity

Children of different ethnicities differ in average intelligence test scores. In the United States, the average intelligence score of European Americans and Asian Americans is about 100 to 102. For African Americans it is about 87 to 90; Latinos score between Whites and African Americans. Keep in mind that these are average scores and say nothing about individuals.

What might account for these differences in intelligence test scores across ethnic groups? There is no single clear explanation (Hunt & Carlson, 2007). Experts agree that there is no evidence for a genetic explanation (Nisbett et al., 2012). Perhaps differences are due to socioeconomic status, because African American and Latino children tend to be of lower SES than Asian American or European American children. Perhaps they are due to differences in opportunities to learn; when groups have equal opportunities to learn, ethnic differences may disappear (Fagan & Holland, 2007). Perhaps they are due to stereotype threat, which refers to a tendency to perform poorly due to fear that one's performance will confirm a negative stereotype. This will be discussed in Chapter 13.

Culture

Different cultures vary in what components of intelligence they value (Photo 5.3). Some national cultures view speed of thought as part of intelligence, while others view slow, deliberate thought as part of intelligence (Sternberg et al., 2001). Some island cultures value the ability to navigate the high seas without electronic equipment, while most people in the United States would find this ability useless. Thus, intelligence is embedded within a cultural setting.

These cultural differences affect measurement of intelligence. Simply translating a test to another language does not necessarily make it a valid test in another culture. Intelligence tests pose questions and tasks. One's success is influenced by whether one understands the question, already has strategies for dealing with the task, or already knows the answer. The influence of cultural background on intelligence tests can be reduced, but not eliminated.

Culture-reduced tests, such as the Universal Nonverbal Intelligence Test or the Raven's Progressive Matrices (see Figure 5.4), reduce reliance on language. For example, the Raven's Matrices display patterns with a piece missing. Children circle the piece that best completes the pattern. Notice that we do not call it a culture-free test; to date, there is no such thing. Even this test requires a mindset of recognizing patterns that move from left to right and top to bottom. Children who have this mindset and are used to viewing two-dimensional patterns have an advantage over children from cultures without this experience. Nevertheless, some nonverbal IQ tests are inappropriately advertised as being culturally fair and unbiased.

Test Bias

Intelligence tests have been accused of being biased because some groups on average score lower than other groups. **Test bias** exists when a test unfairly penalizes a group of test takers because of their gender, SES, cultural background, or other characteristic that is not relevant to the purpose of the test. Tests can be biased if they have culture-specific content. Cultures may vary in their knowledge of sports such as basketball versus rugby, music such as opera versus hip hop, and leisure pursuits such as playing bridge versus

Lihee Avidan/The Image Bank/Getty Images

PHOTO 5.3 Different cultures may value different forms of intelligence and require different measures of intelligence.

test bias
a test has less validity for one group than another group. Predictive bias means members of two groups who have the same score are not predicted to have the same outcome.

FIGURE 5.4 Example of Raven Test Item.

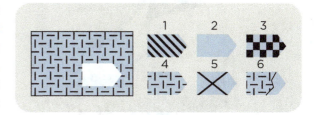

Select the segment on the right that best fits into the larger pattern on the left. Try this item. Does it seem culture-reduced to you? *Source: Bukatko (2008).*

playing poker. When tests refer to culture-specific content, they could disadvantage certain groups. Today's high-quality standardized tests do not have items that are obviously biased, because panels of experts from different groups examine each test item. However, while experts can recognize items that might be offensive to certain groups, they are poor at distinguishing items that are actually biased. In one case, a judge reviewed all the items in two intelligence tests and, after consulting with experts, concluded that eight items might be biased. Later analysis showed that none of them were biased—they did not function differently for White as compared with Black children (Warne, Yoon, & Price, 2014). The difficulty of recognizing biased items is why all high-quality standardized tests today statistically screen for items that function differently for specific groups, like male versus female or Black versus White children.

An important type of test bias is *predictive bias,* which refers to whether members of two groups who have the same score on a test are predicted to have the same outcome, like grades or probability of attending college. Diverse experts agree that intelligence tests do not have predictive bias. In fact, on some standardized tests, for Blacks and Whites who have the same score, Blacks are predicted to have better outcomes (Berry & Zhao, 2015; Warne et al., 2014).

Note that the technical definition of *test bias* is not the same as *unfairness*. If one group consistently scores higher than another group, it does not necessarily demonstrate unfairness in the *test*. Instead, it may demonstrate unfairness in *opportunity to learn* and quality of schools, which historically have been worse for African American and Latino children. But can tests be fair if they affect some groups in a negative way? That is a question that educators, as well as lawyers, judges, and legislators, struggle with.

Cohort Effect—Rising Intelligence

Flynn effect
the worldwide pattern of rising intelligence scores.

You may be surprised to learn that today's youth have higher intelligence scores on the average than their grandparents (Photo 5.4). Researcher James Flynn documented the worldwide pattern of rising intelligence scores, which is now termed the **Flynn effect** (Trahan, Stuebing, Fletcher, & Hiscock, 2014) (see Figure 5.5). For example, U.S. data show IQ scores improving about 30 points between 1900 and 2012. This is a huge gain of about two standard deviations and means that the average person in 2012 has an IQ higher than about 95% of Americans in 1900 (Winer, 2013). Flynn (2007) described similarly strong data for many countries, both so-called developed and undeveloped nations. The effect even pertains to infants and toddlers who are now scoring higher than in previous decades on tests of infant mental development (Lynn, 2009). The Flynn effect applies to all groups, but IQ in Black children has increased at a faster rate than that of White children, so that the IQ gap has narrowed by about five points over the past few decades (Dickens & Flynn, 2006).

However, as Flynn (2007) points out, if real intelligence had increased so substantially, the current generation should be massively outperforming the previous generation, and

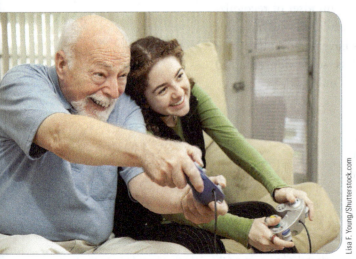

Lisa F. Young/Shutterstock.com

PHOTO 5.4 Youth today have higher intelligence scores than older generations. This is called the Flynn effect.

grandparents should be unable to keep up with their grandchildren in conversation or intellectual activities. No such massive advantage for the young has occurred. He points out that the rising IQ scores are much stronger for tests of abstract reasoning—such as "what do dogs and rabbits have in common?"—than for other types of IQ items. The correct answer is that they are both mammals. This sort of categorical thinking—mammal is a category that contains both dogs and rabbits—is the basis for much scientific reasoning and is much more common today than in the past. Flynn suggests that in 1900, the most common answer would have been that you use dogs to hunt rabbits.

No one knows just what has caused the Flynn effect, but possibilities include changes in the environment such as improved nutrition, less childhood disease, increased complexity of modern life, urbanization, increased SES, reduced family size, increased formal education, and more parental attention to children (Colom, Lluis-Font, & Andres-Pueyo, 2005; Gauvain & Monroe, 2009; Pietschnig & Voracek, 2015).

FIGURE 5.5 Flynn Effect on IQ.

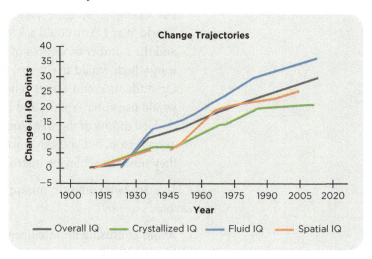

The data from this meta-analysis show rising intelligence since about 1909. Which aspect of intelligence has risen most steeply? *Source: Pietschnig and Voracek (2015).*

5-1d Classroom Implications of Intelligence

While your students' levels of intelligence will influence their success in your classroom, it is important to recognize that intelligence is not the only influence on learning and achievement. Other influences include prior experience and knowledge, SES, cultural value of academic success, cultural capital, self-control, and motivation. In addition, educators should recognize and publicly value students' varied abilities. Sometimes teachers are not even aware of the talents and skills of their students. Understanding Gardner's multiple intelligences can help you recognize and value varied abilities.

Multiple Intelligences in the Classroom

Here are two suggestions that stem from Gardner's model:

1. Become aware of children's different profiles of intelligences. Help individual students succeed by drawing on their strengths, and promoting growth in weak areas. For example, let's take a look at a toddler classroom.

Two-year-old Wyatt has high bodily/kinesthetic intelligence. Wyatt can kick a ball across the room, well-aimed and standing on only one foot. His classmate, Jana, cannot do this, but has high logical/mathematical intelligence. She can already count to 20 accurately. Their teachers' instructional goal is to help each child learn to count better. They have Wyatt throw puff balls into a bucket as he counts from 1 to 10. They then encourage Jana to continue counting to 25 as she throws more puff balls into the bucket. This expands both children's abilities, while drawing on their strengths.

think about **this**

How was your childhood different from that of your grandparents? Which of these differences do you think might account for the Flynn effect?

2. Plan lessons that engage multiple intelligences based on your instructional goals. For example, imagine your instructional goal is for students to understand World War I. You could ask students to write analyses of how population trends and the number of victims of the flu epidemic of 1918 influenced the end of the war, which would use verbal–linguistic and logical–mathematical intelligences. Or students could sculpt relief maps that trace the progress of the war, which would use visual–spatial and bodily–kinesthetic intelligences while still fostering understanding of the war. You should not attempt to engage every intelligence in every lesson, but you can engage a variety across several assignments—as long as they result in achieving instructional goals.

Here are two common misapplications of his theory that Gardner cautions you to avoid:

1. Avoid confusing an intelligence with a domain. Biology is a domain, but there is not a biological intelligence. Intelligences relevant to mastering biology could include verbal, logical–mathematical, spatial, and naturalist. Every domain can draw upon multiple intelligences. In addition, a specific intelligence like spatial intelligence can be relevant to multiple domains, such as sports, sewing, or car mechanics.

2. Avoid confusing an intelligence with a method of learning. An intelligence is an ability, not a technique for learning. For example, children who have bodily–kinesthetic intelligence, like Wyatt, do not necessarily learn best through movement. They are competent at moving in complex ways, but that does not mean they could best learn about the history of the United States through movement.

Gardner's model is valuable because it expands the ideal curriculum. Traditional curriculum emphasizes reading, writing, and computing using mainly two types of intelligence: linguistic and logical–mathematical. Schools emphasize writing, computing, analyzing, comparing, showing cause and effect, and understanding equations. They do not emphasize skilled movement, creating or appreciating music, or understanding other people, nor are these part of state proficiency tests. A curriculum that seriously engages multiple intelligences will support diverse intelligences. For example, there will be more than one roving art teacher with one art cart per elementary school.

You may have students with different intelligences who seek to do assignments in ways that draw on their strengths. For example, in a high school chemistry class, some students ask if they can use graphs or diagrams to answer essay questions. Their teacher lets them, but then asks them to *tell* her what the graph says. Then she says, "OK, write that down." This usually results in a better essay for students whose strengths are not linguistic. Any time her students ask to do an assignment in a different way, she asks them what they think the purpose of the assignment is and whether their alternative approach will fulfill that purpose. If it will, she lets them try it.

Intelligence Tests and the Classroom

Two major classroom purposes of intelligence testing are to diagnose students for special education services—both gifted programs and remedial programs—and to diagnose learning disabilities (see Box 5.2). While intelligence tests are useful as one piece of evidence that could help place a student, you should not rely solely upon one test. Stories abound of children who were clearly struggling with the regular curriculum but were denied remedial services because their intelligence scores were too high; or of children who were exceptionally able, as demonstrated in projects, but who were denied gifted education because their intelligence scores were too low. Multiple pieces of evidence, such as ability manifest in discussions, assignments, or standardized achievement tests, should be used in addition to intelligence tests for placement decisions.

learning disability
discrepancy between a student's achievement and intelligence or as lack of response to instruction that is effective for most other students.

BOX 5.2 challenges in development

Learning Disabilities

A learning disability (LD) refers to a "disorder in one or more of the basic psychological processes involved in understanding or using language, spoken or written.... [T]he disorder may manifest itself in an imperfect ability to listen, think, speak, write, spell or do mathematical calculations" (Individuals with Disabilities Education Act [IDEA], 2004). The legal definition of learning disability (LD) varies by state, but in the past, the most common definition focused on an intelligence-achievement discrepancy, that is, achievement that is lower than what you would expect based on a child's measured intelligence. This definition is based on the assumption that students with a learning disability are cognitively different from students who experience low achievement *and* low intelligence. It is also based on the assumption that they are cognitively different from students who merely experience low achievement due to poor instruction or lack of motivation. However, it is not clear exactly what these cognitive differences are. Most research shows that mere low achievers are *not* different from students diagnosed with a learning disability.

These problems with diagnosing a learning disability have led to the *response to intervention* (RTI) model (Fletcher & Vaughn, 2009). Under this model students are diagnosed with a learning disability if they do not learn from the instruction that most students learn from. Thus, poor instruction does not explain their low achievement, so a disability may be responsible, and specialized intervention may be needed.

Key facts regarding learning disabilities (Cortiella & Horowitz, 2014):

- According to the National Center for Education Statistics, *children with learning disabilities* is the largest category of students who receive special

education services. In 2013 that was 2.24 million, or 35%, of special education students (compared with autism at 8% and emotional disturbance at 6%).
- About 5% of public school students are identified as having learning disabilities under the Individuals with Disabilities Education Act (IDEA).
- In recent years the number of LD students has declined somewhat.
- Two-thirds of LD students are male.
- Students with LD are usually average or above average in intelligence; thus, LD is not linked with intellectual disability.
- The most common characteristic of LD is difficulty reading.

Practicing Inclusion—How to Help Learners with a Learning Disability The answer to this problem depends on which of three RTI tiers your students need. In tier 1, high-quality, evidence-based instruction is provided to all students, and students are frequently assessed to make sure that they are learning adequately. In tier 2, in-class interventions are used to improve achievement for targeted low-achieving students. In tier 3, more intensive small group or one-on-one services are provided for students who do not respond to tier 2 interventions. A large study in Florida showed that an RTI model was linked to reductions in the number of students identified as having learning disabilities and to improvements in reading scores (Torgesen, 2009). However, critics of the RTI model argue that it is unproven and does not detect all the students who may benefit from services; they claim that some students with intellectual disability or emotional disorders can be mistakenly identified as having learning disabilities (Reynolds & Shaywitz, 2009).

5-2 Talent and Expertise

Midway through 8th grade, Bill Gates's school started a computer club. Gates remembers, "They put three thousand dollars into a computer terminal down in this funny little room that we subsequently took control of." From that moment forward, Gates all but lived in the computer room. Soon a company asked would the computer club like to test out the company's software in exchange for free computer time? Absolutely! After school, Gates took the bus to the company offices and programmed long into the evening to earn his free computer time. In one 7-month period in 1971, Gates and his friends used 1,575 hours of mainframe computer time, which averages out to 8 hours a day, 7 days a week. "It was my obsession," Gates says of his early high school years. "I skipped athletics. I went up there at night. We were programming weekends. It would be a rare week that we wouldn't get 20 or 30 hours in." (Adapted from Gladwell, 2008, pp. 50–55)

A central goal of education is to improve learners' expertise. But how is that done? Research shows that *time spent in practice* is critical, just as it was for Bill Gates. Expertise requires practicing correctly over and over. For a swimmer, it might mean making every turn correctly. For a toddler learning to talk, it might mean talking constantly until your teachers finally understand you. For a teacher, it might mean practicing lessons and seeking feedback.

Some people believe expertise is more about genetics than practice. After all, aren't some children just born talented? Don't they find it easy to become expert? The answer depends on what you mean by *expertise* and *talent*.

Expertise refers to having a high level of skill or knowledge. *Talent* also refers to having a high level of skill, but it is often used to refer to natural or innate ability. Some scientists have rejected this notion of talent. They say that talent is not just an innate attribute; it is a product of intense practice. This does not mean there are no innate differences among children, but rather that innate differences are not the only explanation for expertise.

5-2a Age Trends in Talent and Expertise

Talent is defined as having more skill at some activity than do others of the same age, so there are no age trends. In some domains, it takes at least 10 years of intensive practice to attain an international or eminent level of expertise (Ericsson & Ward, 2007). This seems to hold true for chess players, musicians, composers, writers, and scientists. For this reason, eminence is not likely to be reached before the teens, and may not be reached until middle age or beyond.

Some talents or areas of expertise are age-related in the sense that a late start may prevent the development of world-class expertise. For example, some skating coaches agree that age 8 is the latest one could begin skating and hope to become an expert skater (Starkes, Deakin, Allard, Hodges, & Hayes, 1996). So 10 years of practice starting at age 18 could result in a highly competent skater, but not a world-class skater. However, a late start is not a handicap, but a necessity, in some domains. For example, great surgeons do not begin practicing surgery at age 8.

5-2b Individual Diversity in Talent and Expertise

By definition, talent is an individual difference. That is, some children are more talented than others in a given domain. Let's look at what talent and expertise mean for children, and where talent may come from.

What Do Individual Differences in Expertise Predict?

There are obvious outcomes of expertise. Youth who have greater expertise than their classmates perform at higher levels. Their skills can result in new creations in music or technology or winning competitions like science fairs, sports, or quiz bowls. Children who show unusual verbal or math ability, by high scores on the SAT, are more likely to have publications or patents for inventions by middle age (Lubinski, Benbow, & Kell, 2014). Another outcome is enjoyment, because expertise can be inherently rewarding. A calculus student may thoroughly enjoy differential equations. An art student may delight in producing statues.

A less obvious outcome of expertise is improved thinking and memory in the area of expertise. For example, child chess experts have better memory for chess patterns than do adult novices. Researchers showed a pattern of chess pieces on chess boards to child and adult chess experts and novices, then removed the boards and asked the participants to reproduce the pattern of chess pieces (Schneider, Gruber, Gold, & Opwis, 1993). The child chess experts remembered arrangements of chess pieces better than did the adult novices, and as well as the adult experts, *if* the pieces were in the pattern of a real game. The researchers repeated the study with nonchess pieces and with chess pieces in a random pattern. These were remembered equally poorly by child and adult experts and novices. So the chess experts' advantage was only for meaningful chess patterns; they did not have superior memory for random patterns or for nonchess items.

Research on experts has also revealed that experts recognize patterns that novices do not (Chi, 2006). They generate better solutions to problems, and they do it faster and more accurately. Experts generate better strategies than nonexperts, from how to solve a math problem to how to manage misbehaving students. A key question, of course, is how do experts become expert?

What Predicts Individual Differences in Expertise?

Researchers who study talent as the *development of expertise* tend to view ability as caused by practice (Photo 5.5). In contrast, researchers who study talent as an aspect of *giftedness* tend to view ability as innate. Some view the concept of innate talent as destructive because if people believe that they are either born with talent or not, it could discourage the less obviously talented from practicing enough to become expert. What is your perspective? Among your most talented friends, did they learn their particular talent or were they just born with it? Research suggests that talent is a result of long years of deliberate practice combined with genetics,

Jim Commentucci/Syracuse Newspapers/The Image Works

PHOTO 5.5 Children develop expertise through practice.

personality, and physical properties (height, strength) that are relevant to the talent (Hambrick et al., 2014; Mosing, Madison, Pedersen, Kuja-Halkola, & Ullén, 2014; Ullén et al., 2016). The component that teachers can influence the most is deliberate practice. Let's discuss this and other factors that predict expertise next.

Deliberate practice

deliberate practice
activities specifically designed to increase competence that are effortful, use specialized facilities or materials, and require expert feedback.

Deliberate practice is critical to the development of expertise. Deliberate practice refers to activities that are specifically designed to increase competence and that: (1) are goal-directed; (2) require effort and concentration; (3) require teachers who structure the practice, analyze performance, and provide feedback; (4) involve repetition with refinement; and (5) are not inherently motivating.

In a classic study, scientists selected violin students at the Music Academy of West Berlin, including remarkable violinists who would likely go on to play in the best orchestras in Germany (Ericsson, Krampe, & Tesch-Römer, 1993). All had started playing at about the same time and all had spent at least 10 years practicing the violin, yet there were big differences in their expertise, their success at music competitions, and how much music they knew.

Were the best students more talented? Yes, if you define talent as level of expertise. However, if you define talent as innate ability, it is not clear that they were more talented. It was clear that the groups differed in deliberate practice (not just playing, but *deliberate* practice). The best students were practicing the most. The same pattern was seen in their history of practice up to age 18 (see Figure 5.6). The best students reported having practiced an average of 7,410 hours, while the less accomplished students had practiced about 3,420 hours. Rather than saying the best students were "more talented," is it more accurate to say that the best students practiced thousands of hours more? Other studies have found that extensive practice is required for high levels of expertise, as Bill Gates's story illustrates (e.g., Jabusch, Alpers, Kopiez, Vauth, & Altenmüller, 2009). Imagine if your students studied a single topic 4 hours per day!

Practice plays a role in developing skill in all domains. Let's consider reading, for example. While reading practice may not have all the attributes of deliberate practice, it affects later expertise. Some children enter kindergarten with more than 1,000 hours of practice in joint storybook reading with their parents. Other kindergarteners may have only 10 to 20 hours (Adams, 1990). These children enter school with different levels of expertise in pre-reading skills. Differences in amount of reading practice occur through the school years as well. Although the average 5th-grader reads about 1 million words of text per year, there are great individual differences. Some would rather clean their room than read. Youth who read more become more skilled readers. This

FIGURE 5.6 **Deliberate Practice.**

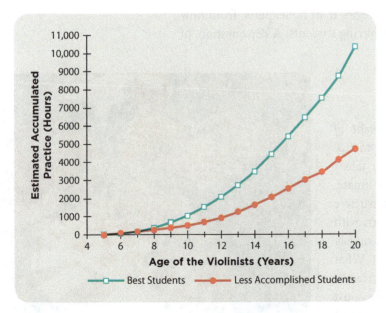

Total hours of violin practice for the best violin students and less accomplished students. *Source: Adapted from Ericsson, Krampe, and Tesch-Römer (1993).*

difference in reading practice may account for the difference between Alex's and Chuck's performance on the homonym worksheets in the opening vignette.

Use of time

A classic study of teens who were talented in art, athletics, music, math, and science found that they were well disciplined in using time (Csikszentmihalyi, Rathunde, & Whalen, 1993). For example, they engaged in more productive activities and spent less time than other teens hanging out with friends. They were less likely to engage in sexual activity. They wasted less time and understood that hanging out does not lead to skill development.

Genes and innate ability

Some chess experts need more practice time to reach mastery than others, and some children who practice will not become chess masters. Perhaps practice is necessary, but not sufficient, for expertise (Hambrick et al., 2014). Research suggests that in some cases expertise arises from an interaction between the environment (e.g., practice, access to expert teachers) and genetically based predispositions (Ullén et al., 2016).

Motivation

Motivation is a key ingredient in the development of expertise. Children who become expert may have a higher level of drive to improve and a greater willingness to practice. While it is hard to get some children to practice, it may be hard to get talented children to quit practicing. We knew a mathematically gifted 4th-grade boy who got algebra books from the public library. His mother struggled to get him to go to bed on time because he would beg to do "just one more" problem. However, researchers have not been able to determine exactly where such motivation comes from. It is possible that inherited talent and practice may be linked. That is, children who work the hardest and earliest may do so because they have more ability.

Remember 2-year-olds Wyatt and Jana? Wyatt has athletic parents and three older siblings who are avid soccer players. He has attended soccer games since birth. Is his remarkable kicking due to practice, or does he have inherited bodily-kinesthetic intelligence? Similarly, Jana's parents are both math teachers. Is her remarkable counting ability due to a math-rich environment that provides her with lots of opportunity to practice or inherited logical–mathematical intelligence? It is probably an interaction of practice, genes, and motivation (review Chapter 1 for gene–environment correlation).

5-2c Group Diversity in Talent and Expertise

Cultures vary in how much they value specific talents, such as skill in mathematics or art. This is reflected in which talents are developed, how expertise is taught, and at what age children begin practicing. For example, Chinese children are taught from early childhood how to produce traditional Chinese paintings. They copy scenes of bamboo, goldfish, roosters, and so on, and ordinary Chinese children become very competent at this sort of art (Winner, 1996). Chinese children would appear gifted compared to American children because Chinese culture emphasizes art in a way

FIGURE 5.7 Art by 6-Year-Old Chinese Child.

This is an example of a brush-and-ink painting by a typical, nongifted Chinese 6-year-old. Traditional painting is a skill that is valued in the culture, and directly taught to children at young ages.
Source: Winner (1996).

that American culture does not (see Figure 5.7). Similarly, chess players in Moscow join chess clubs at younger ages than players in Berlin or Toronto and become better players, which reflects the value of chess in Russia (Charness, Krampe, & Mayr, 1996). Japanese children trained in the Suzuki method of violin teaching appear gifted compared to other young violin players. Talents that are valued in a culture are often introduced at younger ages, and children spend more time practicing them.

Another example of how cultures influence talent is found in sports among African American youth. Historically, African Americans were very interested in baseball, and by the early 1970s, African American ballplayers held 25% of the slots in Major League Baseball. By 2012, the percentage was down to 9% (Lapchick, 2012). Contrast that with the National Basketball Association, which is currently about 80% Black. Today, African American youth are more likely to develop their talents in basketball than in baseball because basketball is more highly valued within their current culture.

5-2d Classroom Implications of Talent and Expertise

In schools, *giftedness* is typically defined as academic talent and high intelligence, yet this is only one form of giftedness. Giftedness can include high ability in any area. Learners can have expertise in some domains without having high general intelligence.

There is disagreement about how academically talented learners should be educated, although some evidence suggests they benefit from being in classrooms with other academically talented learners (Winner, 2000). Thus, most schools have "gifted and talented" programs. You may be asked to nominate learners for such programs. Be careful to give everyone a fair chance. Research suggests that Black students with high test scores who have Black teachers are about 3 times more likely to be assigned to gifted services than if they have non-Black teachers (Grissom & Redding, 2016).

Whether schools directly support placing talented students together, it happens indirectly at the high school level through advanced classes such as calculus, Advanced Placement (AP) classes, and honors classes. AP classes allow academically talented students to take advanced classes for college credit while still in high school. AP classes are linked to greater school enjoyment for academically talented students. Students who take AP classes report that the lack of challenge in non-AP classes is distressing and that AP classes are their favorites. They are more satisfied with the intellectual climate of their school and attain more education over the next 15 years as compared with talented peers who do not take AP classes (Bleske-Rechek, Lubinski, & Benbow, 2004). Thus, AP classes are one large-scale way to provide curriculum that is commensurate with the abilities of academically talented youth.

PHOTO 5.6 Youth who practice can show an amazing level of skill.

A key implication for your classroom from the research on talent is the need to convince learners that deliberate practice is required for expertise (Photo 5.6). If learners believe that talent is innate, and that people who have innate talent do not have to practice hard, they will tend to avoid effort. To counter these beliefs and help all your students—whether gifted or not—to develop expertise, follow these guidelines:

1. *Provide time to practice.* If learners do not put in the time, they will not gain the skill. To help 2-year-old Wyatt learn math skills, his teachers provide many opportunities to practice besides throwing puff balls, such as counting snack items, making patterns with blocks, and singing songs ("Five little monkeys jumping on the bed...."). However, mere time is not sufficient to develop high expertise.

2. *Make sure practice is deliberate.* Assign challenging and complex tasks that require effort and mindfulness. Provide feedback so learners accurately understand what it takes to be successful. Make sure adequate materials and facilities are available.

3. *Help learners feel motivated to engage in deliberate practice.* Motivation is discussed in Chapter 13.

4. *Explain to learners the importance of deliberate practice.* Share stories of people who appear to be supremely talented, but who practiced intensely, from Bill Gates to Michael Jordan to Mozart. This can be done through examples. One teacher used the example of a Korean-born student who, when in Korea during elementary school, was determined to learn English. She studied English 7 hours per day and developed considerable skill in the language!

Expert Teaching

Expert teachers are made, not born. You can apply principles of deliberate practice to your own teaching skill. Deliberate practice for you might include participating in (not just attending) workshops, observing other teachers' classrooms, revising lesson plans based on reflection, and practicing delivery of lessons. Feedback is critical to deliberate practice. Because teaching tends to be private, you will need to make a concerted effort to get feedback from observers. In China, teachers practice by giving public lessons to real students in front of fellow teachers (Han & Paine, 2010). They carefully prepare exactly what they will say and what tasks they will give the students. They anticipate student misconceptions and have appropriate strategies prepared. They receive feedback from the observers that includes lengthy discussions of student responses and misconceptions.

A school in New York City uses a similar approach in which several teachers plan a lesson together, observe each other teaching, discuss how it went, improve the lesson, and try again. There could be 20 teachers observing the revised lesson and giving feedback (Kenny, 2012). Peter, a math teacher, said that this practice transformed the way he taught: "I used to deliver information to students about mathematical formulas: some of them got it, others didn't. Now I facilitate a process where they have to do the work of discovering and understanding the concepts so deeply that they are able to devise the formulas" (p. 214; notice the constructivism in this comment). All of his students passed the state proficiency test; they said the test was easier than their class work. The public lesson helps the performing teacher *and* the observing teachers to improve.

Table 5.2 shows differences between expert and novice teachers. Expert teachers tend to focus on student deep *learning* while novice teachers focus more on *behavior* (Wolff, van den Bogert, Jarodzka, & Boshuizen, 2015). Expert teachers promote achievement in their students, our next topic.

TABLE 5.2 Attributes of expert and novice teachers

Expert teachers	Novice teachers
• Focus on student *learning*	• Focus on student *behavior*
• Perceive unique individuals in the class	• Perceive the class as a whole
• Use unique strategies that address individual learning needs	• Teach to the entire class
• Plan different strategies, including multiple demonstrations	• Use one strategy
• Make long-term and short-term plans	• Focus on short-term plans
• Are skilled at making student thinking public in order to probe for lack of understanding	• Miss signs of lack of understanding
• Present lessons focused on a repeated theme or topic	• Appear disorganized and wander from topic to topic without a theme
• Perceive deep structures of problems	• Perceive surface features of problems
• Are able to adapt and modify if changes to lesson are required	• Have difficulty modifying instruction during a lesson

Source: Adapted from Hogan and Rabinowitz (2009); Hogan, Rabinowitz, and Craven (2003); and Wolff et al. (2015).

5-3 Achievement

One morning in November, during a student Geography Bee, I listened as teenagers from privileged families identified Jamaica as an island in the Pacific … then to their teachers defend that ignorance by arguing, "We don't waste time on simple memorization. We'd rather spend it on 'higher orders' of thinking." But the next afternoon, I watched … Calculus students perform mathematical feats that were dazzling … later, I was horrified to read students' papers and realize that even the best hadn't mastered basic grammar, punctuation or spelling—or to hear scores of students blithely inform me, perhaps even boast to me, that they had never read a complete book. (Burkett, 2001, p. 310)

This is an account from journalist Elinor Burkett (2001), who spent a year observing a typical suburban high school in the Minneapolis area. Both educators and the public are interested in how to explain both appalling and impressive academic achievement.

Academic achievement is usually measured in one of two ways: (1) Teacher-assigned grades or grade point average (GPA). Grades are subjective and can vary by teacher, school, and district. That is, an A might be much easier to earn from one teacher or in one school than another. (2) Standardized test scores. Tests are *standardized* when everyone has the same testing materials, time, instructions, and scoring standards. Standardized tests allow comparison of students' knowledge across teachers, schools, and districts. The achievement tests listed earlier in the chapter are standardized tests, as are college entrance exams like the ACT and SAT. Achievement tests are different from intelligence tests; *they are designed to measure what children already know, rather than capacity to learn*, although this is difficult to separate and, as you learned earlier, they are highly correlated.

Teachers constantly base instructional decisions—such as what content to cover, and the type and difficulty level of learning activities—on their own assessment of student achievement rather than on students' performance on standardized tests. How accurate are teacher assessments? A meta-analysis of many studies found that the average correlation between teacher assessment and standardized test scores was 0.63 (Südkamp, Kaiser, & Möller, 2012). This means that they overlap, but not completely; they measure similar but not identical performance.

academic achievement
a measure of knowledge based on grades or standardized tests.

5-3a Age Trends in Achievement

Standardized tests are typically customized for each grade, so they are not designed to reveal age trends. However, *grades* tend to decline from 6th to 12th grade. The decline is particularly noticeable at major transitions, like the transition from elementary school to junior high and from junior high to senior high (Eccles et al., 1993; Ryan, 2001). This may be partly due to students' perceptions that the teachers in their new school do not care about them in comparison to teachers at the previous school, especially among minority students (see Chapter 6). The decline may also be partly due to increasing demands on personal responsibility and organization—doing your homework on your own, showing up for class, keeping track of when homework is due, and completing assignments on time (Gregory, 1995).

What is the difference between grades and standardized test scores, which are modestly correlated? Do they measure the same thing? How might intelligence affect the correlation?

5-3b Individual Diversity in Achievement

Students vary in their academic achievement. This variation is relatively stable and predicts later outcomes, like dropping out of school.

Stability of Individual Differences in Achievement

Can you remember who were the highest or lowest achievers in your 1st-grade class? If you stayed in the same school district, you probably saw these same peers maintain their academic status through high school. Achievement rank tends to be fairly stable across childhood, whether measured by standardized tests or by GPA (e.g., Ladd & Dinella, 2009; Mok, McInerney, Zhu, & Or, 2015). That is, children who are high achievers at one age tend to be high achievers at another age. However, this does not mean that children never change. Even though achievement is quite stable, it does change for some students.

What Do Individual Differences in Achievement Predict?

To the extent that grades and test scores reflect meaningful knowledge, high academic achievement is its own reward. Greater knowledge helps children be more informed citizens and better problem solvers. High achievement also opens doors of opportunity for a college education, which becomes an avenue for high-status employment that requires advanced training. Research shows that high achievers tend to have greater career success and higher income than lower achievers (Lubinski et al., 2014; Ritchie & Bates, 2013).

You may be interested to know that achievement in *college* also predicts career success. College grades have a small to moderate relationship with adult salary, promotions, job performance, and success in graduate school, with grades in one's major having the greatest predictive power (Roth, BeVier, Switzer, & Schippmann, 1996).

In contrast, *low achievement,* as early as elementary school, is associated with dropping out of school, particularly when low achievement is combined with other factors such as low classroom engagement and low parental expectations. Retention in grade is one of the consequences of low achievement. Retention is also associated with later dropping out, even when it occurs in 1st grade (Stearns, Moller, Blau, & Potochnick, 2007). Dropping out, in turn, is associated with lower wages, higher rates of welfare dependency, and increased criminality (Alexander, Entwisle, & Kabbani, 2001).

underachievement
earning grades that are substantially below those of other students with similar cognitive ability as measured by standardized tests.

A special form of low achievement, known as **underachievement**, is also linked to negative outcomes. Underachievement refers to receiving grades that are substantially below those of other students *with similar cognitive ability*. Research suggests that underachievers participate less in extracurricular activities, date more, and tend to have either extremely close or extremely distant relationships with their parents. After high school they hold lower-income first jobs, complete fewer years of college, are not promoted in their jobs as fast, change jobs more frequently, and are more likely to divorce than normal achievers and overachievers (McCall, Evahn, & Kratzer, 1992). However, some underachievers catch up to their same-ability peers after high school. Those who catch up may have higher educational aspirations, better-educated parents, and less-serious underachievement in high school. They may be exceptions. For most students, underachievement may be chronic.

What Predicts Individual Differences in Achievement?

A variety of factors contribute to children's achievement in school—the child, family, culture, and school. You've read about several factors in earlier chapters and will read about more in each of the subsequent chapters. For example, child factors that contribute to higher achievement include emotional and social competence, which will be discussed in Chapters 6 through 11. Child behaviors that contribute to academic failure include poor behavior at school, low attendance, low homework completion, flunking a grade, not expecting to complete high school, and academic disengagement (Lucio, Hunt, & Bornovalova, 2012).

Several family characteristics are associated with academic achievement. You have already seen that maternal depression, parental substance use, family stress, and family investment are linked to children's achievement. So are frequent family moves that involve changing schools, which also predict low self-control and greater inattention and impulsivity (Friedman-Krauss & Raver, 2015; Ziol-Guest & McKenna, 2014). In Chapter 1 you learned that accumulation of risk factors predicts lower achievement. In Chapter 6 you will learn that secure attachment between parent and child is linked to higher achievement. In Chapter 7 you will learn that parenting style and discipline are linked to achievement. Other factors that affect academic achievement, such as divorce, social skills, and motivation, will also be discussed in later chapters. Thus, you will keep revisiting the issue of child and family characteristics linked to achievement throughout this text.

5-3c Group Diversity in Achievement

Gender, SES, and ethnicity are linked to achievement, with SES having the largest effect. Let's begin with gender differences. Some popular books claim that schools short-change boys and others claim the same for girls. Just how do boys and girls differ in achievement?

Gender

Girls tend to earn higher *grades* than boys at all grade levels, including in math and science; the effect size is small (0.23) but consistent (Valla & Ceci, 2011; Voyer & Voyer, 2014). The female advantage is larger for language courses than for math and science courses. The advantage has existed for 100 years, so despite media hype, there is not a new crisis for boys. Girls also tend to earn higher *standardized test scores* in language, but boys do better on some math tests, especially the SAT math test. Boys tend to stack at the highest end of math tests so that there are more male than female top scorers (Stoet & Geary, 2015). The male math advantage is more pronounced on items that require spatial ability, and the female language advantage is more pronounced for tests that require writing (Halpern et al., 2007). Girls tend to do more homework than boys, which might explain the gender gap in achievement (Gershenson & Holt, 2015). While gender differences are mostly small, SES differences can be large.

Socioeconomic Status

Hundreds of studies have shown that on the average, low-SES children tend to have lower academic achievement than higher-SES children (Sirin, 2005). In Chapter 1 you learned that the effects of SES emerge in the preschool years and get larger with age. For example, in one study, 75% of the children in an upper-middle-income school already had informal arithmetic knowledge before entering school (see Chapter 4), whereas only 7% of children in a lower-income school had this knowledge (Case, Griffin, & Kelly, 2001). By the time they enter school, impoverished children have lower math and reading abilities, and do not catch up to nonpoor children (Pianta, Belsky, Vandergrift, Houts, & Morrison, 2008; Votruba-Drzal, Li-Grining, & Maldonado-Carreno, 2008). These differences may be driven by mother's education; children with college-educated mothers enter kindergarten with higher academic skills, and make greater gains once in school (Grimm, Steele, Mashburn, Burchinal, & Pianta, 2010).

The SES achievement gap occurs across countries (Akiba, LeTendre, & Scribner, 2007). The Program for International Student Assessment (PISA) monitors achievement in many countries throughout the world. This program finds that the achievement gap in the United States is moderate; some countries have larger and some have smaller achievement gaps. Again, parental education, rather than income, is particularly powerful in predicting children's academic achievement across countries.

How does SES affect academic achievement? In Chapter 1 you learned that two plausible explanations are the family stress and family investment models. These models suggest that SES influences children through quality of parenting and opportunities that parental income and education make possible, such as owning books, visiting museums, and travel. However, some high-SES parents do *not* provide such experiences, and some low-SES parents do. Achievement-promoting family activities include things like reading to the child, discussing complex topics, attending church, helping with homework, going to the library, and encouraging achievement. Both high- and low-income families do these things, so some of your low-SES students will do well in school and some high-SES students will be underachievers.

While low achievement among poor children may be partially explained by family factors, it is also explained by less *opportunity to learn* (OTL) at school. A key part of OTL is having high-quality teachers (O'Connor & Fernandez, 2006). Poor children are less likely to have high-quality teachers who are effective at presenting information and using time. Part of becoming a high-quality teacher is knowledge of child development (Darling-Hammond, 2007)—so keep reading! The higher the percentage of high-quality teachers in a school, the higher the achievement test scores of students. Tuerk (2005) estimates that in a school of 400 students in 8th grade, for every percentage point gain in qualified teachers, 10 to 20 more students would pass their proficiency tests.

Unfortunately, as the percentage of poor children in a school rises, so does the percentage of classes taught by teachers who are not certified in the area in which they teach (Tuerk, 2005). Thus, inequality of education exacerbates differences in family resources between high- and low-SES learners. The achievement gap is lower in countries that assign the best teachers to the poorest students (Akiba et al., 2007).

The SES achievement gap has become larger than the ethnic achievement gap between Black children and White children (Reardon, 2011), but ethnic differences remain. We will look at those next.

Ethnicity

Some children in all ethnic groups do well in school. However, in Chapter 1 you learned that there are large average differences in achievement among ethnic groups in America. From kindergarten to high school, on average, students of Asian descent tend to have high achievement and African American and Latino students tend to have relatively low achievement (Palacios, Guttmannova, & Chase-Lansdale, 2008; Raudenbush, 2009). White students are in between. The average 17-year-old African American or Hispanic student can do math and read as well as an average White 13-year-old (Rampey, Dion, & Donahue, 2009). The National Assessment of Educational Progress (NAEP) has been tracking student achievement in the United States at the 4th-, 8th-, and 12th-grade level for more than 35 years. NAEP has found that Black and Latino children's achievement has risen since the late 1990s, slightly narrowing the achievement gap. Graduation rates also vary. Nationwide, the graduation rate is about 50% for African American students, 53% for Hispanic students, and 75% for White students (Orfield, Losen, Wald, & Swanson, 2004).

The achievement gap raises issues of social justice and equity. Why is there an achievement gap? Researchers have tried to answer this question for decades, teachers have tried to close the gap, and the federal government has outlawed the gap. Yet the gap remains. This suggests there is no single large cause, but probably many subtle causes working together. One cause is that SES and ethnicity are linked. Research consistently shows that low-income students are disproportionately minority students (Kim & Sunderman, 2005). Thus, the same factors explaining the SES achievement gap may largely, but not completely, explain the ethnicity gap.

Classroom skills such as attentiveness, persistence, and organization may explain part of the achievement gap. In a national study of literacy, children with these classroom skills learned more. African American boys tended to have the lowest achievement, but those with attentiveness, persistence, and organization had achievement similar to higher-SES students from homes with richer literacy environments (Matthews, Kizzie, Rowley, & Cortina, 2010). These classroom skills are learned at home and have little genetic basis, so students can be trained in them in your classroom (Roisman & Fraley, 2012). Throughout this text you will learn how to promote such cognitive, emotional, and social skills in your learners.

Still another plausible cause of the achievement gap is that schools with predominantly ALANA (African, Latino, Asian, and Native American) students tend to be overcrowded, lack textbooks, and have fewer qualified teachers (Darling-Hammond, 2007). Minority students may also experience overly harsh discipline and low expectations from teachers (O'Connor & Fernandez, 2006; Stinson, 2006; Wiggan, 2007). For example, one study showed that Black and Latino students who perceived that

EVERETT COLLECTION, INC.

PHOTO 5.7 Actor Edward James Olmos and Jaime Escalante on location at Garfield High School in East Los Angeles in 1988.

their teachers played favorites and held lower expectations for minority students achieved substantially less than same-ability White or Asian students (McKown & Weinstein, 2008).

Other plausible causes were discussed in Chapter 1. To review, one explanation is differences in school-related *cultural capital,* which refers to knowledge and relationships that foster opportunity to learn and ability to move through the system. For example, ALANA students tend to be tracked out of honors or AP classes, regardless of standardized test scores, partly because of the lack of mentors or knowledge about how the system works (Darling-Hammond, 2007). Another explanation is *cultural mismatch*—a pattern of incompatibilities between home and school in language and narrative style. Students who experience more compatibility between home and school are at an advantage for school achievement.

Teachers who succeed with low-SES and ALANA students tend to be highly engaging and very demanding. For example, Garfield High School, a primarily Latino school in East Los Angeles, became extraordinarily successful at preparing students to pass the AP Calculus exam. Jaime Escalante, a teacher whose story was made into the film *Stand and Deliver,* was instrumental in this success (Photo 5.7). At his school, students performed better than at any nonmagnet inner-city high school in the country. "Garfield produced 27% of all Mexican Americans in the country who scored 3 or higher in Calculus AB [typical exam], and 22% of Mexican Americans who scored at that level on the BC [more advanced exam]" (Mathews, 1988, p. 301). The AP test is scored from 1 to 5, with 3 being a passing grade that receives credit at most colleges and universities. You can personally help narrow the achievement gap by developing expertise as a teacher—which this text is designed to help you do.

Cross-National Comparisons

Two sets of standardized assessments are conducted in countries across the world. The TIMSS (Trends in International Mathematics and Science Study) is conducted every 4 years with 4th- and 8th-graders. The PISA (Program for International Student Assessment) is conducted every 3 years with 15-year-olds. Table 5.3 ranks 12 countries that participated in both TIMSS and PISA. According to the 2011 TIMSS, 4th- and 8th-graders in the United States are above average in math and science as compared with students in all countries, but do worse than children in most Asian and many European countries. It is interesting that for industrialized countries, achievement is not related to spending; the United States spends more per pupil than many higher-achieving countries.

National differences appear early. Chinese children have better math skills than U.S. children as early as preschool (Siegler & Mu, 2008). Finland, which had mediocre schools in the 1980s, has quickly moved to the top on international achievement

TABLE 5.3 Ranking for mathematics among twelve countries

Country (alphabetical)	Rank		
	TIMSS grade 4	TIMSS grade 8	PISA age 15
Australia	9	8	7
Finland	5	6	4
Hong Kong	3	3	2
Italy	8	10	10
Japan	4	4	5
Korea	2	1	3
New Zealand	11	11	6
Russian Federation	6	5	11
Singapore	1	2	1
Sweden	10	9	8
Turkey	12	12	12
United States	7	7	9

Highlights from TIMSS 2011 and PISA 2012. Results for 12 countries that participated in both assessments.

Source: OECD PISA 2012 Database and TIMSS 2011 International Results in Mathematics

tests like PISA and TIMSS (see Figure 5.8), which has directed a lot of attention to Finnish schools. A key aspect of Finnish success is that the students learn more *and* display low variation (i.e., most students are doing well). The United States has mediocre achievement *and* huge variation in achievement (with a large percentage of low achievers). What might cause Asian and Finnish students to perform so well? Researchers have identified some explanations:

- Asian parents give greater emphasis to the role of effort, rather than innate ability, in achievement (see Chapter 13). So Asian students study more.

- Math ability is more highly valued in Asia than in the United States, and Asian children spend more time practicing math. In contrast, beginning in kindergarten, U.S. teachers spend much more time on reading than math (Claessens, Engel, & Curran, 2014).

- Asian children spend more time in school and spend more time-on-task during class (Photo 5.8). They are also often enrolled in after-school cram schools. In contrast, Finnish students spend less time in school than other high-achieving countries.

- Generally, countries that use high-stakes tests tend to have higher achievement (Fuchs & Wößmann, 2007; Rindermann & Ceci, 2009). However, Finland has high achievement without high-stakes tests (Sahlberg, 2011).

FIGURE 5.8 TIMSS Science Performance of 4th-Grade Students.

Country	Average Scale Score		4th-Grade Science Achievement Distribution
Korea, Rep. of	587	●	
Singapore	583	●	
Finland	570	●	
Japan	559	●	
Russian Federation	552	●	
Chinese Taipei	552	●	
United States	544	●	
Czech Republic	536	●	
Hong Kong SAR	535	●	
Hungary	534	●	
Sweden	533	●	
Slovak Republic	532	●	
Austria	532	●	
Netherlands	531	●	
England	529	●	
Denmark	528	●	
Germany	528	●	
Italy	524	●	
Portugal	522	●	
Slovenia	520	●	
Northern Ireland	517	●	
Ireland	516	●	
Croatia	516	●	
Australia	516	●	
Serbia	516	●	
Lithuania	515	●	
Belgium (Flemish)	509	●	
Romania	505		
Spain	505		
Poland	505		
TIMSS Scale Centerpoint	500		
New Zealand	497		
Kazakhstan	495		
Norway	494	○	
Chile	480	○	
Thailand	472	○	
Turkey	463	○	
Georgia	455	○	
Iran, Islamic Rep. of	453	○	
Bahrain	449	○	
Malta	446	○	
Azerbaijan	438	○	
Saudi Arabia	429	○	
United Arab Emirates	428	○	
Armenia	416	○	
Qatar	394	○	
Oman	377	○	
Kuwait	347	○	
Tunisia	346	○	
Morocco	264	○	
Yemen	209	○	

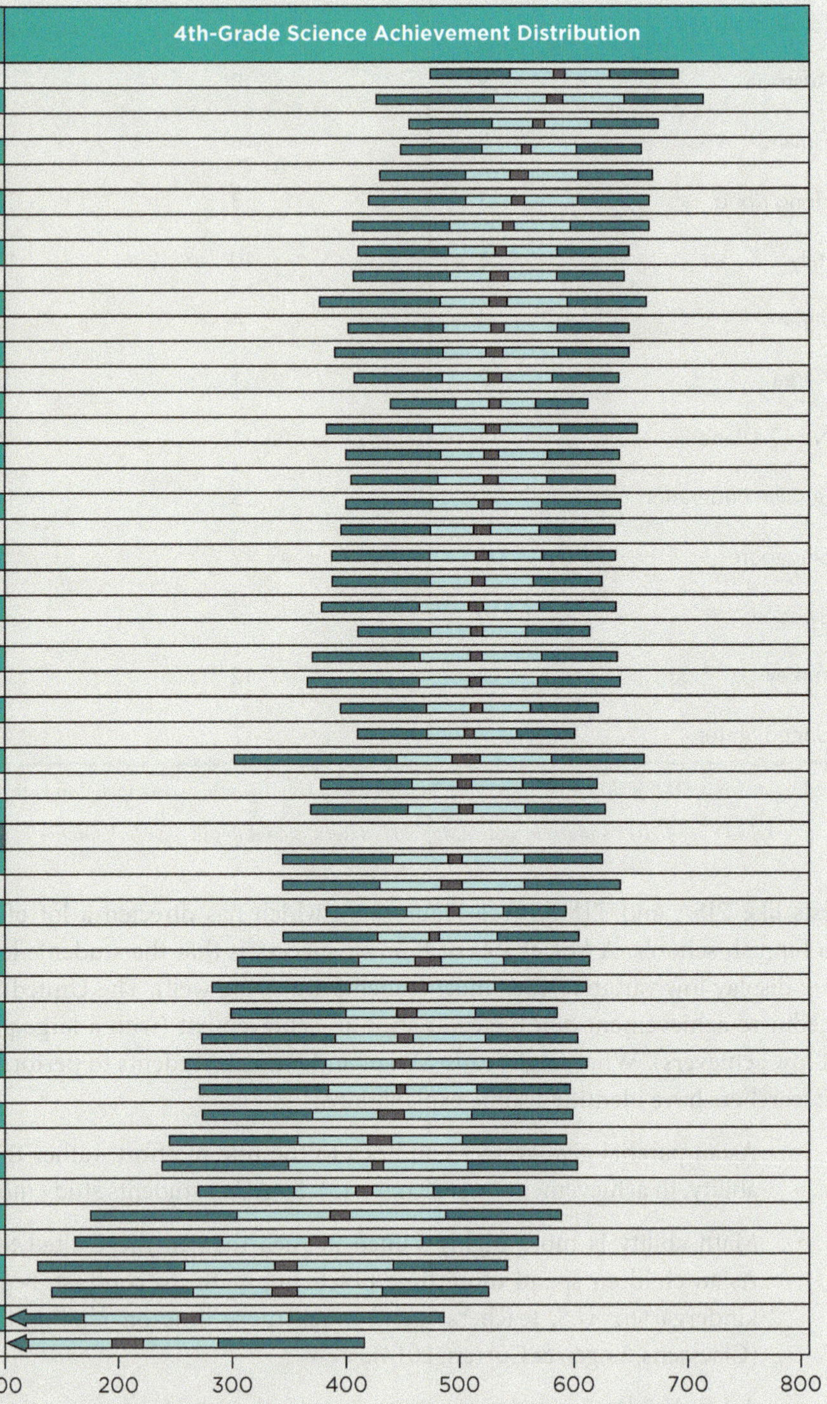

● Country average significantly higher than the centerpoint of the TIMSS 4th-grade scale

○ Country average significantly lower than the centerpoint of the TIMSS 4th-grade scale

Percentiles of Performance
5th 25th 75th 95th
95% Confidence Interval for Average (±2SE)

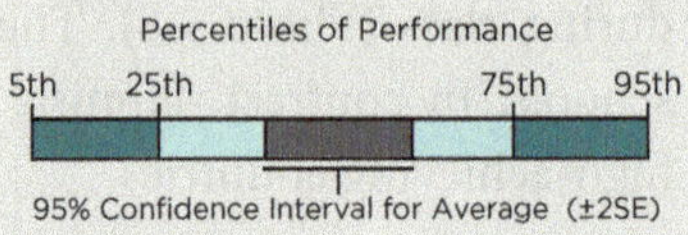

How would you describe the U.S. placement? *Source: TIMSS 2011 International Results in Science.*

- In Finland, teaching is a highly desirable profession. About 10% of applicants are admitted to teacher education, and they must complete a research-based master's thesis (Sahlberg, 2011).

- Finnish and Asian teachers teach fewer hours compared to U.S. teachers, and they have time to craft their lessons more carefully.

A key cause of achievement is teaching expertise. A classic study compared 5th-grade math lessons in the United States and Asia (Stevenson & Stigler, 1992). In one Asian class, the teacher entered with containers of different sizes and asked the class which container would hold the most water. The children disagreed with each other, so she asked them how to solve the problem. They suggested putting water in the containers and measuring it. They divided into small groups to do this, and then graphed the results on the board together. The teacher reviewed what they had done, introduced the concept of graphing, and posed the original question again before the class ended. In a comparable U.S. class, the teacher sent some children out of the room for band or other activities before beginning the math lesson with the remaining children. He went over a problem assigned for homework the previous day, and then had the children silently go over a new assignment in their books. He walked about the room quieting children. These differences were typical of the two cultures. Many (47%) of the U.S. 5th-grade classrooms were interrupted by irrelevant activities (e.g., presenting lunch choices), whereas only 0 to 10% of Asian classrooms were.

PHOTO 5.8 Asian classes tend to be large, but achievement is high.

Asian teachers teach only 3 to 4 hours, or 50 to 60% of the school day. The rest of the day is spent doing other tasks and polishing the next day's lessons. Asian expert teachers are given leave from the classroom to coach novice teachers. Teachers work with colleagues to perfect lesson plans. In contrast, U.S. teachers have little discretionary time to plan lessons and spend too much time in the classroom. U.S. curriculum is also "an inch deep and a mile wide," meaning too many topics are covered, and hence are covered superficially (Stedman, 1997).

5-3d Classroom Implications of Research on Achievement

We can learn from the research on cross-national achievement. For example, U.S. teachers could improve by polishing their lessons more; however, U.S. schools should not necessarily imitate other countries in ways that are not compatible with their culture. We can also learn from the research on SES and ethnic differences within the United States. Teachers could be more tuned in to the cultural capital of their students and find ways to help those with few resources. Sometimes providing cultural capital can be as simple as helping learners get into the right classes for the next year. It can be explaining to learners what is required to become a firefighter, teacher, or lawyer. It can be providing school resources like access to computers or books so that learners can be successful at school tasks.

Research has identified many school factors that affect achievement. Earlier in this chapter, you learned that deliberate practice and feedback are critical to developing expertise. Seven additional school factors that are linked to achievement will be discussed next: testing, study skills, time-on-task, homework, retention in grade, class size, and high-stakes tests.

Testing

In Chapter 4 you learned that students remember content better when they have been tested on it. You can enhance your students' learning by testing frequently (Brown, Roediger, & McDaniel, 2014). The quizzes need not be graded, but students must commit to an answer; otherwise, when they hear the answer, they are likely to think that they already knew it. You could use paper-and-pencil quizzes, questions that you project on a screen, or electronic clickers. You can use similar, but not identical, test items on several different days (spaced practice). Using different wording prevents students from just memorizing the answer rather than understanding the concept and helps them transfer their understanding to different situations, which improves later performance (Glass & Sinha, 2013). Testing improves performance for students of all ages (Lipowski, Pyc, Dunlosky, & Rawson, 2014). Remember that students tend to *believe* that restudying is more effective than testing, even though it usually is not.

Study Skills

It may surprise you, but many students do not develop good study skills. You can improve your students' achievement by teaching them effective study skills (Dunlosky et al., 2013; Pashler et al., 2007). What skills should you teach? Research suggests the following:

1. Self-testing, which helps students determine whether they have understood and will remember what they studied, may result in deeper conceptual learning than rereading. *Delayed* self-testing is best. Teach your students to wait a little while rather than self-testing right after studying.

2. Spaced, or distributed, practice rather than cramming. Cramming does little to improve long-term learning and retention.

3. Asking and answering complex or deep questions about the material, such as *What caused X to occur? What if Y had occurred instead? What are similarities and differences in X and Y?* For example, a student trying to understand that distance from the sun does *not* cause the seasons could ask questions like *In the Northern Hemisphere, what is the difference between shadows at noon in winter and summer? Why?*

Some common study skills—such as underlining and highlighting or merely re-reading—are not particularly effective.

Time-on-Task

Time-on-task, or *academic learning time,* is the amount of time spent learning at school after subtracting time for taking attendance, messing around, lunch, recess, daydreaming, and so forth. Thus, time-on-task is much less than *allocated learning time,* which is the time that is set aside for a particular topic. Time-on-task is linked to the amount of academic growth children experience, after controlling for prior achievement (Pianta, Belsky, Vandergrift, Houts, & Morrison, 2008). Time-on-task tends to be low in U.S. schools, and varies greatly from class to class.

Off-task time can be due to learners' inability to control their attention. It can also be the result of student sabotage, such as when students get the teacher talking about his or her dating life, in order to avoid discussing the course topic. Off-task time can also be the result of poor teaching. In a junior high we observed a teacher spend 40 minutes of a 50-minute class going over instructions for an assignment, like breaking down how many points each component was worth, how to turn it in if it was late, and so on. No content was taught. In contrast, another teacher put children to work solving a geometry problem at their desks as soon as they entered the room. When most had finished, she had three students solve the same problem on the board. As a class, they compared different approaches and discussed better ways to solve it. The teacher modeled how to solve one problem, and students modeled how to solve others. Only 5 minutes of 50 were spent discussing the next assignment. We also observed a preschool where an 18-month-old boy repeatedly asked to be read a book on airplanes. One teacher merely read the book verbatim. A second teacher helped him count the seven airplanes on the page. The second teacher provided more time-on-task for math learning. Typically preschoolers spend almost half (44%) of their time in noninstructional activities such as waiting in line to wash hands (Early et al., 2010). Thus, a key classroom variable that you, the teacher, will directly influence is time-on-task.

One way to increase time-on-task is by offering academic instruction after school or during the summer. Evidence shows that these sorts of interventions, if well implemented with high-quality curriculum, can increase achievement (Bergin, Hudson, Chryst, & Resetar, 1992; Zvoch & Stevens, 2013).

Homework

Does homework facilitate achievement? Not as robustly as you might think. The relationship between achievement and homework is complex because, for example, diligent but low-ability students might do lots of homework yet earn low grades. Some high-ability students with good grades boast about doing almost no homework; they finish their schoolwork on the bus or during easy, boring classes. Still others take several AP classes and have a crushing load of homework. Overall, research shows almost no relationship between homework and achievement for kindergarten to 6th-grade students and a consistently positive relationship for junior and senior high school students (Cooper, Robinson, & Patall, 2006; Eren & Henderson, 2011). Effects are stronger for math than for other subjects.

Homework is more effective if it is of high quality and supports classroom learning objectives (Photo 5.9). That is, it is not busy work, is interesting, requires concentrated thought, but is not so difficult that students cannot figure out what to do (Dettmers, Trautwein, Lüdtke, Kunter, & Baumert, 2010; Rosário et al., 2015). High-quality homework can serve as deliberate practice and as time-on-task.

Homework can be overdone. Students in privileged, high-performing high schools have reported averaging over 3 hours of homework per night. These students tended to be engaged in school, but also reported academic stress, poor sleep patterns,

PHOTO 5.9 Homework can promote achievement, if it is of high quality.

physical health problems, and inadequate time for family and friends. For example, one student said, "If I go to bed before 1:30 I feel like I'm slacking off, or just screwing myself over for an even later night later in the week.... There's never a break. Never." Students described some homework as a "waste of time," "trivial," "repetitive," and "mindless" (Galloway, Conner, & Pope, 2013).

The National PTA (a parent–teacher organization), the NEA (national teachers' union), and researchers recommend that appropriate homework is about 10 to 20 minutes per day in grades K–2, and about 30 to 60 minutes per day in grades 3–6 (Cooper & Valentine, 2001). They did not make a specific recommendation for junior or senior high school. In summary, as Marzano (2007, p. 71) recommends:

- Assign less homework to younger students.

- The amount of homework should not be a burden to parents or students. This may require communication among teachers.

- Homework should have a clear learning purpose.

Retention in Grade

One way that schools attempt to improve learning of low-achieving students is by having them repeat a grade. Some believe retention is a "gift of time" for late-developing children to catch up to their peers. Others believe it harms children because it is viewed as punishment and makes children feel inferior. What does the research say?

Retention predicts later dropping out and a lower likelihood of attending college (Alexander et al., 2001; Ou & Reynolds, 2010). It also predicts worsening achievement, greater anxiety, increased disruptive behavior, and increased inattentiveness across elementary school, beyond preexisting problems. However, the research is correlational so it is not clear whether retention causes the behavior and achievement problems.

Students who are retained are more likely to be male and to have other risk factors such as low SES, low birth weight, and poor social skills (Pagani, Tremblay, Vitaro, Boulerice, & McDuff, 2001). Minority students are more likely than White students to be retained, and subsequently to drop out.

A study of students retained in 1st grade found that over the next 4 years, they showed some improvement in achievement, but also erosion of their improvement, suggesting an unhealthy pattern of failure, success, and failure, yet greater likelihood of passing the 3rd-grade proficiency test. They had reduced hyperactivity and improved academic confidence (Hughes, Chen, Thoemmes, & Kwok, 2010; Wu, West, & Hughes, 2010). Staying in kindergarten an extra year means that the student will likely be 19 at graduation, not 18, and being older is a risk factor for not graduating at all.

Thus, retention is an expensive intervention (about $12,400 per student per year of school) with mostly small effects (Allen, Chen, Willson, & Hughes, 2009; Cham, Hughes, West, & Im, 2015). Struggling students, whether retained or not, may need more intensive, targeted support.

Class Size

Some studies find that small classes of about 12 to 17 are linked to achievement gains in the primary and middle grades. The longer students are in small classes, the greater the effect. However, some studies find the effects occur only up to 1st grade, and primarily for high-achieving students.[1] Other studies find positive effects primarily for low-SES and African American students (Winne & Nesbit, 2010). Furthermore, not all studies find a positive effect, and when positive effects are found, they are small (Whitehurst & Chingos, 2011). The effects may be small because teachers do not change their teaching approach much when they move from large to small classes (Winne & Nesbit, 2010). The small positive findings may not generalize to districts that cannot hire additional *qualified* teachers (due to a shortage) and that lack additional classrooms. Districts with these limitations may "reduce" class size by adding teachers to a classroom, so that instead of a 15:1 student–teacher ratio, it is 30:2. In these situations, teachers may simply trade off teaching 30 students at a time—one does clerical work while the other teaches—without altering their teaching approach (Graue, Hatch, Rao, & Oen, 2007). Thus, small class size may sometimes help, but is not robustly linked, to improved achievement (Finn et al., 2001).

High-Stakes Tests

To raise the achievement of all students and to close the achievement gap between SES and ethnic groups, the federal government requires schools to test all students to determine whether the gap is closing and to ensure that all students have grade-level proficiency in core content. These are **high-stakes tests**, designed to create strong incentives to improve achievement. Based on test scores, schools are designated as *in need of improvement* or as making *annual yearly progress*. When a school is designated as needing improvement for a few years or more, drastic measures can be taken such as replacing teachers, giving students the option to transfer to another school, or even the takeover of the school by the state or other group. This is an example of *standards-based reform*, which refers to attempts to improve achievement by setting standards and holding educators accountable for achieving those standards.

high-stakes tests
tests used to make decisions that have educational or financial impact.

In some states, these mandated tests are not high stakes for students because nothing happens to individual students who get low scores. There is little reason for students to try hard on the tests. However, other states make the tests high stakes for students because they cannot graduate or be promoted if they do not achieve a specific score.

Is this approach working? The data so far suggest that there is a small increase in math and reading scores on the NAEP, but it is not closing the achievement gap (Lee, 2008). Schools designated as needing improvement tend to have a majority of poor or ALANA students enrolled. The high-stakes testing approach is more effective for math than for reading, and for elementary than for secondary students. Some have suggested that children who are just at the border of proficiency are nudging up, but there is no change for higher and lower achievers (Porter & Polikoff, 2007). States that respond to accountability testing by raising teacher certification

[1] Many studies have documented this, just a few of which are listed here: Ehrenberg, Brewer, Gamoran, and Willms (2001); Finn, Gerber, Achilles, and Boyd-Zaharias (2001); Hanushek (1999); Konstantopoulos (2008); Nye, Hedges, and Konstantopoulos (2001).

Westend61/Red Chopsticks Images/Jupiterimages

PHOTO 5.10 You can teach your students test-taking skills.

standards, improving professional development, and increasing school resources are more successful (Lee, 2008).

You can prepare your students for high-stakes tests by teaching test-taking skills such as the following (adapted from Kubiszyn & Borich, 2003, pp. 38–42):

1. Follow directions carefully.

2. Read test items, passages, and related information carefully; this may require highlighting, rereading, and double-checking.

3. Manage test-taking time. You can provide practice with timed assignments.

4. Attempt easier items first. Some students quit when they come to a difficult item, assuming they will not be able to get further items correct. You can provide practice on classroom tests so that students get used to tests *not* being ordered from easy to difficult.

5. Eliminate obviously incorrect options before choosing an answer.

6. Check answers if there is time.

7. Take advantage of preparation materials that are available. For example, many states provide practice tests.

However, avoid overemphasizing proficiency tests. You can undermine your students' motivation if you hold the test up as the primary reason for learning. According to one 7th-grade girl:

All the teachers care about is the proficiency test. They don't care if we learn anything. They're always saying stuff like, "Now, you'd better restate the question, because if you don't, you'll lose points on the proficiency test." Who cares? In life, do you have to restate the question?

In summary, school factors associated with academic achievement include testing frequently, teaching study skills (Photo 5.10), and fostering more time-on-task. Sometimes assigning homework is useful. Retaining low-achieving students in grade is not generally associated with improved achievement. Small class size is sometimes found to be associated with higher achievement. High-stakes testing has not yet demonstrated strong positive effects on achievement, although that is the intent. In the next chapters you will see how emotional well-being contributes to achievement and other child outcomes.

My Teaching

Children differ in cognitive abilities such as intelligence, talent, and achievement. While intelligence may have some basis in genes, all cognitive development is influenced by the environment, which includes the quality of education a child receives. As a teacher you can improve each student's cognitive ability by asking yourself the following:

1. How do I define intelligence? Do I view it as changeable?

2. What does it mean to be intelligent within the culture of my students? Do my views place them at a disadvantage?

3. Do my instruction and assessments include analysis, creativity, and practical applications? Do I value all types of "intelligence"? Which types of intelligence best fit my mode of instruction and assessment? How can I better accommodate all my students?

4. What do I view as the cause of talent? What talents do I value? Do the families of my students value the same talents? Does my school recognize forms of giftedness besides high intelligence? Does my school use multiple pieces of evidence to place students in gifted or remedial programs?

5. How am I helping to develop talents in my students? Do I provide opportunities for deliberate practice? Do I maximize time-on-task?

6. How can I apply principles of deliberate practice to improve my teaching? Have I sought feedback from others about my teaching? Do I frequently reflect on the quality of my teaching?

7. Am I careful to be tuned in to underachievers? Is my school doing all it can to prevent retention in grade?

8. Do I teach effective study skills within the content I teach?

9. Which practices of high-achieving countries might I adopt to enhance achievement—such as emphasizing effort rather than ability, spending more time-on-task, collaborating with colleagues to polish lessons, or eliminating interruptions?

Professional Resource Download

Summary of Age Trends in Cognitive Ability

	Intelligence	Talent and Expertise	Achievement
Infancy & Toddlerhood (Birth–2 Years)	• Individual differences in speed of habituation predict intelligence years later. • Habituation and recognition memory studies demonstrate that 3- to 5-month-olds have many cognitive abilities like object permanence, a sense of time and quantity, understanding of causation, reasoning, and categorization.	• Some talents may begin to emerge during toddlerhood.	• Achievement is not measured in infants and toddlers.
Early Childhood (3–5 Years)	• There are few reliable and valid measures of intelligence in early childhood.	• There is no age trend in talent because talent refers to having greater competence than age-mates. • Talents valued by a culture are often introduced in early childhood, and children are given more practice in those talents.	• The achievement gap emerges in preschool. • Grades are not given in preschool.
Middle Childhood (6–12 Years)	• There are no age trends in intelligence test scores because intelligence tests are designed for comparison to same-age peers. • Intelligence scores have risen across the world over the past several decades.	• Children who are experts in a domain have better memory for new experiences in that domain than do adult novices. • Middle childhood may be the latest one can start in some, but not all, domains in order to develop world-class expertise.	• Small class size in the primary grades may promote a slight increase in achievement. • National and international trends in achievement begin to be tracked in 4th grade. • Homework has little effect on elementary school achievement.
Adolescence (13–19 Years)	• Intelligence scores are largely stable after age 11, but are least stable before age 11.	• Expertise is the result of practicing hundreds of hours, for several years, so it is seldom manifest before the teens.	• The SES and racial achievement gaps are largest in high school. • Grades tend to get worse from late elementary through high school. • Homework is weakly related to achievement in junior high and somewhat stronger in high school. The relationship is complex because weaker students might do more homework but earn lower grades.

≫ Professional Resource Download

Chapter Summary

5-1 Intelligence

- Intelligence is a general mental capability that includes the ability to reason, solve problems, think and learn quickly, and deal with abstraction and complexity.

- Tests of cognitive abilities and academic achievement tend to correlate with each other, suggesting a *g* factor.

- According to Sternberg's Theory of Successful Intelligence, there are three components to intelligence: (1) analytic, (2) practical, and (3) creative. According to Gardner there are multiple intelligences—linguistic, logical–mathematical, spatial, musical, kinesthetic, natural, interpersonal, and intrapersonal. His theory has been criticized and has little research support. However, the theory helps teachers reconsider their perceptions of what ability is, and their decisions about what to teach and how to teach it.

- Intelligence is measured with individual or group tests. Intelligence test scores typically have a mean of 100 and a standard deviation of 15.

- Nativists believe innate knowledge in core domains, such as number and language, may be hardwired into the brain. However, mature competence in core domains requires learning, suggesting an interactionist view.

- Through habituation and recognition memory studies, we know that infants only a few months old have greater cognitive abilities than previously believed.

- Intelligence in influenced by genes and by the environment. The genetic contribution to intelligence is greater for high-SES children and older youth.

- Higher intelligence is associated with higher school achievement, higher SES, and better job performance in adulthood. Intelligence protects children from life stresses and poor health.

- Low-SES children have lower average intelligence test scores than high-SES children.

- There are few gender differences in *general* intelligence. However, on average, males score higher on tests of spatial ability.

- Differences in intelligence test scores across ethnic groups may be a function of socioeconomic status, differences in opportunity to learn, and cultural differences in abilities that are valued. Generally, tests are equally good predictors of future performance across ethnic groups.

- The Flynn effect is a worldwide cohort effect of rising intelligence scores.

- Intelligence tests are commonly used to diagnose students for remedial or gifted education. However, they should not be used as the sole basis for program admission.

5-2 Talent and Expertise

- Talent and expertise both refer to having great skill compared to peers. Deliberate practice, good instruction, and feedback are critical for developing talent.

- In some domains, world-class performance typically requires at least 10 years of intensive practice, and a late start may prevent its development.

- Talented students use their time more productively than do their peers and have greater motivation to practice.

- Experts have better memory and pattern recognition for their domain of expertise than do nonexperts.

- Cultures vary in how much they value specific talents and how they introduce young children to talent development.

- Schools tend to take a narrow view of giftedness, equating it with high intelligence. However, students can be talented in some domains without having high *g*.

- Teachers can apply principles of deliberate practice to improve their students' expertise (e.g., increase time-on-task and provide feedback) and their own teaching (e.g., seek feedback and prepare to adapt lessons as appropriate).

5-3 Achievement

- Achievement is measured by grades or standardized tests. Achievement tends to be fairly stable across time, though some students do change their achievement levels.

- High achievement is linked to career success. Low achievement predicts retention and dropping out, and later, erratic employment.

- School factors associated with higher achievement include frequent testing, teaching study skills, and providing more time-on-task. Small class size and homework are sometimes found to be associated with higher achievement.

- Cross-national studies indicate that U.S. students are low-average in science and math. Asian and Finnish students are higher achieving. These differences begin in elementary school and may be due to more time-on-task, more effort, and more teacher time spent polishing lessons.

chapter **6**

digitalskillet/E+/Getty Images

Attachment and Personality

Does the attachment relationship students have with their parents influence the relationships they have with teachers or the grades they earn in school? In this chapter, we will discuss attachment at length, because it sets the stage for children's academic and social success from preschool through high school. Then we will discuss temperament, which combines with attachment to form children's personalities. **After you read this chapter, you will be able to:**

6-1 Apply knowledge of the different types of attachments and what they mean for learners' well-being to promote secure attachment and school bonding in your classroom.

6-2 Analyze how temperament and personality influence learners' success at school and provide a good fit for the personalities in your classroom.

6-1 Attachment

Audrey is a 10th-grader who drops in on the counselor frequently for long visits that typically involve tears as she describes things her parents have done that hurt her feelings. Audrey was recently diagnosed with ADHD. Her school counselor identified the ADHD, not her parents. The counselor is also concerned about anorexia. Audrey is very thin. She proudly tells the counselor, "I am not fat like my mom." Yet Audrey also tells the counselor that her parents are "awesome" and that she wants to be "just like them." Her homeroom teacher says Audrey does not seem to have close friendships with other girls but has a new boyfriend every couple months. She does her work in class, yet her test scores are surprisingly low.

attachment
a deep and enduring affectionate bond that connects one person to another across time and space.

Why does Audrey criticize and then praise her parents? Why does she seem distant from girlfriends? Audrey's puzzling behavior could be explained by her attachment history. **Attachment** is a deep, enduring emotional bond between people (Ainsworth, 1973). Typically, the most powerful attachments children have are with their parents. Parent–child attachment forms the foundation for children's personality and emotional well-being in the classroom.

Psychologists began to understand the importance of attachment in the early 1900s. At that time, orphanages had high death rates—in some orphanages an astounding 70 to 100% of infants died (Spitz, 1945). With improved conditions, death rates decreased, but many surviving infants failed to grow normally (see Chapter 2) and became cognitively delayed or delinquent as adolescents. Psychologists puzzled over why these children fared so poorly. Orphanage caregivers were purposely rotated so that children would not get overly attached to them and experience the trauma of separation. Suspecting that these rotations might be the problem, Renee Spitz compared two institutions. One was a nursery for infants of incarcerated mothers who were typically young and mentally ill or delinquent. The infants had full access to their mothers in jail, and they developed normally. The other institution was a foundling home for infants of mothers too poor to keep them. Many children became delayed because, according to Spitz, they would do nothing but lie on their backs for months, wearing a hollow into their mattresses so deep that they could not even roll over (p. 63). Social interaction was rare. By the time infants were a year old, they would silently huddle and rock themselves. They had bizarre reactions to strangers—either extreme friendliness or blood-curdling screams. Spitz's films of these children are sad to watch (you can watch them on YouTube) and helped convince people that attachment is a basic need in children. So did the work of John Bowlby and Mary Ainsworth, discussed in Box 6.1.

attachment hierarchy
the vertical organization of primary and secondary attachment figures for a specific child, with a preferred attachment figure at the top.

Most children are attached to more than one person, but they are highly selective. They typically attach to just a few people. Together these attachments form an **attachment hierarchy**, with a preferred person at the top. That preferred person is commonly the mother. Attachments can include nonfamily members, such as a teacher or babysitter. We will refer to a target of the child's attachment as an *attachment figure*.

secure base
an attachment figure who engenders a child's confidence and security, because of willingness to be available when needed while the child explores novel environments.

Children show preference for attachment figures. Children go to them when upset, protest separation from them, and use them as a **secure base** from which to explore the world. Toddlers protest separation from their primary attachment figure more than from other attachment figures and prefer that person when hungry, tired, or ill.

BOX 6.1 theories & theorists

John Bowlby and Mary Ainsworth

John Bowlby (1907–1990) treated 150 children at the famous Tavistock clinic in London. The children were aggressive, destructive, and thieving and had night terrors that he believed were the result of separation from their mothers (Bowlby, 1940). At that time, scholars in different countries from Scotland to Africa were reporting the effects of mother–child separation due to World War II, incarceration, hospitalization, and employment. Bowlby wrote a synthesis of these other scientists' reports for the World Health Organization, concluding that children who are separated from their mothers suffer physical and mental illness. His report led to changes in the care of children in hospitals and orphanages. He wrote:

The mother-love which a young child needs is so easily provided within the family, and is so very very difficult to provide outside it. … In no other relationship do human beings place themselves so unreservedly and so continuously at the disposal of others. This holds true even of bad parents—a fact too easily forgotten. … Children thrive better in bad homes than in good institutions. (Bowlby, 1952, pp. 67–78)

Before Bowlby, psychologists believed that children could be too attached, such as when they were clingy and cried at separation. The negative term *dependent* was commonly used to refer to attachment. Instead, Bowlby argued that attachment was not just a phase of dependency to be outgrown. He wrote: "whereas *dependence is maximum at birth and diminishes more or less steadily until maturity is reached, attachment is altogether absent at birth and is not strongly in evidence until after an infant is past six months*" (1969, p. 228). Secure attachment *liberates* children and should *not* be considered dependency. Bowlby shaped the current view that attachment: (1) is a

characteristic of the relationship, not the child; (2) is normal; (3) is innate with biological underpinnings; and (4) is essential to mental health.

Mary Ainsworth (1913–1999) focused psychologists' attention on *differences* in attachment security. She was hired by Bowlby to work at the Tavistock clinic with school-aged children who had lengthy separations from their parents for tuberculosis treatment. She noticed that the separation affected their personalities. In the 1950s, Ainsworth went to Uganda, where she observed babies in their village homes. She was struck by how much infants *actively* initiate attachment relationships—seeking proximity to, smiling toward, and responding preferentially to their mothers. Several years later she replicated the Uganda study in Baltimore (Ainsworth, 1973). She saw the same array of attachment behaviors in the U.S. infants as those in Uganda, although they were from very different cultures.

Ainsworth's great insight was that children who display what appear to be intense attachment behaviors, like clinging, are not more attached. The happy, secure child may *seem* to take mother for granted, while the anxious child may *seem* to be more strongly attached, but the anxious child who will not get off mother's lap to explore is actually insecurely attached.

Ainsworth was among the first to connect quality of mothering with differences in security of attachment and to point out that it is exploration and reunion behavior—not separation distress—that distinguishes secure from insecure children. Her contributions included the design of the Strange Situation Procedure, which allowed attachment to be measured in a reliable way, placing it within the realm of science. This fostered thousands of studies on how early attachment relates to later development.

However, a child might prefer a different attachment figure, such as a sibling or father, when ready to play (Bowlby, 1969). Having a strong preference for an attachment figure is normal. In fact, children who show attachment behaviors toward almost anyone and demonstrate no clear, strong preference may develop psychological problems.

Why is attachment important for children? Ethology (see Box 6.2) helps answer this question. Ethology seeks to describe the *function* of behavior from an evolutionary perspective. Attachment serves two important functions:

1. It provides a *safe haven* from danger by keeping children close to an adult protector.
2. It provides a *secure base* for moving outward to explore the world.

BOX 6.2 theories & theorists

Ethology and Critical Periods

Attachment behavior is innate and universal, suggesting that it is biologically programmed into children. Adults do not have to teach attachment behaviors; they simply have to respond to children. Typical children seek to be attached. In fact, seeking an attachment figure when frightened is such a strong innate response that children will even seek out an abusive parent.

Ethology, the subdiscipline of biology concerned with the study of animal behavior, helps explain attachment. From an evolutionary perspective, the ultimate purpose of animal (including human) behavior is to pass on genes. This means that species develop attributes that help closely related kin survive to pass on their shared genes. Attachment behavior, like staying close to the mother, protects the young, ensuring their survival and ability to pass on genes (Geary & Bjorklund, 2000).

Ethology often provides insight into child development (Hofer, 2006). However, behavior in animals is not always relevant to behavior in humans. For example, critical periods may apply to attachment in animals, but not humans.

Are There Critical Periods in Attachment? Konrad Lorenz (1903–1989) found that young geese follow their mother soon after hatching. If raised in an incubator, they follow the first creature they see, which is called *imprinting*. Once this imprinting takes place, they cannot be made to attach to another goose, even their own parents. Lorenz believed that imprinting takes place within

minutes of hatching and is irreversible. Thus, there is a *critical period* for imprinting. Attachment is considered a type of imprinting by ethologists. Human children become attached regardless of the quality of care, implying that it is simply the presence of the caregiver that matters. (It is not attachment, but the *security* of attachment, that is affected by quality of care.) For their research, Lorenz and two other ethologists won the Nobel Prize in 1973.

Konrad Lorenz

Bowlby was struck by Lorenz's early studies of imprinting. Bowlby believed that the first years of life are a critical period for human attachment and that later good mothering could not make up for bad or absent mothering in infancy. He was only partly right. Research has confirmed that attachment in infancy does indeed predict later development; however, parenting matters throughout childhood. Change in attachment security is possible. Thus, a critical period for attachment probably does not exist in a strong form for humans. Nevertheless, there appears to be a *sensitive period* for attachment in the first 18 to 24 months. A "sensitive period" means the effect of experience is strongest during a relatively brief period in the lifespan.

ethology
a subdiscipline of biology that seeks to understand the cause and function of animal (including human) behavior.

Do these seem like conflicting functions? Children want to feel secure. If this were their only goal, they would never leave their parents' side. Fortunately, they are also curious and want to explore. Yet, exploration puts them in potential danger, making them feel wary. Children balance wariness and curiosity by using the attachment figure as a secure base when there is no threat and as a safe haven when they feel threatened. Let's take a look at how these functions operate at different ages.

6-1a Age Trends in Attachment

Children's attachment behaviors change dramatically with age, but the function of attachment—feeling secure—continues across the life span.

Infancy and Toddlerhood (Birth to 2 Years)

Infants show attachment as they cling to caregivers when frightened or greet caregivers with delight, like kicking excitedly when Daddy smiles at them. As infants begin to crawl or walk and seek their parents, the *parents'* attachment to the infant deepens. It is gratifying to parents to be preferred and sought out.

Infants become wary of strangers at around 8 to 9 months of age (Sroufe, 1996). This change surprises some parents because when younger, their baby seldom protested when held by strangers. However, *stranger wariness* is part of normal attachment development. It occurs across widely diverse cultures at the same age. Stranger wariness typically lasts several months, peaking at about 12 months, and then gradually decreasing.

How can you approach a toddler who is wary of you? First, give the child time to gradually become familiar with you. Play a familiar game, like peek-a-boo, or offer something familiar, like a favorite blanket. Second, give the child control over the interaction (Sroufe, 1996). If the child backs away, you back away. If the child offers you a toy, take it and then offer it back. Third, recruit the parent's help. If the parent looks happy to see you, rather than worried, the child is more likely to react positively to you. This effect, known as *social referencing,* will be discussed in Chapter 8.

Separation distress, which is part of normal attachment development, peaks between 1 and 2 years of age, and then decreases (Photo 6.1). Thus, most toddlers cry and cling when their attachment figure tries to leave. Most toddlers will explore new environments if their attachment figure is nearby, occasionally looking at or touching the attachment figure.

PHOTO 6.1 Young children feel distress when separated from their attachment figure.

Early and Middle Childhood (3 to 12 Years)

Typically, between 3 and 4 years children outgrow separation distress. In addition, after age 3 most children are comfortable in strange places with secondary attachment figures, like a sibling or a teacher. They need less physical contact with attachment figures; nonphysical contact, like a phone call, can make them feel secure. By 5th or 6th grade, children who frequently seek physical contact with their attachment figure may be overly anxious (Crittenden, 1992). Children still want to be close, but their behavior is normally subtle and might simply involve drifting toward the attachment figure while engrossed in another activity. For example, while Dad cooks dinner, a toddler might be right under his feet banging pans, while her older sister absent-mindedly moves into the kitchen and sits at the table to draw. Thus, attachment *behaviors,* such as clinging to the attachment figure, are not as frequent or intense, but the attachment *relationship* continues. The attachment figure's availability—physical presence, willingness to talk, and awareness of the child's needs—remains very important.

Adolescence (13 to 19 Years)

Adolescents sometimes avoid their parents. They often withhold information about school activities because they don't want their parents to show up at school, so savvy teachers communicate directly with parents. When our 14-year-old daughter was rollerblading with friends in the neighborhood and saw that we were strolling in their direction, she turned around and skated away. This active avoidance of parents in the presence of peers typically lasts for a year or two. (Wise parents and teachers do not take it personally.)

PHOTO 6.2 The attachment relationship remains very important through adolescence.

Does such avoidance mean that adolescents are not attached to their parents? Quite the opposite. Adolescents' age-appropriate independence may be the *result of feeling secure attachment.* That is, secure teens become independent because they know that their parents will be available to them despite their behavior. This knowledge is the bedrock of healthy personality in adolescence. The infant's experience of being comforted by Daddy becomes the adolescent's belief that "Dad is always there for me" (Bretherton & Munholland, 1999; Photo 6.2). Teenagers "touch base" by gravitating toward where their parents are. Even when our daughter avoided us when rollerblading, at home she would drift into the kitchen, help us make dinner for a few minutes, and then disappear again. Attachment even persists into adulthood. When you experience a crisis, you probably seek out your attachment figures.

Do teens shift their primary attachments to peers rather than parents? Most do not. Mothers are usually the primary attachment figure through adolescence for teens with secure attachments (Markiewicz, Lawford, Doyle, & Haggart, 2006). But not all teens have secure attachments. A best friend or boyfriend/girlfriend may be the primary attachment figure for adolescents who feel unsupported by their parents (Freeman & Brown, 2001). Next we consider how secure attachment develops.

6-1b Individual Diversity in Attachment

Strange Situation Procedure (SSP)
a 22-minute laboratory task designed to test quality of attachment in which children under age 6 are stressed by maternal separation and stranger presence.

All typical children have attachment relationships; however, the *quality* of attachment varies. Scientists assess quality of attachment with the **Strange Situation Procedure (SSP)**. The SSP begins with a child and parent entering an unfamiliar room full of toys (Ainsworth, Blehar, Waters, & Wall, 1978). The child plays with the toys while the parent sits in a chair. After 3 minutes, a stranger enters the room, chats with the parent, and then plays with the child. Every 3 minutes thereafter, one of the adults leaves or returns in this order: the parent leaves, the parent returns and the stranger leaves, the parent leaves the child all alone, the stranger returns, and finally the parent returns. The entire SSP takes only 22 minutes, but it provides a remarkably good snapshot of attachment. It reveals whether the child prefers the parent to the stranger and whether the child's distress is soothed by the parent's return. Quality of attachment is determined primarily by what happens during the two reunion episodes, not the separation episodes. We will describe typical child reactions later.

The SSP is the most common way to assess attachment in toddlers; it has been used with children up to age 6 by increasing separation time to more than an hour (Stevenson-Hinde & Verschueren, 2002). Yet how would you assess attachment in adolescents who do not fall apart when their parent leaves the room for an hour? Scientists use the **Adult Attachment Interview (AAI)**. They ask questions about early attachment memories. For example, they ask adolescents to list five adjectives that describe their relationship with each parent and tell about specific experiences that support each adjective. They determine quality of attachment by how coherently the adolescents talk about the relationship. A different method involves asking a parent and teen to discuss an emotionally charged topic, like curfew time, and watching how they interact.

Using the SSP, AAI, and other assessments, attachments can be classified as either secure or one of three insecure types. These four types do not capture all the variation in attachment relationships, but they will help you understand attachment.

Adult Attachment Interview (AAI) a lengthy interview designed to determine adolescents' or adults' "state of mind" regarding the quality of attachment to each parent.

Secure Attachment

During the SSP, toddlers with **secure attachment** freely explore the toys while their parent is present. They may or may not cry when separated, but play less when their parent is gone. When reunited, they show delight and readily go to their parent and are quickly soothed (Ainsworth, 1979). They clearly prefer their parent over a stranger. As preschoolers, they continue to explore new environments more while their parent is present than when absent (McElwain, Holland, Engle, & Ogolsky, 2014).

Older secure children are referred to as *balanced*. They openly negotiate about their parent's availability, like asking, "How long will you be gone?" After separation, they greet their parent with genuine pleasure, converse pleasantly, invite the parent to join in their play, and move closer (Behrens, Hesse, & Main, 2007). They clearly communicate positive, *as well as negative*, feelings toward the parent. Anger and distress are readily resolved or soothed.

Secure adolescents are referred to as *autonomous*. During the AAI, they coherently discuss their parents' positive and negative influence. They value relationships. During disagreements with their parents over hot topics like money, grades, or curfews, they are civil and come to mutual solutions (Beijersbergen, Bakermans-Kranenburg, Van IJzendoorn, & Juffer, 2008).

secure (balanced, autonomous) attachment a form of attachment characterized by feelings of security, open communication, and mutual delight.

Insecure Avoidant Attachment

During the SSP, toddlers with **avoidant attachment** explore the room while ignoring their parent. They do not seem to care when their parent leaves, nor do they clearly prefer their parent over a stranger. When their parent returns, they *ignore or turn away*, appearing to avoid their parent. Ironically, at home these same children are quite distressed if their parent simply moves to another room (Ainsworth, 1979).

Older avoidant children are referred to as *defended* because they hide emotions, like anger, from their parent. This defends them from rejection by their parent. After an hour's separation they may stiffen when the parent returns and subtly try to exclude the parent from their activities (Behrens et al., 2007). They might avoid their parent by appearing engrossed with a toy, or by using it as an excuse to move away. Avoidant children may be prematurely friendly with strangers rather than wary.

avoidant (defended, dismissing) attachment a form of insecure attachment characterized by anxiety, emotional distancing, rejection, and anger.

Avoidant adolescents are referred to as *dismissive.* In the AAI, they dismiss the importance of relationships. They idealize their parents in global ways, like "My parents are the best!" that are contradicted by memories of specific events, like "They locked me out of the house." When they describe events of rejection, they say "it was no big deal." They might not stop what they are doing to greet their mother after a week's absence (Hodges, Finnegan, & Perry, 1999). They avoid discussions of emotionally hot topics with their parents, but their rare discussions are quite angry (Allen & Land, 1999).

resistant (coercive, preoccupied) attachment
a form of insecure attachment characterized by exaggerated emotions, clinginess, and intense attachment behaviors.

Insecure Resistant Attachment

During the SSP, toddlers with **resistant attachment** hover near their parent, exploring very little. They are distressed by separation and difficult to soothe after the parent returns. They seem *ambivalent* because when their parent returns, they go to their parent but act angry and sulky. They might ask to be picked up, but then arch away, or hit the parent.

Older resistant children are referred to as *coercive.* They coerce their parents with tantrums, helplessness, pouting, whining, or coy babyishness (Stevenson-Hinde & Verschueren, 2002). They seek contact with their parent, but are not comforted by it. They may show subtle signs of hostility, such as sitting on their parent's lap but wriggling to make their parent uncomfortable. After an hour's separation, they might hug their mother but then swat her (Behrens et al., 2007). They appear immature, hyperactive, and unsettled in play, as they move from object to object.

Think about Audrey in the opening vignette. With which type of attachment is her behavior congruent? Defend your conclusion through logic supported by your readings.

Resistant adolescents are referred to as *preoccupied.* They have excessive concern over their parent's whereabouts, express a strong need for their parent in stressful situations, and have trouble separating and recovering from distress. For example, after losing their mother at the mall and finding her again, such teens take a long time to calm down and continue to worry about losing her again (Hodges et al., 1999). Their responses on the AAI are incoherent, with rambling and excessive, irrelevant detail. They convey anger, as well as preoccupation with trying to please the parent (Hesse, 1999).

disorganized (controlling, unresolved) attachment
a form of insecure attachment characterized by no coherent pattern of response to the parent.

Disorganized Attachment

Toddlers with **disorganized attachment** are strongly conflicted by a desire to be with their parents and to avoid them at the same time. When their parent returns in the SSP, their stress intensifies and they behave bizarrely. For example, they may approach the parent, then suddenly run away, or freeze in a trancelike state. Some children rock back and forth or walk sideways toward their parent. Sometimes this behavior is subtle and not easily identified by novices.

Older disorganized children are referred to as *controlling* because they take control in an overly cheerful way or by punishing the parent (Behrens et al., 2007). For example, when their parent returns, they may jump and clap in extreme cheerfulness, or they might say "Don't bother me!" Because they take control they appear confident, but they are actually brittle and anxious (Stevenson-Hinde & Verschueren, 2002). They make up stories filled with catastrophic events, like the mother being killed when she went shopping and left the child at home. Their play involves themes of unusual violence and helplessness.

TABLE 6.1	Types of attachment by age group		
Toddlerhood	**Early and middle childhood**	**Adolescence and adulthood**
Secure	Secure/balanced	Autonomous
Avoidant	Defended	Dismissing
Resistant	Coercive	Preoccupied
Disorganized	Controlling	Unresolved

Disorganized adolescents are referred to as *unresolved*. During the AAI, they may report past traumas involving loss. Their reasoning may break down or become incoherent. For example, they might suddenly become silent in the middle of a sentence or discuss a parent who is dead in the present tense. They may be strongly hostile in talking about a parent, or frequently say they feel fearful (Bernier & Meins, 2008). Table 6.1 summarizes the four attachment types across childhood.

How Stable Is Attachment?

Attachment is fairly stable. This means you probably have the same type of attachment now as you had when you were a toddler. Most toddlers will stay secure, or stay insecure, throughout childhood. However, *secure children can become insecure* because of negative events, such as divorce, that might diminish parents' sensitivity. Even common stresses, such as changing from 10 to 20 hours per week of child care, have sometimes been linked to becoming insecure (Booth-LaForce et al., 2014; Lewis, Feiring, & Rosenthal, 2000; Weinfield, Sroufe, & Egeland, 2000). Children with multiple risk factors are most likely to become insecure. It is also possible, but not as common, for children to become *more secure* over time, if family functioning and parents' sensitivity improves (e.g., Beijersbergen, Juffer, Bakermans-Kranenburg, & van IJzendoorn, 2012). Thus, attachment is typically stable, but if situations in a child's life change substantially, attachment can change, for better or worse.

Attachment in Adult Romantic Relationships

Remarkably, mothers' sensitivity toward their children in the first 3 years of life predicts the adult attachments of those children (Raby, Roisman, Fraley, & Simpson, 2015). You may have seen different types of attachment in the romantic relationships of your friends. *Ambivalent* adults tend to be jealous, worry about abandonment and disapproval, and lack trust in their partners, yet are dependent and eager to be in relationships. They share personal information too early in a relationship, fall in love quickly, and frequently break up and reunite. *Avoidant* adults tend to be uncomfortable with closeness or sharing personal information and disinclined to be in long-term relationships. *Unresolved* adults, particularly those unresolved because of abuse, tend to be aggressive early in their marriages (Cooper, Shaver, & Collins, 1998; Crowell, Treboux, & Waters, 2002; Joel, MacDonald, & Shimotomai, 2011).

Secure adults tend to form stable, long-term romantic relationships. They tend to be satisfied in relationships, which are trusting, committed, and interdependent.

They are a secure base for their partners to openly express worries and receive reassurance when distressed. Secure couples have fewer arguments, feel greater intimacy, and are less likely to threaten to leave than insecure couples.

Which of your friends is likely to have a secure romantic relationship? Those who had a secure attachment in childhood (Holland & Roisman, 2010). However, both one's *history* of attachment to parents and one's *current* attachment to a spouse influence the quality of a relationship (Simpson, Collins, & Salvatore, 2011). A secure attachment to a spouse can help compensate for an insecure parent–child attachment. Still, people who are securely attached both to their parents and to their spouse tend to have the most satisfying relationships (Treboux, Crowell, & Waters, 2004). Next we turn to other outcomes predicted by childhood attachment.

What Do Individual Differences in Attachment Predict?

You might be wondering why attachment appears in this section on the "emotional" child. Doesn't it really belong in the section on the social child, because it is a relationship? It is here because attachment is the foundation of personality, self-control, and emotional well-being. Attachment predicts many other outcomes as well. For now let's focus on two that are important in the classroom—academic achievement and social competence.

Academic achievement

Secure learners are likely to be curious, have good verbal ability and academic skills, and earn high grades (e.g., Aviezer, Sagi, Resnick, & Gini, 2002; Granot & Mayseless, 2001). (See Photo 6.3.) In contrast, *insecure* preschoolers are more likely to have poor prereading skills and negative attitudes toward reading. Insecure school-age youth are more likely to have lower math and reading test scores and lower grades (e.g., Bus & Van IJzendoorn, 1997; Diener, Isabella, Behunin, & Wong, 2007; Weinfield, Sroufe, Egeland, & Carlson, 1999). Insecure students are anxious, which interferes with learning (see Chapter 8), and they have difficulty getting along with teachers and classmates.

moodboard/Getty Images

PHOTO 6.3 Learners with secure attachment to their parents tend to have higher achievement in school and are well-liked.

Social competence

Children learn behavior and emotional skills in parent–child attachment that are applied to friendships and later romantic relationships (see Figure 6.1). *Secure* learners are more likely than insecure classmates to have harmonious friendships, empathy for others, and resistance to negative peer pressure. Peers and teachers are more likely to view them as socially competent from preschool through high school.[1] Even in college, secure freshmen may feel more cared for and have a better social support network than insecure students (Grabill & Kerns, 2000).

---

[1] There are many studies that support these conclusions, just a few of which are listed here: Allen, Porter, McFarland, McElhaney, and Marsh (2007); DeMulder, Denham, Schmidt, and Mitchell (2000); Doyle, Lawford, and Markiewicz (2009); Englund, Kuo, Puig, and Collins (2011); McElwain, Booth-LaForce, Lansford, Wu, and Dyer (2008).

FIGURE 6.1 Early Attachment Predicts Later Social Competence.

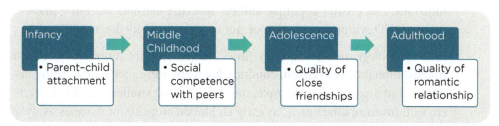

A famous longitudinal study of attachment in Minnesota found the sequence of development depicted here. How might early attachment have these long-term effects? *Source: Simpson, Collins, and Salvatore (2011).*

Insecure learners are more likely to have poor relationships with peers. In a classic study, some insecure 10-year-olds reported having many friends but were unable to name one (Grossmann & Grossmann, 1991). Peers and teachers tend to view insecure learners as angry, mean, dishonest, disruptive, withdrawn, or anxious. *Disorganized* and *avoidant* learners may be the most at risk for serious aggression and behavior problems (e.g., Fearon, Bakermans-Kranenburg, Van Ijzendoorn, Lapsley, & Roisman, 2010; Madigan, Brumariu, Villani, Atkinson, & Lyons-Ruth, 2015).

Other outcomes

Besides social competence and academic achievement, attachment quality predicts other outcomes:

- *Growth.* Insecure attachment is linked to poor physical growth, but earlier puberty (e.g., Belsky, Houts, & Fearon, 2010; St. Petersburg-USA Orphanage Research Team, 2008).

- *Compliance.* Secure learners are more compliant with adults. This doesn't mean they are meekly submissive; they may challenge adult directives, but ultimately they are more cooperative with reasonable demands (Laible, Panfile, & Makariev, 2008).

- *Independence.* Secure learners are more likely to work independently and make their own decisions than insecure learners, from preschool through high school (Sroufe, Fox, & Pancake, 1983; Weinfield et al., 1999).

- *Emotional openness.* Secure learners can express anger or say "I hate you" without fear that they will be rejected or abandoned. In contrast, avoidant learners tend to have trouble discussing emotions (Laible & Thompson, 2000).

- *Emotion regulation.* Secure children tend to have good emotion regulation, as early as 4 months of age. As they get older, they tend to discuss hot topics without anger, take on difficult challenges, and remain composed when distressed (Braungart-Reiker, Garwood, Powers, & Wang, 2001; Sroufe, 1996).

- *Stress.* Insecure learners tend to be stressed, easily excited, and anxious (e.g., Kerns & Brumariu, 2014). This may explain why insecurity is linked to health problems (Maunder & Hunter, 2001) and sleep problems (Bernier, Matte-Gagné, Bélanger, & Whipple, 2014).

- *ADHD.* Secure learners tend to have longer attention spans, better executive functions, and greater cognitive ability.[2] Insecure learners are more likely to show ADHD symptoms whether or not they are formally diagnosed.

- *Psychopathology and delinquency.* Insecure learners are more likely to have suicidal thoughts, depression, conduct disorders, substance abuse, eating disorders, and anxiety.[3] For example, one review of 60 studies found that learners with insecure attachment in early childhood were about twice as likely as secure children to have anxiety disorders and depression later in childhood (Madigan, Atkinson, Laurin, & Benoit, 2013).

Clearly, secure attachment is an important asset for children, and insecure attachment is a risk factor. However, as you learned in Chapter 1, risk factors are about probability, not certainty. For example, although insecure youth are *more likely* to have eating disorders than secure youth, most insecure youth do not develop this problem. The development of children and teens depends on the full array of risk and protective factors they experience.

What Predicts Individual Differences in Attachment?

Ideally all children would be securely attached. In reality about half (50% to 60%) are secure, another quarter (20% to 23%) are avoidant, and the rest are resistant (8% to 10%) or disorganized (10% to 24%) (O'Connor & McCartney, 2007). How do children come to be secure?

Sensitivity and supportiveness

Sensitive and supportive parents are more likely to have secure children (Verhage et al., 2015). Sensitive parents respond with reassurance when their child is distressed. They attend to and accurately interpret the child's signals, respond promptly, and understand the child's feelings. Supportive parents help their child explore their world. When the child is attempting a task just beyond their zone of proximal development (Chapter 3), the parent might adapt the task a little, let the child make choices, follow the child's pace, and provide encouragement, feedback, and just enough scaffolding for success (Bernier et al., 2014). They do this *only when the child indicates need,* not according to the parents' own agenda. For example, if a baby grunts in frustration while trying to grasp an out-of-reach toy, the parent attends to the grunt, realizes the baby wants the toy, and promptly moves it just within reach. An *insensitive* parent might not notice the grunt or not realize what the baby wants. An *unsupportive* parent might notice, but not respond to the baby. For another example, if a teenager begins acting overly irritable, a sensitive, supportive parent notices the change in behavior, realizes the teen is anxious about an upcoming performance, and helps the teen prepare for the performance.

Parents of *avoidant* children tend to be unresponsive and intrusive, meaning they frequently interrupt the child's activities with their own agenda (Ainsworth, 1979).

think about **this**

Some people advise new mothers not to pick up their babies when they cry because they will become dependent and clingy. Based on what you know about sensitive responsiveness, is this good advice? Is it possible to be overly responsive? Does responsiveness create a dependent, clingy child? What does?

[2] There are many studies that support this conclusion, just a few of which are listed here: Bernier, Matte-Gagné, and Bouvette-Turcot (2014); Clarke, Ungerer, Chahoud, Johnson, and Stiefel (2002); Goldwyn, Stanley, Smith, and Green (2000); Moss and St-Laurent (2001).

[3] There are many studies that support this conclusion, just a few of which are listed here: Allen and Land (1999); Branstetter, Furman, and Cottrell (2009); Groh et al. (2012); Hesse (1999); Lewis et al. (2000); Madigan et al. (2015); Morley and Moran (2011).

For example, a father might wave a toy in front of his baby's face when the baby is engrossed with a different toy. They may also withdraw when their child needs help with difficult tasks. Parents of *resistant* children tend to respond inconsistently or only to strong signals from the child (Stevenson-Hinde & Verschueren, 2002). For example, a 5-year-old could show many signs of exhaustion that the mother does not notice until the child has a tantrum.

Other parent behaviors

Although parent sensitivity and supportiveness are considered key to secure attachment, other behaviors are also important. Parents of *secure* children tend to communicate openly and directly with their children and to show interest and enjoyment in them (Photo 6.4). In contrast, parents of insecure children are often negative, depressed, anxious, and dissatisfied with family life. Parents of *avoidant* children may be angry and reject their children. Parents of *resistant* children may be relatively accepting, but vacillate between irritation and empathy with their child and may inappropriately need their child's approval (Leerkes, Parade, & Gudmundson, 2011; Scher & Mayseless, 2000; Stevenson-Hinde & Verschueren, 2002).

Parents of *disorganized* children may be the least sensitive. They are more likely to be single parents, intrusive, psychologically unavailable, or neglectful. However, most importantly, they may be *frightening* (Bernier & Meins, 2008; Stevenson-Hinde & Verschueren, 2002). How does this happen? Parents frighten children through fearful facial expressions, trancelike behavior, approaching the child in an aggressive way, and handling the child like a bag of groceries. They also frighten children through abuse. The child's need for nurturing and protection is constant, whereas incidents of abuse are typically brief, so the child turns to the parent for safety but is frightened by the parent. This terrible paradox results in the bizarre behavior characteristic of disorganized attachment. Parents may behave in frightening ways because of drug use, depression, their own history of experiencing abuse, or loss through death or divorce.

Improving Attachment

Can we help parents create secure attachments? Yes, according to studies using randomized experiments (see Chapter 1). While you cannot randomly assign children to parents, you can randomly assign parents to different training classes and investigate whether they change their behavior and their children's attachment. Interventions that improve parents' sensitivity also improve children's security, suggesting that parents' sensitivity *causes* child attachment. Successful interventions include making home visits to the parent, educating the parent about child development, and keeping the parent and child in physical contact (Bakermans-Kranenburg, van IJzendoorn, & Juffer, 2003). For example, the Kangaroo Care you learned about in Chapter 2 has been linked to improved attachment for low birth weight infants (Baley & Committee on Fetus and Newborn, 2015). In another approach, mothers of highly irritable infants were visited four times at home before their infant's 1st birthday. They were taught about infants' needs,

think about this

Sue arrived at the library with her three children, ages 3 to 7 years. Sue went to the children's section and sat down to read her own book. The children wandered about looking at books. One child asked Sue, "Wanna read me dis one?" Sue said, "Momma's gonna sit here and read her book." Looking over the child's book, she continued, "That's a scary one. Why don't you put that back and get another one?" Her oldest boy several times brought a book to show Sue. She would look at it briefly, chuckle or comment, and return to her own reading. When the children were out of sight, Sue would look up from her book, quietly call out their names until they answered, and then return to reading.

How would you rate Sue on these four dimensions: sensitive or insensitive? accessible or neglecting? cooperative or interfering? accepting or rejecting? How might you judge the attachment behaviors of her children?

PHOTO 6.4 Parents of secure children communicate clearly with them and express interest and delight in them.

how to recognize infants' signals, soothe distress, and promote exploration without being intrusive. How did it work? More infants were secure (89%) as compared with those in the control group (62%) (Cassidy, Woodhouse, Sherman, Stupica, & Lejuez, 2011).

Attachment to Father

Most research has been on *mother*–child rather than *father*–child attachment. Nevertheless, fathers are typically an important part of children's attachment hierarchy. Infants may protest separation from fathers, explore less when separated, and feel comforted when the father returns. Father–child attachment has similar, but somewhat smaller, effects than mother–child attachment. Fathers may uniquely influence their children, such as encouraging more bold exploration because their interactions emphasize rough-and-tumble play, while mothers tend to emphasize teaching and caregiving (Newland, Freeman, & Coyl, 2011). However, in many families mother and father roles overlap to some degree.

Children are more securely attached to sensitive fathers (Lucassen et al., 2011). Just over half of children are securely attached to their fathers. Children can be securely attached to their father but insecurely attached to their mother, or the reverse, but they tend to have similar attachment to both. Children who have secure attachment to both their mother and their father have the best outcomes, while children who have two insecure attachments have the worst outcomes (e.g., Diener et al., 2007).

How Does Attachment Have Such Far-Reaching Consequences?

Scores of studies show that attachment is linked to many important outcomes—aggression, GPA, depression, growth, ADHD, and so forth. Why might this be? One explanation is internal working models.

internal working models (IWMs)
memories and expectations of the self and others that influence whether children approach or avoid others, with either positive or hostile emotions.

Internal working models (IWMs) are memories and expectations—based upon thousands of daily interactions with attachment figures—that children carry into new situations (Dykas & Cassidy, 2011). They are models of both the self and others. A secure child's internal working model is that the *self* is valuable, socially successful, and worthy of love and that *others* are trustworthy, responsive, and caring. In contrast, an insecure child's internal working model is that the self is unworthy and that others are hostile, rejecting, or inconsistent. For example, in one study, secure preschoolers approached new peers expecting positive, enjoyable interaction (McElwain et al., 2014). They were responsive and complied with suggestions (e.g., "let's play with play dough"), but less controlling than insecure children. However, if the new peer was difficult and anger-prone, secure children dampened their responsiveness and became more controlling toward that child over time (see Figure 6.2). They were adaptive. Learners show evidence of their internal working models every day at school. Let's see how a secure model works in a kindergarten:

The children are sitting on the floor in a circle. Janie gets up to get a tissue. When she returns, she says to Lilly, "Thank you for saving my seat." Janie assumes Lilly has saved her seat, but actually Lilly has not noticed she was gone.

FIGURE 6.2 Attachment and Responsiveness to New Anger-Prone Playmates.

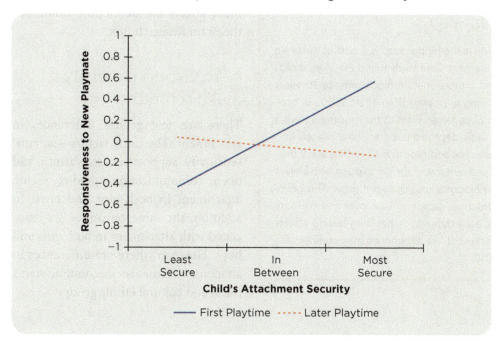

Secure children were more responsive to new anger-prone peers than insecure children in their first playtime together. By their third playtime, secure children were no longer more responsive to the difficult peer; they dampened their responsiveness. This dampening did not occur if the peer was not difficult. Insecure children had the opposite pattern, starting out less responsive and becoming more responsive and obedient toward an intimidating, anger-prone peer. *Source: McElwain et al. (2014).*

Because Janie has a secure internal working model, she expects caring from others, and treats them accordingly.

Internal working models may be apparent by infancy, although they are still developing (Johnson, Dweck, & Chen, 2007). By age 3, they are fairly stable. Although change is possible, internal working models are resistant to change because they are not conscious. They are also resistant to change because children behave in ways that confirm their models. In contrast to Janie, insecure children tend to alienate others, preventing the very social experiences that might help them change their internal working models. Insecure adolescents also "reconstruct" memories of interactions with others that are more negative than reality, whereas secure adolescents have a rosier memory bias (Dykas, Woodhouse, Ehrlich, & Cassidy, 2012). Thus, views of other people become self-fulfilling prophecies that become more validated as children grow older.

Another explanation for why attachment is linked to so many child outcomes is that sensitive parents who promote secure attachment in infancy continue to be sensitive through the child's adolescence. This ongoing good parenting promotes the child's competence, not just secure attachment. Research suggests that both early and current parenting are important. That is, early parent sensitivity and secure attachment have long-term effects beyond current parenting (Raby et al., 2015). In a large national study, parents' sensitivity in the first 3 years of life predicted both achievement and social competence at age 15 (Fraley, Roisman, & Haltigan, 2013).

think about **this**

Can you explain attachment types from a behaviorist perspective? A behaviorist would argue to an ethologist that any behavior that promotes survival has consequences and therefore can be conditioned. Based on what you learned in Chapter 3, discuss how resistant attachment might result from an intermittently responsive parent, or avoidant attachment from a punishing parent.

brain research

Secure Brains Learn Better

Attachment affects neuron growth in the hippocampus, a part of the brain that is involved in memory and learning. One study found that 4-year-olds who had nurturing mothers had a more mature hippocampus 10 years later, at age 13 to 16, despite living in poverty (Rao et al., 2010). In contrast, research on rats finds that pups raised without their mothers have a smaller hippocampus. If these sadly deprived pups are later placed into the care of nurturing mothers who lick and groom their babies a lot, they will develop the ability to learn and remember similar to pups who always had nurturing mothers, but their hippocampus does not grow. This probably means that other brain structures adapt to take over the memory work of the hippocampus. Thus, early deprivation has long-lasting effects on brain structure, but later attachment-like experience may compensate (Bryck & Fisher, 2012; Meany, 2010).

Still another explanation is that attachment affects the developing brain. See the Brain Research Box.

6-1c Group Diversity in Attachment

There are few gender differences in attachment. The same factors—parents' sensitivity, supportiveness, warmth, and open communication—predict secure attachment in both girls and boys. In addition, the same outcomes are associated with attachment in both girls and boys. However, there are differences in attachment across socioeconomic status (SES) and cultural ethnic group.

Socioeconomic Status and Ethnicity

Low-SES and minority children are more likely to be insecurely attached than other children (Tarabulsy et al., 2005). They are almost twice as likely as middle-SES children to have disorganized attachment. They are also more likely to have insensitive parents (Mesman, van IJzendoorn, & Bakermans-Kranenburg, 2012). Perhaps this is due to family stress and the accumulation of risk factors linked to low SES (see Chapter 1) that may lead to insensitive parenting, such as drug use, little education, and father absence. However, *secure attachment occurs in spite of poverty or minority status when parents are sensitive* (Mesman et al., 2012).

At the other end of the spectrum, both Bowlby and Ainsworth felt that high-SES parents who try to produce super-achieving children place their children at risk for insecure attachment by being intrusive. These parents may not understand that **sensitive responsiveness** *does not mean devoting complete attention to children*. For example, in a classic study, mothers of highly competent children interacted with them only 10 to 30 seconds at a time, briefly responding to the child but seldom spending even 5 minutes "teaching" something (White & Watts, 1973). After a question had been answered, help rendered, or applause given, both the parent and child returned to their tasks. If it was inconvenient to attend to the child at a particular moment, the mother said so, but she was available at other times. Thus, these mothers were consistently available and sensitively responding to the child, with limits, but were not intrusively imposing their own agenda onto the child.

Taken together, the research on group diversity in attachment suggests that whether boys and girls grow up in a low-SES or high-SES household is not as important as the quality of parenting they receive. If parents are sensitive, supportive, and positive, their children are likely to be securely attached regardless of group membership.

sensitive responsiveness
a style of interaction in which an adult reads the child's cues accurately and responds promptly and appropriately.

6-1d Classroom Implications of Attachment

You learned earlier that achievement and social competence in the classroom are linked to parent–child attachment. They are also linked to teacher–child attachment and school bonding. Teachers are not simply dispassionate deliverers of information; good teachers develop positive relationships with learners.

Teacher–Student Relationships

There are differences in the quality of relationships between learners and teachers, just as there are with parents. Learners do not always attach to teachers because the structure of some schools provides too little opportunity for a relationship to develop. When relationships are possible, learners who feel *secure* with their teachers accept comfort from their teachers when upset, communicate affection, readily share activities, and seem genuinely happy to see the teacher. In *avoidant* relationships learners may act as if they do not hear or notice the teacher, quickly leave after being requested to come to the teacher, and move away if the teacher tries to comfort them. In *resistant* relationships learners may frequently act frustrated, cry over every little irritation, and demand teacher attention, yet resist classroom routines like cleanup. They may constantly seek help or reassurance and be possessive, clingy, and overly reliant on the teacher (Howes & Ritchie, 1999; Pianta, Nimetz, & Bennett, 1997).

Do secure relationships help learners? Your learners are likely to have greater academic and social competence if you develop close, positive relationships with them (Photo 6.5). Secure, positive teacher–student relationships may protect learners from social problems like aggression, misbehavior, drug use, violence, and early sexual activity.[4] From preschool through high school, they may also reduce retention and special education referrals and improve GPA and test scores.[5] For example, in one study, low-SES students who had a positive teacher–student relationship in 1st grade were more engaged and effortful in 2nd grade and had higher test scores in 3rd grade (Hughes, Luo, Kwok, & Loyd, 2008). In another study, high school teachers who became more sensitive and supportive of students had students who learned more (Allen, Pianta, Gregory, Mikami, & Lun, 2011). Boys tend to report feeling less close and experiencing more conflict with teachers than girls, yet teacher–student relationships may have a larger effect size for boys, so special effort may be needed to connect with boys (Spilt, Hughes, Wu, & Kwok, 2012).

PHOTO 6.5 Positive teacher–student relationships are linked to greater learning as students feel safe to take learning risks and cooperate in learning tasks.

monkeybusinessimages/iStock/Getty Images Plus/Getty Images

---

[4] There are many studies that support this conclusion, just a few of which are listed here: NICHD Early Child Care Research Network (2002); O'Connor, Dearing, and Collins (2011); Stipek and Miles (2008); Wang and Fredricks (2014).

[5] There are many studies that support this conclusion, just a few of which are listed here: Curby, Rimm-Kaufman, and Ponitz (2009); Jia et al. (2009); Leyva et al. (2015); O'Connor and McCartney (2007); Roorda, Koomen, Spilt, and Oort (2011).

How do positive relationships with teachers promote achievement? Students are more engaged in learning activities and motivated to work hard for teachers who care for them, which in turn predicts higher achievement (Hughes, Wu, Kwok, Villarreal, & Honson, 2012; Spilt et al., 2012). Positive teacher–student relationships provide learners with a secure base to adjust to school and explore and master difficult school tasks. Sensitive teachers may be better at scaffolding learners in their zone of proximal development. They also reduce anxiety, which interferes with learning, as you'll learn about in Chapter 8. (If you recognize close teacher–child relationships as a protective factor, and poor relationships as a risk factor from Chapter 1, give yourself a gold star!)

The effect size (see Chapter 1) of teacher–student relationships for school-age children is quite large, suggesting that it may be more significant than which curriculum or instructional approach you use (Cornelius-White, 2007). For preschoolers, the effect of teacher–student interaction on academic, language, and social skills is larger than teacher–student ratio, curriculum, class size, or space and furnishings (Mashburn et al., 2008). At any age, teaching quality centers on positive teacher–student relationships.

Figure 6.3 shows that children can have better, or worse, relationships with different teachers as they progress through elementary school. Studies find that teacher–student closeness and warmth tend to decrease steadily from 1st grade to the end of elementary school, and across middle school, but may stabilize in high school (Hughes et al., 2012). If you teach upper grades, you may need to put extra effort into cultivating positive relationships.

How do you develop secure relationships with learners? One of the most powerful predictors of teacher–student relationships is attachment at home. Learners with

FIGURE 6.3 Teacher–Student Relationships in Elementary School.

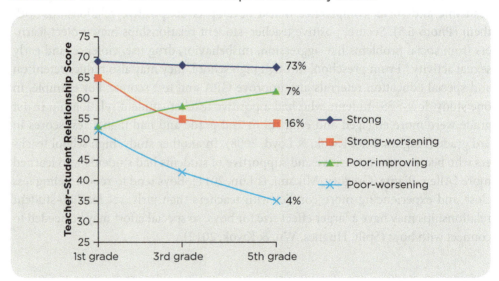

A large national study found that most (73%) elementary students had a strong relationship with their teacher. However, 16% started out strong but became worse across grades, 7% started out poor and improved, and 4% started out poor and got substantially worse. Overall, teacher–student relationships tend to be worse after children leave elementary school. *Adapted from O'Connor, Dearing, and Collins (2011, p. 141). See Spilt et al. (2012) for similar results.*

insecure parent–child attachment are likely to have insecure teacher–student relationships (DeMulder, Denham, Schmidt, & Mitchell, 2000). This is because insecure learners draw negativity from teachers. Teachers tend to be angry and rejecting with *avoidant* learners, viewing them as defiant. Teachers tend to be more tolerant and nurturing toward *resistant* learners, viewing them as immature and needy. In contrast, teachers tend to be sensitive and warm toward *secure* learners and expect good behavior from them (Pianta, Mashburn, Downer, Hamre, & Justice, 2008). Thus, you may find it more difficult to develop a positive relationship with your insecure learners, like Audrey in the opening vignette. In addition, the way you perceive your students' attachment needs may reflect your own attachment history (James, 2012). Nevertheless, it is possible to overcome an insecure history; in one study of thousands of children, about one-third of insecure children developed secure teacher–student relationships (Howes & Ritchie, 1999). How might this happen?

The *teacher's behavior* contributes to the teacher–student relationship. If caring teachers disconfirm insecure learners' internal working model that adults are hostile, rejecting, or unresponsive, then secure teacher–student relationships can develop. If you can develop a secure relationship with learners who are insecure with their parents, like Audrey, those students are likely to do better socially and emotionally and have higher achievement in your classroom (O'Connor & McCartney, 2007). A bonus is that you are also likely to be happier as a teacher if you feel more connected to your learners (Klassen, Perry, & Frenzel, 2012). To promote a secure relationship with your students follow these guidelines (adapted from Bergin & Bergin, 2009):

1. Be sensitive and have frequent positive interactions. Sensitive teachers accurately detect and interpret learners' cues, respond to learners' distress, and are warm.

2. Be responsive to learners' agendas by providing choices whenever possible. Learners feel greater rapport with teachers who give them some control over what they do. When you cannot provide choices, give a reason.

3. Study this textbook carefully. Teachers with greater knowledge of child development are more sensitive toward learners.

4. Be well prepared for class and hold high expectations for learners. This shows you care about their achievement.

5. Use noncoercive discipline. Coercive discipline involves threats and control of resources, like taking away recess for misbehavior. Good discipline builds positive relationships so the learner is motivated to obey. You will learn how to do this in Chapter 7.

6. Try interventions designed to repair poor teacher–student relationships when you feel challenged by a particular learner. In one such intervention, called banking time, you "save up" positive experiences in relationship "capital" that can later be "drawn upon" (Pianta, 1999). For example, 5 to 15 minutes each day the teacher gives the learner undivided attention and follows the learners' lead in an activity the learner chooses. (This can be done during gym, free time, lunch, recess, or small-group instruction.) The teacher conveys interest in the learner.

Conveying interest is easiest in preschool or elementary school, but a junior high teacher did his own form of banking time. He spent half an hour every day after school phoning a portion of his students and their parents to tell them what he liked about having them in his class. Another high school teacher phoned ill students from his classroom so that he and the rest of the class could tell the absent students they were missed. Let's see what happened with another teacher, Mr. Mali, and Caleb, a difficult 7th-grader who challenged him on a poorly written geometry quiz item. Mr. Mali told Caleb to prove his point for homework. That evening, Mr. Mali called Caleb's mother.

> *It was not the first time one of his teachers had ever called home—I got the sense that she was used to fielding such calls—but it was the first time anyone had ever told her anything good. I wanted her to know that the intellectual curiosity and vivacity that her son had displayed in class reminded me why I chose to teach in the first place. I told her that I loved my job because of kids like Caleb. The quality of silence on the other end of the phone told me that she was crying. By reaching out to her that night I had created an ally."* (Mali, 2012, p. 36)

In schools where many learners are at risk for insecure attachment, schoolwide interventions can help. Successful interventions involve all teachers in the school being consistently positive in order to disconfirm learners' internal working models of adults as inconsistent, neglectful, or harsh (Hamre, Hatfield, Pianta, & Jamil, 2014; Ottmar, Rimm-Kaufman, Larsen, & Berry, 2015). When they have multiple positive relationships at school, learners bond to the school.

School Bonding

school bonding
a sense of belonging at school and having a network of relationships with peers and teachers.

School bonding refers to a student's attachment to teachers and peers at school. School bonding includes liking school and engaging in school activities, which tend to go together (Hallinan, 2008). School bonding protects learners against delinquency and dropping out, and promotes achievement (Dynarski et al., 2008; Wang & Fredricks, 2014). In contrast, students who are not bonded to school feel that school is an uncaring place. They may say that they have no friends and that no one talks to them at school, they do not know the principal, and their teachers do not notice their absences or care about their learning.

Although school bonding is important at any school, it is most important in schools with high rates of poverty and other risk factors (Osterman, 2000). School bonding may be particularly important, but less likely, in middle schools. Transitions from elementary to junior high or middle school, and then again to high school, are linked to lower grades, less school interest, and less extracurricular involvement (Juvonen, 2007; Skinner, Furrer, Marchand, & Kindermann, 2008). This is particularly true for students experiencing other changes. such as divorce, and for students with multiple risk factors (Burchinal, Roberts, Zeisel, & Rowley, 2008; Zanobini & Usai, 2002). While school bonding declines from childhood through middle school, it may stabilize in high school (Gillen-O'Neel & Fuligni, 2013).

Students in K–8 systems, who do not have to transition to middle/junior high school, fare better. Why? Just when students are seeking greater freedom and autonomy, middle/junior high schools emphasize teacher control and de-emphasize student choice. Ironically, students tend to have greater autonomy at the end of elementary school than in middle/junior high school. In addition, teacher–student relationships in middle/junior high are less personal and positive. Some students see teachers as less friendly, and some teachers see students as less trustworthy. People enjoy blaming "raging hormones" for negativity in middle school, but the real problem may be school factors. Adolescents in other countries do not necessarily decrease in school bonding. In the United States, 11- to 15-year-olds feel markedly less bonded and dislike school more than in other countries (Juvonen, 2007). What can you do to promote school bonding?

1. Develop secure teacher–student relationships. The primary ingredient of school bonding is close relationships. Students like school better when they think their teachers care about them and praise them for hard work. This may be especially important for students at risk for school disengagement, like those who move a lot or are recent immigrants (Green, Rhodes, Hirsch, Suarez-Orozco, & Camic, 2008; Gruman, Harachi, Abbott, Catalano, & Fleming, 2008).

2. Promote other adult–student relationships, such as with coaches or counselors. In the opening vignette, Audrey's relationship with the counselor helped her feel more connected to school.

3. Advocate keeping peers and teachers together long enough to form relationships, which can take several months to a few years. Classroom management problems may decrease, and motivation and achievement may increase, when a teacher stays with the same students for multiple years (Pianta, 1999).

4. Advocate keeping schools small. The optimal size for bonding in high school is 300 students, although the optimal size for providing strong academic programs may be 600 to 1,200 (McNeely, Nonnemaker, & Blum, 2002). Some secondary schools partially mimic the positive effects of smaller schools by creating small learning communities, which may also be called teams, pods, or schools-within-schools (Felner, Seitsinger, Brand, Burns, & Bolton, 2007).

5. Manage your classroom well. Eliminate overly harsh discipline, like expelling students for relatively minor infractions. Students like school better when they perceive teachers as fair. Classroom management will be discussed in Chapter 7.

6. Provide extracurricular activities. Youth who participate in a variety of activities (e.g., debate club, jazz band, sports) tend to be less depressed and get into less trouble (Simpkins, Eccles, & Becnel, 2008). Students report feeling happier and more motivated during extracurricular activities than during classes (Mahoney, Harris, & Eccles, 2006).

7. Help students be kind, helpful, and accepting of one another. How to do this will be discussed in Chapter 10.

These factors may be especially important for students who are in the ethnic minority at your school. Adolescents are less likely to feel school bonding when most of the other students at school do not share their ethnic background (Johnson, Crosnoe, & Elder, 2001). Does this mean segregated schools are ideal? No. Segregated schools present a different array of problems. It does mean that in multiethnic schools you will need to work to make sure all students feel attached to school.

think
about this

There is a drop in bonding each year in middle school. However, a large study found no discernible change across the 4 years of high school for boys (Gillen-O'Neel & Fuligni, 2013). Girls start out high school with a little higher bonding than boys and have a slight drop over 4 years. What factors are different between middle school and high school that might explain these patterns? What was your experience as a student? What might be some implications for your classroom as a teacher?

In summary, students vary in the security of their attachment, which influences their school success. Parents, teachers, and schools can influence security of attachment. Attachment is also important because it is foundational to healthy personality in children. Let's turn next to temperament and personality.

6-2 Temperament and Personality

Eric is a very shy toddler. He is late to talk and walk, but when he does begin talking, it is in full sentences. In preschool, he will not join group time. Instead he presses his back to the furthest wall and intently, but silently, watches the group while twirling a strand of hair. He cries and puts himself in time-out when he breaks a household rule, even before his mother knows he has misbehaved.

Eric never speaks to his kindergarten teacher. During 1st grade, a baby sister is born whom he adores. Each morning he heads straight to his teacher's desk to tell her about the cute things his baby has done, then goes to his seat and does not say another word the rest of the day. When other teachers greet him, he looks down and does not respond. His 1st-grade teacher says, "He certainly isn't like his older sister!" who is buoyant and extraverted and often has to be told not to talk during class. Eric's teacher suspects he is not quite as bright as his older sister, although his vocabulary is exceptional.

Several years later, Eric's 6th-grade teacher asks him to be a buddy to a new student because Eric is the most popular boy in the class, and he is compassionate. He is a leader at recess, organizing large groups of boys in fantasy play (as Jedi knights). He is at the top of his class academically and exudes self-confidence.

In high school Eric ranks in the top 1% for achievement nationally. He has a network of good friends who particularly enjoy his witty sense of humor. However, he remains relatively quiet and seems as content to play solitary games as to be with his friends. He goes to the homecoming dance because a very popular, outgoing girl invites him. However, he generally does not go to dances or other large social gatherings where there might be people he does not know.

behavioral inhibition
the tendency to be wary and restrict one's approach to new people, events, or objects.

As a toddler Eric has **behavioral inhibition**, which refers to strong, negative reactions to *new* people, events, or objects. Was he born with this trait? Why do children in the same family—like Eric and his sister—have such different personalities? In a famous study, researchers Thomas and Chess observed 141 infants from 85 families beginning in 1956 when they were 2 to 3 months old (Thomas, Chess, & Birch, 1970). After following the children for 14 years, they concluded that temperament explained why some children from dysfunctional families develop problems but others fare well. For example, cold, demanding parents make one child submissive but another defiant. Let's see whether current research supports this view.

temperament
individual differences in reactivity (in emotions, motor activity, or attention) and the ability to control this reactivity.

Temperament refers to individual differences children have in the intensity and pattern of their reactions to their environment. Temperament is typically thought of as a collection of psychological traits (such as shyness) and physiological traits (such as activity level) that have a genetic basis, are present early in life, remain stable over time, and predict later personality. This is only partly correct. Temperament traits are present early in life and do predict later personality, but are not necessarily highly heritable or stable.

Psychologists do not fully agree on which traits are part of temperament, but four traits appear in most definitions of temperament (Shiner et al., 2012):

1. *Activity*, which refers to how much children move.

2. *Effortful control*, which refers to controlling attention and behavior, such as inhibiting impulses, concentrating, following instructions, and resisting distractions. If you recognize this as "executive functions" from Chapter 4, you get another gold star! They are largely the same construct but have different labels because they come from different fields of research (Allan & Lonigan, 2011; Liew, 2012). Scientists who study personality call it effortful control and scientists who study cognitive development call it executive functions.

PHOTO 6.6 Children with behavioral inhibition are cautious about new objects, events, and people.

3. *Negative emotionality*, which refers to how easily children become irritated, angry, or scared; how intense the emotions are; and how well they control the emotions. Children who are emotionally negative also tend to have problems with effortful control (Zhou, Lengua, & Wang, 2009).

4. *Behavioral inhibition.* Inhibited children, like Eric, react strongly to potential threats, so they are wary of novel things, whereas bold, uninhibited children embrace novelty (Photo 6.6). This opposite pattern of boldness is known as "surgency."

Temperament is the activity and emotion core of personality. Personality, however, includes much more. **Personality** refers to enduring behavior and traits and can be thought of as a hierarchy (see Figure 6.4). Temperament and attachment form the foundation for specific personality traits, which are organized into a few personality types.

What personality do you have? There are thousands of words you might use to describe yourself—outgoing, kind, patient, explosive, talkative, or creative. Psychologists have identified five broad **personality traits** that account for most of the words people use to describe adults and children. They are known as the five-factor model (FFM) or the *Big Five.*

1. **Openness to experience**. Open people are smart (but may not necessarily get good grades), creative, and curious. They enjoy exploring new situations, express themselves well, and get lost in thought and wrapped up in projects.

2. **Conscientiousness**. Conscientious people are neat, orderly, and reliable. They get things done, do not give up easily, set high standards for themselves, and think before acting.

3. **Extraversion**. Extraverts are energetic, talkative, sensation seeking, and full of life. They react quickly and show emotions openly.

personality
a constellation of traits that distinguishes one person from another.

personality traits
the tendency to behave, think, and feel in certain consistent ways. Five traits that account for much of the variation in personality are openness, conscientiousness, extraversion, agreeableness, and neuroticism (OCEAN).

openness to experience
a personality trait that includes curiosity, exploration, imaginative dreaming, creativeness, good self-expression, and being smart.

conscientiousness
a personality trait contrasted with lack of direction. It includes getting things done, not giving up easily, being dependable, planning ahead, and orderliness.

extraversion
a personality trait contrasted with social inhibition. It includes high energy; talkativeness; emotional expressiveness; and being fast-paced, reactive, and full of life.

FIGURE 6.4 **Hierarchical Organization of Personality.**

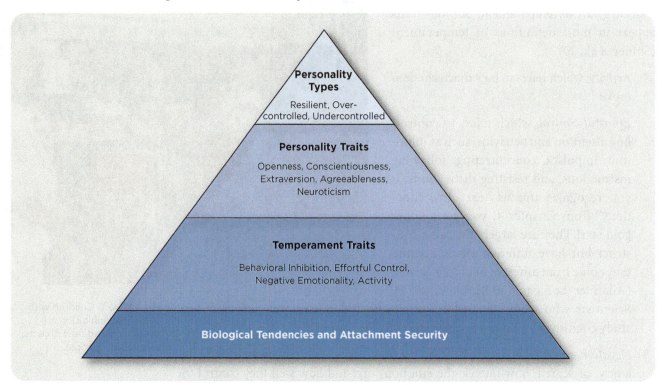

Can you describe your own personality as you begin at the bottom and progress up the pyramid?

agreeableness
a personality trait contrasted with antagonism. It includes thoughtfulness, warmth, kindness, cooperation, and getting along with and pleasing others.

neuroticism
a personality trait contrasted with emotional stability. It includes nervousness, worry, perseverating or falling apart under stress, insecurity, and needing reassurance.

personality types
clusters of personality traits that tend to occur together. The most commonly identified in children are resilient, overcontrolled, and undercontrolled types.

resilient
a personality type characterized by very high levels of openness and conscientiousness, above average levels of extraversion and agreeableness, and very low levels of neuroticism.

4. **Agreeableness.** Agreeable people are thoughtful of others, warm, kind, helpful, and cooperative. They are liked by others.

5. **Neuroticism** (versus emotional stability). Neurotic people are anxious, worry excessively, go to pieces or get sick under stress, and feel hurt easily.

(You can remember these five traits with the mnemonic "OCEAN.") These five traits do not include all personality dimensions, but they are inclusive enough to predict important outcomes (Kline, 2001). These traits are somewhat independent. That is, a person may score high in one trait but low in another. However, the five *traits* tend to cluster together to form three personality *types*.

Research has identified three distinct **personality types**—**resilient**, **overcontrolled**, and **undercontrolled**. This doesn't mean that there are only three types, but rather that these three are easily identifiable. More than 75% of children—across ages, ethnicities, and countries—readily fit into one of these personality types, with most having the resilient type. Table 6.2 shows the traits that comprise each personality type.

6-2a Age Trends in Temperament and Personality

Scientists tend to study *temperament* in early childhood (birth to age 7) and *personality* in older youth (age 3 to adult). You have probably noticed links between temperament and the Big Five personality traits: Negative emotionality is the core of neuroticism; activity and lack of inhibition are the core of extraversion;

TABLE 6.2 Personality types by personality traits

Personality type	Resilient	Overcontrolled	Undercontrolled
Percentage of children	50%–70%	10%–30%	20%–30%
Big Five traits	High openness High conscientiousness Low neuroticism	Low extraversion High agreeableness High neuroticism	High extraversion Low agreeableness Low conscientiousness
Other traits	Confident, competent, verbally fluent, concentrates well, reasonable, compliant, and helpful. Not fearful or anxious.	Helpful, obedient, well-liked, quiet, inhibited, compliant, and indecisive. Not aggressive, assertive, or competitive.	Energetic, restless, antisocial, impulsive, active, cheerful, indecisive, assertive, and unable to concentrate.

Note: The percentage of children in each type comes from studies in the United States and Europe.

Adapted from Asendorpf and Van Aken (1999); Hart, Atkins, and Fegley (2003); Robins, John, Caspi, Moffitt, and Stouthamer-Loeber (1996); and van Lieshout (2000).

effortful control is the core of conscientiousness (Andersson & Bergman, 2011; Rothbart, 2007). See Figure 6.5.

There are age trends in personality. In Chapter 2 you learned that activity level *increases* until 7 to 9 years of age, and *then decreases*. In Chapter 4 you learned that executive functions (i.e., effortful control) *increase* with age, with dramatic increases in early childhood and adolescence. In Chapter 8 you will learn that children become better able to regulate emotions with age, so that emotional negativity *decreases*. Behavioral inhibition is common in young children, and also *decreases* with age. Most inhibited children overcome their inhibition in school settings by 4th grade, particularly intelligent children with social skills, like Eric (Murray et al., 2008).

Overall, from toddlerhood to old age, there is change toward more positive personality (Soto & Tackett, 2015). One exception is that in early adolescence there may

overcontrolled a nonresilient personality type characterized by high agreeableness and neuroticism, and particularly low extraversion.

undercontrolled a nonresilient personality type characterized by particularly low agreeableness and conscientiousness, but also low-average neuroticism and openness.

FIGURE 6.5 The "Big Five" Personality Traits and Their Core Temperament Traits.

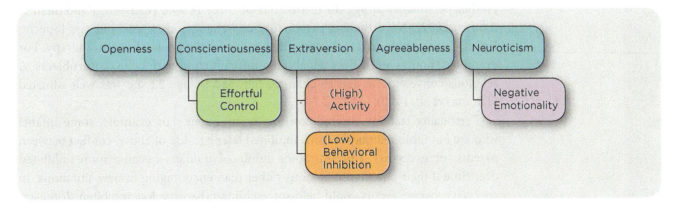

Read the descriptions of each of the Big Five traits. Can you see why each core temperament trait might lead to a specific personality trait?

be a temporary dip in agreeableness, openness, and conscientiousness. There is a particularly steep increase in positive personality traits in young adulthood, perhaps linked to maturing that comes from entering the workforce and romantic relationships (Bleidorn, 2015; Klimstra, 2013). However, not all learners mature in personality. Let's look at individual differences next.

6-2b Individual Diversity in Temperament and Personality

Thomas and Chess believed that temperament has a large effect on children's long-term adjustment. We will look at whether research confirms this in the classroom and beyond, but first let's examine whether temperament and personality are stable across childhood.

How Stable Are Individual Differences in Temperament and Personality?

Stability of individual differences refers to learners maintaining their rank-order as compared with their peers. For example, is shy 3-year-old Eric likely to be more behaviorally inhibited than peers at age 25 as well? Stability depends on: (1) intensity of the trait, (2) which trait, (3) age, and (4) environment. Stability is greater for children with intense traits. For example, in a study that followed inhibited infants to age 15, roughly 15% of children at the extreme stayed inhibited over time but the rest did not (Kagan, Snidman, Kahn, & Towsley, 2007).

Some traits are more stable than others. *Activity* is more stable, *negative emotionality* moderately stable, and *inhibition* less stable (Degnan et al., 2011; Wachs, 2006). Positive traits (e.g., agreeableness and conscientiousness) and types (e.g., resilient) tend to be more stable than their negative counterparts (Andersson & Bergman, 2011; Meeus et al., 2011). This is due to natural maturation (i.e., age trends discussed above) and to pressure from the child's social environment to improve behavior.

Personality becomes more stable across childhood. Attachment theory predicts that personality stabilizes after attachment security is incorporated into personality, perhaps around age 3. Research confirms that personality in infants and toddlers is less stable (Beekman et al., 2015), but it is reasonably stable by middle childhood. For example, one study found that by age 8 researchers can accurately predict personality at age 36 in two out of three people (Laursen, Pulkkinen, & Adams, 2002). Nevertheless, personality can change, even into old age (Specht, Egloff, & Schmukle, 2011). Indeed, that is one of the goals of psychotherapy. For example, Thomas and Chess tell about a difficult child with behavior problems. A religious conversion at age 16 changed her, and by age 22 she was well adjusted (Thomas et al., 1970).

Personality stability depends on the environment. For example, some infants who are not inhibited may become inhibited later because of abuse, conflict between parents, or excessive criticism. Some inhibited toddlers become more inhibited over time if their parents act anxious rather than encouraging in new situations. In contrast, positive events could help some children become less inhibited. *If the environment is stable, personality tends to remain stable* (Wachs, 2006). In summary, personality may remain the same for some children who have extreme traits or whose environment sustains their traits, but many children's personality changes, generally improving, across childhood.

How Stable Is Personality Across Situations?

Would you be surprised to find that a timid learner in your classroom is bossy at home with siblings? An individual's personality can change from situation to situation. A famous 1971 study, known as the Stanford University Prison Experiment, showed that situations can powerfully affect behavior. For 2 weeks, 20 male Stanford students were randomly assigned to be either inmates or guards at a pretend prison in the basement of the psychology building. All the students were chosen for their stable, healthy personalities, yet the experiment had to be cut short after just a few days because the "guards" changed from being agreeable to being cruel to the "inmates." This experiment shows how personality can change based on the situation.

Both personality traits and the situation contribute to how a child will behave at any given moment. This means that your learners' personalities are not a simple collection of traits, but depend on the kind of classroom you create. Throughout this text, and later in this chapter, we'll discuss how to create a classroom that brings out the best in your learners' personalities.

What Do Temperament and Personality Predict?

Your learners' personalities predict important outcomes, often *more strongly than IQ* or *SES* (Meyer et al., 2001). Personality traits in childhood have been linked to physical and mental health, obesity, length of life, happiness in marriage, and career success in adulthood. In particular, high conscientiousness and agreeableness, and low neuroticism, are linked to better outcomes.[6] Personality is also linked to academic achievement and social competence (Photo 6.7).

PHOTO 6.7 Your learners' personalities may predict their academic success more strongly than intelligence or SES. You can create a classroom that fits different personalities so that diverse learners flourish.

Academic achievement

Three personality *traits*—conscientiousness, agreeableness, and openness—predict achievement, regardless of intelligence (Noftle & Robins, 2007). In fact, *the effect of conscientiousness is about as large as that of intelligence* (Poropat, 2009). Effortful control—the foundation of conscientiousness—predicts literacy and math skills as early as 3 to 6 years old, better grades through adolescence, and college completion.[7] Highly agreeable students tend to have higher GPAs. Highly open students tend to have higher SAT scores, but not necessarily good grades. Two other Big Five

[6] There are many studies that support this conclusion, just a few of which are listed here: Andersson and Bergman (2011); Chapman and Goldberg (2011); Hampson (2008); Jackson, Connolly, Garrison, Leveille, and Connolly (2015); Lahey (2009); Sackett and Walmsley (2014); Sutin, Ferrucci, Zonderman, and Terracciano (2011).

[7] There are many studies that support this conclusion, just a few of which are listed here: Allan and Longigan (2011); Andersson and Bergman (2011); Valiente, Lemery-Chalfant, and Swanson (2010); Véronneau, Racer, Fosco, and Dishion (2014).

FIGURE 6.6 Personality Type and Achievement over Time.

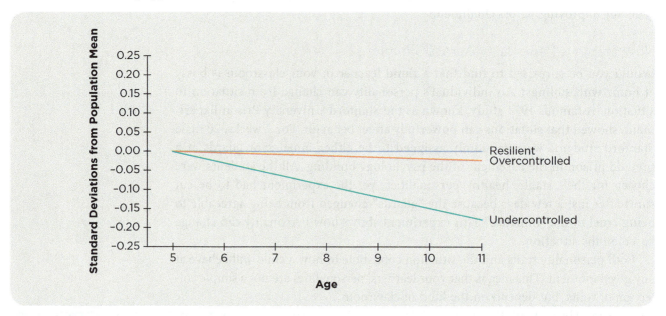

In this graph, zero is the average of all children. Positive numbers indicate achievement that is above average, and negative numbers indicate achievement that is below average. When children are followed from ages 5 to 11, those with resilient and overcontrolled personality types remain near average. What happens over time for children with undercontrolled personalities? *Source: Hart et al. (2003).*

personality traits—extraversion and neuroticism—are not consistently linked to achievement. Extraverted or neurotic learners may be either good or poor students.

Personality *types* also predict achievement. Resilient and overcontrolled students tend to have higher achievement than undercontrolled students. For example, in one study the achievement of undercontrolled students declined steadily across elementary school; the decline was equivalent to missing a full year of school (Hart et al., 2003). (See Figure 6.6.) Undercontrolled students often miss out on much of what happens in the classroom because they are off-task and disorganized.

Social competence

Personality predicts whether learners have social success or behavior problems. *Negative emotionality* is a risk factor for behavior problems over time. Learners with negative emotionality are more likely to experience drug use, depression, anxiety, aggressiveness, peer rejection, and low achievement (Rothbart, 2011; Sanson, Hemphill, & Smart, 2004; Schmitz et al., 1999; Thomas et al., 1970). *Effortful control and behavioral inhibition*, on the other hand, are both protective factors for some of the same problems. Inhibited, cautious learners are less prone to aggression and injuries than uninhibited, sensation-seeking learners (e.g., Davies, Cicchetti, Hentges, & Sturge-Apple, 2013; Schwebel & Plummert, 1999).

Paradoxically, *behavioral inhibition* can also be a risk factor for social problems, but only for nonsociable children. This is a key distinction—inhibited children can be sociable or nonsociable. Remember that inhibition has to do with novelty. Inhibited, nonsociable children avoid social settings. Inhibited, sociable children avoid social settings with strangers, but enjoy social settings with people they know; they only appear shy with strangers. In one study, shy children were less assertive in play with new acquaintances in a new setting, but by the third visit were not distinguishable from other children (McElwain et al., 2014). One of our children was a shy-sociable child. When we moved, she was silent in her new 5th-grade class and did not speak to any of her new peers at lunch for 3 months. She was miserable. However, some months later she was leading noisy "choo-choo trains" of children while waiting to board the school bus; they had become familiar peers. This distinction is important because nonsociable children are likely to be lonely and rejected by peers, while shy-sociable children have social skills and friends (Coplan et al., 2013; Schmidt & Fox, 2002).

Behavioral inhibition can also be a risk factor if the child remains quite shy until 9 to 10 years of age. Shyness in younger children is generally not a cause for concern. Some inhibited young children continue being mildly uncomfortable around new people into adolescence, like Eric, but not to the point of poor social skills. However, about half of children who continue to be extremely shy *are* more likely to develop anxiety disorders (Prior, Smart, Sanson, & Oberklaid, 2000). Thus, inhibition is a protective factor for aggression and injury, and only extreme shyness toward familiar others that persists through middle childhood is a risk factor for problems (Coplan & Armer, 2007; Sanson et al., 2004).

The opposite of inhibition, or extraversion (also called surgency and exuberance), can be positive or negative. Let's take a look at Peter:

> *Two-year-old Peter loves to play with other children. He runs up to a new playmate, shoves him in the stomach with a big grin, and waits for a return smile. This is his way of saying "Let's play!" He is puzzled when the new playmate cries and backs away.*

Extraverted children like Peter have low behavioral inhibition, high activity, are quick to approach novelty with no hesitation, and respond with strong pleasure to rewards (Blandon, Calkins, Keane, & O'Brien, 2010). From infancy to age 5, exuberant children are more impulsive, aggressive, and quick to anger, as well as more friendly, outgoing, and socially competent (Degnan et al., 2011). With age, they learn to control their exuberance so that they don't distress playmates, as Peter did. On the other hand, they tend to develop behavior problems if they have low-quality parenting (Davies, Cicchetti, & Hentges, 2015).

Among older youth, highly *conscientious, agreeable* learners tend to have fewer behavior problems at school (Caspi, 1998; Laursen et al., 2002). In contrast, adolescent boys low in conscientiousness and agreeableness, but high in *extraversion,* are more likely than other youth to be seriously delinquent, like selling drugs, breaking and entering, and joy riding (John, Caspi, Robins, Moffitt, & Stouthamer-Loeber, 1994). Undercontrolled boys tend to be aggressive, while overcontrolled boys tend to be socially withdrawn (Asendorpf & Van Aken, 1999; Hart, Hofmann, Edelstein, & Keller, 1997). Let's look next at the factors that might lead to these diverse personalities.

What Predicts Temperament and Personality?

According to attachment theory, personality is primarily the result of temperament and attachment history. As early as 4 months of age, infant's temperament is apparent (Kagan et al., 2007). Does this mean temperament is genetic? Not necessarily. Even at this early age, temperament could be a result of social experience.

Physiology and genetics

One trait, behavioral inhibition, is known to have a physiological basis. In Chapter 2, you learned that inhibited children have faster heart rates, increased pupil dilation, more muscle tension, and higher levels of cortisol (a stress hormone) when they encounter a new situation. Where do such physiological responses come from? They may be inherited.

Personality is an area in which much heritability research has been conducted (Plomin, DeFries, Knopik, & Neiderhiser, 2016). Research suggests that 20% to 60% of the Big Five personality traits may be heritable (Saudino & Micalizzi, 2015; Turkheimer, Pettersson, & Horn, 2014). *Openness, inhibition, negative emotionality, activity level,* and *extraversion* have moderate-to-strong heritability. In contrast, other traits, like *positive emotionality, effortful control,* and *agreeableness* appear to have little heritability (Bokhorst et al., 2003; Ganiban, Saudino, Ulbricht, Neiderhiser, & Reiss, 2008). Agreeableness is strongly influenced by the family environment; nice children are made, not born (Laursen et al., 2002).

One caution to keep in mind is that heritability estimates are probably inflated because of **sibling-contrast bias**. That is, many studies of personality in childhood use mothers' reports, and mothers tend to exaggerate differences among their children. This results in higher estimates of heritability and lower estimates of shared-environment contribution. But when observers' reports on objective measures (like activity meters) are used, the shared-environment contribution may be substantial (Ganiban et al., 2008; Saudino & Zapfe, 2008).

What might cause such bias? Parents may have two children who are *less active than average,* but they view one child as highly active and the other as very calm because their frame of reference is their own children, rather than all possible children. Such comparison between siblings is a powerful component of the nonshared family environment, or factors that make siblings different (see Chapter 1).

Another important caution is that even when personality traits have a physiological base, this does not mean they are controlled by specific genes. Physiological systems, including the brain, change with experience (see Brain Research box). Thus, there is room for substantial contribution from parents and teachers. See Box 6.3 for remarkable research on how parenting and genes may interact.

sibling-contrast bias
the tendency of family members to report greater difference among siblings than actually exists by evaluating them relative to each other.

 **brain research**

Brain Differences in Personality

Learners with behavioral inhibition have a highly active right frontal lobe. In contrast, extraverted, exuberant learners have a highly active left frontal lobe, which is linked to approaching novelty and responding positively to rewards (Degnan et al., 2011). These physiological differences are apparent in infancy (Hane & Fox, 2006; Laurent, Ablow, & Measelle, 2012). Do these brain differences mean that personality is "wired" in the brain? Not necessarily. Recall from Chapter 2 that the brain changes with experience. For example, infants whose mothers are insensitive and intrusive develop a brain pattern characteristic of behavioral inhibition by 9 months of age, regardless of how their brain started developing earlier in life (Hane & Fox, 2006).

Parenting and attachment

Parenting and attachment predict personality. Earlier we discussed how children, on average, outgrow negative personality traits. However, quality of parenting influences the rate and success with which this happens. For example, children with insecure attachment and punitive, controlling, rejecting parents tend to become *more*, not less, emotionally negative over time (e.g., Blandon et al., 2010). For another example, children with insecure attachment and intrusive, overprotective parents tend to become more inhibited over time and develop social anxiety (e.g., Hastings, Kahle, & Nuselovici, 2014; Lewis-Morrarty et al., 2015; Volbrecht & Goldsmith, 2010). On the positive side, children with warm, responsive mothers become less overly exuberant with time (Blandon et al., 2010) and develop resilient personalities (de Haan, Deković, van den Akker, Stoltz, & Prinzie, 2013).

These data are correlational (see Chapter 1). Thus, you could argue that the child's personality causes parent behavior, or vice versa. Perhaps parents have difficulty securely attaching to infants who are irritable or highly active. Yet, research supports Ainsworth's view that secure attachment is primarily driven by parent behavior, and the child's temperament makes only a small or no contribution. Many difficult infants become securely attached and less difficult over time with sensitive parenting (Bokhorst et al., 2003; Pauli-Pott, Haverkock, Pott, & Beckmann, 2007). Furthermore, differential susceptibility pertains to temperament. That is, some children are more susceptible to their environments—for good or ill. For example, infants with negative emotionality tend to grow into toddlers with poor self-control if they have insensitive mothers, but grow into toddlers with exceptional self-control if they have sensitive mothers (Kim & Kochanska, 2012). Figure 6.7 presents a model for how parenting and personality may combine to influence a child's emotional and social well-being.

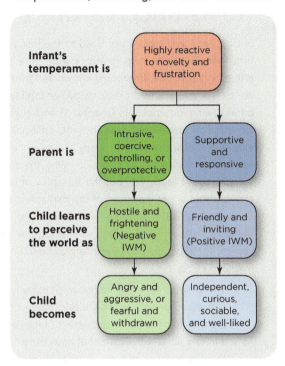

FIGURE 6.7 The Relationship among Temperament, Parenting, and Child Outcomes.

Which side of the model do Eric's experiences and development follow? Describe a child you have known who may have developed according to the other side of the model (IWM = internal working model).

6-2c Group Diversity in Temperament and Personality

Have you heard others claim that there are group differences in personality, like boys are more active than girls? Let's see if research confirms this.

Gender

Gender differences in personality are small to nonexistent. One clear exception is that girls tend to be higher in effortful control, meaning they are less distractible or impulsive (Allan & Lonigan, 2011). In addition, parents report that boys are more active than girls; motion detectors sometimes, but not always, confirm this (e.g., Saudino, 2012). These differences may help explain boys' higher rate of ADHD. They may also explain why preschool boys have more surgency, and adolescent boys are more likely to be undercontrolled, whereas girls are more likely to be overcontrolled (Degnan et al., 2011; Meeus et al., 2011). Other gender differences have been reported, but not confirmed.

Socioeconomic Status

SES is linked to personality types. Students with low SES are more likely to change from resilient to undercontrolled over time, presumably because risk factors make it

BOX 6.3 theories & theorists

Revisiting Nature and Nurture—Epigenetics

In Chapter 1 you were introduced to the interplay of nature (genes) and nurture (environment). One of today's interesting scientific mysteries, known as "missing heritability," is that scientists who study heritability by comparing twins (described in Chapter 1) find high levels of genetic contribution to development, especially personality, whereas scientists who study the genome find very low levels of genetic contribution. Why the difference? We don't fully know yet, but the interplay of genes and environment are at least part of the explanation (Manuck & McCaffery, 2014). This interplay applies to temperament and attachment, as well as many other child outcomes. Three principles of this interplay build on what you learned in Chapter 1.

1. *The environment may influence whether genes are expressed or not.* Genes are seldom destiny. In fact, many genes are never expressed. Genes are like a library filled with books that have the potential to influence you, but they have to be read to have their effect (Champagne & Mashoodh, 2009). Social experience can determine whether a gene is read or not. How might this work? One possibility is called *methylation*. Ongoing stressful experiences, such as having a hostile parent, can cause a methyl group to bind to some genes, which blocks the gene from being read. (A pat on the back if you remember methyl groups from chemistry class!) Methylation of genes can alter neurotransmitters in the brain, which can alter behavior. Through methylation, social experience becomes biologically embedded in genes across generations (Meany, 2010). This is how early childhood experiences can influence you in adulthood—and perhaps even your grandchildren. This process is called epigenetic, which means "upon genetics."

2. *Genes may only influence child outcomes when acting together with environmental factors.* Genes alone seldom explain complex child behavior.

For example, children have a gene called *DRD4*. One version of this gene—or allele—predisposes children to be insecurely attached and to be highly reactive (e.g., their heart rate speeds up) to arousing events, like being separated from their mother. Whether children with this allele actually become insecure or highly reactive depends on their mothers' sensitivity (Propper et al., 2008). If their mothers are sensitive, they tend not to be any more reactive than children without the allele, and they tend to be secure. However, if children have the risk allele *and* poor parenting, they are 19 times more likely to become insecure than children without the allele (Bernier & Meins, 2008). Other studies have found that children may only develop problems if they have a combination of both high-risk genes and a poor environment (e.g., Davies et al., 2015; Kim-Cohen & Gold, 2009; Wiebe et al., 2009).

3. *Genes may make some children more susceptible to their environment—for good or ill.* Children with high-risk genes may have below-average outcomes in negative environments, but above-average outcomes in positive environments because they react to their experiences more strongly than other children (Pluess, 2015). This concept is known as differential susceptibility. For example, children with the "high-risk" *DRD4* allele tend to have more behavior problems and lower achievement than other children if they have insensitive parents. However, they tend to have higher achievement and behave exceptionally well, if their parents are sensitive, emotionally positive, and use positive discipline (Bakermans-Kranenburg, Van IJzendoorn, Pijlman, Mesman, & Juffer, 2008). In other words, *some children are more susceptible to both good and bad parenting*. Perhaps this is why two children in the same family turn out differently—one is more susceptible to the family environment than the other.

difficult to remain resilient. Yet, low-SES students who are resilient are likely to do well because personality type can be as powerful a predictor of academic achievement as SES (Hart et al., 2003). Thus, helping your low-SES learners develop resilient personalities is important.

Some psychologists borrow the Swedish expressions *orkidebarn*, meaning "orchid child," to describe children who are more sensitive to their environment, and *maskrosbarn*, meaning "dandelion child," to describe children who thrive in whatever environment they are in, even poor soil and too much or too little rain. Eric, in the vignette, may be an orchid child. His life story fits research

Orchids are exquisite, but only thrive in the right environment. Resilient dandelions thrive in many environments.

showing that temperamentally challenging children fare not just average, but exceptionally well when their environmental fit is good (e.g., Dich et al., 2015).

Figure 6.8 illustrates these last two principles. Children with high-risk genes often have harsh or insensitive parents, perhaps because of a gene–environment correlation. Notice the red arrow, which indicates that even when children have both

a negative environment and genetic risk, some may develop well. What might lead to such resiliency? Two possibilities are: (1) interventions to help the child and (2) a supportive relationship with an adult, such as a teacher (Kim-Cohen & Gold, 2009). Thus, your students' social environment—including how you interact with them—powerfully shapes their development and may even modify their genes.

FIGURE 6.8 Genes and Environment Interact to Influence Child Outcomes.

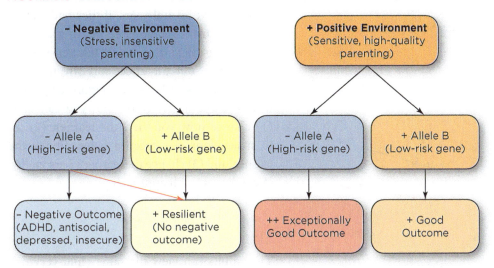

Describe how an "orchid child" with a sensitive parent would proceed through this chart. Do it again for a "dandelion child" with an insensitive parent. (Note: This model has been tested on multiple genes and on child outcomes such as ADHD, antisocial behavior, depression, sensation seeking, and insecure attachment.)

epigenetic
a process in which phenotype, or gene expression, is altered through social experience, or other mechanisms, rather than a change in DNA.

allele
a variation of a gene. For example, a gene that influences dopamine in the brain may have different alleles, one that leads to high levels of dopamine and another that leads to low levels.

differential susceptibility
children differ in the extent to which they are susceptible to a good or bad environment based on their genotype.

Cohort Effect

Have you ever heard veteran teachers say, "Kids today just aren't like they used to be?" Children do vary in personality depending on when they were born. Society-wide changes can result in personality differences in birth cohorts, or children

think
about this

A well-known saying in personality psychology is "every child is like all other children, like some other children, and like no other children" (we've liberally paraphrased). Can you apply attachment, temperament, and personality to this phrase? In what way is every child alike or different?

born at one time compared with children born at another time. For example, in the United States anxiety/neuroticism increased steadily from the 1950s to the 1980s among 9- to 17-year-olds (Twenge, 2000). The increase was large; the *average* scores in the 1980s were equivalent to scores for children with psychiatric problems in the 1950s. This increase in anxiety/neuroticism may be related to social changes—like more divorces, fewer siblings, less trust in others, and more crime. This is an example of the chronosystem in the bioecological model (see Chapter 1), which suggests that children will change as their culture changes over time.

In summary, students in your classroom may have different personalities depending on their gender, SES, and cohort. Girls, on average, may be better able to control their attention and behavior than boys. What are other implications for your classroom?

6-2d Classroom Implications of Temperament and Personality

The personality of your learners can have a large effect on their social and academic success in your classroom. Having a variety of personalities in the classroom is one of the delights of teaching. However, if a learner's personality is problematic, do your best to create a positive teacher–student relationship, as discussed earlier. This can compensate for difficult temperament. For example, in one study Black and White students with low effortful control had less depression and delinquency over the next several years, if they had a close teacher–student relationship in 7th grade. All students benefited from a close teacher–student relationship, but the effect was strongest for at-risk youth and boys (see Figure 6.9). Let's discuss three other approaches you can take: (1) change how you view the learner, (2) try to make your classroom a better fit for the learner, and (3) change the learner's personality. We'll discuss each approach.

Change Your Perceptions of the Learner's Personality

Two adults can view the same child very differently. Research on parents indicates that perceptions of their child's temperament reflect their own internal working models. Insecure mothers tend to perceive their babies as more difficult than secure mothers, and parents who are depressed, unhappily married, or have little social support view their children's personalities more negatively (Harrison & Ungerer, 2002; Priel & Besser, 2000). Thus, when a parent describes one of your learners as difficult, this could mean that the parent

FIGURE 6.9 Teacher–Student Relationship Combines with Personality to Predict Misbehavior.

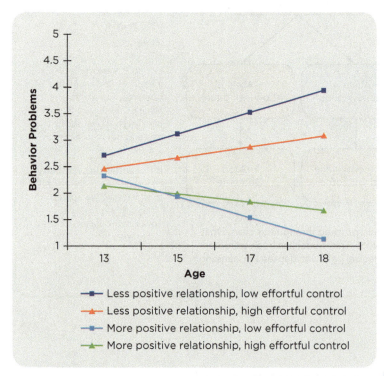

— Less positive relationship, low effortful control
— Less positive relationship, high effortful control
— More positive relationship, low effortful control
— More positive relationship, high effortful control

Seventh graders with low effortful control (a risk factor) fared better over time, if they had a close teacher–student relationship (a protective factor). *Source: Wang, Brinkworth, and Eccles (2013), p. 700.*

has a negative bias rather than that the learner really is difficult. It also suggests that when you find a learner's personality challenging, you may need to reflect about your own biases and whether your perception is accurate. In one program, kindergarten teachers were taught to change their perceptions of their learners' temperament so that they appreciated the strengths of different personalities and to create a "good fit" by scaffolding (Chapter 3) the child's success in situations that challenged their personality, such as helping shy children join a group. As a result, the children were more engaged in class and learned more (O'Connor, Cappella, McCormick, & McClowry, 2014). Let's discuss good fit next.

Create a Good Fit

Personality can change across situations. A student can be open, agreeable, and conscientious in one teacher's room, but not in another teacher's room. Different teachers may evoke different personality traits in the same learner, because one has good fit and one does not. Learners' success in the classroom depends on the match, or **goodness of fit**, between personality and the environment, not personality alone. Learners whose personality fits their teacher's expectations earn better grades, have better relationships with the teacher and classmates, and have higher self-esteem than students with poor fit. Let's discuss what "goodness of fit" is, and then discuss how you can create a good fit for two personality traits—high activity and shyness.

A *good fit* exists when learners' personality matches the demands of their environment. Even if learners have a genetic propensity toward a negative temperament trait, a good fit may result in learners not manifesting the trait or manifesting it to a small degree, whereas a poor fit may magnify the trait.

To illustrate the concept of goodness of fit, Thomas and Chess (1984) give the example of two difficult little girls. One had a warm, but firm father. She developed positively until her father died when she was 13. Her mother felt overwhelmed and could not set limits for her four children. The girl developed severe behavior problems in her teens as the fit went from good to bad. The second difficult girl had a rigid, critical, and punitive father; she became intense and explosive. Around age 10, she developed musical talent that her father admired. He became more positive toward her as he changed from thinking she was "rotten" to thinking she had an "artistic" temperament. She improved through adolescence and was well adjusted by age 22 as the fit went from bad to good.

One aspect of goodness of fit is agreement between the child's "real" personality and the adults' view of the "ideal" personality. Imagine asking parents or teachers what child behaviors they find most annoying and then to rate a specific child on those annoying behaviors. Adults who see the child as having few annoying behaviors have a good fit. You can do the same exercise. Ask yourself what behaviors you find most annoying and which learners in your classroom display those behaviors. This will reveal which learners you have a good fit with, and which you may need to adapt to.

Learners fare best when parents and teachers adapt to them. For example, difficult children may develop more emotion and behavior problems if their parents are punitive (De Clercq, Van Leeuwen, De Fruyt, Van Hiel, & Mervielde, 2008). Similarly, children with low effortful control and high negativity may learn less

goodness of fit
the degree of match between temperament and environmental demands, values, or expectations.

think
about **this**

How do the concepts of "genotype" and "phenotype" and "gene–environment interaction" from Chapter 1 pertain to the concept of goodness of fit? How does the concept of differential susceptibility align with the concept of goodness of fit?

when teachers use guilt-inducing discipline (e.g., telling them you are disappointed in them), compared to teachers who use a redirecting discipline style (e.g., reminding them to do something) (Viljaranta et al., 2015). One approach is a good fit and the other is not. We will discuss effective discipline in the next chapter, so stay tuned!

Let's look at Eric again. Eric's parents seldom disciplined him because he was overly harsh on himself. His parents gently drew him into activities after modeling how to do things that Eric hesitated to do. At preschool he clung to his mother, so she stayed with him each day until he said that he was ready for her to leave—giving him control over the separation. The preschool teachers disapproved of this. They tried coercing Eric into participating in group time by giving him stickers, fearing that he was not learning anything. His mother did not worry, because at home Eric repeated everything that was said during group time, verbatim. Because of the good fit between parenting and child temperament, Eric developed strong academic and social skills and self-confidence. However, Eric did not become a dramatically outgoing adolescent. A good fit may result in optimal development of children, but not in movement to the opposite extreme of temperament traits.

Create a good fit for highly active learners

Teachers tend to prefer less active learners. However, *highly active* learners may have higher test scores despite this trait *not* being valued by teachers (Lerner, 1983). Let's look at Kevin's experience.

> *Kevin is in a team-taught 7th-grade class with two teachers. He is a good student, but never takes his seat at the beginning of class. Instead, he goes to the bookshelf to flip through an atlas, look through a kaleidoscope, and talk to classmates for a few minutes. This annoys one of his teachers, who scolds him and, as a result, the two are constantly irritated with each other. His other teacher, in contrast, appreciates Kevin's curiosity and high energy level. She allows him the few minutes at the beginning of class to "travel" the room while she puts other students to work. They have an agreement that in return for this privilege, he will not get out of his seat during the lesson.*

Kevin's temperament is a poor fit with his first teacher's expectations, whereas it is a good fit with his second teacher who values, or at least accommodates, high activity in her classroom. Guidelines to provide a good fit for highly active learners include:

1. Avoid mistakenly assuming learners who cannot sit still do not want to learn or are intentionally disobeying you. They may simply find sit-still demands overly difficult.

2. Ensure that highly active learners have an outlet for their energy, like adequate recess or freedom to move about the room, as Kevin's second teacher did.

3. If available, use more computer-directed instruction. Distractible, active learners may spend more time-on-task with computer-directed instruction because it is game-like, provides immediate feedback, and engages attention.

Create a good fit for shy learners

Teachers tend to develop distant relationships with shy learners and underestimate their abilities (Viljaranta et al., 2015). This is less likely to happen if you create a good fit in your classroom for shy learners by following these guidelines:

1. Avoid confusing shyness with low ability or low self-esteem. Anxiety in novel situations is not the same as being anxious about one's personal worth. Shy toddlers are less likely to talk, but this may be due to reticence to speak, not a language delay (Watts et al., 2014). Unfortunately, American teachers tend to assume that shy learners are not as intelligent as exuberant learners (Coplan, Hughes, Bosacki, & Rose-Krasnor, 2011), as Eric's 1st-grade teacher mistakenly did. Although shy learners may not show off their intellect, this does not mean they know less than extraverted learners.

2. Avoid confusing shyness with poor social or emotional skills. Shy-sociable learners have friends. However, some shy learners may need intervention. These include: (1) toddlers who are frightened about things that do not frighten age-mates (e.g., a puppet asking them to come play; Buss, 2011), (2) shy-nonsociable learners, who are shy even with known peers, and (3) youth who remain extremely shy beyond 4th grade. We'll discuss how to build their social and emotional skills in Chapters 8 to 11.

3. Give shy learners control whenever possible. Allow them to pace their approach to new situations. Do not be overzealous, intrusive, or pushy with shy learners. Shyness is a way of coping with strong physiological reactions, like a racing heart. Intrusive teachers interfere with the learner's coping mechanism of gradual comfort and cause the learner to feel greater stress (Nachmias, Gunnar, Mangelsdorf, Parritz, & Buss, 1996).

4. Reduce shy learners' stress by giving them repeated exposure to a new task or situation and by keeping them with their friends when making group assignments.

think about this

David was a shy-sociable, cautious child. His younger brother, Raul, was a sociable, highly active, boisterous, risk-taking child. David earned primarily A's in high school, and scored at the 94th percentile on the SAT. Raul earned primarily C's in the same classes, and scored at the 95th percentile on the SAT.

What do you suspect about the goodness of fit at school for these brothers? Do their different achievements fit the research?

Shape the Student's Personality

Some personalities are not well suited to school settings and are linked to low achievement. For example, learners with low effortful control and conscientiousness are unable to concentrate on their work, become occupied with irrelevant things, daydream, give up quickly, and work for a few minutes but then are off-task again. Thus far, we have discussed how you may need to change your expectations and create a good fit for learners' with challenging personalities. A different approach is to shape a student's personality. This may be the kindest approach if a student's personality is creating social or academic problems, but is it doable? Personality can change, as it did for Eric in the opening vignette. You can shape learners' personalities, bringing out their best traits. In other chapters we'll discuss how to promote greater effortful control (Chapters 4 and 7) and agreeableness (Chapter 10) and less emotional negativity (Chapter 8).

In summary, the major lessons on temperament and personality for teachers are that: (1) many aspects of temperament are not heritable, and even those that are heritable are influenced by the environment; (2) while personality may stay the same over time, some traits are not very stable; (3) negative emotionality and poor control are associated with adjustment problems, but inhibition and high activity level may not be; and (4) even learners with challenging personalities can develop secure attachment, social competence, and high academic achievement when there is good fit with classroom demands. Thus, you can help your students become more resilient.

Now that we are at the conclusion of this chapter, you should have a deeper understanding of the importance of attachment, and how you can serve as an attachment figure to learners and influence their personalities. However, you will find that some students will make this challenging because of their misbehavior. Managing misbehavior is a focus of the next chapter.

---

reflections on practice

My Teaching

To consider whether you are promoting secure attachment and positive personality traits in your students, periodically reflect on your classroom practices. Ask yourself the following:

1. What is my attachment to my own parents? How does it affect my expectations of my students and my sensitivity toward them?

2. Do I have a sense of the kind of relationship my students have with their parents and its effect on the relationship they have with me? Can I recognize possible insecure or secure attachment in my students? What attachment behaviors are age-appropriate for my students?

3. What sort of relationship do I have with each student? Could it be considered secure?

4. Am I sensitive and supportive with each student? Is it clear that I care for each student? What kind of internal working model might my students develop about relationships based on their interaction with me?

5. What am I doing to promote school bonding? Are most learners likely to report that they feel cared for at my school?

6. Am I aware of the temperament and personality of each student in my class?

7. Is there a good fit with my teaching approach? (You can test this by listing the traits you expect in your classroom. Then rate each child on those traits.) Am I giving very shy or inhibited learners control and allowing them to warm up slowly to novel situations? Am I sensitive to the needs of highly active learners?

Professional Resource Download

Summary of Age Trends in Attachment and Personality

	Attachment Behaviors	Consequences of Secure Attachment	Temperament and Personality
Infancy & Toddlerhood (Birth–2 years)	• Infants' attachment becomes apparent between 6 and 12 months by their smiling and orienting toward the attachment figure (AF). • Stranger wariness is typically apparent about 8–9 months, and wanes after 12 months. • Internal working models (IWMs) are apparent by 12 months.	• Good emotion-regulation ability (frustration tolerance, persistence, flexibility, compliance, enthusiasm, and cheerfulness). • Longer attention span and less hyperactivity.	• Temperament may be synonymous with personality in infancy. • Temperamental traits are reliably observed by 4 months. • Temperament is not very stable.
Early Childhood (3–5 Years)	• After age 3, IWMs tend to be stable. Children's attachment to their teacher and others is likely to reflect the quality of their primary attachment. • Secure base behaviors are activated less easily and are less intense after age 3. • By 3–4 years, extreme separation distress has waned. Children can feel secure in a strange place with subordinate AFs.	• Good emotion-regulation ability. • Longer attention span and less hyperactivity. • More inclination to stay on mother's lap and be attentive to a book while reading. Better prereading skills and attitudes toward reading. • Social competence. More liked by teachers and peers. More harmonious and intimate friendships. Less anger and aggression. Less likely to start fights and victimize others or be victims.	• The "Big Five" personality factors have been identified in 3-year-olds. • The three personality types—resilient, undercontrolled, and overcontrolled—have also been identified in preschoolers. • Early childhood shyness does not predict later outcomes, but early negativity does predict later antisocial behavior.
Middle Childhood (6–12 Years)	• Children still enjoy proximity to their AF but need less physical contact, explore more widely, and tolerate greater separation. • Attachment behaviors are more subtle, and a larger range of conditions can make children feel secure. • The AF's availability remains very important.	• Social competence. More friends. Less anger, aggression, dishonesty, argumentativeness, disruptiveness, withdrawal, and anxiety. Less likely to be ridiculed or excluded by peers. Less likely to start fights, be victims, or victimize others. • Less likely to be either clingy or defiant with teachers. • Less likely to have ADHD symptoms and academic problems.	• Extreme behavioral inhibition that persists through middle childhood predicts social anxiety in adolescence. • Conscientiousness, agreeableness, and openness all predict achievement. • Each personality type has been associated with a specific pattern of school achievement and social competence.

Summary of Age Trends in Attachment and Personality

	Attachment Behaviors	Consequences of Secure Attachment	Temperament and Personality
Adolescence (13–19 Years)	• "Touching base" behaviors are less frequent and more subtle. • Self-reliance and independence result from feeling secure. • Mother, rather than peers, remains at the top of the hierarchy for most. • Teens who were securely attached as infants are likely to be securely attached in adolescence, unless negative events occur. • Secondary schools are less likely to meet teens' needs for attachment and bonding than elementary schools. Participation in extracurricular activities becomes important.	• Social competence and independence. Less anger and aggression. Less likely to start fights and be victims or victimize others. • Less likely to experience depression, suicidal thoughts, substance use, conduct disorders, eating disorders, or social withdrawal. • More likely to have higher math scores, better reading comprehension, and higher GPAs. • Security of attachment is associated with quality of romantic relationships.	• Personality becomes more stable. • Behavioral inhibition in toddlerhood generally does not predict inhibition in adolescence. • Conscientiousness and agreeableness predict achievement. • Overall, there is change toward more positive personality with a temporary dip in agreeableness, openness, and conscientiousness in early adolescence. • There is a particularly steep increase in positive personality traits in young adulthood.

≫ **Professional Resource Download**

Chapter Summary

6-1 Attachment

• Attachment keeps the parent and young child in proximity to each other, and the older child feeling secure. Ethologists believe attachment promotes survival and exploration of new environments. John Bowlby pointed out that attachment is normal, innate, and necessary for healthy development. Mary Ainsworth pointed out that clingy or avoidant behavior indicates insecure attachment and that quality of care predicts security of attachment.

• Attachment varies in quality. Children with secure attachment are readily soothed, emotionally open, and able to use their attachment figure as a secure base from which to explore. There are three types of insecure attachment. Resistant children have exaggerated emotions and are not able to use their attachment figure as a secure base. Avoidant children appear emotionally indifferent to their attachment figure. Disorganized children have no coherent response to their attachment figure. Quality of attachment is fairly stable across childhood but can change if risk factors change.

• Secure children have sensitive, supportive parents. Resistant children have confusing, inconsistent parents. Avoidant children have intrusive, rejecting parents. Disorganized children are frightened by their parents.

- Across SES and ethnic groups, there are differences in the rate of secure attachment, which are related to differences in quality of caregiving.

- Security of attachment predicts social competence, academic achievement, and many other outcomes. Attachment is thought to have such wide effects through internal working models that become a part of the child's personality by age 3.

- Learners can securely attach to teachers who are sensitive and supportive. Attachment to teachers and bonding with school affect social and academic success in school.

6-2 Temperament and Personality

- Temperament traits are observed early in infancy. Four temperament traits have been identified: activity level, effortful control, behavioral inhibition, and negative emotionality.

- Five personality traits account for much of the variation in personality: openness, conscientiousness, extraversion, agreeableness, and neuroticism (OCEAN). The Big Five traits tend to cluster together into three personality types: resilient, overcontrolled, and undercontrolled.

- Temperament and attachment are the basis of personality. They are both moderately stable, but modifiable, so personality is only moderately stable— unless children have extreme traits, and their environments sustain the traits.

- Some, but not all, aspects of temperament are partially heritable. What is inherited may be differences in physiological arousal, which are also influenced by attachment. Parenting and culture influence personality.

- Genes and the environment interact to determine a child's temperament and attachment in three ways: (1) The environment may influence whether genes are expressed. (2) Genes may influence child outcomes only when acting together with environmental factors. (3) Some genes may make some children more susceptible to both a good and bad environment.

- Some temperament traits have long-term consequences for children. Emotional negativity is a risk factor for antisocial behavior, while inhibition is a protective factor. Inhibition is linked to social or emotional problems, but only for nonsociable children who are extremely shy past early childhood.

- Personality traits and types are linked to social and academic competence. Agreeable and conscientious traits and resilient types predict school success.

- Development depends on the goodness of fit between the child's temperament and the environment. Children whose temperamental traits match the teacher's expectations may have greater social and academic success at school. Teachers can help learners with different personalities by providing a good fit.

Daniel Jedzura/Shutterstock.com

Self-Control and Discipline

How can you help a student who disrupts your class develop more self-control? What is the best way to handle discipline so that learning is not derailed? These are questions teachers face daily. In this chapter we will discuss self-control, effective discipline, and parenting/teaching styles. **After you read this chapter, you will be able to:**

7-1   Describe how students develop self-control and why it matters.

7-2   Implement effective classroom management and discipline to maximize learning.

7-3   Analyze how styles of parenting and teaching influence students' self-control.

7-1 Self-Control

Clint, who is in 8th grade, talks with his classmates before class starts. His teacher, Mrs. Reinhardt, asks him to be quiet. Later in the class, Clint joins a conversation of students sitting behind him. Mrs. Reinhardt tells him he should know the rules and stop acting up. He asks, "Why do you pick on me when everyone else is talking?" Mrs. Reinhardt gives him a red card, as a warning for misbehavior, and tells him that if he misbehaves again, she will send him to the principal's office. In irritation Clint snarls, "This sucks!" He is sent to the office.

When Clint arrives at the principal's office, he is too angry to speak coherently. The principal tells him to sit in the hallway until he calms down. Instead, Clint walks away. The principal catches Clint. They discuss what happened and the principal tells Clint to apologize to Mrs. Reinhardt, which he does.

Clint has difficulty resisting impulses or anticipating the consequences of his behavior. He has low self-control. Will Mrs. Reinhardt's approach to discipline improve Clint's self-control? This chapter will help you answer this question and clarify how your use of discipline influences your students' self-control. First let's discuss what self-control is and how it develops.

self-control
the ability to control one's own behavior and emotions, obey rules, inhibit inappropriate action, and focus attention.

Self-control is the ability to inhibit impulses, obey rules, ignore distractions, be patient, and stay focused on a task. Children with self-control are also able to regulate their emotions. Instead of talking back to the teacher, like Clint, they would cope with their anger in a more acceptable way. You might want to excuse Clint, saying he was provoked, but he still acted without self-control. You will learn more about emotion regulation in Chapter 8. In this chapter we will focus on inhibiting impulses and delaying gratification. **Delay of gratification** means delaying what you desire in the moment in order to get something more desirable in the long term.

delay of gratification
an aspect of self-control in which children delay what they desire right now in order to get something more desirable later.

7-1a Age Trends in Self-Control

Students are asked to inhibit impulses and delay gratification many times every day at school. Toddlers are asked to inhibit the impulse to stand on their chairs during snack time. Adolescents are asked to inhibit the impulse to talk during class. Impulsivity decreases and self-control increases dramatically with age.

Infancy and Toddlerhood (Birth to 2 Years)

Infants' and toddlers' behavior is impulsive. For example, when they are hungry, they want to be fed *immediately*. Their ability to restrain behavior is measured in *seconds*. In one study, when told not to touch a toy, only 11% of 14-month-olds could hold off touching it for 30 seconds, whereas 65% of 3-year-olds could do so (Friedman, Miyake, Robinson, & Hewitt, 2011).

Early Childhood (3 to 5 Years)

In a series of classic studies sometimes called the marshmallow studies, scientists measured young children's ability to delay gratification by placing a tempting pair of items in front of them—for example, one marshmallow versus two, or marshmallows versus pretzels—and telling the children they could have the less preferred item now or the preferred item if they waited, usually about 15 minutes (Mischel, Shoda,

& Rodriguez, 1989). These studies have been replicated many times.

What do such studies find? Older toddlers can wait longer than younger toddlers. Preschoolers can wait even longer. However, even though preschoolers have more self-control than toddlers, their capacity to wait is fairly short-lived, lasting a matter of minutes. Three- and four-year-olds can wait longer if the preferred item is really big compared to the less-preferred item, while size does little to improve 2-year-olds' limited delay (Steelandt, Thierry, Broihanne, & Dufour, 2012). Few children under the age of 4 are able to wait a full 15 minutes. This is why young children need your help to wait for a snack or for their turn to use a toy (Photo 7.1).

PHOTO 7.1 Young children need help controlling their impulses.

Middle Childhood (6 to 12 Years)

Children in elementary school have better self-control than preschoolers, and their self-control increases with time. In one study children were told not to peek at an answer to a test question while the adult was out of the room. Most (78%) 1st-graders, 43% of 3rd-graders, and 31% of 5th-graders peeked (Talwar, Gordon, & Lee, 2007). The situation was too taxing for most 1st-graders but not for most 5th-graders. On average, older children are better at resisting distractions to stay on task and controlling impulses than younger children (Vazsonyi & Huang, 2010).

Adolescence (13 to 19 Years)

Youth continue to become less impulsive from age 10 to age 30 (see Figure 7.1). Self-control requires executive functions. In Chapter 4 you learned that executive functions increase into adolescence. This is probably because the prefrontal cortex, which is activated during tests of self-control, matures in late adolescence or early adulthood (Shamosh et al., 2008).

Adolescents are so skilled at delay of gratification that the tests used with young children are simply too easy for adolescents. They are given more challenging tests, like hypothetically choosing between having $200 now or $1000 a month from now (Steinberg et al., 2009). In their daily lives, adolescents are capable of remarkable delay of gratification. For example, they can delay hanging out with friends in order to study for a test that will help them get into college in order to become an engineer, which is years away. However, adolescents are not good at resisting the allure of electronic devices. Researchers found that during a short 15-minute study period, youth averaged less than 6 minutes of study before switching to something else, usually an electronic activity such as texting (Rosen, Carrier, & Cheever, 2013). Let's look at individual differences next.

FIGURE 7.1 Age Differences in Self-Reported Impulsivity.

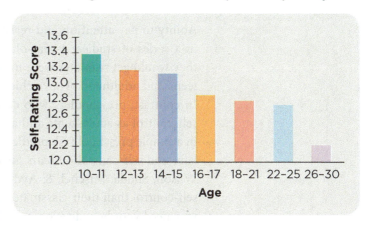

Where are you on this graph? *Source: Steinberg et al. (2008).*

Some Teen Brains Find Risk Rewarding

If self-control steadily increases and impulsivity decreases from infancy to adolescence, thanks to maturing of the prefrontal cortex, then why do teens have a bad reputation as more impulsive risk-takers than younger children? There are three possible answers: (1) Teens have a reputation that is undeserved because they may not be more risk-taking than adults; in fact, they are following the example of adults who also engage in risky behavior (Males, 2010). (2) Impulsiveness and risk taking are not the same thing. Teens may engage in risky behavior as a choice, not as an impulse. (3) Teens find risky behavior more rewarding than adults or younger children as a result of brain development. Adolescents experience heightened brain activation when they receive or expect rewards, such as food (especially sweets), money, and thrills (Galván, 2013). The reward center of the brain matures a little faster than the control center. In teens the reward center is fully mature, while the control center is still developing, so that these systems are temporarily out of balance (Bjork et al., 2012). See Figure 7.2. This sensitivity to rewards can be adaptive if it helps adolescents approach new experiences instead of avoiding them, but it can be a problem if it leads to overly risky behavior.

There are large individual differences such that *most teens do not engage in risky behaviors*, but some do.

FIGURE 7.2 **The Brain and Reward.**

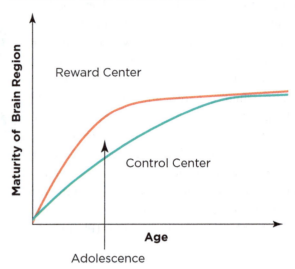

The reward center (nucleus accumbens) of the brain matures a little faster than the control center (prefrontal cortex). What does this suggest about the importance of promoting self-control early in children? *Source: Adapted from Casey, Getz, and Galvan (2008), p. 64.*

Those who do tend to underestimate potential negative consequences (e.g., "nothing bad is going to happen") and tend to have a highly active reward center (e.g., "this is going to be GREAT fun!"). In a competition between the control and reward centers, their reward center wins (Bjork et al., 2012).

7-1b Individual Diversity in Self-Control

Even if they are the same age, children vary widely in their levels of self-control. Are these differences stable? Is Clint likely to have had self-control problems in preschool and elementary school?

Stability Across Time

Ability to pay attention and resist impulses is a relatively stable trait. For example, in a series of studies, 4-year-olds who chose not to eat one marshmallow so that they would get two later were more self-controlled and less distractible in their late teens and adulthood. They achieved higher SAT scores and reported less drug use. In contrast, preschoolers who could not delay gratification continued to have less self-control as adolescents and adults. Remarkably, the number of seconds of delay in a simple preschool task predicts with a fair degree of accuracy overweight 30 years later and self-control *40 years later* (Casey et al., 2011; Mischel et al., 2011; Schlam, Wilson, Shoda, Mischel, & Ayduk, 2013)! This means that your students with less self-control than their classmates are not likely to simply outgrow the problem and may need your help developing self-control.

Stability Across Situations

Self-control varies depending on the situation. It is easier for learners to inhibit their impulses if their attention is diverted from temptations. For example, your students may be able to refrain from touching a forbidden object, like a colorful piñata or equipment in physics class, if other interesting activities are occurring. Children may be able to wait longer to eat a treat if they think about something other than the treat, like playing with a favorite toy. Preschoolers who are particularly good at delay-of-gratification tests generate their own diversions, like singing songs to themselves.

Removing temptations from sight increases self-control. In delay-of-gratification tests, if treats are removed from view and the children have to request them, they can wait much longer than if the treats are in view (see Figure 7.3). Some parents and teachers mistakenly believe that giving children a small taste of a treat, or telling them to keep the treat in mind, will help them delay gratification. This actually undermines their self-control. However, for children with low self-control, whether treats are in view or not may not matter. Some children have low self-control regardless of the situation.

What Do Individual Differences in Self-Control Predict?

Self-control helps learners benefit more from instruction. Imagine if learners acted on every impulse. Preschoolers might scribble in books and youth might text-message their friends instead of participating in a class activity. Thus, it is not surprising that self-control is linked to academic achievement and social competence.

Academic achievement

Learners of all ages who have high self-control tend to have higher academic achievement, probably because they have less trouble paying attention, staying on task, and ignoring distractions (Ponitz, McClelland, Matthews, & Morrison, 2009). In fact, some research shows that self-control *predicts GPA better than intelligence* does (Duckworth & Seligman, 2005). This pattern is stable across time: 4-year-olds who were more self-controlled had higher math and reading achievement at age 21 than other students; in addition, they were more likely to graduate from college by age 25 (McClelland, Acock, Piccinin, Rhea, & Stallings, 2013).

FIGURE 7.3 **Number of Minutes Preschoolers Delayed Gratification.**

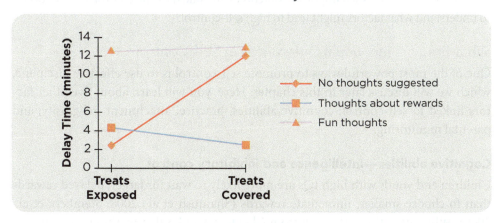

Children who think about fun things, other than the treat, are able to delay the longest. Can you describe what effect having the treats exposed or not has? *Source: Adapted from Mischel, Shoda, and Rodriguez (1989).*

FIGURE 7.4 Childhood Self-Control Has Long-Term Implications.

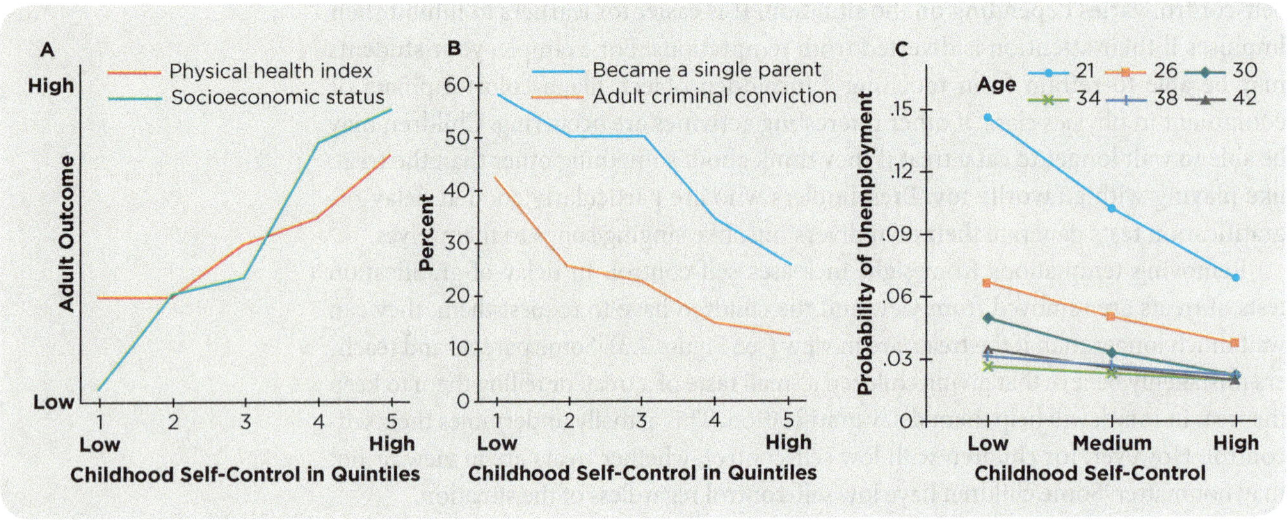

These graphs show adolescent and adult outcomes for children based on their level of childhood self-control. *Source: Adapted from Moffitt et al. (2011) and Daly et al. (2015).*

Social competence

Learners with high self-control may also have higher achievement because they tend to be less aggressive and less prone to behavior problems at school than learners with low self-control. They participate more in class, are more cooperative, and have better relationships with teachers and classmates (Eisenberg et al., 2003; Valiente, Lemery-Chalfant, Swanson, & Reiser, 2008).

Over time, learners with high self-control grow up having better physical health, lower substance dependence, lower rates of teen parenthood, lower rates of family violence, better financial situations, fewer criminal offenses, and less unemployment (Daly, Delaney, Egan, & Baumeister, 2015; Finkenauer et al., 2015; Moffitt et al., 2011). See Figure 7.4. In contrast, learners with low self-control tend to be delinquent. In one study kindergarteners who had low self-control were more likely to have used alcohol or other drugs by age 12 (Kaplow, Curran, Dodge, & Conduct Problems Prevention Research Group, 2002). Because such important outcomes are linked to self-control, it is important to understand what factors might lead to high self-control.

What Predicts Individual Differences in Self-Control?

One of the most powerful ways to promote self-control is to use effective discipline, which we will discuss later in this chapter. Here, you will learn about five other factors linked to self-control: cognitive abilities, practice, attachment, religiosity, and parental monitoring.

Cognitive abilities—intelligence and inhibitory control

Children and youth with high IQs are more likely to wait for larger, delayed rewards than to choose smaller, immediate rewards (Shamosh et al., 2008; Steinberg et al., 2009). Why might this be? Recall from Chapters 4 and 5 that working memory and executive functions are key parts of intelligence and that inhibitory control is part of executive functions. Inhibitory control refers to the ability to suppress inappropriate behavior or irrelevant thoughts. So inhibitory control and intelligence share the same underlying executive functions and brain circuits. Such brain functions can result from experience (see Chapter 2). The next four factors show that experience is linked to differences in self-control.

Practice and fatigue

Every child's self-control has limits, just as yours does. You know this if you have tried to stick to a diet or keep a resolution to study harder. In fact, self-control is like a muscle in that you can only exert so much self-control, just as you can only lift so much weight (Baumeister, Vohs, & Tice, 2007). Like muscles, self-control can be fatigued by resisting temptation (Hagger, Wood, Stiff, & Chatzisarantis, 2010). Thus, if students are asked to sit still and pay attention in class for a long time, their self-control may become fatigued. The more self-control is exercised without rest, the more likely it will fail. The part of the brain responsible for self-control is less capable just after it has been exercised (Inzlicht & Gutsell, 2007). Even students who have age-appropriate self-control may need a break, such as free time to move about or be noisy. One interesting caveat is that youth who believe that willpower is *unlimited* do not exhibit less self-control after exercising their self-control (Job, Dweck, & Walton, 2010). So you might want to keep the fatigue effect a secret!

Over time, the more self-control is exercised, the more it grows, just like exercising a muscle causes it to become stronger. For example, one teacher describes how her preschool students get "stronger" as they "exercise" their self-control:

> *The children eagerly line up when I tell them it's time for PE, but once in the gym, they cannot wait in line for more than a few minutes without trying to play with the tempting equipment. They can't wait for balls to be passed out. They get better as the school year progresses, however. For example, one little girl would push and poke to get a ball or jump rope. She would cry if she did not get one right away. Months later, she is able to wait her turn.*

This little girl is growing in self-control partly by exercising it. Thus, in your classroom you may want to avoid demanding more self-control than students can maintain without a break, but you may also want to stretch them just a little.

Attachment

In Chapter 6 you learned that secure attachment predicts social competence, academic achievement, and other positive outcomes in children, like compliance with adults. This may be due to attachment's link with self-control. Children who have secure attachment and who have mothers who are sensitive and positive are more likely to develop high self-control than insecure children (e.g., Gilliom, Shaw, Beck, Schonberg, & Lukon, 2002; Laible & Thompson, 2000). In fact, difficult infants who are quick to become angry grow into toddlers with poor self-control if their mothers are relatively insensitive, but grow into toddlers with exceptionally good self-control if their mothers are sensitively responsive (Kim & Kochanska, 2012). (You probably thought, "Ah, differential susceptibility"—you were right!)

Religiosity

Research shows that religiosity is linked to less drinking, smoking, gambling, and depression. It is linked to more seat-belt wearing, greater well-being, longer wait before first intercourse, longer life span, and higher academic achievement. Notice that each of these outcomes has a self-control component. A review of dozens of studies found that youth who are religious, on the average, exhibit more self-control than those who are not (McCullough & Willoughby, 2009). Religiosity may affect self-control through its emphasis on self-mastery.

Parental monitoring

How closely parents monitor their children also plays a role in self-control. For young children, parental monitoring includes things like influencing with whom the child plays and restricting television viewing. For adolescents, parental monitoring includes knowing what homework the child has been assigned, how the child spends money, where the child is, and what the child does away from home. Notice that a key aspect of monitoring is *parental knowledge* (Stattin & Kerr, 2000).

Parents monitor their children to different degrees. Parents whose teens are securely attached are more likely to know what their teenage children are doing (Branstetter, Furman, & Cottrell, 2009). Parents with their own risk factors are less likely to monitor their children. For example, parents who are single, low SES, high school dropouts, and who have a history of substance abuse, depression, or other mental illness are less likely to monitor their children (Evans, 2004).

Lack of parental monitoring is linked to low self-control, as well as aggression, depression, dislike of school, drug use, sexual activity, and delinquency.[1] Parental monitoring is even linked to driving. Teens whose parents do not monitor their driving are more likely to have a traffic violation or crash (Hartos, Eitel, Haynie, & Simons-Morton, 2000). The importance of parental monitoring may depend on the neighborhood. Lack of monitoring may be especially detrimental in impoverished, unsafe neighborhoods where youth hang out after school, unsupervised by adults (Pettit, Laird, Bates, & Dodge, 1997). However, wealthy suburbs can be detrimental as well, if there are no adults home after school to monitor the children (Luthar, 2003).

The research on parental monitoring is correlational. As with all correlational data, you can ask which comes first; does parental monitoring *cause* self-control in children, or do well-behaved children *cause* their parents to be better monitors? Research suggests that parents' knowledge of teens' activities is largely due to children freely telling their parents about their activities, but also to parents carefully observing and listening to their children (Crouter, Bumpus, Davis, & McHale, 2005; Stattin & Kerr, 2000). Youth who tell their parents what they are doing tend to study more and earn higher grades than youth who do not keep their parents informed (Cheung, Pomerantz, & Dong, 2013). When parents have to question their children, or rely on others for information (e.g., siblings, neighbors, teachers, friends' parents), the children are likely to become more delinquent over time. In fact, children who feel overly scrutinized by their parents tend to have low self-esteem, depression, and expectations of failure. Thus, skillful monitoring may need to be subtle and may be motivated by the child as well as the parent. Now that we have discussed individual differences in self-control, let's turn our attention to differences across groups.

think about **this**

Some psychologists use the term *parental knowledge* rather than *parental monitoring,* to highlight that children contribute information, instead of the process being driven only by parents. What was your experience? How did your parents know what you were doing throughout your youth, or did they know? How did their monitoring or lack of monitoring affect your behavior?

---

[1] Many studies support this finding, just a few of which are listed here (e.g., Branstetter et al., 2009; Coley, Votruba-Drzal, & Schindler, 2009; Lac & Crano, 2009; Laird, Pettit, Bates, & Dodge, 2003; Morales-Campos, Markham, Peskin, & Fernandez, 2012; Pettit, Laird, Dodge, Bates, & Criss, 2001).

7-1c Group Diversity in Self-Control

There are both gender and SES differences in self-control. As early as preschool, girls tend to have more self-control than boys (Duckworth & Seligman, 2006; Moffitt et al., 2011). In addition, children who come from middle- or high-SES backgrounds, on average, have more self-control than low-SES children, and this difference in self-control predicts school grades and cognitive development (Evans & Rosenbaum, 2008).

There are also cultural differences in one aspect of self-control, which is conformity to authority, rules, and peer pressure. Asian cultures value conformity more than U.S. culture (Fischer & Schwartz, 2011). When youth are immigrants from Asian countries, or if they have a cultural heritage that values conformity, they report greater respect for parental authority and less expectation for making their own decisions than European American youth (Hardway & Fuligni, 2006). This may be due to a greater emphasis on collectivism in their heritage cultures (see Box 7.1). Understanding these group differences may provide insight into your students, but you will also need to be careful not to stereotype based on gender, SES, or ethnicity.

7-1d Classroom Implications of Self-Control

Learners with low self-control are likely to misbehave and have low achievement in your classroom. You can help such learners by teaching them the following self-control strategies[2]:

1. Select the situation: Help students understand that their behavior is strongly influenced by the environment around them, so they need to select adaptive environments. For example, this could include finding study spaces without distractions, spending time with friends who have good self-control, or choosing classes or teams with demanding teachers/coaches.

2. Modify the situation so that it is more adaptive. For example, sit in the front of the room instead of the back, put your cell phone where it is not tempting, or turn off the wireless connection on your computer when studying.

3. Look directly at the teacher.

4. Change the way that you think about a situation. For example, think about mistakes as information about how to improve rather than as devastating information about incompetence, or think about a big, intimidating project as a series of smaller, easier tasks.

5. Set goals and monitor them. When you begin to pursue behavior that does not fit your goals, stop yourself. Be sure to have a plan for when you get off track, and how to get back on track. For example, "if I start to text my friend, I will put the phone in another room so I am not tempted to use it." We will discuss goal setting more in Chapter 13.

Teach these strategies gradually with practice, reminders, and repetitions of when and how to use them. As you learned in Chapter 4, children tend to gradually replace less-effective with more-effective strategies over time. In Chapter 8 you will learn strategies specific to helping learners cope with strong emotions so that they do not lash out at others.

think about this

Imagine that you have a student in your classroom who regularly misbehaves. Would your response be "How can I help this student have greater self-control?" This response is typical for North American or European teachers. They place blame for misbehavior within the student. Japanese teachers are more likely to place blame for misbehavior within the classroom. Their response might be "How can we create a greater sense of community so that this student wants to cooperate in class more?" (Hoffman, 2009). Would the strategies you use to eliminate the misbehavior be different depending on which response you had? Explain.

---

[2] This list is adapted from Duckworth, Gendler, and Gross (2014, 2016); Gollwitzer and Oettingen (2012); and Inzlicht, Legault, and Teper (2014).

BOX 7.1 theories & theorists

Collectivism and Individualism

How do cultures differ in ways that influence children's development? One difference is collectivism versus individualism. In *collectivist* cultures, the needs of the group are more important than individual needs. Interdependence among people and harmonious relationships are emphasized (Brewer & Chen, 2007). Identity stems from the group, and life satisfaction stems from meeting group obligations. In contrast, *individualist* cultures emphasize independence, self-reliance, personal freedom, rights, and liberty above duties. Identity stems from personal accomplishments. One's obligation to one's family is freely chosen (Giles-Sims & Lockhart, 2005). *Independence* means that one wants to be an individual who is unique, who can influence outcomes, and who is free of group pressure; in contrast, *interdependence* means that one wants to be similar to, adjusting to, and rooted in the group (Markus & Conner, 2013). The following examples give you a flavor of such cultural differences:

- The American acceptance of a "lively discussion" in which people argue their points does not exist in Japan because it could disrupt group harmony (Nisbett, 2003, p. 73).
- In some Asian and Pacific Island cultures, respect for elders is so strong that students are unlikely to assert an opinion different from the teacher's or to point out an error (Lee Hang & Bell, 2015).
- Latinos value *familism*, giving priority to family interdependence, support, and obligations. Thus, Latino youth are more likely to prefer living at home during college than White or Black youth (Desmond & Turley, 2009), and they are more likely to cook, clean, and help with siblings (Tsai, Telzer, Gonzales, & Fuligni, 2015).
- European Americans think that talking is good for thinking, while Koreans think that talking can undermine thinking (Markus & Conner, 2013, p. 4). This is relevant in using active, constructivist approaches to instruction that require student talk.
- In Ghana, children report that "letting me do things my own way" seems neglectful (Marbell & Grolnick, 2012), while in the United States it tends to be viewed as normal.

Some psychologists assert that northern European and American nations are individualistic while Asian nations such as China, Korea, Japan, Pakistan, and India, and also African and Latin nations, are collectivistic (e.g., Rudy & Grusec, 2006). However, this may be an oversimplification. Most cultures are a mixture, and cross-national differences tend to be small (Giles-Sims & Lockhart, 2005). Researchers are increasingly critical of assertions that groups are either collectivist or individualist. Groups may value individual autonomy and also value close relationships, the welfare of the group, and cooperation (Tamis-LeMonda et al., 2008).

Nevertheless, you may find that your students from collectivist cultures show fewer strong emotions like jumping and shouting, engage less publicly in class, prefer that you (as the authority) make important decisions, and prefer not to argue, especially with authority figures. However, be careful not to stereotype, because these general patterns may not always apply.

Ethnicity in North America Psychologists generally assert that European Americans are less collectivistic than other ethnic groups within North America. Collectivism has been used to explain why Asian American children have relatively *high* achievement on average, which is that they are obligated to their family to work hard in school. Paradoxically, collectivism has also been used to explain why Latino children have relatively *low* achievement on average, which is that obligations to the family divert them from school work (Desmond & Turley, 2009; Vázquez García, García Coll, Erkut, Alarcón, & Tropp, 1999). Collectivism has been used to explain why the consequence of authoritarian parenting is not as negative among other ethnic groups as it is among European American children; that is, authoritarian parenting is thought to be less detrimental because deference to authority is emphasized in collectivist cultures (Rudy & Grusec, 2006).

In Chapter 1 you learned that some children experience mismatch between their heritage culture and the culture of the school. One cause of mismatch can be differences in collectivism and individualism. For example, in a famous study, Asian American children learned more and preferred learning situations in which important others (like their parents or teachers) made decisions for them, such as what task to do or what level of difficulty to attempt, while European American children learned more and preferred learning situations in which they made their own decisions (Iyengar & Lepper, 1999). To be an effective multicultural teacher, you will need to become aware of your students' cultures, as well as your own culture and teaching style.

You, the teacher, can do the following to structure the environment to foster self-control:

1. Reduce distractions and interruptions. For example: encourage the central office not to use the public address system during the day; have orderly procedures to address common disruptions like late arrivals; do not give instructions and then constantly interrupt the class to clarify; keep tempting objects out of sight, such as glass beakers in science class, until they are needed (Mauro & Harris, 2000).

2. Exercise learners' self-control, like a muscle, but without fatiguing it. If a child with low self-control manages to behave well for a while, give a short rest from self-control. Try to keep learners out of situations that overtax their self-control. For example, one boy was always touching other students—hitting, kicking, punching, and pushing. His teacher put him at the front of every line to limit temptations to touch. She had him put his hands in his pockets while in the hallway or cafeteria. These simple tactics helped substantially.

3. Provide healthy foods. Self-control uses up glucose, the brain's fuel. Learners have more self-control when they have adequate glucose supplies in their bodies (Baumeister et al., 2007).

4. Plan to do the classroom activities that require the most self-control earlier in the day. Self-control tends to be highest early in the day and lowest in the evening (Gailliot, 2008). (Your wise parents probably knew this, which is why they insisted on an early curfew!)

5. Use statements like "You are patient" to communicate positive expectations. A randomized study with preschool boys and girls found that if they were told to imagine that they were Superman and that Superman has lots of patience and can wait really well, they were better able to delay gratification (Karniol et al., 2011).

6. Refer students with serious self-control problems to the school counselor for intervention.

In summary, research suggests that self-control increases steadily with age, so secondary teachers can expect more self-control from their students than can preschool teachers. Even among students of the same age, there are large individual differences in self-control. These differences in self-control are linked to information-processing ability, practice exercising self-control, and parenting. They are also linked to gender, SES, and culture. One of the most powerful things you can do to promote your students' self-control is to use *effective* discipline. We will focus on how to do this next.

7-2 Effective Discipline

In a preschool classroom, 4-year-old Sammy has scattered the blocks across the room. He leaves them there as he moves on to do a puzzle. Mrs. Sanchez asks him to clean up, but he refuses at first.

Mrs. Sanchez: *Sammy, please pick up the blocks before you start your puzzle.*
Sammy: *No.*

Mrs. Sanchez:	*We have to clean up one mess before we start a new activity.*
Sammy:	*[Shakes his head "no."] Not gonna clean up. Don't wanna.*
Mrs. Sanchez:	*These blocks are dangerous. Someone could trip and fall on them. Pick them up.*
Sammy:	*[Shakes his head "no."]*
Mrs. Sanchez:	*[Still speaking kindly, but firmly] Sammy, you know that you should clean up the blocks. Let's do it now.*

Sammy ignores her. Mrs. Sanchez tries again, as she places two blocks in the container.

Mrs. Sanchez:	*Come on. Would you like me to help you with the first blocks? Come on. Let's get this picked up.*

Sammy watches her, and then silently begins to pick up blocks.

Mrs. Sanchez:	*Thank you, Sammy. You are a helpful boy.*

internalization
the child adopts the adult's values and rules as his or her own guide for behavior. The child complies or behaves appropriately without being monitored.

committed compliance
children accept the authority figure's agenda as their own.

Was this effective discipline? Is Sammy likely to develop greater self-control as a result of this discipline episode? As a teacher, you will face these important questions every day because misbehavior is common in classrooms. *Discipline* refers to attempts to correct misbehavior; it is a subset of classroom management, which includes discipline and also attempts to structure the classroom in a way that avoids the necessity of disciplining. We discuss discipline next, and then classroom management.

Most children do not obey every rule all the time—you probably did not when you were a child. Thus, you will probably need to discipline children on a daily basis.

We will discuss different approaches you can use to support good behavior, but first let's be clear about the goal of discipline.

PHOTO 7.2 The long-term goal of effective discipline is to promote self-control.

fine art/Alamy stock photo

7-2a The Goal of Discipline

The short-term goal of discipline is to influence children to behave appropriately right now, but the more important long-term goal of discipline is to instill values and promote self-control (Photo 7.2). If children are to become responsible adults who contribute to society, they must learn the values of their culture. A child's value system is learned in everyday discipline encounters because discipline teaches children the boundaries of socially acceptable behavior. How adults discipline influences whether children learn to become compassionate and self-controlled.

The goal of discipline should not merely be compliance, but rather *internalization* of positive values. **Internalization** means that children personally adopt the values and rules of society, believing that they are important and worth using as guides for behavior. Their compliance is **committed** if they endorse and accept the authority figure's agenda as their own, even when they are not being supervised. Children who have *not* internalized values may behave well when they are being watched, but break the rules when authority figures are out of sight. In this case, children's compliance is **situational**, which means that they lack sincere commitment to the rule. For example, if a student kicks classmates whenever the teacher is not looking, he has not internalized the value of not hurting others. *Self*-control emerges out of committed compliance, not situational compliance.

Compliance is obedience to a specific request or rule, or long-term adherence to a set of general rules. There are four ways a child can respond to adult directives: (1) compliance; (2) direct *defiance* or refusal; (3) *passive noncompliance,* which means the child ignores the directive; and (4) *negotiation,* which means the child asserts his or her own agenda and negotiates a compromise.

Direct defiance is a marker of behavior problems in older children, but not in 1- to 2-year-olds. Well-adjusted toddlers can occasionally be quite defiant, although they are generally positive (Dix, Stewart, Gershoff, & Day, 2007). Research has found that mothers and toddlers argue roughly 20 to 25 times per hour on average, with a range of 4 to 55 times (Laible & Thompson, 2002; Laible, Panfile, & Makariev, 2008). A study of 1- to 2-year-olds found that they initially disobeyed a request 39% of the time (Dahl & Campos, 2013). Between ages 2 and 5, direct defiance and passive noncompliance decline, but negotiation increases as children develop social skills (Kuczynski & Kochanska, 1990). Is 4-year-old Sammy's defiance age-appropriate? Not if he consistently defies adults. However, there is no need for concern if he is usually compliant and has good social skills.

You might think that compliance is always the ideal response, but negotiation may be more appropriate in many situations. For example, when a child is told to clean up, she might say, "I'll clean up after I finish this puzzle." Negotiation, rather than unquestioning compliance, marks the child's emerging ability to balance autonomy with social responsibility. Toddlers who say no to their parents and then engage in negotiation are likely to be securely attached and developmentally advanced (Crockenberg & Litman, 1990). They are more likely to become socially competent several years later (Laible & Thompson, 2002). Successful negotiation requires sophisticated social skills on the child's part. Thus, adults who are open to negotiation during discipline may provide an opportunity for children to develop social skills. In addition, the *type* of discipline that adults use can promote children's social skills and emotional well-being.

7-2b Types of Discipline

We will discuss three types of discipline: induction, psychological control, and power assertion. Both psychological control and power assertion are linked to *negative* child outcomes. Induction is more likely to result in internalization, so let's begin with induction.

Induction

Induction is a type of discipline in which an adult explains the reason for rules and points out the consequences of breaking rules (Photo 7.3).

situational compliance
children comply with demands, but lack sincere commitment and require sustained control by the authority figure.

induction
a form of discipline in which the adult gives the child a reason for why behavior must change or a rule must be complied with.

PHOTO 7.3 Induction is the most effective form of discipline for promoting self-control.

Discipline is more effective when accompanied by a good rationale (Maccoby, 1992). Giving children reasons for doing the right thing helps them understand why a rule is important. For example, when you say, "If everyone wrote in the library books, the pictures would not look nice and other people might be disappointed," you help the child understand your reasons and share in your goals. A particularly important form of induction is *victim-centered induction,* in which the adult points out how the child's behavior has made someone else feel. For example, you might say, "You really hurt Juanita's feelings when you didn't let her join you."

Induction is linked to self-control and social competence. Children who are disciplined with induction rather than other types of discipline are more likely to internalize values and obey rules even when adults are not present. They are more likely to negotiate about, rather than defy, directives. They also are more likely to be empathic, be kind to others, and have fewer behavior problems (Kerr, Lopez, Olson, & Sameroff, 2004; Krevans & Gibbs, 1996; Paulussen-Hoogeboom, Stams, Hermanns, & Peetsma, 2007).

Induction may be the most effective form of discipline *regardless of age of the child.* It makes sense that induction would be effective with teenagers, but what about 1-year-olds? If a toddler approaches the parking lot, shouldn't you just firmly say "No!" rather than "Don't go there; you'll get run over!"? Apparently not. Much of the research on the positive effects of induction has been conducted with toddlers, indicating that even toddlers learn from induction. While the first part of the communication—Don't go there—may be the most important for preventing disaster, the second part—you'll get run over—is also important for training future behavior.

Simply saying, "No!" or "Stop that!" in response to misbehavior is the opposite of induction, and may be effective at stopping a behavior (or not), but it does not guide the child with reasons. One mother was concerned about her toddler's strange behavior; he would freeze when he approached walls. It turned out that his mother slapped his hand or yelled "Stop!" whenever he got near an electrical outlet. He did not understand the reason for the punishment and developed a generalized fear of walls!

Unlike induction, which appeals to children's reason, psychological control appeals to children's need for approval and affection. Although some disapproval of the child is communicated in any discipline, it is minimal in induction. In contrast, disapproval of the child is a central focus of psychological control.

Psychological Control

psychological control
a coercive form of discipline in which the adult attempts to control the child's behavior by inducing guilt or fear of loss of love and affirmation.

Psychological control is a type of discipline in which an adult attempts to manipulate a child's behavior by expressing anger and disapproval, by withdrawing love and affection, or by trying to make the child feel guilty (Barber, Xia, Olsen, McNeely, & Bose, 2012; Wang, Pomerantz, & Chen, 2007). Psychological control manipulates children's emotions and attempts to coerce them in a way that prevents children from developing as individuals. Psychological control includes a broad array of behaviors such as ignoring the child, stating dislike for the child, or asking the child why he or she is so bad. For example, a coach might say, "Get out of here. I don't want to see you when you behave like that." Psychological control includes frequent criticism or trying to make children feel excessive guilt. For example, a teacher might say, "Are you trying to bring this whole class down?" Learners who are disciplined with psychological control tend to have more depression and misbehavior and less self-confidence (Barber, Stoltz, & Olsen, 2005; Rakow et al., 2011). Children prefer induction over psychological control techniques; they particularly disapprove of shaming as they grow older, such as "you are not as good as other children" or "you bring shame upon your family" (Helwig, To, Wang, Liu, & Yang, 2014).

Power Assertion

Power assertion is a form of discipline in which the adult relies on power or resources to control behavior, as Mrs. Reinhardt did with Clint in the opening vignette. Power assertion can take four forms: (1) physical punishment, like spanking; (2) deprivation of material objects or privileges, like taking the car keys away from a teenager; (3) direct application of power, like carrying the child away from a conflict; or (4) threats to use forms 1, 2, or 3. Power assertion is common in schools, particularly removal of privileges. An easy way to recognize power assertion is the presence of an "or else" clause, either explicit or implied, in the command. For example, a teacher might say, "Quit talking or else I'll move your desk."

Costs of power assertion

There are five serious costs to using power-assertive discipline.

1. Children become less compliant. Adults using power-assertive discipline often achieve *immediate* compliance, which reinforces the adults' use of power assertion in the future. However, it results in less compliance over the long run (Erath, El-Sheikh, & Cummings, 2009; Gershoff, 2013).

2. Children do not internalize values (Kochanska, Aksan, & Joy, 2007). Even if misbehavior improves, the emotions and thoughts that are influencing that behavior do not necessarily change. Situational compliance may be achieved, but not committed compliance.

3. Children resent the disciplinarian. Power assertion jeopardizes the caring relationship between adult and child. How do you feel toward someone who threatens you if you don't do what they want? Children often have similar negative feelings toward those who wield power over them, just as Clint did.

4. Children need more and more coercion. When children are constantly threatened until they comply, they begin to ignore mild threats and comply only for stronger threats. They come to *expect* overt power assertion and threats *before* they will comply (Patterson & Bank, 1989).

5. Children imitate the aggression of power-assertive adult models. Children who experience power-assertive discipline are more likely to be aggressive and delinquent later (Bender et al., 2007). This is especially a problem with corporal punishment, a subset of power-assertive discipline.

Research robustly shows that heavy-handed, power-assertive discipline leads to angry, resentful children who are likely to become aggressive. This effect occurs for children of all ages, toddlers to teens. Secure attachment is a protective factor. This means that even when parents are power assertive, if they have a secure attachment with the child, the child is less likely to become aggressive (Kochanska, Barry, Stellern, & O'Bleness, 2009).

think about this
What type of discipline is "time-out"? Is it an effective form of discipline? Base your answers on what you have learned about discipline in this chapter.

power assertion
a coercive form of discipline in which the adult controls the child's behavior by virtue of greater power or resources. It often includes an "or else" clause.

Corporal punishment

corporal punishment
power-assertive discipline that
involves bodily harm to the
child, ranging in severity from
light spanking to abuse.

Corporal punishment, a form of power assertion, is physical punishment such as hitting or spanking. Spanking is common. About 35% to 45% of parents of children ages 1 through 9 spank their children weekly, though many parents choose not to spank (Berlin et al., 2009; Straus, Sugarman, & Giles-Sims, 1997). About 85% of teens report that they had been spanked or slapped at some point (Gershoff, 2013). People hold strong, opposite opinions on whether spanking and other forms of corporal punishment are appropriate. What does the research say?

Like other forms of power assertion, corporal punishment is associated with *less* obedience in the long term (Gershoff, 2013; Lansford et al., 2009; MacKenzie, Nicklas, Waldfogel, & Brooks-Gunn, 2012). This is ironic given that adults spank children because they want the spanking to function as punishment and decrease a behavior (see Chapter 3).

In addition, children who are spanked become aggressive and antisocial over time, even if they were not prone to misbehavior to begin with. Spanked children tend to increase in aggression in the long term (Gershoff, 2013). Severe corporal punishment that goes beyond spanking, including punishment that could be considered abuse, is linked to later violence against dating partners in young adults, like shoving, slapping, and beating up the partner (Swinford, DeMaris, Cernkovich, & Giordano, 2000). Parents who were physically abused as children may be more likely to spank their own children, including 1-year-olds (Chung et al., 2009). See Box 7.2 for more information on child abuse.

As children grow into adolescence, harsh parents tend to switch from corporal punishment to harsh verbal punishment (e.g., shouting, swearing, calling the child dumb). Harsh verbal punishment has effects similar to corporal punishment. In one study, parents' harsh verbal discipline at age 13 predicted an increase in adolescent misbehavior and depression a year later (Wang & Kenny, 2014). Referring to corporal punishment, former president of the American Psychological Association Alan Kazdin summarized the research by saying, "We are not giving up an effective technique. We are saying this is a horrible thing that does not work" (Smith, 2012, p. 60).

How can you decide which is the best disciplinary approach? There are three principles of effective discipline that can guide your decision.

7-2c Principles of Effective Discipline

The first principle of effective discipline is that *you must achieve compliance.* If you can get a child to obey you today, that child is more likely to obey you tomorrow, and so are observing classmates. Conversely, if you do not achieve compliance in one encounter, it will be even harder to achieve compliance in the next encounter. You can never completely ensure compliance. No matter how much power you have, you cannot force children to do what you want. Without taping his mouth shut, you cannot force Clint or any other student to stop talking. You cannot force Sammy to pick up the blocks. Children must choose to obey you. However, there are ways to increase the likelihood of compliance.

BOX 7.2 challenges in development

Child Abuse

Child abuse is related to discipline because over half of physical abuse instances may have started as attempts to correct behavior using corporal punishment (Gershoff, 2013). Child abuse takes four forms: physical, emotional, and sexual abuse and criminal neglect. *Physical* abuse refers to harming children physically, like hitting them with an object, or burning them with cigarette butts. *Emotional* abuse refers to nonphysical harm such as excessive criticism, blaming, or telling them they are not loved or wanted. *Sexual* abuse refers to any type of sexual violation against a child, including fondling, exhibition, or exposure to pornography. *Criminal neglect* refers to ignoring children or depriving them of food, shelter, and adequate hygiene.

Prevalence Each year in the United States, about 800,000 children are abused or neglected and about 1700 may die of that abuse or neglect. As distressing as these numbers are, they are probably underestimates. Much abuse is never reported. Among reported cases, neglect is most common, followed by physical abuse (see Figure 7.5). Notice in Figure 7.5 that multiple maltreatments are more common than physical abuse alone and can include physical abuse.

Physical and emotional abuse and neglect begin anywhere from infancy to adolescence. Sexual abuse occurs most often at about ages 4 to 5 and 14 to 15 (Snyder, 2000). Some children experience a single incident of abuse, whereas others experience many years of abuse. Neglect is the most likely to begin early and last a long time. Girls are more likely to be reported as sexually abused than boys (Dong, Anda, Dube, Giles, & Felitti, 2003). Boys and girls are about equally likely to be victims of other kinds of abuse.

Who Abuses? Most children know the person who abuses them. About 80% of abuse and neglect perpetrators are parents or stepparents. The exception is that *sexual* abusers are more likely to be friends and neighbors, followed by relatives, and then child care providers (U.S. Department of Health and Human Services, 2009). Men are more likely than women to murder children, and killers are most likely to be the father or the mother's boyfriend (Fujiwara, Barber, Schaechter, & Hemenway, 2009).

What Factors Predict Child Abuse? Children resulting from unwanted pregnancy are more likely to be abused. Children with vulnerabilities, such as low birth

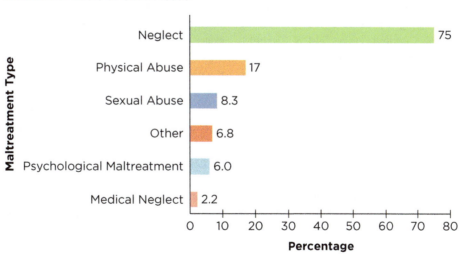

FIGURE 7.5 **Rates of Child Abuse.**

This graph depicts child abuse in the United States in 2007. Of all types of maltreatment, what is the single most common? The second most common? *Source: U.S. Department of Health and Human Services (2009), p. 26.*

Child Abuse (continued)

weight, poor health, and developmental delays are more likely to be abused, although this does not mean that children invite their own abuse (Sidebotham, Heron, & The ALSPAC Study Team, 2003). Mothers who suffer from depression or who feel they have little control as parents and who think power assertion is the best way to discipline are more likely to abuse (Bugental & Happaney, 2004). Most (90%) families in which a child is abused report significant financial hardship (Bolger & Patterson, 2001). Families are likely to be poor, live in subsidized housing, and have an unemployed father. Poverty may explain why maltreatment varies by neighborhood. For example, in Washington DC, one neighborhood had 0.3 victims of substantiated maltreatment per 1000 population, while another neighborhood had 35.4 (Murphey & Cooper, 2015).

What Are the Long-Term Consequences of Child Abuse? Abuse is linked to lower academic achievement. Physically abused children are more likely to be distractible and inattentive than nonabused classmates because they are always on the lookout for others' aggression. Abused children are more likely to be in special education, to have low achievement test scores, to fail a grade, and to have poor work habits at school (Shonk & Cicchetti, 2001).

Abuse is also linked to emotional and social problems. Abused children may have less empathy, lack warmth toward others, and not read others' emotions as well as nonabused students. They may experience poor emotion regulation, such as being depressed or falling to pieces under stress (Kim & Cicchetti, 2006; Teisl & Cicchetti, 2008). Children who are maltreated often have disorganized attachment, and may become aggressive, or overly compliant and too eager to please adults (Cullerton-Sen et al., 2009). Mothers who were abused as children show lower levels of responsiveness and empathy toward their infants (Bert, Guner, & Lanzi, 2009).

Abuse is also linked with poor physical development and poor health through adulthood. Recall what you learned about adverse childhood experience in Chapter 2. Both physical and emotional problems may result from brains that are altered by the chronic, uncontrollable stress of maltreatment (Hanson et al., 2013; Pollak, 2008). Stress can cause chronic inflammation and undermine the immune system, resulting in illnesses such as depression, heart disease, and asthma (Jaffee & Christian, 2014).

However, some children survive abuse reasonably well. The degree of negative outcomes depends on the risk and protective factors operating in their lives. Outcomes depend on how severe, frequent, and early the abuse and how much shame, depression, and stress the child feels.

Implications for Teachers Teachers are mandated reporters. Mandatory reporting laws, which vary by state, require professionals who work with children to report evidence of child abuse. School personnel are the largest single source of abuse reports, responsible for 17% of reports (U.S. Department of Health and Human Services, 2009). The most obvious signs of *physical* abuse you may see are bruises, broken bones, and burn marks that are unlikely to have happened through normal accidents. The main evidence of sexual abuse is when a child tells someone of the abuse (Goodman, Emery, & Haugaard, 1998). Emotional abuse and neglect are difficult to detect. Can children accurately report their own abuse? They can, although memories are subject to distortion (Bruck, Ceci, & Principe, 2006; Goodman & Quas, 2008). There is a widespread belief that anatomically correct dolls help children report abuse, but there is little evidence to support the use of such dolls, and they can increase erroneous reports of inappropriate touching (Poole, Bruck, & Pipe, 2011).

Some teachers assume they should involve parents when a student in their class needs discipline. However, if parents are abusive or have very poor child management skills, they may respond by harshly punishing the child. This could undermine the child's self-control, and cause the child to resent you, while making them vulnerable to further abuse. Thus, caution is called for when involving some parents in disciplining learners. If you suspect abuse, work with the school counselor, who should be trained in appropriate questioning (Brubacher, Powell, Skouteris, & Guadagno, 2015). Some schools have implemented child sexual abuse prevention programs that attempt to teach students how to recognize abuse, appropriate touching, and good versus bad secrets. Such programs may have some positive effects, but the evidence is sparse (Topping & Barron, 2009). Maltreated children are particularly prone to want a close relationship with their teachers, even though they may be more challenging to bond with (see Chapter 6). Attachment to teachers may foster resiliency in abused children.

One way to increase the likelihood of compliance is to use *high-probability requests,* or requests that you know the child will obey, before working up to requests that are low-probability (Lee, 2005). For example,

> *Five-year-old Jesse's teacher told him he could not go outside to play without his coat on because it was too cold. Jesse refused to put his coat on. For several cold days, the conflict over the coat grew. The teacher decided to try using high-probability requests. Jesse loved to clap his hands when asked. The teacher said, "Jesse, clap your hands!" He did, and she clapped hers. She asked again. He did again. She asked a third time. He did it again. She said, "Jesse, put your coat on!" He did.*

Compliance with high-probability requests creates a cooperative mindset in the child that increases the likelihood of complying with low-probability requests (Williams & Forehand, 1984). Another way to increase the likelihood of compliance is to ask nicely, in the context of a warm teacher–student relationship, which brings us to the next principle.

The second principle of effective discipline is to *keep the emotional tone positive during the discipline encounter.* Commands are more effective when adults give them accompanied by positive acts, such as smiling or complimenting the child. Children in a positive mood are more likely to comply with requests (Feldman & Klein, 2003). Children in a warm, secure relationship are more likely to respond with committed compliance (Kochanska, Aksan, & Carlson, 2005). Keeping the tone positive is particularly important for difficult, anger-prone children.

One way to keep discipline emotionally positive and to promote compliance is to cooperate with your students. Whenever it is reasonable, cooperate with their agendas, allowing them control of activities, rather than always imposing your agenda on them. (Recall from Chapter 6 that this is one way to promote secure relationships with students.) One concrete strategy to help you become more cooperative with students is to say no less often. Instead of saying, "No, you can't read your book now," you could say "OK. As soon as you finish your spelling words, you can read your book." The message is the same—you must practice spelling before doing free reading—but the second approach acknowledges the student's agenda, is cooperative, and is more likely to elicit compliance. The more you say no, the more often you will hear it come back to you.

The third principle of effective discipline is to *use the least amount of power that is sufficient to achieve compliance.* All discipline involves some form of power. Yet, when power is minimal in discipline encounters, children are more likely to believe that they complied because they chose to (Lepper, 1983). The child may think, "I'm doing this because it's the right thing to do and I chose it." On the other hand, when power is blatant and excessive, children will likely believe they complied because of the teacher's show of power. The children may think, "I'm doing this because if I don't, I will be punished. I don't want to do it, but I will to avoid punishment." In this case, the children's compliance is situational. The children will probably feel free to change their behavior when the teacher is out of sight.

This helps explain why power assertion tends not to foster internalization. You can promote internalization by helping your students think in a way that emphasizes motives for good behavior. For example, you might say, "You feel bad because you hurt Teresa's feelings" rather than saying, "You feel bad because I caught you."

One way to minimize the power you exert in a discipline encounter is to use subtle rather than obvious forms of control. For example, you can whisper so a noisy class

mandated reporters
people who must by law report suspicion of child abuse and neglect. Laws vary by state, but in most states, teachers are mandated reporters.

must be quiet to hear you instead of threatening them with a late lunch if they don't quiet down. Similarly, if Clint is being noisy and distracting nearby students, you could simply stand near Clint and gently tap his shoulder rather than scolding from the front of the room. In each case, your behaviors are likely to reduce noise, but one draws attention to your power and the other minimizes awareness of your power.

In summary, effective discipline leads to internalization and self-control, whereas ineffective discipline leads to defiance and undermines long-term self-control. *Even if you achieve compliance for the moment, if you have not moved the child toward internalization, your discipline encounter has not been fully effective.* Of course, you are not interested solely in promoting self-control in the classroom; you must also teach academic content. You cannot allow misbehavior to detract from the group's learning time. Effective discipline will achieve both purposes.

What can you do if you prefer to use induction but feel trapped into power assertion because some children are already angry and defiant, come from families that emphasize power assertion, and have already adapted to high levels of coercion? You need a form of discipline that is powerful enough to encourage compliance but subtle enough to allow children to believe they obeyed because of personal choice. The discipline should also foster a positive relationship. One approach you could use is to persuade children, in a persistent way, until they obey. Let's look at how this works.

Applying the Principles of Effective Discipline: Persistent Persuasion

When a child in your classroom is not complying, you can continually restate the command until the child complies, but without increasing the level of power assertion (Bergin & Bergin, 1999). You don't need to use threats or increasingly hostile tones. Instead, present commands in a reasonable or friendly tone of voice. You don't need to use an "or else" clause (either implicitly or explicitly) as in "you better do this or else. . . ." Avoiding threats helps lower expectations for coercion. You can reframe the command, or give additional rationales for compliance with each repetition. You should respond to the child's negotiation and remain in control until compliance is achieved. Afterward, you can attribute the compliance to the child's good intentions. For example, you might say, "You are so helpful; I knew you wanted to do what is right!"

persistent persuasion
an approach to discipline that uses induction repeatedly until the child complies, but without using power assertion.

The critical aspects of this **persistent persuasion** approach are: (1) you *do not quit* making the request *until compliance is achieved*, and (2) you *do not escalate* demands by getting louder or by making threats. Thus, you achieve compliance without encouraging the child to expect coercion and threats. Mrs. Sanchez used it with Sammy. Does it work with older, defiant students? Let's look at an example in a residential facility for difficult teens.

> Counselor: *Michelle, you need turn off the TV.*
> Michelle: *No, b---.*
> Counselor: *Michelle, you need to turn off the television so you can do your chores. (Michelle ignores the counselor.) Michelle, the other girls are doing their chores. (Other girls are standing holding brooms and cleaning supplies, watching the television.) Well . . . they are supposed to be. The TV is distracting.*
> Michelle: *So?*
> Counselor: *I can help you get started.*

> Michelle: No! (Slumps down in sofa and glares at television.)
> Counselor: C'mon. You know the rules. No television during chore time.
> Michelle: (Gets up slowly, swaggers over to the television, and turns it off.)

You can follow up persistent persuasion by *reminding the child of previous compliance* when the same or similar rules are broken later. "Do you remember yesterday, when I asked you to turn off the TV, and you did it?" Children are more likely to obey in the next encounter with *less effort* on the part of the adult. Recall that with power assertion the opposite is true.

You may have noticed that induction takes patience, effort, and time. Yet it can take less time away from instruction than other, less effective, forms of discipline. Consider a 5th-grade classroom, where Peter has a history of aggression.

> Ms. Schwab tells the students to get out their books. Peter picks up Marcus's book and tosses it on the floor, laughing. Marcus pushes Peter. Ms. Schwab shouts, "Boys, that is enough. Out in the hallway now!" (Neither boy moves.) "I said out in the hallway, and when I say now, you better move. Now!" (Neither boy moves.)
>
> Peter: "I don't have to!"
> Ms. Schwab: (Shouting louder) "Get out there now."
> Peter: "No."
> Ms. Schwab: (Still shouting) "Get out in the hallway now!" (Peter sits in his seat, ignoring the teacher. Marcus goes to the hallway.) Ms. Schwab stands over Peter's seat, lowers her voice to a hard edge, and says, "I said get out in the hallway."
>
> Peter finally goes to the hallway. Ms. Schwab follows. The boys begin to laugh. Ms. Schwab says they better do what she says. They look down and giggle. In frustration, she tells them to get back in the classroom and get out their books. They do.

Ms. Schwab eventually achieved compliance, but her approach cost instructional time, damaged her relationship with Peter and Marcus, and damaged her relationship with the rest of the class who were watching. Neither Peter nor Marcus is likely to internalize appropriate values from this encounter. Had Ms. Schwab used persistent persuasion, she would have achieved compliance, with similar or less time and effort, still maintained her authority in the classroom, and fostered a positive atmosphere.

Why Persistent Persuasion Should Work

Some teachers might disapprove of Sammy's teacher and Michelle's counselor because they appeared to ignore student disobedience. However, remember that effective discipline has two goals. The first is to obtain compliance. The second, more important goal is to teach *self*-control, or help children internalize positive values. The persistent persuasion used by Mrs. Sanchez incorporates all three principles of effective discipline that lead to internalization:

1. *The discipline does not rely upon obvious power.* While teachers do have more power than students, in persistent persuasion the display of power is weak, unclear, and not enough to account for students' compliance. This allows students to interpret their compliance as the result of choice, rather than force. Students are not obeying just to avoid a threat of punishment because there is no clear threat.

2. *The interaction is not negative.* Too often disciplinary encounters become struggles for control between an angry teacher and an angry student, like Ms. Schwab and Peter, or Mrs. Reinhardt and Clint. Contrast their experiences with that of Mrs. Sanchez and Sammy; neither was angry. Persistent persuasion helps teachers maintain a positive feeling in the classroom. One teacher said that she had not realized how negative her classroom had become until she tried persistent persuasion. She said that the classroom became more pleasant, she liked the students more, and she was less exhausted at the end of the day.

3. *The child can negotiate.* Some teachers believe that negotiation with students shows weakness, and students should obey simply because they are students. However, allowing students to negotiate with you during discipline has three positive effects: (a) it creates a more reciprocal relationship, (b) it increases the likelihood of committed compliance, and (c) it provides you with opportunity to develop increased empathy for students as you listen to them. The process of negotiation can also reveal to you when your requests are inappropriate. One teacher found that when he tried to give a reason why the student had to comply with his command, he could not think of one. He abandoned the command.

Persistent persuasion is a form of induction that has a sound theoretical basis derived from research. You may find other discipline approaches that you are comfortable with. Whatever approach you adopt, evaluate it to be sure it improves compliance, internalization, and emotions in your classroom.

Applying the Principles of Effective Discipline: Skill Development

While persistent persuasion can help you achieve compliance in a positive atmosphere, sometimes the problem underlying the learner's misbehavior is lack of skill, not a lack of motivation to behave well. Often learners want to behave well, but don't know how (Greene, 2011; Ollendick et al., 2015). If this is the case, rather than focusing on rewards and punishment, it will be more effective to figure out what skills are missing and then teach those skills. The missing skills could be academic (e.g., how to write correct sentences or how to add fractions), or self-management (e.g., difficulty handling transitions or uncertainty), or social skills.

This approach, called "collaborative and proactive solutions" (Greene, 2011), has three key components:

- *Empathy.* You have a deep desire to understand the problem from the learner's point of view. You listen without criticism or suggestions. You might state, "I am still confused," or "Can you say more about that?"

- *Define the problem.* Introduce your concerns into the conversation, for example, how will the problem affect the learner, and how will it affect others. Don't bring up solutions yet.

- *Invitation.* You and the learner brainstorm solutions that are realistic and satisfactory to both. Instead of telling what should happen, you wonder what the learner thinks should happen, and together you generate a plan. You might say, "I wonder if there is a way . . . ."

This approach does not assume that learners lack motivation to behave well, it maintains a positive relationship, and it generates solutions to the problem behavior.

7-2d Group Diversity in Discipline

What kind of discipline did you receive when you were growing up? Your answer may be influenced by your gender, SES, and cultural background. Boys get in more trouble at school than girls. For example, boys are more likely to be suspended or expelled than girls (see Figure 7.6). What about SES and ethnicity?

Socioeconomic Status

Research consistently shows that low-SES learners are more likely than high-SES learners to experience and approve of power assertive or harsh discipline at home, including corporal punishment (e.g., Evans, 2004; Kochanska et al., 2007). This is true across cultures and countries (Douglas, 2006; Erkman & Rohner, 2006; Tang, 2006). One reason for this may be that low-SES families are more likely to live in unsafe neighborhoods and use power-assertive discipline in order to protect their children.

Ethnicity

Rules about how children should behave during discipline encounters may vary by ethnicity. For example, in some ethnic communities children are taught to look a parent in the eye when they are being disciplined to show that they are paying attention. In other ethnic communities, including some African and African American

FIGURE 7.6 School Discipline Rates by Gender.

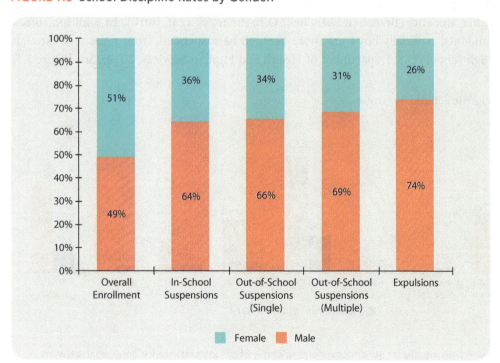

Males make up about half of the student population but 74% of students expelled. *Source: Office for Civil Rights, Civil Rights Data Collection (2009–2010), http://ocrdata.ed.gov.*

communities, looking an authority figure in the eye is a sign of disrespect. For another example, in some (but not all) East Asian cultures, students may smile or even giggle while being disciplined. American teachers may think the child is laughing at them, and become angry if they do not realize that smiles in this situation can mean that the students admit guilt (Weinstein, Tomlinson-Clarke, & Curran, 2004).

Corporal punishment also varies by ethnicity. Spanking is used more and viewed more favorably by Black than White and Latino parents in the United States, although spanking is linked to behavior problems in children (Berlin et al., 2009; Lansford et al., 2009; Lorber, O'Leary, & Slep, 2011). In countries outside the United States, mothers who believe that men are justified in hitting their wives are also more likely to endorse hitting children as useful for child rearing (Lansford, Deater-Deckard, Bornstein, Putnick, & Bradley, 2014). You may have students from U.S. subcultures, or immigrant students from other countries, where corporal punishment is common.

Understanding diversity in discipline is important because you might have students from backgrounds quite different from your own. You and your students may misunderstand each other during discipline if you are not aware of the differences. You will need to find a discipline approach that both you and your students are comfortable with, but that still involves principles of effective discipline and promotes self-control.

Discipline Gap

There are also ethnic differences in punishment within U.S. schools. Among students with low literacy skills, being African American predicts increasing conflict with teachers from 1st to 5th grade, which in turn predicts lower achievement (Spilt & Hughes, 2015). Black students tend to be referred for more minor offenses than other students (Bradshaw, Mitchell, O'Brennan, & Leaf, 2010). In addition, Black students, especially boys, are more likely to be suspended, from preschool through high school (U.S. Department of Health and Human Services, 2014). See Figure 7.7.

FIGURE 7.7 Out-of-School Suspension Rates by Group.

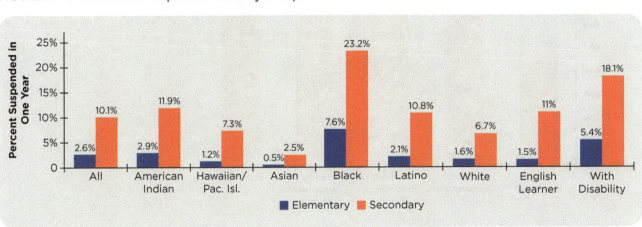

This graph represents suspensions, which are usually for minor nonviolent violations of school rules, not for breaking the law or engaging in dangerous behavior. Expulsions, which are not presented, occur for more serious misbehavior. Describe the rate of suspensions by ethnicity and by disability. Schools are prohibited from suspending students whose misbehavior is caused by their disability, but that prohibition is not always obeyed. *Source: Losen, Hodson, Keith II, Morrison, and Belway (2015).*

In high school, the Black suspension rate may be double the White rate (Gregory, Cornell, & Fan, 2011). This is known as the **discipline gap**.

Suspension is a problematic intervention because it removes students who tend to be low achieving from the very instruction they need, and it is not clear that suspensions improve the learning environment. In fact, suspension-oriented schools tend to have lower academic quality and pay less attention to school climate (Lamont et al., 2013). More suspensions predict lower achievement and higher probability of dropping out (Noltemeyer, Marie, McLoughlin, & Vanderwood, 2015). Overall, this discipline gap results in less opportunity to learn for Black students.

Teachers may contribute to this discipline gap. They report feeling more troubled by second infractions committed by Black male students than by White male students (reactions to first infractions are nearly identical). They recommend more severe disciplinary action for Black male students for the second infraction (Okonofua & Eberhardt, 2015) (see Figure 7.8).

Let's turn next to a discussion of how you can apply research on discipline to your classroom. You can apply principles of effective discipline that promote learners' self-control while minimizing the discipline gap.

7-2e Classroom Implications of Discipline

Discipline is one of the primary tasks of teachers. Learning to use effective discipline is important. You may eliminate about 75% of the misbehavior in your classroom if you use effective discipline, even if you teach difficult-to-manage learners (Balfanz, Herzog, & MacIver, 2007).

discipline gap
disparity in suspension rates based on group membership, primarily ethnicity, but also gender, SES, and disability.

FIGURE 7.8 Teachers' Responses to Misbehavior of Black and White Male Students.

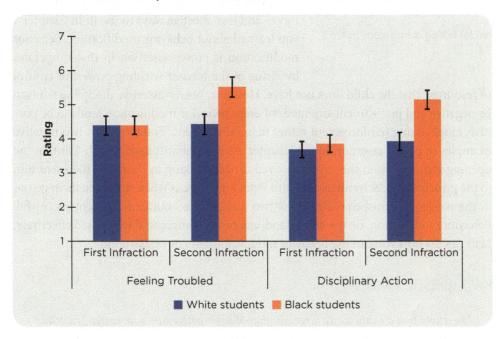

Mean ratings of how troubled teachers felt by male students' misbehavior (left) and how severely they felt students should be disciplined (right). Note that reactions to the first infraction were about the same for Black and White males, but reactions to the second infraction were stronger for Black male students. *Source: Okonofua and Eberhardt (2015).*

FIGURE 7.9 Punishment?

David Bergin

This is a 13-year-old girl's punishment for talking during study hall. Was this effective discipline?

think about this

See Figure 7.9. A 13-year-old girl was told to write "This is a quiet study hall" 50 times as punishment for talking during study hall. Is this effective discipline? Explain your response. Think about the principles of effective discipline and the goal of discipline as you answer this question. What would you do if students talked during study hall?

How do you know if your discipline is effective? Ask yourself: "What did I teach?" If the answer is good values and self-control, you are on the right track. Think of discipline encounters as teaching moments. You will hear about many approaches to classroom discipline—Positive Behavior Interventions and Supports (PBIS), Behavior Intervention Support Team (BIST), Assertive Discipline, Discipline with Dignity, Positive Discipline, and Teacher Effectiveness Training, to name just a few. Before you select an approach, confirm whether it has been evaluated using good science (see Chapter 1). You will be an effective disciplinarian if you follow these guidelines suggested by research:

1. When deciding how and when to use discipline in your classroom, keep in mind that effective discipline: (1) results in compliance, (2) is positive in tone, and (3) uses the least amount of power possible.

2. Use induction as your primary approach to discipline because it promotes self-control. However, power assertion may be appropriate when students are physically hurting each other and you need to forcibly separate them quickly.

If you choose to use power assertion, there are more- and less-effective ways to use it. In Chapter 3 you learned about behavior modification. Behavior modification is power assertion in that it operates by virtue of the teacher wielding power, or control of resources, that the child does not have. However, power-assertive discipline tends to be negative and punishment-oriented, whereas behavior modification tends to be positive, emphasizing reinforcement rather than punishment. You have seen two negative examples of power assertion in this chapter. Mrs. Reinhardt used it with Clint, in the opening vignette, when she gave him a red card for talking in class, and then sent him to the principal. Ms. Schwab used it with Peter and Marcus when she made them go out in the hallway for misbehaving. These two discipline encounters were not successful. Behavior modification, on the other hand, can be quite successful when used effectively. Let's discuss how you can use behavior modification in your classroom.

Revisiting Behavior Modification

My school had an unusually large number of hyperactive, uncooperative 3rd grade children one year. The principal took all the unmanageable kids and formed one class. I was assigned to teach these 18 children, many of whom were on medication for hyperactivity. The next 5 months can be described only as a nightmare. Each day's class was filled with fights, yelling, throwing chairs, and comments like "Try and make me do that!" Many mornings I cried as I anticipated going to school. I often called in sick. In January I told the principal I was quitting because I could not take it any more. He talked me into staying.

I went to a psychologist for help. He told me how to implement tactics that would redirect their aggressive, antisocial hyperactivity into achievement-oriented, socially acceptable activities. Within 3 weeks my students were doing their schoolwork. In class they studied vocabulary words, read books, and helped each other learn. Many even asked to take schoolwork home. The principal, the other teachers, and I could not believe our eyes. (Adapted from Robinson, Newby, & Hill, 1981, pp. vii–viii)

What did the psychologist help this 3rd-grade teacher do? Implement behavior modification in her classroom. Behavior modification is largely based on operant conditioning. That is, as behavior becomes associated with certain consequences, behavior will increase or decrease. Reinforcement refers to a consequence that *increases* the probability of a specific behavior. Punishment refers to a consequence that *reduces* the probability of a specific behavior.

School psychologists and special education teachers often use behavior modification because it is a powerful method for quickly changing behavior even among quite challenging students (Photo 7.4). You can also use it successfully with typical students. Behavior modification is most successful when used in a deliberate, analytical way. In fact, it is also called *applied behavior analysis* because you must analyze the child's behavior to develop a solution. To effectively use behavior modification in your classroom, follow these guidelines:

1. Before you begin an intervention, document a base rate for behaviors. Count the misbehaviors. Note the events that occur before the behavior (antecedents), and the consequences that follow the behavior that may be reinforcing it. Then, systematically alter the antecedents and consequences and observe what happens. Figure out what combination of antecedents and consequences best changes the target behavior (Epstein, Atkins, Cullinan, Kutash, & Weaver, 2008).

2. Apply the principles of effective behavior modification deliberately:

   - Provide positive consequences for positive behavior.

   - Change the child's behavior in small steps (i.e., shaping).

   - Give immediate feedback.

   - Be consistent.

   - Set explicit goals.

   - Allow adequate practice or rehearsal.

3. Reinforce good behavior, rather than punishing misbehavior. Most advocates of behavior modification are critical of

PHOTO 7.4 Effective classroom discipline reduces misbehavior and increases time-on-task.

using punishment because it can elicit aggression, fear, or resentment; it does not teach anything new; and it provides a negative model that students may imitate.

4. If you feel you must use punishment, tell your students exactly what behavior will result in punishment and exactly what the punishment is. Administer the punishment as soon as possible after the infraction. Do this in the context of a warm, caring environment. Combine the punishment with induction; that is, give reasons for why the behavior is prohibited.

Punishment is quite challenging to use effectively in classrooms. Let's take a look at Paul, a 10th-grader, who was punished for tossing a condom onto a girl's desk. He and his friends thought it was funny. His group of friends often plays inappropriate practical jokes, so they are often sent to in-school suspension (ISS). Today he enters his social studies class following three days of ISS:

> His teacher says, "Nice to see you are finally out of ISS." Paul smiles and says, "Yeah, but it won't be long until I am back there—it's only Thursday." Paul says ISS is not a punishment, but rather, "like a time-out except my friends are in there and I don't have to see teachers that I don't like. The teacher never pays attention to what we are doing. We can do anything we want as long as we are quiet."

Paul's experience illustrates important pitfalls you want to avoid in your classroom:

1. Avoid punishing students in ways that remove them from opportunities to learn. Paul is missing substantial instructional time.

2. Make sure that intended rewards are actually reinforcing. For example, is praise a reinforcer? Only if it *increases the probability of a behavior.* Some students would rather disappear than be praised in front of peers by a teacher. Praise for them would function as a punishment, or decrease the probability of a behavior, even though the teacher intended to reward the student.

3. Avoid punishments that send a negative message about doing productive things. For example, don't use homework as punishment or homework exemptions as rewards.

4. Make sure that intended punishment is not reinforcing. Because Paul and his friends enjoy each others' company immensely, the supposed punishment is actually reinforcing. With preschoolers, if time-out is intended to punish by removing the child from sources of reinforcement, verify that the child is not being reinforced with attention or being removed from a situation the child wants to escape.

Time-out is a widely used behavior-modification approach in which a misbehaving child is removed from ongoing activity and from access to reinforcement. It does not require isolation; time-out works through a contrast between the normal, presumably attractive, environment and the time-out environment, which is devoid of reinforcers. It does reduce misbehavior (Morawska & Sanders, 2011). How do children feel about being in time-out? In one study 2- to 4-year-olds said they felt lonely, disliked by their teacher, and scared. Some children were put in time-out for trivial infractions, suggesting it may be overused by preschool teachers (Readdick & Chapman, 2000). A criticism is that time-out does little to teach appropriate behavior.

If you apply behavior-modification principles effectively in your classroom, you are likely to see improvement in student behavior. However, there are important criticisms of behavior modification, even when the focus is on reward rather than punishment. One criticism is that behavior change may be short-lived and may not generalize to other situations. Another criticism is that controlling consequences may undermine students' feelings of autonomy in a way that makes them want to rebel. Finally, while behavior modification changes behavior, attitude change and internalization of values may not accompany behavior change.

This last problem—lack of internalization—is particularly linked to use of material reinforcement. Some teachers reward good behavior with objects like a sticker or candy. Although this may seem positive, there can be subtle, unintended negative effects on internalization. In a famous experiment, preschoolers who liked to draw were randomly assigned to a group that was rewarded for their drawing or to a control group that was not rewarded (Lepper, Greene, & Nisbett, 1973). Later, the children who received the reward showed *less* interest in drawing. The reward appeared to *undermine intrinsic interest* in the task. This effect has been replicated many times with children, teens, and adults doing many different tasks (Lepper, Keavney, & Drake, 1996; Ryan & Deci, 1996). This suggests that rewarding learners for good behavior can undermine their intrinsic motivation for the behavior, possibly short-circuiting their development of self-control.

However, the undermining effect of rewards generally applies only to activities that learners already like. It is difficult to undermine intrinsic motivation if there is none to begin with. Rewards can be useful to get students to do things they do not like. In addition, subtle reinforcers are less likely to undermine motivation than material rewards. That is, a pat on the back or word of praise is less likely to undermine motivation than candy or stickers.

Another problem with using rewards is that it is remarkably difficult to distribute them fairly in real classrooms. Not all deserving learners may get recognized. For example, in one elementary school students are rewarded for positive traits such as caring, respect, or responsibility. Their names are placed in a drawing for a prize. One well-behaved boy had his name placed in the drawing many times, but never won in 6 years. He told his mother he didn't know why he even tried. At another school, an astute, well-behaved 5th-grader told us, "They only give the prizes to the bad kids so that they'll behave better. I'll never get one."

How do you balance the pros and cons of behavior modification? One approach is to use explicit behavior modification only in situations in which learners' behavior is substantially out of control. Use it for the short term until behavior is back to reasonable levels, and then discontinue it, or use it intermittently over time, while gradually increasing use of induction. Be sure to assess whether the underlying problem is a lack of some skill that needs to be taught. You may have to problem solve to see what discipline approach works best in your classroom, but keep in mind that short-term compliance is not the only goal of effective discipline; you want to help learners internalize good behavior and develop self-control.

Whenever a school nurse acquired a confiscated cell phone, she would text all of that student's friends from the phone with this message: "OMG! Make up an excuse to get out of class and meet me in the nurse's office ASAP!" Then the nurse would wait in her office ready to assign detentions (Mali, 2012, p. 112). What do you think about this approach to discipline?

classroom management
all aspects of managing the classroom, including but not limited to, discipline.

Effective classroom management is a key to avoiding disciplinary confrontations. If you manage your classroom well, there should be less need for discipline. That is the next topic.

Classroom Management

Before the class bell rings, Ms. Callahan stands at the door to her 11th-grade English class. As students enter her room, she greets each by name with a smile. Objectives for the day's lesson are written on the board, with instructions for students to begin an activity as soon as they sit down. Ms. Callahan remains at the door until the bell rings, but occasionally calls to students who have already sat down and begun their assignment. She says, "Lin, I'm glad to see that you have begun writing," and "Graciela, would you please show Kayla where to start?" Within minutes after the bell rings, every student is engaged in writing, and they are smiling.

Ms. Callahan is a skilled classroom manager. The casual observer cannot see her skill because it looks like the students are naturally obedient. In fact, Ms. Callahan carefully organized appealing classroom procedures that would prevent misbehavior and foster achievement. Discipline is a part of classroom management, but classroom management goes beyond discipline. **Classroom management** refers to all aspects of managing the classroom, from setting clear rules, to scheduling daily events, to the emotional relationship between teacher and students.

Skillful classroom management can reduce the need for discipline by preventing misbehavior before it happens. Children misbehave less when they perceive their school as orderly, focused on academics, and characterized by positive relations among children and teachers (Wang, Selman, Dishion, & Stormshak, 2010). Students in classrooms that are well managed tend to have better self-control, engagement, and achievement (Freiberg, Huzinec, & Templeton, 2009; Rimm-Kaufman, Curby, Grimm, Nathanson, & Brock, 2009). Teachers who are confident in their ability to manage student behavior are less likely to experience emotional exhaustion and burnout (Aloe, Amo, & Shanahan, 2014). Here are some guidelines for managing your classroom effectively:

1. Establish procedures or routines for common classroom activities like arriving in the morning, handing in homework, dividing into groups, and passing out materials, as Ms. Callahan did (Emmer, Evertson, & Worsham, 2000).

2. Provide an interesting curriculum. (In Chapter 13 we will discuss interest in the classroom.) Boredom fosters distraction and misbehavior.

3. Avoid competitive activities that make some learners feel that no matter how hard they try, they won't be successful. Activities to avoid include giving prizes for reading the most books, displaying only the best papers, and rewarding the fastest math problem solvers.

4. Have a *few* clear rules that everyone knows, such as "respect other persons and their property" and "listen quietly while others are speaking." You can have learners help develop the rules.

5. Create a physical environment that fosters appropriate behavior. This can include removing distracting objects, placing desks in patterns that foster attention and collaboration, and seating learners with nondistracting peers.

6. Avoid negative control (e.g., yelling at or embarrassing individuals, punishing the entire class, or making sarcastic comments). These techniques backfire, creating resentful and distracted learners (Romi, Lewis, Roache, & Riley, 2011).

Effective classroom management can be implemented in all grades, from preschool to high school. Let's listen to a veteran teacher in elementary school:

> We begin class with sustained silent reading (SSR). My students come into the room, put homework on my desk for me to check, and find a place to read. While they read, I check their homework and record attendance and lunch money. The children want to read their books, so they get right to work. I also end the school day with reading, but I read aloud to them. The children dawdle less so that they have more time for the read-aloud. I can tell how much the children like the book by how fast they quiet down. I wish I had started this years sooner.

This teacher and Ms. Callahan both work with challenging students, yet manage their classrooms in ways that help their students experience success at school.

Teachers who are good classroom managers spend time at the beginning of the school year establishing rules and procedures. Teachers who are less-effective classroom managers set rules but do not clearly explain or enforce them. When teachers give vague rules or do not teach students how they should behave, students use their own impulses to guide their behavior. Students may want to please the teacher but do not know exactly what they should be doing.

Classroom management is important because when teachers effectively manage classrooms, learning tends to rise. This is probably because students spend more time on-task and there is less disruptive behavior in well-managed classrooms.

Culturally Responsive Classroom Management

Cultural mismatch can occur in classroom management when teachers and students have different ideas about appropriate behavior. For example, African American students may have little experience with the "indirect commands" that White middle class teachers use, like "Don't you think we should get started?" or "Would you like to get out your book?" African American students may misinterpret the commands as optional and may respond better to direct instructions like "Take out your book and read Chapter 2" (Cartledge, Lo, Vincent, & Robinson-Ervin, 2015).

The same students can be behavior problems in one classroom but not another, depending on fit. These guidelines may help you make your classroom a better cultural fit for more students (Weinstein et al., 2004):

1. Recognize your own cultural biases. You have expectations about language use, profanity, obedience, punctuality, classroom participation, and strictness that are based on your background experience.

2. Use management strategies that fit your students' cultural backgrounds. Cultures differ in their preference to be singled out for achievement versus not being singled

think
about this

The president of the National Association for the Education of Young Children visited a school in China, where she witnessed forty 3-year-olds sit still at their desks for 40 minutes watching a peer performance. In India, she saw sixty 1st-grade boys sit on the floor (only the teacher had a desk) in rapt attention during a lesson. There was no misbehavior in either class (Katz, 1999). What might explain these children's self-control? Base your response on what you know about the development of self-control, cultural differences, and classroom management.

David Grossman/Alamy Stock Photo

PHOTO 7.5 In some schools, students of color are less likely to feel cared for than White students.

out, for independence versus dependence on adult authority, for unsupervised play versus play supervised by adults, for group versus solitary work, and so forth. Such preferences are often related to collectivist versus individualist cultural backgrounds (see Box 7.1). You can learn your students' culture through reading books, observing closely, talking with parents, and visiting neighborhoods. At the same time, you may need to shape students' behavior so they can function effectively in the culture of the school.

3. Recognize patterns of institutional bias, like penalizing an African American male for wearing pants that sag while allowing White students to wear pants with holes in the thighs (Nieto, 2000).

4. Help all students feel cared for. Students of color are less likely to feel cared for than White students, and this undermines their achievement and attitude toward school (Photo 7.5). In one study, Black high school students who were suspended from one teacher's classroom were cooperative and engaged in the classrooms of teachers who focused on building positive relationships with them. Thus, building relationships may narrow the distance between teachers and students who have different social class and ethnicity (Gregory & Ripski, 2008). "Students want to know how much you care before they consider how much you know" (Freiberg et al., 2009, p. 66). A meta-analysis of many studies found that teachers who had high-quality relationships with students had 31% fewer behavior problems over the course of a school year as compared with teachers who did not have high-quality relationships (Marzano, Marzano, & Pickering, 2003).

Your approach to discipline and classroom management is the foundation of your teaching "style." You can learn from the research on parenting styles about how different teaching styles may affect self-control in your students.

7-3 Teaching Self-Control: What Parenting Styles Tell Us

Mr. Dunlop, a 7th-grade science teacher, enforces rules strictly. One rule is that he does not accept late homework. When Anita hands in homework a day late, Mr. Dunlop says, "Keep it. You know I do not accept late homework." Anita pleads, "I was sick yesterday." Mr. Dunlop responds, "Sick does not count as an excuse. You knew 2 weeks ago this would be due." When Anita protests, Mr. Dunlop talks over her until she turns and walks back to her desk in disgust.

As the class begins, she looks annoyed and is not paying attention. During the science lesson, Owen calls out an answer without raising his hand. Mr. Dunlop writes Owen's name on the board. When Owen breaks his pencil in a show of anger, Mr. Dunlop places a check mark next to his name. Mr. Dunlop gives advice to a new teacher: "You've got to rule them, or they'll rule you!"

What do you think of Mr. Dunlop's style of controlling his classroom? Teachers who rigidly enforce rules in power-assertive ways are unlikely to promote self-control in students. At the same time, teachers who are lax with rules are also unlikely to promote self-control. So what teaching style is the best for promoting self-control? Research on parenting style suggests some answers.

7-3a Four Styles of Parenting

Parenting style is defined primarily by two dimensions: (1) the degree to which parents are *warm, accepting,* and *responsive* toward their children and (2) the degree to which parents are *controlling* and *demand mature behavior* of their children (Maccoby & Martin, 1983). You might mistakenly think "controlling" is always negative, such as when parents are intrusive or domineering. However, it also refers to positive control such as guidance, firmness, and structure (Grolnick & Pomerantz, 2009). Many decades of research have found that both parenting dimensions—warmth and control—are critical to children's well-being. Four parenting styles have been identified based on whether parents are high or low on the two dimensions (see Table 7.1). We describe each style and the child outcomes associated with them next.

Indifferent Style

Indifferent parents are *low on both control and acceptance.* They do not set rules for their children, nor do they show much affection, support, or responsiveness. In a child's everyday life, indifferent parents show little interest in events at the child's school, seldom converse with the child, do not consider the child's opinion, and often do not know where their child is or who their child is with. Parents are self-centered rather than child-centered (Maccoby & Martin, 1983). Indifferent parents may use a lot of harsh discipline, but also yield to their children's demands (Fletcher, Walls, Cook, Madison, & Bridges, 2008). At the extreme, they are considered *neglectful.* Severe depression or drug use may cause some parents to be neglectful.

Children with indifferent parents tend to have the lowest self-control and poorest academic performance of the four groups. They are more likely to be obese (Kakinami, Barnett, Séguin, & Paradis, 2015). They are the most likely to engage in delinquent behavior, including smoking, drug use, violence against dating partners, and sexual activity (Baumrind, 1991; Clark, Yang, McClernon, & Fuemmeler, 2015; Steinberg, Blatt-Eisengart, & Cauffman, 2006; Straus & Savage, 2005). One study found that the less responsive and demanding the parents, the more likely their adolescents had hit or beat up a peer, carried a weapon to school, or threatened a peer with a weapon (Jackson & Foshee, 1998).

indifferent parenting style parents are low on both control and acceptance. They are not affectionate or responsive and have few rules. They are self-rather than child-centered. Also called neglectful or uninvolved.

indulgent parenting style parents are low on control, but high on acceptance. They have few rules and avoid controlling their children. Also called permissive.

Indulgent Style

Indulgent, or permissive, parents are *high on acceptance and responsiveness,* but *low on control* of their children. They have few rules governing their children's schedules, like regular mealtime or bedtime. They seldom discipline and avoid asserting authority or imposing restrictions on their child. For example, they may not require their children to follow through on assignments. But they are warm and supportive toward their children.

TABLE 7.1 Parenting styles based on control and acceptance

		Control and Demandingness	
		Low	High
Acceptance and Responsiveness	Low	Indifferent style	Authoritarian style
	High	Indulgent style	Authoritative style

Children of indulgent parents have relatively low self-control and poor academic performance (Clark et al., 2015; Durbin, Darling, Steinberg, & Brown, 1993; Steinberg & Silk, 2002). They are more likely to engage in delinquent behavior, such as smoking, drug use, and sexual activity, than are children of authoritative and authoritarian parents. At the same time, they may feel self-confident and be socially skilled. They tend to be peer-oriented and involved in activities valued by adolescents but not adults, like partying.

Authoritarian Style

authoritarian parenting style parents are high on control but low on acceptance. They discourage verbal give-and-take, value their authority, and tend to be power assertive.

Authoritarian parents are *high on control* of their children, but *low on acceptance and responsiveness* to the child's agenda. In authoritarian households, rules are not discussed or negotiated; in fact, negotiation with children is often viewed as a threat to the parent's authority. Authoritarian parents do not welcome input from their children or give reasons why something should be done. They use phrases like "Because I say so." Authoritarian parents tend to be more punitive than other parents, and use power-assertive discipline (Maccoby & Martin, 1983).

Children of authoritarian parents are somewhat obedient and often conform to rules set for them. For example, at age 12 they are more likely to abstain from alcohol than children of other parenting styles (Clark et al., 2015). They have been pressured into obedience, but may misbehave when the pressure is absent or they get older. They perform adequately in school, but they tend to lack self-confidence (Steinberg & Silk, 2002). They also are more likely to be obese (Kakinami et al., 2015).

Authoritative Style

authoritative parenting style parents are high on control, acceptance, and autonomy support. They maintain authority and enforce rules, but are responsive to their children.

Authoritative parents are *high on both acceptance* and *control* of their children. A key attribute of authoritative parents is that they *support autonomy* in their children (Steinberg & Silk, 2002). How can parents be highly controlling and still support their children's independence and self-direction? They do so by having clear standards and high expectations for mature, polite behavior, but without taking away choice (Grolnick, 2003). They firmly enforce rules, using commands and sanctions when necessary, but give reasons for their decisions. They provide household structure, like set bedtimes. However, there is also open communication between parents and children, with encouragement of verbal give-and-take. Authoritative parents are interested in what their children have to say. While children are required to be responsive to parental demands, parents are as responsive as possible to their children's reasonable demands and points of view (Maccoby & Martin, 1983).

think about this

Think back to two classes you had in school—one that was managed very well and one that was not. What attributes of the classes were different? Did they result in different amounts of learning or elicit different behavior from you? Could you categorize the teachers as indifferent, indulgent, authoritarian, or authoritative? Explain your response.

A 3rd-grade girl provided an example that will help you understand how parents can be both highly controlling and responsive. She told her teacher she had a bedtime of 8:10 p.m. Why such an odd time? She said that if she had to be in bed by 8:00, she would have to start brushing her teeth at 7:50 in order to be in bed on time, and she would always miss the end of her favorite television show. By setting the bedtime at 8:10, the parents maintained control by enforcing a strict bedtime but were responsive to their daughter's desire to watch the program.

Children of authoritative parents tend to have the highest self-control of the four groups. They tend to be securely attached (Karavasilis, Doyle, & Markiewicz, 2003). They also tend to be highest in self-esteem, social competence, and academic achievement (Fletcher et al., 2008; Padilla-Walker, Carlo, Christensen, & Yorgason, 2012; Spera, 2005; Steinberg et al., 2006). Children's decision-making autonomy, which is provided by authoritative parents, is especially important as they grow into adolescence because it is related to improved emotional functioning (Qin, Pomerantz, & Wang, 2009).

There are four possible reasons for positive child outcomes of authoritative parenting:

1. Authoritative parents tend to use inductive discipline, which promotes self-control. Furthermore, parents who use induction typically remain in control of themselves when disciplining their children, which serves as a model for the child.

2. Authoritative parents' warmth and respect for their children's views makes the children more willing to adopt their parents' views.

3. Authoritative parents are very clear about rules or standards for behavior, so children know how to behave in a variety of situations.

4. Authoritative parents permit negotiation and compromise, when appropriate, which fosters their children's development of these important social skills, even in very young children (Kuczynski & Kochanska, 1990).

In adolescence, when parents jointly make decisions with them, teens have better self-control than when parents either impose decisions or leave the decision to their children (Fletcher, Darling, Steinberg, & Dornbusch, 1995).

Parents do not always fit clearly into a single parenting style, and parents may change across time. For example, parents may be authoritarian with their older children but become indulgent with the youngest. In addition, there can be considerable variation within each of the four parenting styles. For example, some authoritarian parents are consistently harsh, while others are occasionally warm toward their children. Furthermore, parents may have a somewhat different style with different children; some children may draw more control or more warmth from their parents. Unfortunately, children whose parents treat them differently from the way their siblings are treated tend to have more risk factors and behavior problems (Meunier, Boyle, O'Connor, & Jenkins, 2013). This sort of favoritism has negative repercussions for the entire family.

The Adolescent Challenge

Across cultures adolescents develop a greater desire for autonomy. Regardless of parenting style, from age 11 to 17 children view their parents' authority as less legitimate and feel less obligated to obey parents than do younger children. It is normal for teens to moderately resist parental authority, particularly in early adolescence. Yet, *authoritative* parents are more likely to be viewed by adolescents as legitimate authorities—and deserving of obedience (Darling, Cumsille, & Martinez, 2008).

In contrast, *authoritarian* parenting becomes a problem during adolescence. The power imbalance between children and their authoritarian parents diminishes, and authoritarian parents lose control over adolescents. For example, when children are able to hold their own jobs, have friends who drive, and can run fast, parents can no longer control their children by withholding money, hiding car keys, or chasing them down. As children enter adolescence, both parents and children become increasingly frustrated as authoritarian parents continue to try to assert their dwindling control. As we will see next, this frustration is more common in some groups than in others.

7-3b Group Diversity in Parenting Style

Religion, socioeconomic status, family structure, and ethnicity are associated with parenting style. Authoritative parents are more likely to be religious, at least among Protestants, Mormons, Catholics, and Jews (Gunnoe, Hetherington, & Reiss, 1999). This may not be true for other religious groups. Authoritative parents are also more likely to be middle class than working class or impoverished and more likely to be part of an intact family than of a single-parent family or stepfamily (Carlson, Uppal, & Prosser, 2000; Deater-Deckard, 2000). Parents who lack a stable relationship, adequate income, and social support may find it more difficult to be authoritative. In addition, parents who fear the future, because they think the world is unsafe or that they cannot make a decent living, are more likely to be highly controlling with their children (Gurland & Grolnick, 2005). Thus, parenting style is a reflection not just of parents' personality, but also the context in which they live.

Indifferent parents are most likely to be at the two SES extremes—low and high. In some high-SES neighborhoods, there are no adults home after school to monitor the children. One teacher, at an expensive private school, tells the story of Kent.

Kent has high test scores, but he never completes his homework on time. He is barely passing his classes. When I call his parents, they tell me they are getting a tutor and he will be doing his homework, but nothing changes. Kent's parents work long hours so that sometimes he does not see them for days. I have never met the parents because they do not attend school events. Kent has started smoking, and other students say he uses drugs.

Kent's parents are wealthy with demanding jobs, and they have an indifferent parenting style. Indifferent parenting is linked to drug and alcohol use in such families (Clark et al., 2015; Luthar, 2003).

Ethnicity

Authoritarian parenting is linked to more behavior problems and lower achievement, as compared with authoritative parenting, for all children, but the effects are weaker for Black or Asian American children than for White and Latino children (Hill, Bush, & Roosa, 2003; Ho, Bluestein, & Jenkins, 2008; Pittman & Chase-Lansdale, 2001). African American parents tend to be more authoritarian and make more decisions for their adolescents than do European American parents (Gutman & Eccles, 2007). In addition, although authoritarian parenting is linked to lower academic achievement among Latino children, it is also linked to respect for elders and family cohesion, which are highly valued outcomes within the culture (Halgunseth, Ispa, & Rudy, 2006).

What might explain ethnic differences in authoritarian parenting? Perhaps quality of neighborhood. Parents who raise children in difficult settings, such as unsafe neighborhoods, or in societies that are racist or foreign to them, may be more restrictive in an attempt to protect their children (Supple & Small, 2006). African

American children living in high-crime neighborhoods are not as negatively affected by restrictive parenting as children of other ethnicities or in other neighborhoods. However, even in this subgroup, by the time children finish elementary school, restrictive parenting becomes linked to depression and lower academic achievement (Dearing, 2004).

Another explanation is that the *meaning* of parenting behavior may vary by culture (Soenens, Vansteenkiste, & Van Petegem, 2015). For example, Chinese mothers are more controlling and critical than European American or African American mothers; they are quite involved in their children's learning and criticize weaknesses even after success (Ng, Pomerantz, & Deng, 2014; Pomerantz, Ng, Cheung, & Qu, 2014). Although Asian American high school students report more pressure from their mothers, they do not find it negative. In contrast, European American students report that the more pressure from their mothers, the less support they feel (Fu & Markus, 2014). Nevertheless, among Chinese parents, higher levels of control are linked to lower academic performance in their children (Pomerantz et al., 2014). Note also that strict Asian American and Latino parents are often more indulgent and warm than strict European American parents. This hybrid style is primarily authoritative, but with some authoritarian components, and the warmth seems to diminish negative effects of the strictness.

Golden Pixels LLC/Shutterstock.com

PHOTO 7.6 Authoritative parents set limits but are warm and listen to their children.

In summary, authoritative parenting predicts more culturally valued child behavior across ethnicities as compared with authoritarian parenting (Photo 7.6). However, in cultures in which restrictive, undemocratic parenting is prevalent and accepted, *if combined with warmth,* children may not develop the behavior problems associated with authoritarian parenting. Therefore, how your students respond to their parents' style depends on nuances in that style and the values of the community in which they live.

7-3c Classroom Implications of Parenting Style

A critical lesson from this discussion on parenting styles is that *the effect of discipline depends on whether it takes place within the context of a warm adult–child relationship.* The same lesson applies to teaching. Teachers have patterns of control and warmth that parallel parenting styles. The following are descriptions of real teachers. Can you identify their styles?

1. Mr. Graham has no classroom rules and low expectations for his students. He has said to other teachers, "Rules will be broken by these monsters, so why set them?" He does not assign homework and is consistently late to class. Students leave during class; he does not know or care where they go. He allows students to threaten each other during class—fights have broken out in his class. In his class, students are slackers who do not care about their grades; most were not like that before Mr. Graham's class.

2. Mrs. Sinclair is always kind-hearted. She wants people to like her. She will do anything parents demand of her. Her kids run the class. She begs them to behave, but they ignore her. She struggles to get papers graded and exams written on time. Her students are slackers who do not care about their grades and do as they please, but they are kind to each other.

3. Mr. Dunlop you have already met. He has high standards for his students. They learn what they are supposed to learn. His students do not step out of line for fear of punishment. His room is neat and orderly. He spends a lot of after-school time in his classroom.

4. Ms. Loeb has high standards for her students. She also has a good personal relationship with most. Students feel she cares for them and is fair to all in both her grading and her discipline. She has total control over her classroom, but in a way that students don't even notice. She is well organized. Papers are graded in a timely way.

Which teaching style do you think is most effective? What style characterizes you at this time? Teachers who are warm, but lax, are not likely to help their students develop self-control or learn much, although the students may like them and be happy in class. Teachers who are harsh and overly controlling are also not likely to help their students develop self-control, or enjoy school, although the students may learn. Teachers who are indifferent to their students and exert no classroom control may be the least effective. Effective teachers behave like authoritative parents. They are demanding, have high expectations, and are perceived as fair and caring by their students (Wentzel, 2002).

Authoritative teaching may be beneficial for all children, but particularly for African American students for whom the discipline gap is linked to less opportunity to learn and poor school bonding. How can this trend be reversed? Students are more obedient toward authoritative teachers, whom they view as having more legitimate authority. Recall from Chapter 6 that personality can be situation-specific. In one study, African American students who were quite defiant with some teachers behaved better in authoritative teachers' classes. They felt that the authoritative teachers cared for them and expected more of them, and they felt obligated to cooperate with that teacher. They were more engaged, paid attention, and skipped class less for authoritative teachers. Listen to what three 11th- and 12th-graders said about their teachers:

- *She nice, but she strict . . . nobody, like, try to go against her judgment.*

- *Well, actually, it is not that he enforces his rules cause he don't have to because all the students respect him . . . if he ask the class, you know, be quiet so that we could get our class discussion started, they automatically be quiet.*

- *When she talk to you with seriousness, she mean it, but then she also have a smile like "I'm on your side." I mean, "I feel where you're coming from but I'm still your teacher." (Gregory & Weinstein, 2008, pp. 469–470)*

The authoritative, respected teachers were equally likely to be male or female, and White, Black, Asian American, or Latino (and so were the teachers who drew defiance).

A veteran high school teacher shared the story of her movement toward a more authoritative style (Armstrong, 1999). For years she had either played the role of judge, evaluating the merits of each sob story for late papers, or taken the dictator stance. She decided to opt out of both roles. After 29 years of teaching, she decided to give students more choice about homework deadlines, as long as students were reasonable and met her clear standards. She now gives students a recommended due date. If they fall behind, all they have to do is write her a note explaining when she can expect their papers. One student wrote: *"I'm really sorry I haven't finished those essay questions yet . . . . For the past 2 weeks I've had to work until 9 each night. I want to hand in my best work . . . but I don't want to inconvenience you too much. Could you please accept them on Monday?"* (Armstrong, 1999, p. 50). Her students are low-SES with after-school jobs, some are parents, and most are sleep-deprived because of hectic schedules. The result of responding to student needs has not been chaos, but better teacher–student relationships, and more conscientious students who accept responsibility for their own achievement.

This approach may not work in every classroom; however, the research presented throughout this chapter suggests that in most situations learners do not need a power-assertive "or else" threat in order to behave responsibly. In fact, consistent use of power assertion may undermine students' self-control in the long run. Reasoning with learners and respecting their agendas, while holding them to high standards, may be a better teaching style. You foster high achievement, as well as self-control, in your learners by being appropriately demanding and controlling, but also by displaying substantial warmth, acceptance, and respect.

Authoritativeness applies to schools as well as to teachers. Authoritative schools have caring and helpful staff and rules that are enforced consistently and fairly. This combination of support and structure is linked to lower suspension rates, less bullying and victimization, and less racial disparity in discipline (Gregory et al., 2011; Gregory et al., 2010). This suggests that it is important for schools to be *both* warm and demanding, just as it is for parents.

At the conclusion of this chapter you should have a clear understanding that, as a teacher, you promote or undermine students' self-control through the way you discipline them and through your interaction style. One aspect of self-control that affects students' functioning is their ability to control their emotions. This is the topic of the next chapter, the final chapter in this section on the emotional child.

My Teaching

Are you using effective discipline with your students and promoting their self-control? Periodically ask yourself the following questions to gauge your mastery of these skills:

1. How was I disciplined in my family of origin? How is this linked to my culture and my own disciplinary style?

2. What was the goal of my last disciplinary action? What values did I teach? Do I analyze whether the problem is a skill deficit (the student doesn't know what to do) before assuming it is a motivational problem (the student does not want to obey)?

3. Am I open to negotiating and compromising with my students during discipline encounters? Or do I expect instant obedience? Do I demand compliance even when it does not matter?

4. Have I used psychological control techniques like trying to make children feel guilty or saying "I am not happy with you today" and then ignoring a child?

5. Do I avoid using an "or else" clause that threatens consequences such as red cards, keeping students in from recess, or calling the office?

6. Do I avoid using extrinsic rewards that learners expect?

7. Do I explain the rules and consequences of misbehavior to my students? Do I give reasons for obeying? Do I avoid saying "no" without explanation?

8. When seeking compliance, do I continually restate a command until the child complies, but without increasing the level of power or using threats (persistent persuasion)?

9. Do my students have committed compliance or situational compliance? Do they break class rules or misbehave when I am not present?

10. Do I maintain a positive emotional tone even during discipline? Do I have a warm relationship with students?

11. Do I recognize that some situations could make anyone lack self-control, and therefore create a classroom that avoids such situations? For example, do I keep temptations out of sight if they are likely to distract?

12. Am I appropriately controlling or lax? Am I warm, accepting, and responsive toward my students or cold and distant?

13. What am I doing to close the discipline gap?

14. Do I understand my legal obligations as a mandated reporter? Do I know the reporting procedure that I should follow?

Professional Resource Download

Summary of Age Trends in Self-Control and Discipline

	Self-Control and Compliance	Discipline and Parenting Style
Infancy & Toddlerhood (Birth–2 Years)	• Infants have little self-control or ability to perceive or comply with demands. • The ability to comply with demands emerges in toddlerhood. • Toddlers argue with their mothers on average about 20 times per hour and disobey many commands. • Toddlers are just beginning to develop self-control. Their delay of gratification is measured in seconds.	• Discipline is generally not relevant to infants. • Toddlers benefit from induction, which is associated with more compliance and prosocial behavior despite their limited verbal skills. • For all age groups, authoritative parenting is most beneficial. • Time-out is effective in controlling behavior, but it makes children feel lonely and rejected.
Early Childhood (3–5 Years)	• Delay of gratification is measured in minutes. It is greater for larger treats. • Children are able to generate their own strategies of self-distraction to increase delay of gratification. • Gender differences emerge; girls have more self-control. • Individual differences in self-control predict important outcomes in adolescence and adulthood. • Direct defiance and passive noncompliance, which are less skilled strategies, decline but negotiation, which is a more skilled strategy, increases.	• The principles of effective discipline pertain to all ages. • Induction is more effective than power assertion or psychological control at any age, including preschool. • Authoritative parenting is most beneficial. • Adults' use of rewards undermines intrinsic motivation in preschoolers. • Time-out is effective in controlling behavior, but makes children feel lonely and rejected. • Children in early childhood are among the most likely to be sexually abused.
Middle Childhood (6–12 Years)	• Delay of gratification is measured in more minutes, suggesting greater ability than preschoolers to control impulses. • Children increase ability to control attention despite distractions. • Individual differences in ability to resist impulses become stable.	• The principles of effective discipline pertain to all ages. • Induction is more effective than power assertion or psychological control at any age. • Authoritative parenting is most beneficial. • Racial disparities in school discipline emerge.
Adolescence (13–19 Years)	• Adolescents have increased ability to control their impulses. • By early adolescence, youth have increased ability to consider the consequences of their immediate actions for the near future. By late adolescence, they can consider the consequences of their actions far into the future, but this is still not fully developed.	• The principles of effective discipline pertain to all ages. • Induction is more effective than power assertion or psychological control at any age. • Authoritative parenting is most beneficial. • Power-oriented parents lose their control over adolescents who develop their own sources of power. • Teen brains may find risks more rewarding. • Children this age are among the most likely to be sexually abused.

⌄ Professional Resource Download

Chapter Summary

7-1 Self-Control

- Self-control is the ability to inhibit impulses, control one's behavior, and follow rules. It includes the ability to delay gratification.

- There are large individual differences in self-control, even in preschoolers. These differences tend to be stable over the course of childhood and predict later outcomes, including academic achievement and social competence.

- The antecedents of self-control include: (1) effective discipline, (2) practice (without taxing the self-control "muscle"), (3) secure attachment, (4) parental monitoring, and (5) authoritative parenting style. In addition, the structure of the situation can affect self-control.

- Girls and higher-SES children tend to be more self-controlled than boys and lower-SES children.

- There are cultural differences in emphasis on conformity to rules and self-control. U.S.-born Americans tend to place less emphasis on conformity than do immigrants. Asian parents tend to emphasize self-control to fulfill group obligations.

- You can promote learners' self-control by teaching them self-control strategies and by carefully structuring the environment.

7-2 Effective Discipline

- There are different kinds of compliance and noncompliance. The goal of effective discipline is committed, not just situational, compliance. Committed compliance is also known as "internalization."

- Induction is a type of discipline in which the adult gives the child a reason for changing misbehavior. Induction seems to be the most effective form of discipline for promoting internalization, social skills, and self-control.

- Psychological control is a type of discipline in which the adult withdraws love or attention from the child for misbehavior and makes critical statements. It is linked to low self-esteem and high anxiety in children, which interfere with learning.

- Power assertion is a type of discipline in which the adult directly controls the child physically or by withholding resources. Power assertion is a common form of discipline, but it has serious drawbacks: it increases angry defiance, reduces internalization, damages relationships, models aggression, and raises expectation for more coercion. Corporal punishment, a form of power assertion, is associated with increased antisocial behavior.

- Physical abuse often begins as corporal punishment. Other forms of abuse include emotional abuse, sexual abuse, and neglect. Abuse is distressingly common and often perpetrated by family or acquaintances. Effects of abuse depend on its severity but can include academic, emotional, social, and health problems.

- The three principles of effective discipline are to: (1) achieve compliance because present compliance predicts future compliance, (2) use the minimum power needed to obtain compliance so that children attribute their compliance to internal motives, and (3) keep the emotional tone of the interaction positive and cooperate with the child whenever possible.

- Persistent persuasion is a type of discipline that uses all three principles. It involves calmly restating the command, giving reasons for compliance, and not escalating the level of coercion until the child complies.

- Sometimes children want to behave well but don't know how. Skill-based instruction, rather than discipline, is called for.

- Behavior modification is commonly used in classrooms to control behavior. It can be effective for controlling behavior, but there are two cautions: (1) rewards can be detrimental to children's intrinsic motivation and self-control, and (2) punishment should be avoided because it has negative side effects.

- Classroom management includes discipline, classroom structure, and routines. In well-managed classrooms, there is less need for overt discipline. Students spend more time on-task and experience higher achievement.

- There are ethnic differences in punishment at school leading to a discipline gap in which Black students, especially boys, are more likely to be disciplined than non-Black students.

7-3 Teaching Self-Control: What Parenting Styles Tell Us

- Adults vary in their level of desire for control and their level of warmth, acceptance, and responsiveness. These two dimensions combine to form four distinct parenting styles.

- Indifferent parents are low on both control and acceptance. Their children fare the worst and tend to be low in self-control and academic achievement and high in delinquent behavior.

- Authoritarian parents are high on control but low on acceptance. They are more likely to use power-assertive discipline. Their children tend to be externally controlled, average in achievement, and low in self-confidence. There are cultural and ethnic differences in the extent to which authoritarian parenting has negative effects.

- Indulgent parents are low on control, but high on acceptance. Their children tend to have low self-control, low academic achievement, minor delinquency, and relatively strong self-confidence.

- Authoritative parents are high on both control and acceptance. Their children fare the best. They tend to be high in academic achievement, self-confidence, social competence, and self-control. Teachers who adopt this style may have students who behave better in class and learn more.

Lynne Carpenter/Shutterstock.com

Emotional Development

Do you know a student who is almost always happy and sensitive to others' feelings? Do you know a student who is easily upset or often angry? Which student is more successful in the classroom? In this chapter we will discuss how learners' emotional competence is relevant to your classroom. **After you read this chapter, you will be able to:**

8-1 Explain the importance of emotions for learners' success in the classroom, and create an emotionally healthy classroom.

8-2 Recognize age-appropriate ability to regulate emotion, and analyze how to coach your students to more effectively regulate their emotions.

8-3 Understand the importance of reading others' emotions, and apply strategies for improving your students' empathy.

8-1 Emotions

As Hailey's 5th-grade class begins a math worksheet, she cannot find her pencil. Her classmate Evan has a pencil on his desk, so Hailey snatches it. Evan grabs it back. Hailey is consumed with anger. She slugs Evan and shoves his friend, Roshni, out of his chair. As Roshni gets up, other children join the melee shouting at Hailey, "He had it first!" Hailey turns red, screams at Evan, and then begins sobbing and hiccupping.

The teacher, Mrs. Ng (pronounced like "ing"), quickly walks to Hailey's side. Although she is angry with Hailey, she says in a soothing but firm tone: "OK. Let's all calm down now. Roshni, are you all right?" Roshni nods yes as he glares at Hailey. Mrs. Ng then tells Hailey: "Why don't you go wash your face in the bathroom and get a drink of water. That will help you feel better." As Hailey leaves the room, Mrs. Ng tells the students, "Everything is all right. Take a deep breath and relax. Turn around and finish your work." With the class focused on the assignment, Mrs. Ng goes to the door to catch Hailey returning. She quietly asks Hailey how she made Evan and Roshni feel and how she might have behaved differently. Hailey begins to relax and adopt Mrs. Ng's calm demeanor as they talk. When Mrs. Ng sees that Hailey has her emotions under control, she pats Hailey on the back, smiles, and says, "I know you'll behave better next time. Now get a pencil from my desk, and get to work."

emotional competence
the ability to regulate your own emotions, and read others' emotions, so that you emerge from an emotional event having accomplished your goals.

Hailey is frequently unable to control her anger and has little empathy for others' feelings. She lacks **emotional competence**—the ability to regulate one's own emotions and to understand others' emotions. Mrs. Ng is helping Hailey develop emotional competence through the way she manages Hailey's outbursts. Effective teachers, like Ms. Ng, promote children's emotional competence as well as their academic skills. Emotional competence is a powerful factor in classroom success from preschool to high school because emotion is foundational to behavior and thought.

emotion
a subjective reaction to an important event, involving physiological or observable behavioral change.

An **emotion** is a subjective reaction to an important event and involves physiological change, readiness to act, and appraisal of the event (Gross, 2015). Notice that there are four components to this definition. First, the event must be *important*. If you do not have strongly held values or goals in an event, then you are unlikely to feel emotion about it. Second, emotions involve *physiological changes* in heart rate, brain activity, hormone levels, and temperature—which are linked to outward signs of emotions, like flushed cheeks or sweaty hands. Third, emotion involves *readiness for action*. Fourth, emotions depend on how you *appraise*, or interpret, an event. For example, imagine Hailey is in your classroom. Another teacher tells you, "I had that troublemaker last year. She is just plain mean!" You might feel angry toward Hailey. But if the other teacher tells you: "I had her last year. Her father left the family, and the poor child is so distraught that she lashes out at others," you might feel compassion instead of anger. Changes in your **appraisal** of an event lead to different emotions.

appraisal
the meaning given to an event.

Different emotions have unique patterns of these four components. For example, you feel anger when you appraise an event to be demeaning, such as a student cursing at you. Physiologically, your face flushes, eyebrows furrow, and heart races. You feel a desire to counterattack. In contrast, you feel shame when you appraise an event as your failure, such as when your term paper gets a low grade. Physiologically, your cheeks flush, posture collapses, eyes lower, heart slows, and you smile weakly. You feel a desire to withdraw or hide.

8-1a What Emotions Do Children Have?

Early Basic Emotions

More than a century ago, Charles Darwin (see Box 8.1) noted that some facial expressions are recognized by people across the world. Carroll Izard (2007) took

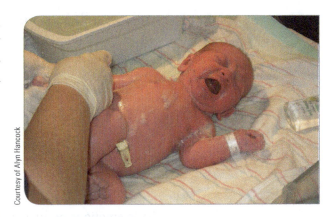

Courtesy of Alyn Hancock

PHOTO 8.1 Less than an hour old, this newborn communicates through emotion. Which does he feel about his first bath—anger, joy, sadness, or interest?

BOX 8.1 theories & theorists

Charles Darwin

Charles Darwin (1809–1882) is among the most famous scientists in history. In 1872, thirteen years after his famous book *The Origin of Species* was published, he published a book about emotion expression. He took an ethological perspective. Recall from Chapter 6 that *ethology* is a science concerned with explaining animal behavior. In his book, Darwin asked thought-provoking questions such as the following: Do we have to learn which expressions to make when sad, frightened, or happy? Do all people, regardless of geography or culture, express the same emotion in the same way? After painstaking documentation of animals and humans in widely different cultures, he concluded that emotion expression is not learned, but innate and universal. Humans even share many expressions with cats, dogs, horses, and monkeys. For example, primates' expressions of fear, anger, sadness, and happiness are similar to those of humans. Like humans, gorillas laugh in response to tickling. Darwin believed that we communicate within and *between* species through emotional expression.

Darwin sought to explain facial expressions. For example, he pondered why the brows contract when we concentrate:

Now, when anyone with no covering on his head (as must have been aboriginally the case with mankind) strives to the utmost to distinguish in broad daylight, and especially if the sky is bright, a distant object, he almost invariably contracts his brows to prevent the entrance of too much light; . . . There is, indeed, much analogy, as far as the state of the mind is concerned, between intently scrutinizing

Charles Darwin

a distant object, and following out an obscure train of thought. (Darwin, 1965/1872, pp. 222–224)

Darwin thus suggested that furrowed brows have become an innate part of our response to concentration.

In the 1960s, Paul Ekman set out to prove that Darwin was wrong about universal emotional expressions by studying an isolated people in Papua New Guinea (Ekman, 1973). To his surprise, his work and that of later scientists largely confirmed Darwin's views, though not entirely (Barrett, 2006; Ekman, 2016; Hess & Thibault, 2009). There are some subtle differences in facial expressions of emotion across cultures. In addition, culture influences aspects of emotion besides expression, such as how we regulate emotions. Thus, both nature and nurture influence our emotional lives.

Contemporaries admired Darwin as a scholar because he expressed gratitude for thoughtful criticism of his work. Darwin spent the last 42 years of his life confined to his home by illness. T. H. Huxley said that Darwin's condition would have made 9 out of 10 men aimless invalids. Rather than languish, Darwin wrote books that would foster debate into a second century.

basic emotions
universal, innate emotions appearing in the first months of life (interest, joy, sadness, anger, disgust, and fear).

Darwin's work a step farther and identified six **basic emotions** that he claims are innate to the human species:

1. Interest
2. Joy/happiness
3. Sadness
4. Anger
5. Disgust
6. Fear

Basic emotions occur rapidly and automatically; they may be built into the human species because they promote the survival of infants (Photo 8.1). For example, fear protects the infant from dangers like crawling down a steep flight of stairs. The joy infants feel when seeing their father motivates them to stay near. Infants display basic emotions within the first months of life.

However, there is controversy over how many different emotions actually exist. Some scientists would expand Izard's list to include love, pride, hope, gratitude, compassion, jealousy, and anxiety. Others would narrow the list to just a few emotion dimensions, like positive versus negative and high versus low activation (amount of energy). They argue that during infancy, distress, anger, sadness, and disgust would all fall under the umbrella of a single basic negative emotion. As children grow cognitively, gain experience, and learn emotion labels, specific emotions emerge out of the basic negative or positive emotions (e.g., Barrett, Mesquita, & Gendron, 2011; Lindquist, Satpute, & Gendron, 2015). For example, if you feel negative, but activated, you would call this anger. If you feel negative, but deactivated, you would call this boredom. Despite this controversy, most current researchers agree with Darwin that there are universal basic emotions (Ekman, 2016).

Scientists disagree about early emotions partly because it is difficult to tell when an infant feels a particular emotion. To shed light on this, scientists recorded infants' faces during emotional events like getting a shot, tasting something sour, or seeing their mother smile. They developed a system to measure infants' emotions from facial expression. Test your ability to recognize infant emotions by covering the answers in Figure 8.1 while you decide which emotion the infant is expressing.

FIGURE 8.1 Infant Emotion Expression.

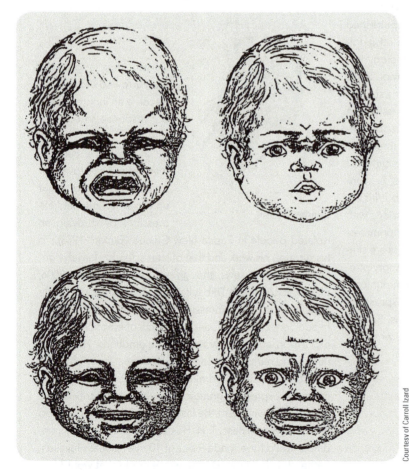

Courtesy of Carroll Izard

These photos depict infants expressing emotions according to Izard's categories. Can you tell what emotion each infant is expressing? They are anger, distress, joy, and fear.

FIGURE 8.2 Emergence of Basic and Complex Social Emotions.

Age	Positive Emotions	Negative Emotions	
Birth	Interest Pleasure	Disgust Distress	Basic Emotions
3–7 Months	Surprise Joy	Sadness Anger Fear	
Self-Awareness Develops			
15–24 Months		Embarrassment Envy	Complex Social Emotions
Awareness of Rules & Responsibility Develops			
30–36 Months	Pride	Guilt Shame	

Have you seen infants or toddlers you know express each of these emotions? Do they fit these research-based age trends?

Complex Social Emotions

Social emotions emerge during the toddler years. These include envy, embarrassment, shame, guilt, and pride (see Figure 8.2). Envy and embarrassment emerge between 15 and 24 months. Shame, guilt, and pride emerge at about 30 to 36 months. Social emotions are more complex and emerge later than basic emotions because they require at least four cognitive abilities in children: (1) awareness that they are a separate self from their attachment figures, (2) awareness that rules exist, (3) ability to evaluate their self against those rules, and (4) ability to judge whether they caused something. If children do not believe they caused something, they are unlikely to feel guilt, shame, or pride about it. For example, 3-year-olds may feel guilt if they snatch a toy from an infant and the infant cries, but not if the infant cries because of hunger.

Young children may feel social emotions, but they are not always accurate in their judgments about guilt. Piaget devised an interesting way to test this ability. He told preschoolers stories of Mary and John. Mary was trying to help by carrying dishes. She dropped and broke eight dishes by accident. John did not want to eat his peas, so he threw his dish and broke it. Who was naughtier? Most preschoolers believe Mary was naughtier than John because she broke more dishes. To preschoolers, greater damage often means more guilt; they may not consider Mary's and John's intentions.

Children get better at judging guilt with age. Most 2nd-graders can accurately judge the contrast between Mary and John. However, most cannot accurately judge between shame and guilt. Guilt results from morally wrong behavior over which you have control. Shame results from a social blunder over which you may or may not have control (Tangney, Stuewig, & Mashek, 2007). The ability to judge between

social emotions
complex emotions that emerge later than basic emotions (shame, embarrassment, guilt, pride, and envy). Also called "self-conscious" or "moral" emotions.

shame and guilt emerges by 5th grade. That is, children know they are likely to feel shame after clumsily falling in the hallway but feel guilt after telling a lie. An important lesson for teachers is that younger children's inability to judge guilt may lead them to feel guilty for events that are not their fault, making them *vulnerable to unrealistic expectations or misplaced blame.*

8-1b Why Do Children Have Emotions?

Emotions serve important functions. They help focus your attention, motivate you, and enable you to take action. For example, fear *focuses* your attention on the frightening object. You are *motivated* to change behavior, like run away. Your heart rate and blood flow will increase, helping you run fast. In Hailey's example, her anger toward Evan focused her attention on him, motivated her to attack him, and physiologically prepared her for the exertion of slugging him. In contrast, positive emotions like interest and joy motivate you to continue, not change, your behavior.

Emotions help you communicate. Infants use emotion to communicate as soon as they are born. Infants cannot talk, but their emotions signal their needs. As children grow into adulthood, they continue to use emotions to communicate. Hailey was clearly *communicating* to Evan that she did not want him to take back his pencil.

The social emotions help you adhere to the norms of your social group. Guilt motivates repairing harm to others and inhibits aggression. Pride motivates achievement. Shame motivates conformity to class rules. For example, during a museum tour a teacher scolded an 8th-grader for talking with friends and interrupting the docent. The student's shame kept her from talking out of turn for the rest of the field trip. Thus, social emotions are helpful, but learners who experience too much shame are not emotionally healthy; they are likely to become aggressive and feel worthless. Any emotion can be a problem if it is out of control, like Hailey's explosive anger.

8-1c Emotions Influence Learning and Thought

Hailey's anger hijacked her thoughts and affected her learning. Although most emotions are not as intense as Hailey's, emotions are ever present and constantly influencing thought. Emotions influence thought in multiple ways:

- As discussed above, emotions focus attention (Huntsinger, 2013). Learners pay more attention to things with emotional significance. For example, when learning about civil rights, students will pay rapt attention to a debate on the emotionally charged topic of school shootings and the right to bear arms. However, too much emotion can swamp attention and executive functions, as you'll learn below.

- Emotions organize recall and memory. Learners tend to remember details of emotionally strong experiences (Kensinger, 2007). For example, they might remember disgust over dissecting a frog more than other lessons in the same class.

- Emotions determine whether learners approach or avoid a learning task, and how much effort they put into learning. For example, a learner who enjoys the topic will expend more effort writing a research paper.

Emotions can have different effects on learning and thought, depending on what emotion is experienced. Let's compare positive and negative emotions.

Positive Emotions

Positive emotions—like interest, happiness, or excitement—promote learning and creativity (Valiente, Swanson, & Eisenberg, 2012). Happy learners are more productive, perform better on projects and tasks, and solve problems more creatively than learners in a negative mood (Nadler, Rabi & Minda, 2010). Are positive emotions always beneficial? *Intensely* positive emotions can result in worse performance on tasks that require detailed analytic processing, like some physics problems. However, when a task is important to the individual, exuberant emotions do not interfere with the task at hand (Liu & Wang, 2014). In other tasks, neutral or *mildly* positive emotions, like interest or amusement, may be ideal for focused attention and fast information processing (Rose, Futterweit, & Jankowski, 1999). Thus, whether your learners perform better in a highly versus a mildly positive mood may depend on the task.

Why does positive emotion enhance productivity and creativity? Mild, positive emotions broaden thought (Fredrickson, 2001; Huntsinger, 2013). When you feel positive, you are motivated to learn, to be open to new information, to generate ideas, and to participate in activities. When you feel interest, you are motivated to focus attention on pursuing a goal (Gable & Harmon-Jones, 2008). Positive emotions may have these effects by altering neurotransmitters in the brain. Positive emotions are linked to small increases of dopamine in the part of the brain responsible for working memory and creativity (Ashby, Isen, & Turken, 1999). A different set of outcomes is linked to negative emotions.

Negative Emotions

Negative emotions—like anger, sadness, and anxiety—can impair learning. When students feel intense or chronic negative emotions, they have difficulty attending to classroom tasks, as Hailey did. Perhaps this is because emotion regulation and executive functions use the same brain systems (Brock, Rimm-Kaufman, Nathanson, & Grimm, 2009; Compton et al., 2008). Recall that executive functions (see Chapter 4) and effortful control (see Chapter 6) predict academic achievement. When learners are intensely angry, sad, or anxious, their emotions swamp their executive functions and undermine their ability to pay attention and remember (Ramirez & Beilock, 2011; Schmeichel & Tang, 2015). For example, while Hailey was trying to contain her anger, she had less working memory space available to process the lesson. For another example, instead of attending to the task at hand, highly anxious learners worry about irrelevant things or attend to potential threats, such as "my dad will go ballistic if I fail this assignment" or "what will happen if my mom doesn't get well?" Anxiety can make learners appear less intelligent because they are so consumed by anxious thoughts that they may not remember, learn, or make good decisions. Thus, *teaching children to regulate their emotions may be as important to school success as helping them develop better executive functions* (Ursache, Blair, & Raver, 2012; Valiente, Lemery-Chalfant, & Swanson, 2010).

A cautionary note is that you do not need to be concerned about all negative emotions. The occasional, mild episode of negative emotions can be beneficial. For example, a little anxiety can motivate learners to study for a test. For another example, a little sadness can help learners process information in systematic, detailed ways that can be helpful in some tasks, such as drawing a picture or doing a karyotype in biology class. Research suggests that when people are in temporary sad moods they are less gullible, make fewer stereotyped judgments, are more polite and generous, and have better memory (Forgas, 2013; Sussman, Heller, Miller, & Mohanty, 2013). Thus, negative emotions can be beneficial, but your students are likely to learn less if they experience intense or chronic negative emotions.

We have discussed how *emotion influences thought*. In the next section, we will see how *thought influences emotion*. For example, learners can control emotions by how they think about an event. Some learners are able to use emotions to guide thinking and to think intelligently about emotions. Psychologists call this ability **emotional intelligence** (Mayer, Roberts, & Barsade, 2008). This term may be over-used in the media to refer to the same abilities that comprise *emotional competence*— to accurately perceive, understand, express, and regulate emotions. In this text, we will use the term *emotional competence* to refer to this broader array of abilities. Let's turn to control of emotions next.

8-2 Regulating One's Own Emotions

> *Shonese, a 2nd-grader, calmly gets off the school bus and walks toward her house. When she sees her mother waiting at the door, she bursts into tears. Between sobs Shonese tells her mother that some mean kids on the bus ridiculed her name. Shonese's mother lovingly rubs her back and says, "Calm down. The best way to handle kids like that is to ignore them. Pretend you didn't hear a thing. They'll quit eventually, because it won't be fun." The next day, when the ridicule starts again, Shonese follows her mother's advice and ignores them. Seeing that they are not getting a reaction, the kids leave Shonese alone.*

Shonese is able to control her emotions until she is safely home, where she bursts into tears. Contrast Shonese's behavior with Hailey's. Although Shonese is only a 2nd-grader, she is better at regulating her emotions than Hailey, a 5th-grader.

Emotion regulation is the ability to control one's emotions. Children with good emotion regulation can alter the *intensity* and *duration* of their emotions so that goals are met. Shonese dampens her distress to meet her goal of stopping the ridicule. Mrs. Ng dampens her anger to preserve a good relationship with Hailey. Emotion regulation does not always involve dampening emotions; it can also involve maintaining or increasing emotions (Gross, 2015). For example, Roshni may need to increase anger in order to stand up to Hailey's aggression.

8-2a Strategies to Regulate Emotion

Her mother helps Shonese develop emotion regulation by suggesting strategies for coping with distress. Mrs. Ng helps Hailey develop emotion regulation by suggesting strategies for coping with anger—leave the room, wash her face, think about

emotional intelligence
the ability to use emotions to guide thinking and to think intelligently about emotions. Sometimes defined more broadly to mean emotional competence.

emotion regulation
the capacity to control the intensity and duration of emotions.

how others feel, relax, and then solve the problem of where to get a pencil. **Coping strategies** are deliberate attempts to change thoughts or behavior when you are overwhelmed by emotion. Coping strategies can be either *problem-focused* or *emotion-focused*. **Problem-focused coping strategies** are action-oriented and involve *trying to change the situation*. For example, if you feel shame over a bad grade, you decide to study the textbook better. **Emotion-focused coping strategies** involve *trying to change emotions*, such as changing one's thoughts about the situation or seeking comfort from others. For example, if you feel shame over a bad grade, you may tell yourself the grade isn't that important or talk with friends about how the teacher is unfair. *Which strategy is best depends on the situation.* In situations that are controllable, problem-focused strategies may be more helpful. For example, academic achievement is controllable—if you work harder, you achieve more. In situations that are not controllable, emotion-focused strategies may be more helpful.

Scientists have identified several strategies that children use to cope with daily emotions in situations like getting a bad grade, having a toy snatched away, or being ridiculed. You will find these in Table 8.1. Some strategies are consistently less constructive ways of coping than others, such as aggression or escaping through drugs. Reappraisal is often the best strategy when you can't change the situation. A key benefit of reappraisal is that is doesn't cost as much mental energy or self-control as some other strategies. Thus, if learners need your help getting their emotions under control, coach them in the best choice among these strategies, as Mrs. Ng and Shonese's mother both did. Your students will fare better if they are able to flexibly draw upon different strategies (Bonanno & Burton, 2013; Gross, 2015).

coping strategies
deliberate attempts to change thoughts or behavior to try to manage strong emotions. They are usually divided into problem-focused or emotion-focused strategies.

problem-focused coping strategies
action-oriented strategies that involve trying to change the situation.

emotion-focused coping strategies
strategies that involve trying to change emotions, such as changing one's thoughts about the situation or seeking comfort from others.

TABLE 8.1 Coping strategies commonly used by children

Less Constructive	1. Do nothing
	2. Aggress—to resolve the problem (e.g., grab a pencil away)
	3. Aggress—to release pent-up feelings (e.g., kick the chair)
	4. Use alcohol or drugs to escape the emotions, or eat "comfort" foods
	5. Cry—to release pent-up feelings
	6. Cry—to elicit help from others
	7. Ruminate (rehash and dwell on negative thoughts)
More Constructive	8. Avoid the situation or leave; just walk away
	9. Talk to friends, teachers, or parents, or pray
	10. Distract yourself or try not to think about the problem
	11. Exercise (for low-arousal emotions like sadness)
	12. Relax (for high-arousal emotions like anger or anxiety)
	13. Seek help from friends, teachers, or parents
	14. Take constructive action to improve the situation (e.g., study harder when anxious about a test)
	15. Reappraise—try to think about the situation in a positive way, or change your goal (e.g., it's better that I wasn't elected to student council because I'll have more free time now)

Compiled from Gross (2015); Seiffge-Krenke, Aunola, and Nurmi (2009); and Zimmer-Gembeck and Skinner (2008).

8-2b Emotional Dissemblance—Faking It

Shonese practiced emotional dissemblance when she did not respond to the children teasing her. **Emotional dissemblance** refers to expressing no emotion or expressing an emotion that is different (but more acceptable) from what you actually feel. Emotional dissemblance helps children fit into their culture because cultures have rules about expressing emotions. For example, it may be acceptable to show anger toward a classmate at recess but not toward the teacher in class. To be a successful member of any culture, children must know the rules for emotional display, anticipate how others will react to their emotions, and control their emotional display. Although this is a sophisticated ability, even young children dissemble. For example:

> *In preschool, 4-year-old Jason builds a car from Duplo blocks and gives it to his friend Daniel. Daniel acts excited about getting the car, but when he is beyond hearing distance, Daniel tells his teacher that he does not really like the car.*

Emotional dissemblance can be positive or negative. Daniel's was positive because he was protecting Jason's feelings. It is negative when children give false impressions for dishonest reasons, such as looking innocent so they will not get into trouble for misbehavior.

Dissemblance goes hand in hand with emotion regulation. Darwin argued that hiding emotions dampens them and expressing emotions intensifies them (Darwin, 1965/1872). Research generally confirms Darwin's view. When you express an emotion, your facial muscles provide feedback to the brain, which then alters your experience of the emotion (Kraft & Pressman, 2012). For example, if you are having a sad day, but you pretend to smile and show happiness, you will come to feel a little happier. So remember the adages "fake it 'til you make it" or "grin and bear it" apply to emotion regulation. This is contrary to a popular volcano myth that if you do not let your negative emotions out, they will explode.

8-2c Age Trends in Emotion Regulation

There is dramatic improvement in emotion regulation across childhood. Infants have minimal coping ability, but by age 10, good coping ability is in place for most children.

Infancy and Toddlerhood (Birth to 2 Years)

Infants cannot yet voluntarily control their emotions, but they do have a few basic coping strategies for overwhelming situations. For example, when infants are passed from relative to relative at a noisy family gathering, they may cope in three ways: (1) sucking on their cheeks or a pacifier, (2) appearing to sleep, their eyes closed and their brows furrowed, and (3) averting their gaze, or looking away (Braungart-Rieker, Hill-Soderlund, & Karrass, 2010). When you play with infants, they may become overstimulated. When this happens, infants look away while they get their emotions back to a comfortable level, at which point they turn back toward you.

Toddlers have more control of their emotions than do infants. This is due to brain maturation that allows them to delay emotional responses and to shift between emotions. Toddlers who were born prematurely may lag in emotional development

emotional dissemblance altering the expression of felt emotion by expressing no emotion or expressing a different emotion.

in the first 2 years of life until their brain development catches up (Malatesta, Culver, Tesman, & Shepard, 1989).

Toddlers can sometimes dissemble. For example, some 2-year-olds can hold back tears—although their lips may tremble—when left with a babysitter. While this shows some self-regulation ability, toddlers often need your help to regulate their emotions. They need hugging, rocking, or other forms of soothing to calm down when they are upset. Because such emotion regulation involves a partnership between caregiver and toddler, it is referred to as *guided self-regulation* (Photo 8.2).

This need for help to regulate emotions can make toddlers challenging. Are the "terrible twos" real? Anger, fussiness and irritability steadily increase from 4 months to 2 years, then diminish (Braungart-Rieker et al., 2010; Lipscomb et al., 2011). See Figure 8.3. Tantrums emerge at 16 months and crest around 18 to 21 months. By age 2 tantrums begin to abate, such that the worst is over for most children. Tantrums are episodes of intense sadness, with peaks of anger (Green, Whitney, & Potegal, 2011). Children may scream, yell, kick, cry, and throw themselves on the floor. Toddler negativity might be due to parents becoming more negative as the child begins to be mobile and get into forbidden things (Lipscomb et al., 2011).

PHOTO 8.2 Adults guide toddlers' emotion regulation until they are able to regulate their own.

Early Childhood (3 to 5 Years)

Preschoolers are increasingly able to regulate their own emotions without adult help. General negativity levels off or decreases from age 2 to age 5 (Lipscomb et al., 2011). However, preschoolers occasionally have breakdowns in emotion regulation, particularly if they are tired, stressed, or hungry. Roughly 80% of preschoolers may have tantrums in any given month, but daily tantrums are not typical (Wakschlag et al., 2012).[1] Tantrums continue to abate and then disappear between age 3 to 5. As young as age 3 or 4, children understand that coping strategies help them regulate emotions. For example, they know that distraction helps relieve sadness. However, they tend to engage in poor strategies, like venting or stamping feet, more than older children (Dennis & Keleman, 2009).

Preschoolers also become more capable of emotional dissemblance, but their ability is still limited. For example, they are better at exaggerating than squelching an emotion, such as howling as though in great pain over a trivial hurt. They may choose to cry after an injury only if a caregiver is watching, but not if they are alone. Preschoolers can "fake a smile," in simple situations, like Daniel did. However, in more complicated situations

FIGURE 8.3 Negative Emotions in Infants and Toddlers.

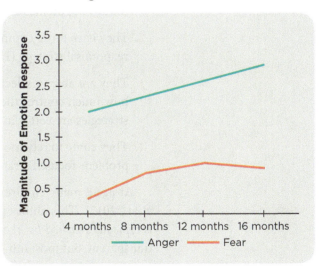

How would you describe the difference in the development of fear and anger? When does the steepest increase in fear occur? Could it be linked to the onset of stranger wariness? *Source: Braungart-Rieker et al. (2010).*

[1] Extreme tantrums that are long, involve aggression, are "out of the blue," are aimed at nonparental adults, and are followed by intense shame or guilt may suggest emotional disorders in preschoolers (Cole, Luby, & Sullivan, 2008; Wakschlag et al., 2012) and may merit professional help.

they can't simultaneously squelch disappointment and fake happiness. Scientists study this by giving children a disappointing gift, such as a baby toy. They then ask the child to "trick" an adult into thinking they got an attractive gift. Most 4-year-olds just can't do this, but most 6-year-olds can (Kromm, Färber, & Holodynski, 2015)

Preschoolers develop regulation ability when they "try on" different emotions during play. A girl who pretends to be an angry mother spanking her doll, and then comforts the crying doll, is practicing feeling and controlling anger. Preschoolers also develop emotion regulation as they use their increased language abilities to talk about emotion.

Middle Childhood (6 to 12 Years)

By 1st grade, children can regulate their emotions in settings away from a caregiver, as Shonese did on the school bus, and they continue to improve across the elementary years (Blandon, Calkins, Keane, & O'Brien, 2008). However, until they reach adolescence children continue to show better emotion regulation when their mother is present, if they have a positive relationship (Gee et al., 2014). They become better at coping in four ways:

1. They use social support less, like talking less to others about their distress. Social support shifts somewhat from parents to peers, but even 12-year-olds are likely to turn to parents for help with emotions.

2. They have more coping strategies. Starting around age 5 they are able to use the reappraisal strategy (Davis, Levine, Lench, & Quas, 2010).

3. They are able to select the best strategy to use because they are better judges of how much control they have over a situation. Remember that emotion-focused strategies are better in situations in which a child has no control.

4. They come to rely more on emotion-focused strategies, but they continue to use problem-focused strategies as well.

At age 8 many children pass the "disappointing gift" tests successfully (Kromm et al., 2015). This ability grows during elementary school so that *adult-like ability is typically reached by about 5th grade.* Thus, kindergarteners' emotions are largely transparent, but most 6th-graders can readily conceal their emotions.

Adolescence (13 to 19 Years)

Adolescents report feeling a lot of daily stress, usually about relationships with friends, sweethearts, or parents, and pressure to do well in school (Gutman & Eccles, 2007; Seiffge-Krenke, Aunola, & Nurmi, 2009). This might explain a common stereotype that adolescents are moody and negative, implying poor emotion regulation. Is this stereotype true? No, according to beeper and diary studies. For example, in a classic study, adults, adolescents, and elementary students were given beepers to wear for a week and asked to report their feelings when the beeper sounded at random times (Larson & Richards, 1994). Adolescents reported more frequently feeling bored, tired, and sleepy (see Chapter 2). They also reported more frequently feeling social discomfort, like awkwardness and loneliness, than their parents. Perhaps this is because adolescents tend to be sensitive to emotions from social evaluation, such

FIGURE 8.4 Age Trends in Embarrassment.

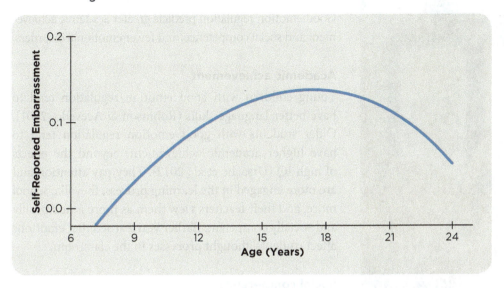

Youth of different ages were in an fMRI scanner. They were told a peer could see them through a camera in the scanner. Afterwards they were asked how they felt. At about what age did participants report feeling the most embarrassment? *Source: Somerville et al. (2013).*

as feeling embarrassment if they think someone is looking at them (see Figure 8.4). They reported less frequently feeling extremely happy than elementary students. However, *most of the adolescents reported being fairly happy most of the time.* In a diary study, adolescents reported having good moods and positive interactions with others more than negative moods and interactions (Flook, 2011).

Although most adolescents are not moody, some are frequently angry, anxious, or sad. In the diary study, adolescents who had a higher ratio of positive to negative events were happier. In the beeper studies, only adolescents who had a pileup of stressors—a family move, a new school, or parents' divorce—were moody. Moodiness was *not* associated with puberty or the "raging hormones" that are often blamed for negativity in adolescents. An important lesson for secondary teachers is that *you should not simply dismiss emotional negativity as a normal phase, but should address the needs of teenagers who are chronically unhappy or moody.*

8-2d Individual Diversity in Emotion Regulation

Shonese has good emotion-regulation ability for her age, but Hailey does not. In an emotionally charged situation, these girls would differ in emotional response, intensity of their emotions, and recovery time. Learners with poor emotion regulation either experience too little emotion or too much emotion; that is, they can be overregulated or underregulated. Underregulated learners, like Hailey, experience chronic negative emotions, or rapidly change from one extreme emotion to another.

Negative emotionality is a temperament trait (see Chapter 6). Individual differences in this trait appear in the first months of life and remain somewhat stable. This means that children who are irritable are not likely to simply outgrow negativity at a later age, unless their environment improves substantially. This is a problem because poor emotion regulation is a risk factor, whereas good emotion regulation is a protective factor, as we will discuss next.

Mark Lewis/Photodisc/Jupiter Images

PHOTO 8.3 Learners with good emotion regulation are happier and have more friends.

What Does Emotion Regulation Predict?

Good emotion regulation predicts greater academic achievement and social competence, and fewer emotional disorders.

Academic achievement

Young children with good emotion regulation tend to have better language skills (Robinson & Acevedo, 2001). Older students with good emotion regulation tend to have higher academic achievement, beyond the effects of high IQ (Ursache et al., 2012). They pay attention and are more engaged in the learning process, they like school more, and their teachers view them as more academically and socially competent. Earlier you learned that emotions affect students' thought processes in the classroom.

Social competence

Learners with good emotion regulation are liked better by both teachers and peers (McDowell, O'Neil, & Parke, 2000; Penela, Walker, Degnan, Fox, & Henderson, 2015; Rydell, Berlin, & Bohlin, 2003). This is because they may use their ability to protect others' feelings, such as Daniel pretending to like Jason's car. This is also because they *typically express more positive than negative emotions,* which leads to less aggression and more positive behavior (Bartlett & DeSteno, 2006; Denham et al., 2003). When learners are happy, they greet others warmly, engage in class activities enthusiastically, and make activities fun for others (Photo 8.3). This attracts classmates and keeps interactions running smoothly, which leads to friendship.

In contrast, learners with poor emotion regulation are often angry. They are at risk for being disliked by peers and teachers because anger makes peers uneasy and because chronically angry learners cope by being aggressive. Classmates prefer peers who use problem-focused coping strategies rather than aggression. Teachers, on the other hand, prefer learners who use avoidant coping strategies, such as backing out of anger-filled situations (Kliewer, 1991). Teachers prefer such learners because they are not likely to act out at school, which makes them easier to handle. However, avoidant strategies are not always best because students do not learn to stand up for themselves or problem solve.

Emotional disorders

Learners with chronic negative emotions approach new situations with a negative bias and use destructive coping strategies. For example, Hailey's negative bias led her to view Evan's reasonable behavior—taking his pencil back—as an attack. She was so overwhelmed by anger that she physically attacked two of her classmates. Such overwhelming negative emotions can lead to emotional disorders.

Emotional disorders are classified as either externalizing or internalizing. **Externalizing disorders** involve aggression and anger. Learners with externalizing disorders "act out." We will discuss these problems in Chapter 10. **Internalizing disorders** involve withdrawal or sadness. The two most common internalizing disorders in childhood—depression and anxiety—are discussed later in this chapter. Learners with poor emotion regulation can have *both* internalizing and externalizing disorders, such as being both depressed and aggressive (Rhee, Lahey, & Waldman, 2015). Internalizing disorders may get less attention from teachers because they do not usually disrupt schooling for anyone but the student, yet sad or anxious students may need intervention.

Emotional disorders are prevalent. Figure 8.5 shows prevalence of the most common disorders, for both moderate and serious cases. Problems tend to go together; 40% of learners with one disorder have another disorder as well. About 22% of all learners have at least one serious disorder before reaching adulthood (Merikangas et al., 2010). Yet most do *not* receive the treatment they need to develop better emotion regulation. Beginning treatment early increases its success. Thus, teachers should address emotional problems as early as possible. Even children who do not have diagnosable disorders, but have poor emotion regulation, may need intervention. Let's discuss next how to help learners develop good emotion regulation.

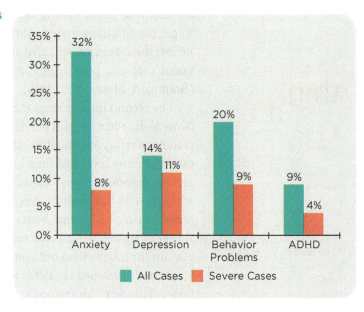

FIGURE 8.5 Mental Health Problems in Youth.

Percent of adolescents in a national U.S. study who meet criteria for a mental health problem up to that point in their lives.
Source: Merikangas et al. (2010).

externalizing disorders emotional disorders based on anger, characterized by aggression and other antisocial behaviors.

internalizing disorders emotional disorders based on sadness or anxiety, characterized by withdrawal.

What Predicts Emotion Regulation?

Learners who have better executive functions (see Chapter 4) also have better emotion regulation. How quickly you can accurately do the Stroop test—where you say the color in which a word is printed, rather than the word, as in Figure 4.5—predicts your ability to cope with stress! This is because good inhibitory control and working memory help you contain emotions and use reappraisal strategies instead of brooding (Diamond, 2013; Schmeichel & Tang, 2015). Genes may influence emotion regulation through differences in executive functions or through the temperament trait of negative emotionality (see Chapter 6) (Clifford, Lemery-Chalfant, & Goldsmith, 2015), but the way parents interact with children may have a larger influence. Let's discuss seven parenting factors next.

Attachment

Children learn emotion regulation from attachment figures during routine activities like feeding, bathing, and playing in infancy. To help you understand, imagine two infants are playing peek-a-boo with their mothers. The first infant is giggling, but turns his face away from his mother when the game gets too intense. His mother does not wait for him to return to the game. Instead, she looms over him making

think about this

A mother was preparing to leave her 4-year-old with a babysitter. The child pleaded with his mother not to leave, but she silently continued putting her coat on. Finally he shouted, "I hate you!" She sighed, rolled her eyes, and said, "You can't hate me. I'm your mother" and left. What type of attachment is this child likely to have? How might this affect his emotion regulation? What about his behavior with peers? Defend your conclusions using what you have learned in this chapter and in Chapter 6.

noises, trying to get him to come back to the game. This overstimulation causes the infant to begin fussing and makes him turn even further away as he struggles to get his emotions under control. The mother ignores emotional signals from her infant; she is being insensitive and intrusive. This infant may develop an angry emotional core and poor regulation if his mother continues to be intrusive over time (Braungart-Rieker et al., 2010).

The second mother stops the game when her infant turns away and waits until he turns to face her again. Then she smiles and says, "Oh, now you're back!" and they resume playing. When adults stimulate young children to an almost, but not quite, overwhelming level and then back off, as this mother did, children learn to control intense emotion. Many repeated experiences like this alter networks in the brain, which results in a brain that regulates emotions well. This may be why infants with sensitive parents become better at emotion regulation (Blair et al., 2008; Braungart-Rieker et al., 2010). Research suggests this kind of parenting may be particularly important for infants with difficult temperament (Leerkes, Blankson, & O'Brien, 2009).

Securely attached children, whose parents are sensitive, tend to have good emotion regulation (Morris, Silk, Steinberg, Myers, & Robinson, 2007). They learn that others are readily available to soothe their emotions. They are more likely to have constructive coping strategies that help them express their emotions, receive others' emotions, take on emotionally charged situations, and talk about hot topics without anger. As adolescents they are less likely to become depressed (Allen, Porter, McFarland, McElhaney, & Marsh, 2007).

By comparison, *resistant* children are more likely to underregulate their emotions. They learn that others will not soothe them until their emotions reach overwhelming levels. For example, parents may ignore subtle signs of distress and wait until children are sobbing loudly before attempting to soothe them. This trains children to have a rapid rise of intense emotions in order to attract attention. They become increasingly difficult to soothe and frequently feel frustrated and anxious (Thompson, 1991).

Avoidant children are more likely to overregulate their emotions. They learn that others are unresponsive, emotionally unavailable, or hostile. For example, parents may ignore intense distress in children. To cope, children may suppress emotions and not seek help, which prevents their learning better coping strategies (Cassidy, 1994). They may particularly suppress emotions that make them feel vulnerable and avoid emotional closeness to others, appearing hostile or detached.

Response to children's emotions

Accepting and responding appropriately to children's negative emotions may help them be more positive (Davidov & Grusec, 2006). For example, an appropriate response to an infant's cry might be soothing; an inappropriate response might be anger. For another example, an appropriate response to a teenager in tears over a bad grade might be, "I can see you're upset. Let's talk about what you can do about it." (Photo 8.4). Inappropriate responses might be dismissing the child's emotions ("It's nothing to get upset about"), mocking or belittling the child ("Don't be a crybaby"), placating the child ("You can have ice cream if you'll stop crying"), eye rolling, or yelling. Parents who routinely use inappropriate, negative responses tend to have children who have poor emotion regulation, are angry, are insecurely attached, and behave badly at school (e.g., Leerkes, Parade, & Gudmundson, 2011; Lipscomb et al., 2011; Swanson, Valiente, Limery-Chalfont, Bradley, & Eggum-Wilkens, 2014).

Responding appropriately to children's exuberant positive emotions is important also. Imagine a child is playing happily with friends in a boisterous way on the front porch. Some parents would invalidate the child's emotions by reprimanding the child or acting embarrassed. Other parents would be comfortable allowing the child to have fun. In one study, children whose parents invalidated their positive emotions tended to have poor emotion regulation and depression (Yap, Allen, & Ladouceur, 2008).

 **brain research**

Extreme Stress Alters Brains

In Chapter 2 you learned about brain plasticity, which means the brain adapts to the environment. Plasticity is usually an asset, but not always. It may make some children vulnerable to toxic levels of stress (Bryck & Fisher, 2012). Stress is not inherently harmful; most children cope with it just fine. However, chronic stress can impair the brain's ability to respond to stress and to learn. As a result, stressed children are vulnerable to physical and mental illnesses (e.g., depression, anxiety, conduct disorder), they become overly reactive to stress, and are less able to regulate their emotions (Blair, 2010; Shonkoff et al., 2012). For example, the chronic anxiety of insecure attachment alters brain chemistry, leading to a poorly developed cortex, where emotion regulation takes place (Schore, 2000). Animal studies show that stress can turn some genes on and off, such as genes that control myelination. (Kudos if you recognize this as epigenetics from Chapter 6!)

Stress may be particularly harmful in the first 2 years of life. It is more harmful if it is intense and chronic and if children do not have protective factors. An important protective factor is having a secure attachment with a supportive adult who helps the child cope (Shonkoff et al., 2012). You can be a protective factor to your students.

Expression of emotions

Parents' emotions influence their children's emotion regulation. Parents who are often cheerful have children who control their own negative emotions and have more coping strategies. Parents who are often negative and model poor emotion regulation—such as frequently yelling or acting depressed—have children with poor emotion regulation. Their children tend to have fewer, primarily aggressive, coping strategies and feel depressed or anxious (Blandon et al., 2008; Stocker, Richmond, Rhoades, & Kuang, 2007).

Parents should not completely avoid expressing negative emotions; rather, they should express substantially more positive than negative emotions. In fact, parents who are more emotionally expressive, with both positive and negative emotions, have children who are well liked (Cassidy, Parke, Butovsky, & Braungart, 1992). As a teacher, you may want to also express a wide range of emotions, but be primarily positive.

Robert Brenner/PhotoEdit

PHOTO 8.4 When adults respond appropriately to children's emotions, children learn to regulate their emotions better.

Talk about emotions

Parents who talk with their children about their own and others' emotions tend to have children who are more positive than negative (Denham, Mitchell-Copeland, Strandberg, Auerbach, & Blair, 1997). For example, during a conflict the parent might say, "Ahmad hit you because he was *angry* that you and Bill were playing without him, and he *felt* left out." Language is a tool for managing emotions.

There are several reasons why talking about emotions is helpful. First, parents are responding calmly, which helps children get their emotions under control. Second, conversations provide children with information about why people behave in certain ways, like why Ahmad hit. Third, conversations teach coping strategies, like reappraising whether Ahmad meant to be hurtful. Fourth, conversations raise children's awareness of emotions and ability to label emotions. Learners who can label specific emotions (e.g., I felt sad; then I became angry) rather than just global feelings (e.g., I felt bad) are better at regulating their emotions (Kashdan, Barrett, & McKnight, 2015). Perhaps this is because emotion labels are a tool to help children "step out" of the feeling and "look upon" it with some distance and control (Bernstein et al., 2015). Fifth, when adults converse with children, they feel valued and worthy of attention, which leads to positive emotions. You will have opportunities to talk with your students about emotions. If you take these opportunities, you may help them learn to regulate their emotions.

Coaching

Parents can directly coach children in coping strategies. Which strategies should they focus on? Comforting works with infants and toddlers, but is less effective after age 4. Distraction, or diverting children's attention, still works but becomes less effective between ages 4 and 8. Reappraisal is effective in preschool and beyond. That is, children whose parents coach them in reappraisal learn to control their emotions better (Morris et al., 2011). For example, when a 10-year-old was afraid to go to theater class, she told her mother, "I'm kinda afraid because of the time I was in dance and I forgot my routine in front of the judges." Her mother helped her reappraise the situation: "You're older now. Everybody forgets routines sometimes. Give it a chance." The girl did—and enjoyed her class. Children whose parents coach them in more effective strategies (see Table 8.1) are better able to cope with distress, such as being excluded by peers, and have better emotion regulation, health, impulse control, attention, and social competence (Abaied & Rudolph, 2011; Lunkenheimer, Shields, & Cortina, 2007; Morris, Silk, Steinberg, Myers, & Robinson, 2007). You can coach your students by suggesting coping strategies, as Mrs. Ng did with Hailey.

think about this

What might be the implication for youth whose parents are not home or available to coach the child in regulating emotions when the youth is exposed to violent, sexually explicit, or emotionally intense movies or video games?

Effective discipline

Discipline influences children's emotion regulation. When an adult overreacts to a child's misbehavior, the child can be overwhelmed by emotion. For example, imagine a toddler is gleefully rolling grapefruit down the basement stairs. He has some sense that he is misbehaving because when he sees his mother, he says "ut oh." His mother can use induction, as she frowns and firmly says, "No. You'll bruise them. Let's get a ball instead." Or, she can use power assertion as she grabs the child, spanks him, and says, "bad boy!" while he cries. In the first case, the child learns that he can cope with disapproval and repair mistakes. In the second case, the child learns that disapproval leads to overwhelming emotions. Adults who overreact with angry, power-assertive discipline make it difficult for children to regulate their own emotions. This effect has been found in infancy through adolescence (e.g., Lipscomb et al., 2011).

Abuse

Abuse influences children's emotion regulation. Some abused children are under-regulated; they have substantial anger, fear, and shame. They may rapidly shift from positive to negative emotions. However, other abused children are overregulated; they are emotionally unresponsive and difficult to engage. They may have blank or sober expressions.

Suppressing emotions, or refusing to "feel," helps abused children cope when they cannot get help or avoid the abuser. However, this suppression prevents them from learning good coping strategies for typical emotions, like frustration at school, so that when their tight emotion control fails, they are explosive. This was characteristic of a teenager who was hospitalized for aggression (Cole, Michel, & Teti, 1994). After many weeks of good behavior, he earned a weekend visit home. He eagerly awaited his mother, but she never came to get him. When he phoned her, she lightheartedly told him she was too busy to come. He showed no emotions when he hung up the phone. He acted like his mother's rejection did not hurt. Shortly afterward, he was caught hurting another child as he vented despair and anger. In therapy, he learned strategies for coping with his grief that his mother would never care for him. If maltreated children are helped to develop emotion regulation skills, they are likely to fare better and not develop internalizing disorders (Kim-Spoon, Cicchetti, & Rogosch, 2013).

In summary, when adults are sensitive and secure attachment figures, express mostly positive emotions, respond well to children's emotions, talk with children about emotions, directly coach them in coping strategies, and use effective discipline, they provide children with the tools to develop good emotion regulation. In contrast, when adults are negative, harsh, rejecting, or abusive, children are likely to develop poor emotion regulation. Two of the most common emotion-regulation problems are depression and anxiety.

8-2e Depression and Anxiety: Emotion Regulation Gone Awry

> *Shelly, a 4th-grader, is described by her teacher as "quiet, spacey, and overly sensitive to others' feelings." Shelly often says she does not feel well, but the school nurse finds nothing physically wrong. Shelly comes from a middle-class, intact family. Shelly's mother helps at school, yet her own childhood history of abuse leads to bouts of depression and interferes with her emotional availability to Shelly. Shelly occasionally says she wishes she were dead. Shelly has behaved this way since preschool, but no teacher has referred her for help.*

Shelly has classic symptoms of **depression**: social withdrawal, poor concentration, lack of interest in school, and feeling worthless. Other symptoms of depression that you might see in learners include changes in appetite, self-criticism, irritability, poor hygiene, can't-sit-still behavior, frequent crying, and sleep problems (American Psychiatric Association, 2013). These symptoms occur across ages; however, in teens depression usually involves too much sleep, and in young children too little sleep. Any learner might have these symptoms occasionally, but if symptoms are severe for at least 2 weeks, or less severe but last for a year or more, learners may have clinical depression, like Shelly.

depression
a common internalizing disorder in which feelings of sadness are severe for at least 2 weeks or are milder but chronic.

Jetta Productions/Lifesize/Getty Images

PHOTO 8.5 Depression is one of the most common psychological disorders in youth, particularly among teenage girls.

anxiety disorder
a common internalizing disorder in which the child feels worried about future threats, or threats to the sense of self.

test anxiety
a dispositional proneness toward anxiety in test situations that interferes with performance.

math anxiety
a dispositional proneness toward anxiety at the prospect of doing math or taking a math test

Anxiety has some symptoms that overlap with depression. Anxiety is a feeling of helplessness focused on future threats or threats to the sense of self. Do not confuse anxiety with fear, which is a response to present threats. Classic symptoms of anxiety include poor concentration and can't-sit-still behaviors such as foot kicking, hair twirling, mouth touching, lip licking, lip twisting, crying, chewing on objects, and nail biting. Both the frequency and intensity of these behaviors may indicate the learner's degree of anxiety. You'll see these symptoms across ages and ethnic groups. Any learner can occasionally feel anxiety strong enough to interfere with learning. However, some learners have chronic intense anxiety that results in an **anxiety disorder**. Two types of anxiety disorders that interfere with success in school are test anxiety and math anxiety (see Box 8.2).

Prevalence of Depression and Anxiety

In Figure 8.5 you saw that depression and anxiety are two of the most common emotional disorders. In a given year, an astounding 8% of U.S. adolescents may have a major depressive episode and 11% have experienced severe depression at some point in their lives (Avenevoli, Swendsen, He, Burstein, & Merikangas, 2015). The rates for severe anxiety are similar. More youth may have milder cases or go undiagnosed. Schools commit substantial resources to reducing substance use and behavior problems, yet very little to the more prevalent depression and anxiety (Photo 8.5).

The median age for onset of depression is 11, meaning that depression develops in half of children at younger ages (Merikangas et al., 2010). Depression is rare among infants, but more common among preschoolers. As children enter school and grow into the teens, the prevalence of depression increases, peaking around 15 to 17 years, and then decreases (Gutman & Eccles, 2007). Thus, teachers in secondary schools are more likely to observe depression in their students, but teachers in preschools should be attuned to it because the earlier the intervention the better (Luby, 2010).

Anxiety disorders emerge earlier; the median age at onset is 6 (Merikangas et al., 2010). As many as one-third of children are anxious in kindergarten, but will gradually overcome it by the end of elementary school (Duchesne, Larose, Vitaro, & Tremblay, 2010). Unfortunately, a sizable percentage of children do not overcome it. Because they are among the most common childhood disorders, some of your students are likely to have anxiety disorders.

Antecedents and Consequences of Depression and Anxiety

Depression and anxiety co-occur partly because they have overlapping causes. Both are disorders of emotion regulation. Children with these internalizing disorders feel less happiness and more sadness, anger, and worry than other children. They have trouble up-regulating positive emotions and down-regulating negative emotions and may not be able to flexibly use different coping strategies (Bonanno & Burton, 2013; Gross & Jazaieri, 2014). So it won't surprise you that the same factors that

BOX 8.2 challenges in development

Test and Math Anxiety

Stefanie, a 10th-grader, has been a self-described wor-rywart since preschool. She is chronically anxious about a lot of things, but especially about doing well in school. She gets so nervous before a test, worrying that she will fail it, that she gets physically sick. She has poor test scores, but earns adequate grades because she does her homework and extra assignments.

Test anxiety is a negative emotional reaction toward test situations. It is rare in the primary grades, rises from 3rd to 5th grade, stabilizes through adolescence, and drops in college (Hembree, 1988). Some psychologists believe this age trend indicates it is learned, rather than innate.

Why Does It Matter if Children Are Test-Anxious? Test anxiety is linked to reduced test scores as early as 3rd grade, and the linkage becomes stronger with age (Fer-rando, Varea, & Lorenzo, 1998). Anyone might feel anxi-ety during a test, but test-anxious learners like Stefanie engage in so much worry that it consumes much of their working memory, leaving less space for processing test items (Beilock & Carr, 2005). This "choking under pres-sure" probably results from cortisol, the stress hormone. A little cortisol enhances executive functioning and working memory (see Chapter 4), but too much reduces capacity (Blair, Granger, & Razza, 2005). Test anxiety is not a lack of ability, but difficulty in trying to show ability. This is impor-tant to understand because teachers form expectations about learners' abilities based on test scores, and teacher expectations can affect learner performance. It is clear that for some learners, test anxiety is not merely a lack of ability because, when test anxiety is reduced through intervention, test scores increase (Lang & Lang, 2010).

What Can Be Done about Test Anxiety? You help your test-anxious students when you have reasonable expecta-tions and reasonable tests and do the following:

1. Help learners reappraise their feelings of anxiety as something positive. A little anxiety can help focus attention and improve performance.
2. Help learners experience academic success. Anxiety is linked to repeated failure in exams.
3. Improve the testing situation. Test-anxious learners will perform better if you give low-stress instructions, give cues to trigger recall, have

minimal distractions, and have more-frequent tests so that each test counts for less.
4. Provide training for test-taking skills.
5. Avoid drawing attention to poor performance, and de-emphasize grades. Anxiety is linked to emphasis on competition or social comparison and standards that are based on how other learners perform (i.e., grading on the "curve").
6. Avoid attributing success or failure to the student's innate ability.
7. Avoid time limits during testing. Timed tests promote anxiety.

The school counselor may suggest additional inter-ventions. One common therapy helps learners change worrisome thoughts. For example, a learner might be worried about failing an exam, and thereby failing school, and never being able to find a job. The counselor might counter this by asking, "What is the *worst* possible thing that might happen if you fail this exam?" The learner might have to take the class over again—which does not doom anyone to a life of unemployment. This approach has a large effect, when combined with teaching study or test-taking skills (Tuncay, 2003). There are other effective treatments, like writing about test worries prior to taking a test, which may help learners "set aside" their worries during the test (Ramirez & Beilock, 2011).

How did Stefanie survive her test anxiety? Her con-cerned teachers sent her to talk to the school counselor, who asked her "What is the *worst* possible ... ?" She re-alized that failing an exam would not ruin her life. She learned to cope with her anxiety, and is now a teacher who is very sensitive about her own students' test anxiety. She does not give surprise tests, and instead of using the "test" word, she tells her students, "show me what you know."

Math anxiety is related to test anxiety. It is a nega-tive emotional reaction to math. Despite normal thinking abilities in other domains, learners with math anxiety tend to perform poorly on math tests. They also tend to avoid math classes and learn less in math classes they do take (Maloney & Beilock, 2012).

Math anxiety can be caused by deficits in basic foun-dational math skills, which results in falling further behind as learners progress through more advanced classes, which causes increasing anxiety. Math anxiety can also be learned from teachers and parents. In one study, if 1st

Test and Math Anxiety (continued)

and 2nd graders had math-anxious parents who helped them with math homework, the children became more math anxious over time. Parents managed to convey their anxiety even though the math the parents were helping with was just adding and subtracting numbers under 20 (Maloney, Ramirez, Gunderson, Levine, & Beilock, 2015).

Interventions for math anxiety include some of the same interventions as test anxiety: boost basic skills,

teach reappraisal coping strategies, and write about math worries (Maloney & Beilock, 2012). Teach that anxiety is not always bad. Figure 8.6 shows that moderate amounts of anxiety can focus attention and be motivating for some children (Wang et al., 2015). Severe cases may involve psychotherapy to help learners understand their emotions, frame the problem realistically, and face their fear through progressive exposure to math.

FIGURE 8.6 **Mathematics Anxiety and Performance.**

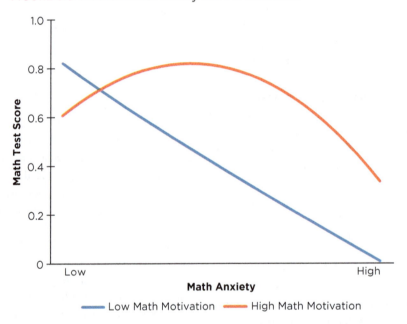

This figure conveys the "inverted U law," which is that moderate amounts of anxiety are beneficial for most students. Which groups of students does this law pertain to? How would you describe the correlation between anxiety and performance for the other group? Learners were ages 9 to 15. Motivation refers to beliefs that math is valuable and interesting. *Source: Wang et al. (2015).*

predict poor emotion regulation (discussed earlier) are risk factors for depression and anxiety—parents who are negative, do not accept children's emotions, and do not coach children on how to cope with their emotions (Katz & Hunter, 2007; Stocker et al., 2007). Additional important risk factors are given in Table 8.2.

The first risk factor is one of the most common antecedents (Hammen, 2009). Dozens of studies have found that insecure attachment predicts anxiety and depression from infancy to adulthood (Madigan, Atkinson, Laurin, & Benoit, 2013; Madigan, Brumariu, Villani, Atkinson, & Lyons-Ruth, 2015). This is thought to occur for at least two reasons: (1) children who do not believe their caretakers are available and protective feel chronic anxiety, and (2) insensitive caretakers do not help children learn to regulate their emotions (Kerns & Brumariu, 2014). Insecure children are three times as likely to have internalizing disorders. However, the effect

TABLE 8.2 Antecedents of depression and anxiety

Antecedent	Depression	Anxiety
Insecure attachment, particularly avoidant or disorganized	X	X
Chronic stress, particularly stress within relationships in the family or rejection by peers	X	X
Parental criticism and overreaction to the child's failures	X	X
Having a parent with depression or anxiety, which may affect children through emotion contagion and lower-quality parenting. (Having a depressed parent doubles or quadruples the risk of a child's becoming depressed.)	X	X
Family problems, such as conflict, lack of closeness, harsh discipline, and disregard for the child's view	X	
Pessimistic explanation style, such as "I got lucky" rather than "I am smart" to explain a good grade or "I am unlikable" rather than "she is unfriendly" to explain a classmate's snub	X	
Low self-esteem	X	
Negative life events, such as death or divorce in the family	X	
Feeling helpless to do anything about negative events	X	X
Having close friends who are depressed, because friends co-ruminate and rehash or dwell on problems together	X	X
Using poor coping strategies, such as thinking over and over again about negative events, or listening to music in order to avoid dealing with the situation	X	X
Genetic propensity toward temperament of negative emotionality	X	X
Extreme behavioral inhibition; shy nonsociability		X

Note: Each of these factors is well documented in research. Just a few studies are listed here (e.g., Buss & McDaniel, 2016; Duchesne et al., 2010; Feng et al., 2009; Gotlib, Joormann, & Foland-Ross, 2014; Hammen, 2009; Laurent, 2014; Milan, Snow, & Belay, 2009; Miranda, Gaudreau, & Morizot, 2010; Schwartz-Mette & Rose, 2012; Van Zalk, Kerr, Branje, Stattin, & Meeus, 2010).

size is modest and many children with insensitive parenting will not become depressed. Thus, is it only one risk factor.

Children with multiple risk factors are more likely to become depressed or anxious than children with a single risk factor. Risk factors may accumulate (see Chapter 1). For example, intrusive, overcontrolling, and emotionally overinvolved parenting leads to insecure attachment in toddlerhood, which leads to a negative internal working model of the self, resulting in helpless responses to challenges, that when combined with negative life events leads to depression in adolescence (Morley & Moran, 2011).

Depression and anxiety may share an underlying genetic propensity (Rhee et al., 2015). In fact, prominent researchers argue that "from a genetic perspective they are the same disorder" (Plomin, DeFries, Knopik, & Neiderhiser, 2016, p. 7). Genes may make some children more vulnerable to the effects of negative parenting or life stress. However, *genes alone probably do not cause internalizing disorders* (Haeffel et al., 2008; Monroe & Reid, 2008). Recall what you learned in Chapters 1 and 6 about how genes and environments work together. For example, anxious parents tend to be overprotective toward anxious children (Narusyte et al., 2008). Right now you are thinking, "Ah ha! A classic gene–environment correlation." Good thinking! In addition, studies find that infants and preschoolers with genetic predisposition may become emotionally negative only if they also have depressed, unresponsive, or unhappily married parents (e.g., Hayden et al., 2010; Natsuaki et al., 2010). In contrast, children with high-risk genes may be especially *low* in internalizing disorders if their parents are happy, which suggests *differential susceptibility*. In addition, research shows that quality of parenting affects methylation of genes, altering how they function, which suggests an *epigenetic effect* (Dadds, Moul, Hawes, Mendoza Diaz, & Brennan, 2015).

What are the consequences of depression and anxiety for children? Unhappiness and distress are serious enough consequences, but in addition, these disorders are linked to other disorders, such as ADHD, learning disorders, and, mostly in teens, eating disorders (Rhee et al., 2015). Depressed learners, particularly boys, may also be angry and act out. Depression and anxiety are also linked to illness, school absence, low academic achievement, inability to pay attention, slow mental processing, unpopularity as a friend or play or work partner, loneliness, and drug abuse.[2] Not all depressed or anxious learners will have these problems; many recover before these problems develop. Those who use good coping strategies, like exercise or going to a movie with friends (depression), or relaxation (anxiety), rather than dangerous escapist strategies, like alcohol abuse, are more likely to recover. However, intervention may be needed. School-based interventions will be discussed later.

8-2f Group Diversity in Emotion Regulation

Research suggests there are gender, socioeconomic status (SES), and ethnic differences in emotion regulation. In addition, immigration and culture influence emotion regulation. Let's look at gender differences first.

Gender

As early as infancy, girls are more skilled at regulating emotions. In one study, 6-month-old boys showed anger, cried, or turned away more than girls when their mothers were unresponsive to them (Weinberg, Tronick, Cohn, & Olson, 1999). In the primary grades, girls are better at emotional dissemblance—appearing happy when they are not. Girls also smile more than boys, which helps regulate emotions and keep interactions pleasant (Saarni, 1999).

Paradoxically, despite better emotion regulation, girls are more likely than boys to be anxious. They are also twice as likely to be depressed (Hammen, 2009). This gender difference is not apparent in early childhood, but emerges by 7th grade and becomes dramatic by midadolescence. Why might girls be more depressed than

---

[2] Many studies have demonstrated these effects, just a few of which are listed here: Duchesne, Larose, Vitaro, and Tremblay (2010); Foersterling and Binser (2002); Kochel, Ladd, and Rudolph (2012); Pomerantz and Rudolph (2003); Verboom, Sijtsema, Verhulst, Penninx, and Ormel (2014); and Van Zalk et al. (2010).

boys? Research supports two possibilities: (1) they have more relationship stress, and (2) they cope in ways that result in depression (Hamilton, Stange, Abramson, & Alloy, 2014). In one study, 8th- and 10th-graders reported the worst thing that had happened that day. Girls reported interpersonal events, like a fight with a friend, whereas boys' reported school-related events, like an F on a quiz or losing a football game (Hanish & Guerra, 2000). Adolescent girls are more likely than boys to have both negative and positive interactions with family and friends (Flook, 2011). Girls for whom the balance tips toward more negative events are at risk for depression.

Girls are more likely to cope by ruminating, or thinking about the situation and their feelings over and over (Smith & Rose, 2011). Ruminating can lead to depression. Girls are also more likely to use *emotion-focused strategies* (Seiffge-Krenke et al., 2009). This is a drawback in situations in which *problem-focused strategies* are more helpful, like studying more after getting a bad grade.

Socioeconomic Status

Low-SES learners tend to be less able to regulate their emotions than middle-SES learners, although the differences are small. Learners living in poverty have more distress to cope with, often have new stressors emerge before they have had time to cope with existing ones, and have fewer supportive people to help them cope (Zimmer-Gembeck & Skinner, 2008). Among low-SES learners, those whose parents provide the positive experiences discussed earlier—secure attachment, positive emotions in the home, discussions about emotions, coaching, appropriate responses to emotion, and effective discipline—develop good regulation despite their economic disadvantage (Raver, 2004).

Ethnicity

A national U.S. study found that Black learners are more likely to have anxiety disorders and Latino learners are more likely to have depression as compared with White learners (Merikangas et al., 2010). Immigrant youth, who must accommodate multiple cultures, might be expected to have more mental health issues, but on average they have similar or better mental health and school behavior than their nonimmigrant peers (Morris, Chiu , & Liu 2015). Two factors are linked to whether immigrants become depressed: family and acculturation. Like other youth, immigrant youths' primary source of stress is within the family. If they have dysfunctional families, they are at higher risk of depression (Flook & Fuligni, 2008). Immigrant youth have additional sources of stress: severed relationships from their heritage country, the struggle to speak English at school, and hearing derogatory ethnic jokes (Romero & Roberts, 2003).

Acculturation refers to adaptation to a new culture. Children can adapt in different ways; they can maintain their heritage culture while adopting the new culture (biculturalism), or they can reject one or both cultures. Immigrant youth are less likely to be depressed if they become bicultural. Bicultural youth tend to be more extraverted and open to new experiences (Ryder, Alden, & Paulhus, 2000). In Chapter 12 you will learn that children who maintain their heritage language *and* learn English fare well. Thus, helping your immigrant learners maintain their heritage culture may foster their well-being if they are also open to their new culture.

A group that must also adapt to new cultures in ways you may not be aware of are military-connected children. Box 8.3 discusses the special needs of these children and what you can do to help them.

acculturation
the long-term process of adapting to a new culture.

BOX 8.3 challenges in development

Military-Connected Children

At a school concert in which the students sang Ave Maria, one young girl burst into tears. Her teacher guided her off the stage and comforted her. Through the tears the teacher learned that the song had been sung at her father's funeral and that this girl was a "Gold Star" child. This term refers to a child whose parent was killed in action.

As Second Lady of the United States, Jill Biden's crusade has been to get educators to do more for military-connected children (Biden, 2016). Children whose parents are active duty, veterans, or reservists have special challenges to cope with, including: (1) missing a deployed parent for months or years, (2) fear for the safety of the parent, (3) taking on adult responsibilities while a parent is gone, (4) re-integrating the family after deployment, and (5) coping with a physically or psychologically traumatized parent who survives or with a parent's death. In addition, military-connected children change schools frequently, on average moving nine times before high school graduation (Astor et al., 2012). In one study, military youth reported feeling significant stress about moving to a new school, trying to maintain past friendships and make new ones, and feeling lost in class because they hadn't covered the same content (Bradshaw, Sudhinaraset, Mmari, & Blum, 2010). Nonmilitary families face some of these same challenges (e.g., police officers face injury, homeless families move often), but generally not to the same extent.

How can you help military-connected children facing these challenges? Try the following approaches:

- Build on their strengths. For example, you are likely to find they are mature for their age as a result of taking on adult responsibilities during a parent's deployment (Bradshaw et al., 2010). You might use their maturity in special roles as classroom helpers. You might also draw upon their experience having lived in other countries to enhance your lessons.
- Honor the many layers of sacrifice their families have made to defend others. Some schools have a "hero wall" with pictures of deployed parents. Recognize

the values of honor, courage, loyalty, and integrity in military culture. Refrain from stating your opinion about the merit of a particular operation.
- Recognize that children and parents are crossing cultural boundaries between military and civilian communities (e.g., differences in language, in clarity of chain of command and social status, or emphases on individuality vs. teamwork).
- Be prepared to support children who may have internalizing or externalizing disorders linked to parent stress. You will learn how to do this in this chapter and in Chapter 10.
- Be patient with the parent "left behind" who may become less involved in school when a deployed parent leaves. Communicate with the deployed parent using technology (e.g., Skype, Facebook).
- Facilitate transitions for newly arriving students. For example, assign a "tour guide" and buddy to help the new students feel comfortable. Make transferring credits and curriculum as smooth as possible. Help the students join extracurricular activities, even if they moved in after the "try outs."
- Facilitate transitions for departing students. For example, send them with a portfolio and letter to their new teacher explaining what the student knows or can do, so the student doesn't lose momentum in the new class.

The Department of Defense operates schools in various parts of the world for a small percentage of military-connected students (most are in regular civilian schools). In DoD schools, despite very high turnover and a large percentage of minority students, there is comparatively high achievement and a smaller achievement gap, partly because these approaches are taken (Astor et al., 2012).

Your school can be a safe haven for military-connected children. As their teacher, you are an important factor in how they adjust to a new school (Esqueda, Astor, & De Pedro, 2012).

8-2g Classroom Implications of Emotion Regulation

Emotion regulation skills influence learners' success in your classroom. Learners who are able to regulate their emotions will tend to be happier, better liked, and better able to pay attention and learn. This may be why some interventions that reduce learners' emotional distress also *raise their grades and test scores significantly* (Durlak, Weissberg, Dymnicki, Taylor, & Schellinger, 2011).

You have learned that negativity in the home predicts poor emotion regulation in children. There is a spillover effect to school. Learners who experience negativity at home tend to feel distress at school and have behavior problems, such as skipping class, failing a quiz, or not doing homework (Timmons & Margolin, 2015). (If you recognized this spillover effect as part of the mesosystem in the bioecological model, you have been paying attention!) The more learners feel such daily stressors, at school or home, the lower their GPA becomes over the years (Flook & Fuligni, 2008). You cannot control the emotional climate of your students' homes, but there are four ways you can help your students develop good emotion regulation in your classroom: (1) talk about emotions, (2) be sensitive to learner's emotions, (3) directly teach emotion regulation, and (4) create a positive classroom.

Talk About Emotions

Seize opportunities to talk about emotions. Help students label, describe, and understand the emotions they experience. Mrs. Ng talked with Hailey about how Evan was *surprised* and *angry* with her, and that Hailey should feel *guilt*. This is especially important for some special education students and very young children who have trouble identifying emotions in themselves or others.

You can also create opportunities to talk about emotions through curriculum. For example, in one experiment 5th- and 6th-grade teachers asked "feeling questions" (e.g., "how would you feel if …") rather than just critical thinking questions as they taught literature. Their students, compared to a control group, learned the content better, were more motivated to learn, were more supportive of one another, felt the classroom was a friendlier place, and decreased fourfold in off-task or aggressive behavior (Shechtman & Yaman, 2012).

Be Sensitive to Learners' Emotions

You can tell whether your students have good emotion regulation or not as you become more sensitive to their emotions. Use these guidelines:

1. Notice whether each student is emotionally positive or negative most of the time. Well-regulated learners should be predominantly positive, and only occasionally negative. Chronic negativity or exaggerated moodiness is not normal, even among 2-year-olds and teenagers.

2. Notice whether each of your students has age-appropriate emotion regulation (review the Age Trends section). Hailey does not have age-appropriate abilities, but Shonese does.

3. Be aware of emotional disorders, especially internalizing disorders like depression and anxiety. Although they are more common in girls, do not overlook them in boys. Notify a counselor if you suspect an emotional disorder. The sooner they are detected the better, because treatment is more successful with young children.

4. Be aware of dissemblance, or emotions that learners may be hiding.

Dissemblance can be positive if done out of kindness, as in the story of Daniel. However, it can also lead to misunderstanding. For example, when you discipline students, some who do *not* show regret or embarrassment may actually feel these emotions, and some who *do* show these emotions may actually be faking to appease you. Learners may pretend they are not distressed by something that they actually

think
about this

In a 9th-grade class, the teacher says, "Sangita, you were talking! I'm taking a point off your assignment." Actually, Sangita was not talking; she is wrongfully accused. Sangita becomes angry. She does not defend herself because her heritage culture dictates that children do not argue with teachers. However, she silently smolders with thoughts of how unfair it is, how the teacher doesn't like her, how she will tell her friends about it at lunch, and so on. Sangita does not hear the rest of the lesson. What coping strategy is Sangita using? How does it affect her executive functions (see Chapter 4)? What discipline strategy might have been more effective (see Chapter 7)?

find quite distressing. Dissemblance ability is well developed by 4th or 5th grade, but even younger learners can hide distress from you. Let's look in a preschool:

> *A girl was bullied by a boy and bit him in self-defense. She had never hurt another child before and was deeply distressed. However, she did not let her teacher see how upset she was. The teacher phoned her mother and said, "she's dealing with it just fine." However, a few hours later when her mother entered the classroom at the end of the school day to take her home, she burst into tears.*

This traumatized little child had been holding back tears for two hours. Learners are more likely to dissemble with an authority figure, like a teacher (Saarni, 1999). However, parents are not always aware of children's emotions either. It is common for divorcing parents to think their children are coping well because they are not acting out and are relatively compliant. In reality, the children may feel depressed or blame themselves for the divorce, but may feel too vulnerable to show these feelings.

Scaffold and Teach Emotion Regulation

Infants and toddlers may need your help to regulate their emotions when they cry intensely. How can you calm an infant? One of the most effective methods is to carry the infant while you walk (Esposito et al., 2013). (This also works with mice pups, in case you need to know.) Try these other age-old remedies: (1) snuggly swaddle them with arms at the side, the legs flexed, and no head covering; (2) hold them on their side, so their startle reflex is not triggered; (3) shush loudly; (4) sway, rock, or jiggle gently while providing head support; and (5) give them something to suck. In one experiment, infants calmed much faster after getting immunizations when doctors used these techniques (Harrington et al., 2012).

How should you handle a toddler's tantrum? Remember that tantrums are intense sadness with peaks of anger. Do nothing (unless the child is in danger) until the peaks of anger abate and mere sadness is left. Sad children seek comfort. However, if you try to comfort or reason with the child during an anger peak, you will prolong the anger.

You can help your older students develop emotion regulation by directly teaching coping strategies and by responding appropriately to their emotions. Draw upon the more constructive strategies in Table 8.1. Reappraisal is one of the best strategies for many situations and can be taught to children as young as 5 (Davison & Birch, 2002). Remember how Mrs. Ng taught Hailey effective ways of coping with anger—distract yourself with a walk to the bathroom and a drink of water. Mrs. Ng also taught Hailey that anger must be contained and not allowed to disrupt other activity in the classroom. Imagine if, instead, Mrs. Ng had scolded, "I'm giving you a demerit!" or sent her to the office. By taking this action, Mrs. Ng would have modeled escalation in angry encounters. She would not have taught Hailey effective ways of coping with anger.

Similarly, in an 8th-grade English class, a teacher helped Raj cope with anxiety about giving a book report in front of his classmates. She told Raj to take slow, deep breaths:

> *During his report Raj pushed and pulled at his shirt sleeves, dragged his hand through his hair, rocked back and forth, and averted his gaze. At one point he tried to control his anxiety by taking slow deep breaths and closing his eyes until he regained his composure and could carry on.*

In this case Raj, who is older than Hailey, was generating his own coping strategies, like rocking and closing his eyes. However, he still needed a little help from his teacher. Her advice to take slow, deep breaths helped him. Help your students identify their coping strategies, and then encourage them to adopt more constructive strategies if needed.

Create a Positive Classroom Climate

A positive classroom atmosphere helps students feel safe communicating their real feelings. Positive emotions also help reenergize self-control when students' self-control is spent (Baumeister, Vohs, & Tice, 2007). Furthermore, positive emotions promote creative problem solving and, for some tasks, analytic thought. Thus, if you induce positive emotions in your students you may help improve their learning (Photo 8.6). Studies have found that 5th- and 6th-graders who felt emotionally supported in a positive classroom were more engaged in class and earned higher grades and test scores (Pianta, Belsky, Vandergrift, Houts, & Morrison, 2008; Reyes, Brackett, Rivers, White, & Salovey, 2012).

You may think that creating a positive classroom climate would be easy in early childhood, but challenging in secondary classrooms. However, in six large studies of early childhood classrooms, teachers' emotional support was about a 5 on a scale of 1 to 7. A score of "7" meant that there was a positive classroom climate, that is, teachers and children had good relationships, enjoyed being together, and seldom were negative with each other. Thus, while classrooms typically were fairly positive, there was also plenty of room for improvement (Hamre, 2014). To create a positive climate with any age group, use the following guidelines:

PHOTO 8.6 Learners have higher achievement in positive classrooms.

1. Express positive emotions. Students need to see adults express a wide range of emotions, but positive emotions more often than negative. Students may learn less from teachers who feel depressed (McLean & Connor, 2015). Wise teachers sometimes act happy even if they don't feel happy, and often their dissemblance improves their mood. Listen to one 1st-grade teacher:

> *During recess Tim complains that Kurt won't let him have a ball. I see that Kurt is carrying two balls. He is not playing with them, but keeping them from other children. My spirits sink. I know from past experience that Kurt will defy my authority. As I head for the showdown, I decide to force myself to feel happy. I smile at Kurt (as genuinely as I can) and ask him to give one of the balls to Tim. Kurt begins to resist, but I keep smiling. Surprisingly, I do not feel angry. Kurt hands Tim a ball. I smile more broadly and say, "That was a nice thing to do!" Amazingly, Kurt smiles back.*

2. Use effective, positive discipline. In Chapter 7 you learned that ineffective discipline harms relationships and makes students angry.

3. Establish secure teacher–student relationships. In Chapter 6 you learned how to do this by sensitively supporting students. Classroom climate is affected by teacher–student

relationships and how much a teacher enjoys students. A close teacher–student relationship protects children from negative parenting, whereas students who have a negative relationship with both parents and teachers (i.e., risk accumulates) are most likely to become depressed and delinquent (Wang, Brinkworth, & Eccles, 2013).

4. Have fun in your classroom. Positive emotions strong enough to affect thinking are remarkably easy to induce. In research, brief interventions as simple as giving participants an unexpected reward results in faster learning during laboratory experiments. Applying this to your classroom, you can induce positive emotions when you celebrate learners achieving a goal or succeeding on a difficult task. Occasionally, reward learners unexpectedly for good effort. (However, keep in mind that when rewards are routine, they no longer induce positive emotions.) Share happy stories or jokes with learners, as Mr. Pugh did in his 6th-grade science class on electricity:

> *The students were out of their seats, excitedly using the Van de Graaf machine and balloons to make their hair stand on end. When one boy began jumping up and down, begging to be next to perform the experiment, Mr. Pugh said he was already too "charged" up. The boy and his classmates laughed. The classroom climate was fun and engrossing. The children were also learning—when asked why their hair was standing up, they could explain static electricity.*

Games that make students think fast can be fun and energizing. Thinking fast is linked to better moods (Pronin & Jacobs, 2008). This may be why fast, upbeat music sometimes has positive effects on test performance in the moment, although not all studies find this "Mozart effect" (e.g., Schellenberg, 2005).

We have discussed what you can do to promote emotion regulation in typical learners. Next let's focus on how you might help learners with depression and anxiety.

Helping Depressed Students

Depressed students tend to have lower achievement than you would expect based on their intelligence. Schools can make a difference in rates of depression; a large national study found that which school an adolescent attended predicted whether the learner was depressed or not, beyond other factors (Dunn, Milliren, Evans, Subramanian, & Richmond, 2015). You can help your depressed students develop good emotion regulation and coping strategies just as you would any student, using the approaches discussed in the previous section. You will also minimize depression when you:

1. Help learners feel more capable. Teach skills and provide realistic goals. Striving for unrealistic goals makes learners feel less capable.

2. Help learners reappraise situations. Challenge their pessimistic thoughts and suggest more optimistic thoughts; help them see the silver lining. Attribute their failure and success to effort, not innate ability, like "You got that B because you worked hard" rather than "because you are smart." Learners who can explain, and control, their successes feel less depressed.

3. Help learners find an activity to lift the depressed mood, such as an activity at which the student is good or enjoys. Also consider pleasant music, a funny book, or exercise. Youth who are physically active are less likely to be depressed or anxious (Monshouwer, ten Have, van Poppel, Kemper, & Vollebergh, 2013).

Teachers are not therapists; you should rely on school counselors for help with learners who are at high risk for depression. The counselor may implement school-based interventions that research suggests are effective (Muñoz, Beardslee, & Leykin, 2012). These are programs designed to teach coping strategies and optimistic thinking. Some depressed learners may need professional interventions. Medication is a possibility, but has serious side effects; some medications have been linked to a risk of suicide. For this reason, experts recommend psychotherapy first, which often involves training parents to use the same techniques you have learned about in this chapter (Dougherty et al., 2015; Weisz, McCarty, & Valeri, 2006). Some psychologists advocate mindfulness training (e.g., meditation, yoga), but there is not yet enough research to know whether this is effective for children (Arkowitz & Lilienfeld, 2014; Greenberg & Harris, 2012).

Helping Anxious Students

Just as with depression, you can help your anxious students develop good emotion regulation and coping strategies using the approaches discussed in the previous section. You will also minimize anxiety when you provide a predictable classroom and give learners as much control over activities as possible. The most important part of a predictable classroom is a teacher who is consistent and responsive. When teachers are responsive, rather than critical or detached, learners are more positive and less anxious (Hestenes, Kontos, & Bryan, 1993).

You can also reduce anxiety by minimizing daily hassles at school. These are small stressors—such as hearing teachers yell at other learners, getting low grades for trivial errors, or having to sit still for too long. Daily hassles can also be time related, such as not having enough time to eat lunch, get from class to class, or play at recess. A group of honors students said their single biggest concern about starting high school was getting to class on time. This may seem trivial to you, but it caused anxiety in these 14-year-olds because the school was large, and they had only five minutes between classes. See Box 8.2 for suggestions on how to reduce test and math anxiety.

In summary, you have learned that emotions are present from birth and serve important functions. Yet, emotions must be regulated. Learners who are better at regulation tend to be liked by others and academically successful; learners who are poor at regulation sometimes develop emotional disorders that interfere with classroom learning. However, regulating their own emotions is half of learners' emotional competence. They must also learn to read others' emotions.

8-3 Understanding Others' Emotions

Shaunt'a (pronounced "Shawn-tae") has recently moved to a new high school. She is quiet and has few friends. In French class, a boy makes fun of her clothes. Shaunt'a acts as though she doesn't hear. However, another classmate, Dirk, knows she hears. Dirk says that he likes Shaunt'a's clothes, which silences the other boy. Dirk then tries to make Shaunt'a more comfortable by talking with her about whether she is going to try out for show choir.

Dirk understood how Shaunt'a felt. The ability to accurately perceive another person's emotions is called **affective perspective-taking**. Affective perspective-taking is an

affective perspective-taking perceiving the emotions of another person.

important part of emotional competence because it influences success in social settings, including classrooms. However, as with any ability, it can be put to good or bad use. The con artist may read others' emotions well but does not share their feelings. When affective perspective-taking includes sharing others' feelings, we call it **empathy**.

When learners have empathy for another person, they may respond in one of three ways:

1. **Sympathy** is feeling concern for the *other's* feelings.

2. **Personal distress** is a negative emotional reaction to someone else's distress where learners focus on *their own* feelings. While Dirk felt sympathy for Shaunt'a, other classmates felt so uncomfortable in the situation that they focused on their own distress and moved away from Shaunt'a.

3. **Empathic distress** is feeling distressed *along with* another person.

These distinctions are important because they have different results. Empathic distress may lead to deeper friendships (Smith & Rose, 2011). Sympathy may lead to helping the person in distress, as Dirk did. In contrast, personal distress may lead to a desire to relieve one's own distress. Learners might help a distressed person in order to alleviate their own distress, but they are more likely to try to avoid the distressed person, as other classmates did with Shaunt'a (Losoya & Eisenberg, 2000). Affective perspective-taking is related to two other important concepts: emotion contagion and social referencing. **Emotion contagion** occurs when the emotion of one person causes a similar emotion in another person. For example, a teenage girl laughed heartily over a joke that her friends thought was lame, but they began laughing too because her mirth was contagious. This mimicking of others' emotions is unintentional and actually changes the emotion you feel.

Social referencing refers to reading another person's emotional expression to decide how you should respond. For example, a 4-year-old boy looked at his teacher's face before approaching a dog. The teacher smiled, so the child petted the dog. If the teacher had looked worried, the child would have backed away. *Social referencing is especially influential in ambiguous situations*, in which the child is not sure what to do or feel. Social referencing provides children with information about a situation, including what emotions are appropriate in that situation.

An interesting apparatus often used to study social referencing in infants is the visual cliff (see Figure 8.7), which is a platform with an abrupt drop-off. Crawling infants are placed on the platform, but typically refuse to cross the cliff because they think they might fall. (Plexiglas covers the deep end, so that infants cannot actually fall off.) The cliff can be

empathy
an emotional state similar to what another person is feeling that results from perceiving the other's emotions.

sympathy
an emotional response that consists of feeling concern for a distressed other.

personal distress
a self-focused, aversive emotional reaction to someone else's negative emotion.

empathic distress
a self- and other-focused experience of taking on a friend's distress and experiencing it as one's own.

emotion contagion
the emotions of one person, through facial, vocal, or gestural cues, generate a similar emotion in another person.

social referencing
children read another's emotional expression to determine how they should respond in an ambiguous situation.

 **brain research**

Mirror Neurons

How does emotion contagion work? One theory is that some (meaning millions, not just a few) neurons respond the same whether you personally do something or watch someone else do it—so scientists call them mirror neurons. For example, mirror neurons respond the same way when you laugh or you watch someone else laugh (Iacoboni, 2009). This helps you bond with other people. Mirror neurons may also be involved in reading others' thoughts (see Chapter 9) and in false memories (see Chapter 4). False memories may be formed by either imagining yourself doing something, or watching someone else do it. For example, in one study people watched someone else shake a bottle of chocolate milk; then two weeks later misremembered themselves shaking the bottle (Lindner, Echterhoff, Davidson, & Brand, 2010). Your brain simulates the real experience. Fortunately this doesn't always happen, and most neurons are not mirror neurons, or you would have few accurate memories. Scientists are working to understand mirror neurons better.

FIGURE 8.7 **The Visual Cliff.**

The baby is hesitating about crawling over the drop-off and is reading the emotional signal from a parent about whether it is OK to continue. In what situations have you seen children exhibit social referencing?

raised so there is only a short drop-off, making it ambiguous to infants whether it is safe to cross or not. In a classic study, mothers were asked to stand at the far end of the cliff and express joy or fear. If mothers expressed joy, most (75%) infants crossed the cliff. If mothers expressed fear, none of the infants crossed the cliff. This experiment demonstrates social referencing because the infants were directly influenced by their mothers' emotion expressions (Sorce, Emde, Campos, & Klinnert, 1985).

8-3a Age Trends in Understanding Others' Emotions

Empathy, emotion contagion, and social referencing are present in children at all ages, but they change as childhood progresses. Let's look at this development next.

Infancy and Toddlerhood (Birth to 2 Years)

Emotion contagion is present at birth. Infants' brains respond to emotion expressions in ways similar to adult brains (Leppanen, Moulson, Vogel-Farley, & Nelson, 2007).

FIGURE 8.8 **Emotion Imitation.**

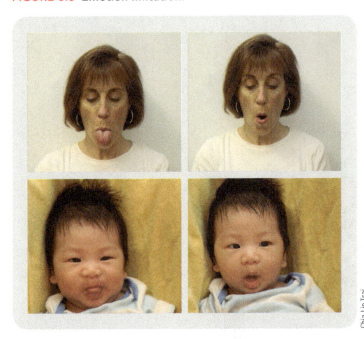

Within the first days of life, infants can imitate the facial expressions of others. *Source: Meltzoff and Moore (1977).*

Infants pay particular attention to expressions in the eye region. Within the first days of life, infants can imitate the facial expression of others. Happy expressions particularly capture attention, presumably because they grease the wheels of social interaction (Becker & Srinivasan, 2014).

Within the first months of life, infants can distinguish different emotions, like happiness or sadness, from your face, tone of voice, and body movement (Zieber, Kangas, Hock, & Bhatt, 2014). We know they are distinguishing emotions because they respond differently. For example, infants may look away or move their mouths (forms of self-soothing) if you look sad, or open their eyes wide and kick excitedly if you look happy (see Figure 8.8). We also know they are distinguishing emotions from habituation studies (see Chapter 5). Infants will look longer at unpleasant (angry, sad, fearful) faces after habituating to happy faces, but they don't distinguish between different unpleasant emotions. Not until toddlers begin to acquire words for "sad," "anger," and "fear" do they distinguish among unpleasant emotions (Lindquist et al., 2015).

Clearly, infants react to others' emotions, but do they understand what emotions mean? Social referencing suggests that they do (Egyed, Király, & Gergely, 2013). Social referencing emerges between 6 and 10 months of age. It increases over the next year, so that by 18 to 20 months old, toddlers are not likely to approach a stranger or a scary toy, like a smoking robot, until *after* they have a reassuring look from a parent, and they will not approach if the parent expresses fear. By 18 months, toddlers also show empathy as they attempt to comfort distressed others, such as hugging a crying sibling.

Early Childhood (3 to 5 Years)

Preschoolers often use social referencing to see if a joke is funny or if their behavior is acceptable. They can also deliberately ignore adults' emotional information if they convey disapproval for misbehavior that the child is enjoying.

As they learn to talk, preschoolers become better at understanding others' emotions because they can label and discuss emotions. They use more emotion labels with age. At age 2, most children correctly use the words *happy* and *sad.* Later they use *angry,* still later *scared* and *surprised,* and lastly labels for less common emotions, like *disgust.* By age 4, children can sort pictures of angry, sad, disgusted, and fearful pictures of faces into different boxes (Lindquist et al., 2015; Widen, 2013).

By age 3, most children talk about consequences and causes of emotions. For example, when one of our sons was almost 3, he said, "Mommy, if you tells peoples you love them, them happy!" By age 4, children know what emotions are typical of common situations, such as feeling happy if you get a treat (Bamford & Lagattuta, 2012). Understanding complex social emotions develops later. By age 5, but seldom younger, children understand that victims forgive others more if they express guilt, indicating they understand the social function of guilt (Vaish, Carpenter, & Tomasello, 2011).

Middle Childhood (6 to 12 Years)

Social referencing continues in middle childhood but occurs less often with age because children use social referencing primarily in ambiguous events, and fewer events are ambiguous for older children. Sixth-graders do not carefully watch their teachers' faces for emotional reactions as much as 1st-graders do, because they know more about which events make their teachers happy or angry.

By age 6, many children understand complex emotion labels like nervous, embarrassed, jealous, and miserable. However, during middle childhood they add variety, accuracy, and complexity to their talk about emotions. For example, a classmate teased 6th-grader Hector for getting a perfect score on his math test. Hector said, "I was *surprised* to find myself *embarrassed* about being a good student, but I knew he was just *jealous*." Hector's 6-year-old sister may know what these words mean, but she is not likely to use them with such skill. The ability to talk about emotions helps older children understand others' emotions better. (See Figure 8.9 for an essay on feelings by an elementary student.)

By age 5 children know that beliefs or memories can cause emotions (e.g., remembering a pet died) and that "positive thinking" in a bad situation can lead to happier emotions (e.g., she broke her arm and gets to have a cool cast that her friends can sign!). However, not until age 7 or older do they emphasize beliefs, rather than the situation, as causing emotions (Bamford & Lagattuta, 2012). Thus, not until middle childhood are they likely to use reappraisal to cope with negative emotions.

During middle childhood children become better at taking into account *multiple, even competing, emotions*. For example, most 12-year-olds can understand feeling both good and bad emotions after misspelling a familiar word during a spelling contest, but still winning a ribbon, while few 6-year-olds can (Larsen, To, & Fireman, 2007).

Adolescence (13 to 19 Years)

Both social referencing and emotion contagion continue in adolescence. Social referencing occurred on the day after Halloween when Mr. Murray barked at a student in his biology class, "Empty your bulging pockets and hand over the candy immediately!" The other students quickly looked at Mr. Murray. They noticed his eyes were twinkling and he was trying to repress a smile. They began smiling, and sharing their favorite candy with Mr. Murray.

You might expect adolescents and elementary-age children to be substantially more empathic than preschoolers because of their greater ability to read others' emotions. However, research does *not* clearly show they feel more strongly for someone in distress, and some studies even find a decrease in empathy with age (Hastings, Zahn-Waxler, Robinson, Usher, & Bridges, 2000; Zahn-Waxler, Kochanska, Krupnick, & McKnew, 1990). Perhaps this is because empathy competes with older children's growing self-protection. Take a peek in a 1st-grade classroom:

> *A boy is sent to the bathroom after wetting his pants in class. When he returns to the classroom, a girl loudly says, "That happened to me once." Several other children affirm that it has happened to them. The boy visibly relaxes at this empathic outpouring.*

What are the implications of emotion contagion for teens who listen to hostile, angry music? Should such media be allowed at school functions? What about soothing, or upbeat energizing music? Defend your conclusions drawing on research discussed in this chapter.

FIGURE 8.9 Essay on Feelings.

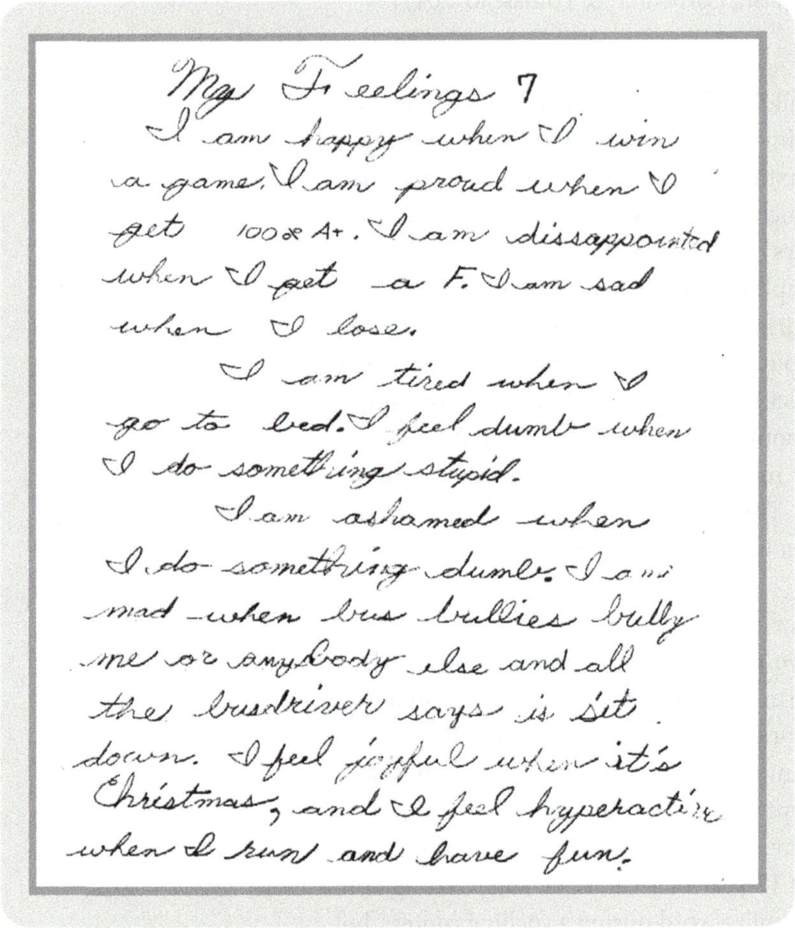

My Feelings 7

I am happy when I win a game. I am proud when I get 100% A+. I am disappointed when I get a F. I am sad when I lose.

I am tired when I go to bed. I feel dumb when I do something stupid.

I am ashamed when I do something dumb. I am mad when bus bullies bully me or anybody else and all the busdriver says is "Sit down." I feel joyful when it's Christmas, and I feel hyperactive when I run and have fun.

This is from the classroom journal of a 6th-grade boy. He is able to label a wide variety of emotions and readily link them to experiences. Would it surprise you to know that he is well liked by classmates?

David Bergin

Would 5th- or 10th-graders do the same when empathy competes with possible embarrassment? In Chapter 9 you will learn that adolescents can be self-centered in their moral judgments, and in Chapter 10 you will learn that adolescents can choose not to help others because they understand the cost of helping better than do younger children.

However, when adolescents choose to behave empathically, their greater knowledge helps them respond in more genuinely helpful ways than younger children. If they see a peer in distress, they can help solve the problem or help the peer cope by reappraising the situation. For example, a girl was distraught that she didn't get selected for the school play. A friend helped her see the advantages of not spending hours and hours in rehearsals with the cranky director. Adolescents' greater knowledge also helps them to empathize with the plight of unfortunate people in distant countries. They are able to intentionally imagine the feelings of others they cannot see. This is why some adolescents become zealous about compassionate causes, such as raising money for far-away victims of natural disasters.

8-3b Individual Diversity in Understanding Others' Emotions

Individual differences in the ability to read others' emotions remain fairly stable over time. That is, children who are especially good at reading emotions and being empathic at one age tend to be better than their peers at a later age (Losoya & Eisenberg, 2000). Dirk is likely to have been more empathic than average since he was a preschooler. This ability has important consequences for learners like Dirk.

What Does Understanding Others' Emotions Predict?

Learners who are good at labeling and reading others' emotions have higher academic achievement, have greater self-control, and are more cooperative (Izard et al., 2001). They are also sought out by peers (Fabes, Eisenberg, Hanish, & Spinrad, 2001). This is because they accurately interpret others' perspectives and easily establish rapport, as Dirk did with Shaunt'a. Dirk is well liked by both boys and girls, as well as teachers.

In contrast, learners who are poor at reading emotional cues are less liked by peers. They tend to be aggressive and have behavior problems in the classroom (Arsenio, Cooperman, & Lover, 2000; Coie & Dodge, 1998). They may confuse sad and angry expressions or not notice when others are irritated with them. For example, a group of 6th-grade boys avoided a classmate who kept telling the same joke over and over. The classmate could not tell that the other boys were irritated by his repetition. His inability to read emotion cues led to social rejection.

What Predicts Understanding Others' Emotions?

Learner's emotion regulation makes a strong contribution to understanding others' emotions, as do the same parent factors that are linked to emotion regulation. Let's discuss these next.

Emotion regulation

Learners understand more about others' emotions and are more sympathetic if they can regulate their own emotions (Denham et al., 2003; Eisenberg et al., 1997). When learners witness someone else's distress, they will feel *sympathy* if they can keep their own emotions at a moderate level, but they will feel *personal distress* if their own emotions are overly intense.

Attachment

Learners with secure attachment tend to be better able to understand and discuss others' emotions and to be more empathic than insecure learners, who tend to respond to others' distress with personal distress rather than sympathy (Dykas & Cassidy, 2011; Mikulincer & Shaver, 2005). Secure attachment may contribute to empathy because attachment promotes emotion regulation ability.

Parent response to children's emotions

Parents who respond compassionately to their children's negative outbursts serve as role models of empathy (Denham et al., 1997). However, parents should not accept children's negativity when it hurts someone else. In one study, parents who allowed their children to express anger when frustrated, but not if it might hurt another's feelings, had more sympathetic children (Eisenberg, Fabes, Schaller, Carlo, & Miller, 1991). Parents who prohibited all displays of anger had children who were more likely to experience personal distress rather than sympathy.

Expression of emotions in the family

Empathy is linked to emotions expressed in the family. Preschoolers whose mothers communicate warmly and are seldom negative toward them are more likely to become adolescents who are sympathetic toward others (Michalik et al., 2007). In contrast, children raised in families with mostly negative emotions may have low levels of sympathy.

Parent–child talk about emotions

Talking about emotions helps children understand others' emotions (Denham, Zoller, & Couchoud, 1994). Some families talk a lot about emotions and some almost never do (Dunn, Brown, & Beardsall, 1991). Conversations about negative emotions

think about this

Think about a child you know well. How would you respond if the child:

1. Looked annoyed at receiving an undesirable gift?
2. Looked shaky while waiting to get a shot?
3. Won a race and jumped around boasting about it?
4. Were very angry, muttered threats, and slammed doors?

How should you respond in order to promote the child's emotional competence? Defend your choices. (Adapted from Saarni, 1999)

are especially helpful because they focus more on the causes of emotions and involve more extensive vocabulary than conversations about positive emotions (Lagattuta & Wellman, 2002). Conflict between siblings provides a rich opportunity to talk about emotions. It may seem ironic that sibling conflict contributes to children's emotional competence, but keep in mind that these are normal family conflicts, not intense conflicts. The emotions may be negative, but they are contained enough to allow (mostly) civil conversation.

Abuse

Abused children are less likely to read others' emotions as accurately as nonabused children. At the same time, they can be overly sensitive to negative emotions. For example, *neglected* children have a bias toward perceiving sadness in others, perhaps because their mothers tend to be depressed. *Physically abused* children have a bias toward perceiving subtle anger cues in others and are quick to identify angry faces (Frankenhuis & de Weerth, 2013; Strang, Hanson, & Pollak, 2012). More of their brains' processing capacity may be consumed by attending to signals of anger, which interferes with learning tasks (Strang et al., 2012).

Abused children may not be as empathic as nonabused children. They are more likely to respond to peers' distress with either personal distress or attack. They might laugh, hit, or withdraw when they see another child in distress. These inappropriate responses occur even after spending considerable time with nonabusive caregivers and peers in child care. Nonabused children, by comparison, are more likely to watch, help, or comfort the other (Klimes-Dougan & Kistner, 1990).

Abused adolescents may not want to talk about emotions, particularly negative emotions (Pollak, Cicchetti, Hornung, & Reed, 2000). Some teens with a history of abuse claim they are not affected by the abuse, but they act out through substance use, abusive relationships with peers, and other problem behaviors. Such teens are unable to acknowledge or discuss their emotions. One purpose of therapy is to help traumatized youth communicate emotions. This can help them recover from abuse and develop emotional competence.

8-3c Group Diversity in Understanding Others' Emotions

Research has not found robust differences in affective perspective-taking across groups. However, small gender and cultural differences may exist. Let's look at these next.

Gender

Are girls more empathic than boys? Some studies have found that girls show more concern for others and are better at reading distress in others, but other studies find no gender differences (Hastings, Zahn-Waxler, Robinson, Usher, & Bridges, 2000; Saarni, 1999). Studies that use self-report rather than physiological measures, such as heart rate, are more likely to find that girls are more empathic. This means that girls may think they should be more empathic and therefore report that they are, or girls may actually be more empathic than boys. The best summary of research to date is that gender differences in empathy are not consistently found, but when differences are found, girls are more empathic. Generally empathy is good, but it is possible that taking on others' distress could have costs for one's own well-being. Girls' vulnerability to depression may be linked to their greater empathic distress (Smith & Rose, 2011).

Culture

As you learned earlier, Darwin argued more than a century ago that facial expressions are universal. Recent research confirms that people can read emotions across cultures through facial expressions, tone of voice, and body language (Ekman, 2009; Shariff & Tracy, 2011). People express emotion in basically the same way across cultures, but some subtle cultural differences exist, much like different dialects of the same language. As a result you are a little more accurate at reading emotions expressed by members of your own culture. Thus, you may need to work at creating emotion understanding when you or your students must cross cultural boundaries.

8-3d Classroom Implications of Understanding Others' Emotions

Skill at reading others' emotions influences success in the classroom. Learners with this skill tend to be less aggressive, higher achievers, and more popular among teachers and classmates. There are several strategies you can use to help your students develop sensitivity to others' emotions:

1. Use victim-centered discipline. Victim-centered discipline is a type of induction (see Chapter 7) that involves pointing out to children during the discipline encounter how their misbehavior made someone else feel. This trains empathy in children.

2. Use emotion contagion and social referencing to your students' advantage, such as vividly conveying enjoyment of them and of the content you teach. Learners will catch your emotions. Learners are more likely to catch the emotions of those they like, such as a favorite teacher. Learners are also more likely to accurately read and catch the emotions of those who clearly and strongly express their emotions (Zaki, Bolger, & Ochsner, 2008). Unfortunately this can also work in a negative way, such as learners catching "math anxiety" from their teachers, so be careful what you communicate (Beilock, Gunderson, Ramirez, & Levine, 2010).

3. Use literature to help learners imagine the emotions of others. Novels help your learners experience empathy for those of other cultures and give you a context for talking about emotions (Kidd & Castano, 2013; Lysaker, Tonge, Gauson, & Miller, 2011).

4. Help learners improve emotion regulation. Factors that predict emotion regulation also predict affective perspective-taking skills. This means you can help learners control their own emotions and understand others' emotions better by following the suggestions given in the previous section.

Mrs. Ng did each of these things with Hailey. She established a warm relationship with Hailey and maintained a positive classroom climate. She accepted Hailey's rage, but did not tolerate her behavior. She sent Hailey to the bathroom to wash her face and calm down, teaching Hailey a coping strategy. Then she used the opportunity to talk with Hailey about emotions. She used inductive, victim-centered discipline by pointing out how Hailey's behavior affected others. As a result, Hailey may become better at both controlling her own anger and understanding the feelings of others.

In addition to the strategies just discussed, there are dozens of curriculum programs designed to help learners understand others' emotions. One example is Promoting Alternative Thinking Strategies (PATHS) for young children. This program includes 60 lessons on how feelings are acceptable, how feelings provide information, how to recognize feelings, and how one's behavior can affect others' feelings. The intent of this program is to raise children's awareness of their own and others' emotions. PATHS has resulted in greater ability to talk about emotions, less negative emotion, less aggression, greater social skills, and more classroom involvement. The greatest gains were made by children who initially had behavior problems (Greenberg & Kusche, 2006).

Figure 8.10 provides a visual summary of the ways you can affect learner's ability to regulate their own emotions and understand others' emotions. It also shows the

FIGURE 8.10 Model of Emotional Competence.

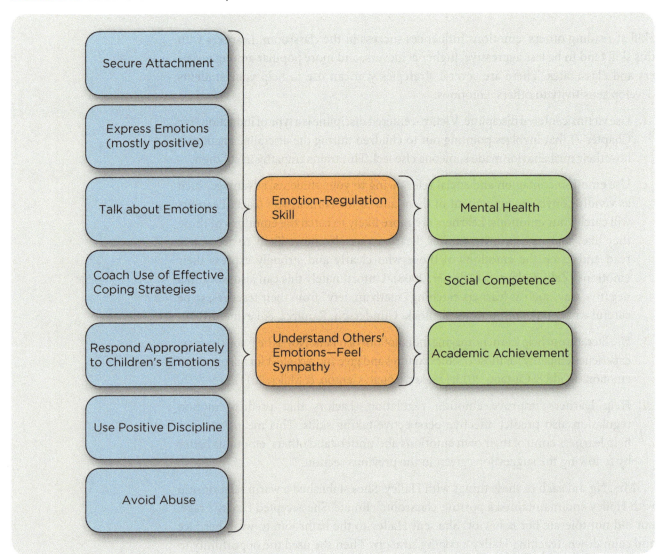

This model summarizes the seven teacher and parent behaviors (in blue) that predict learners' emotional competence (in orange) and the outcomes linked to emotional competence (in green). Use this model to think about your own behavior and your students' emotional competence.

outcomes linked to emotional competence. Use this figure as a quick guide to help you think about ways you can help your students, like Hailey, become more emotionally competent.

We close this chapter, and this section on the emotional child, by reiterating the importance of emotional competence for school success. Promoting learners' emotional competence is central—not merely an add-on—to the teacher's role. Compared with learners who struggle with their emotions, emotionally competent learners like school more, have higher achievement, and are liked better by peers and teachers. As a bonus, when you promote your learners' emotional competence, not only will you be a more effective teacher, but you will enjoy teaching more (Jennings & Greenberg, 2009).

---

reflections on practice

My Teaching

A positive teacher and school climate promote emotional competence in learners and might compensate for, or at least not worsen, challenges faced by learners in negative homes. Two powerful factors associated with both greater emotion regulation and empathy have been discussed in previous chapters:

- Develop a secure teacher–student relationship. How to do this is described in Chapter 6.
- Use victim-centered inductive discipline. How to do this is described in Chapter 7.

In addition, to promote emotional competence, periodically ask yourself the following:

1. Is there a positive emotional climate in my classroom and the school? This will be evident if learners in your classroom are predominantly in a positive or neutral, but not negative, mood.

2. Do I express emotions of moderate intensity and wide range, although primarily positive? Do I model good regulation and coping when I am emotional?

3. Are there simple interventions I can use to create positive moods, like helping learners succeed at a task, asking them to think about happy things, or playing upbeat music?

4. Am I aware of the coping strategies used by each of my learners, particularly those with poor regulation? Do I teach appropriate coping strategies? Do I help learners reappraise emotional situations in a positive light and challenge their pessimistic explanations?

5. Do I respond promptly when learners are overly aroused, before they lose control? Do I validate their negative emotions (but not accept hurtful behavior)?

6. Do I converse with learners about their own and others' emotions? Do I use learners' emotions, conflicts, or stories as opportunities to talk about emotions?

7. Am I aware of military-connected children in my class or school? Do I know what they are coping with?

8. Do I watch for internalizing disorders like anxiety or depression?

⌄⌄ Professional Resource Download

Summary of Age Trends in Emotional Competence

	Emotions Experienced	Emotion Regulation	Understanding Others' Emotions
Infancy & Toddlerhood (Birth–2 Years)	• Basic emotions such as distress, interest, and disgust are exhibited by newborns. • Complex emotions such as envy and embarrassment emerge at about 15–18 months. Social emotions that involve moral judgment—pride, shame, guilt—emerge soon afterward.	• Newborns cope with strong emotions by sucking, appearing to sleep, and gaze aversion. • Toddlers are able to delay emotional expression. However, they need help from adults to regulate their emotions. • Anger increases from age 4 months to 2 years. Tantrums emerge at 16 months and peak at 18–21 months.	• Emotion contagion is present at birth. Newborns mimic others' facial expressions. • Infants can tell one emotion from another and respond uniquely to different emotions. • Social referencing appears at about 8 months and peaks around 22 months. • Toddlers understand a few basic emotion words. Positive emotion words are learned before negative.
Early Childhood (3–5 Years)	• Preschoolers are vulnerable to guilt even when not responsible for events. • Gender differences in anxiety emerge (girls are more anxious). • Depression is identifiable.	• Preschoolers are able to regulate their own emotions under normal conditions. • Intense crying and tantrums abate. • They can dissemble to protect others' feelings. • They are better at exaggerating than at squelching an emotion. • They try on and practice emotions in pretend play. • Preschoolers understand that coping strategies help relieve strong emotions.	• Preschoolers often use social referencing. • Empathy and affective perspective-taking improve as preschoolers learn to label and talk about emotions. • They begin to talk about the cause of others' emotions. Understanding causes of others' emotions is indicated by their comforting distressed others and teasing.
Middle Childhood (6–12 Years)	• Children become able to accurately judge responsibility, and therefore guilt. • Test anxiety rises until 5th grade, then stabilizes. • Average onset of anxiety disorders is age 6 and of mild depression is age 11.	• Adultlike coping ability should be in place by age 10. • Children are able to generate more coping alternatives and begin to use peers to cope, but still primarily use parents. • Ability to judge controllability of the situation allows them to select the best coping strategy. • They are better able to use emotion-focused strategies, but prefer problem-focused strategies. • Ability to dissemble grows dramatically.	• Use of social referencing diminishes, but is still present. • The ability to accurately discuss and label emotions continues to grow. • Children emphasize others' beliefs and attitudes when judging the cause of emotions. • Understanding of multiple and competing emotions in the same situation is manifest by 8–10 years.

Summary of Age Trends in Emotional Competence

	Emotions Experienced	Emotion Regulation	Understanding Others' Emotions
Adolescence (13–19 Years)	• Adolescents are more vulnerable to social evaluation emotions, such as embarrassment. • Rate of depression rises in adolescence. Average age of onset of serious depression is 13. Gender differences in depression emerge (girls are more depressed).	• Most teens are not moody. • Teens feel positive most of the time, although less happy than 10-year-olds. They report more boredom, drowsiness, and social discomfort than their parents do.	• Emotion contagion and social referencing are reduced but still exist. • Teens are not more empathic than younger children, perhaps because of competing impulses toward self-protection • Teens can be empathic toward victims in faraway places.

≫ Professional Resource Download

Chapter Summary

8-1 Emotions

- Emotions involve physiological arousal, tendency to act, and appraisal (or thought). The functions of emotion are to focus attention, motivate behavior, prepare for action, and communicate.

- Charles Darwin argued that emotional expression is innate and universal. Basic emotions are present in early infancy, but complex social emotions do not appear until toddlerhood.

- Emotions influence memory and thought processes. Positive emotions promote creativity, problem solving, attention, and fast information processing. Neutral or mild negative emotions promote detailed, analytic thought, but strong negative emotions interfere with thought.

8-2 Regulating One's Own Emotions

- Emotion regulation is the ability to control emotions. Children do this by using coping strategies, some of which are more adaptive than others. Children also do this through emotional dissemblance. Negative emotions fade if they are not expressed.

- Children who are good at emotion regulation are better liked by teachers and classmates. They have better language skills, better academic achievement, and fewer emotional disorders.

- Antecedents of good emotion regulation include parents who foster secure attachment, express mostly positive emotions, avoid harsh discipline, directly coach coping strategies, and respond appropriately to and talk with children about their emotions.

- Two prevalent emotional disorders are depression and anxiety. They often occur together. Children with these disorders are at additional risk for ADHD, substance use, poor school performance, dropping out, and loneliness.

- Children are likely to be depressed or anxious if they have poor coping strategies, insecure attachment, stressful relationships, a depressed or anxious parent, and negative life events about which they feel helpless.

- Test anxiety results in a working memory overload during testing. Teachers can minimize test anxiety by helping learners experience academic success, using frequent assessment, improving the test situation, avoiding timed tests, training learners in test-taking strategies, attributing failures to effort rather than ability, and avoiding comparison between learners. Math anxiety is related and can be minimized in some of the same ways.

- Girls may be somewhat better at emotion regulation and dissemblance than boys, yet girls experience more depression and anxiety.

- Military-connected children have an unusual array of chronic stressors to cope with and must cross cultural boundaries. Teachers are an important factor in how they adjust.

- Teachers can promote learners' emotion regulation by talking about emotions, being sensitive to learners' emotions, directly coaching learners in coping strategies, responding appropriately to their emotions, and improving classroom climate. Teachers can minimize anxiety by reducing daily hassles and making classrooms predictable.

8-3 Understanding Others' Emotions

- Affective perspective-taking is the ability to read other's emotions and is linked with empathy. This ability is present in infancy, as indicated by emotion contagion and social referencing.

- Learners may respond to another's distress with sympathy, with personal distress, or with empathic distress. Learners who are sympathetic and skilled at understanding others' emotions are liked better by peers and less aggressive.

- Antecedents of affective perspective-taking skill include good emotion regulation and secure attachment. Skilled children have parents who accept their emotional displays without overreacting, express positive emotions at home, talk about emotions during sibling conflict, and are not abusive. Teachers can apply the same behaviors to promote emotional competence in the classroom.

chapter **9**

Konstantin Chagin/Shutterstock.com

Social Cognition

Do you know individuals whom everyone seems to enjoy being around because they have exceptional social skills? Chances are that they are skilled at "reading" other people and have a good sense of humor. They probably also abide by widely held moral rules. All three of these key aspects of social cognition will be discussed in this chapter. **After you read this chapter, you will be able to:**

9-1 Describe the development of students' ability to read other people and create classrooms that foster social cognition.

9-2 Analyze humor in the classroom and how to use it to create a positive learning environment.

9-3 Discuss how morality develops and how you can promote student's moral judgment.

9-1 Theory of Mind

Wally:	*Mrs. Crites said I wasn't doing my math today, just because I was looking out the window.*
Counselor:	*She probably thought you were daydreaming.*
Wally:	*Yeah, but I wasn't. I was thinking about the problem I didn't know how to do. But I fooled her! In social studies I had my book open on my desk, and I looked like I was reading, but I wasn't! I was dreamin'.*

Although only 9 years old, Wally is pretty smart about people; he has good social cognition. You learned in Chapter 3 that cognition refers to thought processes like reasoning and problem solving. **Social cognition** refers to cognition applied to social situations. A goal of schools is to help children think clearly and solve problems. In what domain is clear thinking and problem solving more important than the social domain? In this chapter, you will learn how to foster three aspects of your students' social cognition: theory of mind, humor, and moral judgment (including academic dishonesty).

Wally knew that Mrs. Crites would assume he was learning from his textbook if he looked like he was reading. He cleverly led her to a *false belief* by acting as though he were in one mental state (reading), while actually being in another mental state (daydreaming). He deliberately manipulated Mrs. Crites's mind. Wally has developed a landmark ability of childhood called *theory of mind*.

Theory of mind (ToM) refers to the understanding that other people have mental states—beliefs, desires, knowledge, and intentions—that are different from their own and to the ability to infer or figure out others' mental states. Thus, a simple definition of ToM is "people reading." It is a "theory" because it helps children explain and predict others' behavior. ToM makes it possible to learn from others, which is essential according to Vygotsky's sociocultural theory (see Chapter 3).

ToM is usually studied using two types of false-belief tests. In one test, children observe George leaving an object, like a candy bar, in one location. While George is gone, someone else moves the object to a new location. Children are asked where George will first look for the object upon return. In the second test, children are shown a box, like a crayon box, and asked what they believe will be inside (e.g., crayons). Children are shown that something unexpected is inside (e.g., buttons). Children are then asked what George would think is inside the box. In each test George has a reasonable but *false belief* about where the candy bar is or what is inside the crayon box.

ToM is also assessed with "appearance versus reality" tests. Children are shown a deceptive object, such as a sponge that looks like a rock. After playing with the object, children are asked what the object looks like (e.g., a rock) and what the object really is (e.g., a sponge). Then children are asked what George would think it is.

Typically, young children fail these tests. They claim that George would look in the new location for the candy bar, would know that there were buttons in the crayon box, and would think that the rock-like object is really a sponge. Success on these tests requires ToM because children must separate their own knowledge of the true condition from George's belief in the false condition. This ability develops with age. Failure to develop age-appropriate ToM is a key feature of **autism spectrum conditions** (see Box 9.1).

social cognition
thought processes applied to the social domain.

theory of mind (ToM)
the ability to infer mental states in others, such as beliefs, desires, knowledge, and intentions. Also called "people reading."

autism spectrum conditions
conditions characterized by a continuum of markedly abnormal social interaction; poor language ability; and restricted, repetitive behavior patterns. It commonly occurs with low cognitive ability.

BOX 9.1 challenges in development

Autism Spectrum Conditions

James was a bubbly 2-year-old who loved "mashed to-tatoes" and playing with swords. But he soon became a nearly silent, unhappy child who "pulled cowboy boots on and off until his feet were raw." His father described the change as "falling out of the world." James forgot his name. After intensive one-on-one treatment (at home, at preschool, and with a speech therapist), James began to talk again. By kindergarten, he was able to enroll in a regular classroom but also went to a resource room and had an in-class aide. By 3rd grade, he was told that he had autism. He raged, cried, and denied it—and then began to come to terms with it. James continues to adjust to school, with the help of parents and teachers—and best of all, a friend. His friend has provided a giant step toward helping James develop social skills. (Adapted from O'Neil, 2004)

Autism is a condition characterized by abnormal social cognition. There is a wide spectrum of functioning among children with autism, so it is referred to as autism spectrum conditions (ASC). It is characterized by challenges in three areas: social interaction, poor verbal ability, and repetitive behavior such as flapping the hands or putting on and removing cowboy boots. Children with autism may have trouble comprehending emotions in others and have poor emotion regulation, like giggling for no reason. They may have preoccupation with a narrow interest like maps or light switches.. They may have temper tantrums, self-injury like head banging, and difficulty controlling their movements. Some may be overly sensitive to sights, smells, or sounds (e.g., a dog barking) and others may seek out sensory stimulation such as flickering lights (Pellicano, 2013). Some (8 to 25%) may have seizures (American Psychiatric Association, 2013).

About 41% of children with ASC have low cognitive ability—that is, an IQ below 70 (CDC, 2009a). They also tend to have poor executive functions (Pellicano, 2007). However, low scores on IQ and executive-function tests may be due to language problems. On IQ tests like the Raven's Matrices (see Chapter 5), which do not require much verbal ability, some children with autism may score in the average to high range (Dawson, Soulières, Gernsbacher, & Mottron, 2007). Furthermore, children with autism may have a strong ability that stands out, like reading at a very young age. They may have excellent long-term memory for facts. Some have exceptional ability to focus attention, resist distractions, and pick out objects in a field of other objects, like in Figure 9.1 (Gernsbacher, Stevenson, Khandakar, & Goldsmith, 2008).

FIGURE 9.1 **Visual Search Tasks That Distinguish Children with and without Autism.**

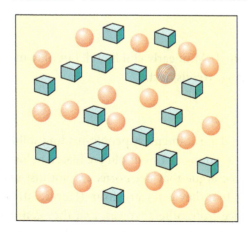 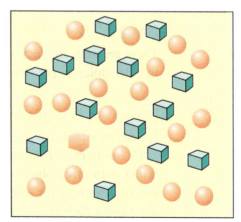

If asked to find the striped ball in the left panel, most children experience a sense of "pop out." They do not need to examine each object to locate the striped ball. But if asked to find the orange cube in the right panel, children without autism typically examine each item until they find the target. In contrast, children with autism easily search the field and are little thwarted by the distracters. Children with autism are nearly twice as fast as other children at these sorts of tasks. *Source: Gernsbacher, Stevenson, Khandakar, and Goldsmith (2008).*

Autism Spectrum Conditions (continued)

Autism and Theory of Mind Children with autism, regardless of cognitive ability, have ToM deficits. With limited ToM, children are not motivated to communicate with others, which could explain why children with autism have language delays. They are less likely than other children to look at faces and follow another person's gaze, which prevents them from sharing attention and experience with other people.

Asperger's Condition While Asperger's condition is no longer an official diagnosis, it is commonly used to refer to some children at the high-functioning end of the autism spectrum. These children have impairment in social interaction and have restricted, repetitive patterns of behavior and interests but *do not* have delays in language, cognitive abilities, self-help skills, or curiosity about the environment (American Psychiatric Association, 2013). Children with Asperger's often want to interact socially, but don't know how. They may perseverate on topics or emotions. For example, a 12-year-old with Asperger's became distressed about worms being crushed on the sidewalk near his school and could think of nothing else for days; he cried, he went outside to protect the worms, and even got in fights with children who cared less about the worms (Mazefsky, Pelphrey, & Dahl, 2012).

Prevalence of ASC Severe autism is clearly recognizable by 3 years of age, but may be diagnosed at a younger age because symptoms may appear by 1 year of age (Gilga, Jones, Bedford, Charman, & Johnson, 2014). You may be asked to help with the diagnosis, because teachers are accurate reporters of symptoms of autism. Diagnosis of autism has increased in recent years (see Figure 9.2). As of 2012, the Centers for Disease Control and Prevention (CDC) estimated that 1 in 68 children has some form of ASC (1 in 42 boys and 1 in 189 girls). The increase in ASC may be due to changes in diagnosis or to real increases in ASC related to cohort effects such as increasing age of first-time parents or environmental toxins. Families with a child with ASC are more likely than other families to have another child with the condition (Ingersoll, 2011).

Children with severe autism are not likely to be able to live and work independently as adults. However, adults with milder forms of ASC can lead independent lives and have successful careers, although they may have social oddities and problems with empathy. Youth with autism who are capable of insight can become depressed when they realize their limitations, and they may need support from you.

Practicing Inclusion—How Can You Help Learners with Autism? Intervention can help many children with autism improve in behavior, social interaction, and language

---

Asperger's condition
a term commonly used to refer to a condition on the autism spectrum characterized by impaired social interaction and restricted, repetitive behavior patterns, but with normal language and cognitive abilities.

9-1a Age Trends in Theory of Mind

There are dramatic increases in ToM in early childhood, but only modest increases in older children. Let's look at age trends next.

Infancy and Toddlerhood (Birth to 2 Years)

Infants have biases that may lead to rudimentary people-reading ability (Liszkowski, 2013; Ruffman, 2014). Infants as young as 1 hour old are biased to look toward faces rather than other objects. Some argue that newborns are not just searching faces, but are searching for teachers that they can learn from (Heyes, 2016). Infants also distinguish their mother's voice from others' voices, and they can match a happy voice with a happy face (Flavell, 1999). Infants imitate others' emotional expressions (see Chapter 8). They will call to people who disappear but not to objects that disappear. If they see an adult look with interest at an object, they express surprise if the adult picks up a different object (Wellman, Lopez-Duran, LaBounty, & Hamilton, 2008). This suggests that they recognize others' intentions and predict their behavior. They also distinguish intentional from accidental actions, and

ability. The younger the child when the intervention begins, the more successful it is; it should, preferably, begin in toddlerhood. One common approach is behavior modification (also called applied behavior analysis, see Chapter 3) to reduce problem behaviors and teach new skills such as how to converse, make eye contact, or read emotional cues in others. This was the approach used with James. A second common approach is to be highly responsive during social interaction, such as imitating the child and scaffolding joint play (Smith & Iadarola, 2015). Sometimes the two approaches are combined. In addition, exercise has helped improve social skills and reduce repetitive behaviors in children with ASC (Pontifex et al., 2014).

You can help children with autism function in your classroom by keeping the physical environment stable (e.g., don't move chairs around); providing lecture notes and extra time for writing; and capitalizing on the good rote memory and intense, obsessive interests (e.g., dinosaurs, astronomy, maps) of some children with autism (Brownell & Walther-Thomas, 2001). You can also help promote their ToM by talking to them about others' emotions, thoughts, and desires, which will help your other students as well (Slaughter, Peterson, & Mackintosh, 2007). You can help

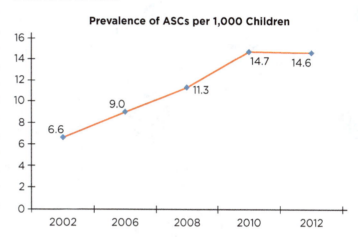

FIGURE 9.2 Prevalence of Autism Spectrum Conditions from 2002 to 2012.

The CDC monitors prevalence of autism spectrum conditions across the United States. These are the most recent data available. The 2012 rate is over double the rate of 1 in 152 in 2002. *Source: Centers for Disease Control and Prevention and the Autism and Developmental Disabilities Monitoring Network (2016).*

them form friendships with particularly warm, kind, and socially mature classmates (Mendelson, Gates, & Lerner, 2016). You will need to collaborate with parents and therapists to provide an optimal classroom environment for each learner.

distinguish other people's inability to help them from unwillingness to help them (e.g., Dunfield & Kuhlmeier, 2010).

You look at others' eyes to infer what they are paying attention to. Infants do the same (Jessen & Grossmann, 2014). Infants are attracted to eyes and will follow other's gaze and look with interest at objects that others are looking at as young as 4 months (Heyes, 2016). Gaze following makes joint attention possible. **Joint attention** occurs when child and caregiver look together at an object and talk about it (Photo 9.1). Joint attention is a rudimentary form of the infant's sharing something in the caregiver's mind. Infants will use this skill to get their needs met. They will wait to reach for an object they want but can't reach until you meet their eye. They expect you to follow their gaze and understand their intention (Liszkowski, 2013).

joint attention
the child and another person visually explore an object together.

Toddlers (1 to 2 years) are better at gaze following than infants, but are not yet fully skilled. Most (67 to 75%) 2-year-olds cannot successfully answer the question "Which one is Sam looking at?" in a drawing like Figure 9.3, but most 3-year-olds can (McGuigan & Doherty, 2002). Yet toddlers are able to infer the mental state (i.e., a preference) of someone else. Imagine a toddler is watching you take toy frogs from a box of all frogs or from a box of almost all ducks. You leave the room while someone

PHOTO 9.1 Even infants are capable of understanding joint attention: that when they look at the same thing as another person, they share something in the other person's mind.

FIGURE 9.3 What Is Sam Looking At?

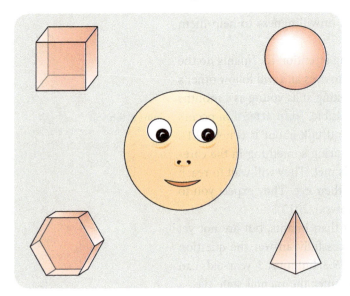

Children are asked to point to the shape that "Sam" is looking at.
Source: Based on McGuigan and Doherty (2002).

gives the toddler a small bowl of frogs and a separate bowl of ducks. You return and silently extend your hand between the bowls. What is the child likely to hand to you, a frog or duck? If you took frogs from a box of all frogs, the toddler is equally likely to give you a frog or a duck, concluding you took a random sample. However, if you took frogs out of a box of almost all ducks, the toddler would give you a frog, concluding you preferred frogs (Kushnir, Xu, & Wellman, 2010). The toddler is inferring your mental state from a statistical pattern. (In Chapter 12 you will learn more about infants' capacity for statistical learning of language.) In fact, recent research shows that toddlers can pass false-belief tasks if they do not have to answer questions. For example, toddlers may point to the correct location of an object that was moved when an adult returns to look for it (Liszkowski, 2013).

Early Childhood (3 to 5 Years)

Children rarely pass typical false-belief tests before age 4 (Rubio-Fernández & Geurts, 2013). Yet 3-year-olds' behavior suggests the ability to read people. They tease siblings. They comfort a crying baby by bringing a blanket. They feign injury to get sympathy (Newton, Vasudevi, & Bull, 2000). One 3-year-old told her mother she was sick and faked coughing so that she would get a sweet-tasting cough drop. Such deception requires understanding others' mental states.

So why do 3-year-olds fail false-belief tests? The tests may overwhelm their language and information-processing abilities. As children develop language skills they are better able to converse about others' mental states. Children develop dramatically better executive functions as the prefrontal cortex of the brain matures (see Chapter 4), and they are better able to think about the false-belief test. ToM tests require the child to hold information in mind (e.g., George will think there are crayons in the box) in the presence of conflicting information (e.g., there are actually buttons in the box). By 5 to 6 years of age, children perform similarly to adults on false-belief tests (Wellman & Liu, 2004).

Middle Childhood (6 to 12 Years)

By middle childhood, most children have fully mastered false-belief tests, but their ToM continues to improve. Children become able to distinguish

iStockphoto.com/andipantz

 brain research

The Puzzle of Autistic Brains

The brains of children with ASC, particularly the frontal lobe of the cortex, are overly large. Their brains grow faster in the first few years than other children's. Researchers do not yet know why, or whether this causes or results from autism. One possibility, based on animal research, is that ASC-related genes control migration of neurons in the developing fetus and the size of brain regions. Genes can affect the brain by altering the amount of neurotransmitters, neuron connections, cell survival, or degree of myelination. Genes can also shift the delicate balance between neuron excitement and quieting

at synapses so that neurons cannot easily distinguish important signals from background noise. There probably is not a single path of brain development for ASC (Rubenstein, 2011).

One puzzle about ASC (and ADHD) is why boys are more susceptible. Some neuroscientists describe ASC as the "extreme male brain" (Rubenstein, 2011). As you learned in Chapter 6, genes must be expressed to affect development. Why are autism-related genes expressed in some susceptible children, especially boys? To date, this remains a mystery.

intentional from unintentional acts, like intentionally versus accidentally breaking a dish. This ability is critical for moral judgment, discussed later in this chapter. Children also become better able to use others' beliefs to make persuasive arguments. For example, 3rd- and 6th-graders are more likely to use belief-oriented arguments to convince their mother to buy a bird, such as telling her "I'll keep the cage clean," whereas preschoolers and 1st-graders are likely to use belief-irrelevant arguments, such as telling her "I want one" (Bartsch & London, 2000).

Children become better at inferring the intent of story characters (see Figure 9.4). For example, children might hear a story about Peter who thought his aunt looked silly in her new hat, but said she looked nice. Why did he say that? Or, Katy wanted to play on the swings but would have to pass a mean dog to get there. She told her mother she did not want to play on the swings. Why did she say that? Inferring intent in stories is more complex than simple false-belief tasks. During middle childhood the ability to infer intent increases steadily (O'Hare, Bremner, Nash, Happé, & Pettigrew, 2009).

Finally, children also begin to understand that they know more about their inner thoughts and feelings than do other people. Five-year-olds mistakenly believe parents and teachers know what they are thinking better than they themselves do, but 10-year-olds realize that they are the best judge of what they are thinking (Burton & Mitchell, 2003). Wally, who pretended to be studying, clearly realized this, and he used it to his advantage with Mrs. Crites.

Adolescence (13 to 19 Years)

Adolescents' continued development of ToM enables greater understanding of irony, sarcasm, humor, negotiation, counseling, argument, and so forth. Yet even adolescents

FIGURE 9.4 Age Trends in Ability to Infer Mental States from Stories.

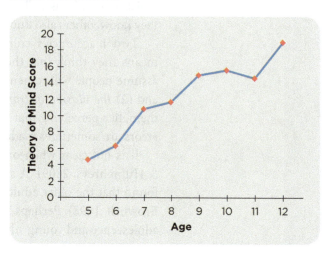

Children were asked to infer why the characters in stories said or did certain things. For example, "Peter thought his aunt looked silly in her new hat, but said she looked nice. Why did he say that?" Or, "Katy wanted to play on the swings but would have to pass a mean dog to get there. She told her mother she did not want to play on the swings. Why did she say that?" Try this task with a few children of different ages and see if you get a steady increase in ability with age. *Source: O'Hare, Bremner, Nash, Happé, and Pettigrew (2009).*

think about **this**

ToM research is an indirect product of Piaget's research—that is, modern scientists were testing whether his view of young children's egocentrism was true. Review egocentrism in Chapter 3. Does the research on ToM support Piaget's view? Explain.

FIGURE 9.5 **Theory of Mind Test for Adolescents and Adults.**

First, you are shown a picture of a house, and then the picture is covered so that just one corner of it shows (purple square). What would a new person believe the mostly covered picture is of, among the 5 options to the right? Try this task on friends to see whether they believe that what they know, others also know. *Source: Adapted from Lagattuta, Sayfan, and Harvey (2014).*

sometimes make mistakes in people reading, so there is still room for improvement. In adolescents and adults, ToM can be measured using partial pictures (see Figure 9.5). That is, you might be shown a picture of a house, and then the picture is covered so that just one corner shows. When asked what a new person might believe the mostly covered picture represents, you are likely to assume the new person would think it was a picture of a house. Thus, even adults tend to be egocentric in assuming that what they know, others also know (Lagattuta, Sayfan, & Harvey, 2014).

Two inaccuracies common to adolescents are: (1) the *spotlight effect,* which means they think that they are the center of everyone's attention and mistakenly assume people will remember what they are wearing or notice their "bad hair" day; and (2) *the illusion of transparency,* which means they think others can easily read them, like perceiving that they are nervous when making a presentation. These same errors are sometimes made by adults (Gilovich & Savitsky, 1999).

It is not clear when or if ToM ability ever stops developing (Apperly, Samson, & Humphreys, 2009). A study comparing college students with 60- to 80-year-olds found that the older adults had significantly better ToM ability (Happe, Winner, & Brownell, 1998). Perhaps ToM should be thought of as "still under construction" in adolescence and young adulthood.

9-1b Individual Diversity in Theory of Mind

All typical children will eventually pass false-belief tests. However, some children are more skilled than age-mates at people reading.

What Do Individual Differences in Theory of Mind Predict?

Theory of mind ability predicts *language development.* By 4 months, infants use another person's gaze to know what to look at as they learn. Imagine a child is looking at a novel object. His father speaks a new word while looking at a different object (Baldwin, 2000). What keeps the child from applying the label to the wrong object? The child follows the father's gaze. This is why joint attention is foundational to language learning.

Theory of mind ability also predicts *social competence.* Young children with better ToM skills tend to have high-quality play with friends; they are better at joint planning, such as "pretend you are squirting me again," and role assignment, such as "let's be fire fighters now" (Jenkins & Astington, 2000). The same is true of older children. A meta-analysis of many studies found that from ages 2 to 10, children who had better ToM abilities were better liked (Slaughter, Imuta, Peterson, & Henry, 2015). ToM helps children take another person's perspective when trying to resolve conflict, consider what kind of help someone needs, decide how to tell a joke, and so on. To function socially, a child must take into account the mental state of others.

In addition, ToM ability predicts *deception,* or intentionally giving someone a false belief. Deception is among the earliest indicators of ToM. In one study, 3-year-olds played a hide-and-seek game with candy. If they lied to an adult about where the candy was, they got to keep it. If the adult found it, the adult got to keep the candy. Despite strong motivation, none could lie successfully. However, after ToM training they became much better at deception (Ding, Wellman, Wang, Fu, & Lee, 2015). Young children are eager to play similar games of deception. Deception is a positive skill when it is used to make others feel good, such as telling a joke. When deception involves controlling emotions it is called *emotional dissemblance,* which you learned about in Chapter 8.

Sadly, ToM also predicts the loss of joyful performance we see in very young children. Contrast inhibited tweens, who hunker down on the sidelines at school dances, with preschoolers, who will dance with relish and confidence anywhere. Preschoolers' joyful performance disappears as they come to read others' mental states and understand that others may be negatively judging them (Chaplin & Norton, 2015).

What Predicts Individual Differences in Theory of Mind?

Genes may play a small role in ToM ability, probably through their influence on information processing and verbal ability. We will examine these abilities next, and then three influences from the social environment.

Information processing

Children who have better executive functions (see Chapter 4), especially inhibitory control and greater working memory capacity, have better ToM.[1] Executive functions make it possible for children to reflect on their thoughts, to distance themselves from the immediate situation, and to ignore false information (e.g., what the crayon box appears to hold but does not), which all contribute to ToM. Greater working memory capacity helps children keep all this relevant information in mind at once. Wally had to keep in mind what behavior his teacher expected and monitor whether he looked like he was reading, while his mind was busy daydreaming. Some researchers think that executive functions are the foundation of ToM (Diamond, 2013).

Verbal ability

Verbal ability is strongly related to whether children pass false-belief tests (Milligan, Astington, & Dack, 2007). The relationship is bidirectional (see Chapter 1). This means that good verbal ability predicts children's ToM ability and that ToM ability predicts children's verbal ability. Infants who are better at gaze following tend to become toddlers who talk more about mental states (e.g., forget, pretend, want, wish, angry, scared), and tend to become preschoolers who are more skilled at false-belief tasks (Brooks & Meltzoff, 2015).Why is verbal ability correlated with ToM? One possibility is that conversation with others exposes children to different points of

---

[1] Many studies support this conclusion, just a few of which are listed here: Apperly, Samson, and Humphreys (2009); Devine and Hughes (2014); Hughes and Devine (2015); Hughes and Ensor (2007).

In Chapter 1 you learned that a correlation means that two variables go together, but not necessarily that one causes the other. Discuss how this might apply to the link between verbal ability and ToM.

view, helping them learn about others' mental states while also helping them become verbally fluent (Ensor & Hughes, 2008). This may be why deaf children who converse with people fluent in sign language have normal ToM development, but deaf children who are unable to converse are significantly delayed in ToM (Schick, de Villers, de Villers, & Hoffmeister, 2007). Similarly, children with language impairment tend to be delayed in ToM (Nilsson & de López, 2016). Lack of opportunity to converse with others may slow development of ToM.

Parent's mind-mindedness and attachment

Parents sometimes say "you want . . ." or "you know . . ." in pseudo-conversation with their infants. These parents are making mind-related comments about their infants' desires and thoughts. This may seem like a silly way to talk to an infant, but parents who do this tend to have children with better ToM and verbal ability (Hughes & Devine, 2015). Psychologists call this *mind-mindedness*.

Parents' mind-mindedness may foster ToM because it helps them perceive their children's experience, respond sensitively, and form a secure attachment. Attachment predicts theory of mind. ToM requires an understanding of emotional states in others, which grows from the attachment relationship (De Rosnay & Harris, 2002). Insecurely attached children struggle to read others' minds and to make meaning of others' behavior, perhaps because their attachment figures are unpredictable in caring for them (Dykas & Cassady, 2011).

Talking about others

Children whose parents frequently talk about others' mental states have greater ToM (Hughes & Devine, 2015). With 1-year-olds, parents may talk mainly about the child's own desires, like "You *want* juice?" As children's ability to understand their own desires grows and they start to use *I* and *me*, sensitive parents get more challenging—talking about others rather than the child, and talking about thoughts as well as desires (Taumoepeau & Ruffman, 2008). "She doesn't realize . . ." "They are really pretending . . ." "He remembers . . ."—these are all ways that families talk about others' mental states with older children. (If you recognize this as scaffolding in the child's zone of proximal development, which moves as the child's competence increases, you go to the head of the class!)

Families vary considerably in how much they use words like *think, know, believe, wonder,* and *understand.* Let's consider two different mothers showing their preschoolers a picture book with no words in which a dog named Carl babysits a toddler:

> Mother 1: *[Carl the dog is] all happy because the baby's in bed, nice and clean, and he's cleaned up and Mom doesn't know that they had fun in the house.*
>
> Mother 2: *Oh, here she comes! And there's Carl waiting for her. Look at that! She's home. And the baby's still safe in bed. (Slaughter, Peterson, & Mackintosh, 2007, p. 846)*

The first mother talks about the mental states of Carl and mother, but the second does not. This may seem subtle, but over time the first mother may use thousands more mental-state words with her child than the second mother. Better-educated mothers talk more about others' mental states, which may explain why their children have greater ToM ability (Jenkins, Turrell, Kogushi, Lollis, & Ross, 2003). See Photo 9.2.

Remarkably, researchers have been able to improve preschoolers' ToM after just a few training sessions in which they give them false-belief tasks with feedback ("No, he thought there were pencils in the box because….") and read stories emphasizing mental state words (Ding et al., 2015; Lecce, Bianco, Demicheli, & Cavallini, 2014).

Seeing others' reactions may contribute to ToM. Blind children tend to be delayed in ToM, passing false-belief tests much later, at about 12 years of age (Peterson, Peterson, & Webb, 2000). Their inability to use social referencing, joint attention, or emotional displays as they hear talk about others may delay their people-reading abilities.

PHOTO 9.2 Children develop ToM ability when their parents talk about others' mental states during storybook reading.

Peers and siblings

Younger children in large families develop ToM earlier than do other children (McAlister & Peterson, 2013). Preschoolers with older siblings are exposed to more talk about mental states than only or eldest children (Jenkins et al., 2003). Siblings and peers provide children with the opportunity to talk about others during humor, conflict, and play. Thus, interacting with minds that are different from their own may promote children's ToM. However, the beneficial effect of siblings occurs mostly in families with positive sibling relationships and in middle-class homes (Lewis & Carpendale, 2002; Recchia & Howe, 2009). Let's look at other group differences next.

9-1c Group Diversity in Theory of Mind

Gender and SES may be linked to ToM. From preschool through high school, studies generally find that girls and boys perform similarly on ToM tests, but when there is a difference, girls do better.[2] This may help to explain why girls generally have higher ratings of social competence than boys. In addition, children whose parents have higher-status jobs and higher education levels perform better on ToM tests. This has been found across countries (Shatz, Diesendruck, Martinez-Beck, & Akar, 2003).

9-1d Classroom Implications of Theory of Mind

The ability to understand others' mental states is one of the crowning achievements of childhood. Theory of mind helps learners navigate their social worlds, including school. Yet, learners (and teachers) sometimes misinterpret the mental states of others, particularly when different cultures come together. For example, in a midwestern high school, misunderstandings about others' intentions led to strong racial tension between Black and Asian American students (Lei, 2003). Black girls were viewed as loud. Some onlookers assumed their loudness was intended to be obnoxious and to convey an aggressive attitude. The girls, however, said they only intended to have fun or express themselves. In contrast, Asian males were viewed as overly quiet. Some assumed their quietness was intended to convey a rejection of U.S. culture. The boys, however, said they were quiet to avoid being teased about their limited English. Teachers did not discuss these behavioral differences for fear of being accused of racism, yet an open discussion might have helped the different groups understand each other's mental state. That is, greater ToM across ethnic groups could improve school atmosphere.

---

[2] Many studies find this, a few of which are listed here: Bosacki and Astington (1999); Cutting and Dunn (1999); Grazzani and Ornaghi (2012); Milligan, Astington, and Dack (2007); Nelson, Adamson, and Bakeman (2012); Suway, Degnan, Sussman, and Fox (2012).

Greater ToM could also improve individual's well-being. Learners in your classroom who have better ToM are likely to get along well with peers and teachers. There are four things you can do to promote each learner's ToM skills:

1. Help learners develop good verbal ability. You'll learn how to do this in Chapter 12.

2. Converse with learners about others' mental states. Use words like *think, know, believe, wonder, remember, forget, guess, expect, meant, ignore, pretend,* and *understand.* This can be done when discussing content in class, such as *"Do you think John Adams believed the French foreign minister?"* or *"Is Joel guessing, or does he know* 317 + 42 = 359*?"* This can also be done when learners have conflict, during social interactions in class, or when reading stories, like the first mother in the earlier vignette reading the book about Carl the dog.

3. Provide learners with the opportunity to interact with peers who might have different perspectives. For example, you can encourage social interaction during noninstructional time, such as lunch, or you can organize cooperative learning during instruction, as will be discussed in Chapter 11.

4. Establish a secure, positive relationship with learners. You learned how to do this in Chapter 6. Secure attachment is linked to greater ToM ability.

ToM ability also promotes humor, or the ability to make others laugh, which is one of the most pleasurable aspects of classroom social interaction.

9-2 Humor

> In a 7th-grade honors algebra class, the teacher wrote a problem on the SMART board. She asked the students to use their calculators to find the solution. After a few minutes she called out, "Joseph, what does your calculator say?" Joseph promptly replied with a deadpan face, "Battery low. Suggest replacement." Both the teacher and students laughed.
>
> This class is in the oldest school building in the city. It is overcrowded and insufferably hot on the third floor. Yet, the ambience is pleasant because the students often use humor, but not in destructive ways. For example, they know the teacher wants them to show all the steps of their problem solving. They resist because "showing your work" takes effort. They prefer shortcuts. Kyle is called to the board to solve a problem where he takes an "extra" step. In friendly teasing, a classmate says, "Kyle's such a hard worker!" Everyone smiles.

Many teachers believe humor enhances classroom climate, improves student motivation, and increases learning. On the other hand, some teachers view students' clowning around as disruptive. Which view is correct? Let's see what the research suggests, but first we will clarify some basic concepts about humor.

9-2a What Is Humor?

Humor is a kind of social-cognitive play that produces smiling or laughing and feelings of amusement. Humor can be intentional or accidental. It can be verbal like a joke, pun, or witticism, or nonverbal like a funny face.

Not all smiles or laughs are caused by humor. In fact, most laughter occurs during day-to-day social interaction, such as "I'll see you guys later," which is not humorous but is often accompanied by a small laugh (Provine, 2000). People also giggle when they are socially uncomfortable. Only about 15% of laughter occurs in response to humor or a joke. Thus, laughter helps create positive feelings between people, in addition to being a response to humor.

Causes and Functions of Humor

In the parking lot of a hospital, one of our preschool-aged children asked what a sign said. Mom replied, "Patient Parking." Our child promptly asked, "Then where do the daddies and impatient people park?"

Adults find this question funny, but our child did not. (Daddy did, sort of.) One cause of humor is processing information with one interpretation (e.g., patients park in one place and medical staff in another), encountering incongruent information (e.g., the meaning of patience), and then rapidly reinterpreting it (Hurley, Dennett, & Adams, 2011). Our child's question is humorous if you can interpret the contrast between "patients" and "patience." Young children with limited language and information-processing ability would not find this humorous. Good ToM ability helps you further comprehend that our child believed daddies have less patience than mommies, which adds to the humor. That is, cognitive insight triggers humor.

Humor has many social functions: to entertain, to make others feel good, to save face, to give information, to communicate liking or disliking, to smooth awkward situations, and to put others in their place. Freud said that humor channels hostility in less harmful ways (see Box 9.2). However, humor can be quite harmful. Antisocial humor involves dirty or gross jokes and jokes that are disparaging to other people.

Playful Teasing

Teasing is commentary that is playful, intentional, and provocative (Keltner, Capps, Kring, Young, & Heerey, 2001). It often involves humorous taunts or mock insults, threats, or challenges, but it can also be nonverbal. Teasing is generally humorous and for fun, like Kyle's classmate teasing him for taking an extra step to solve the math problem. Much like rough-and-tumble play (see Chapter 11), you distinguish teasing from aggression by its playful qualities, like good-natured facial expressions. However, teasing can go too far. It can be used in a hostile way, like to belittle someone. If a child is teased repeatedly in a hostile way, that would constitute bullying. Ridicule and sexual teasing that border on harassment, such as teasing about sexual orientation, also constitute bullying (Espelage, Aragon, Birkett, & Koenig, 2008), and are different from playful teasing. We'll discuss bullying and sexual harassment in Chapter 10.

Playful teasing is pervasive in social interactions. It serves the same functions as other forms of humor: it strengthens social bonds, communicates information, and helps resolve conflicts in a nonconfrontational way. For example, in a school lunchroom, 10- to 14-year-old girls may use teasing to draw positive attention to a friend who has a new haircut. Among elementary children, teasing often occurs when a child talks to someone of the opposite sex. Thus, teasing is used to strengthen gender boundaries (see Chapter 11). Generally, children are more likely to tease those to whom they feel close. Popular high-status children are more likely to tease than low-status children (Keltner et al., 2001).

BOX 9.2 theories & theorists

Sigmund Freud

Sigmund Freud (1856–1939) is among the most famous theorists in history, like both Darwin (see Chapter 8) and Skinner (see Chapter 3), with whom his life overlapped. He was born in the Austro-Hungarian Empire to a Jewish family (Isbister, 1985). The family moved to Vienna when he was a young child, where he lived until just before his death. (Hitler also lived in Vienna when Freud was in his 40s.) In the 1930s, the Nazis burned his books and sent his sisters to death camps. In 1938, he fled to London, where he died as World War II was beginning. He was an obsessive smoker who suffered from mouth cancer, which was linked to his death.

Sigmund Freud

Freud came to believe that unconscious memories of trauma often have an energy that remains dammed up because the memories cannot be expressed in a socially acceptable way, so they are converted to physical symptoms. The symptoms are relieved when the repressed memories are made conscious. Freud made memories conscious through *free association*, in which patients lay on a couch and said whatever passed through their minds. He called his approach *psychoanalysis*.

Freud made some revolutionary contributions to psychology and coined many terms you may have heard, such as *sibling rivalry*. One of his greatest contributions is the concept of the *unconscious*. He asserted that the unconscious often holds destructive or sexual impulses that are repressed, but occasionally leak out, such as a *Freudian slip* that occurs when you say something that is symbolic of an unconscious attitude that you have repressed. For example, the groom asks what time the funeral is, when he means the wedding.

A second great contribution is his assertion that dreams have meaning. To Freud, dreams represented fulfillment of wishes that are hidden from consciousness. Even in dreams, wishes may be hidden by symbols of real wishes, known as *Freudian symbols*. Sometimes they have to do with a child's jealousy of the father and love of the mother, which Freud called the *Oedipus complex*, named after the Greek character Oedipus who kills his father and marries his mother.

The Id, Ego, and Super-Ego Freud devised a model of the psyche with three components: the Id, Ego, and Super-ego. The *Id* is present at birth and consists of drives that seek pleasure. The *Ego* seeks to control the Id. He said the Id was like a horse, and the Ego like the rider. The horse supplies the locomotive energy but the rider decides on the goal and guides the animal.

9-2b Age Trends in Humor

What children think is funny changes with age. You can think of children's humor as a window to their cognitive development. For example, the shift from the 3-month-old who smiles in response to Daddy talking, to the toddler's smile of satisfaction after successfully solving a puzzle, to the 10-year-old's smile at a play on words is a reflection of cognitive development. Children produce and appreciate humor that is neither too easy nor too difficult for them to understand. When they have just mastered a concept, they enjoy jokes about it.

Infancy and Toddlerhood (Birth to 2 Years)

Laughter emerges at about 4 months of age. Infants' first laugh is often in response to physical stimulation, like blowing on the tummy. Laughter in response to tickling emerges at about 6 months and almost disappears in adult middle age (Provine,

The Ego produces anxiety and repression, which keep impulses out of consciousness (Freud, 1905/1960). The *Super-ego* is the conscience that castigates the Ego for failing to control the Id. Moral behavior is the result of a strong Super-ego. The Super-ego is a "substitute for a longing for the father.... As a child grows up, the role of father is carried on by teachers and others in authority; their injunctions and prohibitions remain powerful... and continue, in the form of conscience, to exercise the moral censorship" (Freud, 1923/1961, p. 37). Thus, in Freud's view, you have a dual nature—amoral gratification of instincts and the moral Super-ego.

Humor Freud believed that jokes, like dreams, can have hidden meaning. The purpose can be simply to make others happy and laugh, or it can be to snub them, show aggression, or defend oneself. "By making our enemy... comic, we achieve in a roundabout way the enjoyment of overcoming him" (Freud, 1905/1960, pp. 102–103). Through jokes you can say things that are forbidden, or displace anger with laughter. Jokes allow the sneaky Id to evade control by the Ego.

Morality Freud believed that morality comes from emotions experienced within the family. Children identify with their parents as a result of love and attachment. Children transfer emotions that they feel toward parents to other authority figures such as teachers. Emotions, particularly guilt, regulate behavior because children behave morally in order to control emotions (Tangney, Stuewig, & Mashek, 2007). Research supports Freud's view that emotions and attachment are foundational to moral development. Notice that Freud's view is different from that of Piaget, who viewed morality as constructed by the child through cognitive development, or that of Skinner, who viewed moral behavior as learned through reinforcement.

Freud died when Skinner was 35. They are often portrayed as polar opposites. Freud focused on the mind and the meaning of behavior, while Skinner ignored mind and focused on environmental consequences that shape behavior mechanically. Despite their differences, they both believed that child development is controlled by the environment. They also both believed that people suffer when they are not aware of the forces that control behavior, and both applied their theories to improve society. In fact, Skinner often cited Freud's work and tried to get psychoanalyzed himself (Overskeid, 2007).

While Freud had some far-fetched ideas, like the universal fear of castration in little boys, other aspects of his theory have provided insight into human nature. In addition, psychoanalysis can be productive for healing emotional problems. Freud suggested that teachers should be analyzed and trained in psychoanalysis in order to appropriately help children control their Id (Freud, 1933/1964). Do you want to give it a try?

2000). By 12 months, laughter results more from the infant observing unusual behaviors, like putting a dishcloth on your head, than from physical stimulation.

Toddlers, who are beginning to use language, find word distortions amusing, like calling Daddy "doodoo." They may make jokes by mislabeling (e.g., calling a kitty a lion) or misinforming (e.g., lions say neigh or kitties drink water with a spoon). They may "clown," that is, repeat an act over and over, like walking strangely, in order to make you laugh. Toddlers may laugh hysterically after making a joke, and by age 2 can label their efforts as jokes (Cameron, Kennedy, & Cameron, 2008). Pretend play may be a type of joke, such as when a toddler pretends to fix soup for you, and you loudly slurp it, saying, "very good!" The toddler will laugh and rush to make more.

Early Childhood (3 to 5 Years)

From 3 to 5 years, children find incongruities in appearances and distortion of the physical world humorous, like a cow brushing its teeth or rabbit ears on a child.

Preschoolers are more likely to laugh at their own spontaneous distortions than others' distortions (Bariaud, 2013). Unfortunately for teachers and parents, "poop"-oriented jokes emerge. By age 4, children may begin to intentionally draw funny pictures. They find games involving "tricking" delightfully fun as their burgeoning ToM allows them to intentionally mislead others (Poulin-Dubois & Brosseau-Liard, 2016).

Middle Childhood (6 to 12 Years)

What children find funny shifts in middle childhood (Bariaud, 2013). They still find exaggerated movements and facial expressions funny. However, they move from word distortion, which preschoolers find funny, to interpretation of word meaning as they begin to understand puns and wordplays. For example, 1st-graders are enthusiastic about jokes like *Knock knock. Who's there? Orange. Orange who? Orange you glad I knocked?* Such jokes require phonetic awareness, which 1st-graders are busy learning. Younger children do not understand such jokes, and older children do not find them funny anymore. Many 3rd- to 7th-graders enjoy the incongruity of a verbal joke like *"Order! Order in the Court!"* *"Ham and cheese on rye, please, Your Honor"* that most 1st-graders do not yet "get" (Dowling, 2013). This explains why books of riddles are popular reading material among elementary-age children (Semrud-Clikeman & Glass, 2010).

There is a movement toward antisocial jokes around 4th grade, whereas such jokes are seldom heard in younger children (Socha & Kelly, 1994). At this age, children also begin to understand sarcasm. An observer who watches a driver run into a mailbox might say, "You're a great driver!" Five-year-olds are likely to take the sarcastic remark as truthful—he really is a good driver. Ten-year-olds realize the speaker means the opposite, and would likely find it funny. This is partly a result of a growing ToM; indeed, ToM is assessed in older children by their understanding of sarcasm (Peterson, Wellman, & Slaughter, 2012).

Children's understanding of teasing shifts in middle childhood. Because they do not always understand when a peer is kidding, 1st-graders are more likely to react negatively to teasing than 3rd-graders. By 3rd grade, children are reasonably good at recognizing teasing, irony, and sarcasm, but cannot articulate how they recognize it until about 5th or 6th grade (Keltner et al., 2001). Children also get better at communicating playfulness, so that they less often have to say, "I was just kidding." Perhaps for this reason, 6th-graders view teasing more positively than do younger children (Photo 9.3). With age, children change the issues that they tease about. For example, there is more teasing about the opposite sex among late elementary than early elementary children.

Adolescence (13 to 19 Years)

In the teens, particularly among boys, put-downs become popular across cultures. Teens use humor to soften commands and criticisms, like saying "Thanks for taking off your shoes" to a visitor who had not removed shoes. They make off-the-wall comments like "Check out the abs on

PHOTO 9.3 Playful teasing promotes social cohesion. Children grow in their ability to recognize, appreciate, and pull off playful teasing.

Highwaystarz-Photography/Getty Images

that seagull!" (Cameron, Fox, Anderson, & Cameron, 2010). In addition, adolescents' humor includes broader social topics than the humor of younger children. For example, many teens find the *Darwin Awards* amusing (Northcutt, 2000). The awards are given to people who die as a result of their own foolishness and "improve the gene pool by removing themselves from it." Younger children do not understand such satirical humor. Adolescents are capable of understanding puns and double entendres, like the song title "If I Said You Had a Beautiful Body, Would You Hold It against Me?" and other witticisms. This is what draws some teachers to work in secondary schools—adolescents' humor is imaginative, clever, and fun from an adult's perspective.

9-2c Individual Diversity in Humor

Humor is so widely valued in many cultures that it is an insult to accuse someone of having no sense of humor. However, you probably know people with a great sense of humor and others with a paltry sense of humor. Let's look at a 2-year-old with an unusually good sense of humor:

> Akiva hands her teacher a toy phone. The teacher puts the phone to her ear and says, "Hello? Uh huh, Uh huh, Uh huh, Uh huh, Uh huh, Uh huh. Goodbye!" Akiva giggles at this absurd conversation with such enthusiasm that some of her classmates begin laughing too.

Akiva consistently laughs more than most of her classmates. Her good sense of humor may affect her success in school. Let's look at this next.

What Do Individual Differences in Humor Predict?

Humor helps learners cope with difficult situations by taking a lighthearted view of stressful events (Dowling, 2013). Imagine two children are getting acquainted, and one tells the other that he is repeating 3rd grade. The second child responds, "You must be pretty dumb." In one study, most 8- to 12-year-olds agreed that the best response to this stressful situation is to use humor, like, "You have an interesting way of making friends." Unfortunately, the children were not very good at generating humorous responses for themselves; the only coping strategy most could think of was to ignore the remark (Lightner, Bollmer, Harris, Milich, & Scambler, 2000). Thus, children sometimes need help to use humor as a coping strategy.

Humor also facilitates social acceptance. Children with a good sense of humor are liked better by both teachers and peers. In a study of more than 5,000 2nd- through 12th-graders, children who were popular leaders were described as having a sense of humor (Zeller, Vannatta, Schafer, & Noll, 2003). Adolescents who are humorous are less likely to be socially withdrawn, but they are also more likely to occasionally misbehave in class (Sletta, Sobstad, & Valas, 1995). Humor used effectively, and at the right time, in social interaction is a key part of social competence. However, antisocial, derisive humor can undermine social acceptance. Thus, playful humor contributes to social acceptance, but antisocial humor does not.

What Predicts Individual Differences in Humor?

At least two factors might lead some learners to have a better sense of humor: information-processing ability and creativity. Appreciation of verbal humor is related to working memory, verbal ability, intelligence, and cognitive flexibility (Greengross & Miller, 2011). ToM ability is required for jokes involving others' mind states. Knowledge of one's culture is required for puns, jokes with hidden meanings, and incongruities. For example, children must understand how doorstep dialogue is supposed to occur in order to find "knock knock" jokes funny. Thus, it takes both knowledge and rapid information processing to "get" jokes.

Humor is often delayed in learners with delayed cognitive abilities (Short, Basili, & Schatschneider, 1993). In contrast, cognitively advanced learners tend to have advanced humor, like 2-year-old Akiva. For example, in a 9th-grade English class, the teacher was explaining when to use "good" or "well." One boy raised his hand and said, "I just use whichever sounds well." The teacher chuckled with this bright boy, but many of the other students missed the joke. Medications for ADHD that alter information processing may reduce sense of humor or readiness to laugh in children (Panksepp, 2000).

Humor is also linked to creativity. This is because humor is triggered by incongruity, like seeing an idea or object out of its normal place or seeing something familiar with new eyes. Generating this incongruity is a creative activity, a type of mental gymnastics. In one study, 10th- and 11th-graders who were nominated by their peers as being unusually humorous were also more creative (Ziv, 2013). In Chapter 8 you learned that positive emotions may promote creativity. Thus, creativity may be both a cause and a consequence of humor.

9-2d Group Diversity in Humor

There are some gender differences in humor. Boys may be more humorous than girls in some ways; for example, they write funnier captions for cartoons and laugh more (Greengross & Miller, 2011). However, they tend more toward somewhat antisocial humor. In a study of elementary and middle school students, tickling was a common source of humor among girls, whereas the minor misfortunes of others was a common source of humor among boys (Dowling, 2013). Boys and girls tease about the same amount, but girls are more likely to back off if the target reacts negatively, by saying, "I was just joking," or by cajoling the target to laugh. Boys, on the other hand, may escalate the teasing to a higher level when the target reacts negatively, laughing and enjoying it more, while they duck as the target swings at them (Eder, 1991). In a study of 3rd-graders, boys were more likely to cross the line from teasing to ridicule, particularly when the target was a girl (Voss, 1997). Thus, boys may go too far with teasing more often than girls.

9-2e Classroom Implications of Humor

Humor in the classroom enhances attention, makes learning enjoyable, and creates more positive relationships as well as a positive classroom climate

Marmaduke St. John/Alamy Stock Photo

PHOTO 9.4 Humor in the classroom can enhance attention and make learning enjoyable.

(Fitzsimmons & McKenzie, 2003). See Photo 9.4. Humor may also improve learning (Banas, Dunbar, Rodriguez, & Liu, 2010; Martin, Preiss, Gayle, & Allen, 2006). Sprinkling textbooks with cartoons may increase comprehension and motivation to read (Chua, 2014). You can promote humor in your classroom by initiating your own humor, and by accepting children's humor.

Be Humorous Yourself

Being humorous may be more challenging for secondary teachers, who tend to use less humor than elementary teachers. Reviews of several studies found that humor occurs on average about six times per hour in upper elementary school, but two to three times per hour in junior high and high school (Banas et al., 2010; McGhee, 2013). Use these guidelines to incorporate more humor in your classroom:

1. Keep humor positive. Sarcastic, antisocial humor can damage teacher–student relationships. Humor based on gross-out comments, sex, bodily functions, or obscenity has no place in the classroom.

2. Plan humor, especially if it does not come naturally to you. Build humor into lessons. Practice being humorous, field-test material, and memorize jokes. Use props like food and toys. Use cartoons and TV clips to illustrate concepts or dramatize material. For example, when you teach new material, you could use theme music or clothing from familiar television shows (Berk, 2002).

Accept Children's Humor (When Appropriate)

You do not need to be the primary source of humor in your classroom. Your students will generate humor if you encourage it. Just as with teacher-initiated humor, child-initiated humor may be more common in elementary than in secondary school. In a classic study, smiling and laughter occurred two to three times more in a 3rd-grade versus an 11th-grade classroom (Fabrizi & Pollio, 1987). If you want to increase children's humor in your classroom, use these guidelines:

1. Respond positively to humor. Elementary teachers tend to respond more positively than secondary teachers. In addition, teachers tend to respond more positively to the humorous remarks or behavior of children with whom they have a better relationship (Fabrizi & Pollio, 1987). Thus, you may have to try harder to appreciate the humor of students with whom you have a difficult relationship.

2. Be aware of the culture-based humor of your students if they are from a different ethnic group than you.

3. Invite children to share humor. One of our children's favorite elementary teachers enthusiastically encouraged children to share jokes with her at the beginning of each school day. This set a positive tone for the class, and also kept jokes within teacher-set bounds.

4. Clearly distinguish between playful teasing and antisocial humor. One adult recalled how distressing it was to be called "banana nose" because of his large nose: "I would go home or in the bathroom at school and cry and cry" (Kowalski, 2000, p. 234). In Chapter 10 you will learn how to decrease antisocial behavior among students.

Child-initiated humor can sometimes disrupt class and may need limits. In middle school, humorous students are likely to call out, be out of their seats, not do their schoolwork, and interact with other students. That is, they are highly active and social. By high school, humorous students are more skillful at abiding by classroom rules while still being humorous (Fabrizi & Pollio, 1987). Most learner-initiated humor is only mildly disruptive to class. For example, Joseph's response—"battery low"—in the opening story briefly disrupted the algebra lesson. It also added zest to class. Joseph was a good class clown—a delightful, upbeat child who made teaching fun. He was also a good person in the moral sense, which is our next topic.

9-3 Moral Judgment

The impressions you form of another person (e.g., is this someone you want to work with, marry, or live next door to?) tend to be based on three overarching dimensions: (1) moral character (e.g., honest, trustworthy, just, equitable), (2) prosocial behavior (e.g., kindness, warmth, friendliness), and (3) competence. These are universal dimensions in the way we think about others (Goodwin, 2015). Of the three dimensions, moral character may be the most powerful in shaping our impressions of others (Uhlmann, Pizarro, & Diermeier, 2015). In this section we'll discuss how children come to be honest and just. In Chapter 10 we'll discuss how they come to be kind.

> *I was standing in the classroom, looking out the window, and I saw Ruby coming down the street, with the federal marshals on both sides of her. The crowd was there, shouting, as usual. A woman spat at Ruby but missed; Ruby smiled at her. A man shook his fist at her; Ruby smiled at him. Then she walked up the stairs, and she stopped and turned and smiled one more time! You know what she told one of the marshals? She told him she prays for those people, the ones in that mob, every night before she goes to sleep! (Coles, 1986, pp. 22–23)*

This is the account of a teacher watching 6-year-old Ruby Bridges, the African American child who initiated school desegregation in New Orleans in 1960. Ruby was the only student in the entire school for a while because the other students' parents kept them home. She even received death threats.

How does a 6-year-old come to know what is morally right, and act on it in spite of threats, including from authority figures? See Photo 9.5. There are different views on what motivates moral behavior. The ethologist view is that humans have an inborn tendency to care for others because it promotes their survival (Krebs, 2008). The behaviorist view is that children acquire values through imitation and reinforcement (see Chapter 3). Freud's view was that children identify with and internalize their parents' values (see Box 9.2). Yet another view is that rather than learning morality from external sources, children internally construct principles of right and wrong as they develop cognitively. The last view emphasizes moral judgment, which we discuss next.

PHOTO 9.5 Ruby Bridges was a moral exemplar at age 6.

9-3a Different Views of Moral Judgment

Moral judgment refers to how children *reason* about moral issues and laws. Notice that this is not the same as moral *behavior* because it focuses on *thinking*, not *behaving*. Cognitive developmental theorists believe that with age, children develop increasingly advanced reasoning about justice, which leads to increased morality. That is, children are not morally mature until they are cognitively mature. Piaget was a leader of this view.

moral judgment
reasoning about moral dilemmas that involve justice in a context where rules, laws, formal obligations, and authority are emphasized.

Piaget's View

Piaget believed that children do not simply copy the moral standards of their culture, but rather that conflict during interaction with peers leads children to *construct* their own notions of right and wrong. Piaget viewed *justice* as the essence of morality. To study children's concepts of justice, Piaget told them stories of misbehavior, like playing with a ball in the house and breaking a lamp. Then he asked children what would be fair and unfair punishment. Based on their responses, Piaget concluded that children have two kinds of moral reasoning:

1. Heteronymous morality is authority-oriented. Rules are viewed as fixed and unalterable, and should be rigidly followed. Heteronymous children behave well in order to avoid punishment and because of the pressure of external authority.

2. Autonomous morality is based on reciprocity, mutual respect, and cooperation, rather than external pressure. (Piaget, 1965, p. 196)

Kohlberg's View

Lawrence Kohlberg developed a stage-based model of moral development that followed Piaget's ideas. He gave children hypothetical dilemmas and asked them to make a judgment about the morality of an act. The most famous is the *Heinz dilemma*, which involves stealing:

> *In Europe, a woman was near death from a special kind of cancer. There was one drug that the doctors thought might save her . . . but the druggist was charging 10 times what the drug cost him to make. He . . . charged $2,000 for a small dose of the drug. The sick woman's husband, Heinz, went to everyone he knew to borrow the money, but he could only get together about $1,000 . . . He told the druggist that his wife was dying and asked him to sell it cheaper or let him pay later. But the druggist said, "No, I discovered the drug and I'm going to make money from it." So Heinz gets desperate and considers breaking into the man's store to steal the drug for his wife. (Colby, Kohlberg, Gibbs, & Lieberman, 1983, p. 77)*

Children would then be asked a series of questions such as "Is it morally wrong to steal the drug?" Kohlberg outlined six stages in the development of moral judgment following the pattern of Piaget's stages you learned in Chapter 3, although Piaget did not emphasize stages of morality (Piaget, 1965). Kohlberg believed the stages occur in the same sequence across cultures, as follows (Colby et al., 1983):

Level I: Preconventional Morality: Punishment and Obedience to Authority

Stage 1: "Right" is being obedient, not breaking laws, and not damaging others or property. The reason for doing right is to avoid punishment.

Stage 2: "Right" is fairness, or following rules when it is to your advantage. The reason for doing right is to serve your own interests.

Level II: Conventional Morality: Laws Are Supreme

Stage 3: "Right" is living up to what is expected of you, being loyal, trustworthy, and supporting your family or friends. The reason for doing right is to be viewed as a "good" person, caring for others, or living the Golden Rule.

Stage 4: "Right" is fulfilling duties you've agreed to, contributing to society, and upholding laws (except in extreme cases). This is the "law-and-order" stage. The reason for doing right is to keep society functioning.

Level III: Postconventional Morality: Abstract Principles of Justice and Rights

Stage 5: "Right" is acknowledging that values and rules are relative, but should be upheld to support society. Some absolute values exist (e.g., life, liberty). The reason for doing right is protection of rights, doing the "greatest good for the greatest number," and commitment to contracts.

Stage 6: "Right" is following self-chosen ethical principles. If principles and laws conflict, follow the principles. The reason for doing right is a commitment to universal moral principles of justice, equality, and dignity.

The stages are hierarchical. That is, higher stages represent higher moral reasoning, because justifications are more philosophically sound (Carpendale, 2000).

There are a few key criticisms of Kohlberg's model, one of which is his restricted view of morality. Stages 1, 2, and 3 are intuitively recognized by people as hierarchical. That is, most people would agree that stage 1 reasoning is of lower quality than stage 3 reasoning. However, there is disagreement with Kohlberg's ranking of supposedly higher stages. In addition, it is not clear where some values, such as obligation to one's elders or religious faith, fit in the model. Furthermore, in Kohlberg's model, caring is in stage 3, which is lower than the law-and-order stage 4. Is upholding laws morally higher than caring? This issue is related to gender differences that we will discuss later. The tension between justice and caring has been a key philosophical and religious issue throughout history. A treatment of this tension is beyond the scope of this text, but clearly Kohlberg's view of morality is limited, although most would agree that justice is an important part of morality (Goodwin, 2015; Uhlmann et al., 2015).

think about **this**

Do you agree with the sequence of stages Kohlberg proposed? Do you see any biases that Kohlberg may have had in what he considered "higher" levels of morality? Ask a few friends to describe the attributes of the most moral person they know. Do the attributes fit with Kohlberg's, or your own, notion of morality?

Prosocial Reasoning

prosocial reasoning
reasoning about moral dilemmas in which one person's needs or desires conflict with another's, but in a context in which laws, rules, or formal obligations are minimal.

Prosocial reasoning is reasoning about dilemmas in which caring about others is pitted against self-interest, rather than dilemmas about justice and laws (Eisenberg, Hofer, Sulik, & Liew, 2014). Many real-world dilemmas involve prosocial reasoning, rather than moral judgment. To study prosocial reasoning, psychologists give children hypothetical dilemmas, such as keeping food versus sharing with others, playing with friends versus helping a classmate study for a test, or standing up for a peer being teased. One commonly used dilemma involves a birthday party:

> *On the way to a party, Emmalee saw a girl who had fallen down and hurt her leg. The girl asked Emmalee to go get her parents. But if Emmalee did run and get the girl's parents, Emmalee would be late to the party and miss the fun with her friends. (Adapted from Carlo, Koller, Eisenberg, Da Silva, & Frohlich, 1996, p. 233)*

Children are asked what they should do, and why. In addition, researchers sometimes observe children's natural moral behaviors and then ask them why they behaved that way. Five different types of reasoning have been identified:

1. *Hedonistic.* The focus is on self-oriented consequences, such as "I like her," or "She'll do the same for me."

2. *Needs-oriented.* The focus is on the other's need, such as "She needs my help."

3. *Approval.* The focus is on others' approval, such as "Her parents will thank me."

4. *Stereotyped.* The focus is on what "good" people do and a desire to be considered "good," such as "People will think I'm a good person if I help."

5. *Internalized.* The focus is on how being good makes one feel, such as "I would feel better if I help."

These types of reasoning are hierarchical in that the fifth is considered a higher form of prosocial reasoning than the first. This sequence is subject to criticism, as with Kohlberg's stages, because focusing on how Emmalee would feel if she did not help (level 5) may not be morally higher than focusing on the other girl's needs (level 2).

Honesty and Lying

In addition to being just and fair, moral character includes being honest and refraining from lying (Goodwin, 2015; Uhlmann et al., 2015). Lies are intentionally false statements. False statements that are not intentional, like mistakes, are not lies. One caveat about the morality of lying is that most people believe trivial lies that benefit others or are humorous are not immoral, such as "We're glad the principal is visiting our classroom today." These are known as *white lies, altruistic lies,* and *trick lies.* They are viewed differently from malicious lies or lies to cover up misdeeds.

9-3b Age Trends in Moral Judgment

Piaget (1932) studied how children understand and evaluate lying. Not surprisingly, he found age trends in understanding lies that parallel age trends in moral judgment and prosocial reasoning. Let's discuss these age trends next.

Infancy and Toddlerhood (Birth to 2 Years)

Moral development builds on an early sense of fairness. Toddlers expect resources to be shared equally and will look longer at events that are not fair. For example, in one study, 19-month-olds looked longer at events in which puppets were not given equal

FIGURE 9.6 Toddlers Have a Sense of Fairness.

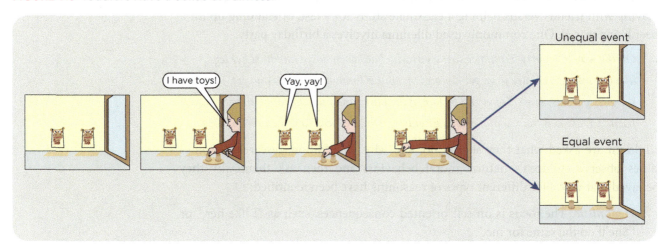

Toddlers looked longer at the unequal distribution of toys and cookies, than the equal distribution, suggesting that they expected fairness. *Source: Sloane et al. (2012).*

amounts of toys or cookies (see Figure 9.6). In a follow-up study, 21-month-olds looked longer at a situation in which equal rewards were given to two people, after one had helped clean up but the other did not. They seemed to expect more reward for the worker than for the slacker; that is, a just, rather than equal, distribution (Sloane, Baillargeon, & Premack, 2012). Studies such as these suggest that infants have an innate moral sense when they are too young to talk and too young to have experienced enough of the world to "construct" a moral sense (Hamlin, 2013).

While they may expect fairness, toddlers are not necessarily honest. They begin to lie as soon as they are able to talk. Two-year-olds intentionally deceive others, such as erasing footprints leading to a hiding place or saying they did not peek when they did (Chandler, Fritz, & Hala, 1989; Evans & Lee, 2013), and they are capable of emotional dissemblance, such as fake crying to get sympathy (see Chapter 8). Lying is normal among toddlers, who typically do not understand what constitutes a lie.

Early Childhood (3 to 5 Years)

Moral reasoning builds upon other developing skills—executive functions, reading others' emotions, and theory of mind—that allow preschoolers to begin to know right from wrong (Decety & Howard, 2013). See Photo 9.6. By age 3 they tend not to violate parents' prohibitions, they are distressed if they do, and they confess wrongdoing (Emde, Biringen, Clyman, & Oppenheim, 1991). They become upset when resources are not allocated fairly, and they try to fix inequity. For example, in a study in which one puppet had two cups of playdough and another had just one, 4-year-olds gave playdough to the deprived puppet (Li, Spitzer, & Olson, 2014). Preschoolers will strongly protest violations and enforce rules ("it goes here!"). This is true even for rules of games, which 3-year-olds see as unalterable facts handed down by supreme authorities, just as Piaget described for heteronymous morality (Köymen et al., 2014). However, by age 5 children see game rules as negotiable.

By age 4 or 5, children distinguish between social convention and morality. **Social conventions** are standards of behavior dictated by culture. Preschoolers know that a breach of social convention, like calling a teacher by her first name, is wrong only if there is a rule against it, and the rule can be changed. They also know that it is wrong to hit someone in order to get a swing even if they are told the school has a rule saying it is all right (Helwig & Turiel, 2011). They believe that a **moral transgression** is wrong regardless of rules, and its wrongness is unchangeable. This is contrary to Piaget's views of 5-year-olds as egocentric and externally oriented in their moral judgments (Thompson, 2012).

Preschoolers do not fully understand what a lie is. They equate exaggeration, "naughty" words, incorrect statements, and mistaken guesses with lies. They may think of "lies" as statements about negative acts and truths as statements about positive acts (Wandrey, Quas, & Lyon, 2012). They have an overly generous view of what a lie is. Yet, they recognize the difference between "good" and "bad" lies. They view lying to cover up a misdeed as morally wrong and judge white lies less harshly than lies intended to harm others (Evans & Lee, 2013; Jambon & Smetana, 2014; Talwar & Lee, 2008).

Despite recognizing lies as morally wrong, preschoolers are quite willing to lie. Children lie more from the toddler to preschool years (Evans & Lee, 2013). See Figure 9.7. Scientists have a sneaky way of testing this. They put a secret toy behind young children and say, "Do not turn around and peek at the toy. I'll be back soon" and leave the room. Hidden cameras reveal that about 80% of young children peek

PHOTO 9.6 Rudimentary morality is present by age 3.

Mel Yates/Stone/Getty images

social conventions
standards of behavior dictated by culture.

moral transgression
behavior that is inherently wrong, independent of culture, and regardless of rules.

FIGURE 9.7 Age Trends in Lying.

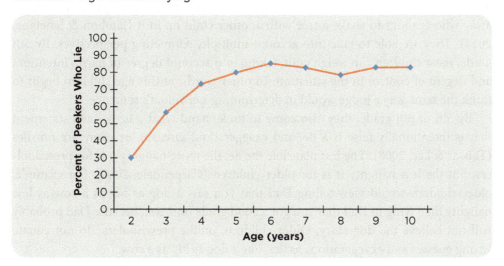

In experiments in which children are asked not to peek, most peek but some do not. Among the peekers, the percentage of those who lie, or deny that they peeked, increases with age. Where is the steepest increase? *Source: Lee (2013).*

at the toy. Among the peekers, 2- to 3-year-olds confess, but most 4- to 5-year-olds lie, saying they did not peek (Lee, 2013).

Preschoolers are not always successful at lying. In these experiments, follow-up conversations with preschoolers often go something like this:

Experimenter:	*Did you peek at the toy?*
Child:	*No.*
Experimenter:	*What do you think the toy is?*
Child:	*A Barney doll because it was purple.*

The truth often leaks out because preschoolers do not have sufficient ToM or executive functions to maintain the lie. Even when researchers offer them a reward for lying, 3-year-olds are not very successful (Ding et al., 2015). The ability to successfully lie develops rapidly between ages 3 and 7, as does the prevalence of lying (Lee, 2013).

In summary, children behave as though they have some moral sense by 3 years of age. They are able to distinguish social conventions from moral issues. They are prolific, but not very successful, liars even though by age 3 they believe lying is wrong.

Middle Childhood (6 to 12 Years)

Elementary children are able to reason about morality and do not rigidly adhere to laws the way that Kohlberg suggested they do. For example, 6- to 10-year-olds can reason about whether it would be all right to violate harmful laws (Helwig & Jasiobedzka, 2001). In addition, they believe lies are morally wrong because they interfere with trust and social justice, not simply because authority figures prohibit them (Carpendale, 2000).

In middle childhood, children become better at taking intention into account when judging others' behavior. They come to view "prosocial lies" as less harmful and more acceptable. For example, they would judge Sariah more positively if she lies to Peter that she is too sick to play with him because she wants to shop secretly to buy a present for him, than if she lies because she wants to shop for herself. They also come to view "necessary harm" as more acceptable, such as pushing a friend away who is about to shake a tree with another child up in it (Jambon & Smetana, 2014). They are able to take into account multiple, competing perspectives. By 5th grade, most children can weigh guilt, taking into account degree of harm, intention, and degree of control in the situation. In other words, at this age children begin to think the same way a judge would in determining a criminal's sentence.

By 5th or 6th grade, they also come to understand what a lie is—any statement that is intentionally false is a lie, and exaggeration, sarcasm, or irony are not lies (Talwar & Lee, 2008). The less plausible the lie, the more naughty it is for preschoolers, but the less naughty it is for older children (Carpendale, 2000). For example, older children would view telling Dad that you saw a dog as big as a cow as less naughty than lying to Dad that you got a good grade on a test, because Dad probably will not believe the dog story. Older children, unlike preschoolers, do not equate wrong guesses and exaggerations as lies, like a dog as big as a cow.

Frequency of lying tends to increase into the early elementary years, but then diminishes. From ages 8 to 16, children who peeked at test answers become increasingly less likely to lie about it (Evans & Lee, 2011). Sophistication of lying continues to increase. By 1st or 2nd grade, children have the ToM and executive functions to maintain a lie, so that the truth doesn't leak out.

Adolescence (13 to 19 Years)

Adolescents are less likely to lie than younger children (Evans & Lee, 2011). Some believe this is because they have internalized moral norms. Kohlberg's view was that in adolescence youth may reach stage 3. Stage 4 is typically reached by college students. Stages 5 and 6 are reached by only some adults. Thus, according to Kohlberg, adolescents and most adults are unlikely to be reasoning at the highest levels of morality. Research confirms that adolescents are better than younger children at judging complex issues of justice (Wainryb, Brehl, & Matwin, 2005), though children as young as 3rd grade distribute resources based on deservingness (e.g., who worked hardest) and special needs (Gummerum, Keller, Takezawa, & Mata, 2008).

In contrast to moral judgment, prosocial reasoning does not improve much in adolescence. In fact, many adolescents regress in prosocial reasoning. When involved in conflict between self-interest and others' needs, teens may be *more hedonistic* and young adults *more stereotyped* in their reasoning, and no more other-oriented than younger children (Carlo et al., 1996; Eisenberg et al., 2014). Adolescents may be more willing to excuse not helping if cost is high and need is low compared to younger children (Sierksma, Thijs, Verkuyten, & Komter, 2014). Some adolescents become skilled at generating self-serving justifications for their misdeeds or decisions not to help others, and even moral disengagement in which they distance themselves from their misdeeds (Bandura, 2015; Recchia, Wainryb, Bourne, & Pasupathi, 2015; Shalvi, Gino, Barkan, & Ayal, 2015). Thus, with age youth may become more logical when discussing laws and justice, but they are not necessarily more selfless.

On the other hand, as adolescents get older, they are more likely to report feeling good after making a moral, rather than a selfish, decision, such as helping a friend with homework rather than playing basketball (Casey et al., 2011). Still, a small minority report feeling good after acting in self-interest. Let's discuss this individual variation next.

think about **this**

If children become better at moral judgment with age, as cognitive developmental theorists would assert, how can you explain adults who spit on 6-year-olds, as some did to Ruby? What factors might lead to such behavior?

9-3c Individual Diversity in Moral Judgment

A famous study was conducted by Hartshorne and May (1928) during the 1920s to address the question of how religious education affected cheating, stealing, and lying. More than 11,000 1st- through 12th-graders from diverse communities were tested in ordinary classrooms using 29 different tasks that challenged children's moral behavior. For example, the researchers would give children the answer key and tell them to score their own tests (after a copy of the original answers had secretly been made). They gave the children athletic tests, like pull-ups, and told them to record their own results. They planted a dime in a puzzle box to see if children returned the dime.

Two major conclusions came from this famous study. One was that religious instruction did not keep children from behaving immorally in the face of temptation, which was very disappointing to their Sunday school teachers. The second was that moral behavior is quite situation-specific, and some situations can tempt almost any child into dishonesty. For example, 92% of children cheated at least once on timed

iStockphoto.com/sjlocke

PHOTO 9.7 The classic Hartshorne and May study found that there were large individual differences in moral behavior, but some situations could tempt almost anyone.

arithmetic tests. However, there were also large individual differences in cheating; some children seldom cheated, and others cheated at every opportunity.

These results are still relevant today (Photo 9.7). Research indicates that honesty is influenced by the situation and that individual differences in honesty appear by early childhood. For example, in studies of toy peeking, more than one-third of guilty 3-year-olds confess and tell the truth, but the rest do not (Talwar & Lee, 2008). In a study of elementary children, half peeked at a test and half did not. Of those who peeked, 93% lied about it (Talwar, Gordon, & Lee, 2007). Are such differences in moral *behavior* the result of differences in moral *judgment*? That is, are children who discuss moral dilemmas at a more sophisticated level than their peers also more honest, just, and compassionate? Let's see what the research says.

What Do Individual Differences in Moral Judgment Predict?

There is no clear relationship between *prosocial reasoning* and moral behavior among older children. Among preschoolers, *needs-oriented* and *internalized* reasoning are related to more kind behavior (Carlo et al., 1996; Eisenberg et al., 2014). There also is no clear relationship between *moral judgment* and moral behavior. Children with *above-average* moral judgment and understanding of lying are not consistently more honest, fair, generous, or compassionate than average children, although *below-average* moral judgment is linked to aggression and delinquency (Gummerum et al., 2008; Talwar & Lee, 2008). In addition, compassion emerges in the first years of life (see Chapter 10), but sophisticated moral judgment does not appear before adolescence. Furthermore, some adolescents engage in antisocial activities, like shoplifting, even though they have greater moral judgment than younger children who do not engage in antisocial activities (Kuther & Higgins-D'Alessandro, 2000).

Fifteen-year-old Heather exemplifies this disconnect. She is old enough to reason about moral issues, but she cheats in school. She feels bad about cheating, but she feels pressure to get good grades. She also lies to her parents. She says that she believes in right and wrong, but her views of morality are based on not getting caught. She recalls drinking alcohol: "The first time I did it, I was a wreck, like paranoid [about getting caught], but other times when I think I won't get caught it's taken a lot of pressure off, so a lot depends on if I think I'm gonna get caught." Heather cannot explain what makes things right and wrong beyond the consequences. She says, "I don't really think about this stuff too much! . . . I don't really know where morality comes from" (adapted from Smith & Denton, 2005, p. 198).

The lack of a strong relationship between moral judgment or prosocial reasoning and moral behavior is called the moral judgment–action gap. What might explain this gap? There are other components to moral behavior besides reasoning. When faced with a moral issue, a student must:

- see the situation as being moral in nature.

- judge which action is morally right (this is what Kohlberg emphasizes).

- give priority to moral values.

- have the integrity, courage, and skill to act on the values.

For example, if adolescents view drug use or sexual activity as issues of personal choice—or falling in the "social convention" domain—rather than moral issues, there will be no link between moral judgment and these behaviors. Even if a student sees a situation as moral in nature (component 1) and knows what is right (component 2), he or she may not care (component 3), or may succumb to self-interest (component 4). Moral principles are supposed to keep people from acting in their own self-interest over the interests of others. Yet self-interest is a powerful motive, even for adults (Shalvi et al., 2015).

What Predicts Individual Differences in Moral Judgment and Behavior?

In the 1920s study, children with higher socioeconomic status (SES) and higher intelligence cheated less. In contrast, children with poor manners, like not tipping their hats at women they passed, cheated more. No single variable distinguished cheaters, but cheaters had a greater number of risk factors. Similar factors are still associated with differences in morality today. Let's discuss these next.

Theory of mind

Theory of mind is foundational to moral judgment (Thompson, 2012). Whether or not you blame someone for misbehavior (moral judgment) depends on whether you view the misbehavior as intentional (ToM judgment). Humans are unique in their ability to assess *intentional* states that allow moral judgment. Children with better ToM are more likely to have mature moral reasoning (Smetana, Jambon, Conry-Murray, & Sturge-Apple, 2012).

Children with better ToM may also be better liars because lying is the deliberate attempt to instill false beliefs in someone else. Children have been found to lie and deceive before they are able to pass false-belief tasks, meaning full-blown ToM is not necessary for dishonesty. However, individual children with better ToM are better liars in that they do not let the truth leak out as much as other children; they can maintain their lies despite questioning by an adult (Talwar & Lee, 2008). One scientist said that lying is ToM in action (Lee, 2013).

In young children, moral behavior is also related to inhibitory control. Preschoolers with good inhibitory control are more likely to obey the rule to clean up their mess or not cheat in a game when unsupervised. They also give less-selfish responses to prosocial dilemmas, like Emmalee helping an injured child and missing the birthday party, than children with less inhibitory control. Both inhibitory control and prosocial reasoning are linked to authoritative parenting.

Quality of parenting

Secure attachment and authoritative parenting are both foundational to development of conscience (Thompson, 2012). This is partly because parent–child relationships that are warm motivate the child to be receptive to parents' influence and to embrace their values (Kochanska, 2002). In addition, children whose parents are authoritative have higher levels of moral reasoning than other children because their parents are likely to use induction rather than power assertion (see Chapter 7). Induction is a form of discipline in which the adult explains the need for a rule and points out the consequences for others of the child's misbehavior. Parents are more likely to express anger and use induction (rather than commands) in response to *moral* transgressions as compared with other kinds of transgressions, such as making a mess (Dahl & Campos, 2013). Induction leads to internalization, or conscience, which refers to doing the right thing because it is right, not to avoid punishment. Induction promotes guilt, a moral emotion that inhibits immoral behavior (Tangney et al., 2007). Children whose parents use induction are more likely to feel bad if they cheat at a game, grab a toy, or do not help someone. Other-oriented induction conveys to children that the needs of others are important.

The way parents talk with children in nondiscipline encounters that involve moral events is also important. In one study 7- to 16-year-olds discussed with their mothers episodes of helping or harming a friend; the mothers praised their helping and pointed out how good it made the child feel (Recchia et al., 2015). In contrast, the mothers pointed out the inappropriateness of the harmful behavior, but still found a way to affirm the child as a moral person (e.g., "you don't usually behave like that," or "you feel bad because you care about others"). They used the opportunity to teach moral principles and help the child develop a moral identity, which is the next topic.

Moral identity

moral identity
the degree to which being a moral person is central to a person's self-identity.

Individuals with a strong **moral identity** feel that being moral is core to their self-identity. They tend to anticipate feeling positive about their good deeds and are more likely to behave in moral ways (Dinh & Lord, 2013; Hardy, Walker, Olsen, Woodbury, & Hickman, 2014). As young as age 5 children differ in their moral identity (Thompson, 2012). For example, in one study 5-year-olds were able to report whether they are the kind of person who is likely to tell someone right away when they break something, as opposed to trying to hide it so no one finds out. The children who self-identified with a strong moral compass were rated as better behaved 2 years later by their teachers (Kochanska, Koenig, Barry, Kim, & Yoon, 2010).

Education

Scores on Kohlberg's moral judgment interview are correlated with education level. Typically, only college graduates score at stage 4 or 5, which is not surprising because scores are based on the ability to make a logically coherent argument about abstract concepts. This is a problem for Kohlberg's model because common sense tells you that morality and education are not synonymous. As Ruby Bridges's "uneducated" mother said, there are some folk who "just put their lives on the line for what's right, and they may not be the ones who talk a lot . . . they just do a lot!" (Coles, 1986).

Ruby could not read or write when she started school, and may not have made it past Kohlberg's stage 2 during an interview, but she had moral integrity. Piaget pointed out that "intelligence alone might suffice to sharpen the child's evaluation of conduct without necessarily inclining him to do good actions . . . an intelligent scamp would perhaps give better answers than a slow-witted but really good-hearted little boy" (1965, p. 116).

Religiosity

Kohlberg stated that "religion is not a necessary or highly important condition for the development of moral judgment and conduct" (1981, p. 304). He distinguished morality from religiosity. He argued that because children in all religions proceed through the same invariant sequence of stages in moral judgment, religion cannot be a source of moral development. In Kohlberg's model, people who justify moral behavior based on conformity to God or their religion score at lower levels than those who use more justice-oriented reasoning.

Many adults and youth do not share this view. Research confirms that religious faith motivates moral behavior and forms the basis for judging whether a behavior is moral or not (Cohen, 2015). Ruby Bridges said that every Sunday she went to church, where she said people were admonished "to pray for everyone, even the bad people, and so I do" (Coles, 1986, p. 23).

Research robustly links both parents' and children's religiosity with moral behavior.[3] Parents' religiosity predicts their children's moral behavior and the children's own religiosity. Youth who frequently participate in religious activities are less likely to be depressed, delinquent, or violent, to cut classes, to drop out, to lie and cheat, to watch TV excessively, to play video games excessively, to view pornography, to use drugs, or to be sexually active at a young age. They are more likely to feel cared for, spend time with adults, get higher grades, get along with parents and siblings, attend college, feel guilt for transgressions, behave kindly, help others, perform community service, and express concern about racism and poverty—actually giving more of their own money to causes. Religious participation may especially contribute to the resilience of inner-city youth.

On the other hand, there is also evidence that some religious people are not more honest and are more discriminatory toward people who threaten their values (Cohen, 2015; Goldfried & Miner, 2002). Some people commit acts of violence motivated by their religion. Thus, in general religiosity is linked to greater moral behavior, but the beneficial effects of religiosity do not apply to all situations.

9-3d Group Diversity in Moral Judgment

Gender and SES are linked to moral judgment. Can you guess whether boys or girls have "higher" levels of moral judgment? Let's see what the research says.

Gender

There are no gender differences in the attributes that people ascribe to morally exemplary women or men, like honesty, loyalty, or religiosity (Walker & Pitts, 1998).

---

[3] Many studies support this conclusion, a few of which are listed here: King and Furrow (2004); Loury (2004); Petts (2009, 2014); Rostosky, Wilcox, Wright, and Randall (2004).

However, there may be some gender differences in moral reasoning. Early research showed that females scored lower than males in Kohlberg's model. Gilligan (1982) criticized Kohlberg's theory as a male version of morality and, based on interviews with women, suggested that women have a different moral voice. They focus more on *care reasoning*—giving priority to maintaining relationships and meeting others' needs—and men focus more on *justice reasoning*. Research shows the effect size for girls favoring care reasoning is 0.28, and for boys favoring justice reasoning is 0.19. This means that while there are small gender differences in moral orientation, most boys and girls use *both* care and justice reasoning (Jaffee & Hyde, 2000). Girls' judgments of morality may be more influenced by relationships than boys' judgments (Eisenberg, Zhou, & Koller, 2001). For example, adolescent girls are more likely than boys to say it is all right to let a friend copy one's homework, but not a nonfriend (Singer, 1999). Boys' judgments are the same for friends and nonfriends. Ironically, despite the focus on justice, more boys than girls may be frequent liars (Gervais, Tremblay, Desmarais-Gervais, & Vitaro, 2000).

Socioeconomic Status

Scores on Kohlberg's moral-judgment interview are correlated with SES. This is not surprising, because education is a component of SES, and education affects moral judgment scores. The higher-SES advantage is true for prosocial reasoning as well (Eisenberg et al., 2014). Most research linking SES and prosocial reasoning has been conducted in the United States, but the same pattern was found in Brazil, where 7th- and 10th-graders with highly educated, prosperous parents scored higher in prosocial reasoning (Eisenberg et al., 2001).

9-3e Classroom Implications of Moral Judgment

Moral education goes on in every classroom—indeed in every social group. It is unavoidable; you teach values to your students through the rules you choose to enforce and the way you behave. You make moral decisions when you decide what text to read and whom to hold up as an example. In U.S. schools today, moral education is typically haphazard rather than deliberate; it is a part of the hidden curriculum. In the past people believed education should be deliberately moral. For example, the McGuffey readers—a widely used text series in the 1800s—used moral stories to teach reading and arithmetic. However, deliberate moral education was avoided in U.S. schools during the latter half of the twentieth century. Recently, there has been a resurgence of interest, partly fueled by concerns about declining civility and rising aggression.

Many teachers are not comfortable with deliberate moral education. Yet, educator-philosopher Nel Noddings (1992) argued that, "Teachers should not be allowed to avoid their responsibilities as moral educators by claiming that they are not prepared for this work. All decent adults are, or should be, prepared for this work. It is a human responsibility—one that belongs to all of us" (p. 69).

So how should you approach moral education? Piaget and Kohlberg believed children's morality is *constructed* out of social interaction and principled reasoning. Behaviorists and Freud hold a different view; morality is *handed down* from elders to children. The term *moral education* is often used to refer to programs based on the first view, and the term *character educa-tion* is often used to refer to programs based on the second view (Berkowitz & Grych, 2000). However, both terms are sometimes applied to any education aimed at promoting morality. Let's take a look at what a moral teacher might do from each approach.

Moral Education (Constructing Morality)

Kohlberg believed the purpose of moral education is to stimulate development of moral judgment, but not to push specific values. He did not approve of indoctrination. Instead, children should be encouraged to examine the pros and cons of their behavior. He argued that moral education should promote autonomy. For example, to force children to agree that cheating is dishonest when they do not really believe it will only teach them to comply when it is expedient. Kohlberg later decided it was all right for teachers to advocate a particular moral view as long as they respected the child as an autonomous moral agent and did not appeal to their authority over the child. Justice is the main moral value that teachers should try to stimulate (Kohlberg, 1981).

PHOTO 9.8 Active discussion of moral issues can promote moral judgment from preschool to high school.

Kohlberg advocated creating "just community" schools at the secondary level. A just school emphasizes discussion of moral issues and joint decision making (Photo 9.8). His approach adheres to the principles of constructivist education that you learned about in Chapter 3. To promote moral judgment from this perspective, use these guidelines:

1. Be democratic, be cooperative, and share power with students. Create an atmosphere of mutual respect in adult–student relationships. Allow students to help make classroom rules and have a voice in decision making. Kohlberg advocated that just community schools hold weekly small-group meetings, of 10 to 12 students, to discuss issues and form bonds, as well as weekly all-school meetings to discuss and vote on school policies, such as how to deal with stealing.

2. Encourage classroom discussion about moral issues. An *active* discussion style, in which students request clarification, justification, and feedback, is associated with greater moral reasoning than is a passive discussion style, simple disagreement, or an opinionated lecture. Small-group debate promotes moral reasoning in students from kindergarten to college (Mayhew & King, 2008; Walker, Hennig, & Krettenauer, 2000).

This approach can even be used in preschool when reading stories. For example, a teacher fostered moral discussion while reading a well-known book to preschoolers called *Heckedy Peg*, wherein a witch has abducted children and their mother is trying to get them back. The witch tells the mother she cannot come into her house because the mother's feet are dirty, so the mother pretends to cut off her feet, but really just hides her legs (DeVries, Hildebrandt, & Betty, 2000). Here's how the dialogue went:

Teacher:	*Do you think that what the mother is saying is OK?*
Edward:	*Uh-uh, it's—she's lying.*
Teacher:	*Is it OK to lie in this case?*
Children:	*No!*
Teacher:	*No? Why? Can you tell me why it's not OK?*
John:	*It's bad, and she will look at her and say, "You have feet," and she'll say, "Yes I do." That's a lie, right?*
Amanda:	*I think that she's just trying to trick the witch. I think that she's just trying to get her children back.*
Teacher:	*OK, Edward has a disagreement. Tell us what you think. Do you think…it's OK to lie to save your children?*
Edward:	*Uh-uh, it's not.*
Teacher:	*Well, we have a difference of opinion. (Adapted from DeVries, Hildebrandt, & Betty, 2000, pp. 26–28)*

In this constructivist approach adults are not supposed to impose their values on children, yet critics point out that in constructivist practice adults typically do impose their values by indicating which response is acceptable (Goodman, 2000). If adults remain truly neutral, then what values should children internalize? Critics would further argue that a traditional approach in which the teacher clearly states a rule (e.g., "Telling lies is wrong—except to a witch who has stolen your children") is more honest.

Character Education (Handing Down Morality)

In contrast to Kohlberg, proponents of character education believe that character is a collection of virtues like honesty, kindness, courage, politeness, and obedience. These virtues are not innate, but are inculcated in the child. To promote moral behavior in your students from this perspective, use these guidelines:

1. Identify the virtues that you hope students will learn, and make them an explicit goal for students and teachers. Some teachers even post their goals on the wall.

2. Provide opportunities for students to practice the virtues. Some advocate volunteerism or service learning as one approach, but there are plenty of opportunities for students to be kind, helpful, and honest in routine classroom activities. Students need to practice and develop well-worn scripts for moral behavior.

3. Praise students who behave in accord with the virtues. This can be done privately or publicly in school ceremonies. However, keep in mind that extrinsic rewards for virtuous behavior can be coercive and may not produce moral students, although rewards might elicit temporary compliance with school rules (see Chapter 7).

4. Prohibit undesirable behavior and punish misbehavior, like cheating. However, keep in mind the costs of punishment that you read about in Chapter 7. If you must use punishment, combine it with other-oriented induction.

5. Discuss honesty with students and inculcate the value of honesty as a virtue. Asking students to promise to tell you the truth results in greater honesty (Talwar, Arruda, & Yachison, 2015). Reassure them that they will not be punished for honesty; they are less likely to tell the truth if they think they will be punished for transgressions.

6. Highlight virtuous role models. Use literature with moral heroes and virtuous deeds. In one study, children who heard the story of George Washington and the ever-suffering cherry tree, which extols the virtues of truth-telling, and were told "I want you to be like George Washington and tell the truth," were more truthful than children who heard stories about the negative consequences of lying, such as *Pinocchio* (Lee et al., 2014). Emphasizing honest behavior, rather than dishonest behavior, was more effective. However, be aware that elementary-age students, even as old as 5th grade, may not understand the theme of a moral story unless you make it explicit (Narvaez, 2002), or they may take a different message from the story than you intended, such as identifying with the bad character.

Critics of the character-education approach argue that behavior without principled reflection is not moral—indeed, that this may be the goal of totalitarian regimes. Rote obedience should not be the aim of moral education, because principled objection to oppressive rules is also moral. Proponents would counter that while self-determination based on moral principles is important, moral judgment is meaningless without habits of moral behavior.

Does Moral or Character Education Work?

Effective moral education should foster all four components of morality discussed earlier: (1) awareness that morals are involved in a situation, (2) ability to judge which action is morally right, (3) desire to do what is morally right, and (4) strength of character to act. However, few programs focus on all the components. The constructivist approaches focus on components 1 or 2, and traditional character education programs focus on 3 or 4.

Currently, there is not enough research to know which methods are most effective for any of these components, except perhaps component 2 (moral judgment). That is, studies find that moral education improves moral *judgment,* particularly for older students (Schlaefli, Rest, & Thomas, 1985). The two types of programs that are most effective, although they have small effects, are: (1) intense self-reflection after engaging in activities that serve others, such as cross-age tutoring, and (2) peer discussion of moral dilemmas, such as in high school civics classes. After just a few months of discussing moral issues and being exposed to the next higher stage of reasoning, approximately one-third of students will move up a stage in moral judgment. Without such experience, it typically takes several years to move up a stage. Academic courses in the humanities, literature, or social studies (like the Great Books program) that highlight moral issues generally do *not* have an effect on moral judgment.

Does moral education affect moral *behavior?* Research on just community high schools finds that students reason at a higher level than at comparison schools, but there is no difference in delinquency rates (Kuther & Higgins-D'Alessandro, 2000). Many companies have produced character-education curricula that schools

think
about this

Imagine that your school implemented a moral-education program. What would you measure in order to decide whether the program was a success or not? What kind of evidence would you want to see before deciding to adopt it? (Review Chapter 1.)

BOX 9.3 **challenges in development**

Academic Dishonesty

In a high school biology class, some students got copies of the final exam just before the test. At least one student bragged about it to another student, Todd, who mentioned test items to his mother. Misunderstanding, Todd's mother called the teacher to find out why her son had not been given a practice test like other students. The teacher figured out what had happened, but was never able to determine who had cheated. Students knew, based on the glares they gave to the cheaters, but no one confessed. The teacher gave the entire class an alternative, more difficult, exam at the beginning of the next semester. This left bad feelings all around. Students who legitimately had high scores were suspected. Some honest students' grades were worse after the time lag. One of the cheaters actually did better on the retest.

Did these students cheat because they did not understand that other students want a level playing field? If so, they lack theory of mind. Or, did they fully appreciate the fact that cheating hurts others, and simply not care? If so, they lack moral principle.

You may have heard a teacher tell students, "When you cheat, you only hurt yourself." This is not true. Cheating is an assault on students who behave honestly. It is an immoral act because it is uncaring toward others. Cheating undermines fairness, equity, and trust. It also undermines the validity and purpose of tests. Cheating hurts the whole community.

This example is not the only form of cheating. Cheating in school, or academic dishonesty, can take many forms. These include copying answers for a test, lying about why homework was not turned in, and plagiarism, which is presenting someone else's intellectual work (or words) as your own.

How can you tell if a child is cheating or lying? You probably cannot. Most adults are not skilled at detecting lying (Ekman, O'Sullivan, & Frank, 1999). Similarly, detecting cheating on tests is very difficult (Cizek, 1999). Todd's

teacher would not have known students had cheated if Todd's mother had not accidentally let the teacher know. Most cheating is not detected.

So how do you know how prevalent cheating is? It is not clear how common cheating really is. Most studies use self-report to determine cheating, which may underestimate the real prevalence. In one study of 23,000 adolescents, 51% admitted they had cheated on a test during the past year, with 28% doing so at least twice, and 32% admitted plagiarizing an assignment by using the Internet (Josephson Institute of Ethics, 2012). In another study, 20 to 25% of 7th- to 11th-graders reported cheating on a science-fair entry—they made up data, copied someone else's work, or received inappropriate help (Syer & Shore, 2001). In still another study, 89% of high school students had copied off someone else's homework within the past year (Jensen, Arnett, Feldman, & Cauffman, 2002). Thus, cheating is common and may vary by task, such as exams versus projects.

What predicts cheating?

- Knowledge that others are cheating (O'Rourke et al., 2010; Rettinger & Kramer, 2009).
- Lax attempts to prevent cheating.
- Belief that the teacher is unreasonably difficult, unfair, or has not taught the material that will be tested (Murdock & Stephens, 2007).
- Learning mainly for grades or extrinsic rewards (e.g., cash rewards from parents, desire to get into an elite college or maintain athletic eligibility) instead of for the sake of learning or interest (Anderman, Griesinger, & Westerfield, 1998; Rettinger & Jordan, 2005; Schraw et al., 2007).

Reasons for cheating vary. Some cheat because they want to enter elite colleges. "There's so much pressure now just for your college application. You have to do a sport but you also have to do other extracurriculars, and you also have to have a job and then you also have to have all A's in honors classes." Others cheat because they want to graduate

purchase, but there is remarkably little evidence that they improve moral behavior. A major study of seven different programs in elementary schools found no effects of the programs (Social and Character Development Research Consortium, 2010). However, you can make a difference through everyday interactions with students.

from high school. They do not want to fail or be kept back (Stephens & Nicholson, 2008, p. 369).

Here are three students' views of cheating.

Student 1:   If . . . cheating is going to get you the grade, then that's the way to do it.

Student 2:   People cheat. It doesn't make you... worse of a person. There are times when you just are in need of a little help.

Student 3:   I guess the first time you do it, you feel really bad, but then you get used to it. You keep telling yourself you're not doing anything wrong. . . . Maybe you might know in your heart that it's wrong, but it gets easier after a while to handle it.

These quotes are from three college-bound high school students (McCabe, 1999, pp. 682–683). The first two are remarkably tolerant of dishonesty. The third is less tolerant of dishonesty, but finds a way to appease her conscience.

There are individual differences in tendency to cheat. Students who are tolerant of cheating, who believe "everyone else is doing it," and believe there is little disapproval for it are more likely to cheat (Jensen et al., 2002). Students who have low confidence in their academic ability, focus on how they compare with other students, feel disconnected to school, have low GPA or low IQ, and have low self-control are more likely to cheat than other students (Brown-Wright et al., 2012; Jensen et al., 2002; Paulhus & Dubois, 2015).

How can you reduce cheating? The nature of the situation that you create is a powerful influence on cheating. In a classic study (Hartshorne & May, 1928), some classrooms had virtually no cheating and others had almost universal cheating. There are several things that you can do to make cheating less likely in your classroom:

1. Challenge the belief that "everybody does it." Define cheating and make it clear that cheating is not acceptable.

2. Be a role model of honesty. Make the fact that you value honesty very clear. There have been allegations of teachers giving students answers to proficiency tests in order to raise test scores in low-achieving schools. Such negative modeling is likely to increase students' academic dishonesty.

3. Develop a warm, mutually respectful relationship with students. Students who view the teacher as disrespectful of students and who do not respect the teacher are more likely to cheat (McCabe, 1999; Murdock & Stephens, 2007).

4. Care about student learning. When students believe the teacher cares about teaching them the subject, students are less likely to cheat (Murdock et al., 2001; Schab, 1991).

5. Avoid negative competition. Cheating is less likely when there is an emphasis on improvement and learning, rather than on doing better than others or on extrinsic rewards like grades or athletic eligibility (Anderman et al., 1998; Schab, 1991).

6. Enforce serious consequences for dishonesty. Most cheating that is detected is not punished, and high school students are blasé about cheating if they know they will not be punished and if they think the teacher does not care (Cizek, 1999; McCabe, 1999). When you come across paragraphs or phrases that do not seem like your students' writing, copy some phrases and paste them into an Internet search engine to check their source.

7. Be fair. Students cheat more in classes that they see as unfair. Give assignments well ahead of deadlines so there is time to honestly study or write. Give fair tests that do not test material that was not taught.

8. Make cheating more difficult (IES, 2013). Remove temptations. Carefully proctor exams, but without making students feel like prisoners.

If you follow each of these guidelines, you should be able to greatly reduce dishonesty in your classroom and help your students become morally principled.

Teach Morality through Everyday Interactions

The way you interact with your students may be more important in promoting morality than a moral education program. Among the most important parenting factors associated with moral development are *modeling, authoritative* parenting, a *democratic* family structure in which parents show respect for children, and *induction* (Berkowitz & Grych, 2000). The same factors can be applied to your classroom. That is, moral teachers model moral behavior. Authoritative teachers are democratic and allow verbal give-and-take with students, including discussing moral issues. They are demanding and set high standards for moral behavior, but are also warm and caring.

Let's focus next on two factors we have not yet discussed in this section:

1. Use inductive discipline and be careful about what you discipline students for. As you learned in Chapter 7, inductive discipline results in internalization, or students who obey even when no one is looking. Recall that discipline is a teaching act. It is during discipline that students learn adults' core values. Students are able to infer that the issues you are most demanding about, like hitting someone, are core values and nonnegotiable. The issues that you are flexible about are not core values and choices are acceptable, like whether to raise your hand before answering. Teachers tend to present students with choices about personal issues but state rules and give commands about moral issues (Killen & Smetana, 1999).

2. Care for students. You learned how to foster teacher–student attachment and school bonding in Chapter 6. Some schools have infrequent cheating, and other schools have almost universal cheating. Cheating tends to be lower in classes with positive teacher–student relationships and where the atmosphere of the class is cordial and cooperative. Such academic honesty is a moral issue that is especially important to teachers (see Box 9.3).

Noddings (1992) asserts that the first job of schools is not to enhance academic ability, but to care for students because morality comes from the memory of being cared for. Every student should feel cared for by you and by classmates. Effective ways you can encourage kind, helpful behaviors, inhibit aggression, and resolve conflicts peacefully among your students will be discussed in the next chapter. Stay tuned.

My Teaching

The way that you interact with students can influence their people-reading skills, sense of humor, and morality. Several factors that promote social cognition have been discussed in previous chapters; you should review the "Reflections on Practice" sections from these other chapters. They include:

- Developing secure attachment with students, which is associated with ToM and morality (see Chapter 6).
- Creating a positive classroom atmosphere, which is associated with less cheating (see Chapter 8).
- Promoting students' information processing ability, which is associated with ToM and humor (see Chapter 4).
- Being authoritative and warm, encouraging give-and-take, and using induction, which are associated with morality (see Chapter 7).

In addition, to make sure you are promoting your students' social cognition, periodically ask yourself the following:

1. Do I talk with students about others' perspectives, thoughts, and beliefs? Do I use words like *think* and *know* in these conversations? Do I provide students with opportunities to interact and talk with peers who have different perspectives?

2. Do I initiate jokes and humor in the classroom to promote creativity, problem solving, and positive emotions?

3. Do my students initiate humor in my classroom? Do I respond positively? Am I able to respond positively to the humor of students with whom I have a difficult relationship?

4. Do I promote small-group debate of moral issues among peers, making sure the discussion style is "active" (i.e., participants request

clarification, elaboration, justification, and feedback) rather than passive?

5. Do I discuss moral issues when the opportunity arises, such as in literature, history, or when conflict erupts? Do I expose students to higher levels of moral reasoning? Do I help students recognize moral issues?

6. Do I share power with students when it is feasible? Do students help set classroom rules?

7. Do I recognize virtuous or moral behavior? Do I inadvertently reinforce immoral behavior?

8. Do I make it clear that I value honesty? Am I a model of honesty? Are there serious consequences for cheating in my class?

9. Am I aware of the virtues I would like to inculcate in students? Do I provide opportunity for students to practice virtues? Do I highlight virtuous role models for students, making their virtues explicit?

10. Do I give students the opportunity to care for others in my classroom? If so, do I foster self-reflection about it?

11. Do I give respect to students, and earn their respect? Are my tests, assignments, and other aspects of the classroom fair?

12. What is the culture of morality in my classroom? What rules do I actually enforce? Are they the same as the ones that I claim to enforce? Which rule violations really upset me? What does this communicate to students about my core values?

Summary of Age Trends in Social Cognition

	Theory of Mind	Humor	Moral Judgment and Prosocial Reasoning
Infancy and Toddlerhood (Birth–2 Years)	• Infants are innately predisposed to look at human faces, distinguish facial expressions, and follow others' gazes. • Toddlers understand that others have feelings, intentions, and desires. • Before age 3, children fail typical false-belief tasks and appearance-reality tasks. However, they may pass them if pointing or looking is used instead of language.	• Social smiling emerges at about 1 month of age. • Laughter emerges at about 4–6 months. • Toddlers laugh at word distortions, unusual behaviors, and pretend play. • Children find concepts they have just mastered most amusing (e.g., word distortions are funny to toddlers who have just acquired language abilities).	• Toddlers feel guilt and try to repair their transgressions. • Toddlers expect fairness and justice. • Both Piaget and Kohlberg underestimated young children's moral development. Children this young are not even tested in Kohlberg's model. • Children are adept at lying by 2–3 years.
Early Childhood (3–5 Years)	• Children's everyday behavior suggests they have ToM. • Most children pass false-belief tasks by age 5. • Autism is often diagnosed by 3 years of age.	• Preschoolers laugh at unusual appearances and distortions of the physical world. • Causes of laughter become more subtle and varied with age and require increasing ToM.	• Children are "moral" beings by age 3. • Preschoolers often use more-advanced needs-oriented, rather than just punishment-oriented, prosocial reasoning. • Individual differences in honesty are manifest by age 3. • Preschoolers are able to distinguish social convention from moral rules. • They often lie. • They mistake exaggerations and mistakes for lies. The more exaggerated the lie, the naughtier it is. • By 4–5 years, they can distinguish "white" lies from antisocial lies, and view white lies as less naughty.

Summary of Age Trends in Social Cognition

	Theory of Mind	Humor	Moral Judgment and Prosocial Reasoning
Middle Childhood (6–12 years)	• By 5–6 years, children perform at adult levels on ToM tasks. • Children become better able to use ToM to generate persuasive arguments. • They come to understand that they know more about their own inner thoughts and feelings than others do. • They become better at distinguishing intentional from unintentional acts. They become increasingly able to figure out why people say or do things, like why someone would say that an ugly hat looks nice.	• Complex verbal jokes become funny. Children enjoy puns, wordplays, and knock knock jokes. • Joke and riddle books become popular for 3rd- to 5th-graders. • They become better at reading others' intent so that they understand when someone is joking or serious, teasing or not. • They enjoy teasing more. They tease about different subjects—in upper elementary grades they tease about boyfriends or girlfriends. • They are able to see the benefit of using humor to cope with stress, but need help doing so. • By age 10, children understand sarcasm. • Children and teachers initiate more humor in elementary than in secondary classrooms. • Humorous children are likely to act out somewhat in class because they are highly active, social children.	• Children are typically in Kohlberg's stage 1 or 2. • They may be slightly more likely to use "internalized" and less likely to use "approval" prosocial reasoning, but they are still likely to use hedonistic reasoning. • They are able to coherently discuss whether laws are good or bad and whether a white lie is acceptable or not. • They are able to judge in a deliberate way how bad an act is based on both intent and degree of damage. • They develop an adult-like concept of what constitutes a lie. The more believable a lie, the naughtier it is (in contrast to preschoolers).
Adolescence (13–19 years)	• Adolescents have better ToM ability than do younger children, but they still tend to believe that others know what they know. • They overestimate whether people will notice and remember something about them (*spotlight effect*). • They overestimate how easily others can read them (the *transparency illusion*). • ToM continues to develop—older adults have better ToM ability than do young adults.	• Adolescents find humor in the wider world and enjoy puns, double entendres, and witticisms that younger children would not understand. • Put-downs become popular, especially among boys. • Both teacher-initiated and child-initiated humor is less common in high school than elementary school. • Humorous students are no longer as disruptive in class because they have learned to use their humor appropriately.	• Adolescents have reached Piaget's autonomous morality. • They may be in Kohlberg's stage 3. Only well-educated adults score a 5 or 6. • Young adolescents may increase in stereotyped prosocial reasoning. They may slightly increase in hedonistic reasoning. Needs-oriented reasoning may decline slightly, indicating moral regression. • Cheating is more prevalent in secondary school than elementary school.

Professional Resource Download

Chapter Summary

9-1 Theory of Mind

- Social cognition refers to cognition applied to the social domain.
- Theory of mind (ToM) is the ability to read other people's mental states. It is commonly tested with false-belief or appearance-reality tests.
- Poor ToM is a hallmark of autism spectrum conditions (ASC). Autism often occurs with other cognitive and language delays, but may also occur with exceptional interests and talents.
- Children who have better ToM ability tend to have advanced language ability, be more socially competent, and better at deception.
- Factors that predict good ToM ability include genes, perhaps acting through executive functions and verbal ability, as well as conversations about others' thoughts, secure attachment, and interaction with siblings and peers. Teachers can promote learner's ToM through each of these factors.
- Girls and high-SES children tend to have better ToM than boys and low-SES children.

9-2 Humor

- Humor is social-cognitive playfulness. It can be caused by physical play, or by encountering information that is puzzling and then suddenly resolved by insight. Humor can serve several functions, such as insulting others or creating social bonds.
- Teasing is playful and provocative commentary on others. It can be physical, and it can be positive or antisocial.
- Children with a good sense of humor are better liked by others. Individuals with better information processing abilities often have a better sense of humor than their peers.
- Positive (nonsarcastic) humor in the classroom promotes positive teacher–student relationships and enhances creativity and positive emotions. It may have positive effects on learning. Humor is less frequent in secondary than in elementary schools.
- Freud emphasized the power of unconscious feelings, and that dreams have meaning. He developed a form of therapy, psychoanalysis, which is widely used today. He believed jokes, like dreams, have hidden meanings and allow people to express forbidden feelings. He believed emotions and attachment are the basis of morality.

9-3 Moral Judgment

- Piaget believed that children construct their own sense of justice, rather than adopting others' moral standards, through social-cognitive conflict with others. He believed that children progress from heteronymous (authority-oriented) to autonomous morality.

- Kohlberg believed that children's moral judgment develops in an invariant, universal sequence of stages. The lowest level is authority-punishment oriented, and the highest level is justice oriented. Not everyone agrees that justice is a higher form of morality compared with other values, such as caring.

- Prosocial reasoning refers to reasoning about dilemmas in which needs conflict but no laws are involved. Hedonistic reasoning is considered lower than internalized reasoning.

- Scores on Kohlberg's stages are not strongly related to moral *behavior*. Prosocial reasoning is related to moral behavior in younger, but not older, children.

- Children who have better ToM, secure attachment, authoritative parents who discuss moral events with them, moral identity, and strong religious beliefs tend to have higher levels of moral judgment and behavior.

- High-SES learners, and boys, tend to score higher on moral judgment. Girls have a slight tendency to be more caring-oriented in their moral judgment, whereas boys are more likely to be justice-oriented. However, boys do not behave with greater honesty.

- Moral education, based on Piaget's and Kohlberg's views, emphasizes peer discussion of moral dilemmas and a democratic school. Character education emphasizes indoctrination of virtues and providing practice, rewards, and models of virtue. There are critics and proponents of each approach.

- Academic dishonesty is prevalent. Students who view cheating as no big deal, who have low ability, who observe others cheating, and who do not respect the teacher are more likely to cheat. Teachers can diminish cheating by being fair, conveying that dishonesty is not acceptable, emphasizing learning for intrinsic rather than extrinsic reasons, punishing cheating, and effectively teaching material that will be tested.

- Teachers' use of induction, caring for students, and creation of a positive classroom atmosphere foster moral behavior.

chapter 10

Cengage Learning

Social Behavior

Why are some learners kind and helpful, but others are aggressive? How should you handle aggressive learners who defy authority? In this chapter we will discuss three aspects of social behavior—prosocial behavior, antisocial behavior (which includes bullying), and conflict resolution. **After you read this chapter, you will be able to:**

10-1 Describe age trends in prosocial behavior and create classroom environments that increase prosocial behavior.

10-2 Describe age trends in antisocial behavior and create classroom environments that reduce antisocial behavior.

10-3 Identify types of conflict resolution and teach conflict-resolution skills to your students.

10-1 Prosocial Behavior

> *In a 3rd-grade class, Patrick feels frustrated; he pleads for Ted's help on an assignment: "I don't know what to do. Can you please help me?" Ted says, "No! Leave me alone; I got to get my own done." Lizzie overhears them. She says to Patrick, "I don't know how to do it either, but maybe Lauren can help us. She always knows what to do." She asks Lauren for help, and the two get their assignment done.*

Classrooms present plenty of opportunities for learners to be kind and helpful, like Lizzie. However, some not only decline to be nice, like Ted, but they are actively aggressive toward classmates. Lizzie is more likely to earn high grades than Ted because *success in the classroom depends on social competence as well as academic ability.* A socially competent learner is often prosocial and seldom antisocial. *Prosocial* refers to positive interactions and *antisocial* to negative interactions with others. You might mistakenly assume that antisocial means "nonsocial," but it does not. Nor does prosocial mean "outgoing." Rather, these terms refer to the *type,* not the *amount,* of interaction.

The term *prosocial* was coined to reflect the opposite of antisocial behavior (Wispe, 1972). **Prosocial behavior** is voluntary behavior that benefits others or promotes harmonious relations with others. Sometimes it is confused with altruism. **Altruism** refers to behavior that benefits someone else *at the expense of the self,* such as giving up time, fun, or money. Prosocial behavior can include altruism, but it can also include behaviors with little cost to the self. Lizzie was prosocial, and more socially competent than Ted, because she found a way to benefit Patrick as well as herself.

In what types of prosocial behavior do learners engage? In one study, 6th-graders said their prosocial classmates do the following (Bergin, Talley, & Hamer, 2003):

- Comfort distressed peers.

- Help others with sports, schoolwork, or social difficulties.

- Make others smile or laugh with their humor.

- Share things, such as food or jewelry.

- Compliment and encourage others.

- Invite others to join in the group and are friendly.

- Confront those who have done wrong, and stand up for those who have been wronged.

- Admit mistakes and apologize.

- Use good manners and behave politely.

- Break up fights, give in to avoid fights, and broker peace among peers.

- Are honest.

- Avoid hurting others' feelings, and avoid bragging.

Other studies have found similar kinds of prosocial behaviors in 2- to 18-year-olds (Bergin, Bergin, & French, 1995; Caldarella & Merrell, 1997; Greener & Crick, 1999; Paulus, 2014). As you can see, prosocial behavior encompasses a variety of positive

prosocial behavior
voluntary behavior that benefits others or promotes harmonious relations with others.

altruism
behavior that benefits others at the expense of the self *without expectation of a gain or reward.* It is a subset of prosocial behavior.

social behaviors that include social convention, such as saying "thank you," and morality, such as being honest. It requires a blend of self-assertion, such as standing up for victims, and conceding to others, such as giving in to avoid fights.

10-1a Age Trends in Prosocial Behavior

Do children become more prosocial as they get older? The *frequency* of prosocial behavior does not appear to increase with age, but *competence* at enacting prosocial behavior does improve with age.

Infancy and Toddlerhood (Birth to 2 Years)

Infants have a universal tendency to help and share that is apparent by 8 months of age (Eisenberg, Fabes, & Spinrad, 2006; Warneken, 2015). By 9 months, before they are mobile enough to help, they expect others to help those in need and show surprise when they do not (Köster, Ohmer, Nguyen, & Kärtner, 2016). By 12 months, sharing and cooperating with parents is so common that the absence of these behaviors indicates developmental disorders, like autism. By 18 months, toddlers try to help their parents with chores without being asked (Photo 10.1). They will also help an experimenter with simple tasks—such as reaching for a clothespin he dropped or opening a closet door when his hands are full—without being asked or rewarded. They will help the experimenter even if they have to leave their own play and climb over obstacles (Warneken & Tomasello, 2009).

Compassion is also present very early in life (Dunfield & Kuhlmeier, 2013). Toddlers express compassion and sympathy as soon as they are able to talk. They try to comfort others who are sad or upset. In one study, toddlers from different cultures (Berlin and Delhi) comforted an experimenter by bringing another toy, or hugging her, when her teddy bear's arm fell off and she began sobbing (Kärtner, Keller, & Chaudhary, 2010). In another study, 18-month-olds gave a stranger a balloon to cheer her up after an actor had been mean to her by tearing her picture (Vaish, Carpenter, & Tomasello, 2009). The mistreated stranger did not express any emotion, so the toddlers were using their theory of mind (see Chapter 9) to infer that she needed comforting, which shows a remarkable level of sensitivity to others (Thompson, 2012).

The strong natural tendency of 1-year-olds to be prosocial may change as they near age 2; they share less, they are more selective about helping, and their motives shift toward self-interest. Two-year-olds are more likely to help someone who has tried to help them rather than someone who has not (Dunfield & Kuhlmeier, 2010). They are also more likely to share with a friend than with a mere acquaintance and less likely to share just because a peer has asked. They are more likely to share a treat they do not especially like. Sharing begins to be used as a tool, such as to resolve a dispute with a peer. Thus, *self-interest and selectivity*

PHOTO 10.1 Very young children have a universal impulse to be kind and helpful.

begin to inhibit the universal impulse to share by 2 years of age, and possibly younger (Martin & Olson, 2015).

Early Childhood (3 to 5 Years)

Preschoolers, compared with toddlers, may become even more selective about their prosocial behavior, directing it primarily toward friends and family. They also are discriminating; 3-year-olds do not show concern for others whose distress is not justified, such as crying over a minor inconvenience rather than real hurt (Hepach, Vaish, & Tomasello, 2013). Yet, they are fair and egalitarian with others. When 3-year-olds work together to earn a treat, most will share the treat evenly (Warneken, Lohse, Melis, & Tomasello, 2011). They also begin to be genuinely helpful when others are distressed—a toddler might simply cry when another child cries, but a 4-year-old might fetch the child's comfort blankie. By age 4, children have a wide range of helping behaviors that they can draw upon.

Interestingly, preschoolers who are highly prosocial are often highly aggressive as well. They are very sociable children, and they have lots of both positive and negative interactions with others. Thus, preschoolers who share are also likely to snatch (Hay, 2009). By middle childhood, children tend to specialize, becoming predominantly positive or negative with others.

Middle Childhood (6 to 12 Years)

In middle childhood, children become more attuned to the norms of their social group, so that they increasingly share only with familiar others who belong to their "in-group" (Warneken & Tomasello, 2009). They also become more skilled at comforting others who are upset. For example, 6th-graders are more likely than younger children to reassure peers. They become more competent than preschoolers at expressing positive emotions toward sad peers in order to cheer them up (Saarni, 1999). This increase in skill partly explains why a classic study of several cultures found that children were typically assigned to care for younger siblings starting at about 6 to 8 years of age (Whiting, 1983).

Elementary school children can be organized and charming in their prosocial behavior. A teacher reported that one day she saw:

> *a little battered automobile festooned with flowers in the school parking lot. Red, pink, orange, yellow, purple flowers were stuck in every crevice of that car, into keyholes and cracks around the doors, the windows, the hood, the gas cap. . . . The car belonged to one of the Puerto Rican teachers. Many of her fourth-grade students had recently come from the island. They had sneaked out at lunchtime to decorate the car of their* maestra. *(Kidder, 1989, pp. 61–62)*

Adolescence (13 to 19 Years)

Adolescents become even more skilled at prosocial behavior. For example, 2-year-olds comfort others by bringing their own favorite blanket, whereas adolescents comfort others by trying to solve the problem or helping them control their emotions. Adolescents are able to help their peers in many ways, such as help with schoolwork, sports, or disagreements (Bergin et al., 2003).

Despite this greater skill, the *frequency* of prosocial behavior does not increase from toddlerhood to adolescence in natural settings, and may even decrease in early adolescence, and then rebound (Carlo, Padilla-Walker, & Nielson, 2015; Eisenberg et al., 2006). (However, in artificial laboratory studies that involve strangers—such as having children donate prize winnings to an anonymous charity—older youth tend to behave more prosocially than younger children.) How is this lack of increased prosocial behavior possible, given the effort adults put into teaching children to be kind and polite?

There are at least four reasons children may not become more prosocial with age:

1. Adults sometimes train children to inhibit their natural prosocial impulses, such as telling them it is the teacher's job to take care of distressed classmates, not theirs.

2. Children have many antisocial models, both live and in the media, that may counter their prosocial tendencies.

3. Children become better able to regulate their own emotional response, so that they do not impulsively respond to others' distress.

4. Children become more aware of the costs of prosocial behavior and learn to protect their self-interests better. After all, if you give away your cookie, you won't have one.

You learned in Chapter 9 that hedonistic prosocial reasoning, which focuses on "what's in it for me?" may *increase* for some adolescents. As prosocial behavior shifts from being a universal impulse of toddlers to a more controlled choice for older youth, individual differences in prosocial behavior become apparent. Let's look at this next.

10-1b Individual Diversity in Prosocial Behavior

Prosocial behavior is almost universal in the first year of life, but by 2 to 3 years of age, there are clear individual differences that remain fairly stable (e.g., Romano, Babchishin, Pagani, & Kohen, 2010; Vaish et al., 2009). That is, toddlers who are more prosocial than their peers will likely be the most prosocial adolescents. Lizzie is more likely to be prosocial than Ted across childhood. Remarkably, one study even found that sharing in preschool predicted prosocial behavior when those children were in their early 30s (Eisenberg, Hofer, Sulik, & Liew, 2014). Some individuals were consistently more prosocial across three decades. These individual differences have important consequences for learners.

What Do Individual Differences in Prosocial Behavior Predict?

Prosocial behavior is linked to academic achievement. Prosocial preschoolers tend to have better emergent literacy skills (Doctoroff, Greer, & Arnold, 2006). Prosocial kindergarteners develop better reading and math skills by 3rd grade (Romano et al., 2010). At-risk prosocial kindergarteners are less likely to be retained a grade or placed in special education before they graduate from high school (Jones, Greenberg, & Crowley, 2015). Prosocial 1st- to 12th-graders tend to have higher grades and test scores than less prosocial students (Bergin, 2014).

think about this

Why do you think prosocial behavior is linked to achievement? Base your argument on what you have learned in previous chapters. (Hint: See Chapter 8 on positive emotions or Chapter 6 on secure attachment, or agreeable and conscientious personality traits). The research linking prosocial behavior and achievement is correlational (Chapter 1). What does that mean about causation? How might this alter your argument?

Prosocial behavior is also linked to happiness. For example, adolescents who help their parents with cleaning and cooking or with tending younger siblings are happier (Fuligni & Telzer, 2013). They may be happier because they feel that they are a better son/daughter and brother/sister. Anticipating feeling good about helping predicts more helping behavior (Malti & Krettenauer, 2013). Prosocial youth may also be happier because behaving kindly reduces the effects of daily stress (Raposa, Laws, & Ansell, 2015). Prosocial children are better at maintaining a state of calm (Miller, Kahle, & Hastings, 2015). They may also be happier because they are better liked by others.

Prosocial behavior is also linked to popularity with peers and teachers. For example, in a famous study, 3- and 4-year-olds were asked to place pictures of their classmates into one of three boxes: like a lot, kinda like, and do not like (Denham, McKinley, Couchoud, & Holt, 1990). The best predictor of whether a child was liked a lot was prosocial behavior. This is true for older youth as well. Prosocial students may be better liked by peers, less depressed, and have fewer behavior problems in elementary and secondary schools (Bandura, Barbaranelli, Caprara, & Pastorelli, 1996).

Is it possible for learners to be overly prosocial? Yes, when they must take on a parenting role because parents are substance users, depressed, or emotionally dependent on their children. For example, preschoolers with severely depressed mothers may be substantially more prosocial than other children (Radke-Yarrow, Zahn-Waxler, Richardson, Susman, & Martinez, 1994). Similarly, elementary school children who worry excessively about family members (e.g., hurrying home from school to check on their mothers) are also substantially more prosocial than other children (Hay & Pawlby, 2003). Children who feel excessive, chronic, misguided guilt for the distress of others, which in fact is not their fault, might be overly prosocial. Some children who are abused or abandoned may also become too eager to please (Klimes-Dougan & Kistner, 1990). Thus, exceptionally high levels of prosocial behavior in your students may result from difficult home situations; however, as you will see next, in most families prosocial behavior is the result of positive parenting.

What Predicts Individual Differences in Prosocial Behavior?

Prosocial behavior is innate and universal initially, but individual differences emerge quite early in life. Does this mean some children inherit kindness? There is a modest genetic component to prosocial behavior (Gregory, Light-Häusermann, Rijsdijk, & Eley, 2009). However, as you learned in Chapters 1 and 6, genes interact with experience. Whether children become more, or less, prosocial depends on their experience (Paulus, 2014; Van Ryzin et al., 2015). Let's discuss important experiences next.

Emotional competence and empathy

In Chapter 8 you learned that emotional competence involves both the ability to control one's own emotions and the ability to read others' emotions. Both abilities are linked to prosocial behavior. Children who are more accurate in reading other's emotions are more prosocial (Denham, Mason, & Couchoud, 1995; Wentzel, Filisetti, & Looney, 2007). Children who can control their own emotions, and fake their emotions in order to protect other's feelings, are more prosocial than other children (Fabes et al., 1999). Those who have trouble with emotion regulation (e.g., are easily upset, or overreact) tend to be less prosocial (Carlo, Crockett, Wolff, & Beal, 2012).

These abilities work together because good emotion regulation allows children to respond to others' distress with sympathy, rather than with personal distress. Recall from Chapter 8 that when children feel empathy for someone in distress, they can react with either sympathy or personal distress. In the opening vignette, Lizzie was able to perceive Patrick's distress and felt enough sympathy to come to his aid. In contrast, Ted seemed to feel personal distress.

You might expect that sympathy leads to prosocial behavior. Some studies confirm this, but sympathy is not strongly or consistently linked to more prosocial behavior (Decety & Cowell, 2014; Paulus, 2014). In contrast, personal distress is clearly linked to *less* prosocial behavior. Does it seem puzzling to you that sympathy is not a strong motivating force for prosocial behavior? Consider that in Chapter 9 you learned that moral reasoning also is not always linked to moral behavior. There are forces, such as self-interest, that compete with sympathy and reasoning to prevent a child from behaving prosocially. However, when the mind and the heart work together, children are more likely to be prosocial. Children who have high levels of *both* moral reasoning and sympathy may be the most prosocial (Malti, Gummerum, Keller, & Buchmann, 2009).

Parental responsiveness and attachment

You learned in Chapter 8 that parents' responsiveness to children's emotions is linked to the children's emotion regulation. It won't surprise you, then, that sensitive, supportive parents have more prosocial children (Davidov & Grusec, 2006; Houltberg, Morris, Cui, Henry, & Criss, 2014; Van Ryzin et al., 2015). When parents meet children's emotional needs, their children become able to meet others' needs. You also learned in Chapter 6 that parents' responsiveness is linked to children's attachment. Secure attachment, in turn, is linked to prosocial behavior. Securely attached children are more affectionate and helpful toward parents and more prosocial toward peers (Bohlin, Hagekull, & Rydell, 2000; Eberly & Montemayor, 1998).

Parents' values

Some parents espouse prosocial values more than other parents (Wray-Lake, Flanagan, & Maggs, 2012). They may tell their children "stand up for others, not just yourself." Parents who value prosocial behavior and respond supportively when their child behaves prosocially tend to have prosocial children with similar values (Eisenberg, Wolchik, Goldberg, & Engle, 1992; Hardy, Carlo & Roesch, 2010). For example, a classic study found that 5th-graders are more likely to stand up for others and to be careful not to hurt other's feelings if both their mother and father rank prosocial behavior as highly important (Hoffman, 1975). Warmth enhances the effects of parents' values. Parents who are warm *and* who hold prosocial values have children who are more prosocial than others (Bergin, 1987). How do children learn their parents' values? One way is during discipline.

Discipline

Learners' prosocial behavior is influenced both by what they are disciplined for and the type of discipline. In Chapters 7 and 9 you learned that parents communicate core values to children during discipline encounters based on what they become

TIM LAMAN/National Geographic Creative

PHOTO 10.2 Children become more prosocial when adults accept their offers of help or assign them chores that benefit others.

victim-centered induction
a form of inductive discipline in which the adult points out how the child's behavior made the victim feel.

upset about. If they become upset about unkind behavior, they communicate that kindness is important.

Parents who are authoritative and use discipline, such as induction, that leads to internalization (see Chapter 7) have more prosocial children (Kochanska, Koenig, Barry, Kim, & Yoon, 2010; Padilla-Walker, Carlo, Christensen, & Yorgason, 2012). Using victim-centered induction when children misbehave may be particularly important. During victim-centered induction, the parent: (1) points out how the child's misbehavior affects others, (2) asks the child to imagine being in the others' place, and (3) suggests concrete acts of reparation. Thus, during victim-centered discipline children learn to focus on *others'* well-being. In contrast, power assertion and psychological control turn the child's attention to the *self* because they arouse resentment and anxiety.

Reinforcement

Recall from Chapter 3 that behaviorism asserts that reinforcement increases behavior. However, recall from Chapter 7 that tangible rewards can sometimes undermine intrinsic motivation. Does this apply to prosocial behavior? Research confirms that tangible rewards may *decrease* prosocial behavior in the long term (Martin & Olson, 2015). In contrast, praise is linked to increased prosocial behavior, particularly if the praise comes from a respected adult (Mussen & Eisenberg, 2001).

Research finds that most (but not all) parents thank and praise children for their help (Dahl, 2015; Rechhia et al., 2014). The way adults talk to children shapes children's identity and self-definition. Praise may help children develop a positive moral identity (see Chapter 9). For this reason praise may be more powerful if it is directed at the child rather than the act, such as "*You are a good boy,*" rather than "*That was a good thing to do.*" It is also more powerful to tell children "*You could be a helper*" rather than "*You could help*" (Bryan, Master, & Walton, 2014). The difference is subtle, yet important (see Figure 10.1).

FIGURE 10.1 Children Want to "Be a Helper."

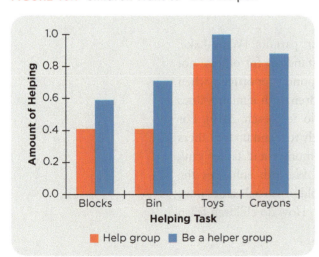

When 4- and 5-year-olds were told "you could be a helper" rather than "you could help" they were later more likely to spontaneously help with four tasks: picking up blocks, opening a bin for someone whose hands were full, putting away toys, and picking up spilled crayons. *Source: Bryan et al. (2014).*

Practice

Many situations that call for prosocial behavior do not require sophisticated moral reasoning but simply well-rehearsed habits. After behaving prosocially once, children are more likely to behave prosocially again (Chernyak & Kushnir, 2013). Learners who are given opportunities to practice prosocial behavior become more prosocial (Mussen & Eisenberg, 2001). Even as young as age 2, if parents let their toddlers help with tasks, like folding clothes, the children become more prosocial than their peers (Photo 10.2). Older children become more prosocial and feel more valued in the family if they are assigned household tasks that benefit others rather than just themselves, like preparing dinner or cleaning (Fuligni & Telzer, 2013; Grusec, Goodnow, & Cohen, 1997). However, in conflict-ridden homes with poor parent–child relationships, chores may lead to increased conflict rather than prosocial behavior.

You may think that adults always encourage children to practice prosocial behavior. However, if you watch carefully, you will notice that some adults reject children's offers of help because it is faster and easier to do it themselves. They may reject children's offers to wash dishes, bag groceries, or hold the baby. Fortunately, other adults graciously accept such offers.

All of the positive parenting factors discussed tend to go together. Parents who are warm, hold prosocial values, use victim-centered discipline, and praise their children also tend to provide them with opportunities to practice prosocial behavior.

10-1c Gender Diversity in Prosocial Behavior

Girls are more likely than boys to be nominated when researchers ask teachers or learners, "Who is nice to others?" Are girls really more prosocial than boys? Most, but not all studies, find clear gender differences favoring girls, from preschool through adolescence (e.g., Caprara, Barbaranelli, & Pastorelli, 2001; Davidov & Grusec, 2006; Pagani, Tremblay, Vitaro, Boulerice, & McDuff, 2001).

Girls and boys may engage in different kinds of prosocial behaviors, and for different reasons. In many societies, for example, nurturing children is the province of women, whereas rescuing people from fires is the province of men. Prosocial behaviors such as providing physical assistance and sharing may be more salient for boys, whereas providing emotional support, keeping confidences, and including everyone may be more salient for girls (Bergin et al., 2003).

10-1d Classroom Implications of Prosocial Behavior

Prosocial behavior is worth cultivating in the classroom for its own sake. You and your students will be happier in a classroom filled with kindness, politeness, and cooperation. Prosocial behavior is also worth cultivating because it is linked to achievement. Indeed, the concept of "kindergarten readiness" partly refers to having appropriate social behavior. For example, a large study found that Latino preschoolers who were respectful (*bien educado, respeto*), cooperative, and caring (*cariño*) were more academically successful after entering kindergarten (Galindo & Fuller, 2010). Prosocial behavior is linked to academic achievement because prosocial youth are more likely to show interest in schoolwork, work independently, take turns, listen, and stay on task (McClelland & Morrison, 2003).

In addition, learners fare better *if their classmates are prosocial*. In Chapter 6 you learned that students with caring teachers have higher GPAs. So do students with caring, prosocial classmates (Jia et al., 2009). Indeed, having prosocial classmates is a protective factor for learners who are poor. For example, a study found that 1st-graders from impoverished, unstable homes were less likely to develop behavior

FIGURE 10.2 Age Trends in Prosocial Behavior in Classrooms.

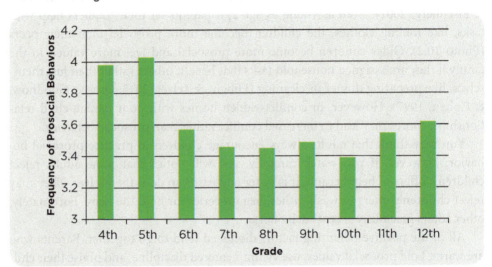

Over 3,400 students in 4th to 12th grade reported how frequently their classmates' behaved prosocially. A score of 3 means monthly and 4 means weekly. Can you describe the age trend? *Source: Bergin, Wang, and Bryant (2011).*

problems compared to other students in poverty if they were in highly prosocial classrooms (Hoglund & Leadbeater, 2004). This is noteworthy because generally students in poverty develop more behavior and emotional problems across the school year.

What is the pattern of prosocial behavior across school grade levels? Secondary students report being less prosocial at school than elementary students (Bergin, Wang, & Bryant, 2011; see Figure 10.2).

How can you promote more prosocial behavior in your classroom? You have learned part of the answer in previous chapters:

1. *Reinforce prosocial behavior* (see Chapters 3 and 7). However, avoid tangible rewards because they can undermine motivation. For example, in a classic study, tangible rewards undermined 3rd-graders' later willingness to tutor 1st-graders and made their tutoring more tense and hostile (Szynal-Brown & Morgan, 1983). Instead, praise learners when they are prosocial.

2. *Provide models of prosocial behavior* (see Chapter 3). Point out the virtuous acts of others—in news, literature, and movies or within your classroom. Witnessing or learning of others' virtuous acts inspires and motivates more prosocial behavior (Schnall, Roper, & Fessler, 2010). The more students perceive their classmates as prosocial, the more prosocial they may be themselves (Spivak, White, Juvonen, & Graham, 2015).

3. *Use victim-centered induction* (see Chapter 7). During discipline, suggest to learners how to make reparation. This reduces guilt and teaches learners to value others' well-being. It also provides practice of prosocial behavior. In one study, after preschool teachers were trained to use induction, prosocial behavior increased dramatically (Ramaswamy & Bergin, 2009). In cases in which one child hurts another, discipline may not be necessary if the transgressor appears

to feel guilty and tries to make reparation. Let's take a peek in Ms. Kathy's preschool:

Three-year-old Tanner shoves one-year-old Vince in the stomach. Vince begins crying. Ms. Kathy gives Tanner an exaggerated look of horror and says with gusto, "Look at Vince! You made him cry. We NEVER make others cry!" Ms. Kathy then begins to pat Vince on the back, making sympathetic noises, and telling Tanner "Let's try to make Vince feel better. Throw him the ball. That might make him happy again." Tanner does, and Vince quits crying. For the rest of the day Tanner becomes Vince's self-appointed helper, holding his hand during group time, and protecting him from another 3-year-old aggressive boy.

This brief victim-oriented discipline worked powerfully on Tanner's compassion and oriented him toward Vince's feelings, helping Tanner become more prosocial.

4. *Increase learners' emotional competence* (see Chapter 8). Focus on creating an emotionally positive classroom (Jennings & Greenberg, 2009). Help learners feel and express gratitude in your classroom. Gratitude is linked to increased prosocial behavior toward others, whether they were the cause of the gratitude or not (Bartlett & DeSteno, 2006; McCullough, Kimeldorf, & Cohen, 2008).

5. *Increase learners' moral reasoning and identity* (see Chapter 9). While reasoning alone is a poor predictor of moral behavior, when combined with sympathy it is linked to prosocial behavior. Identity as a moral person is also linked to prosocial behavior.

6. *Establish a warm, secure relationship with learners* (see Chapter 6). Secure attachment to the teacher is associated with greater prosocial behavior (Bergin & Bergin, 2009). Emotionally supportive classrooms may be particularly effective for promoting prosocial behavior in at-risk, impoverished learners (Johnson, Seidenfeld, Izard, & Kobak, 2012).

7. *Espouse prosocial values.* Talk about your values and model prosocial behavior. Learners feel cared for by teachers who behave prosocially. Table 10.1 provides students' descriptions of caring and noncaring teachers. Notice that students think of teaching well as an expression of caring, even though teachers tend to think of caring and teaching as separate roles (Jeffrey, Auger, & Pepperell, 2013).

Let's next discuss two additional ways you can promote prosocial behavior in your students: Help them feel responsible for others and provide opportunities to practice prosocial behavior. Then, we will take a look at school-based interventions to enhance prosocial behavior.

Help Learners Feel Responsible for Others

Learners do not help each other if someone else is available, but if they are the only ones present, they respond promptly (Plötner, Over, Carpenter, & Tomasello, 2015). In preschools, teachers respond so swiftly to distress that preschoolers can rarely do anything other than watch a distressed peer. Older students may not go to the aid of

TABLE 10.1 Student descriptions of caring and noncaring teachers

Caring Teacher Behavior	Noncaring Teacher Behavior
Helps each student academically. Asks if I need help, calls on me, makes sure I understand.	Doesn't explain things or answer questions, doesn't try to help.
Makes special effort, teaches in a special way, makes class interesting.	Gets off task, teaches while students aren't paying attention, boring.
Talks to me, pays attention, listens, asks questions.	Screams, yells, ignores, interrupts.
Asks what's wrong, talks to me about my problems, acts as a friend.	Forgets my name, doesn't ask why I'm sad, doesn't care if I do something wrong.
Compliments and encourages, checks work, tells me when I do a good job, praises me.	Sends me to the office, gives bad grades, doesn't correct work.
Trusts me, tells the truth, keeps promises, respects students, avoids hurting students' feelings.	Embarrasses, insults, or picks on students.

Source: Adapted from Jeffrey et al. (2013) and Wentzel (1997).

another unless given permission to do so, because they would get in trouble if they did. For example, let's look at Mrs. Hessy's elementary classroom:

> *Anna accidentally spills her colored pencils on the floor. Students around her scurry to help her pick them up. Mrs. Hessy says, "Please get back in your seats. Anna can do it." Later, when another student needs help with an assignment, Blake asks, "Can I help him?" Mrs. Hessy says, "No. I will help him."*

Mrs. Hessy posted a list of classroom rules on the wall that included "Help Others." Yet, she rejected students' overtures of help, making them feel it was not their responsibility. Students learn these subtle lessons early. When asked why they do not help, students indicate that they are not supposed to do anything when adults are available (Caplan & Hay, 1989). You can reverse this lesson by telling learners they are responsible for what happens to others in your classroom and accepting their offers to help, even if it is a little inconvenient.

Provide Opportunities to Practice Prosocial Behavior

Practice builds learners' prosocial habits. Learners should be given opportunities to care for each other (Noddings, 1992). These can include just day-to-day events, as in Mrs. Hessy's classroom, or can be part of a formal school program, such as tutoring other students. Such opportunities can also include community-based service, like food drives. Roughly half of adolescents do volunteer service in their community (Hart, Donnelly, Youniss, & Atkins, 2007). Learners who volunteer in the community are more prosocial in the classroom. They are also more likely to have high GPAs; be idealistic, sociable, and religious (much volunteerism is through church); and have prosocial parents.

Is volunteerism good for students? Youth volunteerism predicts many positive outcomes such as self-esteem, responsibility, acceptance of diverse groups, commitment to the community, school bonding, less delinquency, life goals of civic involvement, and advanced moral reasoning (Hart et al., 2007; van Goethem, van Hoof, Orobio de Castro, Van Aken, & Hart, 2014). Because of these benefits, many high schools and organizations, like the National Honor Society, require community service from students. But do the benefits of volunteerism extend to *mandatory* service? Is it logical to coerce students to behave prosocially? Perhaps. Some studies find that mandatory service is linked to greater disengagement from school and less intention to volunteer in the future, but others find it is beneficial (Hart et al., 2007;

Frances Roberts/Alamy Stock Photo

Planty, Bozick, & Regnier, 2006; Wilson, 2012). Students benefit from mandatory service when it is a high-quality experience. The same is true for voluntary service.

What constitutes a high-quality experience? Service is most beneficial when students meet real needs, interact with recipients (versus anonymous service), serve regularly, have challenging responsibilities, have choice, have a good relationship with those at the service site, work in a group (versus alone), and have opportunities to reflect on the experience such as during class discussions (van Goethem et al., 2014; Youniss, McLellan, Su, & Yates, 1999). See Photo 10.3.

PHOTO 10.3 Students benefit from voluntary or mandatory service when it is a high-quality experience.

School-Based Interventions

School-based interventions have been designed to promote prosocial behavior. An example is the Caring School Community (CSC) for elementary schools. The U.S. Department of Health and Human Services has recognized the CSC as an exemplary program. The CSC has two components: (1) building a strong sense of school community through activities like cross-grade buddy relationships and family activities at school; and (2) developing caring classrooms. Teachers are encouraged to be warm and supportive, use inductive discipline, promote prosocial behavior, and use an authoritative teaching style (Solomon, Battistich, Watson, Schaps, & Lewis, 2000; What Works Clearinghouse, 2007). You learned how to do these things in Chapters 6 through 9. The CSC results in increased prosocial behavior, particularly for high-poverty schools. In highly caring schools, the poorest students have attitudes toward school as positive as those of the most affluent students. An analysis of many studies found that similar programs—in elementary through high schools—can increase prosocial behavior *and raise grades and test scores, even when there is no academic emphasis to the program* (Durlak et al., 2011). A win–win situation!

In summary, there are several things you can do to help your learners become more prosocial, which in turn may help them be better liked and academically successful. You should recognize substantial overlap with moral and character education from Chapter 9. This is because prosocial behavior *encompasses* morality but goes *beyond* it. Moral behavior means abiding by obligatory, universal laws in order to do what is right. For example, honesty is both moral and prosocial. However,

think about this

Does forcing learners to do any activity result in intrinsic motivation for that activity? Could mandatory service promote moral development under any conditions? Draw on what you learned in Chapters 7 and 9 to defend your answer.

complimenting another child does not involve moral judgment, but it is prosocial. Such kind behavior is vitally important because it enhances relationships and happiness in others. Next we turn to behavior that has the opposite effect.

10-2 Antisocial Behavior and Aggression

> *As Josh and his mother enter the office at his high school, his mother loudly swears at him. She threatens Josh: "Your behavior had better stop! If this principal tells me you've done something else that you haven't told me about, I'm gonna let you have it! Is that clear?" Josh, humiliated, says in an undertone laced with profanity, "Would you shut up? I heard you. They just don't like me at this school." His mother then begins swearing profusely at the principal and threatening him because he had suspended Josh. Before her visit is over, other school personnel and a police officer join the confrontation.*

Josh is often in trouble at school and has repeated a grade. Josh is an antisocial child. If the thought of having learners like Josh in your classroom makes you want to switch careers fast, keep reading. In this section, you will come to understand and learn how to help learners like Josh. He needs you, because he is not going to learn social skills from his mother.

Behavior is antisocial if it is aversive, annoying, or harmful to others. Some students annoy classmates almost daily, but have never been suspended. In contrast, Josh has demonstrated more serious antisocial behavior, has often been suspended, and may not graduate. **Antisocial behavior** includes delinquency (breaking the law, truancy, running away from home, vandalism), substance abuse, and inappropriate sexual activity. It is called *antisocial* because it disrupts the functioning of society. Aggression is a subset of antisocial behavior.

Aggression and other antisocial behaviors are comorbid, meaning they often go together. That is, the same youth tend to be violent, sexually promiscuous, and drug using. However, this pattern is not true of all antisocial youth; some are mildly delinquent for a limited time during adolescence and are not aggressive (Burt & Neiderhiser, 2009). Aggression and ADHD are also comorbid; about half of hyperactive learners are aggressive (Saylor & Amann, 2016). Aggression, hyperactivity, inattention, and impulsivity together form a cluster called *externalizing* disorders. This may surprise you, but aggressive learners also tend to have *internalizing* disorders (see Chapter 8), such as depression and anxiety. Seriously antisocial learners may be diagnosed with **oppositional defiant disorder** (ODD) and **conduct disorder** (CD). See Box 10.1.

In Chapter 6, we asked if you had ever heard veteran teachers say, "Kids today just aren't like they used to be." We discussed how neuroticism has increased. Antisocial behavior in the United States has also increased. Since the 1950s, children have become more argumentative, disobedient, anxious, depressed, delinquent, aggressive, and tired. More 7- to 16-year-olds have clinical levels of behavior problems (Achenbach, Dumenci, & Rescorla, 2003). The increase in antisocial behavior occurred across gender, ethnicity, and socioeconomic status (SES) and in rural and suburban areas. Antisocial behavior among youth peaked in the 1990s but has

antisocial behavior
behavior that disrupts the functioning of society, such as aggression and delinquency.

oppositional defiant disorder
a clinical diagnosis given to children who are excessively defiant and hostile for at least 6 months.

conduct disorder
a clinical diagnosis given to youth who are excessively delinquent or aggressive for at least 6 months.

BOX 10.1   challenges in development

Conduct Disorder

Adara is a 10th-grade bully. In the hallways, she punches other students or deliberately bumps into them. In the classroom, she gives nicknames to classmates based on physical flaws, like "Zit Face." She criticizes her teacher's appearance and personality, like "That's an ugly sweater." She breaks class rules, is often tardy, and annoys other students by writing in their notebooks.

Adara has conduct disorder (CD), a clinical diagnosis given to children who consistently violate social norms and the rights of others. Children with CD have hostile attribution bias and little guilt or empathy and are aggressive. CD can range from mild (lying, truancy, staying out after curfew) to severe (rape, physical cruelty, breaking and entering).

Oppositional defiant disorder (ODD) is a clinical diagnosis given to children who are defiant, are hostile toward authority figures, do not accept blame for misbehavior, deliberately annoy others, and are verbally aggressive. ODD is less focused on aggression than conduct disorder, and more on defiance. For both ODD and CD diagnoses, antisocial behavior must last for 6 months and be severe enough to disrupt social or academic functioning (American Psychiatric Association, 2013)—brief or typical levels of antisocial behavior do not qualify.

How Prevalent Is CD? You are likely to have learners with ODD or CD in some of your classes. Conduct disorder is a prevalent psychiatric diagnosis, occurring in 2 to 16% of children. Both ODD and CD have increased over the past few decades (Achenbach et al., 2003; Farrington, 2009). Boys are two to three times more likely to have CD than girls.

What Does CD Predict? As compared with peers, learners with CD are four times more likely to be friendless and

have achievement below what you might expect for their IQ. They are often reckless and prone to injuries. ODD and CD are strongly comorbid with ADHD, meaning that they often occur in the same child (e.g., Trzesniewski, Moffitt, Caspi, Taylor, & Maughan, 2006). How these learners fare in adulthood depends on the severity of their CD and what other problems they have. Boys who struggle with *both* CD and depression or ADHD are two to three times as likely to commit crimes or develop mental illness in adulthood as compared with typical boys (Sourander et al., 2007).

What Predicts CD? The most powerful risk factor for ODD and CD is family dysfunction, combined with genetic predisposition (Dodge, 2009). Family dysfunction refers to parental rejection; harsh discipline; abuse; frequent change of caregivers; marital discord; and antisocial, alcoholic, or depressed parents. Adara missed several months of school because her mother and aunt were fighting over custody.

Practicing Inclusion—How Can You Help Learners with Conduct Disorder? The answer is to apply the principles you learned in this chapter and in Chapter 7. Indeed, therapy for CD typically focuses on training parents to do the same, that is, reinforce prosocial behavior and enforce clear and consistent limits on misbehavior without escalating conflict (Dishion & Kavanagh, 2002). Adara's teacher decided to implement these principles, in addition to using humor. As a result, Adara quit skipping class and became less disruptive. She even became kind and thoughtful toward her teacher; one snowy day Adara offered her coat to her teacher who was headed out the door for bus duty.

declined a little since then; now youth are less likely to commit violent crime, to use drugs, and have sex than in the 1990s (FIFCFS, 2009). Still, most learners are not antisocial, and those who are can be helped. Because substance use is discussed in Chapter 2 and sexual behavior in Chapter 11, we will focus primarily on aggression next.

10-2a Types of Aggression

Aggression is behavior intended to harm another person. You could also consider forceful attempts to dominate someone else as aggression, even if no obvious harm is done. There are different forms (physical, verbal, social) and different motives

aggression
behavior that harms others, or is intended to dominate others. It is a subset of antisocial behavior.

(proactive and reactive) for aggression. Understanding these differences is important because they predict different outcomes.

Physical, Verbal, and Social Aggression

physical aggression
behavior that harms others through physical means such as hitting, pushing, or kicking.

verbal aggression
behavior that harms others through verbal means such as threatening or name calling.

social aggression
behavior that harms others through manipulating their relationships or peer-group status, such as spreading rumors or excluding the victim from a social clique. Also called relational aggression.

reactive aggression
aggression that is aimed at retaliation for a provocation, usually involving anger or frustration.

proactive aggression
aggression that is directed at achieving personal objectives, but that was not clearly provoked.

instrumental aggression
a type of proactive aggression in which the primary aim is to obtain an object, territory, or privilege, but not to hurt the victim.

Physical aggression is hitting, pushing, or fighting. **Verbal aggression** is threatening, name calling, or insulting, such as "your face is ugly." Both physical and verbal aggression are sometimes called *direct* or *overt* because they are easily observed. **Social aggression** involves undermining someone else's relationships or social status (Archer & Coyne, 2005). This might include spreading rumors, refusing to talk to the victim, and excluding the victim from a clique. Social aggression can be conveyed through body language, like rolling the eyes. Social aggression is sometimes called *indirect*, covert, or *relational* aggression. Teachers are better at detecting overt than social aggression, although you may sometimes be aware of your learners' social aggression.

Physical, verbal, and social aggression are highly correlated (Meehan, Hughes, & Cavell, 2003; Murray-Close, Crick, & Galotti, 2006). This means that most learners who use one type of aggression use the others as well. However, the correlations are not perfect, so a learner can be high in one but low in other types of aggression. For example, Josh used all forms of aggression. Other students may use verbal and social aggression, but rarely physical aggression.

Reactive Aggression and Bullying

Aggression can be either reactive or proactive. **Reactive aggression** is provoked retaliation, accompanied by anger or frustration. **Proactive aggression** is a means to achieve personal goals. There are two types of proactive aggression: instrumental and bullying. **Instrumental aggression** is the use of threat or force to obtain something. It is usually goal-oriented rather than person-oriented. For example, in a school lunchroom, Andrew was making an irritating noise by blowing across a straw. Another child threw a small plastic container and hit Andrew's head. Andrew stopped making the noise. The primary goal was not to hurt Andrew, but to stop the noise.

Bullying is proactive aggression that is intended to intimidate and humiliate (Juvonen & Graham, 2014). Both reactive aggression and bullying are considered **hostile aggression** because the *intent is to harm the other*. You might think of reactive aggression as "hot-headed" and bullying as "cold-hearted." In contrast, instrumental aggression is not hostile. Sometimes it is hard to distinguish between these types of aggression, and certainly an act of aggression can have multiple motives. Figure 10.3 helps you understand the types of aggression.

Not all aggression is bullying. Aggression is bullying when there is an imbalance of power in a relationship

FIGURE 10.3 Types of Aggression.

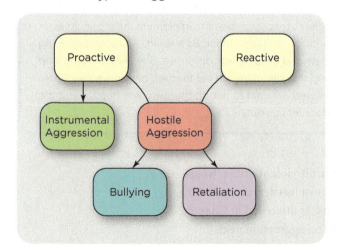

Proactive and reactive aggression are defined by whether they are in response to a provocation or not. Either can be hostile. Bullying is hostile, proactive aggression. Retaliation is hostile, reactive aggression, or a "hot-headed" response to provocation. Instrumental aggression is nonhostile and proactive. Try to generate an example of each to test your understanding.

and the aggressor intends to harm, seeks power, and is not remorseful (Rodkin, Espelage, & Hanish, 2015). Typically bullying is repeated, although a one-time event can be considered bullying (Juvonen & Graham, 2014). If two learners of similar size have a one-time fight, this is not bullying. If a large student who has a gang of deviant friends standing behind him repeatedly threatens a smaller child, this is bullying. Bullying can be psychological rather than physical, such as when a high-status student shames or ostracizes a low-status student. The most common forms of bullying are making fun of others and spreading rumors (Robers, Kemp, Rathbun, & Morgan, 2014). Box 10.2 discusses the effects of bullying on victims.

bullying
a type of proactive aggression in which the goal is intimidation or dominance over another person that typically occurs repeatedly over time and involves someone of greater power victimizing someone of lower status or power.

hostile aggression
a type of reactive or proactive aggression in which the primary aim is to harm another person.

BOX 10.2 challenges in development

Victims

First-grader Arya is very small and young for her grade. She appears to be an easy victim. During the first week of school, a large and older boy bullies her at recess. He pushes her around the playground. Arya tells him to stop, she tries to avoid him, she tells the playground supervisors, but still he bullies her. Finally, she bites him, hard. The bullying ends. Apparently Arya is not an easy victim.

The boy continued to bully other children, but Arya was not bullied again. Being a victim is a common experience. In elementary, middle, and high schools, roughly one-third of the students may be victimized each year, like being called names or having items stolen from a locker (Dinkes, Kemp, & Baum, 2009; Nylund, Bellmore, Nishina, & Graham, 2007; Robers et al., 2014).

Victimization is most often short-lived, particularly for young children, as it was for Arya. However, as many as 5 to 20% of students are regularly victimized (Dinkes et al., 2009; Juvonen & Graham, 2014). Victims and bullies are often in classes together for years, so students can be chronically victimized. When children transfer from primary to secondary school, so that they become the youngest and smallest at school, there is a brief surge in victimization even among those who are typically not victims (Nylund, Bellmore, Nishina, & Graham, 2007). Despite the media hype, cyberbullying is rare; only about 9% of adolescents report being the victims of cyberbullies (Robers et al., 2014). Thus, most students are seldom victimized, some are occasionally, and a smaller number are chronically victimized.

Who Is Victimized? Most chronic victims are submissive. *Submissive victims* tend to be physically weak, insecure, and friendless; they may cry easily and worry excessively. A minority of victims are aggressive. *Aggressive victims* tend

to have poor emotion regulation and be hot-headed. They provoke bullies because they irritate. The more aggressive they are, the more victimized they may become over time. Some of these aggressive victims are themselves bullies. Over time they may shift from being victims to being bullies, and vice versa (Juvonen & Graham, 2014).

What Might Lead to Victimization? Victims tend to be friendless. Bullies need fear no retaliation from friends of the victim, and the victim is often alone, making victimization easy. Quality of parenting also predicts victimization. Victims tend to have insecure attachment (Smith & Myron-Wilson, 1998). *Submissive victims* tend to have either hostile mothers or overly protective, intensely close mothers, or fathers who are negative and distant. *Aggressive victims* tend to have hostile, aggressive parents, and a history of abuse or father absence (Ladd & Pettit, 2002; Vlachou, Andreou, Botsoglou, & Didaskalou, 2011).

What Are the Consequences of Victimization? The same factors may be both cause and consequence of victimization—depression, low self-esteem, anxiety, friendlessness, and peer rejection. Being a victim increases risk for each of these problems, as well as for suicide (Kljakovic & Hunt, 2016; Kowalski, Giumetti, Schroeder, & Lattanner, 2014; Schwartz, Lansford, Dodge, Pettit, & Bates, 2015). Victims feel humiliated, anxious, and angry while at school (Nishina & Juvonen, 2005). In Chapter 8, you learned that *these emotions interfere with learning.* Victims earn lower grades and feel less academically competent (Busch et al., 2014; Thijs & Verkuyten, 2008). Cyberbullying may be especially traumatic because it can be anonymous and make learners feel vulnerable even in their homes (Raskauskas & Stoltz, 2007). *Aggressive bully-victims* fare worse than

Victims (continued)

other victims because they have all the negative outcomes of both bullies and victims (Juvonen & Graham, 2014). When these victims can no longer tolerate the bullying, they may perpetrate serious violence at school.

Should a Victim Seek Your Help? Victims may respond by seeking adults' help, becoming aggressive themselves, or passively ignoring or walking away from the bully. Seeking help can be good or bad. Not seeking help when they need it can put victims in danger. Yet seeking help when they should be able to handle the situation themselves may lead peers to view victims as weak or tattletales. Ideally, victims should seek help *only when it is necessary* (Newman, 2008). Adolescents who ignore bullies fare better than those who seek help (Waasdorp & Bradshaw, 2011). Ignoring bullies may be difficult for young or socially unskilled victims. Notice that Arya sought help only after she had tried to stop the bully herself. She did not get help, so she solved the problem as most young children would—with counteraggression.

What Can You Do to Help Victims? The first step is to perceive victimization. Less than 50% of elementary and 25% of secondary students report victimization, so you have to watch for it (Petrosino, Gugkenburg, DeVoe, & Hanson, 2010; Troop-Gordon, 2015). When you identify a victim, do not simply tell him or her to just ignore it or stand up to the bully, because this can make things worse (Troop-Gordon, 2015). Instead, teach effective (rather than anger-venting) coping strategies (see Chapter 8). Help the victim establish friendships at school (see Chapter 11). Recruit your school counselor to help address any other problems that may have led to victimization.

Stop the culture of bullying. Teach learners to stand up together when they see a peer being bullied, then tell you (you must be willing to do something about it), and then befriend the victim. When victimization stops, the victim's psychological well-being does not necessarily improve (Kochenderfer-Ladd & Wardrop, 2001). This means some victims need help to regain feelings of belonging at school. See Chapter 6 for how to do this.

One form of bullying that occurs in schools is sexual harassment. For example, the following incident occurred in a rural middle school:

> *A boy hung out in the high school restroom. When other boys entered he would say, "I'm your husband," slap their bottoms, or tell them they had nice bodies, and that he wanted to "get some of that." Several boys complained to teachers about this harassment. Nothing changed, so a victim decided to "take care of the problem" himself. Fortunately, a teacher stopped him before anyone was hurt.*

Most (70 to 95%) secondary students have been a witness to or a victim of sexual harassment at least once (Lichty & Campbell, 2012). Schools have a legal and moral obligation to stop sexual harassment (Cornell & Limber, 2015). The Supreme Court (*Davis v. Monroe County Board of Education*, 119 S.Ct. 1661) ruled that a school's "deliberate indifference" to known harassment is prohibited by Title IX because it undermines victims' education, effectively denying equal access to education. In the legal case, a 5th-grade girl told her teacher that a male classmate was repeatedly touching her, rubbing against her, and speaking to her lewdly. The principal was aware of the problem. The girl was not moved away from the bully for 3 months. The bully was not disciplined, and his offensive behavior escalated until the case went to court. The court indicated that an isolated instance of name-calling does not constitute victimization, but continued harassment does, and should not be tolerated in schools.

Schools also have a legal and moral obligation to stop cyberbullying. **Cyberbullying** takes place on the Internet through aggressive text messages, derogatory websites, and display of compromising pictures. For example, youth have taken cell-phone photos of peers undressed in the locker room and posted them on websites. However, this is a complex problem because schools cannot overstep their authority and limit free speech off school grounds. Courts have sometimes, but not always, ruled that schools can stop cyberbullying if it substantially disrupts learning and infringes on other students' civil rights (Hinduja & Patchin, 2011).

cyberbullying
bullying that occurs through interactive technologies.

10-2b Age Trends in Antisocial Behavior

The type and frequency of aggression changes with age. What is normal for 2-year-olds may not be for 14-year-olds. Let's look at age trends next.

Infancy and Toddlerhood (Birth to 2 Years)

Infants are not capable of aggression, but they are capable of anger at as young as 4 months of age (Sullivan & Lewis, 2003). Try taking away food or restraining an infant's arms and you are likely to see anger. In fact, scientists study infant anger by restraining them in a car seat (this won't surprise most mothers). Infants who are anger-prone are likely to be more physically aggressive at age 3 than infants who are not anger-prone (Hay et al., 2014).

Aggression toward peers, such as fighting over toys, is apparent by 12 months (Alink et al., 2006; Hay et al., 2011). *Physical* aggression grows from age 1 to 2. Toddlers primarily engage in *instrumental* aggression that is short-lived. Let's take a peek in a toddler classroom:

> *The children are happily catching and throwing balloons, until Payton decides the yellow balloon is his alone. As Luke catches the yellow balloon, Payton yells, "Mine!" He shoves Luke in the chest and snatches the balloon away. Payton smiles, but Luke begins to cry. Payton looks at Luke in surprise, baffled at what is wrong. Payton brings Luke his sippy cup to cheer him up.*

Payton did not intend to hurt Luke. He simply wanted the balloon. In toddlers, such instrumental aggression toward a peer is normal in that it does not portend later conduct disorder (Hay, Castle, & Davies, 2000).

Early Childhood (3 to 5 Years)

On average, *2- to 4-year-olds are the most aggressive of any age group*, but aggression diminishes by kindergarten (Vlachou et al., 2011). See Figure 10.4. Around age 3, *physical* aggression begins decreasing. This is partly because it is replaced with *verbal* aggression as children learn to talk. It is also partly because children are becoming less aggressive overall. Language reduces the need for instrumental aggression. For example, while 2-year-old Payton may shove Luke to get the balloon, by age 4 he can ask for it. Preschoolers may also become less aggressive as they develop self-control, emotional perspective-taking, and theory of mind (see Chapters 7, 8, and 9). However, approximately 13% of 3-year-olds still physically fight with peers (Underwood, 2002). In addition, preschoolers are often "happy victimizers,"

FIGURE 10.4 Age Trend in Aggression and Noncompliance in Early Childhood.

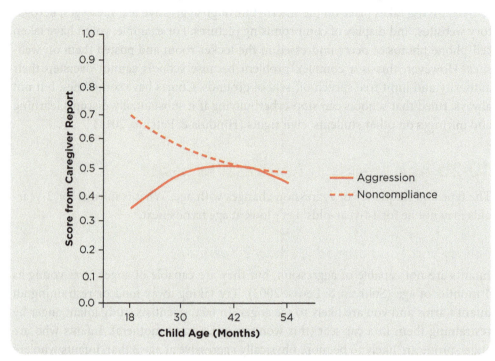

At what age does aggression peak and then begin to taper off? How does this pattern differ for noncompliance? *Source: Sulik et al. (2012).*

meaning they feel happy after successfully aggressing (Arsenio, 2014). Among older school-age children, only antisocial children are happy victimizers (Shalvi, Gino, Barkan, & Ayal, 2015).

Middle Childhood (6 to 12 Years)

Physical aggression diminishes even more in middle childhood and becomes rare when adults are present (Underwood, 2002). Behaviors that may be considered normal in 2-year-olds—temper tantrums, defiance, argumentativeness, irritability—are indicative of serious behavior problems if they are still present at age 8. A diagnosis of conduct disorder is given to children who continue to show frequent physical aggression into middle childhood.

Social aggression may become more apparent in middle childhood (Photo 10.4). Some researchers believe physical, verbal, and social aggression represent a developmental continuum. Physical aggression is the most immature form, and social aggression is the most mature, not developing until children understand they can harm others through manipulating social status, around age 8 (Bjorkqvist, 2001; Vlachou et al., 2011). Thus, 1st-graders tend to use less social aggression than 4th-graders, who tend to use less than 7th-graders (Xie, Farmer, & Cairns, 2003). The opposite pattern is found for physical aggression, as it is replaced by the more subtle verbal and social aggression.

While children are generally less aggressive during middle childhood than during the preschool years, when they are aggressive, it is more likely to be *hostile rather than instrumental.* This is because the major cause of aggression is no longer dispute over toys but threat to self-esteem, which generates hostility (Hartup, 1974).

Bullying emerges at school entry, and then declines between 7 years of age and adolescence (Rigby, 2002). However, there may be a temporary resurgence in bullying when children first transition to middle/junior high school (Nansel et al., 2001). In elementary school, bullies are not liked, but in middle school some may attain a type of high status. For example, some jocks are bullies with high status. In addition, some girls who are cool because they act and dress older than their age are bullies. Their social status allows them to get away with bullying (Juvonen & Graham, 2014).

PHOTO 10.4 Social aggression becomes apparent in elementary school. Girls who are aggressive are more likely to use social aggression than physical aggression.

Adolescence (13 to 19 Years)

Aggression steadily decreases from early childhood through adolescence—other than the temporary spike at the middle school transition (Grunbaum et al., 2002; Nansel et al., 2001). In contrast, delinquency tends to increase in early adolescence, peaking around ages 14 to 15, and then decreases from 15 to 19 years (Gutman & Eccles, 2007).

Despite the overall decrease in aggression, most adolescents are mildly aggressive occasionally, like bickering with siblings or calling someone a name. A few adolescents continue to be highly aggressive. In a national study of high school students, 6% had carried a weapon to school in the past 30 days and 12% were in a physical fight on school property in the past year (Dinkes et al., 2009).

The aggressive acts of these youth may be criminal. Behaviors that are somewhat tolerated in very young children, like hitting someone, can result in the arrest of an 18-year-old. Crimes are most commonly perpetrated in the late teens and young adulthood. Half of criminals commit their first offense between ages 14 and 17. Some researchers believe this is because families with teens are disproportionately poor compared to other age groups, and poverty is linked to high rates of crime (Males & Brown, 2014).

10-2c Individual Diversity in Antisocial Behavior

Some children are more aggressive, and more victimized, than others. An individual child's level of aggression is stable; children who are more or less aggressive than their peers tend to stay that way over time. In fact, *aggression may be one of the most stable personal traits; its stability is as great or greater than the stability of IQ.* This is the case across ethnic groups in the United States and across countries.[1]

What Do Individual Differences in Antisocial Behavior Predict?

About half of children are consistently low in aggression (see Figure 10.5). Another 15 to 20% are moderately aggressive in early childhood but taper off to almost no

[1] Many studies support this conclusion, a few of which are listed here: Broidy et al. (2003); Ettekal and Ladd (2015); Guerra, Huesmann, and Spindler (2003); Hay et al. (2014); Rigby (2002); Rubin, Burgess, Dwyer, and Hastings (2003).

FIGURE 10.5 Trajectories of Children with Different Patterns of Antisocial Behavior.

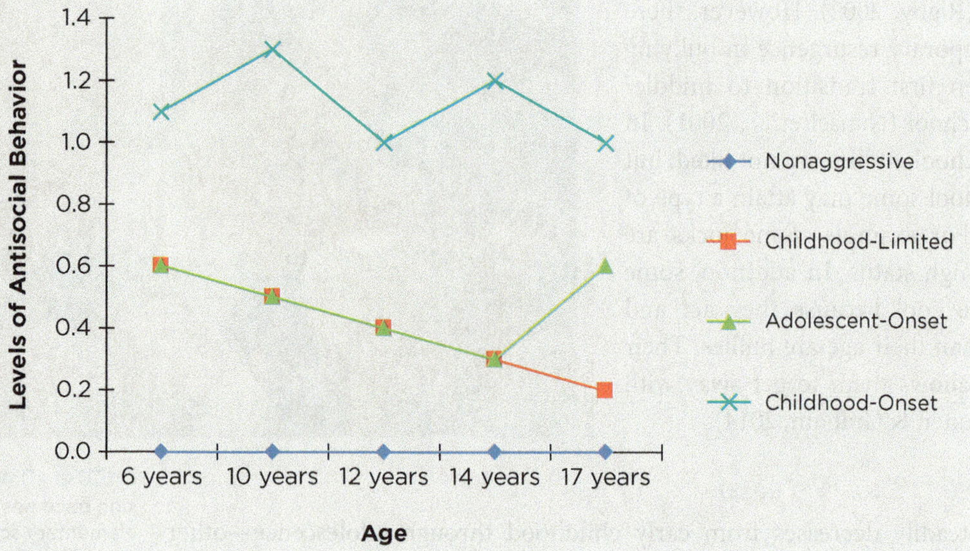

Nonaggressives are children who seldom show aggression throughout childhood. *Childhood-limited* refers to children who are aggressive early in childhood, but taper off with age. *Adolescent-onset* refers to youth who are temporarily delinquent in adolescence. *Childhood-onset* refers to children who are aggressive early and persistently throughout childhood. Note that the lines do not cross; even when children increase or decrease over time in aggression, they tend to maintain their relative rank. Can you think of someone you know, or a literary or movie character, who followed each pattern? *Source: Adapted from Broidy et al. (2003), Piehler and Dishion (2007), and O'Connor, Dearing, and Collins (2011).*

aggression later (Pepler, Jiang, Craig, & Connolly, 2008; O'Connor et al., 2011; Xie, Drabick, & Chen, 2011). However, some children (about 5 to 15%) begin early with behavior problems that persist throughout childhood. This pattern is called *childhood-onset.* Thus, an aggressive teen, like Josh, was probably an aggressive preschooler. Some nonaggressive learners engage in a *brief* episode of antisocial behavior in the teens. This pattern is called *adolescent-onset.* This pattern tends to occur when there is a significant increase in life stress during adolescence and lack of parental monitoring and unsupervised socialization with delinquent peers (Aguilar, Sroufe, Egeland, & Carlson, 2000; Brennan, Hall, Bor, Najman, & Williams, 2003; Xie et al., 2011). These patterns have academic and social consequences.

Academic achievement

Antisocial behavior is both a cause and a consequence of low academic achievement. That is, low achievement leads learners to act out at school, and acting out leads to low achievement. It is a *bidirectional* effect that has been found across ethnicities. Toddlers with substantial behavior problems are likely to have lower achievement when they are in elementary school (Bub, McCartney, & Willett, 2007). From kindergarten through high school, aggressive students are likely to have attention problems, reading and learning difficulties, lower GPAs, and lower test scores (e.g., Grimm, Steele, Mashburn, Burchinal, & Pianta, 2010; Trzesniewski, Moffit, Caspi, Taylor, & Maughan, 2006; Xie et al., 2011). However, aggression is more strongly linked to low achievement in high school than in primary grades.

How might antisocial behavior affect academic achievement? Teachers are likely to develop negative relationships with antisocial learners (see Chapter 6). The learners may then do less homework, disengage from classroom tasks, put less effort into class work, develop poor academic skills, and avoid school (Kiefer & Ryan, 2008; Stipek & Miles, 2008). Antisocial learners tend to have low achievement even when other risk factors, such as low IQ or family problems, are statistically controlled (Masten et al., 2005).

Social competence

Antisocial behavior is also a cause and a consequence of social rejection (Ettekal & Ladd, 2015). A child who is aggressive may not be rejected immediately in the classroom. However, over time peers become less able to tolerate the aggression. Some aggressive learners, particularly girls, feel lonely, but other aggressive learners are not lonely and actually feel overly optimistic about their ability to attract friends (Nansel et al., 2001). They believe they have plenty of friends in class—which is not true.

One of the problems with social rejection is that antisocial learners are precluded from opportunities to develop social skills with normal peers who ignore or avoid them. Antisocial behavior may follow the pathway depicted in Figure 10.6. First, the child has models of aggression at home in parents and siblings and is treated harshly. The child becomes aggressive, entering school with behavior problems. As a result, the child has low achievement and is rejected by normal peers. Parents withdraw

FIGURE 10.6 Developmental Path of Antisocial Behavior.

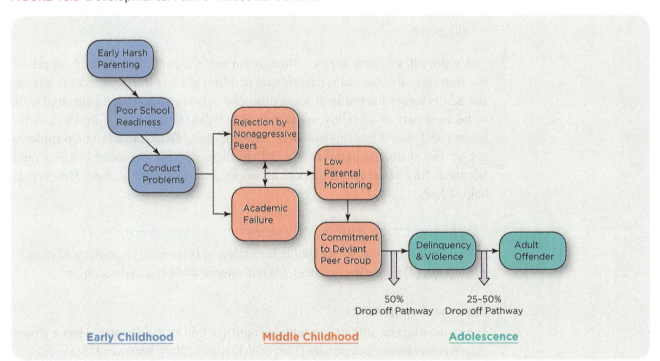

Notice the two points at which learners may drop out of this negative pathway. About 50% of learners in deviant peer groups as they leave childhood will not become delinquent as teens, and 25% to 50% of delinquent teens will not become adult criminals. *Source: Adapted from Dodge et al. (2008), Patterson et al. (1989), and Rudolph et al. (2014).*

from monitoring the child. Then the child, as early as 10 years of age, begins to associate predominantly with other antisocial peers, who promote delinquency. Minor delinquency is followed by alcohol and marijuana use, then hard drug use and serious violent offenses. This progression is partly fostered by schools, which tend to group learners together based on academic performance, sometimes creating a pool of antisocial peers.

Aggressive children tend to grow into adults with many problems, such as criminality, substance use, drunk driving, teen parenthood, low job status, periods of unemployment, spouse abuse, divorce, and harsh parenting of their own children (e.g., Kokko & Pulkkinen, 2000; Nansel et al., 2001; Serbin & Karp, 2003; Xie et al., 2011).

Fortunately, children can drop off this pathway; not all delinquent teens become antisocial adults. They are more likely to become antisocial adults if they have the childhood-onset pattern and are *proactive* rather than reactive aggressors. Let's take another look at Josh.

> Josh is hot-headed. Some classmates call him "fatso" to get a rise out of him. He reacts by fighting them every time, so he is often in trouble. His mother can barely tolerate him. She says he is "stupid" and "good for nothing." His father left after abuse charges; he punched Josh for complaining about his dinner. Josh is an angry boy who hates school. He feels accepted only among his friends. Together, they smoke marijuana and steal things. One of Josh's teachers, Mrs. Wentz, decides to form a secure relationship with him. At the same time, Josh begins to attend church, where he adopts the youth minister as a father figure. Today, as a young adult, Josh is a skilled tradesman, an involved father of two, and physically fit. He is also divorced—the aggression has not stopped altogether.

Josh's story has a fairly happy, although not perfect, ending. How did Josh get off the trajectory to criminality? Antisocial children are less likely to become antisocial adults if they have at least some prosocial behaviors, develop an admired skill, or become part of a healthy social network (Pulkkinen, 2001). In Josh's case, his teacher and church became his social network. As a teacher, you can help students get off the antisocial pathway if you help them develop prosocial behavior and talents or find better social support networks. Later, you will see how Mrs. Wentz helped Josh.

What Predicts Individual Differences in Antisocial Behavior?

Let's examine four major risk factors for antisocial behavior: (1) genetic and epigenetic factors, (2) parenting practices, (3) self-esteem, and (4) social cognition.

Genes and epigenetics

Twin and adoptive studies in multiple countries find that *delinquency* has a strong shared environment component (Burt & Neiderhiser, 2009; Roisman & Fraley, 2006). This means that siblings, regardless of their genetic relatedness, have similar levels of vandalism, truancy, and lawbreaking. In contrast, *aggression* has a moderate to strong genetic component; it is about 50% heritable.[2] However, heritability is complicated in three ways:

1. As you learned in Chapter 1, genes and environment may be correlated. For example, antisocial parents may pass on their genes for aggression to a child whose aggressive behavior evokes harshness from the parents, which creates a hostile family environment (Marceau et al., 2013).

2. The environment influences whether genes are expressed (see Chapter 6). Several studies have found that children with genes that predispose them to aggression may become aggressive only in certain environments, such as having antisocial friends, low-quality parenting, or parents who don't monitor them (Dick, 2011; Latendresse et al., 2011). This has been found for infants as well as teens (e.g., Leve et al., 2010). Notably, these *epigenetic effects have been found for teachers*. For example, one study found that 1st-graders with a high-risk gene did not become aggressive if they had a positive teacher–student relationship, whereas a negative relationship with their teacher exacerbated their aggressive predisposition (Brendgen et al., 2012).

3. Genes can make some children more susceptible to their environment. For example, toddlers with a high-risk gene (SLC6A4 allele) may become preschoolers who are *more* defiant than their peers only if they have low-quality parenting, but *less* defiant if they have high-quality parenting (Sulik et al., 2012). Their "dandelion" peers without the high-risk gene are less affected by quality of parenting (see Chapter 6). These epigenetic effects occur early in life. As children get older, they may become more antisocial if they have low-quality parenting regardless of their genetic makeup.

These epigenetic effects form the basis of individual differences in antisocial behavior. Epigenetic effects can be temporary or permanent, and may extend across generations (Meany, 2010). Genetic effects alone cannot explain the rise in children's aggression over the past few decades because there has not been time for genes to evolve, but epigenetic effects could.

Parenting factors

In previous chapters, you learned about several parenting factors that are associated with antisocial behavior in children. Table 10.2 shows which are protective and which are risk factors. Remember that risk factors are not certainties. For example, while abused children have a heightened tendency to become antisocial, many do not. Unfortunately, risk factors tend to go together. An accumulation of risk factors (see Chapter 1), rather than a single factor alone, more strongly predicts chronic antisocial behavior (Pettit, 2005; Xie et al., 2011).

Coercive families are particularly problematic. A **coercive family cycle** is created when negative parenting leads to aggression in a child, which causes parents to respond with hostility, which causes the child to retaliate more aggressively, and so on. For

think about this
How do the concepts of "genotype" and "phenotype" and "gene–environment interaction" from Chapter 1 pertain to antisocial behavior? Scientists have found that adopted children with antisocial biological parents evoke harsher parenting from their adopted parents than do other adoptees (Moffitt, 2005). Can you explain this as a gene–environment correlation?

think about this
How would an attachment theorist (Chapter 6) explain how parenting causes aggression in children? How would a social learning theorist (Chapter 3) explain how parenting causes aggression in children? Defend your assertions.

coercive family cycle
a cycle of negative reinforcement in hostile families in which negative parenting leads to child aggression, which leads to more parental hostility, which leads to more child aggression, and so on.

---

[2] Heritability is larger if self-report or parent report is used and smaller if behavior is observed (Brendgen et al., 2008; DiLalla, 2000; Roisman & Fraley, 2012; Trzesniewski et al., 2006; Wertz et al., 2016).

TABLE 10.2 Protective and risk factors for antisocial behaviors

Protective Factors	Risk Factors
1. *Parental warmth.* Infants with sensitive, positive parents are likely to be less aggressive into young adulthood.	1. *Insecure attachment*—at all ages. The effect is weaker for children from two-parent families because stable families are a protective factor.
2. *Firm control.* For example, parents who do not let children stay up late, or do not let 7th-graders decide whether they can date, have children who are less likely to be antisocial.	2. *Power assertive discipline, spanking, and authoritarian parenting.* These factors undermine self-control and create angry, defiant children, even as early as age 4. Secure attachment may protect children from power assertion.
3. *Parental involvement,* such as monitoring, taking interest in, and spending time with children (unless the parent is antisocial).	3. *Maternal depression.* This is particularly a risk factor for early-onset antisocial behavior.
4. *Religiosity.* This is also linked to children forgiving aggressors rather than retaliating.	4. *Parental smoking.*
	5. *Abuse and domestic violence.*

Sources: Barber, Stolz, and Olsen (2005); Blatt-Eisengart, Drabick, Monahan, and Steinberg (2009); Bowes et al. (2009); Choe, Olson, and Sameroff (2014); Degnan, Calkins, Keane, and Hill-Soderlund (2008); Goldstein, Davis-Kean, and Eccles (2005); Hay et al. (2011); Joussemet et al. (2008); Kochanska, Barry, Stellern, and O'Bleness (2009); Lorber and Egeland (2009); Madigan, Brumariu, Villani, Atkinson, and Lyons-Ruth (2015); Michiels et al. (2008); Snyder, Cramer, Afrank, and Patterson (2005); Sulik et al. (2015); and Wakschlag et al. (2006).

example, a parent (or sibling) may yell at Josh, modeling aggression and anger. Josh may retaliate with yelling. The exchange escalates with the parent threatening and hitting. Josh fearfully quits misbehaving, which *negatively reinforces* the parent to use aggression in the future (see Chapter 3). In coercive families, parents often reinforce aggression, but seldom reinforce prosocial behaviors. These coercive cycles may be set in motion as early as toddlerhood (Lorber & Egeland, 2011). Siblings can also contribute to the cycle because they train each other in aggression and delinquency (Natsuaki, Ge, Reiss, & Neiderhiser, 2009). Parents can learn to be more positive with their children through intervention, which in turn leads to improvement in the child's behavior (Connell, Dishion, Yasui, & Kavanagh, 2007; Dishion et al., 2008). This means the cycle can be broken; the earlier it is broken the better, so that children do not develop childhood-onset aggression.

Self-esteem

You might assume that low self-esteem causes learners to behave aggressively. This may be partially true for some learners. There is a small correlation between low self-esteem and antisocial behavior (Donnellan, Trzeniewski, Robins, Moffitt, & Caspi, 2005). However, bullies may have *unrealistically high self-esteem.* They may be narcissistic, feeling more superior, deserving, and likable than others see them (Juvonen & Graham, 2014; Salmivalli, Ojanen, Haanpaa, & Peets, 2005). They may rationalize their aggression by derogating, blaming, or belittling their victims (Madhavi et al., 2007). It makes sense that bullies would have high self-esteem because it takes confidence to attack someone. Bullies' self-esteem is based on power.

However, aggression can also result from *threatened self-esteem.* Learners with high self-esteem, but whose self-image is fragile, may act aggressively to protect their self-image (Baumeister, Bushman, & Campbell, 2000; Pauletti, Menon, Menon, Tobin, & Perry, 2012). These learners' self-image is grandiose and vulnerable at the same time. Gaining respect and admiration are all-important. An important lesson for teachers is that *programs to enhance self-esteem that simply make aggressive learners feel more entitled could lead to more aggression.* Programs that help them learn skills and feel cared for will be more productive.

Social cognition—hostile attribution bias

Antisocial behavior often occurs because of misguided social cognition—that is, faulty thinking about others. In Chapter 9, you learned that low levels of moral judgment are linked to aggression. Another type of social cognition that is linked to aggression is **hostile attribution bias**, where learners assume hostile intent on the part of others when it is not clear whether there is actually hostile intent. It is akin to a "chip on the shoulder." For example, 1st-grader Allen was not paying attention to where he was going and accidentally bumped into Evan. Evan immediately tackled Allen to the floor and tried to punch him. Evan assumed that Allen ran into him on purpose. A less aggressive child would have assumed it was an accident.

Learners with hostile attribution bias, like Evan, have many negative peer interactions. As a result, they develop a bad reputation, so that their *own* ambiguous behavior is interpreted by *others* as hostile. For example, a 5th-grade girl explained why there was a fight at school one day:

> *Jenny threw a basketball at Cassie in gym. She was supposed to be throwing it to her, but instead it hit the wall behind Cassie and hit her in the face. Cassie told Jenny to apologize and she wouldn't. So Cassie and her friends threatened to beat Jenny up. At least Jenny says they did—I don't really believe it. Besides, it wasn't an accident. Well, it could be an accident, but Jenny is mean. I mean, like if it was me, nobody would think I did it on purpose. But everyone knows Jenny did it on purpose.*

Jenny is an aggressive child who attracts bias against her—"Jenny is mean." Thus, hostile attribution bias becomes a self-fulfilling prophecy. Aggressive learners overreact, then meet with aggression from others, which confirms their belief that others are hostile, which leads to more aggression on their part.

Hostile attribution bias is a type of faulty thinking in social situations. What causes such bias? One possibility is insecure attachment. Notice the similarity between this bias and internal working models from Chapter 6? When parents are hostile and rejecting, their children may develop negative working models of others, so they expect peers at school to be hostile (Michiels et al., 2008). Another possibility is poor skills in reading others' minds and emotions (Choe, Lane, Grabell, & Olson, 2013; see Chapters 8 and 9). The social information processing (SIP) model reveals additional thought processes that occur in a child's mind that determine whether the child will behave aggressively (see Box 10.3).

In summary, there are many risk factors for antisocial behavior. In Figure 10.6, we gave you a fairly simple model of how risk factors cascade over time. It begins

hostile attribution bias
the tendency to assume hostile intent on the part of others in situations in which it is not clear whether there is actually hostile intent.

BOX 10.3 theories & theorists

The Social Information Processing Model

Dozens of students are eating lunch in the high school's outdoor courtyard. Rob and Marshall are horsing around. Rob throws his apple core at Marshall. Marshall ducks, so the core hits Katie instead. Katie immediately picks up her drink and throws it at Rob, splattering it all over his clothes.

Why did Katie retaliate? Partly because she assumed Rob did it on purpose. Other student witnesses said they assumed it was an accident, and that Katie was "a jerk." Children's behavior is influenced by their interpretation of the situation or by their *processing of social information.* Figure 10.7 shows one model of social information processing (SIP). The figure makes it appear that each step happens sequentially, but in reality the steps are rapid, occurring at the same time, with each step looping back to inform the previous step. Most processing is probably not conscious. Table 10.3 explains the steps of the model.

Hostile attribution bias occurs at step 2, when learners attribute intent to others' behavior. Attributing intent

is easy to do when the cues are clear. However, in many social situations, intent is not clear and has to be inferred. Learners then fill in missing information from their database of memories from past social experience. Usually this database is helpful because learners do not have to decide what to do in every new encounter. However, this database is a problem if it is hostile. Rob's intent when throwing the apple was not clear to Katie, but she assumed hostile intent. The more ambiguous the situation, the more children have to rely on their database, distortions and all.

What Difference Does Social Information Processing Make? Appropriate processing leads to social competence, but distorted processing or bias can lead to aggression. Aggressive learners have biases at several steps. They pay more attention to aggressive cues and attribute hostile intent to others. They generate fewer possible responses, and the responses they generate are more likely to be aggressive. Bullies are more likely

FIGURE 10.7 **Social Information Processing Model.**

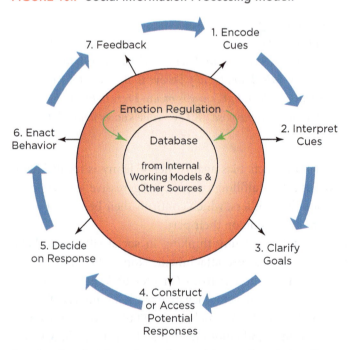

Step 2 is where hostile attribution bias and theory of mind take effect. Step 5 is where empathy and moral judgment take effect. Use one of the vignettes in the chapter and follow the child's thinking through this model. *Source: Adapted from Crick & Dodge (1994) and Lemerise & Arsenio (2000).*

TABLE 10.3 Components of the social information processing model

Step	Description	Example
1. Encode cues	Learners read others' emotions and the situation. In any social situation, there are more cues than can be processed, so each learner must select which to attend to.	I am waiting for a classmate to pass my test back to me. The classmate drops the test on the floor.
2. Interpret cues	Learners use their *theory of mind* and *internal working models* to infer the other's intention, and generate emotions.	He did it on purpose. I feel anger.
3. Clarify goals	Goals come from emotions, instruction, modeling (What would my dad do?), cultural norms, the media (What would Harry Potter do?), and so forth. Learners can have multiple, competing goals.	Do I want to maintain my relationship with him? Get even? Stay out of trouble?
4. Construct or access potential responses	Learners can access responses from memory, or a new behavior may be generated.	Glare at him and roll my eyes. Or act like I don't care. Or tell the teacher. Or slug him.
5. Decide on response	Learners evaluate the selected response. *Moral judgment* may be activated. Learners have expectations about the outcomes of each response, and their ability to pull it off. This can be conscious, but is more likely based on well-worn scripts. Impulsive learners may not consider options, but simply act on the first response that comes to mind.	It is morally OK to slug him if he deserves it. I don't have good enough emotion regulation ability to act like I don't care. My teacher won't help; she doesn't like me. I'm good at slugging.
6. Enact behavior	Learners' behavior can be simply a display of emotion (e.g., a glare) or more active.	Slug him.
7. Feedback	Learners evaluate the outcome. If it wasn't successful, they may repeat the effort, select a different strategy, or abandon the goal.	I feel successful. I showed him not to mess with me.
8. Encode cues	The cycle begins again.	Here comes the teacher!

to view aggression as morally acceptable, such as "it is OK to beat someone up who deserves it" (Paciello, Fida, Tramontano, Lupinetti, & Caprara, 2008). They believe the benefits of aggression outweigh possible punishment. If aggression is successful, they may become even more aggressive. These information processing biases have been found from preschool to adolescence (Arsenio, Adams, & Gold, 2009; Dodge, Godwin, & Group, 2013; Werner & Hill, 2010).

On the positive side, *prosocial* children have the opposite pattern of biases. They are more likely to assume kind intent in ambiguous situations. They are also more likely to think that aggressive solutions are morally bad and that prosocial solutions are best. They hold goals of maintaining relationships, even with a provoking peer. For example, when another child takes their seat at lunch, they are more motivated to maintain good relationships than to get their seat back.

with harsh parenting and ends with an antisocial youth. Reality is a little more complicated. Imagine combining Figure 10.6 with the bioecological model. According to the bioecological model, at each point in time the child's aggression is influenced by: (1) biology; (2) thoughts about others and the self; (3) social experiences besides parenting, like low-quality child care; and (4) cultural factors, like violent media. Harsh parenting has a larger effect than biological risk factors in predicting serious aggression (Brennan et al., 2003). However, in later chapters you will learn that peers, media, child care, and divorce also play a role in predicting antisocial behavior.

10-2d Group Diversity in Antisocial Behavior

Both gender and poverty are linked to antisocial behavior. Let's take a look at group differences in aggression next.

Gender

Perhaps the single most robust gender difference in child development is that boys are more aggressive than girls (Photo 10.5). This difference holds across SES groups and across nations, from Britain to Ethiopia to Mexico (Joussemet et al., 2008; Lansford et al., 2012). This difference occurs early and persists through adulthood. In infancy, boys show more precursors of aggression, such as biting, hitting out at people, and anger (Hay et al., 2014). By age 2, boys grab, push, shove, and hit more than girls (Alink et al., 2006; Baillargeon et al., 2007). Gender differences get larger with age. Boys continue to be more aggressive, dishonest, disruptive, and delinquent than girls from preschool through high school (Autor, Figlio, Karbownik, Roth, & Wasserman, 2015; Ho, Bluestein, & Jenkins, 2008; Xie et al., 2011). While these differences are real, teachers tend to amplify them, overattributing aggression to boys (Pellegrini, 2011). Thus, you may need to guard against bias in your classroom.

Some people believe that while boys are more physically aggressive than girls, girls are more socially aggressive, like gossiping or excluding peers. Where might this "mean girls" stereotype come from? There is a subset (about 15%) of girls who specialize in social aggression. In addition, although girls overall are *less often aggressive,* by 4th grade, *when girls are aggressive,* they are more likely to use social aggression than physical aggression, especially gossip (Ettekal & Ladd, 2015; Putallaz et al., 2007). However, dozens of studies across countries have found that boys are socially aggressive as often, if not more often, as girls (Card, Stucky, Sawalani, & Little, 2008; Lansford et al., 2012). This makes sense because physical, verbal, and social aggression are highly correlated.

Socioeconomic Status

On average, learners from low-SES homes are more likely to be antisocial than high-SES learners (Bradley & Corwyn, 2002). Recall from Chapter 2 that one exception is that high-SES learners tend to use more alcohol and other drugs. Low-SES learners have higher rates of aggression in preschool and when they begin school; they increase in antisocial behavior across the school years (Aber, Brown, & Jones, 2003; Hay et al., 2014). The link between SES and antisocial behavior has been found in many countries like the United States, England, Scotland, and the Netherlands, but not in all European countries (Rigby, 2002).

Why is there a link between SES and antisocial behavior? One reason may be exposure. Low-SES learners tend to use more-violent media, live in more-violent neighborhoods, and experience harsher parenting than middle- or high-SES learners (Dodge, Pettit, Bates, & Valente, 1995; Evans, 2004). For example, in one study low-SES parents were hostile toward their kindergarteners on average every 2 minutes while playing and reading together. The more hostile the parent, the more aggressive the child was on the school playground (Snyder et al., 2005). Parents who feel financial stress when they are not able to pay the bills tend to treat their children with more hostility (Williams, Conger, & Blozis, 2007). This fits the family stress model from Chapter 1. Children who have hostile parents are likely to develop hostile attribution bias. They tend to have stronger physiological reactions, like a rapidly beating heart, in ambiguous situations (Chen, Langer, Raphaelson, & Matthews, 2005). Effects are particularly strong for children who have both an emotionally negative temperament and stress-filled families (Schermerhorn et al., 2013).

PHOTO 10.5 Boys are more aggressive than girls. This is the most robust gender difference in behavior.

Many low-SES learners are not aggressive. Those who are *not* aggressive have less-harsh parents with less substance use than their aggressive peers (Ackerman, Brown, & Izard, 2003). Learners' aggression may change when risk factors change, such as a mother's boyfriend moving in or out or parental drug use increasing or decreasing.

Ethnicity

In many countries, belonging to an ethnic minority is associated with aggression. Adults of minority status tend to be victims of discrimination, have low income, and have less education. Minority children are more likely than majority children to have harsh or single parents and other risk factors. Minority children tend to aggress toward other minority children (Rigby, 2002).

In the United States, large studies of thousands of youth have found that African American youth are more likely than White youth to be both physically and socially aggressive (Blum et al., 2000; Putallaz et al., 2007). The same is found for Latino youth, although this varies by country of origin (Galindo & Fuller, 2010). Furthermore, African American youth are more likely to be arrested than White youth for crimes. This may be largely explained by the link between ethnicity and poverty. That is, impoverished youth are more likely to be arrested (Males & Brown, 2014). On the other hand, extreme violence at school, like school shootings, are most likely to be perpetrated by White males (Brown, Osterman, & Barnes, 2009).

10-2e Classroom Implications of Antisocial Behavior

> *Three girls are working at a table. Gretchen (the victim) joins them. As she approaches the table, Kay (the bully) says, "I can't wait until recess, because I hate you, and I am going to beat you up." Gretchen threatens to tell the teacher. Kay responds, "Tell her. I don't care," and then chases Gretchen away. A classmate warns Kay: "You better not. You'll get in all the trouble." Gretchen comes back to the table. Kay tries to hit her across the table. A classmate says, "Leave her alone." Gretchen tells the teacher. The teacher says, "Don't worry because if Kay hurts you, she will get in trouble." (Adapted from Atlas & Pepler, 1998, p. 99)*

This bullying is occurring in an elementary classroom. As many as two aggressive incidents per hour may occur in elementary classrooms; they occur even more often in the lunchroom and playground (Grossman et al., 1997; Pellegrini & Bartini, 2000). Because of age trends in aggression, preschool classrooms are likely to have more incidents of aggression, like Payton shoving Luke for the balloon. In contrast, secondary classrooms are likely to have fewer incidents. Recall that one exception to the downward trend in aggression is that there is a temporary spike in bullying at the transition to middle school.

Most bullying incidents (80 to 90%) are witnessed by other learners (Polanin, Espelage, & Pigott, 2012). Often witnesses do not intervene to help victims. They may feel it is not their business, or fear they may become the target, or don't care, or simply don't know what to do (Saarento & Salmivalli, 2015). Compared to passive witnesses, the prosocial 20 to 25% of learners who defend victims tend to have better emotion regulation, secure attachment, empathy, prosocial orientation, and high self-esteem and to belong to a peer group that values defending others (Espelage et al., 2012; Nickerson, Mele, & Princiotta, 2008; Vlachou et al., 2011). Teachers often do not intervene to stop aggression; for example, the teacher did nothing to stop Kay's aggression (Xie et al., 2003). Thus, *aggressors often get away with misbehavior at school.*

Levels of aggression vary widely by school and by classroom. In some classrooms, as few as 1% of the interactions are aggressive, but in other classrooms as many as 20% are aggressive (Cairns & Cairns, 1994; Kuppens, Grietens, Onghena, Michiels, & Subramanian, 2008). You might assume that larger schools have more bullying, but research does not support this. However, schools with more low-SES learners tend to have more bullying and physical aggression (Bowes et al., 2009; Klein & Cornell, 2010). Yet, some schools are oases of peace despite being in poor communities, because of caring relationships among staff and learners (Astor, Benbenishty, & Estrada, 2009).

think about **this**

Many parents endorse fighting back when their children are bullied at school. However, most schools prohibit fighting back. Are schools imposing their values on parents and students? Is this appropriate? Justify your responses based on what you have learned in this chapter.

Reducing Bullying and Aggression

How can you stop bullying, reduce aggression, and create such an oasis of peace? Once again, you have learned part of the answer in previous chapters—that is, by addressing the larger issue of promoting your students' emotional and academic competence, as well as their prosocial behavior. This includes:

1. *Avoid using retention* (see Chapter 5). Some teachers assume that if given an extra year to mature, aggressive learners will behave better. However, retention is associated with *increased* aggression at school (Pagani et al., 2001).

2. *Eliminate hunger and tiredness* (see Chapter 2). Hunger and tiredness foster aggression (Anderson, 2001). For example, allow a snack if learners must wait too long for lunch. Let parents know when learners are overtired in your class.

3. *Be thoughtful about what behavior you reinforce* (see Chapter 3). Aggressive learners are reinforced when they get what they want through aggression. Witnesses can inadvertently reinforce bullies by becoming an audience for them. Instead, find ways to reinforce prosocial behaviors among aggressive learners (see, for example, Ellis, Volk, Gonzalez, & Embry, 2015).

4. *Build academic skills* (see Chapters 3 to 5). Earlier you learned that aggression and low achievement are bidirectional; each can cause the other. Over time learners with higher achievement become less aggressive (Romano et al., 2010). In fact, interventions that target academic skills may be as effective at reducing aggression as interventions that specifically target aggressive behavior (McEvoy & Welker, 2000; Wilson, Lipsey, & Derzon, 2003).

5. *Establish a warm teacher–student relationship* (see Chapter 6). High-quality teacher–student relationships are linked to less aggressive, more positive behavior; greater classroom participation; and liking school, regardless of how aggressive learners are to begin with and regardless of a genetic predisposition (Brendgen et al., 2012; Meehan et al., 2003; O'Connor, Dearing, & Collins, 2011; Thomas, Bierman & Powers, 2011). It is difficult to establish positive relationships in a classroom with several highly aggressive learners, but if you can be sensitive and supportive, they are likely to become less aggressive (Thomas et al., 2011).

6. *Promote a positive school and classroom climate* (see Chapters 6 to 8). School climate can have a strong effect on school aggression. Positive school climate is a protective factor that reduces victimization and bullying (Harel-Fisch et al., 2011; Kowalski et al., 2014).

7. *Avoid power-assertive discipline* (see Chapter 7). Power assertion causes resentment and models aggressive interaction. In particular, avoid using suspension because it undermines learners' academic skills and may lead to dropping out.

These factors should be familiar to you by now. They are powerful factors that influence many child outcomes. Five more guidelines apply more narrowly to stopping bullying and other forms of aggression:

1. *Involve all learners in lessons.* It is natural to want to interact more with prosocial learners. However, when teachers do not attend to their more aggressive learners, call on them, or provide information to them, those learners become even less engaged in the classroom (Stipek, 2001).

2. *Do not accept bullying.* Make school rules against bullying explicit, and enforce them. Don't gloss over aggression, like letting star athletes or teachers' pets get away with bullying. Schools that consistently enforce discipline, *in the context of plenty of caring adults,* have the least amount of bullying (Gregory et al., 2010). See Figure 10.8.

3. *Teach witnesses to stand up for victims* or report bullying, and not to passively watch or reward bullies with attention (Saarento & Salmivalli, 2015). You can do this by promoting empathy (see Chapter 8), moral judgment (see Chapter 9),

FIGURE 10.8 School Climate Predicts Bullying.

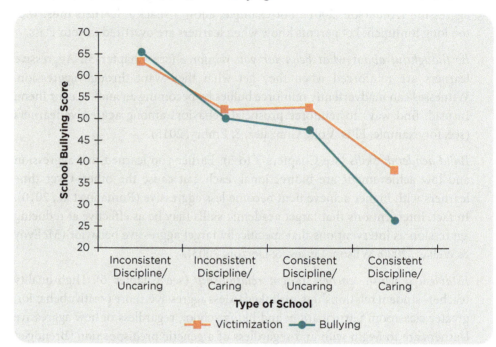

Authoritative schools—those that use consistent discipline and have warm, caring teachers—have the least bullying and victimization. Which may matter more, consistency of discipline or caring, or do they have to occur together? *Source: American Educational Research Association (2013).*

and prosocial behavior. Some school-based programs also do this through role-playing and feedback. Such programs are effective from grades K–12, but effects may be larger in high school (Polanin et al., 2012).

4. *Provide supervision.* Most aggression takes place where there is less teacher supervision. In preschools, it occurs more at the cubbies, sand/water table, and blocks area (Vlachou et al., 2011). In elementary schools, it occurs on the playground or in class when learners work on solitary or small-group tasks, like Gretchen and Kay were doing, but seldom during teacher-led activities. In secondary schools, it occurs more in the hallway, stairwell, or classroom (Robers et al., 2014).

5. *Screen for behavior problems early, preferably before age 8.* Aggression becomes stable at an early age and is difficult to change, although even adolescents can benefit from intervention. Learners who are at high risk for conduct problems can be identified as early as age 3 because at that age they are impulsive, irritable, and noncompliant. Early childhood teachers should be especially concerned about learners who have a high ratio of negative to positive behaviors.

These guidelines will help you reduce aggression in your learners, even in bullies like Kay. Let's see how Josh's biology teacher, Mrs. Wentz, applied some of these guidelines:

When Josh returned from a 3-day suspension, a classmate made a derogatory remark about having Josh back. Mrs. Wentz stopped the class and held an impromptu discussion about how such remarks would make Josh feel. She said their role was not to hold mistakes over each other, but rather to model better behavior and help each other.

Mrs. Wentz began talking with Josh about things that interested him. He began hanging out in her classroom, sometimes straightening chairs and feeding the pets. Mrs. Wentz said he "soaked up positive attention," yet he would suddenly test her by misbehaving, as though he wanted her to yell at him. Mrs. Wentz refused to give in; she used induction instead. Josh was the most difficult child Mrs. Wentz had in her 25 years of teaching. However, she knew she had made a difference on the day he came to her to help him resolve a conflict with a classmate, rather than fighting his way through it.

The majority of learners are not aggressive like Josh; a small number enact most of the aggression at school. Many schools have a "tiered" system of intervention for antisocial behaviors. *Universal* (or primary) interventions promote social competence in all learners. They are led by regular teachers who follow the guidelines discussed above. *Targeted* (or secondary) interventions focus on learners who show signs of problems and are led by counselors. *Indicated* (or tertiary) interventions focus on learners with intensive need and are provided by a professional therapist (Merrell, Levitt, & Gueldner, 2010). Let's take at look at school-based interventions.

School-Based Interventions

Targeted interventions typically focus on promoting more positive parent–child interaction, reducing learners' hostile attribution bias, and increasing emotion-regulation ability, prosocial behavior, and conflict-resolution skills (Connell et al., 2007; Hudley, Graham, & Taylor, 2007; Juvonen & Graham, 2014). Schools with high levels of bullying may implement a universal, or schoolwide, anti-bullying program. A famous program was implemented nationwide in Norway. It resulted in a 50% reduction in antisocial behaviors (Olweus, 1994). How did they reduce bullying? By implementing the same guidelines discussed above.

Programs similar to Norway's have been adopted in Canada, England, the United States, and Europe. However, most anti-bullying programs are not as successful as Norway's. One review of research found that programs can reduce bullying by about 20%, but some programs have negligible or *negative* effects (Ttofi & Farrington, 2011). Negative effects? Interventions that are implemented in a halfhearted way, or that *group deviant youth together* (who then promote each others' problems) can actually be harmful (Juvonen & Graham, 2014). Effective interventions may reduce aggression, but they usually do not eliminate it completely. Despite this cautionary note, some school-based interventions are successful (Ansary, Elias, Greene, & Green, 2013; Bradshaw, 2015). The website accompanying this text summarizes effective interventions that have been evaluated with rigorous scientific methods. This resource may help you select a program appropriate for your school. Let's turn next to how to resolve one cause of aggression: conflict.

10-3 Conflict Resolution

Two Latina high school students are talking in Spanish. An African American girl asks them not to use Spanish, and they agree. However, two other African American students defend the rights of Latinos to speak Spanish, and a fight nearly erupts before a teacher intervenes. The teacher talks with each student individually in the hall to quell the conflict. (Adapted from Lustig, 1997, p. 583)

Cindy Charles/PhotoEdit

PHOTO 10.6 You can teach your students to have better conflict-resolution skills.

conflict
the behavior of one person interferes with the goals of another person who resists or protests the behavior. It is not the same as aggression.

These girls experienced conflict. **Conflict** occurs when the behavior of one person interferes with the goals of another person, who then resists or protests. Conflict is inherent in all social relationships. Conflict can be as harmless as two children disagreeing on what to play, or it can involve serious aggression. *Conflict and aggression are not the same* because aggression involves intent to harm, but conflict does not. However, conflict can be the result or cause of aggression, as it almost was for these girls, and as it was for 2-year-old Payton who wanted his balloon back.

Do you think of conflict as bad? Actually, nonaggressive, day-to-day conflict—such as disagreeing whether to play soccer or dodgeball during recess—can be good for students because it helps children learn to negotiate and problem-solve (Photo 10.6). It helps them understand justice, fairness, and equality. It helps them refine social skills and emotion regulation. Nonaggressive conflict does not interrupt relationships or even activity much; children go back to playing together following conflict episodes. However, conflict can be disruptive if it is not resolved well.

10-3a How Should Conflict Be Resolved?

There are three main types of conflict resolution: (1) *compromise,* which means to negotiate, share, or take turns, as each side concedes something; (2) *disengagement,* which means to walk away, stop the discussion, and change the activity or topic; and (3) *coercion,* which means to command or aggress so that one side submits (Laursen, Finkelstein, & Betts, 2001).

The two goals in most conflict situations are to: (1) achieve your own aims and (2) maintain the relationship. The optimal way to resolve a conflict depends on the importance of each goal. A *constructive* conflict resolution occurs when each person is satisfied with the outcome, the relationship between them is improved, and their ability to resolve future conflicts is enhanced.

10-3b Age Trends in Conflict Resolution

The amount of conflict children have, its source, and how they resolve it changes with age.

Infancy and Toddlerhood (Birth to 2 Years)

Conflict is present early in life. By 8 months, infants protest others' behavior. Among toddlers, conflict is brief and primarily over objects, like Payton's balloon. Toddlers tend to resolve conflict in a win–lose way—holding firm or giving in—but seldom with compromise (Ashby & Neilsen-Hewett, 2012). Their ability to solve conflicts improves rapidly. Two-year-olds resolve disputes with words and use more prosocial solutions than 1-year-olds, like offering one toy in exchange for another (Caplan, Vespo, Pederson, & Hay, 1991).

Early Childhood (3 to 5 Years)

Between ages 1 and 7, children may have conflict every 3 to 12 minutes, depending on the age and setting (Chen, Fein, Killen, & Tam, 2001; Miller, Danaher, & Forbes, 1986). Thus, if you think young children are often in conflict, you are right.

Among preschoolers the sources of conflict are often social control, like who has to be the "baby" during play and who can join the group (Chen et al., 2001). When children try to enter an ongoing playgroup, the group resists about half of the time (Shantz, 1987). Preschoolers are more skilled than toddlers at resolving these conflicts. About half of 4-year-olds, but only a quarter of 2-year-olds, can resolve their own conflicts, and 4-year-olds use more-sophisticated strategies such as saying, *"How about we share it?"* rather than just saying, *"No! Mine!"*

Middle Childhood to Adolescence (6 to 19 Years)

Taking turns, a form of *compromise*, is well established in American children by middle childhood (French et al., 2011). *Coercion* is used less often and *disengagement* is used more often than among preschoolers. Even adolescents most often resolve conflicts with disengagement rather than compromise or coercion. Not until young adulthood are conflicts more often resolved with compromise. Thus, ability to resolve conflicts continues to improve throughout childhood (Laursen et al., 2001).

In summary, from toddlerhood to young adulthood, there is a decrease in coercion that is first replaced with disengagement and finally with compromise. At all ages, learners say they prefer compromise in hypothetical situations, but in actual conflict they may resort to coercion. Thus, preference for compromise does not translate into actual behavior until young adulthood, with the exception of taking turns, which emerges at a much younger age.

10-3c Individual Diversity in Conflict Resolution

Some children master compromise at young ages, while some adults still rely on coercion. In this section we will address what these individual differences mean and how they might come about.

What Do Conflict Resolution Skills Predict?

Children with good conflict-resolution skills achieve their personal goals while also maintaining healthy relationships. Not surprisingly, such children are liked by peers more than are learners with poor skills. From preschool on, well-liked children use more compromise, while rejected children use more coercion in peer conflict (McElwain, Olson, & Volling, 2002).

Children who can resolve conflict without "giving in" tend to be the most socially competent (French et al., 2011). For example, in one classic study, when a conflict involved a peer taking something the child had, well-liked 4th- and 5th-graders were most likely to endorse verbal—but not physical—assertiveness. They said they would not share, but they would politely request the object back (Asher & Hopmeyer, 1997). Good conflict resolution does not involve caving in to another, but it also does not involve escalating conflict.

What Predicts Conflict-Resolution Skills?

Home is a training ground for conflict resolution. Some of the parenting factors that have been discussed in Chapters 6 through 9 are related to conflict-resolution skills. Specifically, *authoritative parents* model negotiation and compromise. In

PHOTO 10.7 When parents teach their children to resolve conflict through compromise, sibling conflict becomes a training ground for good social skills.

addition, parents of *securely attached* children are more likely to compromise and justify their side of an argument without aggravation (Laible, Panfile, & Makariev, 2008). Furthermore, parenting that promotes *empathy, emotion regulation, theory of mind,* and *moral judgment* also promotes conflict-resolution skills, because each of these abilities is needed to constructively resolve conflict. In Chapter 8, you learned that siblings provide opportunity to learn emotional competence. They also provide opportunity to learn conflict resolution skills. Sibling conflict tends to be more frequent and intense than conflict in other relationships, but also tends to involve more remorse and moral reflection (Recchia, Wainryb, & Pasupathi, 2013).

What is the primary cause of sibling conflict? Most sibling conflict is about sharing personal possessions, like one child using another's bike. The next most common cause of conflict is physical aggression and general annoyance with the sibling (McGuire, Manke, Eftekhari, & Dunn, 2000; Recchia et al., 2013). Contrary to common beliefs, concern about who is being treated better by parents is the least common source of conflict, even though siblings are exquisitely aware of and willing to remind parents of any unfairness. Rivalry is reported by only about 9% of children. Sibling rivalry may be limited to families in which parents mishandle sibling conflict or play favorites.

What happens when siblings squabble? *Both* older and younger siblings say that the *other* sibling usually initiates the conflict, but that the older sibling most often wins (McGuire et al., 2000). Compromise, rather than coercion, is more likely when siblings have a good relationship (Recchia & Howe, 2009). Yet, sibling conflicts rarely involve spontaneous compromise, and about half the time end with parent intervention (Ross, Ross, Stein, & Trabasso, 2006). Following parent intervention, children are more likely to compromise. Thus, skilled parents scaffold conflict-resolution skills during sibling conflict (Photo 10.7). However, parents who have limited resolution skills themselves cannot do this. When unskilled parents are trained to mediate their children's conflicts, children develop theory of mind, read others' emotions better, and solve conflict more constructively (Smith & Ross, 2007).

10-3d Classroom Implications of Conflict Resolution

Major and minor conflicts occur frequently at school. If your students learn to resolve conflict quickly and effectively, there will be both social and academic payoffs. Learners with good conflict-resolution skills are liked better, spend more time on classroom tasks, and have higher achievement. How can you help your students develop good conflict-resolution skills?

Promoting Conflict-Resolution Skills

Some methods of helping learners develop conflict resolution skills were discussed in previous chapters:

1. *Be authoritative* (see Chapter 7). Authoritative teachers model negotiation, give-and-take, fairness, and respect for others' views.

2. *Promote emotional competence* (see Chapter 8). Learners who can regulate their own emotions, not respond in hot-headed ways, and read others' emotions will resolve conflicts more constructively.

3. *Promote social cognition* (see Chapter 9). Learners with better people-reading skills, sense of humor, and moral judgment will resolve conflicts more constructively. *It is important that both empathy (concern for the others' perspectives) and equitable goals are discussed.* Trying to promote empathy alone may soften discord, but can perpetrate injustices that cause more conflict (Zaki & Cikara, 2015).

In addition, you may need to directly address conflict-resolution skills. Many teachers do not feel confident about handling conflict and may opt for quick, short-term fixes to achieve peace rather than focusing on building long-term skills (Jenkins, Ritblatt, & McDonald, 2008). In the earlier vignette that involved inter-ethnic conflict between Latina and African American girls, the teacher was able to maintain order, but he did not help the students grapple in a respectful way with issues of ethnicity, language, and feeling excluded, nor did he help them develop better conflict-resolution skills. He promoted disengagement, but his students would have benefited more had he promoted compromise. You may be more effective if you follow these guidelines:

1. *Carefully observe your students' conflict-resolution abilities.* Learners may not tell you about their conflicts. Older learners are less likely to seek teacher help for peer conflict than are younger learners (Newman, Murray, & Lussier, 2001). Typically, learners try to resolve conflict with coercion before going to the teacher, using the teacher only as a fallback strategy. They are more likely to go to the teacher if their goal is to achieve justice, or if the aggressor is bigger than themselves.

2. *Do not intervene in conflicts unless it is necessary or someone is victimized.* Give learners the opportunity to develop conflict-resolution skills.

3. *Scaffold compromise and negotiation, rather than disengagement, when intervention appears necessary.*

You may also want to adopt a specific program designed to enhance conflict-resolution skills across your school. We'll discuss such programs next.

Conflict-Resolution Education

Conflict-resolution education in schools can be part of the curriculum and be designed to train skills that prevent conflict, or it can involve peer mediation and be designed to help learners deal with existing conflict. Such programs might target the entire student body, or only a subset of learners.

Conflict-resolution education can be an alternative to punishment. One supposed punishment—suspension—seldom works, as evidenced by the fact that most students who are suspended are repeat offenders. Suspension puts students at further risk of low achievement and dropping out, as it did for Josh. Students do not learn skills from such punishment. In one Chicago-area high school, students were given the option of a reduced suspension in return for joining a conflict-resolution program. Those who chose to join the program were less likely to get a repeat suspension for fighting later, compared to a control group (Breunlin, Bryant-Edwards,

Hetherington, & Cimmarusti, 2002). The program involved four 90-minute sessions on negotiation, listening, anger management, and problem solving.

Other programs have similar results. Research shows that conflict-resolution education helps learners use more-constructive strategies and reduces office referrals and suspensions. It is also linked to higher achievement and improved school climate. In addition, high-risk learners (and their teachers!) feel less depression, less anxiety, and higher self-esteem after improving conflict-resolution skills at school. The effects may be largest for adolescents, but children can benefit from such programs as early as preschool (Garrard & Lipsey, 2007; Johnson & Johnson, 2006). One example of an effective program is the "I Can Problem Solve" program.

The I Can Problem Solve (ICPS) program

This program is designed to help children from preschool through middle school solve everyday social problems. It focuses on: (1) thinking of *alternative solutions* and (2) *thinking about the consequences* of those solutions. In daily 20-minute lessons, the teacher discusses hypothetical conflicts, such as a child being excluded from play by others. The teacher asks the class to explain the problem and how the child feels and to brainstorm alternative solutions. The teacher asks what might happen if the child used each solution. The same procedure is used when students actually misbehave in the classroom.

This is akin to the inductive discipline you learned about in Chapter 7. However, ICPS dialogues go beyond induction (Shure, 2001). There are four levels (from bad to best) of discipline quality. Only the fourth constitutes an ICPS dialogue, but the third would constitute induction:

1. Demand, threaten, belittle, punish (e.g., *Do you want a referral?*)

2. Offer suggestion without explanation (e.g., *Why don't you ask him for it?*)

3. Explain and reason (e.g., *He will feel angry if you grab.*)

4. Problem-solving dialogue (e.g., *What's the problem? How do you think she felt when . . . ? Can you think of a different way to solve this problem?*)

When learners think through conflicts by talking with an adult as the problem is occurring, they learn to problem-solve better. Let's eavesdrop on a 1st-grade classroom:

> *Allen complains, "Max kept trying to take our ball. When I told him to stop it, he kicked me." Mrs. Wang asks Max his side of the story. Max says, "I wanted to play with them, but they ignored me." Mrs. Wang asks, "How would you feel if Allen took your ball and kicked you?" Max admits, "I guess I'd be mad." Mrs. Wang asks the class for suggestions of how to solve the boys' problem. Three suggestions are given: (1) Allen should kick him back; (2) Max should tell Allen how he feels; and (3) Max should walk away when he feels like kicking. Mrs. Wang turns to Max, "OK, which of these suggestions will you use next time?" Max decides to try walking away.*

In one study, after just 3 months in the ICPS program, low-SES kindergarteners were less impulsive, more cooperative, and shared more than control-group children

(Shure, 2001). In another study, 6th-graders had half as many violence incidents and five times fewer in-school suspensions than a control group (Farrell, Meyer, & White, 2001). Older learners who participate in ICPS also have improved academic skills and test scores, but it takes longer to achieve effects in older learners.

Similar skills can be taught at the high school level. Typically, conflict-resolution curricula are used during advisory periods, or in literature and social studies classes. For example, reading *A Midsummer Night's Dream* could be used as an opportunity to discuss different ways to resolve conflict. The website accompanying this text provides a list of programs that address aggression and bullying. Many of the programs also address conflict-resolution skills. Use this resource to help you select a program appropriate for your school. Another approach to conflict resolution is peer mediation.

think about **this**

In the vignette with Max, which of the solutions provided by the other learners are coercion, disengagement, or compromise? Is Max's preference typical for his age? Is he likely to actually use it? Explain.

Peer mediation

Mediation occurs when a neutral third party facilitates compromise. Mediation involves four steps (Johnson & Johnson, 2006):

1. Set ground rules, like escalation of hostility is not allowed.

2. Identify the issues and define the problem.

3. Make each learner's beliefs, views, or emotions clear.

4. Find a solution that satisfies both learners.

mediation
a neutral, impartial third person facilitates negotiation between two learners in conflict.

You will recognize these as similar to the components of ICPS. In peer mediation at school, either a small cadre of learners is trained to be the mediators for peers or the whole student body is trained. Proponents like peer mediation because it replaces punishment; punishment may stop misbehavior but does not teach learners positive social skills.

Peer mediation is successful in that most problems brought to peer mediators are resolved constructively (Photo 10.8). Learners trained as mediators become better able to generate positive conflict resolutions. Disciplinary referrals and suspensions sometimes decline after peer mediation programs are implemented in schools. In addition, instructional time may increase because teachers do not have to spend as much time disciplining (Garrard & Lipsey, 2007; Smith, Daunic, Miller, & Robinson, 2002). However, programs must be well implemented and mediators must be well trained or they come to be viewed as negative police.

In this chapter you have learned how to help your students become more prosocial, control their aggression, and resolve conflicts constructively. You have heard the stories of both Josh and Adara,

Richard Hutchings/Digital Ligh/Newscom

PHOTO 10.8 Peer mediation programs can reduce conflict and increase instructional time.

who were quite difficult, yet both learned to be less aggressive and more prosocial at school. They each developed a positive relationship with a teacher because that teacher deliberately practiced the guidelines in this chapter. Learners who develop more positive social behavior have better relationships, which is the topic of the next chapter.

---

reflections on practice

My Teaching

There are many things that you can do to increase prosocial behavior, decrease antisocial behavior, and promote conflict-resolution skills in your students. Several of these have been discussed in previous chapters; review the "Reflections on Practice" sections from these other chapters. They include:

- Developing a secure teacher–student attachment (see Chapter 6).
- Being authoritative (see Chapter 7).
- Using inductive discipline, especially victim-centered induction (see Chapter 7).
- Promoting learners' emotional competence (see Chapter 8).
- Promoting learners' social cognition (see Chapter 9).

In addition, periodically ask yourself the following questions:

1. Are my students prosocial toward each other? Do I make them feel responsible for others' well-being?

2. Do I provide opportunities for my students to practice being prosocial? Do I accept offers of help even when it is inconvenient for me? When service opportunities are provided to learners, are they meaningful and is there time for group reflection?

3. Do I clearly communicate prosocial values? Do I model kind and polite behavior? (Teachers who combine warmth with valuing and modeling prosocial behavior are most effective.) Would my students characterize me as a caring teacher?

4. Do I refrain from using extrinsic rewards for prosocial behavior (e.g., stickers) but use praise instead? Do I emphasize praising prosocial behavior rather than punishing antisocial behavior?

5. Am I aware of aggression and bullying among my students? (This is especially important for early childhood teachers because early intervention is important.) Am I aware of which learners are being victimized?

6. Is my school anti-bullying? Do high-status learners get away with bullying? Do I teach learners how to stand up for and befriend victims? Are all areas of the school, and my own classroom, well supervised?

7. Am I helping aggressive learners increase their academic skills by including everyone in classroom learning?

8. Do I intervene in conflicts only when necessary? When I do intervene, do I promote compromise, rather than just suggest disengagement (e.g., leave the area)?

9. Does our school offer conflict-resolution skills training as an alternative to suspension for unruly students? Would our school benefit from a peer mediation program?

Summary of Age Trends in Social Behavior

	Prosocial Behavior	Aggression	Conflict Resolution
Infancy and Toddlerhood (Birth–2 Years)	• A universal tendency to share is apparent by 8 months. At 12 months, an absence of sharing indicates serious developmental delay. • At 18 months toddlers spontaneously help parents and experimenters with tasks. • Toddlers will compassionately try to cheer up distressed others, including strange adults in experiments. • There is a decline in sharing from infancy to toddlerhood as self-interest becomes manifest. • By age 2, children use prosocial behavior as a tool in social interactions. • A variety of prosocial behaviors are exhibited by 2-year-olds, such as comforting, helping, and sharing. • Individual differences in prosocial behavior are apparent and stable by 2–3 years of age.	• By 4 months, infants are capable of anger. Differences in anger predict later aggression. • Aggression toward peers is observed by 12 months. Toddlers exhibit other antisocial behaviors like defiance and tantrums. • Physical aggression peaks at age 2. • Aggression is most likely to be instrumental. • Coercive family cycles can begin in toddlerhood.	• Infants protest others' behavior by 8 months. • Toddlers' conflicts are brief. • Toddlers' conflicts are mostly about objects. • Two-year-olds resolve disputes with words and use more prosocial solutions than do 1-year-olds.
Early Childhood (3–5 Years)	• Preschoolers are more discriminating than toddlers, directing prosocial acts toward family and friends. • By age 3, most children are egalitarian about sharing treats. • By age 4, children have extensive prosocial repertoires. Highly prosocial preschoolers are often aggressive as well. • Gender differences in prosocial behavior emerge.	• Preschoolers, from ages 2–4, are the most aggressive of any age. • Physical aggression decreases (but does not disappear) as verbal aggression increases. • Young children tend to express happiness when they are victimizing others. • Children with severe behavior problems may be diagnosed with oppositional defiant disorder.	• Older preschoolers tend to argue over group play activity. • More 4-year-olds than 2-year-olds are able to resolve their own conflicts, and use better strategies.
Middle Childhood (6–12 Years)	• Children become better at soothing others' distress and cheering them up. They are able to do this verbally, rather than physically. • By ages 6–8 children are often given caretaking responsibilities of younger children. • They develop a better sense of what prosocial behaviors are expected of them, and make donations to anonymous charities in laboratory studies.	• Physical aggression continues to diminish. • Aggression is more likely to be hostile than instrumental. • Social aggression becomes apparent. • Bullying emerges, and then declines. • If physical aggression persists beyond age 8, children may be diagnosed with conduct disorder (CD). Children with CD have childhood-onset antisocial behavior.	• Ability to resolve conflict improves. Coercion is used less and compromise and disengagement are used more as compared with early childhood, although they still are not common. • Children are able to serve as peer mediators in elementary school. • As they grow older, they are less likely to seek teachers' help in resolving conflict.

Summary of Age Trends in Social Behavior

	Prosocial Behavior	Aggression	Conflict Resolution
Adolescence (13–19 Years)	• Adolescents are more competent at helping than younger children. • They are less affectionate and helpful in the family, but helpfulness rises again in late adolescence. Adolescents who provide needed help to their family tend to be happier. • Adolescents are not prosocial more frequently than younger children, perhaps because they are better at suppressing impulses to help others, are motivated by self-interest, learn from antisocial models, and have been trained not to help. • Prosocial behavior is more a controlled choice than an impulse.	• Rate of aggression declines in adolescence, although most young adolescents do engage in mild aggression occasionally. • Bullying may briefly spike in middle school. Bullies are not liked in elementary school, but may have higher status in middle school. • A minority of adolescents may have a temporary surge in antisocial behavior, known as adolescent-onset. This typically includes delinquency more than aggression. • Aggression becomes more dangerous in adolescence. Criminals begin their career in, or before, adolescence. Crime peaks at about age 17.	• Adolescents have less conflict than preschoolers. • The most conflicted relationship is with siblings. • Adolescents engage in less coercion than do younger children, typically using disengagement. • Young adults typically use more compromise than do adolescents, including with siblings.

⌄ Professional Resource Download

Chapter Summary

10-1 Prosocial Behavior

- Prosocial behavior is behavior that benefits others. Altruism is prosocial behavior that involves personal cost.

- Individual differences in prosocial behavior emerge in toddlerhood and are stable. Across cultures, prosocial learners are liked better by teachers and peers and have higher achievement. Yet, excessive prosocial behavior can indicate problems.

- Girls tend to be more prosocial than boys.

- Parents promote children's prosocial behavior by espousing prosocial values, using victim-centered inductive discipline, being warm, being authoritative, and having secure attachment. Tangible rewards can undermine long-term prosocial behavior, but praise promotes it. Opportunity to practice promotes prosocial behavior.

- Teachers can do the same things parents do to promote prosocial behavior. In addition, teachers can promote prosocial behavior by making learners feel responsible for others' well-being and providing high-quality opportunities to serve. The Caring School Community project increased prosocial behavior and academic achievement by making the school a more caring place.

10-2 Antisocial Behavior and Aggression

- Antisocial behavior is behavior that disrupts social functioning. It is comorbid with ADHD and internalizing disorders. Aggression is a subset of antisocial behavior that involves harming others.

- Aggression can be physical, verbal, or social. Learners who use one type are likely to use the other types. Aggression can be instrumental or hostile. Aggression can be proactive or reactive.

- Bullying is a type of proactive, hostile aggression.

- Children's misbehavior has increased over the past few decades, including clinical levels of behavior problems.

- Individual differences in aggression are stable over time. Learners with childhood-onset aggression have the most negative outcomes, including adult criminality. Learners with severe behavior problems are diagnosed with conduct disorder or oppositional defiance disorder.

- Aggressive learners have distorted social cognition, such as hostile attribution bias, as explained by the social information processing model.

- Individual differences in aggression may have a genetic component, but expression of genes is influenced by the environment.

- There are several parenting factors that are associated with aggression. When negative parenting factors co-occur, families form coercive cycles of interaction.

- Antisocial behavior is linked to both low academic achievement and social rejection, but not necessarily to low self-esteem.

- Occasional victimization is common, but some learners are chronic victims. Chronic victims may or may not be aggressive themselves. They are likely to have either overprotective parents, or hostile, intrusive parents. They are also likely to be friendless.

- Boys are more aggressive than girls. Gender differences are greater for physical than social aggression. Boys are more likely than girls to have conduct disorder and to be victims of aggression. Low-SES learners are more likely to exhibit antisocial behaviors.

- Teachers may reduce aggression when they build warm teacher–student relationships, avoid using power-assertive discipline, promote academic skills, supervise activities, avoid retention, and avoid reinforcing aggression.

10-3 Conflict Resolution

- Conflict occurs when one learner's behavior interferes with another learner's goals. Conflict can be resolved through compromise, disengagement, or coercion.

- Learners who have good conflict-resolution skills are more likely to have authoritative parents who promote emotional competence and social cognition in their children.
- Sibling relationships often involve conflict, mostly over possessions but seldom over parental love. Sibling conflict is typically resolved with coercion, unless parents intervene and scaffold compromise.
- Learners who have good conflict-resolution skills are better liked by peers.
- Learners do not often seek a teacher's help to resolve conflict and are less likely to do so with age. If teachers intervene in conflict, they should scaffold compromise.
- Effective conflict-resolution programs result in increased academic achievement and better school climate. Such programs can be an effective alternative to suspension.

chapter 11

Christopher Futcher/Getty Images

Peers, Friends, and Play

Should you be worried about a student in your class who does not appear to have any friends? What about a student who does not play? Is play important for your students? In this chapter we answer these questions as we discuss three aspects of social behavior—peer status, friendships, and play. **After you read this chapter, you will be able to:**

11-1 Evaluate your students' popularity with peers, analyze what it means for their success in your classroom, and help those who are disliked.

11-2 Understand the importance of friendships, judge which learners have friends, and help those who are friendless.

11-3 Explain the role of play and foster playful learning in your classroom.

11-1 Peer Status

In a 3rd-grade classroom, Paul pushes other students, breaks their pencils, steps on their homework, and calls them stupid. When he sits at a table, children move to avoid sitting by him. One day Paul says, "I am having a birthday party and everyone wants to come because I am the most popular boy in this class." A girl sitting nearby says, "Paul, no one likes you. You say nasty things. And you hit." Paul replies, "You're just jealous." His inflated self-esteem seems genuine.

In contrast, his classmate Nadya is well liked. When the teachers are busy, students go to Nadya for help. She always stops what she is doing to help. She is remarkably patient. Several of the children in the class consider Nadya their "best friend." She is consistently cheerful and happy.

Two other classmates, Lydia and Eleanor, are best friends. A new girl asks Lydia a question. Lydia says, "We don't talk to newbies," and turns her back. She whispers to Eleanor and they begin giggling. Nadya tells the new girl, "Don't be sad. They're not nice to anyone." Lydia and Eleanor control a part of the classroom where others can come only with their permission. Some girls follow them every-where and imitate what Eleanor says. Yet, these girls do not actually interact with Lydia and Eleanor. Eleanor says that she and Lydia are popular. A girl later says, "Lots of girls want to be their friends, but lots of girls don't like them either. Some kids are scared of them. I don't know why anyone would want to be their friend. They are rude."

These four children are in the same 3rd-grade classroom, yet they are having very different peer experiences. Why are some learners popular while others are rejected, and what effect will this have on them? In this chapter you will see that peers make a substantial contribution to learners' well-being. First, we will focus on learners' place in the peer group (i.e., peer status) and their friendships. Then we will discuss play, a primary activity of friends.

Paul, Nadya, Lydia, and Eleanor have different peer status. **Peer status** refers to how children are received by the social group. One way scientists assess this is to ask children which classmates they like, or prefer to play or work with, and which they dislike. This is known as a *sociometric* method. This method is used with children from preschool to high school. It results in five categories of peer status as indicated in Figure 11.1.

peer status
a measure of how accepted children are in a peer group.

1. *Popular* children (about 15%) are liked by many peers and disliked by few.

2. *Rejected* children (about 15%) are disliked by many and liked by few.

3. *Neglected* children (about 10%) receive few liked or disliked votes; they go unnoticed by most children.

4. *Controversial* children (about 6%) receive many liked and disliked votes.

5. *Average* children (40 to 60%) are moderately liked and disliked.

Notice that rejection involves active dislike, avoidance, and exclusion by peers, not mere neglect. Most children are average, and the fewest are controversial (see, for example, DeRosier & Thomas, 2003).

FIGURE 11.1 Types of Peer Status.

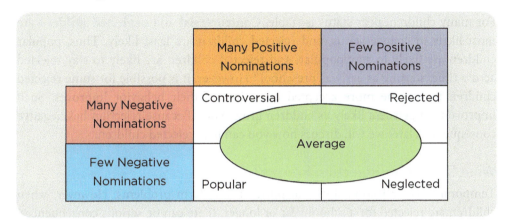

think about this

Based on the opening vignette, which category of peer status best fits Paul, Nadya, Lydia, and Eleanor? Justify your conclusions.

Most learners are average, and the fewest are controversial. Think about a classroom you are familiar with. Do you know specific children who fit each type?

Peer status is also measured with sociograms or social maps of the classroom. Figure 11.2 is an example of a social map of a 3rd-grade classroom. Observers map which learners interact or hang around together. About 2 to 10% of learners are isolated from the social networks in their classroom (Cairns & Cairns, 1994). Can you find isolates in Figure 11.2?

Learners who are well liked and preferred by peers have **sociometric popularity**. In contrast, when teachers or learners are asked who is popular, they nominate some children who are *not* well liked, like Lydia and Eleanor. These learners have **perceived popularity**. Although they are more disliked than average children, they manage to have high social impact and prominence.

If you think perceived popular learners are more common in high school than in elementary school, you are right. Among younger children, sociometric and perceived popularity are correlated, but this decreases over time and by high school the correlation is negative for girls; that is, high school girls with perceived popularity often are not widely liked. Still, learners who are disliked but have high status are readily identified by 2nd grade, and sometimes as early as kindergarten (Farmer et al., 2010; Vlachou, Andreou, Botsoglou, & Didaskalou, 2011).

According to sociometric measures, perceived popular children may actually be *controversial* (especially girls) or *rejected* (especially boys). Throughout this chapter we will use the term "popular" to mean sociometric popularity, or being well liked.

sociometric popularity being well liked and accepted by peers. Also called social preference.

perceived popularity having high social impact and prominence.

FIGURE 11.2 Sociogram of a 3rd-Grade Classroom.

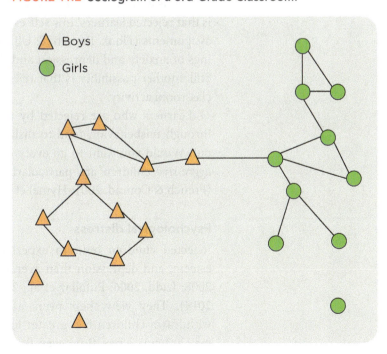

Lines represent regular interaction between learners. Notice that only one girl has interaction with boys. Which learners are the most connected with others?

11-1a Individual Diversity in Peer Status

controversial children
children who are liked by many and also disliked by many peers. They have high social impact.

neglected children
children who are neither liked nor disliked by many peers. They have low social impact.

For many children, peer status is stable. **Controversial** and **neglected children** are most likely to change status, and rejected children are least likely. Thus, popular children are likely to stay popular, and rejected children are likely to stay rejected across time, starting as early as preschool.[1] However, it is possible for some rejected children to become more accepted over time, if their behavior improves. Such improvement gets less likely as children grow older. Because rejection has negative consequences, later we will discuss how you can help rejected children.

What Does Peer Rejection Predict?

rejected-aggressive children
children who are actively disliked by many peers and are highly aggressive.

rejected-withdrawn children
children who are actively disliked by many peers, are not aggressive, but tend to avoid social interaction.

Temporary peer rejection does not portend long-term problems. However, when children are rejected for a school year or longer, there can be serious consequences, such as low academic achievement, psychological distress, and increased aggression. Consequences vary based on whether a rejected child is aggressive. **Rejected-aggressive children** account for about 25 to 50% of rejected children and **rejected-withdrawn children** account for about 10 to 25% (Hymel et al., 2002; Ladd et al., 2014). Rejected-*withdrawn* children see themselves as socially incompetent, which matches their peer status, but rejected-*aggressive* children think they are more popular than they are. In the opening vignette, Paul mistakenly believed he was the most popular boy in the class. In contrast, average and popular children tend to underestimate their social competence (Cillessen & Bellmore, 2002).

Low academic achievement

Rejected learners tend to have lower GPA, IQ, and test scores than well-liked learners (Buhs & Ladd, 2001; Zettergren, 2003). How might this happen? One possibility is that rejected learners' low self-esteem leads them to give up on challenging school assignments (Flook, Repetti, & Ullman, 2005). Another possibility is that their feelings of anxiety and depression and their behavior problems interfere with learning. Still another possibility is that rejection from peers causes them to disengage from classroom activity.

Learners who are rejected by their peers, even if they provoked the rejection through misbehavior, tend to dislike and avoid school, and some eventually drop out. Would you want to go every day to a place where you are disliked? Rejected-*aggressive* children are particularly at risk, with as many as 50% dropping out (French & Conrad, 2001; Hymel et al., 2002).

Psychological distress

Rejected children tend to experience more victimization, loneliness, low self-esteem, and depression than average children (Burt, Obradovic, Long, & Masten, 2008; Ladd, 2006; Putallaz et al., 2007; Spilt, van Lier, Leflot, Onghena, & Colpin, 2014). They view their peers as less prosocial (Ladd et al., 2014). Rejected-withdrawn children feel greater loneliness than rejected-aggressive children; they may anticipate rejection, even from friends, and feel helpless and stressed by mild

---

[1] Many studies support this conclusion, a few of which are listed here: Cillessen and Mayeux (2004); Hymel, Vaillancourt, McDougall, and Renshaw (2002); Ladd, Ettekal, Kochenderfer-Ladd, Rudolph, and Andrews (2014); Santos, Vaughn, Peceguina, Daniel, and Shin (2014).

rejection (Asher & Paquette, 2003; Gazelle & Druhen, 2009). They have higher levels of cortisol (the stress hormone) while at school, which can interfere with learning (Peters, Riksen-Walraven, Cillessen, & de Weerth, 2011).

Although it is not immediately obvious, there may also be a cost to being "perceived popular." These children may engage in pseudomature behavior like minor delinquency and early dating, which earns them some short-term peer status and likability in early adolescence. But their status wanes over adolescence (see Figure 11.3), and by young adulthood they are more likely to use alcohol and other drugs, commit crimes, and have relationship problems compared to other youth (Allen, Schad, Oudekerk, & Chango, 2014; Choukas-Bradley, Giletta, Neblett, & Prinstein, 2015).

Popular children may fare best. However, even if children are not popular, they fare well as long as they feel confident and comfortable among their peers (McElhaney, Antonishak, & Allen, 2008). That is, learners' *feelings* about their peer status matter in addition to their actual status.

FIGURE 11.3 Relationship of Pseudomaturity to Popularity in Adolescence.

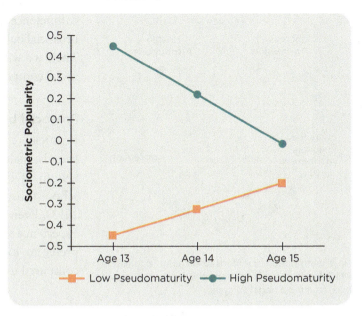

Pseudomaturity was a combination of minor delinquency (e.g., sneaking into a movie without paying), having attractive friends, and early romantic involvement. Sociometric popularity was based on the number of nominations from peers when asked who they would "most like to spend time with on a Saturday night." *Source: Allen et al. (2014).*

Aggression

Rejection may cause students to become aggressive, disruptive in class, hyperactive and distractible, and delinquent (see, for example, Stenseng, Belsky, Skalicka, & Wichstrøm, 2016; Sturaro, van Lier, Cuijpers, & Koot, 2011). Rejected students often watch closely for any sign of others' hostility (hostile attribution bias). They may expect and quickly overreact to perceived rejection, whether it is real or not. They may respond with aggression, which leads to more rejection. Thus, they create a self-fulfilling prophecy of rejection (see Figure 11.4).

Rejection for just 1 year in the primary grades can predict antisocial behavior 5 years later (Dodge et al., 2003). Children rejected for 2 to 3 years by 2nd grade have a 50% chance of having serious behavior problems before adolescence, compared with only a 9% chance for nonrejected children. The degree of rejection matters. Highly rejected and highly controversial children tend to develop more problem behavior than mildly rejected children (DeRosier & Thomas, 2003).

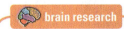 **brain research**

Social Rejection Hurts

How do you feel when that second date doesn't happen? Or your friends leave you out? Rejection hurts. In fact, the brain processes it like physical pain. In one study, the brains of adults who had just broken up with a romantic partner were scanned (fMRI) while they looked at pictures of their "ex" and thought about their break-up experience. They were later subjected to intense heat on their arm. The same regions in their brains were activated in both situations (Kross, Berman, Mischel, Smith, & Wager, 2011). Similar studies find that being excluded from play during a video game also activates part of the "pain matrix" in the brain. Furthermore, painkiller drugs, like Tylenol, reduce the pain of social rejection (Eisenberger, 2012). Although this research has not yet focused on rejection at school, it suggests that rejected children may feel real pain.

FIGURE 11.4 Cycle of Aggression.

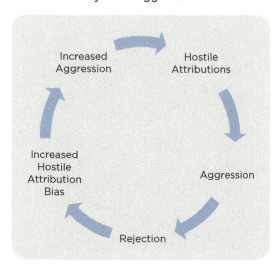

Hostile attribution bias leads to increased aggression, which leads to peer rejection, which leads to increased bias, creating a negative cycle.

What Predicts Peer Status?

Children are accepted or rejected for a reason—usually their social competence. Let's first discuss four aspects of social competence: prosocial behavior, aggression, social withdrawal, and social skills. Then we will discuss parenting factors that contribute to both social competence and peer status.

Prosocial behavior

Prosocial children are liked by nearly everyone, have many friends, make new friends easily, are listened to, and are leaders (Photo 11.1). Prosocial behavior predicts popularity from preschool through high school (Rodkin, Ryan, Jamison, & Wilson, 2013). Even as young as 3 months, before infants have personal experience with the repercussions of good or bad behavior, they prefer to look at puppet characters who behave in prosocial, compared to antisocial, ways (Hamlin, Wynn, & Bloom, 2010).

Aggression

Earlier you learned that rejection may cause children to behave aggressively, but the reverse is also true; aggression causes rejection. Aggressive children tend to be rejected by their peers from preschool through high school.[2] Children do not like peers who hit them, snatch their belongings, or insult them. The greater the aggression, the greater the rejection. Rejected and controversial children are more aggressive than average children, who are in turn more aggressive than well-liked, popular children (Putallaz et al., 2007). Figure 11.5 shows the relationship among prosocial behavior, aggression, and peer status.

Stockbyte/Photos.com

PHOTO 11.1 Prosocial children have greater sociometric popularity in all age groups.

While most aggressive children are rejected, as we discussed earlier, there is a subset of aggressive children who have high social impact or perceived popularity. Why do they have high social status despite aggression? They may have attributes that compensate for their aggression, such as attractiveness, cool clothes, athletic prowess (especially for boys), and involvement in extracurricular activities (Borch, Hyde, & Cillessen, 2011; Farmer, Estell, Bishop, O'Neal, & Cairns, 2003). They may also display less-irritating behavior (less argumentativeness, disruption, hyperactivity, and inattention) and be more covert in their aggression. They may use social aggression, such as pointedly excluding some children in order to maintain their social status, rather than overt physical aggression. Lydia did this when she turned her back on the new girl.

---

[2] Many studies support this conclusion, a few of which are listed here: Ettekal & Ladd (2015); French & Conrad (2001); Pedersen, Vitaro, Barker, & Borge (2007); Xie, Drabick, & Chen (2011).

FIGURE 11.5 Relations between Peer Status and Social Behavior.

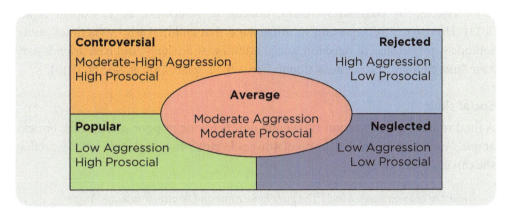

How are aggression and prosocial behavior related to peer status?

Compared to rejected children, these high-status aggressive children are more prosocial when it suits them; they strategically use both prosocial and aggressive behavior *to attain social dominance*. They *read others well* and play by the rules when it is expedient, but have *little guilt, shame, or empathy* and are able to *talk teachers out of punishing* them for misbehavior (Hawley, 2014). Although it is morally reprehensible, aggression can sometimes be functional for them (Rodkin, Espelage, & Hanish, 2015). They may be particularly prominent in middle school (Ettekal & Ladd, 2015). Yet, despite their social prominence, many peers prefer to avoid them (Lansu, Cillessen, & Karremans, 2011).

Social withdrawal

Some rejected children are not aggressive, which means that there are other routes to rejection (French & Conrad, 2001). Rejected-withdrawn children withdraw from social interaction. They may be depressed (see Chapter 8) or extremely shy even *in the context of familiar peers* (see Chapter 6). Rejected-withdrawn children may be sad, play alone, watch peers play, seldom talk, have easily hurt feelings, and have trouble making friends. For example, Tara has just moved to a new kindergarten class because she is now in foster care after being abused. Her behavior leads her to be rejected:

> *Tara seldom speaks, does not know the alphabet, and clings to adults. The other children are caretaking of her, at first. They treat her like a toddler. For example, one girl said, "Hi Tara! Can you find a T for Tara? Let's see if we can find one in your book." Tara does not respond to these overtures; she says nothing and makes no eye contact. Over time, her peers' response to her is quite different. They reject her instead of babying her. During a class project, some children hide her paper and scissors. Tara slowly states, "That's not funny!" so they mimic her poor speech. She leaves the work area. When the teacher tries to get her to return, she kicks the teacher and folds herself into a ball.*

Children reject withdrawn peers as early as preschool if their timid, nervous behavior is extreme, like Tara's. Young children are fairly tolerant toward more moderately withdrawn peers. By 3rd grade on through high school, withdrawn students tend to be rejected by classmates (Avant, Gazelle, & Faldowski, 2011; Coplan et al., 2013). However, it is important to understand that children who sometimes prefer solitude—not because of rejection, social oddities, or anxiety—and have friends may have "just enough" social interaction to fare well (Coplan, Ooi, & Nocita, 2015).

Social skills

A final route to peer rejection is through odd behavior or poor social skills. For example, Angie tries to enter a group of 4th-grade girls who are already talking, so that she can tell them a story.

> *I want to tell you something!" The girls ignore her and continue talking. Angie does not try to figure out what the conversation is about. Instead, she says, "I have something to say!" but the girls continue to ignore her. She gets louder: "Stop talking! Listen to me!" Some girls glance at her, but continue talking. Hands on her hips, she shouts, "Listen to me!" The other girls ignore her, so she stamps her foot and leaves.*

Entering the ongoing activity of a group requires social skill, and many entry bids are rebuffed. Learners' skill in group entry affects their peer acceptance. Popular, well-liked children listen to the group, figure out what they are doing, and make comments relevant to ongoing activities as they enter the group. Unpopular children call attention to themselves, try to take control, or appeal to adult authority. Like Angie, they are disruptive and self-centered during group entry. They may have poor theory of mind skills (see Chapter 9), and their rejection isolates them from opportunities to acquire these skills (Banerjee, Watling, & Caputi, 2011; Slaughter, Imuta, Peterson, & Henry, 2015). Sadly, Angie has few friends.

Children may be rejected for other reasons as well, such as physical unattractiveness or hyperactivity (Hymel et al., 2002; Stormshak et al., 1999). They may behave oddly, like making strange noises, talking to themselves, or making odd faces.

Parenting factors

Parenting factors that influence children's prosocial or antisocial behavior, discussed in Chapter 10, also influence peer status. Parental risk factors for rejection include: (1) marital conflict and divorce; (2) harsh and power-assertive discipline; (3) father's negativity—such as anger, frustration, or irritability—while playing with his children; and (4) maltreatment and abuse. Parental protective factors that reduce rejection include authoritative parenting and secure attachment.

Parents also influence their children's peer status by the way they *select their child's peer world*. Parents choose—within limits—neighborhood, school, child care, lessons, and community activities for their children. Safe neighborhoods with sidewalks, playgrounds, and closely spaced houses provide more opportunity for peer interaction than do wealthy neighborhoods in which each house is its own castle, rural settings without recognizable neighborhoods, or dangerous urban neighborhoods where people are afraid to go out.

Parents can also *directly coach* their children's social skills. Popular children have parents who direct their toddler's peer play, but by preschool age they direct play *only when needed*, in contrast to parents who are overly involved and intrusive. How do parents coach social skills? The same ways you learned in Chapter 10. They might stop their child's aggression; show how to take turns; suggest strategies for entering a play group; frame conflict in a positive way, such as "he didn't mean to knock your tower down"; and encourage resilience, such as "you can build another one" (Colwell, Mize, Petit, & Laird, 2002). By middle childhood or adolescence, parents of well-liked popular children mostly monitor their children's peer interactions, rather than directly intervening.

11-1b Group Diversity in Peer Status

Up to this point you have learned that, in general, prosocial learners are popular, and aggressive or withdrawn learners are rejected. However, learners are rejected by peers only if they are more aggressive or withdrawn than is *normal for their group*. That is, aggressive learners may not be as rejected in aggression-filled classrooms as they are in other classrooms (Powers, Bierman, & The Conduct Problems Prevention Research Group, 2013). Withdrawn learners may not be as rejected in classrooms with lots of solitary play and little social interaction. The more a child fits the group norm, the less rejected the child will be (Mikami, Lerner, & Lun, 2010). One exception is that prosocial behavior is linked to popularity regardless of the classroom norms, because it is valued in almost all cultures and groups (Chang, 2004).

Gender

There may be small gender differences in peer status. Usually learners are accepted or rejected by both boys and girls in the classroom, although learners are slightly more likely to favor same-sex peers (Hymel et al., 2002). While boys are more aggressive than girls, studies do not consistently find them to be more rejected. Perhaps this is because aggression is more normative for boys.

Socioeconomic Status (SES)

On the average, low-SES learners are less popular than middle-SES learners. Perhaps this is because low-SES learners tend to be more aggressive and act out in class (Avant et al., 2011). In addition, low-SES learners have more risk factors that are linked to peer rejection. In one classic study of hundreds of elementary students, only 8% of children without risk factors were rejected, but a whopping 75% were rejected if they had several risk factors, such as an absent mother, unemployed father, divorced parents, low income, or recent move to a new school (Patterson, Vaden, & Kupersmidt, 1991). Still, 25% of children with several risk factors were *not* rejected.

Ethnicity

Characteristics that predict peer status are similar across ethnic groups—learners prefer peers who are more prosocial and less aggressive. Thus, peer status is based on personal characteristics. However, group membership could lead to rejection over time. For example, an Asian child in a predominantly Black school may be excluded and then may withdraw from social interaction, which results in becoming rejected (Killen, Mulvey, & Hitti, 2013). Nevertheless, most studies find that in diverse schools, being a member of one ethnic group does not predict peer status any more than being a member of a different ethnic group.

11-1c Classroom Implications of Peer Status

Peer status influences school success. You might assume that popular learners are ideal in a classroom, but actually neglected learners are often *preferred* by teachers because teachers view them as compliant and easy to manage (Wentzel & Asher, 1995). Learners who are neglected by their peers, but who are liked by teachers, may do fine academically.

Well-liked, popular learners tend to have the highest academic achievement. Note that this pertains to sociometric popularity, not perceived popularity. In fact, by middle school, students with *low* perceived popularity may do better academically (Bellmore, 2011).

In contrast, as you learned earlier, rejection predicts decreasing academic achievement from kindergarten through high school (Bellmore, 2011; Vitaro, Bovin, Brendgen, Girard, & Dionne, 2012). Rejected learners tend to have low test scores, be aggressive, participate less in class activities, and avoid school—all of which make them harder to manage. Their sadness and anxiety about being rejected may interfere with motivation and ability to pay attention in class. Even learners who are temporarily rejected participate less in class during the period in which they are rejected. When the rejection stops, their classroom participation increases (Ladd, Herald-Brown, & Reiser, 2008).

How can you help isolated learners in your classroom? First, you must determine whether the student is neglected or rejected, because neglected students do not necessarily lack social skills or need intervention. Rejected learners are actively disliked and do need intervention. You can help rejected learners by developing positive teacher–student relationships (see Chapter 6). Supportive teachers can buffer children from the consequences of rejection so that they become less anxious or depressed as they might (Spilt et al., 2014). See Figure 11.6. You can also help them by creating a positive emotional climate (see Chapter 8) and positive student–student relationships (see Chapter 10), using good classroom management, and refraining from being overly controlling (see Chapter 7). Learners are less likely to be rejected or victimized in a positive classroom (Avant et al., 2011; Gazelle, 2006).

Three other ways you can improve learners' peer status are: (1) improve their behavior, (2) influence their reputation, and (3) provide more peer interaction, such as through cooperative learning.

Improve Behavior

You may think that moving a rejected student to a new peer group will help the student. Unfortunately, unless the student's behavior improves, the student will soon be rejected in the new group. For example, in a classic study, 1st- and 3rd-grade African American boys who did not know each other played together for 45-minute sessions (Dodge, Coie, Pettit, & Price, 1990). Within one session rejected boys were disliked,

FIGURE 11.6 Supportive Teachers Buffer the Effects of Rejection.

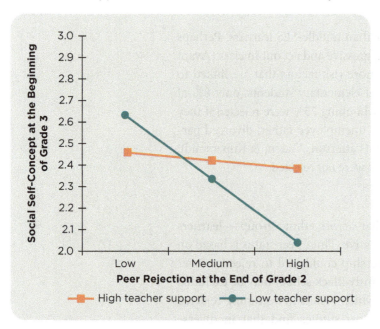

Rejected children who have supportive teachers are less likely to have a poor social self-concept (i.e., feel that they are unable to make friends or that most of their peers do not like them). *Source: Spilt et al. (2014).*

and within three sessions they were as rejected in the new playgroup as they were in their regular classroom. Instead of moving rejected learners, follow these guidelines:

1. *Help the student reduce aggression and increase prosocial behavior* (see Chapter 10). Prominent aggressive children, like Lydia, can create an aggressive classroom climate. In classrooms with high levels of aggression, children become more aggressive over time (Powers et al., 2013). To prevent this, ensure that bullying is not rewarded and promote the leadership of prosocial students. Help children respond to rejection by trying harder to be prosocial rather than retaliating with aggression.

2. *Help the student develop better emotion regulation abilities.* See Chapter 8 for how to do this.

3. *Promote the student's academic skills.* Students who are more academically successful in the classroom are less aggressive and better liked (Véronneau et al., 2010). In addition, prominent aggressive children have less power in classrooms with strong academic emphasis (Garandeau, Ahn, & Rodkin, 2011).

4. *Capitalize on the student's strengths.* An admired skill or talent promotes a student's acceptance. For example, 2nd-grader Rudy seldom plays with other students and is behind in reading skills. He would be a rejected-withdrawn student, except that he has good drawing ability. One classmate said, "Rudy's drawings are so good! He can draw anything. And he makes it look real. He even drew a velociraptor!"

5. *Pair the student up with a buddy.* Ask a prosocial, popular, same-sex student in the classroom to befriend and include the rejected student. This will help the rejected student develop skills, become more accepted, and steer clear of deviant peers (Farmer, Hall, Leung, Estell, & Brooks, 2011). You should plan to support the process as needed.

6. *Arrange for the student to work or play with younger students.* One-on-one activity with younger students is different from classroom interaction with age-mates because it prompts withdrawn students to speak up and direct the activity, which promotes their social skills.

Special education teachers designed an intervention for 2nd-grader Marcel, who was aggressive and working below grade level. He was disciplined frequently, but the discipline was clearly not working. He wore dirty clothes and had recurring infections. Children's protective services had been involved in his home life. What was the intervention and its results?

Marcel was given a star each time he completed academic tasks in his classroom. When he earned enough stars, he could go to the kindergarten room to be a helper. The beginning was rocky because Marcel intimidated the kindergarteners with his aggressive behavior. With a little guidance, Marcel learned to actually help the kindergarteners. He read to a few children from picture books that he practiced each morning. His reading skills improved. Marcel's teacher praised him for being helpful. She phoned Marcel's mother to tell her how well he was doing. After this, his mother attended an Individualized Education Program (IEP) meeting for the first time. Marcel began to do his homework, and his aggression dropped noticeably. His classmates began to view him as a valuable person, and he began to enjoy his own classroom.

PHOTO 11.2 You enhance learners' reputation by pointing out their prosocial behaviors to their peers.

cooperative learning
learning in pairs or small groups, in which the group has a shared learning goal and interdependence is required to achieve the goal.

FIGURE 11.7 "Grading" Classmates.

Sociometric ratings are clearly not only for psychologists. What grade does this self-confident 4th-grader give herself? What attributes earn classmates an A, C, or F?

This intervention combined some of the factors discussed earlier with behavior modification. It also altered Marcel's reputation with his peers, which is the next topic.

Influence Learners' Reputation

Learners are keenly aware of one another's status in the classroom. For example, Figure 11.7 shows the "social grades" a 4th-grade girl and her friends gave to classmates. Learners' attitudes toward peers are affected by your attitudes; classmates like a student better if the student has a good relationship with the teacher (Jennings & Greenberg, 2009; Mikami et al., 2010). Learners' popularity will rise over time, regardless of whether their behavior changes, if the teacher is supportive of them (De Laet et al., 2014). Classmates' judgment of a student depends on teachers' public praise and discipline of the student. (Photo 11.2) This means you can harm a student's status by focusing peers' attention on misbehavior, like saying "Marcel, you are always causing trouble!" *You can also enhance a student's status by focusing on positive behavior, like saying* "Marcel, thanks for helping the kindergarteners." *Through social referencing, children look to you for cues about how to think about classmates.*

Provide Opportunity for Peer Interaction

Another way you can promote learners' peer status is to provide opportunity to learn social skills. It may surprise you, but older students have relatively few opportunities in their classes to socialize. For example, in one suburban high school, students averaged 1.5 interactions with a peer per 50 minutes for midlevel classes and 1.8 for advanced-level classes (Osterman, 2000). You can provide opportunity to learn social skills through strategic seating arrangements and group-based learning activities.

Seating arrangement

The placement of a learner's seat in the classroom determines opportunities to cooperate and interact with others during class. Elementary students who sit closer to each other like each other more and perceive each other as more popular (Neal, Neal, & Cappella, 2014; van den Berg & Cillessen, 2015). Students close to the center of the classroom are liked better. Students who are rejected become better liked over the course of a few months when they are moved next to well-liked classmates. Be deliberate about placement of your students, particularly at the beginning of the year when relationships are developing.

Cooperative learning

Cooperative learning refers to students working together in pairs or in small groups, with a shared learning goal, in which students must work together to achieve the goal. It includes approaches you may have heard of such as peer-mediated learning, peer tutoring, and so on. The main impetus behind cooperative learning is that it promotes academic achievement. Cooperative learning predicts achievement for students in different subjects and grade levels, with an overall effect size of about 0.23 for elementary and 0.85 for high school (Igel, 2015). Some people worry that high achievers are held back by working with lower achievers, but high achievers often actually gain more from cooperative learning because they do more explaining. In addition to promoting academic achievement, an important side effect is that cooperative learning also promotes social interaction, good peer relationships, and motivation (Roseth et al., 2008). Students report that cooperative learning is more fun than traditional classroom learning, and they like one another better during cooperative learning (Gillies, 2003).

While many teachers report using cooperative learning, it is not implemented equally well across classrooms. Some teachers casually state, "You can work together if you like" during an activity, while others organize formal groups that work together on a project for several days or weeks, such as building a mechanical model for a roller coaster or presenting a book report. For effective cooperative learning follow these guidelines:

1. *Hold both individuals and groups accountable.* For example, each student might be required to turn in work or take a quiz, and the group is evaluated on the achievement of each individual, such as giving the group a grade based on the average test score of *each* team member. This makes high achievers less likely to do everything while low achievers loaf.

2. *Actively monitor groups and provide feedback.* Move among the groups, listen to their interaction, and question or prompt them (Emmer & Gerwels, 2002).

3. *Use groups of two to five students.* Pairs result in more collaboration, but small groups produce more discussion (Fuchs et al., 2000). Larger groups, of about 14, may be ideal for electronic discussion boards.

4. *Use tasks that are open-ended or ill-structured,* meaning students do not simply follow a step-by-step sequence to get the one right answer. Open-ended tasks foster better thinking together (Kuhn, 2015).

5. *Make sure each student has a role.* Convince students that each one brings valuable and different abilities to the task. Point out what each student has to contribute. Without this help, rejected students and low achievers may be ignored or barely participate.

6. *Train students to explain.* Students who are instructed to explain the answer, not just state the correct answer, are more successful in cooperative learning (Watkins & Wentzel, 2008).

Do not assume that all your students have adequate social skills to benefit from working with others. Students who are able to manage conflict, behave prosocially (e.g., compliment and encourage others), control their emotions, see others' perspectives, and do their fair share are more productive in cooperative learning. You may need to train less socially skilled students so that they too benefit. One study found that about 37% of elementary school students had high levels of these skills, and other students preferred to work with them (Ladd et al., 2014). They were also high achievers. You learned how to help your students develop these skills in Chapters 8 to 10.

In summary, there are several things that you can do to foster peer acceptance for all learners in your classroom. If a student's rejection is severe, and the student does not respond to any of these in-class interventions, you may need to seek the help of a counselor. Let's turn next to the issue of friendship and peer networks.

11-2 Friendship and Peer Networks

Three elementary boys responded to questions about what a friend is. Mark said, "A friend is someone who thinks you are cool and laughs at the 1st-graders with you. You show off with them."

Joey said, "A friend is someone who talks to you and does things with you. I don't have many friends."

Nick said, "A friend is someone who is nice. I am nice and my friends are nice. We have fun together and don't fight."

Can you predict each boy's peer status based on his understanding of what a friend is? Their answers reveal their social competence. Mark is rejected, Joey is neglected, and Nick is popular. Yet, *peer status* and *friendship* are not the same thing. Typically, popular and average children are most likely to have friends, but a rejected child may have a friend. Having a friend can buffer rejected children from some of the negative effects of rejection (Laursen, Bukowski, Aunola, & Nurmi, 2007). Unfortunately, rejected children sometimes have friends who are mean to them. This raises the question of just what is a friend.

reciprocated friendship
both children nominate each other as a friend.

unilateral friendship
one child nominates another as a friend, but the reverse is not true.

Friends are peers with whom children most like to play or spend time, and can be readily identified even in preschoolers. A **reciprocated friendship** exists when both children nominate each other as a friend. Children can also have one-sided, or **unilateral friendships**, where one child nominates the other as a friend, but the reverse is not true. While you might think reciprocated friendships are the only real friendships, many friendships are not reciprocal. In one study of 7th-graders, only about half their friendships were reciprocated (Ryan, 2001).

clique
a tightly knit group of about 2 to 10 friends, usually of the same sex and same age.

A tightly knit group of about 2 to 10 friends, usually of the same sex and age, is called a **clique**. Most school-age students (70 to 85%) belong to a clique, 5 to 15% are part of an isolated friendship, and 10% may be isolates without friends (Espelage, Holt, & Henkel, 2003; Ryan, 2001). Even rejected students belong to cliques, often of low status (Bagwell, Coie, Terry, & Lochman, 2000). Can you tell which category 16-year-old George falls into?

George is sitting alone at lunch. He has just finished in-school suspension for skipping school. He says he has no friends at school. He claims to have older friends who like to make fun of the "populars" and "jocks." George says, "Outsiders like me, we laugh at the nerds together."

George is an isolate, but he is keenly aware of cliques at school, and even has names for them. He avoids school and is at high risk for dropping out because school is not a friendly place for him.

11-2a Birds of a Feather Flock Together

This is an old adage meaning similar people tend to associate with each other. Psychologists call similarity within a peer group **homophily**. Friends tend to be similar in many ways: ethnicity, religiosity, peer status, physical maturation, athleticism, attractiveness, academic achievement, prosocial behavior, well-being, depression, delinquency, and dropping out of school. Similarities among friends in attractiveness and academic achievement are stronger for teens than for younger children. For example, high school students are more likely to take hard math classes if their friends do so (Crosnoe, Riegle-Crumb, Field, Frank, & Muller, 2008). One of the strongest group similarities is aggressiveness, meaning aggressive children form cliques. Another strong similarity is gender.

homophily
the tendency to prefer and bond with similar others.

Gender segregation refers to the fact that boys affiliate with other boys, and girls with other girls. Gender segregation appears early, by 30 to 36 months of age. Gender segregation is found in cultures across the world. It is driven by children, not adults, and occurs more strongly when adults are *not* in control. This suggests that it may be innate. Gender segregation occurs because children prefer same-sex peers for playmates (Martin et al., 2013).

gender segregation
when given a choice, boys affiliate with other boys and girls with other girls.

11-2b Peer Pressure: Is It Good or Bad?

Friends are similar because they *select* others like themselves and deselect those who are different (Martin et al., 2013; Van Zalk, Kerr, Branje, Stattin, & Meeus, 2010). For example, among identical twins, the one who is more antisocial at age 14 will tend to select more deviant friends at age 17 than will the co-twin (Burt, McGue, & Iacono, 2009). In contrast, prosocial children tend to select prosocial friends. Friends then become more similar over time because they *socialize* or influence each other. This effect occurs from preschool through high school (Dijkstra, Cillessen, & Borch, 2013; Martin et al., 2013). Friends are socialized to conform to the clique's norms through reinforcement, modeling, teasing/joking, and gossip within the clique (Ryan, 2001). This socialization process is what people mean by the term **peer pressure**. Let's look at the peer pressure 8th-grader Justin experiences:

peer pressure
friends exert pressure on each other to conform to group norms. It is typically positive, but can be negative.

> *In algebra class, when exams are returned, students cluster around the high achievers. Several students praise Justin for getting 99%. Later in Spanish class, a substitute teacher says, "Get out your homework." Some students try to trick the sub, saying they did not have homework. Justin says that they did. A girl scolds, "Justin! Let's be smart."*

Peer pressure is usually considered negative. This is misguided. It can be positive or negative, as it was for Justin. Peer pressure is *more likely to be positive*, but that depends on the peer network. For example, in Chapter 2 you learned that while most peers encourage their friends not to use drugs, youth in drug-using cliques promote each other's use. Similarly, most peers encourage their friends to avoid risky sex, but about 5% are a negative influence (Henry, Schoeny, Deptula, & Slavick, 2007). Most peers encourage achievement, as Justin's classmates did, but some students underachieve for fear of being called a nerd, brainiac, or teacher's pet (Fordham, 1996; Tyson, Darity, & Castellino, 2005).

Some children are more powerful at exerting peer pressure, and some are more vulnerable to it. Children who have high status, and cliques that are highly visible, are particularly powerful in influencing average peers (Prinstein, Brechwald, & Cohen, 2011; Ellis & Zarbatany, 2007). Children who are most likely to succumb to *negative* peer pressure tend to: (1) be insecurely attached to their parents; (2) be rejected by the larger peer group, but have delinquent friends; (3) dabble in delinquency, but are not yet fully committed to it; or (4) believe that minor delinquency is common, like "everyone" tries alcohol or sneaks into movies without paying (Allen, Porter, McFarland, McElhaney, & Marsh, 2007; Dodge, 2008). Well-liked, popular children who do *not* believe everyone is delinquent experience more positive peer pressure. Let's turn next to how friendships and peer pressure change with age.

11-2c Age Trends in Friendship and Peer Networks

Learners' choice of friends, number of friends, and time spent with friends all change with age.

Infancy and Toddlerhood (Birth to 2 Years)

Although infants clearly have preferences for playing with specific attachment figures (see Chapter 6), it is not clear how peer friendship applies to infants. However, by age 1 children clearly have regular playmates in their social groups. Are these meaningful friendships or merely playmates? When they have the same qualities as older children's friendships—preference, mutual enjoyment, and comforting each other—they are considered friendships (Howes & Lee, 2006). Toddler friendships tend to be stable across a few years if the social group stays the same. Young toddlers tend to have just one friend, who is just as likely to be of opposite sex as of the same sex, but older toddlers may have more friends.

Early Childhood (3 to 5 Years)

Children first begin using the word *friend* at 3 to 4 years of age. Even then they may not really understand what a friend is (Hartup & Abecassis, 2002). An elderly neighbor used to slowly shuffle by our house on his daily walk. Our 3-year-old son would run to join him, skipping alongside and jabbering nonstop. The neighbor was deaf and never responded. This did not bother our son. He would race back home and exclaim, "Him my friend!" At this age, children typically call anyone they have opportunity to play with their friend, like the next-door neighbor or children of their parents' friends. The opportunity to be together, or proximity, is the foundation of friendship at all ages, but more so for young children.

When they have a choice of playmates, children prefer same-sex peers beginning at about 2½ years of age. Socially competent preschoolers tend to be friends with both boys and girls, but later in childhood having mixed-gender friendships is associated with social incompetence. Typically, preschoolers' best friend is of the same sex and secondary friends are boys and girls (Vaughn, Colvin, Azria, Caya, & Krzysik, 2001).

Roughly 30% of 3- to 7-year-olds may have *imaginary friends* (Taylor, Carlson, Maring, Gerow, & Charley, 2004). Imaginary friends can either be invisible people or objects that have been personified, like our daughter's toy lamb named "Lambykins."

Firstborn and only children are more likely to create invisible people friends, perhaps because of less opportunity for social interaction at home (Gleason, Sebanc, & Hartup, 2000). Children with imaginary friends tend to be more imaginative, happy, and cooperative at preschool and tell higher-quality stories (Trionfi & Reese, 2009). Thus, imaginary friends are an asset, rather than a cause for concern in early childhood (Photo 11.3).

You may think of peer pressure as an adolescent issue, but preschoolers are also subject to peer pressure. For example, in one study 4-year-olds were asked if an animal in a book was big, medium, or small in size. Although they knew the correct answer, if other children gave a different answer, they would agree with the wrong answer (Haun & Tomasello, 2011). Such social conformity has been found as young as age 2 (Haun, Rekers, & Tomasello, 2014). Social conformity helps children adapt to their culture and group norms.

PHOTO 11.3 This 3-year-old is giving piano lessons to her imaginary friend "Moosie."

Middle Childhood (6 to 12 Years)

Most preschoolers (75%) have friends, but even more school-age children do (85%). School-age children average 3 to 8 friends. These friends form networks, or cliques, that average about 5 to 13 children, but can be up to 40 (Espelage, Green, & Polanin, 2012; Farmer et al., 2003; Hartup & Abecassis, 2002; Ryan, 2001). As children get older, they spend substantially more of their after-school time with child companions than with adult companions.

Homophily is stronger in middle childhood than in early childhood as children "shop" for friends (Hartup & Abecassis, 2002). Across elementary grades, children more actively select friends who are similar to them academically (Véronneau, Vitaro, Brendgen, Dishion, & Tremblay, 2010). In addition, aggressive children select each other as friends (Bukowski, Sippola, & Newcomb, 2000; Poulin & Boivin, 2000). In Chapter 10, you learned that some children are genetically predisposed to aggression, but such children tend to become aggressive only if they also have aggressive friends (Brendgen et al., 2008). Aggressive children are usually part of a peer network that supports aggression.

Peer networks are highly gender-segregated during middle childhood. Friends become increasingly same-sex from preschool through early adolescence. At age 4, children play 3 times more with same-sex peers than with opposite-sex peers. At age 6, they play 10 times more with same-sex peers. By 4th grade, 95% of preferred friends are of the same sex. In middle school, 90 to 95% of the cliques are of the same sex (Espelage et al., 2003; Ryan, 2001). Preadolescents are more confident about their social skills with same-sex peers compared to other-sex peers (Zosuls, Field, Martin, Andrews, & England, 2014).

Children not only prefer same-sex peers, but they actively avoid opposite-sex peers. A classic study of 9- to 11-year-olds at a day camp found that not a single child associated primarily with children of the opposite sex, but they did have contact on occasion (Sroufe, Bennett, Englund, Urban, & Shulman, 1993). They seemed to adhere to rules for contact such as "You can say, 'Pass the water' to someone of the other gender, but do not express interest in them" or "You can talk to someone of the other gender as long as it is insulting or you throw something at them as you

FIGURE 11.8 **Change in Time Spent with Peers.**

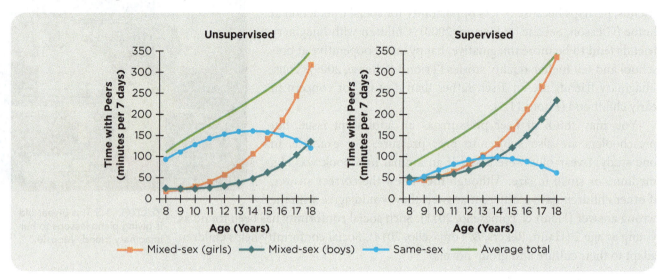

These charts from one study show how youth, ages 8 to 18, spend unsupervised and supervised time with peers across 16 school districts. Time with same-sex peers increases up to age 14, then declines; other-sex interaction rises steeply. Notice that overall the patterns are the same in both charts, but youth spend more time unsupervised with same-sex peers in middle childhood. What other interesting patterns do you see? How does this fit with your personal experience? *Source: Lam et al. (2014).*

pass by." Violation of these rules was associated with having fewer friends and low peer status.

In Figure 11.8 you will see that by 4th grade some students (mostly girls) begin to spend time in mixed-sex settings (Zosuls et al., 2014). Some teachers mistakenly believe that children who cross gender boundaries, such as flirting at a young age, are socially mature. Instead, maintenance of clear gender boundaries in preadolescence is characteristic of socially competent children, whereas early interest in the opposite sex and early dating (pseudomaturity) may forecast problems. Note that this may not apply at home, where children play with whoever is available, including opposite-sex peers, because they have limited playmates in the neighborhood. However, at school, where more playmates are available, same-sex preference is strong.

Adolescence (13 to 19 Years)

> *Allison, a 16-year-old, sits at a crowded lunch table. Other students are trying to find room to squeeze in at her table. Allison says that none of her friends has a boyfriend, but they have lots of male friends with whom they "watch movies together and go to games and stuff." She says teenagers usually have "2 or 3 close friends and 15 to 20 casual friends."*

Is Allison typical? Research shows that most (80 to 90%) teenagers have reciprocal friends, usually with 2 to 4 close friends (Martin-Storey, Cheadle, Skalamera, & Crosnoe, 2015). Adolescent friends exchange things (e.g., clothing or CDs), have shared activities (e.g., watching movies together), and text or talk frequently on the phone.

Adolescents spend more time with friends than younger children do. The average total amount of time with peers steadily increases from age 8 to 18 (see Figure 11.8).

mother, many HIV-infected parents are drug users (Forsyth, 2003). When youth have HIV/AIDS themselves, they may have other problems such as depression, anxiety, ADHD, drug use, and sexual activity while under the influence of drugs. HIV+ children may also have delays in language, motor abilities, cognitive development, and attention regulation (Brown, Lescano, & Lourie, 2001; Mialky, Vagnoni, & Rutstein, 2001; Wachsler-Felder & Golden, 2002). For example, they may have lower IQ, an unusual walking gait, or difficulty holding a pencil and writing. However, the effects vary in severity. Some HIV+ children have normal cognitive development.

What Can Be Done about STDs and AIDS? Some STDs, including AIDS, cannot be cured, but they can be prevented. Prevention may need to start in elementary school because some youth, particularly African American males, report sexual activity as early as 5th grade (Schonfeld, 2000). Prevention can involve informing youth. In Chapter 4 you learned that youth remember fuzzy traces better than detailed verbatim information. Research shows that giving youth details about the risk of sexual behavior is less effective than giving them fuzzy, gist information (Reyna, Weldon, & McCormick, 2015). For example, instead of giving details about STDs, just communicate the gist, such as "Unprotected sex exposes you to viruses, which unlike bacterial infections, cannot be cured." Gist memories of risk are more likely to be remembered and acted upon than difficult-to-retrieve details.

Prevention needs to focus on changing behavior, not just on informing youth. Programs aimed at changing behavior are either abstinence- or safe-sex-oriented. Abstinence programs ask youth to commit to not have sex before marriage or until adulthood. Safe-sex programs try to increase condom use. However, correct condom use may not prevent all STIs, and adolescents may not use condoms correctly (American Academy of Pediatrics, 2013a). Thus, a hierarchy of effective prevention messages would be: unprotected sex is unsafe, condom-protected sex is safer, and abstinence is safest.

Which programs are best? It depends on your goal. Safe-sex programs result in more condom use and do not increase, but sometimes reduce, sexual behavior (Johnson, Scott-Sheldon, Huedo-Medina & Carey, 2011). Abstinence programs result in older age at first sexual experience (see, for example, Jemmott, Jemmott, & Fong, 2010). Unfortunately, benefits of both types of programs are small and decay over time. Thus, it may be more effective to address the risk and protective factors (in Table 11.1) that lead to sexual behavior among youth, such as family functioning and attitudes toward sex (Tinsley, Lees, & Sumartojo, 2004). In a survey by the Centers for Disease Control and Prevention, the most common reason youth gave for not having sex was religion or morals; the least common was to avoid getting an STD (Martinez et al., 2011).

for LGBTQ orientation has been identified. There are most likely multiple biological and environmental pathways.

Some LGBTQ youth have a difficult time establishing healthy friendships. They may experience peer rejection and feel alienated at school—even before they have identified as LGBTQ (Bos, Sandfort, de Bruyn, & Hakvoort, 2008). They may have difficulty dating because they do not know who else feels same-sex attraction. They may be victimized if they make overtures to the wrong person, or their orientation is known, which can lead to depression (Toomey, Ryan, Diaz, Card, & Russell, 2010). They also are at higher risk for substance use, risky sex, violence, lower grades, truancy, and strained parent–child relationships—although most adjust well (American Academy of Pediatrics, 2013c; Robinson & Espelage, 2011).

How can you be supportive? Some teachers mistakenly advise LGBTQ youth to keep their orientation hidden in order to avoid harassment. However, youth who come out at school may have higher self-esteem and less depression, despite harassment (Russell, Toomey, Ryan, & Diaz, 2014). Gay–Straight Alliances, which are youth-driven groups intended to be a supportive setting, can foster resilience (Poteat et al., 2015). LGBTQ youth may be more socially integrated in large, diverse schools, rather than small homogeneous schools (Martin-Storey et al., 2015). School personnel should prevent and address harassment problems and provide social support so that school is welcoming to all youth. Let's turn next to differences in friendships among children.

11-2d Individual Diversity in Friendship and Peer Networks

Did you have the same best friend from preschool to 12th grade? Many adults report having the same best friend across childhood, but this may be a false memory. Among preschoolers, less than 10% of friends are still friends the following school year, even when friends move into a new class together (Vaughn et al., 2001). Roughly half of middle school friendships do not endure into the next year. Friendships in adolescence are more stable, but even in adolescence best friends change from year to year (Dishion & Owen, 2002). Friends who are quite similar (e.g., achievement, aggression, popularity) are the most likely to have more enduring friendships (Hartl, Laursen, & Cillessen, 2015).

The composition of cliques also changes. The most stable cliques retain only about 50% of members from one school year to the next, and other cliques completely dissolve. As children get older there is slightly more stability, so that 7th-grade cliques are more stable than 4th-grade cliques, which are more stable than 1st-grade cliques (Estell, Farmer, Cairns, & Cairns, 2002).

While the specific friends may change from year to year, children who have friends at one age are likely to have friends at a later age. That is, whether a child has friends or is friendless is fairly stable (Hartup & Abecassis, 2002). *Quality* of friendships is also stable. That is, children with high-quality friendships in preschool have high-quality friendships later (Howes & Tonyon, 2000). Quality refers to feeling close and helping each other.

What Do Individual Differences in Friendship Predict?

Some learners have more friends and higher-quality friendships than do others. Friendships can contribute to healthy development, or they can be a source of risk. Let's discuss four outcomes linked to friendships.

Academic achievement

Friends affect school success. Learners with low-quality friendships tend to become less engaged in classroom activities and more disruptive (Berndt, 2002). In contrast, learners with high-quality friendships and whose friends value academics are motivated to do well in class (Nelson & DeBacker, 2008). Homophily occurs less in small private or rural schools because of the limited selection of friends.

From 1st to 12th grade, learners tend to select friends at the beginning of the year who are academically similar and then become even more like their peer network in achievement and motivation over the school year (Estell et al., 2002; Flashman, 2012; Kindermann, 2007). If friends change in achievement over time, they may be deselected from the friendship (Flashman, 2012). Thus, friendships change in ways that maximize academic similarity, or homophily. This perpetuates an achievement gap. Because specific friendships change over time but the clique tends to be more stable, the broader clique more strongly predicts academic achievement.

Emotional well-being

Children with friends are happier and have higher self-esteem than friendless children (Photo 11.5). Prosocial friends buffer children from stresses such as rejection, victimization, loneliness, depression, and divorce (Asher & Paquette, 2003; Bukowski, Laursen, & Hoza, 2010; Ladd, Kochenderfer-Ladd, Eggum, Kochel, & McConnell, 2011). See Figure 11.9.

How do they do this? Friends share enjoyable activities and validate each other's worth. Friends help each other manage, understand, and talk about emotions (Burgess, Wojslawo-wica, Rubin, Rose-Krasnor, & Booth-LaForce, 2006). Friends also reduce stress hormones. For example, one study measured cortisol levels in 5th- and 6th-graders. Those reporting negative events 20 minutes prior to the test had higher cortisol levels. However, *if their best friend was with them,* their cortisol level did not rise (Adams, Santo, & Bukowski, 2011). Thus, friends are a protective factor for emotional well-being. However, a cautionary note is that not all friends are positive. Depressed learners can also socialize their friend into depression, perhaps through emotion contagion (Giletta et al., 2011).

Social well-being

Friends provide opportunities to learn and practice social skills. For example, imagine that your best friend is giving a class presentation, and doing badly. A few students in the class snicker. What would you do? You might kindly reassure your friend that we all mess up sometimes, or hostilely rub it in, or even avoid your friend. In one study, 3rd- to 9th-graders who had more friends became more likely over time to choose helpful, rather than hostile, strategies (Glick & Rose, 2011). They learned to be more prosocial. In another study, 6th-graders became more prosocial by 8th grade if they had a prosocial friend (Wentzel, Barry, & Caldwell, 2004). That is, a single friend's social behavior predicted change in behavior 2 years later.

PHOTO 11.5 Learners with high-quality friends are more engaged in class and happier.

FIGURE 11.9 Growth in Depression of Rejected Children.

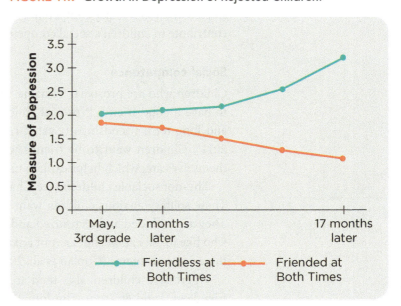

How does depression change for rejected children with and without friends from 3rd to 5th grade? These are correlational data. What are two ways you could interpret this chart in terms of what causes depression and rejection? (Hint: Might the two groups be different from the beginning?) *Source: Bukowski, Laursen, and Hoza (2010).*

What happens when a child does not have friends? One friendless 6th-grade boy said, "I got no friends, but I don't care. When I am nice, they still won't play with me. So I ignore them. Ain't no one gonna take care of you. You gotta take care of yourself. All I need is me. *They* need to change, not me." This boy has little social support for coping with emotions, nor opportunity to develop better social skills.

Delinquency

Learners can have a destructive friendship. Friends can victimize one another. Friends can plot and carry out crime together. Learners who choose antisocial friends become even more antisocial. This is particularly true of early-onset anti-social children. Youth whose antisocial behavior starts when they are older and is limited to the adolescent years are more likely to have typical friendships (Piehler & Dishion, 2007).

How does this negative side of friendship work? Antisocial learners select each other as friends, and then train each other in deviancy. One classic study video-taped teenage boys interacting with their peers for 25 minutes (Dishion, McCord, & Poulin, 1999). When the boys talked about breaking rules, delinquent friends laughed, whereas nondelinquent friends paused or changed the subject. Thus, some friends reinforced delinquency through interest in misbehavior, which led to more substance use, delinquency, and violence 2 years later. Don't assume that training in deviancy pertains only to teenagers—it occurs as young as kindergarten (Snyder et al., 2008). However, the effect of antisocial friends may not be as strong in early elementary grades as in later childhood (Sturaro et al., 2011).

What Predicts Quantity and Quality of Friendships?

Several factors predict whether children will have beneficial or destructive friend-ships. Children's social competence is a key predictor, as are parenting factors that contribute to children's social competence.

Social competence

Children who are prosocial, sociable, and skilled at entering groups are more likely to have a good friend. Prosocial children are especially likely to have reciprocated and long-term friendships (Gest, Graham-Bermann, & Hartup, 2001; Ladd et al., 2011). Children want to be friends with others who are more prosocial than they themselves are, which helps explain unilateral friendships.

Shy-nonsociable children (see Chapter 6) have fewer and less stable friendships. These solitary/anxious children want to interact with others, but they are afraid to. They are excluded and victimized and have easily hurt feelings. In contrast, children who like to play alone, but are not anxious about interacting with others, do not have these same problems (Coplan et al., 2013; Ladd et al., 2011).

Aggressive children also tend to have fewer friends, but are not necessarily friendless (Ladd & Troop-Gordon, 2003). Bullies have friends. Gang members have friends. However, aggressive children tend to have low-quality, conflict-ridden friendships with aggressive or socially marginal peers (Ladd, Buhs, & Troop, 2002).

Keep in mind that there are two patterns of aggressive children. Most follow the pattern that was shown in Figure 10.3. That is, they gravitate into deviant peer

think
about this

Imagine you have a friend whose 15-year-old has "got-ten into the wrong crowd" and is using drugs. Your friend decides to move the child to a different school. Is this a good idea? What would you advise this friend, based on research?

groups because they are rejected by nonaggressive peers. Another, less common, pattern is the perceived popular children who are prominent in classroom social networks (Farmer et al., 2010; Vlachou et al., 2011). They have some nonaggressive friends because they occasionally use prosocial behavior and have valued traits (Farmer et al., 2010). Still, prosocial Nadya, in the opening vignette is not likely to be friends with aggressive Eleanor.

Parenting factors

Parent–child attachment predicts friendship quality. Securely attached children tend to have high-quality friendships and a larger peer network. This effect is found for children of different ethnicities from preschool to young adulthood.[3] Attachment sets the stage for social relationships in general and friendships in particular. How does this happen? Children who are secure openly communicate about emotions, develop better language skills, and have less hostile attribution bias (McElwain, Booth-LaForce, Lansford, Wu, & Dyer, 2008). Their mothers use more "mental state talk," which helps them develop better theory of mind, which promotes high-quality friendships (McElwain, Booth-LaForce, & Wu, 2011).

Several other parenting factors that are linked to children's social competence (see Chapter 10) are also linked to their friendships. These include:

- *Modeling.* Parents who have high-quality friendships and high-quality marriages tend to have children who have high-quality friendships (Allen & Loeb, 2015; Simpkins & Parke, 2001).

- *Coaching friendship skills.* Parents who talk to their children about how to repair relationships during conflicts between friends, rather than just stating rules like *"we always share!"* or simply ending the conflict, have children with more harmonious friendships (Putallaz, Costanzo, Grimes, & Sherman, 1998).

- *Monitoring friendships.* Youth whose parents know their friends and guide them in choosing friends tend to have high-quality friendships. Guidance involves getting to know the friends' parents, telling the child to choose friends carefully, and helping the child recognize bad behavior in friends (Ladd & Pettit, 2002; Mounts, 2001).

- *Supervision.* While friends are beneficial, youth who hang around too much with peers unsupervised have lower grades and more behavior problems than those who are supervised (Goldstein, Davis-Kean, & Eccles, 2005; Updegraff, Whiteman, McHale, Thayer, & Crouter, 2006).

- *Use of effective discipline.* Unfortunately, children whose parents use psychological control have lower-quality friendships and are more influenced by deviant peers (Allen & Loeb, 2015; Oudekerk, Allen, Hessel, & Molloy, 2015). Conflict in the parent–child relationship has a "spillover" effect on conflict with friends (Chung, Flook, & Fuligni, 2011).

---

[3] Many studies find this, just a few of which are listed here: Hartup and Abecassis (2002); Howes and Tonyon (2000); Ladd and Pettit (2002); Schneider, Atkinson and Tardif (2001).

PHOTO 11.6 Where are the boys sitting in this lunch room? Where are the girls sitting?

Adolescents must manage the balance between strong connections with peers (which can promote their well-being) and appropriate autonomy from peer influences. They learn to do this in authoritative families, in which strong connections are balanced with autonomy. Children then carry this balance into relationships with peers (Allen & Loeb, 2015).

11-2e Group Diversity in Friendship and Peer Networks

There are some gender and ethnic differences in peer networks and behavior within friendships.

Gender

Girls tend to have more friends in the classroom than do boys, but cliques may be slightly smaller for girls from preschool through the primary grades (Estell et al., 2002; Hartup & Abecassis, 2002). Young boys tend to hang around with a larger group of friends. However, by middle school, boys' and girls' peer networks are similar in size, and by high school girls' networks are a little larger and less exclusive than boys' (Farmer et al., 2003; Lee, Howes, & Chamberlain, 2007).

Gender segregation results in boys and girls growing up in different peer cultures (Rose & Rudolph, 2006). Boys' friendships tend to be based on shared activities and interests like sports and video games. Girls' friendships tend to be based on emotional closeness and sharing feelings and personal information (Photo 11.6). Girls expect and report greater affection, help, and intimacy from friendships than do boys. Perhaps because of greater expectations, girls may get angrier and sadder over friends betraying them or not being supportive (MacEvoy & Asher, 2012). This may explain why girl friends have just as much conflict and broken friendships, if not more so, than do boy friends from kindergarten through high school (Benenson & Christakos, 2003; Ladd, Kochenderfer, & Coleman, 1996).

Ethnicity

Learners do not segregate by ethnicity as much as they do by gender (Lee et al., 2007). However, if you have been in a multiethnic school, you have probably observed that youth with the same ethnic background tend to associate with each other (Chen & Graham, 2015; Neal et al., 2014). Ethnic homophily is stronger in high school than in elementary school. Boys are more likely to form cross-ethnic friendships than girls, as are prosocial leaders in the classroom (Kawabata & Crick, 2011). Prosocial children are preferred by others regardless of ethnic matching (Wilson & Rodkin, 2011).

Not all classrooms are diverse, which limits opportunities for ethnicity-based friendships. The relationship between ethnicity-based friendships and school diversity is complex. In homogeneous schools, White learners may be least likely to have cross-ethnic friendships (McGill, Way, & Hughes, 2012). Yet, in diverse schools, White learners are more likely to have cross-ethnic friendships than African American or Latino learners; African American children are least likely (Kawabata & Crick, 2011; Wilson & Rodkin, 2011). At the high school level, African American and White learners are least likely to be friends (Quillian & Campbell, 2003). Asian learners are more likely to have cross-ethnic friendships with White, rather than Latino or Black, students (Chen & Graham, 2015).

What about learners whose ethnic group is small in number at your school? Such learners are especially likely to choose same-ethnic friends, as though the small numbers drive them together (Lee et al., 2007; Wilson & Rodkin, 2011). This may be beneficial in some situations. In one study in New York City, Black and Asian students who had only same-ethnic friendships had higher self-esteem and lower depression (McGill et al., 2012). Some educators advocate clustering minority learners in classrooms so that they can form same-ethnic friendships, rather than distributing them across classrooms or schools and forcing them into a lonely existence. However, others argue that this would resegregate schools and result in academic tracking because achievement varies by ethnicity, and schools with academic tracking have the fewest cross-ethnic friendships (Stearns, 2004). They advocate intentionally grouping learners of different ethnicities together. This can increase cross-ethnic friendships, but also racial tension. Thus, educators have to weigh these considerations for the particular ethnic composition of their classroom and school.

11-2f Classroom Implications of Friendship and Peer Networks

You have learned that friendships and peer networks influence academic achievement. Youth who have more friends in school (rather than outside of school) tend to have higher GPAs and feel more bonded to school (Witkow & Fuligni, 2010). Learners with high-quality friendships in the classroom enjoy school and actively participate, which promotes achievement. In contrast, learners who are friendless attend school less, are socially uncomfortable, and achieve less (Thorkildsen, Reese, & Corsino, 2002). Ideally, each child should have at least one good friend in your classroom. You can help your students form high-quality friendships by following these guidelines.

1. *Help learners develop prosocial behavior.* You learned how to do this in Chapter 10.

2. *Promote attachment at school.* Caring teacher–student relationships protect youth from the negative effect of delinquent friends (Crosnoe & Needham, 2004). You learned how to do this in Chapter 6. An additional approach is to use homophily to your advantage. When teachers find they have similarities with specific at-risk students, they develop better teacher–student relationships and those students earn higher grades, narrowing the achievement gap (Gehlbach et al., 2016).

3. *Keep friends together from year to year, if the friendships are not deviant.* Because learners choose friends from among the pool of available classmates, when schools keep learners together in classes from year to year, there is greater stability of friendships, even if the teacher changes. Learners with good friends in their class make smoother transitions to kindergarten, middle school, and junior high (Berndt, Hawkins, & Jiao, 1999; Wentzel et al., 2004).

4. *Place friends together* when forming cooperative learning groups in your classroom or constructing classroom placements for the next school year. Learners without best friends *in their class* are lonelier than others, regardless of their peer status or

whether they have friends in other classes in the school (Parker & Asher, 1993). Some teachers mistakenly assume that learners will be off task if they work with friends, but research suggests the opposite in most situations. Friends tend to spend *more* time on task and work at a more cognitively advanced level than do nonfriends (Hartup & Abecassis, 2002). Friends exchange ideas; explore, remember, write, and help each other more; and have more positive emotions when working together. They work with less conflict and more constructive activity than do nonfriends (Strough, Berg, & Meegan, 2001). These short-term effects are likely to have long-term consequences if they occur frequently.

5. *Promote opportunities to form friendships,* particularly early in the school year. Eliminate school policies that restrict learners' peer interaction outside of class. For example, some schools require learners to walk in a single-file line, without talking, to and from buses. Some schools punish learners for talking with friends at lunch. Such policies promote friendlessness and undermine learners' well-being.

6. *Recruit the help of the school counselor to provide intervention for friendless learners.* Friendship-building skills can be taught in class. Some programs are more effective than others (January, Casey, & Paulson, 2011). Your school counselor should be aware of effective programs.

An important caveat to the preceding guidelines is *don't group aggressive or deviant learners together.* Schools contribute to delinquency when they put such learners together through ability grouping, retaining low-achieving learners, group counseling, alternative classrooms for unruly students, and in-school suspension (Dodge, Dishion, & Lansford, 2006). In Chapter 7, you met Paul, who was sent to in-school suspension (ISS), where his friends could often be found. The boys were given the opportunity to strengthen deviant friendships in ISS. They were also being separated from other peers, who modeled more appropriate behavior.

Learners in classrooms full of aggressive peers become increasingly aggressive over time (Werner & Hill, 2010). In such classrooms, teachers find it difficult to establish a positive class climate and strong teacher–student relationships. However, if teachers manage to be responsive, warm, and supportive despite the odds, the learners are likely to become less aggressive over time (Thomas, Bierman, & Powers, 2011).

You can make a difference. A large national study found that teacher effects on learners' social skills was larger than teacher effects on academic achievement (Jennings & DiPrete, 2010). Furthermore, enhancing learners' social skills contributed to their academic achievement. Clearly a win–win situation. Some teachers were much better at promoting their learners' social skills. Who were these star teachers? Those who were better educated—so study this textbook carefully! In another study, teachers were trained to successfully turn around a negative peer culture in which students pressured each other not to achieve academically. What were they trained to do? The same things you have learned in this textbook—become aware of the peer culture in the classroom and create a positive classroom climate (Hamm, Farmer, Lambert, & Gravelle, 2014).

One of the reasons friendlessness and peer rejection are detrimental is that they restrict learners' opportunity to play. Playing together is a central feature of friendships, from early childhood to adolescence. Let's discuss play next.

11-3 Play

In a 9th-grade science class, the students were told how to do an experiment and then asked to put on their safety goggles. One boy put on three pairs of goggles so that he looked like a scuba diver. He shouted, "Heh, heh! Attack of the scuba monster!" and jabbed at his lab partners with his yardstick. His lab partners retaliated in a mock sword fight with their yardsticks. The teacher told the boys to "settle down and get to work." They did, completing their lab assignment with occasional playful jabs at one another and lots of laughter.

Play is almost inevitable when children are gathered together, even during science class. Play is so much a part of being a child that it is often used to define childhood. Should you encourage play in your classroom? The answer depends on your understanding of play.

Play is easy to recognize, yet difficult to define. Play is characterized by positive emotions (smiling or laughing), fantasy, spontaneity, and flexibility. It has no immediate function and does not involve competition. However, play may not always have all these features. For example, games with rules, like sports, may or may not be considered play because they are often competitive, lack spontaneity, and can involve negative emotion.

play
behavior that has no immediate function and is pleasurable, spontaneous, flexible, and internally controlled.

11-3a Types of Play

How children play helps you understand their development, so let's look at types of play. Play varies along two dimensions: (1) low to high cognitive involvement and (2) low to high social involvement. Table 11.2 displays different types of play.

TABLE 11.2 Cognitive and social dimensions of play from least to most mature

Least mature ————————————————————————————————➤ Most mature

Cognitive dimensions of play				
Functional play	**Physical play**	**Constructive play**	**Pretense (or dramatic) play**	**Game with rules**
Simple movement or a repetitive, practice-like behavior, such as shaking a rattle.	Large movement for the joy of movement, such as climbing, running, or chasing.	Creating, or building something, with a goal in mind, such as building with blocks or drawing with crayons.	Transforming objects and identities. Imaginary friends are a type of pretense.	Play in which children must adapt their behavior to explicit prearranged rules, such as hopscotch or checkers.

Social dimensions of play				
Unoccupied and onlooker	**Solitary play**	**Parallel play**	**Associative play**	**Cooperative play**
Following others around or watching their play, perhaps even talking to them, but not joining the play.	Playing alone when playmates are available, with no reference to what others are doing.	Playing near others with similar toys, but not seeking to interact, that is, children play beside rather than with others.	Borrowing toys or following each other, but the children do whatever each wants to.	Group is organized around a goal, or a formal game, and division of roles (e.g., "I'm the mommy and you're the doggie"). It is clear who belongs to the group and who does not.

TABLE 11.3	Characteristics of rough-and-tumble play compared with aggression	
	Rough-and-tumble play	**Aggression**
Behavior	Soft, open-hand hitting, pushing, chasing, teasing, wrestling. Children help anyone who appears hurt.	Hard hits, shoving, kicking
Emotions	Smiling or laughing	Frowning or scowling
Results	Further shared activities, participants stay together afterward	Participants separate
Intent	Fun, expressing affection	Harm

These types are hierarchical. In the cognitive domain, functional play is the least mature and games with rules the most mature form of play. However, even adolescents engage in functional play, like simply bouncing a ball. In the social domain, higher forms of play involve more social coordination. The most advanced forms of play are pretense and games with rules that involve coordination among multiple children. When pretense play involves cooperation with other children, it is called *sociodramatic play*.

Another type of play, **rough-and-tumble (R&T) play**, or play fighting, combines pretense and **physical play**, like sword fighting in science class (Pellegrini, 2002). *It is not aggression.* This is an important distinction because R&T play is good for children, but aggression is not. R&T play is one way that boys express fondness for one another (Reed & Brown, 2001). Table 11.3 shows how R&T play is distinguished from aggression. R&T play is common on playgrounds, although it can occur in classrooms. Let's look next at how types of play change with age.

11-3b Age Trends in Play

Which age do you think is the most playful? The frequency of play peaks in early to middle childhood and generally follows an inverted U-shape. That is, play is less frequent in infancy/toddlerhood, becomes more frequent in middle childhood, and then becomes less frequent again during adolescence (Pellegrini & Smith, 1998). Type of play also changes with age.

Infancy and Toddlerhood (Birth to 2 Years)

By themselves, infants primarily engage in functional play (see Table 11.2 for definition), like banging a pot over and over, or physical play, like kicking their legs. They are able to engage in social, cooperative play, but only if it is scaffolded by others, such as "peek-a-boo." If others fail to respond during play, infants will vocalize or gesture to get them to take their turn, showing that they have expectations for how the play should proceed.

Toddlers often engage in physical play, such as climbing or chase, and constructive play, such as stacking blocks or coloring. They may do this alone or with the

rough-and-tumble (R&T) play
social, pretense play that involves physically vigorous behavior and often resembles, but is not the same as, aggression.

physical play
play in which children move for the joy of movement, such as climbing, running, or chasing.

scaffolding of others. As early as 10 to 12 months, they may play cooperatively with a familiar friend, such as sharing blocks to stack or taking turns chasing each other (Howes & Lee, 2006). At 15 to 24 months, pretense play first emerges without adult support (Göncü, Patt, & Kouba, 2002). For example, a toddler may pretend to feed a stuffed animal.

Early Childhood (3 to 5 Years)

Physical play and constructive play continue to be common among preschoolers. However, the functional play of infants diminishes and becomes rare by 4 to 5 years. Two other dramatic developments between ages 2 to 5 are: (1) a rise in pretense play, and (2) a shift from parallel to fully cooperative play (Göncü, Patt, & Kouba, 2002). See Photo 11.7. Three-year-olds can sustain play with an unfamiliar peer better than toddlers can, and 5-year-olds are even better. Preschoolers' pretense play involves longer sequences, greater complexity, and more fantasy than toddlers' play. For example, play might shift from toddlers simply feeding a doll to 5-year-olds making an elaborate witch's brew. There is also more agreement among children about the roles, rules, and themes in a play episode as they get older. These changes may be the result of improved perspective-taking ability (see Chapter 8) and theory of mind (see Chapter 9). Pretense play peaks in frequency at about 5 to 6 years of age.

PHOTO 11.7 These children are playing side by side, but not together. What type of play is this?

Children can turn any object into a toy (such as safety goggles and yardsticks), but you should provide age-appropriate, safe toys in your classroom. The website for the National Association for the Education of Young Children lists appropriate toys by age from birth to 6 years.

Middle Childhood (6 to 12 Years)

Each type of play found in preschoolers continues into middle childhood; however, their prevalence shifts. Three kinds of play become more prevalent: R&T play, constructive play, and games with rules. R&T play accounts for about 5% of free play for preschoolers, about 10 to 17% for elementary children, and about 5% for middle school children (Pellegrini, 2002). Preschoolers seldom engage in games with rules, but elementary school children often do, such as playing cards or foursquare at recess. In contrast, pretense play becomes less prevalent in middle childhood, although it still occurs. For example, a group of 6th-grade boys formed a series of large circles in the snow at recess; they were UFO landing sites. Another group played "Jedi Knights." Thus, you will see pretense play in elementary school, but not to the same extent as in preschool.

Play takes on increased complexity with age. Constructive play becomes more complex, like building a Ferris wheel from an erector set. Simple motor activity gives way to complex physical activity like shooting baskets. Simple interactive chase games give way to more complex interactive games, like soccer, basketball, or jump rope (Pellegrini, Blatchford, Kato, & Baines, 2004). Let's visit an elementary playground for a classic example of how play changes over middle childhood.

Will, a kindergartener, spent recess running from place to place—swings, sandbox, and teeter-totter. He played with boys and girls. His teacher tried to keep a kick-ball game going among the kindergarteners, but they had trouble understanding the rules, and the children came and went from the game. In contrast, the 5th-graders quickly organized three games (football, soccer, and foursquare). No adults helped with the games; they were child-run. Will's older brother, Ivan, stayed with the same game (football) the entire recess, as did most other 5th-graders. Ivan's game was boys only. Several girls played jump rope games with complicated rules, rhythms, and songs.

Adolescence (13 to 19 Years)

Teenagers are fun! They can rapidly turn work into play, as the 9th-graders in the opening vignette did. In high school classrooms you will see many forms of play, including the ask-questions-to-get-the-teacher-off-track game. In adolescence, play can be purely mental. Adolescents "play" with ideas much like younger children play with objects—combining them in new ways or substituting one for another. Using the mind as a playground fosters creativity and discovery.

Most types of play continue in adolescence. For example, constructive solitary play occurred when an adolescent built a remote-controlled car. Sociodramatic play occurred when a group of boys stumbled upon a high school storage room where they found two old chairs with wheels, and pretended to be NASCAR drivers in the hallway—until they were caught. Another group was assigned to write a skit for their German class that evolved into a complex pretend sword fight between nations—in German, of course.

R&T play continues, although with less frequency, in adolescence, where it serves at least two purposes:

1. Crossing gender boundaries. Because gender segregation is well entrenched and crossing gender boundaries is socially risky, adolescents use R&T play to do so. A boy might playfully steal a girl's hat so that he can "save face" if the girl rejects his overture. This is known as "poke-and-push courtship."

2. Domination or disguised aggression. In early adolescence, boys who engage in R&T play also engage in more aggression (Pellegrini, 2003). This is not true of younger children.

Playing games with rules, like board games or freeze tag, diminishes in adolescence but does not disappear altogether. Adolescents are more likely to just hang out with friends than play structured games (Blatchford, 1998; Hughes, 1999).

11-3c Individual Diversity in Play

Do you know learners who seem highly playful? Some learners consistently play more, and in more advanced ways, than others. Differences in play provide a window into a child's cognitive and social competence. Let's examine how learners differ in their play.

What Do Individual Differences in Play Predict?

Learners who frequently play in age-appropriate ways have better cognitive abilities and academic achievement. They have greater intelligence, verbal ability, visual-spatial ability, problem-solving ability, creativity, literacy skills, and math achievement.[4] Learners who frequently play in age-appropriate ways also have better social and emotional competence. They have greater self-control, theory of mind, prosocial behavior, emotional perspective-taking, emotion regulation, and happiness, and less aggression.[5] These positive outcomes have been linked to play for all children, from preschoolers through adolescents. These benefits are especially evident in low-SES learners.

Does play *cause* these good outcomes? It seems reasonable. Vygotsky (1978) believed that play promotes development because it allows children to practice and acquire skills beyond their current level, raising their zone of proximal development. For example, a 3-year-old cannot pour a real pot of hot tea or ride a horse, but can pour a pretend pot or ride a stick horse. Video games are similar in that they allow teenagers to be their "ideal self" in a virtual world (Przybylski, Weinstein, Murayama, Lynch, & Ryan, 2012). An 18-year-old may not be a defender of kingdoms, but can imagine being one during a video game. Nevertheless, you could argue that play is the result, not the cause, of social and cognitive abilities. That is, some learners may engage in more-advanced play because they are already more socially skilled and intelligent. This was Piaget's view (Piaget, 1962). How might you answer the question of causation? One approach is an experiment (see Chapter 1). If learners who have poor skills are trained to play more, and then their skills improve, you can conclude that play probably caused the improvement. Let's look at what experiments have revealed.

One stark example of a field experiment occurred at Mother Teresa's orphanage in India. Children's physical needs were met, but the overworked caregivers were reluctant to let children play because they believed it would increase their workload. The children had significant developmental delays, much like the children with hospitalism described in Chapter 6. Researchers convinced the caregivers to try a 90-minute daily playtime. Within 3 months, the children's motor, cognitive, and social skills improved dramatically. Children who could not talk or feed themselves became able to. The children were more active, playful, responsive, and independent, which actually decreased the caregivers' workload (Taneja et al., 2002).

This is a dramatic example, but similar results are sometimes found when at-risk children in preschools or child care centers are trained in sociodramatic play (Roopnarine, Shin, Donovan, & Suppal, 2000). How might you train children to play? One approach is to read fantasy books—like *The Three Little Pigs*—and then help the children enact the story. Another approach is to help the children plan their play—like "Let's play grocery store"—and then back away (withdraw scaffolding), only intervening if the children need help to sustain their play, followed by a debriefing session—like "What did you play? What did you say to...?" (Craig-Unkefer &

---

[4] Many studies support this conclusion, just a few of which are listed here: Cheah, Nelson, and Rubin (2001); Dunn and Hughes (2001); Fantuzzo, Sekino, and Cohen (2004); Jirout and Newcombe (2015); Lloyd and Howe (2003); Wolfgang, Stannard, and Jones (2003).
[5] Many studies support this conclusion, just a few of which are listed here: Bulotsky-Shearer et al. (2012); Cheah et al. (2001); Dunn and Hughes (2001); Elias and Berk (2002); Fantuzzo et al. (2004); Lillard (2002); Pellegrini et al. (2004).

Kaiser, 2002). Research on interventions like these suggests that play causes improvement in language, but there currently is no clear evidence that play causes improvement in other domains (e.g., intelligence, creativity, theory of mind, executive functions, or social skills). More rigorous research to determine whether play *causes* positive outcomes is needed (Lillard et al., 2013). Nevertheless, play clearly has value; it is fun, energizing, and helps solidify relationships.

What Predicts Individual Differences in Play?

Several *child factors* predict playfulness. Learners who are humorous, imaginative, curious, expressive, social, verbal, active, and novelty-seeking play more than other learners. In contrast, learners who have poor emotion regulation and are immature, impulsive, aggressive, and rejected by peers play less. Learners who have physical or mental limitations may be less playful. For example, learners with visual impairment tend to have less mature pretend play (Lewis, Norgate, Collis, & Reynolds, 2000). Their play may be limited because they cannot observe peer models at play and their attention is not visually drawn to play objects. Learners with autism tend to have impoverished functional and pretense play. Play is so characteristic of children that atypical play is often used to diagnose developmental delays.

Several *parent factors* predict playfulness. Parents influence the quality and amount of their children's play by providing opportunities for play and through the type of relationship they have with their children. Children with power-assertive parents are more likely to withdraw from social play, whereas children with authoritative parents are more likely to play cooperatively. Children with secure parent–child attachment initiate more play and have richer, more creative, and more socially complex play. Children with avoidant attachment are more likely to play in ways that involve no people (Cassibba, Van IJzendoorn, & D'Odorico, 2000; Sroufe, 1996).

A Cautionary Note About Solitary Play

In Table 11.2 you learned that solitary play is a less-mature form of play. Solitary play can be a cause for concern, but it depends on the context and whether the play is active or passive. **Solitary-active play** involves either functional play or dramatic pretense play. It is a red flag for poor social skills if a learner plays *alone when others are available to play with*. For example, a learner might play with a ball alone when there are several others playing nearby with a ball. Solitary-*active* play could be a cause and/or consequence of social withdrawal and peer rejection.

In contrast, **solitary-passive play** is not necessarily a cause for concern. It involves constructive play—like doing puzzles, drawing, coloring, or building with blocks. These are activities that are typically done alone, even when playmates are abundant. Solitary-passive play is linked to high academic achievement and social competence. Earlier you learned that children who play alone but are socially skilled and have friends fare well (Coplan et al., 2013). However, learners who play in a solitary-passive way because of social anxiety may have low achievement and internalizing problems (Burgess, Rubin, Cheah, & Nelson, 2005). Thus, solitary-*passive* play warrants careful observation because learners who miss the benefits of social play could lag in social and academic skills. Keep in mind that solitary play is only a concern in the midst of a classroom of playmates, not when there is no one else to play with, such as at home.

solitary-active play
play involving functional or pretense play while alone.

solitary-passive play
play involving construction or exploring objects while alone.

Sports

Whether sports constitute play is debatable because they are organized, competitive, and have rules. Yet they are like play in that youth often participate purely for fun. In fact, many youth say that sports are the most enjoyable aspect of their lives (Larson & Verma, 1999). Participation in sports increases with age. Large national studies indicate that about 25% of kindergarten through 3rd-graders, 40% of 4th- through 8th-graders, and 60% of 10th-graders participate in sports (Broh, 2002; Federal Interagency Forum on Child and Family Statistics, 2008). Sports are the most common type of organized after-school activity, followed by religious activities.

Is participation in sports good for children? It can be. Benefits include increased friendships, psychological well-being, self-esteem as an athlete, improved quality of sleep, fitness, and school bonding (see, for example, Perkins, Jacobs, Barber, & Eccles, 2004). Teen athletes have higher grades, better attendance, and are less likely to drop out of school than nonathletes (Broh, 2002; Busch et al., 2014). However, costs include injuries, overtraining, burnout, less participation in other important activities, and drug use because some sports have a culture of drug use (Fauth, Roth, & Brooks-Gunn, 2007; Gardner, Roth, & Brooks-Gunn, 2009). Thus, whether participation in sports is good for learners depends on the situation. Children who engage in a wider variety of extracurricular activities, not just sports, fare better (Linver, Roth, & Brooks-Gunn, 2009; Simpkins, Eccles, & Becnel, 2008).

11-3d Group Diversity in Play

Differences in play are linked to gender and socioeconomic status. Let's look at these group differences next.

Gender

Gender segregation occurs during play throughout childhood. As boys play with boys and girls play with girls, different play cultures emerge. Preschool girls are more likely to play indoors, near adults. They play house and games that require verbal interaction. They typically play with only two or three others. Their play involves cooperation, discussion, support, and encouragement, with themes oriented around domestic or romantic scripts and maintenance of order and safety (Maccoby, 2002). Boys' play involves dominance, competition, conflict, and risk-taking, with themes of danger, destruction, and heroism. Boys engage in more rough-and-tumble play (Pellegrini, 2003). For example, a teacher of 2- to 3-year-olds described play among the learners in her class:

> *The girls usually draw and play with dolls while the boys usually "drive" toy trucks. Both boys and girls play with the puzzles and books. When I bring out the puppets, the boys immediately begin making their puppets growl and try to gobble each other up. This is funny because the puppets are a turtle and a giraffe—neither of which is known for growling. The girls make their puppets meow, cry, and kiss each other.*

In early elementary school, boys play more games with balls, like soccer, basketball, and football; and girls play more games that involve songs, chants, and rhymes—like jump rope—just as they did at Will and Ivan's school in the earlier vignette

I Love Images/SuperStock

PHOTO 11.8 Can you tell whether this is aggression or rough-and-tumble play? What clues are you using?

(Pellegrini et al., 2004). Boy–girl differences in play have been found during almost a century of research on play (Harper & Huie, 1998).

Where do these gender differences in play come from? Perhaps parents cause them by reinforcing gender-typed play and providing gender-typed toys, like footballs to baby boys. Or, perhaps parents are simply responding to children's innate gender differences, rather than causing them. The peer group, rather than parents, may be more powerful in sustaining gender differences in play. Learners who cross boundaries, especially boys who play in "girl" ways, tend to be rejected by their peer group (Rubin, Bukowski, & Parker, 1998).

Both *selection* and *socialization* are at work in the peer group. Children are exposed to both boy and girl play patterns at school, but they *select* playmates who have play patterns similar to their own (Photo 11.8). Gender differences become more pronounced over time as children *socialize* one another within their same-sex play groups (Martin et al., 2013). This means that at the beginning of the school year, preschool and elementary teachers see fewer gender differences than they do at the end of the school year. Thus, gender segregation may be both a cause and a consequence of differences in play patterns.

Socioeconomic Status

SES affects the amount of space and the range of choices available for play. It is also linked to quality of play. Low-SES children tend to play in less elaborate ways than do middle-SES children. That is, during pretense play they have shorter episodes, fewer different roles, less imaginative use of props, more aggression, and less discussion. Their play involves less reading and writing compared with higher-SES children (Roskos, 2000). These SES differences in play spawned the research on play intervention discussed previously. Scientists hypothesized that if low-SES children could be trained to play in more-advanced ways, they would develop better language, and perhaps cognitive and social skills. They appear to have been correct.

11-3e Classroom Implications of Play

Play is important to your classroom in two ways. First, play is linked to school success and achievement. It predicts cognitive development and creativity. It also predicts social development, communication, and motor skills, such as handwriting. Learners who play cooperatively are liked better by peers, which promotes liking of school and motivation in the classroom (Fantuzzo et al., 2004). Second, play is a legitimate classroom activity because students learn through play (McCune & Zanes, 2001). Playful learning that is carefully designed and challenging is a powerful approach to instruction (Lillard et al., 2013).

Use Play in Your Classroom to Support Learning

As a teacher, you face two difficult challenges:

1. Getting learners to attend to your agenda.

2. Providing practice for skill development while sustaining interest.

Play helps meet both challenges. Play provides opportunities for practice, and mental freshening or physical wakening, so that learners can attend to school work with greater alertness. Play promotes creativity because learners become more alert, more relaxed, more motivated, and more exploratory in their mindset. Thus, you may want to promote play in your classroom, particularly before an activity that calls for creativity. To promote play in your classroom, follow these guidelines:

1. *Provide props, space, and time for pretense play.* This is primarily appropriate for preschools. Such play can facilitate literacy when preschoolers pretend to be a shopper buying items or a waitress taking orders (Roskos & Christie, 2001).

2. *Provide board games and puzzles when appropriate.* Playing with challenging puzzles helps toddlers develop better spatial skills, which are important for math and science ability (Levine, Ratliff, Huttenlocher, & Cannon, 2012). In Chapter 4, you learned that playing board games helped preschoolers learn number sense. Other games, like Scrabble, solidify older students' vocabulary and spelling skills. Games like checkers and Monopoly provide practice for math, problem-solving, and strategic thinking—as well as social skills.

3. *Use games for "drill and practice."* Games like Bingo can be used to review history, physiology, or other topics. For example, practice the order of operations with Bingo; instead of calling out numbers, write expressions (e.g., $2x + 3 = 7$) that when correctly computed will result in the numbers.

4. *Use play centers.* Play centers can help learners become more literate if they include props like books, paper, crayons, and letters. Play centers are common in preschools, but can be adapted to elementary classrooms. Play centers for math and science could include a fix-it shop, a grocery store, or a museum. Two examples follow:

   • In a unit on chemistry, 6th-graders went to the classroom crime lab where they pretended to be detectives who had to analyze mysterious substances found on an envelope and in footprints in order to determine who was at the crime scene (Jarrett, 1997).

   • In a unit on early explorers (e.g., Columbus, Desoto), 5th-graders could go to a "time machine," created by enclosing an area with file cabinets. Inside the time machine they could play with a compass, goggles, protractor, map, journals, travel brochures, and reference books. The learners enjoyed it more than covering the same content in lecture. Some chose to do worksheets in the time machine, but said it "doesn't feel like doing Social Studies" (Romeo & Young, 1999).

5. *Incorporate mind-play into your lessons* (Conklin, 2014). This is primarily appropriate in late elementary and secondary classrooms. Mind-play includes storytelling and imagining. For example, in history class you can role-play (e.g., reenact a battle) or play "what if" games, in which a statement contrary to fact is held as true and learners are asked to imagine the result (e.g., what if Napoleon had not sold Louisiana to the United States?). In science class, you can ask what would happen if the sun split in half or ask learners to picture themselves in an atom and describe what they would see. Such mind-play promotes critical thinking and requires learners to acquire and use knowledge, while being fun.

At an elementary school, many learners arrive half an hour before school starts due to bus scheduling. The learners must sit quietly in rows on the gym floor. Adults patrol the gym to quell any attempts at play. Is this a good policy? What do you think the school's rationale is? What would happen if learners were encouraged to play? Defend your answer using the research discussed here.

Play is not just for preschoolers. Classroom activities that are play-like are more interesting and engaging even for adolescents (Conklin, 2014). Too often adults view play as a break from adolescents' real work, instead of viewing play as useful. Play has a place in your classroom. Play also has a place in out-of-class time. Let's discuss serious games and recess next.

Consider Using Educational Electronic Games

serious games
electronic games carefully designed to teach children school-relevant content. They may be used in or out of the classroom.

Serious games are technology-based games designed to teach school-relevant content, both in and out of the classroom. The games usually involve avatars in multi-user virtual environments. For example, in the game *A World Without Oil,* students work together to determine how a global oil crisis might affect their community. In serious games, players can be scientists, writers, and dictators. They can solve real-world problems even though they do not yet have real expertise. Virtual worlds with avatars have even been created for kindergarteners, where they learn content like how to care for pets (Marsh, 2010).

Do serious games promote learning as well as traditional instruction? There is not yet enough research to answer this question. Thus far, results are more promising for learning language and for physical education (PE) (i.e., exergames), than for history, math, or science. Serious games may be most effective when combined with feedback and good instruction that links the virtual world to the real world (Young et al., 2012). They may be more engaging than traditional instruction; students often voluntarily do "homework" to progress in the game (Barab, Gresalfi, & Ingram-Goble, 2010).

Promote Recess

The American Academy of Pediatrics' policy is that recess should not be withheld from children for punitive or academic reasons because it is crucial to their well-being (American Academy of Pediatrics, 2013b). Recess is an opportunity to engage in physical activity, social interaction, and play—all of which are beneficial (Pellegrini & Bohn, 2005). Recess helps focus attention: when learners have longer periods of time before recess, their attention wanes, but immediately following recess, they are significantly more attentive. Recall Figure 2.11, which shows that the brain is more active following mild exercise. Among older learners, sports and PE may have the same effects as recess. Indeed, teens who participate in more sports and PE are likely to earn higher grades than those who do not (Robert Wood Johnson Foundation, 2009).

Lack of recess may be linked to two current epidemics: nearsightedness and attention-deficit/hyperactivity disorder (ADHD). Children who play outside, where they focus on distant objects, during recess are less likely to develop nearsightedness (Wu, Tsai, Wu, Yang, & Kuo, 2013). The rising diagnosis of ADHD may also be partly a result of insufficient recess. Learners with ADHD may need more playtime in the school schedule. Even learners without ADHD need a few hours of frolic each day. Learners who are given ADHD medication increase their attention, but at the cost of playfulness. Attention-promoting drugs diminish desire to play (Panksepp, 1998).

Boys in particular may need more opportunity for R&T play at school. R&T play is one of the few contexts in which boys experience physical contact among friends.

It is an opportunity to demonstrate caring and friendship, as well as have fun. When educators prohibit R&T play at school, they deny boys the opportunity to express caring toward one another, which is important for their development (Reed & Brown, 2001).

There has been a trend in recent decades to devote less time to recess and physical education, although there is great variation across school districts in the United States. African American and low-SES learners are less likely to have recess time than are other learners (Barros, Silver, & Stein, 2009). Countries with higher academic achievement than the United States provide more playtime during the school day. For example, Finland has one of the highest-achieving education systems in the world. Finnish learners are typically given a 15-minute recess after every 45-minute lesson (Alvarez, 2004). Unfortunately, the movement toward less playtime during school in the United States is coupled with less playtime outside of school. For example, learners are more likely to be driven to school rather than walk with friends. They are more likely to replace neighborhood play with TV watching. Thus, fostering play at school is becoming more important, even as it is being increasingly neglected or actively prohibited (Ginsburg, 2007; Singer & Lythcott, 2002).

In summary, in this section on the social child, you have learned how important learners' social competence is to success at school and what you can do as a teacher to promote their competence. In Chapter 9, you learned how to promote learners' people-reading ability, moral character, and humor. In Chapter 10, you learned how to promote prosocial behavior, reduce aggression, and help learners resolve conflicts. In this chapter, you learned how to promote their acceptance in the peer group, their friendships, and their play at school. In Section 5, The Whole Child, you will learn how physical, cognitive, emotional, and social factors work together to influence your students.

My Teaching

Important factors linked to learners' peer status, friendships, and play have been discussed in other chapters. Review the "Reflections on Practice" sections from these other chapters, where you learned how to do the following:

- Promote academic skills. Learners with better skills are more accepted in the classroom (see Chapter 5).
- Develop a secure teacher–student relationship and promote school bonding. Secure relationships protect learners from rejection and support play (see Chapter 6).
- Use effective discipline and an authoritative teaching style. Children who receive harsh, punitive discipline tend to be rejected by peers. Authoritative teaching facilitates the acceptance of poorly behaved learners and promotes mature play (see Chapter 7).
- Promote emotional competence. Emotionally competent learners are more accepted by peers and have more mature play (see Chapter 8).
- Promote social cognition. Theory of Mind ability promotes play and friendship formation. Humor is a form of playfulness linked to popularity (see Chapter 9).
- Promote social competence. Prosocial behavior enhances peer status and promotes high-quality friendships (see Chapter 10).

In addition, to ensure that you promote your learners' peer status, friendships, and play, periodically ask yourself the following:

1. Am I aware of the peer status of each student in my classroom? Do I know which students are neglected and which students are rejected?
2. Do I help rejected learners develop social and academic competence? Do I coach friendship skills when needed? Can the counselor help me with rejected students?
3. Are my behaviors contributing negatively or positively to each learner's reputation among classmates? Do I praise rejected learners' positive behavior or special talents?
4. Am I aware of how the seating arrangement in my classroom affects peer status and friendships?
5. Do I use cooperative learning in my classroom? If so, do I hold both individuals and the group accountable? Do I teach students how to work cooperatively?
6. Am I aware of the friendships in my classroom? Could I draw a sociometric map of my students? Does each of my students have a close friend in class?
7. Does my school make an effort to keep friends together across school years? Do I encourage friends to work together? Do learners have enough opportunity to socialize during the school day?
8. Is negative or positive peer pressure operating in my classroom? Does my school group delinquent learners together unnecessarily?
9. Does my school have an effective STI or HIV/AIDS prevention program?
10. Do I facilitate play in my classroom? Do I use "mind-play" in the classroom?
11. Does our school provide enough recess or "break" time during the school day? Are learners with ADHD in my class getting enough physical play time?

Professional Resource Download

Summary of Age Trends in Peer Status, Friendship, and Play

	Peer Status	Friendship	Play
Infancy & Toddlerhood (Birth–2 Years)	• Peer status is not applied to infants and toddlers.	• Toddlers may have an identifiable friend as early as 10 to 12 months. • Toddlers typically have only one friend. • Gender segregation in friendships is not yet apparent.	• Solitary functional play is the most common type of play in infancy. • Sociodramatic play begins at about age 2.
Early Childhood (3–5 Years)	• Preschoolers can readily identify who they like and dislike in their classroom. • Young children are not rejecting of withdrawn peers unless their behavior is extreme. • Perceived popular children (aggressive leaders) may be identified as early as kindergarten.	• Children use the word "friend" by age 3–4 and can readily identify their friends. • The basis of friendship is primarily proximity. • Preschoolers are subject to peer pressure. • Gender segregation is apparent by age 3. However, it is normal for preschoolers to have male and female friends. • Preschoolers begin to spend more time with child companions than adult companions.	• Sociodramatic play increases dramatically, peaking at about age 5–6. • Play becomes increasingly complex, social, and less realistic.
Middle Childhood (6–12 Years)	• Social competence (especially aggression) is not strongly linked to peer status until 3rd grade, after which it becomes important. • Between 1st and 4th grades, social withdrawal becomes more strongly linked to rejection. • Peer status becomes more stable through elementary school.	• Most children have 3–8 friends, with peer networks averaging 5–13. • Friendships become more stable. • Homophily becomes stronger, particularly for aggression. • Gender segregation peaks. Having both male and female friends is unusual. • Children who cross gender boundaries have fewer friends. Girls' friendships are more intimate than are boys' by age 6. • Girls' networks are smaller and more exclusive than boys' initially, but then they become similar in size.	• Frequency of play peaks in early to middle childhood. Rough-and-tumble (R&T) play, constructive play, and games with rules all increase in frequency. • Sports participation emerges. • Pretend play diminishes but is still present. • Play becomes more complex and rule oriented.

Summary of Age Trends in Peer Status, Friendship, and Play

	Peer Status	Friendship	Play
Adolescence (13–19 Years)	• Peer status tends to remain stable as children transition to high school. • Adolescents who are vulnerable to negative peer pressure tend to be from authoritarian or permissive families. • Teachers have less influence on students' reputation in adolescence than at younger ages.	• Adolescents spend more time with friends than do younger children. • Girls' networks become larger than boys'. • Homophily is stronger in adolescence. • Delinquent youth may form a gang. Some children may temporarily join a gang as they transition to high school, but then leave it. • Gender segregation still exists for friendships, but gender boundaries are crossed more frequently. • Many adolescents have a romantic relationship by 12th grade. • About half of youth report having had intercourse by the end of high school. • Some youth identify as lesbian, gay, bisexual, or questioning. • STDs are among the most common diseases in adolescence.	• Adolescents often turn work into play. • Adolescents often play "mind games." • R&T play may be used to cross gender boundaries or to disguise aggression. • Solitary constructive play and pretense play continue, but play of games with rules such as board games diminishes (but is still present). An exception is that participation in sports grows.

⌄⌄ Professional Resource Download

Chapter Summary

11-1 Peer Status

- Peer status refers to learners' level of acceptance in the group and is typically categorized as popular, neglected, rejected, controversial, or average.
- Peer status is fairly stable. Rejected status is the most stable.
- Prosocial behavior is linked to sociometric popularity. Aggression and withdrawal are linked to rejection. "Perceived popular" learners may be aggressive—they are not well liked, but have high status.
- Parenting factors associated with peer acceptance include promotion of prosocial behavior, providing opportunities for peer interaction, and direct coaching.
- Rejection may lead to aggression, depression, school avoidance, and low academic achievement.
- There are generally no gender differences in peer status. Low-SES learners are more likely to be rejected.
- Teachers can facilitate learners' acceptance by improving their behavior, altering their reputation, and increasing social interaction through deliberate seating arrangements and use of cooperative learning.

11-2 Friendship and Peer Networks

- Most learners, including rejected learners, have friends. Friendships vary in quality. Small groups of friends are cliques.
- Learners select friends who are similar to themselves, and then friends cause one another to become even more similar.
- Gender segregation grows through childhood, but in adolescence gender boundaries begin to be crossed. Romance can have positive or negative effects on adolescents.
- About half of adolescents do not have sex; those who begin sexual activity early and have multiple partners are at risk for STIs. STIs, including HIV/AIDS, have become more prevalent among adolescents. AIDS is associated with psychological, behavioral, cognitive, and motor problems in some learners.
- Learners who have high-quality friendships at one age are likely to have them at a later age, but they are not likely to be the same friends across time.
- Prosocial learners are more likely to have high-quality friendships than are antisocial learners, but antisocial learners are not necessarily friendless. Having low-quality friends is associated with increased delinquency.
- Girls have more emotionally close, intimate friendships, but similar numbers of friends and just as much conflict among friends as boys.
- Learners with friends in the classroom spend more time on-task, participate more, and like school more than do friendless learners.
- Teachers can help learners develop friendships in the classroom in several ways: promote prosocial behavior, promote school bonding, keep friends together within the class and across years, provide opportunities for socializing, and recruit the help of the counselor for needy learners. Teachers should not group aggressive or deviant youth together.

11-3 Play

- Play is behavior that has no immediate function and is pleasurable, voluntary, spontaneous, and flexible. It predicts learners' cognitive, social, physical, and language skills.
- Different types of play reflect different levels of social and cognitive maturity. Learners with greater emotional and social competence play more maturely.
- Most learners engage in sports, which have many benefits but also some costs depending on the situation.
- Play in the classroom, including educational electronic games, is motivating and contributes to skill development. Recess improves achievement by providing learners with opportunity to play.

chapter 12

AlohaHawaii/Shutterstock.com

Language and Literacy

How do children develop a good command of the language and learn to read and write well? Would it surprise you to learn that many teachers feel ill-prepared to teach these skills? Yet you will need to teach these skills *even if you are not an English teacher and have had no specialized training in literacy*. In this chapter, we will discuss how students acquire language and literacy skills. **After you read this chapter, you will be able to:**

12-1 Describe how language develops with age, and how to promote language development.

12-2 Describe how literacy skills develop with age, and how to promote good reading and writing skills.

12-3 Apply the major theories of learning and cognition to teaching literacy.

12-1 Language Development

> *Mrs. Shafer finds out she will have Micah in her 4th-grade class. She is dismayed because she saw Micah being scolded in the hallway throughout 3rd grade; she doesn't want another problem student. Sure enough, as Micah begins 4th grade, he misbehaves constantly. He also arrives late every day. Mrs. Shafer wants to stop this immediately because entering class after activities are under way makes it hard for Micah to catch up. Mrs. Shafer buys Micah an alarm clock. Micah arrives at school on time. After a few weeks, Micah says to Mrs. Shafer, "Can I keep that… um…that… that time-keeper thing?" This simple question reveals that Micah does not know the word for clock. Intrigued, Mrs. Shafer begins noticing other signs of limited language. She arranges for Micah to work with a language specialist. As Micah's speech and vocabulary improve, so does his behavior. Today, Micah is in 9th grade, where his grades have improved substantially, to a B minus GPA, and he is only occasionally misbehaving.*

Micah's language problems undermined his success at school. Why did he have language problems? There could be several reasons, because all aspects of the child—physical, cognitive, emotional, and social—affect complex skills like language. Culture also affects language. We will discuss each of these topics, but let's begin by defining language. **Language** is a collection of words or signs used in a systematic way that allows people to communicate with each other. This can include speech, sign language, and gestures. Thus, language is both verbal and nonverbal.

12-1a Types of Language: Nonverbal and Verbal

Nonverbal language is communication that does not include words, such as posture, gesture, and facial expression. Gesture may be innate language that forms the foundation of speech and thought. Speaking and gesture go hand-in-hand (pun intended). They are paired as early as 7 months (although infant babbling isn't exactly speaking) and on into adulthood (Iverson & Fagan, 2004). In fact, when you constrain adults' hands, their speech is less fluent.

Verbal language, on the other hand, does involve words and speech. It is typically divided into *receptive* and *expressive*. Receptive language refers to understanding others' speech, and expressive language refers to making one's thoughts known to others. Development of expressive language lags behind receptive language. For example, 1-year-olds may obey commands, like "Get your shoes," before they are able to talk. Thus, language-impaired students in your classroom, like Micah, are more likely to have expressive than receptive problems.

There are five key components of verbal language: (1) phonemes, (2) morphemes, (3) semantics, (4) syntax, and (5) pragmatics. At the most basic level is a **phoneme**, or speech sound. The word *dog* has three phonemes: /d/, /o/, and /g/. The letter *g* expresses two phonemes: the hard (e.g., get) and the soft (e.g., gin) pronunciations. There are a limited number of phonemes—roughly 50 in English and 100 to 800 in all the world's languages (Beatty, 2001; Gibbs, 2002). **Phonological awareness** is the ability to identify phonemes or the sounds of language. This is a critically important skill for learning to read (Hulme & Snowling, 2013). Students have phonological

language
a collection of words or signs used in a systematic way that allows people to communicate with each other. Language can be verbal or nonverbal.

nonverbal language
communication that does not include words, such as posture, gesture, and facial expression.

verbal language
communication that involves words and speech, in contrast to nonverbal language.

phoneme
a sound in speech. The most basic unit of language.

phonological awareness
the ability to identify phonemes or the sound structure of language.

awareness if they can do tasks like say *plig* without the *l*, or tell which word doesn't rhyme among "bat, pad, had," or tap the number of sounds in mat: three taps for /m/, /ae/, and /t/.

At the next level, **morphemes** are the smallest language unit that contains meaning. Morphemes refer to units of meaning rather than units of sound. Morphemes can be word roots, suffixes, and prefixes. The word "dogs" has two morphemes: /dog/ and /s/. The /s/ adds the meaning *plural* to the meaning *dog*. The word *unhelpful* has three morphemes: /un/, /help/, and /ful/. If you change just one phoneme in "dog" to "fog" you get a different morpheme. Morphological awareness is also an important skill for learning to read. Students have morphological awareness when they know about the structure of words and how to manipulate them, like changing words from present tense (John feeds the fish) to past tense (John fed the fish).

Semantics refers to making meanings, or the way you use words and word combinations to express ideas. When you teach vocabulary, you build your students' semantic skills. **Syntax** refers to the way words are organized into phrases and sentences, such as a verb followed by a noun, or preceded by an adverb. "He reads the book" is typical syntax in English, but "The book he reads" is typical in Turkish. **Pragmatics** refers to using language appropriately according to sociocultural rules. For example, you adjust your speech based on whether you are asking a favor or giving a command, and whether you are talking to a child or to your boss. To interpret a spoken sentence, you must identify phonemes, segment them into words, interpret their semantic meaning, analyze the syntax, and activate pragmatic rules (Trout, 2003). Your brain is able to process all these components almost instantly in your native language. Let's look at how this remarkable ability develops.

morphemes
the smallest unit of language that contains meaning. It can include word roots, suffixes, and prefixes.

semantics
the meaning of language.

syntax
the way words are organized into phrases and sentences in a language.

pragmatics
how language is used in social context.

12-1b Age Trends in Language

Language develops dramatically in the first 5 years of life. By middle childhood, development is less dramatic, but important developments continue to adulthood.

Infancy and Toddlerhood (Birth to 2 Years)

Children are born with preferences and capacities that help them develop language. For example, infants prefer to listen to human voices that are communicating with them rather than mere background voices or similarly complex, but nonhuman sounds (Shultz & Vouloumanos, 2010). They are capable of learning to take turns as their caretakers respond to the infants' vocalizations, and then the infants respond to the caretaker's vocalizations (Bornstein, Putnick, Cote, Haynes, & Suwalsky, 2015). Taking turns is an essential part of communication. Toddlers also prefer to interact with people who speak their own language (Kinzler, Dupoux, & Spelke, 2012).

Infants first communicate nonverbally through emotional expression, tone of voice, and gesture. Toddlers use gestures like words. For example, they make a grasping gesture to communicate "give me that," and they raise their arms to communicate "pick me up." Pointing is important (see Photo 12.1)—infants and toddlers will look where

PHOTO 12.1 Although this toddler cannot talk yet, she can command her parents' attention using the imperial toddler finger.

Efficient Brains Can Make Language Learning Harder

When you were a newborn you could distinguish all sounds in English, Chinese, Twi, or any world language. However, by the time you were a year old, you could no longer readily distinguish the sounds of nonnative languages. Chinese toddlers can distinguish subtle differences in Chinese better than English, and English toddlers can do the opposite. As an infant, you also babbled using phonemes that could be part of many languages, but after about 1 year of age you emitted phonemes only from your native language (Gervain & Mehler, 2010).

This means that it is more difficult for you to hear subtle differences in words from another language now, as compared with when you were born. Also, as a very young child you could develop native-like accents, cadence, and grammar in another language, whereas today you would find it difficult to obtain proficiency and a native-like accent (Fox, Levitt, & Nelson, 2010).

Does this mean you were smarter as a baby? Not in most ways, hopefully. Instead, your brain is more efficient now. Recall from Chapter 2 that your brain prunes synapses that are not used. The remaining circuits are more efficient and fine-tuned (Blakemore & Choudhury, 2006). Is it ever too late to achieve native-like ability in another language? There is no magic cut-off age, but it gets harder after early childhood.

adults point, and they will point to direct adults' attention (Tomasello, Carpenter, & Liszkowski, 2007). Pointing to share interest in something is a uniquely human action. For example, a toddler might point at ducks because she wants her dad to look at them.

Toddlers then begin to combine gestures and words. When you talk with toddlers, gestures help them understand your speech. For example, you might say, "Hand me the book" while pointing at the book. If your speech and gesture are mismatched, like pointing at a crayon, toddlers will follow the gesture and hand you the crayon, whereas older children will follow the speech and hand you the book. Older children give primacy to speech (see Chapter 3).

Early Childhood (3 to 5 Years)

Speech replaces gesture during the first 3 years (Iverson & Goldin-Meadow, 2005). The newborn is unable to speak, but the typical preschooler speaks almost fluently. The sequence of this dramatic development is outlined in Table 12.1. This sequence is universal, meaning that it occurs across cultures and languages and even in deaf children who are exposed to sign language. This sequence is also followed by 2- to 6-year-olds learning a new language when they are adopted into another country, such as from Russia to the United States, although they go through the sequence more quickly than infants (Snedeker, Geren, & Shafto, 2007). The ages in Table 12.1 are approximations, because some variation is normal.

When you talk to young children, you probably use a higher pitch, exaggerated ups and downs in pitch, slower tempo, limited vocabulary, and more rhythm than usual. This is known as **child-directed speech** (also called *motherese*). Adults across many cultures use child-directed speech. Even preschoolers use it toward younger children. Infants only a few days old prefer hearing child-directed speech to adult-directed speech (Eaves, Feldman, Griffiths, & Shafto, 2016). Child-directed speech activates the child's brain and fosters learning more than adult-directed speech (Golinkoff, Can, Soderstrom, & Hirsh-Pasek, 2015).

Middle Childhood (6 to 12 Years)

Before 1st grade, children typically master phonemes, or the sound patterns, of their native language. They also master the basics of morphemes and syntax, or the grammatical rules for putting sentences together. Indeed, by 1st grade their use of language is so masterful that they begin to play with language, and much of their humor centers on language such as "knock knock" jokes (see Chapter 9). However, their semantic skills are still developing dramatically, particularly vocabulary.

child-directed speech
a style of speech used with young children that involves higher pitch, exaggerated ups and downs in pitch, slower tempo, and more rhythm than other speech. Also called *motherese*.

TABLE 12.1 Development of language abilities in the first 3 years

Age	Emergent Ability
Birth	Prefer human voices to other complex sounds. Prefer female voices over male voices. Prefer mother's voice over other females' voices. Cries have different sound properties, conveying different meanings.
1–4 months	Cooing begins, which means that infants produce sounds that resemble vowels such as "ooh" and "ahhh."
3–8 months	Babbling begins. Infants produce strings of consonant–vowel syllables (e.g., ma-ma-ma-ma). Babbling provides practice for making speech sounds. At 6 months, babbling includes phonemes that are not part of the native language. Deaf children also babble. Infants are able to discriminate most sounds in the world's languages. Receptive language for family names begins. At 6 months, infants recognize their own name and know that "daddy" pertains to their own dad, not mom and not other men. Around 7–8 months, infants begin to segment individual words from the stream of fluent speech.
9–10 months	Receptive language for objects begins. If someone says "blankie," the infant will look at the object. Infants also understand "no." Infants may comprehend about 50 words, but say none. Deaf children stop babbling. *First gestures* emerge and are used to communicate, most often pointing.
10–15 months	Receptive language grows dramatically. *First words* emerge around 12 months. First words are highly social, such as "bye-bye," "hi," and the names of favorite people. Typically, a repeated phoneme is used to refer to an object (e.g., "baba" means bottle). Ability to discriminate all the phonemes in foreign languages is lost.
15–18 months	Toddlers can follow simple commands, such as "Get your shoes." Toddlers may produce sentence-long utterances with nonsense words that are expressed in meaningful tones, so that you cannot tell what the child is asking, but you can tell it is a question. Speech occurs in *holophrases*, or single-word utterances with multiple meanings (e.g., "cookie" may be used to mean "I want a cookie" or "Look, there is a cookie!"). The 50-word milestone is reached; the average expressive vocabulary is about 50 words. Word learning begins slowly at about 2 words per week. Sometime during this period a *vocabulary spurt* begins, when about 9 words per day are learned.
18–24 months	*First sentences* emerge, where more than one word is combined in a meaningful way. This does not typically occur until toddlers know 50 to 200 words. The average length of utterances is only 2 words. This is the beginning of syntax and *telegraphic speech*, which refers to sentences that sound like a telegram because there are no function words (e.g., "Want cookie" instead of "I want a cookie."). For example, one toddler asked "Where did mommy go?" in the following sequence, from single word utterance, to telegraphic speech, to full sentence: 12 months: Mommy? 17 months: Mommy go? 21 months: Where did mommy go? Common phrases (e.g., "thank you" or "stop it") are treated as one big word. Fast mapping (learning a new word from a single exposure) is evident, but children may need multiple exposures for the learning to stick.
24–30 months	Average vocabulary is about 500 to 600 words. Grammatical words (e.g., "of," "the") are now used as children begin to speak in full sentences. Only 10–15% of 24-month-olds use the words "the" and "these" but 50–60% of 30-month-olds do.

Source: Adapted from Bion, Borovsky, and Fernald (2013); Bornstein et al. (2015); Conboy and Thal (2006); Gervain and Mehler (2010); Graham, Nayer, and Gelman (2011); Jusczyk (2002); Kucker et al. (2015); Snedeker et al. (2007).

Elementary students experience a vocabulary explosion, which is more dramatic than toddlers' vocabulary spurt. For example, in a classic study, the average vocabulary for 1st-graders was roughly 10,000 words, for 3rd-graders 20,000, and for 5th-graders 40,000 (Anglin, 1993). These estimates were calculated conservatively, yet they suggest a rate of 20 words learned per day in elementary school. Do you think you could learn that many now?

Direct instruction probably accounts for only a few hundred words learned in a year—not thousands. Instead, children figure out most words by reasoning. For example, children can figure out what "treelet" means by reasoning that if a piglet is a small pig, a treelet must be a small tree. While 1st-graders are capable of this kind of inference, they do not engage in it to the extent that older children do (Anglin, 1993; Carlisle & Fleming, 2003).

Adolescence (13 to 19 Years)

Vocabulary continues to grow in adolescence. Adolescents, like younger children, learn vocabulary through reasoning, which is usually effective but sometimes leads to wrong conclusions. A 9th-grader assumed that *vocational* education meant "choir or voice training" because she reasoned that it must have to do with *vocal*. Days later she heard an adult praise the district's vocational computer programming class—"Oh, is *that* what vocational means?" she asked. Notice that she used memory and problem solving to correct herself.

Syntax also continues to develop into adolescence. Between kindergarten and 12th grade, sentences become longer and more complex. For example, 3rd-graders might say, "I got a book from the library," but 11th-graders are more likely to say, "When I went to the library, I got the book Linda recommended" (Nippold, Hesketh, Duthie, & Mansfield, 2005).

Pragmatics also continue to develop as adolescents learn to manipulate their listeners. They know that when they explain to the teacher why their homework is not done, they must use a different approach than when they gossip with their friends. Adolescents also process language more rapidly than do elementary school students. These skills combine to produce humor that includes sophisticated wordplay, like double entendres and puns.

Language Learning Is Remarkable

To master language, young children must link words with objects or events; learn words that are abstract (e.g., *truth*) or are purely grammatical (e.g., *the, a, that*); segment words from the stream of speech; distinguish nouns, verbs, and prepositions; and put them in the correct order in a sentence. What a task! Add to this complexity the sheer volume of language—a 2-year-old typically listens to 20,000 to 40,000 words a day (Kuhl, 2000). Yet toddlers manage to learn their native language with remarkable ease from casual interaction, without formal training. How is this possible? Very young children already have several abilities that help them learn language:

- *Ability to hear language in the womb.* At 30 weeks' gestation, infants can tell the difference between male and female speakers, their mother's voice from those of other females, and different consonant and vowel sounds (Kisilevsky et al., 2003).

- *Ability to distinguish grammatical from lexical words* (Shi, 2014). Lexical words are verbs and nouns like *chew*, *hide*, *chair*. Grammatical words provide skeletal structure to a sentence, like *the, a, and, you, that.*

- *Ability to remember and learn* (see Chapters 3 and 4). Toddlers are capable of remembering a new word from a single exposure (Jaswal & Markman, 2001). This remarkable ability is known as **fast mapping**. In a famous experiment, adults asked preschoolers, "You see those two trays over there? Bring me the chromium one, not the red one, the chromium one." The preschoolers knew red, but had never heard the word *chromium* before. After this single indirect exposure to the word, when tested a week later, half the preschoolers could correctly identify the color chromium, which was olive green in the experiment (Carey & Bartlett, 1978). Deep understanding of a word, however, requires multiple exposures (Kucker et al, 2015).

fast mapping
the ability to learn a new word from a single, or very minimal, exposure without deliberate instruction or corrective feedback.

- *Ability to construct rules* without direct instruction (see Chapter 3). If told a bird is a "wug," preschoolers will tell you two birds are "wugs," showing they have constructed basic rules for syntax (Gleason, 1958). They also mistakenly apply syntax rules to irregular words. For example, they might say "goed" instead of "went." Goed is a logical application of the rule to add "ed" to make past tense. Such mistakes are called *overregularization*.

- *Ability to reason* (see Chapter 4). Fast mapping is partly the result of reasoning. In the chromium study, the preschoolers reasoned that the not-red tray must be chromium. Toddlers also infer what a word means using the rules of syntax. For example, if you say, "She blicked the baby," they infer that "blick" is something you do to someone else (Yuan & Fisher, 2009). This ability to infer the meaning of words using syntax is called **syntactic bootstrapping**.

syntactic bootstrapping
a process in which young children figure out the meaning of a new word, without explicit instruction, based on the syntax of the sentence in which the word is used.

Despite these abilities, some argue that language is simply too complex for children to learn at such a young age, suggesting that language must be prewired into human brains. The question of how young children master language has been hotly debated (see Box 12.1). While all typical children will become language users, there are differences in ability among individual children. Let's turn to this topic next.

12-1c Individual Diversity in Language

You have just read about typical age trends in language. Some children have language delays, meaning their development falls *well outside of these age trends*. Language delays can have physical, cognitive, emotional, or social causes, such as hearing impairment, cognitive disability, autism, disorganized attachment, and genetic predisposition (Bishop, 2006).

In addition, some children have lower verbal ability than others, even though they may not have delayed language. Differences in verbal ability are stable from age 20 months to 14 years; however, stability is higher after age 4 (Bornstein, Hahn, Putnick, & Suwalsky, 2014). This suggests that intervention before age 4 may be ideal. Yet, it is difficult to know whether to worry about a young child who talks "funny" or "late." Generally, as long as children clearly articulate words by 1st grade, talking a little funny in preschool is not a concern (Bishop & Snowling, 2004). Toddlers who begin talking a little late will typically develop normal language abilities by

BOX 12.1 theories & theorists

Language as Core Knowledge—The Great Debate

How do children learn language in just a few short years? Historically, there have been two dramatically different views—the environmentalist (nurture) and the nativist (nature) views. B. F. Skinner was a champion of the environmentalist view. He believed that language is learned. According to behaviorists, all behavior is influenced by the environment (see Chapter 3). Children's behavior results from a combination of their current and past history of reinforcement. Thousands of studies have shown that reinforcement shapes all kinds of behavior in humans and other animals. Why would verbal behavior be different? Children learn to speak when their infant babblings are reinforced. Children learn to speak like those around them. Children in Japan learn to speak Japanese, not Finnish. Skinner published a fascinating 1957 book on the topic, called *Verbal Behavior*.

Noam Chomsky is a champion of the nativist view. He believes that the rules of how words are put together to create meaning is innate, or biologically determined, not learned (Chomsky, 2006). Thus, syntax is core knowledge (see Chapter 5), which he calls the "universal grammar." Chomsky believes it is part of the human genotype that evolved through natural selection. Nevertheless, you learn the specific words in your native language. In 1959 he wrote a famous, scathing review of Skinner's book, which launched a debate that is still ongoing (Chomsky, 1959). Chomsky did acknowledge that behaviorism could adequately explain other domains of behavior, just not language.

What Is the Evidence for the Nativist View? First, children do not merely imitate what they hear—given a limited vocabulary, using grammar, children can generate an infinite number of sentences that they have never heard before. Such sentences were not learned through conditioning. Second, typical children across the world proceed through the same sequence outlined in Table 12.1 at roughly the same time. Third, language is remarkably uniform across the human species. Vocabulary and phonetics vary from one language to another, but syntax does not vary much. Chomsky views all humans as having one language, with small variations. Fourth, lower animals have a biologically determined ability to communicate, so why not humans? Fifth, perhaps the most compelling evidence is that language is too big a task for young children to learn through operant conditioning. Chomsky wrote: "The great fact that all normal children acquire essentially comparable grammars of great complexity with remarkable rapidity suggests that human beings are somehow specially designed to do this . . ." (Chomsky, 1959, p. 57).

Grammar is very complex, with abstract rules. No one deliberately teaches these rules to children. In fact, you probably cannot articulate the grammatical rules of your own language, but 3-year-olds can apply them. Why attribute language ability to a meager few years of learning rather than to millions of years of evolution (Chomsky, 2006)?

Skinner thought that Chomsky's argument was illogical. Anything that cannot be learned cannot be selected for through evolution, because anything that does not have consequences for the individual cannot confer a selective advantage. As one theorist put it, "Both evolution and reinforcement theory provide that what survives

5 or 6 years of age. Recall from Chapter 6 that shy Eric began to talk late but went on to be a high achiever. However, some children who do not begin talking until 24 to 30 months may have problems into adolescence, such as poor grammar, vocabulary, and reading comprehension (Rescorla, 2005). If you are concerned about a particular child, seek the help of a language specialist. The federal Individuals with Disabilities Education Act (IDEA) mandates that screening services be available to all children.

What Do Individual Differences in Language Ability Predict?

Low verbal ability affects children's success in the classroom, as it did for Micah. He was difficult to understand in class and talked in a strange way. For example, when describing his dog, he might say, "A lot times he bark the kids. Sometimes he eat and drink." His inability to communicate clearly led to isolation from peers, so Micah

behaviorally is what increases survival chances, or, roughly, what reinforces" (MacCorquodale, 1970, p. 94). If grammar has consequences for the individual, then it can be learned.

What Are Contemporary Views? Today, the behaviorist view that vocabulary depends on practice and modeling is widely accepted. However, the behaviorist view that children are passive learners is not. Instead, children are seen as active learners who figure out language using their information-processing abilities. They *reason by analogy* (Ninio, 2006). For example, toddlers learn specific patterns of word combinations, like the verb–noun pattern "get blankie." They then apply the patterns to new combinations, like the verb–noun "want cookie" (Bannard & Matthews, 2008). They also *reason using statistics* based on how often they hear one set of sounds versus another set (Aslin & Newport, 2012). For example, if an infant hears "Whataprettybaby!" in the stream of speech, how does she know "pretty" and "baby" are words, but their intersection "tyba" is not? Because "pre" is the first syllable in words more often than "ty." "Tyba" is not likely to be a word, statistically speaking (Pelucchi, Hay, & Saffran, 2009). Infants notice that the /nt/ sound usually occurs at the end of words (e.g., went, want, point, plant), so when they hear /nt/, they anticipate the start of a new word (Gervain & Mehler, 2010). You may not think of them as statisticians, but 8-month-olds can find words in a stream of speech in a novel language based on frequency alone. An infant who hears "Mommylovesherlittlegirlareyoumommyslittlegirl?" would recognize that "mommy" was repeated.

Once infants have identified words in the stream of speech, they can begin to link words with meanings (Estes, Evans, Alibali, & Saffran, 2007). They do this using statistics as well. Although children can "fast map" a word to an object when they clearly go together, children usually hear so many words at once that it is not clear which word goes with the object. They learn concrete nouns like *cat* before verbs like *go*. Infants assume that the word that is paired with an object more often is the name of that object (Yu & Smith, 2007). Infants learn both vocabulary and syntax by actively pulling patterns from the speech they hear (Gentner & Namy, 2006).

This statistical learning occurs beyond infancy. For example, 6- to 8-year-olds learn the active structure *"the boy is pushing the girl"* earlier than the passive structure *"the girl is being pushed by the boy"* because the active structure is more common in English (Kidd & Arciuli, 2016). You will find that younger students have more trouble understanding passive sentences.

The ability to learn through statistics and analogy, coupled with children's other amazing learning abilities, supports a more environmentalist than nativist view. That is, much of language learning can be explained by the same general processes involved in all learning (Gentner & Namy, 2006). However, this does not rule out the possibility of biologically endowed abilities that combined with learning develop into full language ability (Spencer et al., 2009; Toro, Nespor, Mehler, & Bonatti, 2008).

often played alone at recess. He also struggled to read. His language problems had both academic and social consequences, until he received intervention.

Academic achievement

Poor *nonverbal* language ability predicts low academic achievement. Students who don't read others' nonverbal cues tend to have lower standardized test scores (Nowicki & Duke, 1992). Similarly, poor *verbal* ability predicts academic problems and learning disabilities. Verbal ability is even linked to math ability, perhaps because the same areas of the brain are involved in both (Gelman & Butterworth, 2005). This may also occur because poor language ability predicts poor executive functioning (Kuhn et al., 2014) and slower processing speed, which predict low academic achievement (see Chapter 4).

One aspect of verbal ability—vocabulary size—may be particularly important because it influences reading. Two-year-olds with larger vocabularies have higher reading and math achievement several years later in kindergarten as compared with other toddlers (Morgan, Farkas, Hillemeier, Hammer, & Maczuga, 2015). Vocabulary size is related to how fast students can process information, measured in milliseconds (Marchman & Fernald, 2008), which is important for fluent reading. Students with large vocabularies learn to read more easily, enjoy reading, and read a lot, which increases their vocabulary even more. Imagine being Micah and trying to read 4th-grade books if you do not know words like "clock."

Social competence

Both nonverbal and verbal ability predict social competence. Students who don't read others' *nonverbal* cues tend to be friendless and rejected by peers. Similarly, children who have problems expressing themselves *verbally* tend to have behavior problems, like Micah (see, for example, Dionne, Boivin, Tremblay, Laplante, & Perusse, 2003). You can see how this would work with 4-year-old Keegan:

> *Keegan was coloring with a pile of five crayons next to him. Another boy picked up the blue crayon. Keegan tried to tell him to put it back, but he began stuttering and couldn't get the words out. Frustrated, he slugged the boy and snatched the crayon back.*

Some children who have trouble communicating verbally may communicate with aggression. Others may withdraw from peers rather than aggress. In contrast, students with high verbal ability are likely to play cooperatively, resolve conflicts, and communicate effectively with peers (NICHD Early Child Care Research Network, 2001a; Morgan et al., 2015).

What Predicts Individual Differences in Language Ability?

Verbal ability is predicted by genes (Christopher et al., 2015). Verbal ability is also predicted by information-processing skills. Learners with good *memorizing* and *problem-solving* ability tend to have high verbal ability, whereas learners with slow processing, poor executive functions, and poor working memory are likely to have language impairments (Im-Bolter, Johnson, & Pascual-Leone, 2006; Rose, Feldman, & Jankowski, 2009).

Learners who are deaf or hearing-impaired develop sign language in a pattern that is similar to how hearing learners develop spoken language, but they may be language-delayed. In particular, they may struggle with grammar (Lederberg, Schick, & Spencer, 2013). They benefit from intervention, and the earlier the better. In addition to these genetic, cognitive, and physical factors, social cognition also predicts language development.

Social cognition

Children use their social cognition to learn language. In fact, some scientists think *joint attention* is critical for language learning (Tomasello et al., 2007). This is because children's ability to figure out what others are looking at helps them learn new words. Imagine a toddler pointing at the ducks in a pond when one suddenly takes flight. Father watches the duck and says, "There he goes. Bye-bye, duck." The child, seeing her father watch the duck, also watches the duck and imitates "Bye-bye." Through joint attention, she links words with objects and actions. Infants who use more joint attention than other infants develop better language skills (Munday et al., 2007). Parents who talk with children during joint attention have children with better language skills than parents who talk a lot but not in joint attention with their children (Tomasello et al., 2007).

Children's *theory of mind* (ToM) allows them to go beyond joint attention to infer what an adult is talking about. If toddlers hear their mother use a new word while she is on the phone, they do not apply the word to whatever Mother is looking at. However, if toddlers hear their mother use a new word while she is touching, looking at, or using an object, toddlers will apply the new word to the object (Golinkoff & Hirsh-Pasek, 2006). They could not do this without ToM—that is, without knowing what their mother is thinking about. Children with better social cognition, particularly *joint attention* and *theory of mind,* have better verbal ability. What promotes strong ToM abilities? One answer, as you learned in Chapter 9, is interaction with others, including peers and adults.

Social interaction

In the preceding chapters you learned how social interaction contributes to children's language development:

- In Chapter 6, you learned that attachment is strongly associated with verbal ability. Secure children tend to have greater verbal ability. Children with sensitive, responsive, nonintrusive parents acquire language faster (Pungello, Iruka, Dotterer, Mills-Koonce, & Reznick, 2009). Responsiveness includes saying, "OK, I'll put bubbles in your bath water" when a toddler says "Ba ba in wa wa." Toddlers with unresponsive, depressed mothers tend to have limited vocabularies (Pan, Rowe, Singer, & Snow, 2005). For example, Figure 12.1 shows that in one study almost all toddlers whose mothers were highly responsive had a vocabulary of 50 words by 13 months, but only 20% of children with less-responsive mothers did.

- In Chapter 7, you learned that parents who use induction tend to have children who are more competent communicators, presumably because they are allowed to negotiate during discipline. Also, when parents foster self-control in young children, the children develop better verbal ability (Lunkenheimer et al., 2009).

- In Chapter 8, you learned that children with good emotion regulation have better verbal ability. Children may develop language disorders in environments that are emotionally negative or unresponsive.

- In Chapter 11, you learned that children who engage in frequent, age-appropriate sociodramatic play also have better verbal ability. When young children with low verbal ability are trained to play more, they develop better verbal ability. Play provides motivation to use language with peers and opportunity to learn from them. You also learned that children learn language better when they attend preschool with peers who have high verbal ability (Mashburn, Justice, Downer, & Pianta, 2009).

FIGURE 12.1 Maternal Responsiveness Predicts Toddlers' Verbal Ability.

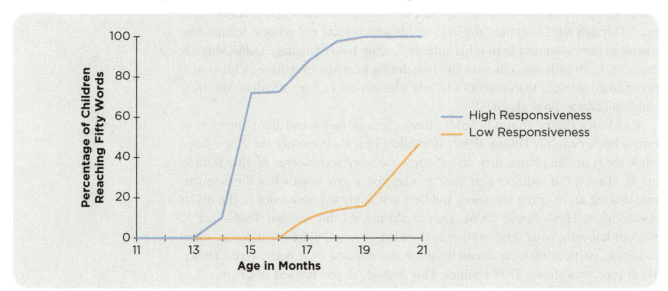

Children whose mothers are highly responsive to their play and vocalizations reach the 50-word vocabulary mark earlier than children with low-responsive mothers. The 50-word vocabulary mark signals the vocabulary spurt and beginning of sentences. At what age did 40% of the children with highly responsive mothers reach the 50-word mark? When did 40% of the children with low-responsive mothers reach this mark? *Source: Tamis-LeMonda, Cristofaro, Rodriguez, and Bornstein (2006).*

In addition to these factors you have learned about in previous chapters, two types of social interaction are particularly important for language development—verbal interaction and joint book reading.

Verbal interaction

Children learn language from verbally interacting with adults (Warlaumont, Richards, Gilkerson, & Oller, 2014). This needs to be interactive, not just passive listening. Merely sitting in front of a television or overhearing language at home does little to promote young children's language development (Schneidman, Arroyo, Levine, & Goldin-Meadow, 2013; Weisleder & Fernald, 2013). Video chat can be helpful, if it involves interactive back-and-forth conversation with eye contact (Roseberry, Hirsh-Pasek, & Golinkoff, 2014).

Both quality and quantity of verbal interaction are important. However, although quantity is important in infancy, by age 2 quality may matter more (Hirsh-Pasek et al., 2015; Rowe, 2012). Quality refers to use of different words, complex words, and complex grammar. For example, research has found that mothers' general talkativeness does not predict children's vocabulary, but the number of words *directed at young children* and the variety of words mothers use does (Hirsh-Pasek et al., 2015; Pan et al., 2005). Parents who use uncommon words have children with higher verbal ability. The typical adult vocabulary is about 40,000 to 100,000 words, but only 3,000 of those words are used frequently. In one study, 99% of the talk between low-socioeconomic status (SES) parents and their preschoolers involved only the 3,000 most common words (Weizman & Snow, 2001). Some children heard no uncommon words, but others heard dozens. Preschoolers whose parents tended to use uncommon words had better vocabulary in 2nd grade.

Joint reading

Another powerful predictor of verbal ability is joint reading. Children who are read to develop better vocabulary and cognitive ability than children who are not (Raikes et al., 2006). Book reading is not driven entirely by the parent. Children with higher verbal ability ask parents to read to them. There is probably a cascading effect, in which parent book reading leads to children's larger vocabulary, which causes children to seek out book reading, which leads to improved vocabulary and knowledge. For families at risk, parents often need training in joint storybook reading in order to provide interaction that fosters children's learning (Landry et al., 2012).

12-1d Group Diversity in Language

There are group differences in nonverbal and verbal ability, but they tend to be smaller than individual differences within groups. For example, studies discussed earlier found substantial diversity within low-SES groups. Keep this *within*-group diversity in mind as you read about *between*-group diversity.

Gender

Girls generally have an advantage in language as compared with boys (Morgan et al., 2015). Girls tend to read nonverbal cues more accurately (Ambady, Bernieri, & Richeson, 2000). They also achieve language milestones a little earlier. For example, toddler girls in one study achieved a 50-word speaking vocabulary on average about a month earlier than did boys (Tamis-LeMonda, Bornstein, & Baumwell, 2001). Such gender differences in language ability are not consistently found, but when found, they favor girls (Halpern, 2011).

Socioeconomic Status

Low-SES children tend to have lower verbal ability than high-SES children (Morgan et al., 2015). Children whose mothers did not graduate from high school are more likely to have a language delay (Campbell et al., 2003). By the age of 3, children in welfare-receiving homes have vocabularies that are half the size of those of their more affluent peers, and the gap persists through childhood (Pungello et al., 2009).

Why are there SES differences in verbal ability? One possibility is opportunity to learn at school and home (see Chapter 1). At school, low-SES students are segregated, beginning with preschool programs like Head Start, where they are exposed to peers with low verbal ability (Mashburn et al., 2009). In kindergarten, low-SES students may receive less vocabulary instruction than their higher income peers (Wright, 2012). At home, low-SES parents tend to speak less often and in less complex ways, use fewer words, use fewer uncommon words, and be less responsive to their children's talk (Golinkoff et al., 2015; Hirsh-Pasek et al., 2015). In contrast, educated parents are more likely to read to and talk with their children. For example, in one study Mexican American middle-class mothers discussed complex concepts (e.g., "Why do we need the flour?") and gave positive feedback (e.g., "Good job!) more than did working-class mothers while cooking with their children (Eisenberg, 2002). A classic study estimated that by age 3, middle- and high-SES children have heard about 40 million words, low-SES children have heard 20 million, and children in poverty only 10 million (Hart & Risley, 1995). The gap in exposure to words between high- and low-SES children is sometimes called the "30 million word gap."

African American English

Standard English (SE)
the form of English used in classroom instruction and textbooks, sometimes called School English.

African American English (AAE)
a dialect of English spoken predominantly by African Americans, sometimes called Ebonics or Black English.

The predominant dialect used in classroom instruction and textbooks is **Standard English (SE)**, also called School English or Formal English. *Most* students experience mismatch between the way informal language is used in the home compared with the more formal usage at school. However, the mismatch is larger for students who speak a dialect other than SE. One such dialect is **African American English (AAE)**, sometimes called Ebonics or Black English. Teachers who are not used to AAE need to guard against forming negative expectations toward students who use AAE (Pearson, Conner, & Jackson, 2013).

AAE is a full dialect that has its own rules. Many language forms that are incorrect in Standard English are accepted in AAE. There are different versions of AAE, but some commonalities include the following (Champion, 2003):

- Saying *ax, bidness,* and *posed to* for *ask, business,* and *supposed to.*

- Stressing the first syllable in words like *PO-lice* and *DE-troit.*

- Omitting possessive /s/ as in *That man hat is on the table.* (*That man's hat is on the table* in SE.)

- Omitting final /ed/ as in *They talk yesterday.* (*They talked yesterday* in SE.)

- Omitting contractions as in *She done well.* (*She's done well* in SE.)

- Omitting final consonants as in *las* for *last.*

- Unique use of *done* as in *I done did her hair* or *I done her hair.* (*I did her hair* in SE.)

- Unique use of *be* as in *He be happy.*

- Using *f* for *th* as in *toof* for *tooth.*

Thus, when AAE-using students say, "My dog name Lady," they are not using incorrect Standard English, but rather are using the home dialect correctly.

Should you force students to use Standard English at school? You should respect students' right to maintain their heritage dialect. However, students also need to learn Standard English because it allows them to participate fully in school, commerce, and society.

code switching
using different language varieties for different situations, such as Standard English at school and African American English at home.

How should you teach Standard English? Simply correcting informal usage is not effective. Instead, teaching students about **code switching** may help. This refers to using different language varieties for different situations, such as SE at school and AAE at home. Point out to students that they code switch as they move between settings, like from the classroom to the playground or sports field. Discuss different patterns of speech without labeling them as correct or incorrect. Invite students to code switch and teach you aspects of their language that differ from SE. This makes them co-discoverers with you of their own language patterns. You can create charts that list the informal version of a phrase next to the SE version and discuss when to use each (see Table 12.2).

TABLE 12.2 Samples for teaching code switching

	AAE	Formal SE
Showing possession	"Yes," said Annie mom.	"Yes," said Annie's mom.
	My dog name is Caesar.	My dog's name is Caesar.
Subject–verb agreement	She work hard.	She works hard.
Using "be"	She my best friend.	She is my best friend.
	Jesse be goin' to the store	Jesse is going to the store.
Showing past time	Yesterday I turn on the TV.	Yesterday I turned on the TV

Source: Adapted from Wheeler and Swords (2010).

This approach can be applied to varied dialects and languages of immigrants. For example, an Appalachian speaker might say "we have 20 mile to go" instead of "20 miles to go." Learners benefit when they can code switch between the home and school language, depending on which is most appropriate.

Immigrant Students and Bilingualism

According to the 2010 U.S. Census, more than one in five children is an immigrant, meaning either the child or at least one parent was born outside the United States. Immigrant children are likely to speak a language other than English at home. Today, about half of immigrant children speak Spanish. The next largest group speaks Chinese. However, immigrant children in the United States have many different heritage languages, such as Russian or Arabic (Photo 12.2).

Most U.S. immigrant children are **bilingual**, meaning they speak both English and their heritage language fluently. Some children are **English language learners (ELL)**[1], meaning they are not yet proficient in English. It takes an average of 3 to 7 years for ELL students to reach proficiency in the new language; younger students take longer but achieve greater fluency (Dixon et al., 2012). In 2013 about 9% of public school students were ELL (U.S. Department of Education, 2015). California has roughly half of the ELL students in the nation. In some districts in California, 60 to 70% of students are ELL.

ELL students are not all immigrants. Many ELL students are born in the United States, but their parents were born outside the United

bilingual
the ability to speak two languages fluently.

English language learner (ELL)
a student whose first language is not English and who is less than proficient in English.

Troy Aossey/Getty Images

PHOTO 12.2 Classes in some schools can have English language learners who speak many different native languages, such as Russian, Spanish, Vietnamese, or Chinese.

---

[1] Other terms you will hear are "language minority (LM) learners" and "English speakers of other languages (ESOL)." These are students who come from homes in which a language other than English is spoken, whether they are fluent in English or not. ELLs and "Limited English Proficients (LEPs)" are also students who come from homes in which a language other than English is spoken, but they are not yet fluent in English. "Dual Language Learner" usually refers to preschoolers who are learning two languages at once, that is, the language of their parents and English.

States. One study found that 60% of 9th-grade ELL students were born in the United States, meaning they had spent many years in school without becoming fluent in English. Some reached an intermediate level of English competence but then stopped making progress. *Foreign*-born ELL students tend to catch up with U.S.-born ELL students by high school (Slama, 2012).

Skill in English is important because it predicts academic achievement (Parker, O'Dwyer, & Irwin, 2014). A study in Boston and San Francisco found that high-achieving ELL students tended to have greater English proficiency than low-achieving ELL students (Suárez-Orozco et al., 2010). There were five patterns of achievement (see Figure 12.2). Two-thirds of students had low or declining achievement across 5 years, and one-third had high or improving achievement. Some low achievers believed their undocumented status would prevent them from attending college, which undermined their attitudes toward school. A protective factor that nearly every improver had was a mentor (see Chapter 1), which is a role you could play for your immigrant students.

When first immersed in a second language, it is common for children to have a temporary silent period that lasts from weeks to months, as they focus on listening and comprehending. It is also common for children to be slightly delayed in language when mastering two languages simultaneously. Many ELL students exclusively speak their home language until age 3, when they enter preschool. Often their progress in the home language slows, but their growth in the new language is rapid. Do not be concerned about temporary delays—in the long term, bilingual students often have better language abilities than their monolingual peers.

Bilingualism has cognitive benefits. Bilingual students are better at tests of executive functions, working memory, inhibitory control, math skills, and theory of mind than monolingual students. This has been found across several languages and as early as age 3 (see, for example, Adesope, Lavin, Thompson, & Ungerleider, 2010; Bialystok, 2015). They are also less egocentric and better able to understand a speaker's meaning and perspective (Fan, Liberman, Keysar, & Kinzler, 2015). It appears that switching

FIGURE 12.2 Patterns of Academic Achievement Among Immigrant Adolescents.

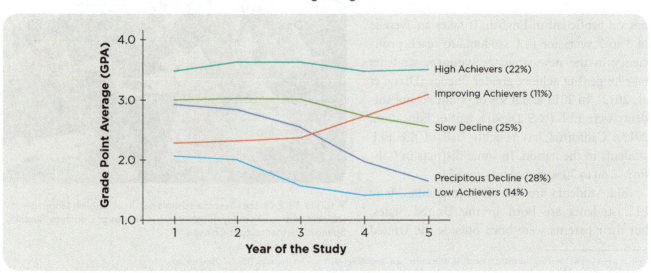

The students were between 9 and 14 years old at Year 1. How many groups of immigrant children show declining grades over 5 years? *Source: Suárez-Orozco, Gaytán, Bang, Pakes, O'Connor, and Rhodes (2010).*

between languages may improve information-processing skills, although not all research supports this claim (de Bruin, Treccani, & Della Sala, 2014).

12-1e Classroom Implications of Language

In a kindergarten classroom, the teacher asked Jared, the meteorologist for the day, to report on the weather. Jared said it was rather brisk. When an observer asked him why he chose such an unusual word to describe the weather, he replied, "Well, it's colder than cool, but it's a long way from frigid." (Adapted from Lane & Allen, 2010, p. 363)

Many high school teachers wish their students had the vocabulary of this 5-year-old. How did he come to be so verbally precocious? His teacher, Ms. Barker, deliberately taught verbal ability in her class. She selected novel words that she scaffolded for her students, building on familiar class routines. Ms. Barker's students "distributed" rather than passed out paper, they lined up "adjacent" rather than next to the wall, and they "provided nutritional sustenance to our rodent friends" rather than fed the hamsters. Despite teaching in a high-poverty school, Ms. Barker demanded extraordinary vocabulary from her students and provided them with the support to use it competently. This is important because strong language skills are linked to academic achievement and appropriate classroom behavior for learners of all ages (Forget-Dubois et al., 2009). To help your students develop better language ability, follow these guidelines:

1. *Be responsive to children's talk.* If you teach infants, encourage them to make sounds. If you teach preschoolers, build on and expand what the child says. If a child says "sock on," you could say, "Do you want your sock on?" This is known as *elaboration.* Elaboration can also be used with adolescents who have limited proficiency in Standard English.

2. *Encourage children to use Standard English*, while respecting their heritage language or dialect. Ask questions that require more than a yes/no response. Pause to let students contribute to classroom talk. To help students speak SE, one high-poverty high school that has narrowed the achievement gap requires students to give all answers in full sentences without slang. The teens initially resisted, but their ability to use SE has improved rapidly.

3. *Read to children, or encourage them to read to themselves.* Exposure to reading builds vocabulary and background knowledge that foster language development. Nonfiction books are particularly useful for language development (Mol, Bus, & de Jong, 2009).

4. *Explicitly teach vocabulary.* For preschoolers, this can mean modeling language and explaining what words mean; for literate students, it can mean memorizing vocabulary. Help learners use mnemonic strategies to memorize vocabulary, as discussed in Chapter 4. For example, to help 9th-graders remember "archaic" using the keyword method, have them visualize an *old* weathered arch.

5. *Help students use new words in multiple ways.* Give the definition of a new word, use it in a context that makes its meaning clear, and then have students use it. Students need repeated exposure to words, as well as the opportunity to use them in context.

6. *Use academic language.* Most learners, including ELL learners, will pick up day-to-day language. They struggle much more with technical vocabulary and complex language use, such as making inferences and hypotheses, summarizing, using analogies, and comparing/contrasting (DiCerbo, Anstrom, Baker, & Rivera, 2014).

Let's take a peek at a teacher using some of these guidelines to teach vocabulary to preschoolers.

Mr. Myers:	*When it* (pointing to butterfly) *was inside, its wings were together, but once it got out, it could splay, or spread out, its wings.*
Aquala:	*Ya!*
Mr. Myers:	*Splay means to spread out.*
Aquala:	*Yeah, like peanut butter. Like spread with a knife.*
Mr. Myers:	*Yes, but the peanut butter doesn't really get splayed because it doesn't have parts. Splay means to spread something that has parts. You have body parts that you can splay. You can splay your arms, legs. And spread out all over like this* (gestures).
Aquala:	(spreading arms apart) *This splay?*
Mr. Myers:	*Yes, you are splaying your arms.*
Aquala:	(to another child) *And you are splaying your whole body.* (Collins, 2012, p. 68).

Tactics like explaining word meanings or elaborating on what learners say may seem easy to do. Yet studies in which teachers are trained to follow these guidelines find that many do not implement the training (Dickinson, 2011; Justice, Mashburn, Hamre, & Pianta, 2008; Piasta, Justice, McGinty, & Kaderavek, 2012). One study found that kindergarten teachers averaged only eight episodes of vocabulary instruction per day, and teachers of low-SES students did less of it, which would tend to perpetuate the vocabulary disparity between high- and low-SES children (Wright, 2012). Thus, you may need to deliberately practice promoting language skills in your classroom.

Nonverbal Language in the Classroom

Parents who use more gestures with their preschoolers tend to have children who develop better vocabulary, which predicts school achievement (Rowe & Goldin-Meadow, 2009). Nonverbal language is also important in your classroom in two ways. First, gestures help students learn and teachers teach. Second, teachers' expectations can be unconsciously conveyed through nonverbal language.

Gestures and instruction

Gestures help students learn, understand, and problem-solve (Goldin-Meadow & Alibali, 2013). Gestures include movements like inclining one's arm to indicate different slopes of lines, pointing at a series of objects to indicate counting, or pointing with both hands at numbers on either side of an equal sign. See Figure 12.3. Perhaps gestures foster learning

FIGURE 12.3 Gesture Helps this Child Understand the Equivalence Concept in Mathematics.

© 2018 Cengage Learning

because they lighten the cognitive load as students talk about concepts they cannot fully articulate yet. Gestures serve as a bridge between concrete experiences and abstract concepts. As students become more expert, there is less need for gesture when they talk about abstract ideas.

Gestures can tell you about students' readiness for instruction. They are particularly ready to learn when gestures suggest accurate thinking despite inaccurate spoken language. For example, a boy explained his incorrect solution to the equivalence problem $7 + 6 + 5 = \underline{} + 5$ as follows:

> "I added 13 plus 10 equals 23" (an incorrect add-all-numbers strategy) while holding his whole hand under the 7 and the 6, pointing at the blank, and then pointing at the 7 and 6 (a correct grouping strategy).

Verbally, this boy is communicating that he does not understand that the equal sign separates the two halves of the equation. However, his gestures communicate that at some level he does understand. He is ready for instruction because he is on the verge of change. His teacher built on his gestures, forcing him to notice that there was a 5 on each side:

> I am going to cover this up (while covering up the 7 and 6 with her hand). Now what do you see on both sides? Five and five, right?" (Goldin-Meadow & Singer, 2003, p. 516)

Teachers convey information through gesture. For example, 7- to 10-year-olds were taught, with or without gestures, about equivalence across an equal sign (e.g., $8 + 6 + 2 = \underline{} + 2$). The group whose teacher used gestures learned more (Cook, Duffy, & Fenn, 2013). See Figure 12.4. Students are more likely to learn concepts when instruction includes *both* speech and gesture—from teaching preschoolers how to count to teaching high school students physics concepts (Ping & Goldin-Meadow, 2008). For example, in teaching the preceding equivalency problem, you might point at the 7 and 6, then flick away at the 5s.

Pygmalion in the classroom

When teachers hold high expectations for their students, their students tend to learn more. This is called the *Pygmalion effect* (named after a Greek myth) or the *teacher expectation effect* (Rosenthal & Jacobson, 1966). This effect has been found in many studies.[2] In one experiment, teachers recorded a lesson to analyze how their own nonverbal behavior communicated expectations of students. Over a year, students' math achievement increased in the intervention as compared with the control group (Rubie-Davies, Peterson, Sibley, & Rosenthal, 2015).

FIGURE 12.4 Gesture Facilitates Learning.

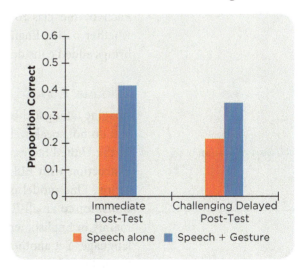

Proportion of problems correct for second and third graders who were taught math equivalence with speech alone compared with speech plus gesture. *Source: Cook, Duffy, and Fenn (2013).*

---

[2] Many studies support this conclusion, a few of which are listed here: de Boer, Bosker, and van der Werf (2010); Friedrich, Flunger, Nagengast, Jonkmann, and Trautwein (2015); Rosenthal (2002); Rubie-Davies et al. (2014).

How might teacher expectations affect learner's achievement? One explanation is that teachers communicate their expectations to students nonverbally without being aware of it. Even when teachers try to hide low expectations and are good at emotional dissemblance, their real expectations leak out in body language and behavior (Porter & ten Brinke, 2008). Teachers tend to do the following at higher rates for students toward whom they have high expectations: express warmth, smile at, call on, teach, wait for answers, and give informative feedback (Rosenthal, 2003). In contrast, when teachers have low expectations of students, they ask easy questions, place students in low-ability groups, use competitive motivation and grading strategies so losers are obvious, and make negative comments about certain students (Bohlmann & Weinstein, 2013).

Classroom implications of nonverbal language

Implications for your classroom from research on nonverbal language include:

1. *Encourage students to use gestures* during explanations and problem-solving tasks. After activities, encourage students to describe their experience using gestures rather than just asking them to "write it up." This promotes deeper understanding and gives you a chance to clarify misunderstandings.

2. *Use gestures in your instruction.* You can convey problem-solving strategies to students by combining speech and gestures as the teacher described earlier did.

3. *Convey high expectations to every child.* Show warmth, demand strong answers, and provide plenty of feedback to all students, particularly low-SES and minority boys who may be most vulnerable to low teacher expectations (Hinnant, O'Brien, & Ghazarian, 2009).

Each of the classroom implications discussed thus far pertains to all students, whether native English speakers or not. However, teaching students who are ELL brings added considerations.

Bilingual Education

Imagine taking a chemistry class in Twi (a language in Ghana), or another language you do not speak well. You would not learn as much as if the class were in English. In the United States, **bilingual education** refers to the use of heritage language for instruction with ELL students. There are many different models of bilingual education. One model is to provide all instruction in the heritage language and then transition to an all-English classroom. Another model is to teach academic content mainly in English, with occasional tutoring for that same content in the heritage language. Yet another model is to teach academic content only in English and then teach English as a second language (ESL). Still another, nonbilingual, model is to simply immerse students abruptly in English-only classrooms. The first two models are not an option in small school districts where few teachers are fluent in other languages, but they are feasible in large districts with high concentrations of a single heritage language, such as Spanish in Arizona.

Which approach is best? The answer to this politically charged question is not completely clear. Some studies show an advantage for bilingual education over immersion,

bilingual education
instruction that is provided in more than one language.

but some show no differences. Rarely do studies show an advantage for immersion. Research supports the following guidelines for working with ELL students (Baker et al., 2014; Dixon et al., 2012):

1. *Devote time to teaching English* (see Chapter 5 for discussion of deliberate practice). This provides opportunities to practice speaking. Make sure students use full sentences in their responses, although they may resist. It may surprise you, but in many ELL classrooms students have little opportunity to speak English.

2. *Integrate oral and written English language instruction into content-area teaching.* Engage students in academic discussions about the course content, such as language arts, science, or math. You could encourage speech through cooperative learning and viewing short video clips that are then discussed.

3. *Directly teach vocabulary.* This includes everyday words and academic words in content areas like math, science, or history (Jansen, 2008). For example, students may struggle with comparative words like *probably, very likely,* and *almost certain,* or math words like *estimate.*

4. *Teach Standard English grammar and syntax explicitly.* Do not expect students to become proficient in English by chance as you teach math, social studies, or other content areas. Provide clear, frequent feedback on grammar and syntax.

5. *Teach language skills as early as possible.* Students who enter kindergarten with adequate English skills tend to do as well as native speakers, but students who do not may lag in achievement throughout elementary school (Kieffer, 2008).

6. *Build strong skills in the heritage language among preschoolers.* Having a strong foundation in their first language helps young students develop skills in English (their second language) faster and transition to English-only classrooms faster (Proctor, August, Carlo, & Snow, 2006).

7. *Encourage English use in informal settings at school.* Students who use English in the hallway, cafeteria, and with friends are more successful (Carhill, Suárez-Orozco, & Paez, 2008).

8. *Remember that Standard English lags behind conversational English.* Students who can converse in English with you and who seem English-proficient may struggle to follow academic content and score poorly on standardized tests. When possible, test students in their dominant language. ELL students may know more math, science, and history than they can demonstrate in English (Abedi, 2004).

9. *Support **additive bilingualism**.* This is where students maintain proficiency in their heritage language while becoming proficient in English. **Subtractive bilingualism** occurs when students learn a second, majority language in a context that does not value their heritage language, which they eventually lose. Students who are fluent in *both* English and their heritage language fare better academically and emotionally.

additive bilingualism acquiring a second language while still maintaining and valuing the heritage language.

subtractive bilingualism acquiring a second, majority language in a way that undermines ability in the heritage language.

Students who must cross cultural borders may be inclined to choose one culture over the other. You can encourage them to be comfortable in English U.S. culture without losing their heritage culture; they can learn to feel positive about both cultures.

ELL students tend to participate more in classes where they feel welcome and where they share aspects of their heritage cultures, compared to classes where they feel like outsiders or invisible (Yoon, 2008).

These issues also apply to nonimmigrant students who have a mismatch between language at school and at home. You have already seen that dialects like AAE are different from Standard English. In addition, many students, like Micah in the opening vignette, have limited opportunity to learn school vocabulary. Furthermore, the ways that students use language at home may differ from the way it is used at school (Hemphill & Snow, 1996). At home, family members scaffold, butt in, and clarify what a child is saying; children talk when they have something to say. In contrast, at school, the teacher controls who gets to talk and what the talk is about. Speaking in class often consists of one-word comments, with very little elaboration. Expository talk, rather than conversation, is used. **Expository talk** is formal, precise, and used to display information—like when a child is asked to summarize a text. You may need to help your students develop expository talk. This can be done through direct instruction and indirectly through exposure to reading and writing. Let's turn to the development of literacy next.

expository talk
formal, precise talk that is used to display information, in contrast to conversational talk.

literacy
narrowly defined, it is the ability to communicate in printed language through reading and writing, particularly in school settings.

decoding
figuring out how to read or spell unknown words by applying phonetic rules.

phonetic
rules regarding how written letters are linked to sounds and how a string of letters is correctly pronounced.

12-2 Literacy

The heartwarming note in Figure 12.5 is from 6-year-old Nora, at the end of kindergarten. At this age, Nora knows all her letters and can write some correctly. In this section, we will follow Nora's literacy progress from budding abilities in preschool to full literacy in 12th grade as we address how students become literate—but first let's clarify what literacy is.

Literacy can be defined broadly as any sort of communication or narrowly as communication in printed language. We will use the narrower definition in this chapter, focusing on reading and writing in school. However, this isn't the only kind of literacy. Children can have multiple literacies in contexts other than school. For example, some of your students may be more literate than you at decoding gangsta messages or at texting emoticons and abbreviations, like :), :(, BBL, or L8R (for *smile*, *sad*, *be back later*, and *later*).

Reading skill has five components: (1) phonological awareness, (2) vocabulary, (3) decoding, (4) fluency, and (5) comprehension. Recall that *phonological awareness* is the ability to distinguish phonemes, or the sounds in language. *Vocabulary* is the number of words you know. Understanding the meaning of words helps with reading them (Taylor, Duff, Woollams, Monaghan, & Ricketts, 2015). **Decoding** is the ability to identify words you have never seen. You decode by applying **phonetic** skills, which

FIGURE 12.5 Nora's Heartwarming Note.

David Bergin

Nora's note reads: "I really, really like you and I hope you have a happy Mothers' Day."

include recognizing letters, knowing their sounds, and pronouncing a string of letters correctly. In English, irregular words, like *choir* or *yacht*, do not follow phonetic rules and must simply be memorized. *Fluency* is the rapid, automatic decoding of novel words or recognition of memorized words. It is typically measured in words accurately read per minute and abbreviated as *wpm*. *Comprehension* is the ability to understand text. Comprehension is the ultimate goal of reading. Next we examine how these components, as well as writing, develop with age.

12-2a Age Trends in Literacy

Literacy development begins in infancy and continues across the lifespan. The most dramatic growth occurs during the early years, but growth continues as adolescents become able to read and write complex expository prose. (Hill, Bloom, Black, & Lipsey, 2008; Quinn, Wagner, Petscher, & Lopez, 2015). See Figure 12.6.

Infancy and Toddlerhood (Birth to 2 Years)

Toddlers' literacy emerges as they develop skills that are precursors to reading and writing. By age 3, most children have several **emergent literacy** skills; they can say the alphabet, name a letter and tell what sound it makes, tell a story back to you, write their name, and recognize familiar words in the environment (such as a stop sign). They also have basic notions of how print stands for language, known as **print concepts** (or print knowledge). Children have print concepts when they know that books are read from left to right, books begin with a title, there is space between words, pictures are different from print, and so forth. Toddlers' "writing" is scribbles or unrecognizable forms. Emergent literacy skills prepare children to learn to read and write; they emerge before formal literacy instruction begins.

emergent literacy
abilities that are precursors to reading and writing, such as good verbal ability, knowing letter names, phonological awareness, and print concepts.

print concepts
basic concepts of how print symbolizes language, such as English books are read from left to right and spaces separate words. A key part of emergent literacy.

FIGURE 12.6 Average Annual Gain in Reading and Math Competence from Kindergarten to Grade 12.

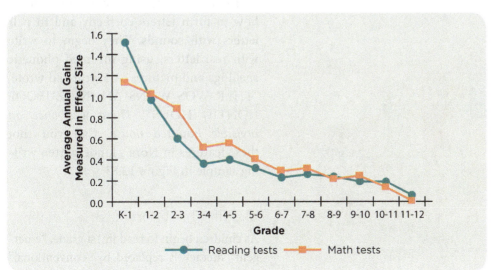

This graph represents change in reading and math competence through the school years. How does rate of growth change across the years? How do math and reading growth rates compare? How would the graph look different if it showed total knowledge of math and reading at each year instead of growth per year? *Source: Data from Hill et al. (2008).*

FIGURE 12.7 **Preschool Writing Sample.**

Nora's grocery shopping list at age 4. If her mother put something wrong in the cart, she said, "That's not on my list!" Notice that although there are no letters, she wrote from left to right in lines that resemble cursive. This demonstrates print concepts.

FIGURE 12.8 **Kindergarten Writing Sample.**

"Dad. Mom. Sister. Brother. Baby" At the beginning of kindergarten, age 5½, Nora can write some letters and common words correctly. She reverses some letters and spells phonetically. "Brother" begins backward on one line and proceeds forward on the second line. Writing is brief and drawings dominate "stories."

Early Childhood (3 to 5 Years)

In early childhood, most children are not yet reading to themselves. However, their emergent literacy skills continue to grow as parents or teachers read to them. Between 18 months and 3 years old, parents shift from commenting on pictures, to conversing about the story, to actually reading the text (Fletcher & Reese, 2005). Researchers estimate that at the rate of one book per day, preschoolers would hear more than 219,000 words in 1 year from books (Montag, Jones, & Smith, 2015). However, some children hear more than one book per day, and others may not experience a single book in a year. Words in books are more diverse and complex than everyday speech, so children who are read to are exposed to both greater quantity and quality of language.

At about age 3, children's writing still may not include real letters, but it begins to look like letters and is written in left-to-right lines. Children believe they are writing, but no one else can read it (Levin & Bus, 2003). For example, Figure 12.7 displays a "shopping list" written by 4-year-old Nora. She has print concepts—that writing translates to speech, it occurs left to right in lines, with motions that are cursive-like—but her writing is not yet divided into words. The first real word children write is usually their own name.

In kindergarten, most children learn how to form letters correctly and to pair letters with sounds. They begin to write with real letters, using invented phonetic spellings and pictures. A 5-year-old wrote, "THER WOS WONS AN INVIZUBOOL HONTID HOUS"—*There was once an invisible haunted house.* Can you spot these features in Nora's kindergarten writing sample in Figure 12.8?

Middle Childhood (6 to 12 Years)

As children begin to read in 1st grade, "emergent" literacy is replaced by "conventional" literacy. Joint storybook reading changes; the child takes on responsibility for reading while parents watch for errors (Bergin, 2001). Joint storybook reading becomes rare

FIGURE 12.12 Twelfth-Grade Writing Sample.

Title: "High School Athletes and Enhancing Substances"

Abstract:
Athletes have been using enhancing substances for hundreds of years to improve their performance. Currently athletes still use substances to give them an edge over their competitors. With modern advances, there are many more products on the market. High school athletes have started taking advantage of such products. The hypothesis is that performance enhancing substances for student athletes are prevalent in high school. The rationale is that many students see professional athletes boosting their performance by taking such substances and the students assume that they would also improve. A survey will be administered to a sample population of students at a mid-west suburban high school. The survey will deal with sports, drugs, and performance enhancers.

David Bergin

This is an abstract written for a science-fair entry. Nora is not only fully literate for day-to-day writing needs, but she has also learned to write in a specialized, academic style for a scientific audience. She is ready for college and professional training. Look back at her earliest writings. What a change in twelve years!

Despite the stability of literacy skills, struggling readers can improve. In a study in which roughly two-thirds of low-SES children who were struggling in 1st grade remained struggling readers in 4th grade, one-third dramatically improved, becoming average readers by 4th grade (Spira, Bracken, & Fischel, 2005). Which struggling readers improved? Children with better phonological awareness, emergent literacy skills, and classroom behavior.

What Do Individual Differences in Literacy Predict?

Literacy predicts academic achievement in school subjects. This effect begins with emergent literacy skills in kindergarten or earlier, and continues as conventional literacy develops (Duncan et al., 2007). This is not surprising, because literacy helps children learn. Reading allows children to take information from text. Writing improves thinking, helping children transform fuzzy thoughts into clear concepts. Literacy allows children to complete worksheets, take tests, and understand assignments. However, it might surprise you that literacy also predicts achievement in math—as early as 2nd grade, before children are doing math word problems (Lee, Ng, & Ng, 2009; Swanson, Jerman, & Zheng, 2008). Perhaps this is because literacy and math skills share the same causes, such as general intelligence or a stimulating home (Hart, Petrill, Thompson, & Plomin, 2008).

FIGURE 12.13 Average words per minute read across 2nd to 12th grade.

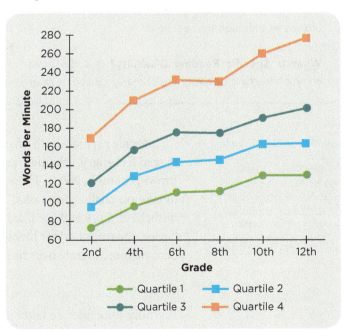

This graph represents number of words per minute that students can read with good comprehension. How does words per minute compare for students in the four quartiles? *Source: Spichtig et al. (2016).*

BOX 12.2 challenges in development

Specific Reading Disability

In 3rd grade, Veronica is in the lowest reading group. Her classmates are reading "chapter books," but she is still struggling with beginning readers. At the school library, after children select a book, the librarian asks them to read a random page and hold up a finger for each word they can't read. If five fingers go up, the children are to choose an easier book. In 5th grade, Veronica is still using the five-finger method, but her classmates no longer need to. Veronica cannot read the social studies textbook, so an aide reads it to her. Her parents are both college-educated and perplexed by the problem. In desperation, her mother buys a phonics program and drills Veronica in sounding out words. It works. In 10th grade, Veronica is in an Honors English class, but she still avoids reading when possible.

Veronica is not unusual. As many as 40% of children have reading problems, which run in families (Snowling & Melby-Lervåg, 2016). Reading problems can result from low IQ, neurological problems, low motivation, poor vocabulary, or inadequate instruction in phonics (Ferrer, Shaywitz, Holahan, Marchione, & Shaywitz, 2010). When these problems are ruled out, but a child still has difficulty learning to read, the child has **specific reading disability**, commonly called *dyslexia*, or reading disorder. About 5 to 15% of children have dyslexia. Veronica was never referred for reading intervention, although she needed it.

What Is Specific Reading Disability? It is the most common learning disability. It is primarily caused by poor oral language abilities, specifically poor vocabulary and phonological awareness (Hulme, Nash, Gooch, Lervåg, & Snowling, 2015; Melby-Lervåg, Lyster, & Hulme, 2012). Students with dyslexia have difficulty linking letters with sounds, blending sounds together, or judging whether two words rhyme. These phonological problems result in labored decoding, poor word recognition, and weak spelling.

There is debate over the identification of dyslexia, just as there is with other learning disabilities. Recall that learning disability is sometimes defined by an IQ-achievement discrepancy (see Chapter 5). Some educators object to a discrepancy definition of dyslexia for three reasons:

1. Low-IQ or ELL students, and those who lack opportunity to learn, cannot qualify for intervention.
2. It suggests that either you have dyslexia or you do not, yet in reality difficulties fall along a continuum. The cutoffs for defining dyslexia are arbitrary (Snowling & Melby-Lervåg, 2016).
3. It results in diagnoses too late. An alternative way to identify dyslexia is to use test scores for reading or phonological awareness that are in the bottom 10th to 25th percentile.

Although dyslexic children have normal intelligence, they may have some information-processing problems, particularly slow processing speed, poor executive functions, and limited working memory (Im-Bolter et al., 2006; Sexton, Gelhorn, Bell, & Classi, 2012; Swanson & Jerman, 2006).

specific reading disability
a learning disability in which a child with normal intelligence and exposure to print has difficulty learning to read. It is characterized by difficulty decoding and recognizing words accurately and/or fluently. It is also called dyslexia.

Literacy predicts both emotional and social competence. Children who struggle to read feel angry, ashamed, anxious, and sad by 5th grade (Ackerman, Izard, Kobak, Brown, & Smith, 2007). These emotions reduce enjoyment of school and willingness to take on challenging tasks. This may explain why struggling readers also tend to misbehave more and are liked by fewer classmates over time. Unfortunately, misbehavior undermines their literacy development. In contrast, students who behave well become more literate over time (Miles & Stipek, 2006).

What Predicts Individual Differences in Literacy?

Learning to be literate takes a coming together of several skills. Thus, there can be a variety of reasons why some children become more literate than others. Students who have an unusually hard time learning to read may have dyslexia (see Box 12.2). Next we discuss characteristics of the child and of the environment that contribute to literacy.

Scientists believe this may explain why dyslexia co-occurs with other problems such as math disabilities, attention-deficit/hyperactivity disorder (ADHD), and delayed language, each of which may result from underlying information-processing problems (Bishop & Snowling, 2004; Sexton, Gelhorn, Bell, & Classi, 2012). This means that your students with dyslexia may learn concepts adequately, but have difficulty with tasks that ask them to rapidly process multiple pieces of information at the same time.

Dyslexia and the Brain Some differences in the brains of dyslexic and nondyslexic children have been found. Infants who later have dyslexia show a very early speech-processing deficit and abnormal brain functioning (van Zuijen, Plakas, Maassen, Maurits, & van der Leij, 2013). However, recall that the brain is modified by experience. After many hours of intervention, the brains of dyslexic children more closely resemble those of good readers (Shaywitz & Shaywitz, 2005).

What Can Be Done about Dyslexia? Intervention for dyslexia is the same high-quality reading instruction we hope all students get, but more of it. Interventions focus on letter knowledge, phonological awareness, decoding, and word-recognition strategies. Word-recognition strategies include simply memorizing common words and figuring out a new word by analogy ("like" is similar to "bike") or by taking off suffixes (change "looked" to "look"). Interventions also focus on guided oral reading with feedback. Experiments show that these interventions help dyslexic students become more fluent readers. Unfortunately, not all students readily respond to intervention. Early childhood interventions for children at family risk of dyslexia have not shown strong results (Snowling & Melby-Lervåg, 2016). Struggling readers who become more fluent are likely to have received better instruction, be of higher SES, and come from literate homes, like Veronica (Shaywitz, Mody, & Shaywitz, 2006). In addition to intervention, you can help dyslexic students by accommodating them in three ways: (1) provide extra time for tasks that involve reading, (2) use recorded books, and (3) allow oral test-taking (Shaywitz, Morris, & Shaywitz, 2008).

Professional rugby player Kenny Logan said that as a young adult he could not read or write. "If there was ever a team meeting involving reading, I would turn up 15 minutes late and hide in the toilets. . . . I wasn't brave enough to tell anyone my secret" (Rooke, 2016). Logan said, "School was awful. For years I would have this horrible stomach ache, a dull pain inside me. . . . I looked confident on the outside and was terrified on the inside. Words and letters confused me from the very beginning of primary school to the end of high school. I saw the other children progress while I was left drowning" (p. 119). Later, his future wife recognized his disability and sought help for him. As a teacher, you can be the one who recognizes and helps students with specific reading disability.

Verbal ability

Children with good verbal ability learn to read more easily than their peers. Good verbal ability includes a large vocabulary, ability to retell a story coherently, letter-sound knowledge, and phonological and morphological awareness. These abilities help children become better readers and spellers (see, for example, Bowers, Kirby, & Deacon, 2010; Caravolas, Lervåg, Mousikou, et al., 2012; Kieffer & Lesaux, 2012; Melby-Lervåg, Lyster, & Hulme, 2012; Quinn et al., 2015). Children with poor vocabulary and poor phonological and morphological knowledge tend to have reading problems.

Physical factors

Differences in brain structure are linked to literacy. For example, Box 12.2 explains that the neural system that connects speech to print is different for students with dyslexia. These brain differences may be genetic and may explain why reading ability has a genetic component (Logan et al., 2013). Genes may influence literacy through their effect on general cognitive abilities like processing speed, working memory, and attention control. Or, genes may influence literacy through how much children are read to, which is partly heritable and partly shared environment (Oliver, Dale, & Plomin, 2005). How do children inherit being read to? A genetic predisposition may lead some toddlers to respond more to books and show more interest, so their parents read more to them.

Brain differences may also be due to experience. Experience alters brain circuitry (see Chapter 2). In Box 12.2 also explains that intense instruction alters the brains of dyslexic children as they become more fluent readers. In addition, the areas of the brain that process sound are altered by music lessons, by hearing different languages like Mandarin versus English, and by phonetic instruction (Kraus & Banai, 2007). This is important because children whose brains are slow to process sound have difficulty learning to read.

Cognitive factors

Reading and writing require general cognitive abilities, like working memory, knowledge, reasoning, and processing speed. Students with good cognitive abilities become fluent readers earlier and with more ease. However, literacy also requires language-specific cognitive abilities, like phonological awareness, print knowledge, vocabulary, and decoding ability.

Emotional factors

Children with secure attachment tend to develop better literacy skills and attitudes toward reading than do insecure children. Secure children have pleasant encounters with print because their parents are sensitive, which makes them better literacy coaches (Clingenpeel & Pianta, 2007). Pleasant interaction during parent–child storybook reading predicts reading fluency and positive attitudes as children begin to read on their own (Bergin, 2001). In contrast, negative emotions, like anger or anxiety, interfere with the information processing needed for reading and writing (see Chapter 8). This may occur when parents aggressively command "Sound it out!" as their children are learning to read.

Social factors

Literacy is social; it is acquired through social interaction and is used to connect with others. Preschoolers who are socially skilled and cooperative tend to have stronger language and literacy development than children who are not (Arnold, Kupersmidt, Voegler-Lee, & Marshall, 2012).

Joint storybook reading (also called shared reading) is an important social factor that predicts literacy. Joint storybook reading is initially about using the book as a tool to converse; toddlers generally look at the pictures, not the print. So how does it help with literacy? It builds oral language, print concepts, phonological awareness, and vocabulary. As early as 18 months, toddlers who are read to develop a larger vocabulary than other children, and they tend to have higher reading achievement as they grow older (Fletcher & Reese, 2005). As children begin to read on their own, parents promote their literacy by listening to them read and providing feedback (Sénéchal & Young, 2008).

Play is another important social factor that predicts literacy. Preschoolers who use literacy in their play—like reading to dolls, writing a shopping list, and putting letters in a mailbox—develop greater literacy. So do elementary school children who make their own books, write a play for their puppets, write out rules for games they make up, or try to find letters in billboards during car trips. This is also true for adolescents who play games, like *Scrabble* and *Boggle,* that involve literacy.

Play is beneficial because it provides practice and authentic reasons to read or write. **Authentic literacy activities** refers to reading for information one wants or writing to inform a reader (Duke, Purcell-Gates, Hall, & Tower, 2006). Nonauthentic literacy tasks are done for the purpose of learning to read or write, or just to complete an assignment. Besides play, authentic tasks may include text-messaging friends and reading the newspaper sports page to see how your team did.

> **authentic literacy activities** reading for information one wants, or writing to inform a reader, as opposed to activities done for the purpose of learning to read or write or just to complete an assignment.

12-2c Group Diversity in Literacy

On the average, students' literacy varies by gender, class, and ethnicity. Let's look at these differences next.

Gender

Recall from Chapter 5 that girls tend to have higher literacy achievement than boys. This gender difference begins in preschool, when girls have slightly higher emergent literacy abilities, and continues into high school. Gender differences are international; 4th-grade girls outperform boys in 35 countries (Baer, Baldi, Ayotte, & Green, 2007). However, in the United States, by high school the difference between boys' and girls' reading ability is small, although writing differences get larger. Research consistently shows that girls like reading more than boys (McKenna, Conradi, Lawrence, Jang, & Meyer, 2012).

Socioeconomic Status

Low-SES learners tend to have lower literacy than other learners. Parents' education, a key component of SES, is particularly important. Parents with more years of education have children with better reading ability. Even among low-income children, those whose mothers have more education tend to have better literacy skills (Dickinson, McCabe, Anastasopoulos, Peisner-Feinberg, & Poe, 2003). This also pertains to internet literacy. In one study, higher-SES learners had better reading comprehension on internet-based text (effect size = 1.5), and they also had a large advantage on regular text (effect size = 1.9) (Leu et al., 2015).

SES differences in literacy may be due to opportunity to learn, as with spoken language. Some families have dozens of children's books, and others have none at all. Some preschoolers are read to several times a day, culminating in thousands of hours before entering school, whereas others are not read to. College-educated parents are more likely to read to their children, to talk with them during storybook reading, and to take them to the public library (Aikens & Barbarin, 2008; Raikes et al., 2006). For example, a national report found that 74% of college-educated mothers read to their preschoolers daily, as compared with 40% of high school–educated mothers and mothers living in poverty (Federal Interagency Forum on Child and Family Statistics, 2009). Thus, children vary by SES in their print exposure, which refers to

think about this
Do SES-related differences in verbal ability and literacy fit the "family investment" or "family stress" model of poverty you read about in Chapter 1? How do they fit the bioecological model?

activities related to print and reading. Print exposure predicts reading comprehension, spelling, and academic achievement (Mol & Bus, 2011). Differences in print exposure continue into adolescence, as high-SES students spend more non-school-time reading than low-SES students (Larson & Verma, 1999). However, your low-SES students will become literate if they like to read and have good instruction.

Ethnicity

On the National Assessment of Educational Progress (NAEP), White and Asian American students have consistently higher reading scores than Black or Latino students in 4th, 8th, and 12th grades. In Chapter 5, you learned about possible causes of this achievement gap. In addition, ethnic differences may be due to print exposure at home. White children (64%) are more likely to be read to daily than Black (48%) or Latino (42%) children (Raikes et al., 2006).

Ethnic differences may also be due to language mismatch. For example, students who speak AAE may hear different letter–sound pairs than those in Standard English (SE). To understand this, imagine that a student is reading the sentence, "Their hands are cold." In AAE this could sound like "Deir han' a' co'." The student has to learn that the letters *th* can spell the sound for *d* as in "their." The student also has to learn to spell the word "hand" with a *d*, even though there is no spoken sound for the *d* in the student's speech (Charity, Scarborough, & Griffin, 2004). Learning letter–sound pairs is simpler for SE-using students or for AAE-using students who can readily code switch to SE.

Another aspect of language mismatch is that some languages, like AAE and Asian languages, do not indicate time with verb tense like Standard English does. For example, an AAE speaker might say, "I be going to school and seen Devin." It is not clear whether this sentence means, in SE, "I went to school and saw Devin" or "I was going to school and saw Devin" or "I go to school everyday and see Devin." Some students need to be taught verb conjugation to master SE. For example, Hong is a U.S.-born 9th-grader with Vietnamese parents who lives in a neighborhood where Vietnamese and AAE are spoken:

> *Hong cannot speak or write fluently in Standard English. She has low achievement, but gets passing grades on papers because she has friends edit them. When it becomes clear she will not pass the high school exit exam, she is referred to a language intervention teacher. Ms. Cole identifies a key problem: Hong does not distinguish different forms of verbs, like walk, walks, walked, and walking. Ms. Cole helps Hong learn to conjugate verbs by asking Hong to hold up a card with the correct ending (ed, ing, s) as Ms. Cole says a variety of verbs.*

After just four training sessions, Hong conjugates verbs correctly in both her speech and her writing. Although all students experience some language mismatch between spoken English and written, formal English, students whose spoken language is a greater mismatch may have more difficulty with school literacy.

Ethnic differences may also be due to cultural mismatch. One aspect of cultural mismatch, introduced in Chapter 1, is different notions of what is a good story. African American children may write stories that appear less coherent in other cultures, but that include multiple narratives, vivid imagery, complexity, and rhythmic language, making them equally competent although of a different style (Gardner-Neblett, Pungello, & Iruka, 2012).

In addition, students who struggle with school literacy can be highly literate in out-of-school peer culture, such as in graffiti and tagging. For example, girls of color who were in gangs in Salt Lake City wrote notes that followed elaborate rules, such as crossing out the letter *O* because a rival gang's name began with *O* (see Figure 12.14). Some of these girls were indifferent to in-school writing but were meticulous in their note writing to friends (Moje, 2000). Other youth cross cultural borders, becoming skilled in both in-school and out-of-school literacy. For example, Maria, a Mexican American, was a tagger (i.e., graffiti writer) and was in AP classes; she said that *The Old Man and the Sea* was a favorite book (MacGillivray & Curwen, 2007). The challenge for teachers is to channel the abilities of these talented youth.

FIGURE 12.14 **Writing Sample from a Gang Member.**

David Bergin

Adolescents can have well-developed out-of-school literacies.
Source: Moje (2000).

12-2d Classroom Implications of Literacy Development

You learned earlier that literacy affects achievement in other subjects. Because of this, literacy skills are emphasized in the early grades in the United States. However, some schools are more successful in promoting literacy than others (see Figure 12.15).

FIGURE 12.15 Schools Make a Difference in Literacy Development.

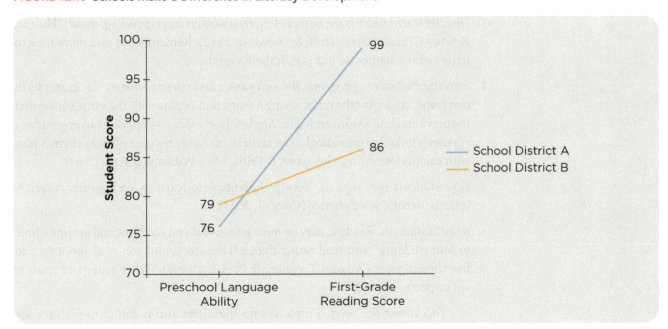

This chart shows two groups of students from the same Head Start preschool program. Those who went on to school district A developed better reading ability in 1st grade than students who went on to school district B. District A students were at grade level, and a whole standard deviation above their peers in district B. *Source: Adapted from Whitehurst and Lonigan (1998).*

What makes them more effective? The same general practices you read about in previous chapters—more time on task, positive teacher–student relationships, opportunity to engage in rich discussions rather than working alone, deliberate practice, and so forth.

Nancy Atwell, winner of the Global Teacher Prize, wrote "In my 40-year career as a middle school English teacher, the simplest and most powerful innovation was to give my students *time* and *choice* as writers and readers" (Atwell, 2015). Giving choice allowed students to follow their interests, which resulted in extensive practice. The students read books that they liked and wrote poetry, memoirs, short fiction, parodies, and profiles. One of her former students wrote from law school, "In the spring we were required to write an appellate brief, and the process included peer editing. I was astonished to see the drastic differences between my writing and that of my classmates—the errors, confusion, and clutter. I was taught from a very young age…to love writing and to practice, regularly and passionately."

Let's look at how literacy practices improve the five components of reading—phonological skills, decoding, fluency, vocabulary, and comprehension—and writing for all students. Then, we will discuss students who cross cultural and language boundaries.

Typically, in preschool through 2nd grade, schools emphasize phonological awareness, decoding, and beginning writing. From 3rd grade through high school, the emphasis shifts to fluency, comprehension, and advanced writing. Thus, the importance of the following guidelines will vary depending on the ages you teach.

Promote Phonological Awareness and Decoding Skills

Phonological awareness is the foundation of reading ability (Dickinson et al., 2003). You promote your students' phonological awareness when you:

1. *Directly teach students the names of letters and their corresponding sounds* (Hulme, Bowyer-Crane, Carroll, Duff, & Snowling, 2012). Remember to give more time to letters whose names do not match their sounds.

2. *Sensitize students to phonemes through games and nursery rhymes.* For example, in one game, students take turns saying a word that begins with the same sound that the previous child's word ended in: Apple—Lion—Nap—Pepper. Learning nursery rhymes is linked to phonological awareness, probably because nursery rhymes play with sounds (Snowling, Gallagher, & Frith, 2003; Williams & Rask, 2003).

3. *Give students spelling lists.* Young students who learn to spell words correctly learn to decode words better (Conrad, 2008).

4. *Read to students.* Reading may be most effective if you read in small groups (three to four students), you read rather than tell the story, and you read about four to five times a week (Adams, Treiman, & Pressley, 1998). Other aspects of reading are important as well:

   - *Talk about the book.* Simple yes/no questions and pointing to pictures are appropriate with toddlers. Ask older students to predict events or analyze characters before and after reading, but not during the story, such as, "How do you think he feels?" Talk about new vocabulary words.

- *Read a balance of familiar and unfamiliar books.* When you read the same story a few times (there are diminishing effects after the second time), students comment more on the story, particularly low-ability students. However, new books expose students to new vocabulary.

- *Read information books,* like books on weather or animals. Expository books tend to elicit more child talk than storybooks (Fletcher & Reese, 2005).

Promote Print Concepts

When you read to preliterate children, draw their attention to the words on the page by pointing or asking questions like "Do you know this word?" A randomized experiment found that when preschool teachers emphasize print concepts during shared reading, children have better reading skills 2 years later (Piasta et al., 2012). The following are examples of emphasizing print concepts (quoted from Piasta et al., 2012):

1. This is a box of cereal. It says, "Corn Flakes."

2. I am going to read this page first and then this page over here next.

3. This is the top of the page. This is where I begin reading.

4. Do you see a letter that is in your own name?

5. This is the letter K. K is in the words *kangaroo* and *kick.*

Promote Fluency

Even if students can decode words, they may not read fluently. Yet, teachers may not give enough attention to fluency. You will help your students become fluent readers when you:

1. *Provide guided oral reading.* Providing immediate feedback as students read out loud improves literacy at all ages (Rasinski et al., 2005). It is ideally done one-on-one. To make this practical, some schools have senior citizens tutor struggling readers.

2. *Provide frequent practice reading.* You can provide regular time in the school day for reading, or ask students to read when they finish assignments early, or ask students to read at home each day.

Some educators advocate independent silent reading, sometimes known as SSR (sustained silent reading) or DEAR (drop everything and read). However, just having students read more does not necessarily lead to better reading because students may not be comprehending (Kim, 2007). A major shortcoming of independent silent reading is that there is no feedback.

Promote Vocabulary and Comprehension

The ultimate goal of reading is comprehension. Good vocabulary is critical to comprehension. When students know the words they read, they comprehend more. In the preceding section on language, you learned how to build students' vocabulary. To quickly review, this includes exposing students to literature, using unusual words in the classroom, and teaching vocabulary. When you build your students' vocabulary,

Marmaduke St. John/Alamy Stock Photo

PHOTO 12.3 When you build your students' vocabulary, you promote both their verbal ability and literacy.

you promote their comprehension. In addition, you promote your students' comprehension when you:

1. *Teach decoding skills through phonological awareness and knowledge of letters and their sounds* (Melby-Lervåg & Lervåg, 2014). Decoding and knowing the relevant phonemes are foundational to reading comprehension.

2. *Directly teach vocabulary*, especially with low-income students before age 6 (Hadley, Dickinson, Hirsh-Pasek, Golinkoff, & Nesbitt, 2016; Marulis & Neuman, 2013; Quinn et al., 2015). (See Photo 12.3.) Poverty is a risk factor that strongly predicts poor vocabulary knowledge.

3. *Directly teach comprehension strategies* (Edmonds et al., 2009), including overviewing before reading, encouraging students to make predictions, asking what the author is trying to communicate and why, asking what the more important ideas are, stopping periodically to clear up confusion (e.g., by going backward in the reading), summarizing, and applying the KWL approach (see Chapter 4). Students who summarize are better at judging whether they comprehend the text and are ready for a test (Dunlosky & Lipko, 2007).

4. *Discuss texts.* Students comprehend more and develop better reasoning ability when they critique and question texts in group discussion (Murphy, Wilkinson, Soter, Hennessey, & Alexander, 2009). However, you need to facilitate the discussion for it to be productive; mere student talk doesn't necessarily lead to deep thinking.

Some evidence suggests that comprehension strategies are best taught embedded in content areas such as science and social studies (Kamil et al., 2008). For example, high school students who study history using multiple, conflicting texts, and who are taught to think about who, why, and when their texts were written learn more content and learn to think more like historians (Nokes, Dole, & Hacker, 2007). That is, these *guidelines are not just for language arts teachers.*

Promote Writing Skills

To become competent writers, students need many of the skills discussed earlier—good verbal ability, phonological awareness, spelling ability, adequate vocabulary, and exposure to print. Thus, as you follow the preceding guidelines, you will help your students become better writers. However, you will also need to provide writing instruction. You will help your students become better writers when you:

1. *Provide handwriting instruction.* Teaching handwriting improves the quality, length, and fluency of students' written work (Santangelo & Graham, 2015). Less legible written work gets considerably lower scores (Graham, Harris, & Hebert, 2011). Using word processing software also tends to improve writing quality (Graham, Harris, & Santangelo, 2015).

2. *Provide instruction in writing strategies*, like how to generate and organize ideas before starting a draft and how to provide supporting arguments for a persuasive

essay. An evidence-based technique is to have students revise a draft and add at least three new ideas, then address both sides of the argument with three or more reasons to support their own side and at least two reasons from the opposing side (Graham et al., 2015).

3. *Teach specific steps of writing, give feedback, and guide revision.* Weak writers benefit from instruction in step-by-step writing. However, writers who are already capable of monitoring their own writing process may not (Pritchard & Honeycutt, 2006).

4. *Provide opportunity to write, especially using authentic activities.* For example, after a lesson on volcanoes, 3rd-graders had many questions about where lava comes from and how hot it is, so their teacher assigned small groups to report the answers in writing to the class. In another class, students wrote about pond life in a brochure to be used at a nature center. Students given such authentic literacy assignments develop better writing skills (Purcell-Gates, Duke, & Martineau, 2007). Merely increasing time writing tends to improve writing skill (Graham, McKeown, Kiuhara, & Harris, 2012).

Even with good instruction, some students will struggle. Seek the help of language intervention specialists for such students. There are effective literacy interventions for struggling students from 1st to 12th grade (Connor et al., 2013). Many struggling students are crossing cultural borders and are English language learners. Let's take a look at classroom implications for these students next.

Bridge Cultural Borders

One way to bridge cultural borders is to use multicultural literature. For example, one Black 5th-grade boy tried to avoid literacy assignments until he discovered the biography of Fannie Lou Hamer, an African American voting advocate. Suddenly he couldn't read enough African American biographies (Smith, 1995). A Chinese American high school student wrote that reading *The Joy Luck Club* made her proud of her culture (Athanases, 1998). At the same time, students should be encouraged to identify with people of other genders, ethnicities, and times. For example, a White adolescent read *House of Dies Drear* and said that when a runaway slave named Thomas dropped his light in a cave, she imagined that she was with him. Literature helps students understand others who are different (Mar & Oatley, 2008). Thus, students should be exposed to diverse literature, but also to literature that is personally relevant.

Teachers may also bridge cultural borders by engaging students' ethnic culture during instruction. For example, Ms. Lee, a teacher, used signifying to teach literary analysis to African American seniors. *Signifying* is verbal teasing that uses double meaning and irony, with clever twists and surprises (Smitherman, 2000). For example, a pregnant woman told her sister, "Yes, I guess I am putting on a little weight." In response, the sister signified on her: "Now look here, girl, we both standing here soaking wet and you still trying to tell me it ain't raining" (Gates, 1988, p. 83). Signifying is evident in rap and hip-hop music. Signifying is also part of Twitter literacy, where tweets can mark Black identity. For example, there are groups that signify on specific Black artists, like this tweet signifyin' on the R&B singer and rapper Drake:

@charles_star: I got ride like a bicycle. Huffy. Am I the worlds worst rapper? Puffy. #fakedrakelyrics (Florini, 2014, p. 227)

Signifying is interpreted figuratively, not literally. Ms. Lee asked students to interpret samples of signifying and defend their interpretation. She then asked them to do the same with a short story and two novels set in a Black community that used AAE (*Their Eyes Were Watching God* and *The Color Purple*). The students learned about irony and figurative language. They performed better on a literary test than students from the same school who had traditional instruction (Lee, 1995).

When bridging cultural borders, it is important to avoid a deficit view that emphasizes the language and literacy abilities that learners lack; instead, emphasize the strengths and background knowledge they bring from their heritage culture. Depending on their backgrounds, students may have extensive knowledge of topics such as agriculture, building trades, engine repair, language dialects, and music. Draw upon their funds of knowledge in ways that attract their interest and highlight areas of competence (Rios-Aguilar, Kiyama, Gravitt, & Moll, 2011).

Support Bilingual and Biliterate Students

For some students, crossing cultural borders involves learning to use a completely different language. Students who speak English fluently as well as another language, like Vietnamese or Arabic, often have better literacy skills than monolingual students. Thus, being bilingual is not an impediment to becoming literate. Immigrant kindergartners who are not yet bilingual, but who are ELL, may struggle initially, but most will successfully learn to read in English by 4th grade (Lesaux, Lipka, & Siegel, 2006). Indeed, many immigrant students have higher reading and math achievement than native-born students—particularly if they attend schools with high-achieving peers (Han, 2008). What can you do to help your ELL students become biliterate? Research suggests doing the following:

1. *Help ELL students develop literacy in their heritage language.* The importance of some skills—phonological awareness, print concepts, and composition—is similar across languages that use alphabets (Caravolas, Lervåg, Defior, Seidlová Málková, & Hulme, 2013; Fitzgerald, 2006). Note that phonological awareness may be less important for learners whose language is Spanish because the sounds and letters consistently match (Goldenberg et al., 2014). Good literacy skills in a first language help students acquire a second language and achieve in school (Guglielmi, 2008; Sparks, Patton, Ganschow, Humbach, & Javorsky, 2008).

2. *When possible, teach ELL students to read and write in a bilingual setting* (Farver, Lonigan, & Eppe, 2009). Students can simultaneously learn both literacies—it does not necessarily confuse them. However, do not wait for them to become literate in their heritage language. The U.S. Department of Education recommends that kindergarten through 5th-grade ELL students be taught to read English from their first day of school, regardless of whether they are also being taught to read in their native language.

advanced literacy
reading and writing that involves a formal, academic style in particular content areas, such as science lab reports. It includes analyzing text; evaluating arguments; and writing extended, reasoned text.

After ELL students have acquired basic literacy skills in the primary grades, they may still struggle with advanced literacy in the upper grades (Merino & Hammond, 2002). **Advanced literacy** includes being able to summarize texts, evaluate arguments, and write a reasoned essay. It is used in tasks like science lab reports or literary analysis. For example, one college-bound Spanish-speaking student wrote a science lab report that began, "The diffusivity of different solvents at different temperatures are determine by using the SDT experiment" (Schleppegrell, 2002). She is a good science student who speaks English well, but she is still struggling with advanced writing. Advanced literacy is related to academic language, discussed earlier. To help ELL students develop advanced literacy, follow these guidelines:

1. *Recognize that capable ELL students who understand everyday use of Standard English will sometimes falter with advanced school-related reading and writing and academic language.*

2. *Provide explicit instruction in grammar and the specialized writing used in your class.* Provide needed corrective feedback.

3. *Require ELL students to write as much as other students.* Even if they understand the topic, ELL students may write as little as possible in order to avoid getting points deducted for poor writing. Unfortunately, this hampers their ability to become more literate. Instead, encourage longer writing, but with sufficient scaffolding to be successful.

All of these guidelines for teaching ELL students may apply to other students who are at risk for low achievement in school. Thus, the lessons in this chapter are not just for preschool or primary teachers, nor are they just for English teachers.

When these guidelines are combined into a comprehensive program across the school, achievement in all subjects can rise. For example, in one California high school, all teachers in the school (i.e., not just English teachers) work on a schoolwide academic language of words such as *discuss, evaluate, excerpt,* and *analyze.* Every class in the school engages in independent reading when students finish their work early. The entire faculty requires every student to answer questions in full sentences. While these are only some approaches to intervention, this school district has won awards for narrowing the achievement gap for minority, ELL, and low-SES students. Next, let's see what different theories suggest about how to teach literacy.

think about **this**
Imagine that you teach science to an ELL student who writes a grammatically incorrect report. Should you deduct points for low-quality writing, even if the student does the experiment correctly and understands the concepts? What would be your best solution for assigning grades in this situation?

12-3 Putting the Theories to Work: The Case of Literacy

While basic language skills are typically mastered early, universally, and without formal instruction, literacy must be formally taught. But how? This is an important question because NAEP results suggest that only one-third of 8th-graders comprehend text proficiently and only one-fourth of 12th-graders write at or above the proficient level (NCES, 2010). How should you teach literacy?

12-3a Implications for Teachers from Different Theories

As with math (Chapter 4), your view of how literacy should be taught would vary depending on your theory about how students develop. Let's look at the implications for literacy from some major theories (key concepts from past chapters are italicized).

Behaviorism and Literacy

Behaviorists believe that learning (or conditioning) results from a pairing of behavior and its consequence. As a behaviorist teacher you would emphasize *direct instruction,* teaching each skill explicitly with no reliance on discovery learning. You would set goals for your students, watch their *observable behaviors* (such as using correct punctuation in writing), and then *reinforce* behavior toward the goals. You would use much *drill-and-practice,* giving frequent and immediate *feedback.*

As a behaviorist teacher you would teach skills in a *hierarchical sequence.* Learners would first master *prerequisite low-level skills* and then move to more complex, advanced skills. For example, you would first teach young children letter names and sounds. Once children mastered these basic skills, they would progress to blending the sounds to read and spell small words and later move on to reading and writing sentences. Similarly, you would intervene with struggling adolescent readers by building basic skills first.

phonics
an approach to teaching literacy that emphasizes training in phonological awareness and decoding words.

Behaviorists favor a phonics approach to literacy instruction. The **phonics** approach involves directly teaching learners phonological awareness, pairing sounds with spelling, blending sounds together to decode words, and breaking words apart to spell them. Phonics instruction can include a variety of techniques such as learning nursery rhymes, playing games, and using worksheets.

Research supports the behaviorist approach. Learners with good phonological awareness and decoding skills become better at reading and writing than those with weak basic skills (Christopher et al., 2015; Graham, 2000; Spichtig et al., 2016). Research also shows that direct instruction may be the most effective approach for teaching decoding, vocabulary, reading comprehension strategies, writing strategies, and sentence construction (Graham & Perin, 2007). However, many educators do not like the behaviorist approach because it treats learners as passive. They prefer a constructivist view—either Piagetian or Vygotskyan, or a combination of the two.

Piaget's Theory of Cognitive Development and Literacy

In contrast to behaviorists, Piaget believed children are active thinkers who *construct their own knowledge.* Young children *assimilate* new experience with what they already know, creating unique language such as invented spellings (e.g., *lik* for *like*) and grammar (e.g., *footses* instead of *feet*). As a Piagetian teacher, you would teach literacy by providing children with a print-rich environment. You might encourage children to initiate their own literacy activities, such as writing a note to Daddy or a letter to the editor. You might help children read a new word by asking them to use what they already know to figure it out, rather than telling them what it is. With young children, you would also use *hands-on activities* with concrete objects that allow them to reinvent literacy for themselves, rather than by directly teaching basic skills. For example, you could encourage young children to play with magnetic letters, crayons, paper, and books. However, research challenges the effectiveness of *unguided* hands-on play with concrete objects for literacy learning. Play with concrete objects can cause children to focus more on the object than on what it stands for (Uttal, Liu, & DeLoache, 2006).

Children cannot by themselves reinvent the print system. Some children will learn to read without formal schooling, but they are not reinventing literacy. Instead, they are internalizing the literacy experiences they have had during social interaction. This is a key point of difference between Vygotsky's and Piaget's constructivism. Sociocultural constructivists give greater emphasis to social interaction and cultural transmission.

Vygotsky's Sociocultural Theory and Literacy

Socioculturalists believe that literacy is learned through *social interaction* in *culturally organized activities*. Print is a *cultural tool*. To become literate, learners' skills must move from interpsychological (between people) to intrapsychological (within the person). This happens through *apprenticeship*. In an apprenticeship, the expert, or teacher, *scaffolds* the child's literacy by gradually giving more responsibility to the child. The expert first performs the cognitive work and the child participates as a spectator. As the lessons progress, the child becomes more involved in the cognitive work and eventually takes over while the expert becomes the supportive spectator. The degree of scaffolding depends on the child's *zone of proximal development*. Effective teachers provide different types of instruction to the same students across the school year as the zone of proximal development shifts (Connor et al., 2009).

Scaffolding can be done between students during *cooperative learning* or *groupwork*. For example, students can do paired reading, edit each other's writing, memorize vocabulary together, or discuss the meaning of texts. *Reciprocal teaching* (see Chapter 3) is effective for developing comprehension strategies. Let's take a look at how Ms. Cole scaffolds struggling high school students' writing ability:

First, we outline in detail. My students aren't yet skilled enough to think about WHAT to write as well as HOW to write, so the WHAT has to be completely thought out before the first draft is attempted. Second, we write one paragraph at a time. I remind students what the basic components of each paragraph should be. For example, an introduction paragraph should begin with a catchy opening followed by the name of the author, title of the work, and a short plot synopsis. The paragraph should be finished with a thesis sentence that lists the main points of the essay in the correct order. This approach may seem overly prescriptive, but my students learn to write. Third, we do peer editing, also one paragraph at a time as I walk them through it. Two peers go through the same paragraph—the first student for content, the second for grammar errors. We pass the papers on for the next paragraph; eventually students' papers are read by 10 different editors. No student is "stuck" with a weak editor for more than one paragraph, and students see 10 different samples of writing. This is eye-opening for the struggling writer. Then students go on to the next draft. We peer edit again to really polish the piece. I take serious time guiding students through peer editing because it has great benefits, but if not STRICTLY guided, it does not.

Research supports the effectiveness of providing models of writing, and having students work together to plan, edit, and revise their writing—two tenets of sociocultural theory used by Ms. Cole (Graham & Perin, 2007).

The Information-Processing Model and Literacy

The information-processing model is concerned with how information is processed, regardless of whether the information was obtained through direct instruction, constructive thinking, or social interaction. Students tend to be better readers and writers if they have these information-processing skills (Carretti, Borella, Cornoldi, & De Beni, 2009; Fenesi, Sana, Kim, & Shore, 2015):

- Faster *processing speed,* particularly speed in naming letters and identifying words.

- Greater *working memory.* This helps students juggle all the tasks involved in reading or writing, and also helps them learn new vocabulary as they read.

- Greater *executive functions,* or the ability to suppress irrelevant information and control attention, from kindergarteners to older students. This helps writers keep the argument in mind while searching for appropriate words, spelling correctly, monitoring grammatical rules, and keeping out intrusive thoughts (e.g., what's for lunch?).

- Greater *metacognition,* or the ability to monitor their reading or writing process as they are doing it. This helps students pause for reflection and self-monitor.

- Greater *long-term memory,* or prior knowledge. Students who know more in general, and more vocabulary in particular, comprehend more of what they read.

Students also tend to be better readers and writers if they have strategies for *memorizing* and *problem solving,* because literacy requires strategy use, like memorizing vocabulary words or figuring out how to spell a word. Just as with math, *retrieval* is the most efficient strategy.

There are three key implications from the information-processing model for your role as a teacher. First, help students acquire greater knowledge—both literacy-specific knowledge such as letter–sound pairs and vocabulary, as well as general knowledge. Students comprehend what they read and they write better when they know more about the topic (Graham & Perin, 2007; McCutchen, 2006). Second, help students make basic literacy skills, such as decoding, so automatic that they do not tax working memory. When struggling readers use all their working memory to decode words, they cannot comprehend what they are reading. Writing especially taxes working memory. Third, help students acquire efficient strategies for literacy tasks, from decoding *bat* to writing a scientific abstract. One way to help students shift from less-efficient to more-efficient strategies is to have students *explain their strategy,* which facilitates metacognition. Strategies can also be taught through modeling, direct instruction, *spaced practice,* and *frequent testing* with *feedback.*

12-3b Comparing the Theories

As you learned in Chapter 1, the different theories of child development are not so much contradictory as they are unrelated because they explain different pieces of development. But sometimes they conflict. Historically, two approaches to literacy instruction have been at odds. Behaviorists favor a phonics approach. Constructivists favor a whole-language approach—in which reading and writing for meaning are emphasized and drilling students in mechanics, such as phonics and grammar, is de-emphasized. Phonics skills are taught individually as needed, not to the group. Constructivists encourage writing for authentic reasons and ignore invented spelling and nonstandard punctuation in order to focus on the child's meaning.

Which approach is best? Many studies converge on the notion that teaching phonics is critically important, particularly for low-SES students and secondary students who are struggling readers (McArthur et al., 2012; National Reading Panel, 2000; Suggate, 2010). Students with weak emergent literacy or phonological skills may need more phonics instruction than average readers (Connor et al., 2009). Students with strong emergent literacy skills can succeed with either a whole-language or a phonics approach (Xue & Meisels, 2004).

While phonetic skills are necessary, they are not sufficient for a child to become a fluent, skilled reader. Whole-language techniques such as focusing on meaning and using authentic literacy tasks are important. Ideally, teachers would use a combination of approaches (Connor et al., 2009; Steubing, Barth, Cirino, Francis, & Fletcher, 2008).

Each theory is true to some extent and can be applied in your classroom. For example, you can teach comprehension strategies effectively through direct instruction (behaviorism), modeling of more skilled others (social cognitive theory), and scaffolding in the child's zone of proximal development, with guided practice (sociocultural constructivism). Effective instruction draws on the best of each theory.

My Teaching

There are several things from previous chapters that you can do to increase language and literacy skills in your students. Review the "Reflections on Practice" sections from these other chapters. They include:

- Scaffold children in their zone of proximal development during literacy tasks. Use guided practice and feedback to teach strategies. Promote general knowledge so that children write with knowledge and comprehend what they read. Help children overlearn basic skills so their working memory is freed for more-complex skills (see Chapters 3, 4, and 5).

- Develop secure relationships with students. Help children develop self-control and good emotion regulation so they benefit from literacy instruction (see Chapters 6, 7, and 8).

- Encourage play with literacy among younger children. Use cooperative learning, such as peer editing, with older children (see Chapter 11).

In addition, periodically ask yourself the following:

1. Do I have any students with poor verbal ability? When a child misbehaves or performs worse than I expect, do I look for language problems?

2. Do I use uncommon words effectively when I talk to my students? Do I directly teach vocabulary? Do I read to my students or encourage them to read?

3. Do my students have opportunities to talk in the classroom? Do I insist on full-sentence answers?

4. Do my students have a mismatch between home and school language? How can I help them cross language borders? Do I support their heritage language, encouraging additive bilingualism and code switching?

5. Do I provide multicultural literature? Do I build on literacies my students have other than school-based literacy?

6. As a preschool teacher, do I promote play with literacy and sensitize children to phonemes and print concepts? As an elementary teacher, do I provide effective literacy instruction? As a secondary teacher, do I help students learn advanced literacy and academic language for my subject area?

7. Am I aware of students who are struggling readers—girls as well as boys? Do I allow extra time for reading tasks or provide oral testing? What interventions are available in my school?

8. Do I teach effective writing strategies?

9. Am I aware of non-verbal communication? Do my students and I use gestures when explaining?

10. Do I communicate high expectations to my students?

Summary of Age Trends in Language and Literacy

	Language	Literacy
Infancy & Toddlerhood (Birth–2 Years)	• Infants communicate nonverbally. • Toddlers first learn the sounds of their language, then use single-word utterances, then multiword utterances without function words (e.g., *of, the*), and then use complete sentences. • For more detail see Table 12.1. • Adults use child-directed speech toward infants and preschoolers.	• Adults read to infants and toddlers, usually picture books. Infants and toddlers handle books and look at pictures. • They scribble and attempt to write as they begin to learn print concepts. • They begin to develop a concept of what is a story, with a beginning, middle, and end.
Early Childhood (3–5 years)	• Phonological development is nearly complete by age 5. • Size of vocabulary continues to increase. • Pronunciation continues to improve. • Grammatical constructions become more complex and more correct. • Children use complete sentences and use grammatical words like "the" and "these."	• Emergent literacy skills and pseudo writing are evident by age 3. • Children first learn letters that are in their own names; their first real written word is usually their name. Children learn letters whose names match their sounds (e.g., v, k) before letters whose names do not match their sounds (e.g., h, w). • "Reading" begins as pointing and talking about books, gradually becoming more written-word oriented. Print concepts develop, such as understanding that English words are read and written left to right. • Gender differences in literacy emerge. • Most kindergarteners can form letters and write words phonetically, but are not yet reading independently.
Middle Childhood (6–12 years)	• Basic syntax is mastered by 1st grade. • Children now play with language and use it for humor. • Vocabulary is about 10,000 words by 1st grade. • Vocabulary explodes between 1st and 5th grades. Vocabulary is often learned through reasoning, but should be directly taught as well.	• Children develop conventional literacy. They first misspell words phonetically, but most become conventional spellers by 4th grade. • By 4th grade, learning-to-read shifts to reading-to-learn. • Children begin to write longer, more-complex pieces that are reader-friendly. They plan and revise their writing more. • Children who lag in literacy, but catch up by 3rd to 5th grade, may fare well as readers; otherwise, poor literacy remains stable.
Adolescence (13–19 Years)	• Language is processed more rapidly. • Sentences become longer and more complex. • Vocabulary continues to grow. • Skill at manipulating listeners increases. • Humor includes sophisticated wordplay.	• Reading fluency increases. • Abstract and specialized vocabulary is acquired, which increases comprehension. • Writing is better organized, longer, and more persuasive. More complex sentence constructions are used. Yet few students have advanced writing ability. • Gender differences diminish in reading, particularly among college-bound students. • ELL students may struggle with advanced literacy, even if they know Standard English.

❯❯ Professional Resource Download

Chapter Summary

12-1 Language Development

- Nonverbal language develops before verbal language and continues to be used throughout childhood. Expressive language lags behind receptive.

- Some nativist psychologists believe language is innate, core knowledge. Yet research suggests that general cognitive abilities such as reasoning and memory are used to learn language.

- Some children have low verbal ability, which is linked to misbehavior and low achievement.

- Verbal ability is predicted by genes, cognitive ability, social cognition (joint attention and theory of mind), secure attachment, emotion regulation, sociodramatic play, and social interaction using language and joint book reading.

- Girls tend to have better verbal ability than boys. Higher-SES children tend to have better verbal ability than low-SES children.

- Most children's home language is different from school language. Greater mismatches occur for children who speak a dialect other than Standard English, such as AAE, or a non-English language. Such children benefit from direct instruction in Standard English and can learn code switching.

- Teachers can promote children's language ability by elaborating on their talk, using uncommon words, encouraging language use in the classroom, reading to them, and teaching vocabulary.

- Teacher expectations can be communicated nonverbally and can influence student achievement.

12-2 Literacy

- Both reading and writing ability depend on vocabulary, phonological awareness, and decoding skills. Reading also depends on fluency and comprehension.

- Early struggling readers tend to remain struggling readers, but some children improve. Poor reading is linked to emotional distress, misbehavior, and low academic achievement.

- Dyslexia is a learning disability for reading. Interventions focus on phonological awareness and fluency. Dyslexia often co-occurs with other information-processing difficulties.

- Literacy is predicted by verbal ability, brain structure (which could be due to genes or experience), information-processing abilities, emotional well-being, and social experiences with print such as play and joint book reading.

- Girls tend to be more literate than boys, high-SES learners more than low-SES, and White and Asian American learners more than Black or Latino children. Reasons for these group differences include opportunity to learn inside and outside of school and culture mismatch.

- Teachers can help young children become literate by promoting verbal ability, teaching letters, using nursery rhymes and phoneme-based games, drawing attention to print concepts, and reading to children. Teachers can help older youth by providing frequent practice with authentic literacy activities, giving feedback, and teaching reading and writing strategies.

- Children can learn multiple literacies, even if they are not yet literate in their heritage language. Biliterate students who have basic English ability may struggle with advanced literacy.

12-3 Putting the Theories to Work: The Case of Literacy

- Behaviorists emphasize direct instruction, with drill-and-practice of basic literacy skills. Behaviorist theory supports the phonics approach.

- Piagetian constructivists emphasize children as active learners who construct their own literacy from a print-rich environment with hands-on activities.

- Sociocultural constructivists emphasize scaffolding in the zone of proximal development, modeling, guided practice, and cooperative learning.

- The information-processing model emphasizes the role of knowledge, working memory, metacognition, strategy use, memorization strategies, and processing speed in literacy development.

- Each theory contributes to effective classroom practices. Phonics is a necessary, but not sufficient, component of effective literacy instruction. Direct instruction, guided practice, and authentic literacy activities are important.

chapter 13

©bikeriderlondon/Shutterstock.com

The Self-System and Motivation

In previous chapters, you learned that children can do poorly in school for many reasons other than low intelligence, such as lack of self-control or aggression. In this chapter we will discuss two other factors that affect school success—self-concept, including gender and ethnic identity, and motivation. **After you read this chapter, you will be able to:**

13-1 Describe how the self-system functions and promote positive self-concept in your learners.

13-2 Discuss how gender and ethnic identity affect school success and create classrooms that minimize sexism and racism.

13-3 Apply principles of motivation to increase your students' motivation.

13-1 The Self-System

Sadie is an active 3rd-grader. Her teacher, Ms. Heck hands out a worksheet that contains several sentences about the Pilgrims. The instructions are to put the sentences in order to make an accurate paragraph. Sadie raises her hand: "Ms. Heck, I don't understand. I don't have them in order."

"Well, you need to pay attention." Ms. Heck did not answer Sadie's question, so Sadie tries again: "Ms. Heck, do we write the sentences or just the numbers?" Ms. Heck looks at Sadie, and then looks away without answering her. Sadie writes one sentence and then blurts out: "What comes second?"

"If you were to read carefully, maybe you would understand."

"Is it this one? The colony was the second after Jamestown?" Ms. Heck starts clapping and has the rest of the class join her, as she sarcastically says, "Very good! It's about time! Maybe you'll be able to figure out the next one, too." Then Sadie asks if they are supposed to use pen or pencil. Ms. Heck says, "Do we use pen for worksheets? No!" A few minutes later, Sadie asks to sharpen her pencil. When she returns to her seat, Sadie raises her hand a few more times. Ms. Heck looks at Sadie, but does not call on her. Sadie asks a classmate for help.

Ms. Heck has recommended that Sadie be retained next year because she is not capable of doing 4th-grade work, is not a good student, and is unable to pay attention. However, she does not want Sadie in her class again next year.

Ms. Heck is remarkably negative with Sadie, but she is not negative with other students. Sadie is not doing well in school, but she is not doing poorly enough to justify retention (see Chapter 1). How do you think Ms. Heck influences Sadie's self-concept? Your answer depends on what self-concept is and what causes it. The **self** is a group of related thoughts that you hold about yourself (Harter, 2006). The thoughts include self-assessments like "Am I worthy of love?" and "What am I good at?" How might Sadie answer these questions in Ms. Heck's classroom?

Psychologists use the term *self-system* because there are multiple aspects of the self. Part of the self is one's personal identity. The theorist who most popularized the notion of personal identity was Erik Erikson. Box 13.1 discusses his contributions. The aspect of the self that you probably hear about most is self-esteem. Other important aspects of the self-system relevant to your classroom include self-concept and self-efficacy.

13-1a Self-Esteem, Self-Concept, and Self-Efficacy

Self-esteem refers to your general feelings of worth; it is a broad concept. **Self-concept** refers to both your global evaluation of yourself and evaluations of yourself in specific domains. You can have different self-concepts in domains like academics, social skills, sports, appearance, peer relations, romantic appeal, verbal skills, and mathematical skills (Cole et al., 2001; Marsh, Ellis, & Craven, 2002). *Global* self-concept and self-esteem are often considered to be the same.

Self-efficacy (see Chapter 3) is even more specific than self-concept, though both are about competence in a domain. Self-efficacy refers to your confidence that you

self
a group of related thoughts that people hold about themselves.

self-esteem
one's feelings of worth.

self-concept
the differentiated conception of self that includes categories such as academic self-concept, social self-concept, and athletic self-concept. The term *global self-concept* is sometimes used synonymously with *self-esteem*.

BOX 13.1 theories & theorists

Erikson's Psychosocial Theory

Erik Erikson was born in Germany in 1902. During his childhood, he thought his father was the man he grew up with. However, as an adolescent he discovered that his birth was the result of an extramarital affair when his mother was in a previous marriage (Hopkins, 1995). Erikson did not publicly reveal this until he was 68. As you read on, think about how his history may have influenced his ideas.

Erikson developed a psychosocial theory of development that paralleled Freud's psychosexual theory. Their theories were similar in many ways, including outlining stages of development, but different in that: (1) Erickson emphasized a crisis at each stage, (2) his theory covered the lifespan instead of only birth to adolescence, and (3) he emphasized the influence of culture and society. Table 13.1 outlines Erikson's stages (Erikson, 1959, 1963).

TABLE 13.1	Comparison of Erikson's and Freud's stages		
Psychosocial stage	**Age period**	**Description of Erikson's stage**	**Freud's parallel stage**
Basic trust versus mistrust	Birth to 1 year	Infants come to understand the world as trustworthy and safe or threatening and unsafe based on how they are treated. Trust comes from being cared for.	Oral
Autonomy versus shame and doubt	1 to 3 years	Toddlers want to feel that they have some autonomy or control over their environment and their choices. At the same time, they need to experience firm and reasonable control. Children need to feel a sense of self-control, or else they will feel shame and a desire to get away with misbehavior.	Anal
Initiative versus guilt	3 to 6 years	The child attempts to gain the mother's affection and is eager for cooperation with age-mates. If parents demand excessive self-control, children become overcontrolled and lose their identity.	Phallic
Industry versus inferiority	6 to 11 years	The child begins to work and win recognition by producing things. This is linked with systematic instruction, which may occur in schools. If unsuccessful, the child feels inferior and inadequate. The stage is a lull before the storm of adolescence.	Latency
Identity versus identity confusion	Adolescence	The child seeks an identity and a profession or occupation. The child may experience role confusion, including sexual identity, and may become clannish and cliquish.	Genital
Intimacy versus isolation	Emerging adulthood	The young adult seeks intimacy and close friendships and, in their absence, feels isolation and self-absorption.	
Generativity versus stagnation	Adulthood	Adults need to be needed. They wish to guide the next generation, usually their own children. Otherwise, they may feel a need for pseudo-intimacy and may fall into stagnation and personal impoverishment.	
Integrity versus despair	Old age	Elderly adults feel that their lives were worthwhile, or they fear death and that it is too late to start another life.	

Erikson's Psychosocial Theory (continued)

In each stage, the individual experiences internal conflict. Some of these conflicts center on sexuality, bowel movements, and breastfeeding. For example, in the second stage—autonomy versus shame—Erikson believed toddlers fear adults who "attack one's power of autonomy and who would designate as evil those products of the bowels which were felt to be all right when they were being passed" (1963, p. 254). The resolution of each conflict, whether positive or negative, sets the stage for the next conflict.

The concept for which Erikson may be most famous is the *identity crisis*. This refers to a person's difficulty in deciding who to be and in finding meaning in life and work. For Erikson, adolescence was the onset of the identity crisis—and a period of storm. If the crisis "Who am I?" is resolved, then adolescents are

Erik Erikson

© Cengage Learning

ready to take on the challenges of the next stage.

Erikson may have been interested in the identity crisis because of his own struggles with identity. His stepfather was Jewish, but his parents were Danish and he was blond and blue-eyed. Was he Jewish or Nordic? His last name officially changed three times, from Salmonsen to Homburger to Erikson. He also had considerable difficulty choosing a career. He studied art, tried teaching school, and studied psychoanalysis. In his career as a psychologist, he did fieldwork among the Sioux and Yurok Native American groups, engaged in casework in Pittsburgh with poor immigrant families, and wrote books about Gandhi and Martin Luther.

can accomplish a specific behavior, and it is future-oriented, referring to what you are confident you can do in the future. You could have a positive social self-concept but still feel low self-efficacy for meeting new people in strange settings, like shy Eric from Chapter 6. Keep in mind that all three self terms (esteem, concept, and efficacy) have to do with your *perceptions* of worthiness and competence, not your actual worthiness or competence. In this section, we will focus on self-concept and self-esteem. We will focus on self-efficacy later in this chapter.

13-1b Age Trends in the Self

A father saw his daughter splattered with mud. He said, "My, you're pretty dirty!" The girl replied, "Yes, but I'm even prettier clean." Could you guess that this child with a robust physical self-concept was 4 years old? Let's look at age trends in the self.

Infancy and Toddlerhood (Birth to 2 Years)

Some infants learn that they can affect the environment; for example, they learn that kicking causes the crib to bounce and crying brings father. This fosters high self-esteem because they feel capable of influencing others and events. In Chapter 6, you learned that when parents are responsive, their children develop secure attachment and internal working models that "I am worthy of love" and "I am capable of getting important people (my parents) to respond to me." This becomes the bedrock of high self-esteem.

Learning Laffs

Early Childhood (3 to 5 Years)

Young children tend to be overly optimistic about their abilities (Davis-Kean, Jager, & Collins, 2009). Every preschooler on a soccer team may think that he or she is the best player, and every preschooler in a classroom may think that he or she is the smartest. This inflated self-assessment is good because it prevents preschoolers from giving up, which they might do if they knew how incompetent they really are.

One reason young children have inflated self-assessment is that they are not good at social comparison yet. They have difficulty comparing their own competence to that of others. They also are unlikely to understand that if others do something with *less* effort, it means that they are *more* skilled (Nicholls, 1989). For example, they do not understand that if a boy can read only after extensive practice, he is less skilled than another boy who easily reads with little practice.

Middle Childhood (6 to 12 Years)

During middle childhood, children's optimistic self-assessment is replaced with more realistic self-concepts. This occurs as children compare their own competence to that of others (Harter, 2006). This growing social comparison ability affects well-being as children begin to understand how they compare with others in socioeconomic status (SES), weight, and academic competence (Davis-Kean et al., 2009). On average, children's perceptions of competence tend to go down in middle childhood.

Adolescence (13 to 19 Years)

Adolescents continue this downward trend in their self-perceptions of competence (see Figure 13.1). This may occur because their assessment of their competence becomes more accurate. It may also occur because youth increasingly are compared with others, in grading at school and in competitive extracurricular activities. If adolescents become overly self-critical, depression may develop (Kopala-Sibley, Zuroff, Hankin, & Abela, 2015). Paradoxically, despite this overall downward trend, adolescents still tend to have a positive bias about themselves.

13-1c Individual Differences in the Self

Some children have higher self-esteem than others. These differences are fairly stable, meaning children with higher self-esteem are likely to stay that way over time, and become even more stable in adolescence (Donnellan, Kenny, Trzesniewski, Lucas, & Conger, 2012; Kuster & Orth, 2013). Next let's look at how these differences might affect children.

What Do Views of the Self Predict?

Learners with higher self-esteem tend to have higher grades; this effect is small but consistent (Baumeister, Campbell, Krueger, & Vohs, 2003; Marsh & Hau, 2003). The link becomes stronger if you consider *domain-specific* self-concept and academic achievement *in that domain*. For example, students' *mathematical* self-concept correlates strongly with mathematics grades and test scores, but *global* self-concept

FIGURE 13.1 Perceptions of Competence from Grade 1 to Grade 12.

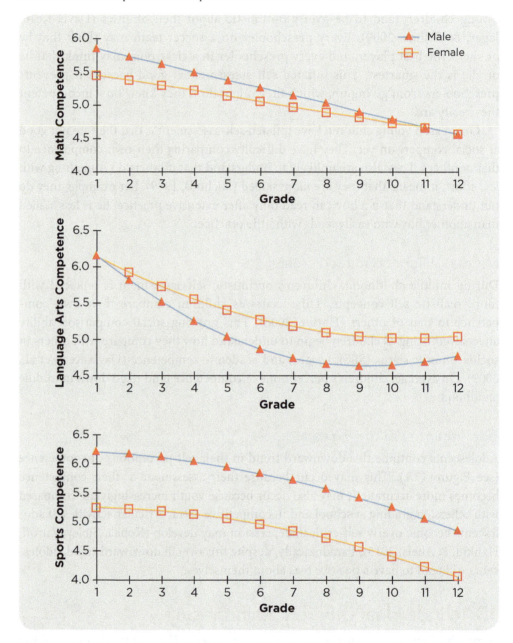

What do these graphs tell you about age trends in self-concept overall, boys versus girls, and specific domains? *Source: Jacobs, Lanza, Osgood, Eccles, and Wigfield (2002).*

correlates weakly with mathematics achievement (Swann, Chang-Schneider, & McClarty, 2007).

Learners with high self-esteem tend to fare better emotionally and socially. High self-esteem is linked to greater happiness, less delinquency, higher probability of graduating from college, and more stable employment (Baumeister et al., 2003; Cheng & Furnham, 2002; Gerard & Buehler, 2004). In contrast, learners with low self-esteem tend to have more depression and anxiety (Orth, Robins, & Meier, 2009; Sowislo & Orth, 2013).

What Predicts Views of the Self?

Figure 13.2 shows a 2nd-grader's essay about what makes her feel important. Does her self-reflection match the research? Self-esteem is influenced by attachment, learners' perceptions of what others think of them, and how their competence compares with others.

Attachment

Attachment figures are particularly powerful in shaping children's self-concepts. *Secure* children tend to have positive self-concepts, with a working model of the self as valued and capable (Verschueren, Marcoen, & Schoefs, 1996). *Ambivalent* children (whose parents may be inconsistently available or critical) tend to have low self-concept. They try to please the parent but seldom succeed (Mayseless, 1996). In contrast, both avoidant and disorganized children can have moderate to high self-concepts. *Avoidant* children may express self-sufficiency, believing they do not need others. They think that they can earn parental regard through high achievement in a valued domain (academics, athletics, wealth), but not unconditional regard, so they defend their self-esteem by becoming workaholics, perfectionists, or materialists. *Disorganized* children may defend their self-esteem by being overly anxious to please others.

FIGURE 13.2 Essay on Feeling Important.

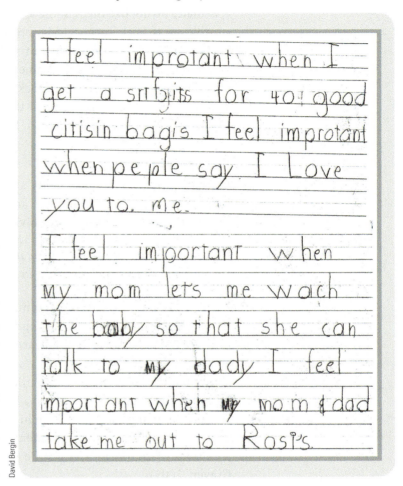

David Bergin

Does this child's views of what leads to self-esteem agree with the research? Translation: *I feel important when I get a certificate for 40 good citizen badges. I feel important when people say* I Love You *to me. I feel important when my* Mom *lets me watch the baby so that she can talk to my* Daddy. *I feel important when my* Mom & Dad *take me out to Rosie's* (restaurant).

Other people's esteem

Learners' sense of self is based largely on how they believe *other people* regard them: "Does my teacher think that I am competent at this activity?" "Do my parents believe that I am worthy of love?" "What do my friends think that I am good at?" When learners are accepted and valued by others, they tend to feel high self-esteem.

Learners' self-concept—particularly academic self-concept—is responsive to both peers' and teachers' views of them from about 3rd grade on. Students with positive school reputations have higher academic self-concept and better grades, and put forth more effort (Gest, Domitrovich, & Welsh, 2005). In Chapter 12, you learned about the Pygmalion effect—that teachers' beliefs about students' competence can alter students' performance. Sadie is likely to develop low self-esteem in her class because Ms. Heck communicates that Sadie is neither competent nor valued.

In Chapter 11, you learned that peer acceptance and friendship help learners feel good about themselves. As long as they have a few good friends, emotionally healthy learners outgrow the need for widespread peer approval sometime in childhood. Yet, some learners continue to be overly vulnerable to peer approval. That is, if a few classmates do not like them, some learners can shrug it off, but others feel shame and worthlessness. Such learners feel more anxiety and depression (Rudolph, Caldwell, & Conley, 2005). Attachment plays a role in this process by influencing the peers with whom learners choose to spend time. Learners with secure attachment tend to seek others who provide positive feedback. Learners with insecure attachment or depression may select peers who confirm their negative self-concepts (Cassidy, Aikins, & Chernoff, 2003; Cassidy, Ziv, Mehta, & Feeney, 2003).

Competence

Learners' actual accomplishments also influence their self-concept. If experience suggests they are good at particular activities, they tend to have high self-concept for those activities (Guay, Marsh, & Boivin, 2003).

> Counselor: Wow! You got a 30 on the ACT. That's great!
> Student: No it's not. Everyone in my class got about the same.

As this brief conversation points out, self-concepts depend on the range of competence learners observe around them. This learner was "average" in a high-achieving school. What if this learner were the best in a low-achieving school? There is a **big-fish–little-pond effect**, which means that learners with the same ability tend to have higher academic self-concept in low-achieving schools than in high-achieving schools (Marsh, Köller, & Baumert, 2001). Thus, attending a school where most students have high standardized test scores and go on to elite universities lowers students' academic self-concept. This pattern has been found in dozens of countries around the world (Marsh et al., 2015; Seaton, Marsh, & Craven, 2009).

13-1d Group Diversity in the Self

One type of group diversity is a cohort effect. Are youth today are more narcissistic and self-aggrandizing than those in past generations? Some research shows a substantial increase in narcissism since the 1980s (Twenge & Campbell, 2010; Twenge, Miller, & Campbell, 2014). Narcissism refers to feeling more important than others, deserving privileged status, and needing admiration. In Chapter 10 you learned that narcissism can lead to aggression or bullying (Pauletti, Menon, Menon, Tobin, & Perry, 2012), so a rise in narcissism is worrisome. During a year in your classroom you won't see cohort effects, but you might see gender and ethnic differences in views of the self.

Gender

Boys may have a little higher global self-esteem than girls, but gender differences are small (Robins & Trzesniewski, 2005). The effect size (see Chapter 1) is about 0.21. However, in some domains, gender differences are larger. Boys tend to have higher self-concept in physical appearance, athleticism, and self-satisfaction (happiness with oneself). See Figure 13.3. Girls tend to have higher verbal and social self-concept (Cole et al., 2001; Marsh, Trautwein, Lüdtke, Koller, & Baumert, 2005).

big-fish–little-pond effect the tendency to experience higher academic self-concept when surrounded by peers whose academic achievement is lower.

think about this
Do you think the timing of the gender difference in self-esteem might be related to puberty? Review Chapter 2 to justify your answer. What other factors might contribute? Do they reflect real gender differences in competence in each domain? Base your answer on a review of gender differences in previous chapters.

FIGURE 13.3 Gender Differences in Self-Concept for Six Domains.

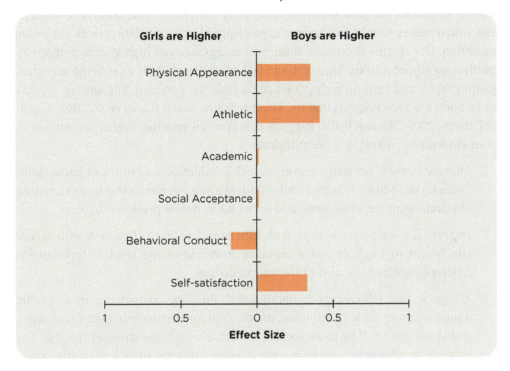

Bars to the right favor boys and to the left favor girls. For social acceptance and academic self-concept, boys and girls do not differ. *Source: Gentile et al. (2009).*

Ethnicity

A consistent finding is that African Americans have slightly higher self-esteem than do Whites (Adams, 2010; Twenge & Crocker, 2002). There is also evidence that African Americans is more impervious to risk factors in their lives; high-risk African American youth tend to have higher self-esteem than high-risk White youth (Gerard & Buehler, 2004). Physical self-concept also varies by ethnicity, with Black children averaging the highest and Asian American children the lowest (Crain, 1996).

13-1e Classroom Implications of the Self

One of my students, 3-year-old Miguel, requires more energy to control than all the other children. He never cooperates with classroom activities or with other children. He screams and cries if another child simply takes a crayon he wants. One day his mother, who knows he has behavior problems, asks me how he is doing. He is standing there listening, so I lie. I turn to Miguel and say, "Miguel is learning to share his crayons nicely with other children. He is learning to wait for his turn. He is learning to be quiet and sit in his chair during sharing time. You are a good boy, aren't you Miguel?" Miguel looks totally confused at first (he is probably wondering who I am talking about), but then beams proudly. I guess he thought about this because over the next week he is transformed. He actually does share, wait his turn, and sit (sometimes) quietly. One afternoon he hands a crayon to another child, and says out loud to himself, "I good. I share. Uh huh."

Miguel is constructing a positive social self-concept, thanks to his teacher's help. This is important because high self-concept is correlated with classroom success. But which causes which? In Chapter 1, you learned that correlation does not prove causation. Does high self-concept *cause* peer acceptance and high grades, perhaps by motivating students to try harder in the face of challenges? Or does being accepted, gaining skills, and earning high grades *cause* high self-concept? The answer appears to be both; research suggests that the effect is bidirectional (Guay et al., 2003; Marsh & Craven, 2006). Research also suggests that you can promote higher self-esteem in your students by following these guidelines:

1. *Improve learners' competence* in areas such as athletics, academics, or social skills. Focus on skills that are valued in the student's culture. For methods of promoting physical, cognitive, emotional, and social skills, review previous chapters.

2. *Improve learners' relationships* with others and yourself. Learners with secure attachment to teachers and acceptance from classmates tend to feel worthy. Review Chapters 6, 10, and 11 for how to do this.

3. *Recognize that self-concept is multifaceted.* Building competence in a specific domain is more likely to influence self-concept for that domain than to influence global self-esteem. The more specific the self-concept, the stronger the link. For example, mathematics performance is more strongly linked to mathematics self-concept than verbal self-concept. Students who are good at math often have good verbal ability as well, yet they may have lower verbal self-concept because of "internal" comparisons—"I'm not good at English because it takes more effort, and I don't get as high test scores in English as I get in math" (Marsh & Craven, 2006). Yet, as you build each component of self-concept, you will contribute to global self-concept.

4. *Be honest about academic achievement.* Do not attempt to protect learners' self-esteem by telling them that they are doing well when they are not. Instead, point out how they have improved and give them supportive feedback about how to improve even more.

Imagine how destructive an impatient and critical teacher could be. Let's look at a trigonometry class:

> *Ms. Kilroy is often impatient with her students. One day she is trying to get a girl to say that the tangent of X is equal to 1 over the cotangent of X. Instead, the girl keeps saying that the tangent of X is equal to 1 over the tangent. Ms. Kilroy raises her voice, grabs a piece of paper roughly off the girl's desk, tells her it is not true, and proceeds to do the problem for the girl. When a boy gives a correct answer, but with more detail than was required, Ms. Kilroy says, "You don't need to tell us all of that extra stuff—we already know it."*

You could see Ms. Kilroy's students deflate when she spoke to them, much like Sadie did in Ms. Heck's class in the opening vignette. As a teacher, you can influence your students' self-concept both by building their competence and by communicating that you value them.

13-2 Social Identity: Gender and Ethnicity

Part of children's sense of self derives from membership in a group. Each child is a member of multiple social groups based on factors such as gender, SES, ethnicity, neighborhood, and religion. Let's next discuss two aspects of this **social identity**: gender and ethnic identity.

13-2a Gender Identity

Among the first questions asked at birth is, "Girl or boy?" Boys and girls often differ in hairstyle, clothes, voice, style of walk, and body shape, so that gender is one of the first things you notice about others. Gender follows you across your lifespan, influencing your name, play, friendships, and activities.

At the simplest level, **gender identity** refers to the ability to accurately label your own sex—are you a boy or a girl? Gender identity also includes more complex concepts—how typical of your gender you feel, how content you are with your gender, how much pressure you feel for gender conformity, and whether you feel that your gender is best (Corby, Hodges, & Perry, 2007). These concepts change with age.

Infancy and Toddlerhood (Birth to 2 Years)

In Chapter 5, you learned that infants spontaneously form categories. Gender is one such category. Infants just a few months old can distinguish male from female faces (Ramsey-Rennels & Langlois, 2006). By age 2, children begin to label people as boys and girls. Girls develop this ability earlier than boys (Zosuls et al., 2009). They are now capable of *gender labeling*. However, they base labels on appearance—if a boy wears a barrette in his hair and a skirt, he is a girl.

Once children figure out their gender, they become "gender detectives" who actively try to figure out how boys and girls differ and what are boy versus girl activities (Martin & Ruble, 2004). They then pay more attention to objects and activities that they think are for their own sex rather than for the other sex (see Photo 13.1).

One cost to this detective work is the development of *gender stereotypes*. As early as 18 months, children judge which toys are for boys and which are for girls. Boys play more with trucks and girls more with dolls by 21 months (Zosuls et al., 2009). If you tell young children that a toy is for girls, then girls are more likely to approach the toy. Parents and teachers sometimes make inappropriate generic statements such as "boys are good at math" with children as young as 2. Young children deduce stereotypes from such statements that are resistant to change (Cimpian & Markman, 2011).

Early Childhood (3 to 5 Years)

Gender constancy emerges between 3 and 4 years of age, but it may not be fully developed until age 7 or later (Golombok & Hines, 2002). This refers to the understanding that

social identity
the part of learners' self-concept that derives from their membership in a group, such as gender, ethnic, religious, national, or other groups.

gender identity
a part of the concept of self that includes ability to accurately label your sex and your feelings about your gender.

PHOTO 13.1 Children become gender detectives, seeking out same-gender activities and friends.

Photodisc/Digital Vision/Jupiter images

gender does not change just because a boy puts on a skirt ("I am a boy and will always be a boy"). We showed our 3-year-old daughter a picture of David when he had long, frizzy hair in the 1970s. A few days later she asked to see "the picture of when Daddy was a girl."

In early childhood, children become gender-typed in appearance and play (see Chapter 11). Girls play more with dolls and boys play more with trucks, and they increasingly resist crossing these gender boundaries (Halim, Ruble, Tamis-LeMonda, & Shrout, 2013; Zosuls, Ruble, & Tamis-LeMonda, 2014). Fathers push their young children toward these gender-typed activities, engaging in more physical play with their sons and more literacy activities with their daughters (Leavell, Tamis-LeMonda, Ruble, Zosuls, & Cabrera, 2012). Preschoolers hold stronger gender stereotypes than toddlers. They describe girls as nice, wearing frilly things, and liking dolls, while they describe boys as having short hair, playing active games, and being rough (Martin & Ruble, 2010). By kindergarten, children have full-blown knowledge of gender stereotypes, such as which occupations and attributes are more male or female (Miller, Trautner, & Ruble, 2006). At this age, they tend to be quite rigid about their stereotypes, such as saying, "*Only* girls can play with dolls," and they become biased toward seeing their own sex as best. It is normal for children to be rigid in applying knowledge they are just solidifying.

A very few children are *gender-variant* or *gender-nonconforming* and do not conform to traditional gender identification. For example, *transgender* children are biologically of one sex but identify with the opposite sex. They might insist that they are the opposite sex as early as preschool (Olson, Key, & Eaton, 2015). There is little rigorous research on the frequency, causes, or outcomes of transgenderism, although the frequency may be increasing (Olson, 2016).

Middle Childhood (6 to 12 Years)

By the early school years, children understand gender constancy, that gender is a fundamental part of someone's identity and is constant across time and situations (Golombok & Hines, 2002). Children understand that even if someone wants to be the other sex, cross-dresses, and behaves like someone of the other sex, he or she does not become the other sex.

Children become more sexist in some ways in early elementary school as gender stereotypes are consolidated. Children begin to understand stereotypes about abilities, not just toys and activities, such as "math is for boys" and girls are less likely to identify with math (Cvencek, Meltzoff, & Greenwald, 2011).

In addition, as you learned in Chapter 11, gender segregation peaks in middle childhood as children seek clear gender boundaries and punish those who cross them. For example, in a class of kindergarteners at the school library, a boy chose a book based on *Beauty and the Beast*. As they lined up to leave:

> *The boy standing behind him spotted the book in his friend's hands and began making gagging noises. Other boys soon joined in with, "Oooh, you're going to read a girls' book?" and taunting, "Ha ha, he's a girl, he's a girl." The accused quickly slipped out of line, ran to a nearby shelf, and exchanged his book. (Dutro, 2002, p. 376)*

Such gender boundaries are often more rigid for boys than for girls. If boys do "girl things," they get more criticism than if girls do "boy things" (Martin & Ruble, 2010; Mulvey & Killen, 2015). Over time, girls tend to focus less on "girl" activities, while boys continue to prefer "boy" activities. For example, a teacher set out a limited number of books to choose from (Dutro, 2002). No boys voluntarily chose babysitting books, though some girls chose basketball books—to the dismay of boys who then had to take the leftover babysitting books.

Toward the end of elementary school, despite a continued preference for their own sex and strong gender segregation, children become less rigid in their stereotypes. Their interest in stereotypically feminine and masculine activities also declines (Crouter, Whiteman, McHale, & Osgood, 2007; McHale, Kim, Dotterer, Crouter, & Booth, 2009). At the same time they are developing understanding of what gender stereotypes might mean in the adult world. From age 7 to 15 there is an increase in children's belief that males get more power and respect than females (Martin & Ruble, 2010).

Adolescence (13 to 19 Years)

In adolescence, feeling typical and content with one's gender are both linked to better adjustment (Corby et al., 2007). For example, girls who experienced atypically *early* breast development tended to report symptoms of depression (Yuan, 2012). Another study found that 4th- through 8th-graders who preferred activities stereotypical for their gender tended to be well adjusted, unless they felt excessive pressure to conform to stereotypes (Egan & Perry, 2001). However, well-adjusted youth also felt that they could try out activities typical of the other gender if they wanted to.

13-2b Ethnic Identity

Your **ethnic identity** is a part of your self-concept that includes a sense of membership in an ethnic group and your attitudes and feelings about that membership (Phinney, 1996). Ethnicity and race are not the same thing. *Ethnic group* refers to a group of people who share ancestry, language, and culture. *Racial group* refers to a group of people who share biological characteristics such as skin color. However, these terms are controversial (Markus, 2008). Many social scientists believe race is not biological but that it is instead a label placed on groups by society (Richeson & Sommers, 2016). In Chapter 1, you were introduced to the largest ethnic minority groups recognized by the U.S. Census, referred to as ALANA (African, Latino, Asian, and Native American). Note that Latino, or Hispanic, is not a race. Latinos can be Black, White, Asian, or Native American. Generally, White youth tend to feel that their ethnic identity is less important than do ALANA youth. In fact, many White youth cannot even conceive of having ethnic identity unless they focus on their family's country of origin, like Ireland or Italy (Phinney, 1989).

In the United States, increasing numbers of children are multiracial, like Barack Obama and actress Cameron Diaz. A multiracial person self-identifies with two or more races. The identity that multiracial children develop may depend on skin color, parentage, social norms, and personal choice. Youth who are Black/White biracial tend to self-identify as Black (Doyle & Kao, 2007). Some multiracial youth feel pressured to "choose sides," that is, to declare that they are of one race or the

ethnic identity
a part of self-concept that includes a sense of membership in an ethnic group and attitudes and feelings about that membership.

other (Gaither, 2015). However, many have a flexible identity, such that they switch between racial identities depending on the situation. This flexibility allows them to function effectively in both minority and majority situations. Developing an ethnic identity can be challenging for multiracial children, but most will develop a positive identity (Herman, 2004).

Age Trends in Ethnic Identity

By 9 months of age, infants distinguish faces from their own race better than those from other races, and they prefer and pay more attention to same-race faces (Pauker, Williams, & Steele, 2016). Their preference for same-race faces is reduced by having experience seeing other-race faces, even if that experience is based on photographs (Anzures et al., 2013).

Between 2 and 4 years of age, children share toys equally with same-race and other-race peers and show no preference when choosing a playmate (Anzures et al., 2013). However, by age 4 to 5 children show a clear preference for their own ethnic or racial group. At this age, most preschoolers are able to correctly label their racial group, but they may not understand the label, and their understanding can be a little muddled (Bernal, Knight, Garza, Ocampo, & Cota, 1990). Listen to multiracial 4-year-old Corrine talk about the class's baby bunnies:

> "How many babies are there?" Sarah asks Corinne.
> "Six!" Corinne announces, "Three boys and three girls."
> "How can you tell if they're boys or girls?" Sarah questions.
> "Well," Corinne begins, "my daddy is White, so the white ones are boys. My mommy is Black, so the black ones are girls."
> Sarah counts: "That's only five." (The remaining bunny is black and white.)
> "Well, that one is like me, so it's a girl," Corinne explains gently. She picks up the bunny and says, "See, this one is both, like me!" (Van Ausdale & Feagin, 1996, p. 784)

Thus, infants' preference for looking at same-race others grows into playmate preferences and ethnic identity in early childhood. This can set the groundwork for experiences of racism.

Around age 6, children use racial features to sort or categorize people (Pauker et al., 2016). This allows them to begin to understand racism at a superficial level. For example, Mexican American children may believe that some people do not like Mexican Americans because they do not like Mexico. Around age 10, they have a more sophisticated understanding—for example, that some people may not like Mexican Americans because of racial stereotypes. At this age, about 80 to 90% of children recognize broadly held racial stereotypes (McKown & Strambler, 2009; McKown & Weinstein, 2003; Quintana & Vera, 1999). For example, 9- to 10-year-olds know that Asians are supposed to be more skilled at math (Cvencek, Nasir, O'Connor, Wischnia, & Meltzoff, 2015).

Once children understand that some groups are stigmatized, they can understand that they themselves could be stigmatized. **Stigma** refers to feeling different and less valued in the community. Perceptions of stigma due to race are not common in elementary school. For example, a study of Puerto Rican children in Boston found

stigma
feeling different and less valued in a community.

that only 12% of 1st-, 2nd-, and 3rd-graders perceived discrimination (Szalacha et al., 2003). However, perceptions of stigma increase through the end of high school (Brody et al., 2006; Seaton, Caldwell, Sellers, & Jackson, 2008). High schools are often more diverse than elementary schools, which can make ethnic identity more salient to high school students and also provide more opportunities for racism.

Individual Differences in Ethnic Identity

Do members of the same ethnic group have similar ethnic identities? Not necessarily. For example, one study found that some African American high school students felt that being African American was central to their identity and were proud to be African American. Others did not strongly identify as African Americans and felt negatively about their racial group (Chavous et al., 2003). Such differences in ethnic identity influence students' well-being.

For ALANA youth, positive ethnic identity is linked to academic success (Caldwell, Zimmerman, Bernat, Sellers, & Notaro, 2002; Smith & Lalonde, 2003). Adolescents with a positive ethnic identity tend to like school, find it interesting and valuable, and feel bonded to school (Fuligni, Witkow, & Garcia, 2005). They are also more likely to complete high school and attend college than those with weak or negative ethnic identities, and may have higher GPAs (Altschul, Oyserman, & Bybee, 2006; Chavous et al., 2003). The specific ethnic group with which a learner identifies does not predict academic achievement or motivation, but a strong, positive identity does. Learners have a positive ethnic identity when they feel good about the people in their ethnic group, see their group as having made major accomplishments, and feel like they derive personal strength from being part of their group (see Photo 13.2).

Ethnic identity is also linked to emotional well-being. ALANA youth who have a strong and positive ethnic identity are more likely to have high self-esteem and be happier, and less likely to be depressed, anxious, or use drugs (Kiang, Yip, Gonzales-Backen, Witkow, & Fuligni, 2006; Mandara, Gaylord-Harden, Richards, & Ragsdale, 2009; Marsiglia, Kulis, & Hecht, 2001; Rogers, Scott, & Way, 2015). It is not psychologically healthy to be ashamed or ambivalent about who you are, and a major component of self-concept for youth of color is ethnic group.

What about bicultural youth? Some research shows that biculturalism, that is, identification with the minority group and also with the dominant group, is positively related with adjustment and well-being (Nguyen & Benet-Martinez, 2013). For immigrant children, their heritage language is a key component of ethnic identity. In Chapter 12, you learned that additive bilingualism, or learners retaining their heritage language, predicts their well-being.

13-2c Sexism and Racism

One potential cost of strongly identifying with any group is the development of prejudice toward other groups. Prejudice refers to negative beliefs or feelings about a group such as an ethnic group. It is human

Cengage Learning

PHOTO 13.2 Children who have a strong, positive ethnic identity and are in a classroom that supports their social identity have greater school success.

nature to categorize others into in-groups ("similar to me") and out-groups ("not like me"), to prefer your in-group, and to exaggerate the similarity of the out-group members. Your in-group may be based on gender, ethnicity, religion, or other factors. To see your in-group in a positive light does not necessarily lead to prejudice, but it may.

Prejudice occurs when people dislike and attach negative stereotypes to the out-group. Sexism and racism refer to judgments based on sex and race that the in-group is inherently superior to the out-group. Racism also refers to assuming that physical differences like skin color, hair texture, or facial features cause differences in behavior, personality, or intelligence. In the following vignette, Riley expresses racial prejudice:

> *Riley is in the office for the third time this year for using racial slurs in class. He is not punished, but is told to never do it again and sent back to class. He was also accused of writing racial slurs in books in the library, but there was no proof and he denied it. Riley is not popular, but he is an exceptional two-sport athlete, which gives him some social status. Riley enjoys flaunting his racism. When his English teacher begins reading* Huckleberry Finn, *Riley and his buddies snicker each time they hear the "n-word." They enjoy the idea that the word is used in class. Riley says his parents use the word on a regular basis and that jokes aimed at other ethnic groups are common at his family dinner table. He says racism is appropriate, because that is what his parents believe.*

Prejudice like Riley's tends to develop when it is accepted in the in-group, the group is threatened by the out-group (whether the threat is real or imagined), competition with the out-group is emphasized, and the learner strongly identifies with the in-group (Nesdale, Maass, Durkin, & Griffiths, 2005).

In North America, discrimination is socially and legally unacceptable. High-status groups do not want to be perceived as prejudiced, and low-status groups do not want to be victims of prejudice. This helps explain why children may become less prejudiced with age. Preschoolers as young as 3 categorize people into in- and out-groups, and attach stereotypes to the groups. Children's prejudice begins between ages 3 and 6, peaks about ages 5 to 7, and then declines slightly (Raabe & Beelmann, 2011). By age 10, some carefully avoid talking about race (Aboud, 2008; Apfelbaum, Pauer, Ambady, Sommers, & Norton, 2008). Few adolescents and adults espouse *explicit* prejudice like Riley. However, some adults retain *implicit* prejudice, or negative feelings about the out-group that are not necessarily conscious or are conscious and hidden (Baron & Banaji, 2006). Those with hidden prejudice may use the anonymity of the Internet to express sexism and racism (Daniels, 2013; Tynes, Umaña-Taylor, Rose, Lin, & Anderson, 2012).

Children can be victims of prejudice. For example, surveys of African American youth show that by age 13, most have experienced racial insults and disrespectful treatment, such as in stores (Martin et al., 2011). Experiencing discrimination can affect children's motivation, peer relationships, and achievement at school. When children experience racism and discrimination, they are at greater risk for depression, low self-esteem, anxiety, illness, and low grades. They are also at greater risk for behavior problems, delinquency, crime, and health risks such as smoking.[1] Negative

---

[1] There are many studies that support this conclusion, a few of which are listed here: Benner and Kim (2009); Martin et al. (2011); Schmitt, Branscombe, Postmes, and Garcia (2014); Sirin et al. (2015); Stein, Supple, Huq, Dunbar, and Prinstein (2016).

effects of discrimination cross generations; African American parents' experience with discrimination predicts their teenage children's depression (Ford, Hurd, Jagers, & Sellers, 2013).

Whether children perceive discrimination depends on at least three factors:

1. Their *social-cognitive abilities*, like theory of mind, perspective-taking, hierarchical classification ability (i.e., people can belong to multiple groups), and moral judgment (Brown & Bigler, 2005). By age 6 or 7, children's social cognition is usually adequate to perceive discrimination, but as you learned earlier, older children tend to perceive more discrimination.

2. The *obviousness of the discrimination*. Young children recognize name calling, racial slurs, or direct comments such as "Girls aren't good at computer games" as discrimination. Older adolescents perceive more subtle forms of discrimination, such as unfair grading, harsher discipline, or specific groups being discouraged from taking higher-level classes.

3. Their *personal vigilance* toward discrimination. People who anticipate being the target of prejudice, and believe that society is prejudiced, tend to be more vigilant about subtle signs of prejudice (Kaiser, Vick, & Major, 2006). People who are part of stigmatized groups are more vigilant. For example, White youth are less likely to perceive subtle discrimination than are youth of color.

think about **this**

Throughout this text, we have advocated respecting children's heritage culture. What is your role as a teacher when your students' heritage culture espouses values contrary to your own—such as racism, sexism, violence, alcohol abuse, child abuse, religious intolerance, or promiscuity? What if cultural mismatches involve moral issues rather than social conventions?

Parents can help their children avoid internalizing discrimination while promoting ethnic pride. Parents who discuss the reality of discrimination and ways to cope with it, point out successful members of their group in the community, and teach pride in their ethnic heritage promote their children's resilience (Hernández, Conger, Robins, Bacher, & Widaman, 2014; Murry, Berkel, Brody, Miller, & Chen, 2009).

Teachers can help, too. However, teachers often feel uncomfortable about discussing ethnic issues because they fear that such discussions might lead to prejudice and stereotypes (Markus, 2008). Nevertheless, discussions can be positive if they lead to greater understanding and empathy for the out-group and help rectify inequities. Throughout this text, you have learned about potential ethnic differences among your students. In the next section, we will focus on how you can promote positive social identities among diverse learners.

13-2d Classroom Implications of Gender and Ethnic Identity

Riley is White and attends a rural high school with little racial diversity, but prejudice can also be found in urban schools with lots of diversity and among ALANA students. As a teacher, you want to eliminate prejudice, while also encouraging your students to develop a strong, positive social identity. One strategy that does not work is claiming color-blindness. Some people find this surprising because they mistakenly think that ignoring differences and treating everyone the same will make race no longer matter. Research shows that we do notice race, in less than a second, and this influences our perceptions of others and our behavior toward them. Pretending to ignore race can leave in place attitudes and policies that disadvantage some groups. Ironically, White individuals who appear to ignore race are viewed as *more* prejudiced by African Americans than Whites who do talk about race (Apfelbaum, Norton, & Sommers, 2012). Let's discuss how to promote healthy social identity without promoting out-group bias, but first let's look at an issue that may affect your students in stigmatized groups—stereotype threat.

Stereotype Threat

stereotype threat
concern that one's performance will confirm negative stereotypes about one's group.

Widely known stereotypes can cause members of stigmatized groups to worry that they will be judged according to stereotypes and that their performance will confirm a negative stereotype. This is called **stereotype threat** (Steele & Aronson, 1995). In school settings, African Americans and Latinos may feel stereotype threat when taking standardized tests because the achievement gap for standardized tests is widely known. Girls may feel stereotype threat on mathematics and science tests.

Scientists study stereotype threat by randomly assigning students to a condition of threat or no threat. In the threat condition, students are told something that will remind them of stereotypes about their group and then they are given a test. For example, 6th- and 7th-graders were given a test that required them to remember a simple line drawing. Half the students were told it was a test of geometry ability, and the other half were told it was a test of memory ability. Girls got lower scores when they thought the test measured mathematical (geometry) ability (Huguet & Regner, 2007; see Figure 13.4). Stereotype threat may help explain why girls get higher grades but lower test scores in "masculine" fields such as mathematics (Kenney-Benson, Pomerantz, Ryan, & Patrick, 2006). Stereotype threat has even been demonstrated with university athletes, especially males, who got lower test scores after being reminded they were athletes (Dee, 2014).

FIGURE 13.4 Girls' Performance and Stereotype Threat.

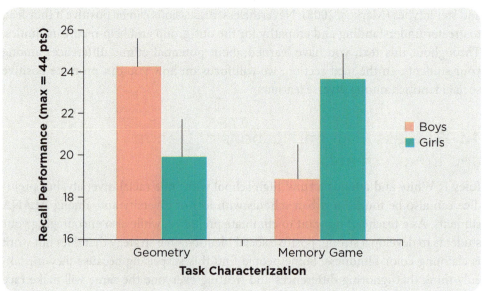

Girls and boys were asked to reproduce a complex geometric figure from memory, but for some it was labeled a memory game and for others a geometry task. Points were awarded for each segment reproduced correctly. When did girls do better? Why might that be? *Source: Huguet and Régner (2007).*

How does stereotype threat work? Attempts to suppress worry about confirming stereotypes may impair information processing and interfere with working memory (Hutchison, Smith, & Ferris, 2013). As learners worry about confirming a stereotype, thoughts like "These math problems are too hard for me" and "I am not good at math" begin to consume working memory space, reduce executive functions, and undermine test performance (Inzlicht, McKay, & Aronson, 2006; Spencer, Logel, & Davies, 2016). Research on stereotype threat suggests that you may help your students by following these guidelines:

1. *Teach learners that intelligence is changeable* and that they can increase their intelligence through effort (Spencer et al., 2016). In a study of this effect, 7th-grade girls scored higher on mathematics tests, and low-SES and minority students scored higher on reading tests, after being encouraged to view intelligence as changeable (Good, Aronson, & Inzlicht, 2003). We'll discuss views of intelligence in the next section.

2. *Teach older students about stereotype threat.* Studies with college students find that a brief lesson on stereotype threat, and a warning that if they feel anxious during the test, it may be due to negative stereotypes that have nothing to do with their actual ability, reduces the effect of stereotype threat (Johns, Schmader, & Martens, 2005). It is likely that the same effect would occur for adolescents.

3. *Be careful not to communicate your own anxieties.* In one study of 1st- and 2nd-grade classrooms, female teachers' math anxiety predicted their female students' math achievement at the end of the school year, regardless of their math ability at the beginning of the school year. The girls also were more likely to endorse stereotypes that boys are good at math and girls are good at reading (Beilock, Gunderson, Ramirez, & Levine, 2010).

Despite the fact that many Western countries have a long history of free schooling for all children, in the past schools contributed to discrimination. Recall from Chapter 9 the experience young Ruby Bridges had with school desegregation. Today, there are legal protections against inequities and discrimination at school, but there is still room for progress. Now let's turn to how you can strengthen your learners' social identity.

Promote Positive Social Identity

You can help your students develop a strong, positive social identity by valuing their group. In contrast, if you do not value your students' social group, this may be sufficient to foster alienation from school; you do not have to be racist or overtly hostile to create a negative environment. Claude Steele (1992), a renowned African American researcher, wrote, "For too many Black students school is simply the place where, more concertedly, persistently, and authoritatively than anywhere else in society, they learn how little valued they are" (p. 78). To prevent this perception, follow these guidelines:

1. *Use a multicultural curriculum.* Select books, software, posters, and samples of work that portray different groups. Comment on the contributions of diverse people to the topic at hand. Depict each group in a positive way across the school year, not only during isolated celebrations like Black History Month and Cinco de Mayo. Clearly communicate appreciation for all cultures—their language, music, history, and current events.

2. *Avoid sex-typed materials in the classroom.* Research shows that gender stereotyping in children's picture books and coloring books has diminished, but is still present (Beilock et al., 2010).

3. *Help each learner feel valued in your classroom.* Communicate that all students are valued no matter what their background (Spencer et al., 2016). When learners feel devalued, or stigmatized, they feel stress, frustration, and anxiety about whether they are being judged. As learners expend mental effort to control these feelings, they have less available for self-control of other behaviors, such as paying attention (Salvatore & Shelton, 2007). Recall that self-control, like a muscle, can fatigue. In contrast, when learners feel emotionally safe, they participate more in class activities.

4. *Hold all learners to high, but reasonable, standards.* When giving feedback to students of stigmatized groups, provide detailed feedback that makes it clear you have high standards and believe the students can reach those standards (Cohen, Steele, & Ross, 1999). Avoid stereotypes that might lead you to hold low expectations, recommend less challenging classes, or overlook talent, such as mathematical ability in girls. Because it is impossible to use group membership to accurately infer learners' abilities, treat learners as though they might be talented at anything, without regard to group. Provide equal opportunities for success to all learners.

5. *Avoid pushing students to represent their race, gender, or ethnic group.* For example, a Black male student wrote, "I feel like I have the weight of all the Black people… [W]henever I open my mouth, I do speak for all Black people here…. I am one of the few glimpses into the Black male perspective that White students get to see" (Gere, Buehler, Dallavis, & Haviland, 2009, p. 828). Can you see how this is related to stereotype threat?

6. *Avoid microaggressions*, which are subtle behaviors that communicate prejudices (Suárez-Orozco et al., 2015). Examples include assuming someone who looks "foreign" does not speak English, showing surprise that a person of color has high achievement, or that a woman is good at math. When microaggressions are brought to their attention, people often deny any intent to offend and may not even realize that they are offending, which makes it particularly difficult to remedy microaggressions.

7. *Be self-reflective about your attitudes toward other groups.* In one survey, one-quarter of Black youth felt their teachers treated them with less respect or thought they were not as smart as other students (Seaton et al., 2008). In another survey, girls reported that some teachers made negative comments about their mathematical, science, or computer abilities (Leaper & Brown, 2008).

Reduce Prejudice

Since the 1954 *Brown v. Board of Education* ruling that repudiated the doctrine of "separate but equal" schools, it has become clear that merely desegregating schools is not enough to reduce prejudice. What can you do to help students like Riley become less prejudiced? Unfortunately, a careful review of thousands of studies found that there are very few rigorous, experimental studies that suggest how to successfully reduce prejudice (Paluck & Green, 2009; see also Aboud et al., 2012). Thus, there is limited research-based guidance for classroom teachers. Nevertheless, you can reduce prejudice when you build skills that were discussed in previous chapters, such as empathy (see Chapter 8), moral judgment (see Chapter 9), and prosocial behavior (Chapter 10). In addition, using a multicultural curriculum tends to promote a spirit of mutual respect for diverse classmates. A multicultural curriculum does not consistently reduce prejudice, but it may make a small contribution (Pfeifer, Brown, & Juvonen, 2007). Additional interventions supported by some evidence include the following:

1. *Use anti-bias training.* There are specific curricula designed to help you discuss prejudice, such as "More Than Meets the Eye," in which students learn to identify differences within their in-group and similarities between them and out-group members. Such curricula can be effective from kindergarten through high school (Pfeifer et al., 2007). In addition, make it clear that you do not tolerate sexual harassment, racial slurs, or other forms of derogatory speech.

2. *Teach about the history of race relations and discrimination.* These lessons can be difficult because they can make stigmatized learners feel angry and privileged learners feel threatened (Bigler & Wright, 2014). However, one study found that White elementary students who learned about famous African Americans and the discrimination that they endured had more positive views of African Americans than students who learned about the famous people but not the discrimination (Hughes, Bigler, & Levy, 2007).

3. *Encourage participation in extracurricular activities, including sports.* Race relations are better when the participants have equal status, and extracurricular activities such as choir and sports can provide a place where learners are on more equal footing (Holland, 2012).

4. *Use cooperative learning,* which also improves achievement when well implemented. How to do this is discussed in Chapter 11. When organized well, cooperative learning can result in greater reduction in prejudice than using a multicultural curriculum (Pfeifer et al., 2007; Slavin & Cooper, 1999).

Research shows that contact between groups can reduce prejudice to a modest degree. However, just because students are in the same classroom or school does not mean they have contact, and mere contact is not enough (Pettigrew & Tropp, 2006). Being in a classroom with Black students is not going to make Riley less prejudiced. Even friendship with out-group others does not necessarily reduce implicit prejudice (Henry & Hardin, 2006). To reduce prejudice, contact should occur in a setting in which the different groups:

- Have equal status within the setting.

- Share goals, which helps create a "super-group" identity.

- Cooperate to pursue those goals.

- Feel support from authority figures (Fiske, 2002; Pettigrew & Tropp, 2006).

Athletics and extracurricular activities often meet these conditions in addition to cooperative learning in the classroom.

think about this

Examine your own gender biases. Do you assign certain tasks to only girls, like taking notes during cooperative learning activities? When handing out jump ropes, footballs, and basketballs, do you give certain items to only boys? Are there other ways that you might convey gender stereotypes?

As an authority figure in your classroom, your students are likely to believe what you tell them about the value of social groups. For example, in one experiment, elementary school students were placed on academic teams. An adult told some teams to like students on both teams, but told others to "stick with their own team." The latter group had greater dislike for the other teams, or out-group (Nesdale et al., 2005). You can use your power to help students feel good about their own in-group identity and also about the out-group.

You have learned that self-concept and social identity can influence success in the classroom. Self-concepts are important for understanding motivation. Self-concepts affect what tasks students are willing to do and the effort they put into tasks. Let's turn to the issue of motivation next.

13-3 Motivation

Vinnie, a sophomore, is required to write an essay on Hawthorne's The Scarlet Letter *in his History/English class. He does not share his teacher's enthusiasm for Hawthorne. He thinks the book is a waste of time and the assignment is "interfering with his life." He is in the middle of building a computer and spends as little time as possible with* The Scarlet Letter. *Later, in the same class, he writes an essay about Alexander the Great, who was "way cool." His grades, a C and an A, reflect his opinion of each assignment.*

motivation
internal states that affect the energy level, direction, vigor, and persistence of behavior toward a goal.

intrinsic motivation
the desire to pursue an activity for its own sake, not for external reasons.

extrinsic motivation
the desire to pursue an activity for reasons external to the activity such as getting a reward, avoiding punishment, or earning a grade.

Vinnie's grades measure his motivation more than his ability. Some students always do their best on assignments, like the compulsive class valedictorian, and others never let school assignments interfere with their lives. Most, like Vinnie, are in the middle—working hard on assignments they view as interesting or important. Your challenge in teaching is to influence those views so that your students are motivated to learn. **Motivation** refers to internal states that affect the energy, direction, vigor, and persistence of behavior toward a goal (Pintrich, 2003).

In an ideal world, your students would engage in class learning activities because each activity itself is rewarding. This is called **intrinsic motivation**. In contrast, **extrinsic motivation** refers to engaging in an activity because of a result outside the activity itself—like getting a scholarship, earning money, avoiding punishment, getting a high grade, pleasing parents, and impressing friends. As you have noticed, this is not an ideal world; promoting intrinsic motivation in each of your students at all times is probably impossible. Your students are likely to feel a mix of intrinsic and extrinsic motivation.

Based on the definition of motivation, nearly every topic discussed in this textbook—reinforcement, background knowledge, stereotype threat, emotion regulation, delay of gratification, self-control, and so forth—affects motivation because each topic affects the energy, direction, vigor, and persistence of behavior at school. However, in this chapter we will focus our discussion of motivation on two key questions: "Can I do this task?" and "Do I want to do this task?" See Photo 13.3.

PHOTO 13.3 Whether students are motivated to engage in learning tasks depends on their answer to two important questions: *Can I do this?* and *Do I want to do this?*

13-3a Can I Do This?

In classrooms, students' answer to this question depends on their self-efficacy, their view of ability such as intelligence, and their attributions for academic success.

Self-Efficacy Affects Learners' Answer to "Can I Do This?"

Self-efficacy refers to your confidence that you can accomplish some behavior. It is a judgment about your competence. Self-efficacy is domain specific. Domains can be broad, such as self-efficacy for schoolwork in general, or narrow, such as self-efficacy to do long division. Students with high academic self-efficacy believe they can master school topics, can regulate their own learning, and can get peers and teachers to help them when needed. Self-efficacy is a key component of social cognitive theory, discussed previously in Box 3.2 (see Chapter 3).

Why does self-efficacy matter? Many studies (Bandura, 1997) have shown that when you feel high self-efficacy, you are more likely to:

- Feel interest.

- Work hard.

- Perform well.

- Persist in the face of difficulty.

- Develop strategies for improvement.

For example, a girl with *high* self-efficacy for mathematics might choose to take calculus in high school, begin the class with low anxiety, work hard, and redouble her efforts when her first test comes back with a low score. Another girl with *low* self-efficacy might avoid taking the class to begin with. If forced to take it, she might enter with high anxiety and give up when the first low test score comes back. These two girls could have similar skill levels, but their self-efficacy influences what they do with those skills. You might think self-efficacy pertains only to older learners, but even 3-year-olds' behavior is affected by self-efficacy (Williamson, Meltzoff, & Markman, 2008).

Where do feelings of self-efficacy come from? There are four main sources (Bandura, 1997; Usher & Pajares, 2008):

1. *Previous experience.* If you have a history of success, you tend to expect success in the future, and if you have a history of failure, you tend to expect failure. This may be the most powerful influence on self-efficacy. You can help your students experience success.

2. *Vicarious experience of models*, or experience that you have through observing someone else. If you observe someone else succeeding or failing, it affects your own self-efficacy. For example, our 6-year-old son quit trying to ride a bicycle because he kept falling over. Then he saw a *younger* neighbor riding a bicycle. He seemed to think, "If that little kid can, I can." Our son got back on his bicycle and quickly learned to ride. His level of skill did not change, but his belief that he could learn to ride did. An important point is that similar-aged models, or *peer models*, are particularly effective. Our son's self-efficacy did not increase from

think about **this**

Parents who have higher self-efficacy about parenting, and who believe that the way their child turns out depends on how well they parent, have children who are more compliant and self-regulated (Feldman & Klein, 2003). Why might this be? Do you think this applies to teachers as well?

seeing adults riding bicycles. Nevertheless, children are sometimes influenced by adult models. This may partly explain why parents with high academic self-efficacy tend to have children with high academic self-efficacy. You can carefully choose models for your students to observe.

3. *Verbal persuasion.* Other people can persuade you to feel more confident about your abilities. The persuader might remind you of previous successes, or point out your strengths and how they apply to the current situation. Respected experts tend to have greater persuasive power. You can be a respected expert for your students.

4. *Physiological reactions.* Emotional arousal, like a racing pulse, can convey information about the probability of success. For example, if you get sweaty palms during an exam, you might attribute the sweaty palms to being incompetent, which would undermine self-efficacy. You learned in Chapter 8 how to help your students regulate their emotions.

Self-efficacy is a powerful component of motivation, but when you ask yourself, "Can I do this?" you are also influenced by your view of ability.

Views of Ability Affect Learners' Answer to "Can I Do This?"

Ability refers to intelligence as well as other forms of aptitude such as artistic talent and athletic skill. You have a **fixed mindset** if you believe ability is unchangeable; you have a certain amount of talent, and that is that. In contrast, you have a **growth mindset** if you believe ability is changeable and can be developed. Which view would lead you to improve your skills? Holding a growth mindset of academic ability can lead to higher achievement, persistence in the face of obstacles, and intrinsic motivation (Paunesku et al., 2015; Yeager & Dweck, 2012). Failure undermines efficacy more if learners hold a fixed mindset than if they hold a growth mindset. Parents move mindset toward growth when they praise the process, rather than the child (e.g., "you worked hard!" or "you did that carefully!" rather than "you are so smart!"). Toddlers whose parents use process praise grow into older children with a growth mindset (Gunderson et al., 2013).

How does mindset influence achievement? Your mindset can change thoughts from "Can I do this?" to "How can I improve at this?" Which of the following thoughts is better for learning? "I failed my chemistry exam because I'm not smart enough and never will be" (fixed mindset) or "I'll study chemistry more so I can become smarter" (growth mindset). Which of the following thoughts is likely to lead to improved athletic ability? "I am just not coordinated" (fixed mindset) or "If I practice, I can improve" (growth mindset). Views of ability influence how learners and teachers think about why they succeed or fail. Learners have a natural tendency to search for such causes, which is the basis of attributions, our next topic.

Attributions Affect Learners' Answer to "Can I Do This?"

Attributions are the causes that you perceive for your own and your students' behaviors, successes, and failures. Attributions that you make for past behavior motivate your future behavior (Weiner, 1985). For example, Vinnie will behave

fixed mindset
a belief that ability is unchangeable; also called an *entity* mindset.

growth mindset
a belief that ability is changeable and can be developed; also called an *incremental* mindset.

attributions
the causes that people perceive for their own and other people's behavior.

differently if he attributes his poor performance on his *Scarlet Letter* essay to low ability, rather than low effort. He will have different motivation if he thinks, "I'm just not good at writing. I might as well not even try" compared to if he thinks, "I did poorly because I didn't try hard."

For most academic situations, attributions to effort are ideal. When you attribute your successes and failures to effort, it means that the cause is under your control because you control your own effort; thus, you are likely to increase effort in the face of failure rather than giving up. In contrast, when you attribute successes to ability, you may feel proud of your ability, but if you begin to fail, you might doubt your ability and give up. When students attribute their school failures to internal, stable shortcomings in themselves, they are more likely to have low grades and to be depressed (Foersterling & Binser, 2002). They are likely to avoid difficult courses or challenging tasks because they do not expect to succeed; they are likely to put in little effort because they do not believe that effort pays off.

Fortunately young children may be oblivious to this effect. Think about toddlers learning to walk. They average 2368 steps and 17 falls per *hour,* yet they get up and keep trying (Adolph et al., 2012). Imagine if learners put that sort of effort into math, art, science, music, or sports. The effect of attributions begins to set in as early as age 5 and is fully developed by age 11 or 12 (Heyman, Gee, & Giles, 2003; Normandeau & Gobeil, 1998).

Some children learn to feel helpless, believing they cannot do something no matter how hard they try. **Learned helplessness** can be the result of an unresponsive environment—that is, the perception that no matter what they do, they cannot get things to change or improve. When learners cannot get the environment to respond, they may attribute it to their own inadequacies, believing that other people could have been successful, but not them. This undermines motivation and self-esteem, which perpetuates a cycle of failure. In one study, helplessness was moderately stable as early as kindergarten, and such feelings in kindergarten predicted helplessness later in 5th grade (Ziegert, Kistner, Castro, & Robertson, 2001). Low-SES students are more vulnerable to helplessness at school than are high-SES children (Evans, Gonnella, Marcynyszyn, Gentile, & Salpekar, 2005).

Can you see how self-efficacy, views of ability, and attributions are linked? Learners who feel high self-efficacy are likely to attribute failure to something other than a lack of ability. For example, if Vinnie has high self-efficacy for writing essays, he may attribute his C grade to bad luck, an off day, low effort, or an unfair teacher. He expects to do better next time. On the other hand, if Vinnie feels low self-efficacy, he is likely to attribute failure to something that fits with his self-image as lacking ability. He may attribute the C to being a mediocre writer who cannot improve. If Vinnie holds a growth mindset, he is likely to attribute his failures to something changeable and believe that he can improve through effort.

think about **this**
Imagine that some teachers attribute learner failure to stable uncontrollable (by the teacher) causes such as bad parenting, too much television, and low intelligence. How might this affect their motivation to improve their teaching?

learned helplessness
the perception developed through experience that no matter what you do, you will not be competent in a domain.

13-3b Classroom Implications of "Can I Do This?"

Your students' answer to the question "Can I do this?" will influence their persistence and willingness to take on challenges, which will then influence their success in your classroom. You can help your students feel more capable by following these guidelines:

1. *Provide models of success.* Models can be live, on video, in books and magazines, or described verbally. You can be a model yourself by demonstrating effective strategies for an activity. You can even model thinking by thinking aloud. This helps learners understand the thinking that is behind successful performance for activities such as solving mathematical problems. Some models are more effective than others:

   - *Peer models* tend to be particularly effective in promoting self-efficacy. When classmates model success, with your scaffolding, other learners are more likely to believe they can be successful also.

   - *Multiple models* are more effective than a single model. Multiple models increase the likelihood that a student will see at least one who seems similar and think, "If they can do it, I can do it."

   - *Coping models* are more effective than watching an expert easily and flawlessly accomplish a task (Zimmerman & Kitsantas, 2002). Watching a renowned mathematician easily prove a theorem may not make you feel efficacious about doing the same. In contrast, when a model copes with difficulty and shows how to overcome failure, you are more likely to believe you might be successful also.

2. *Promote a growth mindset.* In an experiment, when 7th-graders were taught that the brain is like a muscle that gets stronger with use and that the brain forms new connections every time learning occurs, their motivation and grades improved as compared with a control group (Blackwell, Trzesniewski, & Dweck, 2007). In another experiment, at-risk high school students read an article about how the brain changes as a result of effort and then wrote an essay giving advice to an imaginary student who believed he lacked the ability to succeed in school (Paunesku et al., 2015). They later earned higher grades and passed more classes than a control group. In contrast, telling students that boys (or girls) are good at something can reduce the motivation of both boys *and* girls, apparently by creating a fixed mindset about that ability (Cimpian, Mu, & Erickson, 2012).

3. *Attribute success to effort rather than ability.* Your attributions influence learners' beliefs about themselves. If learners do poorly and you say, "It's OK, math isn't my thing either," you are attributing their failure to low ability, and each student may think, "If the teacher thinks I'm no good at math, maybe I'm not." When you attribute their success to effort, your students are more likely to develop a view that ability is changeable (growth mindset), but only if it is true that they worked hard (Dweck, 2010). Be sure to praise for specific effort, not general ability. For example, you might say, "Your hard work paid off," rather than "You are so smart." When learners are praised for ability, they tend to prefer nonchallenging tasks in order to avoid exposing their failures (Dweck, 2006).

4. *Change learners' attribution style.* You can "retrain" learners to make helpful, rather than harmful, attributions. One intervention, called "Best Foot Forward," helped African American and Latino elementary students attribute failure to lack of effort rather than to inability or poor teaching. After the intervention,

they were more motivated and persistent in their schoolwork (Hudley, Graham, & Taylor, 2007). You can improve learners' attributions when you:

- Tell learners that they are sufficiently able; that is, use your position as a knowledgeable person in authority to persuade them (but don't lie).

- Tell learners that they need to try harder, unless of course they are already trying very hard and know it.

- Help them use better strategies and model the strategies.

Even learners who are confident that they are *capable* of learning a skill or topic may wonder if they *want* to learn the skill or topic. This is the other half of motivation.

13-3c Do I Want to Do This?

Vinnie was able to write a good essay on "Alexander the Cool" (his title), but he did not want to write a good essay on *The Scarlet Letter*. What makes a student want to put effort into a learning task at school? Let's focus on three major factors: goals, self-determination, and interest.

Goals Affect Learners' Answer to "Do I Want to Do This?"

Goal setting applies to activities that range from sports to academics to art. Many studies show that goal setting improves motivation and performance (Locke & Latham, 2002). For example, in one experiment, elementary and secondary students were asked to set a "personal best" goal to do better than they had the last year on a standardized test—when they still had time to study (Martin & Elliot, 2016). They scored better than a control group (see Figure 13.5).

Why does goal setting improve performance? There are several reasons:

- *Goals direct attention and action.* They help learners focus on what they want to accomplish, which reduces distraction.

- *Goals mobilize energy.* When learners are tired or feel their attention wandering, they are more likely to generate energy to refocus when they are committed to a goal.

- *Goals prolong effort and persistence.* When learners hold a specific goal for a learning task, they are more likely to persist than when they have no specific goal in mind.

- *Goals motivate problem solving.* When learners start on mathematical problems, for example, and encounter difficulty, they are more likely to try to figure out strategies to solve the problems if they are committed to a goal of mathematical competence, or if they want to become an engineer. They may devise new study strategies like working multiple problems, attending tutoring, and studying with competent friends.

FIGURE 13.5 Goal Setting and Achievement.

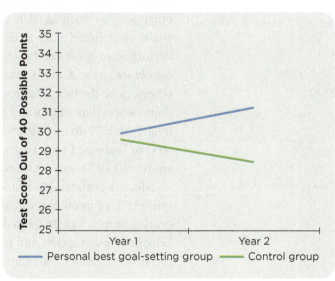

Elementary and secondary students in one group were asked to set a goal to achieve a higher score on a standardized test than they had during the past year. In Year 2, how did they do compared to the control group? *Source: Martin and Elliot (2016).*

TABLE 13.2 Attributes of effective goals

Effective goal attribute	Example
Specific	*I will learn 3 measures of this Beethoven sonata every day this week.* Vague goals such as "do my best" or "try hard" are not effective.
Challenging	*I will beat my last score on the next math test.* Goals should be challenging, but also within one's ability.
Divided into subgoals	*I will choose a topic this week, find references and write summaries of the references by Saturday, and write an introduction by Tuesday.* Subgoals should mark progress toward a long-term goal.
Monitored for progress	*I will record my bench presses on a chart for 3 months.* Ideally, the monitoring should be written.
Committed	*I will tell my Russian teacher that I'll learn 10 new words this week.* Public commitments, for example in front of classmates or teammates, are more effective than unspoken commitments.
Accompanied by feedback	*I will ask my teacher if my weld is uniform and thick enough.*
Accompanied by implementation plans	*I will put my phone in another room while I study so I won't be tempted to text instead.* Plans are important to overcome barriers.

mastery goals
a goal to master a skill or topic.

performance goals
a goal to demonstrate ability by performing better than others.

Not all goals are equally effective. Attributes of effective goals are given in Table 13.2 (Gollwitzer & Oettingen, 2012; Locke & Latham, 2002; Harkin et al., 2016). In one study, when high school Spanish students set goals using some of these techniques, their language learning improved over several years (Moeller, Theiler, & Wu, 2012).

In addition to goal *setting*, *achievement goals* are also important in your classroom. When learners enter an achievement-oriented situation like a classroom or a sports setting, they tend to orient toward one of two types of broad achievement goals: **mastery goals** and **performance goals**. If you hold *mastery* goals, your broad goal is to *develop* your ability; this makes you prefer challenge, want to learn new things even if they are difficult, and focus on comparison with yourself rather than with other people—such as "Am I doing better than I used to?" If you hold *performance* goals, your broad goal is to *demonstrate* your ability and *do better than others*. Performance goals can be separated into performance-*approach* and performance-*avoidance* goals. A performance-approach goal is the desire to perform better than others, or be the best in a group; a performance-avoidance goal is the desire to avoid doing worse than others and to avoid looking dumb or incompetent. Thus, students might think, "I do my history assignment because I want to improve my skills" (mastery) or "because I want to get a higher grade than the other students" (performance-approach), or "because I want to avoid looking dumb" (performance-avoidance).

Mastery goals tend to be more adaptive than performance-avoidance goals. When learners have mastery goals, they are more likely to use effective learning strategies, process deeply, have increased intrinsic motivation and self-efficacy, seek appropriate help, be less disruptive, and feel optimism, with less fear of mistakes—each of which can lead to greater learning.[2] *Performance-approach goals* are mixed. They can be

---

[2] Many studies have demonstrated this, a few of which are listed here: Friedel, Cortina, Turner, and Midgley (2010); Kaplan, Gheen, and Midgley (2002); Pintrich and Schunk (2002); Senko, Hulleman, and Harackiewicz (2011); Shim, Ryan, and Anderson (2008); Turner et al. (2002).

adaptive, especially if combined with mastery goals (Hulleman, Durik, Schweigert, & Harackiewicz, 2008; Senko, Hulleman, & Harackiewicz, 2011); however, they can also undermine performance, especially for low-ability students. In contrast, *performance-avoidance goals* are consistently linked to less-positive attitudes and lower achievement.

Self-Determination Affects Learners' Answer to "Do I Want to Do This?"

Learners have an innate need for self-determination—that is, a need to feel that they have some control over what they do (Deci & Ryan, 2000). You may have noticed infants who insist on feeding themselves, or high school students who want to select which books to read. In Chapter 6, you learned that one reason for the drop in achievement as students transition from elementary to middle/junior high school is that they are given less autonomy, even though they want more autonomy. You also learned that students view teachers as more caring if they provide students with choice and autonomy whenever possible.

When you feel that you chose to do a task rather than having it imposed on you, you are more likely to feel intrinsic motivation for that task. Imagine Sally and Korin are both doing algebra problems. Sally enjoys mathematical problem solving and does extra problems. In contrast, Korin does only the required problems—and only because she wants a good grade. Sally is intrinsically motivated, while Korin is extrinsically motivated. Korin did not choose to do the math problems of her own free will, so she is likely to engage in mathematics at a superficial level.

Teachers may resist giving students autonomy because they feel pressure from principals, parents, the surrounding culture, and their own expectations to "control" students (Reeve, 2009). They think that without structure, students will not achieve. Yet, structure and control are different. Structure refers to clear expectations (e.g., definition of a high-quality paper), guidance during a lesson, step-by-step instructions when needed, and facilitating transitions from one activity to another (Jang, Reeve, & Deci, 2010). Structure, when combined with autonomy support, predicts greater student engagement in classroom learning (Jang et al., 2010).

Interest Affects Learners' Answer to "Do I Want to Do This?"

There are two types of interest (Renninger & Hidi, 2011). **Situational interest** refers to interest generated in a situation, like a classroom. It is sparked by the environment. In contrast, **individual interest** refers to enduring preferences that learners have for certain activities or domains of knowledge. They bring individual interests with them. Let's listen to a teacher describe toddlers in her class:

> *When I play classical music, I set the CD player on the floor. Stuart, our most rambunctious toddler, immediately gets down on the floor with his nose against the CD player and listens intently. In contrast, when I get out books, Stuart is not interested, but Rowan literally drops whatever he is doing and clambers into my lap for reading.*

situational interest
short-lived attention or curiosity that is generated by the conditions in a specific situation.

individual interest
an individual's enduring interest in an activity or domain of knowledge.

These 2-year-olds have distinct individual interests. Both individual and situational interest are relevant to your classroom, but you have more control over situational interest. Situational interest is important because it grabs attention and promotes learning, and if repeated, can promote enduring individual interest.

When learners are interested in something, they work harder at it, persist through challenges, remember it better, process it more deeply, and get better grades (Silvia, 2008). For example, in one study some 9th-grade algebra students received typical word problems and others received problems that were personalized to fit their individual interests in sports, music, and movies. Students who received personalized problems were better at solving the problems, particularly low-ability students (Walkington, 2013). Interest also influences course selection in high school and later career selection. Interest influences how much students comprehend and learn from textbooks. Students feel more interest in texts for which they have individual interest, that they see as valuable, that meet their learning goal, and that connect to prior knowledge (Fox, 2009).

What causes interest? Interest comes partly from your social identity. You are interested in things that are valued by your in-group. Interest could be based on your religion, gender, or SES group (Bergin, 2016). It could also be based on your geography, like deer hunting in rural areas or surfing in coastal areas. Interest could be due to family values; Stuart's mother is a music teacher who values music. It could be due to friends; you might become interested in car mechanics if your friends are. It could also be due to idiosyncratic experiences; you might develop a lifetime interest in minerals if you find a spectacular geode.

Interest also comes from relevance. Learners are interested in topics that are relevant to their goals. You can tell students why classroom topics are relevant to them, but it is also effective to have the *students* generate reasons why a topic might be relevant (Hulleman & Barron, 2015). In one study 9th-graders were asked a day or two before each exam to write a paragraph on how a topic in their science class was relevant to them or to a person they knew (Hulleman & Harackiewicz, 2009). For example, a student whose family ran a dairy farm wrote about the relevance of metric measurement to measuring cheese and milk. Low-ability students felt greater interest in the class and earned higher grades.

Can you see how goals, autonomy, and interest are linked? Students who have initial interest in a topic tend to adopt mastery goals, and then develop increasing interest during a course (Harackiewicz, Durik, Barron, Linnenbrink-Garcia, & Tauer, 2008). Interest is also linked to self-determination. When students are free of external pressures, they tend to become more interested (Ciani, Ferguson, Bergin, & Hilpert, 2010). If Vinnie gets to choose which historical figure he writes about in class, he will be more interested in the task, which will lead him to set a mastery goal to both to learn more about the historical figure and to write a well-crafted essay.

Can you see how answers to "Can I do this?" is linked to "Do I want to do this?" Factors that address the first question—self-efficacy, mindset, and attributions—determine whether you believe you can improve through effort. Factors that address the second question—goals, self-determination, and interest—determine what activities you choose to pursue. Together, these predict whether you will persist through challenges when learning takes effort. You've already learned how to influence answers to "Can I do this?" Now let's see how you can influence answers to "Do I want to do this?"

13-3d Classroom Implications of "Do I Want to Do This?"

You can influence your student's goals, feelings of self-determination, and interest, to some extent, by following these guidelines:

1. *Promote mastery rather than performance goals*, particularly among learners with low self-efficacy. You promote mastery goals when you emphasize learning new skills, working hard, and making mistakes as a vital part of learning. You also promote mastery goals by showing students how they have improved over time. In contrast, you promote performance goals when you emphasize comparing students with each other, demonstrating (rather than developing) ability, and criticizing mistakes.

2. *Help students set high-quality goals.* Use the attributes listed in Table 13.2. An example of a form one 6th-grade math teacher used to do this is provided in Figure 13.6. For another example, in one famous experiment low-ability

FIGURE 13.6 A 6th-Grade Teacher Helped her Learners Set Goals for Learning Geometry using this Form.

Name:_____

Tessellation Unit

My Pretest Score: _____

My Goal for Summative Test: _____

Practice Activity	✔ Check if Completed	Did Not Complete		Score
		Why not?		
		Why not?		
		Why not?		
		Why not?		
		Why not?		

Summative Test Score: _____   Did I Meet My Goal? Yes No

What helped me reach my goal? **OR** What got in the way of reaching my goal, and how will I plan to overcome this next time?

_____

_____

_____

⌄ Professional Resource Download

elementary students who had a series of subgoals improved in arithmetic skills, self-efficacy, and interest in arithmetic. They even chose to do more arithmetic problems outside of the classroom, not for grades, compared to students who had only a long-term goal or no goal (Bandura & Schunk, 1981).

3. *Help learners feel self-determination* (Jang, 2008; Skinner et al., 2008). To do this you can discuss why a task is relevant to your students. You can give your students freedom to pursue their own agendas through opportunities to choose, make decisions, and form their own goals when appropriate. You can take your students' perspectives, respond to their needs and interests, and provide optimal challenges (Jang et al., 2010). In contrast, you undermine perceptions of autonomy when you use overly strict deadlines, surveillance, and messages that emphasize "should" and "ought."

4. *Put your students' individual interests to work.* Students will put more effort into activities they find interesting. For example, Vinnie's teacher might get him to read more history and write better essays by focusing on historical warriors. Similarly, Stuart's teacher might get him to learn the alphabet through song but get Rowan to learn it through picture books.

Unbelievable as it seems, some learners will not have *individual* interest in the topic you are teaching. Vinnie's teacher was quite disappointed that he disliked *The Scarlet Letter*. As a teacher, you have much more influence on *situational* interest. Let's look in a freshman English class. They are studying the parts of speech, which is arguably not everyone's most interesting topic:

> *Several students moaned, "This is BORING!" Ms. Gray, their teacher, said, "I suppose you guys could teach it in an interesting way?" The students responded, "Yes!" Ms. Gray said, "OK, you can teach the figurative language unit." Ms. Gray divided the class into groups of five or six students and gave each group specific concepts to cover and a study guide. They were given 1 week to come up with the lesson. She said they would have a quiz on the material and would get both a group grade for their presentation and an individual grade based on the quiz and the peer evaluations of their contribution to the presentation.*
>
> *The presentations included skits and pop-music examples of key concepts. Each group devised acronyms or songs to help their classmates remember the concepts. Students were attentive and engaged. The class average on the quiz was 94%, higher than on any other quiz during the year.*

Ms. Gray is a master/mentor teacher who does many things to promote interest among her students. She is not unique. A study of 3rd-grade classrooms found that one effective teacher used 43 different motivational practices (e.g., choosing interesting topics, using games, using praise), and did nothing to undermine student motivation (e.g., using criticism or public punishment). A less-effective teacher used only 4 different motivational practices and a whopping 11 that tended to undermine student motivation (Dolezal, Welsh, Pressley, & Vincent, 2003). You can guess whose class was more engaged in learning. There are many ways teachers can trigger situational interest (Bergin, 2016; Renninger & Bachrach, 2015). Table 13.3 discusses several methods that will provide you with a solid foundation for promoting your students' interest in learning tasks.

TABLE 13.3 Methods for promoting situational interest

Method	Explanation
Build competence and confidence	Students feel more interest for domains in which they feel competent—whether English, mathematics, science, sports, or music (Denissen, Zarrett, & Eccles, 2007; Marsh & Craven, 2006). High achievement leads to high self-concept, which leads to high interest, which leads to more effort, which leads to higher achievement.
Build on background knowledge	Students tend to be interested in things that they already know about, and the more they know about something, the more interested they tend to become (Alexander, Jetton, & Kulikowich, 1995). Become informed about your students' background knowledge and activate it so that they realize what they already know about a topic. For example, they may think that they know nothing about World War II until you point out films they might have seen—such as *Atonement, Pearl Harbor, Saving Private Ryan, Band of Brothers, The King's Speech, Fury,* and *Red Tails*—that are set during the war.
Use active learning in which learners DO something	*Students enjoy* hands-on activities, classroom response systems (clickers), and problem-solving activities. Children (and adults) like to build, pour, cut, glue, and hammer. Hands-on activities often include an element of problem solving that engages attention. However, make sure the activity is relevant to learning. Impersonating Elvis does not really help students understand the 1950s better. Active learning needs to also be minds-on, focusing student thinking on the topic to be learned (Bergin, 1999; Prince, 2004; Rotgans & Schmidt, 2011).
Use rewards, but sparingly	Students' interest may be attracted by rewards when they have no prior interest. Sometimes, as students engage in a task for a reward, they develop competence and intrinsic interest. However, as you learned in Chapter 7, rewards can also undermine *intrinsic* interest if students are already interested in a topic (Lepper, Keavney, & Drake, 1996).
Present learners with a discrepancy	Students' curiosity is piqued when they are told something they believe to be true is actually false. They are motivated to resolve the discrepancy. For example, ask what themes the Romantic poets wrote about (*not* romance). Or, show the class a picture of an animal that looks like a tree branch and ask, "Is it an animal or plant?" Students become curious about the definition of animal as they debate what it is. Curiosity leads students to pay attention and to remember what they learn (Kang et al., 2009).
Exploit learners' social goals	Students tend to be more interested, and learn more, during activities with friends (Bergin, 2016). This is one of the reasons cooperative learning is often successful, as it was in Ms. Gray's class.
Tell a good story	Students find narratives and stories more interesting than analytic, expository discourse (Hidi & Anderson, 1992; Slater, Johnson, Cohen, Comello, & Ewoldsen, 2014). Use stories to illustrate key points. Mystery stories are especially engaging, perhaps because they also involve discrepancy. For example, show students amazing pictures of the rings of Saturn and ask what they are made of. Tell stories of how scientists argued and tried to determine if they are made of gas, dust particles, or ice crystals (Cialdini, 2005). However, do not use irrelevant stories that distract students from learning.
Use suspense	Students want to know how the story ended. For example, scientists discovered the rings of Saturn are mostly dust but ice covered. One teacher would read a book to the class, and then quit at a cliffhanger event. The students had to read it themselves to find out what happens. The teacher said, "I see them during lunch reading the book and talking about it with their friends."
Help students find a purpose for the learning task	Students are motivated to make a product they care about. This could be something abstract, like a solution to a problem, or something concrete, like a motor (Ainley, Pratt, & Hansen, 2006). One type of product that motivates some students is a performance for an audience, such as a recital or a publication.
Explain the value or relevance of the activity	Students want to know how they might benefit from a learning task, perhaps by seeing things in a new way or developing a new skill, but not just because it will be on the test. For example, a teacher encouraged Chinese immigrant Alex to maintain his Chinese skill so that he could become a bilingual professional. She encouraged all her students' writing development by pointing out that high-level jobs they might pursue require writing skill.

PHOTO 13.4 When students choose to participate in competitions like debate, robots, and math bowls, they can learn new skills and enhance their feelings of competence. They often put in many more hours of practice than they would have without the competition.

Let's end this chapter with the inspiring story of Juliet Girard, a high school student. With her classmate Roshan Prabhu, Juliet won the Siemens Westinghouse Competition in Math, Science, and Technology—one of the most prestigious academic competitions in the world. She was the first African American to win. She and Roshan helped identify the gene in rice that controls its flowering time. This discovery could help feed more people in poverty-stricken areas.

Winning this competition typically involves 200 to 800 hours of extracurricular work. Juliet would go to school at 7 a.m.—90 minutes early every morning— to work on their project before school. What might lead to such intense motivation? Juliet's parents are not scientists; they are a UPS driver and a cashier. Juliet was a high-achieving, motivated student involved in other extracurricular activities as well, like most students who compete in science fairs. She edited the school newspaper and was in the Drama Club. Yet, Juliet credits Mr. Corcoran's science research class for her intense motivation.

What did Mr. Corcoran's class involve? Many of the guidelines you have just read about. In his class, students develop *explicit, specific goals* for research projects. They see *multiple, coping peers model success* in conducting research. They also have *self-determination;* they choose their own research projects based on *individual interest.* They see a *purpose* for their learning and engage in *hands-on activities,* which increase their interest even further. Mr. Corcoran is described as allowing students "to dance to the beat of your own drummer" and as "a glimmer of hope in a sometimes gloomy" urban school district. In addition, the school rewarded Juliet and Roshan with a "letter" jacket, like those that other schools give to athletes. Further, Juliet and Roshan both participated in the summer research program for ALANA students at the National Aeronautics and Space Administration (NASA). The program helps build *self-concept, social support for achievement,* and *competence* in science. When so many factors work together, students are more likely to be highly motivated. Juliet also credits watching *Bill Nye the Science Guy* on TV for her early interest in science. We will discuss the power of media in the next chapter.

My Teaching

Learners who have a positive self-concept and social identity fare better and have greater motivation than those who do not. Teachers can influence learners' self-concept and motivation through guidelines discussed in previous chapters. They include:

- Promote cognitive abilities and expertise through operant conditioning, scaffolding, and other approaches (see Chapters 3, 4, and 5).

- Promote emotional well-being through a secure teacher–student relationship, coping skills, and self-control (see Chapters 6, 7, and 8).

- Promote social cognition, prosocial behavior, and peer acceptance (see Chapters 9, 10, and 11).

In addition, periodically ask yourself the following:

1. Do I communicate that I value each individual? Do I point out students' accomplishments or strengths, but without overdoing it in a patronizing way?

2. How does my own social identity (such as gender and ethnicity) influence the way I evaluate my students? How do my students' social identities influence how they experience the school and my classroom?

3. Do I avoid pushing sex-typed behavior? Do I avoid making disparaging comments about girls' abilities in mathematics, science, computers, or athletics?

4. Do I avoid stereotyping based on ethnicity? Do I use materials and examples that include people from varied racial, ethnic, and income groups?

5. Do I avoid giving more attention to one group than to others? Do I avoid asking harder, more complex questions of one group than of others?

Do I go out of my way to counter the stereotypes that exist about the groups that I teach?

6. Have I put effort into learning about and talking about my students' social group? For example, can I discuss prominent current and historical members of minority groups in my community (e.g., Art Tatum in Toledo, Cesar Chavez in Yuma)?

7. Do I create a classroom atmosphere in which all students feel emotionally safe? Am I comfortable talking about race and ethnicity in my classroom?

8. Do I use models and persuasion to enhance my students' self-efficacy?

9. Do I help students set high-quality goals for learning in my classroom? Do I foster mastery goals and stay away from performance-avoidance goals? Do I avoid individual competition in the classroom—such as offering a reward to whoever reads the most books?

10. Do I help learners attribute their successes and failures to effort and good/bad strategies rather than innate ability? Do I teach that ability can change?

11. Do I give students choice whenever possible?

12. Do I use interesting activities as much as possible? Do I try to make most lessons spark situational interest? Am I promoting learners' individual interest?

Summary of Age Trends in the Self-System and Motivation

	Self-Concept	Gender Identity	Ethnic Identity	Motivation
Infancy & Toddlerhood (Birth–2 years)	• Infants develop self-concept based on ability to affect the environment.	• Infants distinguish male or female voices and faces. • Toddlers label people as boys or girls. • Toddlers become gender detectives. • Gender stereotypes emerge—toddlers' play is stereotyped and they readily identify toys as being for boys or girls.	• Infants distinguish faces based on ethnicity and prefer same-race faces. • Toddlers play with both same-race and other-race peers.	• Infants and toddlers are naturally motivated to explore their world and learn complex skills (e.g., language). • Toddlers are not deterred by failure (e.g., keep trying to walk despite repeated failure). • Process praise effects growth mindset in toddlers.
Early Childhood (3–5 Years)	• Children are overly positive about their own ability partly due to weak social comparison skills.	• By age 3, children know if they are boys or girls. • Understanding of gender constancy emerges. • Gender stereotypes are robust—certain objects and activities are for girls and others are for boys only.	• Preschoolers prefer same-race playmates. • Preschoolers can label their race or ethnicity, but their understanding is not well developed. • Preschoolers categorize people into in- and out-groups.	• Self-efficacy affects motivation by age 3. • Children do not generally distinguish effort from ability. By age 5 attributions begin to affect motivation. • Learned helplessness begins to appear by age 5.
Middle Childhood (6–12 Years)	• Self-concept declines compared to early childhood. • More-realistic perceptions of self and of competence develop.	• Understanding of gender constancy is fully developed. • Gender stereotypes intensify and then begin to wane. • Gender segregation peaks in intensity.	• Most children can recognize broadly held racial stereotypes, and understanding of racism grows. • Most children in potentially stigmatized groups do not perceive stigma toward themselves. • Stereotype threat can affect achievement.	• Academic intrinsic motivation declines. • Distinction between mastery and performance goals becomes possible.
Adolescence (13–19 Years)	• Self-concept continues to decline, yet adolescents have a positive bias about their abilities. • Self-concept differentiates into different domains, such as academic, athletic, and social. • Erikson believed this is an age of identity crisis.	• Comfort with one's gender identity predicts adjustment. • Most conform to stereotyped activities, but may try out gender-atypical activities.	• Adolescents show a preference for their own ethnic group. • Understanding of prejudice is fully developed. • Perceptions and experiences of stigma increase in adolescence. • Stereotype threat continues to affect achievement.	• Academic intrinsic motivation continues to decline. • Transition from elementary to junior high negatively affects motivation. • Teens develop an orientation that tends to be either mastery- or performance-oriented.

⌄ Professional Resource Download

Chapter Summary

13-1 The Self-System

- The self-system includes self-esteem, self-concept, and self-efficacy, which are related but not identical.

- Self-esteem is relatively stable over time. Academic achievement is only weakly predicted by self-esteem but strongly predicted by domain-specific self-concept in that domain. Self-esteem also predicts social and emotional competence.

- Secure attachment, being valued by important others, and competence in valued skills predict high self-esteem.

- Beyond early childhood, girls tend to have slightly lower self-esteem than boys. This varies by domain. There are few ethnic differences in self-esteem, but African Americans tend to have slightly higher self-esteem than do European Americans.

- Teachers can promote learners' self-esteem by improving learners' social and academic competence, building positive relationships, and realistically pointing out their accomplishments.

13-2 Social Identity: Gender and Ethnicity

- Learners' self-concept is linked to the social group to which they belong, including their gender and ethnic group.

- Learners seek out activities that match their gender. Learners who are content with their gender tend to be better adjusted. Boys may be pressured more than girls to conform to stereotypes.

- Ethnic identity is more important to groups that are a minority. Learners with positive ethnic identity fare better academically and socially.

- It is common to categorize people into "in-group" and "out-group." This may lead to discrimination. Learners who feel discriminated against are more likely to have social, emotional, and academic problems.

- Stereotype threat can lower test scores. Teachers can reduce stereotype threat by teaching what it is and by teaching that intelligence is changeable.

- Teachers can help reduce discrimination and promote positive social identities in all learners by valuing each learner, holding all to a high standard, using a multicultural curriculum, and using well-structured cooperative learning. Simply claiming color-blindness is not effective.

13-3 Motivation

- Learners' motivation is influenced by their answer to the question "Can I do this?" The answer depends on self-efficacy, views of ability, and attributions.

- Self-efficacy predicts goals, persistence, strategy development, achievement, and interest. There are four major influences on self-efficacy: previous experience, vicarious experience (models), verbal persuasion, and physiological experience.

- Learners who have a growth mindset, rather than a fixed mindset, regarding abilities like intelligence and athleticism have greater persistence and intrinsic motivation and are less hurt by failure.

- Learners' view of their own abilities influences their attributions for success or failure. When learners attribute success to effort, they fare better emotionally and academically and are less likely to give up in the face of failure.

- Teachers can increase their students' motivation by providing models of success, encouraging a growth mindset, attributing success to effort rather than ability, and training students to do the same.

- Learners' motivation is also influenced by their answer to the question, "Do I want to do this?" The answer depends on their goals, self-determination, and interest.

- Goal setting can improve performance. High-quality goals are specific, challenging, divided into subgoals, monitored, adopted with full commitment, and accompanied by feedback and plans for implementation.

- Mastery goals reflect a goal to learn new things and a preference for challenge. Performance goals reflect a goal to demonstrate ability and to perform better than other people. Mastery goals are more adaptive in most situations. Performance goals can be divided into performance-approach goals, which are sometimes adaptive, and performance-avoidance goals, which are maladaptive.

- Learners have an innate need for self-determination. They feel greater intrinsic motivation and interest for tasks for which they have some choice.

- Interest predicts achievement in school. Interest can be individual or situational. Interest is linked to holding mastery goals.

- Teachers can increase their students' motivation by promoting mastery goals, helping students set high-quality goals, fostering feelings of self-determination, and exploiting students' individual interests. Teachers can create situational interest in many ways, such as using hands-on activities, discrepant information, and connecting to background knowledge.

chapter 14

Andy Dean Photography/Shutterstock.com

The Child in Context: Family Structure, Child Care, and Media

What were the most powerful influences on how you developed as a child? According to the bioecological model, your answer should be "interactions with my family." In every chapter of this text, you have learned how family interactions affect children (e.g., attachment, parenting style, and talking to children). Yet there were other layers of influence on your childhood. You have learned about some of these in every chapter as well (e.g., genes, culture, and school). In this chapter, we will discuss three additional aspects of the context children live in—family structure, child care, and media. Why these three factors? Because they are pervasive, significant influences on children. **After you read this chapter, you will be able to:**

14-1 Articulate how family structure influences children, create classrooms that support learners from all family structures, and promote parent involvement.

14-2 Differentiate the complex experiences and outcomes linked to maternal employment and child care for various learners.

14-3 Evaluate how media positively and negatively influences learners, and analyze how to help learners minimize negative influences.

14-1 Family Structure

In preschool Reagan pokes and annoys other children. He does not stay focused in play. Instead of building with blocks, he kicks and throws them until the floor is littered, then runs on to activity after activity. His teachers have to hover over him and repeat directions to get him to clean up. In contrast, his classmate K'Shawn is obedient, concentrates intently on tasks like puzzles, and is kind.

Reagan rarely sees his father since his mother "threw him out" for beating her. Reagan's mother works full-time and attends school part-time. She is proud that she supports herself and her son. However, she says that she so seldom sees Reagan that she doesn't understand him. In contrast, K'Shawn lives with his married parents and 1st-grade sister.

family structure
the composition of a child's household.

nuclear family
a family composed of a father and mother who are in their original marriage, and their biological children. Sometimes called a "traditional" family.

K'Shawn and Reagan's teacher assumes their differences in behavior are caused by their family structure. Is this a reasonable assumption? Let's see what the research says, but first we will discuss how typical their families are.

Family structure refers to the composition of a child's household. According to the 2010 U.S. Census, 33% of households have children under age 18 (see Figure 14.1). Among households with children, more children (66%) live in married, two-parent households than in all other family structures combined. Some children in married, two-parent households are stepchildren, but 90% are not. Instead, they live in what is commonly called a nuclear family with only their biological siblings and parents who are in a first marriage (FIFCFS, 2009).

The second most common family structure is single-mother households. Some single mothers are divorced. Other single mothers were never married, like Reagan's

FIGURE 14.1 Household Types in the United States.

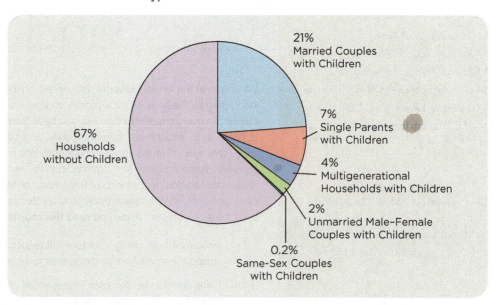

This chart shows the percentage of different types of households according to the 2010 U.S. Census. Where does your family structure fit on this chart?

mother. In the past, unmarried mothers tended to be teenagers, but today they are more likely to be in their 20s. This may be partly because marriage occurs later. In the 1950s, the median age of marriage was 20 for women and 23 for men. Now it is 26 and 28, respectively.[1]

Pregnancies among unwed teens are currently at record lows in the United States, particularly among African American teens (Ventura, Hamilton, & Mathews, 2014). However, teen pregnancy rates remain high in some regions, such as New Mexico, where it is 48 per thousand 15- to 19-year-olds compared to a low of 14 in New Hampshire. Furthermore, U.S. teen birthrates are among the highest in Western industrialized countries.

Other less common family structures in the United States include multigenerational (grandparents live in the home) and cohabiting (parents are unmarried). Most cohabiting parents are opposite-sex couples, but a small number are same-sex. Children of gay and lesbian parents are typically the result of past heterosexual marriages, often before the parent identified as homosexual or bisexual. However, some children enter homosexual families through adoption, sperm donation, or surrogate pregnancy. These children may be biologically related to only one parent, or to neither parent. In the United States, same-sex couples with children are rare, comprising about 0.2% of households (Vespa, Lewis, & Kreider, 2013). In a U.S. national study of 12,000 adolescents, only 44 lived with lesbian mothers and six with gay fathers (Wainright & Patterson, 2008).

14-1a What Does Family Structure Predict?

Although about two out of three children in the United States live in nuclear families, many children do not. Scientists typically compare child outcomes in other family structures with nuclear families because optimal outcomes are linked to living with both biological parents who are married. Let's discuss this research, beginning with divorce.

Divorce

Divorce is not a single event, but rather is a legal marker for a series of events. The series may begin with parents fighting, then a parent moves out, perhaps moves back in and then out again; then families visit counselors and lawyers as they cope with anger or grief and argue about custody, housing, and money. The series may continue after the divorce with renewed arguing about custody and money as children's needs evolve. Divorce brings transitions, and children do not fare well if they experience many transitions. Divorce is linked to several child outcomes[2]:

- Insecure attachment.

- Externalizing disorders such as aggression, impulsivity, drug use, sexual promiscuity, and teenage parenthood.

---

[1] These statistics come from the 2010 U.S. Census at www.census.gov.
[2] There are many studies that support these conclusions, just a few of which are listed here: Amato (2001); Amato et al. (2011); Burt, Barnes, McGue, and Iacono (2008); Joussemet et al. (2008); Kelly (2000); Lansford (2009); Macmillan, McMorris, and Kruttschnitt (2004); Ryan et al. (2015).

- Internalizing disorders such as depression, anxiety, and low self-esteem.

- Medical problems and illnesses. Academic problems such as low test scores, low attendance, and dropping out.

- Relationship problems in adulthood such as divorce and distant relationships with parents.

The effects of divorce may linger across generations; divorce between grandparents, usually before grandchildren are even born, predicts lower educational attainment, more marital problems, and worse parent–child relationships for their children *and* their grandchildren (Amato & Cheadle, 2005). You might expect that divorce without conflict would not have negative effects, but research suggests that it does (Amato, Kane, & James, 2011).

Does the age of the child matter? The effects of divorce occur for children of all ages, though problems may be more pronounced for misbehavior in preschoolers and for low achievement in adolescents (Lansford, 2009; Lewis, Feiring, & Rosenthal, 2000; Woodward, Fergusson, & Belsky, 2000). Several studies have found that, overall, negative effects are strongest for children under 5 years of age (Ryan, Claessens, & Markowitz, 2015).

Does divorce always lead to problems? The link between divorce and these problems is robust, or consistently found in many studies with diverse children. However, *the effect is small*, meaning that many children adjust adequately following divorce (Amato, 2001). An exception to the small effect size is externalizing disorders. There may be a 300% increase in antisocial behavior among boys from divorced families as compared with boys from nuclear families (Pagani, Boulerice, Vitaro, & Tremblay, 1999). Children are more likely to adjust adequately following divorce if their parents: (1) are authoritative, (2) minimize conflict, and (3) provide financial security (Emery, Otto, & O'Donohue, 2005; Lansford, 2009).

think about **this**

You probably know someone who has emerged from childhood divorce fairly well and someone who has not. Compare their risk and protective factors (see Chapter 1). Analyze which factors might explain their different outcomes.

Single-Parent Families and Stepfamilies

Children in single-parent families and stepfamilies tend to have profiles similar to children in divorced families. They experience more transitions and tend to have lower test scores, lower rates of graduation, and lower rates of college attendance (Sun & Li, 2001). They also tend to be more aggressive and have more emotional problems like anxiety or depression (Boyle et al., 2004; Ho, Bluestein, & Jenkins, 2008; Ryan et al., 2015; Turner, Finkelhor, Hamby, & Shattuck, 2013; Xie, Drabick, & Chen, 2011). However, children in stepfamilies may have these problems only if they have other risk factors as well, like a depressed mother or a negative family (Dunn et al., 1998). Children in stepfamilies may do just fine if the parents and the family function well.

Teenage Mothers

Having a teen mother is a risk factor for children. Children of teenage mothers are more likely than other children to have behavior problems, use alcohol or other drugs, have inadequate employment, go to prison (especially boys), and become teen parents themselves (Miller, Bayley, Christensen, Leavitt, & Coyl, 2003). They are also more likely to be placed in special education, be retained a grade, drop out,

FIGURE 14.2 Math and Reading Achievement for Children of Adolescent and Adult Mothers.

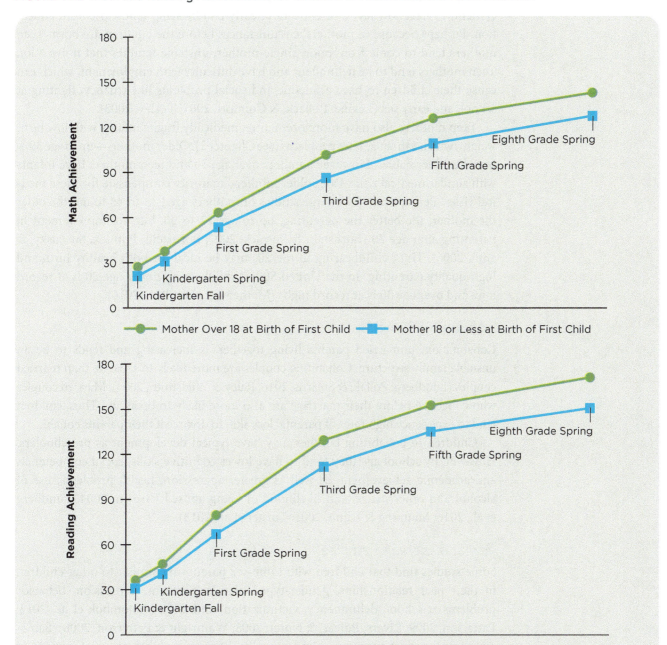

What happens to the gap in achievement for children of adolescent mothers and non-adolescent mothers? Is the pattern different for math and reading? (Note: Achievement measures are estimated means using item response theory and full information maximum likelihood.) *Source: Tang et al. (2016).*

and have lower test scores. As Figure 14.2 shows, they are likely to fall further behind academically with age (Tang, Davis-Kean, Chen, & Sexton, 2016). However, these are group trends. Some children of teenage mothers fare well. One study found that most children of young mothers did well either socially or academically, and 20% did well in both domains (Rhule, McMahon, Spieker, & Munson, 2006).

Why do many children of teen mothers struggle? Perhaps because their mothers tend to have low levels of education; early childbearing tends to curtail education. Perhaps because of mothers' circumstances before the children are born. Teen mothers tend to come from poor, single-mother, unstable families that move a lot. Teen mothers tend to be delinquent and have difficulty with employment, which can cause their children to have academic and social problems like truancy, fighting at school, and early sex (Levine, Pollack, & Comfort, 2001; Turley, 2003).

Teen mothers also have more premature, medically fragile infants with low birth weight, which can cause later problems (see Chapter 2). Older mothers—up to age 30—have healthier babies. However, mothers over age 30 and teen mothers have infants with similar medical risks. Does older mothers' maturity compensate for these medical risks? Perhaps not. Two large studies of mothers aged 15 to 45 found the older the mother, the better the parenting, up to age 27 to 30, but no improvement in parenting after age 30 (Bornstein & Putnick, 2007; Bornstein, Putnick, Suwalsky, & Gini, 2006). Thus, childbearing in the 20s may be ideal for both healthy birth and high-quality parenting. In the United States, childbearing under age 20 is at record lows and over age 30 is at record highs (Mathews & Hamilton, 2016).

Cohabiting Families

Cohabitation, unmarried parents living together, is increasing and tends to be an unstable family structure. Cohabiting couples are more likely to separate than married couples (Lundberg, Pollak, & Stearns, 2016; Raley & Wildsmith, 2004). Married couples who cohabited before their marriage are also more likely to break up. Thus, children tend to experience high rates of parental loss akin to divorce if their parents cohabit.

Children in cohabiting families may have typical development as preschoolers. However, by school age they tend to have lower cognitive skills, social competence, and academic achievement, as well as greater aggression, health problems, use of alcohol and other drugs, and likelihood of being abused (Brown, 2004; Lundberg et al., 2016; Manning & Lamb, 2003; Turner et al., 2013).

Gay and Lesbian Families

Some studies find that children with same-sex parents are similar to other children in their peer relationships, gender-typed play, self-esteem, depression, behavior problems at school, delinquency, victimization, and GPA (Golombok et al., 2014; Patterson, 2009; Rivers, Poteat, & Noret, 2008; Wainright & Patterson, 2008). Same-sex parents report providing similar-quality parenting as heterosexual parents of the same socioeconomic status (SES), with parents in marriage-like relationships providing higher-quality parenting than single parents (Golombok et al., 2003; Wainright Russell, & Patterson, 2004). For example, in a large, national sample of stable households raising their own children, the health and well-being of children of female same-sex parents was similar to that of other children (Bos, Knox, van Rijn-van Gelderen, & Gartrell, 2016). (There were too few male same-sex families to include in the study.) Much of the research on same-sex families is based on small, nonrepresentative samples (Marks, 2012). To date, the research is not adequate for fully confident conclusions about children in this family structure.

In summary, family structure is linked to physical, cognitive, emotional, and social outcomes in children. Children can fare well in any family structure. However, having divorced, unmarried, remarried, or cohabiting parents is a risk factor; happily married parents are a protective factor. Next, let's explore why this might be.

14-1b How Might Family Structure Influence Children?

Family structure may influence children through several paths. Compared to other family structures, nuclear families tend to have: (1) higher parent education; (2) less financial strain (see Figure 14.3); (3) fewer moves; (4) greater parent–child closeness, particularly for adolescents; and (5) less abuse (FIFCFS, 2009; Gruman, Harachi, Abbott, Catalano, & Fleming, 2008; Lundberg et al., 2016; Ryan, 2012). Living with a stepparent or cohabiting adult is one of the largest risk factors for child maltreatment (Daly & Wilson, 2005). However, most stepparents are not abusive; they are more likely to be distant. Let's discuss three other potent paths of influence: father presence, marital conflict, and quality of parenting.

Father Presence

Family structure affects father presence. In nuclear families, like K'Shawn's, children live with their father and mother. In single-parent homes, children typically live with their mothers; only about 24% live with a single father (Livingston, 2013). Many divorced fathers intend to stay involved, but their contact drops off over time. Roughly 40% of nonresidential fathers have no contact with their children in a year's time (Emery et al., 2005). Never-married fathers, like Reagan's, are the least likely to see their children.

When fathers are absent, their children lose economic resources and a father's discipline, supervision, and nurturing. Their children are more likely to feel distressed, use drugs, not finish high school, have worse mental health as adults, and have employment problems (King, Harris, & Heard, 2004; McLanahan, Tach, & Schneider, 2013). Children with absent fathers are at risk for early sex and teen pregnancy (Mendle et al., 2009).

There is an old adage that "The best thing a father can do for his children is love their mother." Does research on family structure support this adage? How might you alter the adage, using research to support your alteration?

FIGURE 14.3 Family Structure and Poverty.

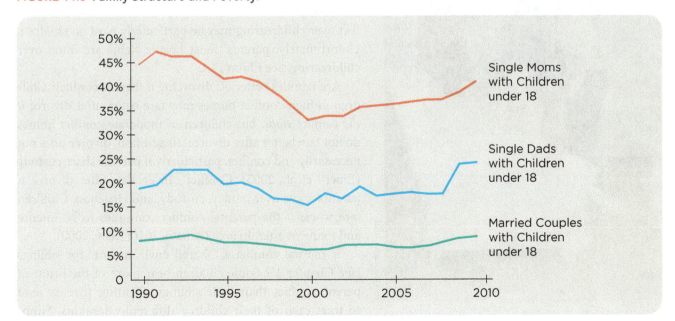

This chart shows the percentage of families living below the poverty level. Single mothers are more likely to live in poverty than single fathers or married couples. *Source: U.S. Census Bureau.*

What if nonresidential fathers stay involved? Fathers who merely take their children to the movies may not contribute to their well-being, but nonresidential fathers who are authoritative, monitor their children, set limits, talk about problems, and help with homework do contribute to their children's well-being. Children do better academically after divorce if their fathers stay involved in their schoolwork (Kelly, 2000).

Other adults can sometimes fill a father's role. Children with father substitutes fare well, particularly African American children, if the substitutes are warm and discipline the children (Coley, 1998). However, stepfathers and cohabiting partners tend to spend less time with children than do biological fathers (Smolensky & Gootman, 2003).

Sometimes children benefit from father absence. Children may be relieved when an abusive father moves out. If fathers are abusive, drug addicts, or criminals, their children may fare better without them. Children are more likely to have behavior problems if they have an antisocial father who lives with them than if he does not live with them (DeGarmo, 2010; Jaffee, Moffitt, Caspi, & Taylor, 2003).

Parental Conflict

Parental conflict is hard on children. It undermines emotional security and increases psychological problems (Davies & Martin, 2014; Davies, Sturge-Apple, Bascoe, & Cummings, 2014). In fact, the child problems linked to divorce may actually result from parents' conflict *before the divorce* (Lansford, 2009). Even if parents do not divorce, their conflict is linked to children's problems. Adolescents' delinquency, hostility, and depression increase when parental conflict increases and decrease when the conflict decreases (Cui, Conger, & Lorenz, 2005). Behavior problems in the child may lead to more parental conflict, creating a vicious cycle (Cui, Donnellan, & Conger, 2007; Schermerhorn, Chow, & Cummings, 2010). Parental conflict over childrearing may be particularly hard on children. Unfortunately, parents' most hostile fights are often over childrearing. See Photo 14.1.

Are families better off divorcing if there is conflict? Children in high-conflict homes may fare better after divorce *if the conflict stops*, but children in moderate-conflict homes do not fare better after divorce. In addition, divorce does not necessarily end conflict, particularly if parents share custody (Emery et al., 2005). Conflict can escalate after divorce if parents argue over money, custody, and visitation. Children fare worse if the parental conflict continues to be intense and frequent after divorce (Amato, 2010; Kelly, 2000).

Is marital conflict a "shared environment" for siblings (see Chapter 1)? Some children bear more of the brunt of parent conflict than their siblings. Fighting parents tend to treat each of their children differently (Jenkins, Simpson, Dunn, Rasbash, & O'Connor, 2005). An angry parent might snap at and criticize one child, while affectionately

PHOTO 14.1 Children's depression, hostility, and antisocial behavior increase when parents' conflict increases.

Goodshoot/Jupiter Images

comforting another child. Thus, parental conflict is often a "nonshared environment." Furthermore, effects vary depending on the temperament of the child. Children with negative emotionality (see Chapter 6) are more likely to develop behavior problems when parents have conflict than other children (Hentges, Davies, & Cicchetti, 2015).

Why is parental conflict hard on children? For several reasons. Conflict may undermine emotional security, or arouse fear, sadness, and anger that children cannot regulate. It may lead to self-blame or feeling helpless. It may alter children's physiological response to stress. It may lead to poor sleep or attention deficits. It may undermine the quality of parenting.[3] When parents are angry with each other, they tend to be less responsive to, affectionate with, and supportive of their children. Each of these factors could lead to emotional disorders and behavior problems (Rhoades, 2008).

Quality of Parenting

Parents in any family structure can be sensitive and authoritative. However, many studies find that never-married, divorced, step, and teen parents tend to provide lower-quality parenting than parents in nuclear families (see, for example, Hay & Nash, 2002; Ho et al., 2008; Jenkins, Rasbash, & O'Connor, 2003). One large national study found that even when the biological parents live together but are not married, mothers tend to be more negative toward their children (Gibson-Davis & Gassman-Pines, 2010). How might family structure influence parenting quality? Parents who feel distress due to financial strain, marital conflict, lack of emotional support, or other challenges are less likely to use effective discipline, be warm, parent authoritatively, and monitor or set limits for children.

Regardless of family structure, children will fare better if parents can maintain high-quality parenting (Rhule et al., 2006). For example, in one study, children of teenage mothers developed good cognitive ability if their mothers were responsive, warm, talked to them, set limits, and read to them (Luster, Bates, Fitzgerald, Vandenbelt, & Key, 2000). When families divorce, if parents use an authoritative parenting style, children fare better (Hay & Nash, 2002). If they continue supervising the children and enforcing household rules, like being home for dinner or limiting TV, then their children are less likely to develop behavior problems. Interventions that help divorced parents stay positive and use effective discipline result in children with better behavior, coping skills, and achievement at school (Forgatch & DeGarmo, 2002; Vélez, Wolchik, Tein, & Sandler, 2011). The key lesson is that *quality of parenting is more important than family structure, but family structure influences quality of parenting.*

Revisiting Risk and Resilience

Some factors discussed earlier, such as father absence and parental conflict, contribute to the risk of problems for children in nonnuclear families. However, in Chapter 1 you learned that protective factors can mitigate risk, leading to resilient

[3] There are many studies that support these conclusions, just a few of which are listed here: Buehler, Lange, and Franck (2007); Davies, Sturge-Apple, Cicchetti, and Cummings (2007, 2008); El-Sheikh et al. (2009); Mannering et al. (2011); Sturge-Apple et al. (2006).

children. For example, Collin, just like Reagan in the opening vignette, had significant risk factors by age 3—when his mother divorced his abusive father. He is now in 7th grade. Let's see how he is doing:

> *Collin's mother became a nurse and was able to financially support the two of them. When he was 8, his mother married a man with two younger daughters. They have since had two more children. Collin's mother is now a homemaker, and the large family barely makes ends meet. However, the home is orderly, and the parents are loving. They set clear limits, like 1 one hour of video games on school days. Collin's stepfather takes him fishing and camping, which Collin loves.*

Collin has several protective factors: an educated mother, adequate (but not plentiful) finances, and limited exposure to media. The marital conflict ended with the divorce. Collin rarely sees his antisocial father, but he has an involved stepfather. Most importantly, his mother and stepfather are authoritative. So how is Collin faring? He earns above-average grades at school, excels in athletics, and is prosocial, but he is a little prone to depression. Overall, he is a resilient child.

14-1c Group Diversity in Family Structure

There are gender differences in how children respond to family structure. There are also SES and ethnic differences in the prevalence of each family structure.

Gender

Both boys and girls have higher achievement and fewer externalizing or internalizing problems in nuclear families than in single-parent, divorced, and stepfamilies (Sun & Li, 2001). In nonnuclear families, boys may be at greater risk than girls for externalizing problems, like aggression and delinquency (Dunn et al., 1998).

In contrast, girls may be more at risk than boys for internalizing problems, like depression, anxiety, and low self-esteem, after divorce. In addition, girls may develop more problems over time, perhaps because nonresident fathers tend to be more involved with boys. However, a subset of girls develops remarkable competence after divorce as they take over parenting responsibility. This may come at a price, because they tend to feel anxiety and low self-esteem despite their competence (Hetherington & Stanely-Hagan, 1999).

Socioeconomic Status

SES is linked to family structure. College-educated married couples are less likely to divorce than less-educated couples (Aughinbaugh, Robles, & Sun, 2013; Martin, 2006). See Figure 14.4. Single motherhood leads to lower income, and mothers who grew up in low-SES homes are more likely to become teen, never-married, or divorced mothers (Bramlett & Mosher, 2002). High-SES teens who do become pregnant are more likely to relinquish the child for adoption, particularly if they aspire to a college education (Miller et al., 2003; see Box 14.1 for a discussion of adoption and related topics). Thus, SES influences the family structure that children enter.

FIGURE 14.4 Divorce Rate by Education Level.

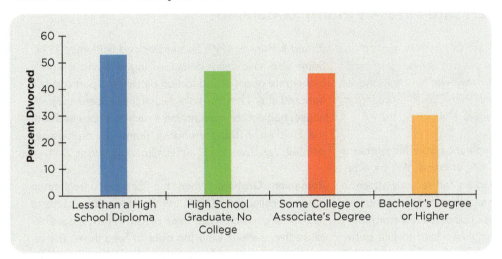

This graph shows the percentage of marriages from 1978 to 2010 by education level. Notice that there is not much difference for the three groups who do not earn bachelor's degrees, but a big difference for the group that does. Why might that be? Which group will you be in? *Source: Aughinbaugh, Robles, and Sun (2013).*

BOX 14.1 challenges in development

Orphanages, Foster Care, and Adoption

Sometimes parents cannot care for children. In the past, children could be put in orphanages because of parents' death, incarceration, abandonment, or poverty. Orphanages were large institutions where caregivers were rotated so that children would not get "too attached." The idea was to spare children the trauma of separation (Rutter, 1995). We now know that never attaching is worse than losing an attachment figure. As Tennyson wrote, "Tis better to have loved and lost, than never to have loved at all." Orphanages are still common in some countries, but in the United States they have been largely replaced by foster care and adoption.

Foster Care In 2014 about 653,000 American children were in foster care (U.S. Children's Bureau, 2015). Children are typically placed in foster care against the parents' will, often because of criminal neglect or parents' drug use. Many foster parents are loving. However, quality of care in 15 to 20% of foster homes may be as bad as in the child's original home (Orme & Buehler, 2001). Foster homes tend to be in low-SES, high-risk neighborhoods with single or cohabiting caregivers (O'Hare, 2008). Foster children are often moved from one home to another, which is distressing to them and is a risk factor (Pears, Kim, Buchanan, &

Fisher, 2015). One child who had lived in five different homes by age 6, was told, "You are a wonderful and special girl." She responded: "Then why does everybody leave me?" (Adam, 2004, p. 211).

Children in foster care tend to have low academic achievement, health issues, and externalizing behavior problems (Font, 2014). Does removing children from their homes lead to more behavior problems, even if it keeps them safer? One national study found no evidence of an increase or decrease in behavior problems (Berger, Bruch, Johnson, James, & Rubin, 2009). Still, decisions about removing children from potentially harmful parents are extremely difficult to make. Attachment needs may conflict with physical safety needs. For example, a toddler in foster care for less than a month was observed at a clinic:

He was playing in a listless way, ignoring his foster mother's attempts to interest him in toys. She signaled to him to come to her, but he turned away. When she left the room, he screamed. When she returned, he walked toward her, but stopped four feet away. When she tried to engage him with toys, he turned away and played several feet away. When his natural mother entered

Orphanages, Foster Care, and Adoption (continued)

the room, he immediately went to her to be picked up. They hugged and he began playing actively and confidently, occasionally smiling. However, later he ignored his mother's overture to pick him up. (Adapted from Gaensbauer, Mrazek, & Harmon, 1981)

This toddler is depressed. Separation from his mother is distressing, but he was not safe at home. Will he eventually become attached? Toddlers can securely attach to foster caregivers if they stay together for several months. However, there are high rates of disorganized attachment among foster children, and children tend to fare better if they are adopted, rather than in foster care (Brand & Brinich, 1999).

Adoption There are three paths to adoption (Grotevant & McDermott, 2014): (1) Adoption from private agencies when parents give up infants they feel others are better prepared to raise. (2) Adoption from the public welfare system when children, on average around age 7, have been removed from abusive homes to which they cannot return. (3) Adoption from birth families, orphanages, or foster families in other countries (e.g., China, Ethiopia, and Russia, or other countries, depending on geopolitics).

Children who are adopted have usually experienced adversity that causes negative outcomes in the short term. Longitudinal studies show that adopted children usually catch up in physical growth except for head circumference. They improve in attachment behaviors, but still suffer from high rates of insecure attachment and avoidance (Palacios, Román, Moreno, León, & Peñarrubia, 2014). Most develop normal IQ and do as well in school as their nonadopted peers. However, a small percentage (12%) of adopted children have substantial behavior problems, such as aggression, delinquency, and mental health issues

(Brand & Brinich, 1999; Deater-Deckard & Plomin, 1999). Some also have minor delays in language and a slightly higher rate of special education placement, particularly if adopted after 12 months of age or if they experience early abuse, neglect, or malnutrition—such as happened with the children in the horrendous Romanian orphanages (McCall, Van IJzendoorn, Juffer, Groark, & Groza, 2011).

Romanian Orphans When the Ceausescu regime in Romania collapsed in 1989, the world found that tens of thousands of children had been placed in orphanages because their parents were too poor to feed them. The orphans were neglected and malnourished. Moved by their plight, many families in America and Europe adopted them.

How have they fared? Children adopted before 6 months of age developed normal attachment. They were physically, socially, and mentally delayed at adoption, but by school entry they were only slightly underweight, had average social skills, and only 18% were still mentally delayed. Children adopted after 6 months of age also made substantial gains, but some problems lingered, such as poor attention and emotion control, behavior problems, and autism-like behavior (Beckett et al., 2006; Kreppner et al., 2007). The longer they were institutionalized, the worse their brain development (Stamoulis, Vanderwert, Zeanah, Fox, & Nelson, 2015).

Children placed in foster care by 15 months of age developed normal language skills, but those left in an orphanage were severely delayed (Windsor et al., 2011). By age 12, the fostered children were doing better than the still-institutionalized children, but worse than never-institutionalized children (Humphreys et al., 2015). An important lesson for teachers is that even severely deprived children can catch up, if not completely recover, in good environments.

Ethnicity

Family structure varies by ethnic group. Asian American children are the most likely to live in a nuclear family (Vespa et al., 2013). About 16% of Asian/Pacific Islander children are born to unmarried mothers, as compared with 36% of White and 53% of Hispanic children (Hamilton, Martin, Osterman, Curtin, & Mathews, 2015). African Americans are much less likely to marry than Whites or Hispanics, and most (71%) African American children are born to unmarried women (Aughinbaugh et al., 2013). Their grandparents and aunts are likely to be actively involved in childrearing, providing extended family stability.

These ethnic differences in family structure are linked to cultural differences in the acceptance of teen parenthood and cohabitation. Many more Latino and African American teens are parents than are Asian American teens. Despite their acceptance, teen parenthood and cohabitation remain risk factors for Latino and African American children.

These ethnic and SES differences may reflect geographic subcultures. Marriage is less likely in urban areas. Marriage is least likely in the Washington, DC, and New York City areas and most likely in the West, in such areas as Utah, Idaho, Phoenix, and Fort Worth (Leonhardt & Quealy, 2015). Interestingly, young people who move increase or decrease their probability of marriage depending on where they move. Paradoxically, married people in religiously conservative counties have higher divorce rates than people in less conservative counties (Glass & Levchak, 2014).

 **brain research**

Deprivation Harms Brains

In Chapter 2 you learned about the power of *enriched* environments to promote brain growth. *Deprived* environments (emotionally, socially, physically) also affect brain development. An extreme example is the Romanian orphanages. Children who were removed to high-quality care made dramatic gains in development. Yet, many continued to have lingering problems despite many years in adoptive homes, particularly those removed after age 1. Deprivation in the first few years of life may cause long-term changes in the brain (Nelson, Bos, Gunnar, & Sonuga-Barke, 2011).

How does this happen? Neurological tests suggest that institutionalized children may have delayed development in the prefrontal cortex and poor connections to other brain areas (Pollak et al., 2010). Brain circuits involved in high-level thinking depend on the quality of information from lower-level circuits, which are shaped by the quality of early experience (Fox, Levitt, & Nelson, 2010). Unstimulating orphanages lead to less brain activity, which may lead to too much synaptic pruning (Nelson, 2007). This does not mean that only early experience is important. It may set the foundation for brain architecture, but enriching experience must continue beyond early childhood for children's brains to reach their full genetic potential.

14-1d Classroom Implications of Family Structure and Parent Involvement

> *I used to get A's and B's because I wanted to make my parents proud. I was happy and my family was happy. Then, when I was 13, I came home from school one day and my mom was crying. My little brother said my parents were fighting and my dad left. I was sad because my dad and I did everything together. I missed him so much. I didn't feel like doing anything; I didn't care no more about my schoolwork. I got D's for like the rest of that year and the next. Now I'm trying to get it together to prove to my dad that I can get on without him.*

This poignant story told by a high school student shows how family structure affected her schoolwork. Research confirms her story; family structure is linked to test scores, attendance, retention, special education placement, graduation rates, educational aspirations, and homework completion, as well as the social and emotional problems you read about earlier. Teachers view learners as less prosocial, less academically competent, and less engaged in class when there is marital conflict at home (Sturge-Apple et al., 2006).

Living in divorced, single-parent, or cohabiting families is a risk factor for learners—but the effect is small. This means many learners in nonnuclear families, like Collin, are successful in school. This is important to realize because if you expect your learners to underachieve or misbehave, they may fulfill your expectations through the Pygmalion effect (see Chapter 12). For your students who are struggling with family problems, there are several things you can do to help that you learned in previous chapters:

1. Help learners develop strong academic skills so that they experience success in your classroom (see Chapters 4, 5, and 12).

2. Serve as an alternative attachment figure (see Chapter 6).

3. Teach them how to cope with their negative emotions and stress (see Chapter 8).

4. Use an authoritative style of classroom management rather than power assertion (see Chapter 7). Encourage parents to be authoritative as well.

5. Help learners replace aggression with prosocial behavior so that their peers will accept them. Friends help buffer the negative effects of divorce (see Chapters 10 and 11).

6. Advocate for learners to continue attending your school even when the family moves out of the attendance area so that their school setting remains stable. Moving is stressful because it disrupts academic development and social ties (Adam, 2004; Gruman et al., 2008).

You can also seek the help of the school counselor, who may provide intervention. School-based interventions are designed to help children of divorce focus on improving social support, coping skills for negative emotions, and parent–child relations. Typically, students meet in a small group at school for several sessions. Such interventions have had success with some skills—such as helping learners be more sociable, less frustrated, less anxious, higher achieving, and less promiscuous and delinquent (Abel, Chung-Canine, & Broussard, 2013; Pedro-Carroll, 2005; Pelleboer-Gunnink, Van der Valk, Branje, Van Doorn, & Deković, 2015; Wolchik et al., 2002; Wolchik et al., 2013). Learners benefit from high-quality intervention programs even if their families divorced several years earlier, because the stress of divorce tends to be ongoing.

Children weather family disruptions if their parents are authoritative, financially stable, and minimize their conflict and if nonresidential fathers remain involved in their children's schooling. Let's focus on this last factor—parental involvement—next.

Involving Parents in Education

While you cannot influence family structure, you can influence parent involvement in school. Parents can be involved in their children's education at school or at home. *School involvement* includes attending parent–teacher conferences, which about 70% of parents do, and volunteering at school, which about 40% of parents do (Noel, Stark, & Redford, 2013). *Home involvement* includes supervising homework, taking children to the library, reading to children, providing study space, and discussing expectations. Parents who are not visible at school may value their children's education and be involved at home. For example, one undocumented immigrant Latino father never went to his sons' school because of his construction job and his fear of deportation. Yet he sat all four sons at the kitchen table after dinner and watched over their homework. He could not help his sons with their homework, but he felt that being present conveyed the importance of education (Carreón, Drake, & Barton, 2005; see also Cruz et al., 2011).

High-SES, White, and Asian American parents are more likely to be visible at school than other groups (Lareau & Calarco, 2012). They tend to actively manage their children's education, like selecting classes. They tend to see themselves as collaborators in their children's education and as being entitled to school involvement. In contrast, teachers are often unaware of the involvement of low-SES parents because it tends to occur at home (Green, Walker, Hoover-Dempsey, & Sandler, 2007; Hill et al., 2004).

Parents who are involved *at school* tend to have children who are socially successful, well behaved, less depressed, and relatively high achieving (El Nokali, Bachman, & Votruba-Drzal, 2010; Hill & Tyson, 2009; Kim & Hill, 2015; Ma, Shen, Krenn, Hu, & Yuan, 2015; Wang, Hill, & Hofkens, 2014; Wang & Sheikh-Khalil, 2014). This research is correlational, so it is not clear whether parents of children who are successful and well behaved in school are more motivated to get involved or if their children are more successful because parents are involved.

While parent involvement is generally welcome at schools, it can also be intrusive. For example, in one elementary school, parents thought the school's administrative assistant was unfriendly and wanted her fired, but the principal refused, saying she needed efficiency and responsibility, not warm and fuzzy (Lareau & Muñoz, 2012). The parents also wanted to have a fund-raising dance for adults, but the principal was concerned it would exclude lower-income families. They had the dance anyway. Thus, parents can be overinvolved or underinvolved at school. They may need your guidance to strike an optimal balance.

When parents are involved *at home*, they also can be involved in *positive or negative ways.* For example, parents might "help" with homework in ways that cause confusion or tension (Patall, Cooper, & Robinson, 2008). In a study of 1st- and 2nd-graders, some parents passed on their math anxiety to their children if they frequently helped their children with math homework (Maloney, Ramirez, Gunderson, Levine, & Beilock, 2015). In addition to passing on anxiety, parents can be overbearing and controlling in ways that cause children to dislike school and homework. Let's peek at 1st-grader Elena at home:

> When they read storybooks, Elena's father insists she sound out every word. Instead of enjoying reading together, her father views it as a time to "practice" reading. When Elena looks at the pictures to figure out hard words—as 1st-graders typically do—her father covers the picture and says she is cheating. Elena does not enjoy reading.

When parents are overly controlling or negative, like Elena's father, their children have lower achievement, particularly if they are already struggling academically. Recall from Chapter 13 that autonomy support is important for promoting motivation. Thus, when parents allow children to take initiative and solve their own problems, help only when needed, and focus on the pleasure of learning, their children have higher achievement (Pomerantz, Moorman, & Litwack, 2007). One exception is that some Asian American parents may be quite controlling, requiring drill and practice at home, yet their children have good grades and enjoy school (Cheung & Pomerantz, 2011; Huntsinger & Jose, 2009). For example, they may require their preschooler to spend an hour a day doing math workbooks or practicing phonics because they do not approve of the school's whole-language approach.

think about this

Teachers tend to believe that parents who are present at the school value their children's education more—which in turn is linked to teachers viewing those learners as more academically capable (Hill & Taylor, 2004). How does this relate to the Pygmalion effect described in Chapter 12?

A powerful form of parent involvement is discussing school topics at home, such as school activities, classroom lessons, which courses to take, and aspirations. Such **academic socialization** predicts school success (Kim & Hill, 2015; Wang et al., 2014). A national study of 8th-graders found that parents who discussed such school issues at home had children who scored the equivalent of a full year's worth of schooling higher than children whose parents who did not do this, regardless of SES (Ream & Palardy, 2008).

How does parent involvement help children? Probably through improved skills and motivation. Children with positively involved parents may be more engaged in school, do more homework, and develop a self-identity as a good student (Oyserman, Brickman, & Rhodes, 2007). If their parents emphasize the fun of learning and the importance of persistence, children feel more motivated than if their parents emphasize extrinsic incentives, such as cash for good grades and grounding for poor grades (Gottfried, Marcoulides, Gottfried, & Oliver, 2009). In addition, involved parents develop cultural capital (see Chapter 1); they learn how to negotiate their children's path through school. Parents learn from teachers and teachers learn from parents what their expectations are. This promotes a cultural match so that children get the same message from home and school.

Why are some parents not involved? There may be barriers, like transportation problems, inflexible work schedules, their own history of school failure, fear of being viewed as incompetent by teachers, and language differences. Their beliefs may also be a barrier. Some believe the parents' job is to send the child to school fed and clothed, with proper manners such as saying "Yes ma'am," and to leave the teaching to the teachers (see, for example, Doucet, 2011). The biggest barrier may be lack of self-confidence about whether they can help their children succeed in school (Green et al., 2007).

When teachers make an effort to engage them, parents are more involved at home and at school (Seitsinger, Felner, Brand, & Burns, 2008). See Photo 14.2. Follow these guidelines to increase parent involvement at your school:

1. *Personally invite parents to be involved.* This is a powerful tactic (Walker, Ice, Hoover-Dempsey, & Sandler, 2011). Whether this is best done through notes, e-mail, or phone depends on the age of your learners, the literacy of their parents, and whether the family has a phone or computer with Internet connection. Adolescents do not take notes home as reliably as younger children do.

2. *Establish a regular forum for communication.* Preschools and elementary schools may use Parent Folders. Secondary schools may have a hotline or website and mass electronic messages.

3. *Develop welcoming activities.* For example, host "Muffins for Mom" or "Doughnuts for Dad" before-school breakfasts. Invite parents with preschoolers to visit kindergarten, or invite 8th-graders to visit high school with their parents.

academic socialization
parents communicating educational goals and expectations to their children and linking schoolwork with future success.

Michael Newman/PhotoEdit

PHOTO 14.2 Parents who feel welcomed are more involved in their children's education at home and at school.

4. *Avoid coercion.* Contracts or policies that require parent involvement are coercive. They are not linked to learners' increased achievement. Instead, develop a strong parent–teacher relationship characterized by trust, support, and mutual respect.

5. *When involving parents, help them remain positive.* Emphasize mastery, not performance goals (see Chapter 13) so that parents do not become overly controlling as they feel pressure to make their children perform. Make sure that they have the skills to help their children. When asking parents to do specific things, such as tutor their child in reading, you may need to directly train parents on how to do it successfully (Sénéchal & Young, 2008).

Generally, preschools and elementary schools are better than secondary schools at involving parents, but parental involvement remains important for adolescents (Hill & Taylor, 2004). Parents' involvement may drop off in secondary schools because schools are bigger, less personal, and more bureaucratic. When schools make parents feel welcomed, and provide opportunities for involvement, learners' achievement increases, particularly for low-SES learners. Unfortunately, schools serving low-SES learners are less likely to reach out to parents (Schulting, Malone, & Dodge, 2005). Thus, if you teach in a secondary or low-SES school, you may need to prod your school to involve parents.

Family structure influences other contexts for children, such as whether the mother works and children are in child care. Reagan's family structure meant that he spent long hours with a babysitter, but K'Shawn did not. Collin's family structure changed from married to divorced to remarried. Each change brought changes in his mother's employment and his child care. Let's discuss these topics next.

14-2 Maternal Employment and Child Care

Eleanor's mother works full-time as an executive and her father is a physician. They have a family income of $500,000 a year. Although they work long hours, both parents take time off to attend their children's activities. Eleanor and her sister have had the same nanny since infancy. Eleanor has personal tutors and coaches whenever she wants them.

Cassie's mother has finally found a job, after months of looking, as an "assisted living" aide who dresses and feeds disabled adults. She makes $12 per hour with no benefits. She works irregular hours and sometimes weekends. They occasionally eat at soup kitchens when money runs out. Cassie's parents are divorced; her father neither visits nor sends child support. Cassie sometimes accompanies her mother to work, but mostly stays home alone watching TV. Cassie has been in many cheap child care arrangements over the years as her mother has found, lost, and regained employment. Cassie's dream is to take piano lessons, but her mother can't afford them.

Jenna's mother has not worked outside the home since Jenna was born. Her mother plans to return to being a schoolteacher when Jenna graduates from high school. Her father is a store manager. Money is often tight, especially now that two brothers are in college, but Jenna has plenty of food and clothing. Her mother takes her to voice lessons and soccer after school. Jenna is seldom home alone.

Eleanor, Cassie, and Jenna are all in the same 9th-grade class, but they have very different experiences with maternal employment and child care. Jenna's experience is becoming less common in the United States because more mothers are in the workforce. More than half of women with children work at least part time: 54% who have infants, 64% who have children under age 6, and 77% who have children 6 to 17 years of age (U.S. Bureau of Labor Statistics, 2009). Most working mothers prefer to work part-time; only 20% feel that working full-time is ideal (Pew Research Center, 2007). Women at all income levels work full-time, or part-time, or stay home with their children. For example, one Latino family opted to have their mobile home foreclosed and move in with the grandparents, rather than have the mother work outside the home. Thus, these issues are deeply significant to many families. What does the research say about how maternal employment and child care may influence children like Eleanor, Cassie, and Jenna?

14-2a Maternal Employment

Research on maternal employment shows that child outcomes depend on the situation. Maternal employment has been linked to positive outcomes, such as good language ability, and to negative outcomes, such as behavior problems and obesity; some research shows neutral outcomes (Cawley & Liu, 2012; Lombardi & Coley, 2014; Ziol-Guest, Dunifon, & Kalil, 2013). Why do outcomes vary? In Chapter 1, you learned about two models used to explain poverty's effects. These same models are used to explain maternal employment's effects. According to the *family investment model*, maternal employment would be positive if it leads to greater income to invest in the child or negative if it leads to less time to invest in the child. According to the *family stress model*, maternal employment would be positive if it enhances the mother's well-being or negative if it leads to stress that diminishes parenting quality. Research supports each possibility, but for different family situations.

Child outcomes tend to be negative when:

- Mothers work during the child's infancy. Full-time maternal employment during the child's first year is linked to later academic and behavior problems (Brooks-Gunn, Han, & Waldfogel, 2010; Lucas-Thompson, Goldberg, & Prause, 2010).

- Mothers work more than 30 hours per week (Goldberg, Prause, Lucas-Thompson, & Himsel, 2008; Hill, Waldfogel, Brooks-Gunn, & Han, 2005; Weiss et al., 2003). However, note that many working mothers work part-time rather than full-time, often entering and exiting the workforce. Part-time employment tends to be linked to higher-quality parenting and positive child outcomes (Brooks-Gunn et al., 2010; Buehler & O'Brien, 2011).

- Mothers must work the night shift or irregular schedules, like Cassie's mother. Nonstandard work hours are linked to parents' depression, sleepiness, divorce, health problems, fewer family routines like eating dinner together, and less sensitive parenting (Han, Miller, & Waldfogel, 2010; Hsueh & Yoshikawa, 2007).

- Mothers have a low-pay, no-benefit job. Mothers' low-quality, unstable employment is linked to children's anxiety, depression, grade retention, dropping out of school, and low self-esteem (Dunifon, Kalil, & Bajracharya, 2005; Kalil & Ziol-Guest, 2005).

Child outcomes tend to be positive when:

- Mother's pay helps the family leave welfare, like Cassie's family. Low-income children have higher academic achievement and improved emotions and behavior when their mothers work (Coley & Lombardi, 2013; Lucas-Thompson et al., 2010). Welfare-leaving mothers feel greater self-esteem and more a part of the community (London, Scott, Edin, & Hunter, 2004).

- Mothers are single. Single mothers who work are more likely to have children with better vocabularies than are single mothers who do not work (Brooks-Gunn et al., 2002; Goldberg et al., 2008).

- Mothers enjoy their work, and believe their employment is good for their children, as compared to mothers who either work but do not feel good about it or do not work but wish they did (Harrison & Ungerer, 2002).

- Mothers make sure that they spend time with their children after work hours. Working mothers spend less time with their children than nonworking mothers, but the differences are not as large as you might expect (Huston & Aronson, 2005).

In summary, there are costs and benefits to maternal employment. In general, among low-income families, the balance tips in the positive direction, particularly if Mom's job has standard hours and has some prestige and if she finds it stimulating. Maternal employment and child care go hand in hand, although not all children in child care have working mothers and not all employed mothers use child care. Let's discuss child care next.

think about **this**

Can you apply each of these findings to the family investment and family stress models to explain outcomes linked to maternal employment?

14-2b Child Care

What are the effects of child care? Like maternal employment, it depends. To understand the research, you need to see how child care varies by: (1) type, (2) amount, and (3) quality. First, child care types include centers, the child's home, and the provider's home. Child care can occur in a group or one-on-one with a nanny. Child care can be provided by relatives for no fee or by strangers for profit. More than half of preschoolers in child care are cared for by relatives (FIFCFS, 2015). Another 13% are in nonrelative, home-based care (family child care provider, nanny, babysitter, or au pair). Even though people tend to think of centers when they think of child care, only about 24% of preschoolers are in center-based care (child care, nursery school, preschool, or Head Start). Children may be in more than one type of care, perhaps going to preschool for a few hours and then to Grandma's for a few hours.

Second, child care varies by amount. Some children spend 60 hours per week in child care, whereas others might spend only 4 hours. National studies have found that preschoolers spend an average of 20 hours per week, and kindergarteners and 1st-graders spend an average of 8 to 9 hours per week in child care (McCartney et al., 2010; NICHD Early Child Care Research Network, 2004).

Third, child care quality varies from excellent to harmful. One ethnography of a child care center described it as having adequate space, toys, and child-caregiver ratios. Yet, adults were often too busy with tasks to talk to children, who were told

PHOTO 14.3 The number of hours and quality of child care vary enormously for children.

Comstock/Getty Images/Jupiter images

"go play." Movies were used daily to keep children occupied (Nelson & Shutz, 2007). Does this constitute high-quality care?

Child care is high quality when caregivers: (1) are sensitive and warm, (2) use rich language, (3) directly instruct children in emergent literacy and informal math in ways that are not overly structured, and (4) are stable so that attachment can form (Burchinal et al., 2008a; Howes & James, 2002). This is more likely if child–caregiver ratios are low and caregivers are educated about child development (de Schipper, Riksen-Walraven, & Geurts, 2006; Marshall, 2004). In the United States, recommended ratios are 3:1 for infants and 8:1 for 4-year-olds.

Why do parents put their children in low-quality care? They may need low-cost care. Yet, surprisingly, there is not a strong link between income and quality of care (Sosinsky & Kim, 2013). Rather, parents may prioritize convenience. They also may not know better. For example, in a classic study, parents were equally satisfied with the worst and the best child care programs; they did not seem to be aware of differences in quality (Miller, 1990). In addition, *there is a shortage of high-quality care* in the United States; research shows that as few as 10 to 17% of settings are high quality (Burchinal et al., 2000; NICHD Early Child Care Research Network, 2006a; Vandell et al., 2010). It is especially difficult to maintain high-quality but affordable care for forty hours per week (see Photo 14.3).

selection bias
children and parents select into or choose certain kinds of experiences based on their preexisting characteristics. This makes it difficult to determine the effect of the experience.

There is **selection bias** in child care. That is, parents who place their children in low-quality care tend to be less educated, more stressed, and less involved with their children. Parents who place their children in high-quality care tend to be educated, psychologically healthy, married, sensitive, authoritative, and have good verbal ability (NICHD Early Child Care Research Network, 2006a). Thus, children in high-quality care have preexisting advantages. Research has to sort out the effects of child care quality from these preexisting differences. Many studies try to control for selection bias, but you should keep this bias in mind whenever you read about child care.

14-2c Age Trends in Child Care

Type, amount, and quality of child care vary by age, as do outcomes linked to child care. You have already learned that child care in the first year of life is a risk factor. How common is early child care?

Infancy to Early Childhood (Birth to 5 Years)

Of the children who will ever be in child care, about a quarter enter by 5 months of age. About 50% will have entered child care by age 2½. These infants and toddlers are more likely to be in part-time, rather than full-time care. They are also more likely to be in home-based care. However, when children reach age 3, they are more likely to be placed in center-based care (FIFCFS, 2009). In the year prior to kindergarten entry, 83% of children are in some kind of group arrangement, but this varies from full-time child care to preschool for just a few hours per week (Flanagan, McPhee, & Mulligan, 2010).

Middle Childhood and Adolescence (6 to 19 Years)

School is the primary source of child care after age 6. School is enough for many families because the mother works only part-time or because the father is home for out-of-school hours. However, many school-aged children need child care before and/or after school. Only 14% of child care center slots go to school-age children (FIFCFS, 2015). This means many school-age children are in after-school programs or self-sibling care, which are discussed next.

After-school programs

After-school programs are diverse; they may be run by schools, churches, organizations such as Boys & Girls Club, or city recreation offices. They have different motives, such as merely keeping kids off the streets, providing academic support, or increasing physical activity (Craig et al., 2013; Schuna, Lauersdorf, Behrens, Liguori, & Liebert, 2013). A high-quality program has warm, supportive staff; multiple activities for children; and opportunity for positive socializing. Some programs use computer-based delivery that improves learning at lower expense than having trained teachers (Craig et al., 2013). About 20% of school-age children are in after-school and enrichment programs (FIFCFS, 2015). More children are in self-sibling care.

Self-sibling care

Self-sibling care refers to children who are home alone or with a sibling under age 18. Self-sibling care typically occurs for 2 hours or less daily—just to fill in the after-school hours. At what age are children old enough to take care of themselves? In some states, it is illegal to leave children under age 13 home alone, but there is a rise in self-sibling care around 9 to 11 years of age, suggesting that some parents believe children can care for themselves and their siblings at this age.

After parental care, self-sibling care is the second most common form of care for school-age children, involving millions of children. National surveys indicate that slightly less than 10% of elementary age, 30% of middle school, and 50% of high school students are in some degree of self-care while their parents work. See Figure 14.5. Self-sibling care is more likely in suburban or rural high-SES, low-risk neighborhoods. However, *long hours* of self-care are more likely for youth living in poverty (Mahoney & Parente, 2009).

Safety is a concern with self-sibling care. Parents teach children not to talk to strangers or let them in the house when children are home alone.

self-sibling care
a prevalent form of nonmaternal care for school-age children, in which children are home alone or with a sibling under age 18.

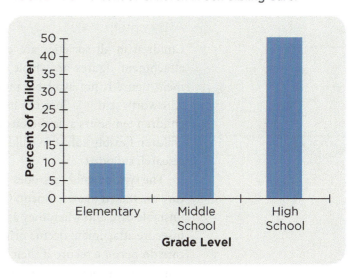

FIGURE 14.5 Percent of Children in Self-Sibling Care.

Half of children are in self-care in high school. Do these percentages reflect the children you know? *Source: Adapted from Mahoney and Parente (2009).*

However, in a classic study, researchers pretended to be strangers phoning elementary students and delivering a package. All but two children readily gave their name during the phone conversation and said they were home alone—and let the stranger deliver the package (Kraizer, Witte, Fryer, & Miyoshi, 1990). *Every* parent predicted beforehand that their child would *not* do either because they had trained their child. Yet, the children were unable to carry out safety instructions when left alone. Let's turn next to what child outcomes are predicted by child care.

14-2d What Does Child Care Predict?

Did you notice in Chapter 1 that "long hours in child care" was listed as a risk factor, but "educational child care" was listed as a protective factor? Is this contradictory? Let's see.

Language and Cognitive Development

Type of care is linked to language and cognitive development. Children tend to have better language and cognitive skills in center-based care than in home-based care and in after-school programs than in self-sibling care, but only if the program has an academic emphasis and well-educated staff (Belsky, Bakermans-Kranenburg, & Van IJzendoorn, 2007; Fredricks & Simpkins, 2012; Laurer et al., 2006; Mahoney, Lord, & Carryl, 2005).

Quality of care is also linked to language and cognitive development. Children in high-quality care and high-quality after-school programs have better language skills, greater school readiness, and higher grades and test scores than children in low-quality care (Burchinal et al., 2000; Burchinal, Lowe Vandell, & Belsky, 2014; Granger, 2008; NICHD Early Child Care Research Network, 2006a). Perhaps this is because care is defined as high quality if caregivers ask children questions, respond to vocalizations, and talk with children, which you learned in Chapter 12 are linked to children's language ability. Remarkably, this effect has been found a full decade after children exited child care, suggesting that it is long-term (Vandell et al., 2010).

Attachment

Children in all societies are cared for by multiple attachment figures. Typically, attachment figures are stable and readily available. What if the primary attachment figure is not available most of the day or the caregiver changes periodically? Ainsworth said it is "hard to be a sensitively responsive mother if you're away from children ten hours a day" (Karen, 1994, p. 69). However, some psychologists believe children flexibly adjust to child care with no attachment problems. Which view does research support?

The type of child care does not appear to matter, but amount and quality of child care are linked to attachment. Children are more likely to be insecure in low-quality, unstable care and when they are in care for more than 10 hours per week. However, insecure attachment occurs primarily when mothers are insensitive; children in child care do become secure if their mothers are sensitive. Perhaps less-sensitive mothers cannot buffer their children from the stress of child care or need more time to establish secure attachment. In addition, when secure toddlers enter child care, they may become insecure, particularly if their mother does not sensitively help them adjust

(Ahnert, Gunnar, Lamb, & Barthel, 2004; Erel, Obermran, & Yirmiya, 2000; NICHD Early Child Care Research Network, 2000b).

Child care may be linked to insecure attachment for three reasons:

1. Many toddlers plead not to be left at child care, yet the mother leaves anyway. This may feel like rejection.

2. Mothers tend to be more responsive than caregivers; mothers soothe, stay near, communicate with, and share emotions more with their children. Mothers are more responsive than caregivers even in countries, like Germany, where child care is higher quality than in the United States (Ahnert, Rickert, & Lamb, 2000).

3. Mothers may fail to develop sensitivity. Long daily separations can interfere with mothers' development of mothering skills (Furman, 1989). Mothers who work full-time in the child's first year tend to be less sensitive (Brooks-Gunn et al., 2002; NICHD Early Child Care Research Network, 1997).

Stress

Bowlby believed that infants separated from their mother would feel stress no matter how well they were cared for. Research shows that young children in child care have high levels of cortisol, a stress hormone (see Chapter 8). Typically, children's cortisol levels peak around wake-up time and then decline slowly over the day, to reach a low at bedtime. But for most children in child care, cortisol levels *rise* over the day—even in high-quality care (Badanes, Dmitrieva, & Watamura, 2012; Bernard, Peloso, Laurenceau, Zhang, & Dozier, 2015; Watamura, Donzella, Alwin, & Gunnar, 2003). See Figure 14.6. Cortisol levels are even higher when: (1) quality of care is low, (2) groups are large, (3) child–caregiver relationships are conflicted, and (4) the caregiver is intrusive and overcontrolling (Gunnar, Kryzer, Van Ryzin, & Phillips, 2011; Lisonbee, Mize, Payne, & Granger, 2008; Rappolt-Schlictmann et al., 2009). Children who live in poverty may be an exception; their cortisol levels may be lower in child care than at home (Rappolt-Schlictmann et al., 2009).

Does stress diminish after children get used to child care? Even after several months, child care remains stressful for some but not all children (Ahnert et al., 2004; Bernard et al., 2015; Gunnar et al., 2011). Cortisol level is linked to being in child care as early as infancy; the link is strongest during toddlerhood, declines at 3 to 5 years, and disappears after age 7 (Bernard et al., 2015). Thus, older children feel less stress while at child care than toddlers.

What does this mean for children? Child care experience may remodel the neural circuits that regulate negative emotions. This may explain why some youth who were in child care as infants and toddlers continue to have abnormal cortisol levels at age 15 (Roisman et al., 2009). Recall from Chapter 8 that cortisol levels affect executive

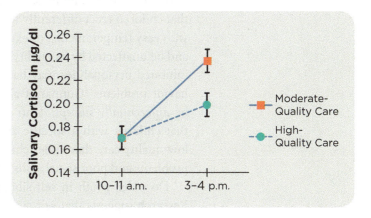

FIGURE 14.6 Cortisol Levels in Child Care.

Children in high-quality care have a smaller daytime rise in cortisol than children in moderate-quality care. Cortisol levels indicate stress. Children who are not in child care have a decrease, rather than rise, in cortisol over the day (Gunnar, 2000). *Source: Tout, de Haan, Campbell, and Gunnar (1998).*

functioning and working memory capacity (Blair, Granger, & Razza, 2005). Furthermore, abnormal cortisol levels are linked to internalizing problems (anxiety, withdrawn behavior, and depression) and aggression among children in child care, our next topic (Tout, de Haan, Campbell, & Gunnar, 1998).

Social Competence

Do young children in center-based care become more socially competent because they have opportunity to play with peers? A large, national study found the opposite. After age 3, and perhaps as early as age 2, children in child care tend to have more behavior problems such as child–caregiver conflict, hyperactivity, aggression, impulsivity, and attention deficits; they tend to have less ability to work independently, use time wisely, or complete work promptly (NICHD Early Child Care Research Network, 2006a). Both center-based and nonrelative care were linked to more behavior problems in young children.

Amount of care is linked to behavior problems; some call this the quantity effect. Researchers reviewing many studies concluded that "the quantity effect is real.... [C]hildren who have experienced many hours in child care prior to school entry, especially center-based care, are rated by their teachers in the early grades as having more externalizing behavior problems, more teacher-child conflict, and lower levels of self-control than their counterparts" (Huston, Bobbitt, & Bentley, 2015, p. 628). Long hours in child care early in life continue to be linked to behavior problems through 6th grade and into midadolescence (Belsky et al., 2007; Vandell et al., 2010). Perceived-popular learners—who have social skills but are aggressive (see Chapter 11)—are likely to have been in longer hours of child care as preschoolers as compared with their peers (Rodkin & Roisman, 2010). Children tend to develop behavior problems even in high-quality care or after-school programs, but the effect is smaller (Howes & James, 2002; Huston et al., 2015; McCartney et al., 2010). The effect is also smaller when the child care occurs in smaller groups—fewer than four for 2-year-olds and fewer than eight for 4-year-olds. Furthermore, the effect is smaller when mothers are sensitive (Burchinal et al., 2014).

Not all studies find that child care is linked to more behavior problems (see, for example, Gormley, Phillips, Newmark, Welti, & Adelstein, 2011). One explanation is that children react differently to child care (Phillips, Fox, & Gunnar, 2011). Children with easy temperaments, or exuberant personalities, may readily adapt to child care, and be unaffected by its quality. In contrast, children with difficult temperament and inhibited personalities may have high levels of cortisol and develop long-term behavior problems (Gunnar et al., 2011; Pluess & Belsky, 2010). Thus, children may be *differentially susceptible* to quality of child care. For example, one study found that children with a specific allele (on the DRD4 gene) were more susceptible to low-quality care than other children; they were more likely to develop externalizing problems and poor social skills (Belsky & Pluess, 2013).

Do older youth in self-sibling care become more responsible and self-reliant? Research suggests that self-sibling care is linked to anxiety and behavior problems. Adolescents in self-sibling care are more likely to commit crime, use drugs, be sexually active, and have sexually transmitted diseases. Adolescent crime peaks at 3 to 4 p.m., just after school, during parents' typical working hours. Just as with younger children, the effects depend on the amount of self-sibling care. Risk is greater when youth spend more than 10 hours per week in self-care, and if self-care starts early in elementary school and continues for years (Mahoney & Parente, 2009). Risk is also greater when youth spend more unsupervised time with peers (Lee & Vandell, 2015). Thus, extended self-sibling care is a risk factor for delinquency. Effects are smaller when parents are authoritative (rather than permissive), monitor the child, and live in a safe neighborhood and when the child does not have preexisting behavior problems (Mahoney & Parente, 2009).

Play

Type and quality of care are linked to play. Children in high-quality care are more likely to play in advanced ways than children in low-quality care (Raspa, McWilliam, & Maher-Ridley, 2001). Children in center-based care with peers are more likely to play in advanced ways than children in home-based care (NICHD Early Child Care Research Network, 2001a). This is important because advanced play promotes social, cognitive, and language skills (see Chapter 11). Children in child care may have a play advantage over home-reared preschoolers at kindergarten entry, but home-reared preschoolers readily catch up once they have abundant classmates (NICHD Early Child Care Research Network, 2005a).

In summary, whether child care is a risk or protective factor depends on the type, amount, and quality of child care and whether you consider cognitive, emotional, or social outcomes. Table 14.1 provides a framework for organizing these factors. What can be done to mitigate the risk linked to child care? You have probably noticed a recurring theme in this research; children fare better when child care is high quality and when they spend less time in child care. Here are three important additional points:

1. Negative outcomes are strongest when child care begins during infancy.

2. Effects of early child care can be long term. Child care during infancy and the preschool years has been linked to behavior and academic problems through elementary school and into high school (Burchinal et al., 2014; Campbell, Lamb, & Hwant, 2000; NICHD Early Child Care Research Network, 2003a, 2005a, 2005b, 2006a).

3. Effects depend on socioeconomic status; child care can be a protective factor for low-SES children. We will discuss this more later.

Does Parenting or Child Care Have a Larger Effect?

You might assume that parenting matters more than child care. To test this, scientists compare the effect size for quality of parenting with the effect size for quality of child care. What does the research show? For *language and cognitive abilities*, parenting quality may be more powerful than child care—the effect size of quality of child care is about 25 to 80% smaller than the effect size of parenting. In contrast, for *behavior problems*, parenting quality may be less powerful than child care—the effect size of quality of child care is more than twice the size of parenting. Thus, child care makes a modest-to-large contribution to behavior problems and a small-to-modest contribution to language and cognitive abilities compared to parenting (NICHD Early Child Care Research Network, 2006a; Peisner-Feinberg et al., 2001).

TABLE 14.1 Summary of research on child care

Child outcomes	Child care attributes		
	Quality	Amount	Type
Language and cognitive ability	High-quality care is linked to better abilities than low-quality care. Effect is strongest for low-SES children.		After age 3, center care is linked to better abilities than home-based child care. Extracurricular activities and high-quality after-school programs are linked to better abilities at school age. Effect is strongest for low-SES children.
Attachment	Low-quality and unstable care are linked to insecure attachment, especially if mother is less sensitive.	More than 10 hours per week is linked to insecure attachment, especially if mother is less sensitive.	There is no effect of type of care, assuming comparable quality. Home care may be higher quality for infants.
Stress	Cortisol levels are high even in high-quality care, but are highest in low-quality care.		Cortisol levels are higher in larger-group care.
Social competence	Low-quality care is linked to long-term behavior problems. So is high-quality care, but effects are smaller. Children in high-quality care have better social skills than children in low-quality care.	More than 10 hours per week is linked to poor social skills and more behavior problems, especially if care began in infancy.	Center-based care is linked to behavior problems. Self-sibling care is linked to antisocial behavior if it is more than ten hours per week.
Play	Children in high-quality care have more-complex peer play than children in low-quality care.		Children in center-based care have more-complex peer play than children in home-based child care.

Child care may reduce the effect of parenting. That is, parenting quality more strongly predicts outcomes for children in less child care than for those in more child care (Adi-Japha & Klein, 2009; Howes, 1990; NICHD Early Child Care Research Network, 1998b). Whether this shift of influence from parent to child care is positive or negative depends on the quality of the home. On the negative side, children do not benefit as much from having two parents or sensitive, authoritative parents if they are in full-time child care. On the positive side, child care helps children from challenging homes. In fact, government programs designed to improve achievement for low-SES children often promote child care. The reason for this will become apparent in the next section.

14-2e Group Diversity in Child Care

The effects of maternal employment and child care may be different for boys and girls and for children with different SES backgrounds. Let's discuss these differences next.

Gender

Most studies find that maternal employment predicts similar outcomes for boys and girls, but when gender differences are found, they favor girls (Goldberg et al., 2008). For example, some studies find that daughters of employed mothers tend to have higher aspirations, while sons tend to have lower achievement (Brooks-Gunn et al., 2002; Smolensky & Gootman, 2003).

Similarly, gender differences in child care effects are not always found (see, for example, Vandell et al., 2010), but when they are found, they mostly favor girls (Bornstein, Hahn, Gist, & Haynes, 2006). Insecure attachment and behavior problems are more strongly linked to child care for boys. One exception to this pattern is that adolescent girls may be at greater risk of delinquency in self-sibling care than boys (Mahoney & Parente, 2009).

Socioeconomic Status

Socioeconomic status is linked to child care in two ways. First, child care tends to be economically segregated in the United States. High-SES children are more likely to be in high-quality care and enriching after-school activities. Middle-SES families tend to be unable to afford high-quality care (NICHD Early Child Care Research Network, 2006a; Smolensky & Gootman, 2003). Impoverished children qualify for high-quality government-subsidized care, but their families may not place them in high-quality care (Johnson, Ryan, & Brooks-Gunn, 2012). Of the 12 million children in child care, about 2 million are subsidized.

Second, child care is more beneficial to low-SES than high-SES children. Low-SES children in high-quality, center-based care tend to have better language ability, school readiness, and academic achievement and fewer behavior problems than low-SES home-reared children (Loeb, Fuller, Kagan, & Carrol, 2004; NICHD Early Child Care Research Network & Duncan, 2003c; Votruba-Drzal, Coley, Maldonado-Carreño, Li-Grinning, & Chase-Lansdale, 2010). For example, one study found that low-SES children who spent more time in *high-quality* child care before age 4 had higher math and reading scores in 3rd and 5th grade than children in low-quality child care—and scored almost as well as higher-SES classmates (Dearing, McCartney, & Taylor, 2009). That is, children from homes with little parental education, few books, little library use, high rates of TV watching, and low rates of reading benefit from being in child care, whereas children with well-educated mothers may not (Bornstein et al., 2006; Cote, Borge, Geoffroy, Rutter, & Tremblay, 2008; Peisner-Feinberg et al., 2001). See Figure 14.7.

FIGURE 14.7 Child Social Outcomes by Quality of Home and Child Care.

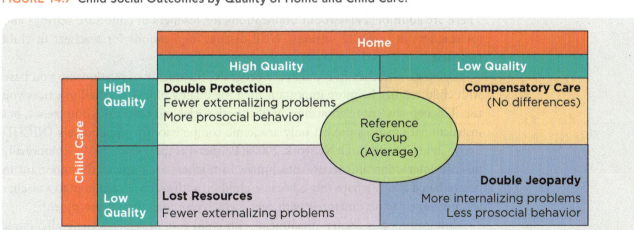

Quality of home refers to maternal sensitivity and home environment. High quality refers to the top third, and low quality to the bottom third. The "reference" group is the middle third of children—those in mid-quality child care and mid-quality homes. Comparisons are to this reference group. Outcomes are based on teachers' ratings of children. *Source: Adapted from Watamura, Phillips, Morrissey, McCartney, and Bub (2011).*

think
about this

A mother moved to a state with free pre-kindergarten child care. Her second child is turning 4. She has planned to keep the child home until kindergarten. The mother is an architect who quit to be a full-time mother. Her husband is a graduate student. Family income is very low. The mother asks you whether she should place the child in the pre-K child care program. Based on research, what would you advise? What additional information would you want to have, and why?

Indeed, many school-readiness programs offer child care as an intervention for children who are at risk because of poverty or low birth weight because high-quality care is a protective factor for them. Keep in mind that this pertains to high-quality care. Children who are in both low-quality homes and low-quality child care experience a "double jeopardy" for behavior problems (Watamura, Phillips, Morrissey, McCartney, & Bub, 2011). Thus, Cassie is more likely to benefit from attending high-quality child care than Jenna. Jenna has the undivided attention of her teacher–mother, an advantage with which even high-quality child care cannot compete.

14-2f Classroom Implications of Maternal Employment and Child Care

Maternal employment influences parents' involvement in your classroom. Mothers who work part-time tend to be more involved in their children's school than mothers who work full-time or not at all (Buehler & O'Brien, 2011). Part-time working mothers may be more likely to talk about school, check homework, restrict TV, promote after-school lessons, be involved in PTA or booster club, and serve as volunteers at school. You can help your students by following these guidelines:

1. Help working parents stay involved in their children's education with creative, flexible solutions. You might suggest that grandparents meet with teachers, or that parents take the child to the workplace where they can supervise homework, or take "lunch hour" in the late afternoon to check on their children after school (Weiss et al., 2003).

2. Advocate for policies that promote part-time work for mothers who desire it and maternal leave during infancy. A creative group of teachers in California did this for themselves; they arranged to have two teachers share one teaching position so that each worked half-time and could be with their children more.

3. Advocate for more high-quality child care. This is important for school-age as well as early childhood care.

There are additional classroom implications for teachers in child care settings and for teachers in preK–12 settings. We'll discuss implications for teachers in child care first.

If you are a teacher in a child care program, the quality of relationship you have with children may be more important than the quality of instructional practices you use. Teacher–student relationships predict both social and academic competence, but instructional practices predict only academic competence for preschoolers (NICHD Early Child Care Research Network, 2000a; Peisner-Feinberg et al., 2001). Emotionally positive interaction and secure attachment to teachers are particularly important in center-based care. Perhaps this is because children with secure attachment to a teacher are more likely to play maturely with peers, which promotes their development.

How common is secure attachment with child care providers? Generally, fewer children develop secure attachments to caregivers than to parents. Many studies across varied cultures show that about 40% of preschool children are securely attached to their caregivers, while about 60% are securely attached to a parent (Ahnert, Pinquart, & Lamb, 2006; Commodari, 2013). Yet children who are insecure with both parents can become secure with a caregiver. In the earlier vignette, Eleanor is more attached to her nanny than to her parents, sharing successes more eagerly with the nanny and seeking her out when tired or sick.

What influences whether a secure relationship develops? In Chapter 6, you learned that sensitive, responsive teachers develop secure relationships with learners. In addition, the structure of child care can make a difference. Children are more likely to develop attachment to a caregiver if they stay with the same caregiver across multiple years and if they are in home-based rather than center-based care (Ahnert et al., 2006). Perhaps this is because caregivers converse and play with children more when they have fewer to care for and when they care for children longer (Elicker, Fortner-Wood, & Noppe, 1999).

An implication for teachers in preK–12 settings is that maternal employment and child care can have positive and negative effects in your classroom. On the positive side, low-SES learners who have been in high-quality care may have better language and cognitive skills. On the negative side, child care during infancy has been linked to behavior problems from elementary through high school. The more students there are in a classroom who have been in child care, the more aggression for the whole classroom (Dmitrieva, Steinberg, & Belsky, 2007). This could alter how much time you spend on discipline. Even small effects are important when many students are involved. If your students are experiencing behavior problems, follow the guidelines from previous chapters that discuss how to help students with these problems.

In summary, the effects of child care depend on the type, amount, and quality of care, as well as on children's gender and SES. High-quality care can promote cognitive abilities in low-SES children, but low-quality care can lead to aggression. Effects are small, but consequences for the classroom and for society could be large because so many children are involved. Prominent psychologists have called for improved child care quality and for policies that allow more parents to stay home or work part-time (Greenspan, 2003; Maccoby & Lewis, 2003). The panel of scientists conducting the largest national child care study concluded, "[O]ur results provide support for policies that reduce the amount of time children spend in child care" (NICHD Early Child Care Research Network, 2006a, p. 114). Let's turn next to media exposure, another powerful context of childhood.

14-3 Television and Other Media

Collin, the resilient 7th-grader you met earlier, has a Wii and a computer, which he plays for an hour a day (a limit set by his parents). He has only sports, fitness, and "tame" electronic games like Mario Brothers. *He has a flip phone, not a smartphone, does not have an iPod or MP3 player, and does not watch TV on school days.*

His classmate, Ricky, takes his iPod to school even though it is against the rules. The songs on his iPod contain profane lyrics about murder, domestic violence, rape, drugs, and sex. He says his favorite song is "The one where he strangles his wife, then throws her in the trunk and drives her into a lake." At home he routinely plays video games like Mortal Kombat, *and watches unlimited TV.*

Most students, like Ricky and Collin, are exposed to a variety of media. Although students use newer technologies, TV still dominates their media use (Hofferth, 2010). Television has a unique niche that is not replaced by newer media. It entered U.S. homes in the 1950s and flooded the market by 1960. Today, 98% of homes have at least one TV. Most families also have video games, a computer, and other media devices.

Do other students use as much violent media as Ricky, or are they more like Collin? Ricky's classmates say he is mean. He doesn't have any friends at school. He sits by himself on the bus and makes fun of others. Would Ricky be equally rejected if he used less violent media? These questions reflect two concerns about media use—time and content. Let's look at these concerns.

14-3a The Issue of Time

Learners spend a great deal of time using media. When you add various media—television, cell phones, tablets, computers—youth consume an average of 7½ hours of media per day (Rideout, Foehr, & Roberts, 2010). This media use displaces other, potentially more important, activities. The more time 1- to 12-year-olds spend watching TV or playing video games, the less time they spend sleeping, playing, reading, or studying (Hofferth, 2010). Time spent using computers and tablets is more complicated because they can be used for studying.

14-3b The Issue of Content

Some TV and computer programs are educational or prosocial. Shows like *Sesame Street* are designed to build academic skills. Shows like *Arthur* are designed to teach social skills, like conflict resolution and kindness to others. Unfortunately, children spend substantially more time with antisocial media.

Antisocial media contains violence. The average child watches tens of thousands of violent acts on TV. The violence is often depicted as glamorous or without traumatic consequences. Aggressors are often heroes with no remorse who go unpunished, and victims often miraculously recover. Video games are even more violent than TV. Some people argue that violent media simply mirror society. This is a myth. Your students will seldom personally witness a murder, even in violent neighborhoods, but they will watch thousands in media. One media critic estimated that if the level of violence on TV were realistic, within 50 days every U.S. citizen would have been murdered, and the last one could turn off the TV (Medved, 1995).

Antisocial media contains sexual content. About 84% of sitcoms have sexual content (Lorch, 2007). TV shows average five sex-related scenes per hour, including shows watched by children during prime time. Sexual content on TV has increased 10-fold since the 1970s, and nearly doubled between 1998 and 2005 (Kunkel, Eyal, Finnerty, Biely, & Donnerstein, 2005). The average student may be exposed to 10,000 to 15,000 media references to sex each year. Women are often portrayed as sex objects. Sex is portrayed as superficial and risk-free. It is portrayed without emotional or physical consequences such as sexually transmitted infections or pregnancy (Ward, 2003).

14-3c Age Trends in Media Use

Most young people today have access to multiple forms of media technology. About 87% have access to a computer, 81% have a gaming console, and 73% have a smartphone (Lenhart & Pew Research Center, 2015). How much and which media children use changes with age.

Infancy and Toddlerhood (Birth to 2 Years)

Young children tend to watch a lot of TV. About 40% live in homes where the TV is on most of the day as "background." On average, toddlers actively watch about 2 hours per day (Courage & Setliff, 2009; Foster & Watkins, 2010). How do infants even know to look at a media screen? Recall from Chapter 9 that infants engage in joint attention with adults. One-year-olds tend to follow their parents' gaze and look at a screen when their parents look, which trains them to pay attention to screens (Demers, Hanson, Kirkorian, Pempek, & Anderson, 2013).

Some videos are specifically designed for children under age 2, and claim to cultivate baby geniuses. Curious scientists decided to test this claim by randomly assigning 1-year-olds to watch an "educational" video daily for 4 weeks. Toddlers who watched with or without a parent did not learn more new words than those who did not watch the video (Deloache et al., 2010). But in another study, toddlers did learn some American Sign Language from video, although they learned more from co-viewing and instruction from their parents (Dayanim & Namy, 2015). Thus, live interaction was more effective. Toddlers do not respond to video as readily as to live interaction. For example, if a videotaped adult tells 2-year-olds that she hid a Piglet doll under the couch, they will not go look for Piglet. If the adult tells them face-to-face, they will go find Piglet (Troseth, Saylor, & Archer, 2006). In a policy statement, the American Academy of Pediatrics (2013a) recommended that parents discourage all screen exposure for children less than 2 years of age.

Early Childhood (3 to 5 Years)

Preschoolers watch about an hour and a half per day of TV (Rideout, 2014). They mostly watch shows designed for adults. However, young children are more likely to watch child-oriented educational or prosocial TV and play educational video games than are older youth (Wartella, Caplovitz, & Lee, 2004). Table 14.2 on the following page shows that media use goes up but *educational* media use goes down from age 2 to 10.

Middle Childhood (6 to 12 Years)

Media use increases during elementary school. At this age, children are more likely to use computers and video games as compared with when they were younger. TV watching and video game use peak among so-called tweens, or children ages 11 to 14 (Hofferth & Moon, 2011; Rideout et al., 2010).

Elementary school students watch less educational and more entertainment TV than preschoolers (Huston, Bickham, Lee, & Wright, 2007). Entertainment TV tends to be violent. Elementary students are more aggressive after watching violent media compared to adolescents (Anderson et al., 2003). See Photo 14.4.

TABLE 14.2 Screen media use by age

	Time spent with screen media (hours:minutes), by age			
	Among all	**2- to 4-year-olds**	**5- to 7-year-olds**	**8- to 10-year olds**
Average amount of time spent per day with:				
Television	1:21	1:20	1:18	1:24
Video games	:17	:03	:20	:27
Computers	:14	:02	:15	:25
Mobile devices	:14	:10	:14	:18
Total screen	2:07	1:37	2:08	2:36
	Proportion of screen time that is educational (hours:minutes), by age			
	Among all	**2- to 4-year-olds**	**5- to 7-year-olds**	**8- to 10-year-olds**
Average amount of time spent using any screen media in a typical day	2:07	1:37	2:08	2:36
Average amount of time spent using any *educational* screen media in a typical day	:56	1:16	:50	:42
Proportion of total screen media time that is *educational*	44%	78%	39%	27%

Notice that that media use goes up but *educational* media use goes down from age 2 to 10.

Source: Rideout (2014).

PHOTO 14.4 Tweens use a variety of media for an average of several hours per day.

Adolescence (13 to 19 Years)

Adolescents spend an average of one to two-and-a-half hours per day watching TV (Larson, 2001). They spend as many hours *per week* watching TV as they do *per month* reading books not assigned in school. They also spend considerable time on the computer and using social media.

Adolescents are more likely to have Internet access at home than are younger children. Almost all adolescents (93%) in the United States use the Internet and most have an e-mail account and a social networking profile (Lenhart, Purcell, Smith & Zickuhr, 2010). Computers are used by teens to visit websites, to communicate, and to study or complete academic tasks more than younger children (Hofferth & Moon, 2011). Most adolescents also own cell phones and report spending an average of 1.5 hours a day texting (Lenhart et al., 2010). One study found that 15-year-olds sent and received roughly 110 texts per day (Underwood, Rosen, More, Erenreich, & Gentsch, 2012). As of 2015, about 71% use Facebook (see Figure 14.8), but what is popular can change rapidly. New platforms spring up and capture interest suddenly. Thus, if you teach high school, your students are likely to use the computer more than you do, but not if you teach early childhood or elementary school.

14-3d Individual Diversity in Media Use

These age trends mask huge individual differences, like Collin compared with Ricky. Children tend to maintain television viewing habits that they start as toddlers—that is, heavy viewers remain heavy viewers (Huston et al., 2007). Some youth seldom, if ever, play video games, and others play many hours each day (and night). Still others are constantly texting and checking Facebook.

What Do Differences in Media Use Predict?

How much media children use and the content of those media are linked to all domains of the child—physical, cognitive, emotional, and social. For example, the American Psychological Association (2007) concluded that the rampant sexualization of girls in the media is linked to impaired cognitive functioning, increased depression, increased eating disorders, and unhealthy sexual development. However, outcomes linked to media use can be positive or negative, depending on content and amount of time using the media. Let's look more closely at specific outcomes next.

Physical development

Media use can undermine physical well-being in four ways:

1. Media use replaces physical activity. Heavy media users tend to be overweight (pun unintended), particularly girls (Lorch, 2007).

2. Media use promotes bad eating habits. TV ads sell high-calorie foods, youth eat more high-calorie foods while watching TV, and metabolism during TV watching is lower than during sleep (Kaiser Family Foundation, 2004).

3. Media use disrupts sleep. Many youth sleep with their mobile devices, which is linked to sleeping fewer hours and feeling more tired (George & Odgers, 2015).

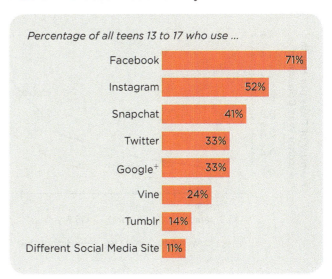

FIGURE 14.8 Social Media Used by Adolescents.

Percentage of all teens 13 to 17 who use …

Platform	Percentage
Facebook	71%
Instagram	52%
Snapchat	41%
Twitter	33%
Google+	33%
Vine	24%
Tumblr	14%
Different Social Media Site	11%

As of 2015, Facebook, Instagram, and Snapchat were the most common social media platforms used by teens. Does that pattern fit your current experience? *Source: Lenhart and Pew Research Center (2015).*

FIGURE 14.9 Alcohol and Mature Video Game Use.

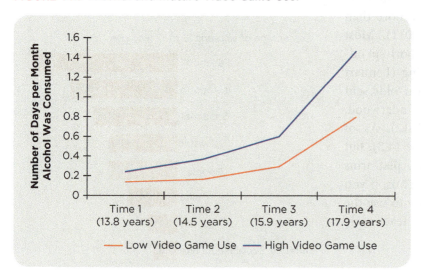

Alcohol use rises more rapidly over 4 years for more frequent users of mature video games than for less-frequent users. *Source: Hull et al. (2014).*

4. Media use glamorizes drug use, portraying smoking and alcohol use as normal, humorous, and risk-free. Heavy viewers use more alcohol and tobacco, even if they do not have other risk factors for drug use (Heatherton & Sargent, 2009; Hull, Brunelle, Prescott, & Sargent, 2014). See Figure 14.9.

On the positive side, video game players tend to develop good hand–eye coordination, better visual processing, enhanced mental rotation skills, and rapid, focused attention (Dye, Green, & Bavelier, 2009; Granic, Lobel, & Engels, 2013). In experiments in which nongamers practice playing action video games, their visual processing improves (Green & Bavelier, 2007). In addition, exergames can help control obesity and promote physical fitness. In fact, some schools are using exergames in PE classes (Staiano & Calvert, 2011).

Cognitive development and achievement

Media use may undermine cognitive ability. Amanda's mother told her teacher, "Amanda don't read no newspapers. She gets her news from the TV, and that's a good thing 'cause I pay 65 dollar' a month for cable!" Heavy TV viewers, like Amanda, read less and talk less with their parents. They have lower verbal and reading ability, lower grades, attention problems, and spend less time studying. These effects occur from preschool through high school (Busch et al., 2014; Ennemoser & Schneider, 2007; Fuligni & Stevenson, 1995; Wright et al., 2001). For example, one study found that adolescents who spend an hour or more per day watching television had lower academic achievement compared to youth who did not watch television (Busch et al., 2014).

One concern is that television viewing may lead to short attention span, limited imagination, and passive children because it is fast-paced with many interruptions. Some research suggests that when toddlers experience several hours per day of TV, they are likely to develop ADHD-like problems later, but not if they watch moderate amounts (Foster & Watkins, 2010). Yet, an experimental study found that just minutes of watching a fast-paced cartoon resulted in short-term deficits in executive functions (see Figure 14.10).

Similar outcomes are linked to video gaming. In one experiment 1st- to 3rd-grade boys who did not own a video gaming system were given one. Half were randomly assigned to receive it immediately, and half to receive it 4 months later. At the end of the 4 months, the boys who were new game players had lower reading and writing scores and more learning problems compared to those who had not yet received their gaming system. The new game players spent

FIGURE 14.10 Watching TV Results in Poor Executive Functioning in the Short Term.

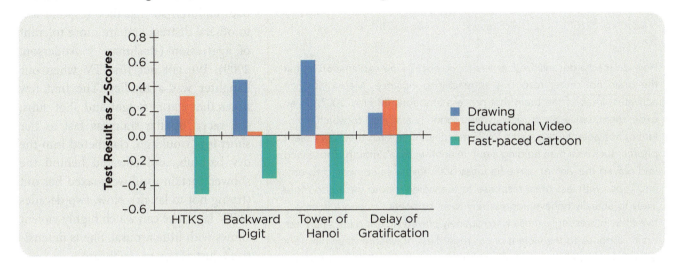

Four-year-olds were randomly assigned to watch a fast-paced cartoon, to watch a slower-paced educational video, or to draw for 9 minutes. They were then given three tests of executive function and a delay-of-gratification test using marshmallows and crackers. (The HTKS test asked children to touch their toes when told to touch their head, and vice versa. This was repeated with shoulders and knees. The backward digit test asked children to repeat a sequence of numbers, such as 4–3–1, in reverse order.) A Z-score is the number of standard deviations above or below the mean. *Source: Lillard and Peterson (2011).*

less time reading, listening to stories, writing, and doing homework (Weis & Cerankosky, 2010).

On the positive side, students who use *educational* media read more and have better reading, math, and vocabulary test scores than those who use *entertainment* media (Schmidt & Anderson, 2007). Watching *Sesame Street* and using educational video games helps low-SES 3-year-olds develop school-readiness skills (Huston et al., 2007; Li & Atkins, 2004). As you learned in Chapter 11, among school-age children serious games (i.e., instruction delivered via computer-based games, simulations, and 3-D virtual worlds) enhance learning (Merchant, Goetz, Cifuentes, Keeney-Kennicutt, & Davis, 2014). Even entertainment media may improve grades depending on what they require of players, such as reading, critical thinking, and cooperation with others in multi-user games (Busch et al., 2014).

Computer use is different from watching TV or video gaming. Computer use is linked to higher achievement, but only up to a point. Among adolescents, both little use and excessive use are linked to lower grades, but moderate use (perhaps 1 to 2 hours per day) is linked to higher grades (Willoughby, 2008). In one study, low-SES students were given a home computer with free Internet, and they developed better reading ability and achieved better grades (Jackson et al., 2006). Effects depend, of course, on how the computer is used (Hofferth & Moon, 2011). Using e-mail with proper grammar is linked to better grades, but surfing the Web is not (Busch et al., 2014).

think about **this**

The American Academy of Pediatrics stated that at no age should children spend more than 2 hours a day in front of any screen, and under age 2, they should watch no screens. Their concern centers on the brain. Explain why they might have this concern based on brain and ADHD research from Chapters 2 and 4.

Emotional development

Media violence is linked to anxiety and fear. Heavy users develop a "mean world" belief that the world is violent and that they are more likely to be victims than is really

brain research

Violent Video Games Alter the Brain's Response to Violence

How do media desensitize learners to violence? One explanation is that the brain no longer responds as readily to violence. Media violence activates areas of the brain that process emotions (Murray, 2007). In an experiment, university students were randomly assigned to watch a violent or nonviolent video game for 25 minutes. Afterwards they saw violent photos, such as a man holding a gun in another man's mouth. Those who had played the violent game had less brain response compared to others. Those with less brain response to the violent photo were also more likely to actually behave aggressively to an opponent during a competitive task. Interestingly, those who routinely played violent games had less brain response to the violent photo regardless of whether they played a game immediately beforehand; their brains were already less responsive to violence (Engelhardt, Bartholow, Kerr, & Bushman, 2011).

the case. Media violence also desensitizes children so that they respond less to others' distress and are more tolerant of aggression (Bushman & Anderson, 2009). We got our first TV when our daughter was a toddler. The first few times that actors fought and shot guns, she raced up the stairs as fast as her short legs would go, clambered into the dry bathtub, and cowered behind the shower curtain until we coaxed her out (trying not to laugh). Now, two decades of TV later, she can watch highly violent shows with little arousal. She is desensitized, just as you probably are.

In addition, emotional development can be affected by compulsive gaming and Internet use. In 2015 a 32-year old male Taiwanese gamer played nonstop for 3 days and died in an Internet café. Less extreme, but compulsive, Internet use can cause mental health problems (Ciarrochi et al., 2016) that arise at least partly through sleep deprivation (see Chapter 2).

Social development

Does computer use replace live interaction, causing isolated, lonely children? Quite the opposite—much of children's online time is used to connect with friends that they see during the day, making friendships closer (Reich, Subrhmanyam, & Espinoza, 2012). See Photo 14.5. However, these social benefits may not apply to solitary use, or chatting with strangers, or excessive use—that is, more than 2 hours daily (Rosen, Cheever, & Carrier, 2008; Valkenburg & Peter, 2009). In addition, children who talk with others face to face, rather than through media, may have better social outcomes (Pea et al., 2010). However, media can promote either prosocial or antisocial behavior.

Prosocial behavior

One of our students had a difficult childhood with an absent father and a drug-addicted mother who was often incarcerated and disappeared for days at a time with boyfriends. Today, he is a tender father and husband, which he credits to watching *Father Knows Best* in childhood. He set a goal that when he grew up, he would imitate the father in the show, rather than his mother. Research supports his life story. Children who watch prosocial TV and play prosocial video games (yes, they do exist) are more likely to share, help, and comfort others, and are less likely to be aggressive, than other children (Gentile et al., 2009; Padilla-Walker, Coyne, Collier, & Nielson, 2015). This effect is not just

iStockphoto.com/Scott Dunlap

PHOTO 14.5 Computer use tends to foster social interaction, rather than isolate children.

correlational. In experimental studies, participants are randomly assigned to play either a prosocial, neutral, or antisocial video game. Those who play prosocial games are more likely to help others after playing the game (Greitemeyer & Osswald, 2010).

Antisocial behavior

Unfortunately, much of the media children experience is antisocial. The Surgeon General of the United States issued a report that violent media leads to aggression in children (Anderson et al., 2003; Wartella et al., 2004). Key points of the report are:

- A variety of types of studies—experimental, laboratory, and correlational— demonstrate that watching violent TV increases children's aggression and acceptance of violence. For example, when young children watch a violent film before playing together, they are more likely to be aggressive during play.

- Similar effects of violence are found for viewing videos, listening to songs, and playing video games. Some, but not all, studies find that video games are more harmful than TV because gamers actually pull the trigger to shoot others and are rewarded for it.

- Most children are affected by TV violence to at least a small degree, but some vulnerable children are affected to a large degree.

Similar effects are found across countries such as Holland, Finland, Germany, Japan, England, and Canada. Thus, violent media is a compelling risk factor for aggression. More recent research continues to support these conclusions (e.g., Anderson et al., 2010; Hull et al., 2014; Verlinden et al., 2012). It has also extended the research from physical aggression to social aggression. Media often portrays social aggression enacted by attractive girls as normal, funny, and effective. Viewing relational aggression on TV predicts relational aggression several years later (Coyne, 2016).

Sexual behavior and attitude

Some research has shown that children who use more sex-filled media initiate sexual behavior at younger ages, but not all research finds this (see, for example, Collins, Martino, Elliott, & Miu, 2011; Steinberg & Monahan, 2011). Causal links are difficult to determine because experimental studies cannot be carried out with youth for ethical reasons. In addition, *selection bias* makes it difficult to establish causal relations. That is, youth who are likely to be sexually active because of other risk factors are also more likely to use sex-filled media. However, youth do report feeling pressure from TV and music to be sexually active. Many report that their attitudes about sex come from media. Children who use more media tend to have callous attitudes toward sex and believe that everyone is doing it. They are also more likely to be promiscuous (Lorch, 2007; Polacek, Rojas, Levitt, & Mika, 2006; Ward, 2003).

The Internet has made pornography easily accessible to youth. In fact, many youth stumble across unwanted pornography (Peter & Valkenburg, 2016; Wolak, Mitchell, & Finkelhor, 2007). The effects of this exposure are not yet known. However, youth who repeatedly *seek* pornography develop reduced concern about rape and child abuse, cynical attitudes about love, less hope for monogamy, a disconnect between love and sex, and a view of marriage as sexually confining (Zillmann, 2001). They also tend to have more experience with intercourse, more permissive attitudes toward sexual activity, more experience of casual sex, and more experience with sexual aggression as perpetrators or victims (Peter & Valkenburg, 2016). Adolescents who view pornography tend to be male, be sensation seekers, experience early puberty, and have problematic family relations.

In summary, both media content and amount of use are linked to children's physical, cognitive, emotional, and social well-being. Nevertheless, some psychologists claim that violent media are simply entertainment, neither helping nor harming children (e.g., Ferguson & Kilburn, 2010). They argue that the scientific evidence discussed herein is not compelling because: (1) effect sizes are small and (2) most of the research is correlational.

Thinking Like a Scientist

These same criticisms apply to most research on child development. In Chapter 1, you learned that today's teachers are expected to be skilled at interpreting research. Let's take a few minutes to hone your scientific skills by examining these criticisms.

Effect sizes

Table 14.3 shows effect sizes for various outcomes linked to media use. Taking aggression as an example, the effect of violent media (0.13 to 0.31) is small-to-moderate in size, just as with child care (Anderson et al., 2010; Wartella et al., 2004). This means not every child who uses violent media will behave aggressively. In Chapter 1, you learned that no single risk factor is likely to have a large effect because so many factors affect children. An effect size of 0.30 for any single factor may be as high as you will see for complex behavior that has multiple causes, which scientists call the "0.30 barrier." The same is true in medical sciences as well (Meyer et al., 2001).

So why pay attention to small effects? Small effects can have practical significance; over large populations, they can alter society. Furthermore, although violent media have a small effect on most children, they have a large effect on vulnerable children. If just 25% of U.S. children are affected by violent media, then more than 10 million would be more violent. To put media effects in perspective, research suggests that TV violence has a stronger effect on children's aggression than low IQ, divorce, child abuse, or antisocial friends (Bushman, Rothstein, & Anderson, 2010). The effect size is larger than the effect for smoking or asbestos exposure on cancer. The government has taken action on these other issues, but has not protected children from violent media.

Correlational versus experimental research

In Chapter 1, you learned that only carefully controlled, randomized experiments can convincingly demonstrate that violent media *causes* aggression. Most parents object to scientists randomly assigning their children to use violent media for years to see if it makes them aggressive. So scientists resort to short-term, artificial experiments. For example, children are randomly assigned to watch a violent or a nonviolent film, then given the opportunity to play with peers, and their aggressive acts like shoving or name-calling are counted. Such studies cannot tell you whether a steady diet of violent media causes long-term aggression in real life. Correlational studies, on the other hand, can tell you whether TV viewing is linked to children's real-life aggression, but they cannot demonstrate causation. Children who are already aggressive may choose to watch more violent TV. Which causes which? Longitudinal

TABLE 14.3 Effect sizes for media use predicting various outcomes

Type of media use	Outcome	Effect size
Physical development		
Television viewing	Obesity	0.08
Video game use	Obesity	0.13
Television viewing	Physical activity	−0.13
Video game use	Physical activity	−0.14
Tobacco use in media	Attitudes toward smoking	0.11
Tobacco use in media	Smoking initiation	0.22
Media use	Male body satisfaction	−0.10
Cognitive development		
Media violence	ADHD symptoms	0.12
Emotional development		
Facebook use	Loneliness	0.17
Exposure to scary television	Fear or anxiety	0.18
Social development		
Media violence	Antisocial behavior	0.31
Media violence	Aggression	0.13
Violent pornography	Aggression	0.22
Video game use	Aggression	0.19
Violent video game use	Aggression	0.15
Video game use	Prosocial behavior	−0.16
Child use of positive media	Positive interaction	0.24
Child use of positive media	Stereotype reduction	0.20

Note: Each row represents a different meta-analysis, and each meta-analysis included many different studies. Negative numbers indicate outcomes and media use are in opposite directions (i.e., the more video game use the less prosocial behavior, but the more aggression).

Source: Valkenburg, Peter, and Walther (2016).

research shows that current TV watching is correlated with aggression years later, but the reverse is not true—current aggression is not correlated with TV watching years later. This helps make a case for causation.

Each form of research has shortcomings, but when many studies using different approaches all converge on the same conclusion, you can have some confidence in that conclusion. You can have further confidence when the conclusion is supported by evidence-based theories, such as social cognitive theory, which focuses on the effects of modeling (see Chapter 13). This is the case for the claim that violent media causes aggression.

think about this

Laws have been proposed to restrict selling violent or sexually explicit video games to minors. Some courts have ruled that protecting First Amendment rights of producers is more important than protecting children and that there is no causal connection between media use and children's antisocial behavior. If you prepared a brief for the court, how would you argue this issue? Is there a parallel with protecting children from purchasing alcohol? Should educational or prosocial TV be mandated?

What Predicts Individual Differences in Media Use?

How much and what media children use depends on parents. Children usually watch what their parents watch. Parents set limits, model media use, and provide alternative activities. If parents encourage playing, reading, or extracurricular activities, their children have less time for TV.

> *Javall's mother has three rules for TV: No more than 1 hour a day, no TV in the summer, and TV is off at 8:30 p.m. for bedtime. Javall is popular in his 4th-grade classroom. He is a good sport, is kind, is already a track star, and is an avid reader of novels and* Boys' Life *magazine.*

Javall's mother's rules about TV are part of her authoritative parenting style. If parents limit TV or video gaming, children tend to be less aggressive, like Javall (Gentile et al., 2004). However, less than half of 3rd- to 12th-graders have household rules about media use (Rideout et al., 2010). If his mother remains authoritative, as Javall becomes a teenager, he is less likely to use the Internet in risky ways, such as disclosing personal information on websites or viewing pornography (Rosen et al., 2008; Wolak et al., 2007).

Keeping computers in family areas where use is monitored also protects against exposure to Internet pornography (Wolak et al., 2007). The same may apply to school where urban youth report watching pornography in areas unsupervised by teachers: "everybody goes to the back of the computers where the teacher can't see nothin'. Like the last computers in the back . . . that's when they start unblockin' Web sites" (Rothman, Kaczmarsky, Burke, Jansen, & Baughman, 2015, p. 740). Girls report that after viewing pornography in school, the boys would sexually harass them and try to touch them inappropriately.

Parents' authoritativeness and monitoring of media use depend on contexts described earlier: family structure and child care. Let's look at other group differences in media use.

14-3e Group Diversity in Media Use

There are gender, SES, and ethnic differences in media use.

Gender

Girls are more likely to use social media, while boys are more likely to play video games (Hofferth & Moon, 2012; Lenhart & Pew Research Center, 2015). See Figure 14.11. Video games tend to be dominated by sports, racing, and violence, which appeal more to boys. As many as 12% of boys ages 8 to 18 are heavy users who feel addicted to video games, but only 3% of girls are heavy users (Gentile, 2009). More girls use a computer for communication, although this is a common use for boys as well. Another common Internet activity is downloading music. There is no gender difference in how much girls and boys text friends (Hofferth & Moon, 2011).

Socioeconomic Status

Educators have been concerned about the *digital divide*, meaning that high-SES students are more likely to have access to technology, like the Internet, which enhances their cultural capital. However, the Internet has flooded the market much in the way TV did; most low-SES youth have access to Internet-supported mobile devices, such as a cell phone.

FIGURE 14.11 **FIGURE 14.11** Gender Differences in Media Use.

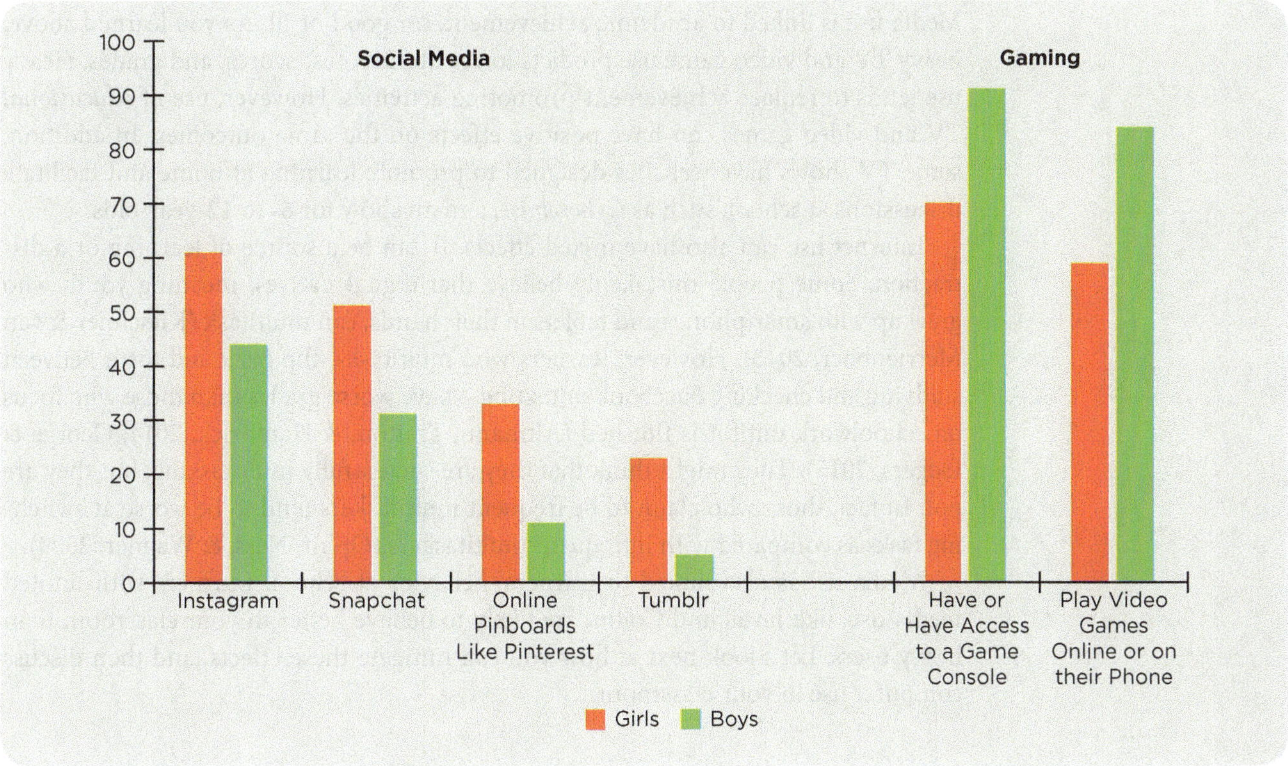

Girls are more likely to use social media platforms while boys are more likely to play video games. Does this fit your experience?
Source: Lenhart and Pew Research Center (2015).

Instead, the digital divide seems to be time. That is, low-SES youth spend more time watching TV and playing video games (Hofferth, 2010). One researcher concluded, "Instead of closing the achievement gap, [technology is] widening the time-wasting gap," and a low-SES 12-year-old said, "I stay up all night, until like 7 in the morning. It's why I'm so tired on Monday" (Richtel, 2012, p. A1). In contrast, students with well-educated mothers and moderate-to-high income spend more time in sports, hobbies, and reading. Low-SES students are more likely to watch violent TV than educational TV, have a TV in their bedroom, and own a video game system (Barr-Anderson, van den Berg, Neumark-Sztainer, & Story, 2008; Ennemoser & Schneider, 2007; Willoughby, 2008). Most students use substantial amounts of media regardless of SES, and there is great variation within SES. Some low-SES children, like Javall, watch very little TV.

Ethnicity

African American and Latino children, particularly adolescents, spend about *4.5 hours more per day* watching TV, playing video games, and listening to music than do Asian American or White children (Hofferth & Moon, 2011; Rideout et al., 2010). These effects hold even when SES is controlled statistically. This gap in media use doubled between 2004 and 2009 (Rideout et al., 2010). Black and Latino youth may spend somewhat less time using the Internet to study, e-mail, or play games as compared with White children and are more likely to access the Internet through cell phones rather than computers (Hofferth & Moon, 2011; Rideout et al., 2010).

14-3f Classroom Implications of Media Use

Media use is linked to academic achievement, for good or ill. As you learned above, heavy TV and video game use predicts lower literacy, test scores, and grades. Heavy use tends to replace achievement-promoting activities. However, use of *educational* TV and video games can have positive effects on the same outcomes. In addition, some TV shows have websites designed to promote learning at home and facilitate discussions at school, such as *Cyberchase*, a math show for 6- to 12-year-olds.

Internet use can also have mixed effects. It can be a source of learning or a distraction. Some people mistakenly believe that digital natives, meaning youth who grew up with smartphones and tablets in their hands, can multitask (Kirschner & van Merriënboer, 2013). However, learners who multitask—flip back and forth between studying and checking Facebook or texting—have worse grades than those who focus on schoolwork until it is finished (Altmann, Trafton, & Hambrick, 2014; George & Odgers, 2015). They might think that they are successfully multitasking, but they are not. In fact, those who claim to be frequent multitaskers tend to be worse at switching tasks as compared with infrequent multitaskers (Ophir, Nass, & Wagner, 2009).

Media use is also linked to learners' behavior at school. Learners with limited media use, like Javall and Collin, are likely to behave better in your classroom than heavy users. Let's look next at how you can mitigate these effects, and then discuss computer use in your classroom.

Reducing the Negative Effects of Violent Media

Researchers have developed classroom interventions that reduce the negative effects of violent media. For example, in a classic experiment, 3rd-graders who watched violent TV were randomly assigned to an intervention or control group (Huesmann, Eron, Klein, Brice, & Fischer, 1983). The intervention group had three lessons about how TV is not real—such as real men cannot fight four other men at the same time and not get hurt—and how real people solve conflicts in nonaggressive ways. The children then made a video to explain this to other kids who had been "fooled by TV." Children in the intervention group became less aggressive. In another school, 3rd- and 4th-graders were challenged to turn off TV for 10 days and to limit themselves to 7 hours per week of media afterward. Over time, the learners became less obese and less aggressive (Robinson, Wilde, Navracruz, Haydel, & Varady, 2001). You could support similar interventions in your school. In addition, you can help your students avoid the negative effects of violent media by following these guidelines:

1. Teach learners about nonaggressive forms of conflict resolution, and promote prosocial behavior (see Chapter 10).

2. Set a good example. Do not model use of violent media. Tell learners about positive media. If learners discuss antisocial media, tell them why you do not use such media.

3. Educate parents about the effects of media. Tell parents that when they watch violent shows without criticizing the violence, their children learn to accept aggression. Notify parents when violent, media-related themes emerge in learners' play.

4. Educate learners about the effects of media. Even an approach as simple as having them count the number of antisocial acts in a show is eye-opening.

Using Computers in Your Classroom

Almost all U.S. classrooms have computers and Internet access (Gray, Lewis, & Tice, 2009). Computers are used for many purposes in classrooms—to post grades and assignments, to access information, to replace textbooks with e-lessons, and to enhance learning. Many states now conduct mandated testing on computers. In some ways computers are simply another tool in the classroom, much like paper or a whiteboard. But they also afford unique opportunities, such as allowing your learners to take virtual field trips across the globe, help each other with homework outside of school, simulate experiments, or contribute to digital books, blogs, and wikis.

Do children learn more in classrooms that use technology as compared with those that do not? Generally yes, with a moderate effect size of 0.30 to 0.35 (Slavin & Lake, 2008; Tamim, Bernard, Borokhovski, Abrami & Schmid, 2011). However, studies find quite varied results because technology can be used in many different effective, and not so effective, ways. There are several trustworthy sources to help you use technology effectively. The International Society for Technology in Education (ISTE) is a widely respected organization that provides guidelines for effective use of digital media in the classroom. In addition, the What Works Clearinghouse provides summaries of research on many computer-based educational programs to help you decide whether to adopt specific programs.

Researchers have proposed guidelines for selecting effective apps (Hirsh-Pasek et al., 2015). First determine whether there is an *overarching learning goal* and then ask four key questions: (1) Does the app require that learners be *actively involved,* such as speaking or writing? Merely swiping a screen does not count. (2) Does the app require that learners be *cognitively engaged* in the learning goal? It should provide feedback to foster engagement. Extraneous animations or sounds should not distract. (3) Does the app support *meaningful learning* with a purpose that is personally relevant? It should activate prior knowledge and take learners beyond rote learning. (4) Does the app support *social interaction,* such as two learners engaged in a similar activity at the same time, video teleconferencing, or screen-sharing? These questions address social constructivism, information processing, and motivation principles that you learned in earlier chapters. Indeed, the questions could be applied to any educational intervention that you consider.

14-4 Farewell

We now come to the end of the section on the whole child. In the previous four sections of the book, you learned how students develop in the physical, cognitive, emotional, and social domains. In this section, you learned how all these domains work together to influence literacy, self-concepts, and motivation, as well as how contexts such as family structure, child care, and media influence child development. Box 14.2 takes you back through the bioecological model, first introduced in Chapter 1, to help you understand multiple layers of influence on each child's development at any point in time. You have learned a great deal in this text—more than can reasonably be mastered in a single class. Refer back to this text in the future in order to improve your teaching, or to solve problems that will arise among your students (and they will). You will become a better teacher if you periodically refer back to the "Reflections on Practice" sections of each chapter over the years to come.

BOX 14.2 theories & theorists

The Bioecological Model Revisited

In Chapter 1 you were introduced to the bioecological model. Let's briefly review the model now that you have learned so much about children's development. According to the model, development is influenced by a hierarchy of systems. At the core are biologically endowed characteristics of the child. Children bring these characteristics to every interaction with others in the environment, particularly the family. These interactions may develop into relationships that become part of the child and part of a system of relationships that are embedded in the larger culture. Let's look at aggression to get a sense of how the model works.

Biological Core Biologically endowed characteristics include gender and temperament. Girls tend to be less aggressive than boys. Children with an emotionally positive temperament tend to be less aggressive.

Microsystem This level refers to settings in which the child is physically present, such as families, classrooms, and child care. Family structure is linked to aggression; children in nuclear families, with parents who are authoritative and seldom fight, are less likely to be aggressive.

Mesosystem This level refers to linkages between microsystems, such as the link between families, schools, and child care. Family structure influences whether parents are involved in school and whether children are in child care. Children are less aggressive if their parents are involved. Children are less aggressive if they are in higher-quality and fewer hours of child care.

Exosystem This level refers to linkages between mesosystems that don't physically include the child. Exosystems include parent's workplace, media companies, institutions that train child care providers, and government agencies that regulate child care or enforce welfare policies that require mothers to work. Good work conditions—such as stable, well-paying jobs with standard, but flexible, hours—may promote parents' involvement at school and placement of their children in high-quality child care for fewer hours. Each of these factors is linked to less aggression.

Macrosystem This level refers to the larger culture. Culture influences the following: acceptability of unwed teenage parenting, preference for violent and sexualized media, father involvement following divorce, whether schools invite parent involvement, whether a parent pays child support, and generosity of maternal leave policies. Each of these aspects of culture, in turn, influences family structure, placement in child care, quality of parenting, and media use, which are linked to children's aggression.

Chronosystem "Chrono" refers to time, or changes over a child's life course. Family structure changes across time for many children, like it did for Collin. For example, Collin's married parents divorced, he lived with a single mother, and then his mother remarried. He experienced less and less contact with his father over time. Even without divorce, changes might have included new siblings, parents losing or gaining employment, and so on.

The chronosystem also refers to historical and societal changes. Today, parents are increasingly disconnecting childbearing with marriage. Television is becoming increasingly violent. Women have increasingly entered the workforce. Welfare-receiving mothers are increasingly required to work. These are huge social changes. Each of these changes influences children's aggression.

The key lesson of the bioecological model is that children's development is influenced by many layers of the context they live in. However, proximal factors—meaning family interaction—are more powerful than the more distant macrosystem (Bronfenbrenner & Ceci, 1994). Family interaction has a powerful effect because it takes place regularly over an extended period of time. However, distant factors can influence quality of parent–child interaction.

reflections on practice

My Teaching

The contexts children live in affect them at school. Children in positive contexts are likely to be successful in your classroom. Unfortunately, some children spend many hours in low-quality child care, use violent media, or live in unstable, conflict-ridden families. In previous chapters, you learned how to help these learners:

- Develop secure teacher–student attachments, which can help compensate for disrupted parent–child relationships (see Chapter 6).

- Help children develop good emotion regulation so that they are able to cope with stress from family disruption, child care, or violent media (see Chapter 8).

- Build children's friendships and conflict resolution skills to counter negative examples at home or on TV (see Chapters 10 and 11).

In addition, periodically ask yourself the following:

1. Am I aware of my students' family structure? (Be aware that while this can help you understand your students, it can also lead to stereotyped expectations.) Are any of my students acting out, anxious, or depressed because of family problems? Is my classroom a safe haven for them?

2. Do I know how involved parents are at home? What barriers to school involvement do parents face? Do I actively invite parents to be involved? Do I give homework assignments that a child could successfully complete without support at home?

3. If I teach in a child care program, are we providing high-quality care with stable staff and a low child–caregiver ratio? Are we educated about child development? Do we have warm relationships and talk with children?

4. If my school has an after-school program, are there opportunities for positive socializing with adults and peers? Can our school provide more before- and after-school care?

5. Am I aware of how much media and which kinds my students use? Do I convey disapproval of negative media and explain its harmful effects?

6. Do I model good media consumption? Do I suggest good TV shows or Internet sites that complement class activities?

7. Do I use digital media effectively to reinforce learning in my classroom? Do I carefully consider the instructional potential of apps and software that I choose for classroom use?

Professional Resource Download

Summary of Age Trends of the Child in Context

	Family Structure	Maternal Employment and Child Care	TV and Media Use
Infancy & Toddlerhood (Birth–2 Years)	• On average, children fare best in nuclear families. • Children adopted by 6 months fare better than later adoptees, but all fare better if adopted rather than left in bad situations.	• Negative effects of maternal employment and child care are greatest before age 1. • Toddlers have high cortisol levels, indicating stress, during child care.	• Toddlers watch an average of 1 to 2 hours per day of TV. Toddlers can learn from media presentations, but not as well as from real life.
Early Childhood (3–5 Years)	• Divorce has similar effects across ages, but effects may be stronger for preschoolers. • Preschool girls with absent fathers are more likely to later become promiscuous.	• About half of mothers with young children work at least part time. • Most children in child care are in part-time care. • Home-based care may be higher quality for infants, but center-based care may be higher for preschoolers. • Preschoolers have high cortisol levels during child care, but this starts to decline. • By age 3, children in child care tend to have more behavior problems.	• Preschoolers watch a higher proportion of educational shows than older children. • Educational media are linked to emergent literacy and later school achievement. • Excessive media viewing may be linked to later ADHD-like symptoms.
Middle Childhood (6–12 Years)	• Children in cohabiting families have social and academic problems that were not apparent as preschoolers. • Divorced fathers' involvement wanes over time. • Parents are more involved with schooling during the elementary school years than later.	• About two-thirds of mothers with elementary school children work at least part time. • Elementary school children in child care tend to be there about 10 nonschool hours per week. • By school age, children no longer have high cortisol levels during child care. • Half of children in child care are in self-sibling care.	• Elementary school children watch more violent media than preschoolers. They are more likely to be aggressive after watching violent media than older children. • Children who watch more entertainment media have lower literacy by 1st grade and fall further behind with age. • Use of educational media is linked to achievement, but less strongly than for preschoolers. • Media viewing and video game playing rise, peaking at age 13.
Adolescence (13–19 Years)	• Children continue to fare better, on average, in nuclear families. Relationships with parents are more distant in divorced than in nuclear families. • Parent involvement in school drops off but is still important.	• About three-fourths of mothers of teenagers work outside the home. • Adolescents in many hours of self-sibling care have higher rates of delinquency.	• Media viewing wanes. Teens watch 1 to 2 hours daily on average. Teens who watch more have lower achievement and do less homework. • SES and ethnic differences in media viewing are pronounced. • Most teens use a computer regularly. School and homework depend more on computers than for younger children. • Use of violent media and pornography is linked with delinquency.

⌄ **Professional Resource Download**

Chapter Summary

14-1 Family Structure

- Children grow up in a variety of family structures, but two-thirds live in nuclear families. The next most common family structure is a single mother and her children.

- Divorce, a process rather than an event, is strongly linked to externalizing problems, particularly for boys. It is also linked to medical, attachment, internalizing, and academic problems for children of all ages. Similar problems are linked to single-parent, teen mother, cohabiting, foster, and stepfamilies. Children fare better if parenting quality remains high and nonresident fathers stay involved in an authoritative way.

- Family structure may affect child outcomes through several factors—parent education, financial stress, parent–child closeness, abuse, rate of moving, father presence, marital conflict, and quality of parenting. Quality of parenting is more important than family structure but is influenced by structure.

- Family structure varies by SES and ethnicity. Higher-SES and Asian American families are most likely to have a nuclear structure.

- Teachers can help learners with distressed families by forming a secure relationship and by teaching academic, emotional, and social skills. Teachers can enhance parent involvement through regular communication and by welcoming parents at school.

- Adopted children fare better than if they have not been adopted out of difficult situations. Adopted children tend to develop similar attachment security and cognitive abilities as nonadoptees. Children from horrendous early conditions may catch up following adoption.

- The younger a child is when removed from difficult conditions, the better the outcome.

14-2 Maternal Employment and Child Care

- Maternal employment has mixed effects on children. Effects are more positive if families leave welfare, mothers are single, mothers believe it is good for children, and they spend more of their nonwork hours with their children. Effects are more negative if mothers are middle class, work long hours, work before children are age 3, find work unrewarding, or have low-quality jobs.

- Child care varies by type, amount, and quality. About half of preschoolers are cared for by relatives. Self-sibling care is the most common nonmaternal care for school-age children.

- Time spent in low-quality child care or in care for more than 10 hours per week is linked to insecure attachment and aggression. Long hours in self-sibling care are linked to delinquency. In the United States, most child care is low quality.

- Child care is linked to elevated stress hormones. The effect of this stress may be long term.

- Low-SES students have better school-readiness skills after being in high-quality child care. Students have better language and cognitive abilities if they are in high- versus low-quality care, and center-based versus family care (for preschoolers) or after-school programs versus self-sibling care (for school-age students).

- Children can become more attached to care providers than to parents.

- Boys are more vulnerable to negative effects of child care and maternal employment than are girls.

14-3 Television and Other Media

- Media, particularly TV, dominate children's free time. Much media content emphasizes violence and sex, although there are prosocial and educational media.

- Heavy TV use is linked to excessive weight, sleep problems, lower academic achievement, desensitization to violence, sexual activity, and a fearful view of the world. Many types of studies show that watching TV violence causes aggression. This effect is small for most children, but large for vulnerable children. Similar effects occur for other media, such as music and video games.

- Exposure to pornography is related to negative outcomes such as casual sex and sexual aggression as perpetrators or victims. There are also positive effects of media use. Educational TV is linked to school readiness and achievement, particularly for preschoolers. Prosocial TV and video games are linked to prosocial behavior. Video gaming is linked to better visual processing.

- Parenting style and parents' media use influence how much and what type of media children use. Low-SES children are exposed to more entertainment media than are middle- and high-SES children. Boys tend to watch more TV and play more video games than girls, and girls tend to use more social media.

- Teachers can protect children from the effects of negative media by educating them about its effects, modeling positive media use, communicating disapproval of negative media, and challenging children to use it less.

- Media can enhance learning in the classroom.

Glossary

A-not-B error children observe an object being moved from hiding place A to hiding place B, but they search in hiding place A. Typical of the sensorimotor stage.

academic achievement a measure of knowledge based on grades or standardized tests.

academic socialization adults communicating educational goals and expectations to children and linking schoolwork with future success.

accommodation the process by which children modify existing mental structures or schemes in order to adapt to new experience, according to Piaget.

acculturation the long-term process of adapting to a new culture.

acquired immunodeficiency syndrome (AIDS) diagnosis given to HIV-positive individuals who develop severe symptoms indicating the immune system is activated.

acronym a mnemonic technique that takes the first letters of words to be remembered and combines them into a word or phrase.

additive bilingualism acquiring a second language while still maintaining and valuing the heritage language.

Adult Attachment Interview (AAI) a lengthy interview designed to determine adolescents' or adults' "state of mind" regarding the quality of attachment to each parent.

advanced literacy reading and writing that involves a formal, academic style in particular content areas, such as science lab reports. It includes analyzing text; evaluating arguments; and writing extended, reasoned text.

adverse childhood experience (ACE) early toxic experience resulting in prolonged and intense stress, which leaves a mark on long-term brain architecture and well-being.

affective perspective-taking perceiving the emotions of another person.

African American English (AAE) a dialect of English spoken predominantly by African Americans. Also called Ebonics or Black English.

aggression behavior that harms others, or is intended to dominate others. It is a subset of antisocial behavior.

agreeableness a personality trait contrasted with antagonism. It includes thoughtfulness, warmth, kindness, cooperation, and getting along with and pleasing others.

ALANA an acronym that stands for the most populous non-White ethnic groups in the United States: African, Latino, Asian, and Native American.

allele a variation of a gene. For example, a gene that influences dopamine in the brain may have different alleles, one that leads to high levels of dopamine and another that leads to low levels.

altruism behavior that benefits others at the expense of the self without expectation of a gain or reward. It is a subset of prosocial behavior.

animism attribution of lifelike qualities, like intention, to nonliving, inanimate objects.

antisocial behavior behavior that disrupts the functioning of society, such as aggression and delinquency.

anxiety disorder a common internalizing disorder in which the child feels worried about future threats, or threats to the sense of self.

apnea a sleep disturbance that consists of repeated periods without breathing, and snoring or gasping for breath.

applied behavior analysis controlled application of behaviorist principles to experimentally alter behavior. Overlaps with behavior modification.

appraisal the meaning given to an event.

apprenticeship a learner actively observes and participates with an expert in order to improve competence.

Asperger's condition a term commonly used to refer to a condition on the autism spectrum characterized by impaired social interaction and restricted, repetitive behavior patterns, but with normal language and cognitive abilities.

assimilation the process by which children incorporate experience into existing mental structures or schemes, according to Piaget.

attachment a deep and enduring affectionate bond that connects one person to another across time and space.

attachment hierarchy the vertical organization of primary and secondary attachment figures for a specific child, with a preferred attachment figure at the top.

attention-deficit/hyperactivity disorder (ADHD) a neurobehavioral disorder characterized by hyperactivity, low impulse control, and inattention.

attributions the causes that people perceive for their own and other people's behavior.

authentic literacy activities reading for information one wants, or writing to inform a reader, as opposed to activities done for the purpose of learning to read or write or just to complete an assignment.

authoritarian parenting style parents are high on control but low on acceptance. They discourage verbal give-and-take, value their authority, and tend to be power assertive.

authoritative parenting style parents are high on control, acceptance, and autonomy support. They maintain authority and enforce rules, but are responsive to their children.

autism spectrum conditions conditions characterized by a continuum of markedly abnormal social interaction; poor language ability; and restricted, repetitive behavior patterns. It commonly occurs with low cognitive ability.

autonomous morality a reciprocity-oriented morality in which cooperation is internally motivated.

avoidant (defended, dismissing) attachment a form of insecure attachment characterized by anxiety, emotional distancing, rejection, and anger.

basic emotions universal, innate emotions appearing in the first months of life (interest, joy, sadness, anger, disgust, and fear).

behavior modification operant conditioning used to change human behavior, frequently applied in special education classrooms. Token economies may be used for reinforcement.

behavioral genetics the study of how genes and the environment contribute to individual differences in behavior.

behavioral inhibition the tendency to be wary and restrict one's approach to new people, events, or objects.

behaviorism the scientific study of overt, observable behavior.

bidirectional variable A influences variable B, while B also influences A.

big-fish-little-pond effect the tendency to experience higher academic self-concept when surrounded by peers whose academic achievement is lower.

bilingual the ability to speak two languages fluently.

bilingual education instruction that is provided in more than one language.

brain plasticity the brain's ability to change structure and function as a result of experience.

bullying a type of proactive aggression in which the goal is intimidation or dominance over another person that typically occurs repeatedly over time and involves someone of greater power victimizing someone of lower status or power.

canalization genetically based restriction or channeling of development to a limited range of outcomes despite differences in environment.

center (or centration) the child focuses on one aspect of a task to the exclusion of other aspects.

child-directed speech a style of speech used with young children that involves higher pitch, exaggerated ups and downs in pitch, slower tempo, and more rhythm than other speech. Also called motherese.

childhood amnesia the inability to recall things that occurred during infancy, typically from birth to about 3.5 years of age.

classical conditioning a form of conditioning in which a neutral stimulus is paired with a stimulus that causes an involuntary response until the neutral stimulus becomes a conditioned stimulus and also causes the response.

classroom management all aspects of managing the classroom, including but not limited to, discipline.

clique a tightly knit group of about 2 to 10 friends, usually of the same sex and same age.

code switching using different language varieties for different situations, such as Standard English at school and African American English at home.

coercive family cycle a cycle of negative reinforcement in hostile families in which negative parenting leads to child aggression, which leads to more parental hostility, which leads to more child aggression, and so on.

cognition mental processes like thinking, planning, reasoning, and remembering.

cognitive flexibility the ability to switch from one cognitive activity or perspective to another. Also called attention shifting.

cohort effect an effect upon development whose cause is specific to the particular time period in which the cohort grew up.

collective monologues children appear to be conversing with each other, but are really not addressing thoughts or adapting speech to their conversation partners.

committed compliance children accept the authority figure's agenda as their own.

computational thinking a particular type of large-scale problem solving using computers.

concrete operational stage children are able to decenter and think logically about concrete objects and experience. Roughly ages 7 to 11.

conditioning learning, or creating conditions conducive to learning.

conduct disorder a clinical diagnosis given to youth who are excessively delinquent or aggressive for at least 6 months.

conflict the behavior of one person interferes with the goals of another person who resists or protests the behavior. It is not the same as aggression.

conscientiousness a personality trait contrasted with lack of direction. It includes getting things done, not giving up easily, being dependable, planning ahead, and orderliness.

conservation understanding that the properties of objects like mass, volume, and number do not change just because the objects' appearance changes.

constructivist one who believes that knowledge acquisition is a process of construction rather than duplication (creating a mental copy of what is observed).

constructivist instruction an approach to instruction in which teachers provide learners with experiences that facilitate their personal construction of knowledge.

continuous reinforcement reinforcement occurs after every correct response.

control group in an experiment, the group that does not receive the special treatment in order to provide a comparison group.

controversial children children who are liked by many and also disliked by many peers. They have high social impact.

cooperative learning learning in pairs or small groups, in which the group has a shared learning goal and interdependence is required to achieve the goal.

coping strategies deliberate attempts to change thoughts or behavior to try to manage strong emotions. They are usually divided into problem-focused or emotion-focused strategies.

core knowledge innate, skeletal conceptual structures that develop early and easily, without instruction, and are universal, but may require experience to fine-tune.

corporal punishment power-assertive discipline that involves bodily harm to the child, ranging in severity from light spanking to abuse.

correlation coefficient a statistic that measures the relationship between two variables.

cortisol a hormone that the body generates as a response to stress.

cross-sectional research design data are collected at one point in time from two or more age groups to investigate age trends.

cultural capital knowledge and social relationships that allow people to reap benefits within their culture.

cultural mismatch a pattern of incompatibilities between home and school.

cultural tools concrete objects and symbolic tools that allow members of a culture to think, build, record, problem solve, and communicate.

cyberbullying bullying that occurs through interactive technologies.

decenter (or decentration) ability to think about multiple aspects of a task simultaneously.

decoding figuring out how to read or spell unknown words by applying phonetic rules.

deferred imitation ability to mentally represent and then imitate an action that was observed in the past.

delay of gratification an aspect of self-control in which children delay what they desire right now in order to get something more desirable later.

deliberate practice activities specifically designed to increase competence that are effortful, use specialized facilities or materials, and require expert feedback.

depression a common internalizing disorder in which feelings of sadness are severe for at least 2 weeks, or milder but chronic.

differential susceptibility children differ in the extent to which they are susceptible to a good or bad environment based on their genotype.

direct instruction a didactic form of instruction largely based on operant conditioning.

discipline gap disparity in suspension rates based on group membership, primarily ethnicity, but also gender, SES, and disability.

dishabituation attention that has become habituated is renewed after a change in the stimulus.

disorganized (controlling, unresolved) attachment a form of insecure attachment characterized by no coherent pattern of response to the parent.

effect size a measure of the strength of the relationship between two variables, or the size of the difference between the treatment and control group

egocentric the tendency to see the world from your own point of view while failing to see other people's point of view.

elaboration a method of enhancing memory that involves creating visual or verbal links or representations to associate two or more items.

emergent literacy abilities that are precursors to reading and writing, such as good verbal ability, knowing letter names, phonological awareness, and print concepts.

emotion a subjective reaction to an important event, involving physiological or observable behavioral change.

emotion contagion the emotions of one person, through facial, vocal, or gestural cues, generate a similar emotion in another person.

emotion-focused coping strategies strategies that involve trying to change emotions, such as changing one's thoughts about the situation or seeking comfort from others.

emotion regulation the capacity to control the intensity and duration of emotions.

emotional competence the ability to regulate your own emotions, and read others' emotions, so that you emerge from an emotional event having accomplished your goals.

emotional dissemblance altering the expression of felt emotion by expressing no emotion or expressing a different emotion.

emotional intelligence the ability to use emotions to guide thinking and to think intelligently about emotions. Sometimes defined more broadly to mean emotional competence.

empathic distress a self- and other-focused experience of taking on a friend's distress and experiencing it as one's own.

empathy an emotional state similar to what another person is feeling that results from perceiving the other's emotions.

encoding the process of forming mental representations of information for storage.

English-Language Learner (ELL) a student whose first language is not English and who is less than proficient in English.

epigenetic a process in which phenotype, or gene expression, is altered through social experience, or other mechanisms, rather than change in DNA.

equilibrium a state of cognitive balance or cognitive comfort.

ethnic identity a part of self-concept that includes a sense of membership in an ethnic group and attitudes and feelings about that membership.

ethology a subdiscipline of biology that seeks to understand the cause and function of animal (including human) behavior.

executive functions the brain's control of its own information processing.

experiment a controlled study comparing outcomes between people randomly assigned to a treatment group and to a control group.

expository talk formal, precise talk that is used to display information, in contrast to conversational talk.

externalizing disorders emotional disorders based on anger, characterized by aggression and other antisocial behaviors.

extinction (classical conditioning) the conditioned stimulus and unconditioned stimulus are repeatedly not paired until the conditioned stimulus no longer elicits the conditioned response.

extinction (operant conditioning) the elimination or decline in response caused by stopping reinforcement.

extraversion a personality trait contrasted with social inhibition. It includes high energy; talkativeness; emotional expressiveness; and being fast-paced, reactive, and full of life.

extrinsic motivation the desire to pursue an activity for reasons external to the activity such as getting a reward, avoiding punishment, or earning a grade.

family structure the composition of a child's household.

fast mapping the ability to learn a new word from a single, or very minimal, exposure without deliberate instruction or corrective feedback.

fixed mindset a belief that ability is unchangeable. Also called entity mindset.

Flynn effect the worldwide pattern of rising intelligence scores.

formal operational stage children are able to think abstractly about hypothetical events and systematically test hypotheses. Roughly age 12 to adulthood.

fuzzy traces a distilled gist of an experience rather than an exact memory.

g general intelligence.

gender identity a part of the concept of self that includes ability to accurately label your sex and your feelings about your gender.

gender segregation when given a choice, boys affiliate with other boys and girls with other girls.

gene–environment correlation genes influence the aspects of the environment that children experience which then further activates the genes.

genotype the set of genes that is directly inherited and transmitted to descendants.

glucose rate the rate of consumption of glucose, an indicator of energy use in the brain.

goodness of fit the degree of match between temperament and environmental demands, values, or expectations.

growth mindset a belief that ability is changeable and can be developed. Also called incremental mindset.

guided participation a novice learns through an expert's scaffolding.

habituation a reduction in attention to a continuously available or repeated stimulus.

heritability estimate the amount of variation in a trait in a population (not individuals) that is attributable to genetic influences. Notated as h^2.

hierarchical classification the ability to classify or place objects into superordinate and subordinate categories.

high-stakes tests tests used to make decisions that have educational or financial impact.

homophily the tendency to prefer and bond with similar others.

hostile aggression a type of reactive or proactive aggression in which the primary aim is to harm another person.

hostile attribution bias the tendency to assume hostile intent on the part of others in situations in which it is not clear whether there is actually hostile intent.

human immunodeficiency virus (HIV) a virus that undermines the immune system, contracted through extended contact with bodily fluids of infected persons.

inclusion creating learning environments that enable learners with special education needs to fully participate in the school community. Some groups (e.g., UNESCO) expand the term beyond students with disabilities to inclusion of marginalized groups, such as religious minorities or impoverished children.

indifferent parenting style parents are low on both control and acceptance. They are not affectionate or responsive and have few rules. They are self- rather than child-centered. Also called neglectful or uninvolved.

individual interest an individual's enduring interest in an activity or domain of knowledge.

induction a form of discipline in which the adult gives the child a reason for why behavior must change or a rule must be complied with.

induction a form of reasoning in which a child detects generalizations, rules, or regularities, often, but not always, through comparison and contrast.

indulgent parenting style parents are low on control, but high on acceptance. They have few rules and avoid controlling their children. Also called permissive.

information-processing model a model of cognition that focuses on how children acquire, store, and use knowledge.

inhibitory control the ability to inhibit processing irrelevant information or to suppress a response.

instrumental aggression a type of proactive aggression in which the primary aim is to obtain an object, territory, or privilege, but not to hurt the victim.

intelligence a general mental capability including the ability to reason, plan, solve problems, think abstractly, comprehend complex ideas, adapt, and learn quickly.

interference existing information in long-term memory prevents accurate retrieval of new information, or information learned recently prevents accurate retrieval of older information.

intermittent reinforcement reinforcement occurs after some, but not all, responses.

internal working models memories and expectations of the self and others that influence whether children approach or avoid others, with either positive or hostile emotions.

internalization the child adopts the adult's values and rules as his or her own guide for behavior. The child complies or behaves appropriately without being monitored.

internalizing disorders emotional disorders based on sadness or anxiety, characterized by withdrawal.

intrinsic motivation the desire to pursue an activity for its own sake, not for external reasons.

joint attention both the child and another person visually explore an object together.

keyword method a mnemonic in which a keyword that *sounds* like the target word is chosen and then an *image* is linked with it.

language a collection of words or signs used in a systematic way that allows people to communicate with each other. Language can be verbal or nonverbal.

learned helplessness the perception developed through experience that no matter what you do, you will not be competent in a domain.

learning according to behaviorists, a relatively permanent change in observable behavior that is the result of experience, not maturation or some other cause.

learning disability discrepancy between a student's achievement and intelligence or lack of response to instruction that is effective for most other students.

literacy narrowly defined, it is the ability to communicate in printed language through reading and writing, particularly in school settings.

long-term memory the relatively permanent storage of information. Duration is long and capacity is very large, perhaps unlimited.

longitudinal research design data are collected from the same individuals two or more times, separated by some period of time (e.g., months or years).

mandated reporters people who must by law report suspicion of child abuse and neglect. Laws vary by state, but in most states, teachers are mandated reporters.

mastery goal a goal to master a skill or topic.

math anxiety a dispositional proneness toward anxiety at the prospect of doing math or taking a math test

mediation a neutral, impartial third person facilitates negotiation between two learners in conflict.

metacognition cognition that reflects on, monitors, or regulates other cognition.

mnemonics techniques for improving memory.

moral identity the degree to which being a moral person is central to a person's self-identity.

moral judgment reasoning about moral dilemmas that involve justice in a context where rules, laws, formal obligations, and authority are emphasized.

moral transgression behavior that is inherently wrong, independent of culture, and regardless of rules.

morpheme the smallest unit of language that contains meaning. It can include word roots, suffixes, and prefixes.

motivation internal states that affect the energy level, direction, vigor, and persistence of behavior toward a goal.

multiple intelligences Gardner's theory of intelligence that proposes that there are various independent intelligences rather than just a dominant *g* factor.

myelin a fatty substance that forms an insulating coating, called a myelin sheath, around axons that allows them to function efficiently.

myelination the development of myelin.

nativists those who believe that competence in core domains is largely innate and little influenced by the environment.

negative reinforcement removal of an aversive stimulus that increases the probability of a response. This is *not* punishment.

neglected children children who are neither liked nor disliked by many peers. They have low social impact.

neuroticism a personality trait contrasted with emotional stability. It includes nervousness, worry, perseverating or falling apart under stress, insecurity, and needing reassurance.

neurotransmitter a chemical that allows neurons to communicate across synapses.

nonorganic failure to thrive failure to grow adequately without any apparent medical reason.

nonshared environment (NSE) factors that make individuals in the same family different from each other.

nonverbal language communication that does not include words, such as posture, gesture, and facial expression.

nuclear family a family composed of a father and mother who are in their original marriage, and their biological children. Also called a "traditional" family.

object permanence the knowledge that objects that are out of view continue to exist.

openness to experience a personality trait that includes curiosity, exploration, imaginative dreaming, creativeness, good self-expression, and being smart.

operant conditioning voluntary behavior is conditioned through its consequences.

operation according to Piaget, mental actions or manipulations that follow rules.

oppositional defiant disorder a clinical diagnosis given to children who are excessively defiant and hostile for at least 6 months.

overcontrolled a nonresilient personality type characterized by high agreeableness and neuroticism, and particularly low extraversion.

peer pressure friends exert pressure on each other to conform to group norms. It is typically positive, but can be negative.

peer status a measure of how accepted children are in a peer group.

perceived popularity having high social impact and prominence.

performance goal a goal to demonstrate ability by performing better than others.

persistent persuasion an approach to discipline that uses induction repeatedly until the child complies, but without using power assertion.

personal distress a self-focused, aversive emotional reaction to someone else's negative emotion.

personality a constellation of traits that distinguishes one person from another.

personality traits the tendency to behave, think, and feel in certain consistent ways. Five traits that account for much of the variation in personality are openness, conscientiousness, extraversion, agreeableness, and neuroticism (OCEAN).

personality types clusters of personality traits that tend to occur together. The most commonly identified in children are resilient, overcontrolled, and undercontrolled types.

phenotype observable characteristics of a person.

phoneme a sound in speech. The most basic unit of language.

phonetics rules regarding how written letters are linked to sounds and how a string of letters is correctly pronounced.

phonics an approach to teaching literacy that emphasizes training in phonological awareness and decoding words.

phonological awareness the ability to identify phonemes or the sound structure of language.

physical aggression behavior that harms others through physical means such as hitting, pushing, or kicking.

physical play play in which children move for the joy of movement, such as climbing, running, or chasing.

play behavior that has no immediate function and is pleasurable, spontaneous, flexible, and internally controlled.

positive reinforcement presentation of a consequence that increases the probability of a response.

power assertion a coercive form of discipline in which the adult controls the child's behavior by virtue of greater power or resources. It often includes an "or else" clause.

pragmatics the study of how language is used in social context.

preoperational stage children are able to use symbolic thought, but unable to think logically, particularly to conserve or decenter. Roughly ages 2 to 7.

print concepts basic concepts of how print symbolizes language, such as English books are read from left to right and spaces separate words. A key part of emergent literacy.

private speech talking to oneself out loud, partially out loud, or silently in one's mind to help regulate one's own behavior or solve problems.

proactive aggression aggression that is directed at achieving personal objectives, but that was not clearly provoked.

problem-focused coping strategies action-oriented strategies that involve trying to change the situation.

prosocial behavior voluntary behavior that benefits others or promotes harmonious relations with others.

prosocial reasoning reasoning about moral dilemmas in which one person's needs or desires conflict with another's, but in a context where laws, rules, or formal obligations are minimal.

protective factor a factor that decreases the likelihood of poor outcomes in children at risk.

psychological control a coercive form of discipline in which the adult attempts to control the child's behavior by inducing guilt or fear of loss of love and affirmation.

puberty physical changes that occur as children move into adulthood, including development of primary and secondary sex characteristics and capacity for reproduction.

punishment consequences that reduce the probability of a response.

qualitative research nonquantitative research characterized by the researcher being the instrument of data collection (rather than a test or questionnaire). May involve observations and interviews as data.

random assignment each research participant has an equal chance of being assigned to the treatment or control group.

reactive aggression aggression that is aimed at retaliation for a provocation, usually involving anger or frustration.

reciprocal teaching students take turns in the teacher role. A student-teacher summarizes, asks questions, clarifies, and predicts the content of a passage of text in a small group of other students.

reciprocated friendship both children nominate each other as a friend.

rehearsal mentally repeating information over and over in working memory.

reinforcer a consequence that increases the probability of a response.

rejected-aggressive children children who are actively disliked by many peers and are highly aggressive.

rejected-withdrawn children children who are actively disliked by many peers, are not aggressive, but tend to avoid social interaction.

reliability consistency of a test or measurement.

resilience positive development despite adversity or risk.

resilient a personality type characterized by very high levels of openness and conscientiousness, above average levels of extraversion and agreeableness, and very low levels of neuroticism.

resistant (coercive, preoccupied) attachment a form of insecure attachment characterized by exaggerated emotions, clinginess, and intense attachment behaviors.

retrieval finding items in long-term memory and placing them into working memory.

reverse operations ability to mentally reverse or negate an operation.

risk factor a variable associated with negative child outcomes.

rough-and-tumble play social, pretense play that involves physically vigorous behavior and often resembles, but is not the same as, aggression.

scaffolding a more competent person helps a child master new skills by breaking the tasks or subskills into small units and guiding performance to a higher level.

schema an organized network of information.

scheme a cognitive structure or piece of understanding constructed through experience.

school bonding a sense of belonging at school and having a network of relationships with peers and teachers.

script a schema for how to do something or for an event.

secure (balanced, autonomous) attachment a form of attachment characterized by feelings of security, open communication, and mutual delight.

secure base an attachment figure who engenders a child's confidence and security, because of willingness to be available when needed, while the child explores novel environments.

segregating genes genes that are free to vary and that dictate individual differences.

selection bias children and parents select into or choose certain kinds of experiences based on their preexisting characteristics. This makes it difficult to determine the effect of the experience.

selective attention attending to task-relevant input while suppressing irrelevant input.

self a group of related thoughts that people hold about themselves.

self-actualization the process of fulfilling one's potential in a way that shows concern for society.

self-concept the differentiated conception of self that includes categories such as academic self-concept, social self-concept, and athletic self-concept. The term *global self-concept* is sometimes used synonymously with *self-esteem*.

self-control the ability to control one's own behavior and emotions, obey rules, inhibit inappropriate action, and focus attention.

self-efficacy belief that you have the capability to perform a specific task.

self-esteem one's feelings of worth.

self-sibling care a prevalent form of nonmaternal care for school-age children, in which children are home alone or with a sibling under age 18.

semantics the study of meaning in language.

sensitive period a biologically determined time period, typically early in life, in which a child readily develops specific abilities. Change is less likely before or after the sensitive period.

sensitive responsiveness a style of interaction in which an adult reads the child's cues accurately and responds promptly and appropriately.

sensorimotor stage children rely on senses and behavioral schemes to acquire knowledge. Roughly birth to 2 years.

sensory register the component of the information-processing model where initial stimuli from the environment are briefly held.

serious games electronic games carefully designed to teach children school-relevant content. They may be used in or out of the classroom.

shaping reinforcement of successive approximations to a target behavior.

shared environment (SE) factors that make individuals residing in the same family similar to each other.

sibling-contrast bias the tendency of family members to report greater difference among siblings than actually exists by evaluating them relative to each other.

situational compliance children comply with demands, but lack sincere commitment and require sustained control by the authority figure.

situational interest short-lived attention or curiosity that is generated by the conditions in a specific situation.

social aggression behavior that harms others through manipulating their relationships or peer-group status, such as spreading rumors or excluding the victim from a social clique. It is sometimes called relational aggression.

social cognition thought processes applied to the social domain.

social constructivism the view that knowledge is not poured into learners' brains, but that knowledge is constructed through social interaction.

social conventions standards of behavior dictated by culture.

social emotions complex emotions that emerge later than basic emotions (shame, embarrassment, guilt, pride, and envy). Also called "self-conscious" or "moral" emotions.

social identity the part of learners' self-concept that derives from their membership in a group, such as gender, ethnic, religious, national, or other groups.

social referencing children read another's emotional expression to determine how they should respond in an ambiguous situation.

sociocultural theory a theory of how children learn, largely based on Vygotsky's writings, that emphasizes social interaction, historical context, and culture.

socioeconomic status (SES) categorization based on parental education, income, and occupational status; often simplified as low, middle, and upper class.

sociometric popularity being well liked and accepted by peers. Also called social preference.

solitary-active play functional or pretense play while alone.

solitary-passive play play involving construction or exploring objects while alone.

source monitoring memory of the source or origin of information.

spaced practice multiple periods of practicing, or studying, over a period of time rather than in a single massed episode. Also called distributed practice.

specific reading disability a learning disability in which a child with normal intelligence and exposure to print has difficulty learning to read. It is characterized by difficulty decoding and recognizing words accurately and/or fluently. Also called dyslexia.

stability a term psychologists use to refer to whether rank-ordering on a trait remains the same across time.

Standard English the form of English used in classroom instruction and textbooks. Also called School English.

stereotype threat concern that one's performance will confirm negative stereotypes about one's group.

stigma feeling different and of little value in a community.

Strange Situation Procedure (SSP) a 22-minute laboratory task designed to test quality of attachment in which children under age 6 are stressed by maternal separation and stranger presence.

subtractive bilingualism acquiring a second, majority language in a way that undermines ability in the heritage language.

sudden infant death syndrome (SIDS) the sudden death of an infant for whom a cause of death cannot be determined.

symbolic thought the cognitive ability to have one thing stand for, or represent, another.

sympathy an emotional response that consists of feeling concern for a distressed other.

synapse a junction where neurons communicate with each other, or with other kinds of cells.

synaptogenesis a spurt in synaptic connections of the brain that occurs from the third trimester of gestation until about 2 years of age.

syntactic bootstrapping a process in which young children figure out the meaning of a new word, without explicit instruction, based on the syntax of the sentence in which the word is used.

syntax the way words are organized into phrases and sentences in a language.

temperament individual differences in reactivity (in emotions, motor activity, or attention) and the ability to control this reactivity.

teratogen an agent that harms the developing fetus.

test anxiety a dispositional proneness toward anxiety in test situations that interferes with performance.

test bias a test has less validity for one group than another group. Predictive bias means members of two groups who have the same score are not predicted to have the same outcome.

theory an organized group of concepts or principles used to explain a particular aspect of human development.

theory of mind the ability to infer mental states in others, such as beliefs, desires, knowledge, and intentions. Also called "people reading."

toddler a child between 1 and 3 years of age; so-called because of recent mastery of walking, often with a wobbly gait.

underachievement earning grades that are substantially below those of other students with similar cognitive ability as measured by standardized tests.

undercontrolled a nonresilient personality type characterized by particularly low agreeableness and conscientiousness, but also low-average neuroticism and openness.

unilateral friendship one child nominates another as a friend, but the reverse is not true.

validity the extent to which a measurement assesses what it is supposed to measure for a specific purpose.

verbal aggression behavior that harms others through verbal means such as threatening or name calling.

verbal language communication that involves words and speech, in contrast to nonverbal language.

victim-centered induction a form of inductive discipline in which the adult points out how the child's behavior made the victim feel.

working memory the component of the information-processing model where items of information are temporarily held for encoding or processing.

zone of proximal development (ZPD) the distance between what learners can do independently and what they can do with the assistance of a competent other.

References

AAP Committee on Nutrition. (2015). Snacks, sweetened beverages, added sugars, and schools. *Pediatrics, 135*, 575–583.

AAP Policy Statement. (2014). School start times for adolescents. *Pediatrics, 134*, 642–649.

Aarnoudse-Moens, C. S. H., Weisglas-Kuperus, N., van Goudoever, J. B., & Oosterlaan, J. (2009). Meta-analysis of neurobehavioral outcomes in very preterm and/or very low birth weight children. *Pediatrics, 124*, 717–728.

Abaied, J. L., & Rudolph, K. D. (2011). Maternal influences on youth responses to peer stress. *Developmental Psychology, 47*, 1776–1785.

Abedi, J. (2004). The No Child Left Behind Act and English language learners: Assessment and accountability issues. *Educational Researcher, 33*, 4–14.

Abel, E. M., Chung-Canine, U., & Broussard, K. (2013). A quasi-experimental evaluation of a school-based intervention for children experiencing family disruption. *Journal of Evidence-Based Social Work, 10*, 136–144.

Aber, L., Brown, J., & Jones, S. (2003). Developmental trajectories toward violence in middle childhood: Course, demographic differences, and response to school-based intervention. *Developmental Psychology, 39*, 324–348.

Aboud, F. E. (2008). A social-cognitive developmental theory of prejudice. In S. M. Quintana & C. McKown (Eds.), *Handbook of race, racism and the developing child* (pp. 55–71). Hoboken, NJ: Wiley.

Aboud, F. E., Tredoux, C., Tropp, L. R., Brown, C. S., Niens, U., & Noor, N. M. (2012). Interventions to reduce prejudice and enhance inclusion and respect for ethnic differences in early childhood: A systematic review. *Developmental Review, 32*, 307–336.

Achenbach, T. M., Dumenci, L., & Rescorla, L. A. (2003). Are American children's problems still getting worse? A 23-year comparison. *Journal of Abnormal Child Psychology, 31*, 1–11.

Ackerman, B., Brown, E., & Izard, C. E. (2003). Continuity and change in levels of externalizing behavior in school of children from economically disadvantaged families. *Child Development, 74*, 694–709.

Ackerman, B., Brown, E., & Izard, C. E. (2004a). The relations between contextual risk, earned income, and the school adjustment of children from economically disadvantaged families. *Developmental Psychology, 40*, 204–216.

Ackerman, B., Brown, E., & Izard, C. E. (2004b). The relations between persistent poverty and contextual risk and children's behavior in elementary school. *Developmental Psychology, 40*, 367–377.

Ackerman, B., Izard, C. E., Kobak, R., Brown, E. D., & Smith, C. (2007). Relation between reading problems and internalizing behavior in school for preadolescent children from economically disadvantaged families. *Child Development, 78*, 581–596.

Adam, E. (2004). Beyond quality: Parental and residential stability and children's adjustment. *Current Directions in Psychological Science, 13*, 210–213.

Adams, G. L., & Engelmann, S. (1996). *Research on direct instruction: 25 years beyond DISTAR.* Seattle, WA: Educational Achievement Systems.

Adams, M. J. (1990). *Beginning to read: Thinking and learning about print. A summary.* Champaign, IL: University of Illinois.

Adams, M. J., Treiman, R., & Pressley, M. (1998). Reading, writing, and literacy. In I. Sigel & K. A. Renninger (Eds.), *Handbook of child psychology: Child psychology in practice* (5th ed., Vol. 4, pp. 275–355). New York: Wiley.

Adams, R. E., Santo, J. B., & Bukowski, W. M. (2011). The presence of a best friend buffers the effects of negative experiences. *Developmental Psychology, 47*, 1786–1791.

Adams, P. E. (2010). Understanding the different realities, experience, and use of self-esteem between black and white adolescent girls. *Journal of Black Psychology, 36*, 255–276.

Adesope, O. O., Lavin, T., Thompson, T., & Ungerleider, C. (2010). A systematic review and meta-analysis of the cognitive correlates of bilingualism. *Review of Educational Research, 80*, 207–245.

Adi-Japha, E., & Klein, P. (2009). Relations between parenting quality and cognitive performance of children experiencing varying amounts of childcare. *Child Development, 80*, 893–906.

Administration for Children & Families. (2007). Head Start Program Fact Sheet. Washington, DC: Department of Health and Human Services. Retrieved April 19, 2007, from http://www.acf.hhs.gov/programs/ohs/about/fy2007.html

Adolph, K. E., Cole, W. G., Komati, M., Garciaguirre, J. S., Badaly, D., Lingeman, J. M., et al. (2012). How do you learn to walk? Thousands of steps and dozens of falls per day. *Psychological Science, 23*, 1387–1394.

Aguilar, B., Sroufe, A., Egeland, B., & Carlson, E. (2000). Distinguishing the early-onset/persistent and adolescence-onset antisocial behavior types: From birth to 16 years. *Development and Psychopathology, 12*, 109–152.

Ahnert, L., Gunnar, M. R., Lamb, M. E., & Barthel, M. (2004). Transition to child care: Associations with infant-mother attachment, infant negative emotion, and cortisol elevations. *Child Development, 75*, 639–650.

Ahnert, L., Pinquart, M., & Lamb, M. E. (2006). Security of children's relationships with nonparental care providers: A meta-analysis. *Child Development, 77*, 664–679.

Ahnert, L., Rickert, H., & Lamb, M. (2000). Shared caregiving: Comparisons between home and child-care settings. *Developmental Psychology, 36*, 339–351.

Aikens, N. L., & Barbarin, O. A. (2008). Socioeconomic differences in reading trajectories: The contribution of family, neighborhood, and school contexts. *Journal of Educational Psychology, 100*, 235–251.

Ainley, J., Pratt, D., & Hansen, A. (2006). Connecting engagement and focus in pedagogic task design. *British Educational Research Journal, 32*, 23–38.

Ainsworth, M. D. S. (1973). The development of infant-mother attachment. In B. Caldwell & H. Ricciuti (Eds.), *Review of child development research* (Vol. 3, pp. 1–94). Chicago, IL: University of Chicago Press.

Ainsworth, M. D. S. (1979). Infant-mother attachment. *American Psychologist, 34*, 932–937.

Ainsworth, M. D. S., Blehar, M., Waters, E., & Wall, S. (1978). *Patterns of attachment.* Hillsdale, NJ: Erlbaum.

Akee, R., Simeonova, E., Costello, E. J., & Copeland, W. (2015). *How does household income affect child personality traits and behaviors?* (Working Paper 21562). Cambridge, MA: National Bureau of Economic Research.

Akiba, M., LeTendre, G. K., & Scribner, J. P. (2007). Teacher quality, opportunity gap, and national achievement in 46 countries. *Educational Researcher, 36*, 369–387.

Akinbami, L. J., Liu, X., Pastor, P., & Reuben, C. (2011). Attention deficit hyperactivity disorder among children aged 5–17 years in the United States, 1998–2009, *NCHS Data Brief* (Vol. 70).

Alaimo, K., Olson, C., Frongillo, E., & Briefel, R. (2001). Food insufficiency, family income, and health in U.S. preschool and school-aged children. *American Journal of Public Health, 91*, 781–786.

Alexander, K. L., Entwisle, D. R., & Kabbani, N. (2001). The dropout process in life course perspective: Early risk factors at home and school. *Teachers College Record, 103*, 760–822.

Alexander, P. A., Jetton, T. L., & Kulikowich, J. M. (1995). Interrelationship of knowledge, interest, and recall: Assessing a model of domain learning. *Journal of Educational Psychology, 87*, 559–575.

Alford, B. L., Rollins, K. B., Padrón, Y. N., & Waxman, H. C. (2015). Using systematic classroom observation to explore student engagement as a function of teachers' developmentally appropriate instructional practices (DAIP) in ethnically diverse pre-kindergarten through second-grade classrooms. *Early Childhood Education Journal*, 1–13.

Alink, L. R. A., Mesman, J., van Zeijl, J., Stolk, M., Juffer, F., Koot, H. M., et al. (2006). The early childhood aggression curve: Development of physical aggression in 10- to 50-month-old children. *Child Development, 77*, 954–966.

Allan, N. P., & Lonigan, C. J. (2011). Examining the dimensionality of effortful control in preschool children and its relation to academic and socioemotional indicators. *Developmental Psychology, 47*, 905–915.

Allen, C., Chen, Q., Willson, V., & Hughes, J. N. (2009). Quality of research design moderates effects of grade retention on achievement: A meta-analytic, multilevel analysis. *Educational Evaluation and Policy Analysis, 31*, 480–499.

Allen, J., Chango, J., Szwedo, D., Schad, M., & Marston, E. (2012). Predictors of susceptibility to peer influence regarding substance use in adolescence. *Child Development, 83*, 337–350.

Allen, J., & Land, D. (1999). Attachment in adolescence. In J. Cassidy & P. Shaver (Eds.), *Handbook of attachment: Theory, research, and clinical applications* (pp. 319–335). New York: Guilford.

Allen, J., & Loeb, E. (2015). The autonomy–connection challenge in adolescent–peer relationships. *Child Development Perspectives, 9*, 101–105.

Allen, J., Pianta, R., Gregory, A., Mikami, A. Y., & Lun, J. (2011). An interaction-based approach to enhancing secondary school instruction and student achievement. *Science, 333*, 1034–1037.

Allen, J., Porter, M., McFarland, C., McElhaney, K. B., & Marsh, P. (2007). The relation of attachment security to adolescents' paternal and peer relationships, depression, and externalizing behavior. *Child Development, 78*, 1222–1239.

Allen, J., Schad, M. M., Oudekerk, B., & Chango, J. (2014). What ever happened to the "cool" kids? Long-term sequelae of early adolescent pseudomature behavior. *Child Development, 85*, 1866–1880.

Al Mamun, A., Lawlor, D. A., Cramb, S., O'Callaghan, M., Williams, G., & Najman, J. (2007). Do childhood sleeping problems predict obesity in young adulthood? Evidence from a prospective birth cohort study. *American Journal of Epidemiology, 166*, 1368–1373.

Aloe, A. M., Amo, L. C., & Shanahan, M. E. (2014). Classroom management self-efficacy and burnout: A multivariate meta-analysis. *Educational Psychology Review, 26*, 101–126.

Altmann, E. M., Trafton, J. G., & Hambrick, D. Z. (2014). Momentary interruptions can derail the train of thought. *Journal of Experimental Psychology: General, 143*, 215–226.

Altman, M., & Wilfley, D. (2015). Evidence update on the treatment of overweight and obesity in children and adolescents. *Journal of Clinical Child & Adolescent Psychology, 44*, 521–537.

Altschul, I., Oyserman, D., & Bybee, D. (2006). Racial-ethnic identity in midadolescence: Content and change as predictors of academic achievement. *Child Development, 77*, 1155–1169.

Alvarez, L. (2004, April 9). Educators flocking to Finland, land of literate children. *New York Times*, p. A4.

Amato, P. R. (2001). Children of divorce in the 1990s: An update of the Amato and Keith (1991) meta-analysis. *Journal of Family Psychology, 15*, 355–370.

Amato, P. R. (2010). Research on divorce: Continuing trends and new developments. *Journal of Marriage and Family, 72*, 650–666.

Amato, P. R., & Cheadle, J. (2005). The long reach of divorce: Divorce and child well-being across three generations. *Journal of Marriage and Family, 67*, 191–206.

Amato, P. R., Kane, J. B., & James, S. (2011). Reconsidering the "good divorce." *Family Relations, 60*, 511–524.

Ambady, N., Bernieri, F. J., & Richeson, J. A. (2000). Toward a histology of social behavior: Judgmental accuracy from thin slices of the behavioral stream. *Advances in Experimental Social Psychology, 32*, 201–271.

Amedi, A., Merabet, L. B., Bermpohl, F., & Pascual-Leone, J. (2005). The occipital cortex in the blind: Lessons about plasticity and vision. *Current Directions in Psychological Science, 14*, 306–311.

American Academy of Pediatrics. (1999). Early brain development and child care. *Healthy Child Care America, 3*, 1–6.

American Academy of Pediatrics (2001). The transfer of drugs and other chemicals into human milk. *Pediatrics, 108*, 776–789.

American Academy of Pediatrics (2011a). ADHD: Clinical practice guideline for the diagnosis, evaluation, and treatment of attention-deficit/hyperactivity disorder in children and adolescents. *Pediatrics, 128*, 1007–1022.

American Academy of Pediatrics (2011b). SIDS and other sleep-related infant deaths: Expansion of recommendations for a safe infant sleeping environment. *Pediatrics, 128*, 1030–1039.

American Academy of Pediatrics. (2012). Breastfeeding and the use of human milk. *Pediatrics, 129*, e827–e841.

American Academy of Pediatrics. (2013a). Children, adolescents, and the media. *Pediatrics, 132*, 958–961.

American Academy of Pediatrics. (2013b). Condom use by adolescents. *Pediatrics, 132*, 973–981.

American Academy of Pediatrics. (2013c). The crucial role of recess. *Pediatrics, 131*, 183–188.

American Academy of Pediatrics. (2013d). Office-based care for lesbian, gay, bisexual, transgender and questioning youth. *Pediatrics, 132*, 198–203.

American Academy of Pediatrics. (2014). Adolescent pregnancy: Current trends and issues. *Pediatrics, 133*, 954–957.

American Educational Research Association (2013). *Prevention of bullying in schools, colleges, and universities: Research report and recommendations*. Washington, DC: American Educational Research Association.

American Psychiatric Association. (2013). *Diagnostic and statistical manual of mental disorders* (5th ed.). Arlington, VA: Author.

American Psychological Association. (2007). *Report of the task force on the sexualization of girls*. Washington, DC: Author.

Amsterlaw, J. (2006). Children's beliefs about everyday reasoning. *Child Development, 77*, 443–464.

Anderman, E., Griesinger, T., & Westerfield, G. (1998). Motivation and cheating during early adolescence. *Journal of Educational Psychology, 90*, 84–93.

Anderson, C. A. (2001). Heat and violence. *Current Directions in Psychological Science, 10*, 33–38.

Anderson, C. A., Berkowitz, L., Donnerstein, E., Huesmann, L. R., Johnson, J. D., Linz, D., et al. (2003). The influence of media violence on youth. *Psychological Science in the Public Interest, 4*, 81–110.

Anderson, C. A., Shibuya, A., Ihori, N., Swing, E. L., Bushman, B. J., Sakamoto, A., et al. (2010). Violent video game effects on aggression, empathy, and prosocial behavior in Eastern and Western countries: A meta-analytic review. *Psychological Bulletin, 136*, 151–173.

Andersson, H., & Bergman, L. (2011). The role of task persistence in young adolescence for successful educational and occupational attainment in middle adulthood. *Developmental Psychology, 47*, 950–960.

Anderson, L. W., & Krathwohl, D. (Eds.). (2001). *A taxonomy for learning, teaching, and assessing: A revision of Bloom's taxonomy of educational objectives*. New York: Longman.

Anglin, J. (1993). Vocabulary development: A morphological analysis. *Monographs of the Society for Research in Child Development, 58* (10, Serial No. 238).

Ansari, D., & Coch, D. (2006). Bridges over troubled waters: Education and cognitive neuroscience. *Trends in Cognitive Sciences, 10*, 146–161.

Ansary, N. S., Elias, M. J., Greene, M. B., & Green, S. (2013). Guidance for schools selecting antibullying approaches: Translating evidence-based strategies to contemporary implementation realities. *Educational Researcher, 44*, 27–36.

Anzures, G., Quinn, P. C., Pascalis, O., Slater, A. M., Tanaka, J. W., & Lee, K. (2013). Developmental origins of the other-race effect. *Current Directions in Psychological Science, 22*, 173–178.

APA. (2015). *Top 20 principles from psychology for preK–12 teaching and learning.* Retrieved from http://www.apa.org/ed/schools/cpse/top-twenty-principles.pdf

Apfelbaum, E. P., Norton, M. I., & Sommers, S. R. (2012). Racial color blindness. *Current Directions in Psychological Science, 21*, 205–209.

Apfelbaum, E. P., Pauer, K., Ambady, N., Sommers, S. R., & Norton, M. I. (2008). Learning (not) to talk about race: When older children underperform in social categorization. *Developmental Psychology, 44*, 1513–1518.

Apperly, I. A., Samson, D., & Humphreys, G. W. (2009). Studies of adults can inform accounts of theory of mind development. *Developmental Psychology, 45*, 190–201.

Archer, J., & Coyne, S. M. (2005). An integrated review of indirect, relational, and social aggression. *Personality and Social Psychology Review, 9*, 212–230.

Archibald, A., Graber, J., & Brooks-Gunn, J. (2003). Pubertal processes and physiological growth in adolescence. In G. Adams & M. Berzonsky (Eds.), *Blackwell handbook of adolescence* (pp. 24–47). Malden, MA: Blackwell.

Arkowitz, H. A. L., & Lilienfeld, S. O. (2014). Is mindfulness good medicine? *Scientific American Mind, 25*, 74–75.

Armstrong, C. (1999, March). The dog ate my . . . : When a teacher gets rid of deadlines, students run out of excuses and do their work. *Teacher Magazine, 10*, 50–51.

Arnold, D. H., Kupersmidt, J. B., Voegler-Lee, M. E., & Marshall, N. A. (2012). The association between preschool children's social functioning and their emergent academic skills. *Early Childhood Research Quarterly, 27*, 376–386.

Arsenio, W. (2014). Moral emotion attributions and aggression. In M. Killen & J. Smetana (Eds.), *Handbook of moral development* (2nd ed., pp. 235–255). New York: Psychology Press.

Arsenio, W., Adams, E., & Gold, J. (2009). Social information processing, moral reasoning, and emotion attributions: Relations with adolescents' reactive and proactive aggression. *Child Development, 80*, 1739–1755.

Arsenio, W., Cooperman, S., & Lover, A. (2000). Affective predictors of preschoolers' aggression and peer acceptance: Direct and indirect effects. *Developmental Psychology, 36*, 438–448.

Asendorpf, J., & Van Aken, M. (1999). Resilient, overcontrolled, and undercontrolled personality prototypes in childhood: Replicability, predictive power, and the trait-type issue. *Journal of Personality and Social Psychology, 77*, 815–832.

Ashby, F. G., Isen, A. M., & Turken, A. U. (1999). A neuropsychological theory of positive affect and its influence on cognition. *Psychological Review, 106*, 529–550.

Ashby, N., & Neilsen-Hewett, C. (2012). Approaches to conflict and conflict resolution in toddler relationships. *Journal of Early Childhood Research, 10*, 145–161.

Asher, S. R., & Hopmeyer, A. (1997). Children's responses to peer conflicts involving a rights infraction. *Merrill-Palmer Quarterly, 43*, 235–254.

Asher, S. R., & Paquette, J. (2003). Loneliness and peer relations in childhood. *Current Directions in Psychological Science, 12*, 75–78.

Aslin, R. N., & Newport, E. L. (2012). Statistical learning. *Current Directions in Psychological Science, 21*, 170–176.

Astor, R., Benbenishty, R., & Estrada, J. N. (2009). School violence and theoretically atypical schools: The principal's centrality in orchestrating safe schools. *American Educational Research Journal, 46*, 423–461.

Astor, R., Jacobson, L., Benbenishty, R., Atuel, L., Gilreath, T., Wong, M., DePedro, K., Esqueda, M., Estrada, J. (2012). *Supporting students from military families.* New York: Teachers College Press.

Athanases, S. Z. (1998). Diverse learners, diverse texts: Exploring identity and difference through literary encounters. *Journal of Literacy Research, 30*, 273–296.

Atlas, R., & Pepler, D. (1998). Observations of bullying in the classroom. *Journal of Educational Research, 92*, 86–99.

Atwell, N. (2015, April 16). The "most powerful" classroom innovation—by the $1 million teaching prize winner. *Washington Post.*

Aughinbaugh, A., Robles, O., & Sun, H. (2013, October). Marriage and divorce: Patterns by gender, race, and educational attainment. *Monthly Labor Review.* Retrieved from http://www.bls.gov/opub/mlr/2013/article/marriage-and-divorce-patterns-by-gender-race-and-educational-attainment.htm

Austin, J. L., & Soeda, J. M. (2008). Fixed-time teacher attention to decrease off-task behaviors of typically developing third graders. *Journal of Applied Behavior Analysis, 41*, 279–283.

Autor, D., Figlio, D., Karbownik, K., Roth, J., & Wasserman, M. (2015). *Family disadvantage and the gender gap in behavioral and educational outcomes.* Evanston, IL: Institute for Policy Research, Northwestern University.

Avant, T. S., Gazelle, H., & Faldowski, R. (2011). Classroom emotional climate as a moderator of anxious solitary children's longitudinal risk for peer exclusion: A child X environment model. *Developmental Psychology, 47*, 1711–1727.

Avenevoli, S., Swendsen, J., He, J.-P., Burstein, M., & Merikangas, K. (2015). Major depression in the National Comorbidity Survey-Adolescent Supplement: Prevalence, correlates, and treatment. *Journal of the American Academy of Child and Adolescent Psychiatry, 54*, 37–44.

Aviezer, O., Sagi, A., Resnick, G., & Gini, M. (2002). School competence in young adolescence: Links to early attachment relationships beyond concurrent self-perceived competence and representations of relationships. *International Journal of Behavioral Development, 26*, 387–409.

Badanes, L. S., Dmitrieva, J., & Watamura, S. E. (2012). Understanding cortisol reactivity across the day at child care: The potential buffering role of secure attachments to caregivers. *Early Childhood Research Quarterly, 27*, 156–165.

Baer, J., Baldi, S., Ayotte, K., & Green, P. (2007). *The reading literacy of U.S. fourth-grade students in an international context: Results from the 2001 and 2006 Progress in International Reading Literacy Study (PIRLS)* (NCES 2008-017). Washington, DC: National Center for Education Statistics, Department of Education.

Bagwell, C., Coie, J., Terry, R., & Lochman, J. (2000). Peer clique participation and social status in preadolescence. *Merrill-Palmer Quarterly, 46*, 280–305.

Bahrick, L. E., & Lickliter, R. (2014). Learning to attend selectively: The dual role of intersensory redundancy. *Current Directions in Psychological Science, 23*, 414–420.

Bailey, J. A., Hill, K. G., Guttmannova, K., Oesterle, S., Hawkins, J. D., Catalano, R. F., & McMahon, R. J. (2013). The association between parent early adult drug use disorder and later observed parenting practices and child behavior problems: Testing alternate models. *Developmental Psychology, 49*, 887–899.

Baillargeon, R. (1987). Object permanence in 3 1/2- and 4 1/2-month-old infants. *Developmental Psychology, 23*, 655–664.

Baillargeon, R. (2008). Innate ideas revisited: For a principle of persistence in infants' physical reasoning. *Perspectives on Psychological Science, 3*, 2–13.

Baillargeon, R., Kotovsky, L., & Needham, A. (1995). The acquisition of physical knowledge in infancy. In D. Sperber, D. Premack, & A. J. Premack (Eds.), *Causal cognition: A multidisciplinary debate.* Oxford, UK: Clarendon Press.

Baillargeon, R., Zoccolillo, M., Keenan, K., Cote, S., Perusse, D., Wu, H.-Z., et al. (2007). Gender differences in physical aggression: A prospective population-based survey of children before and after 2 years of age. *Developmental Psychology, 43*, 13–26.

Baker, S., Geva, E., Kieffer, M., Lesaux, N., Linan-Thompson, S., Morris, J., . . . Russell, R. (2014). *Teaching academic content and literacy to English learners in elementary and middle school (NCEE 2014-4012).* Washington, DC: Department of Education.

Bakermans-Kranenburg, M. J., van IJzendoorn, M., & Juffer, F. (2003). Less is more: Meta-analyses of sensitivity and attachment interventions in early childhood. *Psychological Bulletin, 129*, 195–215.

Bakermans-Kranenburg, M. J., Van IJzendoorn, M. H., Pijlman, F. T. A., Mesman, J., & Juffer, F. (2008). Experimental evidence for differential susceptibility: Dopamine D4 receptor polymorphism (DRD4 VNTR) moderates intervention effects on toddlers' externalizing behavior in a randomized controlled trial. *Developmental Psychology, 44*, 293–300.

Baldwin, D. (2000). Interpersonal understanding fuels knowledge acquisition. *Current Directions in Psychological Science, 9,* 40–45.

Baley, J., & Committee on Fetus and Newborn. (2015). Skin-to-skin care for term and preterm infants in the neonatal ICU. *Pediatrics, 136,* 596–599.

Balfanz, R., Herzog, L., & MacIver, D. J. (2007). Preventing student disengagement and keeping students on the graduation path in urban middle-grades schools: Early identification and effective interventions. *Educational Psychologist, 42,* 223–235.

Bamford, C., & Lagattuta, K. H. (2012). Looking on the bright side: Children's knowledge about the benefits of positive versus negative thinking. *Child Development, 83,* 667–682.

Banas, J. A., Dunbar, N., Rodriguez, D., & Liu, S.-J. (2010). A review of humor in educational settings: Four decades of research. *Communication Education, 60,* 115–144.

Bandura, A. (1965). Influence of models' reinforcement contingencies on the acquisition of imitative responses. *Journal of Personality and Social Psychology, 1,* 589–595.

Bandura, A. (1997). *Self-efficacy: The exercise of control.* New York: Freeman.

Bandura, A. (2007). Albert Bandura. In G. Lindzey & W. M. Runyan (Eds.), *A history of psychology in autobiography* (Vol. IX, pp. 42–75). Washington, DC: American Psychological Association.

Bandura, A. (2012). On the functional properties of perceived self-efficacy revisited. *Journal of Management, 38,* 9–44.

Bandura, A. (2015). *Moral disengagement: How people do harm and live with themselves.* New York: Worth.

Bandura, A., Barbaranelli, C., Caprara, G., & Pastorelli, C. (1996). Multifaceted impact of self-efficacy beliefs on academic functioning. *Child Development, 67,* 1206–1222.

Bandura, A., & Schunk, D. H. (1981). Cultivating competence, self-efficacy, and intrinsic interest through proximal self-motivation. *Journal of Personality and Social Psychology, 41,* 586–598.

Banerjee, R., Watling, D., & Caputi, M. (2011). Peer relations and the understanding of faux pas: Longitudinal evidence of bidirectional associations. *Child Development, 82,* 1887–1905.

Bannard, C., & Matthews, D. (2008). Stored word sequences in language learning: The effect of familiarity on children's repetition of four-word combinations. *Psychological Science, 19,* 241–248.

Barab, S. A., Gresalfi, M., & Ingram-Goble, A. (2010). Transformational play: Using games to position person, content, and context. *Educational Researcher, 39,* 525–536.

Barber, B., Stolz, H., & Olsen, J. (2005). Parental support, psychological control, and behavioral control: Assessing relevance across time, culture, and method. *Monographs of the Society for Research in Child Development, 70* (4, Serial No. 282).

Barber, B., Xia, M., Olsen, J. A., McNeely, C. A., & Bose, K. (2012). Feeling disrespected by parents: Refining the measurement and understanding of psychological control. *Journal of Adolescence, 35,* 273–287.

Barell, J. (1980). *Playgrounds of our minds.* New York: Teachers College Press.

Bariaud, F. (2013). Age differences in children's humor. In P. McGhee (Ed.), *Humor and children's development: A guide to practical applications* (pp. 15–46). London: Routlege.

Barker, J. E., & Munakata, Y. (2015). Time isn't of the essence: Activating goals rather than imposing delays improves inhibitory control in children. *Psychological Science, 26,* 1898–1908.

Barkley, R. A. (2006). *Attention-deficit hyperactivity disorder: A handbook for diagnosis and treatment* (3rd ed.). New York: Guilford.

Barnett, D., Kidwell, S., & Leung, K. H. (1998). Parenting and preschooler attachment among low-income urban African American families. *Child Development, 69,* 1657–1671.

Barnett, S. (1995). Long-term effects of early childhood programs on cognitive and school outcomes. *The Future of Children, 5,* 25–50.

Baron, A. S., & Banaji, M. R. (2006). The development of implicit attitudes: Evidence of race evaluations from ages 6 and 10 and adulthood. *Psychological Science, 17,* 53–58.

Baroody, A. J., Li, X., & Lai, M.-l. (2008). Toddlers' spontaneous attention to number. *Mathematical Thinking and Learning, 10,* 240–270.

Barr-Anderson, D. J., van den Berg, P., Neumark-Sztainer, D., & Story, M. (2008). Characteristics associated with older adolescents who have a television in their bedrooms. *Pediatrics, 121,* 718–724.

Barrett, L. F. (2006). Are emotions natural kinds? *Perspectives on Psychological Science, 1,* 28–58.

Barrett, L. F., Mesquita, B., & Gendron, M. (2011). Context in emotion perception. *Current Directions in Psychological Science, 20,* 286–290.

Barros, R. M., Silver, E. J., & Stein, R. E. (2009). School recess and group classroom behavior. *Pediatrics, 123,* 431–536.

Barrouillet, P., & Camos, V. (2012). As time goes by: Temporal constraints in working memory. *Current Directions in Psychological Science, 21,* 413–419.

Barrouillet, P., Gavens, N., Vergauwe, E., Gaillard, V., & Camos, V. (2009). Working memory span development: A time-based resource-sharing model account. *Developmental Psychology, 45,* 477–490.

Bartlett, M. Y., & DeSteno, D. (2006). Gratitude and prosocial behavior: Helping when it costs you. *Psychological Science, 17,* 319–325.

Bartsch, K., & London, K. (2000). Children's use of mental state information in selecting persuasive arguments. *Developmental Psychology, 36,* 352–365.

Basch, C. E. (2011a). Breakfast and the achievement gap among urban minority youth. *Journal of School Health, 81,* 635–640.

Basch, C. E. (2011b). Physical activity and the achievement gap among urban minority youth. *Journal of School Health, 81,* 626–634.

Basch, C. E. (2011c). Teen pregnancy and the achievement gap among urban minority youth. *Journal of School Health, 81,* 614–618.

Bassett, D. R., John, D., Conger, S. A., Fitzhugh, E. C., & Coe, D. P. (2015). Trends in physical activity and sedentary behaviors of United States youth. *Journal of Physical Activity & Health, 12,* 1102–1111.

Bassok, D. (2010). Do Black and Hispanic children benefit more from preschool? Understanding differences in preschool effects across racial groups. *Child Development, 81,* 1828–1845.

Basten, M., Jaekel, J., Johnson, S., Gilmore, C., & Wolke, D. (2015). Preterm birth and adult wealth: Mathematics skills count. *Psychological Science, 26,* 1608–1619.

Bates, J., Viken, R., Alexander, D., Beyers, J., & Stockton, L. (2002). Sleep and adjustment in preschool children: Sleep diary reports by mothers related to behavior reports by teachers. *Child Development, 73,* 62–74.

Baumeister, R. F., Bushman, B. J., & Campbell, W. K. (2000). Self-esteem, narcissism, and aggression: Does violence result from threatened egotism? *Current Directions in Psychological Science, 9,* 26–29.

Baumeister, R. F., Campbell, J. D., Krueger, J. I., & Vohs, K. D. (2003). Does high self-esteem cause better performance, interpersonal success, happiness, or healthier lifestyles? *Psychological Science in the Public Interest, 4,* 1–44.

Baumeister, R. F., Vohs, K. D., & Tice, D. (2007). The strength model of self-control. *Current Directions in Psychological Science, 16,* 351–355.

Baumrind, D. (1991). The influence of parenting style on adolescent competence and substance use. *Journal of Early Adolescence, 11,* 56–95.

Baydar, N., Reid, J., & Webster-Stratton, C. (2003). The role of mental health factors and program engagement in the effectiveness of a preventive parenting program for Head Start mothers. *Child Development, 74,* 1433–1453.

Beatty, J. (2001). *The human brain: Essentials of behavioral neuroscience.* Thousand Oaks, CA: Sage.

Beck, D. M. (2010). The appeal of the brain in the popular press. *Perspectives on Psychological Science, 5,* 762–766.

Becker, D. V., & Srinivasan, N. (2014). The vividness of the happy face. *Current Directions in Psychological Science, 23,* 189–194.

Beckett, C., Maughan, B., Rutter, M., Castle, J., Colvert, E., Groothues, C., et al. (2006). Do the effects of early severe deprivation on cognition persist into early adolescence? Findings from the English and Romanian adoptees study. *Child Development, 77,* 696–711.

Beekman, C., Neiderhiser, J. M., Buss, K. A., Loken, E., Moore, G. A., Leve, L. D., . . . Reiss, D. (2015). The development of early profiles of temperament: Characterization, continuity, and etiology. *Child Development, 86,* 1794–1811.

Behnke, M., Smith, V., Committee on Substance Abuse, & Committee on Fetus and Newborn. (2013). Prenatal substance abuse: Short- and long-term effects on the exposed fetus. *Pediatrics, 121*, e1009–e1024.

Behrens, K. Y., Hesse, E., & Main, M. (2007). Mothers' attachment status as determined by the adult attachment interview predicts their 6-year-olds' reunion responses: A study conducted in Japan. *Developmental Psychology, 43*, 1553–1567.

Beijersbergen, M., Bakermans-Kranenburg, M. J., Van IJzendoorn, M. H., & Juffer, F. (2008). Stress regulation in adolescents: Physiological reactivity during the adult attachment interview and conflict interaction. *Child Development, 79*, 1707–1720.

Beijersbergen, M., Juffer, F., Bakermans-Kranenburg, M., & van IJzendoorn, M. (2012). Remaining or becoming secure: Parental sensitive support predicts attachment continuity from infancy to adolescence in a longitudinal adoption study. *Developmental Psychology, 48*, 1277–1282.

Beilock, S., & Carr, T. (2005). When high-powered people fail: Working memory and "choking under pressure" in math. *Psychological Science, 16*, 101–105.

Beilock, S., Gunderson, E. A., Ramirez, G., & Levine, S. C. (2010). Female teachers' math anxiety affects girls' math achievement. *Proceedings of the National Academy of Sciences, 107*, 1860–1863.

Bell, S. K., & Morgan, S. B. (2000). Children's attitudes and behavioral intentions toward a peer presented as obese: Does a medical explanation for the obesity make a difference? *Journal of Pediatric Psychology, 25*, 137–145.

Bellmore, A. (2011). Peer rejection and unpopularity: Associations with GPAs across the transition to middle school. *Journal of Educational Psychology, 103*, 282–295.

Bellocchi, A., & Ritchie, S. M. (2015). "I was proud of myself that I didn't give up and I did it": Experiences of pride and triumph in learning science. *Science Education, 99*, 638–668.

Belsky, J., Bakermans-Kranenburg, M. J., & Van IJzendoorn, M. H. (2007). For better and for worse: Differential susceptibility to environmental influences. *Current Directions in Psychological Science, 16*, 300–304.

Belsky, J., Houts, R. M., & Fearon, R. M. P. (2010). Infant attachment security and the timing of puberty: Testing an evolutionary hypothesis. *Psychological Science, 21*, 1195–1201.

Belsky, J., & Pluess, M. (2013). Genetic moderation of early child-care effects on social functioning across childhood: A developmental analysis. *Child Development, 84*, 1209–1225.

Belsky, J., Steinberg, L., Houts, R. M., & Halpern-Felsher, B. L. (2010). The development of reproductive strategy in females: Early maternal harshness → earlier menarche → increased sexual risk taking. *Developmental Psychology, 46*, 120–128.

Belsky, J., Vandell, D. L., Burchinal, M., Clarke-Stewart, K. A., McCartney, K., Owen, M. T., et al. (2007). Are there long-term effects of early child care? *Child Development, 78*, 681–701.

BeLue, R., Francis, L. A., & Colaco, B. (2009). Mental health problems and overweight in a nationally representative sample of adolescents: Effects of race and ethnicity. *Pediatrics, 123*, 697–702.

Bender, H. L., Allen, J. P., McElhaney, K. B., Antonishak, J., Moore, C. M., Kelly, H. O., et al. (2007). Use of harsh physical discipline and developmental outcomes in adolescence. *Development and Psychopathology, 19*, 227–242.

Benenson, J., & Christakos, A. (2003). The greater fragility of females' versus males' closest same-sex friendships. *Child Development, 74*, 1123–1129.

Benner, A. D., & Kim, S. Y. (2009). Experiences of discrimination among Chinese American adolescents and the consequences for socioemotional and academic development. *Developmental Psychology, 45*, 1682–1694.

Beran, M., & Beran, M. (2004). Chimpanzees remember the results of one-by-one addition of food items to sets over extended time periods. *Psychological Science, 15*, 94–99.

Berger, L. M., Bruch, S. K., Johnson, E., James, S., & Rubin, D. (2009). Estimating the "impact" of out-of-home placement on child well-being: Approaching the problem of selection bias. *Child Development, 80*, 1856–1876.

Berger, R. H., Miller, A. L., Seifer, R., Cares, S. R., & LeBourgeois, M. K. (2012). Acute sleep restriction effects on emotion responses in 30- to 36-month-old children. *Journal of Sleep Research, 21*, 235–246.

Bergin, C. (1987). Prosocial development in toddlers: The patterning of mother-infant interactions. In M. E. Ford & D. H. Ford (Eds.), *Humans as self-constructing living systems: Putting the framework to work* (pp. 121–143). Hillsdale, NJ: Erlbaum.

Bergin, C. (2014). Educating students to be prosocial at school. In L. M. Padilla-Walker & G. Carlo (Eds.), *Prosocial development: A multidimensional approach* (pp. 279–301). New York: Oxford University Press.

Bergin, C., & Bergin, D. A. (1999). Classroom discipline that promotes self-control. *Journal of Applied Developmental Psychology, 20*, 189–206.

Bergin, C., & Bergin, D. A. (2009). Attachment in the classroom. *Educational Psychology Review, 21*, 141–170.

Bergin, C., Bergin, D. A., & French, E. (1995). Preschoolers' prosocial repertoires: Parents' perspectives. *Early Childhood Research Quarterly, 10*, 81–103.

Bergin, C., & McCullough, P. (2009). Attachment in substance-exposed toddlers: The role of caregiving and exposure. *Infant Mental Health Journal, 30*, 407–423.

Bergin, C., Talley, S., & Hamer, L. (2003). Prosocial behaviours of young adolescents: A focus group study. *Journal of Adolescence, 26*, 13–32.

Bergin, C., Wang, Z., & Bryant, R. (2011, March). *Prosocial behavior in fourth to twelfth grade classrooms.* Paper presented at the Society for Research in Child Development, Montreal.

Bergin, D. A. (1999). Influences on classroom interest. *Educational Psychologist, 34*, 87–98.

Bergin, D. A. (2016). Social influences on interest. *Educational Psychologist, 51*, 7–22.

Bergin, D. A., Hudson, L. M., Chryst, C. F., & Resetar, M. (1992). An afterschool intervention program for educationally disadvantaged young children. *The Urban Review, 24*, 203–217.

Berk, R. A. (2002). *Humor as an instructional defibrillator.* Sterling, VA: Stylus.

Berkowitz, M., & Grych, J. (2000). Early character development and education. *Early Education and Development, 11*, 55–72.

Berlin, L., Ispa, J. M., Fine, M. A., Malone, P. S., Brooks-Gunn, J., Brady-Smith, C., et al. (2009). Correlates and consequences of spanking and verbal punishment for low-income White, African American, and Mexican American toddlers. *Child Development, 80*, 1403–1420.

Bernal, M. E., Knight, G. P., Garza, C. A., Ocampo, K. A., & Cota, M. K. (1990). The development of ethnic identity in Mexican-American children. *Hispanic Journal of Behavioral Sciences, 12*, 3–24.

Bernard, K., Peloso, E., Laurenceau, J.-P., Zhang, Z., & Dozier, M. (2015). Examining change in cortisol patterns during the 10-week transition to a new child-care setting. *Child Development, 86*, 456–471.

Bernat, D. H., Oakes, J. M., Pettingell, S. L., & Resnick, M. (2012). Risk and direct protective factors for youth violence: Results from the National Longitudinal Study of Adolescent Health. *American Journal of Preventive Medicine, 43*(2, Supplement 1), S57–S66.

Berndt, T. J. (2002). Friendship quality and social development. *Current Directions in Psychological Science, 11*, 7–10.

Berndt, T. J., & Burgy, L. (1996). Social self-concept. In B. A. Bracken (Ed.), *Handbook of self-concept: Developmental, social, and clinical considerations* (pp. 171–209). New York: Wiley.

Berndt, T. J., Hawkins, J., & Jiao, Z. (1999). Influences of friends and friendships on adjustment to junior high school. *Merrill-Palmer Quarterly, 45*, 13–41.

Bernier, A., Carlson, S. M., Bordeleau, S., & Carrier, J. (2010). Relations between physiological and cognitive regulatory systems: Infant sleep regulation and subsequent executive functioning. *Child Development, 81*, 1739–1752.

Bernier, A., Matte-Gagné, C., & Bouvette-Turcot, A.-A. (2014). Examining the interface of children's sleep, executive functioning, and caregiving relationships: A plea against silos in the study of biology, cognition, and relationships. *Current Directions in Psychological Science, 23*, 284–289.

Bernier, A., Matte-Gagné, C., Bélanger, M.-È., & Whipple, N. (2014). Taking stock of two decades of attachment transmission gap: Broadening the assessment of maternal behavior. *Child Development, 85*, 1852–1865.

Bernier, A., & Meins, E. (2008). A threshold approach to understanding the origins of attachment disorganization. *Developmental Psychology, 44*, 969–982.

Bernstein, A., Hadash, Y., Lichtash, Y., Tanay, G., Shepherd, K., & Fresco, D. M. (2015). Decentering and related constructs: A critical review and metacognitive processes model. *Perspectives on Psychological Science, 10*, 599–617.

Berry, C. M., & Zhao, P. (2015). Addressing criticisms of existing predictive bias research: Cognitive ability test scores still overpredict African Americans' job performance. *Journal of Applied Psychology, 100*, 162–179.

Berry, G. L. (2007). Television, social roles, and marginality: Portrayals of the past and images for the future. In N. Pecora, J. P. Murray, & E. Wartella (Eds.), *Children and television: Fifty years of research* (pp. 85–107). Mahwah, NJ: Erlbaum.

Bert, S. C., Guner, B. M., & Lanzi, R. G. (2009). The influence of maternal history of abuse on parenting knowledge and behavior. *Family Relations, 58*, 176–187.

Bessant, J. (2008). Hard wired for risk: Neurological science, "the adolescent brain" and developmental theory. *Journal of Youth Studies, 11*, 347–360.

Best, J. R., & Miller, P. H. (2010). A developmental perspective on executive function. *Child Development, 81*, 1641–1660.

Bethell, C. D., Newacheck, P., Hawes, E., & Halfon, N. (2014). Adverse childhood experiences: Assessing the impact on health and school engagement and the mitigating role of resilience. *Health Affairs, 33*, 2106–2115.

Bialystok, E. (2015). Bilingualism and the development of executive function: The role of attention. *Child Development Perspectives, 9*, 117–121.

Biden, J. (2016, April 11). *Operation Educate the Educators: Recognizing and supporting military-connected students through university-based research, community partnerships, and teacher education programs.* Presentation at the American Educational Research Association, Washington DC.

Bigler, R. S., Brown, C., & Markell, M. (2001). When groups are not created equal: Effects of group status on the formation of intergroup attitudes in children. *Child Development, 72*, 1151–1162.

Bigler, R. S., & Wright, Y. F. (2014). Reading, writing, arithmetic, and racism? Risks and benefits to teaching children about intergroup biases. *Child Development Perspectives, 8*, 18–23.

Bion, R. A. H., Borovsky, A., & Fernald, A. (2013). Fast mapping, slow learning: Disambiguation of novel word–object mappings in relation to vocabulary learning at 18, 24, and 30 months. *Cognition, 126*, 39–53.

Bishop, D. V. (2006). What causes specific language impairment in children? *Current Directions in Psychological Science, 15*, 217–221.

Bishop, D. V., & Snowling, M. J. (2004). Developmental dyslexia and specific language impairment: Same or different? *Psychological Bulletin, 130*, 858–888.

Bjork, J. M., Lynne-Landsman, S. D., Sirocco, K., & Boyce, C. A. (2012). Brain maturation and risky behavior: The promise and the challenges of neuroimaging-based accounts. *Child Development Perspectives, 6*, 385–391.

Bjork, R. A., Dunlosky, J., & Kornell, N. (2013). Self-regulated learning: Beliefs, techniques, and illusions. *Annual Review of Psychology, 64*, 417–444.

Bjorklund, D. F., & Pellegrini, A. (2000). Child development and evolutionary psychology. *Child Development, 71*, 1687–1708.

Bjorkqvist, K. (2001). Different names, same issue. *Social Development, 10*, 272–274.

Blackwell, L. S., Trzesniewski, K. H., & Dweck, C. S. (2007). Implicit theories of intelligence predict achievement across an adolescent transition: A longitudinal study and an intervention. *Child Development, 78*, 246–263.

Blair, C. (2002). School readiness: Integrating cognition and emotion in a neurobiological conceptualization of children's functioning at school entry. *American Psychologist, 57*, 111–127.

Blair, C. (2010). Stress and the development of self-regulation in context. *Child Development Perspectives, 4*, 181–188.

Blair, C., Granger, D., Kivlighan, K. T., Mills-Koonce, W. R., Willoughby, M., Greenberg, M. T., et al. (2008). Maternal and child contributions to cortisol response to emotional arousal in young children from low-income, rural communities. *Developmental Psychology, 44*, 1095–1109.

Blair, C., Granger, D., & Razza, R. (2005). Cortisol reactivity is positively related to executive function in preschool children attending Head Start. *Child Development, 76*, 554–567.

Blair, C., Granger, D., Willoughby, M., Mills-Koonce, R., Cox, M., Greenberg, M. T., et al. (2011). Salivary cortisol mediates effects of poverty and parenting on executive functions in early childhood. *Child Development, 82*, 1970–1984.

Blair, C., & Raver, C. (2014). Closing the achievement gap through modification of neurocognitive and neuroendocrine function: Results from a cluster randomized controlled trial of an innovative approach to the education of children in kindergarten. *PLoS ONE, 9*, e112393.

Blair, C., & Raver, C. (2015). School readiness and self-regulation: A developmental psychobiological approach. *Annual Review of Psychology, 66*, 711–731.

Blakemore, S.-J., & Choudhury, S. (2006). Development of the adolescent brain: Implications for executive function and social cognition. *Journal of Child Psychology & Psychiatry & Allied Disciplines, 27*, 296–312.

Blandon, A., Calkins, S. D., Keane, S. P., & O'Brien, M. (2008). Individual differences in trajectories of emotion regulation processes: The effects of maternal depressive symptomatology and children's physiological regulation. *Developmental Psychology, 44*, 1110–1123.

Blandon, A., Calkins, S., Keane, S., & O'Brien, M. (2010). Contributions of child's physiology and maternal behavior to children's trajectories of temperamental reactivity. *Developmental Psychology, 46*, 1089–1102.

Blatchford, P. (1998). The state of play in schools. *Child Psychology & Psychiatry Review, 3*, 58–67.

Blatt-Eisengart, I., Drabick, D. A., Monahan, K. C., & Steinberg, L. (2009). Sex differences in the longitudinal relations among family risk factors and childhood externalizing symptoms. *Developmental Psychology, 45*, 491–502.

Bleidorn, W. (2015). What accounts for personality maturation in early adulthood? *Current Directions in Psychological Science, 24*, 245–252.

Bleske-Rechek, A., Lubinski, D., & Benbow, C. (2004). Meeting the educational needs of special populations: Advanced Placement's role in developing exceptional human capital. *Psychological Science, 15*, 217–224.

Bliss, L. S., & McCabe, A. (2008). Personal narratives: Cultural differences and clinical implications. *Topics in Language Disorders, 28*, 162–177.

Blum, R., Beuhring, T., Shew, M., Bearinger, L., Sieving, R., & Resnick, M. (2000). The effects of race/ethnicity, income, and family structure on adolescent risk behaviors. *American Journal of Public Health, 90*, 1879–1885.

Blumenthal, H., LeenFeldner, E. W., Babson, K. A., Gahr, J. L., Trianor, C. D., & Frala, J. L. (2011). Elevated social anxiety among early maturing girls. *Developmental Psychology, 47*, 1133–1140.

Blumstein, S., & Amso, D. (2013). Dynamic functional organization of language: Insights from functional neuroimaging. *Perspectives on Psychological Science, 8*, 44–48.

Boaler, J., & Staples, M. (2008). Creating mathematical futures through an equitable teaching approach: The case of Railside School. *Teachers College Record, 110*, 608–645.

Boddy, J., Skuse, D., & Andrews, B. (2000). The developmental sequelae of nonorganic failure to thrive. *Journal of Child Psychology & Psychiatry & Allied Disciplines, 41*, 1003–1014.

Boekaerts, M., & Minnaert, A. (2006). Affective and motivational outcomes of working in collaborative groups. *Educational Psychology, 26*, 187–208.

Bohlin, G., Hagekull, B., & Rydell, A. (2000). Attachment and social functioning: A longitudinal study from infancy to middle childhood. *Social Development, 9*, 24–39.

Bohlmann, N. L., & Weinstein, R. S. (2013). Classroom context, teacher expectations, and cognitive level: Predicting children's math ability judgments. *Journal of Applied Developmental Psychology, 34*, 288–298.

Bokhorst, C., Bakermans-Kranenburg, M., Fearon, P., van IJzendoorn, M., Fonagy, P., & Schuengel, C. (2003). The importance of shared environment in mother-infant attachment security: A behavioral genetic study. *Child Development, 74*, 1769–1782.

Bolger, K. E., & Patterson, C. J. (2001). Developmental pathways from child maltreatment to peer rejection. *Child Development, 72*, 549–568.

Bonanno, G., & Burton, C. L. (2013). Regulatory flexibility: An individual differences perspective on coping and emotion regulation. *Perspectives on Psychological Science, 8*, 591–612.

Bonawitz, E., Shafto, P., Gweon, H., Goodman, N. D., Spelke, E., & Schulz, L. (2011). The double-edged sword of pedagogy: Instruction limits spontaneous exploration and discovery. *Cognition, 120*, 322–330.

Bonuck, K., Freeman, K., Chervin, R., & Zu, L. (2012). Sleep-disordered breathing in a population-based cohort: Behavioral outcomes at 4 and 7 years. *Pediatrics, 129*, e857–865.

Booth, J. L., & Siegler, R. S. (2008). Numerical magnitude representations influence arithmetic learning. *Child Development, 79,* 1016–1031.

Booth-LaForce, C., Groh, A., Burchinal, M., Roisman, G., Owen, M., & Cox, M. (2014). Caregiving and contextual sources of continuity and change in attachment security from infancy to late adolescence. *Monographs of the Society for Research in Child Development, 79,* 67–84.

Borch, C., Hyde, A., & Cillessen, A. (2011). The role of attractiveness and aggression in high school popularity. *Social Psychology of Education, 14,* 23–39.

Borman, G., Hewes, G., Overman, L., & Brown, S. (2003). Comprehensive school reform and achievement: A meta-analysis. *Review of Educational Research, 73,* 125–230.

Bornstein, M. H., Hahn, C.-S., Gist, N. F., & Haynes, O. M. (2006). Long-term cumulative effects of childcare on children's mental development and socioemotional -adjustment in a non-risk sample: The moderating effects of gender. *Early Child Development and Care, 176,* 129–156.

Bornstein, M. H., Hahn, C.-S., Putnick, D. L., & Suwalsky, J. T. D. (2014). Stability of core language skill from early childhood to adolescence: A latent variable approach. *Child Development, 85,* 1346–1356.

Bornstein, M. H., & Putnick, D. L. (2007). Chronological age, cognitions, and practices in European American mothers: A multivariate study of parenting. *Developmental Psychology, 4,* 850–864.

Bornstein, M. H., Putnick, D. L., Cote, L. R., Haynes, O. M., & Suwalsky, J. T. D. (2015). Mother–infant contingent vocalizations in 11 countries. *Psychological Science, 26,* 1272–1284.

Bornstein, M. H., Putnick, D. L., Suwalsky, J. T. D., & Gini, M. (2006). Maternal chronological age, prenatal and perinatal history, social support, and parenting of infants. *Child Development, 77,* 875–892.

Bos, H. M. W., Knox, J. R., van Rijn-van Gelderen, L., & Gartrell, N. K. (2016). Same-sex and different-sex parent households and child health outcomes: Findings from the National Survey of Children's Health. *Journal of Developmental & Behavioral Pediatrics, 37,* 179–187.

Bos, H. M. W., Sandfort, T. G. M., de Bruyn, E. H., & Hakvoort, E. M. (2008). Same-sex attraction, social relationships, psychosocial functioning, and school performance in early adolescence. *Developmental Psychology, 44,* 59–68.

Bosacki, S., & Astington, J. (1999). Theory of mind in preadolescence: Relations between social understanding and social competence. *Social Development, 8,* 237–255.

Bouchard, T. (2004). Genetic influence on human psychological traits. *Current Directions in Psychological Science, 13,* 148–151.

Bowers, P. N., Kirby, J. R., & Deacon, S. H. (2010). The effects of morphological instruction on literacy skills. *Review of Educational Research, 80,* 144–179.

Bowes, L., Arseneault, L., Maughn, B., Taylor, A., Caspi, A., & Moffitt, T. (2009). School, neighborhood, and family factors are associated with children's bullying involvement: A nationally representative longitudinal study. *Journal of the American Academy of Child and Adolescent Psychiatry, 48,* 545–553.

Bowlby, J. (1940). The influence of early environment in the development of neurosis and neurotic character. *International Journal of Psycho-analysis, 21,* 154–178.

Bowlby, J. (1952). *Maternal care and mental health.* Geneva: World Health Organization.

Bowlby, J. (1969). *Attachment* (Vol. I). New York: Basic Books.

Boyle, M., Jenkins, J., Georgiades, K., Cairney, J., Duku, E., & Racine, Y. (2004). Differential-maternal parenting behavior: Estimating within- and between-family effects on children. *Child Development, 75,* 1457–1476.

Bradley, R., & Corwyn, R. (2002). Socioeconomic status and child development. *Annual Review of Psychology, 53,* 371–399.

Bradley, R., & Corwyn, R. F. (2006). The family environment. In L. Balter & C. Tamis-LeMonda (Eds.), *Child psychology: A handbook of contemporary issues* (pp. 493–520). New York: Psychology Press.

Bradley, R., Corwyn, R., Burchinal, M., McAdoo, H., & Garcia Coll, C. (2001). The home environments of children in the United States. Part II: Relations with behavioral development through age thirteen. *Child Development, 72,* 1868–1886.

Bradshaw, C. (2015). Translating research to practice in bullying prevention. *American Psychologist, 70,* 322–332.

Bradshaw, C., Sudhinaraset, M., Mmari, K., & Blum, R. (2010). School transitions among military adolescents: A qualitative study of stress and coping. *School Psychology Review, 39,* 84–105.

Bradshaw, C. P., Mitchell, M. M., O'Brennan, L. M., & Leaf, P. J. (2010). Multilevel exploration of factors contributing to the overrepresentation of black students in office disciplinary referrals. *Journal of Educational Psychology, 102,* 508–520.

Brainerd, C. J. (2013). Developmental reversals in false memory: A new look at the reliability of children's evidence. *Current Directions in Psychological Science, 22,* 335–341.

Brainerd, C. J., Holliday, R., & Reyna, V. F. (2004). Behavioral measurement of remembering phenomenologies: So simple a child can do it. *Child Development, 75,* 505–522.

Bramlett, M., & Mosher, W. (2002). *Cohabitation, marriage, divorce, and remarriage in the United States.* Hyattsville, MD: National Center for Health Statistics.

Brand, A. E., & Brinich, P. M. (1999). Behavior problems and mental health contacts in adopted, foster, and nonadopted children. *Journal of Child Psychology & Psychiatry & Allied Disciplines, 40,* 1221–1229.

Branstetter, S. A., Furman, W., & Cottrell, L. (2009). The influence of representations of attachment, maternal-adolescent relationship quality, and maternal monitoring on adolescent substance use: A 2–year longitudinal examination. *Child Development, 80,* 1448–1462.

Braungart-Reiker, J. M., Garwood, M. M., Powers, B. P., & Wang, X. (2001). Parental sensitivity, infant affect, and affect regulation: Predictors of later attachment. *Child Development, 72,* 252–270.

Braungart-Rieker, J. M., Hill-Soderlund, A. L., & Karrass, J. (2010). Fear and anger reactivity trajectories from 4 to 16 months: The roles of temperament, regulation, and maternal sensitivity. *Developmental Psychology, 46,* 791–804.

Brendgen, M., Boivin, M., Dionne, G., Barker, E. D., Vitaro, F., Girard, A., et al. (2012). Gene-environment processes linking aggression, peer victimization, and the teacher–child relationship. *Child Development, 82,* 2021–2036.

Brendgen, M., Boivin, M., Vitaro, F., Bukowski, W. M., Dionne, G., Tremblay, R. E., et al. (2008). Linkages between children's and their friends' social and physical aggression: Evidence for a gene–environment interaction? *Child Development, 79,* 13–29.

Brennan, P., Hall, J., Bor, W., Najman, J., & Williams, G. (2003). Integrating biological and social processes in relation to early-onset persistent aggression in boys and girls. *Developmental Psychology, 39,* 309–323.

Bremner, J. G., Slater, A. M., & Johnson, S. P. (2015). Perception of object persistence: The origins of object permanence in infancy. *Child Development Perspectives, 9,* 7–13.

Breslau, N., Johnson, E., & Lucia, V. (2001). Academic achievement of low birth-weight children at age 11: The role of cognitive abilities at school entry. *Journal of Abnormal Child Psychology, 29,* 273–279.

Bretherton, I., & Munholland, K. (1999). Internal working models in attachment relationships: A construct revisited. In J. Cassidy & P. Shaver (Eds.), *Handbook of attachment: Theory, research, and clinical applications* (pp. 89–111). New York: Guilford.

Breunlin, D., Bryant-Edwards, T., Hetherington, J., & Cimmarusti, R. (2002). Conflict resolution training as an alternative to suspension for violent behavior. *Journal of Educational Research, 95,* 349–357.

Brewer, M. B., & Chen, Y.-R. (2007). Where (who) are collectives in collectivism? Toward conceptual clarification of individualism and collectivism. *Psychological Review, 114,* 133–151.

Briley, D. A., & Tucker-Drob, E. M. (2013). Explaining the increasing heritability of cognitive ability across development: A meta-analysis of longitudinal twin and adoption studies. *Psychological Science, 24,* 1704–1713.

Brock, L. L., Rimm-Kaufman, S. E., Nathanson, L., & Grimm, K. J. (2009). The contributions of "hot" and "cool" executive function to children's academic achievement, learning-related behaviors, and engagement in kindergarten. *Early Childhood Research Quarterly, 24,* 337–349.

Brody, G. H., Beach, S. R. H., Philibert, R. A., Chen, Y.-F., & Murry, V. M. (2009). Prevention effects moderate the association of 5–HTTLPR and youth risk behavior initiation: Gene-environment hypotheses tested via a randomized prevention design. *Child Development, 80,* 645–661.

Brody, G. H., Chen, Y.-F., Murry, V. M., Ge, X., Simons, R. L., Gibbons, F. X., et al. (2006). Perceived discrimination and the adjustment of African American youths: A five-year longitudinal analysis with contextual moderation effects. *Child Development, 77*, 1170–1189.

Brody, N. (1992). *Intelligence* (2nd ed.). New York: Academic Press.

Broh, B. (2002). Linking extracurricular programming to academic achievement: Who benefits and why? *Sociology of Education, 75*, 69–95.

Broidy, L., Tremblay, R., Brame, B., Fergusson, D., Horwood, J., Laird, R., et al. (2003). Developmental trajectories of childhood disruptive behaviors and adolescent delinquency: A six-site, cross-national study. *Developmental Psychology, 39*, 222–245.

Bronfenbrenner, U., & Ceci, S. J. (1994). Nature-nurture reconceptualized in developmental perspective: A bioecological model. *Psychological Review, 101*, 568–586.

Bronfenbrenner, U., & Morris, P. (1998). The ecology of developmental processes. In W. Damon & R. Lerner (Eds.), *Handbook of child psychology: Theoretical models of human development* (5th ed., Vol. 1, pp. 993–1028). New York: Wiley.

Bronfenbrenner, U., & Morris, P. A. (2006). The bioecological model of human development. In R. M. Lerner & W. Damon (Eds.), *Handbook of child psychology: Theoretical models of human development* (6th ed., Vol. 1, pp. 793–828). New York: Wiley.

Brooks, R., & Meltzoff, A. (2015). Connecting the dots from infancy to childhood: A longitudinal study connecting gaze following, language, and explicit theory of mind. *Journal of Experimental Child Psychology, 130*, 67–78.

Brooks-Gunn, J., Han, W.-J., & Waldfogel, J. (2002). Maternal employment and child cognitive outcomes in the first three years of life: The NICHD Study of Early Child Care. *Child Development, 73*, 1052–1072.

Brooks-Gunn, J., Han, W.-J., & Waldfogel, J. (2010). First-year maternal employment and child development in the first 7 years. *Monographs of the Society for Research in Child Development, 75*, 1–147.

Brown, C. S., & Bigler, R. S. (2005). Children's perceptions of discrimination: A developmental model. *Child Development, 76*, 533–553.

Brown, L., Lescano, C., & Lourie, K. (2001). Children and adolescents with HIV infection. *Psychiatric Annals, 31*, 63–68.

Brown, P. C., Roediger, H. L., & McDaniel, M. A. (2014). *Make it stick: The science of successful learning.* Cambridge, MA: Belknap.

Brown, R. P., Osterman, L. L., & Barnes, C. D. (2009). School violence and the culture of honor. *Psychological Science, 20*, 1400–1405.

Brown, S., Tapert, S., Granholm, E., & Delis, D. (2000). Neurocognitive functioning of adolescents: Effects of protracted alcohol use. *Alcoholism: Clinical & Experimental Research, 24*, 164–171.

Brown, S. L. (2004). Family structure and child well-being: The significance of parental cohabitation. *Journal of Marriage and Family, 66*, 351–367.

Brown, W. H., Pfeiffer, K. A., McIver, K. L., Dowda, M., Addy, C. L., & Pate, R. R. (2009). Social and environmental factors associated with preschoolers' nonsedentary physical activity. *Child Development, 80*, 45–58.

Brownell, M., & Walther-Thomas, C. (2001). Interview with Steven Shore: Understanding the autism spectrum—What teachers need to know. *Intervention in School and Clinic, 36*, 293–299.

Brown-Wright, L., Tyler, K. M., Stevens-Watkins, D., Thomas, D., Mulder, S., Hughes, T., . . . Smith, L. T. (2012). Investigating the link between home-school dissonance and academic cheating among high school students. *Urban Education, 48*, 314–334.

Brubacher, S. P., Powell, M., Skouteris, H., & Guadagno, B. (2015). The effects of e-simulation interview training on teachers' use of open-ended questions. *Child Abuse & Neglect, 43*, 95–103.

Bruck, M., Ceci, S., & Principe, G. (2006). The child and the law. In K. A. Renninger & R. Lerner (Eds.), *Handbook of child psychology* (6th ed., Vol. 4, pp. 776–816). New York: Wiley.

Bryan, C., Master, A., & Walton, G. (2014). "Helping" versus "Being a Helper": Invoking the self to increase helping in young children. *Child Development, 85*, 1836–1842.

Bryck, R. L., & Fisher, P. A. (2012). Training the brain: Practical applications of neural plasticity from the intersection of cognitive neuroscience, developmental -psychology, and prevention science. *American Psychologist, 67*, 87–100.

Bub, K., McCartney, K., & Willett, J. B. (2007). Behavior problem trajectories and first-grade cognitive ability and achievement skills: A latent growth curve analysis. *Journal of Educational Psychology, 99*, 653–670.

Buckhalt, J. A., El-Sheikh, M., Keller, P., & Kelly, R. J. (2009). Concurrent and longitudinal relations between children's sleep and cognitive functioning: The moderating role of parent education. *Child Development, 80*, 875–892.

Buehler, C., & O'Brien, M. (2011). Mothers' part-time employment: Associations with mother and family well-being. *Journal of Family Psychology, 25*, 895–906.

Buehler, C., Lange, G., & Franck, K. L. (2007). Adolescents' cognitive and emotional responses to marital hostility. *Child Development, 78*, 775–789.

Bugental, D., & Happaney, K. (2004). Predicting infant maltreatment in low-income families: The interactive effects of maternal attributions and child status at birth. *Developmental Psychology, 40*, 234–243.

Buhs, E., & Ladd, G. W. (2001). Peer rejection as an antecedent of young children's school adjustment: An examination of mediating processes. *Developmental Psychology, 37*, 550–560.

Bukatko, D. (2008). *Child and adolescent development.* Boston, MA: Houghton Mifflin.

Bukowski, W., Sippola, L., & Newcomb, A. (2000). Variations in patterns of attraction to same- and other-sex peers during early adolescence. *Developmental Psychology, 36*, 147–154.

Bukowski, W. M., Laursen, B., & Hoza, B. (2010). The snowball effect: Friendship moderates escalations in depressed affect among avoidant and excluded children. *Development and Psychopathology, 22*, 749–757.

Bull, R., & Lee, K. (2014). Executive functioning and mathematics achievement. *Child Development Perspectives, 8*, 36–41.

Bulotsky-Shearer, R. J., Manz, P. H., Mendez, J. L., McWayne, C. M., Sekino, Y., & Fantuzzo, J. W. (2012). Peer play interactions and readiness to learn: A protective influence for African American preschool children from low-income households. *Child Development Perspectives, 6*, 225–231.

Bunge, S. A., & Zelazo, P. D. (2006). A brain-based account of the development of rule use in childhood. *Current Directions in Psychological Science, 15*, 118–121.

Burchinal, M., McCartney, K., Steinberg, L., Crosnoe, R., Friedman, S. L., McLoyd, V., et al. (2011). Examining the Black–White achievement gap among low-income children using the NICHD Study of Early Child Care and Youth Development. *Child Development, 82*, 1404–1420.

Burchinal, M. R., Howes, C., Pianta, R. C., Bryant, D., Early, D. M., Clifford, R., et al. (2008a). Predicting child outcomes at the end of kindergarten from the quality of pre-kindergarten teacher–child interactions and instruction. *Applied Developmental Psychology, 12*, 140–153.

Burchinal, M. R., Lowe Vandell, D., & Belsky, J. (2014). Is the prediction of adolescent outcomes from early child care moderated by later maternal sensitivity? Results from the NICHD study of early child care and youth development. *Developmental Psychology, 50*, 542–553.

Burchinal, M. R., Roberts, J., Riggins, R., Zeisel, S., Neebe, E., & Bryant, D. (2000). Relating quality of center-based child care to early cognitive and language development longitudinally. *Child Development, 71*, 339–357.

Burchinal, M. R., Roberts, J. E., Zeisel, S. A., & Rowley, S. (2008b). Social risk and protective factors for African American children's academic achievement and adjustment during the transition to middle school. *Developmental Psychology, 44*, 286–292.

Burgess, K. B., Rubin, K. H., Cheah, C. S. L., & Nelson, L. J. (2005). Behavioral inhibition, social withdrawal, and parenting. In W. R. Crozier & L. E. Alden (Eds.), *The essential handbook of social anxiety for clinicians* (pp. 99–120). New York: Wiley.

Burgess, K. B., Wojslawowicza, J. C., Rubin, K. H., Rose-Krasnor, L., & Booth-LaForce, C. (2006). Social information processing and coping strategies of shy/withdrawn and aggressive children: Does friendship matter? *Child Development, 77*, 371–383.

Burkett, E. (2001). *Another planet: A year in the life of a suburban high school.* New York: HarperCollins.

Burt, K. B., Obradovic, J., Long, J. D., & Masten, A. S. (2008). The interplay of social competence and psychopathology over 20 years: Testing transactional and cascade models. *Child Development, 79*, 359–374.

Burt, S. A. (2009). Rethinking environmental contributions to child and adolescent psychopathology: A meta-analysis of shared environmental influences. *Psychological Bulletin, 135*, 608–637.

Burt, S. A., Barnes, A. R., McGue, M., & Iacono, W. G. (2008). Parental divorce and adolescent delinquency: Ruling out the impact of common genes. *Developmental Psychology, 44*, 1668–1677.

Burt, S. A., McGue, M., & Iacono, W. G. (2009). Nonshared environmental mediation of the association between deviant peer affiliation and adolescent externalizing behaviors over time: Results from a cross-lagged monozygotic twin differences design. *Developmental Psychology, 45*, 1752–1760.

Burt, S. A., & Neiderhiser, J. M. (2009). Aggressive versus nonaggressive antisocial behavior: Distinctive etiological moderation by age. *Developmental Psychology, 45*, 1164–1176.

Burton, S., & Mitchell, P. (2003). Judging who knows best about yourself: Developmental change in citing the self across middle childhood. *Child Development, 74*, 426–443.

Bus, A. G., & Van IJzendoorn, M. H. (1997). Affective dimension of mother-infant picturebook reading. *Journal of School Psychology, 35*, 47–60.

Busch, V., Loyen, A., Lodder, M., Schrijvers, A. J. P., van Yperen, T. A., & de Leeuw, J. R. J. (2014). The effects of adolescent health-related behavior on academic performance: A systematic review of the longitudinal evidence. *Review of Educational Research, 84*, 245–274.

Bushman, B. J., & Anderson, C. A. (2007). Measuring the strength of the effect of violent media on aggression. *American Psychologist, 62*, 253–254.

Bushman, B. J., & Anderson, C. A. (2009). Comfortably numb: Desensitizing effects of violent media on helping others. *Psychological Science, 20*, 273–277.

Bushman, B. J., Rothstein, H. R., & Anderson, C. A. (2010). Much ado about something: Violent video game effects and a school of red herring: Reply to Ferguson and Kilburn (2010). *Psychological Bulletin, 136*, 182–187.

Buss, K. (2011). Which fearful toddlers should we worry about? Context, fear regulation, and anxiety. *Developmental Psychology, 47*, 804–819.

Buss, K. A., & McDaniel, M. E. (2016). Improving the prediction of risk for anxiety development in temperamentally fearful children. *Current Directions in Psychological Science, 25*, 14–20.

Byrge, L., Smith, L. B., & Mix, K. S. (2014). Beginnings of place value: How preschoolers write three-digit numbers. *Child Development, 85*, 437–443.

Cabeza, R., & Moscovitch, M. (2013). Memory systems, processing modes, and components: Functional neuroimaging evidence. *Perspectives on Psychological Science, 8*, 49–55.

Cairns, R. B., & Cairns, B. D. (1994). *Lifelines and risks: Pathways of youth in our time.* New York: Cambridge University Press.

Calarco, J. M. (2011). "I need help!" Social class and children's help-seeking in elementary school. *American Sociological Review, 76*, 862–882.

Caldarella, P., & Merrell, K. W. (1997). Common dimensions of social skills of children and adolescents: A taxonomy of positive behaviors. *School Psychology Review, 26*, 264–278.

Caldwell, C. H., Zimmerman, M. A., Bernat, D. H., Sellers, R. M., & Notaro, P. C. (2002). Racial identity, maternal support, and psychological distress among African American adolescents. *Child Development, 73*, 1322–1336.

Calzo, J. P., Antonucci, T. C., Mays, V. M., & Cochran, S. D. (2011). Retrospective recall of sexual orientation identity development among gay, lesbian, and bisexual adults. *Developmental Psychology, 47*, 1658–1673.

Cameron, E. L., Fox, J. D., Anderson, M. S., & Cameron, C. A. (2010). Resilient youths use humor to enhance socioemotional functioning during a Day in the Life. *Journal of Adolescent Research, 25*, 716–742.

Cameron, E. L., Kennedy, K. M., & Cameron, C. A. (2008). "Let me show you a trick!": A toddler's use of humor to explore, interpret, and negotiate her familial environment during a Day in the Life. *Journal of Research in Childhood Education, 23*, 5–18.

Camos, V. (2015). Storing verbal information in working memory. *Current Directions in Psychological Science, 24*, 440–445.

Camos, V., & Barrouillet, P. (2011). Developmental change in working memory strategies: From passive maintenance to active refreshing. *Developmental Psychology, 47*, 898–904.

Campbell, F. A., Pungello, E. P., Burchinal, M., Kainz, K., Pan, Y., Wasik, B. H., . . . Ramey, C. T. (2012). Adult outcomes as a function of an early childhood educational program: An Abecedarian Project follow-up. *Developmental Psychology, 48*, 1033–1043.

Campbell, J., Lamb, M., & Hwant, P. (2000). Early child-care experiences and children's social competence between 1 1/2 and 15 years of age. *Applied Developmental Science, 4*, 166–175.

Campbell, T. F., Dollaghan, C., Rockette, H. E., Paradise, J. L., Feldman, H. M., Shriberg, L. D., et al. (2003). Risk factors for speech delay of unknown origin in 3-year-old children. *Child Development, 74*, 346–357.

Caplan, M., & Hay, D. F. (1989). Preschoolers' responses to peers' distress and beliefs about bystander intervention. *Journal of Child Psychology & Psychiatry & Allied Disciplines, 30*, 231–242.

Caplan, M., Vespo, J., Pederson, J., & Hay, D. (1991). Conflict and its resolution in small groups of one- and two-year-olds. *Child Development, 62*, 1513–1524.

Cappuccio, F. P., Taggart, F. M., Kandala, N.-B., Currie, N., Peile, E., Stranges, S., et al. (2008). Meta-analysis of short sleep duration and obesity in children and adults. *Sleep, 31*, 619–626.

Caprara, G., Barbaranelli, C., & Pastorelli, C. (2001). Prosocial behavior and aggression in childhood and pre-adolescence. In A. Bohart & D. Stipek (Eds.), *Constructive and destructive behavior: Implications for family, school, and society* (pp. 187–203). Washington, DC: APA.

Caravolas, M., Lervåg, A., Defior, S., Seidlová Málková, G., & Hulme, C. (2013). Different patterns, but equivalent predictors, of growth in reading in consistent and inconsistent orthographies. *Psychological Science, 24*, 1398–1407.

Caravolas, M., Lervåg, A., Mousikou, P., Efrim, C., Litavský, M., Onochie-Quintanilla, E., et al. (2012). Common patterns of prediction of literacy development in different alphabetic orthographies. *Psychological Science, 23*, 678–686.

Card, N. A., Stucky, B. D., Sawalani, G. M., & Little, T. D. (2008). Direct and indirect aggression during childhood and adolescence: A meta-analytic review of gender differences, intercorrelations, and relations to maladjustment. *Child Development, 79*, 1185–1229.

Carey, S., & Bartlett, E. (1978). Acquiring a single new word. *Papers and Reports on Child Language Development, 15*, 17–29.

Carhill, A., Suárez-Orozco, C., & Paez, M. (2008). Explaining English language proficiency among adolescent immigrant students. *American Educational Research Journal, 45*, 1155–1179.

Carlisle, J. F., & Fleming, J. (2003). Lexical processing of morphologically complex words in the elementary years. *Scientific Studies of Reading, 7*, 239–253.

Carlo, G., Crockett, L. J., Wolff, J. M., & Beal, S. J. (2012). The role of emotional reactivity, self-regulation, and puberty in adolescents' prosocial behaviors. *Social Development, 21*, 667–685.

Carlo, G., Koller, S., Eisenberg, N., Da Silva, M., & Frohlich, C. (1996). A cross-national study on the relations among prosocial moral reasoning, gender role orientations, and prosocial behaviors. *Developmental Psychology, 32*, 231–240.

Carlo, G., Padilla-Walker, L. M., & Nielson, M. G. (2015). Longitudinal bidirectional relations between adolescents' sympathy and prosocial behavior. *Developmental Psychology, 51*, 1771–1777.

Carlson, C., Uppal, S., & Prosser, E. C. (2000). Ethnic differences in processes contributing to the self-esteem of early adolescent girls. *Journal of Early Adolescence, 20*, 44–67.

Carpendale, J. (2000). Kohlberg and Piaget on stages and moral reasoning. *Developmental Review, 20*, 181–205.

Carreón, G. P., Drake, C., & Barton, A. C. (2005). The importance of presence: Immigrant parents' school engagement experiences. *American Educational Research Journal, 42*, 465–498.

Carretti, B., Borella, E., Cornoldi, C., & De Beni, R. (2009). Role of working memory in explaining the performance of individuals with specific reading comprehension difficulties: A meta-analysis. *Learning and Individual Differences, 19*, 246–251.

Cartledge, G., Lo, Y.-Y., Vincent, C. G., & Robinson-Ervin, P. (2015). Culturally responsive classroom management. In E. T. Emmer & E. J. Sabornie (Eds.), *Handbook of classroom management* (2nd ed., pp. 411–430). New York: Routledge.

Case, R., Griffin, S., & Kelly, W. (2001). Socioeconomic differences in children's early cognitive development and their readiness for schooling. In S. Golbeck (Ed.), *Psychological perspectives on early childhood education: Reframing dilemmas in research and practice* (pp. 37–63). Mahwah, NJ: Erlbaum.

Casey, B. J., Getz, S., & Galvan, A. (2008). The adolescent brain. *Developmental Review, 28*, 62–77.

Casey, B. J., Somerville, L. H., Gotlib, I. H., Ayduk, O., Franklin, N. T., Askren, M. K., . . . Shoda, Y. (2011). Behavioral and neural correlates of delay of gratification 40 years later. *Proceedings of the National Academy of Sciences, 108,* 14998–15003.

Caspi, A. (1998). Personality development across the life course. In N. Eisenberg (Ed.), *Handbook of child psychology: Social, emotional, and personality development* (5th ed., Vol. 3, pp. 311–388). New York: Wiley.

Caspi, A., Taylor, A., Moffitt, T., & Plomin, R. (2000). Neighborhood deprivation affects children's mental health: Environmental risks identified in a genetic design. *Psychological Science, 11,* 338–342.

Cassibba, R., Van IJzendoorn, M., & D'Odorico, L. (2000). Attachment and play in child care centres: Reliability and validity of the attachment Q-sort for mothers and professional caregivers in Italy. *International Journal of Behavioral Development, 24,* 241–255.

Cassidy, J. (1994). Emotion regulation: Influences of attachment relationships. In N. A. Fox (Ed.), *Emotion regulation: Behavioral and biological considerations. Monographs for the Society for Research in Child Development* (Vol. 59, pp. 228–249).

Cassidy, J., Aikins, J., & Chernoff, J. (2003). Children's peer selection: Experimental examination of the role of self-perceptions. *Developmental Psychology, 39,* 495–508.

Cassidy, J., Parke, R., Butovsky, L., & Braungart, J. (1992). Family–peer connections: The roles of emotional expressiveness within the family and children's understanding of emotions. *Child Development, 63,* 603–618.

Cassidy, J., Ziv, Y., Mehta, T., & Feeney, B. (2003). Feedback seeking in children and adolescents: Associations with self-perceptions, attachment representations, and depression. *Child Development, 74,* 612–628.

Cassidy, J., Woodhouse, S. S., Sherman, L. J., Stupica, B., & Lejuez, C. W. (2011). Enhancing infant attachment security: An examination of treatment efficacy and differential susceptibility. *Development and Psychopathology, 23,* 131–148.

Castelli, D. M., Centeio, E. E., Hwang, J., Barcelona, J. M., Glowacki, E. M., Calvert, H. G., & Nicksic, H. M. (2014). The history of physical activity and academic performance research: Informing the future. *Monographs of the Society for Research in Child Development, 79,* 119–148.

Cawley, J., & Liu, F. (2012). Maternal employment and childhood obesity: A search for mechanisms in time use data. *Economics & Human Biology, 10,* 352–364.

CDC. (2009a). *Prevalence of the autism spectrum disorders (ASDs) in multiple areas of the United States.* Retrieved from http://www.cdc.gov/ncbddd/autism/index.html

CDC. (2009b). *School connectedness: Strategies for increasing protective factors among youth.* Atlanta: Department of Health and Human Services.

CDC. (2010). *The association between school-based physical activity, including physical education, and academic performance.* Atlanta, GA: Department of Health and Human Services.

Ceci, S. J. (2003). Cast in six ponds and you'll reel in something: Looking back on 25 years of research. *American Psychologist, 58,* 855–864.

Cepeda, N. J., Vul, E., Rohrer, D., Wixted, J. T., & Pashler, H. (2008). Spacing effects in learning: A temporal ridgeline of optimal retention. *Psychological Science, 19,* 1095–1102.

Chabris, C. F., Lee, J. J., Cesarini, D., Benjamin, D. J., & Laibson, D. I. (2015). The fourth law of behavior genetics. *Current Directions in Psychological Science, 24,* 304–312.

Chaddock-Heyman, L., Hillman, C. H., Cohen, N. J., & Kramer, A. F. (2014). The importance of physical activity and aerobic fitness for cognitive control and memory in children. *Monographs of the Society for Research in Child Development, 79,* 25–50.

Cham, H., Hughes, J. N., West, S. G., & Im, M. H. (2015). Effect of retention in elementary grades on grade 9 motivation for educational attainment. *Journal of School Psychology, 53,* 7–24.

Champagne, F. A. (2009). Beyond nature vs. nurture: Philosophical insights from molecular biology. *APS Observer, 22,* 3–4, 27.

Champagne, F. A., & Mashoodh, R. (2009). Genes in context: Gene–environment interplay and the origins of individual differences in behavior. *Current Directions in Psychological Science, 18,* 127–131.

Champion, J. E., Jaser, S. S., Reeslund, K. L., Simmons, L., Potts, J. E., Shears, A. R., et al. (2009). Caretaking behaviors by adolescent children of mothers with and without a history of depression. *Journal of Family Psychology, 23,* 156–166.

Champion, T. B. (2003). *Understanding storytelling among African American children: A journey from Africa to America.* Mahwah, NJ: Erlbaum.

Chandler, M., Fritz, A., & Hala, S. (1989). Small-scale deceit: Deception as a marker of two-, three-, and four-year-olds' early theories of mind. *Child Development, 60,* 1263–1277.

Chang, L. (2004). The role of classroom norms in contextualizing the relations of children's social behaviors to peer acceptance. *Developmental Psychology, 40,* 691–702.

Chaplin, L. N., & Norton, M. I. (2015). Why we think we can't dance: Theory of mind and children's desire to perform. *Child Development, 86,* 651–658.

Chapman, B. P., & Goldberg, L. R. (2011). Replicability and 40-year predictive power of childhood ARC types. *Journal of Personality and Social Psychology, 101,* 593–606.

Charity, A., Scarborough, H. S., & Griffin, D. (2004). Familiarity with school English in African American children and its relation to early reading achievement. *Child Development, 75,* 1340–1356.

Charness, N., Krampe, R., & Mayr, U. (1996). The role of practice and coaching in entrepreneurial skill domains: An international comparison of life-span chess skill acquisition. In K. A. Ericsson (Ed.), *The road to excellence: The acquisition of expert performance in the arts and sciences, sports, and games* (pp. 51–80). Mahwah, NJ: Erlbaum.

Chavajay, P., & Rogoff, B. (2002). Schooling and traditional collaborative social organization of problem solving by Mayan mothers and children. *Developmental Psychobiology, 38,* 55–66.

Chavous, T. M., Bernat, D. H., Schmeelk-Cone, K., Caldwell, C. H., Kohn-Wood, L., & Zimmerman, M. A. (2003). Racial identity and academic attainment among African American adolescents. *Child Development, 74,* 1076–1090.

Cheah, C., Nelson, L., & Rubin, K. (2001). Nonsocial play as a risk factor in social and emotional development. In A. Göncü, & E. Klein (Eds.), *Children in play, story, and school* (pp. 39–71). New York: Guilford.

Checkley, K., & Gardner, H. (1997). The first seven . . . and the eighth: A conversation with Howard Gardner. *Educational Leadership, 55,* 8–13.

Chen, D., Fein, G., Killen, M., & Tam, H.-P. (2001). Peer conflicts of preschool children: Issues, resolution, incidence, and age-related patterns. *Early Education and Development, 12,* 523–544.

Chen, E., Langer, D., Raphaelson, Y., & Matthews, K. (2005). Socioeconomic status and health in adolescents: The role of stress interpretations. *Child Development, 75,* 1039–1052.

Chen, X., & Graham, S. (2015). Cross-ethnic friendships and intergroup attitudes among Asian American adolescents. *Child Development, 86,* 749–764.

Cheng, H., & Furnham, A. (2002). Personality, peer relations, and self-confidence as predictors of happiness and loneliness. *Journal of Adolescence, 25,* 327–339.

Chernyak, N., & Kushnir, T. (2013). Giving preschoolers choice increases sharing behavior. *Psychological Science, 24,* 1971–1979.

Cheung, C. S.-S., & Pomerantz, E. M. (2011). Parents' involvement in children's learning in the United States and China: Implications for children's academic and emotional adjustment. *Child Development, 82,* 932–950.

Cheung, C. S.-S., Pomerantz, E. M., & Dong, W. (2013). Does adolescents' disclosure to their parents matter for their academic adjustment? *Child Development, 84,* 693–710.

Chevalier, N. (2015). Executive function development: Making sense of the environment to behave adaptively. *Current Directions in Psychological Science, 24,* 363–368.

Chi, M. (2006). Two approaches to the study of experts' characteristics. In K. A. Ericsson, N. Charness, P. J. Feltovich, & R. R. Hoffman (Eds.), *The Cambridge handbook of expertise and expert performance* (pp. 21–30). New York: Cambridge University Press.

Chien, N. C., Howes, C., Burchinal, M., Pianta, R. C., Ritchie, S., Bryant, D. M., et al. (2010). Children's classroom engagement and school readiness gains in prekindergarten. *Child Development, 81,* 1534–1549.

Choe, D. E., Lane, J. D., Grabell, A. S., & Olson, S. L. (2013). Developmental precursors of young school-age children's hostile attribution bias. *Developmental Psychology, 49*, 2245–2256.

Choe, D. E., Olson, S. L., & Sameroff, A. J. (2014). Effortful control moderates bidirectional effects between children's externalizing behavior and their mothers' depressive symptoms. *Child Development, 85*, 643–658.

Chomsky, N. (1959). Reviews: *Verbal Behavior* by B. F. Skinner. *Language, 35*, 26–58.

Chomsky, N. (2006). *Language and mind* (3rd ed.). New York: Cambridge University Press.

Christensen, D., Baio, J., Braun, K., Bilde, D., Charles, J., Constantino, J., et al. (2016). Prevalence and characteristics of Autism Spectrum Disorder among children aged 8 years — Autism and Developmental Disabilities Monitoring Network, 11 Sites, United States, 2012. *Morbidity and Mortality Weekly Report: Surveillance Summaries, 65*, 1–23.

Christopher, M. E., Hulslander, J., Byrne, B., Samuelsson, S., Keenan, J. M., Pennington, B., . . . Olson, R. K. (2015). Genetic and environmental etiologies of the longitudinal relations between prereading skills and reading. *Child Development, 86*, 342–361.

Chua, Y. P. (2014). The effects of humor cartoons in a series of bestselling academic books. *Humor, 27*, 499–520.

Chugani, H. (1998). A critical period of brain development: Studies of cerebral glucose utilization with PET. *Preventive Medicine, 27*, 184–188.

Chumlea, W. C., Schubert, C., Roche, A., Kulin, H., Lee, P., Himes, J., et al. (2003). Age at menarche and racial comparisons in US girls. *Pediatrics, 111*, 110–113.

Chung, E. K., Mathew, L., Rothkopf, A. C., Elo, I. T., Coyne, J. C., & Culhane, J. F. (2009). Parenting attitudes and infant spanking: The influence of childhood experiences. *Pediatrics, 124*, 278–285.

Chung, G. H., Flook, L., & Fuligni, A. J. (2011). Reciprocal associations between family and peer conflict in adolescents' daily lives. *Child Development, 82*, 1390–1396.

Cialdini, R. B. (2005). What's the best secret device for engaging student interest? The answer is in the title. *Journal of Social and Clinical Psychology, 24*, 22–29.

Ciani, K. D., Ferguson, Y., Bergin, D. A., & Hilpert, J. (2010). Motivational influences on school-prompted interest. *Educational Psychology, 30*, 377–393.

Ciarrochi, J., Parker, P., Sahdra, B., Marshall, S., Jackson, C., Gloster, A. T., & Heaven, P. (2016). The development of compulsive internet use and mental health: A four-year study of adolescence. *Developmental Psychology, 52*, 272–283.

Cillessen, A., & Bellmore, A. (2002). Social skills and interpersonal perception in early and middle childhood. In P. Smith & C. Hart (Eds.), *Blackwell handbook of childhood social development* (pp. 355–374). Oxford, UK: Blackwell.

Cillessen, A., & Mayeux, L. (2004). From censure to reinforcement: Developmental changes in the association between aggression and social status. *Child Development, 75*, 147–163.

Cimpian, A., & Markman, E. M. (2011). The generic/nongeneric distinction influences how children interpret new information about social others. *Child Development, 82*, 471–492.

Cimpian, A., Mu, Y., & Erickson, L. C. (2012). Who is good at this game? Linking an activity to a social category undermines children's achievement. *Psychological Science, 23*, 533–541.

Cizek, G. J. (1999). *Cheating on tests: How to do it, detect it, and prevent it.* Mahwah, NJ: Erlbaum.

Claessens, A., & Dowsett, C. (2014). Growth and change in attention problems, disruptive behavior, and achievement from kindergarten to fifth grade. *Psychological Science, 25*, 2241–2251.

Claessens, A., Engel, M., & Curran, F. C. (2014). Academic content, student learning, and the persistence of preschool effects. *American Educational Research Journal, 51*, 403–434.

Claessens, A., Engel, M., & Curran, C. F. (2015). The effects of maternal depression on child outcomes during the first years of formal schooling. *Early Childhood Research Quarterly, 32*, 80–93.

Clark, C., Sheffield, T., Chevalier, N., Nelson, J., Wiebe, S., & Espy, K. (2013). Charting early trajectories of executive control with the Shape School. *Developmental Psychology, 49*, 1481–1493.

Clark, C. A., Pritchard, V., & Woodward, L. J. (2010). Preschool executive functioning abilities predict early mathematics achievement. *Developmental Psychology, 46*, 1176–1191.

Clark, C. A. A., Woodward, L. J., Horwood, L. J., & Moor, S. (2008). Development of emotional and behavioral regulation in children born extremely preterm and very preterm: Biological and social influences. *Child Development, 79*, 1444–1462.

Clark, T. T., Yang, C., McClernon, F. J., & Fuemmeler, B. F. (2015). Racial differences in parenting style typologies and heavy episodic drinking trajectories. *Health Psychology, 34*, 697–708.

Clarke, L., Ungerer, J., Chahoud, K., Johnson, S., & Stiefel, I. (2002). Attention deficit hyperactivity disorder is associated with attachment insecurity. *Clinical Child Psychology and Psychiatry, 7*, 1359–1045.

Clements, D. H., & Sarama, J. (2008). Experimental evaluation of the effects of a research-based preschool mathematics curriculum. *American Educational Research Journal, 45*, 443–494.

Cleveland, M., Gibbons, F., Gerrard, M., Pomery, E., & Brody, G. (2005). The impact of parenting on risk cognitions and risk behavior: A study of mediation and moderation in a panel of African American adolescents. *Child Development, 76*, 900–916.

Clifford, S., Lemery-Chalfant, K., & Goldsmith, H. H. (2015). The unique and shared genetic and environmental contributions to fear, anger, and sadness in childhood. *Child Development, 86*, 1538–1556.

Clingenpeel, B. T., & Pianta, R. C. (2007). Mothers' sensitivity and book-reading interactions with first graders. *Early education and development, 18*, 1–22.

Coate, D., & Grossman, M. (1985). Effects of alcoholic beverage prices and legal drinking ages on youth alcohol use: Results from the Second National Health and Nutrition Examination Survey. National Bureau of Economic Research.

Coffman, J. L., Ornstein, P. A., McCall, L. E., & Curran, P. J. (2008). Linking teachers' memory-relevant language and the development of children's memory skills. *Developmental Psychology, 44*, 1640–1654.

Cohen, A. B. (2009). Many forms of culture. *American Psychologist, 64*, 194–204.

Cohen, A. B. (2015). Religion's profound influences on psychology: Morality, intergroup relations, self-construal, and enculturation. *Current Directions in Psychological Science, 24*, 77–82.

Cohen, G. L., Steele, C. M., & Ross, L. D. (1999). The mentor's dilemma: Providing critical feedback across the racial divide. *Personality and Social Psychology Bulletin, 25*, 1302–1318.

Cohen, L., Rundell, L., Spellman, B., & Cashon, C. (1999). Infants' perception of causal chains. *Psychological Science, 10*, 412–418.

Coie, J. D., & Dodge, K. A. (1998). Aggression and antisocial behavior. In N. Eisenberg (Ed.), *Handbook of child psychology: Social, emotional, and personality development* (5th ed., Vol. 3, pp. 779–862). New York: Wiley.

Colby, A., Kohlberg, L., Gibbs, J., & Lieberman, M. (1983). A longitudinal study of moral judgment. *Monographs of the Society for Research in Child Development, 48* (1–2, Serial No. 200).

Cole, D. A., Maxwell, S. E., Martin, J. M., Peeke, L. G., Seroczynski, A. D., Tram, J. M., et al. (2001). The development of multiple domains of child and adolescent self-concept: A cohort sequential longitudinal design. *Child Development, 72*, 1723–1746.

Cole, M. (1975). An ethnographic psychology of cognition. In R. W. Brislin, S. Bochner, & W. Lonner (Eds.), *Cross-cultural perspectives on learning*. New York: Wiley.

Cole, P. M., Luby, J., & Sullivan, M. W. (2008). Emotions and the development of childhood depression: Bridging the gap. *Child Development Perspectives, 2*, 141–148.

Cole, P. M., Michel, M. K., & Teti, L. O. (1994). The development of emotion regulation and dysregulation: A clinical perspective. *Monographs of the Society for Research in Child Development, 59* (Serial No. 240).

Coles, R. (1986). *The moral life of children.* Boston: Atlantic Monthly Press.

Coley, R. L. (1998). Children's socialization experiences and functioning in single-mother households: The importance of fathers and other men. *Child Development, 69*, 219–230.

Coley, R. L., & Lombardi, C. M. (2013). Does maternal employment following childbirth support or inhibit low-income children's long-term development? *Child Development, 84,* 178–197.

Coley, R. L., Votruba-Drzal, E., & Schindler, H. S. (2009). Fathers' and mothers' parenting predicting and responding to adolescent sexual risk behaviors. *Child Development, 80,* 808–827.

Collibee, C., & Furman, W. (2015). Quality counts: Developmental shifts in associations between romantic relationship qualities and psychosocial adjustment. *Child Development, 86,* 1639–1652.

Collins, A. (2002). Historical perspectives on contemporary research in social -development. In P. Smith & C. Hart (Eds.), *Blackwell handbook of childhood social development* (pp. 3–23). Oxford, UK: Blackwell.

Collins, M. (2012). The importance of discussing 50-cent words with preschoolers. *Young Children, 67,* 66–71.

Collins, R., Martino, S., Elliott, M. N., & Miu, A. (2011). Relationships between adolescent sexual outcomes and exposure to sex in media: Robustness of propensity-based analysis. *Developmental Psychology, 47,* 585–591.

Collins, W. A., Welsh, D. P., & Furman, W. (2009). Adolescent romantic relationships. *Annual Review of Psychology, 60,* 631–652.

Colom, R., Lluis-Font, J. M., & Andres-Pueyo, A. (2005). The generational intelligence gains are caused by decreasing variance in the lower half of the distribution: Supporting evidence for the nutrition hypothesis. *Intelligence, 33,* 83–91.

Colwell, M., Mize, J., Petit, G., & Laird, R. D. (2002). Contextual determinants of mothers' interventions in young children's peer interactions. *Developmental Psychology, 38,* 492–502.

Commodari, E. (2013). Preschool teacher attachment, school readiness and risk of learning difficulties. *Early Childhood Research Quarterly, 28,* 123–133.

Compton, R. J., Robinson, M. D., Ode, S., Quandt, L., Fineman, S. L., & Carp, J. (2008). Error monitoring ability predicts daily stress regulation. *Psychological Science, 19,* 702–708.

Conboy, B., & Thal, D. (2006). Ties between the lexicon and grammar: Cross-sectional and longitudinal studies of bilingual toddlers. *Child Development, 77,* 712–735.

Conklin, H. G. (2014). Toward more joyful learning: Integrating play into frameworks of middle grades teaching. *American Educational Research Journal, 51,* 1227–1255.

Connell, A. M., Dishion, T. J., Yasui, M., & Kavanagh, K. (2007). An adaptive approach to family intervention: Linking engagement in family-centered intervention to reductions in adolescent problem behavior. *Journal of Consulting and Clinical Psychology, 75,* 568–579.

Connolly, J., Nguyen, H. N. T., Pepler, D., Craig, W., & Jiang, D. (2013). Developmental trajectories of romantic stages and associations with problem behaviours during adolescence. *Journal of Adolescence, 36,* 1013–1024.

Connor, C. M., Morrison, F. J., Fishman, B., Crowe, E. C., Al Otaiba, S., & Schatschneider, C. (2013). A longitudinal cluster-randomized controlled study on the accumulating effects of individualized literacy instruction on students' reading from first through third grade. *Psychological Science, 24,* 1408–1419.

Connor, C. M., Piasta, S. B., Fishman, B., Glasney, S., Schatschneider, C., Crowe, E., et al. (2009). Individualizing student instruction precisely: Effects of child X instruction interactions on first graders' literacy development. *Child Development, 80,* 77–100.

Conrad, N. J. (2008). From reading to spelling and spelling to reading: Transfer goes both ways. *Journal of Educational Psychology, 100,* 869–878.

Cook, S. W., Duffy, R. G., & Fenn, K. M. (2013). Consolidation and transfer of learning after observing hand gesture. *Child Development, 84,* 1863–1871.

Coon, K., Goldberg, J., Rogers, B., & Tucker, K. (2001). Relationships between use of television during meals and children's food consumption patterns. *Pediatrics, 107,* e7.

Cooper, C. E., Osborne, C. A., Beck, A. N., & McLanahan, S. S. (2011). Partnership instability, school readiness, and gender disparities. *Sociology of Education, 84,* 246–259.

Cooper, H. (2008). The search for meaningful ways to express the effects of interventions. *Child Development Perspectives, 2,* 181–186.

Cooper, H., Allen, A. B., Patall, E. A., & Dent, A. L. (2010). Effects of full-day kindergarten on academic achievement and social development. *Review of Educational Research, 80,* 34–70.

Cooper, H., Robinson, J. C., & Patall, E. A. (2006). Does homework improve academic achievement? A synthesis of research, 1987–2003. *Review of Educational Research, 76,* 1–62.

Cooper, H., & Valentine, J. C. (2001). Using research to answer practical questions about homework. *Educational Psychologist, 36,* 143–153.

Cooper, L., Shaver, P., & Collins, N. (1998). Attachment styles, emotion regulation, and adjustment in adolescence. *Journal of Personality and Social Psychology, 74,* 1380–1397.

Coplan, R., Ooi, L. L., & Nocita, G. (2015). When one is company and two is a crowd: Why some children prefer solitude. *Child Development Perspectives, 9,* 133–137.

Coplan, R., Rose-Krasnor, L., Weeks, M., Kingsbury, A., Kingsbury, M., & Bullock, A. (2013). Alone is a crowd: Social motivations, social withdrawl, and socioemotional functioning in later childhood. *Developmental Psychology, 49,* 861–875.

Coplan, R. J., & Armer, M. (2007). A "multitude" of solitude: A closer look at social withdrawal and nonsocial play in early childhood. *Child Development Perspectives, 1,* 26–32.

Coplan, R. J., Hughes, K., Bosacki, S., & Rose-Krasnor, L. (2011). Is silence golden? Elementary school teachers' strategies and beliefs regarding hypothetical shy/quiet and exuberant/talkative children. *Journal of Educational Psychology, 103,* 939–951.

Corby, B. C., Hodges, E. V. E., & Perry, D. G. (2007). Gender identity and adjustment in Black, Hispanic, and White preadolescents. *Developmental Psychology, 43,* 261–266.

Cornelius-White, J. (2007). Learner-centered teacher–student relationships are effective: A meta-analysis. *Review of Educational Research, 77,* 113–143.

Cornell, D., & Limber, S. (2015). Law and policy on the concept of bullying at school. *American Psychologist, 70,* 333–343.

Cortiella, C., & Horowitz, S. (2014). *The state of learning disabilities* (3rd ed.). New York: National Center for Learning Disabilities.

Cote, S., Borge, A. I. H., Geoffroy, M.-C., Rutter, M., & Tremblay, R. E. (2008). Nonmaternal care in infancy and emotional/behavioral difficulties at 4 years old: Moderation by family risk characteristics. *Developmental Psychology, 44,* 155–168.

Council on Community Pediatrics. (2015). Promoting food security for all children. *Pediatrics, 136,* e1431–e1438.

Courage, M. L., & Setliff, A. E. (2009). Debating the impact of television and video material on very young children: Attention, learning, and the developing brain. *Child Development Perspectives, 3,* 72–78.

Coussons-Read, M. E. (2012). The psychoneuroimmunology of stress in pregnancy. *Current Directions in Psychological Science, 21,* 323–328.

Cowan, N. (2010). The magical mystery four: How is working memory capacity limited, and why? *Current Directions in Psychological Science, 19,* 51–57.

Cowan, N., Hismjatullina, A., AuBuchon, A. M., Saults, J. S., Horton, N., Leadbitter, K., et al. (2010). With development, list recall includes more chunks, not just larger ones. *Developmental Psychology, 46,* 1119–1131.

Coyle, T. R., Pillow, D. R., Snyder, A. C., & Kochunov, P. (2011). Processing speed mediates the development of general intelligence (g) in adolescence. *Psychological Science, 22,* 1265–1269.

Coyne, S. M. (2016). Effects of viewing relational aggression on television on aggressive behavior in adolescents: A three-year longitudinal study. *Developmental Psychology, 52,* 284–295.

Craig, S. D., Hu, X., Graesser, A. C., Bargagliotti, A. E., Sterbinsky, A., Cheney, K. R., & Okwumabua, T. (2013). The impact of a technology-based mathematics after-school program using ALEKS on student's knowledge and behaviors. *Computers & Education, 68,* 495–504.

Craig-Unkefer, L., & Kaiser, A. (2002). Improving the social communication skills of at-risk preschool children in a play context. *Topics in Early Childhood Special Education, 22,* 3–13.

Craig, S. D., Chi, M. T., & VanLehn, K. (2009). Improving classroom learning by collaboratively observing human tutoring videos while problem solving. *Journal of Educational Psychology, 101,* 779–789.

Crain, R. M. (1996). The influence of age, race, and gender on child and adolescent multidimensional self-concept. In B. A. Bracken (Ed.), *Handbook of* self-concept: Developmental, social, and clinical considerations (pp. 395–420). New York: Wiley.

Crick, N. R., & Dodge, K. A. (1994). A review and reformulation of social information-processing mechanisms in children's social adjustment. *Psychological Bulletin, 115*, 74–101.

Criss, M., Pettit, G., Bates, J., Dodge, K., & Lapp, A. (2002). Family adversity, positive peer relationships, and children's externalizing behavior: A longitudinal perspective on risk and resilience. *Child Development, 73*, 1220–1237.

Crittenden, P. M. (1992). Quality of attachment in the preschool years. *Development and Psychopathology, 4*, 209–241.

Crockenberg, S., & Litman, C. (1990). Autonomy as competence in 2-year-olds: Maternal correlates of child defiance, compliance, and self-assertion. *Developmental Psychology, 26*, 961–971.

Crockett, L., Raffaelli, M., & Moilanen, K. (2003). Adolescent sexuality: Behavior and meaning. In G. Adams & M. Berzonsky (Eds.), *Blackwell handbook on adolescence* (pp. 371–392). Malden, MA: Blackwell.

Crook, S. R., & Evans, G. W. (2014). The role of planning skills in the income-achievement gap. *Child Development, 85*, 405–411.

Crosnoe, R., & Cooper, C. E. (2010). Economically disadvantaged children's transitions into elementary school: Linking family processes, school contexts, and educational policy. *American Educational Research Journal, 47*, 258–291.

Crosnoe, R., Leventhal, T., Wirth, R. J., Pierce, K. M., Pianta, R. C., & NICHD Early Child Care Research Network. (2010). Family socioeconomic status and consistent environmental stimulation in early childhood. *Child Development, 81*, 972–987.

Crosnoe, R., & Needham, B. (2004). Holism, contextual variability, and the study of friendships in adolescent development. *Child Development, 75*, 264–279.

Crosnoe, R., Riegle-Crumb, C., Field, S., Frank, K., & Muller, C. (2008). Peer group contexts of girls' and boys' academic experiences. *Child Development, 79*, 139–155.

Crouter, A. C., Bumpus, M. F., Davis, K. D., & McHale, S. M. (2005). How do parents learn about adolescents' experiences? Implications for parental knowledge and adolescent risky behavior. *Child Development, 76*, 869–882.

Crouter, A. C., Whiteman, S. D., McHale, S. M., & Osgood, D. W. (2007). Development of gender attitude traditionality across middle childhood and adolescence. *Child Development, 78*, 911–926.

Crowell, J., Treboux, D., & Waters, E. (2002). Stability of attachment representations: The transition to marriage. *Developmental Psychology, 38*, 467–479.

Cruz, J., Emery, R., & Turkheimer, E. (2012). Peer network drinking predicts increased alcohol use from adolescence to early adulthood after controlling for genetic and shared environmental selection. *Developmental Psychology, 48*, 1390–1402.

Cruz, R. A., King, K. M., Widaman, K. F., Leu, J., Cauce, A. M., & Conger, R. D. (2011). Cultural influences on positive father involvement in two-parent Mexican-origin families. *Journal of Family Psychology, 25*, 731–740.

Csikszentmihalyi, M., Rathunde, K., & Whalen, S. (1993). *Talented teenagers: The roots of success and failure*. Cambridge, UK: Cambridge University Press.

Cuevas, K., & Bell, M. A. (2014). Infant attention and early childhood executive function. *Child Development, 85*, 397–404.

Cui, M., Conger, R. D., & Lorenz, F. O. (2005). Predicting change in adolescent adjustment from change in marital problems. *Developmental Psychology, 41*, 812–823.

Cui, M., Donnellan, M. B., & Conger, R. D. (2007). Reciprocal influences between parents' marital problems and adolescent internalizing and externalizing behavior. *Developmental Psychology, 43*, 1544–1552.

Cullerton-Sen, C., Cassidy, A. R., Murray-Close, D., Cicchetti, D., Crick, N. R., & Rogosch, F. A. (2009). Childhood maltreatment and the development of relational and physical aggression: The importance of a gender-informed approach. *Child Development, 79*, 1736–1751.

Curby, T. W., Rimm-Kaufman, S. E., & Ponitz, C. C. (2009). Teacher–child interactions and children's achievement trajectories across kindergarten and first grade. *Journal of Educational Psychology, 101*, 912–925.

Cutting, A., & Dunn, J. (1999). Theory of mind, emotion understanding, language, and family background: Individual differences and interrelations. *Child Development, 70*, 853–865.

Cvencek, D., Meltzoff, A. N., & Greenwald, A. G. (2011). Math–gender stereotypes in elementary school children. *Child Development, 82*, 766–779.

Cvencek, D., Nasir, N. i. S., O'Connor, K., Wischnia, S., & Meltzoff, A. N. (2015). The development of math–race stereotypes: "They say Chinese people are the best at math." *Journal of Research on Adolescence, 25*, 630–637.

Dadds, M. R., Moul, C., Hawes, D. J., Mendoza Diaz, A., & Brennan, J. (2015). Individual differences in childhood behavior disorders associated with epigenetic modulation of the cortisol receptor gene. *Child Development, 86*, 1311–1320.

Dahl, A. (2015). The developing social context of infant helping in two U.S. samples. *Child Development, 86*, 1080–1093.

Dahl, A., & Campos, J. J. (2013). Domain differences in early social interactions. *Child Development, 84*, 817–825.

Dahl, R., & Lewin, D. (2002). Pathways to adolescent health: Sleep regulation and behavior. *Journal of Adolescent Health, 31*, 175–184.

Daly, M., Delaney, L., Egan, M., & Baumeister, R. F. (2015). Childhood self-control and unemployment throughout the life span: Evidence from two British cohort studies. *Psychological Science, 26*, 709–723.

Daly, M., & Wilson, M. (2005). The "Cinderella effect" is no fairy tale: Comment. *Trends in Cognitive Sciences, 9*, 507–508.

Damon, W., & Killen, M. (1982). Peer interaction and the process of change in children's moral reasoning. *Merrill-Palmer Quarterly, 28*, 347–367.

Daniels, J. (2013). Race and racism in Internet studies: A review and critique. *New Media & Society, 15*, 695–719.

Danish, S., Taylor, T., & Fazio, R. (2003). Enhancing adolescent development through sports and leisure. In G. Adams & M. Berzonsky (Eds.), *Blackwell handbook of adolescence* (pp. 92–108). Malden, MA: Blackwell.

Darby, K. P., & Sloutsky, V. M. (2015). When delays improve memory: Stabilizing memory in children may require time. *Psychological Science, 26*, 1936–1946.

Darling, N., Cumsille, P., & Martinez, L. M. (2008). Individual differences in adolescents' beliefs about the legitimacy of parental authority and their own obligation to obey: A longitudinal investigation. *Child Development, 79*, 1103–1118.

Darling-Hammond, L. (2007). The flat earth and education: How America's commitment to equity will determine our future. *Educational Researcher, 36*, 318–334.

Darwin, C. (1965/1872). *The expression of the emotions in man and animals*. Chicago, IL: University of Chicago Press.

Davidov, M., & Grusec, J. (2006). Untangling the links of parental responsiveness to distress and warmth to child outcomes. *Child Development, 77*, 444–458.

Davidson, R. J. (2000). Affective style, psychopathology, and resilience: Brain mechanisms and plasticity. *American Psychologist, 55*, 1196–1214.

Davies, P., & Cicchetti, D. (2014). How and why does the 5-HTTLPR gene moderate associations between maternal unresponsiveness and children's disruptive problems? *Child Development, 85*, 484–500.

Davies, P., Cicchetti, D., & Hentges, R. F. (2015). Maternal unresponsiveness and child disruptive problems: The interplay of uninhibited temperament and dopamine transporter genes. *Child Development, 86*, 63–79.

Davies, P., Cicchetti, D., Hentges, R., & Sturge-Apple, M. (2013). The genetic precursors and the advantageous and disadvantageous sequelae of inhibited temperament: An evolutionary perspective. *Developmental Psychology, 49*, 2285–2300.

Davies, P., & Martin, M. (2014). Children's coping and adjustment in high-conflict homes: The reformulation of emotional security theory. *Child Development Perspectives, 8*, 242–249.

Davies, P., Sturge-Apple, M. L., Cicchetti, D., & Cummings, E. M. (2007). The role of child adrenocortical functioning in pathways between interparental conflict and child maladjustment. *Developmental Psychology, 43*, 918–930.

Davies, P., Sturge-Apple, M. L., Cicchetti, D., & Cummings, E. M. (2008). Adrenocortical underpinnings of children's psychological reactivity to interparental conflict. *Child Development, 79*, 1693–1706.

Davis, C. L., Tomporowski, P. D., McDowell, J. E., Austin, B. P., Miller, P. H., Yanasak, N. E., et al. (2011). Exercise improves executive function and achievement and alters brain activation in overweight children: A randomized, controlled trial. *Health Psychology, 30*, 91–98.

Davis, E., Levine, L., Lench, H., & Quas, J. (2010). Metacognitive emotion regulation strategies: Children's awareness that changing thoughts and goals can alleviate negative emotions. *Emotion, 10,* 498–510.

Davis-Kean, P. E., Jager, J., & Collins, W. A. (2009). The self in action: An emerging link between self-beliefs and behaviors in middle childhood. *Child Development Perspectives, 3,* 184–188.

Davison, D., Susman, E., & Birch, L. (2003). Percent body fat at age 5 predicts earlier pubertal development among girls at age 9. *Pediatrics, 111,* 815–821.

Davison, K., & Birch, L. (2002). Processes linking weight status and self-concept among girls from ages 5 to 7 years. *Developmental Psychology, 38,* 735–748.

Dawson, G., Ashman, S., Panagiotides, H., Hessl, D., Self, J., Yamada, E., et al. (2003). Preschool outcomes of children of depressed mothers: Role of maternal behavior, contextual risk, and children's brain activity. *Child Development, 74,* 1158–1175.

Dawson, G., Frey, K., Panagiotides, H., Yamada, E., Hessl, D., & Osterling, J. (1999). Infants of depressed mothers exhibit atypical frontal electrical brain activity during interactions with mother and with a familiar, nondepressed adult. *Child Development, 70,* 1058–1066.

Dawson, M., Soulières, I., Gernsbacher, M. A., & Mottron, L. (2007). The level and nature of autistic intelligence. *Psychological Science, 18,* 657–662.

Day, K. L., & Smith, C. L. (2013). Understanding the role of private speech in children's emotion regulation. *Early Childhood Research Quarterly, 28,* 405–414.

Dayanim, S., & Namy, L. L. (2015). Infants learn baby signs from video. *Child Development, 86,* 800–811.

Dean, D., & Kuhn, D. (2006). Direct instruction vs. discovery: The long view. *Science Education, 91,* 384–397.

De Angelis, T. (2015, February). Class differences. *Monitor on Psychology,* 62–66.

Dearing, E. (2004). The developmental implications of restrictive and supportive parenting across neighborhoods and ethnicities: Exceptions are the rule. *Journal of Applied Developmental Psychology, 25,* 555–575.

Dearing, E., McCartney, K., & Taylor, B. (2001). Change in family income-to-needs matters more for children with less. *Child Development, 72,* 1779–1793.

Dearing, E., McCartney, K., & Taylor, B. A. (2009). Does higher quality early child care promote low-income children's math and reading achievement in middle childhood? *Child Development, 80,* 1329–1349.

Deary, I. J. (2012). Intelligence. *Annual Review of Psychology, 63,* 453–482.

Deary, I. J., Weiss, A., & Batty, G. D. (2010). Intelligence, personality, and health outcomes. *Psychological Science in the Public Interest, 11,* 53–79.

Deary, I. J., Pattie, A., & Starr, J. M. (2013). The stability of intelligence from age 11 to age 90 years: The Lothian birth cohort of 1921. *Psychological Science, 24,* 2361–2368.

Deater-Deckard, K. (2000). Parenting and child behavioral adjustment in early childhood: A quantitative genetic approach to studying family processes. *Child Development, 71,* 468–484.

Deater-Deckard, K. (2014). Family matters: Intergenerational and interpersonal processes of executive function and attentive behavior. *Current Directions in Psychological Science, 23,* 230–236.

Deater-Deckard, K., & Plomin, R. (1999). An adoption study of the etiology of teacher and parent reports of externalizing behavior problems in middle childhood. *Child Development, 70,* 144–154.

De Boer, H., Bosker, R., & van der Werf, M. (2010). Sustainability of teacher expectation bias effects on long-term student performance. *Journal of Educational Psychology, 102,* 168–179.

De Brauwer, J., & Fias, W. (2009). A longitudinal study of children's performance on simple multiplication and division problems. *Developmental Psychology, 45,* 1480–1496.

de Bruin, A., Treccani, B., & Della Sala, S. (2015). Cognitive advantage in bilingualism: An example of publication bias? *Psychological Science, 26,* 99–107.

de Bruin, C., Deppeler, J., Moore, D., & Diamond, N. (2013). Public school-based interventions for adolescents and young adults with an Autism Spectrum Disorder: A meta-analysis. *Review of Educational Research, 83,* 521–550.

Decety, J., & Cowell, J. M. (2014). Friends or foes: Is empathy necessary for moral behavior? *Perspectives on Psychological Science, 9,* 525–537.

Decety, J., & Howard, L. H. (2013). The role of affect in the neurodevelopment of morality. *Child Development Perspectives, 7,* 49–54.

Deci, E. L., & Ryan, R. M. (2000). The "what" and "why" of goal pursuits: Human needs and the self-determination of behavior. *Psychological Inquiry, 11,* 227–268.

De Clercq, B., Van Leeuwen, K., De Fruyt, F., Van Hiel, A., & Mervielde, I. (2008). Maladaptive personality traits and psychopathology in childhood and adolescence: The moderating effect of parenting. *Journal of Personality, 76,* 357–383.

Dee, T. S. (2014). Stereotype threat and the student-athlete. *Economic Inquiry, 52,* 173–182.

DeGarmo, D. S. (2010). Coercive and prosocial fathering, antisocial personality, and growth in children's postdivorce noncompliance. *Child Development, 81,* 503–516.

Degnan, K. A., Calkins, S. D., Keane, S. P., & Hill-Soderlund, A. L. (2008). Profiles of disruptive behavior across early childhood: Contributions of frustration reactivity, physiological regulation, and maternal behavior. *Child Development, 79,* 1357–1376.

Degnan, K. A., Hane, A. A., Henderson, H. A., Moas, O. L., Reeb-Sutherland, B. C., & Fox, N. A. (2011). Longitudinal stability of temperamental exuberance and social-emotional outcomes in early childhood. *Developmental Psychology, 47,* 765–780.

de Haan, A. D., Deković, M., van den Akker, A. L., Stoltz, S. E. M. J., & Prinzie, P. (2013). Developmental personality types from childhood to adolescence: Associations with parenting and adjustment. *Child Development, 84,* 2015–2030.

De Laet, S., Doumen, S., Vervoort, E., Colpin, H., Van Leeuwen, K., Goossens, L., et al. (2014). Transactional links between teacher–child relationship quality and perceived versus sociometric popularity: A three-wave longitudinal study. *Child Development, 85,* 1647–1662.

DeLoache, J. S., Chiong, C., Sherman, K., Islam, N., Vanderborght, M., Troseth, G. L., et al. (2010). Do babies learn from baby media? *Psychological Science, 21,* 1570–1574.

Delpit, L. D. (1988). The silenced dialogue: Power and pedagogy in educating other people's children. *Harvard Educational Review, 58,* 280–298.

DelPriore, D. J., & Hill, S. E. (2013). The effects of paternal disengagement on women's sexual decision making: An experimental approach. *Journal of Personality and Social Psychology, 105,* 234–246.

Demers, L. B., Hanson, K. G., Kirkorian, H. L., Pempek, T. A., & Anderson, D. R. (2013). Infant gaze following during parent–infant coviewing of baby videos. *Child Development, 84,* 591–603.

Dempster, F. N. (1981). Memory span: Sources of individual and developmental differences. *Psychological Bulletin, 89,* 63–100.

DeMulder, E., Denham, S., Schmidt, M., & Mitchell, J. (2000). Q-sort assessment of attachment security during the preschool years: Links from home to school. *Developmental Psychology, 36,* 274–282.

Denham, S. A., Blair, K., DeMulder, E., Levitas, J., Sawyer, K., Auerbach-Major, S., et al. (2003). Preschool emotional competence: Pathway to social competence? *Child Development, 74,* 238–256.

Denham, S. A., Mason, & Couchoud. (1995). Scaffolding young children's prosocial responsiveness: Preschooler's responses to adult sadness, anger, and pain. *International Journal of Behavioral Development, 18,* 489–504.

Denham, S. A., McKinley, M., Couchoud, E. A., & Holt, R. (1990). Emotional and behavioral predictors of preschool peer ratings. *Child Development, 61,* 1145–1152.

Denham, S. A., Mitchell-Copeland, J., Strandberg, K., Auerbach, S., & Blair, K. (1997). Parental contributions to preschoolers' emotional competence: Direct and indirect effects. *Motivation and Emotion, 21,* 65–86.

Denham, S. A., Zoller, D., & Couchoud, E. A. (1994). Socialization of preschoolers' emotion understanding. *Developmental Psychology, 30,* 928–936.

Denissen, J. J. A., Zarrett, N. R., & Eccles, J. S. (2007). I like to do it, I'm able, and I know I am: Longitudinal couplings between domain-specific achievement, self-concept, and interest. *Child Development, 78,* 430–447.

Dennis, T., & Kelemen, D. (2009). Preschool children's views on emotion regulation: Functional associations and implications for social-emotional adjustment. *International Journal of Behavioral Development, 33,* 243–252.

Der, G., Batty, G. D., & Deary, I. J. (2009). The association between IQ in adolescence and a range of health outcomes at 40 in the 1979 US National Longitudinal Study of Youth. *Intelligence, 37,* 573–580.

DeRosier, M., & Thomas, J. (2003). Strengthening sociometric prediction: Scientific advances in the assessment of children's peer relations. *Child Development, 75,* 1379–1392.

De Rosnay, M., & Harris, P. (2002). Individual differences in children's understanding of emotion: The roles of attachment and language. *Attachment & Human Development, 4,* 39–54.

de Schipper, E. J., Riksen-Walraven, M., & Geurts, S. A. E. (2006). Effects of child-caregiver ratio on the interactions between caregivers and children in child-care centers: An experimental study. *Child Development, 77,* 861–874.

Desmond, M., & Turley, R. N. L. (2009). The role of familism in explaining the Hispanic-White college application gap. *Social Problems, 56,* 311–334.

Desrochers, S. (2008). From Piaget to specific Genevan developmental models. *Child Development Perspectives, 2,* 7–12.

Dettmers, S., Trautwein, U., Lüdtke, O., Kunter, M., & Baumert, J. (2010). Homework works if homework quality is high: Using multilevel modeling to predict the development of achievement in mathematics. *Journal of Educational Psychology, 102,* 467–482.

Devine, R., & Hughes, C. (2014). Relations between false belief understanding and executive function in early childhood: A meta-analysis. *Child Development, 85,* 1777–1794.

DeVries, R., Hildebrandt, C., & Betty, Z. (2000). Constructivist early education for moral development. *Early Education and Development, 11,* 9–35.

DHHS (2008). *Physical activity guidelines for Americans.* Washington, DC: Department of Health and Human Services.

DHHS (2015). U.S. Department of Health and Human Services and U.S. Department of Agriculture. *2015-2020 Dietary guidelines for Americans* (8th ed.). Retrieved from http://health.gov/dietaryguidelines/2015/guidelines

Diamond, A. (2013). Executive functions. *Annual Review of Psychology, 64,* 135–168.

Diamond, A., Barnett, W. S., Thomas, J., & Munro, S. (2007). Preschool program improves cognitive control. *Science, 318,* 1387–1388.

Diamond, A., & Lee, K. (2011). Interventions shown to aid executive function development in children 4 to 12 years old. *Science, 333,* 959–964.

Diamond, L. (2007). A dynamical systems approach to the development and expression of female same-sex sexuality. *Perspectives on Psychological Science, 2,* 142–161.

DiCerbo, P., Anstrom, K., Baker, L., & Rivera, C. (2014). A review of the literature on teaching academic English to English language learners. *Review of Educational Research, 20,* 1–37.

Dich, N., Doan, S. N., & Evans, G. W. (2015). Children's emotionality moderates the association between maternal responsiveness and allostatic load: Investigation into differential susceptibility. *Child Development, 86,* 936–944.

Dick, D. (2011). Gene-environment interaction in psychological traits and disorders. *Annual Review of Clinical Psychology, 7,* 383–409.

Dick, D., & Rose, R. (2002). Behavior genetics: What's new? What's next? *Current Directions in Psychological Science, 11,* 70–74.

Dickens, W. T., & Flynn, J. R. (2006). Black Americans reduce the racial IQ gap. *Psychological Science, 17,* 913–920.

Dickinson, D. K. (2011). Teachers' language practices and academic outcomes of preschool children. *Science, 333*(6045), 964–967.

Dickinson, D. K., McCabe, A., Anastasopoulos, L., Peisner-Feinberg, E. S., & Poe, M. D. (2003). The comprehensive language approach to early literacy: The interrelationships among vocabulary, phonological sensitivity, and print knowledge among preschool-aged children. *Journal of Educational Psychology, 95,* 465–481.

DiClemente, R., & Crosby, R. (2003). Sexually transmitted diseases among adolescents: Risk factors, antecedents, and prevention strategies. In G. Adams & M. Berzonsky (Eds.), *Blackwell handbook of adolescence* (pp. 573–605). Malden, MA: Blackwell.

Diener, M. L., Isabella, R. A., Behunin, M., & Wong, M. S. (2007). Attachment to mothers and fathers during middle childhood: Association with child gender, grade, and competence. *Social Development, 17,* 84–101.

DiFiori, J. P., Benjamin, H. J., Brenner, J. S., Gregory, A., Jayanthi, N., Landry, G. L., & Luke, A. (2014). Overuse injuries and burnout in youth sports: A position statement from the American Medical Society for Sports Medicine. *British Journal of Sports Medicine, 48,* 287–288.

Dijkstra, J., Cillessen, A., & Borch, C. (2013). Popularity and adolescent friendship networks: Selection and influence dynamics. *Developmental Psychology, 49,* 1242–1252.

DiLalla, L. F. (2000). Behavior genetics of aggression in children: Review and future directions. *Developmental Review, 22,* 593–622.

Dilworth-Bart, J. E., & Moore, C. F. (2006). Mercy mercy me: Social injustice and the prevention of environmental pollutant exposure among ethnic minority and poor children. *Child Development, 77,* 247–265.

Dimant, R. J., & Bearison, D. J. (1991). Development of formal reasoning during successive peer interactions. *Developmental Psychology, 27,* 277–284.

Ding, X. P., Wellman, H. M., Wang, Y., Fu, G., & Lee, K. (2015). Theory-of-mind training causes honest young children to lie. *Psychological Science, 26,* 1812–1821.

Dinh, J. E., & Lord, R. G. (2013). Current trends in moral research: What we know and where to go from here. *Current Directions in Psychological Science, 22,* 380–385.

Dinkes, R., Kemp, J., & Baum, K. (2009). *Indicators of school crime and safety: 2009.* Washington, DC: Department of Education and U.S. Department of Justice. Retrieved from http://nces.ed.gov/pubs2010/2010012_1.pdf

Dionne, G., Boivin, M., Tremblay, R., Laplante, D., & Perusse, D. (2003). Physical aggression and expressive vocabulary in 19-month-old twins. *Developmental Psychology, 39,* 261–273.

Dirix, C. E. H., Nijhuis, J. G., Jongsma, H. W., & Hornstra, G. (2009). Aspects of fetal learning and memory. *Child Development, 80,* 1251–1258.

Dishion, T. J., Connell, A., Weaver, C., Shaw, D., Gardner, F., & Wilson, M. (2008). The family check-up with high-risk indigent families: Preventing problem behavior by increasing parents' positive behavior support in early childhood. *Child Development, 79,* 1395–1414.

Dishion, T. J., & Kavanagh, K. (2002). The Adolescent Transitions Program: A family-centered prevention strategy for schools. In J. Reid, G. Patterson, & J. Snyder (Eds.), *Antisocial behavior in children and adolescents: A developmental analysis and model for intervention* (pp. 257–272). Washington, DC: APA.

Dishion, T. J., McCord, J., & Poulin, F. (1999). When interventions harm. *American Psychologist, 54,* 755–764.

Dishion, T. J., & Owen, L. (2002). A longitudinal analysis of friendships and substance use: Bidirectional influence from adolescence to adulthood. *Developmental Psychology, 38,* 480–491.

Dix, T., & Meunier, L. N. (2009). Depressive symptoms and parenting competence: An analysis of 13 regulatory processes. *Developmental Review, 29,* 45–68.

Dix, T., Stewart, A. D., Gershoff, E. T., & Day, W. H. (2007). Autonomy and children's reactions to being controlled: Evidence that both compliance and defiance may be positive markers in early development. *Child Development, 78,* 1204–1221.

Dixon, L. Q., Zhao, J., Shin, J.-Y., Wu, S., Su, J.-H., Burgess-Brigham, R., . . . Snow, C. (2012). What we know about second language acquisition: A synthesis from four perspectives. *Review of Educational Research, 82,* 5–60.

Dmitrieva, J., Steinberg, L., & Belsky, J. (2007). Child-care history, classroom composition, and children's functioning in kindergarten. *Psychological Science, 18,* 1032–1039.

Doctoroff, G. L., Greer, J. A., & Arnold, D. H. (2006). The relationship between social behavior and emergent literacy among preschool boys and girls. *Journal of Applied Developmental Psychology, 27,* 1–13.

Dodge, K. A. (2008). Framing public policy and prevention of chronic violence in American youths. *American Psychologist, 63,* 573–590.

Dodge, K. A. (2009). Mechanisms of gene-environment interaction effects in the development of conduct disorder. *Perspectives on Psychological Science, 4,* 408–414.

Dodge, K. A., Coie, J. D., Pettit, G., & Price, J. (1990). Peer status and aggression in boys' groups: Developmental and contextual analysis. *Child Development, 61,* 1289–1309.

Dodge, K. A., Dishion, T. J., & Lansford, J. E. (2006). Deviant peer influences in intervention and public policy for youth. *Social Policy Report, 20,* 3–20.

Dodge, K. A., Godwin, J., & Conduct Problems Prevention Research Group. (2013). Social-information-processing patterns mediate the impact of preventive intervention on adolescent antisocial behavior. *Psychological Science, 24,* 456–465.

Dodge, K. A., Greenberg, M. T., Malone, P. S., & Conduct Problems Prevention Research Group. (2008). Testing an idealized dynamic cascade model of the development of serious violence in adolescence. *Child Development, 79*, 1907–1927.

Dodge, K. A., Lansford, J., Burks, V., Bates, J. E., Pettit, G. S., Fontaine, R., et al. (2003). Peer rejection and social information-processing factors in the development of aggressive behavior problems in children. *Child Development, 74*, 374–393.

Dodge, K. A., Malone, P. S., Lansford, J. E., Miller, S., Pettit, G. S., & Bates, J. E. (2009). A dynamic cascade model of the development of substance-use onset. *Monographs of the Society for Research in Child Development, 74* (Serial No. 294).

Dodge, K. A., Pettit, G. S., Bates, J. E., & Valente, E. (1995). Social-information-processing patterns partially mediate the effect of early physical abuse on later conduct problems. *Journal of Abnormal Psychology, 104*, 632–643.

Dolezal, S. E., Welsh, L. M., Pressley, M., & Vincent, M. M. (2003). How nine third-grade teachers motivate student academic engagement. *Elementary School Journal, 103*, 239–267.

Donaldson, M. (1978). *Children's minds.* New York: Norton.

Dong, M., Anda, R. F., Dube, S. R., Giles, W. H., & Felitti, V. J. (2003). The relationship of exposure to childhood sexual abuse to others forms of abuse, neglect, and household dysfunction during childhood. *Child Abuse & Neglect, 27*, 625–639.

Donnellan, B., Kenny, D. A., Trzesniewski, K. H., Lucas, R. E., & Conger, R. D. (2012). Using trait–state models to evaluate the longitudinal consistency of global self-esteem from adolescence to adulthood. *Journal of Research in Personality, 46*, 634–645.

Donnellan, B., Trzeniewski, K., Robins, R., Moffitt, T., & Caspi, A. (2005). Low self-esteem is related to aggression, antisocial behavior, and delinquency. *Psychological Science, 16*, 328–335.

Doucet, F. (2011). Parent involvement as ritualized practice. *Anthropology & Education Quarterly, 42*, 404–421.

Douglas, E. M. (2006). Familial violence socialization in childhood and later life approval of corporal punishment: A cross-cultural perspective. *American Journal of Orthopsychiatry, 76*, 23–30.

Dougherty, L. R., Leppert, K. A., Merwin, S. M., Smith, V. C., Bufferd, S. J., & Kushner, M. R. (2015). Advances and directions in preschool mental health research. *Child Development Perspectives, 9*, 14–19.

Dowling, J. (2013). School-age children talking about humor: Data from focus groups. *Humor, 27*, 121–139.

Downing, P. (2000). Interactions between visual working memory and selective attention. *Psychological Science, 11*, 467–473.

Doyle, A., Lawford, H., & Markiewicz, D. (2009). Attachment style with mother, father, best friend, and romantic partner during adolescence. *Journal of Research on Adolescence, 19*, 690–714.

Doyle, J. M., & Kao, G. (2007). Are racial identities of multiracials stable? Changing self-identification among single and multiple race individuals. *Social Psychology Quarterly, 70*, 405–423.

Drover, J., Hoffman, D. R., Castañeda, Y. S., Morale, S. E., & Birch, E. E. (2009). Three randomized controlled trials of early long-chain polyunsaturated fatty acid supplementation on means-end problem solving in 9-month-olds. *Child Development, 80*, 1376–1384.

Duchesne, S., Larose, S., Vitaro, F., & Tremblay, R. E. (2010). Trajectories of anxiety in a population sample of children: Clarifying the role of children's behavioral characteristics and maternal parenting. *Development and Psychopathology, 22*, 361–373.

Duckworth, A., & Seligman, M. (2005). Self-discipline outdoes IQ in predicting academic performance of adolescents. *Psychological Science, 16*, 939–944.

Duckworth, A. L., & Seligman, M. (2006). Self-discipline gives girls the edge: Gender in self-discipline, grades, and achievement test scores. *Journal of Educational Psychology, 98*, 198–208.

Duckworth, A. L., Gendler, T. S., & Gross, J. J. (2014). Self-control in school-age children. *Educational Psychologist, 49*, 199–217.

Duckworth, A. L., Gendler, T. S., & Gross, J. J. (2016). Situational strategies for self-control. *Perspectives on Psychological Science, 11*, 35–55.

Duke, N. K., Purcell-Gates, V., Hall, L. A., & Tower, C. (2006). Authentic literacy activities for developing comprehension and writing. *The Reading Teacher, 60*, 344–355.

Duncan, G., & Brooks-Gunn, J. (2000). Family poverty, welfare reform, and child development. *Child Development, 71*, 188–196.

Duncan, G., Dowsett, C. J., Claessens, A., Magnuson, K., Huston, A. C., Klebanov, P., et al. (2007). School readiness and later achievement. *Developmental Psychology, 43*, 1428–1446.

Duncan, G. J., Morris, P. A., & Rodrigues, C. (2011). Does money really matter? Estimating impacts of family income on young children's achievement with data from random-assignment experiments. *Developmental Psychology, 47*, 1263–1279.

Dunfield, K., & Kuhlmeier, V. (2013). Classifying prosocial behavior: Children's responses to instrumental need, emotional distress, and material desire. *Child Development, 84*, 1766–1776.

Dunfield, K. A., & Kuhlmeier, V. A. (2010). Intention-mediated selective helping in infancy. *Psychological Science, 21*, 523–527.

Dunifon, R., Kalil, A., & Bajracharya, A. (2005). Maternal working conditions and child well-being in welfare-leaving families. *Developmental Psychology, 41*, 851–859.

Dunlosky, J., & Lipko, A. R. (2007). Metacomprehension: A brief history and how to improve its accuracy. *Current Directions in Psychological Science, 16*, 228–232.

Dunlosky, J., Rawson, K. A., Marsh, E. J., Nathan, M. J., & Willingham, D. T. (2013). Improving students' learning with effective learning techniques: Promising directions from cognitive and educational psychology. *Psychological Science in the Public Interest, 14*, 4–58.

Dunn, E. C., Milliren, C. E., Evans, C. R., Subramanian, S. V., & Richmond, T. K. (2015). Disentangling the relative influence of schools and neighborhoods on adolescents' risk for depressive symptoms. *American Journal of Public Health, 105*, 732–740.

Dunn, J., & Hughes, C. (2001). "I got some swords and you're dead!": Violent fantasy, antisocial behavior, friendship, and moral sensibility in young children. *Child Development, 72*, 491–505.

Dunn, J., Brown, J., & Beardsall, L. (1991). Family talk about feeling states and children's later understanding of others' emotions. *Developmental Psychology, 27*, 448–455.

Dunn, J., Deater-Deckard, K., Pickering, K., O'Connor, T., Golding, J., & ALSPAC Study Team. (1998). Children's adjustment and prosocial behavior in step-, single-parent, and non-stepfamily settings: Findings from a community study. *Journal of Child Psychology & Psychiatry & Allied Disciplines, 39*, 1083–1095.

Dupere, V., Lacourse, E., Willms, J. D., Leventhal, T., & Tremblay, R. E. (2008). Neighborhood poverty and early transition to sexual activity in young adolescents: A developmental ecological approach. *Child Development, 79*, 1463–1476.

Durbin, D. L., Darling, N., Steinberg, L., & Brown, B. B. (1993). Parenting style and peer group membership among European-American adolescents. *Journal of Research on Adolescence, 3*, 87–100.

Durlak, J. A., Weissberg, R. P., Dymnicki, A. B., Taylor, R. D., & Schellinger, K. B. (2011). The impact of enhancing students' social and emotional learning: A meta-analysis of school-based universal interventions. *Child Development, 82*, 405–432.

Dutro, E. (2002). "But that's a girls' book!" Exploring gender boundaries in children's reading practices. *The Reading Teacher, 55*, 376–384.

Dweck, C. S. (2006). *Mindset: The new psychology of success.* New York: Random House.

Dweck, C. S. (2010). Even geniuses work hard. *Educational Leadership, 68*, 16–20.

Dye, M. W. G., Green, C. S., & Bavelier, D. (2009). Increasing speed of processing with action video games. *Current Directions in Psychological Science, 18*, 321–326.

Dykas, M. J., & Cassidy, J. (2011). Attachment and the processing of social information across the life span: Theory and evidence. *Psychological Bulletin, 137*, 19–46.

Dykas, M. J., Woodhouse, S. S., Ehrlich, K. B., & Cassidy, J. (2012). Attachment-related differences in perceptions of an initial peer interaction emerge over time: Evidence of reconstructive memory processes in adolescents. *Developmental Psychology, 48*, 1381–1389.

Dynarski, M., Clarke, L., Cobb, B., Finn, J., Rumberger, R., & Smink, J. (2008). Dropout prevention: A practice guide (NCEE 2008-4025). Washington, DC: Department of Education National Center for Education Evaluation and Regional Assistance, Institute of Education Sciences.

Early, D. M., Iruka, I. U., Ritchie, S., Barbarin, O. A., Winn, D.-M. C., Crawford, G. M., . . . Pianta, R. C. (2010). How do pre-kindergarteners spend their time? Gender, ethnicity, and income as predictors of experiences in pre-kindergarten classrooms. *Early Childhood Research Quarterly, 25*, 177-193.

Eaton, W., McKeen, N., & Campbell, D. (2001). The waxing and waning of movement: Implications for psychological development. *Developmental Review, 21*, 205-223.

Eaves, B. S., Jr., Feldman, N. H., Griffiths, T. L., & Shafto, P. (2016). Infant-directed speech is consistent with teaching. *Psychological Review.* April 18, 2016 [Epub ahead of print].

Eberly, M. B., & Montemayor, R. (1998). Doing good deeds: An examination of adolescent prosocial behavior in the context of parent-adolescent relationships. *Journal of Adolescent Research, 13*, 403-432.

Eccles, J. S., Midgley, C., Wigfield, A., Buchanan, C., Reuman, M., Flanagan, C., et al. (1993). Development during adolescence: The impact of stage-environment fit on young adolescents' experiences in schools and in families. *American Psychologist, 48*, 90-101.

Eder, D. (1991). The role of teasing in adolescent peer group culture. *Sociological Studies of Child Development, 4*, 181-197.

Edmonds, M. S., Vaughn, S., Wexler, J., Reutebuch, C., Cable, A., Tackett, K. K., et al. (2009). A synthesis of reading interventions and effects on reading comprehension outcomes for older struggling readers. *Review of Educational Research, 79*, 262-300.

Egan, S. K., & Perry, D. G. (2001). Gender identity: A multidimensional analysis with implications for psychosocial adjustment. *Developmental Psychology, 37*, 451-463.

Egyed, K., Király, I., & Gergely, G. (2013). Communicating shared knowledge in infancy. *Psychological Science, 24*, 1348-1353.

Ehrenberg, R., Brewer, D., Gamoran, A., & Willms, D. (2001). Class size and student achievement. *Psychological Science in the Public Interest, 2*, 1-30.

Eigsti, I.-M., Zayas, V., Mischel, W., Shoda, Y., Ayduk, O., Dadlani, M. B., et al. (2006). Predicting cognitive control from preschool to late adolescence and young adulthood. *Psychological Science, 17*, 478-484.

Eikeseth, S. (2009). Outcome of comprehensive psycho-educational interventions for young children with autism. *Research in Developmental Disabilities, 30*, 158-178.

Eisenberg, A. R. (2002). Maternal teaching talk within families of Mexican descent: Influences of talk and socioeconomic status. *Hispanic Journal of Behavioral Sciences, 24*, 206-224.

Eisenberg, N., Fabes, R. A., Schaller, M., Carlo, G., & Miller, P. A. (1991). The relations of parental characteristics and practices to children's vicarious emotional responding. *Child Development, 62*, 1393-1408.

Eisenberg, N., Fabes, R. A., Shepard, S. A., Murphy, B. C., Guthrie, I. K., Jones, S., et al. (1997). Contemporaneous and longitudinal prediction of children's social functioning from regulation and emotionality. *Child Development, 68*, 642-664.

Eisenberg, N., Fabes, R. A., & Spinrad, T. L. (2006). Prosocial development. In N. Eisenberg (Ed.), *Handbook of child psychology: Social, emotional, and personality development* (6th ed., Vol. 3, pp. 646-718). New York: Wiley.

Eisenberg, N., Hofer, C., Sulik, M. J., & Liew, J. (2014). The development of prosocial moral reasoning and a prosocial orientation in young adulthood: Concurrent and longitudinal correlates. *Developmental Psychology, 50*, 58-70.

Eisenberg, N., Wolchik, S., Goldberg, L., & Engle, I. (1992). Parental values, reinforcement, and young children's prosocial behavior: A longitudinal study. *Journal of Genetic Psychology, 153*, 19-36.

Eisenberg, N., Zhou, Q., & Koller, S. (2001). Brazilian adolescents' prosocial moral judgment and behavior: Relations to sympathy, perspective taking, gender-role orientation, and demographic characteristics. *Child Development, 72*, 518-534.

Eisenberg, N., Zhou, Q., Losoya, S. H., Fabes, R. A., Shepard, S. A., Murphy, B. C., et al. (2003). The relations of parenting, effortful control, and ego control to children's emotional expressivity. *Child Development, 74*, 875-895.

Eisenberger, N. I. (2012). Broken hearts and broken bones: A neural perspective on the similarities between social and physical pain. *Current Directions in Psychological Science, 21*, 42-47.

Ekman, P. (1973). *Darwin and facial expression: A century of research in review.* New York: Academic Press.

Ekman, P. (2009). Darwin's contributions to our understanding of emotion and expression. *APS Observer, 22*, 15-17.

Ekman, P. (2016). What scientists who study emotion agree about. *Perspectives on Psychological Science, 11*, 31-34.

Ekman, P., O'Sullivan, M., & Frank, M. (1999). A few can catch a liar. *Psychological Science, 10*, 263-266.

Elias, C., & Berk, L. (2002). Self-regulation in young children: Is there a role for sociodramatic play? *Early Childhood Research Quarterly, 17*, 216-238.

Elicker, J., Fortner-Wood, C., & Noppe, I. (1999). The context of infant attachment in family child care. *Journal of Applied Developmental Psychology, 20*, 219-336.

Ellis, B. J., & Essex, M. J. (2007). Family environments, adrenarche, and sexual maturation: A longitudinal test of a life history model. *Child Development, 78*, 1799-1817.

Ellis, B. J., Volk, A. A., Gonzalez, J.-M., & Embry, D. D. (2015). The meaningful roles intervention: An evolutionary approach to reducing bullying and increasing prosocial behavior. *Journal of Research on Adolescence.* June 30, 2016.

Ellis, W. E., & Zarbatany, L. (2007). Peer group status as a moderator of group influence on children's deviant, aggressive, and prosocial behavior. *Child Development, 78*, 1240-1254.

El Nokali, N. E., Bachman, H. J., & Votruba-Drzal, E. (2010). Parent involvement and children's academic and social development in elementary school. *Child Development, 81*, 988-1005.

El-Sheikh, M., Bub, K. L., Kelly, R. J., & Buckhalt, J. A. (2013). Children's sleep and adjustment: A residualized change analysis. *Developmental Psychology, 49*, 1591-1601.

El-Sheikh, M., Kouros, C., Erath, S. A., Cummings, E. M., Keller, P., & Staton, L. (2009). Marital conflict and children's externalizing behavior: Interactions between parasympathetic and sympathetic nervous system activity. *Monographs of the Society for Research in Child Development, 74* (1, Serial No 292).

Emde, R., Biringen, Z., Clyman, R., & Oppenheim, D. (1991). The moral self of infancy: Affective core and procedural knowledge. *Developmental Review, 11*, 251-279.

Emery, R. E., Otto, R. K., & O'Donohue, W. T. (2005). A critical assessment of child custody evaluations. *Psychological Science in the Public Interest, 6*, 1-29.

Emmer, E. T., Evertson, C., & Worsham, M. E. (2000). *Classroom management for secondary teachers* (5th ed.). Boston: Allyn and Bacon.

Emmer, E., & Gerwels, M. (2002). Cooperative learning in elementary classrooms: Teaching practices and lesson characteristics. *Elementary School Journal, 103*, 75-91.

Engel, M., Claessens, A., & Finch, M. A. (2013). Teaching students what they already know? The (mis)alignment between mathematics instructional content and student knowledge in kindergarten. *Educational Evaluation and Policy Analysis, 35*, 157-178.

Engelhardt, C. R., Bartholow, B. D., Kerr, G. T., & Bushman, B. (2011). This is your brain on violent video games: Neural desensitization to violence predicts increased aggression following violent video game exposure. *Journal of Experimental Social Psychology, 47*, 1022-1036.

Engelhardt, L. E., Briley, D. A., Mann, F. D., Harden, K. P., & Tucker-Drob, E. M. (2015). Genes unite executive functions in childhood. *Psychological Science, 26*, 1151-1163.

Englund, M., Kuo, S., Puig, J., & Collins, W. (2011). Early roots of adult competence: The significance of close relationships from infancy to early adulthood. *International Journal of Behavioral Development, 35*, 490-496.

Englund, M. M., Luckner, A. E., Whaley, G. J. L., & Egeland, B. (2004). Children's achievement in early elementary school: Longitudinal effects of parental involvement, expectations, and quality of assistance. *Journal of Educational Psychology, 96*, 723-730.

Ennemoser, M., & Schneider, W. (2007). Relations of television viewing and reading: Findings from a 4-year longitudinal study. *Journal of Educational Psychology, 99*, 349-368.

Ennett, S. T., Foshee, V. A., Bauman, K. E., Hussong, A., Cai, L., Luz, H., et al. (2008). The social ecology of adolescent alcohol misuse. *Child Development, 79*, 1777–1791.

Ensor, R., & Hughes, C. (2008). Content or connectedness? Mother-child talk and early social understanding. *Child Development, 79*, 201–216.

Epstein, M., Atkins, M., Cullinan, D., Kutash, K., & Weaver, R. (2008). *Reducing behavior problems in the elementary school classroom*. Washington, DC: National Center for Education Evaluation and Regional Assistance, Department of Education.

Erath, S. A., El-Sheikh, M., & Cummings, E. M. (2009). Harsh parenting and child externalizing behavior: Skin conductance level reactivity as a moderator. *Child Development, 80*, 578–592.

Eren, O., & Henderson, D. J. (2011). Are we wasting our children's time by giving them more homework? *Economics of Education Review, 30*, 950–961.

Erel, O., Obermran, Y., & Yirmiya, N. (2000). Maternal versus nonmaternal care and seven domains of children's development. *Psychological Bulletin, 126*, 727–747.

Ericsson, K. A., & Ward, P. (2007). Capturing the naturally occurring superior performance of experts in the laboratory: Toward a science of expert and exceptional performance. *Current Directions in Psychological Science, 16*, 346–350.

Ericsson, K. A., Krampe, R., & Tesch-Römer, C. (1993). The role of deliberate practice in the acquisition of expert performance. *Psychological Review, 100*, 363–406.

Erikson, E. H. (1959). Identity and the life cycle. *Psychological Issues, 1*, 18–171.

Erikson, E. H. (1963). *Childhood and society* (2nd ed.). New York: Norton.

Erkman, F., & Rohner, R. P. (2006). Youths' perceptions of corporal punishment, parental acceptance, and psychological adjustment in a Turkish metropolis. *Cross-Cultural Research, 40*, 250–267.

Eskritt, M., & Lee, K. (2002). "Remember where you last saw that card": Children's production of external symbols as a memory aid. *Developmental Psychology, 38*, 254–266.

Espelage, D. L., Aragon, S., Birkett, M., & Koenig, B. (2008). Homophobic teasing, psychological outcomes, and sexual orientation among high school students: What influence do parents and schools have? *School Psychology Review, 37*, 202–216.

Espelage, D. L., Green, H., & Polanin, J. (2012). Willingness to intervene in bullying episodes among middle school students: Individual and peer-group influences. *Journal of Early Adolescence, 32*, 776–801.

Espelage, D. L., Holt, M., & Henkel, R. (2003). Examination of peer-group contextual effects on aggression during early adolescence. *Child Development, 74*, 205–220.

Esposito, G., Yoshida, S., Ohnishi, R., Tsuneoka, Y., Rostagno, M. d. C., Yokota, S., . . . Kuroda, K. O. (2013). Infant calming responses during maternal carrying in humans and mice. *Current Biology, 23*, 739–745.

Esqueda, M., Astor, R., & De Pedro, K. (2012). A call to duty: Educational policy and school reform addressing the needs of children from military families. *Educational Researcher, 41*, 65–70.

Estell, D., Farmer, T., Cairns, R., & Cairns, B. (2002). Social relations and academic achievement in inner-city early elementary classrooms. *International Journal of Behavioral Development, 26*, 518–528.

Estes, K. G., Evans, J. L., Alibali, M. W., & Saffran, J. R. (2007). Can infants map meaning to newly segmented words? Statistical segmentation and word learning. *Psychological Science, 18*, 254–260.

Ettekal, I., & Ladd, G. W. (2015). Developmental pathways from childhood aggression–disruptiveness, chronic peer rejection, and deviant friendships to early-adolescent rule breaking. *Child Development, 86*, 614–631.

Evans, A. D., & Lee, K. (2011). Verbal deception from late childhood to middle adolescence and its relation to executive functioning skills. *Developmental Psychology, 47*, 1108–1116.

Evans, A. D., & Lee, K. (2013). Emergence of lying in very young children. *Developmental Psychology, 49, 1958–1963*.

Evans, G. W. (2004). The environment of childhood poverty. *American Psychologist, 59*, 77–92.

Evans, G. W., Gonnella, C., Marcynyszyn, L., Gentile, L., & Salpekar, N. (2005). The role of chaos in poverty and children's socioemotional adjustment. *Psychological Science, 16*, 560–565.

Evans, G. W., & Rosenbaum, J. (2008). Self-regulation and the income-achievement gap. *Early Childhood Research Quarterly, 23*, 504–514.

Evans, G. W., Li, D., & Whipple, S. S. (2013). Cumulative risk and child development. *Psychological Bulletin, 139*, 1342–1396.

Fabes, R. A., Eisenberg, N., Hanish, L., & Spinrad, T. L. (2001). Preschoolers' spontaneous emotion vocabulary: Relations to likability. *Early Education and Development, 12*, 11–27.

Fabes, R. A., Eisenberg, N., Jones, S., Smith, M., Guthrie, I., Poulin, R., et al. (1999). Regulation, emotionality, and preschoolers' socially competent peer interactions. *Child Development, 70*, 432–442.

Fabrizi, M., & Pollio, H. (1987). A naturalistic study of humorous activity in a third, seventh, and eleventh grade classroom. *Merrill-Palmer Quarterly, 33*, 107–128.

Fagan, J. F., & Holland, C. R. (2007). Racial equality in intelligence: Predictions from a theory of intelligence as processing. *Intelligence, 35*, 319–334.

Fagan, J. F., Holland, C. R., & Wheeler, K. (2007). The prediction, from infancy, of adult IQ and achievement. *Intelligence, 35*, 225–231.

Faigenbaum, A. D., Best, T. M., MacDonald, J., Myer, G. D., & Stracciolini, A. (2014). Top 10 research questions related to exercise deficit disorder (EDD) in youth. *Research Quarterly for Exercise and Sport, 85*, 297–307.

Fan, S. P., Liberman, Z., Keysar, B., & Kinzler, K. D. (2015). The exposure advantage: Early exposure to a multilingual environment promotes effective communication. *Psychological Science, 26*, 1090–1097.

Fantuzzo, J., Sekino, Y., & Cohen, H. (2004). An examination of the contributions of interactive peer play to salient classroom competencies for urban Head Start children. *Psychology in the Schools, 41*, 323–336.

Fantuzzo, J. W., LeBoeuf, W. A., & Rouse, H. L. (2014). An investigation of the relations between school concentrations of student risk factors and student educational well-being. *Educational Researcher, 43*, 25–36.

Farber, H., Groner, J., Walley, S., Nelson, K., & Section on Tobacco Control. (2015). Protecting children from tobacco, nicotine, and tobacco smoke. *Pediatrics, 136*, e1439–e1467.

Farmer, T., Estell, D., Bishop, J., O'Neal, K., & Cairns, B. (2003). Rejected bullies or popular leaders? The social relations of aggressive subtypes of rural African American early adolescents. *Developmental Psychology, 39*, 992–1004.

Farmer, T. W., Hall, C. M., Leung, M.-C., Estell, D. B., & Brooks, D. (2011). Social prominence and the heterogeneity of rejected status in late elementary school. *School Psychology Review, 26*, 260–274.

Farmer, T. W., Petrin, R. A., Robertson, D. L., Fraser, M. W., Hall, C. M., Day, S. H., et al. (2010). Peer relations of bullies, bully-victims, and victims: The two social worlds of bullying in second-grade classrooms. *Elementary School Journal, 110*, 364–392.

Farrell, A., Meyer, A., & White, K. (2001). Evaluation of Responding in Peaceful and Positive Ways (RIPP): A school-based prevention program for reducing violence among urban adolescents. *Journal of Clinical Child Psychology, 30*, 451–463.

Farrington, D. P. (2009). Conduct disorder, aggression, and delinquency. In R. M. Lerner & L. Steinberg (Eds.), *Handbook of adolescent psychology* (pp. 683–722). Hoboken, NJ: Wiley.

Farver, J. A. M., Lonigan, C., & Eppe, S. (2009). Effective early literacy skill development for young Spanish-speaking English language learners: An experimental study of two methods. *Child Development, 80*, 703–719.

Fauth, R. C., Roth, J., & Brooks-Gunn, J. (2007). Does neighborhood context alter the link between youth's after-school time activities and developmental outcomes? A multilevel analysis. *Developmental Psychology, 43*, 760–777.

Fay-Stammbach, T., Hawes, D. J., & Meredith, P. (2014). Parenting influences on executive function in early childhood: A review. *Child Development Perspectives, 8*, 258–264.

Fearon, R. P., Bakermans-Kranenburg, M. J., Van IJzendoorn, M. H., Lapsley, A.-M., & Roisman, G. I. (2010). The significance of insecure attachment and disorganization in the development of children's externalizing behavior: A meta-analytic study. *Child Development, 81*, 435–456.

Federal Interagency Forum on Child and Family Statistics. (2002). *America's children: Key national indicators of well-being, 2002.* Washington, DC: Government Printing Office.

Federal Interagency Forum on Child and Family Statistics. (2008). *America's children: Key national indicators of well-being.* Washington, DC: Government Printing Office.

Feigenson, L., Libertus, M. E., & Halberda, J. (2013). Links between the intuitive sense of number and formal mathematics ability. *Child Development Perspectives, 7,* 74–79.

Feldman, R., & Klein, P. (2003). Toddlers' self-regulated compliance to mothers, caregivers, and fathers: Implications for theories of socialization. *Developmental Psychology, 39,* 680–692.

Felner, R. D., Seitsinger, A. M., Brand, S., Burns, A., & Bolton, N. (2007). Creating small learning communities: Lessons from the Project on High-Performing Learning Communities about "what works" in creating productive, developmentally enhancing, learning contexts. *Educational Psychologist, 42,* 209–221.

Fenesi, B., Sana, F., Kim, J., & Shore, D. (2015). Reconceptualizing working memory in educational research. *Educational Psychology Review, 27,* 333–351.

Feng, J., Spence, I., & Pratt, J. (2007). Playing an action video game reduces gender differences in spatial cognition. *Psychological Science, 18,* 850–855.

Feng, X., Keenan, K., Hipwell, A. E., Henneberger, A. K., Rischall, M. S., Butch, J., et al. (2009). Longitudinal associations between emotion regulation and depression in preadolescent girls: Moderation by the caregiving environment. *Developmental Psychology, 45,* 798–808.

Ferguson, C. J., & Kilburn, J. (2010). Much ado about nothing: The misestimation and overinterpretation of violent video game effects in Eastern and Western nations: Comment on Anderson et al. (2010). *Psychological Bulletin, 136,* 174–178.

Ferrando, P. J., Varea, M. D., & Lorenzo, U. (1998). A psychometric study of the Test Anxiety Scale for Children in a Spanish sample. *Personality and Individual Differences, 27,* 37–44.

Ferrer, E., Shaywitz, B. A., Holahan, J. M., Marchione, K., & Shaywitz, S. E. (2010). Uncoupling of reading and IQ over time: Empirical evidence for a definition of dyslexia. *Psychological Science, 21,* 93–101.

Ferry, A. L., Hespos, S. J., & Gentner, D. (2015). Prelinguistic relational concepts: Investigating analogical processing in infants. *Child Development, 86,* 1386–1405.

Field, A., Sonneville, K., Crosby, R., Swanson, S., Eddy, K., Camargo, C., . . . Micali, N. (2014). Prospective associations of concerns about physique and the development of obesity, binge drinking, and drug use among adolescent boys and young adult men. *JAMA Pediatrics, 168,* 34–39.

Field, T. M. (1998). Early interventions for infants of depressed mothers. *Pediatrics, 102,* 1305–1310.

Field, T. M., Hernandez-Reif, M., & Freedman, J. (2004). Stimulation programs for preterm infants. *Social Policy Report, 18,* 3–19.

Field, T. M., Hossain, Z., & Malphurs, J. (1999). "Depressed" fathers' interaction with their infants. *Infant Mental Health Journal, 20,* 3322–3332.

FIFCFS. (2009). *America's children in brief: Key national indicators of well-being.* Washington, DC: Government Printing Office.

FIFCS (2015). *America's children: Key national indicators of well-being.* Washington DC: Government Printing Office.

Fine, C. (2010). From scanner to sound bite: Issues in interpreting and reporting sex differences in the brain. *Current Directions in Psychological Science, 19,* 280–283.

Finkenauer, C., Buyukcan-Tetik, A., Baumeister, R. F., Schoemaker, K., Bartels, M., & Vohs, K. D. (2015). Out of control: Identifying the role of self-control strength in family violence. *Current Directions in Psychological Science, 24,* 261–266.

Finn, A. S., Kraft, M. A., West, M. R., Leonard, J. A., Bish, C. E., Martin, R. E., . . . Gabrieli, J. D. E. (2014). Cognitive skills, student achievement tests, and schools. *Psychological Science, 25,* 736–744.

Finn, J. D., Gerber, S. B., Achilles, C. M., & Boyd-Zaharias, J. (2001). The enduring effects of small classes. *Teachers College Record, 103,* 145–183.

Fischer, R., & Schwartz, S. (2011). Whence differences in value priorities? *Journal of Cross-Cultural Psychology, 42,* 1127–1144.

Fisher, A., Kramer, R., Hoven, C., King, R., Bird, H., Davies, M., et al. (2000). Risk behavior in a community sample of children and adolescents. *Journal of the American Academy of Child and Adolescent Behavior, 39,* 881–887.

Fisher, A. V. (2015). Development of inductive generalization. *Child Development Perspectives, 9,* 172–177.

Fisher, A. V., Godwin, K. E., & Seltman, H. (2014). Visual environment, attention allocation, and learning in young children: When too much of a good thing may be bad. *Psychological Science, 25,* 1362–1370.

Fisher, K. R., Hirsh-Pasek, K., Newcombe, N., & Golinkoff, R. M. (2013). Taking shape: Supporting preschoolers' acquisition of geometric knowledge through guided play. *Child Development, 84,* 1872–1878.

Fiske, S. T. (2002). What we know now about bias and intergroup conflict, the problem of the century. *Current Directions in Psychological Science, 11,* 123–128.

Fitzgerald, J. (2006). Multilingual writing in preschool through 12th grade: The last 15 years. In C. A. MacArthur, S. Graham, & J. Fitzgerald (Eds.), *Handbook of writing research* (pp. 337–354). New York: Guilford.

Fitzsimmons, P., & McKenzie, B. (2003). Play on words: Humor as the means of developing authentic learning. In D. Lytle (Ed.), *Play and educational theory and practice* (Vol. 5, pp. 197–211). Westport, CT: Praeger.

Flanagan, K. D., McPhee, C., & Mulligan, G. (2010). *The children born in 2001 at kindergarten entry* (NCES 2010–005). Washington, DC: National Center for Education Statistics, Department of Education.

Flashman, J. (2012). Academic achievement and its impact on friend dynamics. *Sociology of Education, 85,* 61–80.

Flavell, J. H. (1999). Cognitive development: Children's knowledge about the mind. *Annual Review of Psychology, 50,* 21–45.

Fletcher, A. C., Darling, N. E., Steinberg, L., & Dornbusch, S. M. (1995). The company they keep: Relations of adolescents' adjustment and behavior to their friends' perceptions of authoritative parenting in the social network. *Developmental Psychology, 31,* 300–310.

Fletcher, A. C., Walls, J. K., Cook, E. C., Madison, K. J., & Bridges, T. H. (2008). Parenting style as a moderator of associations between maternal disciplinary strategies and child well-being. *Journal of Family Issues, 29,* 1724–1744.

Fletcher, J. M., & Vaughn, S. (2009). Response to intervention: Preventing and remediating academic difficulties. *Child Development Perspectives, 3,* 30–37.

Fletcher, K., & Reese, E. (2005). Picture book reading with young children: A conceptual framework. *Developmental Review, 25,* 64–103.

Flook, L. (2011). Gender differences in adolescents' daily interpersonal events and well-being. *Child Development, 82,* 454–461.

Flook, L., & Fuligni, A. J. (2008). Family and school spillover in adolescents' daily lives. *Child Development, 79,* 776–787.

Flook, L., Repetti, R., & Ullman, J. (2005). Classroom social experiences as predictors of academic performance. *Developmental Psychology, 41,* 319–327.

Florini, S. (2014). Tweets, tweeps, and signifyin': Communication and cultural performance on "Black Twitter." *Television & New Media, 15,* 223–237.

Flynn, J. R. (2007). *What is intelligence? Beyond the Flynn effect.* New York: Cambridge University Press.

Foersterling, F., & Binser, M. (2002). Depression, school performance and the veridicality of perceived grades and causal attributions. *Personality and Social Psychology Bulletin, 28,* 1441–1449.

Font, S. A. (2014). Kinship and nonrelative foster care: The effect of placement type on child well-being. *Child Development, 85,* 2074–2090.

Ford, K. R., Hurd, N. M., Jagers, R. J., & Sellers, R. M. (2013). Caregiver experiences of discrimination and African American adolescents' psychological health over time. *Child Development, 84,* 485–499.

Fordham, S. (1996). *Blacked out: Dilemmas of race, identity, and success at Capital High.* Chicago, IL: University of Chicago.

Forgas, J. P. (2013). Don't worry, be sad! On the cognitive, motivational, and interpersonal benefits of negative mood. *Current Directions in Psychological Science, 22,* 225–232.

Forgatch, M., & DeGarmo, D. (2002). Extending and testing the social interaction learning model with divorce samples. In J. Reid, G. Patterson, & J. Snyder (Eds.), *Antisocial behavior in children and adolescents: A developmental analysis and model for intervention* (pp. 235–256). Washington, DC: American Psychological Association.

Forgays, D., & Forgays, J. (1952). The nature of the effect of free-environmental experience in the rat. *Journal of Comparative and Physiological Psychology, 45,* 322–328.

Forget-Dubois, N., Dionne, G., Lemelin, J.-P., Perusse, D., Tremblay, R. E., & Boivin, M. (2009). Early child language mediates the relation between home environment and school readiness. *Child Development, 80,* 736–749.

Forster, S., & Lavie, N. (2016). Establishing the attention-distractibility trait. *Psychological Science, 27,* 203–212.

Forsyth, B. (2003). Psychological aspects of HIV infection in children. *Child and Adolescent Psychiatric Clinics, 12,* 423–437.

Foshee, V. A., Benefield, T., Suchindran, C., Ennett, S., Bauman, K. E., Karriker-Jaffe, K. J., et al. (2009). The development of four types of adolescent dating abuse and selected demographic correlates. *Journal of Research on Adolescence, 19,* 380–400.

Foster, E. M., & Watkins, S. (2010). The value of reanalysis: TV viewing and attention problems. *Child Development, 81,* 368–375.

Fox, E. (2009). The role of reader characteristics in processing and learning from informational text. *Review of Educational Research, 79,* 197–261.

Fox, S. E., Levitt, P., & Nelson, C. A. (2010). How the timing and quality of early experiences influence the development of brain architecture. *Child Development, 81,* 28–40.

Fraley, C., Roisman, G., & Haltigan, J. (2013). The legacy of early experiences in development: Formalizing alternative models of how early experiences are carried forward over time. *Developmental Psychology, 49,* 109–126.

Fraley, R. C., Roisman, G. I., Booth-LaForce, C., Owen, M. T., & Holland, A. S. (2013). Interpersonal and genetic origins of adult attachment styles: A longitudinal study from infancy to early adulthood. *Journal of Personality and Social Psychology, 104,* 817–838.

Frankenhuis, W. E., & de Weerth, C. (2013). Does early-life exposure to stress shape or impair cognition? *Current Directions in Psychological Science, 22,* 407–412.

Fredricks, J. A., & Simpkins, S. D. (2012). Promoting positive youth development through organized after-school activities: Taking a closer look at participation of ethnic minority youth. *Child Development Perspectives, 6,* 280–287.

Fredriksen, K., Rhodes, J., Reddy, R., & Way, N. (2004). Sleepless in Chicago: Tracking the effects of adolescent sleep loss during the middle school years. *Child Development, 75,* 84–95.

Fredrickson, B. L. (2001). The role of positive emotions in positive psychology: The broaden-and-build theory of positive emotions. *American Psychologist, 56,* 218–226.

Freeman, H., & Brown, B. (2001). Primary attachment to parents and peers during adolescence: Differences by attachment style. *Journal of Youth and Adolescence, 30,* 653–674.

Freeman, S., Eddy, S. L., McDonough, M., Smith, M. K., Okoroafor, N., Jordt, H., & Wenderoth, M. P. (2014). Active learning increases student performance in science, engineering, and mathematics. *Proceedings of the National Academy of Sciences, 111,* 8410–8415.

Freiberg, H. J., Huzinec, C. A., & Templeton, S. M. (2009). Classroom management—A pathway to student achievement: A study of fourteen inner-city elementary schools. *Elementary School Journal, 110,* 63–80.

French, D., & Conrad, J. (2001). School dropout as predicted by peer rejection and antisocial behavior. *Journal of Research on Adolescence, 11,* 225–244.

French, D. C., Chen, X., Chung, J., Li, M., Chen, H., & Li, D. (2011). Four children and one toy: Chinese and Canadian children faced with potential conflict over a limited resource. *Child Development, 82,* 830–841.

Freud, S. (1905/1960). *Jokes and their relation to the unconscious* (J. Strachey, Trans.). New York: Norton.

Freud, S. (1923/1961). The ego and the id (J. Strachey, A. Freud, A. Strachey & A. Tyson, Trans.). In J. Strachey (Ed.), *The standard edition of the complete psychological works of Sigmund Freud* (Vol. XlX). London: Hogarth.

Freud, S. (1933/1964). New introductory lectures on psycho-analysis. In J. Strachey, A. Freud, A. Strachey, & A. Tyson (Eds.), *The standard edition of the complete psychological works of Sigmund Freud* (Vol. XXll). London: Hogarth.

Frey, M., & Detterman, D. (2004). Scholastic assessment or *g*? The relationship between the Scholastic Assessment Test and general cognitive ability. *Psychological Science, 15,* 373–378.

Friedel, J. M., Cortina, K. S., Turner, J. C., & Midgley, C. (2010). Changes in efficacy beliefs in mathematics across the transition to middle school: Examining the effects of perceived teacher and parent goal emphases. *Journal of Educational Psychology, 102,* 102–114.

Friedman, N. P., Miyake, A., Robinson, J. L., & Hewitt, J. K. (2011). Developmental trajectories in toddlers' self-restraint predict individual differences in executive functions 14 years later: A behavioral genetic analysis. *Developmental Psychology, 47,* 1410–1430.

Friedman, S. L., Scholnick, E. K., Bender, R. H., Vandergrift, N., Spieker, S., Hirsh Pasek, K., . . . NICHD Early Child Care Research Network. (2014). Planning in middle childhood: early predictors and later outcomes. *Child Development, 85,* 1446–1460.

Friedman, W. (2007). The development of temporal metamemory. *Child Development, 78,* 1472–1491.

Friedman-Krauss, A. H., & Raver, C. C. (2015). Does school mobility place elementary school children at risk for lower math achievement? The mediating role of cognitive dysregulation. *Developmental Psychology, 51,* 1725–1739.

Friedrich, A., Flunger, B., Nagengast, B., Jonkmann, K., & Trautwein, U. (2015). Pygmalion effects in the classroom: Teacher expectancy effects on students' math achievement. *Contemporary Educational Psychology, 41,* 1–12.

Fu, A. S., & Markus, H. R. (2014). My mother and me: Why tiger mothers motivate Asian Americans but not European Americans. *Personality and Social Psychology Bulletin, 40,* 739–749.

Fuchs, L. S., Fuchs, D., Kazdan, S., Karns, K., Calhoon, M. B., Hamlett, C. L., et al. (2000). Effects of workgroup structure and size on student productivity during collaborative work on complex tasks. *Elementary School Journal, 100,* 183–212.

Fuchs, T., & Wößmann, L. (2007). What accounts for international differences in student performance? A re-examination using PISA data. *Empirical Economics, 32,* 433–464.

Fuhs, M. W., & Day, J. D. (2011). Verbal ability and executive functioning development in preschoolers at Head Start. *Developmental Psychology, 47,* 404–416.

Fujimoto, K., Unger, J. B., & Valente, T. W. (2012). A network method of measuring affiliation-based peer influence: Assessing the influences of teammates' smoking on adolescent smoking. *Child Development, 83,* 442–451.

Fujiwara, T., Barber, C., Schaechter, J., & Hemenway, D. (2009). Characteristics of infant homicides: Findings from a U.S. multisite reporting system. *Pediatrics, 124,* 210–217.

Fukuda, K., & Vogel, E. K. (2011). Individual differences in recovery time from attentional capture. *Psychological Science, 22,* 361–368.

Fuligni, A. J., & Stevenson, H. W. (1995). Time use and mathematics achievement among American, Chinese, and Japanese high school students. *Child Development, 66,* 830–842.

Fuligni, A. J., & Telzer, E. H. (2013). Another way family can get in the head and under the skin: The neurobiology of helping the family. *Child Development Perspectives, 7,* 138–142.

Fuligni, A. J., Witkow, M., & Garcia, C. (2005). Ethnic identity and the academic adjustment of adolescents from Mexican, Chinese, and European backgrounds. *Developmental Psychology, 41,* 799–811.

Furman, E. (1989). Mothers, toddlers, and care. In S. Greenspan & G. Pollock (Eds.), *The course of life* (Vol. 2, pp. 61–82). Madison, CT: International Universities Press.

Furtak, E. M., Seidel, T., Iverson, H., & Briggs, D. C. (2012). Experimental and quasi-experimental studies of inquiry-based science teaching: A meta-analysis. *Review of Educational Research, 82,* 300–329.

Gable, P. A., & Harmon-Jones, E. (2008). Approach-motivated positive affect reduces breadth of attention. *Psychological Science, 19,* 476–482.

Gable, S., Krull, J. L., & Chang, Y. (2009). Implications of overweight onset and persistence for social and behavioral development between kindergarten entry and third grade. *Applied Developmental Science, 13,* 88–103.

Gaensbauer, T. J., Mrazek, D., & Harmon, R. (1981). Emotional expression in abused and/or neglected infants. In N. Frude (Ed.), *Psychological approaches to child abuse* (pp. 120–135). Totowa, NJ: Rowman & Littlefield.

Gailliot, M. T. (2008). Unlocking the energy dynamics of executive functioning: Linking executive functioning to brain glycogen. *Perspectives on Psychological Science, 3*, 245–263.

Gaither, S. E. (2015). "Mixed" results: Multiracial research and identity explorations. *Current Directions in Psychological Science, 24*, 114–119.

Galindo, C., & Fuller, B. (2010). The social competence of Latino kindergartners and growth in mathematical understanding. *Developmental Psychology, 46*, 579–592.

Galloway, M., Conner, J., & Pope, D. (2013). Nonacademic effects of homework in privileged, high-performing high schools. *Journal of Experimental Education, 81*, 490–510.

Galván, A. (2013). The teenage brain: Sensitivity to rewards. *Current Directions in Psychological Science, 22*, 88–93.

Ganiban, J. M., Saudino, K. J., Ulbricht, J., Neiderhiser, J. M., & Reiss, D. (2008). Stability and change in temperament during adolescence. *Journal of Personality and Social Psychology, 95*, 222–236.

Ganley, C. M., Vasilyeva, M., & Dulaney, A. (2014). Spatial ability mediates the gender difference in middle school students' science performance. *Child Development, 85*, 1419–1432.

Garandeau, C. F., Ahn, H.-J., & Rodkin, P. C. (2011). The social status of aggressive students across contexts: The role of classroom status hierarchy, academic achievement, and grade. *Developmental Psychology, 47*, 1699–1710.

García, E., & Jensen, B. (2009). Early educational opportunities for children of Hispanic origins. *Social Policy Report, 23*, 3–19.

Gardner-Neblett, N., Pungello, E. P., & Iruka, I. U. (2012). Oral narrative skills: Implications for the reading development of African American children. *Child Development Perspectives, 6*, 218–224.

Gardner, A. W., Wacker, D. P., & Boelter, E. W. (2009). An evaluation of the interaction between quality of attention and negative reinforcement with children who display escape-maintained problem behavior. *Journal of Applied Behavior Analysis, 42*, 343–348.

Gardner, H. (1999). *Intelligence reframed: Multiple intelligences for the 21st century.* New York: Basic Books.

Gardner, H. (2006). *Multiple intelligences: New horizons.* New York: Basic Books.

Gardner, M., Roth, J., & Brooks-Gunn, J. (2009). Sports participation and juvenile delinquency: The role of the peer context among adolescent boys and girls with varied histories of problem behavior. *Developmental Psychology, 45*, 341–353.

Garrard, W., & Lipsey, M. W. (2007). Conflict resolution education and antisocial behavior in U.S. schools: A meta-analysis. *Conflict Resolution Quarterly, 25*, 9–38.

Garry, M., & Gerrie, M. P. (2005). When photographs create false memories. *Current Directions in Psychological Science, 14*, 321–325.

Gates, H. L., Jr. (1988). *The signifying monkey: A theory of Afro-American literary criticism.* New York: Oxford University Press.

Gauvain, M., & Monroe, R. L. (2009). Contributions of societal modernity to cognitive development: A comparison of four cultures. *Child Development, 80*, 1628–1642.

Gazelle, H. (2006). Class climate moderates peer relations and emotional adjustment in children with an early history of anxious solitude: A child x environment model. *Developmental Psychology, 42*, 1179–1192.

Gazelle, H., & Druhen, M. J. (2009). Anxious solitude and peer exclusion predict social helplessness, upset affect, and vagal regulation in response to behavioral rejection by a friend. *Developmental Psychology, 45*, 1077–1096.

Ge, X., & Natsuaki, M. N. (2009). In search of explanations for early pubertal timing effects on developmental psychopathology. *Current Directions in Psychological Science, 18*, 327–331.

Geary, D. C. (2011). Cognitive predictors of achievement growth in mathematics: A 5-year longitudinal study. *Developmental Psychology, 47*, 1539–1552.

Geary, D., & Bjorklund, D. F. (2000). Evolutionary developmental psychology. *Child Development, 71*, 57–65.

Gee, D. G., Gabard-Durnam, L., Telzer, E. H., Humphreys, K. L., Goff, B., Shapiro, M., . . . Tottenham, N. (2014). Maternal buffering of human amygdala-prefrontal circuitry during childhood but not during adolescence. *Psychological Science, 25*, 2067–2078.

Gehlbach, H., Brinkworth, M. E., King, A. M., Hsu, L. M., McIntyre, J., & Rogers, T. (2016). Creating birds of similar feathers: Leveraging similarity to improve teacher–student relationships and academic achievement. *Journal of Educational Psychology, 108*, 342–352.

Gelman, R. (2006). Young natural-number arithmeticians. *Current Directions in Psychological Science, 15*, 193–197.

Gelman, R., & Baillargeon, R. (1983). A review of some Piagetian concepts. In J. H. Flavell & E. Markman (Eds.), *Handbook of child psychology: Cognitive development* (Vol. 3, pp. 167–230). New York: Wiley.

Gelman, R., & Butterworth, B. (2005). Number and language: How are they related? *Trends in Cognitive Sciences, 9*, 6–10.

Gelman, R., & Williams, E. (1998). Enabling constraints for cognitive development and learning: Domain specificity and epigenesis. In D. Kuhn & R. Siegler (Eds.), *Handbook of child psychology. Cognition, perception, and language* (5th ed., Vol. 2, pp. 575–630). New York: Wiley.

Gentile, B., Grabe, S., Dolan-Pascoe, B., Twenge, J. M., Wells, B. E., & Maitino, A. (2009). Gender differences in domain-specific self-esteem: A meta-analysis. *Review of General Psychology, 13*, 34–45.

Gentile, D. A. (2009). Pathological video-game use among youth ages 8 to 18: A national study. *Psychological Science, 20*, 594–602.

Gentile, D. A., Anderson, C. A., Yukawa, S., Ihori, N., Saleem, M., Ming, L. K., et al. (2009). The effects of prosocial video games on prosocial behaviors: International evidence from correlational, longitudinal, and experimental studies. *Personality and Social Psychology Bulletin, 35*, 752–763.

Gentile, D. A., Lynch, P. J., Linder, J. R., & Walsh, D. (2004). The effects of violent video game habits on adolescent hostility, aggressive behaviors, and school performance. *Journal of Adolescence, 27*, 5–22.

Gentner, D., & Namy, L. L. (2006). Analogical processes in language learning. *Current Directions in Psychological Science, 15*, 297–301.

Gentner, D., Loewenstein, J., & Hung, B. (2007). Comparison facilitates children's learning of names for parts. *Journal of Cognition and Development, 8*, 285–307.

George, M. J., & Odgers, C. L. (2015). Seven fears and the science of how mobile technologies may be influencing adolescents in the digital age. *Perspectives on Psychological Science, 10*, 832–851.

Georgopoulos, N. A., Roupas, N. D., Theodoropoulou, A., Tsekouras, A., Vagenakis, A. G., & Markou, K. B. (2010). The influence of intensive physical training on growth and pubertal development in athletes. *Annals of the New York Academy of Sciences, 1205*, 39–44.

Gerard, J., & Buehler, C. (2004). Cumulative environmental risk and youth maladjustment: The role of youth attributes. *Child Development, 75*, 1832–1849.

Gere, A. R., Buehler, J., Dallavis, C., & Haviland, V. S. (2009). A visibility project: Learning to see how preservice teachers take up culturally responsive pedagogy. *American Educational Research Journal, 46*, 816–852.

Gernsbacher, M. A., Stevenson, J. L., Khandakar, S., & Goldsmith, H. H. (2008). Why does joint attention look atypical in autism? *Child Development Perspectives, 2*, 38–45.

Gershenson, S., & Holt, S. B. (2015). Gender gaps in high school students' homework time. *Educational Researcher, 44*, 432–441.

Gershoff, E. T. (2013). Spanking and child development: We know enough now to stop hitting our children. *Child Development Perspectives, 7*, 133–137.

Gershoff, E. T., Aber, J. L., Raver, C. C., & Lennon, M. C. (2007). Income is not enough: Incorporating material hardship into models of income associations with parenting and child development. *Child Development, 78*, 70–95.

Gersten, R., Rolfhus, E., Clarke, B., Decker, L. E., Wilkins, C., & Dimino, J. (2015). Intervention for first graders with limited number knowledge: Large-scale replication of a randomized controlled trial. *American Educational Research Journal, 52*, 516–546.

Gervain, J., & Mehler, J. (2010). Speech perception and language acquisition in the first year of life. *Annual Review of Psychology, 61*, 191–218.

Gervais, J., Tremblay, R., Desmarais-Gervais, L., & Vitaro, F. (2000). Children's persistent lying, gender differences, and disruptive behaviours: A longitudinal perspective. *International Journal of Behavioral Development, 24*, 213–221.

Gesell, A. (1933). Maturation and the patterning of behavior. In C. Murchison (Ed.), *A handbook of child psychology.* Worcester, MA: Clark University Press.

Gest, S., Domitrovich, C. E., & Welsh, J. A. (2005). Peer academic reputation in elementary school: Associations with changes in self-concept and academic skills. *Journal of Educational Psychology, 97,* 337–346.

Gest, S., Graham-Bermann, S., & Hartup, W. (2001). Peer experience: Common and unique features of number of friendships, social network centrality, and sociometric status. *Social Development, 10,* 23–40.

Getahun, D., Jacobsen, S., Fassett, M., Chen, W., Demissie, K., & Rhoads, G. (2013). Recent trends in childhood attention-deficit/hyperactivity disorder. *JAMA Pediatrics, 167,* 282–288.

Gibbs, W. W. (2002, August). From mouth to mind. *Scientific American, 287,* 26.

Gibson-Davis, C. M., & Gassman-Pines, A. (2010). Early childhood family structure and mother-child interactions: Variation by race and ethnicity. *Developmental Psychology, 46,* 151–164.

Giedd, J. N., LaLonde, F. M., Celano, M. J., White, S. L., Wallace, G. L., Less, N. R., et al. (2009). Anatomical brain magnetic resonance imaging of typically developing children and adolescents. *Journal of the American Academy of Child and Adolescent Psychiatry, 48,* 465–470.

Giles-Sims, J., & Lockhart, C. (2005). Culturally shaped patterns of disciplining children. *Journal of Family Issues, 26,* 196–218.

Giletta, M., Scholte, R. H., Burk, W. J., Engels, R. C., Larsen, J. K., Prinstein, M. J., et al. (2011). Similarity in depressive symptoms in adolescents' friendship dyads: Selection or socialization? *Developmental Psychology, 47,* 1804–1814.

Gilga, T., Jones, E., Bedford, R., Charman, T., & Johnson, M. (2014). From early markers to neuro-developmental mechanisms of autism. *Developmental Review, 34,* 189–207.

Gillen-O'Neel, C., & Fuligni, A. (2013). A longitudinal study of school belonging and academic motivation across high school. *Child Development, 84,* 678–692.

Gilliam, W., & Zigler, E. (2000). A critical meta-analysis of all evaluations of state-funded preschool from 1977 to 1998: Implications for policy, service delivery and program evaluation. *Early Childhood Research Quarterly, 15,* 441–473.

Gillies, R. (2003). The behaviors, interactions, and perceptions of junior high students during small-group learning. *Journal of Educational Psychology, 95,* 137–147.

Gilligan, C. (1982). *In a different voice: Psychological theory and women's development.* Cambridge, MA: Harvard University Press.

Gilliom, M., Shaw, D., Beck, J., Schonberg, M., & Lukon, J. (2002). Anger regulation in disadvantaged preschool boys: Strategies, antecedents, and the development of self-control. *Developmental Psychology, 38,* 222–235.

Gilovich, T., & Savitsky, K. (1999). The spotlight effect and the illusion of transparency: Egocentric assessments of how we are seen by others. *Current Directions in Psychological Science, 8,* 165–168.

Ginsburg, H., Lee, J. S., & Boyd, J. S. (2008). Mathematics education for young children: What it is and how to promote it. *Social Policy Report, 22,* 3–22.

Ginsburg, K. R. (2007). The importance of play in promoting healthy child development and maintaining strong parent-child bonds. *Pediatrics, 119,* 182–191.

Gissmer, D., Grimm, K., Aiyer, S. M., Murrah, W. M., & Steele, J. S. (2010). Fine motor skills and early comprehension of the world: Two new school readiness indicators. *Developmental Psychology, 46,* 1008–1017.

Gladwell, M. (2008). *Outliers.* New York: Little, Brown and Company.

Glass, A. L., & Sinha, N. (2013). Multiple-choice questioning is an efficient instructional methodology that may be widely implemented in academic courses to improve exam performance. *Current Directions in Psychological Science, 22,* 471–477.

Glass, J., & Levchak, P. (2014). Red states, blue states, and divorce: Understanding the impact of conservative Protestantism on regional variation in divorce rates. *American Journal of Sociology, 119,* 1002–1046.

Gleason, J. B. (1958). The child's learning of English morphology. *Word, 14,* 150–177.

Gleason, T., Sebanc, A., & Hartup, W. (2000). Imaginary companions of preschool children. *Developmental Psychology, 36,* 419–428.

Glick, G. C., & Rose, A. J. (2011). Prospective associations between friendship adjustment and social strategies: Friendship as a context for building social skills. *Developmental Psychology, 47,* 1117–1132.

Goldberg, W. A., Prause, J., Lucas-Thompson, R., & Himsel, A. (2008). Maternal employment and children's achievement in context: A meta-analysis of four decades of research. *Psychological Bulletin, 134,* 77–108.

Goldenberg, C., Tolar, T. D., Reese, L., Francis, D. J., Ray Bazán, A., & Mejía-Arauz, R. (2014). How important is teaching phonemic awareness to children learning to read in Spanish? *American Educational Research Journal, 51,* 604–633.

Goldfried, J., & Miner, M. (2002). Quest religion and the problem of limited compassion. *Journal for the Scientific Study of Religion, 41,* 685–695.

Goldin-Meadow, S., & Alibali, M. W. (2013). Gesture's role in speaking, learning, and creating language. *Annual Review of Psychology, 64,* 257–283.

Goldin-Meadow, S., & Singer, M. (2003). From children's hands to adult's ear: Gesturer's role in the learning process. *Developmental Psychology, 39,* 509–520.

Goldstein, S., Davis-Kean, P., & Eccles, J. S. (2005). Parents, peers, and problem behavior: A longitudinal investigation of the impact of relationship perceptions and characteristics on the development of adolescent problem behavior. *Developmental Psychology, 41,* 401–413.

Goldwyn, R., Stanley, C., Smith, V., & Green, J. (2000). The Manchester Child Attachment Story Task: Relationship with parental AAI, SAT and child behaviour. *Attachment & Human Development, 2,* 71–84.

Golinkoff, R. M., Can, D. D., Soderstrom, M., & Hirsh-Pasek, K. (2015). (Baby) talk to me: The social context of infant-directed speech and its effects on early language acquisition. *Current Directions in Psychological Science, 24,* 339–344.

Golinkoff, R. M., & Hirsh-Pasek, K. (2006). Baby wordsmith: From associationist to social sophisticate. *Current Directions in Psychological Science, 15,* 30–33.

Gollwitzer, P. M., & Oettingen, G. (2012). Goal pursuit. In R. M. Ryan (Ed.), *The Oxford handbook of human motivation* (pp. 208–231). Oxford: Oxford University Press.

Golombok, S., & Hines, M. (2002). Sex differences in social behavior. In P. Smith & C. Hart (Eds.), *Blackwell handbook of childhood social development* (pp. 117–136). Oxford, UK: Blackwell.

Golombok, S., Mellish, L., Jennings, S., Casey, P., Tasker, F., & Lamb, M. E. (2014). Adoptive gay father families: Parent–child relationships and children's psychological adjustment. *Child Development, 85,* 456–468.

Golombok, S., Perry, B., Burston, A., Murray, C., Mooney-Somers, J., Stevens, M., et al. (2003). Children with lesbian parents: A community study. *Developmental Psychology, 39,* 20–33.

Gomez, R., & Edgin, J. (2015). Sleep as a window into early neural development: Shifts in sleep-dependent learning effects across early childhood. *Child Development Perspectives, 9,* 183–189.

Göncü, A., Patt, M., & Kouba, E. (2002). Understanding young children's pretend play in context. In P. Smith & C. Hart (Eds.), *Blackwell handbook of childhood social development* (p. 418). Oxford, UL: Blackwell.

Good, C., Aronson, J., & Inzlicht, M. (2003). Improving adolescents' standardized test performance: An intervention to reduce the effects of stereotype threat. *Applied Developmental Psychology, 24,* 645–662.

Goodman, G. S., Emery, R. E., & Haugaard, J. J. (1998). Developmental psychology and law: Divorce, child maltreatment, foster care, and adoption. In I. Sigel & K. A. Renninger (Eds.), *Handbook of child psychology: Child psychology in practice* (5th ed., Vol. 4, pp. 775–874). New York: Wiley.

Goodman, G. S., & Quas, J. A. (2008). Repeated interviews and children's memory. *Current Directions in Psychological Science, 17,* 386–390.

Goodman, J. (2000). Moral education in early childhood: The limits of constructivism. *Early Education and Development, 11,* 37–54.

Goodson, B., Layzer, J., St. Pierre, R., Bernstein, L., & Lopez, M. (2000). Effectiveness of a comprehensive, five-year family support program for low-income children and their families: Findings from the Comprehensive Child Development Program. *Early Childhood Research Quarterly, 15,* 5–39.

Goodwin, G. P. (2015). Moral character in person perception. *Current Directions in Psychological Science, 24,* 38–44.

Goosby, B. J., & Cheadle, J. E. (2009). Birth weight, math and reading achievement growth: A multilevel between-sibling, between families approach. *Social Forces, 87,* 1291–1320.

Gordon-Larsen, P., McMurray, R., & Popkin, B. (2000). Determinants of adolescent physical activity and inactivity patterns. *Pediatrics, 105,* e83.

Gormley, W., Gayer, T., Phillips, D., & Dawson, B. (2005). The effects of universal pre-K on cognitive development. *Developmental Psychology, 41,* 872–884.

Gormley, W. , Phillips, D. A., Newmark, K., Welti, K., & Adelstein, S. (2011). Social-emotional effects of early childhood education programs in Tulsa. *Child Development, 82,* 2095–2109.

Gotlib, I., Joormann, J., & Foland-Ross, L. (2014). Understanding familial risk for depression: A 25-year perspective. *Perspectives on Psychological Science, 9,* 94–108.

Gottfredson, L. S. (1997). Mainstream science on intelligence: An editorial with 52 signatories, history, and bibliography. *Intelligence, 24,* 13–23.

Gottfried, A. E., Marcoulides, G. A., Gottfried, A. W., & Oliver, P. H. (2009). A latent curve model of parental motivational practices and developmental decline in math and science academic intrinsic motivation. *Journal of Educational Psychology, 101,* 729–739.

Grabill, C., & Kerns, K. (2000). Attachment style and intimacy in friendships. *Personal Relationships, 7,* 363–378.

Graham, S. (2000). Should the natural learning approach replace spelling instruction? *Journal of Educational Psychology, 92,* 235–247.

Graham, S., Harris, K. R., & Hebert, M. (2011). It is more than just the message: Presentation effects in scoring writing. *Focus on Exceptional Children, 44,* 1–12.

Graham, S., Harris, K. R., & Santangelo, T. (2015). Research-based writing practices and the Common Core: Meta-analysis and meta-synthesis. *Elementary School Journal, 115,* 498–522.

Graham, S., McKeown, D., Kiuhara, S., & Harris, K. R. (2012). A meta-analysis of writing instruction for students in the elementary grades. *Journal of Educational Psychology, 104,* 879–896.

Graham, S., & Perin, D. (2007). A meta-analysis of writing instruction for adolescent students. *Journal of Educational Psychology, 99,* 445–476.

Graham, S. A. Kilbreath, C., & Welder, A. (2004). Thirteen-month-olds rely on shared labels and shape similarity for inductive inferences. *Child Development, 75,* 409–427.

Graham, S. A., Nayer, S. L., & Gelman, S. A. (2011). Two-year-olds use the generic/nongeneric distinction to guide their inferences about novel kinds. *Child Development, 82,* 493–507.

Grammer, J., Coffman, J. L., & Ornstein, P. (2013). The effect of teachers' memory-relevant language on children's strategy use and knowledge. *Child Development, 84,* 1989–2002.

Granic, I., Lobel, A., & Engels, R. C. M. E. (2013). The benefits of playing video games. *American Psychologist, 69,* 66–78.

Granger, D. A., Weisz, J. R., McCracken, J. T., & Ikeda, S. C. (1996). Reciprocal influences among adrenocortical activation, psychosocial processes, and the behavioral adjustment of clinic-referred children. *Child Development, 67,* 3250–3262.

Granger, R. C. (2008). After-school programs and academics: Implications for policy, practice, and research. *Social Policy Report, 23,* 3–17.

Granot, D., & Mayseless, O. (2001). Attachment security and adjustment to school in middle childhood. *International Journal of Behavioral Development, 25,* 530–541.

Grant, K., O'Koon, J., Davis, T., Roache, N., Poindexter, L., Armstrong, M., . . . McIntosh, J. (2000). Protective factors affecting low-income urban African American youth exposed to stress. *Journal of Early Adolescence, 20,* 388–417.

Graue, E., Hatch, K., Rao, K., & Oen, D. (2007). The wisdom of class-size reduction. *American Educational Research Journal, 44,* 670–700.

Gray, L., Lewis, L., & Tice, P. (2009). *Educational technology in public school districts: Fall 2008* (NCES 2010–003). Washington, DC: National Center for Education Statistics, Department of Education.

Gray, W. M. (1976). *How is your logic?* (Experimental edition, Form A). Boulder, CO: Biological Sciences Curriculum Study.

Gray-Little, B., & Hafdahl, A. R. (2000). Factors influencing racial comparisons of self-esteem: A quantitative review. *Psychological Bulletin, 126,* 26–54.

Grazzani, I., & Ornaghi, V. (2012). How do use and comprehension of mental-state language relate to theory of mind in middle childhood? *Cognitive Development, 27,* 99–111.

Gredler, M. (2012). Understanding Vygotsky for the classroom: Is it too late? *Educational Psychology Review, 24,* 113–131.

Green, C. L., Walker, J. M. T., Hoover-Dempsey, K. V., & Sandler, H. M. (2007). Parents' motivations for involvement in children's education: An empirical test of a theoretical model of parental involvement. *Journal of Educational Psychology, 99,* 532–544.

Green, C. S., & Bavelier, D. (2007). Action-video-game experience alters the spatial resolution of vision. *Psychological Science, 18,* 88–94.

Green, G., Rhodes, J., Hirsch, A. H., Suarez-Orozco, C., & Camic, P. M. (2008). Supportive adult relationships and the academic engagement of Latin American immigrant youth. *Journal of School Psychology, 46,* 393–412.

Green, J. A., Whitney, P. G., & Potegal, M. (2011). Screaming, yelling, whining, and crying: Categorical and intensity differences in vocal expressions of anger and sadness in children's tantrums. *Emotion, 11,* 1124–1133.

Greenberg, M. T., & Harris, A. R. (2012). Nurturing mindfulness in children and youth: Current state of research. *Child Development Perspectives, 6,* 161–166.

Greenberg, M. T., & Kusche, C. A. (2006). Building social and emotional competence: The PATHS curriculum. In S. R. Jimerson & M. Furlong (Eds.), *Handbook of school violence and school safety: From research to practice* (pp. 395–412). Mahwah, NJ: Erlbaum.

Greene, R. W. (2011). Collaborative problem solving can transform school discipline. *Phi Delta Kappan, 93*(2), 25–29.

Greener, S., & Crick, N. R. (1999). Normative beliefs about prosocial behavior in middle childhood: What does it mean to be nice? *Social Development, 8,* 349–363.

Greengross, G., & Miller, G. (2011). Humor ability reveals intelligence, predicts mating success, and is higher in males. *Intelligence, 39,* 188–192.

Greenspan, S. (2003). Child care research: A clinical perspective. *Child Development, 74,* 1064–1068.

Greenwood, C., Carta, J., Hart, B., Kamps, D., Terry, B., Arreaga-Mayer, C., et al. (1992). Out of the laboratory and into the community: 26 years of applied behavior analysis at the Juniper Gardens Children's Project. *American Psychologist, 47,* 1464–1474.

Gregory, A., Cornell, D., & Fan, X. (2011). The relationship of school structure and support to suspension rates for Black and White high school students. *American Educational Research Journal, 48,* 904–934.

Gregory, A., Cornell, D., Fan, X., Sheras, P., Shih, T.-H., & Huang, F. (2010). Authoritative school discipline: High school practices associated with lower bullying and victimization. *Journal of Educational Psychology, 102,* 483–496.

Gregory, A., & Ripski, M. B. (2008). Adolescent trust in teachers: Implications for behavior in the high school classroom. *School Psychology Review, 37,* 337–353.

Gregory, A., & Weinstein, R. S. (2008). The discipline gap and African Americans: Defiance or cooperation in the high school classroom. *Journal of School Psychology, 46,* 455–475.

Gregory, A. M., Light-Häusermann, J. H., Rijsdijk, F., & Eley, T. C. (2009). Behavioral genetic analyses of prosocial behavior in adolescents. *Developmental Psychology, 12,* 165–174.

Gregory, L. W. (1995). The "turnaround" process: Factors influencing the school success of urban youth. *Journal of Adolescent Research, 10,* 136–154.

Greitemeyer, T., & Osswald, S. (2010). Effects of prosocial video games on prosocial behavior. *Journal of Personality and Social Psychology, 98,* 211–221.

Grimm, K. J., Steele, J. S., Mashburn, A. J., Burchinal, M., & Pianta, R. C. (2010). Early behavioral associations of achievement trajectories. *Developmental Psychology, 46,* 976–983.

Grissom, J. A., & Redding, C. (2016). Discretion and disproportionality: Explaining the underrepresentation of high-achieving students of color in gifted programs. *AERA Open, 2*(1).

Groh, A. M., Roisman, G. I., van IJzendoorn, M. H., Bakermans-Kranenburg, M. J., & Fearon, R. P. (2012). The significance of insecure and disorganized attachment for children's internalizing symptoms: A meta-analytic study. *Child Development, 83,* 591–610.

Grolnick, W. S. (2003). *The psychology of parental control: How well-meant parenting backfires.* Mahwah, NJ: Lawrence Erlbaum.

Grolnick, W. S., & Pomerantz, E. M. (2009). Issues and challenges in studying parental control: Toward a new conceptualization. *Child Development Perspectives, 3,* 165–170.

Gropen, J., Clark-Chiarelli, N., Hoisington, C., & Ehrlich, S. B. (2011). The importance of executive function in early science education. *Child Development Perspectives, 5,* 298–304.

Gross, J. (2015). Emotion regulation: Current status and future prospects. *Psychological Inquiry, 26,* 1–26.

Gross, J., & Jazaieri, H. (2014). Emotion, emotion regulation, and psychopathology: An affective science perspective. *Clinical Psychological Science, 2,* 387–401.

Grossman, D., Neckerman, H., Koepsell, T., Liu, P.-Y., Asher, K., Beland, K., et al. (1997). Effectiveness of a violence prevention curriculum among children in elementary school: A randomized controlled trial. *JAMA, 277,* 1605–1611.

Grossmann, K. E., & Grossmann, K. (1991). Attachment quality as an organizer of emotional and behavioral responses in a longitudinal perspective. In C. M. Parkes, J. Stevenson-Hinde, & P. Marris (Eds.), *Attachment across the life cycle* (pp. 93–114). London: Tavistock/Routledge.

Grotevant, H. D., & McDermott, J. M. (2014). Adoption: Biological and social processes linked to adaptation. *Annual Review of Psychology, 65,* 235–265.

Grover, S., & Pea, R. (2013). Computational thinking in k–12: A review of the state of the field. *Educational Researcher, 42,* 38–43.

Gruman, D., Harachi, T. W., Abbott, R. D., Catalano, R. F., & Fleming, C. B. (2008). Longitudinal effects of student mobility on three dimensions of elementary school engagement. *Child Development, 79,* 1833–1852.

Grunbaum, J. A., Kann, L., Kinchen, S., Williams, B., Ross, J., Lowry, R., et al. (2002). Youth risk behavior surveillance—United States, 2001. *Morbidity & Mortality Weekly Report, 51* (24, SS-4), 1–62.

Grusec, J., Goodnow, J. J., & Cohen, L. (1997). Household work and the development of concern for others. *Developmental Psychology, 32,* 999–1007.

Guay, F., Marsh, H. W., & Boivin, M. (2003). Academic self-concept and academic achievement: Developmental perspectives on their causal ordering. *Journal of Educational Psychology, 95,* 124–136.

Guerra, N., Huesmann, R., & Spindler, A. (2003). Community violence exposure, social cognition, and aggression among urban elementary school children. *Child Development, 74,* 1561–1576.

Guglielmi, R. S. (2008). Native language proficiency, English literacy, academic achievement and occupational attainment in limited-English-proficient students: A latent growth modeling perspective. *Journal of Educational Psychology, 100,* 322–342.

Gummerum, M., Keller, M., Takezawa, M., & Mata, J. (2008). To give or not to give: Children's and adolescents' sharing and moral negotiations in economic decision situations. *Child Development, 79,* 562–576.

Gunderson, E. A., Gripshover, S. J., Romero, C., Dweck, C. S., Goldin-Meadow, S., & Levine, S. C. (2013). Parent praise to 1- to 3-year-olds predicts children's motivational frameworks 5 years later. *Child Development, 84,* 1526–1541.

Gunnar, M. R. (2000). Early adversity and the development of stress reactivity and regulation. In C. Nelson (Ed.), *The effects of early adversity on neurobehavioral development* (pp. 163–200). Mahwah, NJ: Erlbaum.

Gunnar, M. R., Kryzer, E., Van Ryzin, M. J., & Phillips, D. A. (2011). The import of the cortisol rise in child care differs as a function of behavioral inhibition. *Developmental Psychology, 47,* 792–803.

Gunnoe, M. L., Hetherington, M., & Reiss, D. (1999). Parental religiosity, parenting style, and adolescent social responsibility. *Journal of Early Adolescence, 19,* 199–225.

Gurland, S. T., & Grolnick, W. S. (2005). Perceived threat, controlling parenting, and children's achievement orientations. *Motivation and Emotion, 29,* 103–121.

Gutman, L., Sameroff, A., & Eccles, J. S. (2002). The academic achievement of African American students during early adolescence: An examination of multiple risk, promotive, and protective factors. *American Journal of Community Psychology, 30,* 367–400.

Gutman, L. M., & Eccles, J. S. (2007). Stage-environment fit during adolescence: Trajectories of family relations and adolescent outcomes. *Developmental Psychology, 43,* 522–537.

Haden, C., Ornstein, P. A., Eckerman, C., & Didow, S. (2001). Mother-child conversational interactions as events unfold: Linkages to subsequent remembering. *Child Development, 72,* 1016–1031.

Hadley, E. B., Dickinson, D. K., Hirsh-Pasek, K., Golinkoff, R. M., & Nesbitt, K. T. (2016). Examining the acquisition of vocabulary knowledge depth among preschool students. *Reading Research Quarterly, 51,* 181–198.

Haeffel, G. J., Getchell, M., Koposov, R. A., Yrigollen, C. M., DeYoung, C. G., Klinteberg, B., et al. (2008). Association between polymorphisms in the dopamine transporter gene and depression: Evidence for a gene–environment interaction in a sample of juvenile detainees. *Psychological Science, 19,* 62–69.

Hagen, J. W. (2007). Closing remarks. *Developments: Newsletter of the Society for Research in Child Development, 50,* 1, 8.

Hagger, M. S., Wood, C., Stiff, C., & Chatzisarantis, N. L. D. (2010). Ego depletion and the strength model of self-control: A meta-analysis. *Psychological Bulletin, 136,* 495–525.

Haith, M., & Benson, J. (1998). Infant cognition. In D. Kuhn & R. Siegler (Eds.), *Handbook of child psychology: Cognition, perception, and language* (5th ed., Vol. 2, pp. 199–254). New York: Wiley.

Halgunseth, L. C., Ispa, J. M., & Rudy, D. (2006). Parental control in Latino families: An integrated review of the literature. *Child Development, 77,* 1282–1297.

Halim, M. L., Ruble, D., Tamis-LeMonda, C., & Shrout, P. E. (2013). Rigidity in gender-typed behaviors in early childhood: A longitudinal study of ethnic minority children. *Child Development, 84,* 1269–1284.

Hallinan, M. T. (2008). Teacher influences on students' attachment to school. *Sociology of Education, 81,* 271–283.

Halpern, D. F. (1992). *Sex differences in cognitive abilities.* Mahwah, NJ: Erlbaum.

Halpern, D. F. (2011). *Sex differences in cognitive abilities* (4th ed.). New York: Psychology Press.

Halpern, D. F., Benbow, C. P., Geary, D. C., Gur, R. C., Hyde, J. S., & Gernsbacher, M. A. (2007). The science of sex differences in science and mathematics. *Psychological Science in the Public Interest, 8,* 1–51.

Halpern, R. (2000). The promise of after-school programs for low-income children. *Early Childhood Research Quarterly, 15,* 185–214.

Hambrick, D. Z., Oswald, F. L., Altmann, E. M., Meinz, E. J., Gobet, F., & Campitelli, G. (2014). Deliberate practice: Is that all it takes to become an expert? *Intelligence, 45,* 34–45.

Hamilton, B., Martin, J., Osterman, M., Curtin, S., & Mathews, T. J. (2015). Births: Final data for 2014. *National Vital Statistics Reports 64*(12).

Hamilton, J. L., Stange, J. P., Abramson, L. Y., & Alloy, L. B. (2015). Stress and the development of cognitive vulnerabilities to depression explain sex differences in depressive symptoms during adolescence. *Clinical Psychological Science, 3,* 702–714.

Hamlin, J. K. (2013). Moral judgment and action in preverbal infants and toddlers: Evidence for an innate moral core. *Current Directions in Psychological Science, 22,* 186–193.

Hamm, J., Farmer, T., Lambert, K., & Gravelle, M. (2014). Enhancing peer cultures of academic effort and achievement in early adolescence: Promotive effects of the SEALS intervention. *Developmental Psychology, 50,* 216–228.

Hammen, C. (2009). Adolescent depression: Stressful interpersonal contexts and risk for recurrence. *Current Directions in Psychological Science, 18,* 200–204.

Hamond, N. R., & Fivush, R. (1991). Memories of Mickey Mouse: Young children recount their trip to Disneyworld. *Cognitive Development, 6,* 433–448.

Hampson, S. E. (2008). Mechanisms by which childhood personality traits influence adult well-being. *Current Directions in Psychological Science, 17,* 264–268.

Hampton, T. (2008). Researchers seek ways to stem STDs. *JAMA, 299,* 1888–1889.

Hamre, B. K. (2014). Teachers' daily interactions with children: An essential ingredient in effective early childhood programs. *Child Development Perspectives, 8,* 223–230.

Hamre, B. K., Hatfield, B., Pianta, R., & Jamil, F. (2014). Evidence for general and domain-specific elements of teacher–child interactions: Associations with preschool children's development. *Child Development, 85,* 1257–1274.

Han, W.-J. (2008). The academic trajectories of children of immigrants and their school environments. *Developmental Psychology, 44,* 1572–1590.

Han, W.-J., Miller, D. P., & Waldfogel, J. (2010). Parental work schedules and adolescent risky behaviors. *Developmental Psychology, 46,* 1245–1267.

Han, W.-J., Waldfogel, J., & Brooks-Gunn, J. (2001). The effects of early maternal employment on later cognitive and behavioral outcomes. *Journal of Marriage and Family, 63,* 336–354.

Han, X., & Paine, L. (2010). Teaching mathematics as deliberate practice through public lessons. *Elementary School Journal, 110*, 519–541.

Hane, A. A., & Fox, N. A. (2006). Ordinary variation in maternal caregiving influences human infants' stress reactivity. *Psychological Science, 17*, 550–556.

Hane, A. A., Fox, N. A., Henderson, H. A., & Marshall, P. J. (2008). Behavioral reactivity and approach-withdrawal bias in infancy. *Developmental Psychology, 44*, 1491–1496.

Hanish, L., & Guerra, N. (2000). Predictors of peer victimization among urban youth. *Social Development, 9*, 5221–5543.

Hanson, J. L., Adluru, N., Chung, M. K., Alexander, A. L., Davidson, R. J., & Pollak, S. D. (2013). Early neglect is associated with alterations in white matter integrity and cognitive functioning. *Child Development, 84*, 1566–1578.

Hanushek, E. A. (1999). Some findings from an independent investigation of the Tennessee STAR experiment and from other investigations of class size effects. *Educational Evaluation and Policy Analysis, 21*, 143–163.

Happe, F., Winner, E., & Brownell, H. (1998). The getting of wisdom: Theory of mind in old age. *Developmental Psychology, 34*, 358–362.

Harackiewicz, J. M., Durik, A. M., Barron, K. E., Linnenbrink-Garcia, L., & Tauer, J. M. (2008). The role of achievement goals in the development of interest: Reciprocal relations between achievement goals, interest, and performance. *Journal of Educational Psychology, 100*, 105–122.

Harden, K. P., & Mendle, J. (2011). Why don't smart teens have sex? A behavioral genetic approach. *Child Development, 82*, 1327–1344.

Hardway, C., & Fuligni, A. J. (2006). Dimensions of family connectedness among adolescents with Mexican, Chinese, and European backgrounds. *Developmental Psychology, 42*, 1246–1258.

Hardy, S. A., Carlo, G., & Roesch, S. C. (2010). Links between adolescents' expected parental reactions and prosocial behavioral tendencies: The mediating role of prosocial values. *Journal of Youth & Adolescence, 39*, 84–95.

Hardy, S. A., Steelman, M. A., Coyne, S. M., & Ridge, R. D. (2013). Adolescent religiousness as a protective factor against pornography use. *Journal of Applied Developmental Psychology, 34*, 131–139.

Hardy, S. A., Walker, L. J., Olsen, J. A., Woodbury, R. D., & Hickman, J. R. (2014). Moral identity as moral ideal self: Links to adolescent outcomes. *Developmental Psychology, 50*, 45–57.

Harel-Fisch, Y., Walsh, S. D., Fogel-Grinvald, H., Amitai, G., Pickett, W., Mocho, M., et al. (2011). Negative school perceptions and involvement in school bullying: A universal relationship across 40 countries. *Journal of Adolescence, 34*, 639–652.

Harkin, B., Webb, T. L., Chang, B. P. I., Prestwich, A., Conner, M., Kellar, I., . . . Sheeran, P. (2016). Does monitoring goal progress promote goal attainment? A meta-analysis of the experimental evidence. *Psychological Bulletin, 142*, 198–229.

Harper, L., & Huie, K. (1998). Free play use of space by preschoolers from diverse backgrounds: Factors influencing activity choices. *Merrill-Palmer Quarterly, 44*, 423–446.

Harrington, J. W., Logan, S., Harwell, C., Gardner, J., Swingle, J., McGuire, E., et al. (2012). Effective analgesia using physical interventions for infant immunizations. *Pediatrics, 129*, 815–822.

Harrison, J., Bunford, N., Evans, S. W., & Owens, J. (2013). Educational accommodations for students with behavioral challenges: A systematic review of the literature. *Review of Educational Research, 83*, 551–597.

Harrison, K., Bost, K. K., McBride, B. A., Donovan, S. M., Grigsby-Toussaint, D. S., Kim, J., et al. (2011). Toward a developmental conceptualization of contributors to overweight and obesity in childhood: The Six-Cs Model. *Child Development Perspectives, 5*, 50–58.

Harrison, L., & Ungerer, J. (2002). Maternal employment and infant–mother attachment security at 12 months postpartum. *Developmental Psychology, 38*, 758–773.

Harstad, E., Levy, S., & AAP Committee on Substance Abuse. (2014). Attention-deficit/hyperactivity disorder and substance abuse. *Pediatrics, 134*, e293–e301.

Hart, B., & Risley, R. (1995). *Meaningful differences in the everyday experience of young American children.* Baltimore: Brookes.

Hart, D., Atkins, R., & Fegley, S. (2003). Personality and development in childhood: A person-centered approach. *Monographs of the Society for Research in Child Development, 68* (Serial No. 272).

Hart, D., Donnelly, T. M., Youniss, J., & Atkins, R. (2007). High school community service as a predictor of adult voting and volunteering. *American Educational Research Journal, 44*, 197–219.

Hart, D., Hofmann, V., Edelstein, W., & Keller, M. (1997). The relation of childhood personality types to adolescent behavior and development: A longitudinal study of Icelandic children. *Developmental Psychology, 33*, 195–205.

Hart, S. A., Petrill, S. A., Thompson, L. A., & Plomin, R. (2008). The ABCs of math: A genetic analysis of mathematics and its links with reading ability and general cognitive ability. *Journal of Educational Psychology, 101*, 388–402.

Harter, S. (1999). *The construction of the self: A developmental perspective.* New York: Guilford.

Harter, S. (2006). The self. In N. Eisenberg (Ed.), *Handbook of child psychology: Social, emotional, and personality development* (6th ed., Vol. 3, pp. 505–570). New York: Wiley.

Hartl, A. C., Laursen, B., & Cillessen, A. H. N. (2015). A survival analysis of adolescent friendships: The downside of dissimilarity. *Psychological Science, 26*, 1304–1315.

Hartos, J. L., Eitel, P., Haynie, D. L., & Simons-Morton, B. G. (2000). Can I take the car? Relations among parenting practices and adolescent problem-driving practices. *Journal of Adolescent Research, 15*, 352–367.

Hartshorne, H., & May, M. (1928). *Studies in deceit.* New York: MacMillan.

Hartshorne, J. K., & Germine, L. T. (2015). When does cognitive functioning peak? The asynchronous rise and fall of different cognitive abilities across the life span. *Psychological Science, 26*, 433–443.

Hartup, W. W. (1974). Aggression in childhood: Developmental perspectives. *American Psychologist, 29*, 336–341.

Hartup, W. W., & Abecassis, M. (2002). Friends and enemies. In P. Smith & C. Hart (Eds.), *Blackwell handbook of childhood social development* (pp. 285–306). Oxford, UK: Blackwell.

Harwell, M., Post, T. R., Cutler, A., Maeda, Y., Anderson, E., Norman, K. W., et al. (2009). The preparation of students from National Science Foundation-funded and commercially developed high school mathematics curricula for their first university mathematics course. *American Educational Research Journal, 46*, 203–231.

Hastings, P., Zahn-Waxler, C., Robinson, J., Usher, B., & Bridges, D. (2000). The development of concern for others in children with behavior problems. *Developmental Psychology, 36*, 531–546.

Hastings, P. D., Kahle, S., & Nuselovici, J. M. (2014). How well socially wary preschoolers fare over time depends on their parasympathetic regulation and socialization. *Child Development, 85*, 1586–1600.

Hatt, B. (2012). Smartness as a cultural practice in schools. *American Educational Research Journal, 49*, 438–460.

Hattie, J. (2009). *Visible learning: A synthesis of over 800 meta-analyses relating to achievement.* London: Routledge.

Hattie, J., & Timperley, H. (2007). The power of feedback. *Review of Educational Research, 77*, 81–112.

Haun, D. B., & Tomasello, M. (2011). Conformity to peer pressure in preschool children. *Child Development, 82*, 1759–1767.

Haun, D. B. M., Rekers, Y., & Tomasello, M. (2014). Children conform to the behavior of peers: Other great apes stick with what they know. *Psychological Science, 25*, 2160–2167.

Hawley, P. H. (2014). The duality of human nature: Coercion and prosociality in youths' hierarchy ascension and social success. *Current Directions in Psychological Science, 23*, 433–438.

Hay, D. F. (2009). The roots and branches of human altruism. *British Journal of Psychology, 100*, 473–479.

Hay, D. F., Castle, J., & Davies, L. (2000). Toddlers' use of force against familiar peers: A precursor of serious aggression? *Child Development, 71*, 457–467.

Hay, D. F., Mundy, L., Roberts, S., Carta, R., Waters, C. S., Perra, O., et al. (2011). Known risk factors for violence predict 12-month-old infants' aggressiveness with peers. *Psychological Science, 22*, 1205–1211.

Hay, D. F., & Nash, A. (2002). Social development in different family arrangements. In P. Smith & C. Hart (Eds.), *Blackwell handbook of childhood social development* (pp. 238–261). Oxford: Blackwell.

Hay, D. F., & Pawlby, S. (2003). Prosocial development in relation to children's and mother's psychological problems. *Child Development, 74,* 1314–1327.

Hay, D. F., Waters, C. S., Perra, O., Swift, N., Kairis, V., Phillips, R., . . . van Goozen, S. (2014). Precursors to aggression are evident by 6 months of age. *Developmental Science, 17,* 471–480.

Hayden, E. P., Klein, D. N., Dougherty, L. R., Olino, T. M., Dyson, M. W., Durbin, C. E., et al. (2010). The role of brain-derived neurotrophic factor genotype, parental depression, and relationship discord in predicting early-emerging negative emotionality. *Psychological Science, 21,* 1678–1685.

Hayes, L. B., & Van Camp, C. M. (2015). Increasing physical activity of children during school recess. *Journal of Applied Behavior Analysis, 48,* 690–695.

Heatherton, T. F., & Sargent, J. D. (2009). Does watching smoking in movies promote teenage smoking? *Current Directions in Psychological Science, 18,* 63–67.

Hebb, D. O. (1949). *The organization of behavior.* New York: Wiley.

Heberle, A. E., Thomas, Y. M., Wagmiller, R. L., Briggs-Gowan, M. J., & Carter, A. S. (2014). The impact of neighborhood, family, and individual risk factors on toddlers' disruptive behavior. *Child Development, 85,* 2046–2061.

Helwig, C., & Jasiobedzka, U. (2001). The relation between law and morality: Children's reasoning about socially beneficial and unjust laws. *Child Development, 72,* 1382–1393.

Helwig, C., To, S., Wang, Q., Liu, C., & Yang, S. (2014). Judgments and reasoning about parental discipline involving induction and psychological control in China and Canada. *Child Development, 85,* 1150–1167.

Helwig, C., & Turiel, E. (2011). Children's social and moral reasoning. In C. Hart & P. Smith (Eds.), *Blackwell handbook of childhood social development* (2nd ed., pp. 567–583). Hoboken, NJ: Wiley-Blackwell.

Hembree, R. (1988). Correlates, causes, effects, and treatment of test anxiety. *Review of Educational Research, 58,* 47–77.

Hemphill, L., & Snow, C. E. (1996). Language and literacy development: Discontinuities and differences. In D. R. Olson & N. Torrance (Eds.), *The handbook of education and human development* (pp. 173–201). Oxford, UK: Blackwell.

Henry, D. B., Schoeny, M. E., Deptula, D., & Slavick, J. T. (2007). Peer selection and socialization effects on adolescent intercourse without a condom and attitudes about the costs of sex. *Child Development, 78,* 825–838.

Henry, P. J., & Hardin, C. (2006). The contact hypothesis revisited: Status bias in the reduction of implicit prejudice in the United States and Lebanon. *Psychological Science, 17,* 862–868.

Hentges, R. F., Davies, P. T., & Cicchetti, D. (2015). Temperament and interparental conflict: The role of negative emotionality in predicting child behavioral problems. *Child Development, 86,* 1333–1350.

Hepach, R., Vaish, A., & Tomasello, M. (2013). Young children sympathize less in response to unjustified emotional distress. *Developmental Psychology, 49,* 1132–1139.

Herman, M. (2004). Forced to choose: Some determinants of racial identification in multiracial adolescents. *Child Development, 75,* 730–748.

Hernandez, D. J., Denton, N. A., & Macartney, S. E. (2008). Children in immigrant families: Looking to America's future. *Social Policy Report, 22,* 3–22.

Hernández, M. M., Conger, R. D., Robins, R. W., Bacher, K. B., & Widaman, K. F. (2014). Cultural socialization and ethnic pride among Mexican-origin adolescents during the transition to middle school. *Child Development, 85,* 695–708.

Hespos, S. J., Ferry, A. L., Anderson, E. M., Hollenbeck, E. N., & Rips, L. J. (2016). Five-month-old infants have general knowledge of how nonsolid substances behave and interact. *Psychological Science, 27,* 244–256.

Hespos, S. J., Ferry, A. L., & Rips, L. J. (2009). Five-month-old infants have different expectations for solids and liquids. *Psychological Science, 20,* 603–611.

Hess, U., & Thibault, P. (2009). Darwin and emotion expression. *American Psychologist, 64,* 120–128.

Hesse, E. (1999). The adult attachment interview: Historical and current perspectives. In J. Cassidy & P. Shaver (Eds.), *Handbook of attachment: Theory, research, and clinical applications* (pp. 395–433). New York: Guilford.

Hestenes, L., Kontos, S., & Bryan, Y. (1993). Children's emotional expressions in childcare centers varying in quality. *Early Childhood Research Quarterly, 8,* 295–307.

Hetherington, E. M., & Stanely-Hagan, M. (1999). The adjustment of children with divorced parents: A risk and resiliency perspective. *Journal of Child Psychology & Psychiatry & Allied Disciplines, 40,* 129–140.

Heyes, C. (2016). Born pupils? Natural pedagogy and cultural pedagogy. *Perspectives on Psychological Science, 11,* 280–295.

Heyman, G., Gee, C., & Giles, J. (2003). Preschool children's reasoning about ability. *Child Development, 74,* 516–534.

Hickendorff, M., van Putten, C. M., Verhelst, N. D., & Heiser, W. J. (2010). Individual differences in strategy use on division problems: Mental versus written computation. *Journal of Educational Psychology, 102,* 438–452.

Hidi, S., & Anderson, V. (1992). Situational interest and its impact on reading and expository writing. In K. A. Renninger, S. Hidi, & A. Krapp (Eds.), *The role of interest in learning and development* (pp. 215–238). Hillsdale, NJ: Erlbaum.

Hill, C. J., Bloom, H. S., Black, A. R., & Lipsey, M. W. (2008). Empirical benchmarks for interpreting effect sizes in research. *Child Development Perspectives, 2,* 172–177.

Hill, J. L., Waldfogel, J., Brooks-Gunn, J., & Han, W.-J. (2005). Maternal employment and child development: A fresh look using newer methods. *Developmental Psychology, 41,* 833–850.

Hill, N., Bush, K., & Roosa, M. (2003). Parenting and family socialization strategies and children's mental health: Low-income Mexican-American and Euro-American mothers and children. *Child Development, 74,* 189–204.

Hill, N. E., Castellino, D. R., Lansford, J. E., Nowlin, P., Dodge, K. A., Bates, J. E., et al. (2004). Parent academic involvement as related to school behavior, achievement, and aspirations: Demographic variations across adolescence. *Child Development, 75,* 1491–1509.

Hill, N. E., & Taylor, L. C. (2004). Parental school involvement and children's academic achievement. *Current Directions in Psychological Science, 13,* 161–164.

Hill, N. E., & Tyson, D. F. (2009). Parental involvement in middle school: A meta-analytic assessment of the strategies that promote achievement. *Developmental Psychology, 45,* 740–763.

Hillman, C., & Drobes, D. J. (2012). Physical activity and cognitive control: Implications for drug abuse. *Child Development Perspectives, 6*(4), 367–373.

Hillman, C., Pontifex, M., Raine, L., Castelli, D., Hall, E., & Kramer, A. (2009). The effect of acute treadmill walking on cognitive control and academic achievement in preadolescent children. *Neuroscience, 159,* 1044–1054.

Hinde, E., & Perry, N. (2007). Elementary teachers' application of Jean Piaget's theories of cognitive development during social studies curriculum debates in Arizona. *Elementary School Journal, 108,* 63–79.

Hinduja, S., & Patchin, J. W. (2011). Cyberbullying: A review of the legal issues facing educators. *Preventing School Failure, 55,* 71–78.

Hine, J. F., Ardoin, S. P., & Foster, T. E. (2015). Decreasing transition times in elementary school classrooms: Using computer-assisted instruction to automate intervention components. *Journal of Applied Behavior Analysis, 48,* 495–510.

Hines, M. (2011). Prenatal endocrine influences on sexual orientation and on sexually differentiated childhood behavior. *Frontiers in Neuroendocrinology, 32,* 170–182.

Hinnant, J. B., O'Brien, M., & Ghazarian, S. R. (2009). The longitudinal relations of teacher expectations to achievement in the early school years. *Journal of Educational Psychology, 101,* 662–670.

Hipwell, A. E., Keenan, K., Loeber, R., & Battista, D. (2010). Early predictors of sexually intimate behaviors in an urban sample of young girls. *Developmental Psychology, 46,* 366–378.

Hirsh-Pasek, K., Adamson, L. B., Bakeman, R., Owen, M. T., Golinkoff, R. M., Pace, A., . . . Suma, K. (2015). The contribution of early communication quality to low-income children's language success. *Psychological Science, 26,* 1071–1083.

Hirsh-Pasek, K., Zosh, J. M., Golinkoff, R. M., Gray, J. H., Robb, M. B., & Kaufman, J. (2015). Putting education in "educational" apps: Lessons from the science of learning. *Psychological Science in the Public Interest, 16,* 3–34.

Ho, C., Bluestein, D. N., & Jenkins, J. M. (2008). Cultural differences in the relationship between parenting and children's behavior. *Developmental Psychology, 44,* 507–522.

Hodges, E., Finnegan, R., & Perry, D. (1999). Skewed autonomy-relatedness in preadolescents' conceptions of their relationships with mother, father, and best friend. *Developmental Psychology, 35,* 737–748.

Hofer, M. A. (2006). Psychobiological roots of early attachment. *Current Directions in Psychological Science, 15*, 84–88.

Hofferth, S. L. (2010). Home media and children's achievement and behavior. *Child Development, 81*, 1598–1619.

Hofferth, S. L., & Moon, U. J. (2011). Electronic play, study, communication, and adolescent achievement, 2003–2008. *Journal of Research on Adolescence, 22*, 215–224.

Hoffman, D. M. (2009). Reflecting on social emotional learning: A critical perspective on trends in the United States. *Review of Educational Research, 79*, 533–556.

Hoffman, M. L. (1975). Altruistic behavior and the parent–child relationship. *Journal of Personality and Social Psychology, 31*, 937–943.

Hofmann, W., De Houwer, J., Perugini, M., Baeyens, F., & Crombez, G. (2010). Evaluative conditioning in humans: A meta-analysis. *Psychological Bulletin, 136*, 390–421.

Hogan, K., & Corey, C. (2001). Viewing classrooms as cultural contexts for fostering scientific literacy. *Anthropology & Education Quarterly, 32*, 214–243.

Hogan, T., & Rabinowitz, M. (2009). Teacher expertise and the development of a problem representation. *Educational Psychology, 29*, 153–169.

Hogan, T., Rabinowitz, M., & Craven, J. A. (2003). Representation in teaching: Inferences from research of expert and novice teachers. *Educational Psychologist, 38*, 235–247.

Hoglund, W., & Leadbeater, B. (2004). The effects of family, school, and classroom ecologies on changes in children's social competence and emotional and behavioral problems in first grade. *Developmental Psychology, 40*, 533–544.

Holland, A. S., & Roisman, G. I. (2010). Adult attachment security and young adults' dating relationships over time: Self-reported, observational, and physiological evidence. *Developmental Psychology, 46*, 552–557.

Holland, M. M. (2012). Only here for the day. *Sociology of Education, 85*, 101–120.

Holmboe, K., Nemoda, Z., Fearon, R. M. P., Csibra, G., Sasvari-Szekely, M., & Johnson, M. H. (2010). Polymorphisms in dopamine system genes are associated with individual differences in attention in infancy. *Developmental Psychology, 46*, 404–416.

Hopkins, J. R. (1995). Erik Homburger Erikson (1902–1994). *American Psychologist, 50*, 796–797.

Hopkins, W. D., & Cantalupo, C. (2008). Theoretical speculations on the evolutionary origins of hemispheric specialization. *Current Directions in Psychological Science, 17*, 233–237.

Horowitz, T., Cade, B., Wolfe, J., & Czeisler, C. (2003). Searching night and day: A dissociation of effects of circadian phase and time awake on visual selective attention and vigilance. *Psychological Science, 14*, 549–557.

Horvat, E. M., Weininger, E. B., & Lareau, A. (2003). From social ties to social capital: Class differences in the relations between schools and parent networks. *American Educational Research Journal, 40*, 319–351.

Houltberg, B. J., Morris, A., Cui, L., Henry, C. S., & Criss, M. M. (2016). The role of youth anger in explaining links between parenting and early adolescent prosocial and antisocial behavior. *Journal of Early Adolescence, 36*, 297–318

Howes, C. (1990). Can the age of entry into child care and the quality of child care predict adjustment in kindergarten? *Developmental Psychology, 26*, 292–303.

Howes, C., & James, J. (2002). Children's social development within the socialization context of childcare and early childhood education. In P. Smith & C. Hart (Eds.), *Blackwell handbook of childhood social development* (pp. 137–155). Oxford, UK: Blackwell.

Howes, C., & Lee, L. (2006). Peer relations in young children. In L. Balter & C. S. Tamis-LeMonda (Eds.), *Child psychology: A handbook of contemporary issues* (pp. 135–152). Philadelphia, PA: Psychology Press.

Howes, C., & Ritchie, S. (1999). Attachment organizations in children with difficult life circumstances. *Development and Psychopathology, 11*, 251–268.

Howes, C., & Tonyon, H. (2000). Links between adult and peer relations across four developmental periods. In K. Kerns, J. Contreras, & A. Neal-Barnett (Eds.), *Family and peers: Linking two social worlds* (pp. 85–113). Westport, CT: Praeger.

Hsueh, J., & Yoshikawa, H. (2007). Working nonstandard schedules and variable shifts in low-income families: Associations with parental psychological well-being, family functioning, and child well-being. *Developmental Psychology, 43*, 620–632.

Huang, F. L., & Invernizzi, M. A. (2013). Birthday effects and preschool attendance. *Early Childhood Research Quarterly, 28*, 11–23.

Hubbs-Tait, L., Nation, J. R., Krebs, N. F., & Bellinger, D. C. (2006). Neurotoxicants, micronutrients, and social environments: Individual and combined effects on children's development. *Psychological Science in the Public Interest, 6*, 57–121.

Hudley, C., Graham, S., & Taylor, A. (2007). Reducing aggressive behavior and increasing motivation in school: The evolution of an intervention to strengthen school adjustment. *Educational Psychologist, 42*, 251–260.

Huesmann, L. R., Eron, L. D., Klein, R., Brice, P., & Fischer, P. (1983). Mitigating the imitation of aggressive behaviors by children's attitudes about media violence. *Journal of Personality and Social Psychology, 44*, 899–910.

Huey, E. D., Krueger, F., & Grafman, J. (2006). Representations in the human prefrontal cortex. *Current Directions in Psychological Science, 15*, 167–171.

Hughes, C., & Devine, R. T. (2015). Individual differences in theory of mind from preschool to adolescence: Achievements and directions. *Child Development Perspectives, 9*, 149–153.

Hughes, C., & Ensor, R. (2007). Executive function and theory of mind: Predictive relations from ages 2 to 4. *Developmental Psychology, 43*, 1447–1459.

Hughes, F. (1999). *Children, play, and development* (3rd ed.). Boston, MA: Allyn & Bacon.

Hughes, J. M., Bigler, R. S., & Levy, S. R. (2007). Consequences of learning about historical racism among European American and African American children. *Child Development, 78*, 1689–1705.

Hughes, J. N., Chen, Q., Thoemmes, F., & Kwok, O. (2010). An investigation of the relationship between retention in first grade and performance on high stakes tests in third grade. *Educational Evaluation and Policy Analysis, 32*, 166–182.

Hughes, J. N., Luo, W., Kwok, O.-M., & Loyd, L. K. (2008). Teacher-student support, effortful engagement, and achievement: A 3-year longitudinal study. *Journal of Educational Psychology, 100*, 1–14.

Hughes, J. N., Wu, J.-Y., Kwok, O.-m., Villarreal, V., & Honson, A. (2012). Indirect effects of child reports of teacher–student relationship on achievement. *Journal of Educational Psychology, 104*, 350–365.

Huguet, P., & Regner, I. (2007). Stereotype threat among schoolgirls in quasi-ordinary classroom circumstances. *Journal of Educational Psychology, 99*, 545–560.

Hull, J. G., Brunelle, T. J., Prescott, A. T., & Sargent, J. D. (2014). A longitudinal study of risk-glorifying video games and behavioral deviance. *Journal of Personality and Social Psychology, 107*, 300–325.

Hulleman, C. S., & Barron, K. E. (2015). Motivation interventions in education. In L. Corno & E. M. Anderman (Eds.), *Handbook of educational psychology* (3rd ed., pp. 160–171). New York: Routledge.

Hulleman, C. S., Durik, A. M., Schweigert, S. A., & Harackiewicz, J. M. (2008). Task values, achievement goals, and interest: An integrative analysis. *Journal of Educational Psychology, 100*, 398–416.

Hulleman, C. S., & Harackiewicz, J. M. (2009). Making education relevant: Increasing interest and performance in high school science classes. *Science, 326*, 1410–1412.

Hulme, C., Bowyer-Crane, C., Carroll, J. M., Duff, F. J., & Snowling, M. J. (2012). The causal role of phoneme awareness and letter-sound knowledge in learning to read. *Psychological Science, 23*, 572–577.

Hulme, C., Nash, H. M., Gooch, D., Lervåg, A., & Snowling, M. J. (2015). The foundations of literacy development in children at familial risk of dyslexia. *Psychological Science, 26*, 1877–1886.

Hulme, C., & Snowling, M. J. (2013). Learning to read: What we know and what we need to understand better. *Child Development Perspectives, 7*, 1–5.

Humphreys, K. L., Gleason, M. M., Drury, S. S., Miron, D., Nelson, C. A., Fox, N. A., & Zeanah, C. H. (2015). Effects of institutional rearing and foster care on psychopathology at age 12 years in Romania: Follow-up of an open, randomised controlled trial. *Lancet Psychiatry, 2*, 625–634.

Hunt, E., & Carlson, J. (2007). Considerations relating to the study of group differences in intelligence. *Perspectives on Psychological Science, 2*, 194–213.

Hunt, E., Streissguth, A. P., Kerr, B., & Olson, H. C. (1995). Mothers' alcohol consumption during pregnancy: Effect on spatial-visual reasoning in 14-year-old children. *Psychological Science, 6*, 339–342.

Huntley-Fenner, G., & Cannon, E. (2000). Preschoolers' magnitude comparisons are mediated by a preverbal analog mechanism. *Psychological Science, 11,* 147–152.

Huntsinger, C. S., & Jose, P. E. (2006). A longitudinal investigation of personality and social adjustment among Chinese American and European American adolescents. *Child Development, 77,* 1309–1324.

Huntsinger, C. S., & Jose, P. E. (2009). Parental involvement in children's schooling: Different meanings in different cultures. *Early Childhood Research Quarterly, 24,* 398–410.

Huntsinger, J. R. (2013). Does emotion directly tune the scope of attention? *Current Directions in Psychological Science, 22,* 265–270.

Hurley, M. M., Dennett, D. C., & Adams, R. B. (2011). *Inside jokes: Using humor to reverse-engineer the mind.* Cambridge, MA: MIT Press.

Huston, A. C., & Aronson, S. R. (2005). Mothers' time with infant and time in employment as predictors of mother–child relationships and children's early development. *Child Development, 76,* 467–482.

Huston, A. C., Bickham, D. S., Lee, J. H., & Wright, J. C. (2007). From attention to comprehension: How children watch and learn from television. In N. Pecora, J. P. Murray, & E. A. Wartella (Eds.), *Children and television: Fifty years of research* (pp. 41–63). Mahwah, NJ: Erlbaum.

Huston, A. C., Bobbitt, K. C., & Bentley, A. (2015). Time spent in child care: How and why does it affect social development? *Developmental Psychology, 51,* 621–634.

Hutchison, K. A., Smith, J. L., & Ferris, A. (2013). Goals can be threatened to extinction: Using the Stroop task to clarify working memory depletion under stereotype threat. *Social Psychological and Personality Science, 4,* 74–81.

Hymel, S., Vaillancourt, T., McDougall, P., & Renshaw, P. (2002). Peer acceptance and rejection in childhood. In P. Smith & C. Hart (Eds.), *Blackwell handbook of childhood social development* (pp. 265–284). Oxford, UK: Blackwell.

Iacoboni, M. (2009). Imitation, empathy, and mirror neurons. *Annual Review of Psychology, 60,* 653–670.

IES. (2011). *WWC Quick Review of the Report "Achievement effects of four early elementary school math curricula: Findings for first and second graders."* Washington, DC: Department of Education, Institute of Education Sciences.

IES. (2012). *What are districts' written policies regarding student substance-related incidents?* Washington, DC: Department of Education, Institute of Education Science.

IES. (2013). *Testing integrity symposium: Issues and recommendations for best practice.* Washington, DC: Department of Education, Institute of Education Sciences, National Center for Education Statistics.

Igel, C. (2015). *The effect of cooperative learning on student achievement: A meta-analysis.* Paper presented at the American Educational Research Association meeting, Chicago, IL, April 2015.

Iglowstein, I., Jenni, O. G., Molinari, L., & Largo, R. H. (2003). Sleep duration from infancy to adolescence: Reference values and generational trends. *Pediatrics, 111,* 302–307.

Ikonomidou, C., Bittigau, P., Ishimaru, M. J., Wozniak, D. F., Koch, C., Genz, K., et al. (2000). Ethanol-induced apoptotic neurodegeneration and Fetal Alcohol Syndrome. *Science, 287,* 1056–1060.

Im-Bolter, N., Johnson, J., & Pascual-Leone, J. (2006). Processing limitations in children with specific language impairment: The role of executive function. *Child Development, 77,* 1822–1841.

Ingersoll, B. (2011). Recent advances in early identification and treatment of autism. *Current Directions in Psychological Science, 20,* 335–339.

Inhelder, B., & Piaget, J. (1958). *The growth of logical thinking from childhood to adolescence* (A. Parsons & S. Milgram, Trans.). New York: Basic Books.

Inzlicht, M., Legault, L., & Teper, R. (2014). Exploring the mechanisms of self-control improvement. *Current Directions in Psychological Science, 23,* 302–307.

Inzlicht, M., McKay, L., & Aronson, J. (2006). Stigma as ego depletion: How being the target of prejudice affects self-control. *Psychological Science, 17,* 262–269.

Isbister, J. (1985). *Freud: An introduction to his life and work.* Cambridge, UK: Polity Press.

Iverson, J. M., & Fagan, M. K. (2004). Infant vocal-motor coordination: Precursor to the gesture-speech system? *Child Development, 75,* 1053–1066.

Iverson, J. M., & Goldin-Meadow, S. (2005). Gesture paves the way for language development. *Psychological Science, 16,* 367–371.

Iyengar, S. S., & Lepper, M. R. (1999). Rethinking the value of choice: A cultural perspective on intrinsic motivation. *Journal of Personality and Social Psychology, 76,* 349–366.

Izard, C. E. (2007). Basic emotions, natural kinds, emotion schemas, and a new paradigm. *Perspectives on Psychological Science, 2,* 260–280.

Izard, C. E., Fine, S., Schultz, D., Mostow, A., Ackerman, B., & Youngstrom, E. (2001). Emotion knowledge as a predictor of social behavior and academic competence in children at risk. *Psychological Science, 12,* 18–23.

Jabusch, H.-C., Alpers, H., Kopiez, R., Vauth, H., & Altenmüller, E. (2009). The influence of practice on the development of motor skills in pianists: A longitudinal study in a selected motor task. *Human Movement Science, 28,* 74–84.

Jack, F., MacDonald, S., Reese, E., & Hayne, H. (2009). Maternal reminiscing style during early childhood predicts the age of adolescents' earliest memories. *Child Development, 80,* 496–505.

Jack, F., Simcock, G., & Hayne, H. (2012). Magic memories: Young children's verbal recall after a 6-year delay. *Child Development, 83,* 159–172.

Jackson, C., & Foshee, V. A. (1998). Violence-related behaviors of adolescents: Relations with responsive and demanding parenting. *Journal of Adolescent Research, 13,* 343–359.

Jackson, J. J., Connolly, J. J., Garrison, S. M., Leveille, M. M., & Connolly, S. L. (2015). Your friends know how long you will live: A 75-year study of peer-rated personality traits. *Psychological Science, 26,* 335–340.

Jackson, L. A., von Eye, A., Biocca, F. A., Barbatsis, G., Zhao, Y., & Fitzgerald, H. E. (2006). Does home Internet use influence the academic performance of low-income children? *Developmental Psychology, 42,* 429–435.

Jacob, R., & Parkinson, J. (2015). The potential for school-based interventions that target executive function to improve academic achievement: A review. *Review of Educational Research, 85,* 512–552.

Jacobs, J. E., Lanza, S., Osgood, D. W., Eccles, J. S., & Wigfield, A. (2002). Changes in children's self-competence and values: Gender and domain differences across grades one through twelve. *Child Development, 73,* 509–527.

Jaeger, M. M. (2011). Does cultural capital really affect academic achievement? New evidence from combined sibling and panel data. *Sociology of Education, 84,* 281–298.

Jaffee, S. R, & Christian, C. W. (2014). The biological embedding of child abuse and neglect. *Social Policy Report, 28,* 3–19.

Jaffee, S. R., & Hyde, J. (2000). Gender differences in moral orientation: A meta-analysis. *Psychological Bulletin, 126,* 703–726.

Jaffee, S. R., Moffitt, T. E., Caspi, A., & Taylor, A. (2003). Life with (or without) father: The benefits of living with two biological parents depend on the father's antisocial behavior. *Child Development, 74,* 109–126.

Jambon, M., & Smetana, J. G. (2014). Moral complexity in middle childhood: Children's evaluations of necessary harm. *Developmental Psychology, 50,* 22–33.

James, J. H. (2012). Caring for "others": Examining the interplay of mothering and deficit discourses in teaching. *Teaching and Teacher Education, 28,* 165–173.

James, K., & Engelhardt, L. (2012). The effects of handwriting experience on functional brain development in pre-literate children. *Trends in Neuroscience and Education, 1,* 32–42.

James-Burdumy, S., Goesling, B., Deke, J., & Einspruch, E. (2010). *The effectiveness of mandatory-random student drug testing (NCEE 2010-4025).* Washington, DC: Department of Education, Institute of Education Sciences.

Jang, H. (2008). Supporting students' motivation, engagement, and learning during an uninteresting activity. *Journal of Educational Psychology, 100,* 798–811.

Jang, H., Reeve, J., & Deci, E. L. (2010). Engaging students in learning activities: It is not autonomy support or structure but autonomy support and structure. *Journal of Educational Psychology, 102,* 588–600.

Jansen, J. (2008). Teaching English language learners in the content areas. *Review of Educational Research, 78,* 1010–1038.

Jansen, J., de Weerth, C., & Riksen-Walraven, J. M. (2008). Breastfeeding and the mother-infant relationship: A review. *Developmental Review, 28,* 503–521.

January, A., Casey, R. J., & Paulson, D. (2011). A meta-analysis of classroom-wide interventions to build social skills: Do they work? *School Psychology Review, 40,* 242–256.

Jarrett, O. (1997). Science and math through role-play centers in the elementary school classroom. *Science Activities, 34*, 13–19.

Jaswal, V., & Dodson, C. S. (2009). Metamemory development: Understanding the role of similarity in false memories. *Child Development, 80*, 629–635.

Jaswal, V., & Markman, E. (2001). Learning proper and common names in inferential versus ostensive contexts. *Child Development, 72*, 768–786.

Jaušovec, N., & Jaušovec, K. (2012). Sex differences in mental rotation and cortical-activation patterns: Can training change them? *Intelligence, 40*, 151–162.

Jeffrey, A., Auger, R., & Pepperell, J. (2013). If we're ever in trouble they're always there: A qualitative study of teacher–student caring. *Elementary School Journal, 114*, 100–117.

Jemmott, J. B., Jemmott, L., & Fong, G. (2010). Efficacy of a theory-based abstinence-only intervention over 24 months: A randomized controlled trial with young adolescents. *Archives of Pediatrics & Adolescent Medicine, 1645*, 152–159.

Jenkins, J., & Astington, J. (2000). Theory of mind and social behavior: Causal models tested in a longitudinal study. *Merrill-Palmer Quarterly, 46*, 203–220.

Jenkins, J., Rasbash, J., & O'Connor, T. G. (2003). The role of the shared family context in differential parenting. *Developmental Psychology, 39*, 99–113.

Jenkins, J., Simpson, A., Dunn, J., Rasbash, J., & O'Connor, T. G. (2005). Mutual influence of marital conflict and children's behavior problems: Shared and nonshared family risks. *Child Development, 76*, 24–39.

Jenkins, J., Turrell, S., Koguishi, Y., Lollis, S., & Ross, H. (2003). A longitudinal investigation of the dynamics of mental state talk in families. *Child Development, 74*, 905–920.

Jenkins, S., Ritblatt, S., & McDonald, J. (2008). Conflict resolution among early childhood educators. *Conflict Resolution Quarterly, 25*, 429–450.

Jennings, J., & DiPrete, T. A. (2010). Teacher effects on social and behavioral skills in early elementary school. *Sociology of Education, 83*, 135–159.

Jennings, P. A., & Greenberg, M. T. (2009). The prosocial classroom: Teacher social and emotional competence in relation to student and classroom outcomes. *Review of Educational Research, 79*, 491–525.

Jensen, L., Arnett, J., Feldman, S., & Cauffman, E. (2002). It's wrong, but everybody does it: Academic dishonesty among high school and college students. *Contemporary Educational Psychology, 27*, 209–238.

Jessen, S., & Grossmann, T. (2014). Unconscious discrimination of social cues from eye whites in infants. *Proceedings of the National Academy of Sciences, 111*(45).

Jeynes, W. (2002). The relationship between the consumption of various drugs by adolescents and their academic achievement. *American Journal of Drug and Alcohol Abuse, 28*, 15–35.

Jeynes, W. (2012). A meta-analysis of the efficacy of different types of parental involvement programs for urban students. *Urban Education, 47*, 706–742.

Jia, Y., Way, N., Ling, G., Yoshikawa, H., Chen, X., Hughes, D., et al. (2009). The influence of student perceptions of school climate on socioemotional and academic adjustment: A comparison of Chinese and American adolescents. *Child Development, 80*, 1514–1530.

Jirout, J. J., & Newcombe, N. S. (2015). Building blocks for developing spatial skills: Evidence from a large, representative U.S. sample. *Psychological Science, 26*, 302–310.

Job, V., Dweck, C. S., & Walton, G. M. (2010). Ego depletion—is it all in your head? *Psychological Science, 21*, 1686–1693.

Joel, S., MacDonald, G., & Shimotomai, A. (2011). Conflicting pressures on romantic relationship commitment for anxiously attached individuals. *Journal of Personality, 79*, 51–74.

John, O., Caspi, A., Robins, R., Moffitt, T., & Stouthamer-Loeber, M. (1994). The "little five": Exploring the nomological network of the five-factor model of personality in adolescent boys. *Child Development, 65*, 160–178.

John-Henderson, N. A., Stellar, J. E., Mendoza-Denton, R., & Francis, D. D. (2015). Socioeconomic status and social support: Social support reduces inflammatory reactivity for individuals whose early-life socioeconomic status was low. *Psychological Science, 26*, 1620–1629.

Johns, M., Schmader, T., & Martens, A. (2005). Knowing is half the battle: Teaching stereotype threat as a means of improving women's math performance. *Psychological Science, 16*, 175–179.

Johnson, A. D., Ryan, R. M., & Brooks-Gunn, J. (2012). Child-care subsidies: Do they impact the quality of care children experience? *Child Development, 83*, 1444–1461.

Johnson, B. T., Scott-Sheldon, L. A., Huedo-Medina, T., & Carey, M. (2011). Interventions to reduce sexual risk for human immunodeficiency virus in adolescents: A meta-analysis of trials, 1985–2008. *Archives of Pediatrics & Adolescent Medicine, 165*, 77–84.

Johnson, C., & Blasco, P. (1997). Infant growth and development. *Pediatrics in Review, 18*, 224–242.

Johnson, D. W., & Johnson, R. T. (2006). Conflict resolution, peer mediation, and peace making. In C. M. Evertson & C. S. Weinstein (Eds.), *Handbook of classroom management: Research, practice, and contemporary issues* (pp. 803–832). Mahwah, NJ: Erlbaum.

Johnson, J., Im-Bolter, N., & Pascual-Leone, J. (2003). Development of mental attention in gifted and mainstream children: The role of mental capacity, inhibition, and speed of processing. *Child Development, 74*, 1594–1614.

Johnson, L., O'Malley, P., Miech, R., Bachman, J., & Schulenberg, J. (2014). *Monitoring the future: National survey results on drug use 1975–2014.* Ann Arbor, MI: Institute for Social Research, University of Michigan.

Johnson, M. H., Grossmann, T., & Kadosh, K. C. (2009). Mapping functional brain development: Building a social brain through interactive specialization. *Developmental Psychology, 45*, 151–159.

Johnson, M. K., Crosnoe, R., & Elder, G. H. (2001). Students' attachment and academic engagement: The role of race and ethnicity. *Sociology of Education, 74*, 318–340.

Johnson, N. A., Smith, J. J., Pobiner, B., & Schrein, C. (2012). Why are chimps still chimps? *The American Biology Teacher, 74*, 74–80.

Johnson, S. C., Dweck, C. S., & Chen, F. S. (2007). Evidence for infants' internal working models of attachment. *Psychological Science, 18*, 501–502.

Johnson, S., Seidenfeld, A., Izard, C., & Kobak, R. (2012). Can classroom emotional support enhance prosocial development among children with depressed caregivers? *Early Childhood Research Quarterly, 28*, 282–290.

Jones, D. E., Greenberg, M., & Crowley, M. (2015). Early social-emotional functioning and public health: The relationship between kindergarten social competence and future wellness. *American Journal of Public Health, 105*, 2283–2290.

Jordan, N. C., Kaplan, D., Olah, L. N., & Locuniak, M. N. (2006). Number sense growth in kindergarten: A longitudinal investigation of children at risk for mathematics difficulties. *Child Development, 77*, 153–175.

Joseph, R. (2000). Fetal brain behavior and cognitive development. *Developmental Review, 20*, 81–98.

Josephson Institute. (2012). *2012 Report card on the ethics of American youth.* Los Angeles, CA: Josephson Institute of Ethics.

Joussemet, M., Vitaro, F., Barker, E. D., Cote, S., Nagin, D. S., Zoccolillo, M., et al. (2008). Controlling parenting and physical aggression during elementary school. *Child Development, 79*, 411–425.

Jusczyk, P. (2002). How infants adapt speech-processing capacities to native-language structure. *Current Directions in Psychological Sciences, 11*, 15–18.

Justice, L. M., Mashburn, A. J., Hamre, B. K., & Pianta, R. C. (2008). Quality of language and literacy instruction in preschool classrooms serving at-risk pupils. *Early Childhood Research Quarterly, 23*, 51–68.

Juvonen, J. (2007). Reforming middle schools: Focus on continuity, social connectedness, and engagement. *Educational Psychologist, 42*, 197–208.

Juvonen, J., & Graham, S. (2014). Bullying in schools: The power of bullies and the plight of victims. *Annual Review of Psychology, 65*, 159–185.

Kagan, J. (2008). In defense of qualitative changes in development. *Child Development, 79*, 1606–1624.

Kagan, J., Snidman, N., Kahn, V., & Towsley, S. (2007). The preservation of two infant temperaments into adolescence. *Monographs of the Society for Research in Child Development, 72* (Serial No. 287).

Kail, R. V., & Ferrer, E. (2007). Processing speed in childhood and adolescence: Longitudinal models for examining developmental change. *Child Development, 78*, 1760–1770.

Kaiser, C. R., Vick, S. B., & Major, B. (2006). Prejudice expectations moderate preconscious attention to cues that are threatening to social identity. *Psychological Science, 17*, 332–338.

Kaiser Family Foundation. (2004). *The role of media in childhood obesity*. Menlo Park, CA: Kaiser Family Foundation.

Kakinami, L., Barnett, T. A., Séguin, L., & Paradis, G. (2015). Parenting style and obesity risk in children. *Preventive Medicine: An International Journal Devoted to Practice and Theory, 75*, 18–22.

Kalil, A., & Ziol-Guest, K. M. (2005). Single mothers' employment dynamics and adolescent well-being. *Child Development, 76*, 196–211.

Kamberelis, G., & Bovino, T. D. (1999). Cultural artifacts as scaffolds for genre development. *Reading Research Quarterly, 34*, 138–170.

Kamii, C., Pritchett, M., & Nelson, K. (1997). 52 × 8: The importance of children's initiative. *The Constructivist, 12*, 5–11.

Kamil, M. L., Borman, G. D., Dole, J. A., Kral, C. C., Salinger, T., & Torgesen, J. K. (2008). *Improving adolescent literacy: Effective classroom and intervention practices: A practice guide (NCEE #2008-4027)*. Washington, DC: Department of Education, Institute of Education Sciences.

Kanazawa, S. (2015). Breastfeeding is positively associated with child intelligence even net parental IQ. *Developmental Psychology, 51*, 1683–1689.

Kang, M. J., Hsu, M., Krajbich, I. M., Loewenstein, G., McClure, S. M., Wang, J. T., et al. (2009). The wick in the candle of learning: Epistemic curiosity activates reward circuitry and enhances memory. *Psychological Science, 20*, 963–973.

Kaplan, A., Gheen, M., & Midgley, C. (2002). Classroom goal structure and student disruptive behaviour. *British Journal of Educational Psychology, 72*, 191–211.

Kaplan, S., & Berman, M. G. (2010). Directed attention as a common resource for executive functioning and self-regulation. *Perspectives on Psychological Science, 5*, 43–57.

Kaplow, J. B., Curran, P. J., Dodge, K. A., & Conduct Problems Prevention Research Group. (2002). Child, parent, and peer predictors of early-onset substance use: A multisite longitudinal study. *Journal of Abnormal Child Psychology, 30*, 199–216.

Karasick, L. B., Tamis-LeMonda, C. S., & Adolph, K. E. (2011). Transition from crawling to walking and infants' actions with objects and people. *Child Development, 82*, 1199–1209.

Karavasilis, L., Doyle, A. B., & Markiewicz, D. (2003). Associations between parenting style and attachment to mother in middle childhood and adolescence. *International Journal of Behavioral Development, 17*, 153–164.

Karen, R. (1994). *Becoming attached*. New York: Warner.

Karevold, E., Rxysamb, E., Ystrom, E., & Mathiesen, K. S. (2009). Predictors and pathways from infancy to symptoms of anxiety and depression in early adolescence. *Developmental Psychology, 45*, 1051–1060.

Karniol, R., Galili, L., Shtilerman, D., Naim, R., Stern, K., Manjoch, H., & Silverman, R. (2011). Why Superman can wait: Cognitive self-transformation in the delay of gratification paradigm. *Journal of Clinical Child & Adolescent Psychology, 40*, 307–317.

Karpicke, J. D., & Blunt, J. R. (2011). Retrieval practice produces more learning than elaborative studying with concept mapping. *Science, 331*, 772–775.

Kärtner, J., Keller, H., & Chaudhary, N. (2010). Cognitive and social influences on early prosocial behavior in two sociocultural contexts. *Developmental Psychology, 46*, 905–914.

Kashdan, T. B., Barrett, L. F., & McKnight, P. E. (2015). Unpacking emotion differentiation: Transforming unpleasant experience by perceiving distinctions in negativity. *Current Directions in Psychological Science, 24*, 10–16.

Katz, L. (1999). International perspectives on early childhood education: Lessons from my travels. *Early Childhood Research & Practice, 1*.

Katz, L. F., & Hunter, E. C. (2007). Maternal meta-emotion philosophy and adolescent depressive symptomatology. *Social Development, 16*, 343–360.

Kaufman, A. S. (2000). Tests of intelligence. In R. J. Sternberg (Ed.), *Handbook of intelligence* (pp. 445–476). Cambridge, UK: Cambridge University Press.

Kaufman, S. B., Reynolds, M. R., Liu, X., Kaufman, A. S., & McGrew, K. S. (2012). Are cognitive g and academic achievement g one and the same g? An exploration on the Woodcock–Johnson and Kaufman tests. *Intelligence, 40*, 123–138.

Kavšek, M. (2004). Predicting later IQ from infant visual habituation and dishabituation: A meta-analysis. *Journal of Applied Developmental Psychology, 25*, 369–393.

Kawabata, Y., & Crick, N. R. (2011). The significance of cross-racial/ethnic friendships: Associations with peer victimization, peer support, sociometric status, and classroom diversity. *Developmental Psychology, 47*, 1763–1775.

Keen, R. (2011). The development of problem solving in young children: A critical cognitive skill. *Annual Review of Psychology, 62*, 1–21.

Kelly, J. B. (2000). Children's adjustment in conflicted marriage and divorce: A decade's review of research. *Journal of the American Academy of Child and Adolescent Psychiatry, 39*, 963–973.

Keltner, D., Capps, L., Kring, A. M., Young, R. C., & Heerey, E. A. (2001). Just teasing: A conceptual analysis and empirical review. *Psychological Bulletin, 83*, 229–248.

Kemps, E., De Rammelaere, S., & Desmet, T. (2000). The development of working memory: Exploring the complementarity of two models. *Journal of Experimental Child Psychology, 77*, 89–109.

Kenney-Benson, G. A., Pomerantz, E. M., Ryan, A. M., & Patrick, H. (2006). Sex differences in math performance: The role of children's approach to schoolwork. *Developmental Psychology, 42*, 11–26.

Kenny, D. (2012). *Born to rise*. New York: HarperCollins.

Kensinger, E. A. (2007). Negative emotion enhances memory accuracy: Behavioral and neuroimaging evidence. *Current Directions in Psychological Science, 16*, 213–218.

Kerns, K. A., & Brumariu, L. E. (2014). Is insecure parent–child attachment a risk factor for the development of anxiety in childhood or adolescence? *Child Development Perspectives, 8*, 12–17.

Kerr, D. C., Lopez, N. L., Olson, S. L., & Sameroff, A. J. (2004). Parental discipline and externalizing behavior problems in early childhood. The roles of moral regulation and child gender. *Journal of Abnormal Child Psychology, 32*, 369–383.

Kersten-Alvarez, L. E., Hosman, C. M. H., Riksen-Walraven, J. M., Doesum, K. T. M., Smeekens, S., & Hoefnagels, C. (2012). Early school outcomes for children of postpartum depressed mothers: Comparison with a community sample. *Child Psychiatry & Human Development, 43*, 201–218.

Keyes, K. M., Maslowsky, J., Hamilton, A., & Schulenberg, J. (2015). The great sleep recession: Changes in sleep duration among US adolescents, 1991–2012. *Pediatrics, 135*, 460–468.

Khan, N. A., Raine, L. B., Donovan, S. M., & Hillman, C. H. (2014). The cognitive implications of obesity and nutrition in childhood. *Monographs of the Society for Research in Child Development, 79*(4), 51–71.

Khurana, A., Romer, D., Betancourt, L. M., Brodsky, N. L., Giannetta, J. M., & Hurt, H. (2015). Stronger working memory reduces sexual risk taking in adolescents, even after controlling for parental influences. *Child Development, 86*, 1125–1141.

Kiang, L., Yip, T., Gonzales-Backen, M., Witkow, M., & Fuligni, A. J. (2006). Ethnic identity and the daily psychological well-being of adolescents from Mexican and Chinese backgrounds. *Child Development, 77*, 1338–1350.

Kidd, D. C, & Castano, E. (2013). Reading literary fiction improves theory of mind. *Science, 342*(6156), 377–380.

Kidd, E., & Arciuli, J. (2016). Individual differences in statistical learning predict children's comprehension of syntax. *Child Development, 87*, 184–193.

Kidder, T. (1989). *Among schoolchildren*. Boston: Houghton Mifflin.

Kiefer, S. M., & Ryan, A. M. (2008). Striving for social dominance over peers: The implications for academic adjustment during early adolescence. *Journal of Educational Psychology, 100*, 417–428.

Kieffer, M. J. (2008). Catching up or falling behind? Initial English proficiency, concentrated poverty, and the reading growth of language minority learners in the United States. *Journal of Educational Psychology, 100*, 851–868.

Kieffer, M. J., & Lesaux, N. K. (2012). Effects of academic language instruction on relational and syntactic aspects of morphological awareness for sixth graders from linguistically diverse backgrounds. *Elementary School Journal, 112*, 519–545.

Kiley Hamlin, J., Wynn, K., & Bloom, P. (2010). Three-month-olds show a negativity bias in their social evaluations. *Developmental Science, 13*, 923–929.

Killen, M., Mulvey, K. L., & Hitti, A. (2013). Social exclusion in childhood: A developmental intergroup perspective. *Child Development, 84*, 772–790.

Killen, M., & Smetana, J. (1999). Social interactions in preschool classrooms and the development of young children's conceptions of the personal. *Child Development, 70,* 486–501.

Kim, J., & Cicchetti, D. (2006). Longitudinal trajectories of self-system processes and depressive symptoms among maltreated and nonmaltreated children. *Child Development, 77,* 624–639.

Kim, J., & Sunderman, G. (2005). Measuring academic proficiency under the No Child Left Behind Act: Implications for educational equity. *Educational Researcher, 34,* 3–13.

Kim, J. S. (2007). The effects of a voluntary summer reading intervention on reading activities and reading achievement. *Journal of Educational Psychology, 99,* 505–515.

Kim, S., & Kochanska, G. (2012). Child temperament moderates effects of parent-child mutuality on self-regulation: A relationship-based path for emotionally negative infants. *Child Development, 83,* 1271–1289.

Kim, S. W., & Hill, N. E. (2015). Including fathers in the picture: A meta-analysis of parental involvement and students' academic achievement. *Journal of Educational Psychology, 107,* 919–934.

Kim-Cohen, J., & Gold, A. L. (2009). Measured gene-environment interactions and mechanisms promoting resilient development. *Current Directions in Psychological Science, 18,* 138–142.

Kim-Cohen, J., Moffitt, T., Caspi, A., & Taylor, A. (2004). Genetic and environmental processes in young children's resilience and vulnerability to socioeconomic deprivation. *Child Development, 75,* 651–668.

Kim-Spoon, J., Cicchetti, D., & Rogosch, F. A. (2013). A longitudinal study of emotion regulation, emotion lability-negativity, and internalizing symptomatology in maltreated and nonmaltreated children. *Child Development, 84,* 512–527.

Kincaid, C., Jones, D., Sterrett, E., & McKee, L. G. (2012). A review of parenting and adolescent sexual behavior: The moderating role of gender. *Clinical Psychology Review, 32,* 177–188.

Kindermann, T. A. (2007). Effects of naturally existing peer groups on changes in academic engagement in a cohort of sixth graders. *Child Development, 78,* 1186–1203.

King, P. E., & Furrow, J. L. (2004). Religion as a resource for positive youth development: Religion, social capital, and moral outcomes. *Developmental Psychology, 40,* 703–713.

King, V., Harris, K. M., & Heard, H. E. (2004). Racial and ethnic diversity in nonresident father involvement. *Journal of Marriage and Family, 66,* 1–21.

Kinzler, K. D., Dupoux, E., & Spelke, E. S. (2012). "Native" objects and collaborators: Infants' object choices and acts of giving reflect favor for native over foreign speakers. *Journal of Cognition and Development, 13,* 67–81.

Kirschner, P. A., Sweller, J., & Clark, R. E. (2006). Why minimal guidance during instruction does not work: An analysis of the failure of constructivist, discovery, problem-based, experiential and inquiry-based teaching. *Educational Psychologist, 41,* 75–86.

Kirschner, P. A., & van Merriënboer, J. J. G. (2013). Do learners really know best? Urban legends in education. *Educational Psychologist, 48,* 169–183.

Kersten-Alvarez, L. E., Hosman, C. M. H., Riksen-Walraven, J. M., Doesum, K. T. M., Smeekens, S., & Hoefnagels, C. (2012). Early school outcomes for children of postpartum depressed mothers: Comparison with a community sample. *Child Psychiatry & Human Development, 43,* 201–218.

Kisilevsky, B., Hains, S., Lee, K., Xie, X., Huang, H., Ye, H. H., et al. (2003). Effects of experience on fetal voice recognition. *Psychological Science, 14,* 220–224.

Klahr, D., & Chen, Z. (2003). Overcoming the positive-capture strategy in young children: Learning about indeterminacy. *Child Development, 74,* 1275–1296.

Klahr, D., & Nigam, M. (2004). The equivalence of learning paths in early science instruction: Effects of direct instruction and discovery learning. *Psychological Science, 15,* 661–667.

Klahr, D., Zimmerman, C., & Jirout, J. (2011). Educational interventions to advance children's scientific thinking. *Science, 333*(6045), 971–975.

Klassen, R. M., Perry, N. E., & Frenzel, A. C. (2012). Teachers' relatedness with students: An underemphasized component of teachers' basic psychological needs. *Journal of Educational Psychology, 104,* 150–165.

Klauer, K. J., & Phye, G. D. (2008). Inductive reasoning: A training approach. *Review of Educational Research, 78,* 85–123.

Klein, J., & Cornell, D. (2010). Is the link between large high schools and student victimization an illusion? *Journal of Educational Psychology, 102,* 933–946.

Kliewer, W. (1991). Coping in middle childhood: Relations to competence, Type A behavior, monitoring, blunting, and locus of control. *Developmental Psychology, 27,* 689–697.

Klimes-Dougan, B., & Kistner, J. (1990). Physically abused preschoolers' responses to peers' distress. *Developmental Psychology, 26,* 599–602.

Klimstra, T. (2013). Adolescent personality development and identity formation. *Child Development Perspectives, 7,* 80–84.

Kline, P. (2001). Ability and temperament. In J. Collis & S. Messick (Eds.), *Intelligence and personality: Bridging the gap in theory and measurement* (pp. 113–117). Mahwah, NJ: Erlbaum.

Kljakovic, M., & Hunt, C. (2016). A meta-analysis of predictors of bullying and victimisation in adolescence. *Journal of Adolescence, 49,* 134–145.

Kochanska, G. (2002). Mutually responsive orientation between mothers and their young children: A context for the early development of conscience. *Current Directions in Psychological Science, 11,* 191–195.

Kochanska, G., Aksan, N., & Carlson, J. (2005). Temperament, relationships, and young children's receptive cooperation with their parents. *Developmental Psychology, 41,* 648–660.

Kochanska, G., Aksan, N., & Joy, M. E. (2007). Children's fearfulness as a moderator of parenting in early socialization: Two longitudinal studies. *Developmental Psychology, 43,* 222–237.

Kochanska, G., Barry, R. A., Stellern, S. A., & O'Bleness, J. J. (2009). Early attachment organization moderates the parent-child mutually coercive pathway to children's antisocial conduct. *Child Development, 80,* 1288–1300.

Kochanska, G., Koenig, J. L., Barry, R. A., Kim, S., & Yoon, J. E. (2010). Children's conscience during toddler and preschool years, moral self, and a competent, adaptive developmental trajectory. *Developmental Psychology, 46,* 1320–1332.

Kochel, K. P., Ladd, G. W., & Rudolph, K. D. (2012). Longitudinal associations among youth depressive symptoms, peer victimization, and low peer acceptance: An interpersonal process perspective. *Child Development, 83,* 637–650.

Kochenderfer-Ladd, B., & Wardrop, J. (2001). Chronicity and instability of children's peer victimization experiences as predictors of loneliness and social satisfaction trajectories. *Child Development, 72,* 134–151.

Kocken, P. L., Eeuwijk, J., Van Kesteren, N. M. C., Dusseldorp, E., Buijs, G., Bassa-Dafesh, Z., et al. (2012). Promoting the purchase of low-calorie foods from school vending machines: A cluster-randomized controlled study. *Journal of School Health, 82,* 115–122.

Kodak, T., Northrup, J., & Kelley, M. E. (2007). An evaluation of the types of attention that maintain problem behavior. *Journal of Applied Behavior Analysis, 40,* 167–171.

Koerber, S., Mayer, D., Osterhaus, C., Schwippert, K., & Sodian, B. (2015). The development of scientific thinking in elementary school: A comprehensive inventory. *Child Development, 86,* 327–336.

Kohlberg, L. (1981). *The philosophy of moral development. Volume 1. Moral stages and the idea of justice.* San Francisco: Harper & Row.

Kokko, K., & Pulkkinen, L. (2000). Aggression in childhood and long-term unemployment in adulthood: A cycle of maladaptation and some protective factors. *Developmental Psychology, 36,* 463–472.

Kolb, B., & Whishaw, I. (1998). Brain plasticity and behavior. *Annual Review of Psychology, 49,* 43–64.

Konstantopoulos, S. (2008). Do small classes reduce the achievement gap between low and high achievers? Evidence from Project STAR. *Elementary School Journal, 108,* 275–291.

Kontra, C., Lyons, D. J., Fischer, S. M., & Beilock, S. L. (2015). Physical experience enhances science learning. *Psychological Science, 26,* 737–749.

Kopala-Sibley, D. C., Zuroff, D. C., Hankin, B. L., & Abela, J. R. Z. (2015). The development of self-criticism and dependency in early adolescence and their role in the development of depressive and anxiety symptoms. *Personality and Social Psychology Bulletin, 41,* 1094–1109.

Kornell, N., & Bjork, R. A. (2008). Learning concepts and categories: Is spacing the "enemy of induction"? *Psychological Science, 19,* 585–592.

Köster, M., Ohmer, X., Nguyen, T. D., & Kärtner, J. (2016). Infants understand others' needs. *Psychological Science, 27*, 542–548.

Kowalski, R. M. (2000). "I was only kidding!": Victims' and perpetrators' perceptions of teasing. *Personality and Social Psychology Bulletin, 26*, 231–241.

Kowalski, R. M., Giumetti, G. W., Schroeder, A. N., & Lattanner, M. R. (2014). Bullying in the Digital Age: A critical review and meta-analysis of cyberbullying research among youth. *Psychological Bulletin, 140*, 1073–1137.

Köymen, B., Lieven, E., Engemann, D. A., Rakoczy, H., Warneken, F., & Tomasello, M. (2014). Children's norm enforcement in their interactions with peers. *Child Development, 85*, 1108–1122.

Kraft, T., & Pressman, S. (2012). Grin and bear it: The influence of manipulated facial expression on the stress response. *Psychological Science, 23*, 1372–1378.

Kraizer, S., Witte, S., Fryer, G., & Miyoshi, T. (1990). Children in self-care: A new perspective. *Child Welfare, 69*, 571–581.

Kramarski, B., & Mevarech, Z. (2003). Enhancing mathematical reasoning in the classroom: The effects of cooperative learning and metacognitive training. *American Educational Research Journal, 40*, 281–310.

Kramer, M., & Kakuma, R. (2004). The optimal duration of exclusive breastfeeding: A systematic review. *Advances in Experimental Medicine & Biology, 554*, 63–77.

Kraus, M. W., Piff, P. K., Mendoza-Denton, R., Rheinschmidt, M. L., & Keltner, D. (2012). Social class, solipsism, and contextualism: How the rich are different from the poor. *Psychological Review, 119*, 546–572.

Kraus, N., & Banai, K. (2007). Auditory-processing malleability: Focus on language and music. *Current Directions in Psychological Science, 16*, 105–110.

Krebs, D. L. (2008). Morality: An evolutionary account. *Perspectives on Psychological Science, 3*, 149–172.

Kreppner, J. M., Rutter, M., Beckett, C., Castle, J., Colvert, E., Groothues, C., et al. (2007). Normality and impairment following profound early institutional deprivation: A longitudinal follow-up in early adolescence. *Developmental Psychology, 43*, 931–946.

Krevans, J., & Gibbs, J. C. (1996). Parents' use of inductive discipline: Relations to children's empathy and prosocial behavior. *Child Development, 67*, 3263–3277.

Krishnamoorthy, J. S., Hart, C., & Jelalian, E. (2006). The epidemic of childhood obesity: Review of research and implications for public policy. *Social Policy Report, 19*, 3–17.

Kristof, N. D. (2012, January 22). How Mrs. Grady transformed Olly Neal. *New York Times*, p. SR13.

Kromm, H., Färber, M., & Holodynski, M. (2015). Felt or false smiles? Volitional regulation of emotional expression in 4-, 6-, and 8-year-old children. *Child Development, 86*, 579–597.

Kross, E., Berman, M. G., Mischel, W., Smith, E. E., & Wager, T. D. (2011). Social rejection shares somatosensory representations with physical pain. *Proceedings of the National Academy of Sciences, 108*, 6270–6275.

Krumboltz, J. D., & Krumboltz, H. B. (1972). *Changing children's behavior.* Englewood Cliffs, NJ: Prentice Hall.

Kubiszyn, T., & Borich, G. (2003). *Educational testing and measurement* (7th ed.). New York: Wiley.

Kucker, S. C., McMurray, B., & Samuelson, L. K. (2015). Slowing down fast mapping: Redefining the dynamics of word learning. *Child Development Perspectives, 9*, 74–78.

Kuczynski, L., & Kochanska, G. (1990). Development of children's noncompliance strategies from toddlerhood to age 5. *Developmental Psychology, 26*, 398–408.

Kuhl, P. (2000). Language, mind, and brain: Experience alters perception. In M. Gazzaniga (Ed.), *The new cognitive neurosciences* (2nd ed., pp. 99–115). Cambridge, MA: MIT Press.

Kuhn, D. (2006). Do cognitive changes accompany developments in the adolescent brain? *Perspectives on Psychological Science, 1*, 59–67.

Kuhn, D. (2008). Formal operations from a twenty-first century perspective. *Human Development, 51*, 48–55.

Kuhn, D. (2015). Thinking together and alone. *Educational Researcher, 44*, 46–53.

Kuhn, D., Black, J., Keselman, A., & Kaplan, D. (2000). The development of cognitive skills to support inquiry learning. *Cognition and Instruction, 18*, 495–523.

Kuhn, D., & Crowell, A. (2011). Dialogic argumentation as a vehicle for developing young adolescents' thinking. *Psychological Science, 22*, 545–552.

Kuhn, D., & Udell, W. (2003). The development of argument skills. *Child Development, 74*, 1245–1260.

Kuhn, L. J., Willoughby, M. T., Wilbourn, M. P., Vernon-Feagans, L., Blair, C. B., & The Family Life Project Key Investigators. (2014). Early communicative gestures prospectively predict language development and executive function in early childhood. *Child Development, 85*, 1898–1914.

Kujawa, A., Proudfit, G. H., Laptook, R., & Klein, D. N. (2015). Early parenting moderates the association between parental depression and neural reactivity to rewards and losses in offspring. *Clinical Psychological Science, 3*, 503–515.

Kunkel, D., Eyal, K., Finnerty, K., Biely, E., & Donnerstein, E. (2005). *Sex on TV.* Menlo Park, CA: Kaiser Family Foundation.

Kuppens, S., Grietens, H., Onghena, P., Michiels, D., & Subramanian, S. V. (2008). Individual and classroom variables associated with relational aggression in elementary-school aged children: A multilevel analysis. *Journal of School Psychology, 46*, 639–660.

Kushnir, T., Xu, F., & Wellman, H. (2010). Young children use statistical sampling to infer the preferences of other people. *Psychological Science, 21*, 1134.

Kuster, F., & Orth, U. (2013). The long-term stability of self-esteem: Its time-dependent decay and nonzero asymptote. *Personality and Social Psychology Bulletin, 39*, 677–690.

Kuther, T., & Higgins-D'Alessandro, A. (2000). Bridging the gap between moral reasoning and adolescent engagement in risky behavior. *Journal of Adolescence, 23*, 409–422.

La Paro, K., & Pianta, R. (2000). Predicting children's competence in the early school years: A meta-analytic review. *Review of Educational Research, 70*, 443–484.

Laboratory of Comparative Human Cognition. (1998). Culture and cognitive development. In R. M. Lerner (Ed.), *Handbook of child psychology: Theoretical models of human development* (5th ed., Vol. 1, pp. 295–356). New York: Wiley.

Lac, A., & Crano, W. D. (2009). Monitoring matters: Meta-analytic review reveals the reliable linkage of parental monitoring with adolescent marijuana use. *Perspectives on Psychological Science, 4*, 578–586.

Ladd, G. W. (2006). Peer rejection, aggressive or withdrawn behavior, and psychological maladjustment from ages 5 to 12: An examination of four predictive models. *Child Development, 77*, 822–846.

Ladd, G. W., Buhs, E., & Troop, W. (2002). Children's interpersonal skills and relationships in school settings: Adaptive significance and implications for school-based prevention and intervention programs. In P. Smith & C. Hart (Eds.), *Blackwell handbook of childhood social development* (pp. 394–415). Oxford, UK: Blackwell.

Ladd, G. W., & Dinella, L. M. (2009). Continuity and change in early school engagement: Predictive of children's achievement trajectories from first to eighth grade? *Journal of Educational Psychology, 101*, 190–206.

Ladd, G. W., Ettekal, I., Kochenderfer-Ladd, B., Rudolph, K. D., & Andrews, R. K. (2014). Relations among chronic peer group rejection, maladaptive behavioral dispositions, and early adolescents' peer perceptions. *Child Development, 85*, 971–988.

Ladd, G. W., Herald-Brown, S. L., & Reiser, M. (2008). Does chronic classroom peer rejection predict the development of children's classroom participation during the grade school years? *Child Development, 79*, 1001–1015.

Ladd, G. W., Kochenderfer, B. J., & Coleman, C. C. (1996). Friendship quality as a predictor of young children's early school adjustment. *Child Development, 67*, 1103–1118.

Ladd, G. W., Kochenderfer-Ladd, B., Eggum, N. D., Kochel, K. P., & McConnell, E. M. (2011). Characterizing and comparing the friendships of anxious-solitary and unsociable preadolescents. *Child Development, 82*, 1434–1453.

Ladd, G. W., Kochenderfer-Ladd, B., Visconti, K., Ettekal, I., Sechler, C., & Cortes, K. (2014). Grade-school children's social collaborative skills: Links with partner preference and achievement. *American Educational Research Journal, 51*, 152–183.

Ladd, G. W., & Pettit, G. S. (2002). Parenting and the development of children's peer relationships. In M. Bornstein (Ed.), *Handbook of parenting* (2nd ed., Vol. 5, pp. 269–309). Hillsdale, NJ: Erlbaum.

Ladd, G. W., & Troop-Gordon, W. (2003). The role of chronic peer difficulties in the development of children's psychological adjustment problems. *Child Development, 74*, 1344–1367.

Lagattuta, K. H., Sayfan, L., & Harvey, C. (2014). Beliefs about thought probability: Evidence for persistent errors in mindreading and links to executive control. *Child Development, 85*, 659–674.

Lagattuta, K. H., & Wellman, H. (2002). Differences in early parent–child conversations about negative versus positive emotions: Implications for the development of psychological understanding. *Developmental Psychology, 38*, 564–580.

Lahey, B. B. (2009). Public health significance of neuroticism. *American Psychologist, 64*, 241–256.

Laible, D., Panfile, T., & Makariev, D. (2008). The quality and frequency of mother–toddler conflict: Links with attachment and temperament. *Child Development, 79*, 426–443.

Laible, D., & Thompson, R. (2000). Mother-child discourse, attachment security, shared positive affect, and early conscience development. *Child Development, 71*, 1424–1440.

Laible, D. J., & Thompson, R. A. (2002). Mother–child conflict in the toddler years: Lessons in emotion, morality, and relationships. *Child Development, 73*, 1187–1203.

Laird, R. D., Pettit, G. S., Bates, J. E., & Dodge, K. A. (2003). Parents' monitoring-relevant knowledge and adolescents' delinquent behavior: Evidence of correlated developmental changes and reciprocal influences. *Child Development, 74*, 752–768.

Lam, C. B., McHale, S. M., & Crouter, A. C. (2014). Time with peers from middle childhood to late adolescence: Developmental course and adjustment correlates. *Child Development, 85*, 1677–1693.

Lamb, M. (1998). Nonparental child care: Context, quality, correlates, and consequences. In I. Sigel & K. A. Renninger (Eds.), *Handbook of child psychology. Child psychology in practice* (5th ed., Vol. 4, pp. 73–133). New York: Wiley.

Lamborn, S. D., Mounts, N. S., Steinberg, L., & Dornbusch, S. M. (1991). Patterns of competence and adjustment among adolescents from authoritative, authoritarian, indulgent, and neglectful families. *Child Development, 62*, 1049–1065.

Lamont, J. H., Devore, C. D., Allison, M., Ancona, R., Barnett, S. E., Gunther, R., . . . Young, T. (2013). Policy Statement. Out-of-school suspension and expulsion. *Pediatrics, 131*, e1000–e1007.

Lampert, M., Rittenhouse, P., & Crumbaugh, C. (1996). Agreeing to disagree: Developing sociable mathematical discourse. In D. R. Olson & N. Torrance (Eds.), *The handbook of education and human development* (pp. 731–764). Oxford, UK: Blackwell.

Landry, S., Smith, K., Miller-Loncar, C., & Swank, P. (1997). Predicting cognitive-language and social growth curves from early maternal behaviors in children at varying degrees of biological risk. *Developmental Psychology, 33*, 1040–1053.

Landry, S. H., Smith, K. E., Swank, P. R., Zucker, T., Crawford, A. D., & Solari, E. F. (2012). The effects of a responsive parenting intervention on parent–child interactions during shared book reading. *Developmental Psychology, 48*, 969–986.

Landsem, I. P., Handegård, B. H., Ulvund, S. E., Tunby, J., Kaaresen, P. I., & Rønning, J. A. (2015). Does an early intervention influence behavioral development until age 9 in children born prematurely? *Child Development, 86*, 1063–1079.

Lane, H. B., & Allen, S. A. (2010). The vocabulary-rich classroom: Modeling sophisticated word use to promote word consciousness and vocabulary growth. *The Reading Teacher, 63*, 362–370.

Lang, J. W., & Lang, J. (2010). Priming competence diminishes the link between cognitive test anxiety and test performance: Implications for the interpretation of test scores. *Psychological Science, 21*, 811–819.

Lansford, J. E. (2009). Parental divorce and children's adjustment. *Perspectives on Psychological Science, 4*, 140–152.

Lansford, J. E., Criss, M. M., Dodge, K. A., Shaw, D. S., Pettit, G. S., & Bates, J. E. (2009). Trajectories of physical discipline: Early childhood antecedents and developmental outcomes. *Child Development, 80*, 1385–1402.

Lansford, J. E., Deater-Deckard, K., Bornstein, M. H., Putnick, D. L., & Bradley, R. H. (2014). Attitudes justifying domestic violence predict endorsement of corporal punishment and physical and psychological aggression towards children:

A study in 25 low- and middle-income countries. *Journal of Pediatrics, 164*, 1208–1213.

Lansford, J. E., Skinner, A. T., Sorbring, E., Di Giunta, L., Deater-Deckard, K., Dodge, K. A., et al. (2012). Boys' and girls' relational and physical aggression in nine countries. *Aggressive Behavior, 38*, 298–308.

Lansford, J. E., Yu, T., Erath, S., Pettit, G. S., Bates, J. E., & Dodge, K. A. (2010). Developmental precursors of number of sexual partners from ages 16 to 22. *Journal of Research on Adolescence, 20*, 651–677.

Lansu, T. A., Cillessen, A., & Karremans, J. C. (2012). Implicit associations with popularity in early adolescence: An approach-avoidance analysis. *Developmental Psychology, 48*, 65–75.

Lanza, S. T., Rhoades, B. L., Nix, R. L., & Greenberg, M. T. (2010). Modeling the interplay of multilevel risk factors for future academic and behavior problems: A person-centered approach. *Development and Psychopathology, 22*, 313–335.

Lapchick, R. (2012). *The 2012 racial and gender report card: Major League Baseball.* Orlando, FL: University of Central Florida.

Lareau, A. (1989). *Home advantage: Social class and parental intervention in elementary education.* London: Falmer Press.

Lareau, A., & Calarco, J. (2012). Class, cultural capital, and institutions: The case of families and schools. In H. Markus & S. T. Fiske (Eds.), *Facing social class* (pp. 61–86). New York: Russell Sage Foundation.

Lareau, A., & Muñoz, V. L. (2012). "You're not going to call the shots": Structural conflicts between the principal and the PTO at a suburban public elementary school. *Sociology of Education, 85*, 201–218.

Larsen, J. T., To, Y. M., & Fireman, G. (2007). Children's understanding and experience of mixed emotions. *Psychological Science, 18*, 186–191.

Larson, K., Russ, S. A., Nelson, B. B., Olson, L. M., & Halfon, N. (2015). Cognitive ability at kindergarten entry and socioeconomic status. *Pediatrics, 135*, e440–e448.

Larson, R. (2001). How U.S. children and adolescents spend time: What it does (and doesn't) tell us about their development. *Current Directions in Psychological Science, 10*, 160–164.

Larson, R., & Richards, M. H. (1994). *Divergent realities: The emotional lives of mothers, fathers, and adolescents.* New York: Basic Books.

Larson, R., & Verma, S. (1999). How children and adolescents spend time around the world: Work, play, and developmental opportunities. *Psychological Bulletin, 125*, 701–736.

Latendresse, S. J., Bates, J. E., Goodnight, J. A., Lansford, J. E., Budde, J. P., Goate, A., et al. (2011). Differential susceptibility to adolescent externalizing trajectories: Examining the interplay between CHRM2 and peer group antisocial behavior. *Child Development, 82*, 1797–1814.

Laurent, H., Ablow, J., & Measelle, J. (2012). Taking stress response out of the box: Stability, discontinuity, and temperament effects on HPA and SNS across social stressors in mother–infant dyads. *Developmental Psychology, 48*, 35–45.

Laurent, H. K. (2014). Clarifying the contours of emotion regulation: Insights from parent-child stress research. *Child Development Perspectives, 8*, 30–35.

Lauer, P. A., Akiba, M., Wilkerson, S. B., Apthorp, H. S., Snow, D., & Martin-Glenn, M. L. (2006). Out-of-school-time programs: A meta-analysis of effects for at-risk students. *Review of Educational Research, 76*, 275–313.

Laursen, B., Bukowski, W. M., Aunola, K., & Nurmi, J.-E. (2007). Friendship moderates prospective associations between social isolation and adjustment problems in young children. *Child Development, 78*, 1395–1404.

Laursen, B., Finkelstein, B., & Betts, N. (2001). A developmental meta-analysis of peer conflict resolution. *Developmental Review, 21*, 423–449.

Laursen, B., Pulkkinen, L., & Adams, R. (2002). The antecedents and correlates of agreeableness in adulthood. *Developmental Psychology, 38*, 591–603.

Leaper, C., & Brown, C. S. (2008). Perceived experiences with sexism among adolescent girls. *Child Development, 79*, 685–704.

Lear, J. (2003). School-based health centers: A long road to travel. *Archives of Pediatrics and Adolescent Medicine, 157*, 118–119.

Leavell, A. S., Tamis-LeMonda, C. S., Ruble, D. N., Zosuls, K. M., & Cabrera, N. J. (2012). African American, White and Latino fathers' activities with their sons and daughters in early childhood. *Sex Roles, 66*, 53–65.

Lecce, S., Bianco, F., Demicheli, P., & Cavallini, E. (2014). Training preschoolers on first-order false belief understanding: Transfer on advanced ToM skills and metamemory. *Child Development, 85,* 2404–2418.

Lederberg, A. R., Schick, B., & Spencer, P. E. (2013). Language and literacy development of deaf and hard-of-hearing children: Successes and challenges. *Developmental Psychology, 49,* 15–30.

Lee, C. D. (1995). A culturally based cognitive apprenticeship: Teaching African American high school students skills in literary interpretation. *Reading Research Quarterly, 30,* 608–630.

Lee, D. L. (2005). Increasing compliance: A quantitative synthesis of applied research on high-probability request sequences. *Exceptionality, 13,* 141–154.

Lee, H. S., & Anderson, J. R. (2013). Student learning: What has instruction got to do with it? *Annual Review of Psychology, 64,* 445–469.

Lee, J. (2008). Is test-driven external accountability effective? Synthesizing the evidence from cross-state causal-comparative and correlational studies. *Review of Educational Research, 78,* 608–644.

Lee, K. (2013). Little liars: Development of verbal deception in children. *Child Development Perspectives, 7,* 91–96.

Lee, K., Ng, E. L., & Ng, S. F. (2009). The contributions of working memory and executive functioning to problem representation and solution generation in algebraic word problems. *Journal of Educational Psychology, 101,* 373–387.

Lee, K., Talwar, V., McCarthy, A., Ross, I., Evans, A., & Arruda, C. (2014). Can classic moral stories promote honesty in children? *Psychological Science, 25,* 1630–1636.

Lee, K. T. H., & Vandell, D. L. (2015). Out-of-school time and adolescent substance use. *Journal of Adolescent Health, 57,* 523–529.

Lee, L., Howes, C., & Chamberlain, B. (2007). Ethnic heterogeneity of social networks and cross-ethnic friendships of elementary school boys and girls. *Merrill-Palmer Quarterly, 53,* 325–346.

Lee, V., Brooks-Gunn, J., Schnur, E., & Liaw, F.-R. (1990). Are Head Start effects sustained? A longitudinal follow-up comparison of disadvantaged children attending Head Start, no preschool, and other preschool programs. *Child Development, 61,* 495–507.

Lee, V., Loeb, S., & Lubeck, S. (1998). Contextual effects of prekindergarten classrooms for disadvantaged children on cognitive development: The case of Chapter 1. *Child Development, 69,* 479–494.

Lecce, S., Bianco, F., Demicheli, P., & Cavallini, E. (2014). Training preschoolers on first-order false belief understanding: Transfer on advanced ToM skills and metamemory. *Child Development, 85,* 2404–2418.

Lederberg, A. R., Schick, B., & Spencer, P. E. (2013). Language and literacy development of deaf and hard-of-hearing children: Successes and challenges. *Developmental Psychology, 49,* 15–30.

Lee Hang, D., & Bell, B. (2015). Written formative assessment and silence in the classroom. *Cultural Studies of Science Education, 10,* 763–775.

Leerkes, E. M., Blankson, N., & O'Brien, M. (2009). Differential effects of maternal sensitivity to infant distress and nondistress on social-emotional functioning. *Child Development, 80,* 762–775.

Leerkes, E. M., Parade, S. H., & Gudmundson, J. A. (2011). Mothers' emotional reactions to crying pose risk for subsequent attachment insecurity. *Journal of Family Psychology, 25,* 635–643.

Lehmann, M., & Hasselhorn, M. (2007). Variable memory strategy use in children's adaptive intratask learning behavior: Developmental changes and working memory influences in free recall. *Child Development, 78,* 1068–1082.

Legare, C. H. (2014). The contributions of explanation and exploration to children's scientific reasoning. *Child Development Perspectives, 8,* 101–106.

Lei, J. L. (2003). (Un)Necessary toughness?: Those "loud black girls" and those "quiet Asian boys." *Anthropology & Education Quarterly, 34,* 158–181.

Lemelin, J.-P., Boivin, M., Forget-Dubois, N., Dionne, G., Seguin, J. R., Brendgen, M., et al. (2007). The genetic-environmental etiology of cognitive school readiness and later academic achievement in early childhood. *Child Development, 78,* 1855–1869.

Lemerise, E. A., & Arsenio, W. F. (2000). An integrated model of emotion processes and cognition in social information processing. *Child Development, 71,* 107–118.

Lengua, L. J., Bush, N. R., Long, A. C., Kovacs, E. A., & Trancik, A. M. (2008). Effortful control as a moderator of the relation between contextual risk factors and growth in adjustment problems. *Development and Psychopathology, 20,* 509–528.

Lenhart, A., & Pew Research Center. (2015). *Teens, social media & technology overview 2015.*

Lenhart, A., Purcell, K., Smith, A., & Zickuhr, K. (2010). *Social media & mobile Internet use among teens and young adults.* Washington, DC: Pew Internet & American Life Project.

Leonhardt, D., & Quealy, K. (2015, May 15). How your hometown affects your chance of marriage. *New York Times,* http://www.nytimes.com/interactive/2015/05/15/upshot/the-places-that-discourage-marriage-most.html?_r=0

Leppanen, J. M., Moulson, M. C., Vogel-Farley, V. K., & Nelson, C. A. (2007). An ERP study of emotional face processing in the adult and infant brain. *Child Development, 78,* 232–245.

Lepper, M. R. (1983). Social-control processes and the internalization of social values: An attributional perspective. In E. T. Higgins, D. Ruble, & W. Hartup (Eds.), *Social cognition and social development: A sociocultural perspective* (pp. 294–330). Cambridge, UK: Cambridge University Press.

Lepper, M. R., Greene, D., & Nisbett, R. E. (1973). Undermining children's intrinsic interest with extrinsic reward: A test of the "overjustification" hypothesis. *Journal of Personality and Social Psychology, 28,* 129–137.

Lepper, M. R., Keavney, M., & Drake, M. (1996). Intrinsic motivation and extrinsic rewards: A commentary on Cameron and Pierce's meta-analysis. *Review of Educational Research, 66,* 5–32.

Lerner, J. V. (1983). The role of temperament in psychosocial adaptation in early adolescents: A test of a "goodness of fit" model. *Journal of Genetic Psychology, 143,* 149–157.

Lerner, J. V., Lerner, R., & Zabski, S. (1985). Temperament and elementary school children's actual and rated academic performance: A test of a "goodness of fit" model. *Journal of Child Psychology & Psychiatry & Allied Disciplines, 26,* 125–136.

Lesaux, N. K., Lipka, O., & Siegel, L. S. (2006). Investigating cognitive and linguistic abilities that influence the reading comprehension skills of children from diverse linguistic backgrounds. *Reading and Writing, 19,* 99–131.

Lesesne, C., Visser, S., & White, C. (2003). Attention-deficit/hyperactivity disorder in school-aged children: Association with maternal mental health and use of health care resources. *Pediatrics, 111,* 1232–1237.

Leu, D. J., Forzani, E., Rhoads, C., Maykel, C., Kennedy, C., & Timbrell, N. (2015). The new literacies of online research and comprehension: Rethinking the reading achievement gap. *Reading Research Quarterly, 50,* 37–59.

Leve, L. D., Kerr, D. C. R., Shaw, D., Ge, X., Neiderhiser, J. M., Scaramella, L. V., et al. (2010). Infant pathways to externalizing behavior: Evidence of genotype X environment interaction. *Child Development, 81,* 340–356.

Levin, I., & Bus, A. G. (2003). How is emergent writing based on drawing? Analyses of children's products and their sorting by children and mothers. *Developmental Psychology, 39,* 891–905.

Levine, J., Pollack, H., & Comfort, M. E. (2001). Academic and behavioral outcomes among the children of young mothers. *Journal of Marriage and Family, 63,* 355–369.

Levine, S. C., Ratliff, K. R., Huttenlocher, J., & Cannon, J. (2012). Early puzzle play: A predictor of preschoolers' spatial transformation skill. *Developmental Psychology, 48,* 530–542.

Levinson, D. B., Smallwood, J., & Davidson, R. J. (2012). The persistence of thought: Evidence for a role of working memory in the maintenance of task-unrelated thinking. *Psychological Science, 23,* 375–380.

Lewis, A. E. (2001). There is no "race" in the schoolyard: Color-blind ideology in an (almost) all-White school. *American Educational Research Journal, 38,* 781–811.

Lewis, B., Singer, L. T., Short, E., Minnes, S., Arendt, R., Weishampel, P., et al. (2004). Four-year language outcomes of children exposed to cocaine in utero. *Neurotoxicology and Teratology, 26,* 617–627.

Lewis, C., & Carpendale, J. (2002). Social cognition. In P. Smith & C. Hart (Eds.), *Blackwell handbook of childhood social development* (pp. 375–393). Oxford, UK: Blackwell.

Lewis, M., Feiring, C., & Rosenthal, S. (2000). Attachment over time. *Child Development, 71*, 707–720.

Lewis, V., Norgate, S., Collis, G., & Reynolds, R. (2000). The consequences of visual impairment for children's symbolic and functional play. *British Journal of Developmental Psychology, 18*, 449–464.

Lewis-Morrarty, E., Degnan, K. A., Chronis-Tuscano, A., Pine, D. S., Henderson, H. A., & Fox, N. A. (2015). Infant attachment security and early childhood behavioral inhibition interact to predict adolescent social anxiety symptoms. *Child Development, 86*, 598–613.

Leyva, D., Weiland, C., Barata, M., Yoshikawa, H., Snow, C., Treviño, E., & Rolla, A. (2015). Teacher–child interactions in Chile and their associations with pre-kindergarten outcomes. *Child Development, 86*, 781–799.

Li, V., Spitzer, B., & Olson, K. R. (2014). Preschoolers reduce inequality while favoring individuals with more. *Child Development, 85*, 1123–1133.

Li, X., & Atkins, M. S. (2004). Early childhood computer experience and cognitive and motor development. *Pediatrics, 113*, 1715–1722.

Li-Grining, C. P. (2007). Effortful control among low-income preschoolers in three cities: Stability, change, and individual differences. *Developmental Psychology, 43*, 208–221.

Li-Grining, C. P., Votruba-Drzal, E., Maldonado-Carreño, C., & Haas, K. (2010). Children's early approaches to learning and academic trajectories through fifth grade. *Developmental Psychology, 46*, 1062–1077.

Lichty, L. F., & Campbell, R. (2012). Targets and witnesses: Middle school students' sexual harassment experiences. *Journal of Early Adolescence, 32*, 414–430.

Liew, J. (2012). Effortful control, executive functions, and education: Bringing self-regulatory and social-emotional competencies to the table. *Child Development Perspectives, 6*, 105–111.

Light, P., & Littleton, K. (1999). *Social processes in children's learning.* Cambridge, UK: Cambridge University Press.

Lightner, R., Bollmer, J., Harris, M., Milich, R., & Scambler, D. (2000). What do you say to teasers? Parent and child evaluations of responses to teasing. *Journal of Applied Developmental Psychology, 21*, 403–427.

Lilienfeld, S. O. (2007). Psychological treatments that cause harm. *Perspectives on Psychological Science, 2*, 53–70.

Lillard, A. (2002). Pretend play and cognitive development. In U. Goswami (Ed.), *Blackwell handbook of childhood cognitive development* (pp. 189–205). Malden, MA: Blackwell.

Lillard, A. S., Lerner, M. D., Hopkins, E. J., Dore, R. A., Smith, E. D., & Palmquist, C. M. (2013). The impact of pretend play on children's development: A review of the evidence. *Psychological Bulletin, 139*, 1–34.

Lillard, A. S., & Peterson, J. (2011). The immediate impact of different types of television on young children's executive function. *Pediatrics, 128*, 644–648.

Lin, T.-J., Anderson, R. C., Jadallah, M., Kuo, L.-J., Wu, X., Hummel, J. E., . . . Dong, T. (2012). Children's use of analogy during collaborative reasoning. *Child Development, 83*, 1429–11443.

Lindell, A. K., & Kidd, E. (2013). Consumers favor "right brain" training: The dangerous lure of neuromarketing. *Mind, Brain, and Education, 7*, 35–39.

Lindner, I., Echterhoff, G., Davidson, P. S. R., & Brand, M. (2010). Observation inflation. *Psychological Science, 21*, 1291–1299.

Lindquist, K. A., Satpute, A. B., & Gendron, M. (2015). Does language do more than communicate emotion? *Current Directions in Psychological Science, 24*, 99–108.

Linver, M. R., Roth, J., & Brooks-Gunn, J. (2009). Patterns of adolescents' participation in organized activities: Are sports best when combined with other activities? *Developmental Psychology, 45*, 354–367.

Linver, M., Brooks-Gunn, J., & Kohen, D. (2002). Family processes as pathways from income to young children's development. *Developmental Psychology, 38*, 719–734.

Lipowski, S. L., Pyc, M. A., Dunlosky, J., & Rawson, K. A. (2014). Establishing and explaining the testing effect in free recall for young children. *Developmental Psychology, 50*, 994–1000.

Lipscomb, S. T., Leve, L. D., Harold, G. T., Neiderhiser, J. M., Shaw, D., Ge, Z., et al. (2011). Trajectories of parenting and child negative emotionality during infancy and toddlerhood: A longitudinal analysis. *Child Development, 82*, 1661–1675.

Lipsey, M., & Wilson, D. (1993). The efficacy of psychological, educational, and behavioral treatment. *American Psychologist, 48*, 1181–1209.

Lisha, N. E., & Sussman, S. (2010). Relationship of high school and college sports participation with alcohol, tobacco, and illicit drug use: A review. *Addictive Behaviors, 35*, 399–407.

Lisonbee, J. A., Mize, J., Payne, A. L., & Granger, D. A. (2008). Children's cortisol and the quality of teacher-child relationships in child care. *Child Development, 79*, 1818–1832.

Liszkowski, U. (2013). Using theory of mind. *Child Development Perspectives, 7*, 104–109.

Liu, Y., & Wang, Z. (2014). Positive affect and cognitive control: Approach-motivation intensity influences the balance between cognitive flexibility and stability. *Psychological Science, 25*, 1116–1123.

Livingston, G. (2013). *The rise of single fathers.* Washington, DC: Pew Research Center.

Lloyd, B., & Howe, N. (2003). Solitary play and convergent and divergent thinking skills in preschool children. *Early Childhood Research Quarterly, 18*, 22–41.

Locke, E. A., & Latham, G. P. (2002). Building a practically useful theory of goal setting and task motivation. *American Psychologist, 57*, 705–717.

Loe, I. M., Balestrino, M. D., Phelps, R. A., Kurs-Lasky, M., Chaves-Gnecco, D., Paradise, J. L., et al. (2008). Early histories of school-aged children with attention-deficit/hyperactivity disorder. *Child Development, 79*, 1853–1868.

Loeb, S., Fuller, B., Kagan, S., & Carrol, B. (2004). Child care in poor communities: Early learning effects of type, quality, and stability. *Child Development, 75*, 47–65.

Logan, J. A. R., Hart, S. A., Cutting, L., Deater-Deckard, K., Schatschneider, C., & Petrill, S. (2013). Reading development in young children: Genetic and environmental influences. *Child Development, 84*, 2131–2144.

Lombardi, C. M., & Coley, R. L. (2014). Early maternal employment and children's school readiness in contemporary families. *Developmental Psychology, 50*, 2071–2084.

London, A., Scott, E., Edin, K., & Hunter, V. (2004). Welfare reform, work-family tradeoffs, and child well-being. *Family Relations, 53*, 148–158.

Longhi, E., Senna, I., Bolognini, N., Bulf, H., Tagliabue, P., Macchi Cassia, V., & Turati, C. (2015). Discrimination of biomechanically possible and impossible hand movements at birth. *Child Development, 86*, 632–641.

Lopez, S. (February 3, 2016). How a Lincoln High teacher gets all his students to pass the AP calculus exam, *Los Angeles Times*.

Lopez, V., Katsulis, Y., & Robillard, A. (2009). Drug use with parents as a relational strategy for incarcerated female adolescents. *Family Relations, 58*, 135–147.

Lorber, M. F., & Egeland, B. (2011). Parenting and infant difficulty: Testing a mutual exacerbation hypothesis to predict early onset conduct problems. *Child Development, 82*, 2006–2020.

Lorber, M. F., & Egeland, B. (2009). Infancy parenting and externalizing psychopathology from childhood through adulthood: Developmental trends. *Developmental Psychology, 45*, 909–912.

Lorber, M. F., O'Leary, S. G., & Slep, A. M. (2011). An initial evaluation of the role of emotion and impulsivity in explaining racial/ethnic differences in the use of corporal punishment. *Developmental Psychology, 47*, 1744–1749.

Lorch, E. P. (2007). Health, drugs, and values. In N. Pecora, J. P. Murray, & E. A. Wartella (Eds.), *Children and television: Fifty years of research* (pp. 205–231). Mahwah, NJ: Erlbaum.

Lorch, R. F., Jr., Lorch, E. P., Calderhead, W. J., Dunlap, E. E., Hodell, E. C., & Freer, B. D. (2010). Learning the control of variables strategy in higher and lower achieving classrooms: Contributions of explicit instruction and experimentation. *Journal of Educational Psychology, 102*, 90–101.

Losen, D., Hodson, C., Keith, M. A., II, Morrison, K., & Belway, S. (2015). *Are we closing the school discipline gap?* Los Angeles: UCLA Center for Civil Rights Remedies.

Losoya, S. H., & Eisenberg, N. (2000). Affective empathy. In J. Hall & F. J. Bernieri (Eds.), *Interpersonal sensitivity: Theory and measurement* (pp. 21–44). Mahwah, NJ: Erlbaum.

Loury, L. D. (2004). Does church attendance really increase schooling? *Journal for the Scientific Study of Religion, 43*, 119–127.

Love, J., Kisker, E., Ross, C., Raikes, H., Constantine, J., Boller, K., et al. (2005). The effectiveness of Early Head Start for 3-year-old children and their parents: Lessons for policy and programs. *Developmental Psychology, 41*, 885–901.

Lubinski, D., Benbow, C. P., & Kell, H. J. (2014). Life paths and accomplishments of mathematically precocious males and females four decades later. *Psychological Science, 25*, 2217–2232.

Lubman, D., Yucei, M., & Hall, W. D. (2007). Substance use and the adolescent brain: A toxic combination? *Journal of Psychopharmacology, 21*, 792–794.

Luby, J. L. (2010). Preschool depression. *Current Directions in Psychological Science, 19*, 91–95.

Lucas, C. G., Bridgers, S., Griffiths, T. L., & Gopnik, A. (2014). When children are better (or at least more open-minded) learners than adults: Developmental differences in learning the forms of causal relationships. *Cognition, 131*, 284–299.

Lucas-Thompson, R. G., Goldberg, W. A., & Prause, J. (2010). Maternal work early in the lives of children and its distal associations with achievement and behavior problems: A meta-analysis. *Psychological Bulletin, 136*, 915–942.

Lucassen, N., Tharner, A., Van IJzendoorn, M. H., Bakermans-Kranenburg, M. J., Volling, B. L., Verhulst, F. C., et al. (2011). The association between paternal sensitivity and infant–father attachment security: A meta-analysis of three decades of research. *Journal of Family Psychology, 25*, 986–992.

Luce, M., Callanan, M., & Smilovic, S. (2013). Links between parents' epistemological stance and children's evidence talk. *Developmental Psychology, 49*, 454–461.

Lucio, R., Hunt, E., & Bornovalova, M. (2012). Identifying the necessary and sufficient number of risk factors for predicting academic failure. *Developmental Psychology, 48*, 422–428.

Ludwig, D., Peterson, K., & Gortmaker, S. (2001). Relation between consumption of sugar-sweetened drinks and childhood obesity: A prospective, observational analysis. *Lancet, 357*, 505–508.

Lugo-Gil, J., & Tamis-LeMonda, C. (2008). Family resources and parenting quality: Links to children's cognitive development across the first 3 years. *Child Development, 79*, 1065–1085.

Luna, B. (2004). Algebra and the adolescent brain. *Trends in Cognitive Sciences, 8*, 437–439.

Lundberg, S., Pollak, R. A., & Stearns, J. (2016). Family inequality: Diverging patterns in marriage, cohabitation, and childbearing. *Journal of Economic Perspectives, 30*, 79–101.

Lunkenheimer, E. S., Dishion, T. J., Shaw, D., Connell, A., Gardner, F., Wilson, M. N., et al. (2009). Collateral benefits of the Family Check-up on early childhood school readiness: Indirect effects of parents' positive behavior support. *Developmental Psychology, 44*, 1737–1752.

Lunkenheimer, E. S., Shields, A. M., & Cortina, K. S. (2007). Parental emotion coaching and dismissing in family interactions. *Social Development, 16*, 232–248.

Luster, T., Bates, L., Fitzgerald, H., Vandenbelt, M., & Key, J. P. (2000). Factors related to successful outcomes among preschool children born to low-income adolescent mothers. *Journal of Marriage and the Family, 62*, 133–146.

Lustig, D. F. (1997). Of Kwanzaa, Cinco de Mayo, and whispering: The need for intercultural education. *Anthropology & Education Quarterly, 28*, 574–592.

Luthar, S. (2003). The culture of affluence: Psychological costs of material wealth. *Child Development, 74*, 1581–1593.

Luthar, S. S. (2006). Resilience in development: A synthesis of research across five decades. In D. Cicchetti & D. J. Cohen (Eds.), *Developmental psychopathology: Volume Three: Risk, disorder, and adaptation* (2nd ed.). New York: Wiley.

Luthar, S. S., & Latendresse, S. J. (2008). Children of the affluent: Challenges to well-being. *Current Directions in Psychological Science, 14*, 49–53.

Lynn, R. (2009). What has caused the Flynn effect? Secular increases in the Development Quotients of infants. *Intelligence, 37*, 16–24.

Lysaker, J., Tonge, C., Gauson, D., & Miller, A. (2011). Reading and social imagination: What relationally oriented reading insruction can do for children. *Reading Psychology, 32*, 520–566.

Ma, X., Shen, J., Krenn, H. Y., Hu, S., & Yuan, J. (2015). A meta-analysis of the relationship between learning outcomes and parental involvement during early childhood education and early elementary education. *Educational Psychology Review*. December 29, 2015

Maccoby, E. E. (1992). The role of parents in the socialization of children: An historical overview. *Developmental Psychology, 28*, 1006–1017.

Maccoby, E. E. (2002). Gender and group process: A developmental perspective. *Current Directions in Psychological Science, 11*, 54–58.

Maccoby, E. E., & Lewis, C. C. (2003). Less day care or different day care? *Child Development, 74*, 1069–1075.

Maccoby, E. E., & Martin, J. A. (1983). Socialization in the context of the family: Parent–child interaction. In P. H. Mussen (Ed.), *Handbook of child psychology: Vol. 4. Socialization, personality, and social development*. In E. M. Hetherington (Series Ed.) (4th ed., pp. 1–101). New York: Wiley.

MacCorquodale, K. (1970). On Chomsky's review of Skinner's *Verbal Behavior*. *Journal of the Experimental Analysis of Behavior, 13*, 83–99.

MacEvoy, J. P., & Asher, S. R. (2012). When friends disappoint: Boys' and girls' responses to transgressions of friendship expectations. *Child Development, 83*, 104–119.

MacGillivray, L., & Curwen, M. S. (2007). Tagging as a social literacy practice. *Journal of Adolescent & Adult Literacy, 50*, 354–369.

MacKenzie, M. J., Nicklas, E., Waldfogel, J., & Brooks-Gunn, J. (2012). Corporal punishment and child behavioural and cognitive outcomes through 5 years of age: Evidence from a contemporary urban birth cohort study. *Infant and Child Development, 21*, 3–33.

Macmillan, R., McMorris, B., & Kruttschnitt, C. (2004). Linked lives: Stability and change in maternal circumstances and trajectories of antisocial behavior in children. *Child Development, 75*, 205–220.

Madhavi, M., Tobin, D. D., Corby, B. C., Menon, M., Hodges, E. V. E., & Perry, D. G. (2007). The developmental costs of high self-esteem for antisocial children. *Child Development, 78*, 1627–1639.

Madigan, S., Atkinson, L., Laurin, K., & Benoit, D. (2013). Attachment and internalizing behavior in early childhood: A meta-analysis. *Developmental Psychology, 49*, 672–689.

Madigan, S., Brumariu, L. E., Villani, V., Atkinson, L., & Lyons-Ruth, K. (2016). Representational and questionnaire measures of attachment: A meta-analysis of relations to child internalizing and externalizing problems. *Psychological Bulletin, 142*, 367–399.

Magnuson, K., Meyers, M., Ruhm, C., & Waldfogel, J. (2004). Inequality in preschool education and school readiness. *American Educational Research Journal, 41*, 115–157.

Mahoney, J. L., Harris, A. L., & Eccles, J. S. (2006). Organized activity participation, positive youth development, and the over-scheduling hypothesis. *Social Policy Report, 20*, 3–30.

Mahoney, J. L., Lord, H., & Carryl, E. (2005). An ecological analysis of after-school program participation and the development of academic performance and motivational attributes for disadvantaged children. *Child Development, 76*, 811–825.

Mahoney, J. L., & Parente, M. E. (2009). Should we care about adolescents who care for themselves? What we have learned and what we need to know about youth in self-care. *Child Development Perspectives, 3*, 189–195.

Malatesta, C. Z., Culver, C., Tesman, J. R., & Shepard, B. (1989). The development of emotion expression during the first two years of life. *Monographs of the Society for Research in Child Development, 54* (Serial No. 219).

Males, M. (2009). Does the adolescent brain make risk taking inevitable? A skeptical appraisal. *Journal of Adolescent Research, 24*, 3–20.

Males, M. & Brown E. (2014). Teenagers high arrest rates: Features of young age or youth poverty? *Journal of Adolescent Research, 29*, 3–24.

Males, M. A. (2010). Is jumping off the roof always a bad idea? A rejoinder on risk taking and the adolescent brain. *Journal of Adolescent Research, 25*, 48–63.

Mali, T. (2012). *What teachers make: In praise of the greatest job in the world*. New York: Putnam.

Malina, R., Bouchard, C., & Bar-Or, O. (2004). *Growth, maturation, and physical activity* (2nd ed.). Champaign, IL: Human Kinetics.

Maloney, E. A., & Beilock, S. (2012). Math anxiety: Who has it, why it develops, and how to guard against it. *Trends in Cognitive Sciences, 16*, 404–406.

Maloney, E. A., Ramirez, G., Gunderson, E. A., Levine, S. C., & Beilock, S. L. (2015). Intergenerational effects of parents' math anxiety on children's math achievement and anxiety. *Psychological Science, 26*, 1480–1488.

Malti, T., Gummerum, M., Keller, M., & Buchmann, M. (2009). Children's moral motivation, sympathy, and prosocial behavior. *Child Development, 80*, 442–460.

Malti, T., & Krettenauer, T. (2013). The relation of moral emotion attributions to prosocial and antisocial behavior: A meta-analysis. *Child Development, 84*, 397–412.

Mandara, J., Gaylord-Harden, N. K., Richards, M. H., & Ragsdale, B. L. (2009). The effects of changes in racial identity and self-esteem on changes in African American adolescents' mental health. *Child Development, 80*, 1660–1675.

Mannella, J., Jagnow, C. P., & Beauchamp, G. K. (2001). Prenatal and postnatal flavor learning by human infants. *Pediatrics, 107*, e88.

Mannering, A. M., Harold, G. T., Leve, L. D., Shelton, K., Shaw, D. S., Conger, R. D., et al. (2011). Longitudinal associations between marital instability and child sleep problems across infancy and toddlerhood in adoptive families. *Child Development, 82*, 1252–1266.

Manning, W. D., & Lamb, K. A. (2003). Adolescent well-being in cohabiting, married, and single-parent families. *Journal of Marriage and Family, 65*, 876–893.

Mannuzza, S., Klein, R. G., & Moulton, J. L. (2002). Young adult outcome of children with "situational" hyperactivity: A prospective, controlled follow-up study. *Journal of Abnormal Child Psychology, 30*, 191–198.

Manuck, S. B., & McCaffery, J. M. (2014). Gene-environment interaction. *Annual Review of Psychology, 65*, 41–70.

Mar, R. A., & Oatley, K. (2008). The function of fiction is the abstraction and simulation of social experience. *Perspectives on Psychological Science, 3*, 173–192.

Marbell, K. N., & Grolnick, W. S. (2012). Correlates of parental control and autonomy support in an interdependent culture: A look at Ghana. *Motivation and Emotion, 37*, 79–92.

Marceau, K., Horwitz, B. N., Narusyte, J., Ganiban, J. M., Spotts, E. L., Reiss, D., & Neiderhiser, J. M. (2013). Gene–environment correlation underlying the association between parental negativity and adolescent externalizing problems. *Child Development, 84*, 2031–2046.

Marceau, K., Ram, N., Houts, R., Grimm, K. J., & Susman, E. J. (2011). Individual differences in boys' and girls' timing and tempo of puberty: Modeling development with nonlinear growth models. *Developmental Psychology, 47*, 1389–1409.

Marchman, V. A., & Fernald, A. (2008). Speed of word recognition and vocabulary knowledge in infancy predict cognitive and language outcomes in later childhood. *Developmental Science, 11*, F9–F16.

Markiewicz, D., Lawford, H., Doyle, A., & Haggart, N. (2006). Developmental differences in adolescents' and young adults' use of mothers, fathers, best friends, and romantic partners to fulfill attachment needs. *Journal of Youth and Adolescence, 35*, 127–140.

Markovits, H., & Lortie-Forgues, H. (2011). Conditional reasoning with false premises facilitates the transition between familiar and abstract reasoning. *Child Development, 82*, 646–660.

Marks, L. (2012). Same-sex parenting and children's outcomes: A closer examination of the American Psychological Association's brief on lesbian and gay parenting. *Social Science Research, 41*, 735–751.

Markus, H. R. (2008). Pride, prejudice, and ambivalence: Toward a unified theory of race and ethnicity. *American Psychologist, 63*, 651–670.

Markus, H. R., & Conner, A. (2013). *Clash! 8 cultural conflicts that make us who we are*. New York: Hudson Street Press.

Marsh, H. W., Abduljabbar, A. S., Morin, A. J. S., Parker, P., Abdelfattah, F., Nagengast, B., & Abu-Hilal, M. M. (2015). The big-fish-little-pond effect: Generalizability of social comparison processes over two age cohorts from Western, Asian, and Middle Eastern Islamic countries. *Journal of Educational Psychology, 107*, 258–271.

Marsh, H. W., & Craven, R. G. (2006). Reciprocal effects of self-concept and performance from a multidimensional perspective: Beyond seductive pleasure and unidimensional perspectives. *Perspectives on Psychological Science, 1*, 133–163.

Marsh, H. W., Ellis, L. A., & Craven, R. G. (2002). How do preschool children feel about themselves? Unraveling measurement and multidimensional self-concept structure. *Developmental Psychology, 38*, 376–393.

Marsh, H. W., & Hau, K.-T. (2003). Big-fish-little-pond effect on academic self-concept. *American Psychologist, 58*, 364–376.

Marsh, H. W., Koller, O., & Baumert, J. (2001). Reunification of East and West German school systems: Longitudinal multilevel modeling study of the big-fish-little-pond effect on academic self-concept. *American Educational Research Journal, 38*, 321–350.

Marsh, H. W., Trautwein, U., Lüdtke, O., Köller, O., & Baumert, J. (2005). Academic self-concept, interest, grades, and standardized test scores: Reciprocal effects models of causal ordering. *Child Development, 76*, 397–416.

Marsh, J. (2010). Young children's play in online virtual worlds. *Journal of Early Childhood Research, 8*, 23–39.

Marshall, N. (2004). The quality of early child care and children's development. *Current Directions in Psychological Science, 13*, 165–168.

Marsiglia, F. F., Kulis, S., & Hecht, M. L. (2001). Ethnic labels and ethnic identity as predictors of drug use among middle school students in the Southwest. *Journal of Research on Adolescence, 11*, 21–48.

Martin, A., & Olson, K. R. (2015). Beyond good and evil: What motivations underlie children's prosocial behavior? *Perspectives on Psychological Science, 10*, 159–175.

Martin, A. J. (2009). Age appropriateness and motivation, engagement, and performance in high school: Effects of age within cohort, grade retention, and delayed school entry. *Journal of Educational Psychology, 101*, 101–114.

Martin, A. J., & Elliot, A. J. (2016). The role of personal best (PB) goal setting in students' academic achievement gains. *Learning and Individual Differences, 45*, 222–227.

Martin, C., Kornienko, O., Schaefer, D., Hanish, L., Fabes, R., & Goble, P. (2013). The role of sex of peers and gender-typed activities in young children's peer affiliative networks: A longitudinal analysis of selection and influences. *Child Development, 84*, 921–937.

Martin, C. L., & Ruble, D. N. (2004). Children's search for gender cues: Cognitive perspectives on gender development. *Current Directions in Psychological Science, 13*, 67–70.

Martin, C. L., & Ruble, D. N. (2010). Patterns of gender development. *Annual Review of Psychology, 61*, 353–381.

Martin, D. M., Preiss, R. W., Gayle, B. M., & Allen, M. (2006). A meta-analytic assessment of the effect of humorous lectures on learning. In B. M. Gayle, R. W. Preiss, N. Burrell, & M. Allen (Eds.), *Classroom communication and instructional processes*. Mahwah, NJ: Erlbaum.

Martin, G., & Pear, J. (2003). *Behavior modification: What it is and how to do it* (7th ed.). Upper Saddle River, NJ: Prentice Hall.

Martin, M. J., McCarthy, B., Conger, R. D., Gibbons, F. X., Simons, R. L., Cutrona, C. E., et al. (2011). The enduring significance of racism: Discrimination and delinquency among Black American youth. *Journal of Research on Adolescence, 21*, 662–676.

Martin, S. P. (2006). Trends in marital dissolution by women's education in the United States. *Demographic Research, 15*, 537–560.

Martin-Storey, A., Cheadle, J. E., Skalamera, J., & Crosnoe, R. (2015). Exploring the social integration of sexual minority youth across high school contexts. *Child Development, 86*, 965–975.

Martinez, G., Copen, C., & Abma, J. (2011). *Teenagers in the United States: Sexual activity, contraceptive use, and childbearing, 2006-2010, National Survey of Family Growth*. Washington, DC: National Center for Health Statistics.

Marulis, L. M., & Neuman, S. B. (2013). How vocabulary interventions affect young children at risk: A meta-analytic review. *Journal of Research on Educational Effectiveness, 6*, 223–262.

Marzano, R. J. (2007). *The art and science of teaching*. Alexandria, VA: Association for Supervision and Curriculum Development.

Marzano, R. J., Marzano, J., & Pickering, D. (2003). *Classroom management that works*. Alexandria, VA: ASCD.

Mascalzoni, E., Regolin, L., Vallortigara, G., & Simion, F. (2013). The cradle of causal reasoning: Newborns' preference for physical causality. *Developmental Science, 16*, 327–335.

Mashburn, A. J., Justice, L. M., Downer, J. T., & Pianta, R. C. (2009). Peer effects on children's language achievement during pre-kindergarten. *Child Development, 80*, 686–702.

Mashburn, A. J., Pianta, R. C., Hamre, B., Downer, J. T., Barbarin, O. A., Bryant, D., et al. (2008). Measures of classroom quality in prekindergarten and children's development of academic, language, and social skills. *Child Development, 79*, 732–749.

Maslow, A. (1970). *Motivation and personality* (2nd ed.). New York: Harper & Row.

Masten, A., & Reed, M.-G. (2002). Resilience in development. In C. Snyder & S. Lopez (Eds.), *Handbook of positive psychology* (pp. 74–88). London: Oxford University Press.

Masten, A., Roisman, G., Long, J., Burt, K., Obradovic, J., Riley, J., et al. (2005). Developmental cascades: Linking academic achievement and externalizing and internalizing symptoms over 20 years. *Developmental Psychology, 41,* 733–746.

Mathews, J. (1988). *Escalante: The best teacher in America.* New York: Henry Holt.

Mathews, T. J., & Hamilton, B. (2016). *Mean age of mothers is on the rise: United States, 2000–2014. NCHS data brief, no 232.* Hyattsville, MD: National Center for Health Statistics.

Matthews, J. S., Kizzie, K. T., Rowley, S. J., & Cortina, K. (2010). African Americans and boys: Understanding the literacy gap, tracing academic trajectories, and evaluating the role of learning-related skills. *Journal of Educational Psychology, 102,* 757–771.

Maunder, R. G., & Hunter, J. J. (2001). Attachment and psychosomatic medicine: Developmental contributions to stress and disease. *Psychosomatic Medicine, 63,* 556–567.

Mauro, C., & Harris, Y. (2000). The influence of maternal childrearing attitudes and teaching behaviors on preschoolers' delay of gratification. *Journal of Genetic Psychology, 161,* 292–306.

Mayer, J. D., Roberts, R. D., & Barsade, S. G. (2008). Human abilities: Emotional intelligence. *Annual Review of Psychology, 59,* 507–536.

Mayhew, M. J., & King, P. (2008). How curricular content and pedagogical strategies affect moral reasoning development in college students. *Journal of Moral Education, 37,* 17–40.

Mayseless, O. (1996). Attachment patterns and their outcomes. *Human Development, 39,* 206–233.

Mazefsky, C. A., Pelphrey, K. A., & Dahl, R. E. (2012). The need for a broader approach to emotion regulation research in autism. *Child Development Perspectives, 6,* 92–97.

McAlister, A. R., & Peterson, C. C. (2013). Siblings, theory of mind, and executive functioning in children aged 3–6 years: New longitudinal evidence. *Child Development, 84,* 1442–1458.

McArthur, G., Eve, P. M., Jones, K., Banales, E., Kohnen, S., Anandakumar, T., . . . Castles, A. (2012). Phonics training for English-speaking poor readers. *Cochrane Database of Systematic Reviews, 12.*

McCabe, D. (1999). Academic dishonesty among high school students. *Adolescence, 34,* 681–687.

McCaffrey, D. F., Hamilton, L. S., Stecher, B. M., Klein, S. P., Bugliari, D., & Robyn, A. (2001). Interactions among instructional practices, curriculum, and student achievement: The case of standards-based high school mathematics. *Journal for Research in Mathematics Education, 32,* 493–517.

McCall, R., Evahn, C., & Kratzer, L. (1992). *High school underachievers.* Newbury Park, CA: Sage.

McCall, R. B., Van IJzendoorn, M. H., Juffer, F., Groark, C. J., & Groza, V. K. (2011). Children without permanent parents: Research, practice, and policy. *Monographs of the Society for Research in Child Development, 76* (Serial No. 301).

McCartney, K., Burchinal, M. R., Clarke-Stewart, K. A., Bub, K. L., Owen, M. T., & Belsky, J. (2010). Testing a series of causal propositions relating time in child care to children's externalizing behavior. *Developmental Psychology, 46,* 1–17.

McCarty, M. E., Clifton, R. K., & Collard, R. R. (2001). The beginnings of tool use by infants and toddlers. *Infancy, 2,* 233–256.

McClelland, M., & Morrison, F. (2003). The emergence of learning-related social skills in preschool children. *Early Childhood Research Quarterly, 18,* 206–224.

McClelland, M. M., Acock, A. C., Piccinin, A., Rhea, S. A., & Stallings, M. C. (2013). Relations between preschool attention span-persistence and age 25 educational outcomes. *Early Childhood Research Quarterly, 28,* 314–324.

McCormick, M., Brooks-Gunn, J., Buka, S. L., Goldman, J., Yu, J., Saiganik, M., et al. (2006). Early intervention in low birth weight premature infants: Results at 18 years of age for the Infant Health and Development Program. *Pediatrics, 117,* 771–780.

McCullough, M. E., Kimeldorf, M. B., & Cohen, A. D. (2008). An adaptation for altruism? The social causes, social effects, and social evolution of gratitude. *Current Directions in Psychological Science, 17,* 281–285.

McCullough, M. E., & Willoughby, B. L. B. (2009). Religion, self-regulation, and self-control: Associations, explanations, and implications. *Psychological Bulletin, 135,* 69–93.

McCune, L., & Zanes, M. (2001). Learning, attention, and play. In S. Golbeck (Ed.), *Psychological perspectives on early childhood education: Reframing dilemmas in research and practice* (pp. 92–106). Mahwah, NJ: Erlbaum.

McCutchen, D. (2006). Cognitive factors in the development of children's writing. In C. A. MacArthur, S. Graham, & J. Fitzgerald (Eds.), *Handbook of writing research* (pp. 115–130). New York: Guilford.

McDowell, D., O'Neil, R., & Parke, R. D. (2000). Display rule application in a disappointing situation and children's emotional reactivity: Relations with social competence. *Merrill-Palmer Quarterly, 46,* 306–324.

McElhaney, K. B., Antonishak, J., & Allen, J. P. (2008). "They like me, they like me not": Popularity and adolescents' perceptions of acceptance predicting social functioning over time. *Child Development, 79,* 720–731.

McElwain, N. L., Booth-LaForce, C., Lansford, J. E., Wu, X., & Dyer, W. J. (2008). A process model of attachment-friend linkages: Hostile attribution biases, language ability, and mother-child affective mutuality as intervening mechanisms. *Child Development, 79,* 1891–1906.

McElwain, N. L., Booth-LaForce, C., & Wu, X. (2011). Infant–mother attachment and children's friendship quality: Maternal mental-state talk as an intervening mechanism. *Developmental Psychology, 47,* 1295–1311.

McElwain, N. L., Holland, A. S., Engle, J. M., & Ogolsky, B. G. (2014). Getting acquainted: Actor and partner effects of attachment and temperament on young children's peer behavior. *Developmental Psychology, 50,* 1757–1770.

McElwain, N. L., Olson, S. L., & Volling, B. (2002). Concurrent and longitudinal associations among preschool boys' conflict management, disruptive behavior, and peer rejection. *Early Education and Development, 13,* 245–263.

McEvoy, A., & Welker, R. (2000). Antisocial behavior, academic failure, and school climate: A critical review. *Journal of Emotional and Behavioral Disorders, 8,* 130–140.

McGhee, P. (Ed.). (2013). *Humor and children's development: A guide to practical applications.* London: Routledge.

McGill, R. K., Way, N., & Hughes, D. (2012). Intra- and interracial best friendships during middle school: Links to social and emotional well-being. *Journal of Research on Adolescence, 22,* 722–738.

McGraw, M. (1935). *Growth: A study of Johnny and Jimmy.* New York: Appleton-Century.

McGuigan, N., & Doherty, M. (2002). The relation between hiding skill and judgment of eye direction in preschool children. *Developmental Psychology, 38,* 418–427.

McGuire, S., Manke, B., Eftekhari, A., & Dunn, J. (2000). Children's perceptions of sibling conflict during middle childhood: Issues and sibling (dis)similarity. *Social Development, 9,* 173–190.

McHale, S. M., Kim, J.-Y., Dotterer, A. M., Crouter, A. C., & Booth, A. (2009). The development of gendered interests and personality qualities from middle childhood through adolescence: A biosocial analysis. *Child Development, 80,* 482–495.

McKenna, M. C., Conradi, K., Lawrence, C., Jang, B. G., & Meyer, J. P. (2012). Reading attitudes of middle school students: Results of a U.S. survey. *Reading Research Quarterly, 47,* 283–306.

McKown, C., & Strambler, M. J. (2009). Developmental antecedents and social and academic consequences of stereotype-consciousness in middle childhood. *Child Development, 80,* 1643–1659.

McKown, C., & Weinstein, R. S. (2003). The development and consequences of stereotype consciousness in middle childhood. *Child Development, 74,* 498–515.

McKown, C., & Weinstein, R. S. (2008). Teacher expectations, classroom context, and the achievement gap. *Journal of School Psychology, 46,* 235–261.

McLanahan, S., Tach, L., & Schneider, D. (2013). The causal effects of father absence. *Annual Review of Sociology, 39,* 399–427.

McLaughlin, A., Campbell, F., Pungello, E., & Skinner, M. (2007). Depressive symptoms in young adults: The influences of the early home environment and early educational child care. *Child Development, 78,* 746–756.

McLean, L., & Connor, C. M. (2015). Depressive symptoms in third-grade teachers: Relations to classroom quality and student achievement. *Child Development, 86,* 945–954.

McNeely, C., Nonnemaker, J., & Blum, R. (2002). Promoting school connectedness: Evidence from the National Longitudinal Study of Adolescent Health. *Journal of School Health, 72,* 138–146.

McNeil, N. M. (2014). A change–resistance account of children's difficulties understanding mathematical equivalence. *Child Development Perspectives, 8,* 42–47.

Meaney, M. (2010). Epigenetics and the biological definition of gene X environment interactions. *Child Development, 81,* 41–79.

Medved, M. (1995, October). Hollywood's three big lies. *Readers' Digest, 156–157.*

Meehan, B., Hughes, J., & Cavell, T. (2003). Teacher–student relationships as compensatory resources for aggressive children. *Child Development, 74,* 1145–1157.

Meeus, W., Van de Schoot, R., Klimstra, T., & Branje, S. (2011). Personality types in adolescence: Change and stability and links with adjustment and relationships: A five-wave longitudinal study. *Developmental Psychology, 47,* 1181–1195.

Meier, A. M. (2007). Adolescent first sex and subsequent mental health. *American Journal of Sociology, 112,* 1811–1847.

Melby-Lervåg, M., & Lervåg, A. (2014). Effects of educational interventions targeting reading comprehension and underlying components. *Child Development Perspectives, 8,* 96–100.

Melby-Lervåg, M., Lyster, S.-A. H., & Hulme, C. (2012). Phonological skills and their role in learning to read: A meta-analytic review. *Psychological Bulletin, 138,* 322–352.

Mendelson, J. L., Gates, J. A., & Lerner, M. D. (2016). Friendship in school-age boys with Autism Spectrum Disorders: A meta-analytic summary and developmental, process-based model. *Psychological Bulletin, 142,* 601–622.

Mendle, J., Harden, K. P., Turkheimer, E., Van Hulle, C. A., D'Onofrio, B. M., Brooks-Gunn, J., et al. (2009). Associations between father absence and age of first sexual intercourse. *Child Development, 80,* 1463–1480.

Mennen, F. E., Pohle, C., Monro, W. L., Duan, L., Finello, K. M., Ambrose, S., . . . Arroyo, W. (2015). The effect of maternal depression on young children's progress in treatment. *Journal of Child and Family Studies, 24,* 2088–2098.

Merchant, Z., Goetz, E. T., Cifuentes, L., Keeney-Kennicutt, W., & Davis, T. J. (2014). Effectiveness of virtual reality-based instruction on students' learning outcomes in K–12 and higher education: A meta-analysis. *Computers & Education, 70,* 29–40.

Merikangas, K. R., He, J.-P., Burstein, M., Swanson, S. A., Avenevoli, S., Cui, L., et al. (2010). Lifetime prevalence of mental disorders in U.S. adolescents: Results from the National Comorbidity Survey Replication—Adolescent supplement (NCS-A). *Journal of the American Academy of Child & Adolescent Psychiatry, 49,* 980–989.

Merino, B. J., & Hammond, L. (2002). Writing to learn: Science in the upper-elementary bilingual classroom. In M. J. Schleppegrell & M. C. Colombi (Eds.), *Developing advanced literacy in first and second languages* (pp. 227–243). Mahwah, NJ: Erlbaum.

Merrell, K. W., Levitt, V. H., & Gueldner, B. A. (2010). Proactive strategies for promoting social competence and resilience. In G. G. Peacock, R. A. Ervin, E. J. Daly, & K. W. -Merrell (Eds.), *Practical handbook of school psychology* (pp. 254–272). New York: Guilford.

Mesman, J., van IJzendoorn, M., & Bakermans-Kranenburg, M. (2012). Unequal in opportunity, equal in process: Parental sensitivity promotes positive child development in ethnic minority families. *Child Development Perspectives, 6,* 239–250.

Meunier, J. C., Boyle, M., O'Connor, T. G., & Jenkins, J. M. (2013). Multilevel mediation: Cumulative contextual risk, maternal differential treatment, and children's behavior within families. *Child Development, 84,* 1594–1615.

Meuwissen, A., & Carlson, S. (2015). Fathers matter: The role of father parenting in preschoolers' executive function development. *Journal of Experimental Child Psychology, 140,* 1–15.

Meyer, G. J., Finn, S. E., Eyde, L. D., Kay, G. G., Moreland, K. L., Dies, R. R., et al. (2001). Psychological testing and psychological assessment. *American Psychologist, 56,* 128–165.

Mialky, E., Vagnoni, J., & Rutstein, R. (2001). School-age children with perinatally acquired HIV infection: Medical and psychosocial issues in a Philadelphia cohort. *AIDS Patient Care and STDs, 15,* 575–579.

Michalik, N. M., Eisenberg, N., Spinrad, T. L., Ladd, B., Thompson, M., & Valiente, C. (2007). Longitudinal relations among parental emotional expressivity and sympathy and prosocial behavior in adolescence. *Social Development, 16,* 286–309.

Michiels, D., Grietens, H., Onghena, P., & Kuppens, S. (2008). Parent-child interactions and relational aggression in peer relationships. *Developmental Review, 28,* 522–540.

Mikami, A. Y., Lerner, M. D., & Lun, J. (2010). Social context influences on children's rejection by their peers. *Child Development Perspectives, 4,* 123–130.

Mikulincer, M., & Shaver, P. (2005). Attachment security, compassion, and altruism. *Current Directions in Psychological Science, 14,* 34–38.

Milan, S., Snow, S., & Belay, S. (2009). Depressive symptoms in mothers and children: Preschool attachment as a moderator of risk. *Developmental Psychology, 45,* 1019–1033.

Miles, S., & Stipek, D. (2006). Contemporaneous and longitudinal associations between social behavior and literacy achievement in a sample of low-income elementary school children. *Child Development, 77,* 103–117.

Miller, A. (1990). *The day care dilemma: Critical concerns for American families.* New York: Plenum.

Miller, B., Bayley, B., Christensen, M., Leavitt, S., & Coyl, D. (2003). Adolescent pregnancy and childbearing. In G. Adams & M. Berzonsky (Eds.), *Blackwell handbook on adolescence* (pp. 415–449). Malden, MA: Blackwell.

Miller, C. F., Trautner, H. M., & Ruble, D. N. (2006). The role of gender stereotypes in children's preferences and behavior. In L. Balter & C. Tamis-LeMonda (Eds.), *Child psychology: A handbook of contemporary issues* (2nd ed., pp. 293–323). New York: Psychology Press.

Miller, G. E., & Chen, E. (2010). Harsh family climate in early life presages the emergence of a proinflammatory phenotype in adolescence. *Psychological Science, 21,* 848–856.

Miller, G. E., Lachman, M. E., Chen, E., Gruenewald, T. L., Karlamangla, A. S., & Seeman, T. E. (2011). Pathways to resilience: Maternal nurturance as a buffer against the effects of childhood poverty on metabolic syndrome at midlife. *Psychological Science, 22,* 1591–1599.

Miller, J. G., Kahle, S., & Hastings, P. D. (2015). Roots and benefits of costly giving: Children who are more altruistic have greater autonomic flexibility and less family wealth. *Psychological Science 26,* 1038–1045.

Miller, P., Danaher, D., & Forbes, D. (1986). Sex-related strategies for coping with interpersonal conflict in children aged five and seven. *Developmental Psychology, 22,* 543–548.

Milligan, K., Astington, J. W., & Dack, L. A. (2007). Language and theory of mind: Meta-analysis of the relation between language ability and false-belief understanding. *Child Development, 78,* 622–646.

Mindell, J. A., & Owens, J. A. (Eds.). (2010). *A clinical guide to pediatric sleep: Diagnosis and management of sleep problems.* Philadelphia, PA: Lippincott Williams & Wilkins.

Miranda, D., Gaudreau, P., & Morizot, J. (2010). Blue notes: Coping by music listening predicts neuroticism changes in adolescence. *Psychology of Aesthetics, Creativity, and the Arts, 4,* 247–253.

Mischel, W., Ayduk, O., Berman, M. G., Casey, B. J., Gotlib, I. H., Jonides, J., . . . Shoda, Y. (2011). "Willpower" over the life span: decomposing self-regulation. *Social Cognitive and Affective Neuroscience, 6,* 252–256.

Mischel, W., Shoda, Y., & Rodriguez, M. L. (1989). Delay of gratification in children. *Science, 244,* 933–938.

Mix, K. S., Prather, R. W., Smith, L. B., & Stockton, J. D. (2014). Young children's interpretation of multidigit number names: From emerging competence to mastery. *Child Development, 85,* 1306–1319.

Miyake, A., & Friedman, N. P. (2012). The nature and organization of individual differences in executive functions: Four general conclusions. *Current Directions in Psychological Science, 21,* 8–14.

Moeller, A. J., Theiler, J. M., & Wu, C. (2012). Goal setting and student achievement: A longitudinal study. *Modern Language Journal, 96,* 153–169.

Moffitt, T. (2005). The new look of behavioral genetics in developmental psychopathology: Gene-environment interplay in antisocial behaviors. *Psychological Bulletin, 131,* 533–554.

Moffitt, T. E., Arseneault, L., Belsky, D., Dickson, N., Hancox, R. J., Harrington, H., . . . Caspi, A. (2011). A gradient of childhood self-control predicts health, wealth, and public safety. *Proceedings of the National Academy of Sciences, 108,* 2693–2698.

Moilanen, K. L., Crockett, L. J., Raffaelli, M., & Jones, B. L. (2010). Trajectories of sexual risk from middle adolescence to early adulthood. *Journal of Research on Adolescence, 20,* 114–139.

Moje, E. B. (2000). "To be part of the story": The literacy practices of gangsta adolescents. *Teachers College Record, 102,* 651–690.

Mokdad, A., Marks, J., Stroup, D., & Gerberding, J. (2004). Actual causes of death in the United States, 2000. *JAMA, 291,* 1238–1245.

Mok, M. M. C., McInerney, D. M., Zhu, J., & Or, A. (2015). Growth trajectories of mathematics achievement: Longitudinal tracking of student academic progress. *British Journal of Educational Psychology, 85,* 154–171.

Mol, S. E., & Bus, A. G. (2011). To read or not to read: A meta-analysis of print exposure from infancy to early adulthood. *Psychological Bulletin, 137,* 267–296.

Mol, S. E., Bus, A. G., & de Jong, M. T. (2009). Interactive book reading in early education: A tool to stimulate print knowledge as well as oral language. *Review of Educational Research, 79,* 979–1007.

Molina, B. S., Hinshaw, S. P., Swanson, J. M., Arnold, L. E., Vitiello, B., Jensen, P. S., et al. (2009). The MTA at 8 years: Prospective follow-up of children treated for combined-type ADHD in a multisite study. *Journal of the American Academy of Child and Adolescent Psychiatry, 48,* 484–500.

Monroe, S. M., & Reid, M. W. (2008). Gene–environment interactions in depression research: Genetic polymorphisms and life-stress polyprocedures. *Psychological Science, 19,* 947–956.

Monshouwer, K., ten Have, M., van Poppel, M., Kemper, H., & Vollebergh, W. (2013). Possible mechanisms explaining the association between physical activity and mental health; Findings from the 2001 Dutch Health Behaviour in School-aged Children Survey. *Clinical Psychological Science, 1,* 67–74.

Montag, J. L., Jones, M. N., & Smith, L. B. (2015). The words children hear: Picture books and the statistics for language learning. *Psychological Science, 26,* 1489–1496.

Monzó, L. D., & Rueda, R. (2009). Passing for English fluent: Latino immigrant children masking language proficiency. *Anthropology & Education Quarterly, 40,* 20–40.

Moon, R. Y., Patel, K. M., & McDermott Shaefer, S. J. (2000). Sudden infant death syndrome in child care settings. *Pediatrics, 106,* 295–300.

Morales-Campos, D. Y., Markham, C., Peskin, M. F., & Fernandez, M. E. (2012). Sexual initiation, parent practices, and acculturation in Hispanic seventh graders. *Journal of School Health, 82,* 75–81.

Morawska, A., & Sanders, M. (2011). Parental use of time out revisited: A useful or harmful parenting strategy? *Journal of Child and Family Studies, 20,* 1–8.

Moreno, S., Bialystok, E., Barac, R., Schellenberg, E. G., Cepeda, N. J., & Chau, T. (2011). Short-term music training enhances verbal intelligence and executive function. *Psychological Science, 22,* 1425–1433.

Moreno, S., Lee, Y., Janus, M., & Bialystok, E. (2015). Short-term second language and music training induces lasting functional brain changes in early childhood. *Child Development, 86,* 394–406.

Morgan, P. L., Farkas, G., Hillemeier, M. M., Hammer, C. S., & Maczuga, S. (2015). 24-month-old children with larger oral vocabularies display greater academic and behavioral functioning at kindergarten entry. *Child Development, 86,* 1351–1370.

Morland, K., Wing, S., Diez Roux, A., & Poole, C. (2002). Neighborhood characteristics associated with the location of food stores and food service places. *American Journal of Preventive Medicine, 22,* 23–29.

Morley, T. E., & Moran, G. (2011). The origins of cognitive vulnerability in early childhood: Mechanisms linking early attachment to later depression. *Clinical Psychology Review, 31,* 1071–1082.

Morris, A. S., Silk, J. S., Morris, M. D., Steinberg, L., Aucoin, K. J., & Keyes, A. W. (2011). The influence of mother–child emotion regulation strategies on children's expression of anger and sadness. *Developmental Psychology, 47,* 213–225.

Morris, A. S., Silk, J. S., Steinberg, L., Myers, S. S., & Robinson, L. R. (2007). The role of the family context in the development of emotion regulation. *Social Development, 16,* 361–388.

Morris, M. W., Chiu, C.-y., & Liu, Z. (2015). Polycultural psychology. *Annual Review of Psychology, 66,* 631–659.

Morrison, F., Griffith, E., & Alberts, D. (1997). Nature-nurture in the classroom: Entrance age, school readiness, and learning in children. *Developmental Psychology, 33,* 254–262.

Morrow, J., Jackson, A., & Payne, G. (1999). Physical activity promotion and school physical education. *Research Digest: President's Council on Physical Fitness and Sports.* Retrieved January 8, 2010, from http://fitness.gov/digest_sep1999.htm

Mortensen, E., Michaelsen, K., Sanders, S., & Reinisch, J. (2002). The association between duration of breastfeeding and adult intelligence. *JAMA, 287,* 2365–2371.

Moshman, D. (1998). Cognitive development beyond childhood. In D. Kuhn & R. Siegler (Eds.), *Handbook of child psychology: Cognition, perception, and language* (5th ed., Vol. 2, pp. 947–978). New York: Wiley.

Mosing, M. A., Madison, G., Pedersen, N. L., Kuja-Halkola, R., & Ullén, F. (2014). Practice does not make perfect: No causal effect of music practice on music ability. *Psychological Science, 25,* 1795–1803.

Moss, E., & St-Laurent, D. (2001). Attachment at school age and academic performance. *Developmental Psychology, 37,* 863–874.

Mounts, N. (2001). Young adolescents' perceptions of parental management of peer relationships. *Journal of Early Adolescence, 21,* 92–122.

Müller, U., Burman, J., & Hutchinson, S. (2013). The developmental psychology of Jean Piaget: A quinquagenary retrospective. *Journal of Applied Developmental Psychology, 34,* 52–55.

Mulvaney, M. K., & Mebert, C. J. (2007). Parental corporal punishment predicts behavior problems in early childhood. *Journal of Family Psychology, 21,* 389–397.

Mulvey, K. L., & Killen, M. (2015). Challenging gender stereotypes: Resistance and exclusion. *Child Development, 86,* 681–694.

Mummer, D. L., & Fernald, A. (2003). The infant as onlooker: Learning from emotional reactions observed in a television scenario. *Child Development, 74,* 221–237.

Munday, P., Block, J., Delgado, C., Pomares, Y., Van Hecke, A. V., & Parlade, M. V. (2007). Individual differences and the development of joint attention in infancy. *Child Development, 78,* 938–954.

Muñoz, R., Beardslee, W. R., & Leykin, Y. (2012). Major depression can be prevented. *American Psychologist, 67,* 285–295.

Murdock, T., Hale, N., & Weber, M. J. (2001). Predictors of cheating among early adolescents: Academic and social motivations. *Contemporary Educational Psychology, 26,* 96–115.

Murdock, T. B., & Stephens, J. M. (2007). Is cheating wrong? Students' reasoning about academic dishonesty. In E. M. Anderman & T. B. Murdock (Eds.), *Psychology of academic cheating* (pp. 229–251). New York: Academic Press.

Murphey, D., & Cooper, P. M. (2015). *Infants and toddlers in the District of Columbia: A statistical look at needs and disparities.* Bethesda, MD: Bainum Family Foundation.

Murphy, P. K., Wilkinson, I. A. G., Soter, A. O., Hennessey, M. N., & Alexander, J. F. (2009). Examining the effects of classroom discussion on students' comprehension of text: A meta-analysis. *Journal of Educational Psychology, 101,* 740–764.

Murray-Close, D., Crick, N. R., & Galotti, K. (2006). Children's moral reasoning regarding physical and relational aggression. *Social Development, 15,* 345–372.

Murray, J. P. (2007). TV violence: Research and controversy. In N. Pecora, J. P. Murray, & E. A. Wartella (Eds.), *Children and television: Fifty years of research.* Mahwah, NJ: Erlbaum.

Murray, L., de Rosnay, M., Pearson, J., Bergeron, C., Schofield, E., Royal-Lawson, M., et al. (2008). Intergenerational transmission of social anxiety: The role of social referencing processes in infancy. *Child Development, 79,* 1049–1064.

Murry, V. M., Berkel, C., Brody, G. H., Miller, S. J., & Chen, Y.-F. (2009). Linking parental socialization to interpersonal protective processes, academic self-presentation, and expectations among rural African American youth. *Cultural Diversity and Ethnic Minority Psychology, 15,* 1–10.

Mussen, P., & Eisenberg, N. (2001). Prosocial development in context. In A. Bohart & D. Stipek (Eds.), *Constructive and destructive behavior: Implications for family, school, and society* (pp. 103–126). Washington, DC: APA.

Mustanski, B., DuPree, M., Nievergelt, C., Bocklandt, S., Schork, N., & Hamer, D. (2005). A genomewide scan of male sexual orientation. *Human Genetics, 116,* 272–278.

Nachmias, M., Gunnar, M., Mangelsdorf, S., Parritz, R. H., & Buss, K. (1996). Behavioral inhibition and stress reactivity: The moderating role of attachment security. *Child Development, 67,* 508–522.

Nadler, R. T., Rabi, R., & Minda, J. P. (2010). Better mood and better performance: Learning rule-described categories is enhanced by positive mood. *Psychological Science, 21*, 1770–1776.

NAEYC. (2009). Position statement: Developmentally appropriate practice in early childhood programs serving children from birth through age 8. Retrieved October 15, 2009, from NAEYC.org

Nansel, T., Overpeck, M., Pilla, R., Ruan, J., Simons-Morton, B., & Scheidt, P. (2001). Bullying behaviors among US youth: Prevalence and association with psychosocial adjustment. *JAMA, 285*, 2094–2100.

Narusyte, J., Neiderhiser, J. M., D'Onofrio, B. M., Reiss, D., Spotts, E. L., Ganiban, J. M., et al. (2008). Testing different types of genotype–environment correlation: An extended children-of-twins model. *Developmental Psychology, 44*, 1591–1603.

Narvaez, D. (2002). Does reading moral stories build character? *Educational Psychology Review, 14*, 155–171.

National Institute of Mental Health. (2008). *Attention deficit hyperactivity disorder. NIH Publication No. 08-3572*. Washington, DC: Author.

National Mathematics Advisory Panel. (2008). *Foundations for success: The final report of the National Mathematics Advisory Panel*. Washington, DC: Department of Education.

National Reading Panel. (2000). *Teaching children to read: An evidence-based assessment of the scientific research literature on reading and its implications for reading instruction*. Washington, DC: U.S. Government Printing Office.

Natsuaki, M. N., Ge, X., Leve, L. D., Neiderhiser, J. M., Shaw, D., Conger, R. D., et al. (2010). Genetic liability, environment, and the development of fussiness in toddlers: The roles of maternal depression and parental responsiveness. *Developmental Psychology, 46*, 1147–1158.

Natsuaki, M. N., Ge, X., Reiss, D., & Neiderhiser, J. M. (2009). Aggressive behavior between siblings and the development of externalizing problems: Evidence from a genetically sensitive study. *Developmental Psychology, 45*, 1009–1018.

Naylor, A., Gardner, D., & Zaichkowsky, L. (2001). Drug use patterns among high school athletes and nonathletes. *Adolescence, 36*, 627–639.

NCES. (2010). *National Assessment of Educational Progress*, from http://nationsreportcard.gov

Neal, J. W., Neal, Z. P., & Cappella, E. (2014). I know who my friends are, but do you? Predictors of self-reported and peer-inferred relationships. *Child Development, 85*, 1366–1372.

Negriff, S., & Susman, E. J. (2011). Pubertal timing, depression, and externalizing problems: A framework, review, and examination of gender differences. *Journal of Research on Adolescence, 21*, 717–746.

Nelson, C. A. (2007). A neurobiological perspective on early human deprivation. *Child Development Perspectives, 1*, 13–18.

Nelson, C. E., Bos, K., Gunnar, M. R., & Sonuga-Barke, E. J. S. (2011). The neurobiological toll of early human deprivation. *Monographs of the Society for Research in Child Development, 76*(4), 127–146.

Nelson, M. K., & Shutz, R. (2007). Day care differences and the reproduction of social class. *Journal of Contemporary Ethnography, 36*, 281–317.

Nelson, P. B., Adamson, L. B., & Bakeman, R. (2012). The developmental progression of understanding of mind during a hiding game. *Social Development, 21*, 313–330.

Nelson, R. M., & DeBacker, T. (2008). Achievement motivation in adolescents: The role of peer climate and best friends. *Journal of Experimental Education, 76*, 170–189.

Nesdale, D., Maass, A., Durkin, K., & Griffiths, J. (2005). Group norms, threat, and children's racial prejudice. *Child Development, 76*, 652–663.

Newcombe, N. (2002). The nativist-empiricist controversy in the context of recent research on spatial and quantitative development. *Psychological Science, 13*, 395–401.

Newland, L., Freeman, H., & Coyl, D. (2011). *Emerging topics on father attachment: Consideration in theory, context and development*. New York: Routledge.

Newman, R. S. (2008). Adaptive and nonadaptive help seeking with peer harassment: An integrative perspective of coping and self-regulation. *Educational Psychologist, 43*, 1–15.

Newman, R., Murray, B., & Lussier, C. (2001). Confrontation with aggressive peers at school: Students' reluctance to seek help from the teacher. *Journal of Educational Psychology, 93*, 398–410.

Newton, P., Vasudevi, R., & Bull, R. (2000). Children's everyday deception and performance of false-belief tasks. *British Journal of Developmental Psychology, 18*, 297–317.

Ng, F. F.-Y., Pomerantz, E. M., & Deng, C. (2014). Why Are Chinese mothers more controlling than American mothers? "My child is my report card." *Child Development, 85*, 355–369.

Nguyen, A.-M., & Benet-Martinez, V. (2013). Biculturalism and adjustment: A meta-analysis. *Journal of Cross-Cultural Psychology, 44*, 122–159.

NICHD & NCATE. (2007). *Child and adolescent development research and teacher education: Evidence-based pedagogy, policy, and practice*. Washington, DC: National Institute of Child Health and Human Development, National Institutes of Health, Department of Health and Human Services, and National Association for the Accreditation of Teacher Education.

NICHD Early Child Care Research Network. (1997). The effects of infant child care on infant-mother attachment security: Results of the NICHD study of early child care. *Child Development, 68*, 860–879.

NICHD Early Child Care Research Network. (1998). Relations between family predictors and child outcomes: Are they weaker for children in child care? *Child Development, 34*, 1119–1128.

NICHD Early Child Care Research Network. (1999). Chronicity of maternal depressive symptoms, maternal sensitivity, and child functioning at 36 months. *Developmental Psychology, 35*, 1297–1310.

NICHD Early Child Care Research Network. (2000a). Does quality of child care affect child outcomes at age 4 1/2? *Child Development, 39*, 451–469.

NICHD Early Child Care Research Network. (2000b). The relation of child care to cognitive and language development. *Child Development, 71*, 960–980.

NICHD Early Child Care Research Network. (2001a). Child care and children's peer interaction at 24 and 36 months: The NICHD study of early child care. *Child Development, 72*, 1478–1500.

NICHD Early Child Care Research Network. (2001b). Child-care and family predictors of preschool attachment and stability from infancy. *Developmental Psychology, 37*, 847–862.

NICHD Early Child Care Research Network. (2002). The relation of global first-grade environment to structural classroom features and teacher and student behaviors. *Elementary School Journal, 102*, 367–387.

NICHD Early Child Care Research Network. (2003a). Does amount of time spent in child care predict socioemotional adjustment during the transition to kindergarten? *Child Development, 74*, 976–1005.

NICHD Early Child Care Research Network. (2003b). Frequency and intensity of activity in third-grade children in physical education. *Archives of Pediatrics & Adolescent Medicine, 157*, 185–190.

NICHD Early Child Care Research Network, & Duncan, G. (2003c). Modeling the impacts of child care quality on children's preschool cognitive development. *Child Development, 74*, 1454–1475.

NICHD Early Child Care Research Network. (2004). Are child developmental outcomes related to before- and after-school care arrangements? Results from the NICHD Study of Early Child Care. *Child Development, 75*, 280–295.

NICHD Early Child Care Research Network. (2005a). Early child care and children's development in the primary grades: Follow-up results from the NICHD Study of Early Child Care. *American Educational Research Journal, 42*, 537–570.

NICHD Early Child Care Research Network. (2005b). Predicting individual differences in attention, memory, and planning in first graders from experiences at home, child care, and school. *Developmental Psychology, 41*, 99–114.

NICHD Early Child Care Research Network. (2006a). Child-care effect sizes for the NICHD study of early child care and youth development. *American Psychologist, 61*, 99–116.

NICHD Early Child Care Research Network. (2006b). Infant–mother attachment classification: Risk and protection in relation to changing maternal caregiving quality. *Developmental Psychology, 42*, 38–58.

Nicholls, J. G. (1989). *The competitive ethos and democratic education*. Cambridge, MA: Harvard University Press.

Nicholson, J. S., Deboeck, P. R., Farris, J. R., Boker, S. M., & Borkowski, J. G. (2011). Maternal depressive symptomatology and child behavior: Transactional relationship with simultaneous bidirectional coupling. *Developmental Psychology, 47*, 1312–1323.

Nickerson, A., Mele, D., & Princiotta, D. (2008). Attachment and empathy as predictors of roles as defenders or outsiders in bullying interactions. *Journal of School Psychology, 46*, 687–703.

NIDA (National Institute on Drug Abuse). (2010). *Marijuana.*

Nielsen, S., & Popkin, B. (2003). Patterns and trends in food portion sizes, 1977–1998. *JAMA, 289*, 450–453.

Nieto, S. (2000). *Affirming diversity: The sociopolitical context of multicultural education* (3rd ed.). White Plains, NY: Longman.

Nigg, J. T. (2010). Attention-deficit/hyperactivity disorder: Endophenotypes, structure, and etiological pathways. *Current Directions in Psychological Science, 19*, 24–29.

Nikolas, M. A., Klump, K. L., & Burt, S. A. (2015). Parental involvement moderates etiological influences on attention deficit hyperactivity disorder behaviors in child twins. *Child Development, 86*, 224–240.

Nilsson, J., Stien, L. H., Fosseidengen, J. E., Olsen, R. E., & Kristiansen, T. S. (2012). From fright to anticipation: Reward conditioning versus habituation to a moving dip net in farmed Atlantic cod (*Gadus morhua*). *Applied Animal Behaviour Science, 138*, 118–124.

Nilsson, K. K., & de López, K. J. (2016). Theory of Mind in children with specific language impairment: A systematic review and meta-analysis. *Child Development, 87*, 143–153.

Ninio, A. (2006). *Language and the learning curve: A new theory of syntactic development.* Oxford, UK: Oxford University Press.

Nippold, M. A., Duthie, J. K., & Larsen, J. T. (2005). Literacy as a leisure activity: Free-time preferences of older children and young adolescents. *Language, Speech, and Hearing Services in Schools, 36*, 93–102.

Nippold, M. A., Hesketh, L. J., Duthie, J. K., & Mansfield, T. C. (2005). Conversational versus expository discourse: A study of syntactic development in children, adolescents, and adults. *Journal of Speech, Language and Hearing Research, 48*, 1048–1064.

Nisbett, R. E. (2003). *The geography of thought: How Asians and Westerners think differently, and why.* New York: Free Press.

Nisbett, R. E., Aronson, J., Blair, C., Dickens, W., Flynn, J., Halpern, D. F., et al. (2012). Intelligence: New findings and theoretical developments. *American Psychologist, 67*, 130–159.

Nishina, A., & Juvonen, J. (2005). Daily reports of witnessing and experiencing peer harassment in middle school. *Child Development, 76*, 435–450.

Noddings, N. (1992). *The challenge to care in schools: An alternative approach to education.* New York: Teachers College Press.

Noel, A., Stark, P., & Redford, J. (2013). *Parent and family involvement in education (NCES 2013-028).* Washington, DC: National Center for Education Statistics.

Noël, M.-P. (2009). Counting on working memory when learning to count and to add: A preschool study. *Developmental Psychology, 45*, 1630–1643.

Noftle, E. E., & Robins, R. W. (2007). Personality predictors of academic outcomes: Big Five correlates of GPA and SAT scores. *Journal of Personality and Social Psychology, 93*, 116–130.

Nokes, J. D., Dole, J. A., & Hacker, D. J. (2007). Teaching high school students to use heuristics while reading historical texts. *Journal of Educational Psychology, 99*, 492–504.

Noltemeyer, A. L., Marie, R., McLoughlin, C., & Vanderwood, M. (2015). Relationship between school suspension and student outcomes: A meta-analysis. *School Psychology Review, 44*, 224–240.

Nørby, S. (2015). Why forget? On the adaptive value of memory loss. *Perspectives on Psychological Science, 10*, 551–578.

Noritz, G. H., Murphy, N. A., & Neuromotor Screening Expert Panel. (2013). Motor delays: Early identification and evaluation. *Pediatrics, 131*, e2016.

Normandeau, S., & Gobeil, A. (1998). A developmental perspective on children's understanding of causal attributions in achievement-related situations. *International Journal of Behavioral Development, 22*, 611–632.

Norris, A. L., Marcus, D. K., & Green, B. A. (2015). Homosexuality as a discrete class. *Psychological Science, 26*, 1843–1853.

Northcutt, W. (2000). *The Darwin Awards.* New York: Dutton.

Nowakowski, R. S., & Hayes, N. L. (2002). General principles of CNS development. In M. H. Johnson, Y. Munakata, & R. O. Gilmore (Eds.), *Brain development and cognition: A reader* (2nd ed., pp. 57–82). Malden, MA: Blackwell.

Nowicki, S., & Duke, M. P. (1992). The association of children's nonverbal decoding abilities with their popularity, locus of control, and academic achievement. *Journal of Genetic Psychology, 153*, 385–393.

Nuthall, G. (2000). The anatomy of memory in the classroom: Understanding how students acquire memory processes from classroom activities in science and social studies units. *American Educational Research Journal, 37*, 247–304.

Nye, B., Hedges, L. V., & Konstantopoulos, S. (2001). Are effects of small classes cumulative? Evidence from a Tennessee experiment. *Journal of Educational Research, 94*, 336–345.

Nylund, K., Bellmore, A., Nishina, A., & Graham, S. (2007). Subtypes, severity, and structural stability of peer victimization: What does latent class analysis say? *Child Development, 78*, 1706–1722.

O'Brien, K., Daffern, M., Chu, C. M., & Thomas, S. (2013). Youth gang affiliation, violence, and criminal activities: A review of motivational, risk, and protective factors. *Aggression and Violent Behavior, 18*, 417–425.

O'Connor, E., Cappella, E., McCormick, M., & McClowry, S. (2014). Enhancing the academic development of shy children: A test of the efficacy of INSIGHTS. *School Psychology Review, 43*, 239–259.

O'Connor, C., & Fernandez, S. D. (2006). Race, class, and disproportionality: Reevaluating the relationship between poverty and special education placement. *Educational Researcher, 35(6)*, 6–11.

O'Connor, E., & McCartney, K. (2007). Examining teacher–child relationships and achievement as part of an ecological model of development. *American Educational Research Journal, 44*, 340–369.

O'Connor, E. E., Dearing, E., & Collins, B. A. (2011). Teacher–child relationship and behavior problem trajectories in elementary school. *American Educational Research Journal, 48*, 120–162.

O'Connor, T., Rutter, M., Beckett, C., Keaveney, L., Kreppner, J., & English and Romanian Adoptees Study Team. (2000). The effects of global severe privation on cognitive competence: Extension and longitudinal follow-up. *Child Development, 71*, 376–390.

Ogden, C. L., Carroll, M. D., Kit, B. K., & Flegal, K. M. (2014). Prevalence of childhood and adult obesity in the United States, 2011–2012. *Journal of the American Medical Association, 311*, 806–814.

Odgers, C. L., Caspi, A., Nagin, D. S., Piquero, A. R., Slutske, W. S., Milne, B. J., et al. (2008). Is it important to prevent early exposure to drugs and alcohol among adolescents? *Psychological Science, 19*, 1035–1044.

Odgers, C. L., Moffitt, T. E., Tach, L. M., Sampson, R. J., Taylor, A., Matthews, C. L., et al. (2009). The protective effects of neighborhood collective efficacy on British children growing up in deprivation: A developmental analysis. *Developmental Psychology, 45*, 942–957.

Ogden, C. L., Li, Y., Freedman, D., Borrud, L., & Flegal, K. (2011). *Smoothed percentage body fat percentiles for U.S. children and adolescents, 1999–2004.* Hyattsville, MD: National Center for Health Statistics.

O'Hare, A., Bremner, L., Nash, M., Happé, F., & Pettigrew, L. (2009). A clinical assessment tool for advanced theory of mind performance in 5 to 12 year olds. *Journal of Autism and Developmental Disorders, 39*, 916–928.

O'Hare, W. P. (2008). *Data on children in foster care from the Census Bureau.* Baltimore, MD: Casey Foundation.

Okonofua, J. A., & Eberhardt, J. L. (2015). Two strikes: Race and the disciplining of young students. *Psychological Science, 26*, 617–624.

Ollendick, T., & Schroeder, C. (2003). *Encyclopedia of clinical child and pediatric psychology.* New York: Kluwer Academic.

Ollendick, T. H., Greene, R. W., Austin, K. E., Fraire, M. G., Halldorsdottir, T., Allen, K. B., . . . Wolff, J. C. (2015). Parent management training and collaborative & proactive solutions: A randomized control trial for oppositional youth. *Journal of Clinical Child & Adolescent Psychology.* March 9, 2015.

Oliver, B. R., Dale, P. S., & Plomin, R. (2005). Predicting literacy at age 7 from preliteracy at age 4: A longitudinal genetic analysis. *Psychological Science, 16*, 861–865.

Olson, K. R. (2016). Prepubescent transgender children: What we do and do not know. *Journal of the American Academy of Child & Adolescent Psychiatry, 55,* 155–156.

Olson, K. R., Key, A. C., & Eaton, N. R. (2015). Gender cognition in transgender children. *Psychological Science, 26,* 467–474.

Olweus, D. (1994). Bullying at school: Basic facts and effects of a school-based intervention program. *Journal of Child Psychology & Psychiatry & Allied Disciplines, 35,* 1171–1190.

O'Neil, J. (2004, December 29). Slow-motion miracle: One boy's journey out of autism's grasp. *New York Times.*

Ophir, E., Nass, C., & Wagner, A. D. (2009). Cognitive control in media multitaskers. *Proceedings of the National Academy of Sciences, 106,* 15583–15587.

Orfield, G., Losen, D., Wald, J., & Swanson, C. B. (2004). *Losing our future: How minority youth are being left behind by the graduation rate crisis.* Cambridge, MA: Civil Rights Project at Harvard. Retrieved from http://www.urban.org/publications/410936.html

Orme, J., & Buehler, C. (2001). Foster family characteristics and behavioral and emotional problems of foster children: A narrative review. *Family Relations, 50,* 3–15.

O'Rourke, J., Barnes, J., Deaton, A., Fulks, K., Ryan, K., & Rettinger, D. A. (2010). Imitation Is the Sincerest Form of Cheating: The Influence of Direct Knowledge and Attitudes on Academic Dishonesty. Ethics & Behavior, 20, 47–64.

Orth, U., Robins, R. W., & Meier, L. L. (2009). Disentangling the effects of low self-esteem and stressful events on depression: Findings from three longitudinal studies. *Journal of Personality and Social Psychology, 97,* 307–321.

Osterman, K. (2000). Students' need for belonging in the school community. *Review of Educational Research, 70,* 323–367.

Ottmar, E. R., Rimm-Kaufman, S. E., Larsen, R. A., & Berry, R. Q. (2015). Mathematical knowledge for teaching, standards-based mathematics teaching practices, and student achievement in the context of the responsive classroom approach. *American Educational Research Journal, 52,* 787–821.

Ou, S.-R., & Reynolds, A. J. (2010). Grade retention, postsecondary education, and public aid receipt. *Educational Evaluation and Policy Analysis, 32,* 118–139.

Oudekerk, B. A., Allen, J. P., Hessel, E. T., & Molloy, L. E. (2015). The cascading development of autonomy and relatedness from adolescence to adulthood. *Child Development, 86,* 472–485.

Overskeid, G. (2007). Looking for Skinner and finding Freud. *American Psychologist, 62,* 590–595.

Owens, J., & AAP Adolescent Sleep Working Group. (2014). Insufficient sleep in adolescents and young adults: An update on causes and consequences. *Pediatrics, 134,* e921–932.

Oyserman, D., Brickman, D., & Rhodes, M. (2007). School success, possible selves, and parent school involvement. *Family Relations, 56,* 479–489.

Öztekin, I., Davachi, L., & McElree, B. (2010). Are representations in working memory distinct from representations in long-term memory? *Psychological Science, 21,* 1123–1133.

Paciello, N., Fida, R., Tramontano, C., Lupinetti, C., & Caprara, G. V. (2008). Stability and change of moral disengagement and its impact on aggression and violence in late adolescence. *Child Development, 79,* 1288–1309.

Padilla-Walker, L. M., Carlo, G., Christensen, K. J., & Yorgason, J. B. (2012). Bidirectional relations between authoritative parenting and adolescents' prosocial behaviors. *Journal of Research on Adolescence, 22,* 400–408.

Padilla-Walker, L. M., Coyne, S. M., Collier, K. M., & Nielson, M. G. (2015). Longitudinal relations between prosocial television content and adolescents' prosocial and aggressive behavior: The mediating role of empathic concern and self-regulation. *Developmental Psychology, 51,* 1317–1328.

Pagani, L., Boulerice, B., Vitaro, F., & Tremblay, R. E. (1999). Effects of poverty on academic failure and delinquency in boys: A change and process approach. *Journal of Child Psychology & Psychiatry & Allied Disciplines, 40,* 1209–1219.

Pagani, L., Tremblay, R. E., Vitaro, F., Boulerice, B., & McDuff, P. (2001). Effects of grade retention on academic performance and behavioral development. *Development and Psychopathology, 13,* 297–315.

Palacios, J., Román, M., Moreno, C., León, E., & Peñarrubia, M. G. (2014). Differential plasticity in the recovery of adopted children after early adversity. *Child Development Perspectives, 8,* 169–174.

Palacios, N., Guttmannova, K., & Chase-Lansdale, P. L. (2008). Early reading achievement of children in immigrant families: Is there an immigrant paradox? *Developmental Psychology, 44,* 1381–1395.

Palincsar, A. S., & Brown, A. L. (1984). Reciprocal teaching of comprehension-fostering and comprehension-monitoring activities. *Cognition and Instruction, 1,* 117–175.

Paluck, E. L., & Green, D. (2009). Prejudice reduction: What works? A review and assessment of research and practice. *Annual Review of Psychology, 60,* 339–367.

Pan, B. A., Rowe, M. L., Singer, J. D., & Snow, C. E. (2005). Maternal correlates of growth in toddler vocabulary production in low-income families. *Child Development, 76,* 763–782.

Panksepp, J. (1998). Attention deficit hyperactivity disorders, psychostimulants, and intolerance of childhood playfulness: A tragedy in the making? *Current Directions in Psychological Science, 7,* 91–98.

Panksepp, J. (2000). The riddle of laughter: Neural and psychoevolutionary underpinnings of joy. *Current Directions in Psychological Science, 9,* 183–186.

Pape, L., & Ryba, K. (2004). *Practical considerations for school-based occupational therapists.* Bethesda, MD: AOTA Press.

Pargas, R. C. M., Brennan, P. A., Hammen, C., & Le Brocque, R. (2010). Resilience to maternal depression in young adulthood. *Developmental Psychology, 46,* 805–814.

Park, J., Kitayama, S., Markus, H. R., Coe, C. L., Miyamoto, Y., Karasawa, M., . . . Ryff, C. D. (2013). Social status and anger expression: The cultural moderation hypothesis. *Emotion, 13,* 1122–1131.

Parker, C. E., O'Dwyer, L. M., & Irwin, C. W. (2014). *The correlates of academic performance for English language learner students in a New England district (REL 2014-020).* Washington, DC: Department of Education.

Parker, J. G., & Asher, S. R. (1993). Friendship and friendship quality in middle childhood: Links with peer group acceptance and feelings of loneliness and social dissatisfaction. *Developmental Psychology, 29,* 611–621.

Pashler, H., Bain, P., Bottge, B., Graesser, A., Koedinger, K., McDaniel, M., et al. (2007). *Organizing instruction and study to improve student learning.* Washington, DC: Department of Education, National Center for Education Research.

Patall, E. A., Cooper, H., & Robinson, J. C. (2008). Parent involvement in homework: A research synthesis. *Review of Educational Research, 78,* 1039–1101.

Patrick, E., & Abravanel, E. (2000). The self-regulatory nature of preschool children's private speech in a naturalistic setting. *Applied Psycholinguistics, 21,* 45–61.

Patterson, C. J. (2009). Children of lesbian and gay parents: Psychology, law, and policy. *American Psychologist, 54,* 727–736.

Patterson, C. J., Vaden, N., & Kupersmidt, J. B. (1991). Family background, recent life events and peer rejection during childhood. *Journal of Social and Personal Relationships, 8,* 347–361.

Patterson, G. R., & Bank, C. L. (1989). Some amplifying mechanisms for pathologic processes in families. In M. Gunnar & E. Thelen (Eds.), *Systems and development: Symposia on child psychology* (pp. 167–210). Hillsdale, NJ: Erlbaum.

Patterson, G. R., DeBaryshe, B., & Ramsey, E. (1989). A developmental perspective on antisocial behavior. *American Psychologist, 44,* 329–335.

Paulhus, D. L., & Dubois, P. J. (2015). The link between cognitive ability and scholastic cheating: A meta-analysis. *Review of General Psychology, 19,* 183–190.

Pauker, K., Williams, A., & Steele, J. R. (2016). Children's racial categorization in context. *Child Development Perspectives, 10,* 33–38.

Pauli-Pott, U., Haverkock, A., Pott, W., & Beckmann, D. (2007). Negative emotionality, attachment quality, and behavior problems in early childhood. *Infant Mental Health Journal, 28,* 39–53.

Pauleti, R. E., Menon, M., Menon, M., Tobin, D. D., & Perry, D. G. (2012). Narcissism and adjustment in preadolescence. *Child Development, 83,* 831–837.

Paulus, M. (2014). The emergence of prosocial behavior: Why do infants and toddlers help, comfort, and share? *Child Development Perspectives, 8,* 77–81.

Paulussen-Hoogeboom, M. C., Stams, G. J., Hermanns, J. M., & Peetsma, T. T. (2007). Child negative emotionality and parenting from infancy to preschool: A meta-analytic review. *Developmental Psychology, 43*, 438–453.

Paunesku, D., Walton, G. M., Romero, C., Smith, E. N., Yeager, D. S., & Dweck, C. S. (2015). Mind-set interventions are a scalable treatment for academic underachievement. *Psychological Science, 26*, 784–793.

Paus, T. (2005). Mapping brain maturation and cognitive development during adolescence. *Trends in Cognitive Sciences, 9*, 60–68.

Payne, V., & Issacs, L. (1994). *Human motor development: A life-span approach* (2nd ed.). Mountain View, CA: Mayfield.

Pea, R., Nass, C., Meheula, L., Rance, M., Kumar, A., Bamford, H., et al. (2010). Media use, face-to-face communication, media multitasking, and social well-being among 8- to 12-year-old girls. *Developmental Psychology, 48*, 327–336.

Pearce, M., Jones, S., Schwab-Stone, M., & Ruchkin, V. (2003). The protective effects of religiousness and parent involvement on the development of conduct problems among youth exposed to violence. *Child Development, 74*, 1682–1696.

Pears, K. C., Kim, H. K., Buchanan, R., & Fisher, P. A. (2015). Adverse consequences of school mobility for children in foster care: A prospective longitudinal study. *Child Development, 86*, 1210–1226.

Pearson, B. Z., Conner, T., & Jackson, J. E. (2013). Removing obstacles for African American English-speaking children through greater understanding of language difference. *Developmental Psychology, 49*, 31–44.

Pedersen, S., Vitaro, F., Barker, E. D., & Borge, A. I. H. (2007). The timing of middle-childhood peer rejection and friendship: Linking early behavior to early-adolescent adjustment. *Child Development, 78*, 1037–1051.

Pedro-Carroll, J. L. (2005). Fostering resilience in the aftermath of divorce: The role of evidence-based programs for children. *Family Court Review, 52*, 52–64.

Peisner-Feinberg, E., Burchinal, M., Clifford, R., Culkin, M., Howes, C., Kagan, S., et al. (2001). The relation of preschool child-care quality to children's cognitive and social developmental trajectories through second grade. *Child Development, 72*, 1534–1553.

Pelleboer-Gunnink, H. A., Van der Valk, I. E., Branje, S. J. T., Van Doorn, M. D., & Deković, M. (2015). Effectiveness and moderators of the preventive intervention Kids in Divorce Situations: A randomized controlled trial. *Journal of Family Psychology, 29*, 799–805.

Pellegrini, A. (2011). "In the eye of the beholder": Sex bias in observations and ratings of children's aggression. *Educational Researcher, 40*, 281–286.

Pellegrini, A. D. (2002). Rough-and-tumble play from childhood through adolescence: Development and possible functions. In P. Smith & C. Hart (Eds.), *Blackwell handbook of childhood social development* (pp. 438–453). Oxford, UK: Blackwell.

Pellegrini, A. D. (2003). Perceptions and functions of play and real fighting in early adolescence. *Child Development, 74*, 1522–1533.

Pellegrini, A. D., & Bartini, M. (2000). An empirical comparison of methods of sampling aggression and victimization in school settings. *Journal of Educational Psychology, 92*, 360–366.

Pellegrini, A. D., Blatchford, P., Kato, K., & Baines, E. (2004). A short-term longitudinal study of children's playground games in primary school: Implications for adjustment to school and social adjustment in the USA and the UK. *Social Development, 13*, 107–123.

Pellegrini, A. D., & Bohn, C. (2005). The role of recess in children's cognitive performance and school adjustment, *Educational Researcher, 34*, 13–19.

Pellegrini, A. D., & Smith, P. (1998). Physical activity play: The nature and function of a neglected aspect of play. *Child Development, 69*, 577–598.

Pellicano, E. (2007). Links between theory of mind and executive function in young children with autism: Clues to developmental primacy. *Developmental Psychology, 43*, 974–990.

Pellicano, E. (2013). Sensory symptoms in autism: A blooming, buzzing confusion? *Child Development Perspectives, 7*, 143–148.

Pelucchi, B., Hay, J. F., & Saffran, J. R. (2009). Statistical learning in a natural language by 8-month-old infants. *Child Development, 80*, 674–685.

Penela, E. C., Walker, O. L., Degnan, K. A., Fox, N. A., & Henderson, H. A. (2015). Early behavioral inhibition and emotion regulation: Pathways toward social competence in middle childhood. *Child Development, 86*, 1227–1240.

Pennington, B. F., & Bishop, D. (2009). Relations among speech, language, and reading disorders. *Annual Review of Psychology, 60*, 283–306.

Pennington, B. F., McGrath, L. M., Rosenberg, J., Barnard, H., Smith, S. D., Willcutt, E. G., Friend, A., DeFries, J. C., & Olson, R. K. (2009). Gene X Environment interactions in reading disability and attention-deficit/hyperactivity disorder. *Developmental Psychology, 45*, 77–89.

Penrod, B., Wallace, M. D., & Dyer, E. J. (2008). Assessing potency of high- and low-preference reinforcers with respect to response rate and response patterns. *Journal of Applied Behavior Analysis, 41*, 177–188.

Pepler, D., Jiang, D., Craig, W., & Connolly, J. (2008). Developmental trajectories of bullying and associated factors. *Child Development, 79*, 325–338.

Perkins, D., Jacobs, J., Barber, B., & Eccles, J. (2004). Childhood and adolescent sports participation as predictors of participation in sports and physical fitness activities during young adulthood. *Youth & Society, 35*, 495–520.

Peter, J., & Valkenburg, P. M. (2016). Adolescents and pornography: A review of 20 years of research. *Journal of Sex Research, 53*, 509–531.

Peters, E., Riksen-Walraven, J. M., Cillessen, A., & de Weerth, C. (2011). Peer rejection and HPA activity in middle childhood: Friendship makes a difference. *Child Development, 82*, 1906–1920.

Peterson, C., Peterson, J., & Webb, J. (2000). Factors influencing the development of a theory of mind in blind children. *British Journal of Developmental Psychology, 18*, 431–447.

Peterson, C., Warren, K., & Short, M. (2011). Infantile amnesia across the years: A 2-year follow-up of children's earliest memories. *Child Development, 82*, 1092–1105.

Peterson, C., Wellman, H., & Slaughter, V. (2012). The mind behind the message: Advancing theory-of-mind scales for typically developing children, and those with deafness, autism, or Asperger syndrome. *Child Development, 83*, 469–485.

Petrosino, A., Gugkenburg, S., DeVoe, J., & Hanson, T. (2010). *What characteristics of bullying, bullying victims, and schools are associated with increased reporting of bullying to school officials?* Washington, DC: Institute of Education Sciences, REL Northeast & Islands.

Petterson, S., & Albers, A. (2001). Effects of poverty and maternal depression on early child development. *Child Development, 72*, 1794–1813.

Pettigrew, T. F., & Tropp, L. R. (2006). A meta-analytic test of intergroup contact theory. *Journal of Personality and Social Psychology, 90*, 751–783.

Pettit, G. S. (2005). Violent children in developmental perspective: Risk and protective factors and the mechanisms through which they (may) operate. *Current Directions in Psychological Science, 13*, 194–197.

Pettit, G. S., Laird, R., Bates, J., & Dodge, K. (1997). Patterns of after-school care in middle childhood: Risk factors and developmental outcomes. *Merrill-Palmer Quarterly, 43*, 515–538.

Pettit, G. S., Laird, R. D., Dodge, K. A., Bates, J. E., & Criss, M. M. (2001). Antecedents and behavior-problem outcomes of parental monitoring and psychological control in early adolescence. *Child Development, 72*, 583–598.

Petts, R. (2014). Family, religious attendance, and trajectories of psychological well-being among youth. *Journal of Family Psychology, 28*, 759–768.

Petts, R. J. (2009). Family and religious characteristics' influence on delinquency trajectories from adolescence to young adulthood. *American Sociological Review, 74*, 465–483.

Pew Research Center. (2007). From 1997 to 2007: Fewer mothers prefer full-time work. *A Social & Demographic Trends Report*. Retrieved May 22, 2010, from http://pewresearch.org/assets/social/pdf/WomenWorking.pdf

Pfeifer, J. H., Brown, C. S., & Juvonen, J. (2007). Prejudice reduction in schools: Teaching tolerance in schools: Lessons learned since *Brown v. Board of Education* about the development and reduction of children's prejudice. *Social Policy Report, 21*, 3–23.

Pfost, M., Hattie, J., Dörfler, T., & Artelt, C. (2014). Individual differences in reading development: A review of 25 years of empirical research on Matthew effects in reading. *Review of Educational Research, 84*, 203–244.

Phelan, P., Davidson, A. L., & Cao, H. T. (1991). Students' multiple worlds: Negotiating the boundaries of family, peer, and school cultures. *Anthropology & Education Quarterly, 22*, 224–250.

Phillips, D. A., Fox, N. A., & Gunnar, M. R. (2011). Same place, different experiences: Bringing individual differences to research in child care. *Child Development Perspectives, 5*, 44–49.

Phillips, L. M., Norris, S. P., Osmond, W. C., & Maynard, A. M. (2002). Relative reading achievement: A longitudinal study of 187 children from first through sixth grades. *Journal of Educational Psychology, 94*, 3–13.

Phinney, J. S. (1989). Stages of ethnic identity development in minority group adolescents. *Journal of Early Adolescence, 9*, 34–49.

Phinney, J. S. (1996). When we talk about American ethnic groups, what do we mean? *American Psychologist, 51*, 918–927.

Piaget, J. (1926/1959). *The language and thought of the child* (M. Gabain & R. Gabain, Trans. 3rd ed.). London: Routledge & Kegan Paul.

Piaget, J. (1929/1963). *The child's conception of the world* (J. Tomlinson & A. Tomlinson, Trans.). Paterson, NJ: Littlefield, Adams.

Piaget, J. (1932). *The moral judgment of the child (M. Gabain, Trans.).* Glencoe, IL: Free Press.

Piaget, J. (1954). *The construction of reality in the child* (M. Cook, Trans.). New York: Basic Books.

Piaget, J. (1962). *Play, dreams and imitation in childhood* (C. Gattegno & F. M. Hodgson, Trans.). New York: Norton.

Piaget, J. (1965). *The moral judgment of the child* (M. Gabain, Trans.). New York: The Free Press.

Piaget, J. (1970). Piaget's theory (G. Gellerier & J. Langer, Trans.). In P. H. Mussen (Ed.), *Carmichael's manual of child psychology* (3rd ed., Vol. 1, pp. 703–732). New York: Wiley.

Piaget, J., & Inhelder, B. (1956). *The child's conception of space* (F. J. Langdon & J. L. Lunzer, Trans.). London: Routledge & Kegan Paul.

Piaget, J., & Inhelder, B. (1964). *The early growth of logic in the child. Classification and seriation* (E. A. Lunzer & D. Papert, Trans.). London: Routledge & Kegan Paul.

Pianta, R., Mashburn, A., Downer, J., Hamre, B., & Justice, L. (2008). Effects of web-mediated professional development resources on teacher–child interactions in pre-kindergarten classrooms. *Early Childhood Research Quarterly, 23*, 431–451.

Pianta, R. C. (1999). *Enhancing relationships between children and teachers.* Washington, DC: American Psychological Association.

Pianta, R. C., Belsky, J., Vandergrift, N., Houts, R. M., & Morrison, F. J. (2008). Classroom effects on children's achievement trajectories in elementary school. *American Educational Research Journal, 45*, 365–397.

Pianta, R. C., Nimetz, S., & Bennett, E. (1997). Mother–child relationships, teacher–child relationships, and school outcomes in preschool and kindergarten. *Early Childhood Research Quarterly, 12*, 263–280.

Piasta, S. B., Justice, L. M., McGinty, A. S., & Kaderavek, J. N. (2012). Increasing young children's contact with print during shared reading: Longitudinal effects on literacy achievement. *Child Development, 83*, 810–820.

Piehler, T. F., & Dishion, T. J. (2007). Interpersonal dynamics within adolescent friendships: Dyadic mutuality, deviant talk, and patterns of antisocial behavior. *Child Development, 78*, 1611–1624.

Pierce, S., & Lange, G. (2000). Relationships among metamemory, motivation and memory performance in young school-age children. *British Journal of Developmental Psychology, 18*, 121–135.

Pietschnig, J., & Voracek, M. (2015). One century of global IQ gains: A formal meta-analysis of the Flynn Effect (1909–2013). *Perspectives on Psychological Science, 10*, 282–306.

Pike, A. (2002). Behavioral genetics, shared and nonshared environment. In P. Smith & C. Hart (Eds.), *Blackwell handbook of childhood social development* (pp. 27–43). Oxford, UK: Blackwell.

Ping, R. M., & Goldin-Meadow, S. (2008). Hands in the air: Using ungrounded iconic gestures to teach children conservation of quantity. *Developmental Psychology, 44*, 1277–1287.

Pintrich, P. R. (2003). A motivational science perspective on the role of student motivation in learning and teaching contexts. *Journal of Educational Psychology, 95*, 667–686.

Pintrich, P. R., & Schunk, D. H. (2002). *Motivation in education: Theory, research, and applications* (2nd ed.). Upper Saddle River, NJ: Pearson.

Pittman, L. D., & Chase-Lansdale, P. L. (2001). African American adolescent girls in impoverished communities: Parenting style and adolescent outcomes. *Journal of Research on Adolescence, 11*, 199–224.

Planty, M., Bozick, R., & Regnier, M. (2006). Helping because you have to or helping because you want to? Sustaining participation in service work from adolescence through young adulthood. *Youth & Society, 38*, 177–202.

Planty, M., Hussar, W., Snyder, T., Kena, G., KewalRamani, A., Kemp, J., et al. (2009). *The condition of education 2009 (NCES 2009–081).* Washington, DC: National Center for Education Statistics, Institute of Education Sciences, Department of Education.

Plester, B., Wood, C., & Bell, V. (2008). Txt msg n school literacy: Does texting and knowledge of text abbreviations adversely affect children's literacy attainment? *Literacy, 23*, 719–733.

Plomin, R. (2013). Child development and molecular genetics: 14 years later. *Child Development, 84*, 104–120.

Plomin, R., DeFries, J., McClearn, G. E., & McGuffin, P. (2001). *Behavioral genetics* (4th ed.). New York: Worth.

Plomin, R., DeFries, J. C., Knopik, V. S., & Neiderhiser, J. M. (2016). Top 10 replicated findings from behavioral genetics. *Perspectives on Psychological Science, 11*, 3–23.

Plötner, M., Over, H., Carpenter, M., & Tomasello, M. (2015). Young children show the bystander effect in helping situations. *Psychological Science, 26*, 499–506.

Pluess, M. (2015). Individual differences in environmental sensitivity. *Child Development Perspectives, 9*, 138–143.

Pluess, M., & Belsky, J. (2010). Differential susceptibility to parenting and quality child care. *Developmental Psychology, 46*, 379–390.

Polacek, G. J., Rojas, V., Levitt, S., & Mika, V. S. (2006). Media and sex: Perspectives from Hispanic teens. *American Journal of Sexuality Education, 1*, 51–69.

Polanin, J., Espelage, D. L., & Pigott, T. D. (2012). A meta-analysis of school-based bullying prevention programs' effects on bystander intervention behavior. *School Psychology Review, 41*, 47–65.

Polderman, T. J. C., Benyamin, B., de Leeuw, C. A., Sullivan, P. F., van Bochoven, A., Visscher, P. M., & Posthuma, D. (2015). Meta-analysis of the heritability of human traits based on fifty years of twin studies. *Nature Genetics, 47*, 702–709.

Polivy, J., Herman, P., Mills, J., & Wheller, H. (2003). Eating disorders in adolescence. In G. Adams & M. Berzonsky (Eds.), *Blackwell handbook on adolescence* (pp. 523–549). Malden, MA: Blackwell.

Pollak, S. D. (2008). Mechanisms linking early experience and the emergence of emotions: Illustrations from the study of maltreated children. *Current Directions in Psychological Science, 17*, 370–375.

Pollak, S. D., Cicchetti, D., Hornung, K., & Reed, A. (2000). Recognizing emotion in faces: Developmental effects of child abuse and neglect. *Developmental Psychology, 36*, 679–688.

Pollak, S. D., Nelson, C. A., Schlaak, M. F., Roeber, B. J., Wewerka, S. S., Wiik, K. L., et al. (2010). Neurodevelopmental effects of early deprivation in postinstitutionalized children. *Child Development, 81*, 224–236.

Pomerantz, E. M., Moorman, E. A., & Litwack, S. D. (2007). The how, whom, and why of parents' involvement in children's academic lives: More is not always better. *Review of Educational Research, 77*, 373–410.

Pomerantz, E. M., Ng, F. F.-Y., Cheung, C. S.-S., & Qu, Y. (2014). Raising happy children who succeed in school: Lessons from China and the United States. *Child Development Perspectives, 8*, 71–76.

Pomerantz, E. M., & Rudolph, K. (2003). What ensues from emotional distress? Implications for competence estimation. *Child Development, 74*, 329–345.

Ponitz, C. C., McClelland, M. M., Matthews, J. S., & Morrison, F. J. (2009). A structured observation of behavioral self-regulation and its contribution to kindergarten outcomes. *Developmental Psychology, 45*, 605–619.

Pontifex, M., Kamijo, K., Scudder, M., Raine, L., Khan, N., Hemrick, B., . . . Hillman, C. (2014). The differential association of adiposity and fitness with cognitive control in preadolescent children. *Monographs of the Society for Research in Child Development, 79*(4), 72–92.

Poole, D. A., Bruck, M., & Pipe, M.-E. (2011). Forensic interviewing aids: Do props help children answer questions about touching? *Current Directions in Psychological Science, 20*, 11–15.

Poropat, A. E. (2009). A meta-analysis of the five-factor model of personality and academic performance. *Psychological Bulletin, 135*, 322–338.

Porter, A. C., & Polikoff, M. S. (2007). NCLB: State interpretations, early effects, and suggestions for reauthorization. *Social Policy Report, 21,* 3–14.

Porter, S., & ten Brinke, L. (2008). Reading between the lies: Identifying concealed and falsified emotions in universal facial expressions. *Psychological Science, 19,* 508–514.

Posada, G., Lu, T., Trumbell, J., Kaloustian, G., Trudel, M., Plata, S. J., . . . Lay, K.-L. (2013). Is the secure base phenomenon evident here, there, and anywhere? A cross-cultural study of child behavior and experts' definitions. *Child Development, 84,* 1896–1905.

Poteat, V. P., Yoshikawa, H., Calzo, J. P., Gray, M. L., DiGiovanni, C. D., Lipkin, A., et al. (2015). Contextualizing gay–straight alliances: Student, advisor, and structural factors related to positive youth development among members. *Child Development, 86,* 176–193.

Poulin, F., & Boivin, M. (2000). The role of proactive and reactive aggression in the formation and development of boys' friendships. *Developmental Psychology, 36,* 223–240.

Poulin-Dubois, D., & Brosseau-Liard, P. (2016). The developmental origins of selective social learning. *Current Directions in Psychological Science, 25,* 60–64.

Powell, G. F., Brasel, J. A., & Blizzard, R. M. (1967). Emotional deprivation and growth retardation simulating idiopathic hypopituitarism: 1. Clinical evaluation of the syndrome. *New England Journal of Medicine, 276,* 1271–1278.

Powers, C., Bierman, K., & The Conduct Problems Prevention Research Group. (2013). The multifaceted impact of peer relations on aggressive-disruptive behavior in early elementary school. *Developmental Psychology, 49,* 1174–1186.

Price, T., & Jaffee, S. R. (2008). Effects of the family environment: Gene–environment interaction and passive gene–environment correlation. *Developmental Psychology, 44,* 305–315.

Priel, B., & Besser, A. (2000). Adult attachment styles, early relationships, antenatal attachment, and perceptions of infant temperament: A study of first-time mothers. *Personal Relationships, 7,* 291–310.

Prince, M. (2004). Does active learning work? A review of the research. *Journal of Engineering Education, 93,* 223–231.

Principe, G., Kanaya, T., Ceci, S., & Singh, M. (2006). Believing is seeing: How rumors can engender false memories in preschoolers. *Psychological Science, 17,* 243–248.

Prinstein, M., Brechwald, W. A., & Cohen, G. L. (2011). Susceptibility to peer influence: Using a performance-based measure to identify adolescent males at heightened risk for deviant peer socialization. *Developmental Psychology, 47,* 1167–1172.

Prior, M., Smart, D., Sanson, A., & Oberklaid, F. (2000). Does shy-inhibited temperament in childhood lead to anxiety problems in adolescence? *Journal of the American Academy of Child and Adolescent Psychiatry, 39,* 461–468.

Pritchard, R. J., & Honeycutt, R. (2006). The process approach to writing instruction: Examining its effectiveness. In C. A. MacArthur, S. Graham, & J. Fitzgerald (Eds.), *Handbook of writing research* (pp. 275–290). New York: Guilford.

Proctor, C. P., August, D., Carlo, M. S., & Snow, C. E. (2006). The intriguing role of Spanish language vocabulary knowledge in predicting English reading comprehension. *Journal of Educational Psychology, 98,* 159–169.

Pronin, E., & Jacobs, E. (2008). Thought speed, mood, and the experience of mental motion. *Perspectives on Psychological Science, 3,* 461–485.

Propper, C., Moore, G. A., Mills-Koonce, W. R., Halpern, C. T., Hill-Soderlund, A. L., Calkins, S. D., et al. (2008). Gene–environment contributions to the development of infant vagal reactivity: The interaction of dopamine and maternal sensitivity. *Child Development, 79,* 1377–1394.

Protzko, J., Aronson, J., & Blair, C. (2013). How to make a young child smarter: Evidence from the database of raising intelligence. *Perspectives on Psychological Science, 8,* 25–40.

Provine, R. R. (2000). *Laughter.* New York: Viking.

Przybylski, A. K., Weinstein, N., Murayama, K., Lynch, M. F., & Ryan, R. M. (2012). The ideal self at play: The appeal of video games that let you be all you can be. *Psychological Science, 23,* 69–76.

Pulkkinen, L. (2001). Reveller or striver? How childhood self-control predicts adult behavior. In A. Bothart & D. Stipek (Eds.), *Constructive and destructive behavior: Implications for family, school, and society* (pp. 167–185). Washington, DC: APA.

Puma, M., Bell, S., Cook, R., & Heid, C. (2010). *Head Start impact study: Final report.* Washington, DC: Department of Health and Human Services.

Puma, M., Bell, S., Cook, R., Heid, C., & Lopez, M. (2005). *Head Start impact study: First year findings.* Washington, DC: Department of Health and Human Services.

Pungello, E. P., Iruka, I. U., Dotterer, A. M., Mills-Koonce, R., & Reznick, J. S. (2009). The effects of socioeconomic status, race, and parenting on language development in early childhood. *Developmental Psychology, 45,* 544–557.

Pungello, E. P., Kainz, K., Burchinal, M., Wasik, B. H., Sparling, J. J., Ramey, C. T., et al. (2010). Early educational intervention, early cumulative risk, and the early home environment as predictors of young adult outcomes within a high-risk sample. *Child Development, 81,* 410–426.

Purcell-Gates, V., Duke, N. K., & Martineau, J. A. (2007). Learning to read and write genre-specific text: Roles of authentic experience and explicit teaching. *Reading Research Quarterly, 42,* 8–45.

Putallaz, M., Costanzo, P., Grimes, C., & Sherman, D. (1998). Intergenerational continuities and their influences on children's social development. *Social Development, 7,* 389–427.

Putallaz, M., Grimes, C. L., Foster, K. J., Kupersmidt, J. B., Coie, J. D., & Dearing, K. (2007). Overt and relational aggression and victimization: Multiple perspectives within the school setting. *Journal of School Psychology, 45,* 523–547.

Qin, L., Pomerantz, E. M., & Wang, Q. (2009). Are gains in decision-making autonomy during early adolescence beneficial for emotional functioning? The case of the United States and China. *Child Development, 80,* 1705–1721.

Quartz, S., & Sejnowski, T. (2002). *Liars, lovers, and heroes: What the new brain science reveals about how we become who we are.* New York: Morrow.

Quatman, T., Sampson, K., Robinson, C., & Watson, C. (2001). Academic, motivational, and emotional correlates of adolescent dating. *Genetic, Social & General Psychology Monographs, 127,* 211–235.

Quillian, L., & Campbell, M. E. (2003). Beyond Black and White: The present and future of multiracial friendship segregation. *American Sociological Review, 68,* 540–566.

Quinn, J. M., Wagner, R. K., Petscher, Y., & Lopez, D. (2015). Developmental relations between vocabulary knowledge and reading comprehension: A latent change score modeling study. *Child Development, 86,* 159–175.

Quinn, P. C., & Liben, L. S. (2008). A sex difference in mental rotation in young infants. *Psychological Science, 19,* 1067–1070.

Quintana, S. M., & Vera, E. M. (1999). Mexican American children's ethnic identity, understanding of ethnic prejudice, and parental ethnic socialization. *Hispanic Journal of Behavioral Sciences, 21,* 387–404.

Raabe, T., & Beelmann, A. (2011). Development of ethnic, racial, and national prejudice in childhood and adolescence: A multinational meta-analysis of age differences. *Child Development, 82,* 1715–1737.

Raby, K. L., Cichetti, D., Carlson, E., Cutuli, J., Englund, M., & Egeland, B. (2012). Genetic and caregiving-based contributions to infant attachment: Unique associations with distress reactivity and attachment security. *Psychological Science, 23,* 1016–1023.

Raby, K. L., Roisman, G. I., Fraley, R. C., & Simpson, J. A. (2015). The enduring predictive significance of early maternal sensitivity: Social and academic competence through age 32 years. *Child Development, 86,* 695–708.

Radke-Yarrow, M., Cummings, M., Kuczynski, L., & Chapman, M. (1985). Patterns of attachment in two- and three-year-olds in normal families and families with parental depression. *Child Development, 56,* 884–893.

Radke-Yarrow, M., Zahn-Waxler, C., Richardson, D., Susman, A., & Martinez, P. (1994). Caring behavior in children of clinically depressed and well mothers. *Child Development, 65,* 1405–1414.

Rafetseder, E., & Perner, J. (2014). Counterfactual reasoning: Sharpening conceptual distinctions in developmental studies. *Child Development Perspectives, 8,* 54–58.

Raikes, H., Pan, B. A., Luze, G., Tamis-LeMonda, C., Brooks-Gunn, J., Constantine, J., et al. (2006). Mother-child bookreading in low-income families: Correlates and outcomes during the first three years. *Child Development, 77,* 924–953.

Rakow, A., Forehand, R., Haker, K., McKee, L. G., Champion, J. E., Potts, J., et al. (2011). Use of parental guilt induction among depressed parents. *Journal of Family Psychology, 25*, 147–151.

Raley, R. K., & Wildsmith, E. (2004). Cohabitation and children's family instability. *Journal of Marriage and Family, 66*, 210–219.

Ramani, G. B., & Siegler, R. S. (2008). Promoting broad and stable improvements in low-income children's numerical knowledge through playing number board games. *Child Development, 79*, 375–394.

Ramani, G. B., Siegler, R. S., & Hitti, A. (2012). Taking it to the classroom: Number board games as a small group learning activity. *Journal of Educational Psychology, 104*, 661–672.

Ramaswamy, V., & Bergin, C. C. (2009). Do reinforcement and induction increase prosocial behavior? Results of a teacher-based intervention in preschools. *Journal of Research in Childhood Education, 23*, 525–536.

Ramirez, G., & Beilock, S. L. (2011). Writing about testing worries boosts exam performance in the classroom. *Science, 331*, 211–213.

Rampey, B. D., Dion, G. S., & Donahue, P. L. (2009). *NAEP 2008: Trends in academic progress (NCES 2009-479)*. Washington, DC: Department of Education.

Ramsey-Rennels, J. L., & Langlois, J. H. (2006). Infants' differential processing of female and male faces. *Current Directions in Psychological Science, 15*, 59–62.

Rao, H., Betancourt, L., Giannetta, J. M., Brodsky, N. L., Korczykowski, M., Avants, B. B., et al. (2010). Early parental care is important for hippocampal maturation: Evidence from brain morphology in humans. *NeuroImage, 49*, 1144–1150.

Rao, R., & Georgieff, M. (2000). Early nutrition and brain development. In C. Nelson (Ed.), *The effects of early adversity on neurobehavioral development* (pp. 1–30). Mahwah, NJ: Erlbaum.

Raposa, E. B., Laws, H. B., & Ansell, E. B. (2015). Prosocial behavior mitigates the negative effects of stress in everyday life. *Clinical Psychological Science*. December 10, 2015.

Rappolt-Schlictmann, G., Willett, J. B., Ayoub, C., Lindsley, R., Hulette, A., & Fischer, K. (2009). Poverty, relationship conflict, and the regulation of cortisol in small and large group contexts at child care. *Mind, Brain, and Education, 3*, 131–142.

Rasch, B., & Born, J. (2008). Reactivation and consolidation of memory during sleep. *Current Directions in Psychological Science, 17*, 188–192.

Rasinski, T. V., Padak, N. D., McKeon, C. A., Wilfong, L. G., Friedauer, J. A., & Heim, P. (2005). Is reading fluency a key for successful high school reading? *Journal of Adolescent & Adult Literacy, 49*, 22–27.

Raskauskas, J., & Stoltz, A. D. (2007). Involvement in traditional and electronic bullying among adolescents. *Developmental Psychology, 43*, 564–573.

Raspa, M., McWilliam, R., & Maher-Ridley, S. (2001). Child care quality and children's engagement. *Early Education and Development, 12*, 209–224.

Ratcliffe, C., & McKernan, S. (2010). *Childhood poverty persistence: Facts and consequences*. Washington, DC: The Urban Institute.

Raudenbush, S. W. (2009). The Brown legacy and the O'Connor challenge: Transforming schools in the images of children's potential. *Educational Researcher, 38*, 169–180.

Raver, C. C. (2004). Placing emotional self-regulation in sociocultural and socioeconomic contexts. *Child Development, 75*, 346–353.

Raver, C. C., Gershoff, E. T., & Aber, J. L. (2007). Testing equivalence of mediating models of income, parenting, and school readiness for White, Black, and Hispanic children in a national sample. *Child Development, 78*, 96–115.

Raymond, J., Fenskey, M., & Tavassoli, N. (2003). Selective attention determines emotional responses to novel visual stimuli. *Psychological Science, 14*, 537–542.

Readdick, C. A., & Chapman, P. (2000). Young children's perceptions of time out. *Journal of Research in Childhood Education, 15*, 81–87.

Ream, R. K., & Palardy, G. J. (2008). Reexamining social class differences in the availability and the educational utility of parental social capital. *American Educational Research Journal, 45*, 238–273.

Reardon, S. (2013). The widening income achievement gap. *Educational Leadership, 70*, 10–16.

Reardon, S. F. (2011). The widening academic achievement gap between the rich and the poor: New evidence and possible explanations. In G. J. Duncan & R. Murnane (Eds.), *Whither opportunity* (pp. 91–116). New York: Russell Sage.

Recchia, H., Wainryb, C., & Pasupathi, M. (2013). "Two for flinching": Children's and adolescents' narrative accounts of harming their friends and siblings. *Child Development, 84*, 1459–1474.

Recchia, H. E., & Howe, N. (2009). Associations between social understanding, sibling relationship quality, and siblings' conflict strategies and outcomes. *Child Development, 80*, 1564–1578.

Recchia, H. E., Wainryb, C., Bourne, S., & Pasupathi, M. (2014). The construction of moral agency in mother–child conversations about helping and hurting across childhood and adolescence. *Developmental Psychology, 50*, 34–44.

Recchia, H. E., Wainryb, C., Bourne, S., & Pasupathi, M. (2015). Children's and adolescents' accounts of helping and hurting others: Lessons about the development of moral agency. *Child Development, 86*, 864–876.

Reed, T., & Brown, M. (2001). The expression of care in the rough and tumble play of boys. *Journal of Research in Childhood Education, 15*, 104–116.

Reeve, J. (2009). Why teachers adopt a controlling motivating style toward students and how they can become more autonomy supportive. *Educational Psychologist, 44*, 159–175.

Reich, S. M., Subrahmanyam, K., & Espinoza, G. (2012). Friending, IMing, and hanging out face-to-face: Overlap in adolescents' online and offline social networks. *Developmental Psychology, 48*, 356–368.

Reiss, D. (2005). The interplay between genotypes and family relationships: Reframing concepts of development and prevention. *Current Directions in Psychological Science, 14*, 139–143.

Renninger, K. A., & Bachrach, J. E. (2015). Studying triggers for interest and engagement using observational methods. *Educational Psychologist, 50*, 58–69.

Renninger, K. A., & Hidi, S. (2011). Revisiting the conceptualization, measurement, and generation of interest. *Educational Psychologist, 46*, 168–184.

Repetti, R. L., Wang, S.-w., & Saxbe, D. (2009). Bringing it all back home: How outside stressors shape families' everyday lives. *Current Directions in Psychological Science, 18*, 106–111.

Rescorla, L. (2005). Age 13 language and reading outcomes in late-talking toddlers. *Journal of Speech, Language and Hearing Research, 48*, 459–472.

Rescorla, R. A. (1988). Pavlovian conditioning: It's not what you think it is. *American Psychologist, 43*, 151–160.

Resetar, J. L., & Noell, G. H. (2008). Evaluating preference assessments for use in the general education population. *Journal of Applied Behavior Analysis, 41*, 447–451.

Rettinger, D., & Kramer, Y. (2009). Situational and Personal Causes of Student Cheating. Research in Higher Education, 50, 293–313.

Reyes, M. R., Brackett, M. A., Rivers, S. E., White, M., & Salovey, P. (2012). Classroom emotional climate, student engagement, and academic achievement. *Journal of Educational Psychology, 104*, 700–712.

Reyna, V. F., Weldon, R. B., & McCormick, M. (2015). Educating intuition: Reducing risky decisions using fuzzy-trace theory. *Current Directions in Psychological Science, 24*, 392–398.

Reyna, V. F., Wilhelms, E. A., McCormick, M. J., & Weldon, R. B. (2015). Development of risky decision making: Fuzzy-trace theory and neurobiological perspectives. *Child Development Perspectives, 9*, 122–127.

Reynolds, A., Ou, S.-R., & Topitzes, J. (2004). Path of effects of early childhood intervention on educational attainment and delinquency: A confirmatory analysis of the Chicago Child–Parent Centers. *Child Development, 75*, 1299–1328.

Reynolds, A. J., Temple, J. A., Ou, S.R., Arteaga, I. A., & White, B. A. B. (2011). School-based early childhood education and age-28 well-being: Effects by timing, dosage, and subgroups. *Science, 333*, 360–364.

Reynolds, C. R., & Shaywitz, S. E. (2009). Response to intervention: Prevention and remediation, perhaps. Diagnosis, no. *Child Development Perspectives, 3*, 44–47.

Rhee, S. H., Lahey, B. B., & Waldman, I. D. (2015). Comorbidity among dimensions of childhood psychopathology: Converging evidence from behavior genetics. *Child Development Perspectives, 9*, 26–31.

Rhoades, K. A. (2008). Children's responses to interparental conflict: A meta-analysis of their associations with child adjustment. *Child Development, 79*, 1942–1956.

Rhule, D. M., McMahon, R. J., Spieker, S. J., & Munson, J. A. (2006). Positive adjustment and associated protective factors in children of adolescent mothers. *Journal of Child and Family Studies, 15*, 231–251.

Richards, J. E., Reynolds, G. D., & Courage, M. L. (2010). The neural bases of infant attention. *Current Directions in Psychological Science, 19*, 41–46.

Richeson, J. A., & Sommers, S. R. (2016). Toward a social psychology of race and race relations for the twenty-first century. *Annual Review of Psychology, 67*, 439–463.

Rickards, A., Kelly, E., Doyle, L., & Callanan, C. (2001). Cognition, academic progress, behavior and self-concept at 14 years of very low birth weight children. *Journal of Developmental and Behavioral Pediatrics, 22*, e11.

Richtel, M. (2012, May 29). Wasting time is new divide in digital era. *New York Times*, p. A1.

Rideout, V. J. (2014). *Learning at home: Families' educational media use in America.* New York: The Joan Ganz Cooney Center at Sesame Workshop.

Rideout, V. J., Foehr, U. G., & Roberts, D. F. (2010). *Generation M2: Media in the lives of 8- to 18-year olds.* Menlo Park, CA: Kaiser Family Foundation.

Rieger, G., Linsenmeier, J. A. W., Gygax, L., & Bailey, J. M. (2008). Sexual orientation and childhood gender nonconformity: Evidence from home videos. *Developmental Psychology, 44*, 46–58.

Rigby, K. (2002). Bullying in childhood. In P. Smith & C. Hart (Eds.), *Blackwell handbook of childhood social development* (pp. 549–568). Oxford, UK: Blackwell.

Riggins, T. (2014). Longitudinal investigation of source memory reveals different developmental trajectories for item memory and binding. *Developmental Psychology, 50*, 449–459.

Rimm-Kaufman, S. E., Curby, T. W., Grimm, K. J., Nathanson, L., & Brock, L. (2009). The contribution of children's self-regulation and classroom quality to children's adaptive behaviors in the kindergarten classroom. *Developmental Psychology, 45*, 958–972.

Rimm-Kaufman, S., Pianta, R., & Cox, M. (2000). Teacher's judgments of problems in the transition to kindergarten. *Early Childhood Research Quarterly, 15*, 147–166.

Rindermann, H., & Ceci, S. J. (2009). Educational policy and country outcomes in international cognitive competence studies. *Perspectives on Psychological Science, 4*, 551–568.

Rios-Aguilar, C., Kiyama, J. M., Gravitt, M., & Moll, L. (2011). Funds of knowledge for the poor and funds of capital for the rich? A capital approach to examining funds of knowledge. *Theory and Research in Education, 9*, 163–184.

Ristic, J., & Enns, J. T. (2015). The changing face of attentional development. *Current Directions in Psychological Science, 24*, 24–31.

Ritchie, S. J., & Bates, T. C. (2013). Enduring links from childhood mathematics and reading achievement to adult socioeconomic status. *Psychological Science, 24*, 1301-1308.

Rittle-Johnson, B. (2007). Promoting transfer: Effects of self-explanation and direct instruction. *Child Development, 77*, 1–15.

Rittle-Johnson, B., & Star, J. (2009). Compared with what? The effects of different comparisons on conceptual knowledge and procedural flexibility for equation solving. *Journal of Educational Psychology, 101*, 529–544.

Rittle-Johnson, B., Star, J., & Durkin, K. (2009). The importance of prior knowledge when comparing examples: Influences on conceptual and procedural knowledge of equation solving. *Journal of Educational Psychology, 101*, 836–852.

Rivers, I., Poteat, V. P., & Noret, N. (2008). Victimization, social support, and psychosocial functioning among children of same-sex and opposite-sex couples in the United Kingdom. *Developmental Psychology, 44*, 127–134.

Robers, S., Kemp, J., Rathbun, A., & Morgan, R. E. (2014). *Indicators of school crime and safety: 2013* (NCES 2014-042/NCJ 243299). Washington, DC: National Center for Education Statistics, Department of Education.

Robers, S., Zhang, J., & Truman, J. (2012). *Indicators of school crime and safety: 2011.* Washington, DC: National Center for Education Statistics, Department of Education.

Robert Wood Johnson Foundation. (2009). Active education: Physical education, physical activity and academic performance. *Research Brief, Summer 2009.* Retrieved from activelivingresearch.org

Roberts, M. E., Gibbons, F. X., Gerrard, M., Weng, C.-Y., Murry, V. M., Simons, L. G., et al. (2012). From racial discrimination to risky sex: Prospective relations involving peers and parents. *Developmental Psychology, 48*, 89–102.

Roberts, R. E., Roberts, C. R., & Chan, W. (2009). One-year incidence of psychiatric disorders and associated risk factors among adolescents in the community. *Journal of Child Psychology and Psychiatry, 50*, 405–415.

Robins, R., John, O., Caspi, A., Moffitt, T., & Stouthamer-Loeber, M. (1996). Resilient, overcontrolled and undercontrolled boys: Three replicable personality types. *Journal of Personality and Social Psychology, 70*, 157–171.

Robins, R. W., & Trzesniewski, K. (2005). Self-esteem development across the lifespan. *Current Directions in Psychological Science, 14*, 158–162.

Robinson, J. L., & Acevedo, M. C. (2001). Infant reactivity and reliance on mother during emotion challenges: Prediction of cognition and language skills in a low-income sample. *Child Development, 72*, 402–415.

Robinson, J. P., & Espelage, D. L. (2011). Inequities in educational and psychological outcomes between LGBTQ and straight students in middle and high school. *Educational Researcher, 40*, 315–330.

Robinson, P. W., Newby, T. J., & Hill, R. D. (1981). *Manipulating parents: Tactics used by children of all ages and ways parents can turn the tables.* Englewood Cliffs, NJ: Prentice Hall.

Robinson, T. N., Wilde, M. L., Navracruz, L., Haydel, F., & Varady, A. (2001). Effects of reducing children's television and video game use on aggressive behavior: A randomized controlled trial. *Archives of Pediatric & Adolescent Medicine, 155*, 17–23.

Rodkin, P., Espelage, D., & Hanish, L. (2015). A relational framework for understanding bullying: Developmental antecedents and outcomes. *American Psychologist, 70*, 311–321.

Rodkin, P., Ryan, A., Jamison, R., & Wilson, T. (2013). Social goals, social behavior, and social status in middle childhood. *Developmental Psychology, 49*, 1139–1150.

Rodkin, P. C., & Roisman, G. I. (2010). Antecedents and correlates of the popular-aggressive phenomenon in elementary school. *Child Development, 81*, 837–850.

Roebers, C. M., & Kauer, M. (2009). Motor and cognitive control in a normative sample of 7-year-olds. *Developmental Science, 12*, 175–181.

Roediger, H. L., III (2008). Relativity of remembering: Why the laws of memory vanished. *Annual Review of Psychology, 59*, 225–254.

Roehrs, T., & Roth, T. (2008). Caffeine: Sleep and daytime sleepiness. *Sleep Medicine Reviews, 12*, 153–162.

Rogers, L. O., Scott, M. A., & Way, N. (2015). Racial and gender identity among Black adolescent males: An intersectionality perspective. *Child Development, 86*, 407–424.

Rogol, A., Roemmich, J., & Clark, P. (2002). Growth at puberty. *Journal of Adolescent Health, 31*, 192–200.

Rohrer, D., & Pashler, H. (2007). Increasing retention without increasing study time. *Current Directions in Psychological Science, 16*, 183–186.

Roisman, G. I., & Fraley, R. C. (2006). The limits of genetic influence: A behavior–genetic analysis of infant–caregiver relationship quality and temperament. *Child Development, 77*, 1656–1667.

Roisman, G. I., & Fraley, R. C. (2012). A behavior-genetic study of the legacy of early caregiving experiences: Academic skills, social competence, and externalizing behavior in kindergarten. *Child Development, 83*, 728–742.

Roisman, G., Susman, E., Barnett-Walker, K., Booth-LaForce, C., Owen, M. T., Belsky, J., et al. (2009). Early family and child-care antecedents of awakening cortisol levels in adolescence. *Child Development, 80*, 907–920.

Roksa, J., & Potter, D. (2011). Parenting and academic achievement. *Sociology of Education, 84*, 299–321.

Romano, E., Babchishin, L., Pagani, L. S., & Kohen, D. (2010). School readiness and later achievement: Replication and extension using a nationwide Canadian survey. *Developmental Psychology, 46*, 995–1007.

Rome, E., Ammerman, S., Rosen, D., Keller, R., Lock, J., Mammel, K., et al. (2003). Children and adolescents with eating disorders: The state of the art. *Pediatrics, 111*, e98–e108.

Romeo, L., & Young, S. (1999). Using literacy play centers to engage middle grade students in content area learning. In J. A. Dugan, P. Linder, W. Linek, & E. Sturtevant (Eds.), *Advancing the world of literacy: Moving into the 21st century: The twenty-first yearbook of the College Reading Association* (pp. 122–136). Readyville, TN: College Reading Association.

Romero, A. J., & Roberts, R. E. (2003). Stress within a bicultural context for adolescents of Mexican descent. *Cultural Diversity and Ethnic Minority Psychology, 9*, 171–184.

Romi, S., Lewis, R., Roache, J., & Riley, P. (2011). The impact of teachers' aggressive management techniques on students' attitudes to schoolwork. *Journal of Educational Research, 104*, 231–240.

Roopnarine, J. L., Shin, M., Donovan, B., & Suppal, P. (2000). Sociocultural contexts of dramatic play: Implications for early education. In K. A. Roskos & J. F. Christie (Eds.), *Play and literacy in early childhood* (pp. 205–230). Mahwah, NJ: Erlbaum.

Roorda, D. L., Koomen, H. M. Y., Spilt, J. L., & Oort, F. J. (2011). The influence of affective teacher–student relationships on students' school engagement and achievement. *Review of Educational Research, 81*, 493–529.

Rosa, E. M., & Tudge, J. (2013). Urie Bronfenbrenner's theory of human development: Its evolution from ecology to bioecology. *Journal of Family Theory & Review, 5*, 243–258.

Rosário, P., Núñez, J. C., Vallejo, G., Cunha, J., Nunes, T., Mourão, R., & Pinto, R. (2015). Does homework design matter? The role of homework's purpose in student mathematics achievement. *Contemporary Educational Psychology, 43*, 10–24.

Rose, A. J., & Rudolph, K. D. (2006). A review of sex differences in peer relationship processes: Potential trade-offs for the emotional and behavioral development of girls and boys. *Psychological Bulletin, 132*, 1–34.

Rose, R., Viken, R., Dick, D., Bates, J. E., Pulkkinen, L., & Kaprio, J. (2003). It does take a village: Nonfamilial environments and children's behavior. *Psychological Science, 14*, 272–277.

Rose, S., & Feldman, J. (2000). The relation of very low birthweight to basic cognitive skills in infancy and childhood. In C. Nelson (Ed.), *The effects of early adversity on neurobehavioral development* (pp. 31–59). Mahwah, NJ: Erlbaum.

Rose, S. A., Feldman, J. F., & Jankowski, J. J. (2009). A cognitive approach to the development of early language. *Child Development, 80*, 134–150.

Rose, S. A., Feldman, J. F., & Jankowski, J. J. (2015). Pathways from toddler information processing to adolescent lexical proficiency. *Child Development, 86*, 1935–1947.

Rose, S. A., Futterweit, L. R., & Jankowski, J. J. (1999). The relation of affect to attention and learning in infancy. *Child Development, 70*, 549–559.

Roseberry, S., Hirsh-Pasek, K., & Golinkoff, R. M. (2014). Skype me! Socially contingent interactions help toddlers learn language. *Child Development, 85*, 956–970.

Rosen, L. D., Carrier, L. M., & Cheever, N. A. (2013). Facebook and texting made me do it: Media-induced task-switching while studying. *Computers in Human Behavior, 29*, 948–958.

Rosen, L. D., Cheever, N. A., & Carrier, L. M. (2008). The association of parenting style and child age with parental limit setting and adolescent MySpace behavior. *Journal of Applied Developmental Psychology, 29*, 459–471.

Rosenshine, B. (1987). Explicit teaching and teacher training. *Journal of Teacher Education, 38*, 34–36.

Rosenthal, R. (2002). Covert communication in classrooms, clinics, courtrooms, and cubicles. *American Psychologist, 57*, 839–849.

Rosenthal, R. (2003). Covert communication in laboratories, classrooms, and the truly real world. *Current Directions in Psychological Science, 12*, 151–154.

Rosenthal, R., & Jacobson, L. (1966). Teachers' expectancies: Determinants of pupils' IQ gains. *Psychological Reports, 19*, 115–118.

Roseth, C. J., Johnson, D. W., & Johnson, R. T. (2008). Promoting early adolescents' achievement and peer relationships: The effects of cooperative, competitive, and individualistic goal structures. *Psychological Bulletin, 134*, 223–246.

Roskos, K. (2000). Through the bioecological lens: Some observations of literacy in play as a proximal process. In K. Roskos & J. Christie (Eds.), *Play and literacy in early childhood: Research from multiple perspectives* (pp. 125–137). Mahwah, NJ: Erlbaum.

Roskos, K., & Christie, J. (2001). Examining the play-literacy interface: A critical review and future directions. *Journal of Early Childhood Literacy, 1*, 59–89.

Ross, H., Ross, M., Stein, N., & Trabasso, T. (2006). How siblings resolve their conflicts: The importance of first offers, planning, and limited opposition. *Child Development, 77*, 1730–1745.

Rostosky, S. S., Wilcox, B. L., Wright, M. L., & Randall, B. A. (2004). The impact of religiosity on adolescent sexual behavior: A review of the evidence. *Journal of Adolescent Research, 19*.

Rotgans, J. I., & Schmidt, H. G. (2011). Situational interest and academic achievement in the active-learning classroom. *Learning and Instruction, 21*, 58–67.

Roth, P., BeVier, C., Switzer, F., & Schippmann, J. (1996). Meta-analyzing the relationship between grades and job performance. *Journal of Applied Psychology, 81*, 548–556.

Rothbart, M. (2011). *Becoming who we are: Temperament and personality in development.* New York: Guilford.

Rothbart, M. K. (2007). Temperament, development, and personality. *Current Directions in Psychological Science, 16*, 207–212.

Rothman, E. F., Kaczmarsky, C., Burke, N., Jansen, E., & Baughman, A. (2015). "Without porn … I wouldn't know half the things I know now": A qualitative study of pornography use among a sample of urban, low-income, Black and Hispanic youth. *Journal of Sex Research, 52*, 736–746.

Rouse, H. L., & Fantuzzo, J. W. (2009). Multiple risks and educational well being: A population-based investigation of threats to early school success. *Early Childhood Research Quarterly, 24*, 1–14.

Rowe, M. L. (2012). A longitudinal investigation of the role of quantity and quality of child-directed speech in vocabulary development. *Child Development, 83*, 1762–1774.

Rowe, M. L., & Goldin-Meadow, S. (2009). Differences in early gesture explain SES disparities in child vocabulary size at school entry. *Science, 323*, 951–953.

Rubenstein, J. L. (2011). Development of the cerebral cortex: Implications for neurodevelopmental disorders. *Journal of Child Psychology and Psychiatry, 52*, 339–355.

Rubie-Davies, C. M., Peterson, E. R., Sibley, C. G., & Rosenthal, R. (2015). A teacher expectation intervention: Modelling the practices of high expectation teachers. *Contemporary Educational Psychology, 40*, 72–85.

Rubie-Davies, C. M., Weinstein, R. S., Huang, F. L., Gregory, A., Cowan, P. A., & Cowan, C. P. (2014). Successive teacher expectation effects across the early school years. *Journal of Applied Developmental Psychology, 35*, 181–191.

Rubin, K. H., Bukowski, W., & Parker, J. G. (1998). Peer interactions, relationships, and groups. In N. Eisenberg (Ed.), *Handbook of child psychology: Social, emotional, and personality development* (5th ed., Vol. 3, pp. 619–700). New York: Wiley.

Rubin, K. H., Burgess, K., Dwyer, K., & Hastings, P. (2003). Predicting preschoolers' externalizing behaviors from toddler temperament, conflict, and maternal negativity. *Developmental Psychology, 39*, 164–176.

Rubio-Fernández, P., & Geurts, B. (2013). How to pass the false-belief task before your fourth birthday. *Psychological Science, 24*, 27–33.

Ruble, D. N., Martin, C. L., & Berenbaum, S. A. (2006). Gender development. In N. Eisenberg (Ed.), *Handbook of child psychology: Social, emotional, and personality development* (6th ed., Vol. 3, pp. 858–932). New York: Wiley.

Rudolph, K. D., Caldwell, M. S., & Conley, C. S. (2005). Need for approval and children's well-being. *Child Development, 76*, 309–323.

Rudolph, K. D., Lansford, J. E., Agoston, A. M., Sugimura, N., Schwartz, D., Dodge, K. A., . . . Bates, J. E. (2014). Peer victimization and social alienation: Predicting deviant peer affiliation in middle school. *Child Development, 85*, 124–139.

Rudy, D., & Grusec, J. (2006). Authoritarian parenting in individualist and collectivist groups: Associations with maternal emotion and cognition and children's self-esteem. *Journal of Family Psychology, 20*, 68–78.

Ruffman, T. (2014). To belief or not belief: Children's theory of mind. *Developmental Review, 34*, 265–293.

Ruowei, L., Zhao, Z., Mikdad, A., Barker, L., & Grummer-Strawn, L. (2003). Prevalence of breastfeeding in the United States: The 2001 National Immunization Survey. *Pediatrics, 111*, 1198–1200.

Russell, S., Toomey, R., Ryan, C., & Diaz, R. (2014). Being out at school: The implications for school victimization and young adult adjustment. *American Journal of Orthopsychiatry, 84*, 635–643.

Rutter, M. (1995). Clinical implications of attachment concepts: Retrospect and prospect. *Journal of Child Psychology & Psychiatry & Allied Disciplines, 36*, 549–571.

Rutter, M. (2000). Resilience reconsidered: Conceptual considerations, empirical findings, and policy implications. In J. P. Shonkoff & S. Meisels (Eds.), *Handbook of early childhood intervention* (2nd ed., pp. 651–682). New York: Cambridge University Press.

Ryan, A. M. (2001). The peer group as a context for the development of young adolescent motivation and achievement. *Child Development, 72*, 1135–1150.

Ryan, R. M. (2012). Marital birth and early child outcomes: The moderating influence of marriage propensity. *Child Development, 83*, 1085–1101.

Ryan, R. M., Claessens, A., & Markowitz, A. J. (2015). Associations between family structure change and child behavior problems: The moderating effect of family income. *Child Development, 86*, 112–127.

Ryan, R. M., & Deci, E. L. (1996). Intrinsic motivation and extrinsic rewards: A commentary on Cameron and Pierce's meta-analysis. *Review of Educational Research, 66*, 33–38.

Rydell, A. M., Berlin, L., & Bohlin, G. (2003). Emotionality, emotion regulation, and adaptation among 5- to 8-year-old children. *Emotion, 3*, 30–47.

Ryder, A., Alden, L. E., & Paulhus, D. (2000). Is acculturation unidimensional or bidimensional? A head-to-head comparison in the prediction of personality, self-identity, and adjustment. *Journal of Personality and Social Psychology, 79*, 49–65.

Saarento, S., & Salmivalli, C. (2015). The role of classroom peer ecology and bystanders' responses in bullying. *Child Development Perspectives, 9*, 201–205.

Saarni, C. (1997). Coping with aversive feelings. *Motivation and Emotion, 21*, 45–63.

Saarni, C. (1999). *The development of emotional competence.* New York: Guilford.

Sabol, T. J., & Pianta, R. C. (2012). Patterns of school readiness forecast achievement and socioemotional development at the end of elementary school. *Child Development, 83*, 282–299.

Sackett, P. R., & Walmsley, P. T. (2014). Which personality attributes are most important in the workplace? *Perspectives on Psychological Science, 9*, 538–551.

Sadeh, A., Gruber, R., & Raviv, A. (2003). The effects of sleep restriction and extension on school-age children: What a difference an hour makes. *Child Development, 74*, 444–455.

Sahlberg, P. (2011). *Finnish lessons: What can the world learn from educational change in Finland?* New York: Teachers College.

Salmivalli, C., Ojanen, T., Haanpaa, J., & Peets, K. (2005). "I'm OK but you're not" and other peer-relational schemas: Explaining individual differences in children's social goals. *Developmental Psychology, 41*, 363–375.

Salomon, G. (Ed.). (1993). *Distributed cognitions: Psychological and educational considerations.* Cambridge, UK: Cambridge University Press.

Salvatore, J., & Shelton, J. N. (2007). Cognitive costs of exposure to racial prejudice. *Psychological Science, 18*, 810–815.

Sameroff, A. J., Seifer, R., Baldwin, A., & Baldwin, C. (1993). Stability of intelligence from preschool to adolescence: The influence of social and family risk factors. *Child Development, 64*, 80–97.

SAMHSA. (2008). *The NSDUH Report: Underage Alcohol Use.* Rockville, MD: Office of Applied Studies.

Sanders, A., Martin, E., Beecham, G., Guo, S., Dawood, K., Rieger, G., et al. (2015). Genome-wide scan demonstrates significant linkage for male sexual orientation. *Psychological Medicine, 45*, 1379–1388.

Sanson, A., Hemphill, S., & Smart, D. (2004). Connections between temperament and social development: A review. *Social Development, 13*, 142–170.

Santangelo, T., & Graham, S. (2015). A comprehensive meta-analysis of handwriting instruction. *Educational Psychology Review, 1*–41.

Santos, A., Vaughn, B., Peceguina, I., Daniel, J., & Shin, N. (2014). Growth of social competence during the preschool yeaers: A 3-year longitudinal study. *Child Development, 85*, 2062–2073.

Sarver, D., Rapport, M., Kofler, M., Rasiker, J., & Friedman, L. (2015). Hyperactivity in attention-deficit/hyperactivity disorder (ADHD): Impairing deficit or compensatory behavior? *Journal of Abnormal Child Psychology, 43*, 1219–1232.

Saudino, K. J. (2012). Sources of continuity and change in activity level in early childhood. *Child Development, 83*, 266–281.

Saudino, K. J., & Micalizzi, L. (2015). Emerging trends in behavioral genetic studies of child temperament. *Child Development Perspectives, 9*, 144–148.

Saudino, K. J., & Zapfe, J. A. (2008). Genetic influences on activity level in early childhood: Do situations matter? *Child Development, 79*, 930–943.

Saylor, K. E., & Amann, B. (2016). Impulsive aggression as a comorbidity of attention-deficit/hyperactivity disorder in children and adolescents. *Journal of Child and Adolescent Psychopharmacology, 26*, 19–25.

Schab, F. (1991). Schooling without learning: Thirty years of cheating in high school. *Adolescence, 26*, 839–847.

Schaefer, D. R., Simpkins, S. D., Vest, A. E., & Price, C. D. (2011). The contribution of extracurricular activities to adolescent friendships: New insights through social network analysis. *Developmental Psychology, 47*, 1141–1152.

Schellenberg, E. G. (2005). Music and cognitive abilities. *Current Directions in Psychological Science, 14*, 317–325.

Scher, A., & Mayseless, O. (2000). Mothers of anxious/ambivalent infants: Maternal characteristics and child-care context. *Child Development, 71*, 1629–1639.

Schermerhorn, A., Bates, J., Goodnight, J., Lansford, J., Dodge, K., & Pettit, G. (2013). Temperament moderates associations between exposure to stress and children's externalizing problems. *Child Development, 84*, 1579–1593.

Schermerhorn, A. C., Chow, S.-M., & Cummings, E. M. (2010). Developmental family processes and interparental conflict: Patterns of microlevel influences. *Developmental Psychology, 46*, 869–885.

Schick, B., de Villers, P., de Villers, J., & Hoffmeister, R. (2007). Language and theory of mind: A study of deaf children. *Child Development, 78*, 376–396.

Schlaefli, A., Rest, J., & Thomas, S. (1985). Does moral education improve moral judgment? A meta-analysis of intervention studies using the Defining Issues Test. *Review of Educational Research, 55*, 319–352.

Schlam, T. R., Wilson, N. L., Shoda, Y., Mischel, W., & Ayduk, O. (2013). Preschoolers' delay of gratification predicts their body mass 30 years later. *Journal of Pediatrics, 162*, 90–93.

Schleppegrell, M. J. (2002). Challenges of the science register for ESL students: Errors and meaning-making. In M. J. Schleppegrell & M. C. Colombi (Eds.), *Developing advanced literacy in first and second languages* (pp. 119–142). Mahwah, NJ: Erlbaum.

Schliemann, A., & Carraher, D. (2002). The evolution of mathematical reasoning: Everyday versus idealized understandings. *Developmental Review, 22*, 242–266.

Schmeichel, B. J., & Tang, D. (2015). Individual differences in executive functioning and their relationship to emotional processes and responses. *Current Directions in Psychological Science, 24*, 93–98.

Schmidt, L., & Fox, N. (2002). Individual differences in childhood shyness: Origins, malleability, and developmental course. In D. Cervone & W. Mischel (Eds.), *Advances in personality science* (pp. 83–105). New York: Guilford Press.

Schmidt, M. E., & Anderson, D. R. (2007). The impact of television on cognitive development and educational achievement. In N. Pecora, J. P. Murray, & E. Wartella (Eds.), *Children and television: Fifty years of research* (pp. 65–84). Mahwah, NJ: Erlbaum.

Schmitt, M. T., Branscombe, N. R., Postmes, T., & Garcia, A. (2014). The consequences of perceived discrimination for psychological well-being: A meta-analytic review. *Psychological Bulletin, 140*, 921–948.

Schmitz, S., Fulker, D., Plomin, R., Zahn-Waxler, C., Emde, R., & DeFries, J. (1999). Temperament and problem behavior during early childhood. *International Journal of Behavioral Development, 23*, 333–355.

Schnall, S., Roper, J., & Fessler, D. M. T. (2010). Elevation leads to altruistic behavior. *Psychological Science, 21*, 315–320.

Schneider, B., Atkinson, L., & Tardif, C. (2001). Child–parent attachment and children's peer relations: A quantitative review. *Developmental Psychology, 37*, 86–100.

Schneider, M., & Moore, C. (2000). Effect of prenatal stress on development: A nonhuman primate model. In C. Nelson (Ed.), *The effects of early adversity on neurobehavioral development* (pp. 201–244). Mahwah, NJ: Erlbaum.

Schneider, M., Grabner, R. H., & Paetsch, J. (2009). Mental number line, number line estimation, and mathematical achievement: Their interrelations in grades 5 and 6. *Journal of Educational Psychology, 101*, 359–372.

Schneider, M., & Hardy, I. (2013). Profiles of inconsistent knowledge in children's pathways of conceptual change. *Developmental Psychology, 49*, 1639–1649.

Schneider, W. (2000). Research on memory development: Historical trends and current themes. *International Journal of Behavioral Development, 24,* 407–420.

Schneider, W., Gruber, H., Gold, A., & Opwis, K. (1993). Chess expertise and memory for chess positions in children and adults. *Journal of Experimental Child Psychology, 56,* 328–349.

Schneider, W., & Ornstein, P. A. (2015). The development of children's memory. *Child Development Perspectives, 9,* 190–195.

Schneidman, L. A., Arroyo, M. E., Levine, S. C., & Goldin-Meadow, S. (2013). What counts as effective input for word learning? *Journal of Child Language, 40,* 672–686.

Schonfeld, D. (2000). Teaching young children about HIV and AIDS. *Children Affected by HIV/AIDS, 9,* 375–387.

Schore, A. (2000). Attachment and the regulation of the right brain. *Attachment and Human Development, 2,* 23–47.

Schraw, G., Olafson, L., Kuch, F., Lehman, T., Lehman, S., & McCrudden, M. T. (2007). Interest and academic cheating. In E. M. Anderman & T. B. Murdock (Eds.), *Psychology of academic cheating* (pp. 59–85). New York: Academic Press.

Schulting, A. B., Malone, P. S., & Dodge, K. (2005). The effect of school-based kindergarten transition policies and practices on child academic outcomes. *Developmental Psychology, 41,* 860–871.

Schuna, J. M., Jr., Lauersdorf, R. L., Behrens, T. K., Liguori, G., & Liebert, M. L. (2013). An objective assessment of children's physical activity during the Keep It Moving! after-school program. *Journal of School Health, 83,* 105–111.

Schwartz, D., Lansford, J. E., Dodge, K. A., Pettit, G. S., & Bates, J. E. (2015). Peer victimization during middle childhood as a lead indicator of internalizing problems and diagnostic outcomes in late adolescence. *Journal of Clinical Child & Adolescent Psychology, 44,* 393–404.

Schwartz-Mette, R., & Rose, A. (2012). Co-rumination mediates contagion of internalizing symptoms within youth's friendships. *Developmental Psycholoy, 48,* 1355–1365.

Schwebel, D., & Plummert, J. (1999). Longitudinal and concurrent relations among temperament, ability estimation, and injury proneness. *Child Development, 70,* 700–712.

Schwenck, C., Bjorklund, D. F., & Schneider, W. (2007). Factors influencing the incidence of utilization deficiencies and other patterns of recall/strategy-use relations in a strategic memory task. *Child Development, 78,* 1771–1787.

Sciutto, M. J., Terjesen, M. D., & Frank, A. S. B. (2000). Teachers' knowledge and misperceptions of attention-deficit/hyperactivity disorder. *Psychology in the Schools, 37,* 115–122.

Seaton, E. K., Caldwell, C. H., Sellers, R. M., & Jackson, J. S. (2008). The prevalence of perceived discrimination among African American and Caribbean Black youth. *Developmental Psychology, 44,* 1288–1297.

Seaton, M., Marsh, H. W., & Craven, R. G. (2009). Earning its place as a pan-human theory: Universality of the big-fish-little-pond effect across 41 culturally and economically diverse countries. *Journal of Educational Psychology, 101,* 403–419.

Seery, M. D. (2011). Resilience: A silver lining to experiencing adverse life events? *Current Directions in Psychological Science, 20,* 390–394.

Seiffge-Krenke, I., Aunola, K., & Nurmi, J.-E. (2009). Changes in stress perception and coping during adolescence: The role of situational and personal factors. *Child Development, 80,* 259–279.

Seitsinger, A. M., Felner, R. D., Brand, S., & Burns, A. (2008). A large-scale examination of the nature and efficacy of teachers' practices to engage parents: Assessment, parental contact, and student-level impact. *Journal of School Psychology, 46,* 477–505.

Semrud-Clikeman, M., & Glass, K. (2010). The relation of humor and child development: Social, adaptive, and emotional aspects. *Journal of Child Neurology, 25,* 1248–1260.

Sénéchal, M., & Young, L. (2008). The effect of family literacy intervention on children's acquisition of reading from kindergarten to Grade 3: A meta-analytic review. *Review of Educational Research, 78,* 880–907.

Senko, C., Hulleman, C. S., & Harackiewicz, J. M. (2011). Achievement goal theory at the crossroads: Old controversies, current challenges, and new directions. *Educational Psychologist, 46,* 26–47.

Serbin, L. A., & Karp, J. (2003). Intergenerational studies of parenting and the transfer of risk from parent to child. *Current Directions in Psychological Science, 12,* 138–142.

Sexton, C., Gelhorn, H., Bell, J., & Classi, P. (2012). The co-occurence of reading disorder and ADHD: Epidemiology, treatment, psychosocial impact, and economic burden. *Journal of Learning Disabilities, 45,* 538–564.

Shalvi, S., Gino, F., Barkan, R., & Ayal, S. (2015). Self-serving justifications: Doing wrong and feeling moral. *Current Directions in Psychological Science, 24,* 125–130.

Shamosh, N. A., DeYoung, C. G., Green, A. E., Reis, D. L., Johnson, M. R., Conway, A., et al. (2008). Individual differences in delay discounting: Relation to intelligence, working memory, and anterior prefrontal cortex. *Psychological Science, 19,* 904–911.

Shantz, C. (1987). Conflicts between children. *Child Development, 58,* 283–305.

Shariff, A., & Tracy, J. L. (2011). What are emotion expressions for? *Current Directions in Psychological Science, 20,* 395–399.

Shatz, M., Diesendruck, G., Martinez-Beck, I., & Akar, D. (2003). The influence of language and socioeconomic status on children's understanding of false belief. *Developmental Psychology, 39,* 717–729.

Shaw, D., Gilliom, M., Ingoldsby, E., & Nagin, D. (2003). Trajectories leading to school-age conduct problems. *Developmental Psychology, 39,* 189–200.

Shaywitz, S. E., Mody, M., & Shaywitz, B. A. (2006). Neural mechanisms in dyslexia. *Current Directions in Psychological Science, 15,* 278–281.

Shaywitz, S. E., Morris, R., & Shaywitz, B. A. (2008). The education of dyslexic children from childhood to adulthood. *Annual Review of Psychology, 59,* 451–475.

Shaywitz, S. E., & Shaywitz, B. A. (2005). Dyslexia (specific reading disability). *Biological Psychiatry, 57,* 1301–1309.

Shechtman, Z., & Yaman, M. A. (2012). SEL as a component of a literature class to improve relationships, behavior, motivation and content knowledge. *American Educational Research Journal, 49,* 546–567.

Shepard, L. (1997). Children not ready to learn? The invalidity of school readiness testing. *Psychology in the Schools, 34,* 85–97.

Shi, R. (2014). Functional morphemes and early language acquisition. *Child Development Perspectives, 8,* 6–11.

Shim, S. S., Ryan, A. M., & Anderson, C. J. (2008). Achievement goals and achievement during early adolescence: Examining time-varying predictor and outcome variables in growth-curve analysis. *Journal of Educational Psychology, 100,* 655–671.

Shiner, R., Buss, K., McClowry, S., Putnam, S., Saudino, K., & Zentner, M. (2012). What is temperament *now*? Assessing progress in temperament research on the twenty-fifth anniversary of Goldsmith et al. (1987). *Child Development Perspectives, 6,* 436–444.

Shipstead, Z., Hicks, K. L., & Engle, R. W. (2012). Cogmed working memory training: Does the evidence support the claims? *Journal of Applied Research in Memory and Cognition, 1,* 185–193.

Shirtcliff, E. A., Dahl, R. E., & Pollak, S. D. (2009). Pubertal development: Correspondence between hormonal and physical development. *Child Development, 80,* 327–337.

Shneidman, L., & Woodward, A. L. (2016). Are child-directed interactions the cradle of social learning? *Psychological Bulletin, 142,* 1–17.

Shonk, S. M., & Cicchetti, D. (2001). Maltreatment, competency deficits, and risk for academic and behavioral maladjustment. *Developmental Psychology, 37,* 3–17.

Shonkoff, J. P., Garner, A. S., Siegel, B. S., Dobbins, M. I., Earls, M. F., Garner, A. S., . . . Wood, D. L. (2012). The lifelong effects of early childhood adversity and toxic stress. *Pediatrics, 129,* e232–e246.

Short, E. J., Basili, L. A., & Schatschneider, C. W. (1993). Analysis of humor skills among elementary school students: Comparisons of children with and without intellectual handicaps. *American Journal on Mental Retardation, 98,* 63–73.

Short, M., Gradisar, M., Lack, L., & Wright, H. (2013). The impact of sleep on adolescent depressed mood, alertness, and academic performance. *Journal of Adolescence, 36,* 1025–1033.

Shulman, E. P., & Cauffman, E. (2014). Deciding in the dark: Age differences in intuitive risk judgment. *Developmental Psychology, 50,* 167–177.

Shultz, S., & Vouloumanos, A. (2010). Three-month-olds prefer speech to other naturally occurring signals. *Language Learning and Development, 6,* 241–257.

Shure, M. (2001). How to think, not what to think: A problem-solving approach to prevention of early high-risk behaviors. In A. Bohart & D. Stipek (Eds.), *Constructive and destructive behavior: Implications for family, school, and society* (pp. 271–290). Washington, DC: APA.

Sidebotham, P., Heron, J., & The ALSPAC Study Team. (2003). Child maltreatment in the "children of the nineties": The role of the child. *Child Abuse & Neglect, 27*, 337–352.

Siegler, R. S. (1995). How does change occur: A microgenetic study of number conservation. *Cognitive Psychology, 28*, 225–273.

Siegler, R. S. (2000). The rebirth of children's learning. *Child Development, 71*, 26–35.

Siegler, R. S., & Booth, J. (2004). Development of numerical estimation in young children. *Child Development, 75*, 428–444.

Siegler, R. S., Duncan, G. J., Davis-Kean, P. E., Duckworth, K., Claessens, A., Engel, M., . . . Chen, M. (2012). Early predictors of high school mathematics achievement. *Psychological Science, 23*, 691–697.

Siegler, R. S., & Lortie-Forgues, H. (2014). An integrative theory of numerical development. *Child Development Perspectives, 8*, 144–150.

Siegler, R. S., & Mu, Y. (2008). Chinese children excel on novel mathematics problems even before elementary school. *Psychological Science, 19*, 759–763.

Sierksma, J., Thijs, J., Verkuyten, M., & Komter, A. (2014). Children's reasoning about the refusal to help: The role of need, costs, and social perspective taking. *Child Development, 85*, 1134–1149.

Sigman, M., Cohen, S., & Beckwith, L. (1997). Why does infant attention predict adolescent intelligence? *Infant Behavior and Development, 20*, 133–140.

Silver, E. A., Mesa, V. M., Morris, K. A., Star, J. R., & Benken, B. M. (2009). Teaching mathematics for understanding: An analysis of lessons submitted by teachers seeking NBPTS certification. *American Educational Research Journal, 46*, 501–531.

Silvia, P. J. (2008). Interest—The curious emotion. *Current Directions in Psychological Science, 17*, 57–60.

Simon, V. A., Aikins, J. W., & Prinstein, M. J. (2008). Romantic partner selection and socialization during early adolescence. *Child Development, 79*, 1676–1692.

Simpkins, S., & Parke, R. (2001). The relations between parental friendships and children's friendships: Self-report and observational analysis. *Child Development, 72*, 569–582.

Simpkins, S. D., Eccles, J. S., & Becnel, J. N. (2008). The mediational role of adolescents' friends in relations between activity breadth and adjustment. *Developmental Psychology, 44*, 1081–1094.

Simpson, J. A., Collins, W. A., & Salvatore, J. E. (2011). The impact of early interpersonal experience on adult romantic relationship functioning. *Current Directions in Psychological Science, 20*, 355–359.

Simpson, J. A., Griskevicius, V., Kuo, S. I.-C., Sung, S., & Collins, A. (2012). Evolution, stress, and sensitive periods: The influence of unpredictability in early versus late childhood on sex and risky behavior. *Developmental Psychology, 48*, 674–686.

Simpson, R. (2004). Finding effective intervention and personnel preparation practices for students with autism spectrum disorders. *Exceptional Children, 70*, 135–144.

Singer, D. (1999). Imaginative play and television: Factors in a child's development. In J. Singer & P. Salovey (Eds.), *At play in the fields of consciousness: Essays in honor of Jerome L. Singer* (pp. 303–326). Mahwah, NJ: Lawrence Erlbaum.

Singer, J., & Lythcott, M. (2002). Fostering school achievement and creativity through sociodramatic play in the classroom. *Research in the Schools, 9*, 43–52.

Singer, M. (1999). The role of concern for others and moral intensity in adolescents' ethicality judgments. *Journal of Genetic Psychology, 160*, 155–166.

Singh, H., & O'Boyle, M. (2004). Interhemispheric interaction during global-local processing in mathematically gifted adolescents, average-ability youth, and college students. *Neuropsychology, 18*, 371–377.

Sinopoli, K. J., Schachar, R., & Dennis, M. (2011). Reward improves cancellation and restraint inhibition across childhood and adolescence. *Developmental Psychology, 47*, 1479–1489.

Sirin, S. R. (2005). Socioeconomic status and academic achievement: A meta-analytic review of research. *Review of Educational Research, 75*, 417–453.

Sirin, S. R., Rogers-Sirin, L., Cressen, J., Gupta, T., Ahmed, S. F., & Novoa, A. D. (2015). Discrimination-related stress effects on the development of internalizing symptoms among Latino adolescents. *Child Development, 86*, 709–725.

Skinner, B. F. (1948). *Walden two*. New York: Macmillan.

Skinner, B. F. (1957). *Verbal behavior*. New York: Appleton-Century-Crofts.

Skinner, B. F. (1971). *Beyond freedom and dignity*. New York: Bantam.

Skinner, B. F. (1972). *Cumulative record: A selection of papers* (3rd ed.). New York: Appleton-Century-Crofts.

Skinner, E. A., Furrer, C., Marchand, G., & Kindermann, T. A. (2008). Engagement and disaffection in the classroom: Part of a larger motivational dynamic? *Journal of Educational Psychology, 100*, 765–781.

Slama, R. B. (2012). A longitudinal analysis of academic English proficiency outcomes for adolescent English language learners in the United States. *Journal of Educational Psychology, 104*, 265–285.

Slater, M. D., Johnson, B. K., Cohen, J., Comello, M. L. G., & Ewoldsen, D. R. (2014). Temporarily expanding the boundaries of the self: Motivations for entering the story world and implications for narrative effects. *Journal of Communication, 64*, 439–455.

Slaughter, V., Imuta, K., Peterson, C. C., & Henry, J. D. (2015). Meta-analysis of theory of mind and peer popularity in the preschool and early school years. *Child Development, 86*, 1159–1174.

Slaughter, V., Peterson, C. C., & Mackintosh, E. (2007). Mind what mother says: Narrative input and theory of mind in typical children and those on the autism spectrum. *Child Development, 78*, 839–858.

Slavin, R. E., Cheung A., Groff, C., & Lake, C. (2008). Effective reading programs for middle and high schools: A best-evidence synthesis. *Reading Research Quarterly, 43*, 290–322.

Slavin, R. E., & Cooper, R. (1999). Improving intergroup relations: Lessons learned from cooperative learning programs. *Journal of Social Issues, 55*, 647–663.

Slavin, R. E., & Lake, C. (2008). Effective programs in elementary mathematics: A best-evidence synthesis. *Review of Educational Research, 78*, 427–515.

Sletta, O., Sobstad, F., & Valas, H. (1995). Humour, peer acceptance and perceived social competence in preschool and school-aged children. *British Journal of Educational Psychology, 65*, 179–195.

Sloane, S., Baillargeon, R., & Premack, D. (2012). Do infants have a sense of fairness? *Psychological Science, 23*, 196–204.

Smetana, J. G., Jambon, M., Conry-Murray, C., & Sturge-Apple, M. L. (2012). Reciprocal associations between young children's developing moral judgments and theory of mind. *Developmental Psychology, 48*, 1144–1155.

Smith, A., & Lalonde, R. N. (2003). "Racelessness" in a Canadian context? Exploring the link between black students' identity, achievement, and mental health. *Journal of Black Psychology, 29*, 142–164.

Smith, B. (2012). The case against spanking. *Monitor on Psychology, 43*(4), 60.

Smith, C., & Denton, M. L. (2005). *Soul searching: The religious and spiritual lives of American teenagers*. New York: Oxford University Press.

Smith, E. B. (1995). Anchored in our literature: Students responding to African American literature. *Language Arts, 72*, 571–574.

Smith, H., Sheikh, H., Dyson, M., Olino, T., Laptook, R., Durbin, C. E., . . . Klein, D. (2012). Parenitng and child DRD4 genotype interact to predict children's early emerging effortful control. *Child Development, 83*, 1932–1944.

Smith, J., & Ross, H. (2007). Training parents to mediate sibling disputes affects children's negotiation and conflict understanding. *Child Development, 78*, 790–805.

Smith, M. S. (2000). Balancing old and new: An experienced middle school teacher's learning in the context of mathematics instructional reform. *Elementary School Journal, 100*, 351–375.

Smith, P., & Myron-Wilson, R. (1998). Parenting and school bullying. *Clinical Child Psychology and Psychiatry, 3*, 1359–1045.

Smith, R. E., Bayen, U. J., & Martin, C. (2010). The cognitive processes underlying event-based prospective memory in school-age children and young adults: A formal model-based study. *Developmental Psychology, 46*, 230–244.

Smith, R. L., & Rose, A. J. (2011). The "cost of caring" in youths' friendships: Considering associations among social perspective taking, co-rumination, and empathetic distress. *Developmental Psychology, 47,* 1792–1803.

Smith, S., Daunic, A., Miller, D., & Robinson, R. (2002). Conflict resolution and peer mediation in middle schools: Extending the process and outcome knowledge base. *Journal of Social Psychology, 142,* 567–586.

Smith, T., & Iadarola, S. (2015). Evidence base update for autism spectrum disorder. *Journal of Clinical Child & Adolescent Psychology, 44,* 897–922.

Smolak, L., & Thompson, J. K. (Eds.). (2009). *Body image, eating disorders, and obesity in youth: Assessment, prevention, and treatment* (2nd ed.). Washington, DC: American Psychological Association.

Smolensky, E., & Gootman, J. (Eds.). (2003). *Working families and growing kids: Caring for children and adolescents.* Washington, DC: National Academies Press.

Smyke, A. (1997). Theories of spoiling and fear of spoiling: Historical and contemporary perspectives. *The Signal, 5,* 1–9.

Snedeker, J., Geren, J., & Shafto, C. L. (2007). Starting over: International adoption as a natural experiment in language development. *Psychological Science, 18,* 79–87.

Snell, E. K., Adam, E. K., & Duncan, G. (2007). Sleep and the body mass index and overweight status of children and adolescents. *Child Development, 78,* 309–323.

Snowling, M. J., Gallagher, A., & Frith, U. (2003). Family risk of dyslexia is continuous: Individual differences in the precursors of reading skill. *Child Development, 74,* 358–373.

Snowling, M. J., & Melby-Lervåg, M. (2016). Oral language deficits in familial dyslexia: A meta-analysis and review. *Psychological Bulletin, 142,* 498–545.

Snyder, H. N. (2000). *Sexual assault of young children as reported to law enforcement: Victim, incident, and offender characteristics.* Washington, DC: Department of Justice.

Snyder, J., Cramer, A., Afrank, J., & Patterson, G. (2005). The contributions of ineffective discipline and parental hostile attributions of child misbehavior to the development of conduct problems at home and school. *Developmental Psychology, 41,* 30–41.

Snyder, J., Schrepferman, L., McEachern, A., Barner, S., Johnson, K., & Provines, J. (2008). Peer deviancy training and peer coercion: Dual processes associated with early-onset conduct problems. *Child Development, 79,* 252–268.

Socha, T. J., & Kelly, B. (1994). Children making "fun": Humorous communication, impression management, and moral development. *Child Study Journal, 24,* 237–252.

Social and Character Development Research Consortium. (2010). *Efficacy of schoolwide programs to promote social and character development and reduce problem behavior in elementary school children (NCER 2011–2001).* Washington, DC: Department of Education, National Center for Education Research.

Soenens, B., Vansteenkiste, M., & Van Petegem, S. (2015). Let us not throw out the baby with the bathwater: Applying the principle of universalism without uniformity to autonomy—supportive and controlling parenting. *Child Development Perspectives, 9,* 44–49.

Soliday, E. (2007). Infant feeding and cognition: Integrating a developmental perspective. *Child Development Perspectives, 1,* 19–25.

Solomon, D., Battistich, V., Watson, M., Schaps, E., & Lewis, C. (2000). A six-district study of educational change: Direct and mediated effects of the Child Development Project. *Social Psychology of Education, 41,* 3–51.

Somerville, L. H., Jones, R. M., Ruberry, E. J., Dyke, J. P., Glover, G., & Casey, B. J. (2013). The medial prefrontal cortex and the emergence of self-conscious emotion in adolescence. *Psychological Science, 24,* 1544–1562.

Sophian, C., & Madrid, S. (2003). Young children's reasoning about many-to-one correspondences. *Child Development, 74,* 1418–1432.

Sorce, J. F., Emde, R. M., Campos, J. J., & Klinnert, M. D. (1985). Maternal emotional signaling: Its effect on the visual cliff behavior of 1-year-olds. *Developmental Psychology, 21,* 195–200.

Sörqvist, P., & Marsh, J. E. (2015). How concentration shields against distraction. *Current Directions in Psychological Science, 24,* 267–272.

Sosinsky, L. S., & Kim, S.-K. (2013). A profile approach to child care quality, quantity, and type of setting: Parent selection of infant child care arrangements. *Applied Developmental Science, 17,* 39–56.

Soto, C. J., & Tackett, J. L. (2015). Personality traits in childhood and adolescence: Structure, development, and outcomes. *Current Directions in Psychological Science, 24,* 358–362.

Sourander, A., Jensen, P., Davies, M., Niemela, S., Elonheimo, H., Ristkari, T., et al. (2007). Who is at greatest risk of adverse long-term outcomes? The Finnish From a Boy to a Man Study. *Journal of the American Academy of Child and Adolescent Psychiatry, 46,* 1148–1161.

Sowislo, J. F., & Orth, U. (2013). Does low self-esteem predict depression and anxiety? A meta-analysis of longitudinal studies. *Psychological Bulletin, 139,* 213–240.

Sparks, R. L., Patton, J., Ganschow, L., Humbach, N., & Javorsky, J. (2008). Early first-language reading and spelling skills predict later second-language reading and spelling skills. *Journal of Educational Psychology, 100,* 162–174.

Sparks, R. L., Patton, J., & Murdoch, A. (2014). Early reading success and its relationship to reading achievement and reading volume: Replication of "10 years later." *Reading and Writing, 27,* 189–211.

Specht, J., Egloff, B., & Schmukle, S. C. (2011). Stability and change of personality across the life course: The impact of age and major life events on mean-level and rank-order stability of the Big Five. *Journal of Personality and Social Psychology, 101,* 862–882.

Spencer, J. P., Blumberg, M. S., McMurray, B., Robinson, S. R., Samuelson, L. K., & Tomblin, J. B. (2009). Short arms and talking eggs: Why we should no longer abide the nativist-empiricist debate. *Child Development Perspectives, 3,* 79–87.

Spencer, S. J., Logel, C., & Davies, P. G. (2016). Stereotype threat. *Annual Review of Psychology, 67,* 415–437.

Spengler, M., Brunner, M., Damian, R. I., Lüdtke, O., Martin, R., & Roberts, B. W. (2015). Student characteristics and behaviors at age 12 predict occupational success 40 years later over and above childhood IQ and parental socioeconomic status. *Developmental Psychology, 51,* 1329–1340.

Spera, C. (2005). A review of the relationship among parenting practices, parenting styles, and adolescent school achievement. *Educational Psychology Review, 17,* 125–146.

Spichtig, A. N., Hiebert, E. H., Vorstius, C., Pascoe, J. P., David Pearson, P., & Radach, R. (2016). The decline of comprehension-based silent reading efficiency in the United States: A comparison of current data with performance in 1960. *Reading Research Quarterly, 51,* 239–259.

Spilt, J., Hughes, J., Wu, J.-Y., & Kwok, O.-M. (2012). Dynamics of teacher–student relationships: Stability and change across elementary school and the influence on children's academic success. *Child Development, 83,* 1180–1195.

Spilt, J. L., & Hughes, J. N. (2015). African American children at risk of increasingly conflicted teacher–student relationships in elementary school. *School Psychology Review, 44,* 306–314.

Spilt, J. L., van Lier, P. A. C., Leflot, G., Onghena, P., & Colpin, H. (2014). Children's social self-concept and internalizing problems: The influence of peers and teachers. *Child Development, 85,* 1248–1256.

Spira, E. G., Bracken, S. S., & Fischel, J. E. (2005). Predicting improvement after first-grade reading difficulties: The effects of oral language, emergent literacy, and behavior skills. *Developmental Psychology, 41,* 225–234.

Spitz, R. (1945). Hospitalism. *Psychoanalytic Study of the Child, 1,* 53–74.

Spivak, A. L., White, S. S., Juvonen, J., & Graham, S. (2015). Correlates of prosocial behaviors of students in ethnically and racially diverse middle schools. *Merrill-Palmer Quarterly, 61,* 236–263.

Spörer, N., Brunstein, J. C., & Kieschke, U. (2009). Improving students' reading comprehension skills: Effects of strategy instruction and reciprocal teaching. *Learning and Instruction, 19,* 272–286.

Spotts, E. L., Neiderhiser, J. M., Hetherington, E. M., & Reiss, D. (2001). The relation between observational measures of social problem solving and familial antisocial behavior: Genetic and environmental influences. *Journal of Research on Adolescence, 11,* 351–374.

Sroufe, L. A. (1996). *Emotional development: The organization of emotional life in the early years.* Cambridge, UK: Cambridge University Press.

Sroufe, L. A., Bennett, C., Englund, M., Urban, J., & Shulman, S. (1993). The significance of gender boundaries in preadolescence: Contemporary correlates and antecedents of boundary violation and maintenance. *Child Development, 64*, 455–466.

Sroufe, L. A., Fox, N., & Pancake, V. (1983). Attachment and dependency in developmental perspective. *Child Development, 54*, 1615–1627.

Staiano, A., & Calvert, S. (2011). Exergames for physical education courses: Physical, social and cognitive benefits. *Child Development Perspectives, 5*, 93–98.

Stamoulis, C., Vanderwert, R. E., Zeanah, C. H., Fox, N. A., & Nelson, C. A. (2015). Early psychosocial neglect adversely impacts developmental trajectories of brain oscillations and their interactions. *Journal of Cognitive Neuroscience, 27*, 2512–2528.

Stams, G.-J., Juffer, F., & van IJzendoorn, M. (2002). Maternal sensitivity, infant attachment, and temperament in early childhood predict adjustment in middle childhood: The case of adopted children and their biologically unrelated parents. *Developmental Psychology, 38*, 806–821.

Stanovich, K. E. (1992). *How to think straight about psychology* (3rd ed.). New York: HarperCollins.

Starkes, J. L., Deakin, J. M., Allard, F., Hodges, N. J., & Hayes, A. (1996). Deliberate practice in sports: What is it anyway? In K. A. Ericsson (Ed.), *The road to excellence: The acquisition of expert performance in the arts and sciences, sports, and games* (pp. 81–106). Mahwah, NJ: Erlbaum.

Starr, A., Libertus, M., & Brannon, E. (2013). Number sense in infancy predicts mathematical abilities in childhood. *Proceedings of the National Academy of Sciences, 110*, 18116–18120.

Stattin, H., & Kerr, M. (2000). Parental monitoring: A reinterpretation. *Child Development, 71*, 1072–1085.

Stearns, E. (2004). Interracial friendliness and the social organization of schools. *Youth & Society, 35*, 395–419.

Stearns, E., Moller, S., Blau, J., & Potochnick, S. (2007). Staying back and dropping out: The relationship between grade retention and school drop out. *Sociology of Education, 80*, 210–240.

Stedman, L. (1997). International achievement differences: An assessment of a new perspective. *Educational Researcher, 26(3)*, 4–15.

Steelandt, S., Thierry, B., Broihanne, M.-H., & Dufour, V. (2012). The ability of children to delay gratification in an exchange task. *Cognition, 122*, 416–425.

Steele, C. M. (1992, April). Race and the schooling of black Americans. *Atlantic Monthly*, 68–78.

Steele, C. M., & Aronson, J. (1995). Stereotype threat and the intellectual test performance of African Americans. *Journal of Personality and Social Psychology, 69*, 797–811.

Stein, G. L., Supple, A. J., Huq, N., Dunbar, A. S., & Prinstein, M. J. (2016). A longitudinal examination of perceived discrimination and depressive symptoms in ethnic minority youth: The roles of attributional style, positive ethnic/racial affect, and emotional reactivity. *Developmental Psychology, 52*, 259–271.

Steinberg, L., & Monahan, K. C. (2010). Adolescents' exposure to sexy media does not hasten the initiation of sexual intercourse. *Developmental Psychology, 47*, 562–576.

Steinberg, L., & Silk, J. S. (2002). Parenting adolescents. In M. H. Bornstein (Ed.), *Handbook of parenting* (2nd ed., Vol. 1, pp. 103–133). Mahwah, NJ: Erlbaum.

Steinberg, L., Albert, D., Cauffman, E., Banich, M., Graham, S., & Woolard, J. (2008). Age differences in sensation seeking and impulsivity as indexed by behavior and self-report: Evidence for a dual systems model. *Developmental Psychology, 44*, 1764–1778.

Steinberg, L., Blatt-Eisengart, I., & Cauffman, E. (2006). Patterns of competence and adjustment among adolescents from authoritative, authoritarian, indulgent, and neglectful homes: A replication in a sample of serious juvenile offenders. *Journal of Research on Adolescence, 16*, 47–58.

Steinberg, L., Graham, S., O'Brien, L., Woolard, J., Cauffman, E., & Banich, M. (2009). Age differences in future orientation and delay discounting. *Child Development, 80*, 28–44.

Stenseng, F., Belsky, J., Skalicka, V., & Wichstrøm, L. (2016). Peer rejection and attention deficit hyperactivity disorder symptoms: Reciprocal relations through ages 4, 6, and 8. *Child Development, 87*, 365–373.

Stephan, J. L., & Rosenbaum, J. E. (2013). Can high schools reduce college enrollment gaps with a new counseling model? *Educational Evaluation and Policy Analysis, 35*, 200–219.

Stephens, J. M., & Nicholson, H. (2008). Cases of incongruity: Exploring the divide between adolescents' beliefs and behavior related to academic dishonesty. *Educational Studies, 34*, 361–376.

Sternberg, R. J. (1988). *The triarchic mind: A new theory of human intelligence.* New York: Viking.

Sternberg, R. J. (1996). *Successful intelligence: How practical and creative intelligence determine success in life.* New York: Simon & Schuster.

Sternberg, R. J., Grigorenko, E., & Bundy, D. (2001). The predictive value of IQ. *Merrill-Palmer Quarterly, 47*, 1–41.

Sternberg, R. J., Grigorenko, E. L., & Zhang, L.-f. (2008). Styles of learning and thinking matter in instruction and assessment. *Perspectives on Psychological Science, 3*, 486–506.

Sternberg, R. J., & Kaufman, J. (1998). Human abilities. *Annual Review of Psychology, 49*, 479–502.

Sternberg, R. J., Grigorenko, E., & Kidd, K. (2005). Intelligence, race, and genetics. *American Psychologist, 60*, 46–59.

Steubing, K. K., Barth, A. E., Cirino, P. T., Francis, D. J., & Fletcher, J. M. (2008). A response to recent reanalyses of the National Reading Panel report: Effects of systematic phonics instruction are practically significant. *Journal of Educational Psychology, 100*, 123–134.

Stevenson, H. W., & Stigler, J. (1992). *The learning gap: Why our schools are failing and what we can learn from Japanese and Chinese education.* New York: Summit.

Stevenson-Hinde, J., & Verschueren, K. (2002). Attachment in childhood. In P. Smith & C. Hart (Eds.), *Blackwell handbook of childhood social development* (pp. 182–204). Oxford, UK: Blackwell.

Stice, E., & Shaw, H. (2004). Eating disorder prevention programs: A meta-analytic review. *Psychological Bulletin, 130*, 206–227.

Stinson, D. (2006). African American male adolescents, schooling (and mathematics): Deficiency, rejection, and achievement. *Review of Educational Research, 76*, 477–506.

Stipek, D. (2001). Pathways to constructive lives: The importance of early school success. In A. Bohart & D. Stipek (Eds.), *Constructive and destructive behavior: Implications for family, school, and society* (pp. 291–315). Washington, DC: APA.

Stipek, D., & Miles, S. (2008). Effects of aggression on achievement: Does conflict with the teacher make it worse? *Child Development, 79*, 1721–1735.

Stocker, C. M., Richmond, M. K., Rhoades, G. K., & Kuang, L. (2007). Family emotional processes and adolescents' adjustment. *Social Development, 16*, 310–325.

Stoet, G., & Geary, D. C. (2015). Sex differences in academic achievement are not related to political, economic, or social equality. *Intelligence, 48*, 137–151.

Stokes, J., Luiselli, J., & Reed, D. (2010). A behavioral intervention for teaching tackling skills to high school football athletes. *Journal of Applied Behavior Analysis, 43*, 509–512.

Storm, B. C., & Stone, S. M. (2014). Saving-enhanced memory: The benefits of saving on the learning and remembering of new information. *Psychological Science, 26*, 182–188.

Stormshak, E., Bierman, K., Bruschi, C., Dodge, K. A., Coie, J., & Conduct Problems Prevention Research Group. (1999). The relation between behavior problems and peer preference in different classroom contexts. *Child Development, 70*, 169–182.

St. Petersburg-USA Orphanage Research Team. (2008). The effects of early social-emotional and relationship experience on the development of young orphanage children. *Monographs of the Society for Research in Child Development, 73* (Serial No. 291).

Strang, N., Hanson, J., & Pollak, S. (2012). The importance of biological methods in linking social experience with social and emotional development. *Monographs of the Society for Research in Child Development, 77*(2), 61–66.

Straus, M. A., & Savage, S. A. (2005). Neglectful behavior by parents in the life history of university students in 17 countries and its relation to violence against dating partners. *Child Maltreatment, 10*, 124–135.

Straus, M. A., Sugarman, D. B., & Giles-Sims, J. (1997). Spanking by parents and subsequent antisocial behavior of children. *Archives of Pediatric and Adolescent Medicine, 151*, 761–767.

Strauss, R. S. (2000). Childhood obesity and self-esteem. *Pediatrics, 105*, e15.

Strauss, R. S., & Knight, J. (1999). Influence of the home environment on the development of obesity in children. *Pediatrics, 103*, e85.

Strenze, T. (2007). Intelligence and socioeconomic success: A meta-analytic review of longitudinal research. *Intelligence, 35*, 401–426.

Strickgold, R., & Walker, M. (2004). To sleep, perchance to gain creative insight? *Trends in Cognitive Sciences, 8*, 191–192.

Striegel-Moore, R. H., & Bulik, C. (2007). Risk factors for eating disorders. *American Psychologist, 62*, 181–198.

Strough, J., Berg, C., & Meegan, S. (2001). Friendship and gender differences in task and social interpretations of peer collaborative problem solving. *Social Development, 10*, 1–22.

Sturaro, C., van Lier, P. A., Cuijpers, P., & Koot, H. M. (2011). The role of peer relationships in the development of early school-age externalizing problems. *Child Development, 82*, 758–765.

Sturge-Apple, M. L., Davies, P. T., & Cummings, E. M. (2006). Impact of hostility and withdrawal in interparental conflict on parental emotional unavailability and children's adjustment difficulties. *Child Development, 77*, 1623–1641.

Suárez-Orozco, C., Casanova, S., Martin, M., Katsiaficas, D., Cuellar, V., Smith, N. A., & Dias, S. I. (2015). Toxic rain in class: Classroom interpersonal microaggressions. *Educational Researcher, 44*, 151–160.

Suárez-Orozco, C., Gaytán, F. X., Bang, H. J., Pakes, J., O'Connor, E., & Rhodes, J. (2010). Academic trajectories of newcomer immigrant youth. *Developmental Psychology, 46*, 602–618.

Südkamp, A., Kaiser, J., & Möller, J. (2012). Accuracy of teachers' judgments of students' academic achievement: A meta-analysis. *Journal of Educational Psychology, 104*, 743–762.

Suggate, S. P. (2010). Why what we teach depends on when: Grade and reading intervention modality moderate effect size. *Developmental Psychology, 46*, 1556–1579.

Sulik, M. J., Blair, C., Mills-Koonce, R., Berry, D., Greenberg, M., & The Family Life Project, I. (2015). Early parenting and the development of externalizing behavior problems: Longitudinal mediation through children's executive function. *Child Development, 86*, 1588–1603.

Sulik, M. J., Eisenberg, N., Lemery-Chalfant, K., Spinrad, T. L., Silva, K. M., Eggum, N. D., et al. (2012). Interactions between serotonin transporter gene haplotypes and quality of mothers' parenting predict the development of children's noncompliance. *Developmental Psychology, 48*, 740–754.

Sullivan, M., & Lewis, M. (2003). Contextual determinants of anger and other negative expressions in young infants. *Developmental Psychology, 39*, 693–705.

Summer, L. (2003). *Learning joy from dogs without collars.* New York: Simon & Schuster.

Sun, Y., & Li, Y. (2001). Marital disruption, parental investment, and children's academic achievement: A prospective analysis. *Journal of Family Issues, 22*, 27–62.

Sundet, J. M., Eriksen, W., & Tambs, K. (2008). Intelligence correlations between brothers decrease with increasing age difference: Evidence of shared environmental effects in young adults. *Psychological Science, 19*, 843–847.

Supple, A. J., & Small, S. A. (2006). The influence of parental support, knowledge, authoritative parenting on Hmong and European American adolescent development. *Journal of Family Issues, 27*, 1214–1232.

Sussman, T. J., Heller, W., Miller, G. A., & Mohanty, A. (2013). Emotional distractors can enhance attention. *Psychological Science, 24*, 2322–2328.

Sutin, A., Ferrucci, L., Zonderman, A. B., & Terracciano, A. (2011). Personality and obesity across the adult life span. *Journal of Personality and Social Psychology, 101*, 579–592.

Suway, J. G., Degnan, K. A., Sussman, A., & Fox, N. A. (2012). The relations among theory of mind, behavioral inhibition, and peer interactions in early childhood. *Social Development, 21*, 331–342.

Swann, W. B., Chang-Schneider, C., & McClarty, K. L. (2007). Do people's self-views matter? Self-concept and self-esteem in everyday life. *American Psychologist, 62*, 84–94.

Swanson, H. L. (2008). Working memory and intelligence in children: What develops? *Journal of Educational Psychology, 100*, 581–602.

Swanson, H. L. (2014). Does cognitive strategy training on word problems compensate for working memory capacity in children with math difficulties? *Journal of Educational Psychology, 106*, 831–848.

Swanson, H. L., & Jerman, O. (2006). Math disabilities: A selective meta-analysis of the literature. *Review of Educational Research, 76*, 249–274.

Swanson, H. L., Jerman, O., & Zheng, X. (2008). Growth in working memory and mathematical problem solving in children at risk and not at risk for serious math difficulties. *Journal of Educational Psychology, 100*, 343–379.

Swanson, J., Valiente, C., Lemery-Chalfont, K., Bradley, R., & Eggum-Wilkens, N. (2014). Longitudinal relations among parents' reactions to children's negative emotions, effortful control, and math achievement in early elementary school. *Child Development, 85*, 1932–1947.

Swinford, S. P., DeMaris, A., Cernkovich, S. A., & Giordano, P. C. (2000). Harsh physical discipline in childhood and violence in later romantic involvements: The mediating role of problem behaviors. *Journal of Marriage and the Family, 62*, 508–519.

Syer, C., & Shore, B. (2001). Science fairs: What are the sources of help for students and how prevalent is cheating? *School Science and Mathematics, 101*, 206–220.

Szalacha, L. A., Erkut, S., Coll, C. G., Alarcsn, O., Fields, J. P., & Ceder, I. (2003). Discrimination and Puerto Rican children's and adolescents' mental health. *Cultural Diversity and Ethnic Minority Psychology, 9*, 141–155.

Szynal-Brown, C., & Morgan, R. (1983). The effects of reward on tutor's behavior in a cross-age tutoring context. *Journal of Experimental Child Psychology, 36*, 196–208.

Taing, V. (2009). Boy lifts book; librarian changes boy's life [NPR Morning Edition, interview from StoryCorps]. Retrieved October 2, 2009, from http://www.npr.org/templates/story/story.php?storyId=113357239

Talwar, V., Arruda, C., & Yachison, S. (2015). The effects of punishment and appeals for honesty on children's truth-telling behavior. *Journal of Experimental Child Psychology, 130*, 209–217.

Talwar, V., Gordon, H. M., & Lee, K. (2007). Lying in the elementary school years: Verbal deception and its relation to second-order belief understanding. *Developmental Psychology, 43*, 804–810.

Talwar, V., & Lee, K. (2008). Social and cognitive correlates of children's lying behavior. *Child Development, 79*, 866–881.

Tamim, R. M., Bernard, R. M., Borokhovski, E., Abrami, P. C., & Schmid, R. F. (2011). What forty years of research says about the impact of technology on learning: A second-order meta-analysis and validation study. *Review of Educational Research, 81*, 4–28.

Tamis-LeMonda, C., Bornstein, M. H., & Baumwell, L. (2001). Maternal responsiveness and children's achievement of language milestones. *Child Development, 72*, 748–767.

Tamis-LeMonda, C., Cristofaro, T. N., Rodriguez, E. T., & Bornstein, M. H. (2006). Early language development: Social influences in the first years of life. In L. Balter & C. Tamis-LeMonda (Eds.), *Child psychology: A handbook of contemporary issues* (2nd ed., pp. 79–108). New York: Hove.

Tamis-LeMonda, C., Way, N., Hughes, D., Yoshikawa, H., Kalman, R. K., & Niwa, E. Y. (2008). Parents' goals for children: The dynamic coexistence of individualism and collectivism in cultures and individuals. *Social Development, 17*, 183–209.

Taneja, V., Sriram, S., Beri, R., Sreenivas, V., Aggarwal, R., Kaur, R., et al. (2002). "Not by bread alone": Impact of a structured 90-minute play session on development of children in an orphanage. *Child: Care, Health, & Development, 28*, 95–100.

Tang, C. (2006). Corporal punishment and physical maltreatment against children: A community study on Chinese parents in Hong Kong. *Child Abuse & Neglect, 30*, 893–907.

Tang, S., Davis-Kean, P. E., Chen, M., & Sexton, H. R. (2016). Adolescent pregnancy's intergenerational effects: Does an adolescent mother's education have consequences for her children's achievement? *Journal of Research on Adolescence, 26*, 180–193.

Tangney, J. P., Stuewig, J., & Mashek, D. J. (2007). Moral emotions and moral behavior. *Annual Review of Psychology, 58*, 345–372.

Tanner, J. M. (1973). Growing up. *Scientific American, 229,* 34–43.

Tanner, J. M. (1985). Growth regulation and the genetics of growth. *Progress in Clinical & Biological Research, 200,* 19–32.

Tarabulsy, G. M., Bernier, A., Provost, M. A., Maranda, J., Larose, S., Moss, E., et al. (2005). Another look inside the gap: Ecological contributions to the transmission of attachment in a sample of adolescent mother-infant dyads. *Developmental Psychology, 41,* 212–234.

Taumoepeau, M., & Ruffman, T. (2008). Stepping stones to others' minds: Maternal talk relates to child mental state language and emotion understanding at 15, 24, and 33 months. *Child Development, 79,* 284–302.

Taylor, G., Klein, N., & Hack, M. (2000). School-age consequences of birth weight less than 750g: A review and update. *Developmental Neuropsychology, 17,* 289–321.

Taylor, G., Klein, N., Minich, N., & Hack, M. (2000). Middle-school-age outcomes in children with very low birthweight. *Child Development, 71,* 1495–1511.

Taylor, J. S. H., Duff, F. J., Woollams, A. M., Monaghan, P., & Ricketts, J. (2015). How word meaning influences word reading. *Current Directions in Psychological Science, 24,* 322–328.

Taylor, M., Carlson, S., Maring, B., Gerow, L., & Charley, C. (2004). The characteristics and correlates of fantasy in school-age children: Imaginary companions, impersonation, and social understanding. *Developmental Psychology, 40,* 1173–1187.

Teisl, M., & Cicchetti, D. (2008). Physical abuse, cognitive and emotional processes, and aggressive/disruptive behavior problems. *Social Development, 17,* 1–23.

Telzer, E. H., & Fuligni, A. J. (2009). Daily family assistance and the psychological well-being of adolescents from Latin American, Asian, and European backgrounds. *Developmental Psychology, 45,* 1177–1189.

Thelen, E. (1995). Motor development: A new synthesis. *American Psychologist, 50,* 79–103.

Thijs, J., & Verkuyten, M. (2008). Peer victimization and academic achievement in a multiethnic sample: The role of perceived academic self-efficacy. *Journal of Educational Psychology, 100,* 754–764.

Thomas, A., & Chess, S. (1984). Genesis and evolution of behavioral disorders: From infancy to early adult life. *American Journal of Psychiatry, 141,* 1–9.

Thomas, A., Chess, S., & Birch, H. (1970). The origin of personality. *Scientific American, 223,* 102–109.

Thomas, A., Chess, S., & Korn, S. (1982). The reality of difficult temperament. *Merrill-Palmer Quarterly, 28,* 1–40.

Thomas, D. E., Bierman, K. L., & Powers, C. J. (2011). The influence of classroom aggression and classroom climate on aggressive-disruptive behavior. *Child Development, 82,* 751–757.

Thomas, M. S. C., & Johnson, M. H. (2008). New advances in understanding sensitive periods in brain development. *Current Directions in Psychological Science, 17,* 1–5.

Thompson, R. A. (1991). Emotional regulation and emotional development. *Educational Psychology Review, 3,* 269–307.

Thompson, R. A. (2012). Whither the preconventional child? Toward a lifespan moral development theory. *Child Development Perspectives, 6,* 423–429.

Thorkildsen, T., Reese, D., & Corsino, A. (2002). School ecologies and attitudes about exclusionary behavior among adolescents and young adults. *Merrill-Palmer Quarterly, 48,* 25–51.

Tinsley, B., Lees, N., & Sumartojo, E. (2004). Child and adolescent HIV risk: Familial and cultural perspectives. *Journal of Family Psychology, 18,* 208–224.

Timmons, A. C., & Margolin, G. (2015). Family conflict, mood, and adolescents' daily school problems: Moderating roles of internalizing and externalizing symptoms. *Child Development, 86,* 241–258.

Tomasello, M., Carpenter, M., & Liszkowski, U. (2007). A new look at infant pointing. *Child Development, 78,* 705–722.

Toomey, R. B., Ryan, C., Diaz, R. M., Card, N. A., & Russell, S. T. (2010). Gender-nonconforming lesbian, gay, bisexual, and transgender youth: School victimization and young adult psychosocial adjustment. *Developmental Psychology, 46,* 1580–1589.

Topping, K. J., & Barron, I. G. (2009). School-based child sexual abuse prevention programs: A review of effectiveness. *Review of Educational Research, 79,* 431–463.

Torff, B., & Gardner, H. (1999). The vertical mind—The case for multiple intelligences. In M. Anderson (Ed.), *The development of intelligence* (pp. 139–159). East Sussex, UK: Psychology Press.

Torgesen, J. K. (2009). The response to intervention instructional model: Some outcomes from a large-scale implementation in Reading First schools. *Child Development Perspectives, 3,* 38–40.

Toro, J. M., Nespor, M., Mehler, J., & Bonatti, L. L. (2008). Finding words and rules in a speech stream: Functional differences between vowels and consonants. *Psychological Science, 19,* 137–144.

Tout, K., de Haan, M., Campbell, E., & Gunnar, M. (1998). Social behavior correlates of cortisol activity in child care: Gender differences and time-of-day effects. *Child Development, 69,* 1247–1262.

Trahan, L. H., Stuebing, K. K., Fletcher, J. M., & Hiscock, M. (2014). The Flynn effect: A meta-analysis. *Psychological Bulletin, 140,* 1332–1360.

Treboux, D., Crowell, J., & Waters, E. (2004). When "new" meets "old": Configurations of adult attachment representations and their implications for marital functioning. *Developmental Psychology, 40,* 295–314.

Tremblay, M. S., LeBlanc, A. G., Kho, M. E., Saunders, T. J., Larouche, R., Colley, R. C., . . . Gorber, S. C. (2011). Systematic review of sedentary behaviour and health indicators in school-aged children and youth. *International Journal of Behavioral Nutrition and Physical Activity, 8,* 98–98.

Trionfi, G., & Reese, E. (2009). A good story: Children with imaginary companions create richer narratives. *Child Development, 80,* 1301–1313.

Troop-Gordon, W. (2015). The role of the classroom teacher in the lives of children victimized by peers. *Child Development Perspectives, 9,* 55–60.

Troseth, G., Saylor, M. M., & Archer, A. (2006). Young children's use of video as a source of socially relevant information. *Child Development, 77,* 786–799.

Trout, J. (2003). Biological specializations for speech: What can the animals tell us? *Current Directions in Psychological Science, 12,* 155–159.

Trzesniewski, K. H., Donnellan, M. B., & Robins, R. W. (2008). Do today's young people really think they are so extraordinary? An examination of secular trends in narcissism and self-enhancement. *Psychological Science, 19,* 181–188.

Trzesniewski, K. H., Moffitt, T., Caspi, A., Taylor, A., & Maughan, B. (2006). Revisiting the association between reading achievement and antisocial behavior: New evidence of an environmental explanation from a twin study. *Child Development, 77,* 72–88.

Tsai, K. M., Telzer, E. H., Gonzales, N. A., & Fuligni, A. J. (2015). Parental cultural socialization of Mexican-American adolescents' family obligation values and behaviors. *Child Development, 86,* 1241–1252.

Ttofi, M., & Farrington, D. (2011). Effectiveness of school-based programs to reduce bullying: A systematic and meta-analytic review. *Journal of Experimental Criminology, 7,* 27–56.

Tucker-Drob, E. M. (2012). Preschools reduce early academic-achievement gaps. *Psychological Science, 23,* 310–319.

Tucker-Drob, E. M., & Bates, T. C. (2016). Large cross-national differences in gene × socioeconomic status interaction on intelligence. *Psychological Science, 27,* 138–149.

Tucker-Drob, E. M., Rhemtulla, M., Harden, K. P., Turkheimer, E., & Fask, D. (2011). Emergence of a gene × socioeconomic status interaction on infant mental ability between 10 months and 2 years. *Psychological Science, 22,* 125–133.

Tuerk, P. (2005). Research in the high-stakes era: Achievement, resources, and No Child Left Behind. *Psychological Science, 16,* 419–425.

Tuncay, E. (2003). Effective interventions on test anxiety reduction: A meta-analysis. *School Psychology International, 24,* 313–328.

Turkheimer, E., Haley, A., Waldron, M., D'Onofrio, B., & Gottesman, I. (2003). Socioeconomic status modifies heritability of IQ in young children. *Psychological Science, 14,* 623–628.

Turkheimer, E., Pettersson, E., & Horn, E. E. (2014). A phenotypic null hypothesis for the genetics of personality. *Annual Review of Psychology, 65,* 515–540.

Turley, R. N. L. (2003). Are children of young mothers disadvantaged because of their mother's age or family background? *Child Development, 74,* 465–474.

Turner, H. A., Finkelhor, D., Hamby, S. L., & Shattuck, A. (2013). Family structure, victimization, and child mental health in a nationally representative sample. *Social Science & Medicine, 87,* 39–51.

Turner, J. C., Midgley, C., Meyer, D., Gheen, M., Anderman, E., Kang, Y., et al. (2002). The classroom environment and students' reports of avoidance strategies in mathematics: A multimethod study. *Journal of Educational Psychology, 94*, 88–106.

Twenge, J. (2000). The age of anxiety? Birth cohort change in anxiety and neuroticism, 1952–1993. *Journal of Personality and Social Psychology, 79*, 1007–1021.

Twenge, J. M., & Campbell, W. K. (2010). Birth cohort differences in the Monitoring the Future dataset and elsewhere: Further evidence for Generation Me—Commentary on Trzesniewski & Donnellan (2010). *Perspectives on Psychological Science, 5*, 81–88.

Twenge, J. M., Miller, J. D., & Campbell, W. K. (2014). The narcissism epidemic: Commentary on modernity and narcissistic personality disorder. *Personality Disorders: Theory, Research, and Treatment, 5*, 227–229.

Tynes, B. M., Umaña-Taylor, A. J., Rose, C. A., Lin, J., & Anderson, C. J. (2012). Online racial discrimination and the protective function of ethnic identity and self-esteem for African American adolescents. *Developmental Psychology, 48*, 343–355.

Tyson, K., Darity, W., Jr., & Castellino, D. R. (2005). It's not "a Black thing": Understanding the burden of acting White and other dilemmas of high achievement. *American Sociological Review, 70*, 582–605.

Uhlmann, E. L., Pizarro, D. A., & Diermeier, D. (2015). A person-centered approach to moral judgment. *Perspectives on Psychological Science, 10*, 72–81.

Ullén, F., Hambrick, D. Z., & Mosing, M. A. (2016). Rethinking expertise: A multifactorial gene–environment interaction model of expert performance. *Psychological Bulletin, 142*, 427–446.

Underwood, M. (2002). Sticks and stones and social exclusion: Aggression among girls and boys. In P. Smith & C. Hart (Eds.), *Blackwell handbook of childhood social development* (pp. 533–548). Oxford, UK: Blackwell.

Underwood, M., Galen, B., & Paquette, J. (2001). Top ten challenges for understanding gender and aggression in children: Why can't we all just get along? *Social Development, 10*, 248–266.

Underwood, M. K., Rosen, L. H., More, D., Ehrenreich, S. E., & Gentsch, J. K. (2012). The BlackBerry project: Capturing the content of adolescents' text messaging. *Developmental Psychology, 48*, 295–302.

Updegraff, K. A., Whiteman, S. D., McHale, S. M., Thayer, S. M., & Crouter, A. C. (2006). The nature and correlates of Mexican-American adolescents' time with parents and peers. *Child Development, 77*, 1470–1486.

Ursache, A., Blair, C., & Raver, C. C. (2012). The promotion of self-regulation as a means of enhancing school readiness and early achievement in children at risk for school failure. *Child Development Perspectives, 6*, 122–128.

U.S. Bureau of Labor Statistics. (2009). Employment characteristics of families in 2008. Retrieved May 22, 2010, from http://www.bls.gov/news.release/pdf/famee.pdf

U.S. Children's Bureau. (2015). *Trends in foster care and adoption: FY 2005–FY 2014.* Retrieved from http://www.acf.hhs.gov/programs/cb

U.S. Department of Education. (2015). *The condition of education 2015* (NCES 2015-144). Washington, DC: National Center for Education Statistics.

U.S. Department of Health and Human Services. (2009). *Child maltreatment 2007*: Administration on Children, Youth, and Families. Washington, DC: Government Printing Office.

U.S. Department of Health and Human Services. (2014). *Policy statement on expulsion and suspension policies in early childhood settings.* Washington, DC: Department of Education.

Usher, E. L., & Pajares, F. (2008). Sources of self-efficacy in school: Critical review of the literature and future directions. *Review of Educational Research, 78*, 751–796.

Uttal, D., Meadow, N., Tipton, E., Hand, L., Alden, A., Warren, C., & Newcombe, N. (2013). The malleability of spatial skills: A meta-analysis of training studies. *Psychological Bulletin, 139*, 352–402.

Uttal, D., Miller, D. I., & Newcombe, N. S. (2013). Exploring and enhancing spatial thinking: Links to achievement in science, technology, engineering, and mathematics? *Current Directions in Psychological Science, 22*, 367–373.

Uttal, D., Meadow, N., Tipton, E., Hand, L., Alden, A., Warren, C., et al. (2013). The malleability of spatial skills: A meta-analysis of training studies. *Psychological Bulletin, 139*, 352–402.

Uttal, D. H., Liu, L. L., & DeLoache, J. (2006). Concreteness and symbolic development. In L. Balter & C. Tamis-LeMonda (Eds.), *Child psychology: A handbook of contemporary issues* (2nd ed., pp. 167–184). New York: Hove.

Vaish, A., Carpenter, M., & Tomasello, M. (2009). Sympathy through affective perspective taking and its relation to prosocial behavior in toddlers. *Developmental Psychology, 45*, 534–543.

Vaish, A., Carpenter, M., & Tomasello, M. (2011). Young children's responses to guilt displays. *Developmental Psychology, 47*, 1248–1262.

Valenzuela, M. (1990). Attachment in chronically underweight young children. *Child Development, 61*, 1984–1996.

Valiente, C., Lemery-Chalfant, K., & Reiser, M. (2007). Pathways to problem behaviors: Chaotic homes, parent and child effortful control, and parenting. *Social Development, 16*, 249–267.

Valiente, C., Lemery-Chalfant, K., & Swanson, J. (2010). Prediction of kindergartners' academic achievement from their effortful control and emotionality: Evidence for direct and moderated relations. *Journal of Educational Psychology, 102*, 550–560.

Valiente, C., Swanson, J., & Eisenberg, N. (2012). Linking students' emotions and academic achievement: When and why emotions matter. *Child Development Perspectives, 6*, 129–135.

Valkenburg, P. M., & Peter, J. (2009). Social consequences of the Internet for adolescents: A decade of research. *Current Directions in Psychological Science, 18*, 1–5.

Valkenburg, P. M., Peter, J., & Walther, J. B. (2016). Media effects: Theory and research. *Annual Review of Psychology, 67*, 315–338.

Valla, J. M., & Ceci, S. J. (2011). Can sex differences in science be tied to the long reach of prenatal hormones? Brain organization theory, digit ratio (2D/4D), and sex differences in preferences and cognition. *Perspectives on Psychological Science, 6*, 134–146.

Van Ausdale, D., & Feagin, J. R. (1996). Using racial and ethnic concepts: The critical case of very young children. *American Sociological Review, 61*, 779–793.

Vandell, D. L., Belsky, J., Burchinal, M., Steinberg, L., Vandergrift, N., & NICHD Early Child Care Research Network (2010). Do effects of early child care extend to age 15 years? Results from the NICHD Study of Early Child Care and Youth Development. *Child Development, 81*, 737–756.

van den Berg, Y., & Cillessen, A. (2015). Peer status and classroom seating arrangements: A social relations analysis. *Journal of Experimental Child Psychology, 130*, 19–34.

van Goethem, A., van Hoof, A., Orobio de Castro, B., Van Aken, M., & Hart, D. (2014). The role of reflection in the effects of community service on adolescent development: A meta-analysis. *Child Development, 85*, 2114–2130.

van Goozen, S., Fairchild, G., & Harold, G. T. (2008). The role of neurobiological deficits in childhood antisocial behavior. *Current Directions in Psychological Science, 17*, 224–228.

Van Hook, J., & Altman, C. E. (2012). Competitive food sales in schools and childhood obesity. *Sociology of Education, 85*, 23–39.

Van Horn, M. L., Karlin, E. O., Ramey, S. L., Aldridge, J., & Snyder, S. W. (2005). Effects of developmentally appropriate practices on children's development: A review of research and discussion of methodological and analytic issues. *Elementary School Journal, 105*, 325–351.

Van Horn, M. L., & Ramey, S. (2003). The effects of developmentally appropriate practices on academic outcomes among former Head Start students and classmates, Grades 1–3. *American Educational Research Journal, 40*, 961–990.

van Lieshout, C. (2000). Lifespan personality development: Self-organizing goal-oriented agents and developmental outcome. *International Journal of Behavioral Development, 24*, 276–288.

Van Ryzin, M. J., Leve, L. D., Neiderhiser, J. M., Shaw, D. S., Natsuaki, M. N., & Reiss, D. (2015). Genetic influences can protect against unresponsive parenting in the prediction of child social competence. *Child Development, 86*, 667–680.

Van Zalk, M., Kerr, M., Branje, S., Stattin, H., & Meeus, W. (2010). It takes three: Selection, influence, and de-selection processes of depression in adolescent friendship networks. *Developmental Psychology, 46*, 927–938.

van Zuijen, T. L., Plakas, A., Maassen, B. A. M., Maurits, N. M., & van der Leij, A. (2013). Infant ERPs separate children at risk of dyslexia who become good readers from those who become poor readers. *Developmental Science, 16,* 554–563.

Varma, S., McCandliss, B. D., & Schwartz, D. L. (2008). Scientific and pragmatic challenges for bridging education and neuroscience. *Educational Researcher, 37,* 140–152.

Varnhagen, C., McFall, G. P., Pugh, N. P., Routledge, L., Sumida-MacDonald, H., & Kwong, T. E. (2010). lol: new language and spelling in instant messaging. *Reading and Writing , 23, 719–733.*

Vaughn, B. E., Colvin, T., Azria, M., Caya, L., & Krzysik, L. (2001). Dyadic analyses of friendship in a sample of preschool-age children attending Head Start: Correspondence between measures and implications for social competence. *Child Development, 72,* 862–878.

Vázquez García, H. A., García Coll, C., Erkut, S., Alarcsn, O., & Tropp, L. R. (1999). Family values of Latino adolescents. In M. Montero-Sieburth & F. Villarruel (Eds.), *Making invisible Latino adolescents visible.* New York: Falmer.

Vazsonyi, A. T., & Huang, L. (2010). Where self-control comes from: On the development of self-control and its relationship to deviance over time. *Developmental Psychology, 46,* 245–257.

Vecchiotti, S. (2003). Kindergarten: An overlooked educational policy priority. *Social Policy Report, 17,* 3–19.

Vélez, C. E., Wolchik, S. A., Tein, J.-Y., & Sandler, I. (2011). Protecting children from the consequences of divorce: A longitudinal study of the effects of parenting on children's coping processes. *Child Development, 82,* 244–257.

Venables, P. H., & Raine, A. (2016). The impact of malnutrition on intelligence at 3 and 11 years of age: The mediating role of temperament. *Developmental Psychology, 52,* 205-220.

Ventura, S., Hamilton, B., & Mathews, T. J. (2014). National and state patterns of teen births in the United States, 1940–2013. *National Vital Statistics Reports, 63*(4).

Verboom, C., Sijtsema, J., Verhulst, F., Penninx, B., & Ormel, J. (2014). Longitudinal associations between depressive problems, academic performance, and social functioning in adolescent boys and girls. *Developmental Psycholoy, 50,* 247–257.

Verdine, B. N., Golinkoff, R. M., Hirsh-Pasek, K., Newcombe, N. S., Filipowicz, A. T., & Chang, A. (2014). Deconstructing building blocks: Preschoolers' spatial assembly performance relates to early mathematical skills. *Child Development, 85,* 1062–1076.

Verhage, M. L., Schuengel, C., Madigan, S., Fearon, R. M. P., Oosterman, M., Cassibba, R., . . . van Ijzendoorn, M. H. (2016). Narrowing the transmission gap: A synthesis of three decades of research on intergenerational transmission of attachment. *Psychological Bulletin, 142,* 337–366.

Verlinden, M., Tiemeier, H., Hudziak, J., Jaddoe, V., Raat, H., Guzens, M., et al. (2012). Television viewing and externalizing problems in preschool children. *Archives of Pediatrics & Adolescent Medicine, 166,* 191–925.

Véronneau, M.-H., Racer, K., Fosco, G., & Dishion, T. (2014). The contribution of adolescent effortful control to early adult educational attainment. *Journal of Educational Psychology, 106,* 730–743.

Véronneau, M.-H., Vitaro, F., Brendgen, M., Dishion, T. J., & Tremblay, R. E. (2010). Transactional analysis of the reciprocal links between peer experiences and academic achievement from middle childhood to early adolescence. *Developmental Psychology, 46,* 773–790.

Verschueren, K., Marcoen, A., & Schoefs, V. (1996). The internal working model of the self, attachment, and competence in five-year-olds. *Child Development, 67,* 2493–2511.

Vespa, J., Lewis, J., & Kreider, R. (2013). *America's families and living arrangements: 2012. Current population reports, P20–570.* Washington, DC: U.S. Census Bureau.

Viljaranta, J., Aunola, K., Mullola, S., Virkkala, J., Hirvonen, R., Pakarinen, E., & Nurmi, J.-E. (2015). Children's temperament and academic skill development during first grade: Teachers' interaction styles as mediators. *Child Development, 86,* 1191–1209.

Vitaro, F., Boivin, M., Brendgen, M., Girard, A., & Dionne, G. (2012). Social experiences in kindergarten and academic achievement in grade 1: A monozygotic twin difference study. *Journal of Educational Psychology, 104,* 366–380.

Viterbori, P., Usai, C., Traverso, l., & Franchis, V. (2015). How preschool executive functioning predicts several aspects of math achievement in Grades 1 and 3: A longitudinal study. *Journal of Experimental Child Psychology, 140,* 38–55.

Vlachou, M., Andreou, E., Botsoglou, K., & Didaskalou, E. (2011). Bully/victim problems among preschool children: A review of current research evidence. *Educational Psychology Review, 23,* 329–358.

Volbrecht, M., & Goldsmith, H. H. (2010). Early temperamental and family predictors of shyness and anxiety. *Developmental Psychology, 46,* 1192–1205.

von Stumm, S., & Plomin, R. (2015). Socioeconomic status and the growth of intelligence from infancy through adolescence. *Intelligence, 48,* 30–36.

Voss, L. (1997). Teasing, disputing, and playing: Cross-gender interactions and space utilization among first and third graders. *Gender & Society, 11,* 238–256.

Votruba-Drzal, E., Coley, R. L., Maldonado-Carreño, C., Li-Grining, C., & Chase-Lansdale, P. L. (2010). Child care and the development of behavior problems among economically disadvantaged children in middle childhood. *Child Development, 81,* 1460–1474.

Votruba-Drzal, E., Li-Grining, C. P., & Maldonado-Carreno, C. (2008). A developmental perspective on full- versus part-day kindergarten and children's academic trajectories through fifth grade. *Child Development, 79,* 957–978.

Voyer, D., & Voyer, S. D. (2014). Gender differences in scholastic achievement: A meta-analysis. *Psychological Bulletin, 140,* 1174-1204.

Vygotsky, L. S. (1978). *Mind in society: The development of higher psychological processes.* Cambridge, MA: Harvard University Press.

Waasdorp, T. E., & Bradshaw, C. P. (2011). Examining student responses to frequent bullying: A latent class approach. *Journal of Educational Psychology, 103,* 336–352.

Wachs, T. (2000). Nutritional deficits and behavioral development. *International Journal of Behavioral Development, 24,* 435–441.

Wachs, T. D. (2006). The nature, etiology, and consequences of individual differences in temperament. In L. Balter & C. Tamis-LeMonda (Eds.), *Child psychology: A handbook of contemporary issues* (2nd ed., pp. 27–52). New York: Hove.

Wachs, T. D., Black, M. M., & Engle, P. L. (2009). Maternal depression: A global threat to children's health, development, and behavior and to human rights. *Child Development Perspectives, 3,* 51–59.

Wachsler-Felder, J., & Golden, C. (2002). Neuropsychological consequences of HIV in children: A review of current literature. *Clinical Psychology Review, 22,* 441–462.

Wagmiller, R. L. (2015). The temporal dynamics of childhood economic deprivation and children's achievement. *Child Development Perspectives, 9,* 158–163.

Wai, J., Lubinski, D., & Benbow, C. P. (2009). Spatial ability for STEM domains: Aligning over 50 years of cumulative psychological knowledge solidifies its importance. *Journal of Educational Psychology, 101,* 817–835.

Wainright, J. L., & Patterson, C. J. (2008). Peer relations among adolescents with female same-sex parents. *Developmental Psychology, 44,* 117–126.

Wainright, J. L., Russell, S. T., & Patterson, C. J. (2004). Psychosocial adjustment, school outcomes, and romantic relationships of adolescents with same-sex parents. *Child Development, 75,* 1886–1898.

Wainryb, C., Brehl, B., & Matwin, S. (2005). Being hurt and hurting others: Children's narrative accounts and moral judgments of their own interpersonal conflicts. *Monographs of the Society for Research in Child Development, 70* (Serial No. 281).

Wakschlag, L. S., Choi, S. W., Carter, A. S., Hullsiek, H., Burns, J., McCarthy, K., . . . Briggs-Gowan, M. J. (2012). Defining the developmental parameters of temper loss in early childhood: Implications for developmental psychopathology. *Journal of Child Psychology and Psychiatry, 53,* 1099–1108.

Wakschlag, L. S., Leventhal, B., Pine, D., Pickett, K. E., & Carter, A. S. (2006). Elucidating early mechanisms of developmental psychopathology: The case of prenatal smoking and disruptive behavior. *Child Development, 77,* 893–906.

Walker, C., Wartenberg, T., & Winner, E. (2013). Engagement in philosophical dialogue facilitates children's reasoning about subjectivity. *Developmental Psychology, 49,* 1338–1347.

Walker, J., Ice, C., Hoover-Dempsey, K., & Sandler, H. (2011). Latino parents' motivations for involvement in their children's schooling: An exploratory study. *Elementary School Journal, 111,* 409–429.

Walker, L. J., & Pitts, R. (1998). Naturalistic conceptions of moral maturity. *Developmental Psychology, 34*, 403–419.

Walker, L. J., Hennig, K., & Krettenauer, T. (2000). Parent and peer contexts for children's moral reasoning development. *Child Development, 71*, 1033–1048.

Walkington, C. A. (2013). Using adaptive learning technologies to personalize instruction to student interests: The impact of relevant contexts on performance and learning outcomes. *Journal of Educational Psychology, 105*, 932–945.

Wandrey, L., Quas, J. A., & Lyon, T. D. (2012). Does valence matter? Effects of negativity on children's early understanding of the truth and lies. *Journal of Experimental Child Psychology, 113*, 295–303.

Wang, M.-T., Brinkworth, M., & Eccles, J. (2013). Moderating effects of teacher–student relationship in adolescent trajectories of emotional and behavioral adjustment. *Developmental Psychology, 49*, 690–705.

Wang, M.-T., & Fredricks, J. A. (2014). The reciprocal links between school engagement, youth problem behaviors, and school dropout during adolescence. *Child Development, 85*, 722–737.

Wang, M.-T., Hill, N. E., & Hofkens, T. (2014). Parental involvement and African American and European American adolescents' academic, behavioral, and emotional development in secondary school. *Child Development, 85*, 2151–2168.

Wang, M.-T., & Kenny, S. (2014). Longitudinal links between fathers' and mothers' harsh verbal discipline and adolescents' conduct problems and depressive symptoms. *Child Development, 85*, 908–923.

Wang, M.-T., Selman, R. L., Dishion, T. J., & Stormshak, E. A. (2010). A Tobit regression analysis of the covariation between middle school students' perceived school climate and behavioral problems. *Journal of Research on Adolescence, 20*, 274–286.

Wang, M.-T., & Sheikh-Khalil, S. (2014). Does parental involvement matter for student achievement and mental health in high school? *Child Development, 85*, 610–625.

Wang, Q., Pomerantz, E. M., & Chen, H. (2007). The role of parents' control in early adolescents' psychological functioning: A longitudinal investigation in the United States and China. *Child Development, 78*, 1592–1610.

Wang, Z., Lukowski, S. L., Hart, S. A., Lyons, I. M., Thompson, L. A., Kovas, Y., . . . Petrill, S. A. (2015). Is math anxiety always bad for math learning? The role of math motivation. *Psychological Science, 26*, 1863–1876.

Wanless, S. B., McClelland, M. M., Acock, A. C., Ponitz, C. C., Son, S.-H., Lan, X., et al. (2011). Measuring behavioral regulation in four societies. *Psychological Assessment, 23*, 364–378.

Wansink, B., Just, D., Payne, C., & Klinger, M. (2012). Attractive names sustain increased vegetable intake in schools. *Preventive Medicine, 55*, 330–332.

Ward, L. M. (2003). Understanding the role of entertainment media in the sexual socialization of American youth: A review of empirical research. *Developmental Review, 23*, 347–388.

Warlaumont, A. S., Richards, J. A., Gilkerson, J., & Oller, D. K. (2014). A social feedback loop for speech development and its reduction in autism. *Psychological Science, 25*, 1314–1324.

Warne, R. T., Yoon, M., & Price, C. J. (2014). Exploring the various interpretations of "test bias." *Cultural Diversity and Ethnic Minority Psychology, 20*, 570–582.

Warneken, F. (2015). Precocious prosociality: Why do young children help? *Child Development Perspectives, 9*, 1–6.

Warneken, F., & Tomasello, M. (2009). The roots of human altruism. *British Journal of Psychology, 100*, 455–471.

Warneken, F., Lohse, K., Melis, A. P., & Tomasello, M. (2011). Young children share the spoils after collaboration. *Psychological Science, 22*, 267–273.

Wartella, E., Caplovitz, A. G., & Lee, J. H. (2004). From Baby Einstein to Leapfrog, from Doom to the Sims, from instant messaging to Internet chat rooms: Public interest in the role of interactive media in children's lives. *Social Policy Report, 18*, 3–19.

Watamura, S. E., Donzella, B., Alwin, J., & Gunnar, M. R. (2003). Morning-to-afternoon increases in cortisol concentrations for infants and toddlers at child care: Age differences and behavioral correlates. *Child Development, 74*, 1006–1020.

Watamura, S. E., Phillips, D. A., Morrissey, T. W., McCartney, K., & Bub, K. (2011). Double jeopardy: Poorer social-emotional outcomes for children in the NICHD SECCYD experiencing home and child-care environments that confer risk. *Child Development, 82*, 48–65.

Watanabe, H., Forssman, L., Green, D., Bohlin, G., & von Hofsten, C. (2012). Attention demands influence 10- and 12-month-old infants' perseverative behavior. *Developmental Psychology, 48*, 46–55.

Waters, H. (2000). Memory strategy development: Do we need yet another deficiency? *Child Development, 71*, 1004–1012.

Watkins, D. E., & Wentzel, K. R. (2008). Training boys with ADHD to work collaboratively: Social and learning outcomes. *Contemporary Educational Psychology, 33*, 625–646.

Watson, J. B. (1924). *Psychology from the standpoint of a behaviorist* (2nd ed.). Philadelphia, PA: Lippincott.

Watts, A., Patel, D., Corley, R., Friedman, N., Hewitt, J., Robinson, J., & Rhee, S. (2014). Testing alternative hypotheses regarding the association between behavioral inhibition and language development in toddlerhood. *Child Development, 85*, 1569–1585.

Watts, T. W., Duncan, G. J., Chen, M., Claessens, A., Davis-Kean, P. E., Duckworth, K., . . . Susperreguy, M. I. (2015). The role of mediators in the development of longitudinal mathematics achievement associations. *Child Development, 86*, 1892–1907.

Weaver-Hightower, M. B. (2011). Why education researchers should take school food seriously. *Educational Researcher, 40*, 15–21.

Webber, M., Carpiniello, K., Oruwariye, T., Lo, Y., Burton, W., & Appel, D. (2003). Burden of asthma in inner-city elementary schoolchildren: Do school-based health centers make a difference? *Archives of Pediatrics & Adolescent Medicine, 157*, 125–129.

Webster-Stratton, C., & Herman, K. C. (2008). The impact of parent behavior-management training on child depressive symptoms. *Journal of Counseling Psychology, 55*, 473–484.

Weiland, C., & Yoshikawa, H. (2013). Impacts of a prekindergarten program on children's mathematics, language, literacy, executive function, and emotional skills. *Child Development, 84, 2112-2130.*

Weinberg, K., & Tronick, E. Z. (1998). Emotional characteristics of infants associated with maternal depression and anxiety. *Pediatrics, 102*, 1298–1304.

Weinberg, M. K., Tronick, E. Z., Cohn, J. F., & Olson, K. L. (1999). Gender differences in emotional expressivity and self-regulation during early infancy. *Developmental Psychology, 33*, 175–188.

Weiner, B. (1985). An attributional theory of achievement motivation and emotion. *Psychological Review, 92*, 548–573.

Weinfield, N. S., Sroufe, A., & Egeland, B. (2000). Attachment from infancy to early adulthood in a high-risk sample: Continuity, discontinuity, and their correlates. *Child Development, 71*, 695–702.

Weinfield, N. S., Sroufe, A., Egeland, B., & Carlson, E. (1999). The nature of individual differences in infant-caregiver attachment. In J. Cassidy & P. Shaver (Eds.), *Handbook of attachment: Theory, research, and clinical applications* (pp. 68–88). New York: Guilford.

Weinstein, C. S., Tomlinson-Clarke, S., & Curran, M. (2004). Toward a conception of culturally responsive classroom management. *Journal of Teacher Education, 55*, 25–38.

Weis, R., & Cerankosky, B. C. (2010). Effects of video-game ownership on young boys' academic and behavioral functioning: A randomized, controlled study. *Psychological Science, 21*, 463–470.

Weisberg, D. S., Keil, F. C., Goodstein, J., Rawson, E., & Gray, J. R. (2008). The seductive allure of neuroscience explanations. *Journal of Cognitive Neuroscience, 20*, 470–477.

Weisleder, A., & Fernald, A. (2013). Talking to children matters: Early language experience strengthens processing and builds vocabulary. *Psychological Science, 24*, 2143–2152.

Weiss, H., Mayer, E., Kreider, H., Vaughan, M., Dearing, E., Hencke, R., et al. (2003). Making it work: Low-income working mothers' involvement in their children's education. *American Educational Research Journal, 40*, 879–901.

Weisz, J. R., McCarty, C. A., & Valeri, S. M. (2006). Effects of psychotherapy for depression in children and adolescents: A meta-analysis. *Psychological Bulletin, 132*, 132–149.

Weizman, Z. O., & Snow, C. E. (2001). Lexical input as related to children's vocabulary acquisition: Effects of sophisticated exposure and support for meaning. *Developmental Psychology, 37*, 265–279.

Wellman, H., & Liu, D. (2004). Scaling of theory-of-mind tasks. *Child Development, 75*, 523–541.

Wellman, H., Lopez-Duran, S., LaBounty, J., & Hamilton, B. (2008). Infant attention to intentional action predicts preschool theory of mind. *Developmental Psychology, 44*, 618–623.

Wellman, H. M. (2011). Reinvigorating explanations for the study of early cognitive development. *Child Development Perspectives, 5*, 33–38.

Welsh, J. A., Nix, R. L., Blair, C., Bierman, K. L., & Nelson, K. E. (2010). The development of cognitive skills and gains in academic school readiness for children from low-income families. *Journal of Educational Psychology, 102*, 43–53.

Wentzel, K. R. (1997). Student motivation in middle school: The role of perceived pedagogical caring. *Journal of Educational Psychology, 89*, 411–419.

Wentzel, K. R. (2002). Are effective teachers like good parents? Teaching styles and student adjustment in early adolescence. *Child Development, 73*, 287–301.

Wentzel, K. R., & Asher, S. R. (1995). The academic lives of neglected, rejected, popular, and controversial children. *Child Development, 66*, 754–763.

Wentzel, K. R., Barry, C., & Caldwell, K. (2004). Friendships in middle school: Influences on motivation and school adjustment. *Journal of Educational Psychology, 96*, 195–203.

Wentzel, K. R., Filisetti, L., & Looney, L. (2007). Adolescent prosocial behavior: The role of self-processes and contextual cues. *Child Development, 78*, 895–910.

Werner, N. E., & Hill, L. G. (2010). Individual and peer group normative beliefs about relational aggression. *Child Development, 81*, 826–836.

Wertz, J., Zavos, H. M. S., Matthews, T., Gray, R., Best-Lane, J., Pariante, C. M., . . . Arseneault, L. (2016). Etiology of pervasive versus situational antisocial behaviors: A multi-informant longitudinal cohort study. *Child Development, 87*, 312–325.

What Works Clearinghouse. (2007). *Caring School Community. WWC Intervention Report*. Washington, DC: Department of Education Institute of Education Sciences.

Wheeler, R., & Swords, R. (2010). *Code-switching lessons: Grammar strategies for linguistically diverse writers: Grade 3–6*. Portsmouth, NH: Heinemann.

White, B., & Watts, J. (1973). *Experience and environment: Major influences on the development of the young child*. Englewood Cliffs, NJ: Prentice Hall.

White, E. J., Hutka, S. A., Williams, L. J., & Moreno, S. (2013). Learning, neural plasticity and sensitive periods: Implications for language acquisition, music training and transfer across the lifespan. *Frontiers in Systems Neuroscience, 7*, 90.

White, R. M. B., Liu, Y., Nair, R. L., & Tein, J.-Y. (2015). Longitudinal and integrative tests of family stress model effects on Mexican origin adolescents. *Developmental Psychology, 51*, 649–662.

Whitehurst, G., & Chingos, M. M. (2011). *Class size: What research says and what it means for state policy*. Brown Center on Education Policy at Brookings. Retrieved from http://www.brookings.edu/research/papers/2011/05/11-class-size-whitehurst-chingos

Whitehurst, G. J., & Lonigan, C. J. (1998). Child development and emergent literacy. *Child Development, 69*, 848–872.

Whiting, B. B. (1983). The genesis of prosocial behavior. In D. Bridgeman (Ed.), *The nature of prosocial development: Interdisciplinary theories and strategies* (pp. 221–242). London: Academic Press.

Widdowson, E. (1951). Mental contentment and physical growth. *Lancet, 1*, 1316–1318.

Widen, S. (2013). Children's interpretation of facial expressions: The long path from valence-based to specific discrete categories. *Emotion Review, 5*, 72–77.

Wiebe, S. A., Espy, K. A., Stopp, C., Respass, J., Stewart, P., Jameson, T., et al. (2009). Gene–environment interactions across development: Exploring DRD2 genotype and prenatal smoking effects on self-regulation. *Developmental Psychology, 45*, 31–44.

Wiggan, G. (2007). Race, school achievement, and educational inequality: Toward a student-based inquiry perspective. *Review of Educational Research, 77*, 310–333.

Williams, C. A., & Forehand, R. (1984). An examination of predictor variables for child compliance and noncompliance. *Journal of Abnormal Child Psychology, 12*, 491–503.

Williams, J., Smith, V., & Committee on Substance Abuse (2015). Fetal alcohol spectrum disorders. *Pediatrics, 136*, e31395–e31406.

Williams, M., & Rask, H. (2003). Literacy through play: How families with able children support their literacy development. *Early Child Development and Care, 173*, 527–533.

Williams, S. T., Conger, K. J., & Blozis, S. A. (2007). The development of interpersonal aggression during adolescence: The importance of parents, siblings, and family economics. *Child Development, 78*, 1526–1542.

Williamson, R. A., Meltzoff, A. N., & Markman, E. M. (2008). Prior experiences and perceived efficacy influence 3-year-olds' imitation. *Developmental Psychology, 44*, 275–285.

Willoughby, T. (2008). A short-term longitudinal study of internet and computer game use by adolescent boys and girls: Prevalence, frequency of use, and psychosocial predictors. *Developmental Psychology, 44*, 195–204.

Wilson, J. (2012). Volunteerism research: A review essay. *Nonprofit and Voluntary Sector Quarterly, 41*, 176–212.

Wilson, S., Lipsey, M., & Derzon, J. (2003). The effects of school-based intervention programs on aggressive behavior: A meta-analysis. *Journal of Consulting and Clinical Psychology, 71*, 136–149.

Wilson, T., & Rodkin, P. C. (2011). African American and European American children in diverse elementary classrooms: Social integration, social status, and social behavior. *Child Development, 82*, 1454–1469.

Windle, M., & Windle, R. (2003). Alcohol and other substance use and abuse. In G. Adams & M. Berzonsky (Eds.), *Blackwell handbook on adolescence* (pp. 450–469). Malden, MA: Blackwell.

Windsor, J., Benigno, J. P., Wing, C. A., Carroll, P. J., Koga, S. F., Nelson, C. A., et al. (2011). Effect of foster care on young children's language learning. *Child Development, 82*, 1040–1046.

Winer, L. (2013). Smarter than ever? *APA Monitor, 44*, 30–33.

Winne, P. H., & Nesbit, J. C. (2010). The psychology of academic achievement. *Annual Review of Psychology, 61*, 653–678.

Winner, E. (1996). The rage to master: The decisive role of talent in the visual arts. In K. A. Ericsson (Ed.), *The road to excellence: The acquisition of expert performance in the arts and sciences, sports, and games* (pp. 271–301). Mahwah, NJ: Erlbaum.

Winner, E. (2000). Giftedness: Current theory and research. *Current Directions in Psychological Science, 9*, 153–156.

Winsler, A., Carlton, M. P., & Barry, M. J. (2000). Age-related changes in preschool children's systematic use of private speech in a natural setting. *Journal of Child Language, 27*, 665–687.

Winsler, A., Diaz, R. M., Atencio, D. J., McCarthy, E. M., & Chabay, L. A. (2000). Verbal self-regulation over time in preschool children at risk for attention and behavior problems. *Journal of Child Psychology & Psychiatry & Allied Disciplines, 41*, 875–886.

Wispe, L. (1972). Positive forms of social behavior: An overview. *Journal of Social Issues, 28*, 1–20.

Witkow, M. R., & Fuligni, A. J. (2010). In-school versus out-of-school friendships and academic achievement among an ethnically diverse sample of adolescents. *Journal of Research on Adolescence, 20*, 631–650.

Wolak, J., Mitchell, K., & Finkelhor, D. (2007). Unwanted and wanted exposure to online pornography in a national sample of youth Internet users. *Pediatrics, 119*, 247–257.

Wolchik, S., Sandler, I. N., Millsap, R. E., Plummer, B. A., Greene, S. M., Anderson, E. R., et al. (2002). Six-year follow-up of preventive interventions for children of divorce: A randomized controlled trial. *JAMA, 288*, 1874–1881.

Wolchik, S. A., Sandler, I. N., Tein, J.-Y., Mahrer, N. E., Millsap, R. E., Winslow, E., ... Reed, A. (2013). Fifteen-year follow-up of a randomized trial of a preventive intervention for divorced families: Effects on mental health and substance use outcomes in young adulthood. *Journal of Consulting and Clinical Psychology, 81*, 660–673.

Wolff, C. E., van den Bogert, N., Jarodzka, H., & Boshuizen, H. P. A. (2015). Keeping an eye on learning: Differences between expert and novice teachers' representations of classroom management events. *Journal of Teacher Education, 66*, 68–85.

Wolfgang, C., Stannard, L., & Jones, I. (2003). Advanced construction play with LEGOs among preschoolers as a predictor of later school achievement in mathematics. *Early Child Development and Care, 17*, 467–475.

Wolfram, W., & Thomas, E. R. (2002). *The development of African American English*. Oxford: Blackwell.

Wood, D., Bruner, J. S., & Ross, G. (1976). The role of tutoring in problem solving. *Journal of Child Psychology and Psychiatry, 17*, 89–100.

Woodward, L., Fergusson, D., & Belsky, J. (2000). Timing of parental separation and attachment to parents in adolescence: Results of a prospective study from birth to age 16. *Journal of Marriage and the Family, 62*, 162–174.

Wraw, C., Deary, I. J., Gale, C. R., & Der, G. (2015). Intelligence in youth and health at age 50. *Intelligence, 53*, 23–32.

Wray-Lake, L., Flanagan, C. A., & Maggs, J. L. (2012). Socialization in context: Exploring longitudinal correlates of mothers' value message of compassion and caution. *Developmental Psychology, 48*, 250–256.

Wright, J. C., Huston, A. C., Murphy, K. C., St. Peters, M., Piqon, M., Scantlin, R., et al. (2001). The relations of early television viewing to school readiness and vocabulary of children from low-income families: The Early Window Project. *Child Development, 72*, 1347–1366.

Wright, T. S. (2012). What classroom observations reveal about oral vocabulary instruction in kindergarten. *Reading Research Quarterly, 47*, 353–355.

Wu, P.-C., Tsai, C.-L., Wu, H.-L., Yang, Y.-H., & Kuo, H.-K. (2013). Outdoor activity during class recess reduces myopia onset and progression in school children. *Opthalmology, 120*, 1080–1085.

Wu, W., West, S. G., & Hughes, J. N. (2010). Effect of grade retention in first grade on psychosocial outcomes. *Journal of Educational Psychology, 102*, 135–152.

Wu, X., Anderson, R. C., Nguyen-Jahiel, K., & Miller, B. (2013). Enhancing motivation and engagement through collaborative discussion. *Journal of Educational Psychology, 105*, 622–632.

Wynn, K. (1992). Addition and subtraction by human infants. *Nature, 358*, 749–750.

Wyshak, G. (2000). Teenaged girls, carbonated beverage consumption and bone fractures. *Archives of Pediatrics & Adolescent Medicine, 154*, 610–613.

Xie, H., Drabick, D. A., & Chen, D. (2011). Developmental trajectories of aggression from late childhood through adolescence: Similarities and differences across gender. *Aggressive Behavior, 37*, 387–404.

Xie, H., Farmer, T. W., & Cairns, B. (2003). Different forms of aggression among inner-city African-American children: Gender, configurations, and school social networks. *Journal of School Psychology, 41*, 355–375.

Xue, Y., & Meisels, S. (2004). Early literacy instruction and learning in kindergarten: Evidence from the Early Childhood Longitudinal Study—Kindergarten class of 1998-1999. *American Educational Research Journal, 41*, 191–229.

Yan, N., Zhou, N., & Ansari, A. (2016). Maternal depression and children's cognitive and socio-emotional development at first grade: The moderating role of classroom emotional climate. *Journal of Child and Family Studies, 25*, 1247–1256.

Yap, M. B. H., Allen, N. B., & Ladouceur, C. D. (2008). Maternal socialization of positive affect: The impact of invalidation on adolescent emotion regulation and depressive symptomatology. *Child Development, 79*, 1415–1431.

Yeager, D. S., & Dweck, C. S. (2012). Mindsets that promote resilience: When students believe that personal characteristics can be developed. *Educational Psychologist, 47*, 302–314.

Yoon, B. (2008). Uninvited guests: The influence of teachers' roles and pedagogies on the positioning of English language learners in the regular classroom. *American Educational Research Journal, 45*, 495–422.

Yoshikawa, H., & Hsueh, J. (2001). Child development and public policy: Toward a dynamic systems perspective. *Child Development, 72*, 1887–1903.

Young, M. F., Slota, S., Cutter, A. B., Jalette, G., Mullin, G., Lai, B., et al. (2012). Our princess is in another castle: A review of trends in serious gaming for educators. *Review of Educational Research, 82*, 61–89.

Youniss, J., McLellan, J. A., Su, Y., & Yates, M. (1999). The role of community service in identity development: Normative, unconventional, and deviant orientations. *Journal of Adolescent Research, 14*, 248–261.

Yu, C., & Smith, L. B. (2007). Rapid word learning under uncertainty via cross-situational statistics. *Psychological Science, 18*, 414–420.

Yuan, A. (2012). Perceived breast development and adolescent girls' psychological well-being. *Sex Roles, 66*, 790–806.

Yuan, S., & Fisher, C. (2009). "Really? She blicked the baby?" Two-year-olds learn combinatorial facts about verbs by listening. *Psychological Science, 20*, 619–626.

Yumoto, C., Jacobson, S. W., & Jacobson, J. L. (2008). Fetal substance exposure and cumulative environmental risk in an African American cohort. *Child Development, 79*, 1761–1776.

Zacharia, Z. C., Loizou, E., & Papaevripidou, M. (2012). Is physicality an important aspect of learning through science experimentation among kindergarten students? *Early Childhood Research Quarterly, 27*, 447–457.

Zahn-Waxler, C., Kochanska, G., Krupnick, J., & McKnew, D. (1990). Patterns of guilt in children of depressed and well mothers. *Developmental Psychology, 26*, 51–59.

Zaki, J., Bolger, N., & Ochsner, K. (2008). It takes two: The interpersonal nature of empathic accuracy. *Psychological Science, 19*, 399–404.

Zaki, J., & Cikara, M. (2015). Addressing empathic failures. *Current Directions in Psychological Science, 24*, 471–476.

Zanobini, M., & Usai, C. (2002). Domain-specific self-concept and achievement motivation in the transition from primary to low middle school. *Educational Psychology, 22*, 203–217.

Zelazo, P. D., Anderson, J., Richler, J., Wallner-Allen, K., Beaumont, J., & Weintraub, S. (2013). NIH Toolbox Cognitive Function Battery (CFB): Measuring executive function and attention. . *Monographs of the Society for Research in Child Development, 78*(4), 16–33.

Zeller, M., Vannatta, K., Schafer, J., & Noll, R. (2003). Behavioral reputation: A cross-age perspective. *Developmental Psychology, 39*, 129–139.

Zettergren, P. (2003). School adjustment in adolescence for previously rejected, average and popular children. *British Journal of Educational Psychology, 73*, 207–221.

Zhang, X., Anderson, R. C., Morris, J., Miller, B., Nguyen-Jahiel, K. T., Lin, T.-J., ... Hsu, J. Y.-L. (2016). Improving children's competence as decision makers: Contrasting effects of collaborative interaction and direct instruction. *American Educational Research Journal, 53*, 194–223.

Zhang, X., Koponen, T., Räsänen, P., Aunola, K., Lerkkanen, M.-K., & Nurmi, J.-E. (2014). Linguistic and spatial skills predict early arithmetic development via counting sequence knowledge. *Child Development, 85*, 1091–1107.

Zhou, Q., Lengua, L., & Wang, Y. (2009). The relations of temperament reactivity and effortful control to children's adjustment problems in China and the United States. *Developmental Psychology, 45*, 724–739.

Zieber, N., Kangas, A., Hock, A., & Bhatt, R. S. (2014). Infants' perception of emotion from body movements. *Child Development, 85*, 675–684.

Ziegert, D., Kistner, J., Castro, R., & Robertson, B. (2001). Longitudinal study of young children's responses to challenging achievement situations. *Child Development, 72*, 609–624.

Zillmann, D. (2001). Influence of unrestrained access to erotica on adolescents' and young adults' dispositions toward sexuality. *Journal of Adolescent Health, 27* (2 supplement), 41–44.

Zimmer-Gembeck, M. J., & Helfand, M. (2008). Ten years of longitudinal research on U.S. adolescent sexual behavior: Developmental correlates of sexual intercourse, and the importance of age, gender and ethnic background. *Developmental Review, 28,* 153–224.

Zimmer-Gembeck, M. J., & Skinner, E. A. (2008). Adolescents coping with stress: Development and diversity. *Prevention Researcher, 15,* 3–7.

Zimmerman, B. J., & Kitsantas, A. (2002). Acquiring writing revision and self-regulatory skill through observation and emulation. *Journal of Educational Psychology, 94,* 660–668.

Ziol-Guest, K. M., Dunifon, R. E., & Kalil, A. (2013). Parental employment and children's body weight: Mothers, others, and mechanisms. *Social Science & Medicine, 95,* 52–59.

Ziol-Guest, K. M., & McKenna, C. C. (2014). Early childhood housing instability and school readiness. *Child Development, 85,* 103–113.

Ziv, A. (2013). Using humor to develop creative thinking. In P. McGhee (Ed.), *Humor and children's development: A guide to practical applications* (pp. 99–115). London: Routlege.

Zosuls, K. M., Field, R. D., Martin, C. L., Andrews, N. C. Z., & England, D. E. (2014). Gender-based relationship efficacy: Children's self-perceptions in intergroup contexts. *Child Development, 85,* 1663–1676.

Zosuls, K. M., Ruble, D. N., & Tamis-LeMonda, C. S. (2014). Self-socialization of gender in African American, Dominican immigrant, and Mexican immigrant toddlers. *Child Development, 85,* 2202–2217.

Zosuls, K. M., Ruble, D. N., Tamis-LeMonda, C., Shrout, P. E., Bornstein, M. H., & Greulich, F. K. (2009). The acquisition of gender labels in infancy: Implications for gender-typed play. *Developmental Psychology, 45,* 688–701.

Zucker, R. A., Heitzeg, M. M., & Nigg, J. T. (2011). Parsing the undercontrol/disinhibition pathway to substance use disorders: A multilevel developmental problem. *Child Development Perspectives, 5,* 248–255.

Zvoch, K., & Stevens, J. J. (2013). Summer school effects in a randomized field trial. *Early Childhood Research Quarterly, 28,* 24–32.

Name Index

Note: Page numbers followed by italic letters indicate the following: *t* for tables, *f* for figures, and *n* for footnotes.

Subject Index

Note: Page numbers followed by italic letters indicate the following: *t* for tables, *f* for figures, and *n* for footnotes. Page numbers in bold indicate glossary terms.

NAEYC Standards | naeyc

The National Association for the Education of Young Children (NAEYC) published standards for professional preparation in January 2010. The standards describe what teachers of young children (birth to age 8) should know and do when they complete professional preparation programs. They are designed to be comparable to InTASC and NBPTS standards. There are seven standards that are divided into key elements (KE). The following table shows the alignment between content in this text and NAEYC standards.

NAEYC Standards naeyc	Chapter
Standard 1: Promoting Child Development and Learning	
KE 1(a) Knowing and understanding young children's characteristics and needs, from birth through age 8.	All chapters
KE 1(b) Knowing and understanding the multiple influences on early development and learning.	All chapters
KE 1(c) Using developmental knowledge to create healthy, respectful, supportive, and challenging learning environments for young children.	All chapters (classroom implications sections)
Standard 2: Building Family and Community Relationships	
KE 2(a) Knowing about and understanding diverse family and community characteristics.	1, 2, 5, 6, 7, 8, 9, 10, 11, 12, 13, 14
KE 2(b) Supporting and engaging families and communities through respectful, reciprocal relationships.	6, 7, 12, 13, 14
KE 2(c) Involving families and communities in young children's development and learning.	1, 2, 5, 6, 7, 8, 9, 10, 11, 12, 14
Standard 3: Observing, Documenting, and Assessing to Support Young Children and Families	
KE 3(c) Understanding and practicing responsible assessment to promote positive outcomes for each child, including the use of assistive technology for children with disabilities.	5
Standard 4: Using Developmentally Effective Approaches to Connect with Children and Families	
KE 4(a) Understanding positive relationships and supportive interactions as the foundation of their work with young children.	2, 4, 5, 6, 7, 8, 9, 10, 11, 12, 13, 14
KE 4(c) Using a broad repertoire of developmentally appropriate teaching/learning approaches.	3, 4, 5, 6, 7, 8, 10, 11, 12, 13, 14
KE 4(d) Reflecting on own practice to promote positive outcomes for each child.	All chapters (self-reflection checklists)

NAEYC Standards **naeyc**	Chapter
Standard 5: Using Content Knowledge to Build Meaningful Curriculum	
KE 5(a) Understanding content knowledge and resources in academic disciplines: language and literacy; the arts–music, creative movement, dance, drama, visual arts; mathematics; science, physical activity, physical education, health and safety; and social studies.	2, 4, 5, 12
Standard 6: Becoming a Professional	
KE 6(b) Knowing about and upholding ethical standards and other early childhood professional guidelines.	7, 13
KE 6(d) Integrating knowledgeable, reflective, and critical perspectives on early education.	All chapters (self-reflection checklists)